IRISH MENTAL HEALTH LAW

Irish Mental Health Law

ANNE-MARIE O'NEILL

B.A. (Mod.) Legal Science (Trinity College Dublin), LL.M. (London University),
Ph.D. (N.U.I. Galway), (of Gray's Inn) Barrister

Published in 2005 by
First Law Limited,
Merchant's Court,
Merchants Quay,
Dublin 8,
Ireland.'
www.firstlaw.ie

Typeset by Gough Typesetting Services, Dublin.

ISBN 1–904480–20–9

A catalogue record for this book
is available from the British Library.

Printed by Johnswood Press Ltd.

*To those who work towards
the furtherance
of the human rights
of people with
mental disabilities*

Foreword

This text is a welcome addition to the corpus of scholarly work on Irish mental health law. Almost uniquely, it takes a fresh look at the existing law from the perspective of international human rights law as well as comparative law. It provides a clear exposition of the law as it is. More importantly, it provides a clear account of the international and comparative benchmarks against which it should be judged and reformed. It both sets and informs a vigorous law reform agenda.

The analysis provided is animated throughout by the human rights perspective on mental disability. At the heart of the human rights paradigm is a new way of thinking about the human difference of mental disability and the place of those who are different by way of being people with mental disability in our society. In reality, profound difference such as mental disability has often counted as a ground for relative and absolute exclusion from society.

As the author so eloquently expounds, the human rights paradigm demands a new vision of the body politic – one that takes seriously the promise of equal citizenship and social solidarity. People with disabilities and particularly those with mental disability stand to gain as a result of this new thinking. In the past they formed a discrete and insular minority – a minority kept literally out of circulation through civil commitment processes and reduced to passive dependency on the welfare and medical systems. For a variety of reasons their leverage over the political apparatus was minimal. They tended to be viewed as object – and not subject – as the beneficiaries of care and charity and not rights. The vicious circle of exclusion became self-perpetuating in most cultures through the internalisation of society's implicit judgments about the inherent worth of such persons. Perversely the less people with mental disability were seen in public the more plausible came the assumption that they had no rightful place in the mainstream and that policies designed to marginalize them were perfectly acceptable.

The human rights paradigm enables one to more clearly see the reality of the lives of people with mental disability more holistically. Viewing the issue of legal competence as a human rights issue centers the rights and abilities of the individual with mental disability in the determination notwithstanding his or her difficulty or disabilities in personally exercising those rights. The reality is that mental disability complicates but does not ruin human existence. Our law has yet to match this reality.

Further the human rights doctrine provides hard legal criteria against which the reality of the status of people with mental disability may be judged. In a sense they provide authoritative vantage points with which to critique Irish law. Irish law is not self-referencing and self-contained but is part of an evolving cosmopolitan legal order that is characterised by an emphasis on human rights. Accordingly while human rights are instanced often imperfectly in Irish constitutional law they are not exhausted by the Irish constitutional order.

More importantly, the human rights perspective helps to inform a clear reform agenda.

The author has admirably succeeded in bringing together an analysis of the higher ends of the law with a clear exposition of its current failings. This book will be of use to a wide variety of actors in the mental disability field as well as legislators. And the analysis provided can and should lead to more rational and informed debates about disability law reform. I warmly commend it to all who are interested in making the commitment contained in the Declaration of Irish Independence to "cherish all the children of the nation equally" into a reality.

Gerard Quinn
Member of the Irish Human Rights Commission
and
Convenor of its Disability Sub-Committee

Preface

Current Irish law relating to the position of the person with mental health difficulties or with intellectual disability (collectively referred to hereinafter as "people with mental disability") is to be found in a disparate number of sources. As a result a person with mental disability and his/her carer(s) whether professional or otherwise who seeks information as to his/her legal position as a patient in hospital or as a member of society in Ireland may encounter considerable difficulties in finding that information. In the spirit of the new international ethos which seeks to promote the human rights of people with mental disabilities this book aims to provide information for all on the legal rights of the person with mental disability and to provoke discussion about those rights heretofore were regarded primarily as medical issues.

The text commences in Chapter 1 by addressing the concepts of mental illness and intellectual disability collectively described in the term "mental disability" and traces the history of the care of people with mental disability from earliest times to the present day. In this way it seeks to explain why the law comprised elements of seeking to "contain" the problem of mental disability and why the law still contains remnants of a paternalistic ethos. Moving from this basis it describes the organisation of the psychiatric services in operation in the Republic of Ireland today and the nature of services currently available to people with mental health difficulties. It also outlines the individual's entitlements in relation to the services. It then sets out European rights of relevance to the person with mental disability contained in the European Convention for the Protection of Human Rights and Fundamental Freedoms (1950), which is given interpretative effect in Irish law under the terms of the European Convention on Human Rights Act 2003.

Having addressed the matter of the past and the future, the text then sets out to trace the traditional aspects of mental health law which impact on the life of a person with mental disability after diagnosis, i.e. admission to hospital, treatment rights both informational and substantive, and discharge rights.

In the context of admission rights, Chapter 2 discusses the position of the voluntary patient both adult and child and position of the compliant incapacitated patient. It sets out in detail the criteria for involuntary admission and the procedures for the admission of both adults and children as involuntary patients both under the Mental Treatment Act 1945 and the Mental Health Act 2001.

Where information rights of patients are concerned, Chapter 3 addresses the patient's right to information on admission under the 1945 and 2001 Acts, the patient's right of access to medical records at common law, and under the Data Protection and Freedom of Information Acts; the patient's right to privacy and confidentiality; the right to censor a patient's correspondence and the patient's right of access to a lawyer.

Turning to the substantive rights of the patient with mental illness in hospital, Chapter 4 discusses the whether a patient has a positive right to treatment; the need to obtain a patient's consent to treatment; whether a detained patient may refuse consent to treatment;

the circumstances in which treatment may be imposed without consent, the right to restrain a patient, the right to extend detention and the legal mechanisms for maintaining standards of treatment and care.

Dealing with the subject of discharge rights, Chapter 5 addresses the issue of leave of absence, transfer of patients, the situation of detained patients who abscond, the law relating to discharge of patients and the law relating to *habeas corpus*.

In dealing with all of the above issues, the text sets out the principles of Irish law and then comments on them from the new human rights perspective which is found in the laws of other common law jurisdictions such as the UK, Canada, Australia and the USA and in international law.

Chapter 6 outlines and comments on the organisation and structure of the Mental Health Commission and the Constitution, powers and procedures of the Mental Health Tribunals established under the Mental Health Act 2001. At the time of writing, the rules for Mental Health Tribunals had not been published so the discussion was of necessity short and confined to the composition, functions and powers of the Tribunals as outlined in the Act.

The law as it affects the offender with mental disability is discussed in Chapter 7. The chapter addresses and comments on the impact of mental disability on the situation of the offender at all stages from arrest through charge, trial, conviction and sentencing to life in prison and the entitlements of prisoners in relation to psychiatric treatment.

The chapters that follow examine the law as it impacts on the life of the person with mental disability as a member of society.

Chapter 8 discusses the legal capacity of the person with mental disability in private law. It examines the legal capacity to contract and to enter into agency contracts; the law relating to enduring powers of attorney; legal capacity to act as a partner, capacity to execute deeds; capacity to make a will; the law relating to the domicile of the person with mental disability; the liability of the person with mental disability in tort; the law relating to capacity to consent to medical treatment and the wardship jurisdiction of the court exercisable where a person is of unsound mind and incapable of managing his/her property and affairs.

Chapter 9 examines the legal capacity of the person with mental disability to enter personal and family relationships addressing specifically the right to enter personal relationships, marital capacity; the right to bear children; the law of nullity; the position of the person with mental disability in relation to judicial separation, divorce, guardianship of children and adoption

Chapter 10 examines the right of the person with mental disability to exercise of public law rights such as the right to vote; to act as a juror, to practise as a solicitor, pharmacist, or medical practitioner; to act trustee, executor and administrator and the right to participate in the judicial process dealing, inter alia, with the limitation of actions in cases of disability and the position of the person with mental disability as a witness

This text is borne in part of research for a Ph.D thesis entitled *"Irish Mental Disability Law – A Critique from the Perspective of International Human Rights and Comparative Disability Laws"* read at the National University of Ireland, Galway. The research was sponsored by the National Disability Authority and the National Association for the Intellectually Disabled of Ireland (NAMHI) and I am grateful to them for their generosity. I am also indebted to Professor William Duncan of Trinity College, Dublin and Professor Leonard Leigh of London University who supported my research proposal. I should like to thank Dr Vincent Power, Solicitor at A& L Goodbody, Solicitors who assisted me in making my first contact with lawyers involved in the field of disability law and Professor Gerard Quinn and Tom O'Malley B.L. of National University of Ireland, Galway for supervising my thesis.

Throughout the time of writing the text a significant number of lawyers and public servants contributed to the research by generously agreeing to review chapters and making constructive suggestions regarding content among them Mary Keys B.L. of National University of Ireland, Galway; Professor Maeve McDonagh of University College Cork; Geoffrey Shannon of the Law School in the Law Society of Ireland; Dara Robinson, Solicitor of Garrett Sheehan & Co., Solicitors Dublin; William Kennedy, Solicitor of the Irish Medical Council; Robert Pierse, Solicitor, of Pierse and Fitzgibbon Solicitors, Listowel Co. Kerry; Dr Dermot Walsh, Inspector of Mental Hospitals; Noel D. Doherty B.L. Registrar of Wards of Court; the late Joseph Robins formerly of the Department of Health and Geralyn McGarry of Comhairle. To them I extend my sincere thanks.

Many scholarly commentaries by Irish authors both from academia and legal practice on aspects of mental health law have facilitated the writing of this text. I have sought to acknowledge their contributions throughout the text but I should like to express particular thanks to Tom Cooney, Orla O'Neill, Finbarr McAuley, Patricia Casey and Ciaran Craven, Brenda Hoggett (Hale) for their perspectives on major aspects of mental health law. I should also like to thank William Binchy, Brian MacMahon, Alan Shatter, Paul A. O'Connor, and Maeve McDonagh for their substantive works, aspects of which related to the rights of people with mental disabilities.

I should also like to thank my colleagues in the Law Society of Ireland for their helpfulness while the research was being carried out particularly my colleagues in the Law Society Library, Margaret Byrne, Mary Gaynor, Eddie Mackey and Mairead O'Sullivan. I should also like to thank the Law Society's Parliamentary and Law Reform Executive, Alma Clissmann for drawing my attention to human rights materials relevant to my research.

I should like to thank the members of my extended family and my friends both personal and professional who provided moral support and encouragement while the text was being written.

I should like to thank Bart Daly for his direction, patience and perseverance in seeing the text into print. Therese Carrick who edited the final text is owed particular thanks for her professionalism and assistance. I should also like to thank Gilbert Gough for his work in the not inconsiderable task of typesetting this text.

Finally I should like to express my particular gratitude to Gerard Quinn of the Irish Human Rights Commission for writing the foreword. His consistent support and encouragement of the cause of human rights for people with disabilities have been a source of inspiration for not only myself but also many others who embark on research and advocacy in the disability law field.

Developments since text went into print

The law in this text is stated as at September 1, 2004.[1] Since then however a number of legal developments have taken place, which in future may influence the development of

---

[1] With one exception relating to Road Traffic Law. See Chap.10.

the law in Ireland. On September 17, 2004 the *Disability Bill 2004* was presented to the Dail the provisions of which aim, *inter alia*, to enable a person to apply to a health board for an assessment to determine the health needs occasioned by that person's disability and the health services required to meet those needs which the health board may then provide if it is practicable to do so. Simultaneously with the Disability Bill the Government introduced the Comhairle (Amendment) Bill 2004, which aims to empower Comhairle to provide an advocacy service for people with disabilities. Given the interest of non- governmental organisations representing the rights of people with disabilities in this legislation it is to be hoped that the issues raised by the Bills will be fully and forthrightly debated in the Oireachtas.

On September 23, 2004 the Children Act 2001 (Commencement) (No.2) Order 2004 (S.I. No. 548 of 2004) brought into force Parts 2 (other than sections 7(1)(a), 10(2) and 13(2) and 3 of the Children Act 2001 (other than section 23D) of the Children Act 2001. These parts of the Children Act 2001 are referred to in the context of special care orders in Chapter 9 of the text, and regulate family welfare conferencing and the provision of special care services by health boards for non-offending children in need of special care or protection.

On September 24, 2004 the Children (Family Welfare Conference) Regulations 2004 (S.I. No. 549 of 2004) came into force. These regulations are prescribe matters relating to the administration of the family welfare conferences provided for by Part 2 of the Children Act 2001 in order to enable the provisions of Part 2 of the Act to have full effect.

On September 24, 2004 the Child Care (Special Care) Regulations 2004 (S.I. No. 550 of 2004) came into operation. They set out requirements with which a health board must comply before placing a child in a special care unit, requirements in relation to the administration of special care units and the care, supervision, review of cases of children placed in special care units and their discharge from such units, in accordance with section 23 of the Child Care Act 1991 as amended by the Children Act 2001.

On the international front on September 22, 2004 the Committee of Ministers of the Council of Europe adopted *Recommendation Rec(2004)10 of the Committee of Ministers to member states concerning the protection of the human rights and dignity of persons with mental disorder* with aim of promoting "better protection of the human rights and dignity of persons with mental disorder, in particular those subject to involuntary placement or involuntary treatment." Among other matters the recommendation emphasises the principle of least restrictive treatment and care in the least restrictive environment possible (Article 8); and the need for treatment plans to be drawn up in consultation with the person concerned (Article 12). It sets out new and more detailed criteria for involuntary placement (Article 17) and involuntary treatment (Articles 18 and 19), which, inter alia, in addition to the measure being the least restrictive one available require that the person's opinion be taken into consideration. The criteria also require decisions to subject a person to involuntary placement to be taken by a court or competent body which is independent of the person or body proposing an involuntary measure and that can make an independent decision (Article 2.3 and Article 20).

The Recommendation also requires that persons subject to involuntary placement or involuntary treatment should be informed verbally and in writing of their rights and of the remedies open to them (Article 22). Member states are exhorted to minimise the duration of involuntary placement by the provision of appropriate aftercare services

(Article 24). The Recommendation states that "Member states should ensure that appropriate provisions exist to protect a person with mental disorder who does not have the capacity to consent and who is considered in need of placement and does not object to the placement" (Article 26) thus addressing the problem of protection of the rights of compliant incapacitated persons who require treatment. Where minors are concerned the Recommendation states that in all decisions concerning treatment whether provided involuntarily or not the opinion of the minor should be taken into consideration as an increasingly determining factor in proportion to his or her age and degree of maturity (Article 29). The Recommendation also addresses the rights of the person with mental disorder who comes into contact with the criminal law emphasising the need for appropriate police training (Article 32); prompt medical examination at a suitable location to establish a person's need for psychiatric care, capacity to respond to interrogation and whether the person can be safely detained in non-health care facilities (Article 33); equivalence of health care with that outside the penal institution and independent monitoring of treatment and care of persons with mental disorder in penal institutions (Article 35).

On November 10, 2004 the Road Traffic (Licensing of Drivers) (Amendment) Regulations 2004 (S.I. No. 705 of 2004) which amended the categorisation of vehicles for the purposes of driver licensing and certain aspects of the fitness to drive criteria. The text has been amended to take account of this development.

On November 15, 2004 in the case of *O. v St John of God Hospital Stillorgan* the applicant challenged his detention under section 184 of the Mental Treatment Act 1945 by bringing habeas corpus proceedings invoking the provisions of Article 40.4 of the Constitution. It was argued on his behalf that (a) there was not sufficient compliance with section 5(3)(i) of the Mental Treatment Act 1953 in that the applicant was not informed of the nature of the medical certificate and (b) that there was non-compliance with the requirements of the Mental Treatment Act 1953, section 5(3)(i) in that the applicant was not informed that he might request a second opinion. Finnegan P. held in relation to (a) that there was sufficient notification of the effect of the certificate when at Donnybrook Garda Station sergeant attending to the matter in relation to the certificate under section 184 of the 1945 Act informed the applicant who had previously been detained as a temporary chargeable patient: "This entitles me to arrest you under the Mental Health Act". Secondly in relation to (b) although the applicant was not informed of his right to a second opinion "the requirements of the Act were in fact met by a second opinion being obtained with the co-operation of the applicant although he might not in terms have requested a second opinion". Finnegan P. added:

> "I am acutely aware that it is desirable that there should be absolute procedural regularity where a citizen is to be deprived of their liberty. However one must have regard to the circumstances which may affect the invocation of section 184 of the Mental Treatment Act 1945. The person whom it is sought to make a temporary chargeable patient may not be in a position to appreciate the procedures which have been followed but nonetheless the Act requires that they be followed. In such circumstances it would be desirable that a second medical opinion be obtained albeit the same was not requested. If the substantive requirements of the Act are complied with, as in the case by the provision of a second opinion, I am satisfied that this is sufficient compliance."[2]

In reaching his decision in the case the President was strongly influenced by the desirability that the applicant in this case should receive treatment:

> "In this case I have the benefit of the medical report from my own Medical Visitor which confirms the two medical opinions obtained for the purposes of the detention of the applicant. I have regard to the circumstances that on his own account the applicant was in a disturbed condition believing that he was being spoken to and spied upon by his television set and to this extent he destroyed the same and sustained injury in so doing. On the basis of the Medical Visitor's Report it is desirable and indeed essential that he should receive treatment. He appears to have no insight into his condition and is non-compliant with medication. I am satisfied on the applicant's own account as related to his Counsel in instructions that the objectives of section 184 of the Mental Treatment Act 1945 were complied with in substance by the giving to the applicant of the information which he acknowledges he was given in relation to the nature of the certificate and by the obtaining of a second medical practitioner."[3]

However whatever the desirability of treatment in a particular case what is not discussed in the case is the best way treatment could have been delivered in the circumstances so as to achieve therapeutic aims. The regrettable signal sent by the case that where there is a clear need for treatment the rights of a person with mental disability may be compromised. While no one questions that where there is a need for treatment a patient should receive it compromising a patient's rights to achieve that aim must ultimately act to inhibit the establishment of a positive co-operative therapeutic relationship. A patient unaware of his rights however ill is simply not in any position adequately to represent his point of view. A patient who was aware that a second opinion would make the difference between voluntary and involuntary admission is put in a position to represent his point of view on the matter of treatment and when presented with them to address the options and particularly that of voluntary treatment with the doctor giving the second opinion. Indeed in this case it is respectfully submitted that the treatment objectives of the 1945 Act appeared not to have been met. The taking of the action in itself is an indication that there was a failure in the case to establish a positive therapeutic relationship which is normally brought about by informed co-operation and mutual respect of rights between doctor and patient.

On December 7, 2004 in the High Court case of *B. v Minister for Health and Children* Carroll J. made a declaration that section 260 of the Mental Treatment Act 1945 (as amended) was unconstitutional having regard to Article 6 and Article 34 of the Constitution. Section 260 limits the right of access to the courts in cases of civil proceedings instituted in respect of an act purporting to have been done in pursuance of the 1945 Act to circumstances where there are "substantial grounds" for contending that a person acted "in bad faith" or "without reasonable care". Article 6 of the Constitution provides for the separation of powers and Article 34 of the Constitution provides for the administration of justice by the courts. Carroll J. ruled that section 260

---

[2] *O. v St John of God Hospital Stillorgan* at p.3 of the judgment.
[3] *ibid.* at p.4 of the judgment.

constituted an impermissible interference by the legislature in the judicial domain in breach of these provisions of the Constitution by virtue of "the limitation of access to the courts on two specified grounds."

As such the case potentially removes the restriction on the grounds upon which an applicant may challenge the legitimacy of exercise of powers under the Mental Treatment Act 1945 and indeed under the provisions of section 73 of the Mental Health Act 2001 which in effect limits a person's right to challenge an act purporting to have been done under the 2001 Act to cases where it is established there are reasonable grounds for contending that the person against whom the proceedings are brought acted "in bad faith" and "without reasonable care".

The Health Act 2004 which was enacted on December 16, 2004 has reorganised the manner in which the health services are administered. On January 1, 2005 the new Health Service Executive was established.[4] With effect from that date all health services are administered under this one governing body. Whereas the administration of the health services was previously carried out by seven health boards, three area health boards and the Eastern Regional Health Authority the Health Service Executive administrative system is organised more simply. It has four regional divisions: Western, Southern, Dublin-North-East and Dublin/Mid-Leinster with headquarters in Galway city, Cork city, Kells, Co. Meath and Tullamore, Co. Offaly. These regional centres are designed to help co-ordinate services delivered through local offices around the country.

The Health Service Executive has a board which is the governing body of the Executive[5] consisting of 11 members appointed by the Minister as having sufficient experience and expertise relating to matters connected with the Executive's functions.[6] The Board must appoint a chief executive officer with responsibility for carrying on, managing and controlling generally the administration and business of the Executive.[7]

Under the terms of Part 7 the Executive is obliged to prepare and submit a three year corporate plan for the Minister's approval specifying the key objectives of the Executive for the three year period concerned and the strategies for achieving those objectives and the manner in which the Executive proposes to measure the achievement of those objectives and the uses for which the Executive proposes to apply its resources. The Minister for Health and Children is to have a discretion as to whether to approve or refuse to approve the plan.[8] If the plan is approved it is to be laid before both House of the Oireachtas.[9] The Executive is also obliged to prepare a service plan for the financial year or other period as may be determined by the Minister indicating the type and volume of health and personal social services to be provided by the Executive during the period to which the plan relates and indicating any capital plans proposed by the Executive. The Minister may either approve the plan or issue a direction to amend it. The Executive must submit to the Minister with the service plan a statement of the income and expenditure relating to the plan. The Minister must ensure a copy of the service plan is laid before both Houses of the Oireachtas.[10]

---

[4] See Health Act 2004, s.6. Health Act 2004 (Establishment Day) Order 2004 (S.I. No. 885 of 2004).
[5] Health Act 2004, s.12.
[6] *Ibid.*, s.11.
[7] *Ibid.*, s.18.
[8] *Ibid.*, s.29.
[9] *Ibid.*, s.30.
[10] *Ibid.*, s.31.

Under the terms of Part 8 of the Act the Minister may convene a National Health Consultative Forum to advise the Minister on matters relating to the provision of health and personal social services.[11] Under the same part the Minister may by regulation establish regional health forums[12] to make representations to the Executive on the range and operation of health and personal social services provided within its functional area. The regional health forum is to be comprised of members of each city council and each county council within the functional area who are appointed as members of the forum by the relevant city or county council.[13] The Executive is also empowered to take such steps as it considers appropriate to consult with local communities or other groups about health and personal social services and these steps may include the establishment of panels to advise the Executive or to enable it to seek the views of persons who are being or have been provided with a health or personal social service or who are seeking or have sought a health or personal social service, their carers, service providers and such other persons as the Executive considers appropriate.[14]

Part 9 of the Health Act 2004 also provides for a new complaints procedure which subject to certain exceptions may be availed of where there has been an action by the Executive or a service which (a) does not accord with fair and sound administrative practice and (b) adversely affects or affected that person. This part of the Act has yet to come into force.

The text has been amended to take account of the transfer of functions from the Health Boards to the Health Service Executive.

As has been mentioned every care has been taken to state the law as at September 1, 2004. However, no legal responsibility or liability is accepted, warranted or implied by the author or publishers in respect of any errors, omissions or mis-statements. The text is not a substitute for legal advice and all readers are advised to make all necessary enquiries and to consider carefully their own legal advice before taking any decision. That said, the author welcomes comments and suggestions on the text for future reference.

Anne-Marie O'Neill

February 2005

---

[11] Health Act 2004, s.41.
[12] *Ibid.*, s.42. This provision has yet to be brought into force.
[13] *Ibid.*, s.42.
[14] *Ibid.*, s.43.

Table of Contents

Table of Cases

Table of Legislation

Pre–1922 Legislation

Post 1922 Legislation

Child Care Act 1991—*contd.*

Data Protection Act 1988—*contd.*

Freedom of Information Act 1997—*contd.*

Mental Treatment Act 1945—*contd.*

Mental Treatment Act 2001—*contd.*

Mental Treatment Act 2001—*contd.*

Mental Treatment Act 2001—*contd.*

Mental Treatment Act 2001—*contd.*

STATUTORY INSRUMENTS

Rules of the Superior Courts 1986—*contd.*

INTERNATIONAL CONVENTIONS

EUROPEAN DIRECTIVES

ENGLAND, THE COMMONWEALTH AND USA

ENGLAND

NORTHERN IRELAND

SCOTLAND

AUSTRALIA

CANADA

CHAPTER ONE

Introduction

THE LANGUAGE OF MENTAL DISABILITY

Within the disability community most accepted language to refer to people with disabilities is "people first" language.[1] Using this construct a person is not characterised by his/her disability but is rather identified as a person first – someone with many different characteristics only one of which is a disability. Accordingly in this text people are not referred to as mentally ill, or intellectually disabled but as people *with* mental disability, *with* mental illness, *with* mental health difficulties, or people *with* intellectual disability.

Throughout the text the term "mental disability" is used. This is a composite description of a number of mental impairments that are sometimes treated similarly by the law and includes mental illness, intellectual disability and developmental disabilities, cognitive impairments, traumatic brain injury and certain communication disorders.

THE DEFINITION OF MENTAL ILLNESS

The definition of mental illness is a difficult matter both in medicine and law.[2] The dictionary definition of the mind differs from that of the brain and includes "the seat of consciousness, thoughts volitions and feelings."[3] Unlike a physical disease or disability where a medical practitioner can postulate a state of perfect or "normal" bodily health before indicating the ways in which a patient's condition does not measure up to this standard, a state of perfect mental health is difficult to define so that the medical practitioner has to make a diagnosis of mental illness by reference to a deviation from an average standard of mental functioning. Current responses given to the question "What are the characteristics of a mentally healthy person?" are likely to refer to such signs as the capacity to co-operate with others and sustain a close, loving relationship and the ability to make a sensitive, critical appraisal of oneself and the world about one and to cope with everyday problems of living.[4] What degree of deviation from these characteristics is sufficient to amount to a disorder is a difficult matter of clinical diagnosis for the medical practitioner who may at first advance a hypothesis to give an indication as to treatment and may give some direction of the future progression of the illness or disorder.[5] This provisional diagnosis may well have to be modified as more is discerned about the underlying causation of the illness.

---

[1] See "Disability Speak – A Guide to Appropriate Language around Disability", National Rehabilitation Board (now National Disability Authority) pamphlet.
[2] See generall, Hoggett B., *Mental Health Law* (4th ed., Sweet & Maxwell, London, 1996), pp.27–29.
[3] Oxford English Dictionary.
[4] See Gregory, *The Oxford Companion to the Mind* (Oxford University Press, 1978), p.469.

Biological model of mental illness

There is one school of psychiatric thought which postulates that all so called mental illnesses have their origins in physical or organic causes and can treated in the same manner as diseases. Where the cause of a particular mental condition is not known the adoption of this approach will involve a process of minute observation and recognition of clearly perceptible clusters of symptoms, categorising them into distinct syndromes, relieving the distress they cause to the patient and suggesting the future course from similar cases while at the same time searching for some indicator as to the underlying defect.[6] Organic or biological theories falling within this school of thought have drawn

---

[5]   Most medical definitions of mental disorder appear purposive rather than elemental in nature. *The Oxford Companion to the Mind* notes "Arguments rage over the exact limits of mental illness" and as an alternative to definition proffers certain general factors as indicators of diagnostic method viz. "In practice it is possible to discern certain recurring patterns of complaints and disabilities which can be regarded as reasonably discrete entities. These disorders can be divided into two broad groups: organic disorders, in which some demonstrable physical illness including brain disease underlies the psychological symptoms and functional disorders where no definite physical abnormality has yet been replicably demonstrated. Since most forms of mental illness fall into the latter category, the classification of psychiatric disorders is generally based on the clinical distinction between different clusters of symptoms each with a characteristic outcome."

   Alluding to the "usefulness" of distinguishing between the neuroses and psychoses it states "Neurotic symptoms correspond to what is commonly called "nerves" and comprise feelings and thoughts which most normal people have experienced at some time or other albeit in a relatively minor form. However, if they become persistent and severe, such symptoms become markedly disabling and result in frank neurotic illness or "nervous breakdown" Psychotic symptoms, on the other hand are not part of normal experience and are almost invariably severe." See *Oxford Companion to the Mind, op. cit.*, pp.470–471.

[6]   A number of international systems for classification of mental disorders have emerged in recent years. Their objective, however, is less to define mental illness as to "provide a common language in which professional colleagues can inform each other about individual patients and enable investigators in different centres and countries to collate their research findings." See *Oxford Companion to the Mind, op. cit.*, p.465.

   The WHO International Classification of Diseases ICD–10 (1993) divides mental disorders into three classes; psychoses, neurotic disorders, personality disorders and other non-psychotic mental conditions and mental retardation. The psychoses are subdivided into organic psychotic conditions, which include various types of dementia and other brain syndromes; other psychoses, which include schizophrenic psychoses, affective psychoses and paranoid states and psychoses with origins in childhood. Neurotic disorders in the second of the classes include anxiety states, hysteria, phobic state and obsessive compulsive disorders. Also included in this class are several types of personality disorder, sexual deviations, alcohol and drug dependence, non-psychotic disorders specific to childhood and adolescence and a variety of other syndromes. "Mental retardation" in the third of the classes is subdivided according to its degree.

   A more advanced system proposed by the American Psychiatric Association was published in 1994 in "The Diagnostic and Statistical Manual of Mental Disorders: DSM IV". It defines mental disorder by reference to certain key factors viz. "A clinically significant behavioural or psychological syndrome or pattern in an individual" and "not only in the relationship between the individual and society" which is "associated with either a painful symptom (distress) or impairment in one or more important areas of functioning (disability)" It classifies mental disorders as separate entities not as gradations from normal to abnormal. Each case is evaluated on five axes, the first three axes constitute the diagnostic assessment. They are (Axis I) Clinical Disorders, (Axis II) Personality disorders and "Mental Retardation" and (Axis III) General Medical Conditions. Axis IV (Psychosocial and Environmental Problems) describes psychosocial and environmental factors that may affect any ascribed mental disorder. The assessment may be supplemented by a rating on Axis V ("Global

upon the study of electrochemical transmissions between and within the neurons comprising the human brain and as a result medical science have discovered ways in which the rate and substance of neuronal activity can be linked to specific psychiatric disorders. Recent technical advances in the field of investigative techniques have afforded neuroscientists new insights in developing biological theories. Computed Tomography (CT) scans, Positron Emission Tomography (PET) scans, Magnetic Resonance Imaging (MRI) have all contributed to increasing knowledge in this regard.

While the adoption of the organic model of mental illness may, on the one hand, tend to limit the scope of psychiatric intervention by the recognition that psychiatry cannot cure all ills, on the other it may be used to justify the use of treatments whose effects are not fully understood simply on the basis of a hypothesis, in cases where a biological cause has not yet been shown. The imposition of such treatment in cases where the patient objects must be subject to serious question. Moreover the model is inadequate in that it fails to explain why medical practitioners can find biological causes for some conditions but not for others.

Psychotherapeutic model of mental illness

There is a second school of thought based on a psychotherapeutic model which in varying degrees reject the notion of organic causes, distinct disease entities and more radical physical treatments and focus more upon the person's psyche or on its interaction with family or societal pressures. From a legal point of view the disadvantage of this model is that carried too far it may be used to give a spurious scientific objectivity to explanations of behaviour constituting a criminal offence. From the patient's point of view its advantage is that the methods of treatment endorsed by this model can usually only succeed with his co-operation.

Behavioural model of mental illness

A third theory school of thought on the behavioural manifestations of mental disorder rather than its causes. This school describes most adaptive and maladaptive behaviour as learned phenomena and conclude that therapy should focus less on underlying causes and more on observable symptomatic behaviour. By a system of consistent reinforcement of desired behaviour and equally consistent discouragement of the bad it aims to bring about a modification of anti-social or inadequate behaviour.

Developmental model of mental illness

A fourth school of thought – the developmental school describes how human beings evolve psychologically, in a systematic fashion over their lifetimes. Developmental theorists such as Piaget[7] posit that there is an "orderly or patterned" process of stages through which all persons pass, influenced by key factors such a maturation, learning

---

Assessment of Functioning") on a scale of 1–100 of the individual's level of adaptive functioning during past year.

[7] See Jean Piaget, *The Child's Conception of the World* (Littlefield Adams, 1972).

and moral development. Mental illness is ascribed to disruptions in the developmental process. Assessments and diagnoses of persons with intellectual disability also draw to a large extent on developmental perspectives.

The "anti-psychiatrists" view

These models of mental illness have been subject to much criticism not least with the profession of psychiatry. Critics such as Laing have attacked the organic or medical model for failing to enter into the patient's own view of life and to grasp the underlying rational basis of what he says and does. Szasz[8] criticises the same model for distorting the concept of disease or illness to justify the imposition of treatment upon socially inconvenient people for their own objectives and those of society. In response the proponents of the theories have attacked these styled "anti-psychiatrists" of ignoring the problems of the truly ill and concentrating on the more pleasant task of tending to the neuroses of the middle classes.

The point of this analysis from a legal point of view is that where neither the condition nor the cure is universally agreed questions must be asked about the justification for conferring power on psychiatrists alone to confine and treat patients against their will.[9]

OVERVIEW OF THE LEGISLATIVE HISTORY OF REFORM IN IRELAND[10]

The Irish Brehon Laws[11] and Mental Disability

The Brehon laws, which emerged during the pre-Christian and the early Christian period and remained in effect in Ireland until Elizabethan times contained a number of provisions dealing with people with mental disabilities. The laws made a broad distinction between (what appears to have been a person with intellectual disability) (*druth*) and people with mental illness (*mer, dasachtach*). A major criterion in the distinction appears to have been the extent to which the individual was deemed to be capable of doing some work or had the potential to amuse or was in other respects capable of earning his maintenance among his fellows. A child was not presumed to be a *druth* until the end of his seventh year when it was decided whether s/he was a *druth* or a sensible person. Where a person with intellectual disability inherited land it was retained undivided for a period of five successive occupiers and if at the end of a hundred years a sensible son descended from the person with intellectual disability the land was granted to him. A person with mental illness could not be bound by a contract unless at the time making the contract it was made with the consent of their guardians who would presumably be a near kinsman. A contract made by a person with intellectual disability or a woman

---

[8] See Szasz T.S., *The Myth of Mental Illness: Foundations of a Theory of Personal Conduct* (Doubleday, New York, 1961).
[9] See Hoggett, *Mental Health Law* (4th ed., Sweet & Maxwell, London, 1996), pp.27–29.
[10] See generally Robins, *Fools and Mad A History of the Insane in Ireland* (Institute of Public Administration, 1986), Finnane, *Insanity and the Insane in Post Famine Ireland* (Croom Helm, 1981), Commission of Inquiry on Mental Handicap (1965), pp.10–11 Commission of Inquiry on Mental Illness (1966) Pr 9181, pp.5–10.
[11] See generally Kelly, *A Guide to Early Irish Law* (Dublin Institute for Advanced Studies, 2001).

with mental illness was, however, invalid even if authorisation issued from the guardian. In general persons with intellectual disability and men with mental illness were exempt from the penalties for wrongdoing but where people with intellectual disability were concerned the persons responsible for their care were liable to compensate the injured party. Where a person of "half reason or sense" committed a crime the father, mother or stranger who lodged in the house was obliged to compensate the aggrieved party.

A person who failed to provide for the maintenance of a person with intellectual disability who had some land as well as "the power of amusing" could be fined five cows. The fine for not maintaining a woman with mental illness was ten cows as she could neither hold land nor be a minstrel. A person with intellectual disability without land or the capacity to amuse was placed in a similar category.[12]

Other forms of protection were also in evidence. For instance where a man and woman who were both mentally ill had been encouraged to have sexual intercourse by persons making fun of them the persons so doing were made responsible for the fosterage of any children which might result and were also responsible for finding security for and the crimes of those children. If there were no sane adult who could thus be made responsible the fosterage fell equally on the tribes of each of the man and woman with mental illness. If a person with intellectual disability was brought to an ale-house and there became drunk those who brought him there or who treated him while there were responsible for any of his consequent misdeeds.[13]

The ancient laws were however primarily concerned with protection and there is little evidence of a system of special accommodation of persons with mental illness in Ireland prior to the eighteenth century. Such evidence as there is suggests that persons with mental illness were normally looked after by their family or tribe.[14]

The extent to which the Irish monastic system cared for people with mental illness is not clear but there is some evidence to suggest that the wandering person with mental illness was given food and shelter by the monasteries because he was regarded as a wayfarer.[15]

Irish law (1600–1800) – a policy of incarceration of "lunatics"

With the closure of the monasteries as the Reformation progressed during the sixteenth century, the main haven for the sick and the poor disappeared and those seeking assistance had nowhere to turn. Vagrancy gave rise to social order problems and heralded in an era in which the appropriate form of treatment of the people with mental illness was their placement in prisons and other places of detention and, punishment, with the concurrence of medical opinion, in order to bring about socially acceptable conduct.

An Act of 1634 provided for the establishment of houses of correction in each county

---

[12] Senchas Mór (collection of Law texts).
[13] Robins, *op. cit.*, p.15.
[14] *Do brethaib gaire* ("on judgments of maintenance") referred to by Kelly (see above, n.11) is a fragmentary text on the kin's obligation to care for its incapacitated members. The second part entitled *De druthbreathaib* ("on judgments relating to *druth*") deals with the care of people with intellectual disability and people with mental illness.
[15] Robins, *op. cit.*, p.17.

in which specified categories of "rogues"[16] were to be confined.[17] Another Act of the same session of parliament added to the list of vagrants who were subject to imprisonment "cosherers and idle wanderers" intimidating persons into giving lodging and food by threats of "some scandalous rhyme or song."[18] The houses of correction, which subsequently developed, and jails became repositories not only for the statutorily described categories of vagrant but also of persons with mental illness who were regarded a social nuisance and threat to good order. These institutions remained the only centres in which people with mental illness could be confined, with a few exceptions for most of the eighteenth century. Conditions were poor and abuses inevitably arose largely from the fact that those managing the institutions were unpaid and had almost total liberty regarding the treatment of their prisoners.

In a half hearted attempt to deal with the problem of conditions in such institutions two Acts were passed in 1763 with the objective of checking the extortions of jailers and separating people with mental illness from others.[19] The relative failure of the reforming laws was reflected in official reports on prison conditions in subsequent years and led eventually to the passing of an Act of 1786,[20] which provided for the appointment of an inspector general of prisons. The Prisons Amendment Act of 1787, passed in an atmosphere of considerable support for further reforms, extended the powers of the inspector to give him the right to visit all public and private madhouses as often as he thought fit and impose penalties in the event of proprietors or keepers obstructing such visits.

By the end of the eighteenth century prisons had been supplemented by the houses of industry established by a statute of 1772.[21] The statute was enacted to relieve the public of the nuisance of proliferating beggars particularly in the cities and towns and was punitive rather than charitably orientated in its aims. "Undeserving" beggars could be forcibly committed to the houses of industry for up to four years while the "deserving" poor were to be given a badge permitting them to beg. The poor who were ill were to be admitted voluntarily to the institutions. The Act made no reference to people with mentally illness but in practice they were admitted in exceptional circumstances and in time came to comprise a significant proportion of the house of industry population. The government's aim was that every county should provide a house of industry for its own poor. In practice however few were established and, of those, the Dublin House of Industry was most notable.

The growing public demand to control unruly and dangerous persons permitted to wander abroad and lack of local provision led to the enactment in 1787[22] of measures by which the government aimed to establish a county system of special wards. While

---

[16] They included persons calling themselves scholars going about begging, idle persons going about begging or using subtle craft, fortune tellers, fencers, bear-wards and minstrels, jugglers, labourers able but refusing to work at reasonable wages, persons delivered out of jail begging for their fees or otherwise travelling, begging, pretenders to loss by fire and gypsies. 10 & 11 Car. 1, c.4, s.9.

[17] 10 & 11 Car. 1, c.4.

[18] 10 & 11 Car. 1, c.16.

[19] 3 Geo. III, c.5; 3 Geo. III, c.28.

[20] 26 Geo. III, c.27.

[21] 11 & 12 Geo. III, c.30 Ir.

[22] 27 Geo. III, c.39 Ir. stat.

not specific in this regard the legislation implied that the wards should be associated with the infirmaries for each county by rendering surgeons of county infirmaries accountable for public funds spent on the measures. The infirmaries in effect were the only statutory public facilities available for sick people. However as the existing infirmaries were already grossly neglected by the grand juries responsible for their supervision the new legislation was almost completely ignored. In practice if a place could not be found in the local prison the person with mental illness had to be transported to a house of industry willing to take him. In view of the small number of such houses many had to make the harsh and arduous journey to Dublin.[23]

Relief from private benefactors: The will of Jonathan Swift (1745)

When Jonathan Swift died in 1745 he left an estate worth about £12,000. In his will he directed that £11,000 was to be used for the constructtion of a hospital for poor people with mental illness. His will provided for the purchase of lands in any province (with the exception of Connaught) and the income from this was to be applied towards the purchase of a site beside Dr Steevens Hospital on which an asylum would be built for the reception of as many "idiots and lunatics" as the income from the land would be sufficient to maintain. He desired that the hospital be called St Patrick's Hospital. Swift's will directed his executors to apply for a royal charter to incorporate the hospital. This was granted by George II on August 8, 1746.[24]

The original governors acted with considerable expedition in the funding and planning of the construction of the building and facilitated the opening of St Patrick's Hospital, in 1757. Within six years of the opening, however, the governors faced the fact that the annual income from Swift's estate was no more than £4,000 and capable of supporting only about fifty patients and petitioned parliament for support. The House of Commons was receptive to the requests of the hospital and approved a grant of £1,000 for it in November 1763. In 1767 it decided to provide continuing support for St Patrick's. By 1800 as a result of parliamentary grants and further legacies and donations the hospital had been considerably extended and then accommodated 158 patients.

However, faced with the difficulty of running the hospital on a restricted income the governors decided to admit paying patients and by 1800 a third of all residents were paying for their care. The policy of having paying patients was contrary to the hospital's charter, which had interpreted Swift's wishes as intending the hospital to be exclusively for the use the poor. Nevertheless this practice continued until 1842 when the then Lord Chancellor drew attention to its illegality. All paying patients were subsequently transferred to private institutions. In 1888 the governors arranged for an amendment to be made to the hospital's charter authorising the taking of fees and the admission of paying patients was resumed. St Patrick's then became and remained largely a private institution.

In historical terms St Patrick's hospital is of interest because it was not only Ireland's first hospital for the people with mental illness but also the legacy of one of the great figures of the eighteenth century. However while patients during its early history were

---

[23] See Robins, *op. cit.*, Chap.3.
[24] See Orrery, *Remarks on the Life and Writings of Dr Jonathan Swift* (Dublin, 1757), p.266.

undoubtedly cared for in a more humane setting than if they had been confined in prisons and houses of industry the hospital was not pioneering one so far as methods of treatment were concerned. If anything it was a product of and not ahead of its times. However with the dawn of the 19th century St Patrick's was entering a new and more enlightened era.[25]

The development of the asylum system in Ireland

Towards the end of the eighteenth century the treatment of mental illness as a form of moral weakness requiring punishment and terrorisation to make it conform to social norms was troubling those concerned with social reform in Western Europe. Philippe Pinel in the asylum of Bicetre in Paris and William Tuke in York began independently of each other to adopt new care policies described as "moral treatment." The basic elements of this treatment were kindness and comfort. Irons and chains were on the whole rejected and reserved only for the most difficult cases and treatment care and exercise emphasised.

In Ireland the new approach was reflected at official level by the recommendation in 1804[26] by a Select Committee of the House of Commons that a separate asylum system be set up to end the confinement of the insane with criminals and vagrants in the jails and houses of industry. It recommended that there be four provincial asylums for "idiots and lunatics" with one located in Dublin. However a Bill to give effect to the committee's recommendations was dropped because of the expense it would involve.[27] In 1806 minor provision was made when an enactment empowered grand juries to raise annually a sum not exceeding one hundred pounds for the support of a lunatic asylum or a ward associated with a house of industry.[28] However the sums involved were so negligible that the provision was largely ignored.

The first significant measure to implement reform was passed by government in 1810 and provided for a grant to be given to the governors of the Dublin House of Industry to establish a separate asylum "for the reception of lunatics from all parts of the kingdom." This was to become the Richmond Asylum. Before the new asylum opened in 1815 statute had established it as an independent institution and provided a separate board of governors who were appointed by the Lord Lieutenant and obliged to obey his directions.[29] Patients were admitted on the basis of an application based on the certificate of insanity signed by a magistrate, clergyman or medical practitioner and the management pursued the principles of moral treatment in the care of patients. The opening of the new asylum stimulated considerable public enthusiasm for the new approach and overwhelming demand for its services. This in turn made the case for the urgent need for more asylums, a cause that was taken up at Parliamentary level by Thomas Spring Rice, governor of the local house of industry in Limerick.

Spring Rice drafted a Bill, subsequently enacted at the instigation of William Vesey

---

[25] See Robins, *op. cit.*, Chap.4.
[26] *Report of the Select Committee on the Aged and Infirm Poor in Ireland 1804* HC 1803–4 (109), iv.
[27] Hansard IV, paras 66, 206–208.
[28] 46 Geo. III, c.95.
[29] 55 Geo. III, c.107.

Fitzgerald which empowered the Lord Lieutenant to direct the erection of whatever number of asylums he thought appropriate following the recommendations of a Select Committee of the House of Commons which had been established in 1815 to look at better provision for Ireland.[30] This legislation was amended in minor respects by an Act of 1820.[31] Subsequently in 1821 both pieces of legislation were repealed and consolidated in another Act drafted by Spring Rice, which was to become the basis upon which the Irish lunatic asylum system was established and developed.[32] The Lunacy (Ireland) Act 1821 provided for the formation of districts which might include one or more counties or cities or towns and empowered the Lord Lieutenant with the advice of the Privy Council to direct the erection of district asylums for the entire country.[33]

The years 1845–1870 saw the construction, under these powers, of a number of public asylums throughout the country. Since they operated as pauper institutions there emerged a demand for, growth of and a consequent perceived necessity to regulate private institutions throughout the country, which charged for their services. Accordingly the Prison Act 1826 aimed at reforming the Irish prison system required the inspector-general of prisons to visit and report at least once every year on every madhouse kept for profit.[34] Penalties were provided for persons molesting or obstructing a visiting inspector. Further legislation in the form of the Private Lunatic Asylums (Ireland) Act 1842 provided for a compulsory registration system and required private asylums to operate subject to annual licences granted by justices of the peace at quarter sessions subject to revocation by the Lord Chancellor if he was satisfied that the asylum was not properly run.

The 1842 legislation also provided that patients could be detained in private asylums but only on the basis of a certificate signed by two physicians, surgeons or apothecaries. It also required certain records to be kept. Where the asylum was not under the direction of a medical practitioners it had to have a visiting physician. The legislation specifically declared the Inspectors General of Prisons to be Inspectors of Asylums. It also imposed a requirement that the asylums be visited on a six monthly basis by the Inspectors of Asylums.[35] As a measure designed to maintain standards in private institutions it cannot be said that the 1842 Act was particularly effective. It appears that standards in some of the cheaper institutions of the period were very low indeed and were encouraged by the ease with which licences could be obtained and the over tolerant attitude of the inspectors of the period. Further significant changes in the statutory controls had to await the enactment of the Mental Treatment Act 1945.[36]

The obligations imposed upon Inspectors General by the Prison Act 1826 to inspect and report upon private establishments also applied in relation to public asylums. In 1845 the Central Criminal Lunatic Asylum Act empowered the Lord Lieutenant to appoint one or two Inspectors of Lunatics to whom were transferred the functions of the Inspectors General of Prisons so far as they related to people with mental illness. The Local

[30] 57 Geo. III, c.106.
[31] 1 Geo. IV, c.98.
[32] 1 & 2 Geo. IV, c.33; 6 Geo. IV, c.54; 7 Geo. IV, c.14; 7 Geo. IV, c.74; 11 Geo. IV, c.22.
[33] See Robins, *op. cit.*, Chap.5.
[34] The obligation also applied in relation to public asylums.
[35] 5 & 6 Vic., c.123.
[36] See Robins, *op. cit.*, Chap.6.

Government Act of 1898 established a new administrative system in relation to the asylums. The County Councils powers under that Act were exercised through special Committees of Management, which were empowered to make regulations regarding the government and management of the asylums, the admission, detention and discharge of patients and the conditions as to the payment and accommodation for private patients.

Admissions procedures to Irish asylums

The law relating to mental illness continued to develop but in a somewhat haphazard manner throughout the nineteenth century. It focused more upon limiting the financial burden of mental illness upon public funds and controlling admission to already overcrowded accommodation than upon the rights of the individual, the only exception being the chancery jurisdiction over wards of court which protected the property of persons declared to be of unsound mind.

The Lunacy (Ireland) Act 1821[37] provided for the Privy Council to draw up rules for the good conduct and management of asylums. In 1843 the first set of rules was promulgated and required that in order to secure admission to an asylum the application had to be considered by the manager and physician of the asylum and then be put to the asylum board for acceptance. The application had to be accompanied by a medical certificate of insanity and an affidavit from the next of kin declaring the poverty of the patient. The next of kin was required to enter into a bond undertaking to remove the patient from the asylum when they were requested to do so. The rules also provided for admission by the physician of the asylum in cases of emergency. There was no provision for paying patients.

An alternative form of admission was under the Criminal Lunatics (Ireland) Act 1838[38] dealing with the admission of dangerous lunatics. Enacted in response to the killing of a director of the Bank of Ireland by a wandering person with mental disorder it provided for the transfer from prison to an asylum (if accommodation was available) of any person considered to be a dangerous "lunatic" or dangerous "idiot" who had been discovered and apprehended in Ireland "under circumstances denoting a derangement of mind and a purpose of committing crime."[39] The person so found was committed to "strict custody" for an indefinite period on the order of two justices of the peace who were empowered to call medical evidence to their assistance.[40] The detention could be terminated only by an order of two justices (including one who had signed the committal warrant) or on removal to a proper lunatic asylum by order of the Lord Lieutenant.[41] Despite the fact that the person with mental illness was stigmatised with a label of dangerousness and criminality this procedure became to be used quite frequently as an alternative to direct application to a manager of the asylum. For relatives desirous of being relieved of the burden of caring for a person with mental illness it had several

---

[37] Lunacy (Ireland) Act 1821, 1 & 2 Geo. IV, c.33.

[38] 1 Vic., c.27.

[39] *Ibid.*, s.1.

[40] The justices were free not to call for medical evidence if they saw fit and to make the committal on their own judgment or even "from other proof" that is the statement not even sworn of some person who sought the committal.

[41] 1 Vic., c.27, s.1.

attractions over the direct application procedure among them the fact that it was not necessary to make a declaration of poverty or enter into a bond; the fact that the police and not the relatives bore the duty of conveying the mentally ill person to the asylum and the fact that a place in the asylum was guaranteed.

For private asylums which were relatively insignificant in Ireland at this time the Private Lunatic Asylums (Amendment) Act 1842 provided that all admissions should be at the instance of an order made out by a relative or a friend. In this case, however, the admission required certificates from two physicians, surgeons or apothecaries who had separately examined the "patient."[42] Private asylums, it appears, had an infamous reputation as places where profit was made out of mental illness and where wealthy people might be shut up to the pecuniary advantage of their relatives. Accordingly two medical certificates were deemed to be necessary protection against abuse. In contrast one certificate was required for admission to public asylums, it being assumed that no advantage other than a social one would accrue to the partners in committal of a poor person.

During the 30 years of its existence procedures under the Criminal Lunatics (Ireland) Act 1838 became subject to widespread abuse. It appears that committals under the Act could be obtained quite easily given that the legislation left it open for a person to be committed on an information, which was not taken on oath or recorded. The effect of the procedures in practice ran contrary to government policy to reduce the number of persons with mental illness admissions to prisons, the consequence being that an amending statute – the Central Criminal Lunatics Asylum Act – was passed in 1845.[43] It required that a person not be committed as a "dangerous lunatic" unless at least one credible witness presented evidence on oath about the degree of derangement and criminal intent of any person for whom commitment was sought. Despite the amending legislation the abuses continued. It appears from the reports of the inspectors at the time that there was considerable laxity by the magistrates in the administration of the Act some of whom would sign committals without ever seeing the person who was the subject of the order at all.[44]

With the establishment of new asylums and pursuing further its policy of ending committals of persons with mental illness to prison with the discipline problems that it created the government passed the Lunacy Act 1867[45] which provided that where a dangerous "lunatic" or "idiot" was found in the circumstances denoting derangement or mind and a purpose of committing an indictable offence two magistrates could commit him/her to a district lunatic asylum only if they obtained a certificate from a dispensary

---

[42] 5 & 6 Vic., c.123, ss.14, 15.

[43] 8 & 9 Vic., c.107, s.10.

[44] *9th Report*, p.459 HC (1859) Failure to call for a medical opinion during the judicial examination was also widespread. At the instigation of the Inspector of Lunacy certain administrative measures were adopted to deal with the abuses. Thus in 1848 the government issued a standardised warrant of committal hoping this would engender greater compliance with the legal forms. From November 1847 jail governors were asked to forward the details of all committals to the lunatic asylums office to be recorded on a Central Register of Criminal and Dangerous Lunatics. See *Inspectors Report of 1847*, Appendix, pp.19–23, HC (1849), p.xxiii. See also Finnane, *Insanity and the Insane in Post Famine Ireland* (Croom Helm, London, 1981), Chap.3.

[45] 30 & 31 Vic., c.118.

medical officer as to the person's dangerous condition.[46] The Act also simplified the system of discharge so that a person could be discharged from detention on the certificate of the medical superintendent or visiting physician without reference to a higher authority. In essence, with minor amendments this is the system, which was to remain in operation until the passing of the Mental Treatment Act 1945.

In an attempt to prevent a rush of committals to the asylums under the 1867 Act, the Chief Secretary issued a circular[47] to magistrates urging them to observe the importance of obtaining evidence of a purpose of committing an indictable offence and advising them to confine the exercise of their powers to persons likely to commit acts of violence and crime.

In practice there proved to be too few safeguards against abuse of the procedure. Such historical evidence as there is suggests that justices of the peace signed the prescribed forms on vague and unsatisfactory information without any real regard as to the mental condition of the person concerned.[48] This laissez-faire approach combined with a degree of public complacency meant that the asylum became a repository for the unwanted in the community until well into the twentieth century.[49] Such complaints as there were against the practices were treated as involving "uncalled for county expenditure and continuing trouble to the Executive"[50] and not issues of dignity and respect for human rights. Indeed a single attempt at introducing more enlightened procedure in 1887 was discouraged on the basis of cost to the exchequer and failed.[51]

The Lunacy Asylums (Ireland) Act 1875 marked a sea change in the perception of asylums since it authorised the admission of private paying patients to the district asylums.[52] Then in 1891, influenced largely by the passage of the lunacy legislation of 1890[53] in England, a three man commission established by the Lord Lieutenant made a number of significant recom-mendations for change. Among these were the introduction of voluntary admissions; detention on the authority of a magistrate supported by at least two medical certificates that would distinguish between what the medical practitioner had been told by relatives and what he had observed himself and stricter regulation of admissions on grounds of dangerousness. There was also a proposal to end indefinite detention and limit it to a maximum of three years. The recommendations were, however, never acted upon.[54]

---

[46] 30 & 31 Vic., c.118, s.10.

[47] Dated December 30, 1867.

[48] Indeed irregularities in the form of committal were so frequent that the Lunacy Act 1875 provided for the correction of a defective form within 14 days of admission. See 38 & 39 Vic., c.67, s.5.

[49] By 1875 50% of all admissions to district asylums were in the "dangerous lunatic" category. By 1887 this had increased to 60%. Comparable figures in Scotland where the admission procedures were more complex were 4%.

[50] See Robins, *op. cit.*, p.146.

[51] The bill was introduced as a private members bill by EF Litton the member for Tyrone. Its aim was to streamline British and Irish lunacy laws.

[52] 38 & 39 Vic., c.67, s.16. Although paying patients remained a small minority in the district asylums representing in 1894 only 411 out of a total population of 12,771.

[53] 53 & 54 Vic., c.5.

[54] See Robins, *op. cit.*, Chap.10.

Early Irish treatment of offenders with mental disorder

The passage of the Irish lunacy legislation of 1821[55] marked a recognition of the concept of offences caused by people with mental illness. It provided that any person charged with an offence should be acquitted if found to have been insane at the time the crime was committed but it enabled him to be kept in custody during the pleasure of the Lord Lieutenant. It also provided for the indefinite detention at the Lord Lieutenant's pleasure of any person accused of a crime who was found insane at the time of their indictment. In practice the usual place for detention of such persons was prison since asylum accommodation was limited. However a person could be transferred from prison to the asylum as soon as a place became available.

In the Criminal Lunatics (Ireland) Act 1838[56] the concept of "criminal lunacy" was broadened to provide for the transfer to asylums of a criminal already undergoing imprisonment or awaiting transportation where two medical practitioners certified that the person in question was insane. Prisoners who were found to be insane while awaiting trial could also be transferred.

As the laws relating to the offender with mental disorder evolved there was a view that they permitted some criminals who had knowingly committed a crime to avoid punishment. The debate came to a head when Daniel McNaughten was acquitted of the murder of Edward Drummond, the secretary to the then Prime Minister Robert Peel on the grounds of insanity. The controversy surrounding the unpopular verdict led to the definition of insanity by the House of Lords in what have come to be known as the McNaughten Rules and in effect the creation of a new class of criminals who were shown to be insane at the time the offence was committed.

The publicity surrounding the case focused attention on and public objection to the combined housing of people with mental illness (albeit with a label of "dangerousness" affixed) with the "atrocious criminals" in the district asylums and when a Committee of the House of Lords reviewed the Irish lunacy provisions in 1843 it recommended the establishment of a special central asylum which was legislated for in the Central Criminal Lunatic Asylum Act 1845[57] and opened in 1850.

However the statute establishing the new asylum made no distinction between minor and major offences and the number of offenders with mental disorder in the district asylums far exceeded the number of places available in the new institution. Accordingly when it was ready for occupation the inspectors selected the worst offending of those already in detention, a procedure endorsed by the government's law advisors. For a while the criterion for referral was that offenders with mental disorder should have been charged with offences involving a punishment of death, transportation or lengthy imprisonment. Later only those who were clearly homicidal or were regarded as dangerous were admitted.

The law pertaining to the offender with mental disorder was subsequently amended on a number of occasions. Between 1875 and 1884 a number of enactments[58] facilitated the movement of prisoners between asylums and prisons and provided for a special

---

[55] 1 & 1 Geo. IV, c.33, ss.16–18.
[56] 1 Vic., c.27, ss.2 and 3.
[57] 8 & 9 Vic., c.107.
[58] 38 & 39 Vic., c.67; 46 & 47 Vic., c.38; 47 & 48 Vic., c.64.

verdict of guilty but insane where the accused person was found to be insane at the time of the commission of the offence. In the early twentieth century a number of enactments were passed touching upon the offender with mental disorder but did not make any fundamental changes in the law.[59]

When the Irish Free State administration took over on the independence of the state the powers given to the Lord Lieutenant in relation to the trial and custody of offenders with mental illness were transferred to the Minister for Justice.[60] In 1960 the Criminal Justice Act redefined the term "criminal lunatic" used in the legislation[61] and introduced new provisions relating to the conditional discharge[62] and transfer[63] of such patients.[64]

Incapacity and the evolution of the wardship jurisdiction in Ireland

The earliest legislation relating to mental illness applied to people with mental illness who owned property. It was rooted in the medieval principle that all land was held from the crown. Where under the feudal system persons granted estates from the crown became unable to perform their services to the crown through "idiocy" or "lunacy" the lands reverted to the crown. A similar principle applied to estates inherited by children during their minority. Were it not for the influence of the religious chancellors this land would have been distributed at will by the Norman monarchs. However the ecclesiastical presence at the royal courts ensured the development of practices in keeping with equity and conscience.[65]

The original legislation regarding the property of persons of unsound mind was laid down in a statute of Edward I but confirmed by a statute of Edward II in 1324.[66] It applied to the property of "idiots" and "lunatics". Where property was held by a person designated an "idiot" the king took custody of it, cared for the person concerned out of its income and on his death gave it to his heirs. Where property was held by a "lunatic" the king also took it over, kept it "without waste and destruction" maintained the "lunatic" and his household and, if he returned to sanity returned it to him. If the person concerned died without recovering his health the estate was assigned to his heirs and any residual profits "distributed for his soul."

The law in relation to wards of court continued to develop during the centuries and by the middle of the eighteenth century was firmly established under the direction of the Lord Chancellor, head of the judiciary. Heirs and relatives concerned about the mental capacity of a person could petition the Lord Chancellor to inquire into his condition. If

[59] 1 Edw VII, c.17; 4 and 5 Geo. V, c.58.
[60] See Adaptation of Enactments Act 1922 (No. 2 of 1922) and Ministers and Secretaries Act 1924 (No. 16 of 1924).
[61] "Criminal lunatic" is defined as "a person who is detained in a district mental hospital or in the Central Mental Hospital by warrant, order or direction of the Government or the Minister for Justice or under the provisions of s.91 of the Army Act 1881 or of the Defence Act 1954 and, if he is undergoing a sentence of penal servitude or imprisonment or of detention in Saint Patrick's Institution whose sentence has not expired." See s.3(1).
[62] See ss.3 and 4.
[63] See s.8.
[64] See Robins, *op. cit.*, Chap.10.
[65] See Abraham, *The Law and Practice of Lunacy in Ireland* (E. Ponsonby, Dublin, 1886), pp.2–6.
[66] 17 Edw., c.9.

satisfied that there was prima facie evidence of unsoundness of mind the Lord Chancellor issued a writ, *de lunatico inquirendo* to special commissioners who in turn established a jury to carry out an inquiry into the condition of the person concerned. The jury then decided whether his incapacity was such that he be taken into the wardship of the Lord Chancellor who became responsible for the protection and administration of his property.

As the wardship laws evolved in the nineteenth century so did the responsibilities of the Lord Chancellor in relation to the care of wards of court. Most of the chancery patients were in private asylums and legislation in 1842 gave the Lord Chancellor power to revoke a licence issuable under that enactment if he thought it desirable to do so. He was also empowered to direct the inspectors to report to him on any "lunatic", chancery or otherwise irrespective of where he or she was detained and even if in the care of a relative. During 1843 the then Lord Chancellor, Sir Edward Sugden initiated a practice which was to continue during the latter half of the nineteenth century of visiting the asylums either alone or accompanied by the Inspector General. This practice was extended by successive Lords Chancellor to become one of close supervision of all patients in public and private asylums and not just chancery patients. In 1860 an arrangement was put in place whereby special medical visitors also inspected the chancery patients and reported directly to the Lord Chancellor.

This concern for the well-being of the mentally ill also found expression in two pieces of legislation initiated in 1871 and 1880 by the then Lord Chancellor, Lord O'Hagan which were to become the basis for the exercise of the current wards of court jurisdiction. The first, the Lunacy (Ireland) Act 1871[67] rendered the writ *de lunatico inquirendo* obsolete and set out in detail a new administrative structure and legal procedures for dealing with the estates of persons of unsound mind. The position of Registrar in Lunacy was established and the provisions for the supervision of the estates of wards of court included the establishment of the role of the committee for each estate.

In 1880[68] the County Court Jurisdiction in Lunacy (Ireland) Act was passed with the object of protecting the property of persons of unsound mind which was regarded as outside the control of the court of chancery because of its small amount and the expenses which chancery procedures would involve. The Act afforded protection by vesting jurisdiction in such cases in county court judges.

Much of the responsibility for the administration of the asylum system eventually passed in 1898 to newly established county councils and the interest of the Lords Chancellor in the affairs of the asylums diminished. While the Act of 1871 continued to regulate the affairs of wards of court, the Lunacy (Ireland) Act 1901 made this jurisdiction exercisable by any judge of the Supreme Court to whom it might be entrusted. Following the departure of British administration from Ireland the jurisdiction became exercisable under the Government of Ireland Act 1920[69] by the Chief Justice of Ireland and the Chief Justice of Northern Ireland. In 1961 the Courts (Supplemental Provisions) Act provided that the wards of court jurisdiction be exercisable by the President of the High Court or, where the President so directs by an ordinary judge assigned that task by the President.

---

[67] 34 Vic., c.22.

[68] 43 & 44 Vic, c.39.

[69] See Robins, *op. cit.*, Chap.10.

The recognition of intellectual disability as a distinct form of disability in Ireland

Dating back to early times there the law has recognised a distinction between persons with intellectual disability and those with mental illness. The first statute for the protection of the property of persons of unsound mind distinguished between "idiots" and "lunatics".

In the nineteenth century the issues presented by intellectual disability were perceived as being appropriately dealt with primarily under the Poor Law. The Poor Relief (Ireland) Act 1838 authorised the provision of workhouses in which it was lawful to relieve such destitute poor persons as by reason of old age, infirmity or defect might be unable to support themselves, destitute children and such other persons as would be deemed to be destitute poor and unable to support themselves by their own industry or other lawful means.

While the 1838 Act was permissive in nature, the Poor Relief (Ireland) Act 1847 required the provision of "due relief for all such destitute poor persons as are permanently disabled from labour by reason of old age, infirmity or bodily or mental defect."

In 1878 the Poor Afflicted Persons Relief (Ireland) Act[70] authorised the sending of "idiots" and "imbeciles" to any hospital or institution for the reception of such persons and the payment or a sum not exceeding 5 shillings weekly for the maintenance and instruction of such persons.

In addition to provision under the Poor Law the authorities responsible for the administration of asylums and the Lunacy laws also addressed the issue of intellectual disability. In 1843 the rules for the administration of the district asylum system provided that "idiots as well as lunatics properly so called are to be admissible to every asylum." However it was not until overcrowding in asylums became an issue that a decision was taken to make separate provision for people with intellectual disabilities. It was a decision prompted principally by expediency and the avoidance of further public expenditure and less by concern for the establishment of a caring environment for the individual. Therefore it came as no surprise that a Select Committee of the House of Lords which reviewed the provisions for poor persons with mental illness in 1843 expressed strong views as to the unsuitability of the workhouse as a form of accommodation for "idiots" and recommended that the needs of "idiots and incurables" be met either by extending asylum accommodation or erecting separate provincial centres for them.[71] The boards of governors of the existing asylums agreed. However the concept of separate institutions never made any real progress. The need for new district asylums was accorded priority and in any event there was space in the workhouses – an option which would not involve a drain on public funds. The workhouse regime, however, was seriously deficient and no special care was given because the majority of persons admitted as an alternative to the asylums were admitted primarily as paupers and because the workhouse was not organised or staffed to meet the special needs of its occupants.

On the European front a developing knowledge of the problems and needs of people with intellectual disabilities emerged throughout the nineteenth century and with the advent of first ideas of care came the first special asylums. In England small institutions opened in Bath in 1846 and Highgate in 1848 but efforts in Ireland to establish a separate

---

[70] 41 & 42 Vic., c.60.
[71] *Report Select Committee on the Lunatic Poor in Ireland 1843* (625), p.xxv.

centre which would provide education and treatment for children with intellectual disabilities using the English methods received little financial support until 1869 when Dr Henry Hutchinson Stewart handed over the lease of a private asylum at Lucan to a Committee under the Presidency of Lord Charlemont who reorganised it into two separate institutions – the Stewart Institution for "Idiots" and the Stewart Asylum for "Lunatic Patients of the Middle Classes" the former institution catering mainly for the educational needs of "protestant" children with intellectual disabilities on both a fee paying basis and in a certain number of cases free of charge.

In 1879 when the premises at Lucan became overcrowded the residents were transferred to the newly acquired residence of Lord Donoghmore at Palmerstown and the new centre named the Stewart Institution for "Idiotic and Imbecile" Children and Middle Class "Lunatic Asylum". In time the institution dropped the asylum element, shortened its name to Stewart's Hospital and became wholly a centre for children and adults with intellectual disabilities. For the following fifty years it was the only centre making special provision for people with intellectual disabilities in Ireland.

In the public sphere the issues of mental illness and intellectual disability continued in practice to be regarded as elements of the same problem. The question of providing separately for people with intellectual disability received little government attention although official reports continued to draw attention to the need for further provision. The workhouse remained the principal repository for people with intellectual disabilities although conditions there remained unsatisfactory. The principal obstacle to improvement was a financial one. There was growing concern about the cost of mental illness and increased resistance to paying for it. The recommendations of a commission in 1879 that district asylums be classified into two categories: "lunatic hospitals" for those who were mentally ill and curable and "asylums" for "chronically insane requiring special care" (which category appeared to include people with intellectual disabilities); that dispensary doctors be obliged to supervise the well-being of people with intellectual disabilities and other people with mental illness "at large" and that a medical certificate of neglect or improper care be sufficient to require action from the lunacy authorities were largely ignored and by the 1890s there was a reluctant acceptance by the central authorities that for the time being the best that could be done for people with mental illness in the workhouses was to improve their conditions where they were. Accordingly efforts were made to ensure paid not pauper staff looked after them; that less use was made of strait jackets and other restraints and that separate accommodation was provided and "idiot cells" closed.

The pressures applied to workhouse guardians to improve the care of patients accelerated the movement of patients from the workhouse to the asylums. Changes in the local authority system stimulated the flow of transfers further. The Local Government Act of 1898 transferred the financing of the poor law to new county councils. The Act also transferred to them responsibility for the provision and management of the district asylums.[72] The Act also empowered the new authorities to establish auxiliary lunatic asylums in selected workhouse premises for the reception of "chronic lunatics who not being dangerous to themselves or others are certified … not to require care and treatment in a fully equipped lunatic asylum." Any auxiliary so established could be regarded as a

---

[72] 61 & 62 Vic., c.37, ss.9, 76, and Pt III.

separate asylum or as a department of an existing asylum. Under the new arrangements the financing of the asylums and the workhouses became the responsibility of one authority, the local county council. Central government grants however tended to favour asylum patients and accordingly the rate of transfers to asylums increased. Similarly as the grant towards auxiliaries was less than that towards asylum patients the provisions enabling separate accommodation to be provided were being ignored.

Developments regarding the education of children with intellectual disabilities were facilitated towards the end of the twentieth century by the formulations of Alfred Binet's tests of intelligence. These tests enabled a classification of the intellectual capacity of children with intellectual disabilities to be made so as to assess their educability. Public pressure for better provision for children prompted the establishment in 1904 and report of the Royal Commission on the Care and Control of the "Feeble Minded". The Commission conducted the first comprehensive review of the needs of the various categories of persons with congenital mental defects.[73] It reported in relation to Ireland that one of the barriers to making a special educational service available to children with intellectual disabilities was that the national school system for children without intellectual disabilities was still not universally available on a compulsory basis. In addition there was no local educational authority such as in Britain,[74] which could carry out the required planning and organisation. Schools were usually managed by the local clergyman and occasionally admitted children with intellectual disabilities despite difficult conditions. The Commission recommended that local authorities be statutorily obliged to make suitable provision for all mentally ill and "abnormal" persons subject to the direction of a specially constituted central body. This led to the enactment in the United Kingdom of the Mental Deficiency Act 1913 but no action was taken in regard to Ireland. The care of people with mental illness and people with intellectual disability in Ireland continued in practice to be treated as a single issue for the next 50 years.[75]

Irish law relating to mental disorder and policy in transition (1900–1930)

At the turn of the century the prevailing policies in mental health care were those of isolation and safe custody of people with mental disorder. Because its clinical dimension appeared to be minimal the management of mental illness was seen as only peripherally involved with medicine, and people in institutions received, on the whole, care rather than treatment. However with the emergence in continental Europe of psychoanalysis as a technique for assessing and treating the individual patient[76] concepts of the care of

---

[73] The report proposed four classifications: idiots, imbeciles, feeble-minded and moral imbeciles (later described as moral defectives) Idiots were designated the most dependent group and moral imbeciles defined as persons who had a mental defect coupled with 'strong vicious or criminal propensities".

[74] In Britain legislation in 1899 empowered education authorities to arrange special facilities for intellectually disabled children unable to benefit from instruction in the ordinary elementary schools. See 62 & 63 Vic., c.32.

[75] See Robins, *op. cit.*, Chap.11.

[76] Freud's *The Interpretation of Dreams* was first published in Vienna in 1900 and suggested that neurotic behaviour and personality were determined by early childhood experience. His concepts were further elaborated in *Three Essays of the Theory of Sexuality* (1905). In *Mourning and Melancholia* (1917) he outlined his theories on the genesis of depression. The theories were taken up by others such as Carl Jung, Otto Rank and Alfred Adler elaborated and modified.

the disturbed mind moved more rapidly away from assumptions implicit in the term "lunacy" towards the recognition of mental illness as a human condition capable of explanation and treatment in scientific terms.

On the domestic front despite official recognition of the issues the period 1900–1930 could be described as a period of relative inactivity in real terms in the area of mental health care. In 1898, as has already been mentioned, county councils established under the Local Government (Ireland) Act of that year became responsible for the administration of local public services including the district asylums. Their membership was subject to popular election and their attitude on the issue of mental health was influenced by the continued absence of any real public interest in the asylums or their patients. In addition any proposed expenditure on that front was restricted by the fact that the Local Government Act set clearly defined limits to support for asylums from government funds with the capitation grant being proportionately reduced when demands on the local taxation account exceeded its annual income.[77] In effect between 1898 and the departure of British administration central government contributions to the asylum remained static with excesses being met fully from local rates so that little development of a significant nature took place over that period.

Between 1906 and 1910 three separate commissions of inquiry reported on services for people with mental illness in Ireland. The first, the Royal Commission on the Care and Control of the Feeble Minded (1908) was established primarily to made recommendations in relation to the care of idiots and imbeciles but also urged the ending of the words "lunatic" and "asylum." While the term "patient" quickly replaced "lunatic" descriptions of office continued so that the "Inspectors of Lunacy" continued to operate from the "Office of Lunatic Asylums" and to report on the "district asylums" until the ending of British administration in Ireland.

The two other commissions were concerned primarily with the poor law but both made recommendations in relation to the management of asylums. The Vice-regal Commission on Poor Law Reform in Ireland (1906) recommended that all insane persons in the workhouses be transferred either to district or auxiliary asylums. The motivation however was financial rather than humanitarian and it was suggested that disused workhouse buildings be used for this purpose, heavy expenditure being declared "unnecessary and wasteful." While the report expressed admiration for the efforts of the Inspectors of Lunacy to arouse sympathy for the insane they believed the sane sick had more urgent claims on "the practical sympathy of the ratepayers" The third commission the Royal Commission on the Poor Law and Relief of Distress reported in 1909 referred only briefly to the subject of the Irish asylums, pointing out the Vice Regal Commission had already dealt fully with them and simply concurred with the recommendations of the previous Commission.

With the departure of the British administration in 1922 the Minister for Local Government (later Local Government and Public Health) became responsible for public health services and the relief of the poor. The poor law system of the British regime was abolished and general hospitals and workhouses were re-organised into county systems consisting of county homes and county, district and fever hospitals. The mental hospital system at local level remained virtually unchanged but the central policy making for the

---

[77] 61 & 62 Vic., c.37, ss.58 and 76.

system became the responsibility of the Minister. A single Inspector of Mental Hospitals was appointed for the Irish Free State. In the official nomenclature references to lunacy, lunatic and asylums disappeared and statutory sanction was given in the Local Government Act 1925[78] to the change of name from "lunatic asylum" to "mental hospital".

There was little public discussion during the 1920s about mental hospital services. Times were difficult politically and economically and overcrowding in mental hospitals continued. During 1925 the government established a Commission to examine critically the laws and administration relating to provisions for sick and destitute poor people in general with particular reference to people with mental illness and people with intellectual disabilities. The picture that emerged from the report[79] was one of considerable overcrowding and inactivity in district mental hospitals with apathy and pessimism pervading management and its policies and little being done to provide special facilities for children with intellectual disabilities who were largely being accommodated in former workhouses now euphemistically termed "county homes". Some of the recommendations of the report echoed those of previous Commissions that there be a system of auxiliary mental hospitals established in old workhouses to relieve in an economical manner pressure on existing district hospitals and provide for the insane then in county homes. The auxiliaries would be superintended by a matron, there would be no resident medical practitioner and, as the patients would not be violent or dangerous the staff could be entirely female.[80] It also recommended that local authorities be enabled to assist parents financially in sending their children with disabilities for training to an approved institution but expressed no views on the further development of such services.

More progressively, it recommended the introduction of out-patient services for people with mental illness and the treatment in a general hospital setting of short term patients.[81] It drew attention to the fact that some patients were admitted inappropriately under provisions which labelled them "dangerous lunatics" when their actual condition was of a very mild and non violent nature. It recommended the repeal of all existing lunacy laws and the introduction of new and simpler procedures for admission including voluntary admission which would safeguard the rights of the patient.[82]

Set against the wide remit of the report to examine all aspects of provisions for the sick and disadvantaged poor there was little chance of these recommendations receiving immediate attention. In the light of the needs of other groups such as the elderly, people with tuberculosis, single parents and their children, orphans and deserted children the needs of the people with mental illness were not perceived as requiring any special urgency or priority.[83]

In economic terms the 1930s, the war and post-war years were difficult times which were not conducive to the implementation of new healthcare advances. To the extent that advances were made in the area of provision for people with mental illness they

---

[78] S.79.
[79] Report of Commission on the Relief of the Sick and Destitute Poor including the Insance Poor 1927.
[80] Paras 428–436.
[81] Paras 432–434.
[82] Paras 447–470.
[83] See Robins, *op. cit.*, Chap.12.

were due in large part to the creation of the hospital sweepstakes which provided the much needed finance for developments. Statutorily taken over in 1931 by the Minister for Local Government and Public Health the monies of the Irish Hospital Sweepstakes were applied by way of grant to both local authority and voluntary hospitals.[84] In practice however public policy favoured expenditure on general hospitals and the opening of new sanatoria for the treatment of tuberculosis so that expenditure on district mental hospitals was extremely limited.[85]

While not noted for its contribution to the improvement of the fabric of mental hospitals the period marked a real practical recognition by the government of the need for extra provisions for people with intellectual disabilities. 1.25 million was allocated during the years for the creation of new residential centres for people with intellectual disabilities mainly to accommodate children.[86] The centres were nearly all operated by Catholic religious bodies which in some cases contributed substantially to their development – it being generally accepted that many of the orders such as the Daughters of Charity, the Brothers of Charity and the Brothers of St John of God already had a considerable amount of experience in looking after the people with intellectual disabilities which the statutory agencies lacked. The centres themselves were designed to avoid the characteristics of the Victorian institution and in general were planned as a complex of small single storey buildings which recognised the needs of the different degrees of severity of intellectual disability and facilitated courses of social training, physical activation and occupational habilitation. Education was provided for those who were "deemed" educable. Services were based almost entirely upon residential centres until 1957. Subsequently care, education and in some cases sheltered employment were provided in an increasing number of day centres. In Dublin these facilities were provided by St Michael's House and in Cork by the Cork Polio and General After-Care Association and in other parts of the country in day centres operated mainly by voluntary groups of parents and friends of people with intellectual disabilities.[87] In 1961 the National Association for the Mentally Handicapped of Ireland was formed from representatives of voluntary groups and continues to represent the interests of Irish people with intellectual disabilities at national and international level.

The Mental Treatment Act 1945

As time passed the need to change the mental hospital admission laws of 1867 became more pressing. More liberal legislation enacted in the United Kingdom in 1930 had been extended to Northern Ireland in 1932.[88] This legislation had introduced voluntary admissions and a procedure for the reception of patients on a voluntary basis following

---

[84] Public Charitable Hospitals (Amendment) Act 1931; Public Hospitals Act 1933.
[85] Between 1931 and 1935 less than £1.5 million was allocated to mental hospitals from sweepstake funds out of a total distribution of £35 million.
[86] Sheehan and De Barra, *Oispideil na hÉireann 1930–1955* (Dublin Hospitals Trust, 1940), pp.22–62 A report prepared in 1943 on the incidence of mental handicap by Dr Louis Clifford at the incidence of the Hospitals Commission served as a stimulus to the provision of the additional facilities.
[87] See Robins, *op. cit.*, Chap.13.
[88] 20 & 21 Geo. V, c.23; 22 & 23 Geo. V, c.15. (Northern Ireland).

an application by a relative. It was not until 1944 that change was considered at government level in Ireland. Dr Con Ward, parliamentary secretary to Sean McEntee, the Minister for Local Government and Public Health introduced the proposals which eventually became the Mental Treatment Act 1945. In 1947 a separate Minister for Health was appointed to the Cabinet which helped to strengthen the central administration and implementation of the new laws.[89]

The 1945 Act which is still in force despite the partial implementation of a new Mental Health Act 2001 repeals all the earlier unrepealed lunacy laws except those relating to offenders wtih mental disorder and wards of court. On the general administrative front it provides for the formation of mental hospital districts and the appointment of mental hospital authorities. It sets out the duties of mental hospital authorities regarding the provision of hospitals, treatment, maintenance advice and services. It provides for the financing of mental hospital authorities and the acquisition and disposal of land by them and the superannuation of their staff.

More specifically it introduces new admission and discharge procedures. In a complete departure from the process of committal on the order of two peace commissioners it bases the committal process entirely on medical certification. It introduces an informal procedure of voluntary admission and created two categories of detained patient; (a) the temporary patient, who requires up to six months treatment and is unsuitable for treatment as a voluntary patient and (b) "persons of unsound mind" who may be made the subject of indefinite detention. A legal duty is imposed on hospitals to discharge a recovered patient. Certain safeguards were built into the Act for the benefit of the patient. Among these were the appointment of visiting committees for hospitals; the right of a relative or friend to appeal to the Minister for the discharge of the patient and the right of any person to apply to the Minister for Health to have the patient examined by independent medical practitioners. The Inspector of Mental Hospitals is also given special powers to investigate and report suspected abuses of the detention provisions.

These changes in the law assisted in small part in bringing about a change in public perspectives on the mental hospital. The introduction of the concept of voluntary treatment in the procedures helped to challenge attitudinal and physical barriers. The change in perspective on the treatment of people with mental illness was also assisted by the development of psychotherapy as a method of understanding and correcting the distorted communicating process of the psychotic patient. However, the most significant change was effected by the discovery of the chlorpromazine group of drugs as a treatment for schizophrenia and other serious psychotic conditions and of anti-depressants such as imipramine and amitriptyline as an effective means of treating depression. The new chemotherapy made it possible to consider alternatives to the deep rooted policy of isolation and confinement. Out patient clinics increased in number and attendance. The first day hospitals aimed at helping patients to return to the community appeared. Changes in entitlement to free health services also assisted the process of removal of stigma by removing the long-time pauper associations of the mental hospital, placing it on the same basis as other hospitals and broadening eligibility for care.[90] Little by little there followed a decline in the mental hospital population.[91]

---

[89] Ministers and Secretaries (Amendment) Act 1946.
[90] Health Act 1953.
[91] See Robins, *op. cit.*, Chap.13.

Government Commissions of Enquiry (1965–1966) and other official reports

In 1965 and 1966 separate government commissions of inquiry reported on mental handicap and mental illness respectively. The Commission of Inquiry on Mental Handicap recommended the continuation of residential services for people with intellectual disabilities which were the concern mainly on religious and voluntary groups. It also emphasised the establishment of care and education services on a day basis. The report proposed and adopted new descriptive terminology – "mentally handicapped persons" classified according to intelligence quotient. The terms "idiot" and "imbecile" were accordingly discarded from official usage. The Commission of Inquiry on Mental Illness made wide ranging recommendations for non-institutional care and community support for people with mental illness. These included greater training in psychiatry in the curricula of medical schools the inclusion of short-term psychiatric units in general hospitals and planned and purposeful activity for long stay patients in psychiatric hospitals with a view to their rehabilitation and restoration to the community as soon as possible.

In 1970 the establishment of eight health boards to take over the operation of the health services in general from the local authorities facilitated further improvements in the whole area of healthcare. A network of services emerged outside the psychiatric hospital structures. Community psychiatric nursing services emerged which involved home visiting by nurses based in the local psychiatric hospital. Many of the larger general hospitals developed psychiatric units.

From the 1960s onwards residential accommodation and day facilities for persons with intellectual disability expanded considerably. With increasing attention being given to a policy of normalisation and integration of persons with intellectual disability the character of residential care changed to reflect a family setting. The religious and voluntary bodies already working in the area were joined by many others and by various local groups consisting largely of parents and friends of people with intellectual disability. In some instances in the absence of suitable voluntary organisations health boards established residential centres of their own.

On admission to the European Economic Community in 1973 Ireland gained access to financial support for the European Social Fund which facilitated the making of considerable improvements in services for the vocational training and social integration of people with intellectual disability and persons with long term mental illness.[92]

Health (Mental Services) Act 1981

In 1981 the Health (Mental Services) Act was passed with the aim of making "further and better provision for the regulation of the care and treatment of persons suffering from mental disorder" The Act required the written recommendation of two registered medical practitioners if a reception order was to be made[93] without a distinction in requirements between chargeable and private patients. Where a registered medical practitioner proposed to make a recommendation he was required to inform the person to whom it related of his intention.[94]

---

[92] See Robins, *op. cit.*, Epilogue, pp.205–207.
[93] Health (Mental Services) Act 1981, s.9.
[94] *Ibid.*, s.19(6).

The Act required the medical officer in charge of a psychiatric centre to give a person detained a copy of the reception order once made together with the recommendation for reception and a copy of any extension order. He was also required to give the patient a statement of his rights and entitlements under the Act.[95] He was further obliged to provide persons detained with the necessary facilities for writing delivering and posting of letters.[96]

Reception orders were stated to last for a period not exceeding 28 days. The order could only be extended on the order of two medical practitioners who have separately examined the person.[97]

The Act also established psychiatric review boards comprised of three members one medical, one legal and one lay, *inter alia*, to review the detention of persons under the Act.[98]

Although it passed all stages in the Oireachtas the 1981 Act was never implemented partly due to the resistance of members of the psychiatric profession to its implementation.

In 1984 the Department of Health Study Group on the Development of the Psychiatric Services published a report entitled "Planning for the Future" The report made detailed recommendations for a more comprehensive community oriented, sectorised and integrated service for mental health care.

The service was to be comprehensive because it is envisaged that it would cater for the differing needs of people with mental disorder. Its elements covered prevention and early identification; assessment, diagnostic and treatment services; inpatient care; day care; outpatient care; community based residences and rehabilitation and training. The idea was to provide such a service to meet the needs of a particular community and to situate the service within the community it served.

The main focus on this community oriented service was intended to be outpatient treatment and day care predicated on the principle that the patient had a right to be treated in his or her own community. The service was to be sectorised meaning that it would serve a population within a geographical boundary. A multi-disciplinary team would be based in each sector serving a population of 20–25,000 people. The final feature was that the new service would be integrated with general practitioners, community care and voluntary services. Where in-patient care was necessary it would be provided in general hospitals.

It was envisaged that the proposals would be funded by a diversion of current expenditure from institutional to community services. The Report's assumption that proper community based care was necessarily cheaper than institutional care and its initial premise that no additional expenditure will be required has been criticised as unrealistic[99] nonetheless the report has been cited as the psychiatric profession's programme for action whenever the issue of overdue legal reform is raised in Ireland.

In 1992 a Private Members Bill was presented to the Dail by Nuala Fennell T.D. with the aim of establishing a independent body to review cases of reported wrongful

---

[95] *Ibid.*, s.34.
[96] *Ibid.*, s.35.
[97] *Ibid.*, s.24.
[98] *Ibid.*, ss.37–39.
[99] See Kritik I., *Psychiatric Detention Civil Commitment in Ireland* (Baikonur, 1996), p.324.

detention and to repeal section 260 of the Mental Treatment Act 1945. The Bill however was defeated at the second stage.

Green Paper (1992) and White Paper (1995) on Mental Health

Green Paper on mental treatment law reform

In June 1992 the Department of Health published its Green Paper on Mental Health[100] with the dual aims of reviewing the progress that had been made in implementing the Report of the Study Group on the Development of the Psychiatric Services *Planning for the Future* and inviting submissions on reform of the Mental Treatment Act 1945 to keep pace with changes in psychiatry and developments in international law.

The main deficiency in the existing legislation was perceived to be the absence of review of the decision to detain by a body independent of the person taking the decision and the executive.[101] However the Government invited submissions on a number of matters including the wording of the criteria for detention which would be consistent with the *U.N. Principles for the Protection of Persons with Mental Illness and for the Improvement of Mental Health Care*; the definition of mental disorder; the places where people with mental disorder may be detained. It also invited responses to the question of whether there should be provisions in new legislation for the compulsory admission in limited circumstances of children without their parents consent. Further it indicated that it would welcome views as to who should initiate the application for involuntary admission and what is the most appropriate professional training for this role; whether a relative should be disqualified from making an application for the detention of a spouse where certain legal proceedings have been taken or are in train; whether there should be one or two medical recommendations accompanying an application for involuntary admission of a patient; whether recommending doctors should have formal training in psychiatry and whether special provision should be made to detain voluntary patients in hospital under certain circumstances.

Other issues which arose in the Green Paper and in relation to which responses were invited were whether new legislation should provide for an initial period of examination and assessment of detained patients of 48 hours or whether there should be one kind of treatment order for an initial period of seven days extendable to 28 days and the length of subsequent periods of detention; whether the review of the decision to detain a person should be the function of the courts or of an independent Mental Health Review Board; the criteria and procedures for the review of initial detention orders; the frequency of automatic review hearings of long-term detention.

Then the Green Paper dealt with the issue of consent and proposed that there be two types of treatment for mental disorder namely treatment requiring the patient's consent and a second medical opinion which would include psychosurgery and surgical implantation of hormones and treatment requiring consent *or* a second medical opinion which would include the administration of medication for mental disorder after a specified period of medication and electroconvulsive therapy. The Government invited views on

---

[100] Pl. 8918.
[101] See para.17.7.

whether such a scheme provided an adequate safeguard for patients and a workable scheme for practitioners.

Addressing the issue of the offender of mental disorder the Government invited views on whether the courts should be given powers to refer persons to psychiatric hospitals for assessment and/or treatment and if so, what measures should be included in new legislation to govern such referrals. It also welcomed views on what procedures should govern the transfer of patients from psychiatric hospitals to the special psychiatric centre in Dundrum.

The Government proposed the use of supervision order to protect persons with mental illness, severe mental handicap or severe mental infirmity living in the community and invited views on the value of supervision orders, the categories of people with mental disorder which such orders might cover and the procedures for making supervision orders which might be included in new legislation.

Following the terms of rights embodied in the *European Convention on Human Rights, Recommendation No. R(83) 2 of the Committee of Ministers to Member States concerning the legal protection of persons suffering from mental disorders placed as involuntary patients and the UN Principles for the Protection of Persons with Mental Illness and the Improvement of Mental Health Care* the Government invited views on whether procedures should be put in place to inform detained persons of their rights and the most appropriate way to provide this information and the manner in which legal aid and assistance should be provided for detained patients with inadequate means in hearings or appeals involving their detention.

Then addressing the issue of protection of the mentally disordered patient the Government invited views on the role and functions of the Inspectorate of Mental Health Services; the value of a code of practice for the care of the mentally disordered and the contents of any such code; the extent to which the right of mentally disordered persons to correspond and communicate should be limited; the rules which should govern the future use of seclusion and bodily restraint; and whether the provisions of the Clinical Trials Act 1987 are sufficient to safeguard the interests of mentally disordered patients.

Finally the Government invited views on the structure and composition of the proposed Mental Health Review Board; whether the Inspectorate of Psychiatric Services should be attached to the Department of Health or the proposed Mental Health Review Board and whether the post of clinical director for mental health services should have a statutory basis.

White Paper proposals for reform of mental treatment law

The submissions elicited in response to the Green Paper were embodied in a White Paper entitled *A New Mental Health Act*[102] in July 1995 which outlined the Governments proposals for reforming legislation which were designed to comply with Ireland's international obligations in the field of mental health law.

---

[102] Pn.1824.

New criteria for involuntary admission

Drawing on the *UN Principles for the Protection of Persons with Mental Illness and the Improvement of Mental Health Care* and *Council of Europe Recommendation (83)2 on the legal protection of persons suffering from mental disorder placed as involuntary patients* the White Paper made proposals for the criteria for involuntary admission to a psychiatric hospital. It provided that a person may be involuntarily admitted to an approved centre if he or she is suffering from a mental disorder and:

(a) because of that mental disorder there is a serious likelihood of that person causing immediate or imminent harm to himself/herself or to other persons; or

(b) that in the case of a person whose mental disorder is severe and whose judgement is impaired, failure to admit or detain a person is likely to lead to serious deterioration in his or her condition or will prevent the giving of appropriate treatment that can only be given by admission to an approved centre .

The White Paper also proposed a wide definition of mental disorder to include mental illness, significant mental handicap and severe dementia The Government proposed to exclude explicitly personality disorder, social deviance and addiction form the scope of the definition of mental disorder in the new legislation.[103]

Involuntary admission of children – Proposals for new procedures

It was proposed to provide in new legislation for the admission of a child to an approved centre without parental consent or against the wishes of the child, by means of a court order where the child meets the criteria for detention. There would be two kinds of court order, a treatment order permitting the examination, assessment and treatment of a child lasting twenty eight days and an emergency treatment order to allow the placement of a child under the care of an approved centre for a period of up to eight days. Extensions to both orders would be provided for. In both cases the judge would make the order on the basis of the recommendation of the consultant psychiatrist recommending treatment.[104]

Proposals relating to applicants for recommendation for involuntary admission

It was proposed to extend the range of persons who may make an application in respect of a person who appears to meet the criteria for involuntary admission to include (a) an authorised officer of a health board or a person authorised to act in this capacity who is not employed directly in the mental health services at the request of a spouse or a relative or (b) an authorised officer of a health board who is not employed directly in the mental health services where a spouse or relative is unavailable, unwilling or disqualified from making an application.[105]

---

[103] Paras 2.18–2.20.
[104] Para.3.45.
[105] Para.3.11.

The Government proposed to provide in new legislation that the Garda Síochána might make an application for involuntary admission for a person who appeared to meet the criteria for detention where no spouse, relative or authorised officer of a health board was available or willing to make such an application.[106] The Government also proposed in new legislation to disqualify a spouse from making an application for the detention of his or her partner where the couple has separated or was in the process of separating or where an order has been sought or granted under the Family Law (Protection of Spouses and Children) Act 1981. If an application for detention was necessary in such circumstances it was envisaged that it could be initiated by an authorised officer of the health board.[107]

Proposals relating to medical recommendations

The Government stated that in new legislation each application for involuntary admission would be accompanied by one medical recommendation[108] and did not propose to make formal training in psychiatry a requirement of general medical practitioners making recommendations for involuntary admissions.[109]

Proposals relating to holding powers

Under the 1945 Act a person who is the subject of an application for a temporary patient reception order can be held for twelve hours in a hospital while a decision is being taken by the medical officer whether or not to make a reception order. It was proposed in the White Paper to repeat this twelve hour provision in the new Act.[110]

In the White Paper the Government also proposed to give nurses, authorised for this purpose by their employing authority the legal authority to hold a voluntary patient in an approved centre for up to six hours within which time the person had to be examined by a medical practitioner and to provide that a consultant psychiatrist could hold such a patient for a period of forty eight hours within which time procedures for detention had to be completed.[111]

Proposals relating to patient's absence with leave

It was proposed that provision would be made for granting detained patients absence with leave to which conditions might be attached in the interests of the person concerned or for the protection of other people. Any such conditions would be subject to review by the Mental Health Review Board.[112]

Provision was to be made for apprehending and returning to an approved centre a

---

[106] Para.3.12.
[107] Para.3.13.
[108] Para.3.17.
[109] Para.3.18.
[110] Para.3.27.
[111] Para.3.34.
[112] Para.3.36.

detained patient who has left without permission or who has absconded while on leave, by any medical or nursing staff of the centre in which he or she was detained, by an authorised officer of the health board or by a member of the Garda Síochána at the request of the clinical director within twenty eight days or the termination of the term of detention whichever is the sooner. The Garda Síochána at the request of the clinical director and accompanied by a member of the clinical team responsible for the patient would be authorised to enter a premises to apprehend a patient who has escaped or absconded and to return the patient to the approved centre.[113]

Proposals relating to length of period of detention of patient

The Government stated that new legislation would provide that persons involuntarily admitted might be detained for treatment under the new legislation for an initial period of up to twenty eight days. The initial period would be capable of being extended the consultant psychiatrist responsible for the care of the patient by a period of three months, followed by a period of six months and by periods of one year thereafter. The consultant psychiatrist would be obliged to discharge at any time a detained patient who has recovered sufficiently that he or she no longer meets the criteria for detention.[114]

Proposals relating to establishment of Mental Health Review Board

The Government further proposed to provide for the establishment of a Mental Health Review Board. The Board would be responsible for reviewing every initial decision to detain a patient in a psychiatric hospital and each decision to extend detention. The Board would also review by panel the detention of persons whose detention orders had been extended by one year and any subsequent orders for one year at two yearly intervals thereafter. The Board would arrange a hearing if a patient objected to a detention order or the extension of a detention order. The appeal would be heard by a panel consisting of a psychiatrist, lawyer and lay person appointed for each health board area. The Board's decisions could be appealed to the High Court.[115]

Proposals relating to change of law regarding consent to psychiatric treatment

The Government also proposed to provide for new conditions for all mentally disordered patients in relation to consent to irreversible treatments such as psycho-surgery, consent to medication administered without consent after three months to detained patients and consent to electroconvulsive therapy ("ECT") where a detained patient is unable or unwilling to give consent. In the case of psycho-surgery such a procedure could only be carried out if two independent people one of whom had to be a medical practitioner certified that the patient understood the treatment and was capable of giving informed consent. The independent opinion would be given by persons appointed by the proposed Mental Health Review Board and acting on its behalf.

---

[113] Paras 3.39 and 3.48.
[114] Para.4.10.
[115] Para.5.23.

In relation to administration of medication to detained patients after three months without consent a second medical opinion to a treatment plan would be required. The person providing the second opinion would have to be satisfied that the patient lacked the capacity to give or withhold informed consent or that having regard to the patient's own safety or the safety of others the patient was unreasonably withholding such consent. He or she would also have to be satisfied that the treatment was in the best interests of the patient's health. In relation to the administration of ECT a similar second medical opinion would be required to be given by a consultant psychiatrist approved by the proposed Mental Health Review Board for this purpose and acting on its behalf. The approved consultant would be asked to approve a treatment plan for the administration of ECT to a patient who was unwilling or unable to give consent. If approved the treatment plan would permit a maximum of twelve administrations of ECT at no greater frequency than two or three times per week as recommended in the guidelines of the Royal College of Psychiatrists. Where consent was required it was proposed that it should be in writing wherever possible. It was proposed that there would be a right of appeal to the High Court by patients or persons acting on their behalf in relation to consent to treatment.[116]

Proposals regarding the mentally disordered offender and adult care orders

The White Paper also contained proposals in relation to Mentally Disordered Persons before the Courts and in Custody[117] and for the making of Adult Care Orders which could be used to protect mentally disordered persons who are being abused neglected or exploited.[118]

Proposals regarding patient's right to information

It was proposed that the clinical director of a member of staff to whom this function has been delegated would be required to inform patients who had been involuntarily admitted of the nature of their detention, the review procedure, their right to appeal, the nature of proposed treatment while detained; the nature of legal advice and aid available and the right of any detained patient to agree to treatment in the approved centre as a voluntary patient. The Government also proposed that the Scheme of Civil Legal Aid would be extended to include hearings of the Mental Health Review Board.[119]

Proposals relating to the Inspector of Mental Health Services

The Government stated that it intended to retain a system of inspection of the mental health services and to change the name of the Inspector of Mental Hospitals to the Commissioner of Mental Health Services. Quality assurance would remain central to the Commissioner's role and would be given a statutory basis in new legislation. The Commissioner would have a particular responsibility to review the quality of care of all

---

[116] Paras 6.12–6.16.
[117] Chap.7.
[118] Chap.8.
[119] Paras 9.4 and 9.9.

detained patients and long-stay mentally ill patients. Patients would be able to make complaints to the Commissioner who will be obliged to investigate them.

Proposals relating to code of practice for care of detained patients

The Government also proposed to provide in new legislation an obligation on the Minister for Health to publish a code of practice for the care of detained patients and to consult with interested parties in the preparation of the code.

Proposals relating to the patients' right to communicate

The Government further proposed to protect the right of detained patients to correspond and communicate with a lawyer, the authority responsible for his or her care and to send a letter unopened to the Minister for Health, the President of the High Court, the Registrar of Wards of Court, a health board or the Inspector of Mental Hospitals. The only restriction which might be permitted to a detained patient's right to communicate or correspond was, if a complaint is made to the clinical director of the approved centre by the person to whom the communication or letter was directed, that a threat has been made to the health or well-being of the person receiving the communication or correspondence or that of any other person and the clinical director considered that the complaint justified the restriction on the patient's right to communicate or correspond.[120]

Proposals relating to seclusion and restraint of patients

The Government indicated that it would redefine the grounds which justify the use of seclusion and physical restraint in regulations under new legislation.[121]

Proposals relating to participation of patients with mental illness in clinical trials

The Government recommended augmenting the safeguards provided under the Control of Clinical Trials Act 1987 by including in the new mental health legislation a condition that the participation of patients without the capacity to consent to clinical trials be approved by the proposed Mental Health Review Board and that the Board had to satisfy itself that there was a reasonable expectation of benefit direct or indirect to the patient's health.[122]

Proposals relating to patient's right to take civil proceedings to challenge lawfulness of detention

Finally the Government was of the view that the retention of section 260 of the Mental Treatment Act 1945 was warranted explicitly to protect persons engaged in acts

---

[120] Para.10.20.
[121] Paras 10.22 and 10.36.
[122] Paras 10.27 and 10.37.

undertaken in accordance with the terms of mental health legislation from vexatious legal actions. Accordingly it proposed that section 260 be retained and amended to read that a patient applying to the High Court would have to satisfy the court that there were "reasonable grounds" for contending that the person against whom the proceedings were to be brought acted in bad faith or without reasonable care.[123]

The Mental Health Act 2001

In July 8, 2001 the Mental Health Act 2001 was enacted and was to give effect to the proposals contained in the White Paper and consequently Ireland's obligations under the *UN Principles for the Protection of Persons with Mental Illness and the Improvement of Mental Health Care and Council of Europe Recommendation (83) 2 on the legal protection of persons suffering from mental disorder placed as involuntary patients.*

The provisions of the Act are discussed in detail in the Chapters which follow. What is of interest at this point is the fact that the Act is promulgated as a measure which embraces the human rights benchmarks posited in international instruments. As such it invites close scrutiny as to whether it has actually shed the paternalistic philosophies of the past and achieves its stated aims.

On December 16, 2004 the Health Act 2004 was enacted which provides for new management structures in the health service and in particular the establishment on January 1, 2005[124] of the Health Service Executive which as a single national entity will be responsible for the management of the health service including mental health services.

CONCLUSION

It is true to say that the philosophy of the law has progressed significantly from the days of incarceration and control of "lunatics" as a matter of public order when the issue of rights was considered anathema in the light of the "problem" to be solved. It has moved from this stage to a welfare philosophy where the state's intervention was perceived as benign and as in the interests of the welfare of the person with person with mental illness so that the issue of rights was considered irrelevant. Now it is faced with a new challenge that of acknowledging that the recognition of the rights of the person with mental illness is an essential ingredient of the ethical carer/patient relationship[125] and for encouraging full participation of people with mental disability in society as a whole.

---

[123] Para.10.38.

[124] Health Act 2004, s.6; Health Act 2004 (Establishment Day) Order 2004 (S.I. No. 885 of 2004).

[125] Cooney & O'Neill state: "The better view of law and psychiatry is that they share certain basic values. ... Mental health law ... reflects the obligations and duties which carers have to patients or health care service users. ... The concept of a right is pivotal here. It is an ethical and legal concept." See Kritik I., *op. cit.*, p.24.

THE ORGANISATION OF THE PSYCHIATRIC HEALTH AND HOSPITAL SERVICES

The nature of the public health services available to people with mental illness[126]

Public Health Services including public psychiatric services in the state are currently provided by the Health Service Executive established under the Health Act 2004. Traditionally, the Health Boards which preceded the establishment of the Executive divided their work into three broad programmes. These were (a) a general hospital programme comprising in-patient, day care and acute hospital services, and (b) special hospital programme which covered in-patient and out-patient hospital care for the people with mentally illness and intellectual disability, (c) a community care programme, comprising (i) community health services including general practitioner services and community nursing services, (ii) welfare services which include financial support by way of a range of income maintenance schemes; (iii) community support services such as home helps; Responsibility for the administration of each of these programmes was in the charge of a programme manager.

More recently new management arrangements have been developed and regional managers have been appointed provide of services to a population of known size within geographical boundaries. Alternatively managers have been appointed to focus on particular target groups such as services for the elderly and addiction services. Health boards have however continued to provide (a) Hospital Care Services (comprising Acute and Mental Health Hospital Services), and (b) Community Care Services under the direction of Programme Managers for people with mental illness. It remains to be seen whether the newly established Health Service Executive will continue with these management arrangements.

The legislative basis for the establishment and monitoring of psychiatric hospital services

Hospitals established under the Mental Treatment Act 1945 The basic administrative structure of the psychiatric hospital services was contained in the Mental Treatment Act 1945. This Act divides[127] the state into mental hospital districts administered by local mental hospital authorities. It also recognised certain private institutions for the purposes of the provision of psychiatric care.

The mental hospital authorities were obliged to provide treatment, maintenance advice and services to persons with mental illness who were resident in their district where such persons were unable to afford the full cost.[128] They were also obliged to provide proper and sufficient accommodation for carrying out their functions under the Act[129] and in particular to provide and maintain a district mental hospital for their mental hospital district.[130] The chief medical officer of the district mental hospital was to be

---

[126] For a general critique of health service provision for people with disabilities see *Towards Best Practice in Provision of Health Services for People with Disabilities in Ireland* (National Disability Authority, November 2003).

[127] Mental Treatment Act 1945, s.14.

[128] Mental Treatment Act 1945, repealed by the Health Act 1970, s.3.

[129] Mental Treatment Act 1945, s.20.

[130] *Ibid.*, s.21.

known as the resident medical superintendent.[131] The mental hospital authority had a duty to carry on their district mental hospital and all other institutions and accommodation maintained by them under Part V of the Act in a proper manner.[132]

The system of registration of institutions currently in operation under the Mental Treatment Act 1945 The Mental Treatment Act 1945 also currently provides for a system of registration of private institutions, private charitable institutions, the recognition of authorised institutions and the approval by order of institutions to be known as approved institutions.

A private institution is defined as an institution or premises in which one or more persons of unsound mind is or are taken care of for profit, not being (a) district mental hospital or other institution maintained by a mental hospital authority (a) private charitable institution, or (c) an authorised institution.[133]

A private charitable institution is defined as an institution for the care of persons of unsound mind which is supported wholly or partly by voluntary contributions and which is not kept for profit by any private individual, not being (a) a district mental hospital or other institution maintained by a mental hospital authority, or (b) an authorised institution.[134]

An authorised institution is defined as an institution authorised by special Act or other enactment (including a charter) for the care, maintenance and treatment of person of unsound mind not being the Central Mental Hospital.[135]

An approved institution is defined as an institution or premised approved of by order of the Minister under section 158 of the Mental Treatment Act 1945.[136] Under section 158 the Minister may by order approve of any institution or premises as an institution or premises for the reception of persons as temporary patients and/or for the reception of persons as voluntary patients.

The 1945 Act provides for the registration of private institutions.[137] The Act provides that it is not be lawful for any person to carry on a private institution unless it is registered in the register and such person is the registered proprietor thereof.[138] The Act also sets out the grounds for the refusal[139] of registration and the removal[140] of such institutions from the register. The Act also provides for the making of regulations governing the carrying on of private institutions.[141] The Act contains similar provisions in relation to private charitable institutions.[142]

Where authorised institutions are concerned the Minister for Health and Children has power by order to require the person carrying on the institution to do such things

---

[131] Mental Treatment Act 1945, s.94.
[132] *Ibid.*, s.28.
[133] *Ibid.*, s.3.
[134] *Ibid.*, s.3.
[135] *Ibid.*, s.3.
[136] *Ibid.*, s.3.
[137] *Ibid.*, Pt X.
[138] *Ibid.*, s.113.
[139] *Ibid.*, ss.119 and 120.
[140] *Ibid.*, s.121.
[141] *Ibid.*, s.132.
[142] *Ibid.*, s.10.

and take certain steps in the event that (a) the person in charge of the institution is not fit for that position; (b) the persons of unsound mind taken care of in that institution are not under the observation of a registered medical practitioner approved of by the Minister; (c) that the food given to such persons is unsuitable or inadequate; (d) that the number of such persons is too great having regard to the size of the premises of the institution, and (e) that the premises of the institution require repair.[143] Where there is a contravention of the order the person carrying on the institution is guilty of an offence[144] and where there is a conviction for an offence the Minister has power by order to require that the authorised institution not be used after a specified date for the care, maintenance and treatment of persons of unsound mind and if it is so used the person carrying on the institution is guilty of an offence.[145]

Where approved institutions are concerned the 1945 Act provides that no person may be received as a temporary patient or as a voluntary patient in an institution or premises unless the institution or premises is or are approved of under Part XIII of the Act for the reception of temporary or voluntary patients.[146] The Minister for Health and Children is also empowered to make regulations governing the carrying on of approved institutions.[147]

Administrative changes brought about by Health Act 1970 The Health Act 1970 empowered the Minister for Health to establish eight health boards which have been responsible for the administration of the public health services including public psychiatric services in the state since April 1971. The Act empowered the Minister to define the functional area of each health board and to specify its membership.[148]

The Mental Treatment Acts (Adaptation) Order 1971,[149] made by the Minister for Health pursuant to section 82 of the Health Act 1970, purported to amend the Mental Treatment Act 1945 and to transfer authority for the administration of the psychiatric services from the mental health authorities to the health boards with effect from April 1, 1971 by providing that any reference in the Mental Treatment Acts 1945 to 1966 to a mental hospital authority shall be construed as a reference to a health board in its capacity as an authority performing functions under those Acts.[150] References in those Acts to a mental hospital district are, according to the order, to be construed as a reference to the functional area of the health board[151] and references to a district mental hospital as a reference to a district mental hospital maintained or designated as such by a health board under section 38 of the Health Act 1970.[152]

---

[143] Mental Treatment Act 1945, s.156.
[144] *Ibid.*, s.156(2).
[145] *Ibid.*, s.157.
[146] *Ibid.*, s.159.
[147] *Ibid.*, s.161.
[148] Health Act 1970, s.4(1).
[149] S.I. No.108 of 1971.
[150] Mental Treatment Acts (Adaptation) Order 1971 (S.I. No.108 of 1971), art.4(2).
[151] *Ibid.*, art.4(3).
[152] *Ibid.*, art.4(1).

Administrative changes brought about by Health Act 2004 On January 1, 2005 under the terms of the Health Act 2004[152a] the health boards were dissolved and responsibility for the management and delivery of the health services was assigned to one governing body, the Health Service Executive. Whereas the administration of the health services was previously carried out by seven health boards, three area health boards and the Eastern Regional Health Authority the Health Service Executive administrative system is organised more simply. It has four regional divisions: Western, Southern, Dublin North-East and Dublin/Mid-Leinster with headquarters in Galway city, Cork city, Kells Co. Meath and Tullamore Co. Offaly. These regional centres are designed to help co-ordinate services delivered through local offices around the country.

The chief executive officer of the Health Service Executive has responsibility for the day-to-day administration of the business of the Executive. In addition he may be delegated authority from the Executive to perform other functions. Policy decisions on services and expenditure are however the responsibility of the Executive.

New system of registration under the Mental Health Act 2001 The Mental Health Act 2001 (not yet brought fully into force) repeals the 1945 Act with its distinctions between private institutions, private charitable institutions, authorised institutions and approved institutions and requires that "centres" i.e. hospitals or other in-patient facility for the care and treatment of persons suffering from mental illness or mental disorder be registered as "approved centres". It also provides that a person may not carry on a centre unless the centre is registered and the person is the registered proprietor thereof.[153] A person who carries on a centre in contravention of this provision is guilty of an offence[154] and is liable on summary conviction to a fine not exceeding £1,500 (€1,904.61) or to imprisonment for a term not exceeding 12 months or to both, (b) on conviction on indictment to a fine not exceeding £50,000 (€63,486.90) or to imprisonment for a term not exceeding two years or to both.[155]

The Mental Health Commission is obliged to establish and maintain a Register of Approved Centres.[156] The Register must be available for inspection free of charge by members of the public at all reasonable times.[157]

An application for registration must be in a form specified by the Commission.[158] The Commission may request an applicant for registration or, as the case may be, a registered proprietor to furnish it with such information as it considers necessary for the purposes of its functions under Part V of the 2001 Act. A person who, whether in

---

[152a] See Health Act 2004, s.6; Health Act 2004 (Establishment Day) Order 2004 (S.I. No. 885 of 2004).

[153] Mental Health Act 2001, s.63(1).

[154] *Ibid.*, s.63(2).

[155] *Ibid.*, s.68.

[156] *Ibid.*, s.64(1). The particulars entered on the Register in respect of each centre are the name of the person, by whom it is carried on, the address of the premises in which it is carried on, a statement of the number of patients who can be accommodated in the centre, the date on which the registration is to take effect and such other particulars as may be prescribed. See Mental Health Act 2001, s.64(2).

[157] Mental Health Act 2001, s.64(2)(b).

[158] *Ibid.*, s.64(7).

pursuance of a request or otherwise furnishes information to the Commission for the purposes of Part V of the Act that is false or misleading in a material particular shall be guilty of an offence unless s/he shows that, at the time the information was furnished to the Commission, s/he was not aware that it was false or misleading in a material particular.[159]

When an application is made to it by a person who proposes to carry on an approved centre the Commission has discretion as to whether to register the centre.[160] Where the centre is registered the period of registration is three years from the date of registration.[161] Where the Commission registers a centre it must issue a certificate of registration to the registered proprietor of the centre.[162]

The registered proprietor of a centre who proposes to carry on a centre immediately after the expiration of the period of registration of the centre may apply under section 64(3) of the Act to the Commission for registration of the centre not less than two months before the expiration of the period of registration. If the Commission does not notify him/her that it proposes to refuse to register the centre before the expiration of the period of registration then it must register the centre and its date of registration shall be the day following the day of the expiration of the period of registration.[163]

Section 64(10)(a)(i) provides that where an approved centre commences to be carried on by a person other than the registered proprietor the centre thereupon ceases to be registered. The person other than the registered proprietor must apply not later than four weeks after the commencement to the Commission for the registration of the centre, if he or she has not done so before the commencement.[164] A person who does not do so commits an offence.[165] If the application for registration is duly made and is not refused then during the period from the commencement until the centre is registered the centre shall be deemed to be registered and any conditions attached to the previous registration shall be deemed to be attached to the registration.[166] If the application is granted the date of registration of centre shall be the day following the day the centre ceases to be registered under section 64(10)(a)(i).[167]

The Commission has the power to refuse to register,[168] and to remove[169] a centre from the register and to attach conditions to the registration.[170]

The Commission may not refuse to register a centre in relation to which an application for registration has been duly made.[171] In addition it may not remove a centre from the Register unless (i) it is of opinion that (a) the premises to which the application or as the

---

[159] Mental Health Act 2001, s.64(7).
[160] *Ibid.*, s.64(3)(a).
[161] *Ibid.*, s.64(3)(b).
[162] *Ibid.*, s.64(3)(c).
[163] *Ibid.*, s.64(9).
[164] *Ibid.*, s.64 (10)(a)(ii).
[165] *Ibid.*, s.64(10)(b).
[166] *Ibid.*, s.64(10)(a)(iii).
[167] *Ibid.*, s.64(10)(a)(ii).
[168] *Ibid.*, s.64(5).
[169] *Ibid.*, s.64(5).
[170] *Ibid.*, s.64(6).
[171] *Ibid.*, s.64(5).

case may be the registration relates does not comply with the registration, or (b) the carrying on of the centre will not be or is not in compliance with the regulations; (ii) the registered proprietor has been convicted of an offence under Part V[172] of the Act; (iii) the registered proprietor has failed or refused to furnish the Commission with information requested by it pursuant to section 64(8) or has furnished the Commission that is false or misleading in a material particular, or (iv) the registered proprietor has, not more than one year before the date from which the registration or removal from the register would take effect, contravened a condition imposed by the Commission under section 64(6).[173]

The Commission has power (i) at the time of registration or subsequently to attach to registration conditions in relation to the carrying on of the centre concerned and such other matters as it considers appropriate having regard to its functions under Part V of the Act, (ii) to attach different conditions to the registration of different centres, and (iii) to amend or revoke a condition of registration.[174]

Without prejudice to its general power to impose conditions, conditions attached to the registration of a centre may (i) require the carrying out of essential maintenance or refurbishment of a centre or specified areas within a centre; (ii) require the closure, temporarily or permanently of a specified area or areas within a centre; (iii) specify the maximum number of residents[175] who may be accommodated in a centre or in a specified area or areas within a centre; (iv) specify the minimum number of staff required to be employed in a centre; (v) require the introduction or review, as the case may be, of specified policies, protocols and procedures relating to the care and welfare of patients and residents and relating to the ordering, prescribing, storing and administration of medicines; (vi) specify measures to be taken to ensure that patients and residents are informed of their rights under the Mental Health Act 2001.[176]

Conditions imposed and amendments and revocations of conditions must be notified in writing to the registered proprietor of the centre concerned.[177] Where there is a contravention of a condition of registration in relation to an approved centre the registered proprietor shall be guilty of an offence.[178]

Where the Commission proposes to refuse to register a centre, to remove a centre from the register, to attach a condition to or amend or revoke a condition attached to a registration it must notify the applicant or registered proprietor as the case may be of its proposal and of the reasons for it.[179] A notification of such a proposal must include a statement that the person concerned may made representations to the Commission within 21 days of the receipt by him/her of the notification and a notification of the decision must also include a statement that the person concerned may appeal to the District Court under section 65 against the decision within 21 says from the receipt by him/her

---

[172] i.e. Mental Health Act 2001, ss.62–68.
[173] Mental Health Act 2001, s.64(5).
[174] *Ibid.*, s.64(6).
[175] "Resident" is defined by s.62 of the Mental Health Act 2001 as a person receiving care and treatment in a centre. The definition clearly encompasses both voluntary and involuntary patients.
[176] Mental Health Act 2001, s.64(6)(b).
[177] *Ibid.*, s.64(6)(c).
[178] *Ibid.*, s.64(13).
[179] *Ibid.*, s.64(11)(a).

of the notification.[180] A person who has been notified of such a proposal may, within 21 days of receipt of the notification make representations in writing to the Commission and the Commission is obliged: (i) before deciding the matter to take into consideration any representations duly made to it under this paragraph in relation to the proposal, and (ii) notify the person in writing of its decision and of the reasons for it.[181]

Section 65 of the Act provides that the registered proprietor or, as the case may be the person intending to be the registered proprietor of an approved centre may appeal to the District Court[182] against a decision of the Commission to refuse to register the centre, to remove the centre from the register or to attach a condition, or to amend or revoke a condition attached to the registration of a centre. The appeal must be brought within 21 days of the receipt by the person of the notification of the decision by the Commission under section 64.[183]

The Commission must be given notice of an appeal under section 65 and shall be entitled to appear, be heard and adduce evidence on the hearing of the appeal.[184]

The District could has a discretion as it thinks proper to register or to restore the registration of the centre, to withdraw the condition or the amendment to or revocation of a condition, to attach a specified condition to the registration or to make a specified amendment to a condition of the registration.[185] A decision of the District Court under section 65 on a question of fact shall be final.[186]

Where a notification is given then (with the exception of a decision to refuse to register a centre which was not registered or deemed to be registered at the time of a relevant application for registration) during such period from the notification as the Commission considers reasonable and which is not less than 21 days the centre shall be treated as if the decision had not been made and if the decision was to refuse an application for registration under section 64(10)(a) it shall be treated as if it had been registered and the registration had attached to it any conditions attached to the relevant registration that had ceased by virtue of section 64(10)(a) (i).[187]

If an appeal against the decision of the Commission is brought under section 65 then (i) during the period from the end of the period mentioned in the previous paragraph until the determination or withdrawal of the appeal or any appeal therefrom or from any such appeal and (ii) such further period as the court concerned considers reasonable and specifies in its decision the centre shall (a) be treated for the purposes of section 64 as if the appeal had been upheld and (b) if the appeal was against a decision of the Commission to refuse an application for registration under section 64(10)(a) it shall be treated as if the registration had attached to it any conditions attached to the relevant registration that had ceased by virtue of section 64(10)(a)(i).[188]

---

[180] Mental Health Act 2001, s.64(12).

[181] *Ibid.*, s.64(11)(b).

[182] The jurisdiction conferred on the District Court by s.65 must be exercised by the judge of the District Court for the time being assigned to the district court district in which the centre concerned is situated. See Mental Health Act 2001, s.65(2).

[183] Mental Health Act 2001, s.65(1).

[184] *Ibid.*, s.65(5).

[185] *Ibid.*, s.65(1).

[186] *Ibid.*, s.65(3).

[187] *Ibid.*, s.65(4)(a).

[188] *Ibid.*, s.65(4)(b).

Promulgation of standards for approved centres under the Mental Health Act 2001 General obligations regarding the administration of the psychiatric services are contained in the Health Act 1970 and Mental Health Act 2001, but the more detailed rules are to be found regulations made by the Minister for Health and Children, in guidelines and directives issued by the Department of Health and Children and Children and decisions of the Health Service Executive and other executive agencies. For instance section 66 of the 2001 Act (which has yet to be brought into force) empowers the Minister for Health and Children, after consultation with the Mental Health Commission, to make such regulations as he or she thinks appropriate in relation to such centres for the purpose of ensuring proper standards in relation to centres including adequate and suitable accommodation, food and care for residents while being maintained in centres and the proper conduct of centres.[189]

Without prejudice to the generality of this power regulations under section 66 may:

(a) prescribe requirements as to the maintenance, care and welfare of residents,

(b) prescribe requirements as to the staffing including requirements as to the suitability of members of staff of centres,

(c) prescribe requirements as to the design, maintenance, repair, cleaning and cleanliness, ventilation, heating and lighting of centres,

(d) prescribe requirements as to the accommodation provided in centres,

(e) prescribe requirements as to the establishment and maintenance of a register of residents,

(f) prescribe requirements as to the records to be kept in centres and for the examination and copying of any such records or of extracts therefrom by the Inspector,

(g) prescribe requirements as to the drawing up and carrying out by centres, so far as practicable, in consultation with each resident of an individual care plan for that resident including the setting of appropriate goals,

(h) prescribe requirements as to the information to be provided to the Inspector of Mental Health Services,

(i) provide for the enforcement and execution of regulations by the Commission.[190]

Where there is a failure or refusal to comply with the regulations in relation to a centre the registered proprietor shall be guilty of an offence.[191] In addition a person who fails or refuses to comply with the regulations shall be guilty of an offence.[192]

By virtue of section 66(4) where a person is convicted of an offence under section 66 the Circuit Court[193] may, on application of the Commission which is brought not more than six months after the conviction or where there is an appeal against the conviction the final determination of the appeal or of any further appeal (if it is a

---

[189] Mental Health Act 2001, s.66(1).
[190] *Ibid.*, s.66(2).
[191] *Ibid.*, s.66(3)(a).
[192] *Ibid.*, s.66(3)(b).
[193] The jurisdiction conferred on the Circuit Court by s.66(4) must be exercised by the judge of the Circuit Court for the time being assigned to the circuit in which the premises concerned are situated. See s.66(4)(e).

determination affirming the conviction) or the withdrawal of any such appeal therefrom, by order declare that the person shall be disqualified during such period as may be specified in the order from carrying on the centre to which the conviction related or, at the discretion of the court from carrying on any centre.[194] A person in respect of whom such a disqualifying order is made shall not during the period specified in the order carry on the centre specified in the order or, if the order so specifies, any centre.[195] A person who contravenes this prohibition shall be guilty of an offence.[196] Notice of an application by the Commission under section 66(4) must be given to the person convicted of the offence concerned and he or she shall be entitled to appear, be heard and adduce evidence on the hearing of the application.[197]

A person who wilfully obstructs or interferes with the Inspector of Mental Health Services in the performance of functions under the regulations or who fails or refuses to comply with a requirement of the Inspector under such regulations will be guilty of an offence.[198]

A person guilty of an offence under Part V of the Act shall be liable (a) on summary conviction, to a fine not exceeding £1,500 (€1,904.61) or to imprisonment for a term not exceeding 12 months or to both or (b) on conviction on indictment to a fine not exceeding £50,000 (€6,3486.90) or to imprisonment for a term not exceeding 2 years or to both.[199]

The Central Mental Hospital

Prior to 1800 people acquitted on the grounds of insanity were released back into the community. As a result of the Criminal Lunatics Act of that year they began to be detained in prisons and this practice continued until 1821 when provision was made for the transfer of insanity acquittees to district asylums as accommodation became available. This transfer arrangement was criticised on the grounds that offenders with mental disorder were a distinct group requiring specialised treatment. This criticism led to the passing of the Central Criminal Lunatic Asylum (Ireland) Act 1845 and to the establishment in 1850 of a special asylum for criminal lunatics in Dundrum. The hospital's name was changed to the Central Mental Hospital in 1961,[200] and in 1971 its administration was transferred from the Department of Health to the newly established Eastern Health Board.[201] With effect from 1 January 2005 the Health Act 2004 assigned the functions of the Eastern Health Board to the Health Service Executive.

The hospital contains a central secure unit for psychiatric patients, who for a short time during their illnesses need secure accommodation. It also houses a number of patients who have committed an indictable offence in another psychiatric hospital. It has a total population of approximately eighty patients. It is essentially a custodial institution and has largely continued in that vein.

---

[194] Mental Health Act 2001, s.66(4)(a).
[195] *Ibid.*, s.66(4)(b).
[196] *Ibid.*, s.66(4)(c).
[197] *Ibid.*, s.66(4)(d).
[198] *Ibid.*, s.66(5).
[199] *Ibid.*, s.68.
[200] Health (Mental Services) Act 1961, s.39.
[201] Health Act 1970, s.44 and the Central Mental Hospital Order 1971 (S.I. No.236 of 1971).

THE PSYCHIATRIC SERVICES IN PRACTICE – ADMINISTRATIVE ARRANGEMENTS

General duty of the Health Service Executive to provide psychiatric services

Under section 52 of the Health Act 1970 as amended by the Health Act 2004 the Health Service Executive is obliged to make in-patient services available to persons with full eligibility (Medical Card Holders) and persons with limited eligibility. The in-patient services, which must be made available within this obligation, are "institutional services provided for persons while maintained in a hospital, convalescent home or home[202] for persons suffering from physical or mental disability or in accommodation ancillary thereto."[203] The Health Service Executive is also obliged to provide in-patient services for children who are not within the category of people with full or limited eligibility where they are people with diseases and disabilities of a permanent or long-term nature, which are prescribed by the Minister for Health, and Children with the consent of the Minister for Finance.[204]

Under section 56 of the Health Act 1970,[205] as amended by the Health Act 2004 the Health Service Executive is obliged to make out-patient services available to persons with full eligibility and persons of limited eligibility. "Out patient services" is defined to mean "institutional services other than in-patient services provided at or by persons attached to[206] a hospital or home,[207] and institutional services provide at a laboratory, clinic, health centre or other similar premises." "Out patient services" does not include: (a) the giving of a drug, medicine or other preparation except where it is administered to the patient direct by a person providing the service or is for psychiatric treatment, or (b) dental, ophthalmic or aural services.[208] The Health Service Executive is further obliged to make out-patient services available without charge to children in respect of diseases and disabilities of a permanent or long term nature prescribed by the Minister for Health and Children with the consent of the Minister for Finance.[209] The Health Service Executive is further obliged to make out-patient services available to children in respect of defects notice at a health examination held pursuant to the services provided under

---

[202] If under s.52 the Health Service Executive makes available in-patient services in a home for persons suffering from a physical or mental disability which is a home registered under the Health Nursing Homes Act 1990 it must do so in accordance with the provisions of that Act and any regulations made under that Act. See Health (In-Patient Services) Regulations 1993 (S.I. No.224 of 1993), Art. 4.

[203] Health Act 1970, s.51.

[204] *Ibid.*, s.52.

[205] As amended by Health (Amendment) Act 1987 and Health (Amendment) Act 1991, s.56.

[206] S.56 provides for an out-patient service in the normal or ordinary sense of the words at or attached to hospitals or other institutions. It envisages the situation where a person who is otherwise resident at his or her home attends at a hospital, health centre, clinic or other institution to obtain such medical services as x-rays, dressing of minor wounds, clinical tests and the like. It does not provide for a care and maintenance service for a person in his own home. See *CK v. Northern Area Health Board*, unreported, Supreme Court, May 29, 2003, p. 26.

[207] "Home" in this context means "an institutional home, such as a convalescent home or disabled persons home as referred to in s.51 [of the Health Act 1970]". See *CK v. Northern Area Health Board* Supreme Court, May 29, 2003 p. 25.

[208] Health Act 1970, s.56(2) as substituted by Health (Amendment) Act 1987, s.1.

[209] Health Act 1970, s.56(3) as substituted by Health (Amendment) Act 1987, s.1.

section 66.[210] Section 56(5)[211] provides for the making of relevant regulations in relation to these services by the Minister including regulations for the imposition of charges for out-patient services including the giving of any drug, medicine or other preparation for persons who are not persons with full eligibility and are not children who are entitled to free services.

"Institutional services" are mentioned in the context of both "in-patient" and "out-patient" services i.e. in both sections 52 and 56 of the Act and are defined to "include (a) maintenance in an institution (b) diagnosis, advice and treatment at an institution; (c) appliances and medicines and other preparations, and (d) the use of special apparatus at an institution."[212]

The manner of the provision of psychiatric services

For the purpose of the provision of psychiatric services the Health Service Executive area is divided into catchment areas, which in turn are sub-divided into sectors. The designation of areas as sectors is influenced by the population density and demographic characteristics, by public transport networks and by the degree of urbanisation. In-patient public psychiatric services are provided both in psychiatric units attached to general hospitals and in specialist psychiatric hospitals administered by the Health Service Executive or in public voluntary hospitals,[215] which provide the services for persons resident within these catchment areas. Out-patient services in the community are also managed from these hospital bases and are provided on a sectorised basis.

Private psychiatric services are typically provided in private hospitals and clinics, which receive no funding from the state. However, some of the beds in private psychiatric hospitals may be used by public patients by arrangement with the Health Service Executive.

Typically the public psychiatric services are provided by a team comprising a consultant psychiatrist, registrar in psychiatry and psychiatric nurses with the consultant psychiatrist as its leader. In many areas the services of a psychologist, social worker and occupational therapist may also available. Each psychiatric team has responsibility for the provision of in-patient services, the provision of all the community psychiatric services in its sector and manages the out-patient clinics, day care and residential facilities in its sector.

The treatment options available as part of the services provided fall into two broad categories: (a) in-patient care usually within the psychiatric unit of a general hospital or in a psychiatric hospital and, (b) out-patient care which can include out patient clinics,

---

[210] Health Act 1970, s.56(4) as substituted by Health (Amendment) Act 1987, s.1. S.66 obliges the Health Service Executive to make available without charge at clinic, health centres and other prescribed places a health examination and treatment service for children under the age of six years.

[211] As substituted by the Health (Amendment) Act 1987 s.1.

[212] See Health Act 1947, s.2 The Health Act 1970, s.1(3) provides that the Health Acts 1947 to 1970 are to be construed as one.

[215] Public voluntary hospitals are hospitals most of whose income comes from the state. They may be owned by private bodies such as religious orders or incorporated by charter or statute and managed by boards appointed by the Minister for Health and Children.

day hospitals, day centres, home visits form the mental health team, referral to clinical psychological services, access to social work or occupational therapy services.

In-patient psychiatric care services In-patient care refers to psychiatric medical and nursing care provided in hospital. Typically a patient may be admitted to an acute admission ward for assessment and treatment of their condition. After treatment typically the patient will be discharged home and follow-up care is provided by the out-patients' clinic or day hospital.

However, some patients may be referred as appropriate to their needs to a:

(i)   continuing care ward;

(ii) a rehabilitation ward;

(iii) a care of the elderly unit; or

(iv) exceptionally to a special care unit or secure ward.

A continuing care ward is an in-patient facility, which offers care to patients with long-term mental illness. A small percentage of patients in this ward may be discharged to a residential unit. This unit may be used as a respite facility for patients in the community who have a need for respite care.

A rehabilitation ward aims to restore patients' everyday living skills and assist them to regain the independence to live in their own homes or a residential facility.

A care of the elderly unit is a specialised unit providing 24 hour care and treatment of patients usually over the age of 60 with a mental illness or associated problems. The environment is specifically designed to meet the needs of the elderly.

Occasionally it may be necessary to admit a patient to a special care unit or secure ward to care for and treat that patient when s/he presents with a mental illness, which gives rise to disturbed behaviour, which is unresponsive to treatment. The special care unit or secure ward is usually a small unit within a hospital setting staffed by psychiatric nurses. A special care unit provides a safe and restricted environment for the care and treatment of the patient's illness. The unit is locked and the environment is secure.

Out-patient psychiatric care services A number of out-patient community based psychiatric services have been developed within the scope of the hospital care services. They include:

(a) specialist out-patient clinic,

(b) day care facilities (including day hospitals, day centres, combined day facilities and mental health centres),

(c) community based residences, and

(d) community based workshops.

(a) Specialist out-patient clinics are typically attached to the Health Service Executive hospital. These clinics are attended mostly by appointment by people with mental illness from their homes or a care setting. The clinic provides assessment, diagnosis and treatment facilities for people with mental illness and follow-up or continuing

management of the person's mental illness. The clinics are staffed by a consultant psychiatrist, community psychiatric nurses and other members of a mental health team as required. The team is led by the consultant psychiatrist who has responsibility for the treatment of the patient both in hospital and in the community.

The community psychiatric nurse has an important role to play in the community oriented mental health service. The nurses are actually hospital based but act as liaison between the hospital, the consultant psychiatrist, the patients, their families and their general medical practitioner. They cover a geographical area and recently district co-ordination systems with team leaders have developed to facilitate integration of services and cooperative working. The responsibilities of the community psychiatric nurse include (a) family and patient support in the community, (b) crisis intervention, (c) monitoring out-patient long-term therapy in conjunction with day centres, out-patient clinics and the consultant psychiatrists, (d) liaising with general medical practitioners and responding to their requests for any of the aforementioned services.

(b) Day care facilities are available at a number of hospitals and other centres throughout the country. The main aim of day-care is to provide appropriate care and treatment at appropriate intervals to persons with mental illness without the necessity for admission to hospital. The care provided may include a planned treatment programme tailored to individual or group needs and the range of services, assessment and diagnosis, medication, psychotherapy including behaviour therapy, occupational therapy, social support and care, instruction and recreational activities and specialised services. There are four different types of day-care available.

Day hospitals, which provide intensive treatment for acutely ill patients, which is similar to that available to in-patients. They provide all the services available within the hospital to people attending on a daytime basis only. Accordingly people for whom in-patient care is either unnecessary, undesirable or unavailable may avail of a daily hospital service and simultaneously maintain residences in the community. The day hospital facilities are usually available five days a week. Transport is provided by the Health Service Executive for patients who require it.[216]

Day centres that provide social care for patients whose needs cannot otherwise be accommodated. The centres are staffed by psychiatric nurses and occasionally occupational therapists. They offer services such as rehabilitation, occupational therapy and social skills training.

Combined Day facilities may offer the combined services of a day hospital and a day centre.

Mental Health Centres, which provide treatment services similar to those offered in a day hospital but including a small number of twenty four hour, care beds for assessment and crisis intervention purposes. These beds may be in the mental health centre itself or in a house or supervised hostel nearby. The mental health centre provides services, which are similar to those available in a day centre including facilities for out-patient consultation. It may be used by the psychiatric team or by voluntary groups to provide social activities for patients in the evening or for general educational purposes.

---

[216] In some cases patients are required to contribute to the cost of the transport.

(c) Community based residences are also increasing in numbers. These are provided for people with long term mental illness who need medical and other community supports to enable them to live in the community. The Inspector of Mental Hospitals refers to these units as group homes. These may typically be high, medium low support residences.

High support residences cater for people with mental illness who do not need to be in hospital and who can live in the community but who require 24 hour nursing care and support for a variety of reasons. A person with mental illness may spend a period of time in a high support residence and then move on into a medium or low support residence.

Medium support residences cater for people with mental illness who are relatively independent in most areas of their everyday living skills but require some assistance and support in certain areas such as managing finances or cooking skills. The home is typically staffed by a nurse or trained care staff on a daytime basis only.

Low support residences cater for people with mental illness who are independent in most if not all areas of their everyday living skills. The hospital management co-ordinates the overall upkeep and management of the home. A psychiatric nurse or supervisor may be available to be consulted by residents.

(d) Community or sheltered workshops, which aim to enable people with mental illness to work in areas, suited to their skills or needs with support and guidance from trained staff. A person with mental illness may have access to these workshops either from home or in a hospital setting. Some psychiatric hospitals have industrial therapy units, which cater primarily for in-patients.

Care for people with mental infirmity – nursing homes

Nursing homes are designed to provide care and maintenance for persons who require assistance with the activities of daily living by reason of physical or mental infirmity.[217] All nursing homes must be registered by the Health Service Executive, which keeps a list of registered nursing homes available to the public free of charge.[218]

Standards of care in nursing homes The standards of care which must be complied with in nursing homes is set out in the Nursing Homes (Care and Welfare) Regulations 1993.[219] These prescribed standards cover nursing and medical care, occupational and recreational facilities, privacy, information on current affairs, religious facilities, visits, staffing levels, accommodation and facilities, safety and design, kitchen facilities, hygiene and sanitary facilities and nutrition. A contravention of these Regulations is an offence.[220]

The Regulations introduce the concept of a contract of care between the nursing home and the person cared for.[221] This must set out the care and welfare of that person and include details of the services to be provided and the fees to be charged. It must be provided to each person within two months of admission to the nursing home.

---

[217] Health (Nursing Homes) Act 1990, ss.1 and 2.
[218] *Ibid.*, ss.3 and 4.
[219] *Ibid.*, s.6 and Nursing Homes (Care and Welfare) Regulations 1993 (S.I. No. No.226 of 1993).
[220] *Ibid.*, ss.6(3), 11 and 12.
[221] Nursing Homes (Care and Welfare) Regulations 1993 (S.I. No. 226 of 1993), art.7.

A person in a nursing home or somebody acting on his or her behalf may make a complaint to the Health Service Executive in relation to any matter concerning the home or the maintenance, care and welfare and well being of the person.[222] The Executive must investigate the complaint and the proprietor of the person in charge of the nursing home must be notified. If the complaint is upheld the Health Service Executive can direct the nursing home to take specified action in relation to the complaint and the proprietor must comply with this. The Health Service Executive must notify the person in the nursing home of the outcome of the complaint.

Entitlement of nursing home subvention The Health (Nursing Homes) Act 1990, and the Nursing Homes (Subvention) Regulations 1993 introduced a new scheme of entitlement to nursing home care and subventions.[223] Section 7 of the 1990 Act provides for an assessment of dependency of the person and his/her means and circumstances to be carried out by the Health Service Executive on the basis of which the Health Service Executive forms an opinion of the person's need for maintenance and whether s/he is able to pay the costs of such maintenance. If the Executive forms an opinion that the person is in need of maintenance in a nursing home and is unable to pay any or part of the costs of maintenance it may, subject to the compliance by the home with any requirements made by the Executive, pay to the home such amount in respect of the person's maintenance as it considers appropriate having regard to the degree of dependency and the means and circumstances of the person. While section 7 appears to contemplate solely a system of assessment to nursing home subventions, the Nursing Homes (Subvention) Regulations 1993 made under section 7 provide not only for this assessment but also for a system of assessment of access to public nursing homes and private subvented care.

Under the Nursing Homes (Subvention) Regulations 1993 as amended by the Health Act 2004 applications for a subvention must be made to the Health Service Executive before a person's admission to a nursing home. To qualify for a subvention the applicant must be: (a) sufficiently dependent to require maintenance in a nursing home, and (b) be unable to pay any or part of the cost of maintenance in the home. Dependency refers to the level of physical and mental dependency of a person applying for a subvention in relation to the person's need for assistance with the activities of daily living such as

---

[222] *Ibid.*, art.26.
[223] Cousins makes the point that the 1990 Act did not change the fact that nursing home care falls within the definition of "in-patient services" which people were entitled to, (either free, if they were entitled to a medical card or subject to limited charges which could not exceed a person's income) up to September 1, 1993 and continued to be entitled to under s.52 of the Health Act 1970 after that date. He refers to the fact that the Minister for Health recognising this difficulty made the Health (In-Patient Services) Regulations 1993 (S.I. No.224 of 1993) which purport to amend s.52 of the Health Act 1970 so that nursing home services provided under the Health Acts must be provided in accordance with the Health (Nursing Homes) Act 1990 and the regulations made thereunder – entitlement being subject to assessment and additional means testing under that Act and those regulations. Cousins makes the point that "these [Health (In-Patient Services)] Regulations are almost certainly unconstitutional as an attempt by the Minister to amend the primary legislation contrary to article 15.2.1 of the Constitution" (at p.18) and cites *Cooke v. Walsh* [1984] I.R. 710 in support of his point. See "The Health (Nursing Homes) Act 1990", *Law Society Gazette* (January/February 1994), p.15.

dressing, eating, walking, washing and bathing arising from physical or mental infirmity.[224] The Regulations establish three levels of dependency; medium,[225] high[226] and maximum.[227] Each applicant is assessed by the Health Service Executive. This must include an evaluation of the ability of the person to carry out the tasks of daily living, of the level of social support available to the person and of his or her medical condition. On the basis of this assessment the Executive will either offer public accommodation or assess entitlement to subvention.

An assessment of means must also be carried out. Means are the applicant's income and the imputed value of his or her assets and the income and value of the assets of the spouse.[228]

The rates of subvention vary depending on the level of dependency,[229] and the Health Service Executive has a discretion to reduce or increase the amount depending on the outcome of the assessment of means and the extent to which the assessed means of the person are lower than or exceed the rate of the weekly rate payable at the time of the Old Age Non-Contributory Pension.[230] If the person applying for the subvention is dissatisfied with a decision in relation to means and circumstances s/he may appeal to an appeals officer appointed by the Minister for Health. The appeal must be made within 28 days of receiving the notification of the decision. Decisions of the appeal officer are subject to review by the Ombudsman. There is, however, no appeal in relation to the medical aspects i.e. as to the existence of or level of dependency.

Under the Nursing Homes (Subvention) Regulations 1993, as amended,[231] the Health

---

[224] Health (Nursing Homes) Act 1990, s.1.

[225] Medium dependency describes a person whose independence is impaired to the extent that s/he requires nursing home care because the appropriate support and nursing care required by the person cannot be provided in the community. His or her mobility would be impaired to the extent that s/he would require supervision or a walking aid. See Nursing Home (Subvention) Regulations 1993 (S.I. No.227 of 1993), sch.1, para.17(a).

[226] High dependency describes a person whose independence is impaired to the extent that s/he needs nursing home care but who is not bed bound. The person may have a combination of physical and mental disabilities, may be confused at times and be incontinent. He or she may require a walking aid and physical assistance to walk. See Nursing Home (Subvention) Regulations 1993 (S.I. No.227 of 1993), sch.1, para.17(b).

[227] Maximum dependency describes a person whose independence is impaired to the extent that s/he requires constant nursing care. The person is likely to have very restricted mobility, require assistance with all aspects of physical care or be confused, disturbed and incontinent. See Nursing Homes (Subvention) Regulations 1993 (S.I. No.227 of 1993), sch.1, para.17(c).

[228] Nursing Homes (Subvention) Regulations 1993 (S.I. No.227 of 1993), Art.8 and sch.2. There are a number of asset and income disregards set out in the Regulations and if the applicants asset exceeds that set by an asset value ceiling set by the Regulations subvention will not be paid. See also Nursing Homes (Subvention) (Amendment) Regulations 1998 (S.I. No.498 of 1998), Nursing Homes (Subvention) (Amendment) Regulations 1998 (S.I. No.498 of 1998).

[229] See Nursing Homes (Subvention) (Amendment) Regulations 2001 (S.I. No.89 of 2001); sch.4 as amended by Nursing Homes (Subvention) (Amendment) Regulations 2001 (S.I. No.89 of 2001). The current maximum weekly rate of subvention for medium dependency is €114.30, for high dependency is €152.40 and for maximum dependency is €190.50.

[230] Nursing Homes (Subvention) Regulations (S.I. No.227 of 1993), art.10 as amended by the Nursing Homes (Subvention) (Amendment) Regulations 1998 (S.I. No.498 of 1998), art.4.

[231] (S.I. No.227 of 1993), art.17.1 as amended by the Nursing Homes (Subvention) (Amendment) Regulations 1996 (S.I. No.225 of 1996), art.2.

Service Executive having determined that a person qualifies for a subvention may instead of paying that subvention offer that person accommodation in a Health Service Executive institution providing nursing care within the Executive's functional area.

Further under the Nursing Homes (Subvention) Regulations 1993 as amended,[232] the Health Service Executive may enter into an arrangement with a registered nursing home to provide in-patient services under section 52 of the Health Act 1970. This arrangement must be considered to be in accordance with the 1993 Regulations for as long as the home is registered. In making the arrangement the Health Service Executive has a discretion to pay a rate of subvention exceeding the maximum rate payable in respect of each level of dependency set out in the Fourth Schedule to the 1993 Regulations.[233]

Community care services for people with mental disability

People with mental illness may benefit from four specific aspects of Community Care Services provided by the Health Service Executive namely:

(a) the General Medical Service which provides free access to general medical practitioners and free medication;

(b) the Long Term Illness programme which provides free medication to those with a long term illness or disability;[234]

(c) the provision of a home nursing service to people who are ill;[235]

(d) the provision of free home help to assist in the maintenance at home of, *inter alia*, "an infirm person".[236]

The General Medical Services

Free general medical practitioner services Under section 58(1) of the Health Act 1970 as amended by the Health Act 2004, the Health Service Executive is obliged to make available without charge a general practitioner medical and surgical service for persons with full eligibility (Medical Card Holders) under the General Medical Services scheme.

Under the General Medical Services Scheme a person with mental illness who is fully eligible may avail of medical services provided by a general medical practitioner who has a contract with the Health Service Executive to operate within the scheme and whose list of patients participating in the scheme does not exceed the maximum number permissible under the scheme. In so far as is practicable a person availing himself/

---

[232] (S.I. No.227 of 1993), art.22.3 as inserted by the Nursing Homes (Subvention) (Amendment) Regulations 1996 (S.I. No.225 of 1996), art.2.

[233] (S.I. No.227 of 1993), art.22.4 as inserted by the Nursing Homes (Subvention) (Amendment) Regulations 1996 (S.I. No.225 of 1996), art.2.

[234] Health Act 1970, s.59.

[235] *Ibid.*, s.60.

[236] *Ibid.*, s.61(1)(a).

herself of the medical services under the scheme is entitled to have a choice of medical practitioner.[237]

Under the scheme the medical practitioner is obliged to render his patients all proper and necessary treatment of a kind usually undertaken by a general medical practitioner. He must be available for consultation at his surgery for a specified number of hours weekly and for consultation generally and for domiciliary visits for an aggregate of forty hours weekly during normal hours. He must undertake to have suitable arrangements to enable contact with him outside normal hours for emergency cases. He must supply a person on his list with such drugs and appliances as he considers necessary for immediate administration and application. His surgery arrangements may not discriminate between eligible patients and private patients.

Free medicines Under section 59(1) of the Health Act 1970,[238] as amended by the Health Act 2004 the Health Service Executive is obliged to make arrangements for the supply without charge by community pharmacies[239] of approved[240] drugs to persons with full eligibility (Medical Card Holders). The drugs must be prescribed by a registered medical practitioner and the definition of "drugs" in the Act includes medicines and medical and surgical appliances that are so prescribed.[241]

Section 59(4) provides that, subject to the right of the Minister for Health and Children to specify the terms and conditions under which the Health Service Executive may defray the cost of supplying drugs under section 59(6), a registered medical practitioner who is so authorised by an agreement entered into by him or her with the Health Service Executive may, in accordance with the terms of the agreement supply approved drugs to persons with full eligibility (Medical Card Holders) for the purposes of section 59(1).[242]

By virtue of section 59(4)(b) a person granted Ministerial approval under section 59(7) may supply approved drugs (other than medicines) for the purposes of section 59(4).

Section 59(5) provides that, subject to the right of the Minister for Heath and Children to specify the terms and conditions under which the Health Service Executive may defray the cost of supplying drugs under section 59(6), an institution[243] that provides a specialist service under the direct supervision of a medical consultant[244] and is approved

---

[237] Health Act 1970, s.58(2), Health Services Regulations 1972 (S.I. No.88 of 1972), art.5(2).

[238] As substituted by Health (Miscellaneous Provisions) Act 2001, s.1(b).

[239] A "community pharmacy" is a pharmacy the proprietor of which has entered into an agreement with the Health Service Executive for the supply by the pharmacy of drugs for the purposes of s.59. A "pharmacy" is defined as a shop lawfully kept open for the purposes of the dispensing and compounding of medical prescriptions in accordance with the Pharmacy Acts 1875 to 1977. See Health Act 1970, s.59(12) as inserted by Health (Miscellaneous Provisions) Act 2001, s.1(b).

[240] The drugs must be approved by the Minister for Health and Children under s.59(7) of the 1970 Act.

[241] Health Act 1970, s.59(12) as inserted by Health (Miscellaneous Provisions) Act 2001, s.1(b).

[242] Health Act 1970, s.59(4) as substituted by Health (Miscellaneous Provisions) Act 2001, s.1(b).

[243] "Institution" is defined widely to mean a hospital, nursing home or clinic that is maintained wholly or mainly out of funds provided by the Minister for Health and Children, the Executive or a charity or by voluntary prescription. See Health Act 1970, s.59(12) as inserted by Health (Miscellaneous Provisions) Act 2001, s.1(b) and amended by Health Act 2004.

[244] "Medical consultant" is defined as a registered medical practitioner in hospital practice who, by reason of his or her training, skill and experience in a particular specialty is consulted by a registered

by the Minister for Health and Children under section 59(7) may supply approved drugs to persons with full eligibility under section 59(1), where the drugs are prescribed by or under the direction of a consultant for the purposes of that service. Accordingly drugs may be supplied by pharmacies attached to psychiatric units of general hospitals and psychiatric hospitals free of charge to medical card holders, where those drugs are prescribed by or under the direction of the consultant psychiatrist supervising the psychiatric service.

Drugs payment scheme A new Drugs Payment Scheme came into effect from July 1, 1999. It replaces the Drug Refund Scheme and the Drug Cost Subsidisation Scheme, which had been operation prior to that date. Under this new scheme which is statutorily authorised by section 59(2) of the Health Act 1970,[245] where the cost of a person[246] or of his or her spouse or of a dependant member of the family of the person being supplied in any month with drugs, medicines and medical and surgical appliances prescribed by a registered medical practitioner for the treatment of that person or of his or her spouse or of a dependant member of the family of the person[247] exceeds €85.00 the Health Service Executive must meet the cost to the extent that the cost exceeds €85.00.[248]

In so far as the scope of entitlement is concerned "spouse" in relation to a person is defined as including a person with whom the person is living as husband and wife.[249]

"Dependant member of the family" in relation to a person is defined to mean any child[250] under the age of 18 years who is not a person with full eligibility or a child who has attained 18 years of age who is living in the home of the person, and (i) is or will be receiving full-time education or instruction at any university, college, school or other educational establishment and is under the age of 23 years, or (ii) has a mental or physical disability to such extent that it is not reasonably possible for the child to maintain himself or herself fully and is not a person with full eligibility.[251]

To register for the scheme a person must complete the registration form, which is available from pharmacies or from the Health Service Executive. A plastic swipe card is issued for each person named on the registration form. This card is presented whenever the person concerned is having prescriptions filled. Using the same pharmacy throughout

medical practitioners in relation to that specialty. See Health Act 1970, s.59(12) as inserted by Health (Miscellaneous Provisions) Act 2001, s.1(b).

[245] As substituted by Health (Miscellaneous Provisions) Act 2001, s.1(b).

[246] i.e. a person with limited eligibility or a person with full eligibility who does not avail himself of the arrangements for the provision of free drugs under s.59(1). See Health Act 1970, s.59(2) as substituted by Health (Miscellaneous Provisions) Act 2001, s.1(b).

[247] Health Act 1970, s.59(12) as inserted by Health (Miscellaneous Provisions) Act 1970, s.1(b).

[248] Health Services Regulations 1972 (S.I. No. 88 of 1972), art.6 as substituted by Health Services Regulations 2004 (S.I. No.658 of 2004), art.4.

[249] Health Act 1970, s.59(12) as amended by the Health (Miscellaneous Provisions) Act 2001, s.1(b).

[250] "Child" is defined widely to cover: (a) a child of the person and his or her spouse or adopted by both of them under the Adoption Acts 1952 to 1998 or in relation to whom both of them are *in loco parentis* under an arrangement of a permanent nature, (b) of the person or his or her spouse or adopted by either of them under those Acts, or in relation to whom either of them is *in loco parentis* under an arrangement of a permanent nature where the other person being aware that he or she is not the parent of the child has treated the child as a member of the family, or (c) of whom the person or his or her spouse is a foster parent (within the meaning of the Child Care Act 1991).

[251] Health Act 1970, s.59(12) as substituted by Health (Miscellaneous Provisions) Act 2001, s.1(b).

the month the person should bring receipts or evidence to show how much has been spent for that month and will not be obliged to pay more than €78 in any calendar month to the pharmacist.

Under the terms of section 59(5),[252] approved drugs may be supplied under the drugs payment scheme by psychiatric units of general hospitals and psychiatric hospitals to persons entitled to avail of that scheme where those drugs are prescribed by or under the direction of the consultant psychiatrist supervising the psychiatric service.[253]

(a) Medication for long term illness

Section 59(3) of the Health Act 1970 provides that, subject to the right of Minister to determine the terms and conditions under which the Health Service Executive may defray the cost of supplying drugs under section 59(6), the Health Service Executive is empowered to make arrangements for the supply without charge by community pharmacies of approved drugs[254] to persons suffering from a prescribed illness or disability of a permanent or long-term nature for the treatment of those conditions where those persons are persons with limited eligibility or persons with full eligibility who do not avail themselves of the free drugs scheme under section 59(1). Regulations made under section 59(3)[255] specify the illnesses and disabilities to which the drugs for long-term illness scheme applies. They include mental illness in children under the age of 16, intellectual disability, epilepsy and Parkinson's disease.

In order to make a claim under the scheme a person completes an application form, which must be certified by their general practitioner and sent to the local Health Service Executive office. Approved applicants are given a long term illness booklet in which the general practitioner is required to enter details of the drugs/medicines prescribed. The book is presented to a pharmacist by the patient for dispensing of the drugs/medicines as required.

Under the terms of section 59(5),[256] approved drugs may be supplied without charge to persons with illnesses or disabilities of a permanent or long term nature by psychiatric units of general hospitals and psychiatric hospitals where those persons are entitled to obtain the drugs without charge under section 59(3) and those drugs are prescribed by or under the direction of the consultant psychiatrist supervising the psychiatric service.[257]

(b) The home nursing service

Section 60 of the Health Act 1970 as amended by the Health Act 2004 obliges the Health Service Executive to provide without charge a nursing service to persons with full eligibility (Medical Card Holders) and other categories of persons "to give those

---

[252] See p.50 *supra* (under free medicines).

[253] See Health Act 1970, s.59(5) as inserted by Health (Miscellaneous Provisions) Act 2001, s.1(b).

[254] The drugs must be prescribed by a registered medical practitioner and "drugs" includes medicines and medical and surgical appliances that are so prescribed. See Health Act, s.59(12) as inserted by Health (Miscellaneous Provisions) Act 2001, s.1(b).

[255] Health Services (Amendment) Regulations 1971 (S.I. No.277 of 1971), arts 8 and 9 as amended by Health Services (Amendment) Regulations 1975 (S.I. No. 64 of 1975), art.3.

[256] See p.50 *supra* (under free medicines).

[257] See Health Act 1970, s.59(5) as inserted by Health (Miscellaneous Provisions) Act 2001, s.1(b).

persons advice and assistance on matters relating to their health and to assist them if they are sick."[258]

Under the current system a public health nurse is assigned to a district within the community care area and is responsible for the provision of a comprehensive nursing service within that area. Part of his/her work is to provide general domiciliary care and advice for the aged and to identify and visit elderly people living alone or in need of help on a regular basis. The services of the nurse are normally free of charge to all people over the age of 65 and to all Medical Card holders.

In *CK v. Northern Area Health Board*,[259] it was held by the Supreme Court that section 61 does not intend that the health board should have an obligation to provide a "long term virtually full-time (or even extensive part-time) nursing service for disabled persons in their own homes…[W]hat is intended is an advice and assistance service as is at present provided by the Public Health Nurse Scheme."[260]

(c) The home help service

Section 61 of the Health Act 1970 obliges a health authority to make arrangements to assist in the maintenance at home *inter alia*, of (a) a sick or infirm person or a dependant of such a person, (b) a woman availing herself of medical, surgical or midwifery services in connection with motherhood or receiving similar care or her dependant(s) and (c) a person who, but for the provision of a service for him under this section, would require to be maintained otherwise than at home.[261]

The provisions of section 61(a) are wide enough to be availed of by people with mental illness living in the community and the provisions of section 61(c), being a clear endorsement of community care, may be availed of by people with mental illness who would otherwise need to be maintained in institutional care. However, in *CK v. Northern Area Health Board*,[262] it was held that the provision of services under section 61 was not mandatory but a matter of discretion for the health boards and the Minister for Health and Children. The matter of whether any services should be provided and the extent of the services were a matter of policy for the health board and also for the Minister for Health and Children having regard to the terms of the section. However, it was held that the section did empower the Health Board to provide general care assistance to assist a ward of court with severe brain damage and epilepsy to be maintained in his own home where it was not in his interests to be placed in institutional accommodation.[263]

---

[258] Nursing at community level was first introduced by voluntary organisations. Later a corps of public health nurses who were attached to the county medical officers of health with duties mainly in the public health service. S. 44 of the Health Act 1947 empowered health authorities to appoint nurses for district duties and this service developed in the 1950s.

[259] Unreported, Supreme Court, May 29, 2003.

[260] *Ibid.*, p.27.

[261] A woman who is availing herself of medical, surgical or midwifery services in connection with motherhood and who is a person with full or limited eligibility may also avail of the home help service.

[262] *Op. cit.*

[263] It was also observed at the conclusion of the judgment that the course of assisting him at home was probably a more economical course than that of maintaining him in an institution. See p.28 of judgment.

Before a home help is provided an assessment is made of the health and financial, and social circumstances of an applicant. Under the terms of section 61(1) of the 1970 Act the chief executive officer has a discretion to determine whether a charge should be paid for the service. In practice the service is not usually made available to people who do not satisfy the criteria of eligibility for medical cards but exceptions may be made in cases of hardship. Relatives do not, in general, qualify for appointment as a home help and it appears that it is only in cases where no relative is available that the Health Service Executive will appoint a home help.

There is no statutory limit on the number of hours of employment of a home help but in practice the maximum number of hours allotted is usually 18 per week. The home help's work is usually monitored by an organiser and in the absence of an organiser, the local public health nurse.

Under section 65 of the Health Act 1953[264] as amended by the Health Act 2004 the Health Service Executive also has the power to give assistance to bodies providing services "similar or ancillary to" the services of the Executive. Under these provisions the Health Service Executive itself employs home helps and makes grants for voluntary agencies providing home helps. In addition it may make grants to voluntary agencies providing meals on wheels.

Social workers

The Health Service Executive employs social workers who provide advice and guidance on matters of personal concern. Most of the large hospitals also employ social workers with whom patients and relatives may discuss problems arising from the patient's mental illness.

Respite Care

Respite Care services are provided by the Health Service Executive in order to give carers a break from their caring responsibilities, to allow them time for themselves, to have a holiday or to spend time with other family members. Under scheme of services provided the person being cared for is admitted to a Health Service Executive Nursing Home for two weeks.

To apply for respite care a person must contact their local Health Service Executive office, public health nurse, or general medical practitioner.

A respite care grant in respect of the cost of respite care is also payable in June of each year to carers in receipt of certain social welfare payments and by the Health Service Executive to carers of children in receipt of Domiciliary Care Allowance.

Entitlement to avail of the public health (including public psychiatric) services

Under Part IV of the Health Act 1970 as amended by the Health Act 2004 the Health Service Executive is obliged to make available a number of health services to persons deemed fully eligible for the services under the Act. These include free hospital in-

---

[264] As amended by Health (Amendment) (No.3) Act 1996, s.19.

patient[265] and out patient services[266] (including free hospital consultant care,[267] medications and investigations), free general medical services including general practitioner medical and surgical services,[268] free prescribed medicines and drugs,[269] and free home nursing services.[270]

Determination of full eligibility to avail of public health services

The issue of whether an individual is entitled to avail of such health services without charge depends upon his/her financial and family circumstances. Under section 45(1) of the Health Act 1970 as amended by the Health Act 2004 a person will be fully eligible to avail of the health services provided by the Health Service Executive without charge where s/he is ordinarily resident in the State and falls into the category of:"(a) adult persons unable without undue hardship to arrange general practitioner and medical and surgical services for themselves and his/her dependants and (b) dependants of persons mentioned in category (a)".[271]

Decisions as to who has full eligibility entitling them without charge to health services mentioned in Part IV of the Act are in practice generally taken by officers at the local Health Service Executive offices. In deciding upon an application these officers follow national guidelines agreed annually by the Health Service Executive for determining eligibility. These guidelines however have no statutory effect and are issued primarily to inform the Health Service Executive and the public in general of the Executive categories of persons who normally qualify for full eligibility.

The decision as to whether a person has full eligibility is taken by reference to an assessment of means. The means limits are updated every January. Typically the means assessment takes account of whether a person is single living alone, single living with a family, has a spouse and make allowances for children aged under 16 and dependants aged over 16 with no income. The allowance for a child over 16 years is doubled where the child is in full-time third level education and is not grant aided. Outgoings on a house such as rent or mortgage excess over a certain amount per week and cost of travelling to work in excess of a certain amount per week are also taken into account.

Since July 2001, every person ordinarily resident in the State who aged 70 or over is entitled to a Medical Care regardless of his/her income.[272] This medical card which is not means tested covers the applicant only and does not cover dependants. If a person already holds a medical card when s/he reaches the age of 70 s/he will continue to hold that medical card and his/her dependants will be covered. If a person does not hold a medical card when s/he reaches the age of 70 s/he can still apply for a means tested medical card and if granted his/her dependants will be covered.

---

[265] Health Act 1970, s.2.

[266] Health Act 1970, s.56(2), (5) as substituted by the Health (Amendment) Act 1987 Section 1 Health (Out-Patient Charges) Regulations 1994 (S.I. No. 37 of 1994), art.4(1)(a).

[267] Health Services (Out-Patient) Regulations 1993 (S.I. No.178 of 1993), art.3.

[268] Health Act 1970, s.58(1).

[269] *Ibid.*, s.59.

[270] *Ibid.*, s.60.

[271] Health Act 1970, s.45(1) as amended by Health (Amendment) Act 1991, s.2.

[272] Health (Miscellaneous Provisions) Act 2001, s.1.

Widowed and other lone parents with dependants are treated under the same income guidelines as a married couple with dependants. It may be possible for one or more members of a family who would not otherwise qualify to obtain a medical card in their own right if they have high medical expenses.

The Health Service Executive maintains a register of persons with full eligibility which is periodically reviewed. A person on the register is issued with a General Medical Services Card (Medical Card) on presentation of which s/he is entitled to health services referred to in Part IV of the 1970 Act free of charge.[273]

Where a person does not fall within any of statutory categories of eligibility the chief executive officer of the Health Service Executive retains a statutory discretion to deem a person to be a person with full eligibility where s/he is "unable, without undue hardship" to provide a service to which persons with full eligibility would be entitled, for himself or his dependants.[274]

Limited eligibility to avail of public health services

Any person ordinarily resident in the State who does not have full eligibility has limited eligibility for services under Part IV of the Health Act 1970.[275] Persons with limited eligibility are not entitled to free general practitioner services or free prescribed medicines and drugs. They are, however, entitled to avail of the drugs payment scheme. In addition they are entitled to in-patient services (including consultant care and medication) in a public ward of a hospital subject to payment of a charge of €45 per day subject to a maximum of €450 in any period of 12 consecutive months.[276] Persons with limited eligibility may opt to be treated as private patients in a public hospital in which case they must pay for maintenance in the private or semi private accommodation provided at a set rate in addition to the public hospital in-patient charges and the full price of the consultant services and treatment provided.[277] However, private health insurance is an option to cover the cost of these charges.

A long stay patient with limited eligibility who has no dependants and has been in receipt of in-patient services for thirty days or for periods aggregating in total thirty days within the previous twelve months may be subject to a charge towards the cost of in-patient services. The charge is determined by the chief executive officer of the Health Service Executive having regard to the circumstances of the case and must be at a rate

---

[273] See *supra* p.54.

[274] See Health Act 1970, s.45(7) as amended by Health (Amendment) Act 1991, s.2.

[275] Health Act 1970, s.46 as substituted by the Health (Amendment) Act 1991, s.3. This is subject to s.52(3) see n.277 below.

[276] Health Act 1970, Section 53 Health (In-Patient Charges) Regulations 1987 S.I. No.116 of 1987) as amended by Health (In Patient Charges) (Amendment) (No.2) Regulations 2002 (S.I. No.553 of 2002) The charge was increased from €40 to €45 with effect from January 2004 by the January 2004 budget.

[277] S.52(3) of the 1970 Act (as inserted by Health (Amendment) Act 1991, s.5) provides that where a person with full eligibility or limited eligibility for in-patient services does not avail of those services but instead avails of like services not provided under s. 52(1) then the person shall, while being maintained for the said in-patient services, be deemed not to have full eligibility or limited eligibility for those in-patient services. Under s.55 of the 1970 Act (as substituted by Health (Amendment) Act 1991, s.6 the Health Service Executive may charge for these like services.

not exceeding the income of the person less a sum of €3.17 per week or less such larger sum as determined by the chief executive officer.[278] Long stay patients who are subject to this charge are not subject to the €40 charge for in-patient services mentioned in the previous paragraph.[279]

Patients with limited eligibility are generally entitled to avail of out-patient services (including assessment by a consultant or his team and diagnostic assessments). However, a person with limited eligibility who attends at a designated accident and emergency or casualty department of a public hospitals directly without a letter of referral from his/ her registered medical practitioner is liable to a charge of €45.[280] However, this applies only to the first visit for any episode of care.[281] There is no charge if the person attends with a letter of referral from his/her registered medical practitioner or if person's attendance at the department results in admission as an in-patient.[282] Where persons with limited eligibility avails of out-patient services in a private capacity s/he will be obliged to pay the full price for the service provided.

Children suffering from prescribed permanent or long term illness and disabilities who do not fall into the category of persons with full eligibility are exempt from hospital in-patient,[283] and out-patient[284] charges. Children entitled to these exemptions include children with intellectual disabilities and mental illness.[285] Children referred from child health clinics and school health examinations are also entitled to exemptions from these charges.[286]

Private health insurance

The availability of private health insurance is of relevance to any person who wishes to avail of private or semi-private accommodation in hospitals and who has to meet the cost of private medical care (including health professionals services) either in hospital or in the community.

---

[278] Health (Charges for In-Patient Services) Regulations 1976 (S.I. No.180 of 1976) as amended by Health (Charges for In-Patient Services) (Amendment) Regulations 1987 (S.I. No. 300 of 1987), art.3.

[279] Health (In-Patient Charges) Regulations 1987 (S.I. No.116 of 1987), art.4(1)(g) While the legal requirement is that a least €3.17 of a person's income be left after levying the charge in practice allowance is made for items such as rent and insurance and a reasonable amount is left to meet a patient's needs which is more than the statutorily prescribed minimum.

[280] Health Act 1970, s.56(5)(a)(i) as substituted by Health (Amendment) Act 1987, s.1, Health (Out-Patient Charges) Regulations 1994 (S.I. No.37 of 1994) as amended by Health (Out-Patient Charges) (Amendment) Regulations 2002 (S.I. No.366 of 2002), art. 3 The charge was increased from €40 to €45 with effect from January 2004 by the 2004 Budget.

[281] Health (Out-Patient Charges) Regulations 1994 (S.I. No.37 of 1994), art.4(2). Thus if a patient has to return for further visits in relation to the same illness or accident s/he does not have to pay the charge.

[282] Health (Out-Patient Charges) Regulations 1994 (S.I. No.37 of 1994), art.4(1)(j). The person may then be subject to in-patient charges.

[283] Health Act 1970, s.52.

[284] Health Act 1970, s.56(3) as substituted by the Health (Amendment) Act 1987, s.1.

[285] Health Services (Amendment) Regulations 1971 (S.I. No. 277 of 1971), art.6. Health Services (Amendment) Regulations 1987 (S.I. No. 114 of 1987), art.3.

[286] Health Act 1970, s.56(4) Health (In-Patient Charges) Regulations 1987 (S.I. No.116 of 1987), art.4(1)(e).

A number of companies provide voluntary private health insurance in Ireland. The Voluntary Health Insurance Board is the oldest and largest provider of private health insurance. It is a semi state body whose board is appointed by the Minister for Health and Children. It is non-profit making and any surplus on its income must be applied to the reduction of insurance premiums or increases in benefits.

Initially when the VHI was established in 1957,[287] it was designed to provide a means by which those in the higher income group who did not have eligibility for the health services time would be able to insure themselves against the cost of medical care. Now however it is established that some people with full eligibility for free health services also invest in supplementary health insurance cover to enable them to obtain private or semi-private accommodation and private treatment in hospitals.

In accordance with the Health Insurance Act of 1994 the health insurance market in Ireland was opened up to competition and at the beginning of 1997 the British United Provident Association ("BUPA") commenced operating in the Irish market. It is now the second largest provider of voluntary private health insurance in Ireland.

There are a number of long-established health insurance providers that deal only with particular groups of employees. Membership is confined to employees and retired employees and their dependants. These schemes are known as restricted membership schemes and examples include the Gardaí, prison officers and ESB employees. The rules relating to health insurance apply equally to all providers with some limited exceptions for the restricted membership schemes.

All insurance companies providing health insurance must be registered with the Health Insurance Authority which maintains a register of such companies.[288]

Health insurance companies which offer cover for in-patient services must offer a minimum level of benefits.[289] They must provide a minimum level of cover for in-patient/day patient treatment, hospital out-patient treatment, consultants' fees,[290] and psychiatric treatment and substance abuse.[291]

The maximum amount of cover (in terms of time) which all health insurance companies combined are obliged to provide in respect of in-patient services for a psychiatric condition (other than treatment for alcoholism, drug or substance abuse) in any calendar year is 100 days in-patient cover.[292] The maximum amount of cover (in terms of time) which all health insurance companies combined are obliged to provide in respect of in-patient services for alcoholism, drug or other substance abuse in any continuous period of 5 years is 91 days in-patient cover.[293]

The maximum amount of cover which all health insurance companies combined are obliged to provide in respect of in-patient and day patient services (generally) combined in respect of any calendar year is 180 days cover in respect of in-patient and day patient services.[294]

---

[287] Voluntary Health Insurance Act 1957.
[288] Health Insurance Act 1994, s.14.
[289] Health Insurance Act 1994, s.10 as amended by Health Insurance(Amendment) Act 2001, s.13(c).
[290] With the significant exception of consultant's fees relating to eating disorders or weight reduction.
[291] Health Insurance Act 1994 (Minimum Benefit) Regulations 1996 (S.I. No.83 of 1996), art.5.
[292] *Ibid.*, art.5(3).
[293] *Ibid.*, art.5(4).
[294] *Ibid.*, art.5(6).

A health insurance company is not required to make any prescribed minimum payments in respect of prescribed health services provided by a registered nursing home unless (i) such prescribed health services are provided to an insured person immediately following the provision of in-patient services to the insured person, and (ii) the company has received and approved a certificate from the hospital consultant responsible for the treatment of the person to the effect that the prescribed health services to be provided by the registered nursing home are appropriate health services.[295] This certificate must be received and approved prior to the admission of the insured person to the registered nursing home.[296]

Health insurers may also offer contracts in relation to general medical practitioner and out-patient services without having to meet minimum benefit requirements.[297]

Companies offering health insurance must do so in accordance with the principles of (a) open enrolment;[298] (b) lifetime cover;[299] and (c) community rating.[300]

The principle of "open enrolment" obliges health insurance companies to accept anyone under 65 who wishes to take out a health insurance policy regardless of age, sex or status. Restricted membership schemes are obliged to accept anyone who is qualified to join.[301]

The principle of "lifetime cover" means that once a person has joined a health insurance scheme and continues to pay his/her premiums the insurance company cannot refuse to provide him/her with cover.[302]

The principle of "community rating" means that the insurance company must charge the same rate to every policy holder for a given level of service regardless of the policy holders age, sex or health status.[303] However, there may be a lower rate of charges for people aged under 18, people aged 18-23 who are in full-time education, retired people who have a special arrangement within their company's group health insurance scheme and people in group health schemes.[304]

There are exceptions to the general principles in some cases. For example, a health insurance company may restrict the cover given on the basis of health status in certain circumstances. In this regard it may impose a 26 week[305] waiting restriction before it

---

[295] i.e. health services in relation to the diagnosis or treatment of the illness or injury of a patient which would be accepted generally by the medical profession as appropriate and necessary having regard to good standards of medical practice and to the nature and cost of any alternative forms of treatment as well as to all of the circumstances relevant to the patient. See Health Insurance Act 1994 (Minimum Benefit) Regulations 1996 (S.I. No. 83 of 1996), art.3.

[296] Health Insurance Act 1994 (Minimum Benefit) Regulations 1996 (S.I. No. 83 of 1996), art.5(5).

[297] *Ibid.*, art.5(1) These are categorised as "ancillary health services" See Health Insurance Act 1994, s.2.

[298] Health Insurance Act 1994, s.8 as amended by Health Insurance (Amendment) Act 2001, s.8.

[299] *Ibid.*, s.9, Health Insurance Act 1994 (Lifetime Cover) Regulations 1996 (S.I. No. 82 of 1996).

[300] *Ibid.*, s.7 as amended by Health Insurance (Amendment) Act 2001, s.5.

[301] *Ibid.*, s.8 as amended by Health Insurance (Amendment) Act 2001, s.8.

[302] *Ibid.*, s.9; Health Insurance Act 1994 (Lifetime Cover) Regulations 1996 (S.I. No. 82 of 1996).

[303] Health Insurance Act 1994, s.7 as amended by Health Insurance (Amendment) Act 2001, s.5.

[304] *Ibid.*, s.7(4) as amended by Health Insurance (Amendment) Act 2001, s.5.

[305] It may impose a 52 week initial waiting period in respect of a person who is of or over the age of 55 years and under the age of 65 years. See Health Insurance Act 1994 (Open Enrolment) Regulations 1996 (S.I. No. 81 of 1996), art.7(1)(ii).

provides cover.[306] In addition the insurance company may refuse to cover an applicant for insurance in respect of pre-existing conditions for longer periods.[307]

As a matter of insurance contract law an applicant for insurance must disclose all relevant information to the insurance company. Failure to disclose such information or concealment of material facts where the applicant for insurance knows of such facts entitles the insurance company to avoid the contract.[308] Tax relief is available on premiums paid in respect of health insurance.

THE EUROPEAN CONVENTION FOR THE PROTECTION OF HUMAN RIGHTS AND FUNDAMENTAL FREEDOMS AND IRISH LAW

The provisions of the European Convention relevant to the person with mental disability

The *European Convention for the Protection of Human Rights and Fundamental Freedoms* was concluded under the auspices of the Council of Europe on November 4, 1950. States parties to the Convention are bound to accord the rights contained in it to anyone regardless of nationality who is within their jurisdiction.[309] Ireland is a signatory.[310] There are eleven protocols to the Convention,[311] which, *inter alia*, provide for amendments to procedures under the Convention and additional rights and freedoms not provided for in the original text. A twelfth protocol containing a general prohibition on discrimination has recently been proposed.[312] It provides in Article 1.1 that "the enjoyment of any right set forth by law shall be secured without discrimination *on any ground* such as sex, race, colour, language, religion, political or other opinion, national

---

[306] Health Insurance Act 1994 (Open Enrolment) Regulations 1996 (S.I. No. 81 of 1996), art.7. A person will be eligible for minimum payments immediately and during the initial waiting period where prescribed health services are provided to a person as a result of accident or injury which occurred while that person was named as an insured person. Health Insurance Act 1994 (Open Enrolment) Regulations 1996 (S.I. No. 81 of 1996), art.7(3), Health Insurance Act 1994 (Minimum Benefit) Regulations 1996 (S.I. No. 83 of 1996) art.8(1).

[307] Health Insurance Act 1994 (Open Enrolment) Regulations 1996, art.8. The person is entitled to cover during the waiting period in respect of the provision of health services which do not relate to the condition which gave rise to the "pre-existing condition waiting period." See Health Insurance Act 1994 (Minimum Benefit) Regulations 1996 (S.I. No. 83 of 1996), art.8(2).

[308] *Brownlie v. Campbell* (1880) 5 App. Cas. 925 at 954; *Joel v. Law Union & Crown Insurance Co.* [1908] 2 K.B. 863.

[309] Art.1.

[310] Ireland signed on February 4, 1953 and ratified on February 25, 1953.

[311] The First Protocol (1952) contains certain additional rights and freedoms; the second (1963) confers upon the European Court of Human Rights competence to give advisory opinions; the third (1970) amends certain procedural provisions of the Convention; the fourth (1963) contains further additional rights and freedoms; the fifth (1971) further amends the procedural provisions of the Convention; the sixth (1983) concerns the abolition of the death penalty; the seventh (1984) contains further rights and freedoms; the eighth (1990) contains further procedural amendments to the Convention provisions; the ninth (1990) contains further improvements to the procedure under the Convention; the tenth (1992) provides for an amendment to the procedure of the Commission under Art.32 of the Convention; and the eleventh (1994) provides for a restructuring of the control machinery established by the Convention.

[312] Rome 4.XI.200.

or social origin, association with a national minority, property, birth *or other status*". The terms of paragraph 1 speak of discrimination "on any ground" instancing some of the grounds on which discrimination may take place and include discrimination based on "other status." It is submitted that on this basis discrimination grounded on disability including mental disability would fall within the ambit of the terms of the protocol. Article 1.2 states that no one shall be discriminated against by any public authority on any ground such as those mentioned in paragraph 1. It would appear therefore that discrimination by private concerns is not covered by the terms of the Protocol.

Ireland has signed but not yet ratified Protocol No. 12.[313] By the terms of Article 5 of the Protocol it shall enter into force on the first day of the month following the expiration of a period of three months after the date on which *ten* member states of the Council of Europe have expressed their consent to be bound by the Protocol in accordance with the provisions of Article 4 by signature and ratification, acceptance and approval.

Interestingly by Article 3 of the Protocol the provisions of Article 1 are to be regarded as additional articles to the Convention and all the provisions of the Convention shall apply accordingly so that any discrimination in the enjoyment of the rights set forth under the Convention based on disability is prohibited.

Convention rights relevant to the person with mental disability The text to the Convention is set out in Appendix 1 of this text. The rights covered in the Convention which may be of particular relevance to the person with mental disability include the right to life (Article 2); prohibition of torture and inhuman and degrading treatment (Article 3); the right to freedom from slavery, servitude and forced or compulsory labour (Article 4); the right to liberty and security of the person (Article 5); the right to a fair and public hearing within a reasonable time by an independent and impartial tribunal established by law (Article 6); the right to freedom from retrospective criminal law and no punishment without law (Article 7); the right to respect for private and family life and correspondence (Article 8); the right to freedom of thought, conscience and religion (Article 9), the right to freedom of expression (Article 10); the right to freedom of assembly (Article 11); the right to marry and found a family (Article 12); the right to an effective remedy before a national authority if one of the Convention rights or freedoms is violated (Article 13); the right to enjoy the rights and freedoms set forth in the Convention without discrimination. (Article 14).

The First Protocol to the Convention[314] provides for a person's right to the peaceful enjoyment of his possessions (Article 1), the right to education (Article 2)[315] and imposes

---

[313] Ireland signed the Protocol on November 4, 2000.

[314] Ireland signed the first Protocol on March 29, 1952 and ratified on February 25, 1953 making the following declarations "the Government of Ireland do hereby confirm and ratify the aforesaid Convention and undertake faithfully to perform and carry out all the stipulations therein contained, subject to the reservation that they do not interpret article 6(3)(c) of the Convention as requiring the provision of free legal assistance to any wider extent than is now provided in Ireland."

[315] At the time of signing the Protocol the Irish delegate put on record that "in the view of the Irish Government Art.2 of the Protocol is not sufficiently explicit in ensuring to parents the right to provide education for their children in their homes or in the schools of the parents' own choice, whether or not such schools are private schools or are schools recognised or established by the State."

an obligation upon states parties to hold free elections at reasonable intervals by secret ballot (Article 3). The Fourth Protocol contains among other things the right to freedom of movement (Article 2) and also prohibits the individual or collective expulsion of nationals (Article 3).[316] The Sixth Protocol deals exclusively with the abolition of the death penalty and the Seventh Protocol contains procedural safeguards concerning the expulsion of lawfully resident aliens (Article 1), the right of appeal in criminal matters (Article 2), compensation for wrongful conviction (Article 3), the right not to be punished twice for the same offence (Article 4) and equality between spouses (Article 5).[317]

Enforcement of Convention rights at European level

Bringing a case to the European Court of Human Rights The Convention also creates machinery for the enforcement of these rights in the form of the European Court of Human Rights.[318]

The jurisdiction of the European Court of Human Rights extends to all matters concerning the interpretation and application of the Convention.[319] The Court consists of judges elected by the Parliamentary Assembly of the Council of Europe from a list of three nominees put forward by each state.[320] Accordingly there are the same number of judges in the court as States, which have ratified the Convention.[321] The Court seldom sits in plenary session. In general it discharges its duties in Committees of three judges, Chambers of seven judges and occasionally as a Grand Chamber of 17 judges.

Article 34 of the Convention provides for the right of individuals, non-governmental organisations or groups of individuals claiming to be the victim of a violation of the rights set forth in the Convention to apply to the court. In addition to allowing such persons and bodies to bring complaints the Convention obliges states not to hinder in any way the effective exercise of this right.

However, complaints to the court can only be considered if they meet the admissibility criteria set out in Article 35. In essence the complaint must (a) be made by an eligible person; (b) concern a Convention issue; (c) be concerned with a time when the state was bound by the Convention; (d) be in a jurisdiction to which the Convention extends; (e) be made after domestic remedies have been exhausted; (e) have raised Convention arguments in the domestic courts and (f) be made within six months of the exhaustion of the last domestic remedy.

The requirement of exhaustion of domestic remedies means that the applicant must have had recourse to the entire system of legal protection of the member state.[322] The requirement is however, dispensed with where domestic remedies are ineffective or

---

[316] Entered into force on May 2, 1968. Ireland ratified on October 29, 1968.

[317] This Protocol entered into force on 1 November 1988. It was signed by the State on August 3, 2001 and is in the process of formal ratification by it.

[318] European Convention for the Protection of Human Rights and Fundamental Freedoms Art.19. The Eleventh Protocol which came into force on November 1, 1998 merged the functions of two previous institutions of the Convention – the Commission and the Court into a single European Court of Human Rights.

[319] *Ibid.*, Art.32(1).

[320] *Ibid.*, Art.22.

[321] *Ibid.*, Art.20. Forty European States have ratified the Convention.

[322] See *Lawless Case* (1961) 4 *Yearbook*, European Convention on Human Rights 438.

where there are special circumstances.[323] Remedies are not effective if they are theoretically available but are not likely to be effective for the purposes of the case.[324]

In addition the court will not deal with any petition submitted by an applicant under Article 34 that (a) is anonymous or (b) is substantially the same as a matter which has already been examined by the court or has already been submitted to another procedure of international investigation or settlement and contains no relevant new information. The court must also consider inadmissible any petition which it considers incompatible with the provisions of the Convention or the protocols thereto, manifestly ill-founded or an abuse of the right of application.[325]

If the Chamber does not declare the complaint inadmissible it will generally convene an oral hearing before taking its decision on admissibility if either party so requests.[326] The Chamber's decision will be communicated to the state and the applicant and will be published. It must contain reasons [327] as well as a statement as to whether it was taken unanimously or by a majority.[328]

Once the Court has made a positive admissibility decision it will generally undertake an investigation into the merits of the complaint. Article 38 of the Convention provides that if the Court declares the application admissible it shall (a) pursue the examination of the case together with the representatives of the parties, and if need be, undertake an investigation for the effective conduct of which the States concerned shall furnish all necessary facilities; (b) place itself at the disposal of the parties concerned with a view to securing a friendly settlement of the matter on the basis of respect for human rights as defined in the Convention. The procedure therefore follows the twin track of preparing the case for final hearing and at the same time seeking an agreed resolution between the parties to avoid the necessity of a hearing.

If after a final hearing the court finds that there has been a violation of the Convention the Court judgment is required to deal with the question of "just satisfaction" (specific redress including costs) under Article 41. The Court cannot award anything other than compensation and costs. The object of compensation is to place the applicant so far as possible in the position he or she would have been in had the violation not occurred and compensation can be granted for pecuniary which would include such items such as loss of earnings, out of pocket expenses and/or non pecuniary loss which would cover compensation for "stress and anxiety" occasioned by the breach of the Convention and damages for ill-treatment or other such pain and suffering or unlawful imprisonment.

If the applicant succeeds in establishing that a violation of the Convention has occurred then the Court can order that the respondent state pay all or part of the applicant's costs. A detailed breakdown of how these are computed must be provided. The award of costs can only relate to those costs actually incurred, necessarily incurred and which

---

[323] E.g. where the applicant alleges an administrative practice rendering the remedy ineffective in practice and can show official tolerance of that practice (*Donnelly v. UK* 4 D& R 1975) or where strict application of the exhaustion rule would unreasonably subject the applicant to further violation of his rights (*Reed v. UK*, 19 D&R 113 1979).

[324] *W, X, Y, Z v. United Kingdom* (1968) 11 *Yearbook*, European Convention on Human Rights 562.

[325] *Ibid.*, Art.35(2).

[326] *Ibid.*, Rules of Court, November 1998, rule 54(4).

[327] *Ibid.*, rule 45(1).

[328] *Ibid.*, rule 56(1).

are reasonable as to quantum. The applicant's claim for costs can include those of the domestic proceedings taken to exhaust the national judicial remedies prior to submitting the application to the court.[329] However, such costs would only be awarded if the applicant were responsible for their payment in whole or in part.

A Chamber's judgement can be appealed to the Grand Chamber if it raises a serious issue affecting the interpretation of the Convention or of general importance.[330]

The friendly settlement is perhaps at the core of the Convention. The friendly settlement phase runs in tandem with the courts investigation of the merits. After the Court has decided that a complaint is admissible it writes to the parties asking whether or not they wish to explore the possibility of a friendly settlement and if so, inviting any proposals to this end. Negotiations are strictly confidential.[331] In order to encourage the parties to consider a friendly settlement the Court would appear to handle power to deliberate with a view to reaching a provisional opinion on the merits of the case and to communicate this to the parties. Thus if the opinion is strongly of the view that a violation has occurred then a generous friendly settlement would avoid embarrassment and further costs and if on the other hand the opinion is against a violation an early settlement could assist in avoiding the uncertainty and prove cheaper for the State than a contested hearing.

If the parties succeed in effecting a friendly settlement then the court is required by Article 39 to strike the case out of its list by means of a decision which "shall be confined to a brief statement of the facts and the solution reached." In general such statements contain details of the parties and their representatives, an outline of the facts and the terms of the settlement. The report is signed by the President and the Secretary and is then sent to the State concerned, the applicant and the Secretary General of the Council of Europe for publication. Unlike Court judgments the performance of friendly settlements are not supervised by the Committee of Ministers. In practice, States have complied with friendly settlements and so the issue of enforcement has not arisen.

Council of Europe legal aid is available to applicants where the Court is satisfied that it is essential for the proper discharge of the Court's duties and that the applicant has not sufficient means to meet all or part of the costs involved.[332]

Jurisprudence of the European Court of Human Rights on mental health issues

Cases brought under Article 5 of the Convention In the context of mental health issues the European Court of Human Rights has built up a considerable jurisprudence under Article 5 of the Convention albeit critics have argued that the protection it affords is not always watertight.[333] Article 5(1) provides that everyone has the right to liberty and security of person. It states that "No one shall be deprived of his liberty save in the following cases and in accordance with a procedure prescribed by law." Two of the exceptional cases are those set out in Article 5(1)(a) namely the lawful detention of a person after conviction by a competent court and Article 5(1)(e) namely the lawful

---

[329] *Kokkinakis v. Greece* [1993] 17 E.H.R.R. 397.

[330] European Convention on Human Rights, Art.43.

[331] *Ibid.*, Art.38(1) and see Rules of Court, rule 62.

[332] Rules of Court, r.92.

[333] See Gostin, "Human Rights of Persons with Mental Disabilities: The European Convention on Human Rights" (2000), Vol. 23, No. 2, *International Journal of Law and Psychiatry* 125.

detention of persons of unsound mind. Article 5(2) provides that everyone who is arrested shall be informed promptly, in a language, which he understands of the reasons for his arrest. … In addition Article 5(4) states that everyone who is deprived of his liberty by detention shall be entitled to take proceedings by which the lawfulness of his detention shall be decided speedily by a court and his release ordered if the detention is not lawful.

Article 5(1) which guarantees the right to liberty and security of the person appears to apply only to cases of formal detention as opposed to mere restriction of movement. In *Ashingdane v. United Kingdom*[334] the European Court of Human Rights held that a patient was detained in the sense that "his liberty and not just his freedom of movement has been circumscribed both in fact and in law" even though he had been permitted to leave the hospital on frequent occasions.[335] It has been argued that the case of the incompetent, "informally admitted", non-protesting patient[336] may fall outside the scope of the protection of Article 5(1) if the court does not have closer regard to the "factual and legal realities facing the individual" in determining whether s/he is detained.[337]

Albeit the European Court of Human Rights' interpretation of the protection afforded by Article 5(1) is less rigorous than might be wished for the court has imposed stricter criteria for detention under Article 5(1)(e) The conditions under which it is lawful to detain a person of unsound mind were discussed in the leading *Winterwerp v. the Netherlands*[338] in which Mr Frits Winterwerp, a Netherlands national was at the request of his wife committed to a psychiatric hospital under a provisional order made by the local District Court. Subsequently the detention order was renewed periodically by decision of the regional court on the basis of medical reports from the doctor in charge of his case. Mr Winterwerp complained that the various courts never heard him, that he was never notified of the orders concerning his detention, that he did not receive any legal assistance and that he had no opportunity of challenging the medical reports. In his view his deprivation of liberty could not be considered lawful within the meaning of Article 5(1) of the Convention. He further claimed that he was unable to take court proceedings in accordance with Article 5(4) to test the lawfulness of his detention.

The European Court of Human Rights held that for detention to be justified under Article 5(1)(e) it had to be in conformity with the applicable municipal law both as to the grounds for detention and the procedure followed.[339] In addition the detention would not be lawful if it was "arbitrary". The court held that the requirement of lack of arbitrariness meant that three minimum conditions had to be satisfied: (i) except in emergencies the individual concerned must be "reliably shown" by "objective medical expertise" to be of "unsound mind";[340] (ii) the individual's "mental disorder must be of a kind or degree warranting compulsory confinement" and (iii) the disorder must persist throughout the period of detention. Since Mr Winterwerp's initial detention was in the nature of an emergency confinement albeit for as long as six weeks it constituted the

---

[334] [1985] 7 E.H.R.R 528.
[335] *Ibid.*, para.42.
[336] See for example the case of *R v. Bournewood Community and Mental Health NHS Trust, ex parte L. (Secretary of State for Health and others intervening)* [1998] 3 All E.R. 289.
[337] See Gostin, *op. cit.*, p.138.
[338] Series A 33 (1979).
[339] *Ibid.*, para 39.
[340] This condition does not apply in emergencies.

lawful detention of a person of unsound mind within the meaning of Article 5(1)(e). The court however, held that a person who is detained as being "of unsound mind" under Article 5(1)(e) must be allowed "to be heard either in person or where necessary through some form of representation"[341] by a court which is to determine the lawfulness of his detention under Article 5(4). Accordingly the court ruled that Mr Winterwerp's inability to have his detention reviewed by a court and the failure to hear him thus constituted a violation of Article 5(4) of the Convention.

The third criterion outlined in the Winterwerp case viz. that the disorder must persist throughout the period of confinement – does not necessarily mean that patients must be unconditionally released as soon as they cease to be mentally ill but in the case of *Johnson v. United Kingdom*[342] the Court established that the criterion does mean that safeguards must be in place to assure that discharge is not unreasonably delayed. In that case an English Mental Health Review Tribunal found that Johnson no longer suffered from a mental illness but deferred his conditional discharge until arrangements could be made for suitable hostel accommodation. In the event, however, a suitable hospital could not be found and the applicant remained in hospital for an additional three years. The European Court of Human Rights held, that although a deferral of conditional discharge was justified in principle, the applicant's detention was not permitted under Article 5(1)(e) because of the lack of safeguards to ensure that the applicant's discharge was not unreasonably delayed.

Offenders with mental disorder admitted to the Central Mental Hospital are detained on the basis of Article 5(1)(a) – the lawful detention of a person after conviction by a competent court and Article 5(1)(e) – the lawful detention of persons of unsound mind. The European Court of Human Rights has found that where a court initially orders detention of an offender with mental disorder the judicial review required by the Convention is incorporated in the court's decision. The initial court order, however, according, to the court lasts only for the period of time that is proportional to the gravity of the offence. In *Silva Rocha v. Portugal*[343] the court found that a person found not guilty by reason of insanity could be detained under Article 5(1)(a) for three years given the seriousness of the offence and the risk to the public for that period. The review required by Article 5(4) was incorporated in the sentencing court's decision. However, once this "tariff" of three years had expired the applicant had the right to further judicial review.

The scope of Article 5(2) which states that everyone who is arrested shall be informed promptly, in a language which he understands of the reasons for his arrest and Article 5(4) which provides that everyone who is deprived of his liberty by detention shall be entitled to take proceedings by which the lawfulness of his detention shall be decided speedily by a court and his release ordered if the detention is not lawful have also been examined in cases before the European Court of Human Rights.

In *X v. United Kingdom*[344] the applicant who at the time of lodging of his complaint with the Commission was detained in Broadmoor Hospital lodged a complaint against

---

[341] Series A 33 (1979), para.60.
[342] [1999] 27 E.H.R.R. 296.
[343] Judgment, October 26, 1996 (1996) V Eur.Ct. H.R. (Ser. A).
[344] Series A No. 46 (1981).

his recall to Broadmoor Hospital in April 1974 following a three-year period of conditional discharge. He claimed that his recall was unjustified, that he was not promptly given sufficient reasons for his re-detention and that he had no effective way of challenging the authorities' actions. The European Court of Human Rights found that the Government of the United Kingdom was in breach of both Articles 5(2) and Article 5(4) of the Convention. It was in breach of Article 5(2) in that the authorities had not promptly informed the applicant of the reasons for his recall and it was in breach of Article 5(4) in that it failed to provide restricted patients (i.e. those whose discharge is at the discretion of the Home Secretary) with a periodic right of access to a court capable of reviewing the substantive grounds for their continued detention in hospital and of ordering their discharge if these were not satisfied.[345]

In *Van Der Leer v. Netherlands*[346] Mrs Van Der Leer was a voluntary patient in a psychiatric hospital on October 3, 1983. On November 18, 1983 the Cantonal Court judge, without holding a hearing, ordered her compulsory confinement in the same hospital for a period of six months. The applicant became aware of this order only by accident on November 28, 1983. On December 6, 1983 through her lawyer she lodged a request for discharge, which was refused by the Board of the Hospital. Legal proceedings were initiated. She left the hospital without authorisation on 31 January 1984 and without notice to her was granted probationary leave on February 7. The District Court eventually ordered her discharge on May 7, 1984. On application to it, the European Court of Human Rights held that there had been a violation of Article 5(1) of the Convention. The Cantonal Judge had failed to hear the applicant before authorising her confinement and this amounted to a failure to comply with an essential procedural requirement under Article 5(1). There was also a violation of Article 5(2), which provides that everyone who is arrested has the right to be informed promptly of the reasons for his arrest. The term "arrest" in Article 5(2) was to be interpreted "autonomously" in particular in accordance with the aim and purpose of protecting everyone from arbitrary deprivation of liberty. It extended beyond criminal law measures and applied to psychiatric confinement. There was a breach of Article 5(2) in that neither the manner in which Mrs Van Der Leer was informed of the order depriving her of her liberty nor the time it took to communicate the information to her satisfied the requirements of Article 5(2). The court found further that there had been a breach of Article 5(4). The relevant period during which proceedings could be taken ran from the date when her application for release was lodged which step had to be regarded as equivalent to instituting proceedings against a confinement order to the date of the judgment ordering her release. The proceedings thus lasted five months and in the absence of grounds justifying this delay the Court found a violation of Article 5(4).

In *Megyeri v. Germany*[347] it was held in an Article 5(1)(e) case that a person detained as being mentally disordered was entitled to legal representation at the hearing unless

---

[345] In January 1982 in response to the European Court's judgment the Government of the United Kingdom introduced amendments to the Mental Health (Amendment) Bill (now the Mental Health (Amendment) Act 1982) which was then before Parliament designed to empower mental health review tribunals to order the discharge of restricted patients.

[346] Series A No. 170.

[347] A 237–A (1992).

there were special circumstances suggesting otherwise. Moreover the person concerned should not be required to take the initiative to obtain legal representation.

In the case of *Luberti v. Italy*[348] Mr Luberti complained of the failure of the Italian courts to decide "speedily" on his applications for a confinement order to be reviewed or set aside under Article 5(4). The European Court of Human Rights ruled that a delay of 18 months before a court's deciding on the legality of the detention was too long and consequently there had been a breach of Article 5(4). In *Herczegfalvy v. Austria*[349] reviews at intervals of 15 months, and two years meant the decision by the national courts could not be regarded as having been given speedily as required by Article 5(4). In *Koendijbiahre v. Netherlands*[350] a period of four months between lodging of the application to extend the complainant's detention and the communication of the decision on the application to the complainant was held to be unacceptably long. The domestic law of the Netherlands allowed a maximum of three months in exceptional cases and the court could find no good reason why a four-month delay had occurred. Consequently there was a breach of Article 5(4).

Cases brought under Article 3 of the Convention Not only admission procedures but also conditions in psychiatric hospitals have been subjected to examination under the Convention provisions. Article 3 of the Convention states that "No one shall be subjected to torture or to inhuman and degrading treatment or punishment." In *Ireland v. United Kingdom*[351] the European Court ruled that torture must involve an unlawful or invidious purpose. As a consequence the prohibition in Article 3 is unlikely to apply in cases involving mental health issues unless there is some anti-therapeutic or unethical motive.

In *Ireland v. United Kingdom* the criteria for determining whether treatment was inhuman and degrading was set out as follows:

> "Treatment will be inhuman only if it reaches a level of gravity involving con-siderable mental or physical suffering and degrading if the person has undergone humiliation or debasement involving a minimum level of severity"[352]

Whether treatment is inhuman and degrading depends on all the circumstances of the case including its nature and context, the manner and method of its execution, its duration, its physical and mental effects and, in some cases the victim's gender age and state of health.[353]

The application of Article 3 to the case of the conditions of confinement and treatment of a patient with mental health difficulties was examined in the case of *Herczegfalvy v. Austria*.[354] In that case the applicant had been admitted to a psychiatric hospital in a

[348] Series A 75 (1984).
[349] Series A 244 (1992).
[350] Series A 185–B paras 28–30 (1990).
[351] (1978) 25 Eur. Ct. H.R. (Ser A.) paras 66–67.
[352] *Ibid.*, para.162.
[353] *Ireland v. United Kingdom*, para.162; *Tyrer v. United Kingdom* 26 Eur. Ct. H.R (Ser. A) paras 29–30, 2 E.H.R.R. (1979–80); *Costello-Roberts v. United Kingdom*, 247–C Eur. Ct. H.R. (Ser. A) para.30 19 E.H.R.R. 112 (1995).
[354] 24 Eur. Ct. H.R. (Ser. A) (1993) E.H.R.R. 437.

weakened state following a hunger strike. He was forcibly fed and given strong doses of sedatives notwithstanding his refusal to consent. At different times he was also attached to a security bed by a net and straps. Because of his aggressive behaviour he was handcuffed and a belt placed around his ankles. The court stated:

> "The court considers that the position of inferiority and powerlessness which is typical of patients confined in psychiatric hospitals calls for increased vigilance in reviewing whether the Convention has been complied with … The established principles of medicine are admittedly in principle decisive in such cases; as a general rule, a measure which is a therapeutic necessity cannot be regarded as inhuman or degrading. The court must nevertheless satisfy itself that the medical necessity has been convincingly shown to exist…"[355]

The court also stated that while it was for it to make the ultimate determination under Article 3 "it was for medical authorities to decide, on the basis of recognised rules of medical science, on the therapeutic methods to be used, if necessary by force, to preserve the physical and mental health of patients…".[356] Although the court found the prolonged use of handcuffs and the security bed worrying, it found the restraint medically justified. This approach of recognising treatment as justified if it complies with internationally recognised mental health standards pervades many of the cases taken in relation to conditions in psychiatric hospitals under Article 3.[357]

On the other hand in *A v. United Kingdom*[358] the European Commission of Human Rights adopted a report accepting a friendly settlement in a case involving an application under Article 3. In that case a patient at Broadmoor hospital was placed in seclusion for a period that lasted five weeks following his suspected involvement in an arson attack on one of the hospital wards. He alleged that he had been subject to inhuman and degrading treatment. He had very limited opportunities for exercise or association. He was deprived of adequate furnishing and clothing and the conditions in the room were insanitary, inadequately lit and ventilated. The friendly settlement that was secured included an *ex gratia* payment to the applicant and a requirement that new working guidelines for seclusion of patients be introduced at Broadmoor hospital. Thus while the European Court of Human Rights has not been highly sympathetic to claims under Article 3 the provision can still be effective in bringing about improvements in conditions in psychiatric hospitals.

Cases brought under Article 6 of the Convention Article 6(1) of the European Convention is yet another provision that has been called in aid by people with mental disabilities before the European Court of Human Rights. It provides "In the determination of his civil rights and obligations …, everyone is entitled to a fair and public hearing within a reasonable time by an independent and impartial tribunal established by law."

---

[355] Para.8.2.
[356] *Ibid.*, para.82.
[357] Gostin (see above note) cites the examples of *B v. United Kingdom*, (App No. 6870/75, Second Partial Decision of the Commission as to Admissibility, 10 Dec & rep 37 (Eur. Comm. H.R. 1977); *Dhoest v. Belgium*, App. No. 19448/83, para.129 (Eur. Comm. H.R. 1987); *Aerts v. Belgium*, judgment of July 30, 1998 1998–V Eur. Ct. H.R. 1939 [1998] E.H.R.L.R. 777–780 (1998).
[358] App. No. 6840/74 (Eur. Comm H.R. 1977).

In the cases of *Winterwerp v. Netherlands* it was held that " while mental illness may render legitimate certain limitations upon the exercise of a "right to a court" it cannot warrant the total absence of that right as embodied in Article 6(1)."[359] Article 6(1) therefore guarantees people with mental disabilities the right to judicial determination to secure their complete entitlement to civil rights. The European Court of Human Rights has found that there has been a breach of Article 6 in cases where people with mental disabilities were either refused access to a court or there were unreasonable delays. Thus in the *Winterwerp* case it was held that there was a violation of Article 6 in a case of a denial of a patient's right to control property. In the case of *Matter v. Slovakia*[360] Article 6 was breached in a case where the courts took a total of seven years and three months to determine whether the applicant had mental incapacity to acquire rights and undertake obligations. In the case of *Bock v. Germany*[361] the court held there was a breach of Article 6(1) when German courts took nine years to establish that the applicant had the mental capacity to institute divorce proceedings. The hardship caused to the applicant by unfounded doubts cast on his mental health for that length of time amounted to a serious encroachment upon human dignity and finally in *H. v. United Kingdom*[362] it was held that since proceedings which related to a mentally ill parent's access to her child and the latter's adoption could lead to the dissolution of natural ties between mother and child and those ties constituted the very substance of family life the proceedings in question involved the determination of a 'civil right' of the applicant under Article 6(1). In such cases the Court held that the authorities were under a duty to exercise exceptional diligence since there was always the danger that any procedural delay would result in the *de facto* determination of the issue submitted to the court before it had held its hearing. This was what happened in the instant case. The proceedings in question lasted two years and seven months. They were not concluded within a reasonable time and consequently there was a violation of Article 6(1).

Cases invoking Article 8 of the Convention Article 8 of the Convention has also been litigated in the context of mental health care. Article 8 prohibits public authorities from interfering with a persons right "to respect for his private and family life, his home and his correspondence" In *Herczegfalvy*[363] the hospital and a detained patient's guardian had screened all outgoing post and determined which pieces should be forwarded to the addressees including letters of complaint about his medical treatment. The European Court found this to be a violation of the patient's right to freedom of correspondence under Article 8 (as well as a violation of the right to receive and impart information under Article 10)

---

[359] Judgment of November 27, 1981, 47 Eur. Ct. H.R. (Ser. A). (1979) 2 E.H.R.R. 387 para.75.
[360] App. No. 31534/96, Judgment of the Eur. Ct. H.R. July 5, 1999 para.51.
[361] Judgment of February 21, 1989, 150 Eur. Ct. HR (Ser. A) 12 E.H.R.R. 247.
[362] Judgment of July 8, 1987, 121 Eur. Ct. H.R. (Ser. A) 10 E.H.R.R. 95.
[363] (1995) 19 E.H.R.R. 112.

Giving force to the European Convention on Human Rights in Irish law

The recent European Convention on Human Rights Act 2003 that came into force on December 31, 2003[364] gives indirect interpretative force to Articles 2[365] to 14 of the European Convention on Human Rights[366] and Protocols 1, 4, 6 and 7[367] thereof in Irish domestic law subject to the Constitution.

Background to the enactment of legislation The promulgation of the Act was primarily prompted by the Irish Government's commitment to the British-Irish Agreement of April 10, 1998 ("The Good Friday Agreement"). Under the Agreement the State had an obligation to bring forward measures to strengthen the protection of human rights in the State; to introduce proposals that would "draw on the European Convention on Human Rights and other international instruments in the field of human rights" and to "further examine" the question of incorporation in this context. Any measures to be brought forward had to "ensure at least an equivalent level of protection of human rights as will pertain in Northern Ireland" in the light of ongoing developments in human rights there. The United Kingdom had already decided to give effect to European Convention on Human Rights throughout its constituent jurisdictions including Northern Ireland by means of the Human Rights Act 1998 which had full effect from October 2, 2000 and so it fell to the Irish Government to address the incorporation of the European Convention measures into Irish law, Ireland being the only state in the Council of Europe not to have incorporated the Convention into its domestic law.

The choice of methods of incorporation The Convention could, by means of a referendum have been adopted directly as part of our Constitution and declared to be

---

[364] European Convention on Human Rights Act 2003 (Commencement) Order 2003 (S.I. No. 483 of 2003).

[365] At Second Stage in the Seanad the Minister for Justice, Equality and Law Reform stated "Art.1 of the Convention is not included but there is no need to do so. This is due to the fact that the obligation to respect human rights as defined in the Convention and to secure them to everyone within the jurisdiction of the contracting states to the Convention, has already been accepted by the State since the time it ratified the Convention and its coming into effect in 1953. That obligation has been binding on us since that time and that is the reason the Long Title refers to the Bill giving further effect to the Convention." See Vol. 173, No. 10, Seanad Debates, June 18, 2003 Col. 832.

[366] S.1(1) of the Act defines "the Convention" as the "Convention for the Protection of Human Rights and Fundamental Freedoms done at Rome on the 4th day of November, 1950 (the text of which, in the English language, is, for convenience of reference set out in sch.1 to this Act) as amended by Protocol No. 11 done at Strasbourg on the 11th day of May 1994." The Convention as set out in the sch.1 to the Act is set out in Appendix 1.

[367] S.1(1) of the 2003 Act defines "Convention provisions" as meaning "subject to any derogation which the State may make pursuant to Art.15 of the Convention, Articles 2 to 14 of the Convention and the following protocols thereto as construed in accordance with Articles 16 to 18 of the Convention: (a) the Protocol to the Convention done at Paris on the 20th day of March 1952; (b) Protocol No. 4 to the Convention securing certain rights and freedoms other than those already included in the Convention and in the First Protocol thereto done at Strasbourg on the 16th day of September 1963; (c) Protocol No. 6 to the Convention concerning the abolition of the death penalty done at Strasbourg on the 28th day of April 1983; (d) Protocol No. 7 to the Convention done at Strasbourg on the 22nd day of November, 1984 (the texts of which protocols in the English language, are, for convenience of reference, set out in schs 2, 3, 4, and 5 respectively to this Act)." See Appendix 1 for the relevant text.

part of the fundamental law of Ireland. Any subordinate legislation, which was incompatible with Convention rights, would have been unconstitutional and invalid. An incompatible constitutional provision would not automatically be rendered invalid (except where it is also incompatible with Community law) and the courts would have resolved any conflicts.

However, this idea was rejected by the Government accepting the views of the Constitution Review Group in 1996[368] that there was already a high degree of overlap between the Constitution's guarantees in the area of fundamental rights and the provisions of the Convention. Nonetheless, it is submitted that this is not the case in relation to the detention and treatment of persons of unsound mind where it can be cogently argued that the Convention provisions (particularly Articles 3 and 5(1)(e)) afford greater protection than the Irish constitution. Further as to the mechanics of constitutional incorporation it appears that the government did not give much consideration to "a method [*of retaining*] (emphasis added) the current rights enshrined in the Constitution while incorporating the European Convention on Human Rights in a manner that would give some or all the Convention provisions similar constitutional status".[369]

Secondly, the Minister for Justice, Equality and Law Reform argued that incorporation of the Convention into the Irish Constitution would give rise to a question of whether the European Court of Human Rights or the Irish Supreme Court would be the final authority on how the Convention provisions should be interpreted. It being likely that the view of the European Court of Human Rights would prevail the Minister stated:

> "That would mean a cessation of sovereignty in respect of fundamental rights to a court over which we have no direct influence, in the sense we have over our domestic courts, independent though they are."[370]

However, in response to this argument it may be argued that the European Court of Human Rights is in any event under the interpretative system of adaptation the final arbiter on Convention interpretation as Irish nationals retain their right to apply to that court for a remedy.

The alternative method of incorporation, which could have been adopted, would be to make the Convention part of Irish legislation. This approach was not considered by the Constitution Review Group and was not taken by the Government as the view was expressed by the Minister for Justice, Equality and Law Reform at Committee Stage in

---

[368] The group comprised a Chairman Dr T.K. Whittaker the Chancellor of the National University of Ireland and 14 experts drawn from different disciplines with a mandate from the Government "to review the Constitution and in the light of this review to establish those areas where constitutional change may be desirable or necessary, with a view to assisting the all-Party Committee on the Constitution, to be established by the Oireachtas in its work ...". The group met for just over one year from May 1995 until May 1996 and produced a number of reports. The report referred to is the final report in May 1996.

[369] See Murphy R. and Willis S., "The European Convention on Human Rights and Irish Incorporation – Adopting a Minimalist Approach" 2001 Oct/Nov *Bar Review*, p.41 at 42 The Constitution Review Group favoured a form of incorporation where certain provisions of the Convention could be reflected in laws where the European Convention on Human Rights standard was higher than that already contained in domestic law. See Report of Review Group, p.219.

[370] Seanad Debates 2003 Vol. 173 No. 10 (Second Stage) Col. 830.

the Dáil that it would provide for a system whereby courts could declare one piece of legislation valid by reference to another ordinary piece of legislation, namely the 2003 Act. If that happened there would be "a very large risk" that the European Convention on Human Rights Act would be found to be unconstitutional, "as amounting *de facto* to giving the European Convention on Human Rights a status equivalent to the Constitution itself without a corresponding constitutional amendment."[371]

The Minister stated further:

> "We cannot incorporate into Irish law a statute which has the effect of potentially invalidating future statutes under Irish law. That would be surrender by the Legislature to the courts of the right to make law for the State. The only exception to that in our law is the right for the [courts] to strike down Acts which are inconsistent with our Constitution."[372]

Further in the Debate at Second Stage in the Seanad the Minister stated of the approach that would make the Convention part of the law of state:

> "[T]he fatal flaw with such an approach is that it would have the capacity to undermine one of the central pillars of the Constitution, namely the doctrine of separation of powers. It would mean the Oireachtas was investing the Judiciary with a new right to invalidate the laws of the Oireachtas by reference to what was decided by the Court of Human Rights at Strasbourg. In effect the judiciary would become law makers, implementing decisions of that court contrary to the exclusive role of the Oireachtas under Article 15.2.1 of the Constitution."[373]

In the ultimate event an interpretative approach similar to that adopted in the United Kingdom was chosen and the Convention was adopted indirectly as a means of governing administrative practice. While this method was chosen in the United Kingdom in deference their system of parliamentary sovereignty the interpretative method appears to have been adopted in Ireland in order to defer to the "our doctrine of constitutional sovereignty and the supremacy of the will of the people"[374] It was also adopted to defer to the "system of fundamental rights" embodied in the Constitution which the Minister for Justice, Equality and Law Reform stated was:

> "chosen by the people, which are unalterable save by the wish of the people and which are made superior and justiciable at the instance of the individual over all other law both in theory and practice."[375]

The other reason appears to have been to avoid the risk of interference with the legislative supremacy of the Oireachtas or the judicial supremacy of the courts under the

---

[371] See Select Committee on Justice, Equality, Defence and Women's Rights, February 19, 2003, p.8 (Minister for Justice, Equality and Law Reform quoting Dr Gerard Hogan's submission to the Committee).

[372] See Select Committee on Justice, Equality, Defence and Women's Rights, February 19, 2003, p.9.

[373] Seanad Éireann Debates 2003 Vol. 173 No. 10 (Second Stage) Col. 830.

[374] See Seanad Éireann Debates 2003 Vol. 173 No. 10 Col. 830.

[375] Dáil Éireann Debates 2001, Vol. 538 No. 2 Col. 298 In the Seanad the Minister was more categorical.

Constitution.[376] In the course of debates at Committee stage the Minister stated that "it would be ... impermissible to delegate the exposition of human rights in Ireland to the court in Strasbourg without a constitutional amendment"[377] and further that "we have an absolute imperative of constitutional sovereignty."[378]

However, it was pointed out that in certain respects the Convention rights do not supplant but supplement the rights guaranteed by the Constitution and that in this regard a system of direct incorporation subject to the Constitution might have been preferable.[379] In addition it was pointed out at Committee Stage in the Seanad that the interpretative approach may have certain drawbacks because of the rules of interpretation applied by the judges when it is sought to impugn enacted legislation by reference to a higher law. One rule of interpretation – the "double construction" rule – has been applied particularly in cases where it is sought to impugn legislation by reference to the Irish Constitution and is an instance in point. Effectively it means that statutes are presumed to be constitutional and a statute will not be declared invalid where it is possible to construe it in accordance with the Constitution. The presumption of constitutionality applies to both the substance and the operation of a statute. In cases of doubt or where more than one construction is possible an interpretation favouring the validity of an Act must be given. Only if the words of the statute admit of no possible interpretation other than a constitutionally objectionable one is the presumption of constitutionality of the statute rebutted. This has resulted in courts attributing artificial and restrictive meanings to statutes to save them from a finding of constitutional invalidity.[380] Applied in the context of testing compatibility with Convention provisions it was pointed out in the Seanad that:

> "impugned legislation or acts of certain public bodies will enjoy a presumption of compatibility with the ECHR unless and until a litigant rebuts that presumption. This judicial technique ... can lead to quite artificial findings by the courts in their determination to uphold challenged legislation."[381]

Further commentators have pointed out that Ireland's record of applying Convention decisions has not been a happy or convincing one:

> "Irish courts have refused to give effect to decisions of the Strasbourg court – even when the decision was made against Ireland.[382] They have also refused to apply a decision of the Strasbourg court when it concerned exactly the law that

---

[376] Dáil Éireann Debates 2001 Vol. 538 No. 2 Col. 302.
[377] Select Committee on Justice, Equality, Defence and Women's Rights, February 18, 2003, p.6.
[378] *Ibid.*
[379] Select Committee on Justice, Equality, Defence and Women's Rights, February 18, 2003, p.9, 11 (J.O'Keeffe T.D.).
[380] See *Loftus v. Attorney General* [1979] 1.R. 211; *Doyle v. An Taoiseach* [1986] I.L.R.M. 693; *Hegarty v. O'Loughran* [1940] I.R. 148; *In re National Irish Bank Ltd.* [1999] I.L.R.M. 321. See also G. Hogan and G. Whyte (eds.), *J.M.Kelly: The Irish Constitution* (3rd ed., 1994), pp.458–459.
[381] Seanad Éireann Debates 2003 Vol. 173 No. 11 (Committee Stage) Col. 993 (*per* Senator Norris quoting Donncha O'Connell from a lecture delivered in November 2002).
[382] *E v. E* [1982] I.L.R.M. 497 and *Airey v. Ireland* [1979] Series A No. 32.

was before them.[383] When Irish judges do cite the ECHR it is normally only to provide additional back up support for a decision that the Court would have reached any way based on Irish law.[384] They appear anxious to stress the primacy of Irish jurisprudence even when the right in question clearly derives from European jurisprudence."[385]

Further at Committee Stage in the Dáil attention was drawn to the limited nature of the adaptation of the Convention and Protocols by J. Costello T.D. who argued that provision should be made in the 2003 Act for the incorporation of Protocol 12 and future Protocols to the Convention into Irish law. An amendment to the legislation to this effect was rejected by the Minister for Justice Equality and Law Reform who stated that the:

> "appropriate method for further incorporation on an interpretative basis into Irish law of the probable additional protocols to the Convention is to require that the Oireachtas should amend the legislation to give them effect, subject to whatever qualifications are open to it, in a way that is compatible with Irish law".[386]

The provisions of the European Convention on Human Rights Act 2003

Section 2: The interpretative obligation Section 2 of the Act provides that in interpreting and applying any statutory provision or rule of law an [Irish] court shall, in so far as is possible, subject to the rules of law relating to such interpretation and application, do so in a manner compatible with the State's obligations under the Convention provisions. "Statutory provision" is defined widely by section 1 of the Act to mean:

> "any provision of an Act of the Oireachtas or of any order, regulation, rule, licence, bye-law or other like document made issued or otherwise created thereunder or any statute, order, regulation, rule, licence, bye-law or other like document made, issued or otherwise created under a statute which continued in force by virtue of Article 50 of the Constitution"

"Rule of law" is defined by section 1 to include common law.

Section 2(2) gives retroactive and prospective force to the obligation to interpret provisions and rules of law consistently with the State's obligations under section 2 and provides that section 2 applies to any statutory provision or rule of law in force immediately before the passing of the Act or any such provision coming into force thereafter. Further the duty to interpret legislation in this way applies to all courts including the District and Circuit Courts.[387]

---

[383] *Norris v. Attorney General* [1984] I.R. 36.

[384] See for example the dicta of Barrington J. in *Irish Times Ltd v. Murphy* [1998] 2 I.L.R.M. 161 at 193.

[385] See Murphy R. and Willis S., "The European Convention on Human Rights and Irish Incorporation – Adopting a Minimalist Approach" (2001 October/November) *Bar Review* 41 at 42.

[386] Select Committee on Justice, Equality, Defence and Women's Rights, February 18, 2003, p.17.

[387] See Dáil Éireann Debates, 2003 Vol. 568 No. 19 (Report Stage) Col. 76 (*per* Minister for Justice, Equality and Law Reform).

Section 4: Aids to interpretation Section 4 provides a statutory aid to the interpretation of the provisions of the Convention and Protocols and provides that judicial notice must be taken (i.e. proof will not be required) of the Convention provisions[388] and of (a) any declaration, decision, advisory opinion or judgment of the European Court of Human Rights established under the Convention on any question in respect of which that court has jurisdiction, (b) any decision of the European Commission of Human Rights so established on any question in respect of which it had jurisdiction, (c) any decision of the Committee of Ministers established under the Statute of the Council of Europe on any question in respect of which it had jurisdiction and an Irish court must when interpreting and applying the Convention provisions "take due account" of the principles laid down by those declarations, decisions, advisory opinions, opinions and judgments.[389]

During the Debate at Committee Stage in the Seanad the Minister for State at the Department of Justice, Equality and Law Reform stated the words "take due account of the principles" indicated that the principles were to be of persuasive but not binding authority. This was consistent with the fact that the Convention case law represented a minimum threshold, which a given state might wish to exceed, and there was no imperative that Convention countries should adopt a uniform solution to a particular problem. It also recognised that the social values of contracting states might well be different and was consistent with the doctrine of the "margin of appreciation" adopted by the Strasbourg court that there must be a wide discretion as to how rights can be applied given the cultural and social differences between the states.[390] However, viewed from another perspective the fact that the Irish courts are neither bound to follow or apply a precedent of the European Court of Human Rights and related bodies may mean that the Irish courts may exercising their discretion continue to adopt a traditionally restrictive approach to the European Court's jurisprudence and the 2003 Act will have little effect in Irish case law.[391]

Section 4 is of particular significance in the context of Irish Mental Health law in that the jurisprudence of the European Court of Human Rights particularly under Article 3 (prohibition on torture or inhuman or degrading treatment or punishment), Article 5 (right to liberty and security of person), Article 8 (right to respect for private and family life), Article 10 (right to freedom of expression) and Article 14 (prohibition on discrimination) will from the coming into force of the Act have persuasive authority in the context of the interpretation of Irish mental health legislation and case law.

Section 3: Obligation on organs of State to perform functions compatibly with Convention provisions By virtue of section 3(1) of the Act every "organ of state" assumes an obligation, subject to any statutory provision (other than the 2003 Act) or rule of law, to perform its functions in a manner compatible with the State's obligations under the Convention provisions. An "organ of state" is defined by the section 1(1) to include:

---

[388] See definition in s.1(1) above, n.288.

[389] European Convention on Human Rights Act 2003, s.4.

[390] Seanad Éireann Debates 2003 Vol. 173 No. 11 (Committee Stage) Cols. 997–998 (*per* B. Lenihan T.D.).

[391] See Murphy R. and Willis S., "The European Convention on Human Rights and Irish Incorporation – Adopting a Minimalist Approach" (2001 October/November) *Bar Review* 41 at p.43.

"a tribunal or any other body (*other than* the President or the Oireachtas or either House of the Oireachtas or a Committee of either such House or a Joint Committee of both such Houses *or a court*) which is established by law *or* through which any of the legislative, executive or judicial powers of the State are exercised." (Italics added)

To be an organ of state therefore a body must either be a body, which is established by law *or* in the alternative a body through which any of the legislative, executive or judicial powers of the State are exercised. "Functions" are defined by section 1(1) to include:

"powers and duties and references to the performance of functions includes, as respects powers and duties, reference to the exercise of the powers and the performance of the duties."

It is clear from section 3 that people will now enjoy a right of due process (in accordance with Article 6 of the European Convention) in the determination of their entitlements by local authorities, welfare officers, and the Health Service Executive and this will include a right to a fair hearing and a reasoned decision which will be open to challenge in the courts.

The exclusion of the courts from the definition of "organ of the state" is a matter of concern. The European Convention obligations extend to the performance of judicial functions. Thus judicial delay or failure to give adequate reasons could constitute a breach of the Convention provisions. Accordingly there is an argument that the definition of "organ of the state" should be expanded to encompass the courts. In answer to this argument the Minister for Justice Equality and Law Reform at the Second Stage Debate in the Seanad stated:

"The courts are under a duty to administer justice in accordance with law and the Constitution. Furthermore the Convention is primarily a vertically effective instrument – by which I mean that it is designed as a means for redressing human rights violations between the individual and the State – the inclusion of the courts could result in their being drawn into its development as a horizontally effective means of resolving rights-based disputes between individuals. I do not want to create a new set of actionable torts consisting of breaches of Convention rights as between individuals, nor do I want to see a development whereby people under sections 3(1) and 3(2) would be able to sue the courts in respect of court decisions."[392]

At Committee Stage in the Seanad the Minister of State at the Department of Justice, Equality and Law Reform stated in response to a proposed amendment including courts within the definition of "organ of state":

"The courts do not operate as an autonomous area of unregulated power. They are constrained by the Constitution, statutory instruments and the legislation the

---

[392] Seanad Éireann Debates 2003 Vol. 173 No. 10 Col. 832.

Oireachtas has enacted to regulate the conduct of court proceedings. The rules of court constitute a statutory instrument, which the courts are obliged to follow. Under this Bill, all of these provisions will have to be interpreted in the context of the Convention in a manner compatible with it, if at all possible."[393]

However, these arguments do not take account of the fact that the European Convention on Human Rights contains justiciable rights for delay on the part of the courts in hearing the case and failure to give adequate reasons, which may not be contained in domestic legislation. Further if other bodies "exercising judicial powers" (such as tribunals) are included in the definition of "organ of state" the exclusion of the courts is an artificial one.[394]

A further difficulty of interpretation arises as to precisely what bodies would be included within the term "organ of the state". It would appear to be the case that the Health Service Executive would be included as it was established by law. The issue of whether private hospitals were included is more problematic. It would appear that much would depend on whether the hospital was established by law or could be said to be a body through which the executive powers of the state were exercised. Much may turn on the amount of public funding committed to the institution.[395] At Committee Stage the Minister for State at the Department of Justice, Equality and Law Reform, Brian Lenihan TD, stated that the issue was "similar to that pertaining to judicial review proceedings concerning the definition of a public body" and that in this regard "an area of discretion" had been left to the courts but that if was " a form of discretion that the courts [could] use to maximise the protection of persons who [had] an entitlement to invoke the provisions of the Convention."[396]

Under section 3(2) a person who has suffered injury, loss or damage as a result of a contravention of the obligation under section 3(1) may if no other remedy in damages is available, institute proceedings to recover damages in respect of the contravention in the High Court or (subject to the monetary limit of that court's jurisdiction in tort)[397] in the Circuit Court and the court may award to the person such damages (if any) as it considers appropriate.

In the course of debates at the Committee Stage the Minister for Justice, Equality and Law Reform stated that the damages to be awarded under section 3 "are the ordinary compensatory measure of damages available under Irish law". The level of compensation will not be decided according to the principles laid down by the European Court of Human Rights which were "usually 10% or 20% of what one might expect an Irish court to award in similar circumstances".[398]

---

[393] Seanad Éireann Debates 2003 Vol. 173 No. 11 (Committee Stage) Col. 979 (*per* B. Lenihan T.D.).

[394] See Seanad Éireann Debates 2003 Vol. 173 No. 11 (Committee Stage) Col 982 (*per* Senator Norris) See also concession by the Minister of State at the Department of Justice, Equality and Law Reform to the effect that "the courts are, in our constitutional law, an organ of State but not in this proposed legislation" at Col. 987.

[395] See Seanad Éireann Debates 2003 Vol. 173 No. 12 (Report Stage) June 24, 2003 Cols 1126, 1129 (*per* B. Lenihan T.D.).

[396] Select Committee on Justice, Equality, Defence and Women's Rights, March 5, 2003, p.13 (www.gov.ie/committees-29/c-justice).

[397] European Convention on Human Rights Act 2003, s.3(3).

[398] See Select Committee on Justice, Equality, Defence and Women's Rights, March 12, 2003, p.10.

While this is a welcome provision it has been argued that the court's power under the section should be extended to make orders other than orders for damages. In the context of mental health law a power to issue injunctions (including mandatory injunctions) and orders for the release of a person from detention would be of particular relevance. Indeed in the course of the debate at Second Stage in the Seanad reference was made to the conditions in the Central Mental Hospital which had been internationally criticised and which could amount in an individual case to a breach of Article 3 of the European Convention (prohibition on torture or inhuman or degrading treatment or punishment). It was argued that financial compensation would not improve conditions in the hospital or secure the release of the people in it.[399]

However, in the course of the debate at Committee Stage in the Dáil the Minister for Justice, Equality and Law Reform stated that:

> "[s]ections 3(1) and 3(2) do not exclude other equitable relief such as injunctive relief or declarations being given."[400]

At a further stage in the Committee Stage Debates the Minister for State at the Department of Justice, Equality and Law Reform stated:

> "It is important to understand that [section 3] subsection (1) does not preclude the other remedies which may be considered by a court. Subsection (1) allows the court to grant any remedy to a litigant. On the other hand, subsection (2) solely deals with the issue of damages. It may be for example that injunctive relief would be appropriate and subsection (1) does not exclude that in any way. If injunctive relief is desired the section does not limit that or any other option."[401]

However, if it were the case that such remedies were intended to be included by section 3 it is difficult to see why they were not expressly provided for in the provision. Indeed later in the Debate at Report stage the Minister for Justice, Equality and Law Reform appeared to have shifted his position as he argued:

> "In this context if one were to introduce something like an injunction or a declaration one would replicate in large measure the law relating to judicial review. ... [Uniting] section 2 with judicial review as we understand it – the law relating to *mandamus, quo warranto, certiorari* and the declarations and injunctions which go with those will provide [the non damage based remedies argued for].[402] Convention issues will be melded into judicial review law. If one marries our existing law of judicial review to section 2 of this Bill, one will have a very complex system of enforcement of what some might call "Convention-based rights."[403]

---

[399] See Seanad Éireann Debates 2003 Vol. 173 No. 10 Col. 849 (*per* Senator Henry).

[400] See Select Committee on Justice, Equality, Defence and Women's Rights, February 19, 2003, p.12.

[401] See Select Committee on Justice, Equality, Defence and Women's Rights, March 5, 2003, p.12 (Web version).

[402] The argument for non damage based remedies was advanced by J. O'Keeffe T.D. See Dáil Éireann Debates Vol. 568 No. 1 (Report Stage) Col. 83.

[403] Dáil Éireann Debates 2003 Vol. 568 No. 1 (Report Stage) Cols.84–85.

It is noteworthy also that the remedy in section 3 excludes the District Court. It was argued in the course of the Dáil Éireann Debates at Report stage that the remedy provided by section 3 should be available in all courts including the District Court. The Minister for Justice, Equality and Law Reform replied:

> "It may be that in the fullness of time we will consider making it available in the District Court. At present the District Court is under pressure because it has a good deal of work to do in other cases and by definition the cases under which these kinds of damages will be awarded are complex. ... There are some things which it is felt are so complex and require so much attention, that a court which is charged with summary, civil and criminal justice and given significant responsibilities especially for family law, should not have responsibility for this matter. These issues will not be capable of being disposed of in half an hour or an hour like simple car crashes because they will be immensely complex ...
>
> It may be that in the future, once this beds down, someone will suggest extending it to the District Court as it is working so simply and summarily in the Circuit Court that there is a case for giving that jurisdiction to the District Court. I am trying to operate a workable law which does not swamp the District Court with all types of claims that require many hours and many learned lawyers on both sides arguing high points....This is analogous to judicial review because it is damages in respect of actions by the State against its citizens. The District Court does not have a judicial review function at present."[404]

Section 3(4) provides that nothing in section 3 shall be construed as creating any criminal offence.

Under section 3(5)(a) proceedings may not be brought under section 3(1) in respect of any contravention which arose more than one year before the commencement of proceedings but by virtue of section 3(5)(b) this period of limitation may be extended by order made by the court if it considers it appropriate to do so in the interests of justice.

It has been argued that since the claim prescribed by section 3 is analogous to a claim in tort for breach of statutory duty the one-year limitation period should be extended to six years.[405] The response of the Minister of State at the Department of Justice, Equality and Law Reform to an argument at Committee Stage in the Seanad that the limit be extended to just three years is interesting in the context of the State's apparent commitment to vindication of human rights:

> "It is in the public interest that the exposure of the State to potentially large awards and damages should be reasonably short, commensurate with the rights of the individual. For the sake of comparison, if a person wishes to invoke the right of individual petition in Strasbourg the time limit is six months. ..."[406]

---

[404] See Dáil Éireann Debates 2003 Vol. 568 No. 1 (Report Stage) Cols 83– 84.
[405] See Dáil Éireann Debates 2003 Vol. 538 No. 2 (Second Stage) Col. 310 (*per* A. Shatter T.D.).
[406] See Seanad Éireann Debates 2003 Vol. 173 No. 11 (Committee Stage) Col. 996.

However, the Minister of State did give an indication of the circumstances in which it was envisaged the limitation period might be extended:

> "In section 3(5)(b) there is a provision where the court can extend the period if it considers it appropriate to do so in the interests of justice. ... Generally statutes of limitation provide for an absolute limit. There is a very limited category of exceptions to that, generally based on ignorance of matters, disability or minority, as in lack of full age. In this case, while the limit is one year, the period may be extended by order of the court if it considers it appropriate in the interests of justice. In the context of limitation periods this is a very broad discretion to give to a court. If the court believes that justice requires it, the relevant period may be extended."[407]

It would appear from this that a disability which had the effect of incapacitating a person from instituting proceedings within the one year time limit could found a basis for an application to extend it.

Section 5: Declaration of incompatibility Having regard to the court's duty interpret and apply statutory provisions and rules of law in a manner compatible with the State's obligations under the European Convention provisions section 5 of the Act empowers the High Court or the Supreme Court when exercising its appellate jurisdiction to make a declaration of incompatibility that a statutory provision or rule of law (which includes common law)[408] is incompatible with the State's obligations under the Convention provisions. The High Court or the Supreme Court may only grant the declaration where no other legal remedy is adequate and available. It may do so on application to it by a party to the proceedings or of its own motion.

Before a court decides whether to make a declaration of incompatibility the Attorney General and the Human Rights Commission[409] must be given notice of the proceedings in accordance with rules of court.[410] Having been given notice the Attorney General will thereupon be entitled to appear in the proceedings and to become a party thereto as regards the issue of the declaration of incompatibility.[411]

Section 5(2) provides that the declaration will not (a) affect the validity, continuing operation or enforcement of the statutory provision or rule of law in respect of which it is made and (b) it will also not prevent a party to the proceedings concerned from making submissions or representations in relation to matters to which the declaration relates in any proceedings before the European Court of Human Rights.

Section 5(3) provides that the Taoiseach shall cause a copy of the any order containing

---

[407] See Seanad Éireann Debates 2003 Vol. 173 No. 11 (Committee Stage) Col. 996.

[408] European Convention on Human Rights Act 2003, s.1(1).

[409] The giving of notice to the Human Rights Commission is to facilitate its making an application for liberty to appear before either the High or Supreme Court as *amicus curiae* in human rights cases involving the European Convention on Human Rights. See Select Committee on Justice, Equality, Defence and Women's Rights (*per* Minister for Justice, Equality and Law Reform, pp.14–15).

[410] European Convention on Human Rights Act 2003, s.6(1).

[411] European Convention on Human Rights Act 2003, s.6(2).

a declaration of incompatibility to be laid before each House of the Oireachtas within the next 21 days[412] on which that House has sat after the making of the order.

Where (a) a declaration of incompatibility is made, and (b) a party to the proceedings concerned makes an application in writing to the Attorney General for compensation in respect of an injury or loss or damage suffered by him or her as a result of the incompatibility concerned and (c) the Government in their discretion consider that it may be appropriate to make an *ex gratia* payment of compensation to that party the Government may request an adviser appointed by them to advise them as to the amount of such compensation (if any) and may, in their discretion make a payment of the amount aforesaid or of such other amount as they consider appropriate in the circumstances.[413] In advising the Government on the amount of compensation the adviser must take appropriate account of the principles and practice applied by the European Court of Human Rights in relation to affording just satisfaction to an injured party under Article 41 of the Convention.[414]

It is clear from the terms of section 5 that notwithstanding the possibility of availing of the "ex gratia payment" system the party who has obtained the declaration of incompatibility retains the right to apply to the European Court of Human Rights for compensation under Article 41 of the Convention.

In the course of the debates at Report Stage the Minister for Justice, Equality and Law Reform stated that section 5 was designed to apply to the situation where a court will have failed to deal with a provision on an interpretative basis under section 2. It will have examined the Constitution and found the provision constitutional and found that, even so, it is still incompatible with the Convention. He continued that

> "it is only in this extremely narrow area, where the High Court – and possibly the Supreme Court on appeal – comes to a view that the legal provision is fully compatible with the Constitution and yet there is an issue to be determined as to whether it is compatible with the Convention that the jurisdiction under section [5] will be invoked".[415]

It has been argued that section 5 provides for a minimalist approach to the domesticating the European Convention.[416] It contemplates a situation where a litigant may have gone all the way to the Supreme Court to obtain a declaration which may be of little use to him or her since the offending legislation remains in place and s/he may not be entitled to any other relief. In the course of the Dáil Éireann Debates at Second Stage Alan Shatter T.D. took the point further. He stated:

---

[412] In the course of debates at the Committee Stage the Minister for Justice Equality and Law Reform Stated that the reason 21 days was provided was that it would allow the State to appeal the matter to the Supreme Court if it wanted to. 21 days was the normal period for an appeal. If the Attorney General decided not to appeal it and accepted that the High Court was correct that the Act was incompatible with the Convention, it would be for the Government, in the normal course of events to come up with some suggested outcome" See Select Committee on Justice, Equality, Defence and Women's Rights, March 12, 2003, p.7.

[413] European Convention on Human Rights Act 2003, s.5(4).

[414] *Ibid.*, s.5(5).

[415] Dáil Éireann Debates 2003 Vol. 568 No. 1 (Report Stage) Col. 77.

[416] See Dáil Éireann Debates 2001 Vol. 538 No. 2 (Second Stage) Col. 308.

"In effect, we will create a situation within the legal system where a court may make a declaration that a statutory provision is incompatible with the Convention but, nevertheless, be required and compelled to apply that statutory provision to the resolution of a dispute between individuals in a case in which the incompatibility is pronounced and in future cases until such time as the legislation is changed. That type of approach will bring the courts system and the judiciary into disrepute. ..."[417]

He suggested that the preferable approach would have been to provide that statutory provisions or rules of law should be amended to the extent that the violate provisions contained in the Convention subject to the overriding authority of the Constitution.[418]

It has been argued that the making of an *ex gratia* payment for an injury or loss or damage suffered by a person as a result of the incompatibility of Irish law and the European Convention of Human Rights fails to afford full recognition to the rights under the Convention and a court should have power to make an order for monetary payment in the event of injury, loss or damage suffered as a result of the incompatibility. In the course of the Debates at Second Stage in the Seanad Senator David Norris made reference to the fact that the Human Rights Commission had expressed the view that:

"it is unacceptable to place the courts in a position where they can identify a breach of human rights and not be in a position to give an effective remedy".[419]

However, in the course of the Dáil Éireann Debates at second stage the Minister for Justice, Equality and Law Reform stated that the reason any such payment is to be made by the Government and not the courts is that:

"the courts could not award damages where there is compliance with a statutory provision or rule of law which while incompatible with the Convention, remains constitutionally valid."[420]

On the other hand it has been argued that a model which seeks to confer on the Attorney General and the Government:

"adjudicating power in determining issues of compensation for violation of rights under the European Convention on Human Rights".

may violate the concept of separation of powers.[421] At Report Stage in the Dáil it was argued that "there should be a guaranteed system for the payment of compensation as of right by a body, which is independent of the Government."[422] Further it was argued at Committee Stage that a system of *ex gratia* payment for violation of Convention

---

[417] Dáil Éireann Debates 2001 Vol. 538 No. 2 (Second Stage) Col. 308.
[418] Dáil Éireann Debates 2001 Vol. 538 No. 2 (Second Stage) Cols. 308–309.
[419] Seanad Debates 2003 Vol. 173 No. 10 Col. 860.
[420] Dáil Éireann Debates 2001 Vol. 538 No. 2 (Second Stage) Col. 304.
[421] Dáil Éireann Debates 2001 Vol. 538 No. 2 (Second Stage) Col. 311.
[422] Dáil Éireann Debates 2003 Vol. 567 No. 2 (Report Stage) Col. 364 (*per* Mr Cuffe T.D.).

provisions may not provide an "effective remedy before a national authority" as required by Article 13 of the Convention.[423]

The issue of what would happen if the person who had received the declaration of incompatibility was dissatisfied with the amount *ex gratia* payment was also raised in the Seanad.[424] It must be assumed that one's right to reject the amount and apply to the European Court of Human Rights for compensation would remain unaffected.

A further issue raised at second stage was the matter of the identity the adviser on compensation would be and what his/her qualifications would be. This is not specified in the legislation.[425] Further the question was asked as to what the Attorney General's position would be should a case be taken to the European Court of Human Rights for the State's alleged violation of human rights where the High Court or Supreme Court had declared the legislative provision to be incompatible with the Convention. Would the Attorney General be then entitled to argue that the State was in compliance with the Convention?[426]

It has been argued there is no reason why a court should not have the right to issue an injunction or order a release from detention on a finding of incompatibility. The Dáil Éireann Debates addressing this issue focus almost exclusively on the position of prisoners whose detention is constitutional but incompatible with the European Convention and make little reference to the situation a person detained under the Mental Health Act in those circumstances.[427] In the former case it was stated that the appropriate response would be for the Government to exercise its discretion to advise the President to pardon the person under the provisions of the Constitution.[428] However, this discretionary remedy was not acceptable to other members of the Committee.[429]

Further it has been argued that all courts (including the Circuit Court and the District Court) not simply the High Court and Supreme Court on appeal should have power to consider points related to incompatibility of statutory provisions and rules of law with the Convention.[430]

It was argued further in the course of Debates at Committee stage that there was a need to put in place "some statement of intent" that action will be taken by the Oireachtas on the order containing a declaration of incompatibility that had been placed before each House by the Taoiseach in accordance with section 5(3).[431] The Minister for Justice, Equality and Law Reform pointed out that under the Constitution it was not possible by Act of Parliament to say what happens in either House and according to Article 15.10 of the Constitution "Each House shall make its own rules and standing orders".[432] No rules or standing orders have been made to deal with the situation where an order

---

[423] Select Committee on Justice, Equality, Defence and Women's Rights, February 18, 2003 (J. O'Keeffe T.D.).

[424] Seanad Éireann Debates 2003 Vol. 173 No. 10 Col. 866 (*per* Senator Norris).

[425] Dáil Éireann Debates 2001 Vol. 538, No. 2 (Second Stage) Col 312.

[426] Dáil Éireann Debates 2001 Vol. 538, No. 3 (Second Stage) Col. 312.

[427] A brief mention was made by Mr Cuffe T.D. at Report Stage See Dáil Éireann Debates Vol. 567 No. 2 Col. 364.

[428] See Select Committee on Justice, Equality, Defence and Women's Rights, March 12, 2003, p. 1.

[429] *Ibid.*, p.12 (*per* J. O'Keeffe T.D.), p.13 (*per* J. Costello T.D.).

[430] Dáil Éireann Debates 2001 Vol. 538 No. 2 (Second Stage) Cols. 310–311 (*per* A. Shatter T.D.).

[431] See Select Committee on Justice, Equality, Defence and Women's Rights March 12, 2003, p.8.

[432] *Ibid.*, p.7.

containing a declaration of incompatibility has been laid before each House of the Oireachtas. Hence as the position currently stands, the Government does not appear to be bound in any way to introduce amending legislation when the courts have declared that a piece of existing legislation is incompatible with the European Convention on Human Rights and theoretically a situation of legislative limbo could persist where an Act is declared incompatible with the European Convention on Human Rights but is not repealed or replaced. Indeed the Minister for Justice, Equality and Law Reform conceded that this could happen in the Debates at Second Stage in the Seanad:

> "It is theoretically possible that both Houses of the Oireachtas in their wisdom, with the declaration order handed down by the court, will simply say, "We refuse to change the law as we are happy with it the way it is". That is the act of a sovereign Legislature and no more can be said about it. The person in question would then have to go to Strasbourg and argue, before the court established under the Council of Europe Convention, that Ireland was in breach of its obligations to him or her. That is possible."[433]

Placing a person in a position where s/he would have to go to Strasbourg to put pressure on the Government to change legislation, which is incompatible with the European Convention, surely defeats the purpose of the legislation, which was to make Convention right justiciable in Irish courts.

In the course of debates at the Committee Stage, however, the Minister for Justice, Equality and Law Reform accepted that "it would be reasonable for either House [of the Oireachtas] to insert in its Standing Orders a provision" requiring a Minister before the second reading of a Bill to make a statement in writing that in his or her view the provisions of the Bill are compatible with the Convention (a "statement of compatibility") or to make a statement to the effect that although s/he is unable to make a statement of compatibility the Government nevertheless wishes the House to proceed with the Bill.[434] Accordingly the Minister indicated that he would not rule out a system of "Convention proofing" of proposed legislation.[435]

---

[433] Seanad Éireann Debates 2003 Vol. 173 No.10 (Second Stage) Col. 839.

[434] Such a provision is to be found in s.19 of the Human Rights Act 1998 in the United Kingdom. In February 2001 the Westminster Parliament established a Joint Committee on Human Rights to assist it in the function of scrutinising proposed legislation for European Convention on Human Rights compatibility.

[435] See Select Committee on Justice, Equality, Defence and Women's Rights, March 12, 2003, p.16 (in response to an amendment proposed by J. O'Keeffe T.D.) However, in response to a similar proposal to amend the legislation in the Seanad the Minister of State at the Department of Justice, Equality and Law Reform, Brian Lehihan T.D., was not prepared to accept the amendment. He stated that the Human Rights Commission was already empowered under s.8(b) of the Human Rights Act 2001 to examine a legislative proposal and report its views on any human rights implications it might have. Further the Attorney General advises the Government on the compatibility of draft legislation with current law and also with the State's obligations under the European Convention. See Seanad Debates 2003 Vol. 173 No. 11 (Committee Stage) Col. 1016 (*per* B. Lenihan T.D.).

Section 7: Power of Human Rights Commission to institute proceedings under the European Convention on Human Rights Act 2003 Section 7 of the 2003 Act amends section 11(3)(b) the Human Rights Commission Act 2000 to confer on the Human Rights Commission an additional power to institute proceedings in respect of any matter concerning the rights liberties and freedoms conferred on or guaranteed to persons by the Convention provisions within the meaning of the European Convention on Human Rights Act 2003. The Commission may institute proceedings in any court of competent jurisdiction and the proceedings may be instituted for the purpose of obtaining relief of a declaratory or other nature.[436]

Finally the availability of legal aid is an important element in enabling people to exercise rights in practice. It was argued at Report Stage in the Dáil that it should be extended to Convention cases.[437] It was also argued in the course of the Second Stage Debates in the Seanad that the Minister for Justice, Equality and Law Reform should issue a policy directive under section 7 of the Civil Legal Aid Act 1995 to the effect that applications for legal aid will be considered in suitable cases under the Act.[438]

---

[436] Human Rights Commission Act 2000, s.11(1).
[437] Dáil Éireann Debates 2003 Vol. 567 No. 2 (Report Stage) Col. 364 (*per* Mr. Cuffe T.D.).
[438] Seanad Éireann Debates 2003 Vol. 173 No. 10 (Second Stage) Col. 842 (*per* Senator Terry citing the recommendation of the Human Rights Commission).

CHAPTER TWO

Primary Care and Admission to Hospital

INTRODUCTION

In the year 2003 the Report of the Inspector of Mental Hospitals indicated that there were about 23,234 admissions to public and private psychiatric hospitals and acute hospital units in. Of these approximately 2,349 were involuntary admissions representing about 10 per cent of total admissions.

This Chapter examines the law on the admission of persons with mental illness to hospital taking into account both voluntary and involuntary admissions.

THE LEGAL FRAMEWORK

The current law in force is to be found in the Mental Treatment Act 1945 and partly in those parts of the Mental Health Act 2001 which have been brought into force. The Mental Health Act 2001 (Sections 1 to 5, 7, 31 to 55) (Commencement) Order 2002[1] appointed April 5, 2002 as the day on which sections 1 to 5, 7, 31 to 55 inclusive of the Mental Health Act 2001 should come into operation. For the purposes of the present discussion section 2 of the Act contains the definition of terms used in the Act; section 3 defines "mental disorder"; section 4 sets out criteria to be taken into consideration regarding the care or treatment of a person including a decision to admit that person involuntarily to a psychiatric hospital; section 5 confers power on the Minister to make regulations under the Act and section 7 provides for the expenses incurred by the Minister in the administration of the Act to be paid out of moneys provided by the Oireachtas to the extent as may be sanctioned by the Minister for Finance. Interestingly section 6, which provides for repeals of previous legislation, has not yet been brought into force. Sections 31–55 put in place the administrative machinery for review of detention including the establishment of the Mental Health Commission; the establishment of mental Health Tribunals by the Commission and the establishment of the office of Inspector of Mental Health Services.

---

[1] S.I. No. 90 of 2002.

VOLUNTARY ADMISSIONS

Voluntary consent

Criteria for admission under the Mental Treatment Act 1945

The Mental Treatment Act 1945 (which is still in force) provides that where a person wishes to be admitted as an eligible patient[2] and as a voluntary· patient that person should make an application in the prescribed form[3] to the person in charge of the district mental hospital serving the area in which he ordinarily resided[4] or to an approved institution in which voluntary patients of the Health Service Executive may be received pursuant to an arrangement with the Health Service Executive.[5]

Where the person concerned is under sixteen years of age the parent or guardian of the person concerned is obliged to make the application and it must be accompanied by a recommendation by a registered medical practitioner stating that he has examined the person concerned on a date not earlier than seven days before the date of the application and is of the opinion that the person concerned would benefit by the proposed reception.[6]

Where the patient is an eligible patient the registered medical practitioner examining the patient is obliged not to be interested in the payments to be made on account of the taking care of the person, a member of that person's family[7] or his/her guardian or trustee or a medical officer of a district mental hospital.[8]

Where a person desires to be admitted to a private hospital the 1945 Act provides that s/he should make a written application in that regard to the person in charge of the institution.[9] There is no prescribed form but in practice most hospitals have their own standard forms.

---

[2] *i.e.* a person entitled to hospital services without charge under the Health Act 1970 as amended.

[3] See Mental Treatment Regulations 1961, Sch. Form No. 8 Commonly known as the "blue form".

[4] Where however the person is admitted to a public hospital as a voluntary patient and it is discovered that he was not ordinarily resident at the material time in the appropriate mental hospital district the application and reception are expressed by the Act to be "as valid for all purposes as if such person had been ordinarily resident at that time in that district". See Mental Treatment Act 1945, s.192 as amended Mental Treatment Act 1961, s.21.

[5] Mental Treatment Act 1945, s.190(1) as substituted by Mental Treatment Acts (Adaptation) Order 1971 art.5, Sch.

[6] Mental Treatment Act 1945, s.190(3) as amended by the Mental Treatment Act 1961, s.19(1). Where a request for a recommendation is made to the authorised medical officer in respect of a person under the age of sixteen years of age the medical officer concerned is obliged to examine the person who is the subject of the application and to give the recommendation if he is of the opinion that the person would benefit by the proposed reception. Mental Treatment Act 1945, s.190(4) as inserted by the Mental Treatment Act 1961, s.19(2). This provision has no relevance to private patients. The reference to the "authorised medical officer" in s.19(2) was to the medical officer of the patient's dispensary district or of the nearest district. The Health Act 1970, s.81 deleted the definition of "authorised medical officer" in the 1945 Act. Presumably this role is taken over by the registered medical practitioner for whose services the patient is eligible and the requirement of examination etc. is imposed on this registered medical practitioner.

[7] S.190(5) specifies that the practitioner is to be disqualified if the person is "the husband or wife, father, stepfather or father-in-law, mother, step-mother or mother-in- law, son, step-son or son-in-law, daughter, step-daughter or daughter-in-law, brother, step-brother or brother-in-law, sister, step-sister or sister-in-law, or guardian or trustee of the person.

[8] Mental Treatment Act 1945, s.190(5) as inserted by the Mental Treatment Act 1961, s.19(2).

[9] *Ibid.*, s.191.

Where a patient under the age of sixteen is to be admitted as a patient to a private institution similar provisions apply[10] but oddly enough there are no provisions disqualifying a registered medical practitioner on the grounds of financial or professional interest or kinship.

Where a person makes a voluntary application for reception either to a private or a public hospital[11] the hospital concerned may admit him/her if there is accommodation for him in the institution not required for a person of unsound mind and s/he could be treated there and on his recovery discharged.[12]

Criteria for admission under Mental Health Act 2001

The Mental Health Act 2001 contains very few provisions relating to voluntary admissions. Those that it does contain have not yet been brought into force.

Admission as a voluntary partient Section 29 (not yet in force) provides that nothing in the Act shall be construed as preventing a person from being admitted voluntarily to an approved centre[13] for treatment without any application,[14] recommendation or admission order rendering him or her liable to be detained under the Act or from remaining in an approved centre after he or she has ceased to be so liable to be detained. There is no requirement under the 2001 Act that a person who is voluntarily in hospital fills in any admission forms.

Admission of Children as Voluntary Patients

No procedure is prescribed for the voluntary admission of children is prescribed under the 2001 Act. "Child" is defined by section 2 of the Act as "a person under the age of 18 year other than a person who is or has been married". Section 23 of the Non Fatal Offences against the Person Act 1997 that a minor over the age of 16 has capacity to consent to medical treatment on their own behalf and it is not necessary to obtain any consent for it from their parents. "Medical treatment" includes "*any* procedure undertaken for the purposes of diagnosis" and extends "to any procedure", which is "ancillary to

---

[10] *Ibid.*, s.191.

[11] Where the patient is received as an eligible patient and voluntary patient and it is ascertained that s/he was not ordinarily resident at a material time in the appropriate mental hospital district both the reception and the application by reference to which the reception was effected were as valid for all purposes as if the person had been ordinarily resident at that time in that district. See Mental Treatment Act 1945, s.192 as amended by Mental Treatment Act 1961, s.21.

[12] Mental Treatment Act 1945, s.192 The requirements whereby notice of reception, discharge or death must be given to the Minister for Health and Children three days after the relevant event imposed by s.197(1) and the requirement to keep a register of voluntary patients were repealed by Mental Treatment Act 1961, s.42 and sch.2.

[13] Under the terms of s.64 of the Mental Health Act 2001 the Mental Health Commission is to establish and maintain a "Register of Approved Centres." S.63 states that a person shall not carry on a centre unless the centre is registered and the person is the registered proprietor thereof and a centre which is so registered shall be known as is referred to in the Mental Health Act 2001 as "an approved centre". See Mental Health Act 2001, ss 2 and 63.

[14] "Application" is defined by s.2 of the 2001 Act as an application for a recommendation that a person be involuntarily admitted to an approved centre.

any such treatment". Psychiatric treatment involving drug therapy clearly falls within this definition of "medical treatment." There is an immediate clash between the 1997 Act and the 2001 Act and it is not clear what status the consent or refusal of consent of a child to treatment for mental disorder between the ages of 16 and 18 will have.

When the 1945 Act is repealed and the 2001 Act is brought into force then in the case where it is proposed to admit a child under 16 (or 18 years of age if the assumption made by the Mental Health Act 2001 that a person under the age of 18 years who is not married is incapable of consent to treatment for mental disorder is found to supersede the terms of the 1997 Act insofar as it may relate to treatment for mental disorder) as a voluntary patient it appears that common law principles will apply. At common law legally effective consent may be given by a parent where the procedure is in the best interests of the minor[15] and the minor is incapable by virtue of immaturity of consenting on his/her own behalf. The common law does not fix a specific age above which a minor's own consent to treatment is valid but in England it has been held in *Gillick v. West Norfolk and Wisbech Area Health Authority*[16] that a minor under 16 may give valid consent without any need for parental consent if the minor has the capacity fully to comprehend the nature and consequences of the proposed treatment. In the absence of any Irish case law on the point the *Gillick* decision may be relevant in Ireland in relation to minors under the age of 16. Lord Scarman stated, "the parental right to determine whether or not their minor child below the age of sixteen will have medical treatment terminates if and when the child achieves a sufficient understanding and intelligence to enable him or her to understand fully what is proposed".[17]

However, in the later case of *In re R (a minor)*[18] the principle set out in *Gillick* was qualified somewhat with the court taking the view that the required consent could also be obtained even in relation to a competent child from "another competent source" – which could be a parent or a person *in loco parentis*.

It appears that in the Irish jurisdiction Article 41 of the Constitution which recognises the family as the natural primary and fundamental unit group of society and as a moral institution possessing inalienable and imprescriptible rights, antecedent and superior to all positive law and Article 42 by virtue of which the inalienable right and duty of parents to provide for the religious and moral, intellectual, physical and social education of their children is guaranteed may constitute a barrier to a decision similar to *Gillick* being arrived at. In the recent Supreme Court decision of *North Western Health Board v. H.W. and C.W.*,[19] which endorsed the right of parents to refuse the taking of a blood sample from a very young child for the purposes of a PKU test, Hardiman J. remarked:

> "[t]he Constitution plainly accords a primacy to the parent and this primacy in my view gives rise to a presumption that the welfare of the child is to be found in the family exercising its authority as such".[20]

---

[15] Procedures in the best interests of the minor's health may include procedures for the purposes of assessment and prevention as well as those for the treatment of an existing condition.

[16] [1985] 3 All E.R. 402.

[17] *Ibid.*, 423–424.

[18] [1991] 4 All E.R. 177.

[19] Unreported, Supreme Court, November 8 2001.

[20] *Ibid.*, p.49.

These dicta constitute a further endorsement of the constitutional supremacy of Articles 41 and 42 and they may pose an obstacle to an argument for the recognition of the right of a mature child under 16 to consent in his/her own right to medical treatment and (if the Mental Health Act 2001's assumption that a child under 18 is incapable of consent to medical treatment for mental disorder) may pose an obstacle to the recognition of the right of the child under 18 to consent in his/her own right to medical treatment for mental disorder.

Commentary from international and comparative law perspective

1. The 2001 legislation focuses almost exclusively on compulsory admission. Those provisions which address voluntary admission tend be of a relatively minor nature. While at first sight "voluntary admission" may appear self-explanatory difficulties present regarding the validity of consent when a patient is incapable of understanding the nature and consequences of his/her request for admission and difficulties present regarding its voluntariness when a patient is coerced under threat of committal to sign an admission form.

    The 2001 Act as a whole fails to provide adequate checks as to whether a patient has mental capacity to give voluntary consent to treatment on entry into hospital. In contrast in the case of *Zinerman v. Burch*[21] the United States Supreme Court has held that a violation of rights may arise where a clearly incompetent patient is held in a psychiatric hospital under his or her own "consent" without a hearing or any other procedure to determine that he validly had consented to admission. In that situation the consent is legally ineffective and the decision to hold the patient without a proper hearing may deprive the patient of liberty without due process of law.

    The difficulty of determining whether a person voluntarily consents to treatment has been alluded to by Picard who notes:

    > "[w]hile it is true that consent must be the result of freedom of choice, an anxious, ill person, often with a concerned family hovering and advising, will be unable to make a decision without some degree of fear, constraint and duress."[22]

The decision to obtain voluntary psychiatric in-patient treatment is often take after considerable persuasion from a psychiatrist or registered medical practitioner. There are usually good clinical reasons for this approach. Brakel observes:

> "The idea of voluntary admission has much to commend itself. … A person who voluntarily seeks admission recognises his need of medical treatment. He is more prone to co-operate with the treatment staff and to participate conscientiously in the treatment program and therefore more likely to benefit from institutionalisation than an unwilling patient. In addition, the availability of voluntary procedures may encourage a person to seek help for his condition

---

[21] 110 S.Ct 975 (1990).
[22] Picard, *Legal Liability of Doctors and Hospitals in Canada* (2nd ed., Carswell, Toronto, 1984), p.53.

early, when the chances of successful treatment are greatest. To delay treatment until the person's condition reaches crisis proportions has several disadvantages in addition to the fact that his prognosis may then be poor."[23]

As a matter of law however it is sometimes difficult to determine where persuasion ends and coercion begins. If a voluntary patient expressing a desire to leave hospital is informed by a psychiatrist that if s/he insists on leaving s/he is likely to be committed under the mental health legislation whereupon s/he agrees to stay can s/he be described as having made a voluntary decision? It appears that the correct analysis may depend upon whether the grounds for committal indeed exist. If such grounds do exist the psychiatrist's advice may be considered persuasion and not coercion and the patient's decision voluntary. If, however the psychiatrist's statement is in the nature of a false threat and the patient is misled as to the nature of the psychiatrists authority to detain him the reverse is the case and the patient may have an action in false imprisonment. This view is supported by an analysis of Canadian case law dealing with psychological imprisonment.[24] In *R v. Therens*[25] the Supreme Court of Canada held that an accused had been "detained" within the meaning of section 10 of the Canadian Charter of Rights and Freedoms when he had complied with a police officer's demand to accompany him for the purpose of obtaining samples of the accused's breath for alcohol content analysis. In the course of his judgment Mr Justice LeDain indicated the features of involuntary detention, which are equally applicable in the medico-legal context of psychiatric medicine:

> "In my opinion, it is not realistic, as a general rule, to regard compliance with a demand or direction by a police officer as truly voluntary, in the sense that the citizen feels he or she has the choice to obey or not…Most citizens are not aware of the precise legal limits of police authority. Rather than risk the application of physical force or prosecution for wilful obstruction, the reasonable person is likely to err on the side of caution, assume lawful authority and comply with the demand. The element of psychological compulsion in the form of a reasonable perception of suspension of freedom of choice is enough to make the restraint of liberty involuntary. Detention may be effected without the application or threat of application of physical restraint if the person concerned submits or acquiesces in the deprivation of liberty and reasonably believes that the choice to do otherwise does not exist."[26]

This view is also supported by the decision of the High Court of Australia in *Watson v. Marshall*,[27] ruling that a plaintiff was subjected to false imprisonment when he was taken by the defendant (a police officer) to a psychiatric hospital without lawful authority. Although no physical force was used in the circumstances the court held

---

[23] Brakel *et al, The Mentally Disabled and the Law* (3rd ed., American Bar Foundation, 1985) p.178.
[24] *Chaytor v. London, New York and Paris Association of Fashion Ltd* (1961) 30 D.L.R. (2d) 527 (Newfoundland Supreme Court); *Conn v. David Spencer Ltd* [1930] 1 D.L.R. 805 (B.C.S.C.).
[25] [1985] 1 S.C.R. 613.
[26] *Ibid.*, p.644.
[27] [1972] Aust.L.R. 83.

that plaintiff had a justified apprehension that if he did not submit to the police officer's request to accompany him to the hospital he would be compelled by force to do so. Therefore a restraint was imposed on the plaintiff, which amounted to imprisonment.

It is submitted that the Mental Health Act 2001 should be amended to require that an independent check be made to determine whether a voluntary patient has capacity to and has given voluntary consent to the treatment proposed. This role could be performed by an independent advocate. If there is reasonable cause to believe that valid consent has not been given or that the admission is otherwise not in the interests of the person concerned a Mental Health Tribunal should be empanelled to consider the case. This should assist in reducing the risk of mistaken deprivation of liberty under the guise of voluntary admission procedures.

2. Given the conflicting provisions of the Mental Health Act 2001 and the Non Fatal Offences against the Person Act 1993 it is not clear at what age a child may give valid consent to medical treatment for mental disorder. This needs to be clarified. It is pertinent in this regard to note the provisions of Article 12.1 of the Convention on the Rights of the Child 1989 which Ireland has ratified[28] and which provides that states parties to the Convention shall assure to the child who is capable of forming his or her own views the right to express those views freely on all matters affecting the child, the views of the child being given due weight in accordance with the age and maturity of the child. The provisions of the Mental Health Act 2001 which potentially deny the right of the child under 18 years to express his/her views in the matter of voluntary admission to a psychiatric hospital effectively breach the provisions of Article 12.1.

3. If a child under 16 (or indeed a person under 18 years of age if the Mental Health Act definition of a "child" is deemed supersede the terms of section 23 of the Non Fatal Offences against the Person Act 1997) is admitted to a psychiatric hospital as a voluntary patient at the request of his parents that child may be denied the protection which the mental health legislation affords to involuntary patients including the right to apply for review of his/her confinement.[29] The underlying rationale of the legislation is that since voluntary patients are in the hospital by choice and are free to leave if they so decide they do not require the same protection as involuntary patients. This basis is strained when a child is admitted as a consequence of their parent's decision rather than their own particularly when the child is in dispute with his/her parents. On the other hand it is arguable that the approach of the Mental Health legislation is consistent with that of Article 41 and 42 of the Constitution by virtue of which the state accords supremacy to the rights of the family and guarantees to respect the inalienable right of parents of parents to provide for the intellectual, physical and social education of their children. However these provisions of the Constitution are not without their critics. In 1993 a Government appointed tribunal

---

[28] Ireland ratified the Convention on September 28, 1992.

[29] In *A Human Condition: The Mental Health Act from 1959 to 1975: Observations, Analysis and Proposals for Reform* (Vol.1) (London: MIND) Gostin argues that parents should not be able to "volunteer" their children for admission to mental hospitals without some additional check such as an automatic review by a mental health review tribunal.

of enquiry noted "the very high emphasis on the rights of the family in the Irish constitution may be interpreted a giving a higher value to the rights of the parents than to the rights of the child" and recommended a constitutional amendment to provide expressly for a declaration of the rights of the child.[30]

It is also interesting to note that other jurisdictions do not follow the approach of Irish Mental Health legislation in regard to the voluntary admission of children. For instance in contrast to the absence of provisions regarding review of admission of children as voluntary patients in Ireland Ontario's Mental Health Act provides that children between the ages of twelve and sixteen who are admitted to a psychiatric facility as informal (voluntary) patients have the right to apply to a Review Board once every three months. The Act also provides for automatic review by the Board every six months.[31] The Review Board's duty is to determine whether the child needs observation, care and treatment in the psychiatric facility having regard to the factors set out in the Act[32] and it has power to direct that the child be discharged or that he continue as a voluntary patient in the facility.

On the other hand in the US Supreme Court decision in *Parham v. JR*[33] the court upheld the rights of parents to place their children as voluntary patients in mental health facilities on the basis that there the traditional presumption that parents act in the best interests of their parents applied to the situation . The court also held that a physician's independent examination and medical judgment provided sufficient protection against abuse of parental authority. However the assumption made by the court that parents always act in their child's best interests has been questioned[34] and despite the ruling many US states have introduced significant legal protection for children in the context of voluntary commitment.[35]

It is submitted that the Ontario approach has much to commend it in the context of the protection of the civil liberties of children and that Irish legislation should provide that children who are admitted to a psychiatric facility as voluntary patients should have a right to apply to a Mental Health Tribunal once every three months for review of their admission and their continued presence in the hospital should be automatically reviewed once every six months.

4.   The English House of Lords decision in *R v. Bournewood Community and Mental*

---

[30] *Kilkenny Incest Investigation Report* (1993).

[31] RSO 1980, c.262, s.8a [en. 1986, c.64, s.33(6)].

[32] S.8a (3) [en. 1986, c.64, s.33(6)].

[33] 442 US 584 (1979).

[34] See Melton "Family and Mental Hospitals as Myths: Civil Commitment of Minors" in Reppucci *et al* (eds.), *Children, Mental Health and the Law* (Sage, California, London, 1984) 151.

[35] Some states require the consent of the child (e.g. Florida, Mississippi, New Mexico, New York, Texas, Vermont, Washington, West Virginia) and/or mandate a court hearing if he protests (e.g. Colorado, Connecticut, District of Columbia, Illinois, Iowa, Michigan, South Dakota and Wisconsin). Other states require automatic court hearing regardless of the child's consent or his protest (e.g. Alabama, Alaska, Colorado, Connecticut, Washington and Georgia). A number of third party commitment statutes have also provided that after a certain age ranging from 12–18 the minor may no longer be hospitalised on the petition of his parent or guardian alone and he may voluntarily admit himself (e.g. Alaska, Arizona, Connecticut, Illinois, Kansas, Louisiana, Massachusetts, Missouri, New Mexico, New York, Pennsylvania, South Carolina) See Brakel *et al* (eds), *The Mentally Disabled and the Law* (3rd ed., American Bar Foundation, 1985), pp.43–46.

Health NHS Trust ex parte L (Secretary of State for Health and others intervening)[36] has drawn attention to the widespread practice in Ireland of admitting to psychiatric hospitals as "voluntary" patients people with autism, learning disabilities or Alzheimers disease who are incapable of giving consent. In that case a majority of the House of Lords overruling the Court of Appeal held that compliant persons who lacked the capacity to consent and who did not resist admission (in the instant case an autistic man with profound intellectual disability who also had psychiatric difficulties) could be "informally" admitted to hospital under section 131(1) of the Mental Health Act 1983[37] and could be given medical treatment that was in their best interests without being formally detained on the basis that this was justified by the common law doctrine of necessity and there was therefore no need to find justification for the treatment in the statute itself which was silent on the subject. Lords Nolan and Steyn dissenting were of the view that the decision in the case was to leave compliant incapacitated patients without the safeguards enshrined in the 1983 Act which were afforded to patients detained under its provisions.

The House of Lords judgment accordingly represents a worrying development in English law. In Ireland there is no provision for informal admission under either the 1945 Act or the 2001 Act and the 1945 Act contemplates and section 29 of the 2001 Act implicitly states that the alternative to involuntary admission is voluntary admission. It seems clear therefore that if a patient is incapable of giving voluntary consent they must be admitted involuntarily. However it is submitted that an amendment to the 2001 Act should put the matter beyond doubt by setting out clearly the criteria for determining whether a patient's consent is voluntary and stating clearly that if a patient is found incapable of giving voluntary consent then that person must be involuntarily admitted under the Act and afforded the protection which the Act gives to involuntary patients under the Act. The main argument against this approach in England appears to have been the resource implications of increasing the average number of detained patients from 13,000 to 35,000.[38]

Indeed the problem is more extensive than the matter of the issue of admission of persons with intellectual disabilities to psychiatric hospitals. The matter of the legal basis for the admission of persons with intellectual disabilities to residential units generally is a matter of concern. Kennedy has commented as follows:

> "Following on the movement to 'normalise' the care of those with learning disabilities and dementias, most are cared for in residential units which are

---

[36] [1998] 3 All E.R 289.

[37] S.131(1) provides that: "Nothing in this Act shall be construed as preventing a patient who requires treatment for mental disorder from being admitted to any hospital ... in pursuance of arrangements made in that behalf and without any application, order or direction rendering him liable to be detained under this Act and from remaining in any hospital ... in pursuance of such arrangements after he has ceased to be so liable to be detained."

[38] See Eastman N., "Bournewood: an indefensible gap in mental health law" (1998) B.M.J. Vol.317 94–95. Eastman suggests in relation to England that the distinct category of "informal patient" should be retained and that consideration be given to tailoring specific safeguards to this category of patient. These could included extending the remit of the Mental Health Act Commission to these patients or alternatively having "some formal review mechanism (tribunal or otherwise) relating to incapacitated patients".

not hospitals, and most of the carers are not formally qualified as nurses, so detention under mental health law is not possible. However it is not uncommon to hear of the use of seclusion, restraints, psychoactive medication, anti-androgens and other treatments in such settings."[39]

Further the European Committee for the Prevention of Torture and Inhuman and Degrading Treatment or Punishment in its visit to Ireland in 2002[40] expressed the following view:

"The CPT is ... concerned about the current absence of a clear legal or administrative framework for involuntary admission to establishments for mentally disabled persons. Despite being severely mentally disabled, residents are generally regarded as voluntary admissions. Persons are apparently admitted to such facilities by decision of a general practitioner or upon referral from another mental health establishment and it appears that there are no avenues to appeal against such placements.

In the establishments visited there was little or no trace of the decision making process concerning each resident. Residents were examined by a psychiatrist shortly after admission but there were no formal procedures as to the need for the placement to continue nor any supervision by an independent (e.g. judicial) authority."

Accordingly it recommended that the "legal situation of persons placed in mental disability facilities be reviewed as a matter of urgency and that action be taken with a view to providing a comprehensive legal framework for such institutions offering an adequate range of safeguards to persons placed in them."[41]

The Committee further recommended that "an individualised assessment of residents in establishments for mentally disabled persons be carried out with a view to ensuring that they receive the treatment they require or are transferred to a more appropriate establishment".[42] In its response the Irish Government "noted" the Committee's recommendations.[43]

Holding powers in relation to voluntary patients

Position under Mental Treatment Act 1945 Section 194(1) of the Mental Treatment Act 1945 (which is still in force) provides that a person who is not less than 16 years of age and who is being treated in an approved institution as a voluntary patient may give

---

[39] See Kennedy H.G., "Human Rights Standards and Mental Health in Prisons", *Medico-Legal Journal of Ireland* (2002), Vol.8, No.2 p.58 at p.60.

[40] Report to the Government of Ireland on the visit to Ireland carried out by the European Committee for the Prevention of Torture and Inhuman or Degrading Treatment or Punishment (CPT) from May 20–28, 2002 CPT/Inf (2003) 36.

[41] Para.94.

[42] Para.103.

[43] Response of the Government of Ireland to the report of the European Committee for the Prevention of Torture and Inhuman or Degrading Treatment or Punishment (CPT) on its visit to Ireland from May 20–28, 2002 CPT/Inf (2003) 37, p.29, 30.

written notice to the person in charge of the institution that he wishes to leave the institution not earlier than 72 hours from the giving of the notice and he shall be entitled and shall be allowed to leave the institution on or at any time after the expiration of the said 72 hours. Section 194(2) provides that the parent or guardian of a person less than 16 years of age may give written notice to the person in charge of the institution that he wishes to remove such person from the institution and shall be entitled to remove such person from the institution at any time after he gives such notice.

Section 195 of the 1945 Act provides that where a patient who is being treated in an approved institution as a voluntary patient becomes mentally incapable of expressing himself as willing or not willing to remain in the institution he shall be discharged from the institution into the custody of such person as the person in charge of the institution approves of not later than 28 days after becoming so incapable unless he sooner becomes capable of expressing himself or a reception order relating to him is obtained.

In the recent case of *Gooden v. Waterford Regional Hospital*,[44] it was held by the Supreme Court (McGuinness, Hardiman, Geoghegan JJ.), that construing section 194 purposively in the light of the provisions of the Mental Treatment Act 1945 as a whole, it was possible to imply a power on the part of the hospital authorities to make a reception order in respect of a voluntary patient who, contrary to his own medical interests, gave notice of intention to leave the hospital. It was held that a literal interpretation on the provision, to the effect that during the 72 hours period the patient is inviolate and at the end of it must be physically released would give rise to an absurdity in the situation where the patient was so mentally ill as to be a danger either to himself or the public. Hardiman J. sounding a caveat to the implication of such a power stated:

> " I do not know that I would have been prepared to go as far as we have in this direction were it not for the essentially paternalistic character of the legislation as outlined in *In re Philip Clarke* [1950] I.R. 235".[45]

Position under Mental Treatment Act 1945 Section 23 of the Mental Health Act 2001, (although not yet in force) provides expressly for a power to prevent a voluntary patient leaving an approved centre. Section 23 of the 2001 Act states that where a person other than a child who is being treated in an approved centre as a voluntary patient indicates at any time that he or she wises to leave the approved centre then if a consultant psychiatrist,[46] registered medical practitioner[47] or registered nurse[48] on the staff of the approved centre is of the opinion that the person is suffering from a mental disorder[49] he or she may detain the person for a period not exceeding 24 hours or such

---

[44] Unreported, Supreme Court, February 21, 2001.

[45] *Ibid.*, p.4.

[46] "Consultant Psychiatrist" is defined by s.2 of the Act as amended by the Health Act 2004 as meaning "a consultant psychiatrist who is employed by the Health Service Executive or by an approved centre or a person whose name is entered on the division of psychiatry or the division of child and adolescent psychiatry of the Register of Medical Specialists maintained by the Medical Council in Ireland".

[47] "Registered Medical Practitioner" is defined by s.2 as meaning "a person whose name is entered in the General Register of Medical Practitioners".

[48] "Registered nurse" is defined by s.2 as meaning "a person whose name is entered in the register of nurses maintained by An Bord Altranais under s.27 of the Nurses Act 1985".

[49] This is defined by s.3 of the 2001 Act.

shorter period as may be prescribed beginning at the time aforesaid. Where a person (other than a child) is detained pursuant to section 23 the consultant psychiatrist responsible for the care and treatment of the person[50] prior to his or her detention must either discharge the person or arrange for him or her to be examined by another consultant psychiatrist who is not a spouse[51] or relative[52] of the person.[53]

If following such examination the second mentioned consultant psychiatrist (a) is satisfied that the person is suffering from a mental disorder[54] he or she must issue a certificate in writing in a form specified by the Mental Health Commission stating that he or she is of opinion that because of such mental disorder the person should be detained in an approved centre or (b) if the second mentioned consultant psychiatrist is not satisfied that the person is suffering from a mental disorder he or she must issue a certificate in writing in a form specified by the Commission stating that he or she is of opinion that the person should not be detained and the person shall thereupon be discharged.[55] For the purpose of carrying out an examination[56] the consultant psychiatrist concerned is entitled to take charge of the person concerned for the period of 24 hours.[57]

Section 24(3) provides that where a certificate is issued under section 24(2)(a) the consultant psychiatrist responsible for the care and treatment of the person immediately before his or her detention under section 23 shall make an admission order in a form specified by the Mental Health Commission for the reception, detention and treatment of the person in an approved centre.

The provisions of sections 15 to 22 of the 2001 Act apply to a person detained under section 24 as they apply to a person detained under section 14 with any necessary modifications.[58] Thus, *inter alia*, the admission order may be renewed for a further period not exceeding 3 months, then for a further period not exceeding 6 months and for further periods not exceeding 12 months;[59] the consultant psychiatrist must not later than 24 hours after making the admission order send a copy of the order to the Mental Health Commission and give notice in writing of the making of the order to the patient; the notice must include a statement in writing containing certain statutorily prescribed details concerning the patient's detention and treatment in the approved;[60] the admission order must be referred by the Commission to a tribunal; a legal representative must be assigned to represent the patient unless he or she proposes to engage one; the Mental

---

[50] This includes a consultant psychiatrist acting on behalf of the consultant psychiatrist responsible for the care and treatment of the person. See Mental Health Act 2001, s.24(6).

[51] "Spouse" is defined by s.2 as "a husband or wife or a man or a woman who is cohabiting with a person of the opposite sex for a continuous period of not less than three years but is not married to that person".

[52] "Relative" in relation to a person is widely defined by s.2 of the Act to mean "a parent, grandparent, brother, sister, uncle, aunt, niece, nephew or child of the person or of the spouse of the person whether of the whole blood, of the half blood or by affinity."

[53] Mental Health Act 2001, s.24.

[54] Mental Disorder is widely defined by s.3. See below Criteria for Involuntary Admission.

[55] Mental Health Act 2001, s.24(2).

[56] "Examination" in relation to an admission order means a "personal examination of the process and content of though, the mood and behaviour of the person concerned", see s.2.

[57] Mental Health Act 2001, s.24(5).

[58] *Ibid.*, s.24(4).

[59] Mental Health Act 2001, s.15.

[60] *Ibid.*, s.16. See Chap.3 on Informational Rights.

Health Commission must direct a member of the panel of consultant psychiatrists to examine the patient, interview the consultant psychiatrist responsible for the care of the patient, review the records relating to the patient and report in writing to the tribunal;[61] the detention must be reviewed by a Mental Health Tribunal;[62] the patient has a right to appeal to the Circuit Court against a decision of the tribunal to affirm an order in respect of him or her on the grounds that he or she is not suffering from a mental disorder;[63] the patient has the right to request a transfer to another approved centre subject to the approval of the clinical director of that centre;[64] the clinical director of an approved centre may transfer a patient to another approved centre if it would be for his/her benefit or if it is necessary for the purpose of obtaining special treatment for the patient subject to the consent of the clinical director of that centre; where the clinical director of an approved centre is of opinion that it would be for the benefit of a patient detained in that centre or that it is necessary for the purpose of obtaining special treatment for such a patient to transfer him or her to the Central Mental Hospital and proposes to do so the clinical director must notify the Mental Health Commission in writing of the proposal and the Commission must refer the proposal to a tribunal which will decide whether to authorise the transfer;[65] a clinical director of an approved centre may arrange for the transfer of a patient detained in that centre for treatment in a hospital or other place and for his or her detention there for that purpose.[66]

Holding Powers in respect of children contained in the Mental Health Act 2001 Section 23(2) provides for holding powers to be exercised in the case of children admitted as voluntary patients and states that where the parents[67] of a child who is being treated in an approved centre as a voluntary patient or either of them or a person acting *in loco parentis* indicates that he or she wishes to remove the child from the approved centre and a consultant psychiatrist,[68] registered medical practitioner[69] or registered nurse[70] on the staff of the approved centre is of the opinion that the child is suffering from a mental disorder[71] the child may be detained and placed in the custody of the Health Service Executive. Section 2 defines "a child" as a person under the age of 18 years other than a person who is or has been married.

By virtue of section 23(3) where a child is detained in accordance with section 23 then unless the Health Service Executive returns the child to his or her parent(s) or a person acting *in loco parentis*, it must make an application under section 25 (involuntary

---

[61] Mental Health Act 2001, s.17.

[62] *Ibid.*, s.18.

[63] *Ibid.*, s.19.

[64] *Ibid.*, s.20.

[65] *Ibid.*, s.21.

[66] *Ibid.*, s.22.

[67] "Parents" includes a surviving parent and in the case of a child who has been adopted under the Adoption Acts 1952 to 1998 or where the child has been adopted outside the State, whose adoption is recognised by virtue of the law for the time being in force in the State means the adopter or adopters or the surviving adopters. See Mental Health Act 2001, s.2.

[68] See definition above, n.46.

[69] See definition above, n.47.

[70] See definition above, n.48.

[71] This is widely defined by s.3 of the Act. See Criteria for Involuntary Admission below.

admission of children) at the next sitting of the District Court held in the same district court district or in the event that the next such sitting is not due to be held within three days of the date on which the child is placed in the care of the Health Service Executive at a sitting of the District Court which has been specially arranged, held within the said three days. Pending the hearing of the application the Health Service Executive must retain custody of the child.

By virtue of section 23(4) the provisions of section 13(4) of the Child Care Act 1991 shall apply to the making of an application in respect of a child to which section 23 applies with any necessary modifications. This in effect means that (a) any order shall be made by the justice for the District Court in which the child resides or is for the time being; (b) where a justice for the district in which the child resides or is for the time being is not immediately available an order may be made by any justice of the district court; (c) an application for any such order may, if the justice is satisfied that the urgency of the matter so requires be made *ex parte:* (d) an application for any such order may, if the justice is satisfied that the urgency of the matter so requires be heard and an order made thereon elsewhere than at a public sitting of the District Court.

Commentary from international and comparative law perspectives

1. The proposed holding power in the Mental Health Act 2001 represents an implicit hedging about of rights however necessary it may be and it could arguably lead to unnecessary detention taking place in certain cases. It has been noted[72] that where doubt exists about the necessity for detention if the person with mental illness is in the community then the decision tends to lean in the direction of not detaining and leaving well alone. When the person with mental illness is in hospital the opposite is the case. Care providers feel more "responsible" for inpatients and they are less inclined to expose themselves to risks which would be considered tolerable for someone already in the community and they are more inclined to guard against any hint of negligence which consideration looms large when the slightest doubt exists about the safety of a mentally ill person leaving hospital. When this doubt exists the decision tends to lean in the direction of keeping the person with mental illness in hospital and to "play safe." Accordingly a case could be argued for making conditions for holding powers more rigorous so that people in "doubtful" cases have the chance of returning to the community to try again. This might lessen the amount of defensive psychiatric practice where the main motive is not the patient's welfare but the fear of making a mistake.

2. When the nurse, registered medical practitioner or consultant psychiatrist uses the holding power it is submitted that there should be a procedure for scrutiny by a Mental Health Tribunal of how the powers are used and a right of appeal.

3. It is submitted that it should also be a requirement that the registered nurse on the staff of the approved centre have completed his/her training in psychiatry before being permitted to exercise holding powers. This is consistent with the jurisprudence

---

[72] See Ball and Chakrabarti, *Mental Health and the Law in Scotland* (Gordanhill College of Education), p.36.

of the European Court of Human Rights in *Winterwerp v. Netherlands*[73] which requires that except in emergencies, a decision to detain be based on objective medical expertise.

4.   The provisions of the Mental Health Act dealing with holding powers seem to deviate from the terms of the White Paper which proposes that nurses be given holding powers to detain a patient in an approved centre for up to six hours within which time the person must be examined by a medical practitioner and a consultant psychiatrist may hold such a patient for a period of 48 hours within which time procedures for detention must be completed.[74] (The reason for such an extensive detention period in the case of psychiatrists was that an application to have someone compulsorily detained might take longer at weekends and Bank Holidays.).[75] It is interesting to note that when the introduction of a similar holding power was proposed in Scotland pressure groups such as MIND and various Mental Health Associations opposed and were partly responsible for the reduction in its duration form the originally proposed six hours to the two hours now laid down in the Mental Health (Scotland) Act 1984[76] It is submitted that a similar reduction in the length of the "holding" time should be considered in this country.

5.   The evidence in other jurisdictions where holding powers exist is that there is a tendency to abuse them. In some cases they have been used as a substitute for full compulsory procedures e.g. by persuading a patient to enter hospital voluntarily and using holding powers the same day[77] and in others they have been used as a means of persuading long-stay patients to co-operate in their treatment.[78]

PATIENTS ADMITTED UNDER COMPULSORY POWERS

Criteria for involuntary admission under the Mental Treatment Act 1945

The Mental Treatment Act 1945 (which is still in force) creates two main categories of admission the temporary patient and the person of unsound mind category. These categories are further divided into public ("eligible") and private categories.

Broadly speaking a person may be detained as a temporary eligible patient if a registered medical practitioner certifies that he has examined the person in question and is of opinion (a) that such person is suffering from mental illness and (ii) requires for his recovery not more than six months suitable treatment and (iii) is unfit on account of his mental state for treatment as a voluntary patient or (b) that such person (i) is an addict[79]

---

[73] [1980] 2 E.H.R.R. 387.

[74] See para.3.34.

[75] Para.3.33.

[76] In England and Wales nurses have power to hold a patient for a period of six hours s.5(4) of the Mental Health Act 1983.

[77] See Bean P., *Compulsory Admissions to Mental Hospitals* (Chichester: Wiley, 1980).

[78] Hoggett, *Mental Health Law* (Sweet & Maxwell, London, 1990), p.16.

[79] "Addict" is defined as a person who (a) by reason of his addiction to drugs or intoxicants is either dangerous to himself or others or incapable of managing himself or his affairs or of ordinary proper conduct or (b) by reason of his addiction to drugs or intoxicants or perverted conduct is in serious danger of mental disorder See s.3 of the Mental Treatment Act 1945.

and (ii) requires for his recovery at least six months preventive and curative treatment.[80] Where it is proposed to admit a person as a temporary private patient two registered mental practitioners must have separately certified that the conditions for detention exist[81].

A person may be detained as a person of unsound mind and an eligible patient where a registed medical practitioner issues a certificate that the person was of unsound mind and is a proper patient to be taken charge of and detained under care and treatment and is unlikely to recover within six months and of the date of examination[82]. Once again where it is proposed to admit a person as a person of unsound mind in a private institution an order must be signed by two registered medical practitioners who have separately examined the patient.[83]

The terms "mental illness" and "unsound mind" are not defined in the 1945 Act giving broad scope to medical discretion.

The Mental Health Act 2001 revises the criteria for involuntary admission so that a person may be involuntarily admitted to an approved centre and detained there on the grounds that he or she is suffering from "mental disorder".

Criteria for involuntary admission under the Mental Health Act 2001

The Mental Health Act 2001 revises the criteria for involuntary admission. However the sections of the Act which authorise involuntary admission are not yet in force. Section 8 (which is not yet in force) provides that a person may be involuntarily admitted to an approved centre and detained there on the grounds that he or she is suffering from mental disorder. 'Mental disorder' is given a meaning under the Act which combines both the meaning of those terms and the criteria for admission. "Mental disorder" is defined by section 3(1) of the Act (which came into force on April 5, 2002)[84] to mean "mental illness, severe dementia or significant intellectual disability" where:

"(a) because of the illness, disability or dementia there is a serious likelihood of the person concerned causing immediate and serious harm to himself or herself or to other persons; or
(b) (i) because of the severity of the illness, disability or dementia the judgment of the person concerned is so impaired that failure to admit the person to an approved centre[85] would be likely to lead to a serious deterioration in his or her condition or would prevent the administration of appropriate treatment[86] that could only be given by such admission, and

---

[80] Mental Treatment Act 1945, s.163(2).
[81] Mental Treatment Act 1945, s.185(4).
[82] *Ibid.*, s.163.
[83] *Ibid.*, s.178.
[84] S.3 of the Act was brought into force by the Mental Health Act 2001 (Sections 1 to 5, 7, 31 to 55) (Commencement) Order 2002 (S.I. No. 90 of 2002).
[85] S.2 of the Act provides that "approved centre" shall be construed in accordance with s.63 which provides that a person shall not carry on a centre is registered (in the Register of Approved Centres established and maintained by the Mental Health Commission) and the person is the registered proprietor thereof.
[86] "Treatment" in relation to a patient is defined to include "the administration of physical, psychological

(b) (ii) the reception, detention and treatment of the person concerned in an approved centre would be likely to benefit or alleviate the condition of that person to a material extent."

Section 3(2)[87] (which came into force on April 5, 2002) defines the diagnostic terms used in the definition of "mental disorder:

> "'Mental illness' is to be defined as 'a state of mind of a person which affects the person's thinking, perceiving, emotion or judgment and which seriously impairs the mental function of the person to the extent that he or she requires care or medical treatment in his or her own interests or in the interest of other persons'.

> 'Severe dementia' means 'a deterioration of the brain of a person which significantly impairs the intellectual function of the person thereby affecting thought, comprehension and memory and which includes severe psychiatric or behavioural symptoms such as physical aggression'.

> 'Significant intellectual disability' is defined as 'a state of arrested or incomplete development of mind of a person which includes significant impairment of intelligence and social functioning and abnormally aggressive or seriously irresponsible conduct on the part of the person concerned'."

Personality disorder, social deviance and addiction to drugs or intoxicants are in effect excluded from this definition by section 8(2). However section 8(3) provides that the Mental Health Commission shall, from time to time issue guidelines for staff in approved centres in relation to the provisions of this section.

Section 4(1) of the Act which came into force on April 5, 2002[88] adds that in making a decision under the Act concerning the care or treatment of a person including a decision to make an admission order in relation to a person the best interests of the person shall be the principal consideration with due regard being given to the interests of persons who may be at risk of serious harm if the decision is not made.

Section 4(2) provides that where it is proposed to make an admission order in respect of a person or to administer treatment to a person under the Act the person shall so far as is reasonably practicable be notified of the proposal and be entitled to make representations in relation to it and before deciding the matter due consideration shall be given to any representations duly made under section 4(2).

Section 4(3) provides that in making a decision under the Act concerning the care or treatment of a person including a decision to make an admission order in relation to a person due regard shall be given to the need to respect the right of the person to dignity, bodily integrity, privacy and autonomy.

---

and other remedies relating to the care and rehabilitation of a patient under medical supervision, intended for the purposes of ameliorating a mental disorder". See Mental Health Act 2001, s.2.

[87] S.3(2) of the 2001 Act was brought into force on April 5, 2002 by the Mental Health Act 2001 (Sections 1 to 5, 7, 31 to 55) (Commencement) Order 2002 (S.I. No 90 of 2002).

[88] S.4 was brought into force on April 5, 2002 by the Mental Health Act 2001 (Sections 1 to 5, 7, 31, to 55) (Commencement) Order 2002 (S.I. No.90 of 2002).

Commentary form international and comparative law perspectives

1. The definition of "mental disorder" in the White Paper proposals includes "significant intellectual disability." In the opinion of most psychiatrists and psychologists intellectual disability *per se* is not a form of mental illness and is usually not responsive to treatment regimes traditionally available in psychiatric facilities. A person with an intellectual disability may become mentally ill but in such a case involuntary hospitalisation is justified because of the mental illness, not the intellectual disability. It is possible that "significant intellectual disability" is made a ground for committal simply because hospitalisation has often been the only way to provide care in a structured environment to some persons with intellectual disabilities who display abnormally aggressive and seriously irresponsible conduct and involuntary hospitalisation the only means to place such a person in care against his wishes. In principle people with intellectual disabilities should not be hospitalised. Care for those individuals who are too severely mentally impaired to function in the community should be provided in facilities designed for that purpose rather than in psychiatric wards.[89]

2. The definition of "mental illness" in the legislation is circular and based on paternalistic welfare philosophy. Section 3(2) of the Act indicates that "mental illness" is to be defined as "a state of mind of a person which affects a persons thinking, perceiving, emotion or judgment and which seriously impairs the mental function of the person to the extent that he or she requires care or medical treatment in his or her own interests or in the interests of other persons." The circularity of the definition lies in the notion that a person may be committed if he or she needs care or medical treatment because of a mental illness which seriously impairs his/her mental function or her to the extent that he or she needs care or medical treatment.[90] The concept thus also appears professionally self-interested. It is not defined in behavioural or functional terms but by reference to undisclosed diagnostic criteria.

    In *Goldy v. Beal*,[91] a Pennsylvania court struck down as unconstitutionally vague a statute which permitted the state to commit a persons "in need of care and treatment' because of their "mental disability" The court ruled that since the statute failed to define with clarity and precision the grounds of commitment it failed to give individuals fair notice as to the conduct which could lead to loss of liberty. Significantly in the context of the present discussion the court focused in its judgement on the words "in need of care and treatment". It stated:

    > "Such a standard is impermissibly vague, if only because by key phrase "in need of care "is susceptible of several interpretations. How incapacitated must a person be before he needs care within the meaning of the statute? Must he be completely incapacitated of conducting his own affairs or may he be

---

[89] The Report of the Inspector of Mental Hospitals for the year ended 1993 states. "Little progress had been made in the transfer of patients with a mental handicap from psychiatric hospitals to appropriate specialised, residential or community based facilities."

[90] Indeed commitment based on vague standards such as "mentally ill" or "in need of treatment" have been held to be unconstitutional in the US. See *Goldy v. Beal* 429 F. Supp. 640 (M.D. Pa. 1976).

[91] 429 F. Supp. 640 (M.D. Pa. 1976).

committed if simply cannot conduct his affairs as well as most other people? And what is meant by care? Does it mean active medical treatment under the supervision of doctors and other medical personnel or does it simply mean providing for the committed person's basic needs?"[92]

It also found that "such lack of specificity in a statute that authorizes an interference with the constitutionally protected right of physical liberty places insufficient limits on the discretion of officials who are responsible for its implementation, with the result that there is nothing in the statute to prevent it being enforced arbitrarily".[93] Such a result amounted to vagueness that violated due process.

In addition to the vagueness of the "care" criterion the requirement in the definition of "mental illness" in the 2001 Act that a person with mental illness requires involuntary admission "in the interests of others" is open to criticism on the grounds that it goes beyond the *parens patriae* justification which permits committal only in the persons own interests.

Adopting the terms of the Stromberg and Stone's *Model State Law on Civil Commitment of the Mentally Ill*,[94] it is submitted that involuntary admission should be confined to cases where the patient has a "severe mental disorder" defined as:

> "an illness, disease, organic brain disorder or other condition that (1) substantially impairs the person's thought, perception of reality, emotional process or judgment or (2) substantially impairs behaviour as manifested by recent disturbed behaviour. [Intellectual disability,] epilepsy or other developmental disabilities should not in themselves constitute a severe mental disorder."[95]

This definition recognises the serious social decision that underlies involuntary admission. Only a person suffering from a "severe mental disorder" should lose his/her liberty. In the Model Law the definition of 'severe mental disorder" corresponds roughly to a psychotic disorder. In addition the realities of a persons impairment (*viz* "substantial impairment of the persons thought perception of reality emotional process or judgment" or substantial impairment of behaviour") not diagnostic categories alone determine the existence of the mental disorder.

3. The criteria for involuntary admission in the Mental Health Act 2001 are fraught with interpretational difficulties. The criterion of "serious likelihood of the person concerned causing immediate and serious harm" to oneself or to others is an unreliable one. The Mental Health Act does not define "serious likelihood" nor does it define the type of "harm" in question. Is it confined to physical harm or does it extend to mental or emotional harm?. The criterion of "serious likelihood of immediate and serious harm" also tends to assume that psychiatric predictions are rarely inaccurate when evidence suggests that in practice psychiatrists have difficulty

---

[92] *Ibid.*, p.648.
[93] *Ibid.*, p.648.
[94] See (1983) *Harvard Journal on Legislation* (Vol.20) 275.
[95] See Stromberg and Stone, "A Model State Law on Civil Commitment of the Mentally Ill" (1983) 20 *Harvard Journal on Legislation* 275 at p.312.

in diagnosing mental disorder accurately[96] and have a tendency to over-predict dangerousness.[97]

In Northern Ireland recognising the difficulties encountered by psychiatrists when making predictions of dangerousness[98] for the purpose of committal orders the Mental Health Northern Ireland Order 1986 provides that in determining whether the failure to detain a patient would create "a substantial likelihood of serious physical harm to himself" – a criterion for committal for assessment and treatment – regard is to be had "only to evidence (i) that the patient has inflicted or threatened or attempted to inflict serious physical harm on himself or (ii) that the patient's judgment is so affected that he is or would soon be unable to protect himself against serious physical harm and that reasonable provision for his protection is not available in the community."[99] In determining whether the failure to detain a patient would create a "substantial likelihood of serious physical harm to other persons" regard is to be had only to evidence "(i) that the patient has behaved violently towards other persons or (ii) that the patient has so behaved himself that other persons were placed in reasonable fear of serious physical harm to themselves."[100]

In addition to the finding of severe mental disorder Stromberg and Stone in the *Model Law on Commitment of the Mentally Ill* suggest the necessity for a finding that a*s a result of* the severe mental disorder, the person must be (a) likely to cause harm to himself or to suffer substantial mental or physical deterioration or (b) likely to cause harm to others if involuntary admission is to be justified.

Regarding (a) the phrase "likely to cause harm to himself or to suffer substantial mental or physical deterioration" is defined by Stromberg and Stone to mean that:

> "*as evidenced by recent behaviour*, the person (1) is likely in the near future to inflict substantial physical injury upon himself or (2) is substantially unable to provide for some of his basic needs such as food, clothing, shelter, health or safety or (3) will if not treated suffer or continue to suffer severe and abnormal mental emotional or physical distress and this distress is associated with significant impairment of judgment, reason or behaviour causing a substantial deterioration of his previous ability to function on his own"[101]

---

[96] Rosenham, "On Being Sane in Insane Places" (1973) 13 *Santa Clara Law* 379 at 384; Ennis & Litwack, "Psychiatry and the Presumption of Expertise: Flipping Coins in the Courtroom" (1974) 62 Cal. L.Rev. 693.

[97] Monahan J., *The Clinical Prediction of Violent Behaviour* (Washington, National Institute of Mental Health Monograph 1981) 47–49; Steadman and Cocozza, *Careers of the Criminally Insane* (Lexington, Lexington Books, 1974); Thornberry and Jacoby, *The Criminally Insane: A Community Follow-up of Mentally Ill Offenders* (Chicago, 1979) The Law Reform Commission of Canada in its *Report on the Criminal Process and Mental Disorder* (1975) stated: "In the last few years legal and medical journals have been inundated with reports of studies considering various aspects of the reliability and predictive accuracy of psychiatric assessments of dangerousness. More remarkable than the bulk of this literature is its unanimity – it concludes that clinical predictions of dangerousness are at best, suspect and at worst, totally unreliable" (at p.9).

[98] The tendency of psychiatrists to over predict dangerousness is documented in Cooney & O'Neill, *Psychiatric Detention Civil Commitment in Ireland* (Baikower, Ireland, 1995), pp.115–118.

[99] Mental Health (Northern Ireland) Order 1986, art.2(4)(a).

[100] *Ibid.*, art.2(4)(b).

[101] See Stromberg and Stone, *op. cit.*, p.302.

In this definition the prediction of harm cannot be based solely on descriptions of the person's mental processes but must be grounded in the patient's "recent behaviour." In addition the harm must be more than possible it must be probable or "likely". The rest of the definition proposes that the involuntary commitment be justified by reference to three *parens patriae* principles.

The first of these principles is that the person "is likely in the near future to inflict substantial physical injury upon himself." This will require a recent credible threat of or attempt at self-mutilation or suicide accompanied by a mental state indicating a likely recurrence. The time period "in the near future" aims to define the time period more explicitly.

The second *parens patriae* principle is that the person "is substantially unable to provide for some of his basic needs." Lest this ground justify committal on the basis that a person's lifestyle simply offends the majority a person is liable to be involuntarily admitted on this ground only if his alleged inability to care for himself is due to a severe mental disorder.

The third *parens patriae* principle justifying the commitment is that due to a "severe mental disorder" the person is likely to "suffer substantial mental or physical deterioration". This ground applies only to persons who will suffer "severe and abnormal mental, emotional or physical distress" which impairs the person's reason or behaviour so severely as to cause a major decline in his ability to function. By introducing these requirements the proposed reform avoids judging individual lifestyles but permits commitment of severely mentally ill persons who are moving towards sudden collapse.

Regarding (b) he phrase "likely to cause harm to others" is defined by Stromberg and Stone as meaning that:

> "as evidenced by recent behaviour causing, attempting or threatening such harm a person is likely in the near future to cause physical injury or physical abuse to another person or substantial damage to another person's property".[102]

Commitment on the basis of likelihood of causing harm to others is the classic exercise of a police power, i.e. detention for the protection of society. In the proposed Model Law the police power commitments are predicated on "recent behaviour causing, attempting or threatening harm" to others. They are not based simply on a diagnosis of the person's mental state. In addition the potential for harm must arise from a severe mental disorder and the individual must meet the other criteria for commitment outlined in the scheme above.

According it is submitted that to facilitate accuracy in prediction of behaviour it is submitted that there should be a requirement of evidence of recent dangerous behaviour to self or others.[103]

4. In other respects also the *parens patriae*-based justification for involuntary commitment in the Mental Health Act 2001 differ substantially to clinical prognosis. The Mental Health Act 2001 provides for involuntary admission where. because of

---

[102] *Ibid.*, p.305.
[103] See Stromberg and Stone (1983) 20 *Harvard Journal on Legislation* 275 at 302.

the severity of the illness, disability or dementia the judgment of the person concerned is so impaired that failure to admit the person to an approved centre[104] would be likely to lead to a serious deterioration in his or her condition or would prevent the administration of appropriate treatment[105] that could only be given by such admission. The words "would be likely to lead to serious deterioration in his or her condition" and "prevent the administration of appropriate treatment" gives considerable scope to medical prediction and discretion. If a person is to have due notice of committal standards it would be preferable if the basis for the diagnosis and the nature of the deterioration in question were described. Thus adopting the Stromberg and Stone template discussed above a person could be involuntarily admitted if "as evidenced by recent behaviour the person will if not treated suffer or continue to suffer severe and abnormal mental, emotional or physical distress and this distress is associated with significant impairment of judgment reason or behaviour causing a substantial deterioration of his previous ability to function on his own."[106] Further according to the Stromberg and Stone model law a person facing an acute episode or sudden collapse of mental state might be subject to involuntary admission provided this is evidenced "by recent behaviour" and there is "significant impairment of judgment reason or behaviour" causing substantial deterioration of previous ability to function independently and the other criteria are satisfied.

The use of the criterion "that failure to admit the person to an approved centre would prevent the administration of *appropriate treatment* that could only be given by such admission" by failing to define the notion of appropriacy does not provide adequate safeguards against arbitrary decision making. It is therefore submitted that it should be omitted from the criteria.

5. It is submitted that decision makers should be obliged to seek the consent of the person with a view to voluntary admission before considering involuntary admission. Voluntary admission is likely to bring therapeutic benefits with it.[107]

6. In section 3(1) the Act does not require that a person should be incompetent before he or she should be committed. The threshold requirement for committal must be incapacity. It is this factor which justifies substitution of a medical practitioner's judgment for the patient's. In *Colyar v. Third Judicial District Court*[108] a Utah court held unconstitutionally vague and overly broad a statute which permitted involuntary commitment of a person who is "mentally ill" and "in need of custodial

---

[104] S.2 of the Act provides that "approved centre" shall be construed in accordance with s.63 which provides that a person shall not carry on a centre is registered (in the Register of Approved Centres established and maintained by the Mental Health Commission) and the person is the registered proprietor thereof.

[105] "Treatment" in relation to a patient is defined to include "the administration of physical, psychological and other remedies relating to the care and rehabilitation of a patient under medical supervision, intended for the purposes of ameliorating a mental disorder". See Mental Health Act 2001, s.2.

[106] *Ibid.*, p.302–303.

[107] See Winick, "Competency to Consent to Voluntary Hospitalisation" in Durham, *Essays in Therapeutic Jurisprudence* 83 (Carolina Academic Press, 1991).

[108] 469 F. Supp. 424 (D Utah 1979).

care and treatment in a mental health facility and because of illness lacks sufficient insight to make responsible decisions as to the need for care and treatment" The court held that the statute failed to require the state to "show that the individual is incapable of making a rational choice regarding the acceptance of care and treatment."[109] The court pointed out that a "finding of mental illness does not necessarily mean that an individual is deprived of all his capacity to make rational decisions."[110] The court stated that it was not difficult to see that the rational decision in many cases would be to forego treatment particularly if it carries with it stigma, detention, curtailment of rights and interruption of job and family life. It expressed the view that if an individual can make "a meaningful choice not to receive treatment, he must be allowed to make that choice."[111]

In Canada the mental health legislation in several Canadian provinces provides that a person can be committed to a facility only if he is unsuitable for admission as a voluntary patient. In Saskatchewan legislation provides in addition to a requirement of dangerousness ("likely to cause harm to himself or to others") and a *parens patriae* criterion ("likely to suffer substantial mental or physical deterioration") there is a requirement that the examining physician have probable cause to believe that the person is unable because of his mental disorder, "fully [to] understand and to make an informed decision regarding his need for treatment or care and supervision."[112] Incapacity is thus made an essential threshold requirement for committal.[113] It is submitted that this is a desirable judgment as society cannot credibly justify substituting its judgment for that of a competent person. *Parens patriae* commitments can only be justified if the person lacks capacity.

Stromberg and Stone's Model State Law also requires that the person must lack the capacity to make an informed decision concerning treatment. This is defined by the Model Law as meaning that:

> "the person, by reason of his mental disorder or condition, is unable, despite conscientious efforts at explanation, to understand basically the nature and effects of hospitalisation or treatment or is unable to engage in a rational decision making process regarding such hospitalisation or treatment as evidenced by inability to weigh the possible risks and benefits"[114]

This reflects the view that *parens patriae* commitments cannot be justified by mental illness unless the person also lacks capacity. Many mental disorders do not impair a person's ability to assess his desire for hospitalisation or a particular therapy. Moreover unless lack of capacity is made a threshold criterion for all involuntary

---

[109] *Ibid.*, p.431.

[110] *Ibid.*, p.431.

[111] *Ibid.*, p.432.

[112] The legislation also requires that the physician have probable cause to believe that the person "is suffering from a mental disorder as a result of which he is in need of treatment or care and supervision which can be provided only in an in-patient facility". S.S.1984–85–86, c. M-13.1, s.24(2).

[113] See Law Reform Commission of Saskatchewan, *Proposals for a Compulsory Mental Health Care Act* (1985), 15.

[114] See Stromberg and Stone, "A Model State Law on Civil Commitment of the Mentally Ill" (1983) 20 *Harvard Journal on Legislation* 275 at 301.

admissions there is no way to decide which patients retain the right to refuse treatment.

Accordingly it is submitted that the committal criteria in the 2001 Act should require that the patient be found to lack capacity fully to understand and to make an informed decision concerning treatment.

7. To achieve a fair balance between commitment and personal liberty it should be made an express requirement of the Act that decisions to commit be consistent with least restrictive alternative principle. This will at least confront decision makers with the need to consider appropriate placement alternatives. In the case of *Winterwerp v. Netherlands*,[115] now a persuasive authority in the Irish domestic courts,[116] the European Court of Human Rights ruled that before a person could be detained as a person of unsound mind the person must in addition to being shown by objective medical expertise to be of unsound mind also be suffering from a mental disorder "of a kind or degree" as to "warrant continuous confinement." Consistency with the least restrictive alternative principle is also required by Principle 16(b) of the *United Nations Principles for the Protection of Persons with Mental Illness and the Improvement of Mental Health Care* and by Article 3 of *Council of Europe Recommendation (83) 2 of the Committee of Ministers to Member States concerning the legal protection of persons suffering from mental disorder placed as involuntary patients*[117] (which sets out criteria for unvoluntary admission to be applied "in the absence of any other means of giving the appropriate treatment") both of which international instruments formed the basis for the proposals for reform contained in the White Paper leading to the enactment of the 2001 Act. In addition the US Supreme Court in the case of *O'Connor v. Donaldson*[118] enshrined the least restrictive alternative principle as one of constitutional due process mandating in the context of civil commitment that the state may not involuntarily institutionalise an individual if less restrictive settings will suffice.

"Consistent with the least restrictive alternative principle" has been defined by Stromberg and Stone's *Model State Law on Civil Commitment of the Mentally Ill*[119] as meaning that:

> "(1) each patient committed solely on the ground that he is likely to cause harm to himself or to suffer substantial mental or physical deterioration shall be placed in the most appropriate and therapeutic available setting, that is, a setting in which treatment provides the patient with a realistic opportunity to improve and which is no more restrictive of his physical or social liberties than is believed conducive to the most effective treatment for the patient; and (2) each patient committed solely or in part on the ground that he is likely to cause harm to others shall be placed in a setting in which treatment is available

---

[115] [1979] E.H.R.R. 387.
[116] See European Convention on Human Rights Act 2003, ss 2, 4.
[117] Adopted by the Committee of Ministers on February 22, 1983.
[118] 422 U.S. 563, (1975). The court referred to *Shelton v. Tucker* 364 U.S. 479 (1960) in formulating its ruling that it is unconstitutional to confine non-dangerous individuals who are "capable of surviving safely in freedom on their own or with the help of family or friends", *ibid.*, p.576.
[119] See Stromberg and Stone (1983) Vol.20 *Harvard Journal on Legislation* 275.

and the risks of physical injury or property damage posed by such placement are warranted by the proposed plan of treatment"

This definition reflects the various purposes of civil commitment. A patient committed solely on a *parens patriae* basis (for his own good) must be placed in "the most appropriate and therapeutic available setting" that restricts his liberty no more "than is believed conducive to the most effective treatment for the patient." In this case treatment is the key goal and restrictions on patient liberty should not be imposed unless they help to ensure effective treatment. A patient committed on the police power basis (to protect society) must be placed where society will be adequately protected and where any reduction in restrictiveness is "warranted by the proposed plan of treatment".

Further in a recent decision in *Olmstead v. LC ex rel Zimring et al*[120] the United States Supreme Court held that unjustified placement or retention of persons in institutions when community placement was deemed clinically appropriate and could be reasonably accommodated by the state constituted a form of discrimination based on disability prohibited by Title 11 of the Americans with Disabilities Act 1990 which prohibits discrimination with respect to state services. The court stated:

"Recognition that unjustified institutional isolation of persons with disabilities is a form of discrimination reflects two evident judgments. First, institutional placement of persons who can handle and benefit from community settings perpetuates unwarranted assumptions that persons so isolated are incapable or unworthy of participation in community life. ...

Second, confinement in an institution severely diminishes the everyday life activities of individuals, including family relations, social contacts, work options, economic independence, educational advancement, and cultural en-richment. ... Dissimilar treatment correspondingly exists in this key respect: In order to receive needed medical services, persons with mental disabilities must, because of those disabilities, relinquish participation in community life they could enjoy given reasonable accommodations, while persons without mental disabilities can receive the medical services they need without similar sacrifice."

The judgment opens up the possibility of an argument being made in the Irish jurisdiction that placement of a person with mental illness in an institution when a community setting *is* available and deemed clinically appropriate[121] amounts to unlawful discrimination on the grounds of mental disability in relation to the provision of services under section 5 of the Equal Status Act and would be actionable against a public body such as the Health Service Executive.

On the other hand, in *R (on the application of K) v. Camden and Islington*

---

[120] Supreme Court of the United States, June 22, 1999.
[121] Thereby removing the possibility that the decision might be exempt from being discrimination under s.16(2) which states that "treating a person differently does not constitute discrimination where the person is so treated in the exercise of a clinical judgment in connection with the diagnosis of illness or his or her medical treatment".

Health Authority,[122] the English Court of Appeal examining the lawfulness of the continuing detention of a patient under Article 5(1)(e) of the European Convention on Human Rights, as incorporated into English Law by the Human Rights Act 1998, has held that detention in an institution may be lawful, if community facilities are not available, and for as long as the patient remained of unsound mind within the meaning of Article 5(1)(e), even if the patient would also be able to live in the community if properly supported. The Court was reluctant to impose any duty on the State to provide such community facilities. Phillips L.J. stated:

> "Where (i) a patient is suffering from mental illness and (ii) treatment of that illness is necessary in the interests of the patient's own health or for the protection of others and (iii) it proves impossible or impractical to arrange for the patient to receive the necessary treatment in the community it seems to me that the three criteria identified by the European Court of Human Rights in *Winterwerp's case* 2 E.H.R.R. 387 are made out. Whether or not it is necessary to detain a patient in hospital for treatment may well depend upon the level of facilities available for treatment within the community. Neither Article 5 nor Strasbourg jurisprudence lays down any criteria as to the extent to which Member States must provide facilities for the care of those of unsound mind in the community, thereby avoiding the necessity for them to be detained for treatment in hospital."[123]

8. There is no requirement in the Mental Health Act provisions that treatment be available at or through the centre where the person is to be detained but simply at any approved centre. The treatment in question should not simply be capable of being given in theory at any approved centre but be clearly shown to be available to him *de facto* at or through (i.e. capable of being arranged by) the approved centre in question. It is submitted that without a requirement as to treatability the State's justification for acting as *parens patriae* becomes a nullity.

9. While criteria for committal are specified in the 2001 legislation the standard of proof remains unstated. In *Addington v. Texas*,[124] the US Supreme Court ruled that since civil commitment for any purpose constitutes a significant deprivation of liberty and involves a stigma for the individual committed the detention must be justified by a measure of proof that falls somewhere between the civil standard and the criminal standard thus attempting to strike a fair balance between the rights of the individual and the legitimate concerns of the state. Thus any criteria for commitment must be established at least by "clear and convincing evidence." Given the deprivation of liberty and social stigma that the detention process involves it is submitted that the criteria for committal should be established by this standard.

10. Following the commentary above it is submitted that the following criteria should be satisfied in any formulation for involuntary admission: A person should be admitted as an involuntary patient to an approved centre only if: (a) s/he has a

---

[122] [2001] 3 W.L.R. 553.
[123] *Ibid.*, para.33.
[124] 441 U.S. 418 (1978).

severe mental disorder; (b) as a result of severe mental disorder, the person as evidenced by recent behaviour– (i) is likely in the near future to inflict substantial injury upon himself or (ii) to cause physical injury to another person or (iii) will if not treated suffer substantial mental or physical deterioration,[125] i.e. suffer or continue to suffer severe and abnormal mental, emotional or physical distress and this distress is associated with significant impairment of judgment, reason or behaviour causing a substantial deterioration of his previous ability to function on his own;[126] (c) the person lacks the capacity to make an informed decision about treatment; (d) such involuntary admission would be consistent with the least restrictive alternative principle, and (e) his/her disorder is treatable at the psychiatric centre to which he/she is be involuntarily admitted.

10. Finally, section 8(1) of the Act provides that a person may be involuntarily admitted to an approved centre and *detained* there on the grounds that he or she is suffering from mental disorder. It makes no reference to treatment. The detention of a mentally ill person without treatment amounts simply to an arbitrary exercise of state power. A mentally ill person has as a proper *quid pro quo* of confinement a right to treatment which is designed to restore his autonomy. This right to treatment should be embodied expressly in the Act.

Who may apply for involuntary admission

Position under Mental Treatment Act 1945

Applications for a a temporary eligible patient reception order may be made by:

(a) the husband or wife or a relative of the person to whom the application relates,

(b) at the request of the husband or wife or a relative by the appropriate Community Welfare Officer, or

(c) by any other person.[127]

An application may be made for a temporary private patient reception order by (a) the husband or wife or relative of the person to whom the application relates, or (b) by any other person.[128]

An application for an eligible patient reception order (i.e. to have a person admitted to a public hospital as a person of unsound mind) may be made by the same persons who may apply for a temporary eligible patient reception order.[129] A Community Welfare Officer may also apply for an eligible patient reception order in specified circumstances,[130] as may a member of the Garda Síochána.[131] Persons who may apply

---

[125] See Stromberg and Stone (1983) 20 *Harvard Journal on Legislation* 275 at p.330.

[126] *Ibid.*, p.302.

[127] Mental Treatment Act 1945, s.184(2).

[128] *Ibid.*, s.185(2).

[129] *Ibid.*, s.162(2) (3).

[130] *Ibid.*, s.166. See *infra*, p.115.

[131] *Ibid.*, s.165. See *infra*, p.117.

for a private patient reception order are the same persons as may apply for a temporary private patient reception order.[132]

Where private persons are applying for eligibe patient reception orders or private patient reception orders there is a requirement that the applicant must have seen the patient within 14 days before making the application.[133] This requirement does not apply in the case of applicants for temporary eligible patient orders or temporary private patient reception orders.

Position under Mental Health Act 2001

Section 9 of the Mental Health Act 2001 (which is not yet in force) specifies the persons, who subject to sections 9(4), 9(6) and 12, may apply to a medical practitioner for a recommendation for the involuntary admission of a person (other than a child) to an approved centre. These are (a) the spouse or a relative of the person, (b) an authorised officer (c) a member of the Garda Síochána or (b) subject to section 9(2) any other person.

Application by spouse or relative A "spouse" is defined to mean a husband or wife of a man or woman who is cohabiting with a person of the opposite sex for a continuous period of not less than three years but is not married to that person.[134] The Act disqualifies from making an application for a recommendation a spouse who is living separately and apart from the person or in respect of whom an application or order has been made under the Domestic Violence Act 1996[135] In these circumstances the application it is envisaged that an application would be initiated by an authorised officer of the Health Service Executive.[136]

During the debate in the Dáil there were requests for the inclusion of same sex partners as applicants. Minister Hanafin stated that the provisions of the Act provide for applications by "any other person" and that this covers such relationships.[137]

"Relative" in relation to a person is defined to mean a parent, grandparent, brother, sister, uncle, aunt, niece, nephew, or child of the person or of the spouse of the person whether of the whole blood, of the half blood or by affinity.[138] Given the wide definition of "spouse" the definition of relative extends to include relatives of cohabitees.[139]

A spouse or relative of a person must not make an application unless he or she has observed the person the subject of the application not more than 48 hours before the date of making the application.[140]

A spouse or relative of a person who, for the purposes of or in relation to an application makes any statement which is to his or her knowledge false or misleading in any material particular shall be guilty of an offence.[141]

---

[132] *Ibid.*, s.177(3), (4) and (5).
[133] See Mental Treatment Act 1945, s.162(4) (eligible patients); s.177(5) (private patients).
[134] Mental Health Act 2001, s.2.
[135] Mental Health Act 2001, s.9(8).
[136] See White Paper, "A New Mental Health Act" (Department of Health 1995, Pn.1824), para.3.13.
[137] 536 *Dáil Debates* Cols 1375–1378; 167 *Seanad Debates* Col.81.
[138] Mental Health Act 2001, s.2.
[139] *Ibid.*
[140] *Ibid.*, s.9(4).
[141] *Ibid.*, s.9(6).

Commentary from comparative law perspective

In contrast to the provisions of the Irish Mental Health Act 2001 in England and Wales, section 26 of the Mental Health Act 1983 contains an extended list of relatives who are excluded from the category of nearest relative who has power to apply for compulsory admission of a person to hospital either for assessment or for treatment. The excluded relatives include (a) a relative who is not resident in the United Kingdom, Channel Islands or Isle of Man when a patient is ordinarily resident there (b) a spouse of the patient who has deserted or has been deserted by the patient (c) a person other than the husband, wife, father or mother of the patient who is for the time being under the age of 18; (d) a person against whom an order divesting him of authority over the patient has been made under section 38 of the Sexual Offences Act 1956 (which relates to incest with a person under eighteen) and has not been rescinded.[142]

The provision of the Mental Health Act 2001 disqualifying relatives who are living separately and apart from the person or in respect of whom an application has been made or an order has been made under the Domestic Violence Act 1996 are welcome developments. However the category of exclusion does not extend to spouses who are in the process of separating – a scenario which is very likely to give rise to the possibility of unjustified applications. In the light of warnings from the High Court in *Bailey v. Gallagher*[143] general practitioners should be very cautious of making any recommendation on the application of a spouse in a situation where there is marital disharmony. Further it is submitted that the disqualification should be extended to preclude any person who has committed a crime against the person in question from making an application.

Application by officer of the Health Service Executive

Criteria for application under Mental Health Treatment Act 1945 Section 166 of the Mental Treatment Act 1945 (still in force) provides that where the appropriate Community Welfare Officer is informed or knows that a person believed to be of unsound mind is not under proper care or control or is neglected or cruelly treated by any relative or other person having the care or charge of him that officer is obliged apply in the prescribed form[144] to an appropriate registered medical practitioner for a recommendation for the reception and detention of the person in question as a person of unsound mind in a district mental hospital serving the area in which the person ordinarily resides.[145]

Where the person in question has no fixed residence and the Community Welfare Officer reports the matter to the member of the Garda Síochána in charge of the Garda Station for the sub-district in which the person was for the time being that member of the Garda Síochána may take the person into custody and remove him to the Garda Station in question for the purpose of his examination by an appropriate registered medical practitioner.[146]

---

[142] Mental Health Act 1983(UK), s.26(5).
[143] [1996] I.L.R.M. 433.
[144] Mental Treatment Regulations 1961, Sch. Form No. 4.
[145] Mental Treatment Act 1945, s.166(1) as adapted by the Mental Treatment Acts (Adaptation) Order 1971 (S.I. No. 108 of 1971).
[146] Mental Treatment Act 1945, s.166(2).

Criteria for application under the Mental Health Act 2001 Section 9 of the 2001 Act (which has not yet been brought into force) lists "an authorised officer" among the categories of person who may apply to a registered medical practitioner for a recommendation that a person (other than a child) be involuntarily admitted to an approved centre. "Authorised officer" is defined to mean an officer of the Health Service Executive[147] who is of a prescribed rank or grade and who is authorised by the chief executive officer to exercise the powers conferred on authorised officers by section 9.[148] "Prescribed" is defined by section 2 to mean prescribed by regulations made by the Minister for Health and Children.

An authorised officer must not make an application unless he or she has observed the person the subject of the application not more than 48 hours before the date of making the application.[149]

An authorised officer who, for the purposes of or in relation to an application makes any statement which is to his or her knowledge false or misleading in any material particular shall be guilty of an offence.[150]

Commentary from an international perspective

1. The qualifications of the authorised officer of the Health Service Executive are not specified in the 2001 Act. The White Paper which preceded the Act proposed that authorised officers would include public health nurses, clinical psychologists and social workers who had received special training for this purpose.[151] In the course of the Committee Stage of the Bill it was stated by the Minister for Health and Children that the grades of officer who would be prescribed for the purposes of the Act would include paramedical staff such as social workers, therapists, psychologists and district nurses but would exclude clerical or administrative staff.[152] It is submitted that any proposed regulations should set out precisely the qualifications of the authorised officers of the Health Service Executive empowered to exercise powers under the mental health legislation. They should also make it a prerequisite to appointment that the authorised officer have adequate training and experience about the procedures and criteria of admission and the rights of appeal and complaints available to the patient.

2. The duties of the "authorised officer" are not defined in the 2001 Act. The White Paper states that the Government agreed with the view expressed by respondents to the Green Paper that "the role assigned to community welfare officers under the 1945 Act should be reviewed in the light of the availability of a wider range of professional staff … employed by the Health Service Executive skilled in assessment of individual and family problems."[153] It was envisaged in the White Paper that the

---

147 "The Health Act 2004 dissolved the health boards which exercised functions under the Mental Health Act 2001 and assigned these functions to the Health Service Executive.
148 Mental Health Act 2001, s.9(8).
149 *Ibid.*, s.9(4).
150 *Ibid.*, s.9(6).
151 See White Paper, "A New Mental Health Act" (Department of Health 1995, Pn.1824), para 3.10.
152 See Select Committee on Health and Children, October 24, 2000.
153 White Paper, "A New Mental Health Act" (Department of Health 1995, Pn.1824), para.3.9.

authorised officer would make application at the request of a spouse or relative or where a spouse or a relative was unavailable, unwilling or disqualified from making an application.[154] but beyond that no role is specified in the Act. *The Council of Europe White Paper on the protection of the human rights and dignity of people suffering from mental disorder especially those placed as involuntary patients in a psychiatric establishment*[155] states that the social care aspects should be taken into consideration in any proposed involuntary admission and it may be that the purpose of the inclusion of the authorised officer among the applicants is precisely to ensure that the social context of mental disorder is taken into account.

It is submitted that authorised officers of the Health Service Executive should be guided by clear statutory criteria in making applications for admission. As a minimum the authorised officer must be required to interview the person concerned. S/he should also be required to make a thorough investigation of alternative provisions for treatment and care in the community. Application for hospital admission should be made only where it is demonstrated that it is the least restrictive course feasible in the situation and in all the circumstances of the case the most appropriate way of providing the care and medical treatment which the patient needs. It should also be provided by statute that the authorised officer of the Health Service Executive owes a duty of care to the patient concerned which should include a duty to ensure that the law is strictly complied with.

Application by member of An Garda Síochána

Position under Mental Treatment Act 1945 Section 165 of the Mental Treatment Act 1945 provides that where a Member of An Garda Síochána is of the opinion that it is necessary that a person believed to be of unsound mind[156] should be placed immediately under care and control, for the public safety or the safety of the person himself he may take that person into custody and remove him to a Garda station. To this end the member of An Garda Síochána has the right of entry into any house or other premises provided that he has reasonable grounds for believing that the person who was believed to be of unsound mind was for the time being in the premises.[157] Where a member of An Garda Síochána so removes a person to a garda station s/he must apply forthwith to a registered medical practitioner for a recommendation for the reception and detention of the person as a person of unsound mind in a district mental hospital.[158]

The constitutional validity of the Garda Power under the 1945 Act and the subsequent hospital order to detain was challenged in the case of *In re Philip Clarke*[159] where it was argued on a *habeas corpus* application to the High Court that the powers of detention provided for by section 165 of the 1945 Act were unconstitutional as no judicial determination of the applicant's case took place between the time of his arrest and the

---

[154] *Ibid.*

[155] CM(2000) 23, February 10, 2000.

[156] This term was undefined in the 1945 legislation.

[157] Mental Treatment Act 1945, s.165(1) as amended by Mental Treatment Act 1961, s.9(1).

[158] See s.165(2) of the Mental Treatment Act 1945 as amended by s.9(2) of the Mental Treatment Act 1961.

[159] [1950] I.R. 235.

time of detention in a psychiatric hospital. Gavan Duffy P. (Davitt and Dixon JJ. concurring) in the High Court was of the view that:

> "Section 165 of the Act of 1945 empowers a Garda Síochána as a first step, to be followed by two separate medical examinations, to arrest a person believed to be of unsound mind, if he thinks it necessary for the public safety or the safety of the person himself. That seems to be a necessary and proper power for an emergency and the dual medical examination constitutes a reasonable safeguard. The attack here is really an attack on the method of procedure, replacing that under the former law, which, though a district justice or a peace commissioner intervened, was necessarily summary, where a dangerous lunatic or idiot was concerned; and I think the new procedure is an improvement."[160]

On appeal O'Byrne J. delivering the judgment of the Supreme Court stated:

> "The impugned legislation is of a paternal character, clearly intended for the care and custody of persons suspected to be suffering from mental infirmity and for the safety and well being of the public generally. The existence of mental infirmity is too widespread to be overlooked, and was, no doubt, present to the minds of the draughtsmen when it was proclaimed in Article 40.1. of the Constitution that, though all citizens, as human beings, are to be held equal before the law, the State may nevertheless, in its enactments, have due regard to differences of capacity, physical and moral, and of social function. We do not see how the common good would be promoted or the dignity and freedom of the individual assured by allowing persons, alleged to be suffering from such infirmity, to remain at large to the possible danger of themselves and others.
>
> [Section 165] is carefully drafted so as to ensure that the person alleged to be of unsound mind shall be brought before and examined by responsible medical officers with the least possible delay. This seems to us to satisfy every reasonable requirement and we have not been satisfied and do not consider that the Constitution requires that there should be a judicial enquiry or determination before such a person can be placed and detained in a mental hospital.
>
> The section cannot, in our opinion, be construed as an attack upon the personal rights of the citizen. On the contrary it seems to be designed for the protection of the citizen and for the promotion of the common good."[161]

This analysis of the legislation was upheld by the Supreme Court in *Croke v. Smith (No.2)*.[162]

However, it is submitted that the decision in *In re Philip Clarke* fails to address the pivotal issue of procedural due process and tends to assume that the decision to commit is a purely medical process. The matter of review of detention is addressed in the Mental Health Act 2001 by the establishment of Mental Health Tribunals to review detention within a short period of admission to hospital.

---

[160] *Ibid.*, p.237.
[161] *Ibid.*, p.247.
[162] [1998]1 I.R. 101.

Powers of a member of An Garda Síochána under Mental Health Act 2001 Section 12 of the Mental Health Act 2001 (which has not yet been brought into force) places a greater onus on the Gardaí to identify risk factors than under the 1945 Act. Section 12 provides that where a member of the Garda Síochána has reasonable grounds for believing that a person is suffering from mental disorder,[163] and that because of the mental disorder there is a serious likelihood of the person causing immediate and serious harm to himself or herself or to other persons the member may either alone or with any other members of the Garda Síochána (a) take the person into custody and (b) enter if need be by force any dwelling or other premises or any place if he or she has reasonable grounds for believing that the person is to be found there.

Section 12(2) provides that where a member of the Garda Síochána takes a person into custody under subsection (1) he or she or any other member of the Garda Síochána shall make an application forthwith in a form specified by the Commission to a registered medical practitioner for a recommendation.

A Garda must not make an application unless he or she has observed the person the subject of the application not more than 48 hours before the date of making the application.[164]

If a Garda, for the purposes of or in relation to an application makes any statement which is to his or her knowledge false or misleading in any material particular s/he shall be guilty of an offence.[165]

Commentary from international and comparative law perspectives

1. It cannot be doubted that the state may on occasion have a compelling interest in the emergency detention of those who threaten immediate and serious violence to themselves and others. In this regard the Gardaí have a role to play in preserving public safety. However the balance must be struck correctly between the Gardaí having a roving commission to take into custody any person whose mental status they doubt and their fear of tort liability from the absence of specific statutory authority for their actions. It is submitted that the Gardaí's powers in section 12 should be more precisely defined. They should be confined to situations (a) where the person concerned would otherwise be subject to lawful arrest and the Garda believes that the person is in need of emergency psychiatric treatment or (b) the Garda has reasonable cause to believe based on his personal observation and investigation that the person is suffering from *severe* mental disorder as a result of which there is a serious likelihood of the person causing immediate and serious harm to himself or herself or to other persons and that immediate hospitalisation is necessary to prevent the harm to the person or to others.[166]

2. In the interests of the person who is ill and in need of treatment the place to which he should be removed by the Garda should be one which has the facilities to cater

---

[163] This term is defined in s.3 of the Act. See "Criteria for Involuntary Admission".
[164] Mental Health Act 2001, s.9(4).
[165] *Ibid.,* s.9(6).
[166] See Stromberg and Stone, "A Model State Law on Civil Commitment of the Mentally Ill" (1983) 20 *Harvard Journal on Legislation* 315.

for his medical needs. Detention of person who is ill in a Garda Station should be avoided wherever possible.

3.   Where it is necessary to detain a person in custody the maximum possible period of Garda detention permissible should be stipulated in legislation. It should be no longer than is absolutely necessary for an examination to be made of the person's medical condition and for provision to be made for his treatment and care.[167]

4.   The section assumes that a member of the Garda Síochána possesses the required training to form an opinion on the basis of information received that a person is in need of involuntary admission and on that basis to make application himself/herself for a recommendation for reception. It is submitted that the Garda's powers should be confined to the matter of public order and that they should extend no further than arranging forthwith for a medical examination of the person who is detained. Any further arrangements for treatment or care should be made by an appropriately trained social worker.

5.   The Garda powers of entry are framed in similar terms to police powers of entry when a person has committed an offence. However significantly they may be used in respect of a person who is ill and has not done so. It is submitted that a Garda should be accompanied by an authorised officer and a registered medical practitioner where it is proposed to use the powers of entry under the terms of the Act.

6.   Only Garda with special training to deal with people with mental illness be called upon to perform duties under the Act which are para-medical in nature and not related to issues of public safety. In his 1998 Report the Inspector of Mental Hospitals proposed that the training of Gardaí should encompass a mental health module and in each divisional area certain officers should be designated police mental health specialists for the purpose of joint community based mental health activities in co-operation with the statutory services.[168]

Application by any other person

Position under Mental Treatment Act 1945 Under the Mental Treatment Act 1945 (which is still in force) an application is made by someone who is not related to the person concerned and (in the case where a temporary eligible patient reception order or an eligible patient reception order is sought is not the appropriate Community Welfare Officer) the application must contain a statement of (i) the reasons as to why it was not made by this person; (ii) the connection between the applicant and the person to whom the application relates and (iii) the circumstances in which the application is made.[169]

Position under Mental Health Act 2001 Where the application is made by a person

---

[167] In its proposals for reform of the Mental Health Act 1959 Mind proposed a period of 24 hours. See *The Mental Health Act 1959 – Is it fair?* (MIND, London, March 1978) 13.

[168] See Report of the Inspector of Mental Hospitals for the year ending December 31, 1998 Pn 7706 p.2.

[169] See ss 184(3) and 185(3) of the Mental Treatment Act 1945 (Temporary Orders) and ss 162(3) and 177(4) of the Mental Treatment Act 1945 ("PUM" Reception Orders).

other than a spouse or a relative of the person, an authorised officer or a member of the Garda Síochána, section 9(5) of the 2001 Act (not yet in force) requires that the application must contain a statement of the reasons why it is so made, of the connection of the applicant with the person to whom the application relates and of the circumstances in which the application is made.[170]

As mentioned above it is envisaged that in the absence of a comprehensive definition of "spouse" which would include a same sex partner a same sex partner of a person may make an application for a recommendation under this provision. An application must be made in a form specified by the Mental Health Commission.[171]

A person must not make an application under this provision unless he or she has observed the person the subject of the application not more than 48 hours before the date of making the application.[172]

A person who, for the purposes of or in relation to an application makes any statement which is to his or her knowledge false or misleading in any material particular shall be guilty of an offence.[173]

Persons disqualified from making applications

Person under Mental Treatment Act 1945 The Mental Treatment Act 1956 does not specify many disqualified categories of applicants. One category of person impliedly mentioned as disqualified is a person under the age of 21 years.[174]

Position under Mental Health Act 2001 Certain persons are disqualified from making an application in respect of a person under the Mental Health Act 2001, these are (a) a person under the age of 18 years,[175] (b) an authorised officer or a member of the Garda Síochána who is a relative of the person or of the spouse of the person (c) a member of the governing body,[176] or the staff, or the person in charge of the approved centre concerned; (d) any person with an interest in the payments (if any) to be made in respect of the taking care of the person concerned in the approved centre concerned, (e) any registered medical practitioner who provides a regular medical service at the approved centre concerned (f) the spouse, parent, grandparent, brother, sister, uncle or aunt of any of the persons mentioned in (b) to (e) whether of the whole blood or of the half blood or by affinity.[177]

---

[170] Mental Health Act 2001, s.9(5).

[171] *Ibid.*, s.9(3).

[172] *Ibid.*, s.9(4).

[173] *Ibid.*, s.9(6).

[174] See ss.162(4), 177(5) (P.U.M. Orders) and s.184(3A) of the Mental Treatment Act 1945 as added by ss 16 and 185(3A) of the Mental Treatment Act 1961 as added by s.19(1) of the Mental Treatment Act 1961.

[175] The age of the applicant is lowered under the 2001 Act. Under the Mental Treatment Act 1945 the applicant had to be 21 years of age. See Mental Treatment Act 1945, ss.162(4), 177(5), 184(3A) as inserted by Mental Treatment Act 1961, s.16(1), s.185(3A) as inserted by Mental Treatment Act 1961, s.17(1).

[176] This does not include a reference to a member of the Board of the Health Service Executive. See Mental Health Act 2001, s.9(7) as amended by Health Act 2004 Schedule 7 Part 12.

[177] Mental Health Act 2001, s.9(2).

Procedures for making medical recommendations

Position under Mental Treatment Act 1945

Certificate for temporary eligible[178] patient orders Where it is sought to have a person received and detained in a public hospital, pursuant to a temporary patient reception order, under the Mental Treatment Act 1945, the relevant applicant must apply to an appropriate[179] registered medical practitioner[180] for a certificate in the prescribed form,[181] stating that the person concerned is suffering from mental illness; requires for his recovery not more than six months suitable treatment and is unfit on account of his mental state for treatment as a voluntary patient or in the alternative stating that the person is an addict[182] and requires for his recovery at least six months preventive and curative treatment.[183]

When an application is made to a registered medical practitioner, he must certify that he has examined the person to whom the application relates on a specified date not earlier than seven days before the date of the application, and then state his opinion as to whether the grounds for making a temporary order are made out.[184]

Section 184(4) of the 1945 Act required that a registered medical practitioner certify that he had examined the person whom the application relates on a specified date not earlier than seven days before the date of the application for a reception order. In the case of *Bailey v. Gallagher*,[185] the plaintiff was forcibly removed to a Garda Station on the ninth day after the plaintiff was examined under the Act. The plaintiff sought leave to take proceedings under section 260 of the 1945 Act and was refused by the High Court. The Supreme Court allowing the appeal held that the detention of the plaintiff at the Garda station based, as it was, on the spent or expired certificate of the defendant was without legal justification and was due in part to a want of reasonable care on the part of the defendant general practitioner since it was at least arguable the defendant was bound to ascertain whether the certificate upon which the detention was based was still in force. Keane J. remarked:

> "it may be fairly contended that a doctor should be aware, if only in the most general terms of the strict requirements that must be met before citizens can be deprived of their liberty under the 1945 Act".[186]

---

[178] s.81(c) of the Health Act 1970 substitutes the phrase "eligible patient" for "eligible patient" in each case where that occurs. Under s.81(b) of the 1970 Act "eligible patient" means "a patient who is a person with full eligibility or a person with limited eligibility within the meaning of ss 45 and 46 of the Health Act 1970". "Eligibility" relates to entitlement to health services from the State.

[179] The registered medical practitioner must not be disqualified under the provisions of s.184(7).

[180] Mental Treatment Act 1945, s.184(4) as amended by s.16(2) of the Mental Treatment Act 1961.

[181] Mental Treatment Regulations, 1961, sch., Form No. 6.

[182] "Addict" is defined as " a person who (a) by reason of his addiction to drugs or intoxicants is either dangerous to himself or others or incapable of managing himself or his affairs or of ordinary proper conduct or (b) by reason of his addiction to drugs, intoxicants or perverted conduct is in serious danger of mental disorder". See Mental Treatment Act 1945, s.3

[183] Mental Treatment Act 1945, s.184(4).

[184] *Ibid.*

[185] [1996] 2 I.L.R.M. 433.

[186] *Ibid.* at 448.

A registered medical practitioner may be disqualified from issuing a certificate in relation to the person concerned:

(a) if he is interested in the payments (if any) to be made on account of the taking care of the person,

(b) if such practitioner is related to the person concerned as a member of the person's family or marriage[187] or the guardian or trustee of the person,

(c) if the practitioner is a medical officer of a district mental hospital.

It appears however that an authorised medical officer of the Health Service Executive has power to examine a person and issue a certificate where he is opinion that the appropriate grounds are made out.[188]

Where a certificate has been given by the registered medical practitioner concerned the applicant or any person authorised by him have power take the person who is the subject of the certificate and convey him or her to the institution in which it is desired to have him received and detained not later than seven days after the date of the examination.[189]

However, where the applicant proposes to exercise this power s/he must, before exercising it, inform the person to whom the application relates of the nature of the medical certificate and of the fact that that person may request a second medical examination.[189a] Where such a request has been made, the power may not be exercised unless the second examination has been made and the registered medical practitioner has signified in writing that he agrees with the medical certificate.[190] This second medical practitioner may not signify his agreement with the certificate concerned if he is a member of the family of the person concerned[191] or the guardian or trustee of the person.[192]

Certificates for temporary private patient orders Where it is proposed to admit a person to a private institution under a temporary private patient reception order the procedure is in large part similar. However in this case application must be made[193] on

---

[187] Mental Treatment Act 1945, s.184(7)(b) of the Act lists the relationships which will disqualify a registered medical practitioner as follows: "if such practitioner is the husband or wife, father, step-father or father-in-law, mother, step-mother or mother in law, son, step-son or son-in-law, daughter, step-daughter or daughter in law, brother, step-brother or brother in law, sister, step-sister or sister in law … of the person".

[188] Mental Treatment Act 1961, s.184(6) as added by s.16(3) of the Mental Treatment Act 1961.

[189] Mental Treatment Act 1953, s.5(1)(a). The date of the examination is the date as specified in the relevant medical certificate. s.5(2)(a).

[189a] In *O. v. St John of God Hospital* November 15, 2004, Finnegan P. held that this requirement and the objectives of the Act may be satisfied by obtaining a second medical opinion without informing the patient of his/her rights. See Preface.

[190] *Ibid.*, s.5(3).

[191] The medical practitioner is disqualified if he is "the husband or wife, father, step-father or father in law, mother, step-mother or mother in law, son, step-son or son in law, daughter, step-daughter or daughter in law, brother, step-brother or brother in law, sister, step-sister or sister in law of the person. *Ibid.*, s.5(2)(b).

[192] *Ibid.*, s.5(2)(b).

[193] The applicants who may apply are similar to those who may apply in the case of a person in respect of whom a temporary eligible patient order is sought with the exception that there is no provision

the prescribed form[194] to two registered medical practitioners for a certificate stating each of them has examined the person to whom the application relates separately not earlier than seven days before the date of the application.[195]

In the case of a private patient also a registered medical practitioner may not give a certificate if s/he is:

(a) the person in charge of the approved institution in which the person in respect of whom the certificate is given is to be received,

(b) a person in the employment of the person in charge of such institution, or

(c) a person having an interest in the institution.[196]

Applications to admit a person to hospital as a person of unsound mind pursuant to an eligible patient reception order following application by a spouse, relative Community Welfare Officer or other person Where it is proposed to admit a person to hospital as a person of unsound mind pursuant to an eligible patient reception order, application must be made to one registered medical practitioner. If the registered medical practitioner has visited and examined the person to whom the application relates within 24 hours before receipt of the application he may proceed to make the recommendation.[197] In any other case he may within 24 hours after receipt of the application visit and examine the person to whom the application relates and if he is the authorised medical officer he must do so.[198] In either case, the practitioner concerned must make the recommendation if he is satisfied that it is proper to do so and where he is of the opinion that the person to whom the application relates will, if received be an eligible patient.[199]

The registered medical practitioner must not be disqualified from acting in relation to the applicant, under the provisions of the Mental Treatment Act.[200] A registered medical practitioner will be disqualified if:

(a) s/he is interested in the payments if any to be made on account of the taking care of the person,

(b) if the practitioner is the husband or wife, father, step-father or father in law, mother, step-mother or mother in law, son, step-son or son-in-law, daughter, step-daughter or daughter in law, brother, step-brother or brother in law, sister, step-sister or sister in law or guardian or trustee of the person, or

(c) s/he is the medical officer of a district mental hospital.[201]

The recommendation must be made in the prescribed form.[202] It must state the date of

---

for an Community Welfare Officer to make application. Mental Treatment Act 1945, s.185(2), (3A) as inserted by Mental Treatment Act 1961, s.17(1).
[194] Mental Treatment Regulations 1961, Schedule Form No. 7.
[195] *Ibid.*, s.185(4).
[196] *Ibid.*, s.185(5).
[197] *Ibid.*, s.163(1)(a) as amended by Mental Treatment Act 1961, s.7(1).
[198] *Ibid.*, s.163(1)(b) as amended by Mental Treatment Act 1961, s.7(1).
[199] *Ibid.*, s.163(1).
[200] *Ibid.*, s.162(1).
[201] *Ibid.*, s.162(6) as inserted by the Mental Treatment Act 1961, s.6.
[202] *Ibid.*, s.163(1).

the examination of the person to whom the application relates by the registered medical practitioner. It must be signed on the date of receipt of the application, where the application was received after the date on which the examination was carried out or in any other case on the date of the examination. It must contain a certificate that the person who is the subject of the recommendation is of unsound mind, is a proper person to be taken charge of under care and treatment and is unlikely to recover within six months from the date of the examination. It must also contain a statement of facts upon which the registered medical practitioner has formed his opinion that such person is a person of unsound mind, distinguishing between facts observed by himself and facts communicated by others.[203]

Where a registered medical practitioner refuses an application for reception and the applicant makes a further application in relation to the same person he must disclose the fact relating to the previous application and its refusal to the registered medical practitioner to whom he makes the second application.[204] Failure to do so is an offence punishable on summary conviction by a fine.[205]

Recommendations to admit a person to hospital as a person of unsound mind pursuant to an eligible patient reception order following application by a member of the Garda Síochána Where the person is removed to a Garda Station, the member of the Garda Síochána must apply forthwith in the prescribed form[206] to an appropriate registered medical practitioner for a recommendation for the reception of the person as a person of unsound mind, in a district mental hospital serving the area in which the person ordinarily resides. Where an application is made the registered medical practitioner may, or if he is the authorised medical officer, must, examine the person to whom the application relates immediately and either, if he is satisfied that it is proper to do so, make the recommendation in the prescribed form or in any other case refuse it.[207] A registered medical practitioner may not make an order under these provisions where s/he:

(a) is interested in the payments to be made on account of the taking care of the person,

(b) is the husband or wife, father, step-father or father in law, mother, step-mother or mother in law, son, step-son or son-in-law, daughter, step-daughter or daughter in law, brother, step-brother or brother in law, sister, step-sister or sister in law or guardian or trustee of the person concerned, or

(c) if the practitioner is a medical officer of a district mental hospital.[208]

Where the recommendation is made under these provisions, the appropriate assistance order is regarded as the applicant for reception.[209]

---

[203] *Ibid.*, s.163(2) as amended by the Mental Treatment Act 1961, s.7(2).
[204] *Ibid.*, s.164(1).
[205] *Ibid.*, s.164(2).
[206] Mental Treatment Regulations 1961, Schedule Form No. 4.
[207] Mental Treatment Act 1945, s.165(3).
[208] *Ibid.*, s.165(5) as inserted by Mental Treatment Act 1961 s.9(4).
[209] *Ibid.*, s.165(4).

Recommendations to admit a person to hospital as a person of unsound mind pursuant to an eligible patient reception order following an application by a Community Welfare Officer   Where the person in question has no fixed residence and the Community Welfare Officer reports the matter to the member of the Garda Síochána in charge of the Garda Station for the sub-district in which the person is for the time being that member of the Garda Síochána may take the person into custody and remove him to the Garda Station in question for the purpose of his examination by an appropriate registered medical practitioner.[210]

A registered medical practitioner will be disqualified from making a recommendation for reception in relation to a person where the practitioner concerned is:

(a)   interested in the payments (if any) to be made on account of the taking care of the person,

(b)   a spouse, father, step-father or father-in-law, mother, step-mother or mother-in-law, son, step-son or son-in-law, daughter, step-daughter or daughter in law, brother, step-brother or brother in law, sister, step-sister or sister in law or guardian or trustee of the person, or

(c)   if such person is a medical officer of a district mental hospital.[211]

Where an Community Welfare Officer makes an application for a recommendation under these provisions the registered medical practitioner concerned must visit the person immediately and examine him/her and having done so either make the recommendation in the prescribed form if he is satisfied that it is proper to do so or in any other case refuse the application.[212]

It is an offence to obstruct or impede the medical practitioner in visiting and examining the person concerned under these powers.[213] It is also an offence to obstruct, or impede the appropriate Community Welfare Officer in the removal of the person to a district mental hospital, pursuant to a recommendation made by the registered medical practitioner under these powers.[214] Both offences are punishable on summary conviction by a fine.[215]

Order by medical practitioner to admit a person to hospital as a person of unsound mind pursuant to a private patient reception order   Where application is made to admit a person to a psychiatric hospital, as a person of unsound mind pursuant to a private patient reception order, the application must by accompanied by a statement of particulars relative to the person to whom the application relates in the prescribed form,[216] and be made to registered medical practitioner. If the practitioner accepts the application, s/he must arrange with another registered medical practitioner for two separate examinations of the person concerned one by himself/herself, and the other by the second registered medical practitioner. When the examinations have been carried out, the

---

[210] *Ibid.*, s.166(2).
[211] *Ibid.*, s.166(5) added by the Mental Treatment Act 1961, s.10(5).
[212] *Ibid.*, s.166(3).
[213] *Ibid.*
[214] *Ibid.*
[215] *Ibid.*
[216] *Ibid.*, s.177(6).

practitioners may make the order in the prescribed form, if they are satisfied that it is proper to make it or in any other case refuse to make it.[217] The proper grounds for making an order are that the person to whom the application relates is of unsound mind, is a proper person to be taken charge of and detained under care and treatment and is unlikely to recover within six months from the date of the order.[218]

The registered medical practitioners making the order must not be related to each other by being a member of the other's immediate family or family in law,[219] nor must one be a guardian, trustee, partner or assistant of the other. Furthermore, the order must not be made by or on the application of:

(i)   a member of the governing body of or the person carrying on or in charge of the institution,[220]

(ii) any person interested in the payments (if any) to be made on account of the taking care or the person proposed to be received,

(iii) any registered medical practitioner who is a regular medical attendant at the institution or any member of the immediate family or family-in-law of,[221] or the guardian, trustee, partner or assistant of the foregoing persons.[222]

Further, the order may not be signed by the applicant, any member of the immediate family or of the family in law[223] of the applicant or of the person concerned or by his/her guardian or trustee, partner or assistant.[224] The order itself must:

(i)   state the date or dates of the medical examination of the person to whom it relates,

(ii) certify that the person to whom the application relates is of unsound mind, is a proper person to be taken charge of and detained under care and treatment and is unlikely to recover within six months from the date of the order, and

(iii) state the facts upon which the registered medical practitioners signing the order have formed the opinion that the person to whom the order relates is of unsound mind, distinguishing facts observed personally and facts communicated by others.[225]

---

[217] *Ibid.*, s.178(1).

[218] *Ibid.*, s.178(2)(d).

[219] Specifically they must not be related to each other as "husband or wife, father, step-father, or father in law, mother, step-mother or mother in law, son, step-son or son in law, daughter, step-daughter or daughter in law, brother, step-brother or brother in law, sister, step-sister or sister in law." Mental Treatment Act 1945, s.178(2)(aa) added by Mental Treatment Act 1961, s.15.

[220] Members of the Health Service Executive are excepted. Mental Treatment Act 1945, s.178(2) as amended by Health Act 2004

[221] The prohibited family relationships are listed as "the husband or wife, father, step-father or father in law, mother, step-mother or mother in law, son, step-son or son in law, daughter, step-daughter or daughter in law, brother, step-brother or brother in law, sister, step-sister or sister in law." Mental Treatment Act 1945, s.179(1)(d).

[222] *Ibid.*, s.179(1).

[223] The Act lists the family member of the applicant and subject of the order who may not sign the order as follows: "husband or wife, father, step-father or father in law, mother, step-mother or mother in law, son, step-son or son in law, daughter, step-daughter or daughter in law, brother, step-brother or brother in law, sister, step-sister or sister in law".

[224] Mental Treatment Act 1945, s.178(2).

[225] *Ibid.*, s.178(2).

An order may not be made after the seventh day of the date of the application.[226] Where an application for an order is refused, and a further application is made in relation to the same person, the applicant must state the facts of the previous application and its refusal, so far as s/he is aware of them, to the registered medical practitioner to whom the subsequent application is made. Failure to do so is an offence punishable on summary conviction by a fine.[227]

Position under the Mental Health Act 2001

Following the recommendations of the White Paper the Mental Health Act provides an application for involuntary admission be accompanied by one medical recommendation. This, according to the White Paper, is because of the practical difficulties of securing two medical recommendations.[228]

Where an application is made to a registered medical practitioner an examination of the person the subject of the application must be carried out within 24 hours of the receipt of the application.[229] An examination for the purposes of making a recommendation is defined as "a personal examination... of the process and content of thought, the mood and behaviour of the person concerned."[230] The registered medical practitioner concerned must inform the person of the purpose of the examination unless in his or her view the provision of such information might be prejudicial to the person's mental health, well-being or emotional condition.[231]

The definition of examination is a significant factor in the 2001 Act. The nature of the examination was not specified in the 1945 Act and was the subject of judicial consideration in *O'Reilly v. Moroney and the Mid Western Health Board*[232] where the Supreme Court by a 2:1 majority ruled that the statements of the appellant's father that she had threatened to commit suicide and the observation of a registered general practitioner of the appellant's behaviour from a position of about 12 to 15 yards away from her house was sufficient to constitute an examination for the purposes of making a recommendation under the 1945 Act. Blayney J. in a strong dissenting judgment ruled that the medical practitioner should have examined the appellant physically or put a question to her for the purpose of ascertaining direct evidence as to her mental or emotional well-being. In addition he was of the view that the principle of *audi alteram partem* demanded that the appellant should have been given the opportunity to defend herself by putting her side of the case before being removed from her home. The case was subsequently the subject of a friendly settlement by Ireland before the European Court of Human Rights in *O'R v. Ireland*.[233]

In the light of these wide construction of the term "examination" in the 1945 Act the more precise definition in the 2001 Act is, from the perspective of protecting the rights of the patient, to be welcomed.

---

[226] *Ibid.*, s.178(2)(e).
[227] *Ibid.*, s.180.
[228] See para.3.16.
[229] Mental Health Act 2001, s.10(2) which is not yet in force.
[230] Mental Health Act 2001, s.2.
[231] *Ibid.*, s.10(2).
[232] Unreported, Supreme Court, November 16, 1993.
[233] Application NO 24196/94.

Under the 2001 Act a registered medical practitioner is disqualified from making a recommendation if relation to a person the subject of an application (a) if he or she has an interest in the payments (if any) to be made in respect of the care of the person in the approved centre concerned, (b) if he or she is a member of the staff of the approved centre to which the person is to be admitted, (c) if he or she is a spouse[234] or relative[235] of the person or (d) if he or she is the applicant.[236]

Where a registered medical practitioner is satisfied following an examina-tion of the person the subject of the application that the person is suffering from a mental disorder (as defined in the Act)[237] he or she must make a recommendation in a form specified by the Commission that the person be involuntarily admitted to an approved centre (other than the Central Mental Hospital) specified by him or her in the recommendation.[238]

Section 4(2) of the Act (which came into force on April 5, 2002) provides that where it is proposed to make a recommendation in respect of a person the person shall so far as is reasonably practicable be notified of the proposal and be entitled to make representations in relation to it and before deciding the matter due consideration shall be given to any representations duly made under section 4(2).

Section 4(1) of the Act (which also came into force on April 5, 2002) imposes an obligation inter alia on medical practitioners in making a decision concerning the care or treatment of a person to regard the best interests of the person as the principal consideration with due regard being given to the interests of other persons who may be at risk of serious harm if the decision is not made.

Section 4(3) (in force with effect from April 5, 2002) also imposes an obligation on registered medical practitioners by providing that in make a decision concerning the care or treatment of a person due regard must be given to the need to respect the right of the person to dignity, bodily integrity, privacy and autonomy.

When made, the recommendation must be sent by the registered medical practitioner concerned to the clinical director of the approved centre concerned and a copy of the recommendation given to the applicant concerned.[239] A recommendation remains in force for a period of seven days from the date of its making and then expires.[240]

Section 11(1) of the 2001 Act (which is not yet in force) provides that where an application for a recommendation is refused and following such refusal any further application is made in respect of the same person the applicant so far as he or she is aware of the facts relating to the previous application and its refusal must state those facts to the registered medical practitioner to whom the further application is made. A person who contravenes section 11(1) is guilty of an offence.[241]

---

[234] "Spouse" is defined by s.2 of the 2001 Act as "a husband or wife or a man or a woman who is cohabiting with a person of the opposite six for a continuous period of not less than three years but is not married to that person".

[235] "Relative" is defined by s.2 of the 2001 Act as "a parent, grandparent, brother, sister, uncle, aunt, niece, nephew or child of the person or of the spouse of the person whether of the whole blood, of the half blood or by affinity".

[236] Mental Health Act 2001, s.10(3).

[237] See Criteria for Involuntary Admission.

[238] Mental Health Act 2001, s.10(1).

[239] *Ibid.*, s.10(4).

[240] *Ibid.*, s.10(5).

[241] *Ibid.*, s.11(2).

The provisions of the Act relating to medical recommendations, i.e. sections 10 and 11 are stated to apply to application by a member of the Garda Síochána as they apply to an application made by any other application under section 9 with any necessary modifications.[242] If an application under section 12 is refused by the registered medical practitioner the person the subject of the application must be released from custody immediately.[243]

Section 12(5) provides that where following an application under this section a recommendation is made in relation to a person a member of the Garda Síochána shall remove the person to the approved centre specified in the recommendation.

Commentary from an international perspective

1.   The requirement for an independent second medical opinion before a person may be involuntarily admitted as a private patient to a private psychiatric hospital provided for in the Mental Treatment Act 1945 has always been viewed as a safeguard against abuse of powers.[244] It is submitted that it should be retained and extended to apply to both public and private patients.

2.   Under Mental Health Act 2001 there is no requirement that the general medical practitioner called upon to certify a person should have special experience of psychiatry and the White Paper on Mental Health concludes that general practitioners certifying patients under the Mental Treatment Acts need have no formal training. In 1984 a Department of Health Study Group reported that many general practitioners felt that their training in psychiatry did not equip them adequately for dealing with their patients psychological problems and that there was a need for ongoing training.[245] The White Paper however contradicts this finding with a statement that "in this country general practitioners are well equipped by their medical training to deal with a broad spectrum of mental illness and disability including symptoms and behaviour which suggest the need for compulsory admission for psychiatric treatment".[246]

The proposition that certifying doctors need have no formal training in psychiatry is in direct contravention of the ruling of the European Court of Human Rights in the *Winterwerp* case which requires that in cases where detention is in issue the existence of the mental disorder requiring admission must be determined on the basis of objective medical expertise. Since the *Winterwerp* decision is following the coming into force of the European Convention on Human Rights Act 2003[247] a persuasive authority in the Irish courts it is desirable that legislation require that decisions to admit a person involuntarily to a psychiatric hospital only be made by

---

[242] *Ibid.*, s.12(3).

[243] *Ibid.*, s.12(4).

[244] See Niall O'Shea, "Some thoughts on the Law relating to the Admission Procedures to Psychiatric Hospitals in the Republic of Ireland today", *Dlí* (Winter 1993) 77 at 79.

[245] See *Planning for the Future*, Report of a Study Group on the Development of Pschiatric Services (Dublin Stationery Office, December 1984, PL. 3001), paras 5.15 and 5.16.

[246] Para.3.18.

[247] The Act came into force on December 31, 2003. See European Convention on Human Rights Act (Commencement) Order 2003 (S.I. No. 483 of 2003).

practitioners who are specifically approved as having special experience in the diagnosis and treatment of mental disorder.

2. Under section 10 of the Act it appears that the registered medical practitioner issuing the recommendation need not have had any previous acquaintance with the person who is the subject of the application. A requirement that the medical practitioner issuing the recommendation be known to the person who is the subject of the application is a desirable one since such a medical practitioner is likely to be familiar with the applicant's medical history and may afford the person concerned a better opportunity to state his/her case than a person who is unknown to the person concerned as a medical practitioner.

3. Section 10 (2) obliges the registered medical practitioner to "inform the person of the purpose of the examination unless in his or her view the provision of such information might be prejudicial to the person's mental health, well-being or emotional condition." In order to afford the patient concerned an opportunity to state his or her case fully it is submitted that the registered medical practitioner should be required to inform the person of the purpose of the examination as a matter of course unless in his or her view the provision of such information might be *seriously* prejudicial to the person's mental health, well-being or emotional condition.

4. The 2001 Act contains no requirement that the medical recommendation should state the facts upon which the general practitioner has formed his/her opinion, distinguishing facts perceived by him/herself from facts communicated by others. This is a particularly necessary safeguard when the objectivity of applicants is in question. The 1945 Act requires that such a distinction to be made in respect of persons of unsound mind.[248]

Removal of persons to hospital

Procedures under the Mental Treatment Act 1945

Conveyance of temporary patients (eligible and private) to hospital Where it is proposed to make application for a temporary eligible patient reception order, and a certificate has been obtained from the relevant registered medical practitioner, the applicant or any person authorised by him have power take the person who is the subject of the application, and convey him or her to the institution in which it is desired to have him received and detained not later than seven days after the date of the examination.[249]

However, where the applicant proposes to exercise this power s/he must, before exercising it, inform the person to whom the application relates of the nature of the medical certificate and of the fact that that person may request a second medical examination.[250] Where such a request has been made, the power may not be exercised

---

[248] Mental Treatment Act 1945, s.163(2)(c) (persons of unsound mind eligible) and s.178(2)(d) (persons of unsound mind, private).

[249] Mental Treatment Act 1953, s.5(1)(a). The date of the examination is the date as specified in the relevant medical certificate, s.5(2)(a).

[250] *Ibid.*, s.5.

unless the second examination has been made and the registered medical practitioner has signified in writing that he agrees with the medical certificate.[251]

Where it is proposed to apply for a temporary private patient order, then when the applicant has obtained certificates from the relevant registered medical practitioners the applicant for the order or any person authorised by him may, not later than seven days of the earlier of the two examinations take the person to whom the application relates and convey him to the appropriate institution.[252] Where a temporary eligible patient reception order, or a temporary private patient reception order is made at the hospital, the applicant for the order or any person authorised by him may, not later than seven days after the date on which the order is made, take the person to whom the order relates to the approved institution mentioned in the order.[253]

Where a temporary eligible patient reception order is made, the appropriate Community Welfare Officer is obliged to defray the reasonable expenses of conveying the person to whom the order relates to the approved institution mentioned in the order.[254] In the alternative the Health Service Executive maintaining a district mental hospital mentioned in the order may co-operate with the applicant for the order or with any relative or guardian of the person to whom the order relates in making arrangements for the removal of the person concerned to the hospital.[255]

Conveyance of persons of unsound mind (eligible patients) to hospital When a recommendation for the reception of a person as a person of unsound mind in a district mental hospital the applicant, any person authorised by him/her may take and convey the person to the district mental hospital stated in the recommendation. Where a person has been removed to a Garda Station, because a member of the Garda Síochána was of the opinion that it was necessary to place him/her under care and control for the public safety, or the safety of the person himself a member of the Garda Síochána may take and convey the person to the district mental hospital.[256] If the person is not conveyed to the district mental hospital, concerned within seven clear days after the date of the recommendation, the recommendation ceases to have effect.[257] Where, however, the registered medical practitioner making the recommendation certifies that the person will not be fit to be moved until after the expiration of the seven clear days the recommendation remains valid for another seven days but expires at the end of that period if the person has not been conveyed by then.[258]

The Health Service Executive maintaining the district mental hospital mentioned in the recommendation, may co-operate with the applicant for the recommendation or with any relative or guardian of the person to whom the recommendation relates in making arrangements for the removal of the person concerned to the hospital.[259]

---

[251] *Ibid.*, s.5(3).

[252] Mental Treatment Act 1953, s.5(1), (2).

[253] Mental Treatment Act 1945, s.186(1)(a). See also Mental Treatment Act 1953, s.5(1)(b)(ii) which prevents overlapping of powers of conveyance.

[254] Mental Treatment Act 1945, s. 187(1).

[255] *Ibid.*, s.188.

[256] *Ibid.*, s.167(1).

[257] *Ibid.*, s.167(2).

[258] *Ibid.*, s.167(3).

[259] *Ibid.*, s.168.

Where the registered medical practitioner making the recommendation, certifies that the case is one in which an escort is required to ensure the safe conveyance of the person who is the subject of the recommendation, the person to whom the certificate is issued may present it to the member of the Garda Síochána in charge of the Garda station who is obliged to request the resident medical superintendent of the district mental hospital mentioned in the recommendation to arrange for an escort or arrange for whatever escort as in his opinion is necessary himself/herself. If a request is made to the resident medical superintendent s/he has discretion arrange for whatever escort is in his/her opinion necessary. Where the resident medical superintendent indicates that he does not intend to arrange an escort the member of the Garda Síochána must arrange whatever escort as in his opinion is necessary himself/herself.[260] The appropriate Community Welfare Officer is obliged to defray the reasonable expenses of the conveyance of the person to whom the recommendation relates to the district mental hospital, except where a person is conveyed there by a member of the Garda Síochána.[261]

Conveyance of persons of unsound mind (private patients) to hospital Where a private patient reception order is made, the applicant for the order or any person authorised by him may take the person to whom the order relates and convey him/her to the mental institution stated in the order.[262] Where the person concerned is not conveyed to the mental institution in question within seven clear days after the day on which the order is made, it ceases to have effect.[263] However, where a registered medical practitioner[264] certifies that the person to whom the order relates will not be fit to be moved until after the expiration of the seven clear days the order continues in force for a further seven days, but if the person is not conveyed to the institution within the second period it ceases to have effect on its expiry.[265]

Where the registered medical practitioners making the order certify that an escort is required to ensure the safe conveyance of the person to whom the order relates to the institution concerned the person to whom the certificate is issued may present it to the member of the Garda Síochána in charge of any Garda station and upon doing so that member of the Garda Síochána must arrange for whatever escort is necessary.[266]

Commentary

Under the 1945 Act only the applicant for a temporary patient reception order or a person authorised by that applicant has power to take and convey the person to whom the application referred to the hospital once the relevant medical certificate had been

---

[260] *Ibid.*, s.169 as amended by Mental Treatment Act 1961, s.12.

[261] *Ibid.*, s.170.

[262] *Ibid.*, s.181(1)(a).

[263] *Ibid.*, s.181(3).

[264] This may be the registered medical practitioner to whom application for the order was made or in his absence or incapacity any other registered medical practitioner. Mental Treatment Act 1945, s.181(4).

[265] Mental Treatment Act 1945, s.181(4).

[266] *Ibid.*, s.183(2). It appears that the applicant for the escort must meet any expenses incurred by the Garda Síochána in providing one. Mental Treatment Act 1945, s.183(2).

given by the recommending medical practitioner.[267] If the applicant was unable to make arrangements for the transfer or if the person to whom the application refused to go to hospital then there is no specific obligation on the hospital staff or the Gardaí to assist in the removal of the person to hospital. As a result the Inspector of Mental Hospitals reported in 1999 that "an intolerable situation has existed over the last couple of years where neither nurses nor Gardaí will escort patients on temporary reception orders to hospital who are not prepared to come with their relatives. One consequence of this was that in practice the person of unsound mind (PUM) form was used to secure a Garda escort which was discarded on the patient's reaching hospital with the temporary patient form then being used to establish the patient's status."[268]

Procedures under the Mental Health Act 2001

The 2001 Act addresses the anomaly arising from the procedures for conveying a patient to hospital under the 1945 Act. Section 13(1) of (which is not yet in force) provides that where a recommendation is made in relation to a person (other than a recommendation made following an application by a member of the Garda Síochána pursuant to section 12 of the Act) the applicant concerned must arrange for the removal of the person to the approved centre specified in the recommendation.[269]

Where the applicant is unable to arrange for the removal of the person concerned the clinical director of the approved centre specified in the recommendation or a consultant psychiatrist acting on his or her behalf shall, at the request of the registered medical practitioner who made recommendation arrange for the removal of the person to the approved centre by members of staff of the approved centre.[270]

If the clinical director of the approved centre or a consultant psychiatrist acting on his or her behalf and the registered medical practitioner who made the recommendation are of the opinion that there is a serious likelihood of the person concerned causing immediate and serious harm to himself or herself or to other persons the clinical director or a consultant psychiatrist acting on his or her behalf may, if necessary, request the Garda Síochána to assist[271] the members of staff of the approved centre in the removal by the staff of the person to that centre and the Garda Síochána must comply with any such request.[272]

Where any such request is made to the Garda Síochána a member or members of the Garda Síochána may (a) enter if need be by force any dwelling or other premises where

---

[267] Mental Treatment Act 1953, s.5(1)(a). This had to be done not later than seven days after the date of the examination.

[268] See *Report of Inspector of Mental Hospitals for the year ending 31 December 1999*, Pn.8606, p.11. See Keys, "Challenging the Lawfulness of Psychiatric Detention" (2002) 24 *Dublin University Law Journal* 39, n.55.

[269] Mental Health Act 2001, s.13(1).

[270] *Ibid.*, s.13(2).

[271] The meaning of the word "assist" is not clear. It could encompass direct involvement by the Garda Síochána in removing the person or driving behind an ambulance or staff car containing the person.

[272] Mental Health Act 2001, s.13(3). It is interesting to note that the Government White Paper on Mental Health proposed that where a person was resisting admission following attempts at persuasion, the clinical director could seek an order from the District Court permitting the person to be transferred against his/her will. See "A New Mental Health Act" (Department of Health, July 1995, Pn.1824). Clearly the proposal to involve the courts was not favoured in the Act.

he or she has reasonable cause to believe that the person concerned may be and (b) take all reasonable measures necessary for the removal of the person concerned to the approved centre including where necessary the detention or restraint of the person concerned.[273]

Time Limits

Position under Mental Treatment Act 1945

Under the 1945 Act the requirement is for the *examination* to be carried out within 24 hours of receipt of the *application* in the case of persons of unsound mind (who were eligible patients)[274] and not earlier than seven days before the date of the application in the case of temporary patients.[275]

Under the 1945 Act there is no time limit between the *examination* and *recommendation/private patient reception order* in the case of persons of unsound mind. Further under the 1945 Act the parties have another seven days following the making of a *medical recommendation/private patient reception order* within which to convey a person of unsound mind to hospital.[276] In the case of temporary patients while was no time limit specified to govern the span between *examination* and the *medical recommendation* the situation is a little stricter than in the cases of persons of unsound mind given that the 1945 Act specifies that there should be a time limit of seven days between the *examination* and *conveying* the patient to hospital.[277] Further where a temporary patient reception order (whether eligible or private) is made by a medical officer of the hospital on the basis of the application and a medical certificate, the applicant or any person authorised by him/her has seven days from the date on which *the order* was made to *convey* the patient to the institution named in the order.[278]

Position under Mental Health Act 2001

Section 10(2) of the Mental Health Act 2001 (which is not yet in force) requires a registered medical practitioner to *examine* the person in respect of whom application is made within twenty-four hours of receipt of the *application*. No time limit is laid down in the 2001 Act to determine the time which must elapse between the *medical examination* and the *medical recommendation*. The White Paper "A New Mental Health Act"[279] proposed a time limit of 48 hours between the medical examination and subsequent medical recommendation[280] and while no time limit between examination and recommendation is contained in the 2001 Act it is safe to assume that best practice would dictate that the medical recommendation should be made as soon as possible after examination to avoid the liabilities which may arise where a practitioner signs a recom-

---

[273] Mental Health Act 2001, s.13(4).
[274] Mental Treatment Act 1945, s.163(1)(a) as amended by s.7(1) of the Mental Treatment Act 1961.
[275] See Mental Treatment Act 1945, s.184(4) (eligible patients) and s.185(4) (private patients).
[276] *Ibid.*, s.167(2) (persons of unsound mind, eligible) and s.181(3) (persons of unsound mind, private).
[277] Mental Treatment Act 1953, s.5(1)(a) (temporary patients eligible and private).
[278] Mental Treatment Act 1945, s.186(1)(a).
[279] Department of Health, July 1995, Pn.1824.
[280] Para.3.19.

mendation some time after examination recommending the involuntary admission of a person whose illness has since subsided. There is no time frame provided under the 2001 Act between the *examination* and *removal* to hospital.

Arrival at hospital and admission order

The nature of the receiving centre

The Mental Health Act 2001 when fully brought into force will remove the distinction in the Mental Treatment Act 1945 between public and private hospitals and introduce the concept of the "approved centre." A "centre" is defined by section 62 as "a hospital or other in-patient facility for the care and treatment of persons suffering from mental illness or mental disorder" and an "approved centre" is one which is registered on the Register of Approved Centres maintained by the Mental Health Commission (in effect one which is approved as having met certain standards regarding management and accommodation set out in regulations under the 2001 Act).[281]

Examination after arrival

Position under Mental Treatment Act 1945 There is no requirement under the Mental Treatment Act 1945 that a temporary patient be examined on admission to hospital merely that the admitting doctor consider the application and the certificate.[282] In addition there was no requirement that a person referred by a reception order made by a general practitioner for involuntary admission as a person of unsound mind (private) be examined on arrival at hospital. Persons recommended for admission as eligible persons of unsound mind, by contrast, must be examined on their arrival at the hospital.[283]

Position under Mental Health Act 2001 Section 14(1) of the Mental Health Act 2001 (not yet implemented) removes the anomalies under the 1945 Act regarding examination after arrival at hospital and provides for a uniform requirement of examination in all cases. It states that where a recommendation in relation to a person is received by the clinical director of an approved centre a consultant psychiatrist on the staff of the approved centre shall, *as soon as may be*, carry out an examination of the person and if s/he is satisfied that the person is suffering from a mental disorder as defined in the Act s/he must thereupon make an admission order for the reception, detention and treatment of the person and, if s/he is not so satisfied, refuse to make an order.

Detention pending making of order for admission

Position under Mental Treatment Act 1945 The Mental Treatment Act 1945 as amended[284] provides that a person who is the subject of an application for a temporary patient reception order may be detained for up to 12 hours while a decision was being

---

[281] Mental Health Act 2001, s.63.
[282] See Mental Treatment Act 1945, s.184(5) (temporary eligible patient) and s.185(6) (temporary private patient).
[283] Mental Treatment Act 1945, s.171 (Persons of unsound mind, eligible).
[284] Mental Treatment Act 1953, s.5(1)(b)(i).

taken by the medical officer as to whether or not to make a reception order. It is not stipulated whether the holding power is for examination purposes only or whether treatment could be carried out. (Presumably common law principles justify the administration of treatment pending a decision on detention although it is difficult to see how a decision to refuse detention could be made if treatment were necessitated during this period.) The persons entitled to detain the person under the 1945 Act are the person in charge of the approved institution in which it is desired to have such person received and detained and his officers, assistants and servants and any medical officer of the institution.[285] It was proposed in the White Paper to repeat this 12-hour provision in the proposed Act as it gave "medical and nursing staff a reasonable period in which to make an assessment of the need for detention."[286]

Position under Mental Health Act 2001 Section 14(2) (which is not yet in force) states that a consultant psychiatrist, a medical practitioner or a registered nurse[287] on the staff of the approved centre is entitled to take charge of the person concerned and detain him or her for a period not exceeding 24 hours (or such shorter period as may be prescribed after consultation with the Commission) for the purpose of carrying out an examination under subsection (1) or if an admission order is made or refused in relation to the person during that period until it is granted or refused.

Provision for a 24-hour holding period departs from the proposals in the White Paper and was criticised during the Dáil Debates as being too long. As a result the words "or such shorter period as may be prescribed after consultation with the Commission" were added by the Minister for Health to emphasise that 24 hours was an upper limit designed with the "current strains on staff numbers in the health services" in mind and in order "to provide hospital staff with some flexibility". It was envisaged that the Commission should keep the situation under review and advise the Minister when a change became appropriate.[288]

Section 14(2) empowers nurses to exercise holding powers for the first time. In the Seanad Deputy Henry proposed an amendment to ensure that nurses exercising such powers were registered psychiatric nurses. Minister Moffatt replied that any such restriction would inhibit the ability of the services to respond to the shortage of psychiatric nursing staff by employing general nurses in psychiatric hospitals. Currently some psychiatric hospitals include both general and psychiatric nurses on their staff. Many psychiatric hospitals also employ nurses specialising in intellectual disability and consequently maximum flexibility had to be ensured.[289]

In addition concern was expressed by Deputy Henry that doctors who did not have experience in psychiatry might be in a position to refuse to discharge patients. Minister Moffatt replied:

---

[285] Mental Treatment Act 1953, s.5(1)(b) (i), (4).
[286] See White Paper, "A New Mental Health Act" (Department of Health, July 1995, Pn.1824), para. 3.27.
[287] "Registered Nurse" is defined by s.2 as meaning "a person whose name is entered in the register of nurses maintained by An Bord Altranais under s.27 of the Nurses Act 1985".
[288] (HC3 No.2 *Dáil Debates* Cols 96–97).
[289] 167 *Seanad Debates* 130–132.

"… [t]he provisions merely enable the doctor concerned to detain the person for a
period of 24 hours until a consultant psychiatrist is available to examine the patient.
It is entirely appropriate that a decision such as this could be made by a qualified
junior doctor. The crucial decision about whether a person should be deprived of
their liberty by way of an involuntary admission order is reserved for the consultant
psychiatrist."[290]

A consultant psychiatrist is disqualified from making an admission order in relation to
a person the subject of an application (a) if he or she is a spouse[291] or a relative[292] of the
person or (b) if he or she is the applicant.[293]

The admission order

Position under Mental Treatment Act 1945

The temporary eligible patient reception order Where an application for a temporary
eligible patient reception order is made, the person in charge of the institution that
person may, after consideration of the application and of the certificate accompanying
the application if he so thinks proper make the order in the prescribed form.[294] Where a
temporary eligible patient reception order is made, the person in charge of the institution
mentioned in the reception order or any medical officer or employee of the institution[295]
may receive and take charge of the person to whom the order relates and detain him for
six months from the date on which the order is made or his earlier removal, discharge or
death. They also have power to retake him/her within twenty eight days if s/he escapes.[296]

The temporary private patient reception order Where the application for a temporary
private patient reception order is to be made it must be presented to "the appropriate
person" at the institution concerned. The "appropriate person" to make such an order is
the person in charge of the institution,[297] where s/he is a registered medical practitioner
or in any other case the chief medical officer of the approved institution or in the case of
an institution for the reception of one person only, the medical attendant of the person
to whom the application relates.[298] The appropriate person may, after considering the
application and the medical certificate accompanying it, make an order if s/he thinks

---

[290] 167 *Seanad Debates* 129–130.
[291] "Spouse" is defined by s.2 as meaning "a husband or wife or a man or a woman who is cohabiting
with a person of the opposite six for a continuous period of not less than three years but is not
married to that person".
[292] "Relative" in relation to a person is defined by s.2 as meaning "a parent, grandparent, brother,
sister, uncle, aunt, niece, nephew or child of the person or of the spouse of the person, whether of
the whole blood or of the half blood or by affinity".
[293] Mental Health Act 2001, s.14(3).
[294] Mental Treatment Act 1945, s.184(5).
[295] *Ibid.*, s.186(2).
[296] *Ibid.*, s.186(1)(b).
[297] See Mental Treatment Act 1953, s.3. A power or duty of the person in charge of a mental institution
other than a district mental hospital may be exercised or performed by any officer of the institution
authorised in that behalf by the person in charge.
[298] Mental Treatment Act 1945, s.185(6)(b) as inserted by the Mental Treatment Act 1961, s.17(2).

fit.[299] The person in charge of the approved institution, any medical officer or employee of the institution may then receive and take charge of the person to whom the order relates and detain him for six months from the date on which the order is made or his earlier removal, discharge or death.[300]

The eligible patient reception order Where a person is removed to a district mental hospital pursuant to a recommendation for reception the resident medical superintendent of the hospital or another medical officer acting on his behalf must examine the person on his arrival and on presentation of the recommendation. Upon examination s/he must, if s/he is satisfied that the person is a person of unsound mind and a proper person to be taken care of and detained under care and treatment immediately make an order in the prescribed form[301] for the reception and detention of the person as a person of unsound mind in the hospital or in any other case refuse to make such an order.[302]

Where such a eligible patient reception order is made, the the Health Service Executive, resident medical superintendent of the hospital and the employees thereof are entitled to receive and take charge of the person concerned and detain him until his removal or discharge by proper authority or his death and in the case of his escape they may retake him within twenty eight day and again detain him/her.[303]

Where the order is refused by the resident medical superintendent or other medical officer of the hospital, s/he must give the applicant for the relevant recommendation for reception a statement in writing of the reasons for refusal, and send a copy of the statement to the Minister for Health, and give the Minister all such additional information as the Minister may require as to the circumstances of refusal. The Minister may communicate such facts, relative to the refusal as he thinks proper to the person in relation to whom the order was sought or to any other bona fide inquirer.[304]

The 1945 Act provides that where a resident medical superintendent of the hospital or another medical officer of the hospital makes an order for the reception and detention of the patient as a person of unsound mind in the hospital that patient may be received, taken charge of and detained "until his removal or discharge by proper authority or his death."[305] There is no automatic review of the patient's detention under the 1945 Act . In *Croke v. Smith*,[306] Budd J. in the High Court held that detention without any automatic independent review fell below the norm required by the constitutional guarantee of personal liberty and consequently the provisions of section 172 of the Mental Treatment Act 1945 were repugnant to the Constitution. In a judgment which is unquestionably contentious when viewed against the provisions of the European Convention on Human

---

[299] Mental Treatment Act 1945, s.185(6)(a) as inserted by the Mental Treatment Act 1961, s. 17(2).
[300] *Ibid.*, s.186.
[301] If the order or recommendation for reception is found to be in any respect incorrect or defective after it is made a power exists in s.174 of the Mental Treatment Act 1945 to amend the relevant document within twenty one days after the reception of the person. The Minister for Health may also require an amendment to be made within twenty one days and if it is not so amended to his satisfaction within that period he may if he thinks fit direct the discharge of the person.
[302] Mental Treatment Act 1945, s.171(1).
[303] *Ibid.*, s.172.
[304] *Ibid.*, s.173.
[305] *Ibid.*, ss 172, 181.
[306] [1998] 1 I.R. 101.

Rights[307] and Government provisions for automatic review procedures in Mental Health Act 2001 the Supreme Court overruling Budd J. upheld the constitutionality of the section stating that:

> "the sections which permit of such detention do not constitute an attack upon the personal rights of the citizen but rather vindicate and protect the rights of the citizen by providing for their care and treatment."[308]

The Supreme Court added:

> "It must be presumed ... that the Oireachtas intended when giving to the resident medical superintendent the power of detention and to him and the Minister the power of discharge that the permitted discretions and adjudications given to them are to be exercised in accordance with the principles of constitutional justice and that any departure therefrom would be restrained and corrected by the courts."[309]

It stated further:

> "... that the detention of a patient does not require automatic review by an independent tribunal because of the obligation placed on a person in charge of a district mental hospital to discharge a patient who has recovered."[310]

It was noted that:

> "Inherent in [the Act] is the obligation placed on the resident medical superintendent to regularly and constantly review a patient in order to ensure that he/she has not recovered and is still a person of unsound mind and is a proper person to be detained under care and treatment. If such a review is not regularly carried out, in accordance with fair procedures and rendering justice to the patient, then the intervention of the court can be sought because of the obligation on the resident medical superintendent to exercise the powers conferred on him by the Act in accordance with the principles of constitutional justice."[311]

On appeal to the European Court of Human Rights in the case of *Croke v. Ireland*,[312]

---

[307] The Supreme Courts decision on s.172 is in direct conflict with the decision of the European Court of Human Rights in *X v. United Kingdom* [1981] 4 E.H.R.R. 181 that a person of unsound mind who has been detained in a psychiatric institution for an indefinite period is by virtue of Art.5(4) entitled to take proceedings at reasonable intervals before a court to test the lawfulness of his detention and that Art.5(4) requires that the review be automatic and of a judicial character and that it also conflicts with the admission expressed in the Government White Paper entitled "A New Mental Health Act" (1995, Pn.1824) that the current safeguards did not satisfy Ireland's obligations under the European Convention (*ibid.*, p.51).

[308] *Ibid.*, p.114.

[309] *Ibid.*, p.123.

[310] *Ibid.*, p.131.

[311] *Ibid.*, p.131.

[312] Application No. 3326/96.

the applicant invoked Articles 5(1) and 5(1)(e) and 5(4) of the Convention arguing that as a person detained as a person of unsound mind he had the right to have available to him reviews which comply with the requirements of Article 5 of the Convention and that domestic law was deficient in that respect. He referred to *De Wilde, Ooms and Versyp*[313] in support of his argument that he was entitled to a review of his initial and ongoing detention in accordance with Article 5(4). Referring to *Winterwerp v. The Netherlands*[314] he argued that he should not have to take the initiative to obtain legal representation before having access to court. He relied further on *Megyeri v. Germany*[315] in support of the contention that the initial and subsequent review under Article 5(4) should be automatic and the onus should not be on the patient to institute the proceedings. The applicant's case was declared admissible and was subsequently the subject of a friendly settlement in which the State "being conscious of its obligations under the Convention in respect of the rights of persons detained under its Mental Health laws … agreed … with the Applicant to acknowledge, by an agreed compensatory sum, the Applicant's legitimate concerns in relation to the absence of independent formal review of detention under the Mental Health Acts."[316]

The private patient reception order As mentioned above, in contrast to the procedure in relation to the making of eligible patient reception orders, there is no requirement in the case of a person who is the subject of a private patient reception order for a further examination of a person who is the subject of a private patient reception order on arrival at the institution concerned.[317] The order (not a recommendation) has in fact has already been made by the two registered medical practitioners, and its effect is that the person concerned may be immediately detained by the hospital staff.[318] The order for detention is expressed to last until the person's removal or discharge by proper authority or his death.[319] Where a person escapes, any member of the hospital staff has the right to retake the person within twenty eight days and again detain him.[320]

Thus, under the Mental Treatment Act 1945, which is still in force, the decision to detain a person in respect of whom an application including a medical recommendation has been made is the responsibility of a medical officer of the hospital.[321] In the White Paper the Government proposed to limit the decision to detain a person in respect of whom an application for voluntary admission had been made to a consultant psychiatrist on the staff of the approved centre.[322]

---

[313] (1971) Series A, No. 12.

[314] [1979] 2 E.H.R.R. 387.

[315] (1992) (63/1991/315/386).

[316] Judgment (Striking Out) Strasbourg, December 21, 2000. See further Keys M., "Challenging the Lawfulness of Psychiatric Detention under Habeas Corpus in Ireland" (2002) 24 *Dublin University Law Journal* 26.

[317] Mental Treatment Act 1945, s.181(1)(b).

[318] The persons expressed to be entitled to receive, take charge of and detain him are the person in charge of the mental institution mentioned in the order and his officers, assistants and servants and any medical officer of the institution. Mental Treatment Act 1945, s.181(2).

[319] *Ibid.*, s.181(1)(b).

[320] *Ibid.*

[321] See Mental Treatment Act 1945, ss 171,184, 185, Mental Treatment Act 1953, s.3.

[322] See White Paper, "A New Mental Health Act" (Department of Health, July 1995, Pn.1824), para.3.25.

Position under Mental Health Act 2001 Section 14(1) of the Mental Health Act 2001 (yet to be implemented) provides that where a recommendation[323] in relation to a person the subject of an application is received by the clinical director[324] of an approved centre, a consultant psychiatrist[325] on the staff of the approved centre[326] must, as soon as may be, carry out an examination[327] of the person concerned and shall thereupon (a) if he or she is satisfied that the person is suffering from a mental disorder make an order to be known as an involuntary admission order in a form specified by the Commission for the reception detention and treatment[328] of the person (b) if he or she is not so satisfied refuse to make an order.

In making a decision to make an admission order in relation to a person section 4(1) of the Act (which came into force on April 5, 2002) provides that the best interests of the person must be the principal consideration with due regard being given to the interests of other persons who may be at risk of serious harm if the decision is not made.

There is also a requirement under section 4(2) (which came into force on April 5, 2002) the Act that where it is proposed to make an admission order in respect of a person the person shall so far as is reasonably practicable be notified of the proposal

---

[323] S.2 of the Act specifies that "recommendation" is to be construed in accordance with s.10 which states that "where a registered medical practitioner is satisfied following an examination of the person the subject of the application is suffering from a mental disorder he or she shall make a recommendation (in this Act referred to as "a recommendation") in a form specified by the Commission that the person be involuntarily admitted to an approved centre (other than the Central Mental Hospital) specified by him in the recommendation."

[324] S.2 of the Act defines a "clinical director" as a person appointed under s.71 of the Act. S.71(1) provides that the governing body of each approved centre shall appoint in writing a consultant psychiatrist to be the clinical director of the centre.

[325] A "consultant psychiatrist" is defined by s.2 of the 2001 Act as meaning "a consultant psychiatrist who is employed by the Health Service Executive or by an approved centre or a person whose name is entered on the division of psychiatry or the division of child and adolescent psychiatry of the Register of Medical Specialists maintained by the Medical Council in Ireland".

[326] For meaning of "approved centre" see *supra*, n.108.

[327] "Examination" in relation to an admission order is defined by s.2 of the Act as meaning "a personal examination ... of the process and content of thought, the mood and the behaviour of the person concerned". The nature of the examination to be carried out under the 1945 Act was the subject of judicial consideration by the Supreme Court in *O'Dowd v. North Western Health Board* [1983] 1 I.L.R.M. 186 when the point in issue was the requirement of examination for a detention order at a hospital. In that case Griffin J. indicated that when "a doctor speaks of seeing a patient this is equivalent to saying that he examined him" (*ibid.*, p.194) and on this reasoning concluded with the majority (O'Higgins C.J. and Griffin J.) that the chief medical superintendent did examine the applicant and carried out the duty imposed on him by s.171 of the 1945 Act before and at the time he made the order for the reception of the plaintiff notwithstanding that at the time the chief superintendent saw him the plaintiff had been detained for three hours in the hospital and sedated. Henchy J. dissenting held that the chief medical superintendent signed the prescribed form (Form 4 of the Mental Treatment Regulations 1961, S.I. No. 61 of 1961) stating that he had examined the plaintiff on the day of his admission "without having personally carried out any psychiatric examination of the applicant that day" (*ibid.*, p.201). In addition he did not carry out an examination of the plaintiff immediately on his arrival at the hospital as required by s.171 and therefore was disqualified from signing the form. He was of the view that this amounted to a want of reasonable care.

[328] "Treatment" in relation to a patient, is defined by s.2 as including "the administration of physical, psychological and other remedies relating to the care and rehabilitation of a patient under medical supervision intended for the purposes of ameliorating a mental disorder".

and be entitled to make representations in relation to it and before deciding the matter due consideration must be given to any representations duly made.

Further in making a decision to make an admission order in relation to a person section 4(3) (which came into force on April 5, 2002) stipulates that due regard must be given to the need to respect the right of the person to dignity, bodily integrity, privacy and autonomy.

Section 15(1) (which is not yet in force) provides that an admission order shall authorise the reception, detention and treatment of the patient concerned and shall remain in force for a period of 21 days from the date of making the order and shall then expire. This is subject to the consultant psychiatrist responsible for the care and treatment of the patient not making a renewal order extending the order for a further period not exceeding three months provided for in section 15(2) or thereafter making further renewal orders extending the period of detention for a period not exceeding 6 months and thereafter for periods not exceeding 12 months.[329] It is also subject to the Mental Health Tribunal (either of its own motion or at the request of the person concerned) not making an order extending the period for the making of decision in relation to the validity of the detention (and a fortiori the validity of the admission order) and continuing the admission order in force for a further period of 14 days or thereafter for a further period of 14 days on the application of the patient if the tribunal is satisfied that it is in the interest of the patient as provided for in section 18(4).

Section 67 of the 2001 Act (which is not yet in force) provides that subject to section 12 (power of Gardaí to take a person believed to be suffering from a mental disorder into custody where there is a serious likelihood of the person causing immediate and serious harm to himself or herself or to other persons) and subject to section 22 (power of clinical director to arrange the transfer of a patient detained in an approved centre for treatment to a hospital or other place and for his or her detention there for treatment) a person suffering from a mental disorder must not be detained in a place other than an approved centre. "Approved centre" is be construed in accordance with section 63[330] which provides in effect that a person shall not carry on a hospital or other in-patient facility for the care and treatment of persons suffering from mental illness or mental disorder (known as a "centre")[331] unless the centre is registered and the person is the registered proprietor thereof. A centre which is so registered is to be known as "an approved centre." The Mental Health Commission is charged with establishing and maintaining a "Register of Approved Centres."[332]

Where there is a contravention of this provision in relation to an approved centre the person carrying on the centre shall be guilty of an offence[333] and liable on summary conviction to a fine not exceeding £1,500 (€1,904.61) or to imprisonment for a term not exceeding 12 months or to both or on conviction on indictment to a fine not exceeding £50,000 (€6,3486.90) or to imprisonment for a term not exceeding two years or to both.[334]

---

[329] Mental Health Act 2001, s.15(3).
[330] *Ibid.*, s.2.
[331] *Ibid.*, s.62.
[332] *Ibid.*, s.64.
[333] *Ibid.*, s.67(2).
[334] *Ibid.*, s.68.

Rectification of recommendations for reception or eligible patient reception orders

Position under Mental Treatment Act 1945

The Mental Treatment Act 1945 contains a provision which permitted rectification of recommendations for reception or eligible patient reception orders. Section 174(1) provides that where a recommendation for reception is found to be in any respect incorrect or defective within 21 days after the reception of the person to whom the recommendation relates into the district hospital mentioned in the recommendation then the resident medical superintendent of the hospital may refer the recommendation to the person by whom it was made for amendment and that person may with the consent of the Minister for Health and Children amend the recommendation within the period of 21 days. Where an amendment is made in accordance with section 174 then section 174(4) provides that the recommendation had effect as if the amendment had been contained in it when it was signed. Section 174(5) provides, in effect, that notwithstanding the fact that the recommendation is found to be incorrect and defective the resident medical superintendent and the officers and staff of the hospital have power to receive, take charge of and detain the patient during the 21 day period and if the patient absconds they have power to retake him/her within 28 days and again detain him/her. A similar provision relating to rectification of private patient reception orders is to be found in section 182 of the 1945 Act.

Position under the Mental Health Act 2001

The power of rectification contained in the Mental Treatment Act 1945 is not replicated in the Mental Health Act 2001 so general practitioners must be extra vigilant in completing the recommendation for reception. However by implication from section 18(1)(a)(ii) there is a possible relief when there has been a clerical error in completion of the recommendation. It states that where there is a failure to comply with, *inter alia*, section 10 (the procedure relating to the making of a recommendation) and the failure "does not affect the substance [of an admission order] and does not cause an injustice" the Mental Health Tribunal may nonetheless affirm the admission order.

Detention of children

Position under Mental Treatment Act 1945

There is no provision for detention of children with mental illness in the Mental Treatment Act 1945 (which is still in force). A person under sixteen years may be admitted as a voluntary patient where the parent or guardian has made an application to the person in charge of the institution accompanied by a recommendation from a registered medical practitioner stating that he has examined the person concerned on a date not earlier than seven days before the date of the application and is of the opinion that the person concerned will benefit by the reception.[335] A child thus admitted to hospital can not

---

[335] See Mental Treatment Act 1945, s.190.

benefit from any of the safeguards against inappropriate admission afforded to detained patients.

Position under Mental Health Act 2001

Section 25 of the Mental Health Act (which is not yet in force) provides for the extension of detention powers to children and the enactment of legislation to make provision for the admission for treatment without parental consent of a child under the age of eighteen years of age with a mental disorder who meets the criteria for detention.

Section 25(1) provides that where it appears to the Health Services Executive (a) that the child is suffering from a mental disorder[336] and (b) that the child requires treatment which he or she is unlikely to receive unless an order is made under Section 25 then the Health Service Executive may make an application to the District Court for an order authorising the detention of the child in an approved centre.

Section 25(2) provides that subject to section 25(3) the Health Service Executive shall not make an application to the District Court under subsection (1) unless the child has been examined by a consultant psychiatrist who is not a relative of the child and a report of the results of the examination is furnished to the court by the Health Service Executive.

Section 25(3) dispenses with the requirement for prior examination of the child by a consultant psychiatrist where (a) the parent(s) of the child or a person *in loco parentis* refuses to consent to the examination of the child or (b) following the making of reasonable enquiries by the Health Service Executive the parent(s) of the child or a person acting *in loco parentis* cannot be found by the Health Service Executive.

By virtue of section 25(4) where the Health Service Executive makes an application under section 25(1) without any prior examination of the child the subject of an application by a consultant psychiatrist the court may, if it is satisfied that there is reasonable cause to believe that the child the subject of the application is suffering from a mental disorder,[337] direct that the Health Service Executive arrange for the examination of the child by a consultant psychiatrist who is not a relative of the child and that a report of the results of the examination be furnished to the court within such time as may be specified by the court.

Section 25(5) provides that where the court gives a direction under section 25(4) the consultant psychiatrist who carries out an examination of the child the subject of the application must report to the court on the results of the examination and must indicate to the court whether he or she is satisfied that the child is suffering from a mental disorder.

By virtue of section 25(6) where the court is satisfied having considered the report of the consultant psychiatrist referred to in section 25(1) or the report of the consultant psychiatrist referred to in section 25(5) as the case may be and any other evidence that may be adduced before it that the child is suffering from a mental disorder the court must make an order that the child be admitted and detained for treatment in a specified

---

[336] "Mental disorder" is defined by s.3 of the Mental Health Act 2001. See above Criteria for Involuntary Admission at pp.27, 101 *et seq.*
[337] *Ibid.*

approved centre for a period not exceeding 21 days. Section 25(7) permits an application under section 25 to be made *ex parte* if the court is satisfied that the urgency of the matter so requires.

Section 25(8) deals with the issue of custody of the child between the application and the order and provides that between the making of an application for an order under section 25 and its determination the court, of its own motion or on the application of any person may give such directions as it sees fit as to the care and custody of the child who is the subject of the application pending such determination and any such direction will cease to have effect on the determination of the application.

Under the terms of section 25(9) where while an order under section 25(6) is in force an application is made to the court by the Health Service Executive for an extension of the period of detention of the child the subject of an application the court may order that the child be detained for a further period not exceeding 3 months. Section 25(10) permits an extension of the period of detention by providing that on or before the expiration of the three month period of detention referred to in section 25(9) a further order of detention for a period not exceeding 6 months may be made by the court on the application of the Health Service Executive and thereafter for periods not exceeding six months.

Section 25(11) provides that a court shall not make an order extending the period of detention of a child under section 25 unless (a) the child has been examined by a consultant psychiatrist who is not a relative of the child and a report of the results of the examination is furnished to the court by the Health Service Executive concerned on the application of the Executive to the court under section 25(9) or 25(10) as the case may be and (b) following consideration by the court of the report it is satisfied that the child is still suffering from a mental disorder.

Section 25(12) provides that psychosurgery shall not be performed on a child detained under section 25 without the approval of the court. In addition, section 25(13) provides that a programme of electro-convulsive therapy shall not be administered to the child without the approval of the court.

Application of Child Care Act 1991 provisions to detention proceedings in relation to a child under the 2001 Act

Section 25(14) provides that the provisions of sections 21, 22, 24 to 35, 37 and 47 of the Child Care Act 1991 shall apply to proceedings under section 25 as they apply to proceedings under those sections with the modification that references to proceedings or an order under Part III, IV or VI of that Act shall be construed as references to proceedings or an order under section 25 and with any other necessary modifications.

The provisions of the Child Care Act 1991 referred to in section 25(14) of the Mental Health Act 2001 are mostly procedural. Thus under section 21 of the 1991 Act the effect of an appeal from an order under section 25 shall, if the court that made the order or the court to which the appeal is brought so determines (but not otherwise) is to stay the operation of the order on such terms (if any) any as may be imposed by the court making the determination. Section 22 of the 1991 Act empowers the court of its own motion or on the application of any person to (a) vary or discharge an order under section 25 of the Mental Health Act 2001 (b) vary or discharge any condition or direction attaching to the order

Welfare of child in paramount consideration Of the provisions of the Child Care Act 1991 section 24 is probably the most significant. As applied by section 25(14) of the Mental Health Act 2001 it provides, in effect that in any proceedings before a court under section 25 of the Mental Health Act the court, having regard to the rights and duties of the parents whether under the Constitution or otherwise shall (a) regard the welfare of the child as the first and paramount consideration and (b) in so far as is practicable, give due consideration, having regard to his age and understanding to the wishes of the child.

A potential conflict could arise under this section where a child of sufficient age and understanding refuses to undergo psychiatric treatment where this is contrary to the welfare of the child. In such circumstances the fundamental principle of securing the welfare of the child would have to override the child's wishes.

Child may be party to procedings Section 25(1) of the 1991 Act as applied by section 25(14) of the Mental Health Act 2001 empowers the court to join a child as a party to the proceedings and makes provision for the costs of the child as a party. In effect, therefore, if in any proceedings under section 25 of the Mental Health Act 2001 the child to whom the proceedings relate is not already a party the court may, where it is satisfied having regard to the age, understanding and wishes of the child and the circumstances of the case that it is necessary in the interests of the child and in the interests of justice to do so, order that the child be joined as a party to, or order that the child shall have such of the rights of a party as may be specified by the court in, either the entirety of the proceedings or such issues in the proceedings as the court may direct. The making of such an order is stated not to require the intervention of a next friend in respect of the child

Where the court makes an order under section 25(1) of the 1991 Act as applied by section 25(14) of the Mental Health Act 2001 to proceedings under the Mental Health Act 2001 or a child is a party to the proceedings otherwise than by reason of such an order the court may, if it thinks fit appoint a solicitor to represent the child in the proceedings and give directions as to the performance of his duties which may include, if necessary, directions in relation to the instruction of counsel.[338] Section 25(4) provides that where a solicitor is appointed under section 25(2) of the 1991 Act the costs and expenses incurred on behalf of a child exercising any rights of a party in any proceedings under the Act must be paid by the Health Service Executive and the Health Service Executive may apply to the court to have the amount of any such costs or expenses measured or taxed. The court which has made an order under section 25(2) may on application to it of the Health Service Executive order any other party to the proceedings in question to pay the Executive any costs or expenses payable by the Executive under section 25(4).[339]

The making of an order under section 25(1) or the fact that the child is a party to the proceedings otherwise than by reason of such an order shall not prejudice the power of the court under section 30(2) of the Child Care Act 1991 to refuse to accede to a request of a child made thereunder.[340] Section 30(2) provides that where the child requests to

---

[338] Child Care Act 1991, s.25(2).
[339] *Ibid.*, s.25(5).
[340] *Ibid.*, s.25(3).

be present during the hearing or a particular part of the hearing of the proceedings the court shall grant the request unless it appears to the court that, having regard to the age of the child or the nature of the proceedings it would not be in the child's interests to accede to the request.

Court's power to appoint guardian *ad litem* Section 26(1) of the 1991 Act empowers the court to appoint a guardian *ad litem* for the child. As applied by section 25(14) of the 2001 Act in the context of proceedings under section 25 of the Mental Health Act 2001 it provides that if the child to whom the proceedings relate is not a party the court may, if it is satisfied that it is necessary in the interest of the child and in the interests of justice to do so, appoint a guardian *ad litem* for the child.

The role of the guardian *ad litem* is an independent one to safeguard the child's interests and ensure the most positive outcome possible for the child. In *M.H. & J.H., Oxfordshire County Council v. J.H. and V.H, re,*[341] Costello J. remarked that it was significant that a person appointed as guardian *ad litem* is independent of parents and local authorities and acts to advise the court on the infants behalf of what is to happen.

Under section 26(2) any costs incurred by a person acting as a guardian ad litem under section 26 shall be paid by the Health Service Executive. The Health Service Executive may apply to the court to have the amount of any such costs or expenses measured or taxed. The court which has made an order under section 26(1) may on application to it of the Health Service Executive order any other party to the proceedings in question to pay to the Executive any costs or expenses payable by the Executive under section 26(2).[342] Where a child in respect of whom an order has been made under section 26(1) becomes a party to the proceedings in question whether by virtue of an order under section 25 of the 1991 Act or otherwise then that order will cease to have effect.[343]

Court's power to obtain reports on child By virtue of section 27(1) of the 1991 Act the court has power to procure reports on children. Thus, as applied by section 25(14) of the 2001 Act, in any proceedings under section 25 of the Mental Health Act 2001 the court may, of its own motion, or on the application of any party to the proceedings by an order give such directions as it thinks proper to procure a report from such person as it may nominate on any question affecting the welfare of the child. In deciding whether or not to request a report under section 27(1) the court must have regard to the wishes of the parties before the court where ascertainable but shall not be bound by such wishes.[344] A copy of the report under section 27(1) must be made available to the counsel or solicitor, if any, representing each party in the proceedings or, if any party is not so represented, to that party and may be received in evidence in the proceedings.[345]

Where any party prepares a report pursuant to a request under section 27(1) the fees and expenses of that person shall be paid by such party or parties to the proceedings as

---

[341] Unreported, High Court, May 19, 1988.
[342] Child Care Act 1991, s.26(3).
[343] *Ibid.*, s.26(4).
[344] *Ibid.*, s.27(2).
[345] *Ibid.*, s.27(3).

the court shall order.[346] The court, if it thinks fit, or any party to the proceedings, may call the person making the report as a witness.[347]

Jurisdiction of District and Circuit Courts Section 28 of the 1991 Act as applied by section 25(14) of the 2001 Act provides that the District Court and the Circuit Court on appeal from the District Court shall have jurisdiction to hear and determine proceedings under section 25 of the Mental Health Act 2001. Proceedings under section 25 of the 2001 Act may be brought, heard and determined before and by a justice of the District Court for the time being assigned to the district court district where the child resides or is for the time being.[348]

Conduct of proceedings By virtue of section 29(1) of the 1991 Act as applied by section 25(14) of the 2001 Act proceedings under section 25 of the Mental Health Act 2001 must be heard otherwise than in public. Proceedings in the Circuit Court are required to be as informal as practicable and consistent with the administration of justice.[349] Judges, barristers and solicitors must not appear in wigs and gowns before the Circuit Court.[350] Proceedings before the District Court must also be conducted in as informal a manner as practicable and consistent with the administration of justice. Judges, barristers and solicitors must not wear wigs and gowns.[351]

Section 29(3) of the 1991 Act as applied by section 25(14) of the 2001 Act provides that the District Court and the Circuit Court on appeal from the District Court shall sit to hear and determine proceedings for an order under section 25 of the Mental Health Act 2001 at a different place or at different times or on different days from those at or on which the ordinary sittings of the court are held. Proceedings before the High Court in relation to proceedings under section 25 of the 2001 Act must be as informal as is practicable and consistent with the administration of justice.[352]

Court's power to proceed in the absence of the child Section 30(1) of the 1991 Act as applied by section 25(14) of the Mental Health Act 2001 gives the court before whom an application under section 25 of the Mental Health Act 2001 is brought power to proceed in the absence of the child. It provides that it shall not be necessary for the child to whom the proceedings relate to be brought before the court or to be present for all or any part of the hearing unless the court either of its own motion or at the request of any of the parties to the case is satisfied that this is necessary for the proper disposal

---

[346] *Ibid.*, s.27(4).

[347] *Ibid.*, s.27(5).

[348] Child Care Act 1991, s.28(2).

[349] Child Care Act 1991, s.29(2) applying s.33(1) of the Judicial Separation and Family Law Reform Act 1989 to proceedings under the 1991 Act. By virtue of s.25(14) of the Mental Health Act 2001 the provisions of s.29 of the 1991 Act apply to proceedings under s.25 of the 2001 Act.

[350] Child Care Act 1991, s.29(2) applying s.33(2) of the Judicial Separation and Family Law Reform Act 1989 to proceedings under the 1991 Act. By virtue of s.25(14) of the Mental Health Act 2001 the provisions of s.29 of the 1991 Act apply to proceedings under s.25 of the 2001 Act.

[351] Child Care Act 1991, s.29(2) applying s.45 of the Judicial Separation and Family Law Reform Act 1989 to proceedings under the 1991 Act. By virtue of s.25(14) of the Mental Health Act 2001 the provisions of s.29 of the 1991 Act apply to proceedings under s.25 of the 2001 Act.

[352] Child Care Act 1991, s.29(4).

of the case. Section 30(2) provides that where the child requests to be present during the hearing or a particular part of the hearing the court shall grant the request unless it appears to the court that, having regard to the age of the child or the nature of the proceedings it would not be in the child's interests to accede to the request.

It is submitted that the presence of a child will be necessary where the child is directed to undergo psychiatric examination or treatment and the child objects to this.

Prohibition on publication or broadcast of proceedings Section 31(1) of the 1991 Act as applied by section 25(14) of the Mental Health Act 2001 embodies a prohibition on publication or broadcast of certain matters. Section 31(1) provides that no matter likely to lead members of the public to identify a child who is or has been the subject of proceedings under section 25 of the Mental Health Act 2001 shall be published in a written publication available to the public or be broadcast.

"Written publication" is defined to include "a film, a sound track and any other record in permanent form (including a record that is not in a legible form but which is capable of being reproduced in a legible form) but does not include an indictment or other document prepared for use in particular legal proceedings."[353] "Broadcast" is defined as meaning "the transmission, relaying or distribution by wireless telegraphy of communications, sounds, signs, visual images or signals, intended for direct reception by the general public whether such communications, sounds, signs, visual images or signals are actually received or not."[354]

Without prejudice to this prohibition in section 31(1) the court may, in any case if satisfied that it is appropriate to do so in the interest of the child, by order dispense with the prohibitions contained in section 31(1) in relation to him to such extent as may be specified in the order.

If any matter is published or broadcast in contravention of section 31(1) certain specified persons shall be guilty of an offence and be liable on summary conviction to a fine not exceeding £1,000 (€1,269.74) or to imprisonment for a term not exceeding 12 months or both. The persons specified are (a) in the case of publication in a newspaper or periodical any proprietor, any editor and any publisher of the newspaper or periodical; (b) in the case of any other publication the person who publishes it and (c) in the case of a broadcast, any body corporate who transmits or provides the programme in which the broadcast is made and any person having functions in relation to the programme corresponding to those of an editor of a newspaper.[355] Nothing in section 31 is to affect the law as to contempt of court.[356]

Ascertainment of age of child Section 32 as applied by section 25(14) of the 2001 Act provides that in any application for an order under section 25 of the Mental Health Act 2001 the court shall make due inquiry as to the age of the person to whom the application relates and the age presumed or declared by the court to be the age of that person shall, until the contrary is proved for the purposes of the 2001 Act, be deemed to be the true age of that person.

---

[353] Child Care Act 1991, s.29(5).
[354] *Ibid.*
[355] *Ibid.*, s.31(3).
[356] *Ibid.*, s.31(4).

Service of documents Section 33 as applied by section 25(14) of the 2001 Act provides that for the purpose of ensuring the expeditious hearing of applications under section 25 of the Mental Health Act 2001 rules of court may make provision for the service of documents otherwise than under section 7 of the Courts Act 1964 as amended by section 22 of the Courts Act 1971 in circumstances to which section 7 relates. Rules of court may also make provision for the furnishing of information and documents by parties to proceedings under section 25 of the 2001 Act to each other or to solicitors acting for them. Section 33 is expressed to be without prejudice to section 17 of the Interpretation Act 1937. Section 17 of the 1937 Act enables the making of rules of court in relation to the conferring of a new jurisdiction upon the courts or the extension or variation of an existing jurisdiction.

Implications of failure or refusal to deliver up a child Section 34 of the 1991 Act addresses the issue of failure or refusal to deliver up a child. As applied by section 25(14) of the 2001 Act it states that without prejudice to the law as to contempt of court, where the court has made an order under section 25 of the Mental Health Act 2001 directing that a child be placed or maintained in the care of the Health Service Executive then any person having the actual custody of the child, who having been given or shown a copy of the order and having been required by or on behalf of the Health Service Executive to give up the child to the Executive, fails or refuses to comply with the requirement, shall be guilty of an offence and be liable on summary conviction to a fine not exceeding £500 (€634.87) or at the discretion of the court to imprisonment for a term not exceeding six months or both such fine and imprisonment. For the purposes of section 34 a person shall be deemed to have been given or shown a copy of an order made under section 25 of the 2001 Act if that person was present at the sitting of the court at which such order was made.

Section 35 empowers a justice to issue a warrant to search for and deliver up a child. As applied by section 25(14) of the 2001 Act it states that where a justice has made an order directing that a child be placed or maintained in the care of the Health Service Executive a justice may for the purpose of executing that order issue a warrant authorising a member of the Garda Síochána accompanied by such other members of the Garda Síochána or such other persons as may be necessary to enter (if need be by force) any house or other place specified in the warrant (including any building or part of a building, tent, caravan, or other temporary or moveable structure, vehicle, vessel, aircraft or hovercraft) where the child is or where there are reasonable grounds for believing that he is and to deliver the child into the custody of the Health Service Executive.

Health Service Executive obliged to facilitate reasonable access to child Section 37(1) of the 1991 Act as applied by section 25(14) of the Mental Health Act 2001 provides that where a child is in the care of Health Service Executive by virtue of an order under section 25 of the Mental Health Act 2001 the Executive must, subject to the provisions of the Act, facilitate reasonable access to the child by his parents, any person acting *in loco parentis* or any other person who, in the opinion of the Executive has a bona fide interest in the child and such access may include allowing the child to reside temporarily with any such person.

Any person who is dissatisfied with arrangements made by the Health Service Executive under section 37(1) may apply to the court and the court may (a) make such order as it thinks proper regarding access to the child by that person and (b) vary or discharge that order on the application of any person.[357] The court may also on the application of the Health Service Executive and if it considers that it is necessary to do so in order to safeguard or promote the child's welfare may (a) make an order authorising the Executive to refuse to allow a named person access to a child in its care and (b) vary or discharge that order on the application of any person.[358]

Section 37 is expressed to be[359] without prejudice to section 4(2), which concerns children placed voluntarily in care by parents or a person acting *in loco parentis*. Section 4(2) provides that without prejudice to the provisions of Parts III, IV and VI of the 1991 Act[360] nothing in section 4 (voluntary care) shall authorise the Health Service Executive to take a child into its care against the wishes of a parent having custody of him or of any person acting *in loco parentis* or to maintain him in its care under section 4 if that parent or any such person wishes to resume care of him. Thus, the effect of section 37(4) is that where children are placed voluntarily in care by parents or a person acting *in loco parentis* such persons may not have their rights to access interfered with and should the Health Service Executive wish to curtail access the appropriate procedures of obtaining the necessary orders must be complied with.

District Court's powers to give directions, make orders etc. Section 47 of the 1991 Act provides that where a child is in the care of the Health Service Executive, the District Court may of its own motion or on the application of any person, give such directions and make such order on any question affecting the welfare of the child as it thinks proper and may vary or discharge any such direction or order.

Finally, section 25(15) of the Mental Health Act 2001 provides that references in sections 13(7),[361] 18(3)[362] and 19(4)[363] of the Child Care Act 1991 to psychiatric examination, treatment or assessment do not include references to treatment under the 2001 Act.

---

[357] Child Care Act 1991, s.37(2).

[358] *Ibid.*, s.37(3).

[359] *Ibid.*, s.37(4).

[360] Pt III deals with protection of children in emergencies. Pt IV addresses the issues surrounding care proceedings and Pt VI deals with issues surrounding children in the care of the Health Service Executive.

[361] S.13(7) of the 1991 Act provides that where a justice makes an emergency care order, he may, of his own motion or on the application of any person give such directions (if any) as he thinks proper with respect to the medical or psychiatric examination, treatment or assessment of the child.

[362] S.18(3) of the 1991 Act provides that where a care order is in force the Health Service Executive shall have the authority to give consent to any necessary medical or psychiatric examination, treatment or assessment with respect to the child.

[363] S.19(4) of the 1991 Act provides that where a court makes a supervision order in respect of a child it may on the application of the Health Service Executive, either at the time of the making of the order or at any time during the currency of the order give such directions as it sees fit as to the care of the child which may require the parents of the child or a person acting *in loco parentis* to cause him to attend for medical or psychiatric examination, treatment or assessment at a hospital, clinic or other place specified by the court.

Commentary

1. The provisions of Section 25 do not reflect the proposals in the White Paper in a number of respects. Significant among these is the fact that the White Paper proposes that an emergency treatment order be made *ex parte* for a period not exceeding eight days where there are reasonable grounds for believing that urgent treatment is necessary.[364] The Act provides for *ex parte* applications to be made in cases of urgency but in effect permits an order made pursuant to an *ex parte* application to last for 21 days. It is submitted that where an application for an order is made *ex parte* the period of detention should not exceed eight days and an any further period of detention should be authorised at an *inter partes* hearing.

2. Section 25 outlines the circumstances in which the Health Service Executive may make an application to the District Court for an order authorising the detention of a child in an approved centre. However it neither identifies the officer in the Health Service Executive who would be entitled to make such an application nor specifies what his qualifications might be. This is a significant omission from the Act. In addition the White Paper provided that the officer or person of the health board making an application would not be employed by the mental health services.[365] It must be presumed that this was intended as a safeguard against bias in making applications but it is not reflected in the Act. It is submitted that the identity and qualifications of the officer of the Health Service Executive entitled to make an application and the safeguard against bias proposed by the White Paper should be embodied in amending legislation.

3. Section 2 of the Act defines a child as a person under the age of 18 years other than a person who is or has been married. Section 23 of the Non-Fatal Offences Against the Person Act 1997 provides in effect that minors who have attained the age of sixteen years are as competent to refuse medical treatment as if they were of full age. The provisions of Section 25 therefore are inconsistent with section 23 of the 1997 Act. It raises the question as to what status the refusal of a 16–18 year old to consent to treatment for mental disorder will have. It would appear from the terms of sections 2 and 25 that the refusal of the child and the parents to consent to examination could be overridden.

4. Before authorising detention it is submitted that statute should require that the court should be satisfied that there is no less restrictive alternative method of treatment available at the time. In this regard it is pertinent to note that Article 37 of the Convention on the Rights of the Child provides that detention of a child shall be used only as a measure of last resort and for the shortest appropriate period of time.

5. It is further submitted that the court should not direct involuntary admission unless it is satisfied that the child is incompetent to make a decision about the need for hospitalisation; that the hospital to which the child is to be admitted provides treatment appropriate to the child's condition and an individualised treatment plan

---

[364] See White Paper, "A New Mental Health Act" (Department of Health, July 1995, Pn.1824), pp.40–41.
[365] *Ibid.*, p.40.

has been written and presented to the court by the hospital to which the child is to be admitted.[366]

6. It is submitted that in common with adults who are involuntarily admitted to approved centres children who are involuntarily admitted to approved centres should have the right to change to voluntary status.

7. In a recent report entitled *"Mental Illness – The Neglected Quarter"*,[367] Amnesty International examined mental health services for children and made the following observations:

> "The provision of child mental health services is inadequate and those available are severely under-resourced in staff, funding and available therapies; adult psychiatric services and facilities are used inappropriately to treat children; and children with behavioural problems and mental health needs are detained in prisons and places of detention without having those needs addressed, contrary to international human rights law. Service planning is hampered by a lack of systems for the collection of data and research on the needs of and provision for children. Geographical inequities exist in the distribution of services; and while the funding is generally disproportionately low, in less affluent regions, services are more under-resourced."

It is submitted the legislative framework for detention of children must be complemented by proper mental health care facilities for the detention, care and treatment of children.[368]

---

[366] See Division of Child, Youth and Family Services of the American Psychological Association Committee on the Civil Commitment of Minors – A Model Act for the Mental Health Treatment of Minors in Melton Gary B., Lyons Phillip M Jr. and Spaulding Willis J., *No Place to Go – The Civil Commitment of Minors* (University of Nebraska Press, 1998) Appendix A.

[367] Amnesty International (2003).

[368] See Ubaldus de Vries, "The New Mental Health Act – Failing to be Progressive" (2000) *Medico Legal Journal of Ireland* 19 at 26.

CHAPTER THREE

Treatment of Patients while in Hospital – Informational Aspects

INTRODUCTION

A modern mental health law, which recognises the human rights of people with mental disability, should endorse due process values. These are values, which guarantee the individual fairness in criteria and procedures when it is proposed to deprive the individual of other important rights and interests. Three reasons dictate this imperative. First due process promotes accuracy and reasonable predictability in official decision-making when people's rights are subject to deprivation. Secondly due process recognises the individual's interest in participating in decision making processes which affect him or her and thirdly due process endorses the person's interest in being treated as an equal, participating and responsible member of society and affords recognition to the dignity and worth of the individual.[1]

Rights such as a patient's right to information, right of access to medical records, right to communicate without undue censorship, right to confidentiality and privacy, and right of access to a lawyer, are all rights which should be accorded fully to the patient if due process is to be observed in relation to a patient's treatment.

PATIENT'S RIGHT TO INFORMATION

Ensuring a patient has a right to information about his legal and medical position is key if s/he is to be enabled to exercise his/her rights in relation to treatment. The existence of this right is also essential if effect is to be given to the patient's basic right to due process and to self-determination or autonomy. It is also in the patient's interest that these rights be recognised as more positive therapeutic outcomes result from positive recognition of the value of patient involvement in therapy.

---

[1] See Cooney & O'Neill, *Kritik 1 Psychiatric Detention Civil Commitment in Ireland* (Baikonur, 1996).

ACCESS TO LEGAL INFORMATION

Current law

Position under Mental Treatment Act 1945

Under the Mental Treatment Act 1945 (still in force) the right of the patient to legal information about his/her situation in hospital was quite limited. Where a person who was detained as a temporary patient in an approved institution considers himself /herself to be unjustly detained s/he may make a request in writing to the Minister for Health and Children who has a discretionary power to direct the person in charge of the institution to give him/her, free of charge, a copy of the order and of the medical certificate consequent upon which he is detained.[2]

This right is confined to patients currently detained under a temporary certificate in an approved institution and the right to information is not absolute but conditional upon the discretionary power of the Minister to grant it.

Where a person discharged from a mental institution considers that the detention was unlawful s/he may apply for a copy of the reception order authorising the detention provided s/he does so by letter addressed to the person in charge of the mental institution not later than six months after discharge. On receipt of such an application, a copy must be forwarded to the person concerned.[3]

The patient appears to have no right to be informed automatically of his/her legal position during the period of detention under the Act.[4]

Position under Mental Health Act 2001

Section 16 of the Mental Health Act 2001 (not yet implemented) provides that where a consultant psychiatrist[5] makes an admission order[6] or a renewal order[7] he or she shall

---

[2] Mental Treatment Act 1945, s.228.

[3] *Ibid.*, s.271.

[4] By contrast third parties appear to have extensive rights. Under s.204(A) of the 1945 Act as inserted by s.24 of the Mental Treatment Act 1961 any person may apply to the chief executive officer of the Health Service Executive for information as to whether a particular person is detained as a patient of the authority under a reception order and if he is so detained as to the name of the person in charge of the institution named in the reception order and the situation of that institution. The applicant may also apply for (a) a copy of the relevant reception order, (b) the name of the applicant for any relevant recommendation for reception or reception order, (c) the name or names of any registered medical practitioner or practitioners who made any recommendation or signed any certificate in relation to such person. Where such an application is made the Health Service Executive is obliged to grant it unless they decide that the applicant has failed to satisfy them that s/he is a proper person to be given the information for which s/he applies or the relevant documentation. Where the request is refused the applicant has a right of appeal to the Minister for Health.

Under s.200 of the 1945 Act any person may apply to the Minister for Health for information as to whether particulars regarding any particular person have been entered in the register of persons detained in an institution and if the Minister considers the application to be reasonable the Minister is obliged to cause an examination to be made of the register. If satisfied that the applicant is a proper person to receive the information the Minister is obliged to give him/her the name of the person in charge of the institution, its situation and if the Minister thinks fit a copy of the reception order and of any document which accompanied the reception order.

[5] "Consultant Psychiatrist" is defined by s.2 of the 2001 Act to mean "a consultant psychiatrist who

not later than 24 hours thereafter give notice in writing of the making of the order to the patient. A notice must include a statement in writing to the effect that the patient (a) is being detained pursuant to section 14 (admission orders) or 15 (renewal orders) as the case may be (b) is entitled to legal representation[8] (c) will be given a general description of the proposed treatment[9] to be administered to his or her during the period of his or her detention (d) is entitled to communicate with the Inspector[10] (e) will have his or her detention reviewed by a tribunal in accordance with the provisions of section 18; (f) is entitled to appeal to the Circuit Court against a decision of a tribunal under section 18 if he or she is the subject of a renewal order and (g) may be admitted to the approved centre concerned as a voluntary patient[11] if he or she indicates a wish to be so admitted.

By virtue of section 24(4) the provisions of Section 16 also apply when a person is detained after a holding power is exercised.

The Government White Paper which preceded the Act provided that during the course of care and treatment information was to be provided in relation to consent to treatment, about renewal of detention and the powers of the Mental Health Review Board to review decisions to extend detention. There was also to be a requirement that when an authorised nurse exercised the power to hold a voluntary patient for up to six hours, within which time the person must be examined by a doctor, the patient would have to be informed of the nature of the power, the purpose of the medical examination and the possibility that he or she may be detained.[12] These requirements are not reflected in the Act.

---

is employed by the Health Service Executive or by an approved centre or a person whose name is entered on the division of psychiatry or the division of child and adolescent psychiatry if the Register of Medical Specialists maintained by the Medical Council in Ireland".

[6] References to an admission order are stated by s.16(3) to include references to the relevant recommendation and the relevant application. A registered medical practitioner is obliged to make a "recommendation' where s/he is satisfied following an examination of the person the subject of the application that the person is suffering from a mental disorder. S.10 of the Mental Health Act 2001. "Application" is defined by s.2 to mean an application for a recommendation that a person be involuntarily admitted to an approved centre. See s.2 of the Mental Health Act 2001.

[7] This refers to orders made on the expiration of an admission order which remains in force for a period of 21 days. A renewal order may then be made by the consultant psychiatrist responsible for the care and treatment of the patient concerned for a further period not exceeding three months. It may be further extended by order made by the consultant psychiatrist concerned for a period not exceeding six months on the expiration of the three month period. Thereafter it may be further extended by order made by the psychiatrist for periods each of which does not exceed 12 months. See ss.2 and 15 of the Mental Health Act 2001.

[8] "Legal Representative" is defined by s.2 as meaning a barrister or a solicitor.

[9] "Treatment" in relation to a patient is defined by s.2 as including the administration of physical, psychological and other remedies relating to the care and rehabilitation of a patient under medical supervision, intended for the purposes of ameliorating a mental disorder.

[10] i.e. the Inspector of Mental Health Services, see ss.2 and 50.

[11] "Voluntary Patient" is defined by s.2 of the 2001 Act as a person receiving care and treatment in an approved centre who is not the subject of an admission order or a renewal order.

[12] See para.9.6.

Commentary

It is doubtful whether the Mental Health Act goes far enough to secure a persons right of access to information.

International principles relating to the patient's right to information

First *Recommendation 1235 (1994) of the Parliamentary Assembly of the Council of Europe on psychiatry and human rights* not considered in the White Paper which preceded the Act recommends that a code of rights be brought to the attention of patients on their arrival at a psychiatric institution.[13] Secondly, Principle 12 of the *UN Principles for the Protection of Persons with Mental Illness and the Improvement of Healthcare*[14] while providing more vaguely that a patient in a mental health facility "shall be informed as soon as possible after admission" of all his or her rights in accordance with [the] Principles and under domestic law, places emphasis upon the patient's understanding of the information given by stipulating that it be provided, "in a form and language which the patient understands and by requiring that the information regarding rights "include an explanation of those rights and how to exercise them."[15] It also provides that if the patient is unable to understand the information the rights of the patient must be communicated to the personal representative[16] if any and if appropriate and to the person or persons best able to represent the patient's interests and willing to do so.

The *Body of Principles for the Protection of All Persons under any form of Detention or Imprisonment* adopted by the General Assembly of the United Nations on 9 December 1988 contains a number of provisions relevant to the situation of patients involuntarily admitted to psychiatric hospitals. Among these is the right of a detained person and his counsel, if any, to receive prompt and full communication of any order of detention, together with the reasons therefore.[17]

Comparative law

An examination of the authorities of other common law jurisdictions also reveals that legislatures and courts have gone some considerable way towards specific definition of the requirement of notice.

The patient's right to information in England and Wales In England and Wales the Mental Health Act 1983 and Code of Practice contain comprehensive provisions regarding the right to notice. Section 132(1) of the Mental Health Act 1983 provides

---

[13] See recommendation i.d.

[14] Adopted by the General Assembly on December 17, 1991.

[15] Principle 12.1.

[16] Principle 12.3 provides that a patient who has the necessary capacity has the right to nominate a person who should be informed on his or her behalf as well as a person to represent his or her interests to the authorities of the facility. "Personal representative" is defined by the Principles as "a person charged by law with the duty of representing a patient's interests in any specified respect or of exercising specified rights on the patient's behalf and includes the parent or legal guardian of a minor unless otherwise provided by domestic law."

[17] Principle 11.2.

that whenever any patient is detained under the Act the managers of the hospital or mental nursing home in which the patient is detained must take "such steps as are practicable" to ensure that the patient understands his legal position.

The steps must be taken "as soon as practicable" after the detention has begun and again if the section under which the patient is detained changes. The information, which the patient must be given, must enable him to understand under which section he is detained, the effect of that section and the rights of applying to a mental health review tribunal which are available to him under it.[18] The managers of the hospital or mental nursing home must also explain who has the power to discharge him, including the possible bar on a discharge by his nearest relative and the relative's right to challenge this before a tribunal; the hospital's powers to censor his correspondence; the Act's provisions relating to the treatment of detained patients and the extra safeguards where certain treatments are proposed; the protective powers of the Mental Health Act Commission and the effect of the Code of Practice.[19] The required information must be given both orally and in writing.[20]

Unless the patient requests otherwise the managers of the hospital or mental nursing home must also "take such steps as are practicable" to supply his nearest relative (if any) with a copy of this information, either at the same time as it is given to the patient or within a reasonable time afterwards.[21]

The patient's right to information in Canada   In Canada British Columbia Regulations made pursuant to the Mental Health Act provide that[22] every involuntary patient has a right to be informed "immediately on admission or transfer or as soon as the person is capable of comprehension" of the reasons for his detention, his right to retain and instruct counsel without delay, his right to have the validity of the detention determined by way of *habeas corpus* and his right to apply to the Review Panel and to the court for review.

In other provinces the information, which must be given to the patient, is less extensive. Thus some provinces require that the patient be informed of the reason for the detention[23] and of his right to apply for review.[24]

In Saskatchewan, Nova Scotia and Yukon the Act requires in addition that the patient be informed of his right to counsel.[25] Only three provinces require that the patient's

---

[18] Mental Health Act 1983, s.132(1).

[19] *Ibid.*, s.132(2).

[20] *Ibid.*, s.132(3).

[21] *Ibid.*, s.132(4).

[22] B.C. Reg. 145/84, s.7(2).

[23] R.S.A. 1980, c.M-13, s.24: S.S.1984-85-86, c.M-13.1, s.16(1); R.S.O. 1980, c.262, s.30(A) [en. R.S.O. 1980, c.262, s.66; proclaimed in force March 1, 1984)]; R.R.O 1980, Reg. 609, Form 30 [en. Reg. 734/86].

[24] R.S.A. 1980, c.M-13, s.24: S.S.1984-85-86, C-M-13.1 ss.33(1); R.S.O 1980, c.262, s.30a (2) [en. R.S.O. 1980, c. 262, s.66; proclaimed in force March 1 1984; am. 1986, c. 64, s.33(29)]; R.S.N.S.1967, c.249, s.62(8) [en. 1977, c.45, s.8]; R.S.Y.T. 1971, c.M-7, s.6.4 [en. 1984, c.21, s.5].

[25] Sask. Reg. C. M-13.1, Reg. 1, s.10; R.S.N.S.1967, c.249, s.62(8) [en. 1977, c.45, s.8], R.S.Y.T. 1971, c.M-7, s.6.4 [en. 1984, c. 21, s.5]. The right is also to be found in Manitoba's Bill 59 (first reading June 5, 1987) and in Ontario's Bill 190 (third reading June 15, 1987).

next of kin or nearest relative be informed of the existence of a right of review.[26]

Significantly and in contrast to the absence of any similar provision in the Irish Constitution, section 10 of the Canadian Charter of Rights and Freedoms provides:

"Everyone has the right on arrest or *detention*:

> (a) to be informed promptly[27] of the reasons therefor, and
> (b) to retain and instruct counsel without delay and to be informed of that right."[28]

The effect of two decisions of the Canadian Courts is that that a written sign on the wall of a mental health facility will satisfy the requirements of section 10 only if the patient is shown to have read and understood the sign. In *R v. Ahearn*[29] the Prince Edward Island Court of Appeal held that section 10(b) of the Charter is satisfied if is shown that the accused read and understood a sign on the wall of a police station informing him of his right to counsel. In *Lussa v. Health Science Centre*,[30] Kroft J. held that a patient who had been civilly committed had not been informed according to the requirements of section 10 notwithstanding a sign that had been posted in the ward.

Also on the authority of *Clarkson v. R*[31] where a patient is involuntarily admitted to hospital the fact that the patient has been diagnosed as suffering from mental disorder may be sufficient to establish "special circumstances" which import a duty that the physician enquire into the level of the patient's comprehension. Where it is apparent that the patient does not understand the information, the physician must take reasonable steps to assist the patient in understanding it.[32] Indeed it may be advisable for the medical practitioner to document what steps were taken.[33] In cases where a patient in incapable of understanding the information no matter how often or carefully it is explained Kroft J. expressed the view in *Lussa v. Health Sciences Centre*[34] that section 10 would be complied with if it were established that the patient either understood the information or was incapable of such understanding. Robertson however argues that if the patient is

---

[26] R.S.B.C. 1979, c.256, s.28; R.S.A. 1980, c.M-13, s.24; S.S.1984-85-86, c. M-13.1, s.33(1).

[27] In *R v. Kelly* (1985) 17 C.C.C. (3d) 419 (Ont. C.A.), it was held that "promptly" meant "immediately" consequently it would appear that as soon as a person is apprehended under an examination certificate he must be informed of the reasons for his detention.

[28] In *R v. Manninen* (1983) 3 D.L.R. (4th), 541, it was held that the words "without delay" do not mean immediately. If the circumstances (e.g. an emergency admission or the patient's mental state) make it impracticable to inform the person immediately a slight delay might be justified.

[29] (1983) 4 D.L.R. (4th) 171 (P.E.I. C.A.).

[30] (1983) 9 C.R.R. 350.

[31] [1986] 1 .S.C.R 383. In that case the Supreme Court of Canada held that the police ought to have delayed their questioning of the accused until she was sufficiently sober to understand and properly exercise her right to retain and instruct counsel.

[32] It may be advisable for the physician to record the steps taken. In *Lussa v. Health Sciences Centre* [1983] 9 .C.R.R. 350 the court held that s.10 had not been complied with because there was no evidence of whether the patient understood the information which was given to her.

[33] In *Lussa v. Health Sciences Centre* (1983) 9 C.R.R. 350 (Man. Q.B) the court held that s.10 had not been complied with because there was no evidence of whether the patient understood the information which was given to her.

[34] (1983) 9 C.R.R. 350 (Man Q.B.).

incapable of understanding the spirit of section 10 requires the hospital to pass the information on to the patient's nearest relative.[35]

In cases where section 10 is breached the court has discretion under section 24(1) to grant whatever remedy it considered appropriate and just in the circumstances including an award of damages in appropriate cases.[36]

In New Zealand every person has a right to receive a statement in writing of his or her rights "on becoming a patient."[37] Thus *from the time a preliminary assessment has been completed* a patient must be informed of the legal consequences of the Act and their consequent right to review.

Conclusions

1. The Mental Health Act provisions regarding notice of rights do not go far enough. It is submitted that due process requires that notice be given to the patient by (a) an independent advocate, (b) immediately on arrival at the psychiatric hospital and (c) in a form and language which will enable the patient to understand the information given him. Information given in relation to rights should include an explanation of those rights and how to exercise them. Any proposed legislation should require that the information be given orally and in writing.

2. The information which the patient is required to be given should include the section under which the patient is detained *and its effects*, the patient's right to legal representation and how this right may be exercised; details of the powers of the Inspector of Mental Health Services and how s/he may communicate with the Inspector; the hospital's powers of discharge; the provisions of the Mental Health Act in relation to treatment of detained patients and the safeguards applying in relation to certain treatments.

3. While the Act proposes that the patient should be informed that s/he is entitled to legal representation and to communicate with the Inspector of Mental Health Services. The right to legal representation and the right to communicate with the Inspector of Mental Health Services and how it may be exercised are not set out as separate provisions in the Act. Full recognition should be given to these rights by embodying them as separate provisions in the legislation.

4. When the role of the patient advocate is established the details given to the patient should include an explanation of the nature of the role and powers of the advocate and the patient's right to nominate a third party to represent his interests.

---

[35] See Robertson, G.B., *Mental Disability and the Law in Canada* (Carswell Calgary 1987), 376. Robertson cites in support of this argument the case of *R v. Hardisty* (1985) 6 C.R.D. 650, 70-03 (Man. C.A.) in which the Manitoba Court of Appeal held that a minor's right to counsel under s.10 of the Charter cannot be waived by him but only by his guardian or next friend. In Robertson's view this case "recognises the importance of interpreting s.10 in such a way as to protect those who through immaturity or disability are incapable of deciding whether to retain and instruct counsel."

[36] See Pilkington, "Damages as a Remedy for Infringement of the Canadian Charter of Rights and Freedoms" (1984) 62 *Can. Bar Rev.* 517.

[37] S.64 of the Mental Health (Compulsory Assessment and Treatment) Act 1992.

ACCESS TO MEDICAL RECORDS[38]

Patient's right of access to medical records at common law

At present under Irish law a person with mental illness has no unrestricted right at common law to access to medical or other records held by health and other authorities about him/her. In the Canadian case of *McInerney v. McDonald*[39] the Canadian Supreme Court ruled that medical records compiled by the medical practitioner were the property of the clinic, which employed the medical practitioner and not the patient. However, as far as the information stored in the medical records was concerned the court concluded that: "such information remains in a fundamental sense one's own for the individual to communicate or retain as he or she sees fit.[40] In reaching its conclusion the court considered the case of *Halls v. Mitchell*[41] in which it was held that the professional secrets acquired by a medical practitioner from his patient belonged to the patient. Accordingly the Supreme Court formed the view that information stored in the records received by the medical practitioner was effectively the patient's property and subject to his control. The Supreme Court also held that in the fiduciary relationship which exists between medical practitioner and patient the patient by placing his trust in the medical practitioner had established a right of access to his medical records – personal privacy and access to medical information were interchangeable rights. While in the ordinary case these records should be disclosed upon request of the patient it added the proviso that the information could be withheld "if there is a significant likelihood of a substantial adverse effect on the physical, mental or emotional health of the patient or harm to a third party.[42]

The English Courts in *R v. Mid Glamorgan Health Authority, ex parte Martin*, took a more conservative stance.[43] The issue in the case was whether a patient with mental health difficulties had a right of access to his medical records in order to query his treatment by the defendant health authorities. It was held at first instance at common law no general principle of access existed under English law and if such right existed it would be conditional upon their being *no* risk to the mental or physical health of the patient. The court dismissed the legal validity of the concept of the fiduciary relationship giving rise interchangeability of patient's rights to privacy and access to legal records used in the *McInerney* Case. It was also of the view that while the confidential clinical information imparted by the patient did belong to him, the medical interpretation of the information received and subsequent diagnosis did not. Referring to the English precedent of *Sidaway v. Bethlehem Hospital*,[44] Popplewell J. stated that:

> "It is appropriate to point out that in *Sidaway* which is not referred to in this decision the notion of a fiduciary relationship was expressly disavowed. In my

---

[38] See Doran, "The Legal Position Governing Access to Medical Records" (1997) *Medico-Legal Journal of Ireland* 90.
[39] [1993] D.L.R. 415.
[40] [1993] D.L.R. 415 at 422.
[41] [1928] S.C.R. 125.
[42] [1993] 93 D.L.R. 415 at 430.
[43] [1995] 1 W.L.R 110.
[44] [1984] 1 All E.R. 1018.

judgment there is a distinction to be made between the information conveyed by a patient for the benefit of the doctor's consideration and the conclusion to which the doctor comes based on that information. The opinion of the doctor is wholly the property of the doctor. It does not seem to me that the fact that the patient provides the original information entitles him, subject to exception, to seek the conclusions of the doctor based on that information."[45]

The Court of Appeal, dismissing the appeal, did assert a patient's right of access and the doctor's reciprocal duty to disclose but based the patient's right of access on the doctor's duty to act in the patient's best interests at all times not on any proprietary interest on the part of the patient in the records. This was because the files belonged to the local Family Health Services Authority in the case of a general practitioner's patients and were owned by the relevant health authority or NHS Trust in the case of hospital patients. It was held that even if the patient's right of access was based on a fiduciary relationship this would not be an absolute right. The fiduciary relationship had to be adapted into the doctor's obligations to the patient to ensure that the doctor always acted in the patient's best interests. As a result of this provision was made regarding the prohibition of disclosure of details from the records if there was a perceived threat to the patient's physical or mental health in the doctor's opinion. The Court of Appeal's decision has been criticised as endorsing medical paternalism. Feenan states:

"Although the novel recognition in *Martin* of common law based right of access is to be welcomed the decision maintains the paternalistic tradition of privileging medical control over personal health information, exemplified in the *Martin* case by the increasing problematic use in novel medical law cases of a best interests approach, coupled with a broad exception to the newly recognised access right framed in terms of mere detriment to the patient."[46]

Samuel J. Brakel outlines the concerns surrounding the issue of access as follows:

"Many therapists and other managers of confidential information traditionally have been unwilling to provide patients with access in order to protect the patients or third parties who provided the information from harm or liability. The best interests of the patient, as viewed by the patient may come into conflict with the view of the patient's interests held by the therapist, who would be influenced by concerns about malpractice implications of access, control of patients and increased competition for the patient's dollar.

Patients in addition are increasingly concerned about personal interests that may be compromised by faulty records and records containing information that may stigmatise or subject them to discrimination."[47]

However, recently legislation both in England and Ireland has increasingly established a principle of access by individuals to personal information relating to

---

[45] [1994] *Medical Law Review* 355.
[46] See "Common Law Access to Medical Records" (1996) 59 *Modern Law Review* 101.
[47] *The Mentally Disabled and the Law* (American Bar Foundation, 1985).

the individual. Typically however the right tends to be hedged around by exemptions relating to information, which will have a detrimental effect on the mental health of the individual so that the extent to which a person may be said to have a right to information concerning their mental health is potentially quite limited.

A patient's right of access to medical records as a matter of ethics

Paragraph 4–10 of the Medical Council's Guide to Ethical Conduct and Behaviour, which is fundamentally a set of ethical or moral principles which doctors must apply in clinical situations in which they work[48], provides that patients are entitled to receive a copy of their own medical records, provided it does not put their health (or the health of others) at risk. The proviso to the right of access as a matter of ethics is very broad and offers a wide discretion to doctors to refuse access to medical records where there is the slightest risk to the patient's health whether it be his/her physical, mental or emotional health or that of others. So that the right of access as a matter of ethics may prove difficult for a patient with mental disability to insist on. If a patient believes, however, that access is being unreasonably refused and has good grounds for so believing the matter may be referred to the Medical Council for investigation.

Paragraph 4–10 continues that it is in the interest of doctors and patients that accurate records are always kept. It states that they should be retained for an adequate period (this may be for periods of 21 years) and eventual disposal may be subject to advice from legal and insurance bodies.

Legislative measures governing the patient's right of access to medical records

The patient's right of access to information under the Data Protection Acts

Under the provision of the Data Protection Act 1988 as amended by the Data Protection (Amendment) Act 2003 a person or body who controls the contents and use of personal data ("data controller") must comply with the provisions of the data protection legislation and must register[49] with the Data Protection Agency.[50] The 1988 Act as amended applies to automated data and (with some exceptions)[51] is extended to apply to manual data

---

[48] See Introduction, sixth edition, 2004).

[49] The obligation to register does not apply to data controllers or data processors who carry out (i) processing whose sole purpose is the keeping in accordance with law of a register that is intended to provide information to the public and is open to consultation either by the public in general or by any person demonstrating a legitimate interest, (ii) the processing of manual data. (other than such categories, if any, of such data as may be prescribed) or (iii) any combination of the foregoing categories of processing. See Data Protection Act 1988, s.16(1) as amended by Data Protection (Amendment) Act 2003, s.16 and Data Protection Act 1988, s.19(1). However, s.16 of the 2003 Act was not brought into force by the Data Protection (Amendment) Act 2003 (Commencement) Order 2003 (S.I. No.207 of 2003) and consequently as yet has no legal effect.

[50] Data Protection Act 1988, s.19(1).

[51] The obligations imposed by ss.2, 2A and 2B of the 1988 Act come into operation on October 24, 2007 in respect of manual data held in relevant filing systems on the passing of 2003 Act. i.e. April 10, 2003. See Data Protection (Amendment) Act 2003, s.23(4).

from the date of the commencement of the Data Protection (Amendment) Act 2003, i.e. July 1, 2003.[52]

Medical practitioners may fall within the definition of "data controller" Medical practitioners, consultants and other health care professionals working as sole practitioners are data controllers as they manage, control and have primary responsibility for their patients' information and as such they bear the obligation to comply with the Data Protection Acts and to register. Bodies such as hospital, clinics, research bodies and the Health Service Executive are also data controllers. Medical practitioners, consultants and health care professionals employed by health care providers or bodies and who process sensitive information as employees are not data controllers since they process information on behalf of their employers. Where practitioners are organised as partnerships the partnership is the data controller.[53]

Patients may be data subjects A patient may be a "data subject" where s/he is the subject of "personal data" as defined in the 1988 Act (see section 1(1) of the Data Protection Act 1988).

To what information does the Data Protection Acts apply? "Data" in the Act is defined as "automated data and manual data."[54] "Automated data" is defined as "information that (a) is being processed by means of equipment operating automatically in response to instructions given for that purpose or (b) is recorded with the intention that it should be processed by means of such equipment." [55] "Manual data" means "information that is recorded as part of a relevant filing system or with the intention that it should form part of a relevant filing system." "Relevant filing system" means "any set of information relating to individuals to the extent that, although the information is not processed by means of equipment operating automatically in response to instructions given for that purpose, the set is structured either by reference to individuals or by reference to criteria relating to individuals, in such a way that specific information relating to a particular individual is readily accessible."[56] "Personal data" is defined as "data relating to a living individual who is or can be identified either from the data or from the data in conjunction with other information that is in, or is likely to come into the possession of the data controller."[57]

Obligations of data controllers to process information fairly Section 2 of the 1988 Act as amended requires medical practitioners and health professionals as data controllers[58] to comply with certain basic data protection principles. Among these is a

---

[52] See Data Protection (Amendment) Act 2003 (Commencement) Order 2003 (S.I. No. 207 of 2003).
[53] See A & L Goodbody, *A Practical Guide to Data Protection Law in Ireland* (Thompson Roundhall, Dublin, 2003), p.100.
[54] See Data Protection Act 1988, s.1 as amended by Data Protection (Amendment) Act 2003, s.2(a)(ii).
[55] See Data Protection Act 1988, s.1 as amended by Data Protection (Amendment) Act 2003, s.2(a)(i).
[56] See Data Protection Act 1988, s.1 as amended by Data Protection (Amendment) Act 2003, s.2(a)(i).
[57] See Data Protection Act 1988, s.1 as amended by Data Protection (Amendment) Act 2003, s.2(a)(iv).
[58] "Data controller" is defined as "a person who, either alone or with others controls the content and use of personal data". See Data Protection Act 1988, s.1.

requirement that the data or the information constituting the data shall have been obtained and the data shall been processed fairly[59] "Processing" is a term which occurs frequently throughout the Act and in relation to information or data is defined widely as meaning "performing any operation of set of operations on the information or data, whether or not by automatic means, including (a) obtaining, recording or keeping the information or data, (b) collecting, organising, storing, altering or adapting the information or data; (c) retrieving, consulting or using the information or data, (d) *disclosing the information or data by transmitting, disseminating or otherwise making it available* or (e) aligning, combining, blocking,[60] erasing or destroying the information or data."[61]

When is processing "fair"? Section 2D(1) of the Data Protection Act 1988 states the personal data shall not be treated for the purposes of section 2(1)(a) as processed fairly unless (a) in the case of data obtained from the data subject the data controller ensures so far as practicable that the data subject has, is provided with or has made readily available to him or her at least the *information* specified in section 2D(2). This is (a) the identity of the data controller, (b) if he or she has nominated a representative for the purposes of the Act the identity of the representative (c) the purpose or purposes for which the data are intended to be processed and (d) any other information which is necessary, having regard to the specific circumstances in which the data are or are to be processed, to enable processing in respect of the data to be fair to the data subject such as information as to the recipients or categories of recipients of the data, as to whether replies to questions asked for the purpose of collection are obligatory, as to the possible consequences of failure to give such replies and as to the existence of the right of access to and the right to rectify the data concerning him or her.

In a case where data is not obtained from the data subject section 2D(1)(b) requires that the data controller must ensure so far as practicable that the data subject has, is provided with or has made readily available to him or her at least the information specified in section 2D(3): (i) not later than the time when the data controller first processes the data or (ii) if disclosure of the data to a third party is envisaged not later than the time of such disclosure. The information specified in section 2D(3) is (a) the information specified in section 2D(2), (b) the categories of data concerned and (c) the name of the original data controller.

Exemptions from obligation to process information fairly Where the information is obtained from a source other than the data subject section 2D(4) specifies that the requirements of section 2D(1) (b) do not apply (a) where, in particular for processing for statistical purposes or for the purposes of historical or scientific research the provision of the information specified therein proves impossible or would involve a disproportionate effort or (b) in any case where the processing of the information contained or to be contained in the data by the data controller is necessary for compliance with a legal obligation to which the data controller is subject other than an obligation

---

[59] Data Protection Act 1988, s.2(1)(a) as amended by Data Protection (Amendment) Act 2003, s.3(a).
[60] "Blocking" in relation to data means so marking the data that it is not possible to process it for purposes in relation to which it is marked. See Data Protection Act 1988, s.1 as amended by Data Protection (Amendment) Act 2003, s.2(a).
[61] Data Protection Act 1988, s.1(1) as amended by Data Protection (Amendment) Act 2003, s.3(a).

imposed by contract if such conditions as may be specified in regulations made by the Minister for Justice Equality and Law Reform after consultation with the Data Protection Commissioner are complied with.

The manner in which notice of use of data is to be given While the Act states that information regarding the use of data must be given to the data subject it does not specify the manner in which it is to be given. In some cases a written notice may amount to compliance with the requirements. However, in one case the Data Protection Commissioner held that a notice on the wall of a waiting room in an Accident and Emergency Department in a hospital indicating that patient's information would be given to researchers and asking patients to indicate to the receptionist if they did not want their information disclosed to researchers did not amount to the provision of adequate information about how patients details would be used and upheld a complaint by a patient who was contacted by the research team that the hospital had obtained her data unfairly.[62] The Commissioner stated:

> "In this case ... account ought to have been taken of the particular environment in which patients' data were obtained. Many patients presenting themselves to the casualty department of a hospital may be expected to be in a state of some anxiety or discomfort. Consequently they may not be expected to be alert to matters not relating directly to their condition. In such circumstances there is a special need for the data controller to satisfy itself that any uses of the data which are unlikely to be anticipated by the data subject are fully explained."

In a clinical context it best practice would seem to dictate that the patient be given an individual notice of the use to which their data may applies and ask them to sign a section indicating that they had understood its contents.[63]

Duty of data controllers to ensure data is accurate and complete There is an additional requirement under section 2 of the Data Protection Act 1988 for data controllers (which would include medical practitioners) to ensure the data is accurate and complete and, where necessary kept up to date.[64] Other requirements are (i) The data must be obtained for one or more specified, explicit and legitimate purposes and (ii) must not be further processed in a manner incompatible with that/those purpose(s). (iii) The data must be adequate, relevant and not excessive in relation to the purposes(s) for which they were collected or are further processed and (iv) must not be kept longer than is necessary for the purpose(s).[65]

 Requirements (ii) and (iv) do not apply to personal data kept for statistical or research or other scientific purposes and the keeping of which complies with such requirements (if any) as may be prescribed for the purpose of safeguarding the fundamental rights and freedoms of data subjects and the data, or as the case may be the information constituting such data shall not be regarded as having been obtained unfairly by reason

---

[62] Case 1/97.

[63] See A & L Goodbody, *op. cit*, p.102.

[64] Data Protection Act 1988, s.2(1)(b) as amended by Data Protection (Amendment) Act 2003, s.3(a).

[65] Data Protection Act 1988, s 2(1)(c) as amended by Data Protection (Amendment) Act 2003, s.3(a).

only that its use for any such purpose was not disclosed when it was obtained, if the data are not used in such a way that damage or distress is or is likely to be caused to any data subject.[66]

Sections 2A and 2B impose additional obligations in respect of the processing of personal data and sensitive personal data respectively which are discussed at page 169 below.

Section 2 comes into operation on October 24, 2007 in respect of manual data held in relevant filing systems on April 10, 2003 the date of the passing of the 2003 Act.[67]

Right of data subject to access to personal data Section 3 of the Data Protection Act 1988 confers a right on any individual to establish whether a person keeps personal data relating to him/her. Accordingly an individual who believes that a person keeps such data may request that person in writing to inform him/her whether this is the case and if so, to give a description of the data and the purposes for which it is kept.

Section 4(1)(a) of the Data Protection Act 1988 confers a right on an individual, who requests a data controller by notice in writing to be informed by a data controller whether the data processed by or on behalf of the data controller includes personal data relating to the individual and, if it does, to be supplied with a description of (i) the categories of data being processed by or on behalf of the data controller, (ii) the personal data constituting the data of which that individual is the data subject (iii) the purpose or purposes of the processing and (iv) the recipients or categories of recipients to whom the data are or may be disclosed.

In addition the individual is entitled if s/he requests a data controller by notice in writing to have communicated to him or her in intelligible form (i) the information constituting any personal data of which that individual is the data subject and (ii) any information known or available to the data controller as to the source of those data unless the communication of that information is contrary to the public interest.[68] An individual is also entitled if s/he so requests a data controller by notice in writing to be informed free of charge of the logic involved in the processing where the processing by automatic means of the data of which the data is the data subject has constituted or is likely to constitute the sole basis for any decision significantly affecting him or her.[69] These requests by the individual must be acceded to not more than 40 days after compliance by the individual with the requirements of section 4. Where any of the information is expressed in terms that are not intelligible to the average person without explanation the information must be accompanied by an explanation of those terms.

A request that does not relate to all of the matters specified in section 4(1)(a) shall, nevertheless in the absence of any indication to the contrary be treated as relating to all of them.[70]

---

[66] Data Protection Act 1988, s.2(5) as amended by Data Protection (Amendment) Act 2003, s.3(b).

[67] Data Protection (Amendment) Act 2003, s.23(4).

[68] Data Protection Act 1988, s.4(1)(a)(iii) as amended by the Data Protection (Amendment) Act 2003, s.5(a).

[69] Data Protraction Act 1988, s.4(1)(a)(iv) as amended by the Data Protection (Amendment) Act 2003, s.5(a).

[70] Data Protection Act 1988, s.4(1)(b) as amended by the Data Protection (Amendment) Act 2003, s.5.

The individual's request must be complied with by supplying the data subject with a copy of the information concerned in a permanent form unless (a) the supply of such a copy is not possible or would involve disproportionate effort or (b) the data subject agrees otherwise.[71]

Rights of data subject in relation to manual data Section 23(5) of the Data Protection (Amendment) Act 2003 provides that notwithstanding that the 2003 Act insofar as it (a) amends section 2 of the 1988 Act (collection, processing, keeping, use and disclosure of personal data) and applies it to manual data and (b) inserts sections 2A (additional conditions for processing of personal data) and 2B (additional conditions for processing of sensitive personal data) into the 1988 Act comes into operation on October 24, 2007 in respect of manual data held in relevant filing systems on the passing of the 2003 Act, i.e. April 10, 2003, a data controller must if requested in writing by a data subject when making a request under section 4 of the 1988 Act (right of access) (a) rectify, erase, block[72] or destroy any data relating to him or her which are incomplete or inaccurate or (b) cease holding manual data relating to him or her in a way incompatible with the legitimate purposes pursued by the data controller.[73] In effect therefore section 23(5) acknowledges that a data subject has a right of access to personal data held in manual form from the date of the commencement of the 2003 Act, i.e. July 1, 2003[74] and imposes on the data controller the obligation to rectify, erase, block or destroy any incomplete or inaccurate data whether automated or manual or the obligation to cease holding manual data relating to the data subject in a way incompatible with the legitimate purposes pursued by the data controller when so requested by the data subject when exercising the right of access. The data subject thus has no need to prove a breach of section 2(1) to impose these obligations on the data controller.

A reasonable fee may be levied by the data controller for complying with the request.[75]

Refusal of access to data A notification of a refusal of a request made by an individual in compliance with section 4 must be in writing and must include a statement of the reasons for the refusal and an indication that the individual may complain to the Data Protection Commissioner about the refusal.[76]

Where a data controller has previously complied with a request under section 4(1) that data controller is not obliged to comply with a subsequent identical or similar request under section 4(1) by the same individual unless in the opinion of the data controller a reasonable interval has elapsed between compliance with the previous request and the making of the current request.[77] In determining whether a reasonable interval has elapsed regard must be had to the nature of the data, the purpose for which the data are processed and the frequency with which the data are altered.[78]

---

[71] Data Protection Act 1988, s.4(9) as inserted by the Data Protection (Amendment) Act 2003, s.5(d).
[72] "Blocking" in relation to data means so marking the data that it is not possible to process it for purposes in relation to which it is marked. See Data Protection (Amendment) Act 2003, s.2(a)(i).
[73] Data Protection (Amendment) Act 2003, s.23(5).
[74] See Data Protection (Amendment) Act 2003 (Commencement) Order 2003 (S.I. No. 207 of 2003).
[75] Data Protection Act 1988, s.4(1)(c).
[76] *Ibid.*, s.4(7).
[77] Data Protection Act 1988, s.4(10) as inserted by Data Protection (Amendment) Act 2003, s.5(d).
[78] Data Protection Act 1988, s.4(11) as inserted by Data Protection (Amendment) Act 2003, s.5(d).

Right of access of data subject to expressions of opinion Section 4(4A) of the 1988 Act [79] states that where personal data relating to a data subject consists of an expression of opinion about the data subject by another person the data may be disclosed to the data subject without obtaining the consent of that person to the disclosure. However, this provision does not apply if the expression of opinion was given in confidence or on the understanding that it would be treated as confidential. Thus where for example an employer is asked to give a confidential reference about an employee and that reference is restricted to expressions of opinion the reference cannot be disclosed to the employee without the author's consent. However, Kelleher points out:

> "An employer who tries to bring himself within the terms of the exemption contained in section 4(4A) by confining himself to expressions of opinion about a former employee would be going against an emerging consensus of legal opinion that references should be confined to simple statements of fact without the benefit of any opinions whether good or bad." [80]

A person may not require another person to make a request under section 4(1) or to supply him or her with data relating to that other person obtained as a result of such a request in connection with (i) the recruitment of that other person as an employee (ii) the continued employment of that other person, or (iii) a contract for the provision of services to him or by that other person. [81]

Modification of right of access in certain situations Notwithstanding these general rights the Minister for Justice is empowered under section 4(8) of the Act [82] to modify the right of access to personal data relating to physical or mental health where he considers it desirable in the interest of data subjects or in the public interest. Under the terms of the Data Protection (Access Modification) (Health) Regulations 1989, [83] personal data relating to physical or mental health must not be supplied to a data subject if it is likely to cause serious harm to his/her physical or mental health. [84] Where the data controller forms the view that the release of personal data would be likely to cause serious harm to the physical or mental health of the data subject the data controller is nonetheless not relieved of his obligation to supply so much of the information as can be supplied without harm to the person concerned and to edit the data accordingly. [85]

Where the data controller is a "health professional" [86] s/he may decide whether the

---

[79] As inserted by the Data Protection (Amendment) Act 2003, s.5(b).

[80] See D Kelleher, "FOI Reloaded", *Law Society Gazette* (August/September 2003) 22 at p.25.

[81] Data Protection Act 1988, s.4(13) as inserted by the Data Protection (Amendment) Act 2003, s.5(d) This subsection was not brought into force by the Data Protection (Amendment) Act 2003 (Commencement) Order 2003 (S.I. No.207 of 2003) and consequently does not yet have legal effect.

[82] Data Protection Act 1988, s.4(8) as amended by Data Protection (Amendment) Act 2003, s.5.

[83] S.I. No. 82 of 1989.

[84] Art.4(1).

[85] Art.4(2).

[86] A "health professional" is defined by art.3 of the Regulations as: "(a) a person who is a medical practitioner, dentist, optician, pharmaceutical chemist, nurse or midwife and who is registered under the enactments governing his profession" and (b) "a chiropodist, dietician, occupational therapist, orthopaedist, physiotherapist, psychologist, child psychotherapist or speech therapist."

data should be released. Where the data controller is not a health professional then the disclosure of health data to the data subject or a decision to withhold health data, cannot be taken unless the data controller has first consulted the person who appears to him to be the "appropriate health professional".[87] The "appropriate health professional" is defined[88] as either:

(a) the registered medical practitioner, or registered dentist, currently or most recently responsible for the clinical care of the data subject in connection with the matters to which the information the subject of the request relates,

(b) where more than one such person, the person most suitable to advise on those matters,

(c) where no one in (a) or (b) is available, a health professional who has the necessary experience and qualifications to advise on those matters.

A data controller is not entitled to withhold information relating to a data subject where it comprises personal data relating to a third party who is a health professional who has been involved in the care[89] of the data subject and the data relates to him in his capacity as such.[90] Thus the Health Service Executive would not be entitled to refuse to release personal data on the grounds that it contains a health professional's assessment or opinion of the data subject.

Further the Data Protection (Access Modification) (Social Work) Regulations 1989[91] provide that social work data is not to be supplied to a data subject if it would be likely to cause serious harm to the physical or mental health of the data subject or the emotional condition of the data subject.[92] This only applies to "social work data" which is defined in the Regulations as:

> "personal data kept for, or obtained in the course of, carrying out social work by a Minister of Government, a local authority, the Health Service Executive or a voluntary organisation or other body which carries out social work and is in receipt of moneys provided by such a Minister, authority or board, but excludes any health data within the meaning of the Data Protection (Access Modification) (Health) Regulations 1989."[93]

Where the information is likely to cause any of the harmful consequence mentioned the data controller is not excused from the obligation to supply so much of the information requested as can be supplied without causing harm[94] and accordingly to excise the harmful sections.

Where social work data is provided to controllers by persons who are not employees or agents of the data controller the regulations require consultation with the data source

---

[87] Art.5(1).
[88] Art.5(2).
[89] "Care" is defined by art.3 to include examination, investigation and diagnosis.
[90] Art.6.
[91] S.I. No. 83 of 1989.
[92] Art.4(1).
[93] Art.3.
[94] Art.4(2).

before the information can be passed onto the data subject[95] but it appears that consultation in good faith will be sufficient and the data source does not have to give permission before disclosure is made. Where the source of the data is an employee or agent of the data controller no process of consultation is necessary.

The withholding of data relating to an individual other than the data controller or data subject is not permitted where the individual is engaged in carrying out social work and the information relates to him in that capacity.[96] The regulations are also stated to be without prejudice to the power of the court to withhold from a data subject social work data kept by it and constituting information provided in a report supplied to it in any proceedings.[97]

Section 5 of the 1988 Act provides for a number of further restrictions of the right of access. Significantly the right of access under section 4 does not apply, *inter alia*, to personal data in respect of which a claim of privilege could be maintained in proceedings in a court in relation to communications between a client and his professional legal advisers or between those advisers.[98]

Section 22 of the 1988 Act provides that a person who (a) obtains access to personal data or obtains any information constituting such data, without the prior authority of the data controller or data processor by whom the data are kept and (b) discloses the data or information to another person shall be guilty of an offence

Data subject's right to rectification of data Section 6 of the Data Protection Act 1988 confers on the data subject a right of rectification, blocking[99] or erasure. It states that an individual shall, if he so requests in writing a data controller who keeps personal data relating to him be entitled to have rectified or, where appropriate blocked or erased any such data in relation to which there has been a contravention by the data controller of section 2(1) of the 1988 Act . The data controller must comply with the request not later than 40 days after it has been given or sent to him. A data controller shall be deemed to have complied with the request if he supplements the data with a statement (which the individual has assented to) relating to the matters dealt with by the data and if he so supplements the data he will be deemed not to be in contravention of section 2(1)(b).[100] Where a data controller complies or is deemed to have complied with a request under section 6(1) he or she must not later than 40 days after the request has been given or sent to him notify the following of the rectification, blocking, erasure or statement concerned:- (a) the individual making the request and (b) if such compliance materially modifies the data concerned any person to whom the data were disclosed during the period of 12 months immediately before the giving or sending of the request unless such notification proves impossible or involves a disproportionate effort.[101]

---

[95] Art.4(3).

[96] Art.5.

[97] Art.6.

[98] See Data Protection Act 1988, s.5(1)(g).

[99] "Blocking" in relation to personal data, means so marking the data that it is not possible to process it for purposes in relation to which it is marked. See Data Protection Act 1988, s.1(1) as amended by Data Protection (Amendment) Act 2003, s.2(a).

[100] Data Protection Act 1988, s.6(1) as amended by Data Protection (Amendment) Act 2003, s.7(a).

[101] Data Protection Act 1988, s.6(2) as amended by Data Protection (Amendment) Act 2003, s.7(b).

Section 6A of the 1988 Act[102] which confers on a data subject the right to object to processing likely to cause damage or distress is discussed at page 221 below.

Data subject's rights in relation to automated decision taking Section 6B(1) of the 1988 Act[103] confers rights on the data subject in relation to automated decision taking and provides that subject to section 6B(2) a decision which produces legal effects concerning a data subject or otherwise significantly affects a data subject may not be based solely on processing[104] by automatic means of personal data in respect of which he or she is the data subject and which is intended to evaluate certain personal matters relating to him or her such as for example (but without prejudice to the generality of the foregoing) his or her performance at work, creditworthiness, reliability or conduct.

Section 6B(2) provides for exceptions to the general rule in section 6B(1), (a) in a case in which a decision referred to in section 6B(1), (i) is made in the course of steps taken (I) for the purpose of considering whether to enter into a contract with the data subject, (II) with a view to entering into such a contract, or (III) in the course of performing such a contract, (ii) is authorised or required by any enactment and the data subject has been informed of the proposal to make the decision, and (iii) either (I) the effect of the decision is to grant a request of the data subject or (II) adequate steps have been taken to safeguard the legitimate interests of the data subject by, for example (but without prejudice to the generality of the foregoing) the making of arrangements to enable him or her to make representations to the data controller in relation to the proposal, or (b) if the data subject consents to the processing referred to in section 6B(1).

Exemptions for processing for journalistic etc. purposes Section 22A(1)[105] provides that personal data that are processed only for journalistic, artistic or literary purposes shall be exempt from certain provisions of the Act specified in section 22A(2) if (a) the processing is undertaken solely with a view to the publication of any journalistic, literary or artistic material, (b) the data controller reasonably believes that, having regard in particular to the special importance of the public interest in freedom of expression, such publication would be in the public interest, and (c) the data controller reasonably believes that, in all the circumstances, compliance with that provision would be incompatible with journalistic, artistic or literary purposes.

In considering whether for the purposes of (b) above whether publication would be in the public interest, regard may be had to any code of practice approved under section 13(1)[106] or 13(2)[107] of the 1988 Act as amended.[108]

---

[102] Inserted by Data Protection (Amendment) Act 2003, s.8.

[103] Inserted by Data Protection (Amendment) Act 2003, s.8.

[104] The word "processing" is widely defined see pp. 164, 166 and 169.

[105] S.22A was inserted by the Data Protection (Amendment) Act 2003, s.21.

[106] S.13(1) provides that the Data Protection Commissioner shall encourage trade associations and other bodies representing categories of data controllers to prepare codes of practice to be complied with by those categories in dealing with personal data.

[107] S.13(2) provides for the approval of codes of practice by the Commissioner .It states, *inter alia*, that the Data Protection Commissioner shall (a) where a code of practice is submitted to him or her for consideration consider the code and after such consultation with such data subjects or persons representing data subjects and with the relevant trade associations or other bodies aforesaid as appears to him to be appropriate (i) if he or she is of opinion that the code provides for the data

"Publication" in relation to journalistic, artistic or literary material is defined widely to mean the act of making the material available to the public or any section of the public in any form or by any means.[109]

The relevant provisions from which personal data processed for journalistic artistic or literary purposes are exempt by virtue of section 22A(2) are:

(a) section 2 (collection, processing, keeping, use and disclosure of personal data) other than section 2(1)(d) (the requirement to take appropriate security measures against unauthorised access);

(b) section 2A (requirements regarding processing of personal data);[110] section 2B (requirements regarding processing of sensitive personal data);[111] section 2D (criteria for fair processing of personal data);

(c) section 3 (right of individual to establish existence of personal data);

(d) section 4 (right of individual to access to personal data relating to him/her held by a data controller); section 6(right of individual to rectification or erasure);[112]

(e) section 6A (right of data subject to object to processing likely to cause damage or distress);[113] section 6B (rights of data subject in relation to automated decision making).

Powers of Data Protection Commissioner Where enforcement of the right of access is concerned the Data Protection Commissioner has power under section 10 of the 1988 Act to investigate whether any provisions of the Act have been, are being or are likely to be contravened in relation to an individual either where a complaint is made by the individual or he is otherwise of the opinion that there may be such a contravention.[114] When a complaint is made the Commissioner is obliged to investigate the complaint or cause it to be investigated unless he is of opinion that it is frivolous or vexatious.[115] If s/he is unable to arrange within a reasonable time for the amicable resolution by the parties concerned of the matter which is the subject of the complaint the Commissioner must notify the complainant in writing of his or her decision in relation to it. The individual may, if aggrieved by the decision appeal against it to the Circuit Court within 21 days from the receipt by him or her of the notification.[116]

---

subjects concerned a measure of protection with regard to personal data relating to them that conforms with that provided for by s.2, ss 2A–2D and ss.3 and 4 other than s.4(8) and 6 of the 1988 Act approve the code and encourage its dissemination to the data controllers concerned and (ii) in any event notify the association or body concerned of his or her decision to approve or not to approve the code.

[108] S.13 was amended by the Data Protection (Amendment) Act 2003, s.14.

[109] S.22A(4) as inserted by Data Protection (Amendment) Act 2003, s.21(4).

[110] See below under A Patient's Right to Confidentiality and Privacy.

[111] *Ibid.*

[112] *Ibid.*

[113] *Ibid.*

[114] Data Protection Act 1988, s.10(1)(a) as amended by Data Protection (Amendment) Act 2003, s.11(a)(i).

[115] Data Protection Act 1988, s.10(1)(b)(i).

[116] Data Protection Act 1988, s.10(1)(b)(ii) as amended by Data Protection (Amendment) Act 2003, s.11(a)(ii).

The Commissioner has a general power also to carry out or cause to be carried out such investigations as s/he considers appropriate in order to ensure compliance with the provisions of the Act and to identify any contravention thereof.[117]

Where the Data Protection Commissioner is of the opinion that the data controller has contravened or is contravening a provision of the Act (other than a provision the contravention of which is an offence) s/he may issue an enforcement notice. The notice sets out the steps, which must be taken by the data controller within a specified time limit in order to comply with the Act.[118] The enforcement notice could, for example require the data controller to block, rectify, erase or destroy any of the data concerned or insert a supplementary statement approved by the Data Protection Commissioner.[119] The data controller may appeal to the Circuit Court against the requirement specified in the enforcement notice within 21 days of the service of the notice.[120] A person who, without reasonable excuse, fails or refuses to comply with a requirement specified in an enforcement notice will be guilty of an offence.[121]

Rights of access to information under the Freedom of Information Acts[122]

Section 6 of the Freedom of Information Act 1997 confers a right of access on every person to any record held by a public body. A public body is defined in accordance with the First Schedule to the Act and includes Government Departments, a local authority, the Health Service Executive[123] and certain bodies prescribed as public bodies by regulation.[124] The 1997 Act does not apply, however, to information held by private hospitals and clinics, general medical practitioners in relation to private patients or records held by a private consultant and consequently there is not a right of access to records held by such bodies and persons under the Act. By virtue of section 47(8) of the Mental Health Act 2001,[125] the 1997 Act applies to the Mental Health Commission.

---

[117] Data Protection Act 1988, s.10(1A) as inserted by Data Protection (Amendment) Act 2003, s.11(b).
[118] Data Protection Act 1988, s.10(2) as amended by Data Protection (Amendment) Act 2003, s.11(c).
[119] Data Protection Act 1988, s.10(3) as amended by Data Protection (Amendment) Act 2003, s.11(d).
[120] Data Protection Act 1988, s.26(1)(a).
[121] *Ibid*, s.10(9) This provision does not apply where an appeal is brought pending the determination or withdrawal of the appeal. See Data Protection Act 1988, s.10(5).
[122] See Doran and Cusack, "Access to Medical Records: The Effect of the Freedom of Information Act 1997" (1997) *Medico-Legal Journal of Ireland* 106; see also Doran, "The Legislative Position Governing Patient Access to Medical Records" (1998) *Irish Medical Journal* Vol. 91(1) 27.
[123] Freedom of Information Act 1997, s.2.
[124] See Freedom of Information Act 1997 (Prescribed Bodies) Regulations 1999 (S.I. No. 329 of 1999) which prescribes certain bodies and hospitals providing mental health services or services for persons with an intellectual disability as public bodies for the purposes of para.1(5) of the First Schedule. See further S.I. No.67 of 2000 which prescribes the Equality Authority, the Area Health Boards established on the establishment day by s.14(1) of the Health (Eastern Regional Health Authority) Act 1999 and the Health Boards Executive established on the establishment day by s.21(1) of the Health (Eastern Regional Health Authority) Act 1999 as public bodies for the purposes of the First Schedule. See further S.I. No. 355 of 2000 which prescribes the Social Welfare Tribunal as a public body for the purposes of the First Schedule. See further S.I. 359 of 2002 which prescribes the National Disability Authority as a public body for the purposes of the Schedule. See further S.I. No. 530 of 2002 which prescribes the National Drugs Strategy Team as a public body for the purposes of the Schedule.
[125] S.47 was brought into force on April 5, 2002 by the Mental Health Act 2001 (Sections 1 to 5, 7, 31 to 55) (Commencement) Order 2002 (S.I. No. 90 of 2002).

It is the duty of the public body to give reasonable assistance in the making of a request for access to any person who is seeking such a record and if the person has a disability to facilitate the exercise by the person of his or her rights under the Act.[126] The right of access exists primarily in relation to records created after the commencement of the Act.[127] However, a person may have access to records created before such commencement where access to records created before the commencement of the 1997 Act is necessary or expedient in order to understand records created after such commencement.[128] A person may also have access to records created before the commencement of the Act where they relate to personal information[129] about the person seeking access to them.[130]

Exercise of the right of access to information A person wishing to exercise the right of access must make a request in writing or such other form as may be determined addressed to the head of the public body (in the case of the Health Service Executive the Chief Executive Officer) for access to the record concerned (a) stating that the request is made under the Act (b) containing sufficient particulars in relation to the information concerned to enable the record to be identified by the taking of reasonable steps and (c) if the person requires such access to be given in a particular form or manner specifying the form or manner of access.[131] A person is not required to specify the reason for seeking access. A fee is chargeable by the public body in respect of a request which is payable at the time of making the request[132] but is not chargeable if the record(s) contain(s) only personal information[133] relating to the requester.[134] The Chief

---

[127] Freedom of Information Act 1997, s.6(2).

[127] Freedom of Information Act 1997, s.6(4) The Act came into force on April 21, 1998. The date of commencement of the Act in relation to local authorities and health boards is October 21, 1998. See Freedom of Information Act 1997, s.6(11)(a) as inserted by Freedom of Information (Amendment) Act 2003, s.4.

[128] Freedom of Information Act 1997, s.6(5)(a).

[129] "Personal information" is defined as "information about an identifiable individual that (a) would, in the ordinary course of events, be known only to the individual or members of the family, or friends, of the individual or (b) is held by a public body on the understanding that it would be treated as confidential and, without prejudice to the generality of the foregoing, includes information relating to the educational, medical, psychiatric or psychological history of the individual ; information relating to the entitlements of the individual under the Social Welfare Acts as a beneficiary (within the meaning of the Social Welfare (Consolidation) Act 1993 or required for the purpose of establishing whether the individual being a claimant (within the meaning aforesaid) is such a beneficiary; the name of the individual where it appears with other personal information relating to the individual or where the disclosure of the name would or would be likely to establish that any personal information held by the public body concerned relates to the individual; subject to certain exceptions where the individual is an officeholder or an employee of a public body or was providing a service for a public body under a contract for services the views or opinions of another person about the individual". See Freedom of Information Act 1997, s.2(1).

[130] Freedom of Information Act 1997, s.6(5)(b).

[131] *Ibid.*, s.7(1).

[132] Freedom of Information Act 1997, s.47(6A)(a) as inserted by Freedom of Information (Amendment) Act 2003, s.30 The fees chargeable are set out in the Freedom of Information Act (Fees) Regulations 2003 (S.I. 264 of 2003) A fee of €15 is prescribed in respect of a person who makes a request under s.7 with a reduction of €5 in respect of persons who are medical card holder or dependants of medical card holders as defined in the Regulations.

[133] "Personal information" is defined by the Freedom of Information Act 1997, s.2 as meaning

Executive Officer must decide within four weeks of receipt of the request whether to grant or refuse the request and notify the requester accordingly.[135]

Access may be given by the Chief Executive Officer of the Health Service Executive to a medical record by providing the requester:

(a) with a copy of the record,

(b) a transcript of the information concerned, or

(c) a computer disk containing the information,

(d) a reasonable opportunity to inspect the record, access in the form requested may be denied if the Chief Executive Officer is satisfied that access in another form or manner would be significantly more efficient or the giving of access in the form or manner requested would–
  (i)   be physically detrimental to the record,
  (ii) involve an infringement of copyright,
  (iii) conflict with a legal duty or obligation of a public body,
  (iv) prejudice impair, or damage an interest protected by Part III (Exempt Records)[136] or section 46(records held by courts, tribunals etc).[137]

Grounds for refusal of access to information The request may be refused on administrative grounds that (a) the record concerned does not exist or cannot be found after all reasonable steps to ascertain its whereabouts have been taken, or (b) that accessing the records would cause a substantial and unreasonable interference with or disruption of work of the public body concerned, or (c) the request is, in the opinion of the head of the public body frivolous or vexatious or forms part of a pattern of manifestly unreasonable requests from the same requester or from different requesters who, in the opinion of the head of the public body appear to have made the requests acting in concert.[138] A head of a public body may not refuse to grant a request under (b) above

---

information about an identifiable individual that (a) would in the ordinary course of events, be known only to the individual or members of the family or friends of the individual or (b) is held by a public body on the understanding that it would be treated as confidential and, without prejudice to the generality of the foregoing, includes, *inter alia*, information relating to the medical, psychiatric or psychological history of the individual; information relating to the entitlements of the individual under the Social Welfare Acts as a beneficiary (within the meaning of the Social Welfare (Consolidation) Act 1993 or required for the purpose of establishing whether the individual being a claimant (within the meaning aforesaid) is such a beneficiary; the name of the individual where it appears with other personal information relating to the individual or where the disclosure of the name would or would be likely to establish that any personal information held by the public body concerned relates to the individual; subject to certain exceptions where the individual is an officeholder or an employee of a public body or was providing a service for a public body under a contract for services the views or opinions of another person about the individual.

[134] Freedom of Information Act 1997, s.47(6A) (c) as inserted by Freedom of Information (Amendment) Act 2003, s.30.

[135] Freedom of Information Act 1997, s.8.

[136] See below.

[137] Freedom of Information Act 1997, s.12.

[138] Freedom of Information Act 1997, s.10 as amended by Freedom of Information (Amendment) Act 2003, s.7.

unless s/he has assisted or offered to assist the requester concerned in an endeavour so to amend the request that it no longer falls within (b).[139]

Right to rectification of record Section 17(1) of the Act provides that where personal information in a record held by a public body is incomplete, incorrect or misleading the head of the body must on application to him or her by the individual to whom the information relates, amend the record (i) by altering it so as to make the information complete or correct or not misleading as may be appropriate, (ii) by adding to the record a statement specifying the respects in which the body is satisfied that the information is incomplete, incorrect or misleading, as may be appropriate or (iii) by deleting the information from it. "Personal information" is defined as "information about an identifiable individual that (a) would in the ordinary course of events be known only to the individual or members of the family or friends of the individual or (b) is held by a public body on the understanding that it would be treated as confidential and without prejudice to the generality of the foregoing includes, *inter alia*, information relating to the medical, psychiatric or psychological history of the individual ; information relating to the entitlements of the individual under the Social Welfare Acts as a beneficiary (within the meaning of the Social Welfare (Consolidation) Act 1993 or required for the purpose of establishing whether the individual being a claimant (within the meaning aforesaid) is such a beneficiary; the name of the individual where it appears with other personal information relating to the individual or where the disclosure of the name would or would be likely to establish that any personal information held by the public body concerned relates to the individual; and subject to certain exceptions where the individual is an officeholder or an employee of a public body or was providing a service for a public body under a contract for services the views or opinions of another person about the individual."[140]

The head of the body concerned must decide whether to grant or refuse the application within four weeks of receipt by him or her of an application and must give notice of his/her decision to the person concerned. If the decision is to grant the request notice of the manner of the grant must be given to the person concerned.[141] If the application is refused the head of the body (i) must attach the application to the record concerned or a copy of it or if that is not practicable a notation indicating that the application has been made and (ii) must include in the notice given to the person concerned particulars of the right of review and appeal under the Act and the procedures governing the exercise of those rights and any time limits governing such exercise.[142] The requirement of attachment of the application does not apply in relation to a case in which the head of the public body concerned is of opinion that the application concerned is defamatory or the alteration or addition to which it relates to the record concerned would be unnecessarily voluminous.[143] Where the record is amended the public body concerned must take all reasonable steps to notify (a) any person to whom access to the record was granted under the Act and (b) any public body to whom a copy of the record was given

---

[139] Freedom of Information Act 1997, s.10(2).
[140] *Ibid.*, s.2.
[141] *Ibid.*, s.17(3).
[142] *Ibid.*, s.17(4).
[143] *Ibid.*, s.17(4)(b).

of the amendment during the period of one year ending on the date on which the amendment was effected.[144]

Facilitation of Exerise of Right of Rectification by Person with Disability By virtue of section 17(6) the Minister may provide by regulations for the making of an application under section 17 by the parent or guardian of an individual referred to in section 17(1) if the individual belongs to a class specified in the regulations or in a case where such an individual is dead by a member of a class specified in the regulations. Pursuant to these powers the Minister for Finance has made the Freedom of Information Act 1997 (Section 17(6)) Regulations 2003[145] which came into operation on July 7, 2003 and provide that notwithstanding section 28(1) an application under section 17 in relation to a record that includes personal information that is incomplete, incorrect or misleading may subject to the other provisions of the Freedom of Information Act 1997, be made where:

(a) the applicant is a parent or guardian of the individual to whom the information in the record concerned relates and the individual belongs to one of the following classes of individual (i) individuals who, on the date of the request have not attained full age (within the meaning of the Age of Majority Act 1985) or (ii) individuals who on the date of the request have attained full age, and have a mental condition or a mental incapacity or severe physical disability, the incidence and nature of which is certified by a registered medical practitioner and who, by reason thereof, are incapable of exercising their rights under the Act. The individual belonging to the class specified in (i) and (ii) must be an individual as respects whom the granting of the application would, in the opinion of the head of the public body concerned, having regard to all the circumstances and to any guidelines drawn up and published by the Minister for Finance, be in his or her best interests;

(b) the individual to whom the information in the record concerned relates is dead and the applicant belongs to one of the following classes of applicant: (i) a personal representative of the individual acting in due course of administration of his or her estate or any person acting with the consent of a personal representative so acting, (ii) a person on whom a function is conferred in law in relation to the individual or his or her estate acting in the course of the performance of the function, and (iii) the spouse[146] or next of kin of the individual or such other person(s) as the head considers appropriate having regard to all the circumstances and to any relevant guidelines drawn up and published by the Minister for Finance.

Duty to forward statement to individual affected by act of public body Section 18 of the Act provides that where the individual has made an application to the head of the public body (including the Chief Executive Officer of the Health Service Executive)

---

[144] Freedom of Information Act 1997, s.17(5).

[145] S.I. No.265 of 2003.

[146] "Spouse" includes (a) a party to a marriage that has been dissolved, being a dissolution that is recognised as valid in the State or who is living apart form his or her wife or husband pursuant to a deed of separation, or (b) a man or woman who was not married to but cohabited as husband and wife, as the case may be, with the deceased individual. See Freedom of Information Act 1997 (Section 17(6)) Regulations 2003, art.4(2).

he/she has a duty to issue a statement to an individual who is affected by an act of a public body and has a material interest[147] in a matter affected by the act or to which it relates (where the individual has made an application to the head of the public body). The statement must state (a) the reasons for the act and (b) any findings on any material issues of fact made for the purposes of the act. An "act" in relation to a public body is defined to include a decision of the body. [148] However, this obligation does not extend to any record, which is exempt, nor does it require the disclosure of the existence or non-existence of a record if the non-disclosure of the existence or non-existence is required by the Act.[149] Further the obligation does not apply to decisions of Civil Service Commissioners or Local Authority Appointments Commissioners not to offer employment to any individual, if in the opinion of the head of the public body concerned the giving of a statement would be likely to prejudice the effectiveness of the process for selecting a person for appointment to the position.[150]

If the head of a public body decides not to cause a statement to be given to the person who has made an application in that regard the head must cause notice of the decision to be given to the person.[151]

Facilitation of right of access by, inter alia, *persons under disability* By virtue of section 18(5A) of the 1997 Act [152] the Minister for Finance may provide by regulations for the making of an application by (a) the parent or guardian of a person if the person belongs to a class specified in the regulations or (b) in a case where such a person is dead by a member of a class specified in the regulations. Pursuant to these powers the Minister for Finance has made the Freedom of Information Act 1997 (Section 18(5A)) Regulations 2003[153] which came into operation on July 7, 2003 and provide that an application section 18 may, subject to the other provisions of the Freedom of Information Act 1997, be made where:

(a) the applicant is a parent or guardian of the individual who is affected by an act of a public body and has a material interest in a matter affected by the act or to which it relates and the individual belongs to one of the following classes of individual (i) individuals who, on the date of the request have not attained full age (within the meaning of the Age of Majority Act 1985 or (ii) individuals who on the date of the request have attained full age, and have a mental condition or a mental incapacity

---

[147] For the purposes of s.18 a person has a material interest in a matter affected by an act of a public body or to which such an act relates if the consequence or effect of the act may be to confer on or withhold form the person a benefit without also conferring on or withholding it from persons in general or a class of persons which is of significant size having regard to all the circumstances and of which the person is a member. See Freedom of Information Act 1997, s.18(5) "Benefit" in relation to a person, includes (a) any advantage to the person, (b) in respect of an act of a public body done at the request of the person any consequences or effect thereof relating to the person, and (c) the avoidance of a less, liability, penalty, forfeiture, punishment or other disadvantage affecting the person. See Freedom of Information Act 1997, s.18(6).

[148] Freedom of Information Act 1997, s.18(6).

[149] *Ibid.*, s.18(2).

[150] *Ibid.*, s.18(3).

[151] *Ibid.*, s.18 (4).

[152] As inserted by Freedom of Information (Amendment) Act 2003, s.13.

[153] S.I. No. 266 of 2003.

or severe physical disability, the incidence and nature of which is certified by a registered medical practitioner and who, by reason thereof, are incapable of exercising their rights under the Act. The individual belonging to the class specified in (i) and (ii) must be an individual as respects whom the granting of the application would, in the opinion of the head of the public body concerned, having regard to all the circumstances and to any guidelines drawn up and published by the Minister for Finance, be in his or her best interests; or

(b) the individual to whom the information in the record concerned relates is dead and the applicant belongs to one of the following classes of applicant:
  (i) a personal representative of the individual acting in due course of administration of his or her estate or any person acting with the consent of a personal representative so acting,
  (ii) a person on whom a function is conferred in law in relation to the individual or his or her estate acting in the course of the performance of the function, and
  (iii) the spouse[154] or next of kin of the individual or such other person(s) as the head considers appropriate having regard to all the circumstances and to any relevant guidelines drawn up and published by the Minister for Finance.

Exemptions from right of access Part III of the Act specifies a range of records, which are exempt for the purposes of the Act.[155] The most relevant categories of exemptions giving rise to refusal of access in the context of mental health law are as follows:

Deliberate processes of public body etc. Access may be refused if it would disclose material relative to the deliberative processes of a public body (including opinions, advice, recommendations and the results of consultations, considered by the body, the head of the body or a member of the body or of the staff of the body for the purpose of those processes)[156] Access must be refused in respect of a record in relation to which the Secretary General of a department of State has issued a certificate in writing stating

---

[154] "Spouse" includes (a) a party to a marriage that has been dissolved, being a dissolution that is recognised as valid in the State or who is living apart form his or her wife or husband pursuant to a deed of separation, or (b) a man or woman who was not married to but cohabited as husband and wife, as the case may be, with the deceased individual. See Freedom of Information Act 1997 (Section 18(5A)) Regulations 2003, art.4(2).

[155] In brief these are records relating to:
  (1) meetings of the government (s.19); (2) deliberations of public bodies (s.20); (3) functions and negotiations of public bodies; (4) parliamentary court and private papers of representative of the European parliament or a member of the local authority or the Health Service Executive (s.22); (5) law enforcement and public safety (s.23); national security defence and international relations (s.24); information obtained in confidence (s.26); commercially sensitive information (s.27); personal information (s.28); to research being carried out by or on behalf of a public body where disclosure would result in serious disadvantage or information relating to cultural, heritage or natural resource, species of flora or fauna where disclosure would result in prejudice to well-being of same (s.30); financial and economic interests of the State and public bodies (s.31). Ss.19–29 are amended by the Freedom of Information (Amendment) Act 2003.

[156] Freedom of Information Act 1997, s.20(1) as amended by Freedom of Information (Amendment) Act 2003, s.15(a).

that the record contains matter relating to the deliberative processes of a Department of State.[157]

However, the exemption does not apply to a record insofar as it contains matter used or intended to be used by a public body for the purpose of making decisions, determinations or recommendations referred to in section 16 of the 1997 Act,[158] nor does it apply to factual information,[159] the reasons for making of a decision by a public body; and a report, study or analysis of a scientific expert relating to the advice of such an expert and not being a report used or commissioned for the purposes of a decision of a public body made pursuant to any enactment or scheme.[160] This discretion to refuse does not apply to a case which, in the opinion of the head of the public body concerned the public interest, would, on balance be better served by granting than by refusing to grant the request.[161] The definition of "public interest" is left completely to the discretion of the head of the public body (in the case of the Health Service Executive records the Chief Executive Officer).

Adverse effect on management functions of public body Access to the records may also be refused where it would have a significant adverse effect on the performance by the body of any of its functions relating to management.[162] These criteria are undefined in the Act. It seems that whether access to the records would have a significant adverse effect on the management functions of the Health Service Executive would fall to be decided by the Chief Executive Officer. However, the exemption does not apply in a case where in the opinion of the head of the public body concerned the public interest would, on balance, be better served by granting than by refusing to grant the request.[163]

Legal professional privilege applies Access must be refused if the record concerned

---

[157] Freedom of Information Act 1997, s.20(1A) as inserted by Freedom of Information (Amendment) Act 2003, s.15(a).

[158] as amended by the Freedom of Information (Amendment) Act 2003, s.11. S.16 as amended provides that a public body shall cause to be prepared and published and to be made available in accordance with s.16(5)(a) the rules, procedures, practices, guidelines and interpretations used by the body and an index of any precedents kept by the body for the purposes of decisions, determinations or recommendations, under or for the purposes of any enactment or scheme administered by the body with respect to rights, privileges, benefits, obligations, penalties or other sanctions to which members of the public are or may be entitled or subject under the enactment or scheme and (b) appropriate information in relation to the manner or intended manner or administration of any such enactment or scheme.((S.16(1)) "Published" includes published by electronic means (S.16(8)) Such publications must be made available for inspection free of charge and for removal free of charge or at the discretion of the head of the public body concerned for purchase (s.16(5)). S.16 applies to health boards from October 21, 1998.

[159] This includes information of a statistical, econometric or empirical nature, together with any analysis thereof. See Freedom of Information Act 1997, s.2 as amended by Freedom of Information (Amendment) Act 2003, s.2(c).

[160] Freedom of Information Act 1997, s.20(2) as amended by Freedom of Information (Amendment) Act 2003, s.15(b).

[161] Freedom of Information Act 1997, s.20(3) as inserted by Freedom of Information (Amendment) Act 2003, s.15.

[162] Freedom of Information Act 1997, s.21 as amended by Freedom of Information (Amendment) Act 2003, s.16.

[163] Freedom of Information Act 1997, s.21(2).

would be exempt from production in proceedings in a court on the ground of legal professional privilege or if the record is such that the head of the public body knows or ought reasonably to have known that its disclosure would constitute contempt of court.[164]

Endangerment of life or safety of person etc. Access to a record may also be refused by the head of a public body if it could, in the opinion of the head of the public body reasonably be expected to endanger the life or safety of any person[165] or reveal or lead to the revelation of the identity of a person who has given information to a public body in confidence in relation to the enforcement or administration of the civil law or any other source of such information given in confidence.[166] Where the disclosure of the existence or non existence of the record would have the aforementioned effects the head of the public body must refuse to grant the request for access and must not disclose to the requester concerned whether or not the record exists.[167]

Other categories of information exempted from the right of access by third parties these are (i) Information obtained in confidence and (ii) Personal Information.

Information given in confidence Section 26(1)[168] provides that a request for certain information disclosed in confidence must be refused. Accordingly section 26(1) states if (a) a record contains information given to a public body in confidence and on the understanding that it would be treated by it as confidential [169] and in the opinion of the head its disclosure would be likely to prejudice the giving to the body of further similar information from the same person(s) and it is of importance to the body that further similar information should be given to the body or (b) disclosure of the information concerned would constitute a breach of a duty of confidence provided for by a provision of an agreement or enactment,[170] or otherwise by law the head of the public body concerned must refuse the request. If the request relates to a record to which section 26(1) applies and in the opinion of the head of the public body concerned the disclosure of the existence or non-existence of the record would have the effect specified in section 26(1) s/he must refuse to grant the request and must not disclose whether or not the record exists.[171]

Section 26(2) states that the exemption from disclosure of confidential information does not apply to a record which is prepared by a head of a public body or director, member of the staff of public body or a person who is providing a service for a public

---

[164] Freedom of Information Act 1997, s.22 (1) as amended by Freedom of Information (Amendment) Act 2003, s.17(a).

[165] Freedom of Information Act 1997, s.23(1)(aa) as inserted by Freedom of Information (Amendment) Act 2003, s.18.

[166] Freedom of Information Act 1997, s.23(1)(b).

[167] Freedom of Information Act 1997, s.23(2) as amended by Freedom of Information (Amendment) Act 2003, s.18(b).

[168] As amended by the Freedom of Information (Amendment) Act 2003, s.21.

[169] This includes information that a person was required by law or could have been required by the body pursuant to law to give to that body. S.26(1)(a).

[170] Provisions specified in col.(3) to Sch.3 to the Act are excluded. Freedom of Information Act 1997, s.26(1)(b).

[171] Freedom of Information Act 1997, s.26(4) as inserted by Freedom of Information (Amendment) Act 2003, s.21(b).

body under a contract for services in the course of the performance of his or her functions unless disclosure of the information concerned would constitute a breach of a duty of confidence and is owed to a person other than a head of a public body or a director or member of staff of a public body or a person who is providing or provided a service for a public body under a contract for services.[172]

Section 26(3) states that the duty to refuse to disclose confidential information does not apply where in the opinion of the head of public body concerned the public interest would on balance be better served by granting rather than refusing to grant the request under section 7.

Disclosure of personal information involved Section 28(1) of the 1997 Act provides that the head of a public body must refuse to grant a request for access to records if in his/her opinion access to the record concerned would involve the disclosure of personal information (including personal information relating to a deceased individual).

"Personal information" is defined by section 2 of the 1997 Act as "information about an identifiable individual that (a) would, in the ordinary course of events, be known only to the individual or members of the family or friends of the individual or (b) is held by a public body on the understanding that it would be treated as confidential." Without prejudice to the generality of this definition it includes information relating to the medical, psychiatric or psychological history of the individual; information relating to the financial affairs of the individual; information relating to the age, sexual orientation or marital status of the individual; information relating to the entitlements of the individual under the Social Welfare Acts as a beneficiary (within the meaning of the Social Welfare (Consolidation) Act 1993) or required for the purpose of establishing whether the individual being a claimant (within the meaning of the 1993 Act) is such a beneficiary.

Section 28(5A)[173] provides that where a request relates to a record to which section 28(1) applies and in the opinion of the head of the public body the disclosure of the existence or non-existence of the record would have the effect specified in section 28(1) then the heard of the public body must refuse to grant the request and must not disclose to the requester concerned whether or not the record exists.

Section 28(2) provides that the obligation to refuse access to personal information does *not* apply if, (a) subject to section 28(3) the information concerned relates to the requester concerned; (b) any individual to whom the information relates consents to its disclosure to the requester,[174] (c) information of the same kind as that contained in the record in respect of individuals generally or a class of individuals that is (having regard to all the circumstances) of significant size, is available to the general public, (d) the information was given to the public body concerned by the individual to whom it relates and the individual was informed on behalf of the body before its being given that the information belongs to a class of information that would or might be made available to the general public, or (e) disclosure of the information is necessary in order to avoid a serious and imminent danger to the life or health of an individual.

---

[172] S.26(2) of the Freedom of Information Act 1997.

[173] as inserted by the Freedom of Information (Amendment) Act 2003, s.23.

[174] In the case of (a) or (b) the head of the public body concerned must ensure that the identity of the requester or the consent of the individual is established to his/her satisfaction. Freedom of Information Act 1997, s.28(1).

Section 28(5B) of the 1997 Act[175] provides that notwithstanding that personal information may be disclosed where the information relates to the requester concerned under section 28(2)(a) a head of a public body must, subject to sections 28(2)(b) to (e) and sections 28(5) and 28(6) refuse to grant access to a record if, in the opinion of the head, access to the record concerned would, in addition to involving the disclosure of personal information relating to the requester, also involve disclosure of personal information relating to an individual or individuals other than the requester.

Section 28(3) provides that where a request relates to (a) a record of a medical or psychiatric nature relating to the requester concerned or (b) a record kept for the purposes of or obtained in the course of the carrying out of social work in relation to the requester and in the opinion of the head of the public body concerned disclosure of the information to the requester might be prejudicial to his or her physical or mental health, well-being or emotional condition, the head of the public body may decide to refuse to grant the request.

Where the head of the public body refuses to grant such a request there must be included in a notice of the decision issued to the requester a statement to the effect that, if the requester requests the head to do so, the head will offer access to the record concerned and keep it available to such health professional having expertise in relation to the subject matter of the record as the requester may specify. In addition, if the requester so requests the head of the public body concerned he or she must offer access to the record to such health professional as aforesaid and keep it available for that purpose in accordance with section 8(3).[176]

A "health professional" for this purpose means a registered medical practitioner, a registered dentist, a member of any other class of health worker or social worker standing prescribed after consultation with such (if any) other Ministers of the Government as the Minister for Finance considers appropriate.[177] By virtue of the Freedom of Information Act 1997 (Classes of Health Professionals) Regulations 2001,[178] clinical psychologists[179] are prescribed as a class of health worker for the purposes of section 28[180] and social workers[181] are prescribed as a class of social worker for the purposes of the section.[182]

---

[175] As inserted by Freedom of Information (Amendment) Act 2003, s.23.

[176] Freedom of Information Act 1997, s.28(4).

[177] *Ibid.*, s.28(7).

[178] S.I. No. 368 of 2001.

[177] "Clinical psychologist" is defined by art.2 of the 2001 Regulations as "a person holding a qualification in clinical psychology recognised by the Minister for Health and Children and who has been practising as a clinical psychologist for at least three out of the last give years, which practice shall have occurred after the award of the qualification concerned" Art.3 of the Regulations states that in calculating a period of time for the purposes of the Regulations the calculation shall be made by counting back in time from the date on which it is contended by the person concerned that he or she has completed the required period of practice.

[180] See art.4.

[181] "Social worker" is defined in art.2 of the Regulations as a person holding (a) the National Qualification in Social Work (N.Q.S.W.) issued by the National Social Work Qualification Board or (b) the Certificate of Qualification in Social Work (C.Q.S.W.) issued by the National Validation Body on Social Work Qualifications and Training or (c) a letter of accreditation from the National Social Work Qualifications Board. In this context "letter of accreditation" has the same meaning

The application of section 28(3) was recently reviewed by the Information Commissioner in Case 99189 in which the health board had the opinion of four separate psychiatrists that the harm specified in section 28(3) would be occasioned to the applicant in this case. The Information Commissioner expressed the opinion that "he considered that there should be evidence of a real and tangible possibility of harm being caused to the general health, welfare and good of the requester as a result of direct access to the records in question." On this basis he refused access to the records sought.

Section 28(5) provides that where a request would fall to be refused under the exemption in section 28(1) then if in the opinion of the head of the public body concerned on balance (a) the public interest that the request should be granted outweighs the public interest that the right to privacy of the individual to whom the information relates should be upheld or (b) the grant of the request would benefit the individual aforesaid the head of the public body may subject to section 29[183] grant the request.

Facilitation of right of access where person is, inter alia, *under disability* Section 28(6) provides that notwithstanding the general prohibition in section 28(1) on granting access to personal information the Minister for Finance may provide by regulations for the grant of a request for access where the individual to whom the record concerned relates belongs to a class specified in the regulations and the requester concerned is the parent or guardian of the individual or the individual to whom the record relates is dead and the requester is a member of a class specified in the regulations. Pursuant to these powers the Minister for Finance has made the Freedom of Information Act 1997 (Section 28(6)) Regulations 1999[184] which provide that a request in relation to a record access to which involves disclosure of personal information (including personal information relating to a deceased individual) shall, subject to the other provisions of the Freedom of Information Act 1997, be granted where:

(a) the requester is a parent or guardian of the individual to whom the record concerned relates and the individual belongs to one of the following classes of individual (i) individuals who, on the date of the request, have not attained full age (within the meaning of the Age of Majority Act 1985) or (ii) individuals who have attained full age, who at the time of the request have a mental condition or mental incapacity or severe physical disability, the incidence and nature of which is certified by a registered medical practitioner and who, by reason thereof, are incapable of exercising their rights under the Act. The individuals specified in the classes specified in (i) and (ii) must be individuals access to whose records would, in the opinion of the head of

---

as it has in the National Social Work Qualifications Board (Establishment) Order 1997 (S.I. No. 97 of 1997).

[182] See art.5.

[183] S.29 sets out certain procedures to be followed in the event that a request is granted under s.28(5). These include requiring the head of the public body to notify the person to whom the information relates of the request and that it falls in the public interest to be granted and affording the person the opportunity to make submissions to the head of the public body and informing the person to whom the information relates that the head of the public body will consider any such submissions before deciding whether to grant or refuse to grant the request. See s.29(2).

[184] S.I. No. 47 of 1999.

the public body, having regard to all the circumstances and to any guidelines drawn up and published by the Minister for Finance, be in their best interests; or

(b) the individual to whom the record concerned relates is dead and the requester concerned belongs to one of the following classes of requester (i) a personal representative of the individual acting in due course of administration of his or her estate or any person acting with the consent of a personal representative so acting, (ii) a person on whom a function is conferred in law in relation to the individual or his or her estate acting in the course of the performance of the function, and (iii) the spouse[185] or next of kin of the individual or such other person(s) as the head considers appropriate having regard to all the circumstances and to any relevant guidelines drawn up and published by the Minister for Finance.

The persons specified in the 1999 Regulations are entitled to access to records created prior to the commencement of the 1997 Act.[186]

Review of decision to refuse access Where a decision regarding access has been made by a delegate of a head of a public body a person may apply in writing to the head of the public body for internal review of the decision. The head of the public body has power to review the decision and following the review (i) affirm or vary the decision or (ii) annul the decision and, if appropriate, make such decision in relation to the matter as s/he considers appropriate.[187] If the decision is to grant the request in whole or in part notice must be given to the person of the day on which and the form and manner in which access to the record will be offered to the requester concerned and the period during which the record will be kept available for the purpose of such access and the amount of any fee payable.[188] Notice of a decision to refuse a request for access must specify the reasons for that decision.[189] In addition, subject to specified exceptions, [190] the provisions of the Act under which the request is refused must be specified and findings on material issues relevant to the decision as well as particulars of any public interest considerations taken into consideration in making the decisions must be revealed.[191] Where a head of a public body has made a decision appeal lies to the

---

[185] "Spouse" includes (a) a party to a marriage that has been dissolved, being a dissolution that is recognised as valid in the State, or (b) a man or woman who was not married to but cohabited as husband and wife, as the case may be, with the deceased individual. See Freedom of Information Act 1997 (Section 28(6)) Regulations 1999, reg.3(2).

[186] See Freedom of Information Act (Section 6(4)(b)) Regulations 1999 (S.I. No.46 of 1999).

[187] See Freedom of Information Act 1997, s.14(2).

[188] *Ibid.*, s.14(5)(b).

[189] *Ibid.*, s.14(5)(c) as amended by Freedom of Information (Amendment) Act 2003, s.9.

[190] The additional information need not be provided if the refusal is made, inter alia, under s.10(1) (refusal on administrative grounds), s.22(2) (refusal on grounds of legal professional privilege etc); s.23(2) (refusal on grounds of law enforcement and public safety); s.26(4) (refusal where information is obtained in confidence); s.28(5A) (refusal of disclosure of personal information). See Freedom of Information Act 1997, s.14(5) as amended by Freedom of Information (Amendment) Act 2003, s.9.

[191] Freedom of Information Act 1997 14(5)(c) as amended by Freedom of Information (Amendment) Act 2003 s.9 These additional requirements do not apply in situations where disclosure of the existence or non-existence of the record would be contrary to the public interest or would be damaging to certain specified interests.

Information Commissioner.[192] The primary role of the Commissioner is to act as an intermediary between the person requesting access to the record or any part thereof and the head of the public body (in the case of the Health Service Executive the Chief Executive Officer). The Commissioner may affirm, vary or annul the decision of the head of the public body on review.[193] In annulling the decision the Commissioner may "if appropriate make such decision in relation to the matter concerned as he or she considers proper."[194] The Act further provides that a decision on review shall, in so far as it is inconsistent with the decision, which has been reviewed, have effect in lieu thereof.[195] The decision of the Information Commissioner on appeal is binding on the public body.[196] A party to a review or any other person affected by a decision of the Information Commissioner following such a review may appeal to the High Court on a point of law from the decision.[197]

The Interaction of the right of access under the Data Protection Act 1988 as amended and the right of access under the Freedom of Information Act 1997 as amended[198]

1. The definition of personal data in the Data Protection Act 1988 as amended[199] is wider than the definition of personal information[200] which is exempted from disclosure in the Freedom of Information Act 1997. This means that information which falls within the wider definition of personal data in the Data Protection Act 1988 as amended could become subject to disclosure under the Freedom of Information Act

    Personal information, which could include personal data, as defined in the Data Protection Act 1988 could become subject to disclosure under the Freedom of Information Act 1997 where its disclosure is found to be in the public interest.[201]

2. Section 32(1)(a) of the Freedom of Information Act 1997 requires the head of a public body to refuse to grant a request for access to information where disclosure is prohibited by any enactment apart from those provisions listed in the Third Schedule to the 1997 Act. The Data Protection Act 1988 as amended is not listed in the Third Schedule. If the restrictions on processing (which includes disclosure) of personal data in the Data Protection Act 1988 as amended are interpreted as a prohibition on disclosure for the purposes of section 32 of the Freedom of Information Act 1997 the head of a public body would be required to refuse to

---

[192] Freedom of Information Act 1997, s.34 as amended by Freedom of Information (Amendment) Act 2003, s.26.

[193] *Ibid.*, s.34(2)(b).

[194] *Ibid.*, s.34(2)(b)(ii).

[195] *Ibid.*, s.34(14)(a).

[196] *Ibid.*, s.34(14)(b).

[197] *Ibid.*, s.42.

[198] See generally, McDonagh M., *Freedom of Information Law in Ireland* (Round Hall Sweet and Maxwell, Dublin, 1998), pp.373–394.

[199] Data Protection Act 1988, s.1(1) as amended by Data Protection (Amendment) Act 2003, s.2(a)(iv).

[200] Freedom of Information Act 1997, s.2(1).

[201] *Ibid.*, s.28(5).

grant a request for access to such data. Section 2 of the Data Protection Act 1988[202] provides that personal data shall be obtained only for one or more specified, explicit and legitimate purposes and shall not be further processed in a manner incompatible with that purpose or those purposes. For disclosure to be permitted under the Freedom of Information Act, therefore, it would have to be established that disclosure under the Freedom of Information Act was a "legitimate" purpose and it would have to be specified and made explicit to the individual at the time of collection that disclosure under the Freedom of Information Act was one of the purposes for which the data was being collected or such disclosure would have to be listed as one of the purposes of collection of the data in the data controller's entry in the register maintained by the Data Protection Commissioner.[203] On the other hand, section 8 of the Data Protection Act 1988 as amended[204] lists a number of exceptions to the restrictions on processing (including disclosure) of personal data. In particular section 8(e) excepts processing (including disclosures) "required by or under any enactment or by a rule of law or order of a court." McDonagh points out that it could be argued that the right of access to records expressly provided for in section 6 of the Freedom of Information Act 1997 that disclosure of information under the Freedom of Information Act amounts to disclosure "required by or under any enactment"[205] and that accordingly the Data Protection Act 1988 as amended could not be used to restrict disclosure under the Freedom of Information Act 1997 as amended but this position is not free from doubt[206] and much will depend upon how the right to access to information is reconciled with the right to privacy.

It is open to an individual seeking access to personal information to use either the Data Protection Act 1988 or the Freedom of Information Act 1997 to obtain access and if dissatisfied with the outcome of one application to institute an application under the other set of provisions.

3. While the Freedom of Information Act applies only in respect of records held by public bodies the Data Protection Act applies to personal information kept by any data controller.

4. The right of access to personal data under the Data Protection Act 1988 as amended applies to all data kept by a data controller. There is no limit in relation to the age of the data. The Freedom of Information Act 1997 confers a right of access to records created after the commencement of the Act but exceptions to this rule are created in the case of records which (a) are created before the commencement of the Act and access to them is necessary in order to understand records created after the commencement or (b) are created before the commencement of the Act but relate to personal information about the person seeking access to the records. Thus the right of access to personal information applies retrospectively under both pieces of legislation.

5. There are significant differences between the Data Protection Act 1988 as amended

[202] As amended by Data Protection (Amendment) Act 2003, s.3(a).
[203] See Clark, R., *Data Protection Law in Ireland* (The Round Hall Press Dublin, 1990), p.51.
[204] As amended by the Data Protection (Amendment) Act 2003, s.9.
[205] See *Freedom of Information Law in Ireland, op. cit.*, pp.378–379.
[206] See *ibid.*, p.379.

and the Freedom of Information Act 1997 in relation to the question of access to health and social work records. While the refusal of access to records, which, if disclosed, could be damaging to the individual requesting is discretionary under the Freedom of Information Act, it is mandatory under Data Protection (Access Modification) (Health) Regulations[207] and the Data Protection (Access Modification) (Social Work) Regulations.[208]

6.   There is also a difference in the degree of potential harm to the requester, which must exist to bring about a refusal of access. Under the Access Modification Regulations access to health or social work data must be refused "if it would be likely to cause serious harm to the physical or mental health (or, in the case of social work data, the physical or mental health or the emotional condition) of the data subject".[209] Under the Freedom of Information Act there may be a refusal to grant access where, in the opinion of the head of a public body disclosure of the information concerned to the requester "might be prejudicial to his or her physical or mental health or emotional condition."[210] The use of the lower standard "might be prejudicial" in the Freedom of Information Act 1997 means that a refusal of access is more likely under the 1997 Act provisions than under the Data Protection Act.

7.   Where there is a finding that disclosure would be damaging under the Access Modification Regulations the effect is that there may be no disclosure of information . By contrast under the Freedom of Information Act the effect of such a finding does not result in an absolute prohibition of disclosure and provision is made for the release of records to which such access has been denied to "such health professional having expertise in relation to the subject matter of the record as the requester may specify".[211] By implication the health professional will then be able indirectly to release the information to the requester. In both the Access Modification Regulations and the Freedom of Information Act provision is made for the granting of access to an edited version of the health or social work information requested.[212]

The Access Modification Regulations made pursuant to powers in the Data Protection Act 1988 impose an additional general restriction on the disclosure of health or social work data. This restriction applies even where the disclosure would not be damaging to the data subject. The restriction applies first where health data is held by a data controller who is not a health professional and prohibits that data controller from disclosing or withholding such data from an individual to which it relates before consulting with "the appropriate health professional."[213] Where social

---

[207] S.I. No. 82 of 1989.

[208] S.I. No. 83 of 1989.

[209] Data Protection (Access Modification) (Health) Regulations 1989, reg.4(1) and Data Protection (Access Modification) (Social Work) Regulations 1989, reg.4(1).

[210] Freedom of Information Act 1997, s.28(3)(b).

[211] *Ibid.*, s.28(4)(a).

[212] Data Protection (Access Modification) (Health) Regulations 1989, reg.4(2); Data Protection (Access Modification) (Social Work) Regulations 1989, reg.4(2) and Freedom of Information Act 1997, s.13.

[213] "Appropriate health professional" is defined by reg.5(2) of the Data Protection (Access Modification) (Health) Regulations 1989, see above, p.171.

work data includes information supplied to a data controller by a third party (who is not an employee or agent of the data controller) while carrying our social work the data controller is prohibited from disclosing such information to the data subject without first consulting the third party. These additional restrictions are not present in the Freedom of Information Act.

8.   The additional obligations to consult imposed by the Data Protection Act as amended may make it more advantageous and less bureaucratic for a person to apply for access to health or social work records to the head of a public body (in the case of the Health Service Executive the Chief Executive Officer) under the Freedom of Information Act who is not obliged to engage in any consultation process in respect of the release of such records.

9.   There is a difference in the time limits within which access must be granted under both Acts. Under the Data Protection Act 1988 access must be granted within 40 days from the satisfaction by the applicant of the procedural requirements set out un section 4.[214] Decisions under the Freedom of Information Act 1997 regarding access must be made given no later than four weeks after the day on which the request is received.[215]

10. Further a maximum charge of €6.35 can be levied in respect of a request for access to personal data under the data protection legislation,[216] while no charge may be levied in respect of personal information sought under the Freedom of Information Act as amended.[217]

11. Where the right of rectification, blockage or erasure is concerned section 6 of the Data Protection Act 1988 as amended[218] confers in some respects a broader set of rights than section 17 of the Freedom of Information Act. The right of rectification under section 6 of the Data Protection Act as amended applies in respect of data in relation to which there has been a contravention of section 2(1) of the 1988 Act as amended[219] Section 2(1) is a widely framed provision. It provides protection in relation to the obtaining, recording, keeping, collecting, organising, storing, altering, adapting, retrieving, consulting, using, disclosing, aligning, combining, blocking, erasing, destroying, the information or data, the adequacy and relevance of the data, its retention and security. In particular section 6 of the Data Protection Act confers a right of rectification, blockage or erasure where personal data has, in contravention of section 2(1)(a) been unfairly obtained or processed. It also applies in cases where contrary to section 2(1)(c)(ii) personal data kept for certain purpose(s) is processed in a manner incompatible with that/those purpose(s). These rights are not covered within the amendment rights in section 17 of the Freedom of Information Act.

---

[214] Data Protection Act 1988, s.4(1) as amended by Data Protection (Amendment) Act 2003, s.5.
[215] Freedom of Information Act 1997, s.8(1).
[216] Data Protection Act 1988, s.4(1)(c).
[217] Freedom of Information Act 1997, s.47 (6A) (c) as added by Freedom of Information (Amendment) Act 2003, s.30.
[218] The Data Protection Act 1988, s.6 is amended by Data Protection (Amendment) Act 2003, s.7.
[219] The Data Protection Act 1988, s.2(1) is amended by the Data Protection (Amendment) Act 2003, s.3.

12. However, in one significant respect the Data Protection Act rectification rights are more limited than those under the Freedom of Information Act the Data Protection Act does not allow a challenge to be made to the accuracy of a statement of opinion. Section 1(2) of the Data Protection Act 1988 defines "inaccurate" as "incorrect or misleading as to any matter of fact." The Freedom of Information Act, on the other hand appears to cover the amendment of incorrect or misleading opinions in addition to matters of fact.[220]

13. In the case of inaccurate data or data which is out of date the primary remedy under the Data Protection Act is that of the addition to the data of a statement.[221] There is no requirement as there is under the Freedom of Information Act that the statement explains the respects in which the data is inaccurate.[222] The Data Protection Act 1988 does however require that the individual to whom the information relates has assented to the terms of the statement.[223] It is only where agreement cannot be reached that the other remedies of rectification, blockage or erasure come into play. Where data is found to be in adequate under the Data Protection Act 1988 the only remedies available are those of rectification, blockage or erasure. The Freedom of Information Act 1997 provides for a global set of remedies alteration of a record,[224] the addition of a statement to the record[225] and deletion of information from a record,[226] and does not distinguish between the various grounds in the allocation of remedies.

14. Under the Freedom of Information Act where an application for amendment of a record of personal information is unsuccessful, the application or a copy of it must be attached to the record or, if that is not practicable, a notation must be attached indicating that the application has been made unless the application is considered by the public body to be defamatory or the alterations or additions to which it relates would be unnecessarily voluminous.[227] No similar obligation to annotate exists under the Data Protection Act 1988.

15. In terms of time limits the Freedom of Information Act 1997 provides for a decision on amendment to be made within four weeks whereas the Data Protection Act 1988 provides for a time limit of 40 days. However, while the Data Protection Act requires the data controller to comply with the request for rectification blockage or erasure within 40 days of receipt[228] no time limit for compliance is laid down in the Freedom of Information Act 1997.

---

[220] See McDonagh, *op. cit.*, pp.338–340.
[221] Data Protection Act 1988, s.6(1).
[222] Freedom of Information Act 1988, s.17(1) (ii).
[223] Data Protection Act 1988, s.6(1)(a).
[224] Freedom of Information Act 1997, s.17(1)(i).
[225] *Ibid.*, s.17(1)(ii).
[226] *Ibid.*, s.17(1)(iii).
[227] *Ibid.*, s.17(4).
[228] Data Protection Act 1988, s.6(1) as amended by Data Protection (Amendment) Act 2003, s.7.

Commentary on patient's right of access to medical records

Patient's right of access to medical records as reflected in international principles

Principle 19.1 of the *United Nations Principles for the Protection of Persons with Mental Illness and the Improvement of Mental Health Care* begins with the premise that a patient (which term in this Principle includes a former patient) is entitled to have access to the information concerning the patient in his or her health and personal records maintained by a mental health facility. However, this right may be subject to restrictions in order to prevent *serious* harm to the patient's health and avoid putting at risk the safety of others. The Principle then states:

> "As domestic law may provide any such information not given to the patient should when this can be done in confidence be given to the patient's personal representative and counsel. When any of the information is withheld from a patient the patient or the patient's counsel, if any, shall receive notice of the withholding and the reasons for it and it shall be subject to judicial review."

Principle 19.2 provides that any written comments by the patient or the patient's personal representative or counsel must, on request, be inserted in the patient's file.

The Council of Europe *Convention on Human Rights and Biomedicine*[229] provides that everyone has the right to respect to private life in relation to information about his or her health and everyone has the right to know any information collected about his or her health. However, it provides that in *exceptional cases* restrictions may be placed by law on the exercise of the right to know information collected about his or her health in the interests of the patient.

Patient's right of access to medical records in comparative law

Patient's right of access to medical records in English legislation In England in recent years a number of statutes have been enacted conferring on individuals a right to inspect information held by various professionals and bodies about them. The first of these is the Data Protection Act 1984 whose provisions are broadly similar to those of the Irish equivalent enacted in 1988.

The Access to Personal Files Act 1987 entitles an individual to have access to personal information about him/her held by a local authority for the performance of its social services function. The information may be withheld where the local authority believes that access would be likely to result in "serious harm to the person's physical or mental health or emotional condition or that of some other person." The harm must be serious and the Regulations envisage that "withholding of information would be most exceptional." Where a person is dissatisfied with the way the authority has responded representations may be made for the decision to be reviewed by a committee of the authority.

A problem relating to the issue of access to medical records that is not addressed in Irish legislation is the protection of confidential records when the doctor has to prepare

---

[229] Adopted on April 4, 1997 but not yet ratified by Ireland.

a medical report for a third party e.g. an employer or insurance company. The English Access to Medical Reports Act 1988 addresses this by conferring on an individual a right of access to a medical report prepared by a medical practitioner (including a consultant or psychiatrist) which is supplied in connection with employment or insurance purposes relating to that individual.[230] A third party such as an employer or an insurer may only apply to a medical practitioner for such a report where s/he has informed the person concerned that s/he is doing so and has obtained that person's consent.[231] S/he must also inform the person concerned of his/her rights under the Act.[232]

In order to exercise his/her right of access under the Act a person must when giving his consent to the application by the employer or insurance company for a medical report state that he wishes to have access to the report before it is supplied to the third party.[233] "Access" is defined as meaning both a right of inspection and a right to a copy of the report.[234] The medical practitioner is obliged to wait for a period of 21 days before forwarding the report to the third party in the absence of a patient request for access to the report.[235] Where an individual has been given access to a report the report must not be supplied to the third party unless the individual has notified the medical practitioner that he consents to its being so supplied. If the individual considers any part of the report to be inaccurate or misleading s/he may request the medical practitioner to change it. If the latter refuses a statement of the individual's objections must be attached to the report if the person concerned so desires.[236] If the report has been already forwarded to the third party the individual is entitled to access for a subsequent period of up to six months.[237]

As in the 1987 legislation there is an exception to the right of access and a medical practitioner may refuse access to the report where s/he believes that it would "be likely to cause serious harm to the physical or mental health" of the individual or others or would indicate the intentions of the practitioner in respect of the individual or would be likely to reveal the identity of a person who has supplied information about the individual who is not a health professional.[238]

A medical practitioner must keep a copy of the report for a minimum of six months and either make a copy available for inspection by the individual or supply him/her with a copy at a reasonable charge. The medical practitioner must notify the individual if any exempt information is withheld and if it is felt that information is being wrongly withheld or that there is a breach of the provisions application may be made to the court for compliance.[239]

In contrast to the situation in Ireland where there is as yet access to manual records only for specific purposes under the Data Protection (Amendment) Act 2003,[240] the

---

[230] Access to Medical Reports Act 1988, s.1.
[231] *Ibid.*, s.3(1).
[232] *Ibid.*, s.3(2).
[233] *Ibid.*, s.4.
[234] *Ibid.*, s.4(4).
[235] *Ibid.*, s 4(2).
[236] *Ibid.*, s.5.
[237] *Ibid.*, s.6.
[238] *Ibid.*, s.7.
[239] *Ibid.*, s.8.
[240] See s.23(5).

Access to Health Records Act 1990 permits people to see and copy information that has been manually recorded on their health records since November 1991. The Act also offers a definition of a health record which defined as one which (a) consists of information relating to the physical or mental health of an individual who can be identified from that information or from that and other information in the possession of the holder of the record, and (b) has been made by or on behalf of a health professional in connection with the care of that individual.

Both the NHS and private sector fall within the scope of the Act. Where a record is not made in connection with the care of an individual it does not fall within the definition of health records contained in the Act. In this context "care" is defined as including "examination, investigation, diagnosis and treatment."[241]

The 1990 Act also offers a procedural structure regarding patients' rights of access to health records and the doctor's duties in that regard. To obtain access application must be made in writing to the holder of the record, usually the GP or health authority, and access must be given within 40 days.[242] Applicants may inspect a record in person or authorise a representative to do so,[243] and may have photocopies on payment of postage or photocopying costs.

Information which in the record holder's opinion is likely to cause serious harm to the physical or mental health of the patient or of another individual is exempt from disclosure.[244] Applicants do not have the right to be informed where information has been withheld but anyone who suspects that it has may appeal.

A person who has believes part of a record in incorrect, misleading or incomplete may apply for it to be rectified. If the record holder accepts that the information is inaccurate it must be corrected otherwise a note describing the applicant's views is added to the record. In either case a copy of the correction or note must be supplied to the applicant without charge.[245]

An applicant who considers that a record holder is failing to comply with the Act for example by improperly withholding information, refusing to correct information which is inaccurate or acting on the basis of a wholly unreasonable opinion must first exhaust an internal complaints procedure set up by regulations and if having done so is dissatisfied must make application to the court to make an order for compliance.[246]

In the USA the American Psychiatric Association's Model Law on Confidentiality[247] of Health and Social Service Records provides for potentially harmful information to be submitted to a clinical mediator who will decide what will be done with the information. If the patient is dissatisfied with the decision s/he may ask a court to review the material in chambers.

---

[241] Access to Health Records Act 1990, s.11.
[242] *Ibid.*, s.3.
[243] *Ibid.*, s.3(1).
[244] *Ibid.*, s.5(1).
[245] *Ibid.*, s.6(1).
[246] *Ibid.*, s.8.
[247] 136 *Am J. Psychiatry* 137 (1979).

Conclusions in relation to access to medical records

1.   Where the Data Protection Act 1988 is concerned it is submitted that the burden of
     proving a justification for denying a patient access to his or her medical data should
     fall on the person seeking to deny access and the onus should fall upon him/her to
     litigate the matter in the event of a dispute

2.   When a person applies for access to automated medical data s/he also implicitly
     seeks an assurance that that computer data has not been altered in any way. In
     contrast to the static nature of hand-written records new data on computer records
     takes the place of the old without any indication of alteration appearing on the face
     of the record. It is submitted that computer data should be subject to specific
     regulation so that data controllers in the health sector are required to build a
     discernible "audit trail" into the computer programme which would allow previous
     entries and alterations to remain on the record and if required to be recalled. The
     person applying for access should be entitled to the entire trail of information relating
     to him/her.[248]

3.   To prevent the argument arising in the course of a court action that health carers do
     not have an opportunity to defend themselves as records have been destroyed,[249]
     health carers should have a statutory duty to preserve records for a specified length
     of time and if they wish to destroy them they should be obliged to notify the person
     to whom the record relates and offer him/her the opportunity to take a full copy of
     the record.

4.   The 1997 Act gives the important task on deciding on rights of access to medical
     records to the Chief Executive Officer of the Health Service Executive who does
     not have the medical knowledge nor the expertise to make such a decision. It is
     submitted that while the Chief Executive does have power to delegate to a member
     of staff of the Health Service Executive who might be a health professional,[250]
     such a task should primarily be the responsibility of a medical professional with
     expertise in the relevant area of medicine.

5.   It is submitted that section 28(3) of the Irish Freedom of Information Act should be
     amended so that a person may not be denied personal access to information about
     him/her unless it would be likely to result in "serious harm" (as opposed simply to
     being "prejudicial") to the person's health. As presently framed there is a possibility
     that section 28(3) may be applied discriminatorily in practice so as to exclude persons
     with mental illness or intellectual disability as a class from personal access to
     information held about them by a public body.

6.   Regulations made under section 28(6) of the Freedom of Information Act 1997
     permit the parents or guardians to have access to personal information regarding
     their children up to the age of 18. On the other hand under section 23 of the Non
     Fatal Offences Against the Person Act 1997, children over the age 16 may give
     consent to medical treatment and the consent of the parent or guardian is not

---

[248] See Cooney & O'Neill, *op. cit.*, p.289.
[249] See *Toal v. Duignan (No.1)* [1991] I.L.R.M. 135.
[250] See Freedom of Information Act 1997, s.4(1).

necessary. The right to refuse medical treatment is not referred to in this section and it is not clear whether it is implied. It is consequently unclear whether a court would find in favour of parents seeking information under the Freedom of Information Act 1997 about their child aged between 16 and 18 if the child withheld consent.

7.　There is a need for specific legislation dealing with the sensitive issue of access to medical records. This legislation should define what is meant by "medical records" and provide a detailed procedure for exercising the right of access. In this regard the approach of the English Access to Health Records Act 1990 might be adopted.

8.　In general there is also a need for legislation conferring on individuals a right of access to medical records prepared by a medical practitioner which is to be supplied in connection with employment or insurance purposes and a right in appropriate circumstances to apply for rectification of that report.

9.　Also in general where a person is denied access to personal information about him/her on the grounds of the applicant's health the onus should be on the holder of the records to justify the exclusion in court. It is unjust to impose the burden of proof upon the applicant since the information is personal to him/her.

A Patient's Right to Communicate without Undue Censorship

Position under Mental Treatment Act 1945

The Mental Treatment Regulations 1961 provide that where the person in charge of a mental institution "thinks fit" correspondence to or from a patient therein may be examined by him.[251] However, any letter addressed by a patient in a mental institution to the Minister for Health, the President of the High Court, the Registrar of Wards of Court, a mental hospital authority, a visiting committee of a district mental hospital or the Inspector of Mental Hospitals must be forwarded unopened to the addressee.[252] Notices setting forth this right must be kept posted in prominent positions in the mental institution if the Minister for Health so directed or be posted in positions indicated by the Inspector of Mental Hospitals.[253]

　　The Government White Paper acknowledged the wide powers given by the Mental Treatment Act 1961 to restrict a patient's correspondence and recommended that legislation be enacted to protect the right of a detained person to correspond and communicate with a lawyer and with the authority responsible for his/her care. However, the proposals also recommended that the director of an approved centre be empowered to restrict a patient's right to communicate where a complaint is made to the clinical director of the approved centre by the person to whom the communication or letter is directed that a threat has been made to the health or well-being of the person receiving the communication or correspondence or that of any other person.

---

[251] S.I. No. 261 of 1961, art.7.
[252] S.266 of the Mental Treatment Act 1945.
[253] *Ibid.*, s.267.

Position under Mental Health Act 2001

The Mental Health Act 2001 makes no provision whatever for censorship of patient's correspondence. It is possible that this will be provided for in regulations made by the Minister for Health under section 5 of the Act.

Commentary on right to censor patient's correspondence in Irish law

The right to communicate in Irish constitutional law

In domestic law the decisions in *Attorney General v. Paperlink*[254] and *Kearney v Minister for Justice*,[255] recognised that individuals have an unenumerated right to communicate under the Irish Constitution. Article 7 of the Mental Health Regulations 1961, which provides that a person in charge of a mental institution may examine correspondence to, or from a patient detained in a psychiatric institution where he "thinks fit", would appear to breach this constitutional guarantee since it articulates no criteria in terms of public health, public order or public morality for its exercise.

The right to censor patient's correspondence in Irish law and the European Convention on Human Rights and Fundamental Freedoms

Section 2 of the European Convention on Human Rights Act 2003 came into force on December 31, 2003 and requires courts when interpreting and applying Irish domestic legislation to do so in a manner consistently with the Irish state's obligations under the *European Convention on Human Rights*. Article 7 of the Mental Treatment Regulations 1961 would also appear to be inconsistent with Article 10 of the *European Convention of Human Rights 1950,* since it fails to define precisely the scope of the discretionary power to restrict the right to freedom of expression.[256] Article 10 of the *European Convention on Human Rights* provides:

> "Everyone has the right to freedom of expression. This right shall include freedom to hold opinions and to receive and impart information and ideas without interference by public authority and regardless of frontiers. ...
>
> The exercise of these freedoms, since it carries with it duties and responsibilities, may be subject to such formalities, conditions, restrictions and penalties as are prescribed by law and are necessary in a democratic society, in the interests of national security, territorial integrity or public safety, for the prevention of disorder or crime, for the protection of health or morals, for the protection of the reputation or rights of others, for preventing the disclosure of information received in confidence or for maintaining the authority and impartiality of the judiciary."

In *Herczegfalvy*,[257] the European Court of Human Rights held that Article 10 imposes a requirement regarding the quality of the law restricting the right:

---

[254] [1984] I.L.R.M. 373.
[255] [1987] I.L.R.M. 47.
[256] See *Herczegfalvy* (1993) 14 *Human Rights Law Journal* 84 at 88.
[257] (1993) 14 *Human Rights Law Journal* 84 at 88.

"requiring that it should be accessible to the person concerned, who must moreover be able to foresee its consequences for him, and compatible with the rule of law."

It is also necessary that the law specify the scope of the discretion restricting the right. What was said of the provisions in *Herczegfalvy* is equally applicable to Article 7 of the 1961 Regulations:

"These vaguely worded provisions do not specify the scope or conditions of exercise of the discretionary power...but such specifications appear all the more necessary in the field of detention in psychiatric institutions in which the persons concerned are frequently at the mercy of the medical authorities, so that their correspondence is their only contact with the outside world."[258]

A provision such as Article 7 of the 1961 Regulations which gives the person in charge of a mental institution unfettered discretion to withhold patient's mail is too wide and too vague to constitute a justifiable interference with a patient's freedom of expression.

Article 8 of the European Convention on Human Rights provides that everyone is entitled to "respect for his correspondence." Interference by a public body is only permissible where it is:

"necessary in a democratic society in the interests of national security, public safety or the economic well-being of a country, for the prevention of disorder or crime, for the protection of health or morals or for the protection of the right or freedom of others."

In the *Golder* case,[259] the European Court of Human Rights considered this list of exceptions to be finite. The White Paper proposals which permit the restriction of a patient's right to communicate, where a complaint is made to the clinical director of an approved centre that a threat is made to the health or wellbeing of a person other than the recipient of correspondence, would appear to go further than the *Golder* case permits.

The right of the patient to communicate in international law

Article 17 of the *International Covenant on Civil and Political Rights* adopted by the General Assembly in 1966 provides that no one shall be subjected to arbitrary or unlawful interference with his privacy... or correspondence.[260] Principle 19 of the *Body of Principles for the Protection of All Persons under any form of Detention or Imprisonment*,[261] provides for the right of the detained person to adequate opportunity to communicate with the outside world subject to *reasonable* [italics added] conditions and restrictions as specified by law or lawful regulations.

---

[258] *Ibid.*, p.88.
[259] (1975) E.H.R.R. 524.
[260] As mentioned in Chap.2 the machinery for enforcement of this Covenant consists of a procedure whereby the State must report on its legislative and other measures to give effect to the rights by the Covenant to the Human Rights Committee
[261] Adopted by the General Assembly on December 9, 1988.

Article 6 of the *Council of Europe Recommendation R (83)2*[262] *on the legal protection of persons suffering from mental disorder placed as involuntary patients* states that restrictions on personal freedom of the patient should be confined to those which are necessary because of his or her state of health and for the success of the treatment. However, the right of a patient (a) to communicate with any appropriate authority, the person mentioned in Article 4 (i.e. the person designated to advise him on his right of appeal to a court when a decision for involuntary placement is made)[263] and a lawyer, and (b) to send any letter unopened should not be restricted.

This provision recognises that restrictions on communication based on necessity are permitted. However the basic premise of freedom of communication is to be found in *Principle 13 of the UN Principles for the Protection of Persons with Mental Illness and the Improvement of Mental Health Care*[264] which provides that every patient in a Mental Health Facility shall have the right to full respect for his or her freedom of communication which includes freedom to communicate with other persons in the facility; freedom to send and receive uncensored private communications and freedom of access to postal and telephone services.

Comparative law relating to the patient's right to communicate

Restrictions on patient's right to communicate in England and Wales   In England and Wales, a postal packet addressed to any person by a patient detained in a hospital under the Mental Health Act 1983 and delivered by the patient for despatch, may be withheld from the Post Office if the addressee has requested[265] that communications addressed to him by the patient should be withheld.[266] It may also be withheld,[267] subject to certain exceptions, if the hospital is a special hospital and the managers of the hospital consider that the postal packet is likely (i) to cause distress to the person to whom it is addressed or to any other person (not being a person on the staff of the hospital), or (ii) to cause danger to any person.[268] Incoming mail to a patient detained in a special hospital under the Act may be withheld[269] from the patient, if, in the opinion of the managers of the hospital, it was necessary to do so in the interests of the safety of the patient or for the protection of other persons.[270] The managers of the hospital may inspect and open any packet for the purposes of determining whether it is a packet to which any of the above criteria apply and if so, whether it should be withheld.[271]

---

[262] Adopted on February 22, 1983.

[263] Art.4 provides for a person whose duty it is to assist the patient to decide whether to appeal to be designated by the appropriate authority when a decision for involuntary placement is made.

[264] Adopted by the General Assembly on December 17, 1991.

[265] Requests must be made in writing given to the managers of the hospital, the registered medical practitioner in charge of the treatment of the patient or the Secretary of State. See Mental Health Act 1983, s.134(3).

[266] Mental Health Act 1983, s.134(1)(a).

[267] The power to withhold a packet under s.134(1) includes power to withhold anything in it. Mental Health Act 1983, s.134(5).

[268] Mental Health Act 1983, s.134(1)(b).

[269] The power extends to withholding anything in the packet. Mental Health Act 1983, s.134(5).

[270] Mental Health Act 1983, s.134(2).

[271] *Ibid.*, s.134(4).

However, certain specified correspondence may not be withheld. This includes mail from any of the following:

(a) any Minister of the Crown or Member of either House of Parliament,

(b) a Master or officer of the Court of Protection or Lord Chancellor's Visitor,

(c) any of the Ombudsmen (the Parliamentary Commissioner for Administration, Health Service Commissioners for England, or Wales and Local Government Commissioners within the meaning the Local Government Act 1974),

(d) a Mental Health Review Tribunal, a health authority, local social services authority, Community Health Council or probation and after care committee,

(e) the managers of the hospital in which the patient is detained, any legally qualified person instructed by the patient to act as his legal advisor,

(f)   and the European Commission of Human Rights or the European Court of Human Rights.[272]

If a hospital censor does inspect and open a postal packet, but does not withhold anything, the Mental Health (Hospital, Guardianship and Consent to Treatment) Regulations 1983[273] require that he put a written note of that fact along with his name and that of the hospital inside the packet before resealing it. If he decides to withhold the packet or anything in it, he must enclose a note to the same effect describing any item withheld. He must also record in a special register the fact that the packet has been withheld, the date when this was done, the grounds for it, a description of the items and his name.[274]

Where a postal packet or anything in it is withheld on the wider grounds applicable only to special patients the managers of the hospital must give notice of that fact to the patient and to the sender of the packet (if known).[275] The notice must be given in writing. [276] It must also set out the grounds for withholding the packet and the name of the censor and hospital.[277] The notice must also give an explanation of the Mental Health Act Commission's powers of review. All of these details must be included in the note enclosed with the packet in which case they are sufficient notice to the person to whom it is addressed.[278] A separate notice must be sent to the sender.

Where it is requested to do so by the patient or by the person by whom incoming mail was sent the Mental Health Act Commission must review the decision of the manager of a special hospital to withhold mail. [279] Application to the Commission must be made within six months of receipt by the applicant of the notice that the mail was withheld and the application should include that notice.[280] The Commission has power to direct

---

[272] *Ibid.*, s.134(3).
[273] Reg.17(1).
[274] Mental Health Act 1983, s.134(5) and Mental Health (Hospital, Guardianship and Consent to Treatment) Regulations 1983, reg.17(2).
[275] Mental Health Act 1983, s.134(6).
[276] *Ibid.*
[277] Mental Health (Hospital, Guardianship and Consent to Treatment) Regulations 1983, reg.17(3).
[278] *Ibid.*, reg.17(2) and (3).
[279] Mental Health Act 1983, s.121(7).
[280] *Ibid.* See also Mental Health (Hospital, Guardianship and Consent to Treatment) Regulations 1983, reg.17(3).

the production of any documents, information or evidence that they reasonably require including the letter withheld.[281] The Commission has an absolute discretion to overrule the hospital's decision to withhold the packet or anything contained in it.[282]

Restrictions on patient's right to communicate in Canada   In the province of Ontario in Canada, a patient's mail may be examined and withheld only if there is reasonable and probable cause to believe that the contents of the communications would be unreasonably offensive to the addressee or prejudicial to the best interests of the patient (in the case of outgoing mail), or would interfere with the patient's treatment or cause him unnecessary distress (in the case of incoming mail).[283] Written communications between a patient and a barrister and solicitor, a member of the Review Board and a member of the Legislative Assembly cannot be examined or withheld nor can written communications to the Ombudsman.[284] Similar provisions are found in New Brunswick and the Northwest Territories.[285] In Nova Scotia, outgoing mail cannot be examined or withheld but the contents of incoming mail (but not correspondence itself) may be removed if they would be detrimental to the patient.[286]

Conclusions

1. A patient's right to communicate should be protected by legislation. This statutory protection should extend to guaranteeing a patient the right to receive incoming correspondence and to send outgoing correspondence.

2. The clinical director should be permitted to examine incoming correspondence if there is reasonable and probable cause to believe that the correspondence contains substances or devices which may result in harm to the patient or others.

3. Written communications between the patient and a member of the Mental Health Commission or of a Mental Health Tribunal, a member of the Dáil, the Ombudsman, the European Commission on Human Rights and the European Court of Human Rights should not capable of being examined or withheld.

4. Interference should not be permitted with outgoing correspondence unless it is addressed to someone who notifies the clinical director in writing that he or she does not wish to receive correspondence from the patient.[287]

5. Where a hospital censor exercises his discretion to inspect and open a postal packet and/or to withhold its contents, s/he should be required to notify the patient of that fact by note in the packet. This note should indicate the name of the censor, that of

---

[281] Mental Health (Hospital, Guardianship and Consent to Treatment) Regulations 1983, reg.17(3).
[282] Mental Health Act 1983, s.121(8).
[283] R.S.O. 1980, c.262, s.0(2).
[284] Ombudsman Act R.S.O. 1980, c. 325, s.17(2) [re-en. 1984, c.55, s.225].
[285] S.N.W.T. 1985 (2nd), c.6, s.37 (not yet proclaimed).
[286] R.S.N.S. 1967, c.249, s.62(1), (2), (3) [all en. 1977, c.45, s.8].
[287] In other jurisdictions the power to withhold outgoing mail on the ground that it is likely to cause danger to any person (including a member of the hospital staff) or to cause distress to any person (other than a member of the hospital staff) may only be exercised censors in special hospitals. See Mental Health Act 1983 (UK), s.134.

the hospital and contain a description of the item (if any) withheld. The censor should also be required to record in a special register details of the withholding of the packet, a description of the items withheld, the date when it was done, the grounds for it and the censor's name.

6. Current criteria for censorship do not hold the person in charge of a mental institution accountable for his actions. A patient or person by whom incoming mail was sent, should have a right to apply to the Mental Health Tribunal for review of the hospital's decision to withhold incoming mail.

A PATIENTS RIGHT TO CONFIDENTIALITY AND PRIVACY[288]

Current law

A duty of confidentiality arises:

> "when confidential information comes to the knowledge of a person...in circumstances where he has notice or is held to have agreed that the information is confidential, with the effect that it would be just in all the circumstances that he should be precluded from disclosing the information to others." [289]

The medical practitioner's duty of confidentiality arises from three distinct sources. First it may be accepted if s/he voluntarily enters into a contract containing a term imposing a duty of confidentiality; secondly, even if such a contractual term is not agreed upon a medical practitioner has a duty in equity to respect his/her patient's confidences. This arises from the relationship of trust which exists between medical practitioner and patient[290] and thirdly, the practitioner owes a moral duty of confidentiality to his/her patient. This is based of the codes of ethics adopted by the medical profession.

There is an overlap between the legal and ethical duties of a medical practitioner. Indeed it has been judicially stated that the "legal common law duty is nothing else than the enforcing by law of that which is a moral obligation without legal enforcement"[291] The *Guide to Ethical Conduct and Behaviour*, issued by the Irish Medical Council,[292] recognises that:

> "Confidentiality is a time honoured principle of medical ethics. It extends after death and is fundamental to the doctor/patient relationship."

---

[288] See generally O'Neill, "Matters of Discretion – The Parameters of Doctor/Patient Confidentiality" (1995) Vol.1(3) *Medico-Legal Journal of Ireland* 94.

[289] *A.G. v. Guardian Newspapers Ltd (No.2)* [1988] 3 All E.R 545 at pp.658–659 *per* Lord Goff (the Spycatcher case).

[290] See *Stephens v. Avery* [1988] 1 Ch. 449 in which it was held that the duty existed even in the absence of contract between the parties by virtue of an equitable obligation imposed on the receiver of confidential information not to take unfair advantage of it, *per* Browne Wilkinson V.C. at p.456.

[291] Lord Coleridge C.J. in *R v. Instan* [1893] 1 Q.B. 450 at 453.

[292] Fifth Edition 1998, approved by the Medical Council, Ireland at its meeting on June 30, 1998 and published in Dublin, November 1998.

While a medical practitioner's legal duty in relation to confidentiality is not co-extensive with the rules on confidentiality set out in the *Guide to Ethical Conduct* the latter may provide admissible evidence of the standards to which a reasonably careful skilled and informed practitioner should adhere to in an action for breach of confidence, negligence or of the nature of terms which may be implied in a contract between medical practitioner and patient.[293]

Information received by a medical practitioner about a patient in a professional capacity must not be disclosed to any third party without the patient's consent. Similar considerations apply to information about a patient obtained in a professional capacity from a third party,[294] and that in this regard the medical practitioner is effectively regarded as being in a fiduciary relationship with the patient.[295]

The need to protect medical confidences is clear for if a patients' right to confidentiality is not protected, s/he may fear to speak openly to his/her medical practitioner about his/her medical problems. This is essential if the practitioner is to be in a position to make an accurate diagnosis of the patient's condition. This accordingly is the public interest in confidentiality. However, there is a second public interest that in freedom of speech which sometimes conflicts with this. In the event of conflict,[296] the courts have referred to accepted practice in the medical profession in order to delimit the boundaries of these interests.

The *Irish Medical Council's Guide*[297] recognises that there are circumstances when exceptions may be made to the duty of confidentiality. Thus confidential information may be disclosed where a patient gives consent to the disclosure of information to third parties [298] Disclosure may be made in the absence of permission from the patient only in four stated circumstances:

(a) when ordered by a judge in a court of law or by a Tribunal of Inquiry established by an Act of the Oireachtas;

(b) when necessary to protect the interests of the patient;

(c) when necessary to protect the welfare of society;

(d) when necessary to safeguard the welfare of another individual or patient.[299]

---

[293] [1958] N.Z.L.R. 396 at 404.
[294] See *A Guide to Ethical Conduct and Behaviour* (6th ed., 2004), para.16.1.
[295] Newspaper reports in February 1997 indicated that an inquiry had been carried out into the disclosure by a consultant of certain information he had received in respect of a patient from a third party- who was not his patient after that third party's death. It was reported that the consultant had been censured by the Medical Council for the disclosure. The censure was capable of being appealed to the High Court.
[296] The conflict is reflected in Art.10 of the European Convention on Human Rights which states the fundamental freedom of expression but then qualifies it by providing for an exception preventing the disclosure of information received in confidence.
[297] The Guide is not intended to be a Code but rather a "Guide by which individual members of the profession may judge particular situations", see para.1.2.
[298] Para.18.1.
[299] Para.18.3.

Disclosure where the patient has consented to the disclosure to third parties

As a matter of law it has been held that a positive consent to a release of information elides any obligation of secrecy owed by the person receiving the consent.[300] For the consent to be effective, it must be fully informed and freely given and the medical practitioner must not exceed its terms.

Issues regarding a patient's capacity to consent to disclosure may arise in cases where a patient is mentally ill or intellectually disabled. In such cases caution should be exercised. This will include safeguarding against the possibility of undue influence by third parties, obtaining specialist advice as to whether the patient has the capacity to understand the nature of confidentiality and the implications of disclosure, and assuming that the patient has the capacity to consent to the disclosure communicating with him/her in a manner that will enable him/her to understand fully the nature of the proposed course of action.

Where minors are concerned, the Non-Fatal Offences against the Person Act 1997 stipulates that the age of 16 as the age at which the consent of a minor to medical treatment shall be as effective as it would be if s/he were of full age. By implication the consent of a 16 year old to disclosure of confidential information relating to that treatment is also effective. However, below this age common law does not specify any age at which a child is held to have capacity to consent to the disclosure of confidential information. However, on the authority of the House of Lords decision in *Gillick v. West Norfolk and Wisbech Area Health Authority*,[301] it is submitted that a child would be competent to consent to the disclosure without parental consent, if s/he fully comprehended the nature of the secrecy and the consequences of the decision to disclose. Where a child is incapable of understanding the nature of the course proposed but the medical practitioner forms the view that the disclosure would be in the child's best interests then legally effective consent may be given on the child's behalf by a parent.[302]

In the majority of cases it is desirable that the patient's express consent in writing be obtained to the disclosure of clinical information. However, it has been accepted that a patient impliedly consents to the disclosure of clinical information in three distinct situations.

First a medical practitioner treating a patient has implied authority to inform other health care professionals involved in his/her care about his/her condition. The accepted approach appears to be that in these circumstances[303] there should be disclosure only in so far as is required to provide optimum care and steps should be taken to ensure that the health care professionals to whom information has been disclosed are made subject to the same obligation of confidentiality as the treating doctor.[304]

Secondly, a medical practitioner has implied authority to make disclosure in the interests of teaching and medical research. While it is preferable to obtain the express consent of patients where it is proposed to provide confidential information about them

---

[300] *C v. C* [1946] 1 All E.R. 562.
[301] [1985] 3 All E.R. 402.
[302] See Donnelly, "Capacity of Minors to Consent to Medical and Contraceptive Treatment", 1(1) *Medico-Legal Journal of Ireland* (1995) 18.
[303] See Kennedy and Grubb, *Medical Law: Text with Materials* (Butterworths, London, 1994), pp. 644–645.
[304] See *Guide to Ethical Coduct and Behaviour* (6th ed., 2004), para.16.4.

to *bona fide* medical researchers or students, it is likely that no action for breach of confidence would lie if details of a patient's condition from which no personal identification could be made were passed to medical researchers.

Thirdly, doctors are encouraged to report evidence of adverse reactions to drugs administered by them to the National Drugs Advisory Board.[305] In practice these reports are usually made without identification of the patient In exceptional cases where it might be necessary to identify the patient and his/her condition the disclosure is very restricted and the duties and responsibilities of those employed by the Board in relation to the handling of the information are subject to strict guidelines.

Where disclosure is required by a judge in a court of law or by a tribunal established by an Act of the Oireachtas

Discovery of medical records may be ordered either during the course of litigation or during the course of an inquiry, pursuant to the provisions of the Tribunal of Inquiries (Evidence) Acts 1921 and 1979. However, following the enactment of section 45(1) of Court and Court Officers Act 1995 the number of situations in which discovery may be ordered during the course of litigation has been reduced. Pursuant to the power contained in this section an amendment to the Superior Court Rules was made[306] with effect from September 1, 1997 requiring the parties to a personal injuries action[307] to exchange copies of reports[308] from expert witnesses intended to be called at the trial.[309] Where there has been non-compliance with the rules the court has discretion to prohibit the adducing of evidence in relation to which the non-compliance relates or may adjourn the action to permit compliance.[310]

The Irish Medical Council's Guide to Ethical Conduct and Behaviour states that a medical practitioner has a responsibility to supply medical reports to a patient's solicitor on receipt of a request for such a report. However, such reports should not be given without the patient's permission.[311]

The report must be factual and true. It is not to be influenced by pressure from

---

[305] By virtue of the National Drugs Advisory Board (Establishment) Order 1966 (S.I. No.163 of 1966). Art.4(a) the Board is charged with the responsibility of organising and administering a service for obtaining and assessing information as regards the safety of new and reformulated drugs and, in particular their toxicity and other adverse effects.

[306] See Rules of the Superior Courts (No.6) (Disclosure of Reports and Statements) 1988 (S.I. No.391 of 1998).

[307] But not an action to which s.1(3) of the Courts Act 1988 applies so as to entitle a party to trial by jury in that action. S.1(3) applies, *inter alia*, (a) to actions where the damages claimed consist only of damages for false imprisonment or intentional trespass to the person or both and (b) actions where the damages claimed consist of the foregoing and damages for another cause of action in respect of the same act or omission or (c) to a question of fact or an issue arising in an action referred to in (a) or (b). See O.39, r.45(1)(a).

[308] Defined in the rules to include a report or reports or statement from, *inter alia*, doctors, occupational therapists, psychologists, psychiatrists, scientist or any other expert whatsoever intended to be called to give evidence in relation to an issue in an action and containing the substance of the evidence to be adduced. See O.39, r.45(1)(e).

[309] See O.39, r.46(1).

[310] See O.39, r.48.

[311] Irish Medical Council, *A Guide to Ethical Conduct and Behaviour* (2004), para.8.1.

anyone to omit some details or to embellish others and strict accuracy must be observed. It should concentrate on the relevant medical problem.[312]

The confidential information disclosed in medical reports to solicitors is subject to legal professional privilege. This privilege protects the confidentiality of communications between solicitor and client and extends to a medical report sent by a medical practitioner to the solicitor concerning the patient. For legal professional privilege to apply there must be a proposal to instigate legal proceedings or such proceedings must already have been issued. Further, the primary purpose in drafting the medical report must be the purpose of litigation. The privilege does not apply to reports whose primary purpose is for accident investigation and prevention rather than litigation.

Where an order for discovery is made in court it may be made either against an individual who is a proper party to the proceedings or against the institution or persons (such as a medical practitioner) who hold the individual's records. Where a litigant refuses to disclose his medical records which the other party claims to be relevant to the proceedings, an order for discovery may be made if the court is satisfied that the documents sought to be disclosed are relevant. Rarely the records of a person who is not a party to the litigation may be discovered.[313] An institution or person served with such an order might consider it prudent to notify the patient whose records are sought.[314] This would permit the patient who had not been a notice party to the application to make appropriate appeals or objections.

In the cases where a medical practitioner is called to appear as a witness in court he cannot claim any privilege in court in respect of confidences imparted to him by his patient.[315] In *Hunter v. Mann*,[316] Lord Widgery stated:

> "If a doctor is asked in court a question which he finds embarrassing because it involves him in talking about things which he would normally regard as confidential he can seek protection from the judge and ask if answering is necessary. The judge, by virtue of the overriding discretion to control his court which all … judges have, could tell the doctor that he does not need to answer the question. Whether or not the judge would take that line depends largely on the importance of the potential answer to the issue being tried."

While judges may go to considerable lengths to preserve confidences,[317] a medical practitioner *is* bound to answer any question which are put to him as a witness in court

---

[312] *Ibid.*, para.8.2.

[313] The Tribunal of Inquiry into the Blood Transfusion Service Board (The "Finlay" Inquiry March 1997) ordered discovery of the clinical and laboratory records of certain patients who had been treated with the Board's products where those records were considered to be central to the issues the Tribunal had to determine. Similar orders were made by the High Court in related litigation. In such circumstances a masking order such that the identity of the person to whom the records relate cannot be ascertained may also be made.

[314] In any event any practice of not notifying the party concerned must be questionable. See *Haughey v. Moriarty*, unreported, Supreme Court, July 28, 1998.

[315] *Attorney General v. Mulholland and Attorney General v. Foster* [1963] 2 Q.B. 477.

[316] [1974] Q.B. 767.

[317] This may include the judge's first perusing the evidence in private. See Kloss, *Occupational Health Law* (2nd ed., Blackwell Scientific Publications, Oxford, 1994), p.82.

and if the court does not exercise its discretion to excuse the conscientious witness a refusal to answer will expose the practitioner to a charge of contempt.[318] However, as far as exposure to suit for breach of confidence is concerned the medical practitioner's evidence given in the witness box is absolutely privileged. This is "settled in law and cannot be doubted."[319] Moreover this privilege extends to pre-trial conferences but is lost if the communication is malicious the privilege is lost.[320]

When disclosure is necessary to protect the interest of the patient

The word "protect" in this exception suggests that the patients interests must be threatened in some way before the exception may be relied upon and the term "necessary" appears to imply that the nature and amount of information disclosed be proportionate to the protection required. It would also appear to require the disclosure to be made only to such persons who need to know such information if the necessary protection is to be afforded to the patient's interests. In practice the exception may be of some assistance in cases where a medical practitioner suspects parental abuse of a child patient or in cases of abuse of a patient with mental illness or intellectual disability where a doctor is uncertain of the patient's capacity to consent to the disclosure. In general it is preferable in the interests of development of trust in the doctor/patient relationship for the medical practitioner to use all reasonable efforts to obtain the patient's consent to disclosure first and to rely on this exception as a last resort only when all powers of persuasion have failed. Ultimately the decision whether disclosure is necessary to protect the patient's interests is a matter of medical judgment and if challenged the medical practitioner may have to justify his decision by reference to the general and approved professional practice in the circumstances.[321]

Where disclosure is necessary to protect the welfare of society

This is the most controversial exception to the rule of confidentiality perhaps because it its premises are general in nature and undefined. "Welfare" may cover anything which contributes to the well being or is to the benefit of society as a whole and equally "society" comprises a diverse range of different groups whether they be regional, political, economic or based on age. The nature of the harm which must be shown if the exception is to be invoked is not defined nor is the degree of risk which necessitates disclosure. Moreover, it would appear that this ethical exception to the rule of confidentiality is rather narrower than the legal exception which would permit a breach of confidence which is in the "public interest."[322] However, since the latter expression has not been precisely defined it is likely that in cases of breach of medical confidence the courts will have regard to the professional standard and construe it narrowly.

Statutory provisions require the notification to public health authorities of persons

---

[318] *Garner v. Garner* (1920) 36 *Times Law Reports* 196.
[319] *Watson v. McEwan* [1905] A.C. 480.
[320] *AB v. CD* (1904) 7 F. 72.
[321] See *Dunne v. National Maternity Hospital* [1989] I.R. 91.
[322] See *Lion Laboratories Ltd v. Evans* [1984] 2 All E.R. 417.

known or suspected to be suffering from certain infectious diseases.[323] Where communicable diseases are concerned the Medical Council's *Guide to Professional Conduct* provides that (at para.16.9):

> "Certain communicable disease are notifiable by statute. Such notifications should preferably be made with the informed consent of the patient. In cases where informed consent is not provided reporting should be to the relevant authority but should observe the patient's confidentiality in all other respects. Where others may be at risk if not aware that a patient has a serious infection, a doctor should do his/her best to obtain permission from the patient permission to tell them, so that appropriate safeguards can be put in place."[324]

If the patient refuses to consent to the disclosure the Council considers that that those who might be at risk of infection while treating the patient should be informed of the risk to themselves. They in turn would, of course, be bound by the general rules of confidentiality.[325]

Disclosure when necessary to safeguard the welfare of another individual or patient

The fourth exception to the general obligation of confidentiality permits disclosure when necessary to safeguard the welfare of another individual or patient. There appears to be little Irish authority on the freedom of a doctor to disclose a confidence imparted to him by a patient when this is necessary to safeguard the welfare of another individual or patient. However, in the Californian case of *Tarasoff v. Regents of the University of California*,[326] the Supreme Court of California held by a majority that a cause of action could be established against a psychologist and his superior, both employees of the defendant institution in whom a patient had confided an intention to kill the deceased Tatiana Tarasoff on the grounds that their patient presented a serious danger of violence to the deceased and they failed to exercise reasonable care to protect her from that danger.[327]

The question is whether the *Tarasoff* decision would be followed in this country. It is submitted that much would depend upon the courts view of the proximity of the relationship between the injured plaintiff and defendant psychiatrist. The more foreseeable the harm and the more readily identifiable the victim the more likely it is that an Irish court will find that a duty of care arises.[328]

---

[323] Health Act 1947 and the Infectious Disease Regulations, Public Health (Control of Disease) Act 1984.

[324] Para.16.9.

[325] Para.16.9.

[326] Sup. 131 Cal. Rptr. 14 (1976).

[327] Subsequent cases have extended the ambit of the Tarasoff decision so as to impose a duty of a medical practitioner to warn whenever it is foreseeable that persons will be endangered by the patient. See *Davis v. Lhim* (1983) 335 N.W. 2d. 481 (Mich. Sup. Ct). On the other hand other authorities have limited its application to cases where the particular victim is readily identifiable *Thompson v. County Alameda* (1980) 614 P. 2d 728 (California Sup. Ct).

[328] For the English perspective see Michael Jones, *Medical Negligence* (Sweet & Maxwell, London, 1992), paras 2.62–2.66 and 2.68.

The question of whether a medical practitioner has a duty of disclosure where he discovers that his patient has just committed or is about to commit a grave offence in general is a vexing one It appears to be accepted[329] that it may be justifiable for a medical practitioner to provide information to the police if s/he becomes aware that his patient has committed or is likely to commit a criminal offence and if s/he forms the view that on balance that to do so is in the public interest. In making the decision account should be taken of the seriousness of the offence and the potential damage to the public arising from non-disclosure.[330]

The English decision in *W v. Egdell*[331] provides an interesting example of the operation of the principles. In this case W was detained as a patient in a secure hospital after he had shot and killed five people and wounded two others. Ten years after he had been first detained he applied to a mental health review tribunal for discharge or transfer to a regional secure unit with a view to eventual discharge. His application was supported by his responsible medical officer but opposed by the Secretary of State. W's solicitors instructed Dr Egdell to examine W and report on his mental condition with a view to using his report to support W's application to the tribunal. In his report Dr Egdell opposed W's transfer and recommended further tests and treatment drawing attention to W's longstanding interest in firearms and explosives. W subsequently withdrew his application from the tribunal. When Dr Egdell learned that neither the tribunal nor the secure hospital had received a copy of his report he contacted the medical director of the hospital who having discussed the matter with Dr Egdell agreed that the hospital should receive a copy of the report in the interests of W's further treatment. At Dr Egdell's prompting the hospital sent a copy of his report to the Secretary of State who in turn sent the report to the tribunal when referring W's case to them for consideration. W subsequently issued proceedings against Dr Egdell and the recipients of the report seeking, *inter alia*, an injunction to restrain them from using or disclosing the report and damages for breach of confidence. W's proceedings against Dr Egdell and the recipients of the report were dismissed by Scott J. His subsequent appeal to the Court of Appeal was also dismissed. The Court of Appeal held that in the circumstances Dr Egdell was entitled, out of a fear to real risk to public safety, to take reasonable steps to communicate to the appropriate authorities the grounds of his concern relating to the transfer of W from the secure hospital to a regional secure unit.

It is interesting to note the recent decision of the Supreme Court of Canada in *Smith v. Jones*[332] which has broadened the public interest exception to confidentiality to enable disclosure where there is a potential risk not only to an identifiable person to also to a class of victims. In that case "Jones" was charged with aggravated sexual assault on a

---

[329] Mason and McCall Smith, Butterworths *Medico-Legal Encyclopaedia* (Butterworths, London, 1987), p. 115.

[330] Account should also be taken of s.7 of the Criminal Law Act 1997 which provides that where a person has committed an arrestable offence i.e. one punishable by at least five years imprisonment any other person who, knowingly or believing him to be guilty of the offence or of some other arrestable offence does without reasonable excuse any act with intent to impede his apprehension or prosecution shall be guilty of an offence. Note however that the provision only applies to acts, it does not apply to omissions and failures to act.

[331] [1990] Ch. 359.

[332] (1999) 132 C.C.C. (3d.) 225.

prostitute. His counsel referred him to "Dr Smith,"[333] a psychiatrist for the purpose of preparing a defence or drafting a submission for sentencing in the event of a guilty plea. During the examination Jones told Dr Smith that he had deliberately chosen a small woman who could be easily overwhelmed as his victim and that he had planned to rape, kidnap and kill her and that this would be a "trial run" to see whether he could "live with" what he had done. If he could, he planned to carry out further rapes and killings of prostitutes. Following the examination Dr Smith telephoned Jones counsel and told him that in his opinion Jones was a dangerous person who would, more likely than not, commit future offences unless he received sufficient medical treatment. Dr Smith subsequently heard from Jones counsel that he would not be called to give evidence and having discovered this sought a declaration that he was entitled to disclose the information he had in his possession in the interests of public safety. Since the communications between Jones and Dr Smith attracted solicitor-client privilege (given that they were made for the purposes of preparing a possible legal defence or sentencing hearing) the decision was approached by way of public interest exception to solicitor-client privilege. At first instance the judge ruled that Dr Smith was under a duty to disclose both the accused's statements and Dr Smith's own opinions regarding Jones' dangerousness to the police and the Crown. On appeal the British Columbia Court of Appeal allowed Jones appeal to the extent that the mandatory order was changed to a discretionary one permitting rather than requiring Dr Smith to disclose the relevant information. When Jones appealed to the Supreme Court of Canada the court by a majority of six to three dismissed his appeal on the grounds that solicitor-client privilege may be set aside when there is a danger to the public safety and death or serious bodily harm is imminent.

Cory J. delivering the judgment of the majority outlined three factors which should be considered in weighing up whether confidentiality should be breached in the interest of public safety:

First, is there a clear risk to an identifiable person or group of persons? Second, is there a risk of serious bodily harm or death? Third, is the danger imminent?[334]

In relation to the first criterion Cory J. widened the parameters of the public interest exception to include warning a large threatened group provided it was clearly identifiable. He cited examples of a threat to seriously injure children of five years of age and under, or single women living alone in apartment buildings. In relation to the second criterion, Cory J. framed the notion of serious bodily harm in terms of the public interest exception broadly by stating that "serious psychological harm" may constitute serious bodily harm. Thirdly in relation to the factor of the imminence of the danger, Cory J. stated:

"The nature of the threat must be such that it creates a sense of urgency. This sense of urgency may be applicable to some time in the future. Depending on the seriousness and clarity of the threat, it will not always be necessary to impose a particular time limit on the risk. It is sufficient if there is a clear and imminent threat of serious bodily harm to an identifiable group, and if this threat is made in such a manner that a sense of urgency is created." [335]

---

[333] "Smith" and "Jones" were pseudonyms employed by the court.
[334] (1999) 132 C.C.C. (3d.) 225 at 249.
[335] *Ibid.* at 251.

McSherry[336] notes that among the difficulties created by the *Smith v. Jones* decision is the possibility that the broadening of the public interest exception will lead health professionals to "err on the side of caution by breaching confidentiality in many more situations that is absolutely necessary,"[337] and the fact that it is not clear from the decision of the Supreme Court of Canada as to who should be contacted in the public interest.[338]

Medical practitioners undertaking specific obligations to report to third parties

Medical practitioners who are in a position where they undertake obligations to conduct a medical examination and to report to a third party in relation to certain categories of patient encounter particular difficulties in relation to the issue of confidentiality. These include medical practitioners in public health,[339] occupational physicians, prison medical officers, doctors employed by and/or acting for An Garda Síochána,[340] Defence Forces,[341] and the Civil Service.

Paragraph 16.6 of the *Medical Council's Guide to Ethical Conduct* (6th edition, 2004) is relevant to all of the above categories. It states in relation to all situations which require doctors to report to third parties subsequent to medical examinations certain principles must be observed namely:

Before commencing such examinations the doctor should explain the nature, context and reporting implications of the examination and should have consent form from the patient before proceeding. Doctor's reports should be factual and true. They are not to be influenced by the fee or by pressure from anyone to omit some details or to embellish others and strict accuracy must be observed. They should concentrate on relevant medical problems.

Normally the patient's general practitioner should be informed, provided that consent is obtained. The significance rather than the precise details of the medical findings should be conveyed to any third party and under confidential cover.

---

[336] See McSherry, "Confidential Communications between Clients and Mental Health Care Professionals: The Public Interest Exception" (2002) *Irish Jurist* 269.

[337] *Ibid.*, p.279.

[338] *Ibid.*, p.280.

[339] Where a doctor is obliged by statutory requirements to provide doctor in public health medicine with medical information which may be essential if the payment of a financial allowance is to be recommended the public health physician is not obliged to release the specific details but may interpret them to the administrative authority concerned with the patient's consent. See para.18.8 of the *Guide to Ethical Conduct and Behaviour*.

[340] Doctors employed by and/or acting for An Garda Síochána should have regard to the fact that accused persons are presumed innocent and have the same rights of confidentiality as any member of the public . They must accordingly state that the result of their examination will be reported to third parties and cannot proceed to examine if as a result consent is refused.

[341] The obligations of confidentiality owed by medical officers to individual soldiers who are their patients is basically the same as that owed to civilians but in this context the obligation of the doctor to disclose when it is necessary to protect the welfare of society is refocused in terms of a duty of disclosure when it is necessary to protect the welfare of the military unit – since the lives of others may dependent on the patient. Accordingly there is a more compelling justification for disclosure than would exist in civilian practice and the recruit is deemed to accept this on enlisting in the army The disclosures however must still be justified. See Mason and McCall Smith, *op. cit.*, p.189.

The above principles apply to doctors reporting to employers. In addition an occupational physician is entitled to present to an employer the significant aspects of a medical condition which he may discover as a result of an examination and will usually be obliged by contract to do so. In this case, however, as a matter of law the employer may only have access to the patient's *medical record* with the consent of the patient and then only in specifically agreed circumstances. Where the patient refuses to consent to disclosure the patient's confidentiality must be respected.[342] Where an employee is suing in respect of a work related injury or disease it may be necessary to obtain a court order for disclosure.

Where a medical examination is carried out for the purposes of a contract between an individual and an insurance company the following principles should be borne in mind. It is a settled principle of insurance law that the failure of the assured person to disclose any material fact within his actual or presumed knowledge renders the insurance contract voidable at the instance of the insurers.[343] However, where an assured person is unaware of the existence of a medical condition at the time he executes the policy[344] or where the terms of the policy limit the amount of disclosure required so that he completes the policy accurately but does not make full disclosure[345] it appears that the insurance company would not be entitled to avoid the contract.

The Irish Medical Council[346] advises medical practitioners requested by an insurance company to complete a medical record on a patient to ensure that this is not issued without the consent of the patient. Patients should also be informed that such reports will be read by non-medical personnel and as a matter of practice the reports should be sent to the medical officer acting on behalf of the company. As a matter of good practice a patient's consent should be sought in writing and disclosure of the contents of the medical report should be made on a "need to know" basis.[347]

Medical reports on a patient who has died may only be issued to an insurance company by the deceased's doctor only with the consent of the next of kin or the executors to the estate. As a matter of ethical practice these medical reports remain confidential notwithstanding the fact that the patient is deceased.[348]

Because of the far reaching implications of an adverse medical report to insurers and employers it is submitted that there is a case for greater accountability of medical reporters in this area and possibly for the enactment in Ireland of legislation similar to the English Access to Medical Reports Act 1988.[349]

---

[342] *Dunn v. British Coal Corporation* (1993) I.C.R. 597.

[343] *Carter v. Boehm* (1766) 3 Burr 1905.

[344] See *Keating v. New Ireland Assurance Co. Plc.* [1990] 2 I.R. 383.

[345] See *Kelleher v. Irish Life Assurance Co. Ltd* [1993] I.L.R.M. 643.

[346] *A Guide to Ethical Conduct and Behaviour* (6th ed., 2004), para.16.7.

[347] See Mason and McCall, *op. cit.*, p.189.

[348] *A Guide to Ethical Conduct and Behaviour, op. cit.*, para.18.11 While the ethical obligation of confidentiality survives the death of the patient it appears doubtful that the estate of the deceased could maintain an action for breach of the legal obligation of confidentiality since, by analogy with the law of defamation it is unlikely that the right to bring proceedings for breach of confidence is a chose in action which passes to the estate on the death of the deceased. A difficulty would also arise in relation to proof of damage viz. injury to feelings etc. See Kennedy & Grubb, *op. cit.*, p.643.

[349] See Access to Medical Records, *supra*, pp.162 *et seq.*

Confidentiality and medical records

The Medical Council's *Guide to Ethical Conduct and Behaviour*[350] requires that all medical records in whatever format and wherever kept must be safeguarded. Doctors are responsible for ensuring that other health professionals and ancillary staff working with them maintain confidentiality at all times.

The *Medical Council's Guide to Ethical Conduct and Behaviour* makes specific reference to recording and states that identifiable audio-visual or photographic recordings of a patient or a relative of a patient should only be taken with informed and appropriate consent.[351] It continues that where taken for teaching purposes these records should normally remain as part of the patient's medical file. Images may have been recorded during emergency treatment without informed consent but this should be sought as soon as possible and before any teaching or other use of the images. As far as possible photographic, digital and video images should be taken in such a manner that a third party cannot identify the patient concerned. If the patient is identifiable he or she should be informed about the security storage and eventual destruction of the record.[352]

The Guide also provides that doctors working in Ireland have a responsibility to ensure compliance of their record systems with current Irish Data Protection and Freedom of Information legislation.[353]

Data protection and confidentiality

Medical practitioners who control the contents and use of personal data relating to their patients physical or mental health must comply with the provisions of the Data Protection Act 1988 as amended by the Data Protection (Amendment) Act 2003 and register[354] with the Data Protection Agency.[355] The 1988 Act as amended applies to automated data,[356] and (with some exceptions)[357] is extended to apply manual data[358] from the

---

[350] Para.16.4.

[351] Para.16.10.

[352] See para.19.2.

[353] Para.16.4.

[354] S.16 of the 2003 Act amending s.16(1) of the 1988 Act provides that the obligation to register does not apply to data controllers or data processors who carry out (i) processing whose sole purpose is the keeping in accordance with law of a register that is intended to provide information to the public and is open to consultation either by the public in general or by any person demonstrating a legitimate interest, (ii) the processing of manual data. (other than such categories, if any, of such data as may be prescribed) or (iii) any combination of the foregoing categories of processing. See Data Protection Act 1988, s.16(1) as amended by Data Protection (Amendment) Act 2003, s.16, Data Protection Act 1988, s.19(1). However, s.16 of the 2003 Act was not brought into force by the Data Protection (Amendment) Act 2003 (Commencement) Order 2003 (S.I. No.207 of 2003) and consequently as yet has no legal effect.

[355] Data Protection Act 1988, s.16(1)(c)(iii), s.19(1). Note s.16 of the 2003 Act amends this section and applies the obligation to register to persons who are data controllers generally (i.e. not limited to persons who are who keep personal data relating to physical or mental health) subject to certain exceptions but s.16 of the 2003 Act has not yet been brought into force).

[356] See definition of automated data at p.165 *infra*.

[357] The obligations imposed by ss.2, 2A and 2B of the 1988 Act come into operation on October 24, 2007 in respect of manual data held in relevant filing systems on the passing of 2003 Act, i.e. April 10, 2003. See Data Protection (Amendment) Act 2003, s.23(4).

[358] See definition of manual data in p.165 *infra*.

date of the commencement of the Data Protection (Amendment) Act 2003, i.e. July 1, 2003.

Obligation of data controller to comply with data protection principles Section 2 of the 1988 Act as amended obliges medical practitioners who are data controllers to comply with certain basic data protection principles and to ensure, *inter alia,*

(a) that the data, or as the case may be the information constituting the data shall have been obtained and the data shall be processed fairly;

(b) that the data is accurate and complete and where necessary kept up to date;

(c) the data:
  (i)   shall have been obtained only for one or more specified, explicit and legitimate purposes,
  (ii) shall not be further processed in a manner incompatible with that purpose or those purposes,
  (iii) shall be adequate, relevant and not excessive in relation to the purpose or purposes for which they were collected or are further processed, and
  (iv) shall not be kept for longer than is necessary for that purpose or those purposes.[359]

By virtue of section 2(1)(d) medical practitioners as data controllers are obliged to take appropriate security measures against unauthorised access to or unauthorised alteration, disclosure or destruction of , the data, in particular where the processing involves transmission of data over a network and against all other unlawful forms of processing.[360] In determining appropriate security measures, in particular but without prejudice to the generality of section 2(1)(d) where the processing involves the transmission of data over a network, a data controller:

(a) may have regard to the state of technological development and the cost of implementing the measures, and

(b) must ensure that the measures provide a level of security appropriate to
  (i) the harm that might result from unauthorised or unlawful processing, accidental or unlawful destruction or accidental loss of, or damage to the data concerned, and
  (ii) the nature of the data concerned.[361]

A data controller[362] or data processor[363] must take all reasonable steps to ensure that:

---

[359] Data Protection Act 1988, s.2(1)(a) to (c) as amended by Data Protection (Amendment) Act 2003, s.3(a).

[360] Data Protection Act 1988, s.2(1)(d) as amended by Data Protection (Amendment) Act 2003, s.3.

[361] Data Protection Act 1988, s.2C(1) as inserted by Data Protection (Amendment) Act 2003, s.4.

[362] "Data controller" is defined as " a person who, either alone or with others, controls the contents and use of personal data". See Data Protection Act 1988, s.1.

[363] "Data processor" is defined as "a person who processes personal data on behalf of a data controller but does not include an employee of a data controller who processes such data in the course of his employment". See Data Protection Act 1988, s.1.

(a) persons employed by him or her, and

(b) other persons at the place of work concerned are aware of and comply with the relevant security measures mentioned above.[364]

Where the processing of personal data is carried out by a data processor on behalf of a data controller the data controller shall:

(a) ensure that the processing is carried out in pursuance of a contract in writing or in another equivalent form between the data controller and the data processor and that the contract provides that the data processor carries out the processing only on and subject to the instructions of the data controller and that the data processor complies with obligations equivalent to those imposed on the data controller by section 2(1)(d) of the 1988 Act,

(b) ensure that the data processor provides sufficient guarantees in respect of the technical security measures and organisational measures governing the processing, and

(c) take reasonable steps to ensure compliance with those measures.[365]

The Act does not prescribe any set standard of security. However, in practice medical data controllers will need to audit their security needs according to the circumstances of their practices and seek expert advice on the adequacy of their systems. Sensitive information will clearly require a higher level of security than ordinary information because of its confidential nature and the potential damage which unauthorised disclosure or loss of information could give rise to.[366]

Specific obligations of data controller in relation to personal data Personal data may not be processed by a data controller unless the requirements of section 2 of the 1988 Act as amended by the 2003 Act are complied with and at least one of the conditions specified in section 2A are met. "Personal data" is defined as "data relating to a living individual who is or can be identified either from the data or from the data in conjunction with other information that is in or is likely to come into the possession of the data controller."[367] "Processing" of or in relation to information or data means "performing any operation or set of operations on the information or data, whether or not by automatic means, including;

(a) obtaining, recording or keeping that information or data;

(b) collecting, organising, storing, altering or adapting the information or data;

(c) retrieving, consulting or using the information or data;

(d) *disclosing* the information or data by transmitting, disseminating or otherwise making it available; or

---

[364] See Data Protection Act 1988, s.2C(2) as inserted by Data Protection (Amendment) Act 2003, s.4.

[365] See Data Protection Act 1988, s.2C(3) as inserted by Data Protection (Amendment) Act 2003, s.4.

[366] See A & L Goodbody, *A Practical Guide to Data Protection Law in Ireland* (Thompson Roundhall, Dublin , 2003).

[367] Data Protection Act 1988, s.1 as amended by the Data Protection (Amendment) Act 2003, s.2 (a)(iv).

(e) aligning, combining, blocking,[368] erasing or destroying the information or data."[369]

Section 2A(1) of the 1988 Act[370] specifies that at least one of the following conditions must be met if personal data is to be processed (a term which includes disclosure):

(a) the data subject has given his or her consent to the processing or, if the data subject, by reason of his or her physical or mental incapacity or age, is likely to be unable to appreciate the nature and effect of such consent, it is given by a parent or guardian or a grandparent, uncle, aunt, brother or sister of the data subject and the giving of such consent is not prohibited by law;

(b) the processing is necessary—
    (i)   for the performance of a contract to which the data subject is a party,
    (ii) in order to stake steps at the request of the data subject prior to entering into a contract,
    (iii) for compliance with a legal obligation to which the data controller is subject other than an obligation imposed by contract or to prevent—
        (I)   injury or other damage to the health of the data subject or
        (II) serious loss of or damage to property of the data subject or otherwise to protect his or her vital interests where the seeking of consent of the data subject or another person referred to in (a) above is likely to result in those interests being damaged;

(c) the processing is necessary for—
    (i)   the administration of justice,
    (ii) for the performance of a function conferred on a person by or under an enactment,
    (iii) for the performance of a function of the Government or a Minister for the Government,
    (iv) for the performance of any other function of a public nature performed in the public interest by a person;

(d) the processing is necessary for the purposes of the legitimate interests pursued by the data controller or by a third party or parties to whom the data are disclosed except where the processing is unwarranted in any particular case by reason of prejudice to the fundamental rights and freedoms or legitimate interests of the data subject.

Sections 2 and 2A comes into operation on October 24, 2007 in respect of manual data held in relevant filing systems on April 10, 2003.[371]

---

[368] "Blocking" in relation to data, means so marking the data that it is not possible to process it for purposes in relation to which it is marked. See Data Protection Act 1988, s.1 as amended by Data Protection (Amendment) Act 2003, s.2(a).

[369] Data Protection Act 1988, s.1 as amended by the Data Protection (Amendment) Act 2003, s.2(a)(v).

[370] As inserted by the Data Protection (Amendment) Act 2003, s.4.

[371] Data Protection (Amendment) Act 2003, s.23(4). The Data Protection (Amendment) Act 2003 was passed on April 10, 2003.

Irish Mental Health Law

Specific obligations of data controller in relation to sensitive personal data "Sensitive personal data" must not be "processed" (a term which includes disclosure) by a data controller unless sections 2 and 2A of the 1988 Act are complied with and in addition at least one of the conditions specified in section 2B(1)(b) of the 1988 Act[372] are met. "Sensitive personal data" is defined to include "personal data as to the physical or mental health or condition or sexual life of the data subject" and "the commission or alleged commission of any offence by the data subject".[373] Section 2B(1) specifies that in addition to compliance with section 2 and 2A *at least one* of the following conditions specified in section 2B(1)(b) must be met before disclosure of sensitive personal data is made The first condition is that the consent specified in section 2A (1)(a) must be explicitly given. The other conditions specified in section 2B(1)(b) any one of which, in addition to complying with section 2 and 2A, must be met before processing (of which disclosure is an element) may be made are:

(ii) the processing is necessary for the purpose of exercising or performing any right or obligation which is conferred or imposed by law on the data controller in connection with employment;[374]

(iii) the processing is necessary to prevent injury or other damage to the health of the data subject or another person or serious loss in respect of, or damage to, property or otherwise to protect the vital interests of the data subject or of any other person in a case where—

    (I) consent to the processing cannot be given by or on behalf of the data subject in accordance with section 2A(1)(a), or

    (II) the data controller cannot reasonably be expected to obtain such consent or the processing is necessary to prevent injury to or damage to the health of, another person, or serious loss in respect of, or damage to, the property of another person in a case where such consent has been unreasonably withheld; ...

(v) the information contained in the data has been made public as a result of steps deliberately taken by the data subject;

(vi) the processing is necessary for the administration of justice;

    (I) for the performance of a function conferred on a person by or under an enactment, or

    (II) for the performance of a function of the Government or a Minister of the Government,

---

[372] As inserted by the Data Protection (Amendment) Act 2003, s.4.

[373] See Data Protection Act 1988, s.1 as amended by the Data Protection (Amendment) Act 2003, s.2(a)(i) The Minister for Justice Equality and Law Reform is empowered by regulations to make such provision as he considers appropriate for the protection of data subjects in relation to the processing of personal data as to the commission or alleged commission of any offence by data subjects and processing of personal data must be in compliance with any regulations so made. See Data Protection Act 1988, s.2B(3) as amended by Data Protection (Amendment) Act 2003, s.4.

[374] The Minister is empowered by regulations made after consultation with the Data Protection Commissioner to exclude the application of s.2B(1)(b)(ii) in such cases as may be specified or provide that in such cases as may be specified the condition in s.2B(1)(b)(ii) is not to be regarded as satisfied unless such further conditions as may be specified are also satisfied. See Data Protection Act 1988, s.2B(2) as inserted by Data Protection (Amendment) Act 2003, s.4.

(vii) the processing,

(viii) the processing is necessary for "medical purposes" and is undertaken by,
    (I) a health professional,[375] or
    (II) a person who in the circumstances owes a duty of confidence to the data subject that is equivalent to that which would exist if that person were a health professional; "Medical purposes" includes the purposes of "preventive medicine, medical diagnosis, medical research, the provision of care and treatment and the management of healthcare services."[376]

(ix) the processing is necessary in order to obtain information for use, subject to and in accordance with the Statistics Act 1993, only for statistical, compilation and analysis purposes; ...

(xi) the processing is authorised by regulations that are made by the Minister for Justice Equality and Law Reform and are made for reasons of substantial public interest;

(xii) the processing is necessary for the purpose of the assessment, collection or payment of any tax, duty, levy or other moneys owed or payable to the State and the data has been provided by the data subject solely for that purpose;

(xiii) the processing is necessary for the purposes of determining entitlement to or control of, or any other purpose connected with the administration of any benefit, pension, assistance, allowances, supplement or payment under the Social Welfare (Consolidation) Act 1993 or any non statutory scheme administered by the Minister for Social Community and Family Affairs

In circumstances (ii) to (xiii) above consent is not necessary to process the sensitive information. Section 2B comes into operation on October 24, 2007 in respect of manual data held in relevant filing systems on the April 10, 2003.[377]

Disclosures of Medical Information Practice Guide In his Guidelines relating to the *Medical and Health Sector*, the Data Protection Commissioner outlines a number of practical situations where issues of consent may arise and offers guidance on the issue of consent in those circumstances.[378] The following are some typical disclosure situations and the appropriate responses to them:

---

[375] "Health professional" includes a registered medical practitioner, within the meaning of the Medical Practitioners Act 1978, a registered dentist within the meaning of the Dentists Act 1985 or a member of any other class of health worker or social worker standing specified by regulations made by the Minister for Justice Equality and Law Reform after consultation with the Minister for Health and Children and any other Minister of the Government who, having regard to his or her functions, ought, in the opinion of the Minister for Justice Equality and Law Reform to be consulted. See Data Protection Act 1988, s.2B(4) as inserted by the Data Protection (Amendment) Act 2003, s.4.

[376] See Data Protection Act 1988, s.2B(4) as inserted by Data Protection (Amendment) Act 2003, s.4. Some typical examples of situations of disclosure which may arise in medical practice are outlined *infra* at pp.183 *et seq.*

[377] Data Protection (Amendment) Act 2003, s.23(4). The Data Protection (Amendment) Act 2003 was passed on April 10, 2003.

[378] See www.dataprivacy.ie. See also A & L Goodbody, *op. cit.*, pp.103–106.

(a) Explicit consent will not be required for routine processing of a patient's information in connection with his/her treatment and diagnosis; for disclosure to a locum or for referrals to consultants and other specialists or specialist hospitals. In the latter case consent may be implied where the patient agrees to the referral.

(b) The Commissioner advises that secretaries and other administrative staff should only be allowed access to patient files to the extent necessary to enable them to perform their functions. They should have no need to access clinical material as distinct from administrative details and the patient is entitled to an assurance that their medical information will be treated on a need to know basis.

(c) Where a medical practitioner passes patient data on to a person or body acting in an agency capacity such a clinical laboratory then there is no disclosure for the purposes of the Act and there is no need for explicit consent. However, the Data Protection Commissioner advises that the patient should be informed in advance that his/her data will be used in this way.

(d) If information is being passed on to another health professional for guidance and advice on clinical issues this is a non-obvious use of the patient's information and the patient should be informed and the patient data kept anonymous. If full patient details are to be passed on then the patient's explicit consent is required, except in cases of urgent need.

(e) Disclosing patient details to third parties for research purposes will require explicit consent. Where the patient's data is anonymous,[379] consent will not be required however the patient must be informed that their information will be used in this way.

(f) The explicit consent of the patient is not required for disclosure of information to debt collection agencies since they act on behalf of medical practitioners. However, only such information as is necessary to enable the debt to be processed should be revealed. There should be a written data processor agreement between the agency and the data controller.

(g) Information gleaned from a pre-employment medical examination does not fall within the definition of information processed for "medical purposes" and explicit consent of the examinee should be obtained before sending the information to his or her employer.[380]

(h) Examinations carried out by medical practitioners for insurance companies likewise do not come within the definition of "medical purposes" and the explicit consent of the patient is required before the information may be passed on to the insurance company.[381]

---

[379] Information can be anonymised (i.e. all identifiers are removed) or pseudononmysed (i.e. removal of personal identifiers but application of a code to the data). Anonymising or pseudononymising will bring the information outside the scope of the Data Protection Act, but in the latter case it will do so only if the recipient of the information does not have, or have access to, the key to the code. See A & L Goodbody, *op. cit.*, p.106.

[380] See below Medical Council's *Ethical Guidelines* which indicated that "the significance rather than the precise details of the medical findings should be conveyed to any third party", para.16.6.

[381] See para.16.7 of the Medical Council's *Guide to Ethical Conduct and Behaviour* which states that

Right of data subject to object to disclosure likely to cause damage or distress Section 6A confers a limited right on a data subject to object to processing (including disclosure) likely to cause damage or distress. It provides that subject to section 6A(3) and unless otherwise provided by any enactment an individual is entitled at any time to request a data controller by notice in writing served on him or her to cease within a reasonable time or not to begin processing or processing for a specified purpose or in a specified manner any personal data in respect of which the individual is the data subject if the processing falls within certain categories specified in section 6A(2) on the ground that for specified reasons (a) the processing of those data or their processing for that purpose or in that manner is causing or is likely to cause substantial damage or distress to him or her or to another person and the damage or distress is or would be unwarranted.

Section 6A(2) specifies that this right applies to processing that is necessary (a) for the performance of a task carried out in the public interest or in the exercise of official authority vested in the data controller or in a third party to whom the data are or are to be disclosed or (b) for the purposes of the legitimate interests pursued by the data controller to whom the data are or are to be disclosed, unless those interests are overridden by the interests of the data subject in relation to fundamental rights and freedoms and, in particular, his or her right to privacy with respect to the processing of personal data.

By virtue of section 6A(3) the right to object to processing does not apply;

(a) in a case where the data subject has given his or her explicit consent to the processing (including disclosure),

(b) if the processing (including disclosure) is necessary
   (i) for the performance of a contract to which the data subject is a party,
   (ii) in order to take steps at the request of the data subject prior to his or her entering into a contract,
   (iii) for compliance with any legal obligation to which the data controller or data subject is subject other than one imposed by contract,
   (iv) to protect the vital interests of the data subject. …

(d) in such other cases, if any, as may be specified in regulations made by the Minister for Justice Equality and Law Reform after consultation with the Data Protection Commissioner.

The Data Protection Commissioner's powers of enforcement Where a notice under section 6A(1) is served on a data controller, s/he must not later than 20 days after receipt of the notice serve a notice on the individual concerned (a) stating that s/he has complied or intends to comply with the request concerned or (b) stating that s/he is of opinion that the request is unjustified to any extent and the reasons for the opinion and the extent (if any) to which he or she has complied or intends to comply with it.[382]

If the Data Protection Commissioner is satisfied, on application to him/her by an individual who has served a notice under section 6A(1) that appears to the Commissioner

---

"a doctor's asked by an insurance company to complete a medical report on a patient, must ensure that this is not issued without the consent of the patient".

[382] Data Protection Act 1988, s.6A(4) as inserted by Data Protection (Amendment) Act 2003, s.8.

to be justified or to be justified to any extent, that the data controller concerned has failed to comply with the notice or to comply with it to that extent and that not less than 40 days have elapsed since the receipt of the notice by him or her the Data Commissioner may serve an enforcement notice on the data controller ordering him or her to take such steps for complying with the request or for complying with it to that extent as the Commissioner thinks fit and specifies in the enforcement notice and the enforcement notice must specify the reasons for the Commissioner's being satisfied as to the non-compliance.[383]

Section 19(2)(d) of the 1988 Act makes it unlawful[384] for a person to disclose data to a person or body not described in the registration entry,[385] and while this assumes that it is lawful to disclose the information to persons so described a medical practitioner should construe that freedom as being subject to his/her common law obligations of confidentiality.

No restrictions on disclosure in certain circumstances The restrictions on disclosure under section 19(2)(d) do not apply where the information is "processed" (a term widely defined[386] to include disclosure) for any of the purposes mentioned in section 8. These include the prevention, detection and investigation of criminal offences or where the application of the restrictions would be likely to prejudice the assessing or collecting of taxes or monies owed or payable to the state, local authority or the Health Service Executive;[387] or where the processing is required urgently to prevent injury or other damage to the health of a person or serious loss of or damage to property;[388] where processing is required by or under any enactment or by a rule of law or order of a court;[389] where processing is required for the purpose of obtaining legal advice or for the purposes of or in the course of legal proceedings in which the person making the disclosure is a party or a witness;[390] where the processing is at the request or with the consent of the data subject or a person acting on his behalf.[391]

Section 22A(1)[392] provides that personal data that are "processed" (a term which includes disclosure) only for journalistic, artistic or literary purposes shall be exempt from certain provisions of the Act specified in section 22A(2) if (a) the processing is undertaken solely with a view to the publication of any journalistic, literary or artistic

---

[383] Data Protection Act 1988, s.6A(5) as inserted by Data Protection (Amendment) Act 2003, s.8.
[384] Subject to the exceptions mentioned in s.8.
[385] S.9(2)(d).
[386] Data Protection Act 1988, s.1 as amended by the Data Protection (Amendment) Act 2003, s.2. "Processing" of or in relation to information or data, according to the Act as amended means performing any operation or set of operations on the information or data, whether or not by automatic means, including: (a) obtaining, recording or keeping the information or data, (b) collecting, organising, storing, altering or adapting the information or data, (c) retrieving, consulting or using the information or data, (d) disclosing the information or data by transmitting, disseminating or otherwise making it available or (e) aligning, combining, blocking, erasing or destroying the information or data.
[387] Data Protection Act 1988, s.8(b) as amended by the Data Protection (Amendment) Act 2003, s.9.
[388] *Ibid.*, s.8(d) as amended by the Data Protection (Amendment) Act 2003, s.9.
[389] *Ibid.*, s.8(e) as amended by the Data Protection (Amendment) Act 2003, s.9.
[390] *Ibid.*, s.8(f) as amended by the Data Protection (Amendment) Act 2003, s.9.
[391] *Ibid.*, s.8(h) as amended by the Data Protection (Amendment) Act 2003, s.9.
[392] S.22A was inserted by the Data Protection (Amendment) Act 2003, s.21.

material, (b) the data controller reasonably believes that, having regard in particular to the special importance of the public interest in freedom of expression, such publication would be in the public interest and (c) the data controller reasonably believes that, in all the circumstances, compliance with that provision would be incompatible with journalistic, artistic or literary purposes.

In considering whether for the purposes of (b) above whether publication would be in the public interest, regard may be had to any code of practice approved under section 13(1)[393] or 13(2)[394] of the 1988 Act as amended.[395]

"Publication" in relation to journalistic, artistic or literary material is defined widely to mean the act of making the material available to the public or any section of the public in any form or by any means.[396]

The relevant provisions from which personal data processed for journalistic artistic or literary purposes are exempt by virtue of section 22A(2) are:

(a) section 2 (collection, processing, keeping, use and disclosure of personal data) other than section 2(1)(d) (the requirement to take appropriate security measures against unauthorised access),

(b) section 2A (requirements regarding processing of personal data); section 2B (requirements regarding processing of sensitive personal data); section 2D (criteria for fair processing of personal data),

(c) section 3 (right of individual to establish existence of personal data),

(d) section 4 (right of individual to access to personal data relating to him/her held by a data controller); section 6(right of individual to rectification or erasure),

(e) section 6A (right of data subject to object to processing likely to cause damage or distress); section 6B (rights of data subject in relation to automated decision making).

Penalties for non-compliance with data protection principles Non-compliance with the principles of personal data protection may render the medical practitioner liable for breach of confidence, breach of contract or in negligence. In the latter regard, a plaintiff may rely on section 7 of the 1988 Act which establishes that a data controller owes a duty of care to a data subject in respect of his dealings with personal data which relates to the data subject.

---

[393] S.13(1) provides that the Data Protection Commissioner shall encourage trade associations and other bodies representing categories of data controllers to prepare codes of practice to be complied with by those categories in dealing with personal data.

[394] S.13(2) provides for the approval of codes of practice by the Commissioner. It states, *inter alia*, that the Data Protection Commissioner shall (a) where a code of practice is submitted to him or her for consideration consider the code and after such consultation with such data subjects or persons representing data subjects and with the relevant trade associations or other bodies aforesaid as appears to him to be appropriate: (i) if he or she is of opinion that the code provides for the data subjects concerned a measure of protection with regard to personal data relating to them that conforms with that provided for by s.2, ss.2A to 2D and ss 3 and 4 other than s.4(8) and 6 of the 1988 Act approve the code and encourage its dissemination to the data controllers concerned and (ii) in any event notify the association or body concerned of his or her decision to approve or not to approve the code.

[395] S.13 was amended by the Data Protection (Amendment) Act 2003, s.14.

[396] S.22A(4) as inserted by Data Protection (Amendment) Act 2003, s.21(4).

Registers of illness

The *Medical Council's Guide to Ethical Conduct and Behaviour* provides that with the increasing importance of audit in medicine and the necessity for evidence based medicine it is important for doctors to remember that where registers of specific illnesses are being kept the principles of confidentiality must be adhered to and that results from research projects should protect patient anonymity. It adds that Irish Data Protection legislation must also be considered when making use of chemical data for research or audit purposes.

Remedies for disclosure in breach of the obligation of confidentiality

Where a medical practitioner has entered into a contract with a patient a breach of an express or implied term relating to confidentiality will confer on the patient a right of action for damages for breach of contract.[397] There is some dispute as to the type of damages which are recoverable. While it is reasonably clear that a patient may recover damages for foreseeable economic loss,[398] it is less clear whether a patient would also be in a position to recover damages for injury to his feelings arising from the unauthorised disclosure. If it is possible that such injury could reasonably be supposed to have been in the contemplation of the parties at the time they made the contract as the probable consequence of a breach, it is arguable that such damages should be recoverable. However, there is some authority against recovery of damages for social discredit, and loss of prestige and other forms of non-pecuniary loss.[399]

Where a medical practitioner discloses information and it is reasonably foreseeable that this may cause physical harm to a patient the practitioner may be liable in negligence. In the New Zealand case of *Furniss v. Fitchett*,[400] when a certificate that was issued a patient's physician to her husband stating that in the physician's opinion she was suffering from paranoia, was produced during separation and maintenance proceedings the patient was held to be entitled to recover damages for mental shock.

In *AG v. Guardian Newspapers Limited (No.2)*[401] a breach of confidentiality was recognised as a legitimate basis for legal action. However, the remedies for breaches of confidentiality are well defined. In equity the courts may grant injunctions to restrain the disclosure of confidential communications between medical practitioner and patient.[402] In this regard courts in exercise of their equitable jurisdiction may act to restrain not only parties to the relationship but also third parties fixed with actual or constructive knowledge that the information was given in breach of the obligation of confidentiality.[403]

---

[397] *AB v. CD* (1851) 14 Dunlop 177. See Boyle, "Medical Confidentiality – Civil Liability for Breach" (1973) N.I.L. 19.

[398] *Sealer v. Copyedit Ltd* [1967] 1 W.L.R. 923.

[399] *Groom v. Crocker* [1939] 1 K.B. 194; *Bailey v. Bullock* [1950] 2 All E.R. 1167.

[400] [1958] N.Z.L.R. 396.

[401] [1990] 1 A.C. 109.

[402] See *Argyll v. Argyll* [1967] Ch. 302 and *Goddard v. Nationwide Building Society* [1986] 3 All E.R. 264 at 271.

[403] Jacob and Jacob, "Confidential Communications" (1969) 119 N.L.J. 133 at 134.

In the case of *X v. Y*,[404] there was a clear implication in the judgment of Rose J. that damages were available as a remedy for breach of equitable duty of confidence in the absence of a better solution when the identities of two doctors who were allegedly continuing in practice having contracted AIDS were leaked to a newspaper. Arising from the judgment in the case it might be possible to claim considerable damages where the breach of the obligation of confidentiality leads to loss of society, severe injury to feelings, job loss or interference with prospects of promotion. Other possible remedies available for breach of confidence include a declaration, destruction and delivery up and account of profits.

A claim of defamation may be made against a medical practitioner who makes a false statement about a patient, the effect of which is to lower his/her reputation in society. Most medical records and opinions and statements made to professional colleagues will, however, be subject to qualified privilege. Nevertheless qualified privilege will be lost where the speaker or writer knows that his or her statement is false and damaging.

Where the automated[405] information is disclosed in breach of the provisions of the Data Protection Act 1988 a medical practitioner could face the prospect of prosecution under the provisions of section 19 of the Act or an action for damages in tort for breach of the duty of care of the data controller to the data subject established by section 7.

A breach the ethical duty of confidentiality is also regarded as a serious issue, which may expose a medical practitioner to a range of penalties for professional misconduct. The sanctions of the Fitness to Practise Committee of the Medical Council, are however essentially punitive in nature and while they may be effective as a deterrent against future misconduct by the medical practitioner, and it has been questioned whether they give adequate protection to the patient who has suffered damage.

Commentary in relation to obligation of confidentiality from an international law perspective

Article 17 of the *International Covenant on Civil and Political Rights* provides in general terms that no one shall be subjected to arbitrary or unlawful interference with his privacy. Principle 13 of the *UN Principles for the Protection of Persons with Mental Illness and the Improvement of Mental Health Care* provides equally generally that every patient in a mental health facility shall, in particular have the right to full respect of his or her privacy. Neither provision however deals with the extent to which confidential information may be disclosed.

Conclusions

1. It would greatly facilitate accessibility in the law relating to confidentiality if the common law and ethical principles in Irish law were codified in legislation.

---

[404] [1988] 2 All E.R. 648.

[405] The 1988 Act as amended by the Data Protection (Amendment) Act 2003 comes into operation in respect of manual data held in relevant filing systems on April 10, 2003 (the date of passing of the 2003 Act) on October 24, 2007.

2. It is submitted that legislation should provide that confidential information may be disclosed where necessary to safeguard the welfare of another individual or patient only where a patient presents a clear and substantial risk of imminent physical danger to another person.

3. Legislation is required to govern the confidentiality obligations of non-carers such as insurance companies.

4. Computerisation creates the risk of violation of confidentiality where there is transmission of patient identifiable information to the central or outside computer facility and the potential for leakage of information from the system and unauthorised use of that information to embarrass or discredit or injure an individual. Legislation requiring that such information be encoded in such a way as to make it impossible for persons other than data processing personnel within the relevant facility to discern the identity of the patient/client would assist in protecting patient/client confidentiality and in assuring certainty in the law in this regard.

A PATIENT'S RIGHT OF ACCESS TO A LAWYER

The establishment of a right of a patient with mental disability to a lawyer is essential if that patient is to exercise his right to due process, and self-determination effectively. Patients with mental illness are particularly vulnerable to invasion of their legal rights. A number of points must be made in this regard. First patients with mental illness are likely to be economically disadvantaged and not able to afford a lawyer from their own funds. Secondly the stigma of mental illness leaves a person with mental illness uniquely exposed to social prejudice, discrimination and abuse of power. Thirdly by reason of his/her mental illness a person with mental illness faces unique problems in recognising and asserting his/her legal rights because in some cases of impaired insight into his/her condition, impaired ability to communicate or ingrained deference to authority. All of these factors make access to a specialist lawyer essential.

Provision under Civil Legal Aid Act 1995

There is no provision of the Mental Treatment Act 1945 conferring on a patient the right of access to or assistance with the cost of consulting a lawyer. However, a patient wishing to pursue a civil action under section section 260 of that Act (still in force) and under section 73 of the Mental Health Act 2001 (yet to be implemented) to question an act purported to have been done under 2001 Act, potentially has a right to legal advice and legal aid under the provisions of the Civil Legal Aid Act 1995 provided s/he satisfies the financial and other eligibility criteria set out in the 1995 Act.[406]

---

[406] The Civil Legal Aid Act 1995 consolidated in statutory form the 1979 non-statutory scheme as amended. See also Scheme of Civil Legal Aid and Advice as amended Pn. No. 2078. In practice, however, it must be said that while the 1995 Act does include such a right to legal advice and legal aid, the majority of cases assisted under the 1995 Act are family law cases and priority seems to be accorder to such cases in granting legal advice and legal aid under the scheme.

The Legal Aid Board

The 1995 Act establishes the Legal Aid Board to administer the scheme under the Act. The principal functions of the Board are to provide within its resources legal aid and advice in civil cases to persons who satisfy the eligibility criteria of the 1995 Act and to disseminate information concerning its services. In addition the Board is authorised to establish a panel of solicitors and barristers in private practice who are willing to provide legal aid and advice under the Act.[407]

₀ *Criteria for obtaining legal advice and legal aid*

Legal advice is defined by section 25 of the 1995 Act to mean:

> "any oral or written advice given by a solicitor of the [Legal Aid] Board or by a solicitor or barrister engaged by the Board for that purpose on the application of the law of the state[408] to any particular circumstances which have arisen in relation to the person seeking the advice and as to any steps which that person might appropriately take having regard to the application of the law of the state to those circumstances and includes any assistance given by such a solicitor or barrister to any person in taking such steps ... whether by assisting a person in taking any such steps on his or her own behalf or taking any such steps (other than the institution or conduct including defence, of civil proceedings) on the person's behalf."

Section 27 of the Act defines "legal aid" as "representation by a solicitor of the [Legal Aid] Board or solicitor or barrister engaged by the Board in any civil proceedings ... and includes all such assistance as is usually given by a solicitor and, where appropriate, barrister in contemplation of, ancillary to or in connection with such proceedings whether for the purposes of arriving at or giving effect to any settlement in the proceedings or otherwise".

Merits test To obtain legal advice or aid two basic tests of eligibility are laid down, a "merits" test and a "means" test. The basic "merits" test is set out in section 24 of the Act and provides that without prejudice to the other criteria laid down by the Act a person will not be granted legal aid or advice unless in the opinion of the Legal Aid Board a reasonably prudent person would be likely to seek such services in such circumstances at his or her own expense when his/her means were such that the cost of seeking such services at his or her own expense, while representing a financial obstacle to him or her would not be such as to impose undue hardship upon him or her, and a solicitor or barrister acting reasonably would be likely to advise him or her to obtain such services at his or her own expense.

---

[407] Civil Legal Aid Act 1995, s.30.

[408] The Civil Legal Aid Act 1995, s.26(4) provides that where a person would qualify for legal advice but for the fact that the advice sought concerns the application of the law of another State such person shall be entitled to obtain such guidance or assistance in relation to the matter as the Legal Aid Board deems appropriate.

Means test The "means test" is laid down in section 29. An applicant must satisfy certain requirements regarding financial eligibility specified in section 29 and in regulations under section 37 of the Act and pay a contribution to the Legal Aid Board towards the cost of legal aid or advice, the level of contribution laid down in Regulations under the Act.

An applicant's financial eligibility for legal aid is assessed by reference to his/her disposable income (i.e. gross income less items such as income tax, social insurance, actual expenses not exceeding €4,900 per annum incurred in respect of accommodation costs[409] and other items to take account of for example of dependants set out in Regulation 16 of the Civil Legal Aid Regulations 1996)[410] and where applicable, disposable capital (i.e. money, stocks, shares, securities, interests in a company or business, house property, interests in land, life insurance or endowment policies, valuables, debts owed, current value of equipment in a business[411] less certain deductions set out in regulation 19 of the Civil Legal Aid Regulations 1996)[412] The value of the applicants home and household

---

[409] Where spouses are living in separate households the allowance specified applies also to the normal place of residence of the spouse of the applicant, if the accommodation expenses incurred in respect of that residence are paid by the applicant. See Civil Legal Aid Regulations 1996 (S.I. No.273 of 1996), reg.16(7).

[410] €1,100 per annum may be deducted in respect of each of the applicant's dependants. Expenses incurred on child care facilities to enable an applicant to pursue employment subject to a maximum equal to the standard deduction for dependants may also be deducted. "Dependants" includes the applicant's children or step-children who are under 18 years of age, children above that age who are pursuing a full-time course of education and dependent relatives or other persons who are permanently residing with the applicant, who are supported by the applicant and who do not have available to them independent means of support. A sum of €1,900 may be deducted in respect of the applicant's spouse. This is applicable even where a spouse is living apart from the applicant if the applicant is providing maintenance for the spouse. See Civil Legal Aid Regulations 1996 (S.I. No. 273 of 1996), reg.16 as substituted by the Civil Legal Aid Regulations 2002 (S.I. No. 8 of 2002), reg.3(g) Note however a spouses income may be aggregated with that of the applicant where the applicant and the spouse are married or are living together as man and wife. See Civil Legal Aid Regulations 1996 (S.I. No. 273 of 1996.), reg.14(4). This does not apply however where the applicant and his or her spouse are living separate and apart, the spouse or partner has a contrary interest in the matter in respect of which the application is made or it would in the opinion of the Legal Aid Board be unreasonable in all the circumstances of the case to take such resources into account. See reg.14(4). See the Civil Legal Aid Act 1995, s.29(3), Civil Legal Aid Regulations 1996 (S.I. No. 273 of 1996), reg.16 as substituted by the Civil Legal Aid Regulations 2002 (S.I. No. 8 of 2002), reg.3(g).

[411] Civil Legal Aid Regulations 1996 (S.I. No. 273 of 1996), reg.18.

[412] For the purpose of determining the applicant's disposable capital the deductions to be made from his/her capital are set out in Civil Legal Aid Regulations 1996 (S.I. No.273 of 1996), reg.19 as follows: (a) where the capital resources consists of land including farm land its value shall exclude any amount which is attributable to a family home. The full amount of any charge, mortgage, loan or debt outstanding on that land shall also be deducted. (b) where the capital resource consists of a house property other than the applicant's family home, plant or equipment of a business or other equipment of a capital nature (including a car) its value shall be reduced by the full amount of any charge, mortgage, loan or other debt outstanding on it, (c) in the case of a capital resource other than money, the expense which would be incurred in realising the asset, shall be deducted, (d) the amount by which any legally enforceable debts which fall to be paid (and, are in the opinion of the Board, likely to be paid) by the applicant in the twelve month period following the date of application for legal aid or advice (and which have not already been the subject of a deduction from income or capital resources) and (e) capital payments falling to be made in respect of any loan within twelve

chattels are included in the assessment of disposable capital only to extent that such value exceeds €190,500.[413]

The qualifying disposable income limit is reviewed from time to time by reference to the Consumer Price Index. In 2002 the disposable income limit was €13,000 per annum.[414] The disposable capital limit was €320,000.[415]

The amount of contribution which an applicant is expected to pay also assessed by reference to the applicant's disposable income and where relevant disposable capital.[416] In 2002 if the applicant's disposable income was € 8,300 per annum or less the maximum contribution, which he or she would be, required to pay was (a) if legal advice was obtained €6, and (b) if legal aid was obtained €35. If the applicant's disposable income was over €8,300 per annum and not more than €13,000 per annum the maximum contribution which he or she will be required to pay was (a) if legal advice only was obtained, one tenth of the difference between his or her disposable income and €8,300 subject to a minimum contribution of €6 and a maximum of €100, and (b) if legal aid was obtained €35 plus one quarter of the difference between his or her disposable income and €8,300. [417] This is subject to the Board's discretion to grant legal aid or advice to persons who are in receipt of social welfare benefits or allowances as their only source of income for a maximum of €35 for legal aid and €6 for legal advice payable in advance.[418] The 1996 Regulations also provide that the Board is empowered in certain circumstances where severe hardship would be caused to waive the contribution.[419]

No capital contribution was payable in respect of that portion of the applicant's disposable capital which is under €3,200.[420] Regulation 20 of the 1996 Regulations set out in some detail the criteria for the calculation of the capital contribution.[421]

---

months of the date of application for a certificate which have not already been the subject of a deduction from income or capital resources shall be deducted.

[413] Civil Legal Aid Regulations 1996 (S.I No. 273 of 1996), reg.18(4) as amended by the Civil Legal Aid Regulations 2002 (S.I. No.8 of 2002), reg.3(i).

[414] Civil Legal Aid Regulations 1996 (S.I. No. 273 of 1996), reg.13 as amended the Civil Legal Aid Regulations 2002 (S.I. No 8 of 2002), reg.3(b).

[415] Civil Legal Aid Regulations 1996 (S.I. No.273 of 1996 reg.13(4) as amended by the Civil Legal Aid Regulations 1996 (S.I. No. 8 of 2002) Reg.3(c).

[416] See Civil Legal Aid Act 1995, s.29(3).

[417] See Civil Legal Aid Regulations 1996 (S.I. No. 273 of 1996), reg.17 as substituted by Civil Legal Aid Regulations 2002 (S.I. No. 8 of 2002), reg.3(h).

[418] Civil Legal Aid Regulations 1996 (S.I. No. 273 of 1996), reg.21(10).

[419] *Ibid.*, reg.21(9).

[420] *Ibid.*, reg.20(1).

[421] The applicant's maximum capital contributions in respect of that portion of his or her capita resources which consists of farm land shall be based on the market value of the land less any deductions in respect of it which fall to be made under reg.19(1) and the market value thus reduced is referred to as "disposable capital (farm land). See reg.20(2) The applicants maximum capital contribution in respect of that portion of his or her capital resources which consists of farm land shall, subject to the provisions of regs 20(1) and 20(2) is (i) if s/he is a full-time farmer, namely a person who engages in farming and whose gross income from all sources other than farming does not exceed €3,200 per annum: (a) where the disposable capital (farm land) is €79,400 or less, a contribution of €35; (b) where the disposable capital (farm land) is between €79,400 and €320,000 a contribution of one per cent of the amount by which the disposable capital (farm land) exceeds €79,400 plus €35; (ii) if s/he is a person who has farm land but is not a full-time farmer as defined in para.(i) and who also has income from a source other than farm land the maximum capital contribution in respect of that portion of his or her capita resources which consists of farm land shall be the

Significantly the maximum capital contribution payable in respect of the applicant's family home where the unencumbered value of the home exceeds €190,500 is to be one per cent of the amount by which such value exceeds €190,500 provided that the contribution payable in respect of that portion of the unencumbered value which is under €250,000 does not exceed the applicants contribution.[422]

Criteria for obtaining legal advice

Section 26 of the Civil Legal Aid Act 1995 allows the Board to provide legal advice if the applicant satisfies the means test in section 29 of the Act and any Regulations made under the Act. Section 26(2) provides that legal advice may not deal with any criminal law matter unless it concerns how legal aid can be obtained under the Criminal Justice (Legal Aid) Act 1962. Legal Advice may not be provided by the Board in respect of the excluded categories of civil matters referred to in section 28(9)[423] of the Act. Subject to that proviso legal advice may be given in respect of virtually any legal matter. This includes advice to a person who has a case pending before a tribunal. The 1995 Act however prevents the Board granting legal aid to such a person.[424]

---

amount specified in para. (i) plus (a) where the gross amount of the income is over €3,200 but not more than €4,000 a contribution of one tenth of one per cent of the disposable capital (farm land); (b) where the gross amount of the income is over €4,000 but not more than €4,350 a contribution of one fifth of one per cent of the disposable capital (farm land); (c) where the gross amount of the income is over €4,350 a contribution of one per cent of the disposable capital (farm land) plus one fifth of one per cent of the disposable capital (farm land) in respect of each €380 or portion of €380 by which the income exceeds €4,350. See reg.20(3) The maximum capital contribution in respect of that portion of the applicant's capital resources which consists of farm stock or machinery shall be based on the market value of that stock or machinery less any deductions which fall to be made under reg.19(1) and the value thus assessed shall be referred to as "disposable capital (stock and machinery). See reg.20(4). Subject to the provisions of reg.20(1) and reg.20(4) and (6) the maximum capital contribution in respect of that portion of the applicant's capital resources which consists of farm stock or machinery will be one half or one per cent of the disposable capital (stock and machinery). See reg.20(5). Notwithstanding the provisions of reg.20(5) the capital contribution to be paid in respect of dry stock shall be such amount as the Board following consultation with the appropriate authorities shall determine. See reg.20(6). The maximum capital contribution in respect of that portion of the applicant's capital resources which consists of resources other than those referred to reg.20(1) to reg 20(6) shall be based on the value of those resources assessed in accordance with the 1996 Regulations less any deductions in respect of those resources which fall to be made under reg.20(1) and the value thus assessed is referred to as "disposable capital (resources)." See reg.20(7). The maximum capital contribution in respect of that portion of the applicant's capital resources which consists of resources other than those referred to in regs 20(1) to 20(6) shall be as follows (i) where the disposable capital is €79,500 or less, two and a half per cent of the disposable capital (resources) (ii) where the disposable capital is over €79,500 the contribution will be the sum specified in para (i) plus ten per cent of the amount by which the disposable capital (resources) exceeds €79,500. See reg.20(8). See Civil Legal Aid Regulations 1996 (S.I. No.273 of 1996), reg.20 as amended by Civil Legal Aid Regulations 2002, reg.3(j)–(s).

[422] See Civil Legal Aid Regulations 1996 (S.I. No. 273 of 1996), reg.20(9) as amended by Civil Legal Aid Regulations 2003, reg.3(s).

[423] See below, p.231.

[424] See terms of Civil Legal Aid Act 1995, s.27.

Additional criteria for obtaining legal aid

Section 28(2) of the Civil Legal Aid Act 1995 lays down the essential additional criteria under which the Board may grant a legal aid certificate. A certificate must be granted if in the Board's opinion:

(a) the applicant satisfies the financial eligibility criteria in section 29 of the Act;

(b) the applicant has as a matter of law reasonable grounds for instituting, defending or being a party to the proceedings for which legal aid is sought;

(c) the applicant is reasonably likely to be successful in the proceedings, assuming that the facts put forward by him/her in relation to the proceedings are proved before the court or tribunal concerned;

(d) the proceedings for which legal aid is sought are the most satisfactory means (having regard to all the circumstances of the case including the probable cost to the applicant) by which the result sought by the applicant or a more satisfactory one, may be achieved; and

(e) having regard to all the circumstances of the case (including the probable cost to the Board, measured against the likely benefit to the applicant) it is reasonable to grant legal aid.

Section 27 of the Civil Legal Aid Act 1995 provides that legal aid may with some exceptions be given in connection with any civil proceedings in any court from the District Court to the Supreme Court. In general the Board will grant legal aid in the lowest court having jurisdiction in the matter.[425] The Board may also be authorised by Ministerial Order to provide legal aid for proceedings in any prescribed court or tribunal.

Categories of action in respect of which legal aid and legal advice is not available

Section 28(9) of the Civil Legal Aid Act 1995 prohibits the Board from providing legal aid and legal advice in relation to the following matters:

(a) defamation;

(b) disputes concerning rights and interests in and over land;[426]

(c) civil matters within the jurisdiction of the District Court (Small Claims Procedure) rules;

(d) licensing;[427]

---

[425] See s.28(8) of the Civil Legal Aid Act 1995.

[426] Family law proceedings concerning land and landlord and tenant disputes concerning residential property are not excluded. Neither are disputes concerning the applicant's home (or what would be the applicant's home but for the dispute) and the Legal Aid Board considers that the applicant (I) suffers from an infirmity of mind or body due to old age or other circumstances or (II) may have been subject to duress, undue influence or fraud in the matter and that a refusal to grant legal aid would cause hardship to the applicant. See s.28(9)(c) of the Civil Legal Aid Act 1995.

[427] Where hardship would be caused to the applicant by the granting of the licence the subject matter of the dispute licensing disputes are not excluded. See s.28(9)(c)(vi).

(e) conveyancing;

(f) election petitions;

(g) claims made in a representative, fiduciary or official capacity where the Board is of opinion, having regard to any source from which the applicant is or may be entitled to be indemnified in respect of the cost of the proceedings concerned and any resources of the persons who would be likely to benefit from a successful outcome of the proceedings for the applicant, that legal aid should not be granted;

(h) claims brought by a person as a member of and by arrangement with a group of persons to establish a precedent on a particular point of law or any other question in which the members of the group have an interest;

(i) any other matter as respects, which the application for legal aid is made by or on behalf of a person who is a member and acting on behalf of a group of persons having the same interest in the proceedings concerned.

Recovery of costs by Legal Aid Board

The Legal Aid Board is entitled to recover the costs incurred by it in providing legal aid or advice.[428] To this end a person in receipt of legal aid or advice who recovers damages, money (including costs) or property in court or tribunal proceedings or by virtue of a settlement is obliged to pay the sums recovered into or make the property recovered or preserved for him subject to a charge in favour of the Legal Aid Fund. However, the Board is obliged to waive this requirement to the extent that the money or other property consists of a house or portion of it (including the normal household chattels) which is the normal place of residence of the recipient of legal aid or advice or the first €3,174 (£2,500) of any monies payable by way of arrears or lump sum under the Social Welfare Acts, the Health Acts 1947 to 1994, the Unfair Dismissals Acts 1977 to 1993, the Minimum Notice and Terms of Employment Acts 1973–1991, the Employment Equality Act 1977, the Anti-Discrimination (Pay) Act 1974 or the Redundancy Payments Acts 1967 to 1991.[429] In addition the Board has a discretion to waive its entitlement to costs in circumstances where not to do so would be likely to create hardship for the recipient of the legal aid or advice.[430] Subject to this obligation and discretion as to waiver where the total cost incurred by the Legal Aid Board in providing legal aid or advice is less than the total amount paid into the Legal Aid Fund by way of contribution, payment made or charge created in favour of the Fund by the person in receipt of legal aid or advice the balance must be refunded to him/her.[431]

In general costs awarded to a person not in receipt of legal aid against a person in receipt of legal aid are not recoverable from the Legal Aid Fund. However, the Board has a discretion to make an *ex gratia* payment towards such costs if it is satisfied:

(a) that the proceedings were instituted by the unsuccessful litigant;

---

[428] Civil Legal Aid Act 1995, s.33(6).
[429] *Ibid.*, s.33(8)(a).
[430] *Ibid.*, s.33(8)(b).
[431] *Ibid.*, s.35.

(b) the successful litigant has taken all reasonable steps to recover his or her costs from the unsuccessful litigant in person;

(c) the successful litigant will suffer sever financial hardship unless an *ex gratia* payment is made;

(d) the *ex gratia* payment will not exceed the amount that would be allowed if the costs were taxed on a party and party basis; and

(e) the case has been finally determined.[432]

Attorney General's Scheme Civil legal aid is not currently available to challenge the validity of a detention under the Mental Health Act by way of a *habeas corpus* application. A person may however obtain legal representation for a *habeas corpus* application through the non-statutory Attorney General's Scheme. The aim of the scheme is to provide legal representation for persons where it is needed but the applicant cannot afford it. The scheme is not however an alternative to costs and a person who wishes to avail of the scheme must do so at the commencement of the proceedings. The applicant must satisfy the court that s/he is unable to retain legal representation without the benefit of the Scheme.

Provision for legal aid under the Mental Health Act 2001

By virtue of section 33(3) of the Mental Health Act 2001, one of the functions of the Mental Health Commission is to make or arrange for the making, with the consent of the Minister for Health and the Minister for Finance of a scheme or schemes for the granting by the Commission of legal aid to patients. (No mention is made, however, of legal advice.) It is not clear whether this legal aid is to be made available for patients appearing before Mental Health Tribunals only or whether it will have a wider remit.

Under the provisions of section 17 of the Act, the Mental Health Commission must upon receipt of a copy of an admission order or a renewal order assign a legal representative to represent the patient concerned unless he or she proposes to engage one.

By virtue of section 64(6)(b)(vii) conditions attached by the Mental Health Commission to the registration of an approved centre may specify measures to be taken to ensure that patients and residents are informed of their rights under the Act. Although this is in the nature of an administrative power it may if exercised strictly by the Commission have potentially wide ranging effects.

Assistance from Human Rights Commission

Another provision worthy of note in the context of a patient's right of access to a lawyer is section 10 of the Human Rights Commission Act 2000. By virtue of section 10(2), a person may apply to the Human Rights Commission[433] for legal assistance in relation to

---

[432] Civil Legal Aid Act 1995, s.36.

[433] The Commission was established to perform the functions conferred on it by the Act on July 25, 2001. See Human Rights Commission 2000 (Establishment Day) Order 2001 (S.I. No. 340 of 2001).

legal proceedings (a) involving law or practice relating to the protection of human rights which a person has instituted or wishes to institute and (b) legal proceedings in the course of which a person relies or wishes to rely on such a law or practice. "Human Rights" is defined in the Act to mean (a) the rights, liberties and freedoms conferred on or guaranteed to, persons by the Constitution and (b) the rights, liberties or freedoms conferred on, or guaranteed to persons by any agreement, treaty or convention to which the State is a party.[434]

The Commission may decide to grant an application for such assistance as is appropriate on any of the following grounds namely (a) the matter to which the legal proceedings concerned relate raises a question of principle; (b) it would be unreasonable to expect the person to deal with the matter concerned without legal assistance because of its complexity or for any other reason and (c) that there are other special circumstances which make it appropriate for the Commission to grant such assistance.[435]

The assistance which may be granted is (a) the provision or the arranging for the provision of, legal advice to the applicant, (b) the provision, or the arranging for the provision of, legal representation to the applicant, (c) the provision of such other assistance to applicant as the Commission deems appropriate in the circumstances.[436]

The Commission may decide to refuse to grant an application for such assistance as is appropriate if in its opinion (a) the assistance sought could be obtained by the applicant (i) under the Civil Legal Aid Act 1995 (ii) under the Criminal Justice (Legal Aid) Act 1962 or (iii) by any other means, whether or not provided for by or under any enactment or (b) powers to award redress or grant relief in relation to the matter to which the proceedings relate stand vested in any tribunal or other person and the matter, could, in the opinion of the Commission, be more effectively or conveniently dealt with by that tribunal or other person.[437]

Any arrangements made by the Commission under section 10 for the provision of legal advice or representation to the applicant may include provision for recovery of ₀ expenses incurred by or on behalf of the Commission in that behalf from the applicant in specified circumstances.[438]

Institution of actions by the Human Rights Commission

The Commission itself is further empowered by section 11 of the 2000 Act to institute proceedings in any court of competent jurisdiction for the purpose of obtaining relief of a declaratory or other nature in respect of any matter concerning the human rights of any person or class of persons. In this respect "human rights" according to section 11(3) means: (a) the rights, liberties and freedoms conferred on or guaranteed to persons by the Constitution and (b) the rights, liberties or freedoms, conferred on or guaranteed to, persons by any agreement, treaty or convention to which the state is a party and which has been given the force of law in the State or by a provision of any such agreement, treaty or convention which has been given such force. Since the enactment of section 7

---

[434] Human Rights Commission Act 2000, s.2.
[435] *Ibid.*, s.10(4).
[436] *Ibid.*, s.10(5).
[437] Civil Legal Aid Act 1995, s.10(3).
[438] Human Rights Commission Act 2000, s.10(6).

of the European Convention on Human Rights Act 2003 this definition has been expanded by the addition of a paragraph (c) to include the rights, liberties and freedoms conferred on or guaranteed to persons by the Convention provisions within the meaning of the European Convention on Human Rights Act 2003.

The declaratory relief which the Commission may seek to obtain in proceedings instituted in exercise of its powers under section 11 includes relief by way of declaration that a statute[439] or a provision thereof is invalid having regard to the provisions of the Constitution or was not continued in force by Article 50 of the Constitution.[440]

Commentary on right of access to a lawyer

International principles relevant to patient's right of access to lawyer

The *Principles for the Protection of all Persons under any Form of Detention or Imprisonment* adopted by the General Assembly of the United Nations on 9 December 1988 provide that a detained person shall be entitled to have the assistance of a legal counsel. He shall be informed of his right by the competent authority promptly after arrest and shall be provided with reasonable facilities for exercising it.[441] If a detained person does not have a legal counsel of his own choice he shall be entitled to have a legal counsel assigned to him by a judicial or other authority in all cases where the interests of justice so require and without payment by him if he does not have sufficient means to pay.[442]

Principle 1.5 *United Nations Principles for the Protection of Persons with Mental Illness and the Improvement of Mental Health Care* provides that every person with a mental illness shall have the right to exercise all rights as recognised in the Body of Principles for the Protection of All Persons under Any Form of the Detention and Imprisonment. Principle 18 provides that the patient shall be entitled to choose and appoint a counsel to represent the patient as such including representation in any complaint procedure or appeal. If the patient does not secure such services a counsel shall be made available without payment by the patient to the extent that the patient lacks sufficient means to pay. Where access to medical records are concerned Principle 18 continues:

> "the patient and the patient's counsel may request and produce at any hearing an independent mental health report and any other reports and oral, written and other evidence that are relevant and admissible.[443]

---

[439] "Statute" in this context is defined by s.11(3) of the Human Rights Commission Act 2000 as having the same meaning as it has in the Interpretation Act 1937. S.3 of the 1937 Act defines "statute" as including (in addition to Acts of the Oireachtas) Acts of the Oireachtas of Saorstát Éireann, Acts of the Parliament of the former United Kingdom of Great Britain and Ireland, and Acts of a Parliament sitting at any time before the coming into force of the Union with Ireland Act 1800.

[440] Human Rights Commission Act 2000, s.11(2).

[441] Principle 17.1.

[442] Principle 17.2.

[443] Principle 18.3.

Copies of the patient's records and any reports and documents to be submitted shall be given to the patient and to the patient's counsel except in special cases where it is determined that a specific disclosure to the patient would cause serious harm to the patient's health or put at risk the safety of others. As domestic law may provide, any document not given to the patient should, when this is done in confidence, be given to the patient's personal representative and counsel. When any part of a document is withheld from a patient, the patient or the patient's counsel, if any, shall receive notice of the withholding and the reasons for it and it shall be subject to judicial review."[444]

Article 5(4) of the European Convention on Human Rights provides that everyone who is deprived of his liberty by arrest or detention shall be entitled to take proceedings by which a court shall decide the lawfulness of his detention speedily and his release ordered if the detention is not lawful. In *Megyeri v. Germany*,[445] it was held Article 5(4) implied that a person detained as being mentally disordered was entitled to legal representation at the hearing unless there were special circumstances suggesting otherwise and that the person concerned should not be required to take the initiative to obtain legal representation.

The provisions of section 17 of the Mental Health Act go a considerable way towards meeting these obligations. However, as the example of other jurisdictions demonstrates given the special needs of persons with mental illness they could go further towards ensuring that a patient can exercise his/her right to legal representation effectively.

Comparative law relating to detained patient's right of access to a lawyer

Right of access to a lawyer in Canada In Canada, section 10 of the Canadian Charter of Rights and Freedoms provides that:

> "Everyone has the right on arrest or detention … (b) to retain and instruct counsel without delay and to be informed of that right".

The necessity for a person in detention to have assistance with the exercise of the right to retain counsel where s/he wishes to do so but does not know how to do so was addressed in *R v. Williams*,[446] a decision of the Alberta Court of Appeal in which Hetherington J.A expressed the opinion that "[t]he right of a person who is arrested or detained to retain and instruct counsel without delay is an empty and meaningless one if the person does not know and is not told how he can give effect to it." She concluded that if the accused in any manner indicates that he would like to retain and instruct counsel the peace officer is obliged to explain to him how he may do so. The two other members of the panel declined to endorse this view but they conceded that a duty to assist the accused in exercising his right to retain counsel might well arise in the "relatively rare" case where the accused was unable to understand the meaning of his rights. Applied in the context of civil commitment the reasoning in this case and particularly that of the Hetherington J.A. would require the hospital staff to assist patients who wished to obtain legal advice but did not know how to do so.

---

[444] Principle 18.4.
[445] A 237-A (1992).
[446] (1986) 48 Alta.L.R. (2d) 68 (C.A.).

In Saskatchewan there exists an advocacy scheme that is aimed at advising patients of their rights and assisting them with respect to their right to apply for review. Under the scheme an "official representative" must be notified of the patient's detention or transfer.[447] S/he is required to visit patients within 24 hours and advise them of their rights including the right to apply for review.[448] The official representative must also offer to assist patients in exercising their rights and must (as far as is reasonably practicable) provide any assistance that is requested with respect to the prosecution of an appeal or application for review.[449]

Right of access to a lawyer in England and Wales In England and Wales patients are entitled to have anyone represent them before a Mental Health Review Tribunal. The Mental Health Act 1983 Revised Code of Practice[450] requires patients to be informed as to how to apply to a Tribunal; how to contact a suitably qualified solicitor; that free Legal Aid – Advice by Way of Representation may be available and how to contact any other organisation which may be able to help them make an application to a Tribunal.[451] The Mental Health Review Tribunal Rules also provide that if the patient does not want to conduct his own case and has not authorised anyone else to do so the tribunal can appoint someone to act as his representative.[452]

Where entitlement to legal aid is concerned a person proposing to apply to a Mental Health Review Tribunal in England and Wales may subject to satisfying merits test[453] also obtain financial assistance under the Legal Aid Act 1988 with the cost of retaining a lawyer to represent them.

Under the Mental Health Review Tribunal Rules where a patient's authorised representative is either a barrister or a solicitor or a registered medical practitioner or some other person authorised by the patient or applicant whom the tribunal considers to be suitable because of his experience or professional qualifications, that authorised representative has the right to see all the evidence even if there are grounds for withholding some from the patient and to remain throughout the hearing even though the patient or anyone else is excluded.[454]

Conclusions relating to the access of a patient with mental illness to a lawyer

1. In addition to legal aid it is submitted that patients should be entitled to legal advice under the proposed scheme in the Mental Health Act.

---

[447] Sask. Reg. 1984-85, c. M-13.1 S.16(2) The official representatives are appointed by the Minister for each region under s.10 of the Act.

[448] *Ibid.*, s.33(2): Sask. Reg. c. M-13.1 Reg. 1. s.13.

[449] *Ibid.*, c. M-13.1, Reg. 1, ss. 13(1)(c), (h).

[450] March 1999.

[451] Para.14.5.

[452] S.I. No.942 of 1983, r.10.

[453] The means test was abolished by S.I. No. 805 of 1994 inserting reg.5A into the Regulations. The Legal Advice and Assistance Regulations S.I. No. 340 of 1989 provide that approval for legal representation must be refused "unless it is shown that the client has reasonable grounds" for bringing proceedings and may be refused if it appears unreasonable in all the circumstances that it should be granted. Reg. 22.

[454] Mental Health Review Tribunal Rules (S.I. No. 942 of 1983) rr.12(3) and 21(4).

2.   It is not clear from the Mental Health Act whether assistance will be given to a patient to exercise his right to legal representation of his own choosing. The choice appears to be between accepting the lawyer assigned by the Mental Health Commission or relying entirely on one's own initiative in obtaining an alternative one. Assistance should be given to the patient in obtaining a lawyer of his/her choice.

3.   A matter not specifically addressed in the Mental Health Act is the significant issue of the extent of the lawyer's access to the patient's records for the purpose of representation before the Mental Health Tribunal and the extent to which details may be disclosed to his client. It is submitted that in accordance with the *UN Principles for the Protection of Persons with Mental Illness and the Improvement of Mental Health Care*,[455] the patient's counsel should be entitled to receive copies of the patient's records and any relevant reports and documents and to be notified when any part of a document is withheld from a patient. Documents should only be withheld from a patient where it is determined that a specific disclosure to the patient would cause serious damage to the patient's health or put at risk the safety of others and any withholding should be subject to judicial review.

4.   The experience of other jurisdictions is that there is a reluctance on the part of the legal profession both in private practice and through legal aid schemes to become involved in the practice of law relating to patients in psychiatric facilities,[456] and there is a need for a panel of lawyers qualified in mental health law to act on their behalf.[457] It is submitted that to facilitate and encourage representation of patients with mental illness the Bar Council and the Law Society should consider the development of a specialist Mental Health Law panels.

5.   Given the fact that people with mental illness are particularly vulnerable to invasion of their rights and require assistance with their exercise it is submitted that consideration should be given to the establishment and definition by legislation of the role of the Patient Advocate who would be responsible for representing persons in the mental health care setting. It is submitted that any advocacy service so established should be independent of the providers of mental health care. Advocates should be trained in the law and have a sound working knowledge of psychiatry, psychology, and the law relating to the social services. It is submitted that they should be responsible for representing the interests of patients within a given area and also be involved in conciliation and mediation. The advocate should have a duty to visit all persons in any psychiatric hospital in that area so as to inform those persons of the available services and the hospital reciprocally should have a duty to facilitate the advocate in the performance of his/her functions. On admission to

---

[455] Adopted by the General Assembly, December 17, 1991.

[456] Kaiser notes of the Canadian situation. "Although legal services may already by theoretically available through the private bar and legal aid schemes the actual level of involvement by lawyers has been low compared to the obvious needs of the mentally ill." See "Legal Services for the Mentally Ill: A Polemic and a Plea" (1986) 35 U.N.B.J. 89.

[457] Cooney and O'Neill, *op. cit.*, note that the proposal to extend the scheme of civil legal aid to appearances before the mental health review board appears to exclude lawyers who have developed experience under the criminal legal aid scheme protecting personal liberty before the criminal courts. See p.154.

hospital all persons should be entitled to receive written information explaining the person's rights and the advocate's role and powers. The person should also be given details as to how to contact the advocate. The advocate should be entitled by statute to information about the policies, practices, procedures and programmes in hospitals and units and on the individual patient's instructions to access to his/her medical and social records. The advocate should also have a right to be heard when decisions relating to the individual's care and treatment are to be made. In addition the advocate should have power to accept and investigate complaints from third parties interested in the patient's welfare. The service should also be capable of offering advocacy services to people with mental illness at all stages of their contact with the mental health services *i.e.* on admission, while in hospital or in community care, on discharge, during aftercare and also in relation to issues such as social welfare entitlement, and access to employment and education.[458]

---

[458] See Cooney & O'Neill, *op. cit.*, pp.292–297.

CHAPTER FOUR

Treatment of Patients while in Hospital – Substantive Rights

INTRODUCTION

In this chapter the focus is on substantive rights of the person with mental illness whilst in hospital and whether the patient is afforded the right to treatment, the right to self determination in matters relating to consent to treatment, the right to bodily integrity in the matter of the application of constraints; the right to due process in the matter of extension of periods of detention; whether the law is effective in upholding standards of care in psychiatric hospital and whether the patient has appropriate access to the courts in the matter of vindication of rights.

A PATIENT'S AFFIRMATIVE RIGHT TO TREATMENT

If involuntary detention is not to be regarded as the mere arbitrary exercise of state power then a right to treatment must follow as a necessary quid pro quo for the deprivation of liberty of a person with mental illness. In fact, if given its full effect the right to treatment should involve a duty on the part of the state to provide a humane physical and psychological environment, qualified staff in adequate numbers, individualised treatment plans and proper regulation of the various methods of treatment as part of the right to treatment. This argument in favour of a right to treatment would be subject to the right of the competent involuntary patient to refuse treatment.

Further involuntary patients have a right to expect the prevention of deterioration in their condition while detained. Simple detention in a psychiatric hospital may lead to regression and a failure to realise a patient's capacity to improve. Accordingly subject to the patient's right to refuse treatment the hospital should provide a patient with protection from harm while detained, decent and hygienic conditions and appropriate treatment.

Thirdly, the deprivation of liberty of a person with mental illness is frequently justified on the basis that its aim is in fact to restore a person's autonomy by saving him/her from whatever incapacitating mental disorder s/he suffers. It would follow for the degree of deprivation of liberty to be regarded as proportionate to the achievement of that aim a person should not be detained for any longer than is necessary to restore autonomy. Prompt and effective treatment is required to ensure that this is the case. Accordingly a right to treatment should be guaranteed subject to the right of the competent patient to refuse it.

The current law

Position under Mental Treatment Act 1945

The Mental Treatment Act 1945 in its provisions providing for involuntary admission used the fact that the patient requires treatment as the basis for involuntary admission but vested no enforceable right to treatment in the patient after committal.[1] Thus in effect the patient was left in the situation where s/he was left no option but to accept what was currently on offer in the psychiatric hospital.

Position under Mental Health Act 2001

Section 3 of the Mental Health Act 2001 now makes the existence of mental disorder the basis for involuntary admission. "Mental disorder" is defined by section 3(1)(b) as:

> "mental illness, severe dementia or significant intellectual disability where (i) because of the severity of the illness, disability or dementia, the judgment of the person concerned is so impaired that *failure to admit the person to an approved centre* would be likely to lead to a serious deterioration in his or her condition or *would prevent the administration of appropriate treatment that could only be given by such admission* and (ii) *the* reception, detention and *treatment of the person concerned in an approved centre would be likely to benefit or alleviate the condition of that person to a material extent.*" (Italics added)

In this case effective treatment is postulated as the justification for involuntary admission but once again no specific enforceable right to treatment is vested in the patient after involuntary admission. Medical discretion and (inevitably) available resources determines what treatment is given to the patient.

Section 8(1) of the Mental Health Act 2001 provides that a person may be involuntarily admitted to an approved centre and *detained* there on the grounds that he or she is suffering from a mental disorder. No reference is made to treatment, which is the *sine qua non* of the involuntary admission.

However, section 66(1) of the 2001 Act empowers the Minister for Health and Children after consultation with the Mental Health Commission to make regulations as s/he thinks appropriate in relation to approved centres for the purpose of ensuring proper standards in relation to approved centres including adequate and suitable accommodation, food and care for residents while being maintained in centres and the proper conduct of centres. Without prejudice to the generality of these provisions regulations may prescribe requirements as to the drawing up and carrying out by approved centres so far as practicable in consultation with each resident of *an individual care plan* for that resident including the setting of appropriate goals.[2]

---

[1] See ss.163(2) and 178(2) which requires the medical practitioner to certify that the person is of unsound mind and is a proper person to be taken charge of and "detained under care and treatment" and is unlikely to recover within six months from the date of examination before s/he can be involuntarily admitted. See also ss.184(4) and 185(4) which requires a medical practitioner certificate to state that s/he is of opinion that the person the subject of the application requires not more than six months "suitable treatment" for his recovery.

[2] Mental Health Act 2001, s.66(2)(g).

Commentary

The right to treatment reflected in international principles

Recognition of the right to treatment may found in international principles governing mental health care. The *UN Principles for the Protection of Persons with Mental Illness and the Improvement of Mental Health Care*[3] asserts at Principle 1, which is entitled "Fundamental Freedoms and Basic Rights":

> "All persons have the right to the best available mental health care which shall be part of the health and social care system."[4]

Principle 7.3 provides for a right to individualised treatment:

> "Every patient shall have the right to treatment suited to his or her cultural background."

Principle 8 addresses the issues of a patient's entitlement to care of a certain standard and provides:

> "Every patient shall have the right to receive such health and social care as is appropriate to his or her health needs and is entitled to care and treatment in accordance with the same standards as other ill persons."

Principle 9 of the Principles addresses the issue of treatment. Implicit in its provisions is recognition of a right to treatment and it aims to set standards in relation to the quality of that treatment as follows:

> "Every patient shall have the *right to be treated* in the least restrictive environment and with the least restrictive or intrusive treatment appropriate to the patient's health needs and the need to protect the physical safety of others."[5]

The treatment and care of every patient shall be based on an individually prescribed plan, discussed with the patient, reviewed regularly, revised as necessary and provided by qualified professional staff.[6] The treatment of every patient shall be directed towards preserving and enhancing personal autonomy.[7]

At European level, Article 5 of *Council of Europe Recommendations No. R (83) 2 of the Committee of Ministers to member states concerning the legal protection of persons suffering from mental disorders placed as involuntary patients*[8] provides that a patient under placement has the right to receive appropriate treatment and care.

Building upon Recommendation No. R (83) 2, *Recommendation 1235 (1994) of the*

---

[3] Adopted by the General Assembly on December 17, 1991.
[4] Principle 1.1.
[5] Principle 9.1.
[6] Principle 9.2.
[7] Principle 9.4.
[8] Adopted by the Committee of Ministers on February 22, 1983.

Parliamentary Assembly of the Council of Europe on Psychiatry and Human Rights makes a number of recommendations in relation to the standard of treatment of patients among them that there must be adequate nursing staff appropriately trained in the care of such patients;[9] that accommodation in large dormitories should be avoided[10] and that there be accurate and detailed recording of the treatment given to the patient.[11] It also recommends that a distinction be made between handicapped and mentally ill patients.[12]

The right to treatment in comparative law

The right to treatment in American law Comparative support for the existence of a constitutional right to treatment in Irish law may be gleaned from the US decision in *Wyatt v. Stickney*,[13] in which Judge Johnson held that "to deprive any citizen of his or her liberty upon the altruistic theory that the confinement is for humane therapeutic reasons and then fail to provide adequate treatment violates the very fundamentals of due process."[14] In the course of the judgment the court also set out a set of "minimum constitutional standards for adequate treatment of the mentally ill"[15] which have formed the basis of subsequent decisions on the constitutional rights of patients. These included the right to (a) a humane psychological and physical environment, (b) qualified staff in adequate numbers to administer adequate treatment and (c) individualised treatment plans:

(a) Subsumed in the right to a humane psychological and physical environment was the patient's right to privacy and dignity and the right to the least restrictive conditions necessary to achieve the purposes of commitment; freedom from unnecessary or excessive restraint or seclusion; the right to protection against unnecessary or excessive medication and to safeguards against drugs as unwarranted chemical restraints. The court also added other elements such as the rights to wear one's own clothing; to have physical exercise on a regular basis; to go outdoors at frequent intervals; to have interaction with members of the opposite sex; to send sealed mail; and to enjoy visitation and telephone communications with those outside the treatment facilities.[16]

(b) The court in *Wyatt* required that psychiatric facilities have qualified staff in adequate numbers to administer adequate treatment. Although the case of *O'Connor v. Donaldson*,[17] heard after *Wyatt*, was decided on the basis of the applicant's loss of liberty the irregularity and superficiality of the treatment staff's contact with the applicant constituted a major factor in his judicial victory.

---

[9] Para.ii.d.
[10] Para.iii.b.
[11] Para.ii.c.
[12] Para.ii.a.
[13] 325 F. Supp. 781 (M.D. Ala. 1971).
[14] *Ibid.*, p.785.
[15] These included thirty five specific measure for securing individualised treatment plans, adequate and qualified staffing and a humane psychological and physical environment.
[16] *Wyatt v. Stickney*, 344 F. Supp. 373, 379 (Standards 4–5, 11–17).
[17] 422 U.S. 563, 569 (1975).

(c) Specifying the right of the patient to an individualised, written treatment or service plan, the court in *Wyatt* detailed the elements which should be included in such a plan including intermediate and long range treatment goals, projected timetables for their attainment, criteria for release to less restrictive treatment conditions, criteria for discharge and a post-hospitalisation plan.[18] The right to periodic review of treatment and the right to appropriate revision of treatment plans were also recognised. The court required that the treatment plan be "continuously reviewed' by the responsible mental health professional. The findings of periodic reviews should assess the "success and failures of the treatment program" and incorporate in the plan "whatever modifications are necessary."[19]

Conclusions

1.   It is submitted that legislation should be enacted recognising the involuntary patient's right to individually tailored and appropriate treatment as will afford him/her a reasonable chance to recover or achieve improvement in their condition. In particular the patient should be entitled to receive such medical, psychological, social, educational and occupational therapy services as his or her condition requires to bring about a return to his or her community as early as possible. The patient should also be entitled to expect that the treatment s/he receives be provided safely and humanely with full concern and respect for the dignity, personal integrity and rights of the patient.[20]

2.   As a precondition to his/her receiving appropriate treatment the patient should have a statutory right to expect that the psychiatric hospital in which s/he is detained will provide a humane physical and psychological environment in which to recover.[21] In particular because of the adverse psychological effects of involuntary hospitalisation the involuntarily detained patient should have a right to treatment in the least restrictive conditions necessary to achieve the purposes of treatment.

3.   The patient should also have a statutory right to expect that the hospital has a qualified staff in adequate numbers to administer proper treatment. In particular the hospital should be in a position to offer an assurance that there will be appropriate staff-patient ratios in hospitals.

4. The patient should have a statutory right to an individualised treatment plans[22] and proper regulation of the various methods of treatment.

---

[18] See *Wyatt v. Stickney* 344 F. Supp. 373, 384–5 (M.D.Ala) (Standards 26–31): Also *Davis v. Watkins*, 384 F. Supp. 1196, 1203–06 (N.D. Ohio 1974).

[19] See *Wyatt v. Stickney* 344 F. Supp. 373 at 384 (M.D. Ala. 1972) (Standards 29 and 31 g).

[20] See Cooney & O'Neill, *Psychiatric Detention Civil Commitment in Ireland* (Baikonur, 1996), p. 238.

[21] Successive reports of the Inspector of Mental Hospitals have indicated that basic hospital conditions in many hospitals are below an acceptable minimum standard.

[22] Cooney & O'Neill, *op. cit.*, suggest that the treatment plan should include (1) a statement of the least restrictive treatment conditions necessary to achieve the purposes of commitment; (2) a description of intermediate and long-range treatment goals, with a projected timetable for their attainment; (3) a statement and rationales for the treatment for achieving these intermediate and long-range goals; (4) a specification of staff responsibility and a description or proposed staff

5. Finally, all of the above rights in relation to treatment should be subject to the patient's right as a competent involuntary patient to refuse to consent to treatment.

CONSENT AS THE BASIS FOR PSYCHIATRIC TREATMENT

It is a basic rule of medical practice that no treatment should be given to a competent patient without his/her informed consent. This informed consent requirement serves to promote respect for the person's right of autonomy or self determination and his or her welfare or best interests.[23] There are sound therapeutic reasons for adopting this approach. Bandura suggests that individuals who are coerced into carrying out tasks do not feel a commitment to the task and do not have a sense of being personally responsible for its successful outcome.[24] Thus patients who are not involved in medical decision-making tend not to follow medical and psychiatric advice. Conversely enabling a patient to share in the process of decision making about his or her health may stimulate an active commitment to carrying out successfully the necessary therapeutic tasks.[25]

From a rights perspective the right to self-determination inheres in the idea of being a human equal. This in turn plays a vital role in the structure of the carer patient relationship alerting the carer to the fact that the patient has rights which must be respected.[26]

Self-determination involves the capacity of the individual to make important decisions about himself/herself according to his/her own aims and values. Problems arise when the patient is unable to exercise genuine self-determination or autonomy by reason of serious mental disorder such as severe psychotic delusions. It is this situation, which poses a challenge to devise legal standards, which cater precisely for that degree of incapacity without being over inclusive or otherwise discriminating against the interests of the person with mental illness.

VOLUNTARY PATIENTS AND THE REQUIREMENT OF CONSENT

The position as governed by common law

In the case of voluntary patients the criteria for giving consent to treatment for mental disorder are similar to those relating to consent to other forms of treatment and are governed by the common law. In summary they require (a) that the patient's consent be voluntary; (b) that the patient have capacity to understand the nature and likely effects

---

involvement with the patient in order to achieve these treatment goals; (5) criteria for release to less restrictive conditions; and (6) criteria for discharge. (At p.257). See also *Wyatt v. Stickney* 344 F Supp 373 (1972).

[23] Gustafson, "Ain't nobody Gonna Cut My Head!" (1975) *The Hastings Center Report* 49.

[24] See Bandura, *Social Foundations of Thought and Action: A Social Cognitive Theory* (Englewood Cliffs, Prentice Hall, N.J. 1986).

[25] "Restructuring Informed Consent: Legal Therapy for the Doctor-Patient Relationship" (1970) 79 Yale L.J. 1533.

[26] See Shannon, "The Problem of Interests and Loyalties: Ethical Dilemmas in Obtaining Informed Consent" (1976) *Bioethics Digest* 1.

of the proposed treatment; (c) that the patient has been given appropriate information to enable him/her to give informed consent. Exceptionally in emergency circumstances where a voluntary patient is unable to communicate his/her consent s/he may be treated to remove a danger to the life or health of the patient.

(a) The requirement that voluntary patients consent be freely given The consent of the patient must be voluntary and not be induced by force or fraud. In *In re T (Adult: Refusal of Treatment)*,[27] Lord Donaldson stated that to test for the presence of duress in a medical context:

> "The real question in each such case is "Does the patient really mean what he says or is he merely saying it for a quiet life, to satisfy someone else or because the advice and persuasion to which he has been subjected is such that he can no longer think and decide for himself?"

Where consent is alleged to have been induced by fraud the validity of that consent is a question of fact – whether the patient's will was overborne in the circumstances of the case.[28] Where a patient is present in a psychiatric hospital there are dicta of the English Court of Appeal[29] to suggest that medical practitioners should be especially careful to satisfy themselves that consent is freely given. It has been noted that the mere fact of being in hospital assigned to the role of psychiatric patient may be regarded as inherently coercive.[30]

The issue of voluntariness may also raise itself in the context of treatment of a violent patient. In this context the Irish Medical Council's *Guide to Ethical Conduct and Behaviour*[31] provides that as a matter of pratice:

> "A doctor asked to examine or treat a violent patient is under no obligation to put him/herself or other healthcare staff in danger but should attempt to persuade the patient concerned to permit an assessment as to whether any therapy is required"[32]

Accordingly the doctor is clearly under an obligation to persuade the patient to consent to an examination.

Even if a patient gives a valid consent s/he has the right to revoke it at any time. For instance a patient may have consented to a course of drug treatment but may withdraw it before it has been completed. The only exceptions to this rule are circumstances where a patient consents on terms, which restrict his right to revoke.[33]

---

[27] [1992] 3 W.L.R. 782.

[28] *In re T (adult; refusal of medical treatment)* [1992] 4 All E.R. 649.

[29] See *Freeman v. Home Office (No.2)* [1984] Q.B. 524.

[30] See Bartlett and Sandland, *Mental Health Law, Policy and Practice* (2nd ed., Oxford University Press, Oxford), p.343.

[31] 6th edition, 2004.

[32] Para.18.1.

[33] See *Robinson v. Balmain New Ferry Co.* [1910] A.C. 295 and *Herd v. Weardale Steel Coal and Coke Co. Ltd* [1915] A.C. 67.

(b) The requirement that voluntary patients have capacity to consent A voluntary patient must have capacity to consent. In the English decision of *In re C (Refusal of Treatment)*[34] court used a threefold test to determine capacity to consent to medical treatment in that case where a detained patient suffering from chronic schizophrenia refused consent to amputation of a gangrenous leg. The test employed was (a) whether the patient could understand the information relevant to the decision in question, (b) whether the patient could believe the information and (c) whether the patient can weigh that information in the balance to arrive at a choice. The court also ruled that the relevant question as to whether it is established that the patient's capacity is so reduced by his mental illness that he does not fully understand the nature, purpose and effects of the treatment. There is no reason why the test in *In re C*, should not apply equally to determining the capacity of a voluntary patient to consent to psychiatric treatment.

The Irish Medical Council's *Guide to Ethical Conduct and Behaviour*[35] advises doctors that as a matter of practice that in cases of refusal to consent the assessment of competence and the discussion on consent should be carried out in conjunction with a senior colleague.[36]

The issue of capacity was also addressed in Ireland in *A Ward of Court, re*,[37] where the Supreme Court accepted that an individual with capacity could refuse life saving treatment but the fact that capacity was not present did not mean loss of constitutional rights, such as the right to self determination and the right to refuse treatment.

Consent of minors to consent to psychiatric treatment Where the voluntary patient is a minor the issue of capacity looms large. Section 23 of the Non-Fatal Offences 1997 against the Person Act provides that the consent of a minor who has attained the age of 16 years to any surgical, medical or dental treatment, which in the absence of consent would constitute a trespass to his or her person, shall be as effective as it would be if he or she were of full age and where a minor by virtue of section 23 has given an effective consent to any treatment it shall not be necessary to obtain any consent for it from his or her parent or guardian. "Surgical, medical or dental treatment" is defined to include any procedure undertaken for the purposes of diagnosis and extends to any procedure including the administration of an anaesthetic which is ancillary to such treatment. It is clear that "medical treatment" within the section would include psychiatric treatment.

However, section 2 of the Mental Health Act 2001 provides that a "child" means a person under the age of 18 years other than a person who is or has been married and it would appear by implication that a young person under the age of 18 years who is not married cannot give effective consent to psychiatric treatment in his own right. The 2001 Act contains no provisions expressly governing the giving of consent given by a minor who is a voluntary patient. The situation of capacity of a minor under the age of 18 to give consent to psychiatric treatment would therefore appear to be governed by the common law and legally effective consent to treatment for mental disorder may be given by a parent where that treatment is in the best interests of the minor.

However, at common law there is persuasive authority in the form of the English

---

[34] [1994] I. F.L.R. 31.
[35] 6th edition, 2004.
[36] See para.17.1.
[37] [1995] 2 I.L.R.M. 401.

decision of House of Lords in *Gillick v. West Norfolk and Wisbech Area Health Authority*[38] to the effect that a minor who full comprehends the nature and consequences of the proposed medical treatment may give valid consent in his/her own right without requiring parental consent. If this authority were to apply to the situation of a minor's consent to psychiatric treatment in Ireland it would mean that a minor under the age of 18 years who understands the nature and consequences of that treatment could give valid consent to it.

However, in *In re R (A Minor) (Wardship Consent to Treatment)*,[39] Lord Donaldson dealt a serious blow to the autonomy of *Gillick* competent minors when he ruled that that while the refusal of a *Gillick* competent child to consent was a very important factor in the doctor's decision to treat or not to treat that did not prevent the necessary consent being obtained from another competent source such as a parent or person in *loco parentis*. The net effect of this decision is that the refusal of a competent child under 18 to consent to psychiatric treatment can be overridden by his or her parent or person in loco parentis.[40]

In addition it would appear that in Ireland Article 41 of the Constitution which accords supremacy in law to the institution of the family and Article 42.1 which recognises "the inalienable right and duty of parents to provide ... for ... the ... intellectual, physical and social education of their children" would prove a barrier to the application of the *Gillick* principles.

In the recent case of *North Western Health Board v. W(H)*[41] a majority[42] of the Supreme Court (Keane CJ dissenting) found that in most circumstances and in keeping with the family's rights under the Constitution the welfare of the child is best served by deferring to healthcare decisions made by a child's parents. The majority held relying on Article 42.5 of the Constitution that only in "exceptional circumstances" would the child's personal rights supersede family and parental considerations. Denham J. defined such circumstances as circumstances where there was "an imminent threat to life or serious injury."[43] Hardiman J. instanced the situation of where there was "an immediate threat to life".[44] Murray J. referred to circumstances where there was "an immediate and fundamental threat to the capacity of the child to continue to function as a human person, physically morally or socially, deriving from an exceptional dereliction of duty on the part of the parents."[45] Murphy J. defined the circumstances as "such a degree of neglect as to constitute abandonment of the child and all rights in respect of it."[46]

Keane C.J. dissenting and finding that the law in Ireland was effectively stated in the English case of *In re T (A Minor) (Wardship: Medical Treatment)*,[47] held that the best interests of the minor were the paramount consideration of the court under the Constitution and the law and those best interests prevailed over the wishes of the parents.

---

[38] [1985] 3 All E.R. 402.
[39] [1991] 4 All E.R. 177.
[40] See also *In re W (A Minor) (Medical Treatment: Courts Jurisdiction)* [1992] 3 W.L.R. 758.
[41] [2001] 3 I.R. 635.
[42] Denham, Murphy, Murray, Hardiman JJ.
[43] p.26 of judgment.
[44] p.31 of judgment.
[45] p.11 of judgment.
[46] p.8 of judgment.
[47] [1996] 35 B.M.L.R. 63.

The net effect of the application of Articles 41 and 42 in the context of consent of minors to psychiatric treatment in Ireland is that the parental right to give consent to psychiatric treatment where that treatment is in that child's best interests is likely to supersede the rights of the child and continue up to the age of 18.

As a matter of practice the Irish Medical Council's *Guide to Ethical Conduct and Behaviour*[48] advises doctors that:

> "if the doctor feels [as a matter of practice] that a child will understand a proposed medical procedure, information or advice, this should be explained fully to the child. Where the consent of parents or guardians is normally required in respect of a child for whom they are responsible due regard must be had to the wishes of the child."[49]

The Guide does not, however, state how much weight should be attached to these wishes. *The Guide* continues:

> "The doctor must *never* assume that it is safe to ignore the parental/guardian interest" [emphasis added].[50]

The Guide therefore appears to suggest that in accepted medical practice in Ireland parental/guardian interest takes precedence over those of the child in the majority of cases. It avoids outlining the situations in which consideration might be given to giving precedence to the wishes of the child.

Where an adult voluntary patient is found to be incapable of consenting to treatment then steps should be taken to admit him/her as an involuntary patient to the hospital and to treat him/her under section 57 of the Mental Health Act 2001. Where the child lacks competence his/her parent may give consent to psychiatric treatment where this is in his/her best interests and where the child is suffering from mental disorder and the parent is unwilling to consent the child may be admitted to hospital for treatment pursuant to an order of the District Court under section 25 of the Mental Health Act 2001.

(c) The requirement that voluntary patients consent be informed The voluntary patient must have been given appropriate information to enable him/her to give informed consent.

The three approaches to determining whether a patient's consent is adequately informed The question as to what is the proper test for deciding whether a medical practitioner has given sufficient information to a patient has invited three solutions at common law. These are best described in McMahon & Binchy on the *Law of Torts*:[51]

> "The first resolves the question by reference to the generally accepted practice in the medical profession. This test which is an application of the [test in the case of

---

[48] 6th edition, 2004.
[49] See para.18.3.
[50] See para.18.6.
[51] Butterworths, Dublin, 2000, pp.380–381.

Bolam v. Friern Hospital Management Committee[52]] stresses the fact that the decision of what to tell to the patient has traditionally been regarded as primarily a matter of medical judgment and discretion.

The second solution, at the other end of the spectrum, concentrates on the patients right to self-determination in regard to what is to be done to his body. It requires full disclosure of all material risks incident to the proposed treatment, so that the patient rather than the doctor makes the real choice as to whether treatment is to be carried out:

> 'The patient has the right to chart his own destiny, and the doctor must supply the patient with the material facts the patient will need in order to intelligently chart that destiny with dignity'."[53]

The third approach lies between these two extremes. While tilting somewhat towards the first, it applies the *Bolam* test save where the disclosure of a particular risk "was so obviously necessary to an informed choice on the part of the patient that no reasonably prudent medical man would fail to make it."[54]

The tests adopted by the English courts In England the resolution of the appropriate standard of care in disclosure cases has been problematic. In the House of Lords decision in *Sidaway v. Board of Governors of the Bethlehem Royal Hospital and the Maudsley Hospital,*[55] the Law Lords were divided on the correct approach. Lord Diplock favoured the application of the *Bolam* test (the first test), i.e. what to tell a patient is a matter of clinical decision making the standard of disclosure to be determined by the profession itself in matters of diagnosis and treatment. Lord Scarman favoured full disclosure of all material risks incident to the proposed treatment so that the patient rather than the medical practitioner could make the real decision as to whether or not to undergo treatment (the second test) . Lords Bridge and Keith [56] who while favouring the application of the *Bolam* test considered that disclosure of a particular risk was required where it was "so obviously necessary to an informed choice on the part of the patient that no reasonably prudent medical man would fail to make it."[57] (the third test) Lord Templeman took the view that the duty of the doctor who must have regard to the best interests of the patient is to "provide the patient with information which will enable the patient to make a balanced judgment if the patient chooses to make a balanced judgment."[58]

---

[52] [1957] 2 All E.R. 118.
[53] *Miller v. Kennedy* (1975) 85 Wash 2d 151, 530 P 2d 334.
[54] See McMahon & Binchy, *op. cit.*, pp.380–381.
[55] [1985] A.C. 871.
[56] In particular O'Hanlon J. relied on the dicta of Lord Bridge and Lord Keith that a medical practitioner would be negligent where he failed to disclose a particular risk which was so "obviously necessary to an informed choice on the part of the patient that no reasonably prudent medical man would fail to make it." [1985] A.C. 871 at 900 per Lord Bridge.
[57] [1985] A.C. 871 at 900 The *Dunne* test when applied in the context of informed consent is essentially the same as that favoured by Lords Bridge and Keith in *Sidaway*.
[58] [1985] 1 All E.R. 643 at 666.

In the later case of *Bolitho v. City and Hackney Health Authority*,[59] the House of Lords rejected the *Bolam* test and held that if it can be established that a body of medical opinion relied upon is not reasonable or responsible or is not capable of withstanding logical analysis then a finding of negligence cannot be avoided by reliance upon it. However, the House of Lords was careful in that case not to become embroiled in a debate on informed consent. Lord Scarman's approach based on disclosure of material risks has been favoured by the Supreme Court of Canada[60] and the High Court of Australia.[61]

In the later case of *Pearce v. United Bristol Healthcare NHS Trust*[62] which examined the issue of information provision the English Court of Appeal seemed to have moved away from the reasonable medical professional test (the first test) and towards "the reasonable patient" test (the second test). In that case Lord Woolf stated:

> "If there is a significant risk which would affect the judgment of a reasonable patient, then in the normal course it is the responsibility of a doctor to inform the patient of that significant risk, if the information is needed so that the patient can determine for him or herself as to what course she should adopt."[63]

As a matter of basic principle for consent to be regarded as appropriately informed the patient must be "informed in broad terms of the nature[64] of the procedure which is intended."[65] If the patient wishes to complain that s/he was not properly informed of the risks attached to psychiatric treatment then the complaint must now be grounded in breach of statutory duty or negligence.[66]

The Irish tests for determining whether a patient's consent has been adequately informed In the general context of negligence actions in respect of medical treatment Walsh J. in the Irish case of *O'Donovan v. Cork County Council*[67] stated the governing principles as follows:

---

[59] [1997] 4 All E.R. 771.
[60] *Hopp v. Lepp* (1980) 112 D.L.R. (3d) 67 (SC Can); *Reibl v. Hughes* (1980) 114 D.L.R. (3d) 1 (SC Can.).
[61] *Rogers v. Whittaker* (1992) 175 Comm. L.R. 479.
[62] [1999] P.I.Q.R. 53 (CA).
[63] *Ibid.*, p.59.
[64] The word "nature" is intended to include the purpose of the treatment. See *In re C* (1993) N.L.J.R. 1642 where Torpe J. stated the patient must understand the "nature, purpose and effect" of the treatment.
[65] *Chatterton v. Gerson* [1981] Q.B. 432.
[66] Judicial policy appears to lie against trespass claims in informed consent litigation. It has been argued (see G. Robertson, "Informed Consent to Medical Treatment" (1981) 97 L.Q.R. 102) that it has sought to confine claims in battery to deliberate, hostile acts, a situation which most judges would regard as hostile to the doctor-patient relationship – the stigma and damage to professional reputation being probably seen as more serious in an action for battery than in an action for negligence. Secondly there has been a deliberate policy to restrict the doctrine of informed consent by means of the requirement of causation, expert evidence as to accepted medical practice and the "best interests of the patient" principle. Restriction in this manner would not be possible if failure to inform were to ground an action in trespass.
[67] [1967] I.R. 173.

252 *Irish Mental Health Law*

"A medical practitioner cannot be held negligent if he honours general and approved practice in the situation with which he is faced. ... That proposition is not, however, without qualification. If there is a common practice which has inherent defects, which ought to be obvious to any person giving the matter due consideration, the fact that it is shown to have been widely and generally adopted over a period of time does not make the practice any the less negligent. Neglect of duty does not cease by repetition to be neglect of duty."[68]

This view was restated and affirmed in *Dunne v. National Maternity Hospital and others*[69] as follows:

"1.   The true test for establishing negligence in diagnosis or treatment on the part of the medical practitioner is whether he has been provided to be guilty of such failure as no medical practitioner of equal specialist or general status and skill would be guilty of if acting with ordinary care.

2.   If the allegation of negligence against a medical practitioner is based on proof that he deviated from a general and approved practice, that will not established negligence unless it is also proved that the course he did take was one which no medical practitioner of like specialisation and skill would have followed had he been taking the ordinary care required from a person of his qualifications.

3.   If a medical practitioner charged with negligence defends his conduct by establishing that he followed a practice which was general and which was approved of by his colleagues of similar specialisation and skill, he cannot escape liability if in reply the plaintiff establishes that such practice has inherent defects which ought to be obvious to any person giving the matter due consideration.

4.   An honest difference of opinion between doctors as to which is the better of two ways of treating a patient does not provide any ground for leaving a question to the jury as to whether a person who has followed one course rather than the other has been negligent.
       It is not for a jury (or for a judge) to decide which of two alternative courses of treatment is in their (or his) opinion preferable, but their (or his) function is merely to decide whether the course of treatment followed, on the evidence, complied with the careful conduct of a medical practitioner of like specialisation and skill to that professed by the defendant.

5.   If there is an issue of fact, the determination of which is necessary for the decision as to whether a particular medical practice is or is not general and approved within the meaning of these principles, the issue must in a trial held with a jury be left to the determination of the jury."[70]

---

[68] [1967] I.R. 173 at 193 (Supreme Court).
[69] [1989] I.R. 91.
[70] *Per* Finlay C.J., p.109.

The decision in *Dunne* was in turn applied in the context of disclosure of the risks of treatment by Finlay CJ and McCarthy J. in *Walsh v. Family Planning Services and others*,[71] Hence, the disclosure of the risks of treatment was held to be an issue of professional judgment except where the disclosure of a particular risk was so obviously necessary to an informed choice on the part of the patient that no reasonably prudent medical man would fail to make it. This approach was also followed by the Supreme Court but not the High Court[72] in *Bolton v. Blackrock Clinic and others*,[73] and also in the recent case of *Reid v. Beaumont Hospital Board and anor.*[74]

On the matter of the standard of care O'Flaherty J. (with whom Hederman J. agreed) in *Walsh* held that it was a matter for the trial judge to decide whether there was a breach of the duty of care owed by the defendants to a person such as the plaintiffs and that this was to be resolved on the established principles of negligence. This appears to favour the approach of Lord Scarman in *Sidaway*.[75]

In the later Irish case of *Farrell v. Varian*,[76] O'Hanlon J. relied on the dicta of Lords Bridge and Keith in *Sidaway*. In that case O'Hanlon J. stated:

> "With regard to the nature and extent of the warning which should be given to a patient contemplating an operation, I am of the opinion that the doctor's obligation does not extend to enumerating all the possible risks, however, remote, which are involved. Such a procedure could only subject many patients to unnecessary fears and worries and possibly have the effect of deterring many patients from submitting to treatment which it was obviously in their best interests to undergo."

In contrast to the English view expressed in *Gold v. Haringey Health Authority*,[77] there is a greater readiness on the part of the Irish courts to intervene in the area of medical discretion in cases involving elective procedures. Finlay CJ noted in *Walsh v. Family Planning Services and others*:[78]

> "[T]he obligation to give a warning of the possible harmful consequences of a surgical procedure which could be said to be … elective … may be more stringent and onerous. … [I]t may be certainly in relation to very clearly elective surgery that the court might more readily reach a conclusion that the extent of the warning given or omitted contained inherent defects which ought to have been obvious to any person giving the matter due consideration than it could do in a case of complicated medical or surgical procedures, and an allegation that, although generally adopted they were inherently unsafe."

---

[71] [1992] I.R. 496.

[72] The High Court in the *Bolton* case appeared to accept that the standard of care in relation to disclosure was to be determined on ordinary negligence principles. However, on appeal and without reference to the basis for the decision in the High Court the Supreme Court adopted the *Dunne* approach. Therefore the definitive determination of the standard of care in Ireland must await another decision.

[73] Unreported, Supreme Court, January 23, 1997.

[74] Unreported, High Court, Johnson J., July 19, 1997.

[75] [1985] A.C. 871.

[76] Unreported, High Court, O' Hanlon J., September 19, 1994.

[77] [1987] 2 All E.R. 888.

[78] [1992] I.R. 496 at 510–511.

In the recent case of *Geoghegan v. Harris*,[79] Kearns J. subjected the previous Irish authorities on informed consent to critical review. Applying *Walsh*, Kearns J. considered that even though the views of the medical experts were all to the effect that no warning was necessary there was a duty to warn. He thus considered the application of the third *Dunne* principle was unsuited to matters of disclosure. He continued:

> "The application of the reasonable patient test seems more logical (than that of *Dunne*) in respect of disclosure. This would establish the proposition that, as a general principle, the patient has the right to know and the practitioner a duty to advise of all material risks associated with a proposed form of treatment. The Court must ultimately decide what is material. 'Materiality' includes consideration of both (a) the severity of the consequences and (b) statistical frequency of the risk. That both are critical is obvious because a risk may have serious consequences and yet historically or predictably be so rare as not to be regarded as significant by many people. ...
>
> The reasonable man, entitled as he may be to full information of material risks does not have impossible expectations nor does he seek to impose impossible standards. He does not invoke only the wisdom of hindsight if things go wrong. He must be taken as needing medical practitioners to deliver on their medical expertise without executive restraint or gross limitation on their ability to do so. The decision in *Walsh* effectively confines the test of materiality to severity of consequences only. ...
>
> However, [there is a] possibility that at times a risk may become so remote, in relation at any rate to the less than most serious consequences, that a reasonable man may not regard it as material or significant. While such cases may be few in number, they do suggest that an absolute requirement of disclosure in every case is unduly onerous and perhaps in the end counter productive if it needlessly deters patients from undergoing operations, which are in their best interests to have.
>
> As pointed out by Mr Healy 'materiality is not a static concept'.[80] If the assessment of materiality is to "abide by a rule of reason" any absolute requirement which ignores frequency seems much more at variance with any such rule.
>
> Every case it seems to me should be considered in the light of its own particular facts, evidence and circumstances to see if the reasonable person in the plaintiff's position would have required a warning of a particular risk."[81]

While avoiding the central issue of what information should be given to a patient the Irish Medical Council's *Guide to Ethical Conduct and Behaviour*[82] offers the following guidance to doctors which does focus on the need to facilitate the patient's understanding. However its terms do tend to suggest that precisely what is disclosed is a matter for "experienced medical" judgment:

> "Informed consent can only be obtained by a doctor who has sufficient training

[79] Unreported, High Court, June 21, 2000.
[80] Healy, *Medical Negligence Common Law Perspectives* (Sweet & Maxwell, London, 1999), p.99.
[81] pp.31–33 of Kearns J.'s judgment.
[82] 6th edition, 2004.

and experience to be able to explain the intervention, the risks and benefits and the alternatives. In obtaining this consent the doctor must satisfy himself/herself that the patient understands what is involved by explaining in appropriate terminology. A record of this discussion should be make in the patient's notes".[83]

The Medical Council's Guidelines are of interest in the context of what is accepted medical practice.

The problem of the non-disclosure of risks in the field of psychiatry where many medications have not insignificant side effects and capacity to consent may be impaired has yet to be addressed by the Irish courts. However, it appears from the decision of McCarthy J. in *Murphy v. Greene*,[84] that the courts may take what has been described as a somewhat "benign"[85] view of the standard of care in cases involving decisions in the field of psychiatric medicine:

> "When a medical practitioner is called on to deal with such as existed on the night in question [assault, breach of protection order by and arrest of the person the subject of an application for involuntary admission] *the law does not require a standard of precision such as might be appropriate to other aspects of medical practice.* It is for that very reason – the urgency, the danger to others and like circumstances that the limited statutory protection is afforded to a medical practitioner doing an act purporting to have been done in pursuance of the Act of 1945. *The standard of reasonable care under the Act may be quite different from such standard in ordinary medical practice.*"[86]

(d) Circumstances in which voluntary patients may be treated without consent At common law in emergency situations where the voluntary patient (whether an adult or a child not accompanied by a patient) is unable to communicate his/her consent s/he may be treated without consent to protect life, health or well-being.[87] If the patient is temporarily unable to communicate his/her consent the principle of necessity is applied even more strictly and will authorise such treatment as is immediately necessary.[88]

Patients involuntarily admitted and the issue of consent

The issue of consent of patients detained under the Mental Treatment Act 1945

The Mental Treatment Act 1945 as amended is silent on the issue of the requirement to obtain personal or proxy consent to treatment in the case of detained patients. Accordingly it is presumed that given that the criteria for involuntary admission in the case of temporary patients included unfitness "on account of the mental state of the patient for

---

[83] Para.17.1.
[84] [1990] 2 I.R. 566.
[85] See Casey & Craven, *Psychiatry and the Law* (Oaktree Press, Dublin, 1999), p.523.
[86] *Ibid.*, p.581 albeit this view was expressed in the context of a s.260 application.
[87] *Marshall v. Curry* [1933] 3 D.L.R. 260. See also the Irish Medical Council's *Guide to Ethical Conduct and Behaviour* (6th edition, 2004), para.18.4.
[88] See *Devi v. West Midlands AHA* [1980] 7 C.L. 44 (HC), *In re T (Adult: Refusal of Medical Treatment)* [1992] 3 W.L.R. 782; *Murray v. McMurchy* [1949] 2 D.L.R. 442.

treatment of his/her illness as a voluntary patient" such patients are incapable of giving consent and treatment may be given to such patients under the common law doctrine of necessity.[89] The test to be applied to temporary patients involuntarily admitted is the best interests test and the doctor must act in accordance with the a responsible and competent body of relevant professional opinion on the principles set down in *Bolam v. Friern Hospital Management Committee.*[90]

Where a person was detained as "a person of unsound mind"—a description which may be defined to mean that the patient is suffering from mental illness and is incapable of caring for himself/herself or of managing his/her property and a finding which gives rise to the consequence that the person could be detained for more than six months then, since the distinction between a person of unsound mind and a temporary patient was really rather one of degree rather than kind the person of unsound mind may also be treated under the common law doctrine of necessity.

The issue of whether consent is required before a patient involuntarily admitted under the provisions of the Mental Treatment Act 1945 could be treated without consent as a matter of constitutional law was never litigated. The most that could be discerned from the decided cases was the possible approach of the courts to the issue were it ever to arise. Thus in the case of *In re Philip Clarke,*[91] the Supreme Court clearly indicated that the courts would adopt a paternalistic approach to the construction of the Act. O'Byrne J. delivering the judgment of the court stated:

> "[This Act] as shown by the title, was primarily intended to provide for the protection and treatment of mental disorders and the care of persons suffering therefrom and is of a paternal character, clearly intended for the care and custody of persons suspected to be suffering from mental infirmity and for the safety and well-being of the public generally…".

The Supreme Court in the case of *SC v. Smith & others* endorsed this approach[92] when the Chief Justice stated that the Mental Treatment Act provisions, which provide for the detention of persons with mental illness:

> "do not constitute an attack on the personal rights of the citizen but rather vindicate and protect the rights of citizens concerned by providing for their care and treatment and are not repugnant to the constitution".

but the court added,

> "It is important that any person exercising any power or discretion under the Act which touches on the rights of a patient, should be conscious…of the constitutional rights of the patient. …"

Accordingly notwithstanding that a "welfare" approach might have been adopted by

---

[89] *In re F (Mental Patient: Sterilisation)* [1989] 2 All E.R. 545.
[90] [1957] 2 All E.R. 118.
[91] [1950] I.R. 235.
[92] Unreported, Supreme Court, July 31, 1996.

the courts to the construction of the Act the court is likely to be vigilant to ensure that those charged with exercising powers of detention and (it is submitted *a fortiori*) powers of treatment would respect the constitutional rights of the patient.

Whether consent of detained patient required under Mental Health Act 2001
Section 57 of the Mental Health Act 2001 (not yet implemented) provides that:

> "The consent of a 'patient'[93] shall be required for treatment except where in the opinion of the consultant psychiatrist[94] responsible for the care and treatment of the patient the treatment[95] is necessary to safeguard the life of the patient, to restore his or her health, to alleviate his or her condition or to relieve his or her suffering and by reason of his or her mental disorder the patient concerned is incapable of giving such consent."

Section 56 (not yet implemented) defines "consent" in relation to a patient as:

> "consent obtained freely without threats or inducements where (a) the consultant psychiatrist[96] responsible for the care and treatment of the patient is satisfied that the patient is capable of understanding the nature, purpose and likely effects of the proposed treatment[97] and (b) the consultant psychiatrist has given the patient adequate information in a form and language that the patient can understand on the nature, purpose and likely effects of the proposed treatment"

Section 57(2) provides that that section 57 shall not apply to treatment specified in section 58 (psychosurgery), 59 (electro-convulsive therapy) or 60 (the administration of medicine after a period of three months).

It is interesting to note that section 4 of the Act[98] (which came into force on April 5, 2002) also states that in making a decision under the Act concerning the care or treatment of a person due regard must be given to the need to respect the right of the person to dignity, bodily integrity privacy and autonomy

The criteria for the giving of consent under section 56 involves the application of three tests (i) whether the consent is freely given (ii) whether the person has capacity to consent and (iii) whether the consent is adequately informed.

(a) Consent freely given To be valid under section 56 of the Mental Health Act 2001

---

[93] "Patient" is defined by ss.2 and 14 as a person to whom an admission order relates. "Patient" therefore includes patients involuntarily admitted to an approved centre but not voluntary patients.

[94] "Consultant psychiatrist" is defined by s.2 of the 2001 Act as a "consultant psychiatrist who is employed by the Health Service Executive or by an approved centre or a person whose name is entered on the division of psychiatry or the division of child and adolescent psychiatry of the Register of Medical Specialists maintained by the Medical Council in Ireland".

[95] "Treatment" in relation to a patient is defined by s.2 of the 2001 Act to include "the administration of physical, psychological and other remedies relating to the care and rehabilitation of a patient under medical supervision, intended for the purposes of ameliorating a mental disorder."

[96] Consultant psychiatrist is defined by s.2. See *supra*, n.85.

[97] Treatment is defined by s.2. See *supra*, n.86.

[98] Inserted at Report stage of the Act.

(not yet in force), the detained patients consent must be given freely and without threats or inducements. Consent given by force or fraud may be invalid.[99] The common law criteria which apply for testing the voluntariness of a voluntary patient's consent apply equally in the context of the consent give by a detained patient[100] with the *caveat* that the fact that a patient is involuntarily detained in a psychiatric hospital may in itself indicate an element of duress which affects the patient's freedom to consent.

(b) Capacity to consent Section 56(a) of the Mental Health Act 2001 provides that in the cases of patients detained under the Act the consultant psychiatrist responsible for the care and treatment of the patient must be satisfied that the patient is capable of understanding the nature, purpose and likely effects of the proposed treatment.

However, there is no test of capacity in the Act to check the patient's understanding of the matters involved. Accordingly the common law criteria adopted in *In re C (Refusal of Treatment)*,[101] referred to above apply.

The Irish Medical Council's *Guide to Ethical Conduct and Behaviour*[102] states:

> "*Most* [emphasis added] patients with psychiatric illness are competent to provide consent. Where a patient with a psychiatric illness is not competent to give consent the provisions of the Mental Health Act 2001 may nominate a specific process to give consent".[103]

The Guide clearly contemplates that the consent of the patient with mental illness to psychiatric treatment should be sought in the majority of cases.

(c) Informed consent Under section 56 (b) of the Mental Health Act 2001, the consultant psychiatrist must have given the patient adequate information, in a form and language that the patient can understand on the nature, purpose and likely effects of the proposed treatment. In effect the section imposes a statutory obligation on the consultant psychiatrist to ensure that the patient understands the issues surrounding the treatment. Where the patient is incapable of grasping the information due to illness or for other reasons then in practice other methods of imparting the information will have to be found e.g. through an independent advocate or a family member.

Section 56 begs the question as to what is meant by "adequate information." Given the similarity in approach of the statute and the common law to the issue of informed consent it would appear that reference to the common law principles enunciated above[104] in relation to the giving of informed consent by voluntary patients would also apply in determining the adequacy of the information given under section 56.

---

[99] *Sidaway v. Bethlem Royal Hospital Governors* [1984] 1 All E.R. 1018.
[100] See p.246 *supra*.
[101] [1994] 1 F.L.R 31.
[102] 6th edition, 2004.
[103] Para.18.2.
[104] See pp.245 *et seq*.

Commentary

Requirement of consent as an international principle

Principle 11.1 of the *UN Principles for the Protection of Persons with Mental Illness and the Improvement of Mental Health Care* provides that *no* treatment shall be given to a patient without his or her informed consent except as provided in paragraphs 6, 7, 8, 13 and 15 as set out below.

Principle 11.2 provides that informed consent is consent obtained freely, without threats or improper inducements, after appropriate disclosure to the patient of adequate and understandable information in a form and language understood by the patient on:

(a) the diagnostic assessment;

(b) the purpose, method, likely duration and expected benefit of the proposed treatment;

(c) alternative modes of treatment including those less intrusive; and

(d) possible pain or discomfort, risks and side-effects of the proposed treatment.

Principle 11.3 provides that a patient may request the presence of another person or persons of the patient's choosing during the procedure for granting consent.

The UN Principles are more specific that section 56 of the Mental Health Act 2001 in that they require not merely information on the "nature purpose and likely effects of the proposed treatment" but stipulate that the patient be informed of the "diagnostic assessment," the "method, likely duration and expected benefit of the proposed treatment" and "possible pain or discomfort, risks and side-effects of the proposed treatment." They also afford the patient the right to request the presence of another person during the procedure for granting consent.

Paragraph 6 provides:

> "Except as provided in paragraphs 7, 8, 12,[105] 13, 14,[106] 15 below a proposed plan of treatment may be given to a patient without a patients informed consent if the following conditions are satisfied:
>
> > (a) the patient is, at the relevant time held as an involuntary patient;
> > (b) an independent authority having in its possession all relevant information including the information specified in paragraph [11.]2 above is satisfied that at the relevant time, the patient lacks the capacity to give or withhold consent to the proposed plan of treatment or, if domestic legislation so provides that, having regard to the patient's own safety or the safety of others the patient unreasonably withholds such consent; and

---

[105] Para.12 provides that sterilisation shall never be carried out as a treatment for mental illness.

[106] Para.14 provides that psycho-surgery and other intrusive and irreversible treatments for mental illness shall never be carried out on a patient who is an involuntary patient in a mental health facility and, to the extent that domestic law permits them to be carried out, they may be carried out on any other patient only where the patient has given informed consent and an independent external body has satisfied itself that there is a genuine informed consent and that the treatment best serves the health needs of the patient.

(c) The independent authority is satisfied that the proposed plan of treatment is
in the best interest of the patient's health needs."

In contrast to section 57 of the Mental Health Act 2001 which defers to the opinion of
the consultant psychiatrist responsible for the care and treatment of the patient on the
matter of the capacity of the patient to give consent, there is a requirement under the
UN Principles that "an independent authority"[107] make a finding of incapacity before
an involuntary patient can be treated without consent.

Paragraph 7 of Principle 11 sets out another exception to the rule that treatment may
not be given without a patient's informed consent and permits such treatment to be
given to a patient who has a personal representative empowered by law to consent to
treatment for the patient. In that case treatment may be given to such a patient without
his or her informed consent if the personal representative having been given the
information described in paragraph 11.2 consents on the patient's behalf.

Paragraph 8 of Principle 11 outlines a further exception to the general rule and
permits:

"treatment to be given to any patient without the patient's informed consent if a
qualified mental health practitioner authorised by law determines that it is urgently
necessary in order to prevent immediate or imminent harm to the patient or to
other persons. Such treatment must not be prolonged beyond the period that is
strictly necessary for this purpose."

Paragraph 8 therefore permits treatment to be given without a patient's informed consent
in emergencies where it is necessary in order to prevent immediate or imminent harm to
the patient. Section 57 affords a broader discretion to the consultant psychiatrist
responsible for the care and treatment of the patient and permits treatment without consent
to be given not only where it is necessary to safeguard the life of the patient but also
where it is necessary "to restore his or her health, to alleviate his or her condition or to
relieve his or her suffering" where the patient by reason of his or her mental disorder is
incapable of giving consent.

Paragraph 13 of Principle 11 provides that:

"a major medical or surgical procedure may be carried out on a person with mental
illness only where it is permitted by domestic law, where it is considered that it
would best serve the health needs of the patient and where the patient gives informed
consent except where the patient is unable to give informed consent the procedure
shall be authorised only after independent review."

Major medical or surgical procedures may therefore only be carried out on a patient
who lacks capacity to give informed consent after independent review.

---

[107] Although the Principles provide stronger protection for the patient who lacks capacity to consent
they have been criticised on the basis that they do not go far enough. Rosenthal and Sundram point
out that the Principles do not define what would constitute an "independent authority" and the
procedural protections for people whose decision may be to refuse treatment and whose decision
may be overruled by this authority are absent. See "International Human Rights and Mental Health
Legislation" (Paper submitted to the WHO, February 10, 2003), p.37.

Paragraph 15 of Principle 11 outlines the final exception to the rule that informed consent is required. It provides that:

> "Clinical trials and experimental treatment shall never be carried out on a patient without informed consent except that a patient who is unable to give informed consent may be admitted to a clinical trial or given experimental treatment but only with the approval of a competent, independent, review body specifically constituted for this purpose."

A patient who lacks the capacity to give informed consent may therefore be admitted to a clinical trial or given experimental treatment only with the approval of a competent independent review body specifically constituted for this purpose.

Principle 11.9 of the UN Principles also provides that where any treatment is authorised without the patient's informed consent every effort shall nevertheless be made to inform the patient about the nature of the treatment and any possible alternatives and to involve the patient as far as possible in the development of the treatment plan.

Principle 11.10 provides that all treatment shall be immediately recorded in the patient's medical records with an indication of whether involuntary or voluntary.

The general rule under the UN Principles therefore is that treatment may not be given to a patient with mental illness without his or her informed consent. The exceptions are hedged around by safeguards, which apply in the situation where the patient is to be treated without consent. Although the Mental Health Act 2001 purports to bring Irish law into line with the highest international standards as recommended by the UN Principles[108] it falls somewhat short of the standards of those principles.

The *Council of Europe Convention on Human Rights and Biomedicine* adopted on April 4, 1997 which Ireland has not yet ratified sets out general standards regarding obtaining consent and contains provisions similar to those set out in the *UN Principles.* Once again the general rule is that an intervention in the health field may only be carried out after the person concerned has given free and informed consent to it.[109]

Article 6.1 of the Convention provides that subject to Articles 17 (protection of persons not able to consent to research) and 20 (protection of persons not able to consent to organ removal) an intervention may only be carried out on a person who does not have the capacity to consent for his or her direct benefit. Dealing with cases of mental incapacity the Convention provides that where according to law an adult does not have the capacity to consent to intervention because of a mental disability, a disease or for similar reasons the intervention may only be carried out with the authorisation of his or her representative or an authority or body provided for by law and *the individual must as far as possible take part in the authorisation procedure.*[110] The Convention also provides that *the authorisation given to the representative authority or body provided for by law may be withdrawn at any time in the best interests of the person concerned.*[111]

Article 7 of the Convention deals with "protection of persons who have a mental disorder" and provides that subject to protective conditions prescribed by law including

---

[108] See White Paper, *A New Mental Health Act*, Department of Health, July 1995, Pn.1824, para.1.13.
[109] Art.5.
[110] Art.6.3.
[111] Art.6.5.

supervisory, control and appeal procedures a person who has a mental disorder of a serious nature may be subjected without his or her consent to an intervention aimed at treating his or her mental disorder only where without such treatment serious harm is likely to result to his or her health. Interestingly the Convention does not offer harm to other persons as a justification for treatment of a person with mental disorder without consent. Another significant provision of the Convention is Article 9, which provides that *the previously expressed wishes relating to medical intervention by a patient who is not, at the time of the intervention in a state to express his or her wishes shall be taken into account.*

Conclusions

1. The Mental Health Act 2001 does not deal directly with the issues, which may confront a voluntary patient in hospital. Many voluntary patients are unaware of their rights. It is submitted that legislation should be enacted providing expressly that no treatment should be given to a voluntary patient without his or her free and informed consent and where s/he refuses to give consent s/he shall not be treated against his/her wishes.

2. The issue of whether the consent of a patient in hospital to psychiatric treatment is truly "voluntary" or "free" is inherently problematic. It might well be argued that a voluntary patient who gives consent to treatment under threat of committal has been deprived of his freedom to choose. Similarly a patient who is involuntarily admitted to hospital might be prevented from giving free consent under section 57 by reason of the coercive nature of the environment in which s/he is detained.

3. Difficulties are presented by the issue of "adequate information" to enable a patient to give informed consent. The extent of the present obligation of disclosure is quite uncertain and the issue of measures, which should be taken to facilitate a patient's understanding of the issues, need to be addressed in further detail. In this regard it is submitted that a way forward might be for the Medical Council to promulgate detailed guidelines on the practice of obtaining a patient's consent. Cooney & O'Neill make the following suggestions:

    "1. The doctor should explain the proposed intervention or treatment and its inevitable consequences, including the procedures to be followed and the aftercare required in understandable detail.
    2. The doctor should explain the purpose of the proposed intervention or treatment saying why the patient's physical, mental or emotional condition renders the treatment necessary.
    3. The doctor should explain all risks of intervention or treatment, which the patient would consider material. This should include (i) a disclosure of the overall chance or probability of harmful complications and (ii) a disclosure of the risks to be faced from a decision to forego intervention or treatment.
    4. The doctor should explain all the risks which the doctor believes the patient in his or her circumstances and with his or her interests, concerns, commitments, values and relationships would consider relevant in deciding about intervention or treatment.
    5. The doctor should include in his or her explanation of risks the nature,

degree duration and the probability of the side effects of the proposed intervention or treatment.

6. The doctor should offer to provide a more detailed disclosure of risks, which would include the more remote risks of intervention or treatment. He or she should explain which factors (e.g. risk percentage) were used in deciding which risks to disclose.

7. The doctor should describe the potential benefits of the treatment and explain the efficacy of the treatment in producing those benefits.

8. The doctor should describe the alternative interventions or treatments relevant to the patients condition and disclose the risks and potential benefits inherent in those alternatives.

9. The doctor should explain why he or she prefers the proposed treatment and why he or she thinks it would be more beneficial to the patient than alternative interventions or treatment.

10. The doctor should offer to answer any questions from the patient about the proposed intervention or treatment, its risks and side effects or alternatives. This offer should be made several times during the conversation with the patient. The doctor should finish the conversation with a review of the information disclosed.

11. The doctor should point out the difficulty of absorbing medical information and ask the patient whether he or she understands the information provided.

12. The doctor should consult the patient on whether another session would be desirable to review the information.

13. The doctor should inform the patient that he or she is free to refuse treatment or choose one of the alternatives. The doctor should convey his or her willingness to carry out the alternative intervention or treatment that the patient chooses or to assist the patient to find a doctor qualified to carry out the chosen alternative.

14. The patient should be informed of his or her right to withdraw consent at any time up to and during the course of treatment. …

15. Doctors should document and preserve the record of the disclosures made to the patient."[112]

4. Following the standards set out in the UN Principles treatment should not be given to a patient with mental disorder without that patient's consent unless an independent authority has determined that the patient lacks the capacity to give or withhold informed consent and the authority is satisfied that that proposed plan of treatment is in the best interests of the patient's health needs.

5. The power of mental health practitioners to authorise treatment without a patient's consent and without reference to an independent authority should be limited to cases where the treatment is urgently necessary in order to prevent immediate or imminent harm to the patient or to other persons. In accordance with UN principles the treatment should not be prolonged beyond the period that is strictly necessary for this purpose.

---

[112] Cooney & O'Neill, *Kritik 1 Psychiatric Detention Civil Commitment in Ireland* (Baikonur, 1996), pp. 229–231.

Treatment without Consent

Voluntary patients

A voluntary patient cannot as a general rule be treated without his/her consent. The only exception to this rule is in emergencies where the patient due to unconsciousness is unable to communicate his/her consent and the treatment is required to save the life or preserve the health of the patient.[113] Where a voluntary patient is deemed incapable of giving consent by reason of mental disorder steps should be taken to admit him/her to hospital as an involuntary patient whether temporary or as a person of unsound mind under the Mental Treatment Act 1945 (which is still in force) or pursuant to an admission order under the Mental Health Act 2001 (when it comes into force) and to treat him or her under section 57.

Detained Patients

Position under the Mental Treatment Act 1945

Where it is proposed to admit a person as a temporary patient, under the Mental Treatment Act 1945, it must be established that that person is unfit on account of his/her mental state for treatment of his/her mental illness as a voluntary patient.[114] As a consequence, it would appear that for a temporary patient order to be made the person must be incompetent to consent to treatment for his/her mental illness, and in practice, it would appear to be assumed from this the patient subject to a temporary patient order may have medical treatment for that illness administered to him/her without his/her consent for as long as s/he remains incompetent.

The situation is less clear in the case of a person admitted as a temporary patient, on account of his being an addict. An addict is a person who by reason of his addiction to drugs or intoxicants is either dangerous to himself or others, or incapable of managing himself, or his affairs or of ordinary proper conduct.[115] The addict may be involuntarily admitted, but the Act is silent on the issue of treatment without consent. The fact that a person is an addict does not necessarily mean that s/he is incompetent to consent to medical treatment. It has been argued[116] on the one hand that to sanction detention without consent in such circumstances without conferring a right to treat without consent appears to be self defeating. However on the other it is arguable that as the Act does not confer an express power to impose treatment upon detained persons the common law relating to consent probably remains relevant to the circumstances of addicts detained under its provisions and it will be necessary to examine whether that person is competent to consent to medical treatment.

In the context of involuntary detention as a person of unsound mind, the Mental Treatment Act provides no definition of what constitutes "unsoundness of mind". In other contexts, however, it appears to mean mental illness with an inability to care

---

[113] See Denham J. *In the matter of A Ward of Court (Withholding Medical Treatment) (No. 2)* [1996] 2 I.R. 100 and *Marshall v. Curry* (1933) 3 D.L.R. 260.

[114] Mental Treatment Act 1945, s.184(4) as amended by the Mental Treatment Act 1961, s.16(2).

[115] Mental Treatment Act 1945, s.3.

[116] See Casey and Craven, *Psychiatry and the Law* (Oak Tree Press, Dublin, 1999), p.503.

properly for oneself or to deal with one's property.[117] It appears also from the fact that a person of unsound mind may be detained for more than six months, that it connotes a degree of mental illness which is more profound than that of the temporary patient and *a fortiori* that the person concerned is at the time of admission incapable of giving legally effective consent. As such, it would seem that the assumption of the legislation is that treatment for the underlying illness may be instituted, and continued without the consent of the person detained as a person of unsound mind for as long as that person remains incompetent.

Position under Mental Health Act 2001

Section 57(1) of the 2001 Act (not yet in force) authorises treatment of a detained patient without consent where in the opinion of the consultant psychiatrist responsible for the care and treatment of the patient the treatment is necessary to safeguard the life of the patient, to restore his or her health, to alleviate his or her condition, or to relieve his or her suffering and by reason of his or her mental disorder the patient concerned is incapable of giving such consent.

> "Treatment" in relation to a detained patient is defined by section 2 of the Act as "including the administration of physical, psychological and other remedies relating to the care and rehabilitation of a patient under medical supervision, intended for the purposes of ameliorating a mental disorder".

In England in the context of the English definition of treatment in section 145(1) of the Mental Health Act 1983 which defines "medical treatment" as including "nursing ... care, habilitation and rehabilitation under medical supervision" for the mental disorder from which the patient is suffering it was held in *Reid v. Secretary of State for Scotland*[118] that the definition was wide enough to include treatment which alleviated or prevented a deterioration of the *symptoms* of the mental disorder not the disorder itself which gave rise to them. It is submitted that the application of the definition of treatment in section 2 of the 2001 Act would give rise to a similar conclusion.

It is worth noting that the definition of treatment in section 2 of the Mental Health Act 2001 is inclusive and therefore not an exhaustive definition. In England the courts have taken advantage of the expansive nature of the definition under section 145(1) and construing that section widely have ruled that controversial interventions such as the application of force by way of restraint which is necessary to administer treatment to a detained patient incapable of consent amounted to "medical treatment."[119] It is submitted that a similar conclusion may be reached in Ireland by the construction of the words "includes the administration of physical ... and other remedies ... intended for the purposes of ameliorating a mental disorder" under section 2 of the 2001 Act.

When section 2 of the European Convention on Human Rights Act 2003 comes into force section 57 will have to be construed consistently with the requirements of Article 3 of the European Convention on Human Rights. Article 3 provides that "No one shall

---

[117] See O.67, Rules of the Superior Courts 1986.
[118] [1999] 2 A.C. 512.
[119] *Pountney v. Griffiths* [1976] A.C. 314.

be subjected to..inhuman or degrading treatment." In *Herczegfalvy v. Austria*,[120] the European Court of Human Rights stated:

> "The Court considers that the position of inferiority and powerlessness which is typical of patients confined in psychiatric hospitals calls for increased vigilance in reviewing whether the Convention has been complied with...The established principles of medicine are admittedly in principle decisive in such cases; as a general rule, a measure which is a therapeutic necessity cannot be regarded as inhuman or degrading. The Court must nevertheless satisfy itself that the medical necessity has been convincingly shown to exist...".[121]

Thus in relation to section 57 the word "necessary" must when the 2003 Act comes into force be construed as a "therapeutic necessity" which is so demonstrated in accordance with "the established principles of medicine". In addition to this a "therapeutic" or "medical" necessity (the words are used interchangeably by the European Court although it has been argued[122] that a "medical" necessity is wider than a "therapeutic" necessity) must be "convincingly" shown to exist. In *R v. Dr M and others, ex p. N*[123] the English Court of Appeal held that "convincingly shown" was not the same as the criminal burden of proof but stated that the standard was a "high one" which did "not need elaboration or further explanation".[124]

THE RIGHT TO REFUSE TREATMENT

Voluntary patients right to refuse treatment

There are no special provisions in either the Mental Treatment Act 1945 or the Mental Health Act 2001 in respect of the medical treatment of voluntary patients and the common law applies to their treatment for mental disorder in the same way as it does in relation to other types of medical treatment. To be admitted to hospital as a voluntary patient a person must have capacity to consent. Once this capacity is found to exist the fundamental rule is that no psychiatric treatment may be given to a voluntary patient without his or her consent and s/he has a right to refuse any proposed treatment.

In the Irish case of *A Ward of Court (Withholding Medical Treatment) (No.2), re*,[125] Denham J. stated:

> "Medical treatment may not be given to an adult person of full capacity without his or her consent. There are a few rare exceptions to this; e.g. in regard to contagious diseases or in a medical emergency where the patient is unable to communicate. This right arises out of civil, criminal and constitutional law. If

---

[120] [1992] 15 E.H.R.R. 437.
[121] *Ibid.*, para.82.
[122] See Bartlett and Sandland, *Mental Health Law, Policy and Practice* (Oxford University Press, 2003), p.363.
[123] [2003] 1 W.L.R. 562.
[124] At para. 18.
[125] [1996] 2 I.R. 100.

medical treatment is given without consent it may be trespass against the person in civil law, a battery in criminal law and a breach of the individual's constitutional rights. The consent that is given by an adult of full capacity is a matter of choice. It is not necessarily a decision based on medical considerations. Thus, medical treatment may be refused for other than medical reasons, or reasons most citizens would regard as rational, but the person of full age and capacity may make the decision for their own reasons."[126]

In the English case of *In re T (Adult: Refusal of Treatment)*,[127] Lord Donaldson spelt out the extent of the right of the competent patient to refuse treatment:

"Every adult has the right and capacity to decide whether or not he will accept medical treatment, even if a refusal may risk permanent injury to his health or even lead to premature death ... it matters not whether the reasons for the refusal were rational or irrational, unknown or even non existent."[128]

In Ireland the right to refuse treatment may also find its source in the Constitution. In *In re A Ward of Court*, Denham J. characterised the requirement of consent to treatment as a constitutional right:

"The requirement of consent to medical treatment is an aspect of a person's right to bodily integrity under Article 40, s.3 of the Constitution, which right was first recognised by Kenny J. in *Ryan v. Attorney General* [1965] IR 294. ..."[129]

In her judgment Denham J. examined the unenumerated constitutional right to privacy and went on to hold that part of the right to privacy was the giving or refusing of consent to medical treatment, although a component in the decision may relate to personal dignity. Further as part of their constitutional rights a patient had a right to choose whether or not to accept medical treatment. Classified as "a right to choose" Denham J. considered that "this concept is the requirement of consent to medical treatment seen from another aspect"[130]

Thus a voluntary patient's right to refuse treatment in Irish law may derive its source from the common law or from the constitutional rights to bodily integrity, privacy or personal dignity.

The right of patients involuntarily admitted to hospital to refuse treatment

Position under Mental Treatment Act 1945 The traditional assumption of the Mental Treatment Act 1945 was that once that a person was certified for involuntary admission s/he was incompetent to decide upon their medical treatment and matters of treatment were left practically entirely to the discretion of staff and hospital authorities.[131]

---

[126] *Ibid.*, p.156.
[127] [1992] 3 W.L.R. 782.
[128] *Ibid.*, p.799.
[129] [1996] 2 I.R. 100 at 156.
[130] *Ibid.*, p.154.
[131] Gordon & Verdun Jones note that reluctance on the part of commonwealth courts in the past to

Position under Mental Health Act 2001 Section 57 of the Mental Health Act 2001 (not yet in force) introduces a new requirement for the consent of the competent detained patient with mental disorder to be obtained in relation to proposed treatment. The effect of sections 56 and 57 of the 2001 Act taken together when implemented will be that a detained patient who is "capable of understanding the nature, purpose and likely effects of the proposed treatment" will be capable of refusing psychiatric treatment. However, this right to refuse does not extend to electro-convulsive therapy. In this case the unwillingness of a competent patient to consent to ECT can be overridden by the treating consultant psychiatrist's approving the treatment and obtaining a second authorisation for the administration of the treatment from another consultant psychiatrist.[132] Further where a patient to whom medicine has been administered for three months is unwilling to consent to the further administration of medication after the three months has expired his/her unwillingness may be overridden by the treating consultant psychiatrist approving the treatment and obtaining a second authorisation for the continued administration from another consultant psychiatrist.[133]

However, section 57 states that while the consent of a detained patient is required for treatment where a detained patient is, in the opinion of the consultant psychiatrist responsible for the care and treatment of the patient, incapable by reason of his mental disorder of giving consent s/he may be given treatment intended for the purposes of ameliorating a mental disorder without consent where the treatment is necessary to safeguard the life of the patient, to restore his or her health, to alleviate his or her condition or to relieve his or her suffering. Thus where a detained patient is deemed in the opinion of the consultant psychiatrist responsible for his/her care to be incapable of giving consent s/he loses the right to refuse treatment for mental disorder. In the absence of other authority the test of capacity to consent in the case of *In re C (Refusal of Treatment)*,[134] may apply.

The decision of the Ontario Court of Appeal the case of *Starson v. Swayze*[135] may also be of interest. In that case an exceptionally intelligent scientist who suffered from bi-polar disorder was detained in a psychiatric hospital after having been found not criminally responsible because of his mental disorder of uttering death threats. Two psychiatrists at the institution proposed to treat him with mood stabilisers and anti-psychotic, anti-anxiety and anti-parkinsonian medication. He refused treatment. The psychiatrists applied to Consent and Capacity Board who found the patient was incapable of making his own decisions about treatment. The test applied in assessing his capacity was that set out in section 4(1) of the Ontario Health Care Consent Act 1996 which stated that a person was capable if (a) the person was able to understand the information that was relevant to making a decision, and (b) was able to appreciate the reasonably foreseeable consequences of a decision or lack of decision.

The patient appealed the Board's ruling and the court allowed the patient's appeal. The psychiatrists further appealed to the Ontario Court of Appeal. Applying the test of

---

recognise a right of patients to refuse treatment stems from the nature of such mental health legislation. See "The Right to Refuse Treatment Commonwealth Developments and Issues" (1983) 6 *International Journal of Law and Psychiatry* 57 at 63.

[132] See Mental Health Act 2001, s.59.
[133] See Mental Health Act 2001, s.60.
[134] [1994] I W.L.R. 290.
[135] 201 D.L.R. 123.

reasonableness applicable in judicial review cases it found that the Board's finding was unreasonable because the patient met both parts of the test. The patient recognised he had psychiatric problems. The appellants however, could adduce no evidence to the effect that any of the many psychiatric medications forced on the patient in the past had ever helped him. In addition the patient did not think they had and he found the side effects of the treatment extremely unpleasant. The consideration that lay at the root of the patient's refusal was the effect of the medication on his scientific work. He found that the medication would slow his brain to the point where he could not pursue the thing which gave his life meaning namely his scientific research. What the Board thought would be best for the respondent was irrelevant under the statute. The Board and the psychiatrists had adopted a paternalistic approach, which they were not entitled to adopt. The respondent understood through "the screen of his mental illness" all aspects of the decision whether to be treated. He understood the information relevant to that decision and its reasonably foreseeable consequences. He made a decision that could "cost him his freedom and accelerate his illness."

While many would have agreed with the Board that it was a decision which was against his best interests for the respondent it was "a rational decision and not one that reflected any lack of capacity" Accordingly it was a decision which the statute and section 7 of the Charter of Rights and Freedoms permitted him to make. While on the one hand it might be said that the decision represents a high watermark in recognition of the right to self determination of the patient; it might equally be argued that a more satisfactory result may have been obtained with better therapeutic negotiation between doctor and patient regarding types of medication and of that medication appropriate doses.

Commentary regarding the right to refuse treatment in Irish law

International Principles

It is interesting to examine whether the assumptions of Irish legislation and proposals for reform comply with international norms regarding the treatment of persons with mental illness. Principle 11.4 of the *UN Principles for the Protection of Persons with Mental Illness and the Improvement of Mental Health Care*[136] provides that subject certain exceptions provided for in paragraphs 6, 7, 8, 13 and 15[137] a patient has the right to refuse or stop treatment. However, the consequences of refusing or stopping treatment must be explained to the patient.

Comparative law

Right to refuse treatment in Canadian law In Nova Scotia and Ontario, mental health legislation recognises the right of involuntary patients to refuse treatment. In Nova Scotia, legislation provides that no person can be treated without his consent.[138] However, if a

---

[136] Adopted by the General Assembly, December 17, 1991.
[137] These paragraphs are discussed *supra* under the heading "Consent as the basis for Psychiatric Treatment" at pp.245 *et seq.*
[138] S.N.S. 1967, c.249, s.46(1) [en. 1977, c.45, s.8].

patient has been declared after examination by a psychiatrist to be incapable of consenting to treatment, he may be treated with the consent of his guardian or next of kin[139] or with the consent of the Public Trustee if the next of kin is either unavailable or refuses to consent.[140] However, the patient has the right to appeal any declaration of incapacity to the Provincial Review Board. If the issue is resolved in favour of the patient then the right to withhold consent is secured.[141]

Right to refuse treatment in American law The issue of whether a patient involuntarily admitted to a psychiatric hospital has the right to refuse treatment has been the subject of much controversy in the USA. The cases creating new developments in this field were decided in the late 1970s and upheld the right of involuntary patients to refuse prescribed drugs. The decisions were largely influenced by judicial concern about the adverse effects of powerful psychoactive drugs and their misuse for administrative convenience and the control and punishment of patients.[142]

The recognition of this "new" right to refuse treatment was grounded on the guarantee of due process, the guarantee of freedom of thought and the free exercise of religion provision intended to secure personal privacy or autonomy.[143] In addition the courts invoked the right to bodily integrity, which emphasises the value of personal autonomy and underpins the requirement for informed consent.[144]

A civil due process model for deciding the question of the right to refuse was established in a series of decisions known as the *Rogers* litigation. The groundbreaking decision arose after the US Supreme Court refused to decide whether a constitutional right to refuse anti-psychotic medication existed and remanded the case to the state court.[145] Eventually Massachusetts's highest court concluded in the case of *Rogers v. Commissioner of the Department of Mental Health*[146] that under state law involuntarily committed patients who have not been adjudicated as lacking capacity to consent to treatment have a right to refuse anti-psychotic medication in non-emergency situations. Patients adjudicated incompetent have a similar right that must be exercised through court approved independent decision maker endeavouring by substituted judgement to make the same choice the patient would have made if competent.

Perhaps the high point of the due process hearing approach can be traced to the case of *Colorado v. Medina*, in which the Colorado Supreme Court held that an adversary hearing is required before antipsychotic drugs could be administered in a non emergency

---

[139] *Ibid.*, s.46(2) [en. 1977, c.45, s.8].

[140] *Ibid.* See *In re Public Trustee and Boudreau* (1980) 114 D.L.R. (3d) 756 (N.S.T.D.).

[141] R.S.N.S.1967, c.249 s.50 [en. 1977, c.45, s.8].

[142] Plotkin, "Limiting the Therapeutic Orgy: Mental Patients Rights to Refuse Treatment" (1978) 72 *Northwestern University Law Review* 461.

[143] Rhoden, "The Right to Refuse Psychotic Drugs" (1980) 15 *Harvard Civil Rights Civil Liberties Law Review* 363; Tancredi, "The Right to Refuse Psychiatric Treatment; Some Legal and Ethical Considerations" (1980) 5 *Journal of Health Politics, Policy and Law* 514.

[144] Hermann, "The Basis of the Right of Committed Patients to Refuse Psychotropic Medication" (1989) 22 *Journal of Health and Hospital Law* 176.

[145] See *Mills v. Rogers* 457 U.S. 291 (1982) 6 M.D.L.R. 221 remanding *Rogers v. Okin* 634 F. 2d. 650 (1st Cir. 1980) 5 M.D.L.R. 17.

[146] See *Rogers v. Commissioner of the Department of Mental Health* 458 N.E. 2d 308 (Mass. Sup. Jud. Ct. 1093) 8 M.P.D. L.R. 103.

situation. The court held that it must be demonstrated by clear and convincing evidence that (1) the patient is incompetent; (2) without treatment the patient is likely to commit harm to self or others or to undergo significant long-term deterioration in his or her mental condition; (3) a less intrusive treatment is not available and (4) the need for treatment is compelling enough to override any legitimate interest the patient may have in refusing it.

An approach based on the state constitutional right to privacy was adopted in *Jarvis v. Levine*[147] where the Minnesota Supreme Court held that involuntary patients have a right to a hearing before being given neuroleptics. In addition it held that state officials were not immune from liability if they failed to secure judicial approval before such administration. Similarly in *Riese v. St Mary's Hosp. & Medical Center*[148] a California appeals court held that absent a judicial determination of the patient's incapacity to make treatment decisions patients have a right under state law to refuse anti-psychotic medications in non-emergencies.

Basing its decision on grounds of equal protection the Wisconsin Supreme Court ruled in *Wisconsin ex rel. Jones v. Gerhardstein*[149] that the state has no power forcibly to administer anti-psychotic medication in non-emergency situations to patients who have not been adjudged incompetent.

Other courts have promulgated due process approaches, which do not encompass direct judicial review but instead concentrate more on the due process element of the administrative procedures in a given case. In the case of *Rennie v. Klein*,[150] the Third Circuit reviewed New Jersey's three step internal administrative processes whereby a facility's medical director or a designee had the final decision making authority. The court held that involuntarily committed patients had a right to refuse antipsychotic medication as long as their exercising this right does not endanger themselves or others.

Similarly in the New York case of *Project Release v. Prevost*,[151] the Second Circuit approved the approach of allowing anti-psychotic medication to be administered involuntarily without a court finding of dangerousness as long as the treating physician's decision had received three levels of medical review by medical personnel other than the treating physician and the patient had access to counsel at all levels of the appeal process. Subsequently in *Rivers v. Katz*,[152] New York's highest court found that in non-emergency situations the state constitution requires a separate judicial determination that the patient lacks the capacity to make a reasoned decision with respect to the proposed treatment and that the administration of anti psychotic medication would be in the patient's best interests before medication can be administered without his/her consent.

Yet another approach is to be found in the Idaho Supreme Court decision of *Bradshaw v. Idaho*[153] in which the court upheld the involuntary administration of medication to detained patients found to lack the capacity to make treatment decisions. The requirement of lack of capacity to make informed treatment decisions was incorporated into the

---

[147] 418 N.W. 2d. 139 (Minn. Sup. Ct. 1988) 12 M.P.D. L.R. 144.
[148] 243 Cal Rptr. 241 (Cal. Ct. App. 1987), 12 M.P.D. L.R. 145, 255.
[149] 416 N.W. 2d. 883 (Wis. Sup. Ct. 1987) 12 M.P.D. L.R. 31.
[150] 720 F. 2d 266 (3d Cir. 1983) 8 M.P.D. L.R. 18.
[151] 722 F. 2d. 960 (2d Cir. 1983) 8 M.P.D. L.R. 86.
[152] 495 N.E. 2d 337 (N.Y. Ct. App. 1986) 10 M.P.D. L.R. 284.
[153] 816 P. 2d 986 (Idaho Sup. Ct. 1991) 16 MP.D. L.R. 42.

involuntary commitment proceedings and had to be supported by clear and convincing evidence.

Comparative law on advance refusals of treatment

The position of the patient who expresses while competent that s/he does not wish to receive neuroleptic medication and later becomes incompetent and refuses to accept such medication was addressed by the Ontario Court of Appeal in *Fleming v. Reid.*[154] In that case two involuntary patients at a psychiatric facility in Ontario were diagnosed as suffering from schizophrenia and their attending psychiatrist proposed treating them which neuroleptic medication. Both patients were certified as being mentally incompetent to make treatment decisions and so the substitute decision maker (the Official Guardian) was called upon to consent to the proposed treatment. However, as both patients had previously indicated while mentally competent that they did not wish to receive neuroleptics the Official Guardian refused to consent as Ontario legislation provides that when making a treatment decision on behalf of a mentally incompetent patient the substitute must follow any wishes expressed by the patient when apparently mentally competent.[155] Accordingly the attending psychiatrist applied to the Review Board for an order authorising the treatment. The Board granted the order and this was upheld on appeal to the Ontario District Court. However, the order was set aside on appeal to the Court of Appeal on the basis that the governing provisions of the Mental Health Act which permitted and indeed required the Review Board to ignore the wishes of a patient expressed while competent and to authorise the treatment if it considered this to be in the patient's best interests, deprived the patients of their right to security of the person as guaranteed by section 7 of the Canadian Charter of Rights and Freedoms.

This decision would suggest that in Canada an advance directive made by a person while competent regarding treatment, which a patient wishes to receive when incompetent, could allow a patient who becomes incompetent to refuse treatment, which he or she could lawfully refuse while competent.

Conclusions

Given the wide range of comparative options the question remains as to the most appropriate process for implementing a right to refuse treatment in Irish law. The following principles are suggested as a basis for legislation in this area.[156]

1. Mental Health Tribunals in Ireland should have power to review the capacity of patients to consent to and refuse psychiatric treatment. Prior to review of capacity by a Mental Health Tribunal a patient should have a right to refuse treatment of any sort unless the patient is endangering his or her own life or the lives of others prior. Intrusive treatment should not be imposed unless less intrusive means of treatment have been exhausted without success.

---

[154] (1991) 82 D.L.R. (4th) 298.
[155] R.S.O. 1990 c.M.7 s.2(6) [rep. 1992, c.32, s.20(7) and re-en. As 1992, c.31 s.13(1);].
[156] See Cooney & O'Neill, *Kritik 1 Psychiatric Detention Civil Commitment in Ireland* (Baikonur, 1996), pp.273–274.

2. A voluntary patient should have an unqualified right to refuse treatment and this right should be specifically stated in statutory form. Such patients should also be provided with a meaningful range of choice of potential treatments.

3. Where an involuntary patient's competency to decide about treatment for himself or herself is in issue s/he should be given a hearing on the issue before an independent and interdisciplinary Mental Health Tribunal. The patient should be physically present at any hearing, be represented by a lawyer or advocate and afforded the right and opportunity to be confronted with and to cross examine all witnesses alleging the necessity of such treatment. If the patient cannot afford a lawyer he or she should be legally aided. At the hearing the deciding body should consider all relevant matters. These should include the patient's legal status, the treatment setting, the technique of treatment, the motives of the treating carer, the circumstances of the treatment, the intrusiveness of the treatment, the application of legislative restrictions, whether the patient is an inpatient or an outpatient, the irreversibility of the treatment, the qualifications and experience of the treating carer, whether such treatment is life-saving or not, whether or not the treatment is physical or psychiatric and whether the situation is an emergency.[157] Evidence should be taken as to all available alternatives to the treatment in question, as well as the potential efficacy, risk and restrictiveness of such treatment.

4. It is submitted that the Powers of Attorney Act 1996 should be extended to give a person power to execute an enduring power of attorney conferring authority on another person to give or refuse consent on his or her behalf to some or all medical treatment in respect of which the donor of the power has lost his or capacity to make competent decisions. This power should be subject to certain limitations. Thus the attorney so appointed:
    (a) would have no power to refuse pain relief or ordinary hydration and nutrition or to prevent civil commitment when the donor constitutes a danger to others;
    (b) should have no power to consent to a treatment which is prohibited by law or unless the power provides otherwise by an advance directive by the donor;
    (c) should have no power to consent to the taking of any step for which approval of a court or a mental health review tribunal is required; and
    (d) should have no power to consent to a treatment to which the incapacitated person objects. Any objection in the mental health context should be referred to a mental health review board where the issues of competency and appropriateness would be dealt with.

    The President of the High Court should have power to revoke the appointment of a healthcare attorney who fails in his or her duty to act in the best interests of the donor taking into account the values and preferences of the donor.

5. Legislative provision should be made for the making of advance health care directives, which would give legal effect when incompetent to the expression of consent or refusal of consent made by a patient while competent as though the consent or refusal were a present decision of the patient in the circumstances to

---

[157] See Perlin, "The Right to Refuse Treatment in New Jersey" (1976) 6 Psych. Annals 300.

which it is applicable. It should be a requirement that the document be executed in writing and a copy lodged with the patient's medical practitioner and solicitor. The document should be signed by the patient and witnessed by one person who is not the patient's healthcare attorney. The advance directive should be ineffective to refuse involuntary admission to an appropriate centre when the person is dangerous to others.

THE HAZARDOUS NATURE OF CERTAIN FORMS OF TREATMENT

Certain forms of psychiatric treatment are subject to special rules because of their very intrusive nature, the health risks associated with them, their questionable efficacy and historically the potential for abuse of those treatments. Among these treatments are (a) Psycho-surgery (b) Electro-convulsive therapy and (c) Prolonged Administration of Psychoactive drugs.

Psycho-surgery

At present psycho-surgery is not carried out in Ireland. However, in a recent Council of Europe report on psychiatry and human rights the Irish government was reported as stating that patients "are occasionally referred to Britain for this procedure."[158] Psychosurgery is used in the treatment of a range of conditions but appears to be most successful in relation to the treatment of mood disorders, obsessive-compulsive neuroses and schizo-affective psychoses.[159] It has also been used in the treatment of schizophrenia and anorexia nervosa but its efficacy in the treatment of these conditions has, however, been questioned.[160] Moreover its use as a method of controlling violent behaviour seems to be even less justifiable.

Position under Mental Treatment Act 1945

The Mental Treatment Act 1945 contains no provisions governing the carrying out of psycho-surgery and the giving of consent to such surgery, were it to be carried out in Ireland is governed by the common law. Accordingly the issue of the capacity of the person to give such consent presents itself. In the absence of capacity the surgery may be carried out if it is in the best interests of the person concerned as judged by a responsible body of medical opinion even if another might not agree unless the course adopted has inherent defects.[161]

---

[158] A. Rogers, "Legislation on psychiatry in Europe", *Lancet* (1994) Vol. 343, pp.1027 (April 23).

[159] E.O. Goktepe, L.B. Young, P.K. Bridges, "A further review of the results of stereotactic subcaudate tractotomy" *British Journal of Psychiatry* (1975) Vol. 126, pp.270–280 and R. Strom-Olsen & S Carlisle, "Bifrontal Stereodactic Tractotomy" *British Journal of Psychiatry* (1971) Vol.118, pp.141–54.

[160] P.K. Bridges and J.R. Bartlett, "Psychosurgery Yesterday and Today" British Journal of Psychiatry (1977) Vol.131, pp.249–260.

[161] See *Dunne v. National Maternity Hospital* [1989] I.R. 91.

Position under Mental Health Act 2001

Section 58(1) of the Mental Health Act 2001 (which has yet been implemented), however, addresses the issue and provides that psycho-surgery shall not be performed on a patient unless (a) the patient gives his or her consent in writing to the psycho-surgery and (b) the psycho-surgery is authorised by a tribunal.[162]

"Psycho-surgery" is defined by section 58(6) "as any surgical operation that destroys brain tissue or the functioning of brain tissue and which is performed for the purposes of ameliorating a mental disorder." "Patient" in the context of the Act means in effect a person who has been involuntarily admitted to an approved centre.[163] According to section 56, "Consent" in relation to a patient means "consent obtained freely without threats or inducements, where (a) the consultant psychiatrist responsible for the care and treatment of the patient has certified in a form specified by the Commission that the patient is capable of understanding the nature purpose and likely effects of the proposed treatment; and (b) the consultant psychiatrist has given the patient adequate information in a form and language that the patient can understand, on the nature, purpose and likely effects of the proposed treatment."

Section 58(2) provides that where it is proposed to perform psycho-surgery on a patient and the consent of the patient has been obtained the consultant psychiatrist[164] responsible for the care and treatment of the patient must notify the Mental Health Commission in writing of the proposal and the Mental Health Commission must refer the matter to a Mental Health Tribunal. Where such a proposal is referred to a tribunal the tribunal must review the proposal and either (a) authorise the performance of the psycho-surgery if satisfied that it is in the best interests of the health of the patient concerned or (b) if it is not so satisfied refuse to authorise it.[165]

The Tribunal has all the powers of a Tribunal under section 49 when dealing with the matter. Thus it may, *inter alia*, receive submissions and such evidence as it thinks fit; direct the consultant psychiatrist responsible for the care and treatment of the patient to arrange for the patient to attend before the tribunal; direct the production of documents; make provision for enabling the patient the subject of the review to present his or her case to the tribunal in person or through a legal representative; make provision for the examination by or on behalf of the tribunal and the cross examination by or on behalf of the patient the subject of the review of witnesses before the tribunal; make provision for the examination by or on behalf of the patient the subject of the review and the cross examination by or on behalf of the tribunal of witnesses before the tribunal called by the patient the subject of the review; Sittings of the tribunal shall be held in private.

Where a patient is dissatisfied with a decision of a tribunal s/he may appeal the matter to the Circuit Court under section 19.[166] Effect will not be given to a decision of a tribunal before (a) the expiration of the time for the bringing of an appeal to the Circuit Court or (b) if such an appeal is brought, the determination or withdrawal thereof.[167]

---

[162] The Constitution of Tribunals is provided for in s.48 discussed in Chap.8 *infra*.
[163] See ss.2, 13.
[164] "Consultant psychiatrist" is defined in s.2. See n.94 *supra*.
[165] S.58(3).
[166] S.58(4).
[167] S.58(5).

Commentary on Irish law regarding psycho-surgery

Consistency with International Principles The question arises as to whether these safeguards are fully in accordance with international principles on the matter. The *UN Principles for the Protection of Persons with Mental Illness and the Improvement of Mental Health Care*[168] provide that psycho-surgery and other intrusive and irreversible treatments for mental illness shall never be carried out on a patient who is an involuntary patient in a mental health facility and, to the extent that domestic law permits them to be carried out they may be carried out on any other patient only where the patient has given informed consent and an independent external body has satisfied itself that there is a genuine informed consent and that the treatment best serves the health needs of the patient.[169]

Under the terms of Principle 11.16, the patient or his or her personal representative or any interested person has a right of appeal to a judicial or other independent authority concerning any treatment given to him or her under this provision.

It is notable that international principles require that informed consent and the approval of an *independent external body* both that *there is a genuine informed consent and* that the treatment best serves the needs of the patient be obtained before psycho-surgery is carried out. Questions remain as to whether it can be said that there has been approval by a truly independent external body when the Mental Health Tribunals under the Act are appointed by the Mental Health Commission whose membership is in turn appointed by the Minister for Health. In addition under the terms of the Mental Health Act the Tribunal is not required to be satisfied that there has been genuine informed consent to the psycho-surgery as required by the UN Principles.

Comparative law on psycho-surgery In Canada Saskatchewan legislation prohibits the administration of psycho-surgery to an involuntary patient.[170] Ontario legislation provides that the consent of an involuntary patient (or his nearest relative if he is incompetent to consent) is deemed not to include consent to psycho-surgery.[171] In addition a Review Board may not authorise such treatment.[172] Thus this specific type of treatment is excluded altogether in the case of the involuntarily committed patient.

In Nova Scotia, legislation is less stringent and provides that, *inter alia*, the consent of the patient (or substitute consent of a guardian, relative or the Public Trustee if he is incompetent) must be obtained to psycho-surgery. In addition the attending psychiatrist and two independent psychiatrists must recommend the surgery *and* the Review Board must be satisfied that these requirements have been fulfilled.[173]

In New South Wales, the Mental Health Act 1990 provides that psycho-surgery can only be performed if the patient gives informed consent as defined by the Mental Health Act and that consent has been reviewed by the Psycho-surgery Review Board. Among the elements of the required consent are:

---

[168] Adopted by the General Assembly on December 17, 1991.
[169] Principle 11, para. 14.
[170] S.S.1984–85–86, c.M-13.1, s.25(5).
[171] R.S.O. 1980, c.262, s.35(3).
[172] R.S.O. 1980, c.262, s.35(5) [re.en. 1986, c.64, s.33(55)].
[173] R.S.N.S.1967, c.249, s.52 [en. 1977, c.45, s.8].

– the patient has been given a full explanation of the procedure, its risks and proposed
  – benefits;

– the patient has been given a full explanation of alternative treatments available;

– the patient has been given an opportunity to ask questions about the procedure and

– the patient is not a prisoner, an involuntary patient, awaiting trial or under any form of
  legal restraint.

In the USA it was held in *Kaimowitz v. Department of Mental Health*[174] that involuntarily
committed patients cannot give informed consent to psycho-surgery on the basis that
where people are confined against their will, their consent to such an intrusive measure
cannot be considered truly free and voluntary.

Conclusions

International principles require that informed consent and the approval of an *independent
external body both* that there is a genuine informed consent and that the treatment best
serves the needs of the patient be obtained before psycho-surgery is carried out. This
should be reflected in Irish mental health legislation.

Electro-convulsive therapy

Position under Mental Treatment Act 1945

Electro-convulsive therapy is provided in Irish psychiatric units. The Mental Treatment
Act 1945 (which is still in force) does not provide any guidance on the administration
of electro-convulsive therapy. As a result the common law rules in relation to the giving
of consent to medical treatment applied. The main issue with regard to consent to ECT
was that disorders, which it is used to treat such as severe depression, may affect a
patient's ability to give consent. At common law where a patient is found incapable of
giving consent such treatment can be given if it is in that patient's best interests.[175]
What was in the patient's best interests would be that course which was supported by a
responsible body of medical opinion even if another might not unless the course adopted
has inherent defects.[176] The Inspector of Mental Hospital's *Guidelines on Good Practice
and Quality Assurance in Mental Health Services* published in 1998 state that ECT:

> "should be administered to patients only with their fully informed written consent.
> There should be a written protocol for its administration including prescription
> and compliance with all the physical investigations and examinations preliminary
> to its administration. There should be an appropriate consent form for ECT with
> provision for the patient's signature, relative's signature, if appropriate and a section
> indicating that the doctor explained fully the procedure to the patient or relatives,

---

[174] No. 73-19434 AW (Cir. Ct. Wayne County, Michigan, July 10, 1973).
[175] See *In re F* [1988] 1 All E.R. 358.
[176] *Dunne v. National Maternity Hospital* [1989] I.R. 91.

if appropriate. A named consultant should be responsible for the ECT programme and should oversee its administration.

Guidelines for its administration should be displayed prominently in the treatment room including pre-ECT and post-ECT nursing checklists. There should be a specific ECT treatment record form, which contains patient information, i.e. name, date of birth, sex, name of treating doctor and whether the patient is an inpatient or outpatient. The diagnosis, current medication, allergies, outcome of physical/anaesthetic assessment should be clearly stated on the treatment record form. Provision should also be made for recording the signature of the anaesthetist and psychiatrist indicating any complications, comments and clinical response.

The treatment facilities should be adequate and incorporate a waiting room and separate treatment and recovery rooms. It is essential that there be adequate monitoring and resuscitation equipment available in the unit. Staff should have (and not merely for purposes of ECT administration) regular cardio-pulmonary resuscitation and foreign body airway obstruction training that should be carried out at regular intervals. It is particularly important that adequate clinical note taking on the administration and clinical response to ECT be documented in patients' case notes."[177]

Position under Mental Health Act 2001

Under the terms of section 59 of the Mental Health Act 2001 (which has yet to be brought into force) a programme of electro-convulsive therapy may not be administered to a patient[178] unless either: (a) the patient gives his or her consent[179] in writing to the administration of the programme of therapy or (b) where the patient is unable or unwilling to give such consent; (i) the programme of therapy is approved (in a form specified by the Commission) by the consultant psychiatrist[180] responsible for the care and treatment of the patient, and (ii) the programme of therapy is also authorised (in a form specified by the Commission) by another consultant psychiatrist following referral of the matter to him or her by the first mentioned psychiatrist.

Section 4 (which came into force on April 5, 2002) of the Mental Health Act provides that in making a decision under this Act concerning the care or treatment of a person due regard shall be given to the need to respect the right of the person to dignity, bodily integrity, privacy and autonomy.

The Mental Health Commission is empowered to make rules providing for the use of electro-convulsive therapy and a programme of electro-convulsive therapy must not be administered to a patient except in accordance with those rules.[181] In the course of the Debates at Committee stage of the Mental Health Bill 1999, Minister Martin referred

---

[177] Para.4.4. of the Guidelines.

[178] *i.e.* a person admitted to hospital pursuant to an admission order. See s.2.

[179] The requirements in relation to consent specified in s.56 apply. See s.56.

[180] Consultant psychiatrist is defined by s.2 as a consultant psychiatrist who is employed by the Health Service Executive or by an approved centre or a person whose name is entered on the division of psychiatry or the division of child and adolescent psychiatry of the Register of Medical Specialists maintained by the Medical Council in Ireland.

[181] S.59(2).

to the protocol issued by the Royal College of Psychiatrists in Ireland on ECT and the fact that the Inspector of Mental Hospitals had included a section on ECT in the *Guidelines on Good Practice and Quality Assurance in Mental Health Services* (1998). He stated that it was envisaged that the Mental Health Commission's rules will draw on the protocols and guidelines already in existence.[182]

At the time of writing the *ECT Handbook* (1995) published by the Royal College of Psychiatrists addresses the common law position relating to consent to ECT in Ireland in the absence of provisions in the Mental Treatment Act 1945 addressing the issue. A new Handbook is in the course of preparation.

It is worth noting that the Inspector's *Guidelines* provide that ECT should be administered only with the patient's fully informed written consent. He does not appear to envisage a set of circumstances where this treatment is administered to patients competent but unwilling to receive it.

It is also significant that the White Paper which preceded the Mental Health Act 2001 proposed that ECT may be administered to an involuntary patient who refuses to give his or her consent to the treatment if there is a second opinion by a consultant psychiatrist "approved by the proposed Mental Health Review Board for this purpose and acting on its behalf."[183]

Commentary

Principles for authorisation of ECT in International law It is interesting to note that the Mental Health Act provisions in relation to electro-convulsive therapy do not take account of and appear to run contrary to *Recommendation 1235(1994) of the Parliamentary Assembly of the Council of Europe on psychiatry and human rights* which provides that electro-convulsive therapy may not be performed unless informed written consent has been given by the patient or a person, counsellor or guardian chosen by the patient as his or her representative *and* unless the decision has been confirmed by a select committee not composed exclusively of psychiatric experts.[184]

Comparative law relating to administration of ECT

New South Wales In New South Wales electro-convulsive therapy may be given to informal patients with the patient's informed consent. Informed consent is defined in section 183 of the Mental Health Act 1990 and includes such matters as full disclosure of benefits, side-effects and alternative treatments. Where the medical superintendent is unsure as to whether a person is capable of giving informed consent s/he may be able to apply to the Mental Health Review Tribunal to determine whether that consent can and has been given.[185]

Application must be made to the Mental Health Review Tribunal to approve the administration of ECT to an involuntary patient. At least two medical practitioners one of whom is a psychiatrist must certify in writing that ECT is a reasonable and proper

---

[182] HC3 No.3, *Dáil Debates*, Cols 149–150.

[183] See, *A New Mental Health Act* (Department of Health, July 1995) Pn.1824, para.6.12.

[184] See para.7(ii)(b).

[185] S.188 of the Mental Health Act 1990 (NSW).

treatment and necessary or desirable for the safety or welfare of the patient.[186] The tribunal must then hold an inquiry to determine whether the patient is capable of giving informed consent to the treatment, whether that consent has been given and whether, in the absence of informed consent, the treatment is reasonable and proper and is necessary or desirable for the patient's safety or welfare. The views of the patient as well as the medical evidence must be taken into account by the Tribunal.[187]

US law Three general principles may be drawn from US law in relation to ECT. First, in most states of the USA electro-convulsive therapy may be administered without court intervention only if the patient gives voluntary, knowing and competent consent. Secondly in the absence of an incompetency adjudication or an emergency most courts that have reviewed the matter have held that patients have an absolute right to accept or decline ECT. Third, if however, the patient has been adjudicated incompetent generally a court must appoint a substitute decision maker with the specific authority to exercise the patient's right to accept or decline ECT.

In general US courts have tended to restrict the administration of ECT on common law and constitutional grounds. In *Price v. Sheppard*[188] the Minnesota Supreme Court required a due process adversary hearing where a patient is incompetent to give consent or where a patient withheld consent. In the hearing the court would determine the necessity and reasonableness of the prescribed treatment. In *Lillian F v. Superior Court of California*,[189] the California Court of Appeal ruled that there must be clear and convincing evidence that a person lacks the capacity to consent to electro convulsive therapy before honouring a substitute decision that a person needed electro convulsive therapy. The evidential standard applied even in the case of a person already placed under conservatorship. In *Colorado ex rel. M.K.M.*,[190] a Colorado Appeals Court required clear and convincing evidence that such treatment was needed and finally in *In re Detention of Schuoler*,[191] the Washington Supreme Court ruled that in adopting a criterion for decision making regarding the use of electro convulsive therapy the substituted judgment test based on the decision maker's determination of what the patient would want was the test that was required.

Conclusions

1. It is submitted that there is some doubt that the requirement of a second medical opinion will operate as an objective check against intrusive intervention by ECT. It may result in the issue of competence to give consent being treated as an exclusively medical concept when in effect the question of whether it is proper to treat a detained patient against his or her objections is social and legal having a direct bearing on the rights of self determination and privacy of the patient. In addition experience in other jurisdictions where similar provisions operate suggests that second opinions

---

[186] S.188 of the Mental Health Act 1990 (NSW).
[187] S.193 Mental Health Act 1990 (NSW).
[188] 239 N.W. 2d 905 (1976) 1 M.P.D. L.R. 120.
[189] 206 Cal. Rptr. 603 (Cal. Ct. App. 1984) 9 M.P.D. L.R. 25.
[190] 765 P. 2d. 1075 (1988) 13 M.P.D. L.R. 209.
[191] 723 P. 2d 1103 (1986) 11 M.P.D. L.R. 24.

routinely support the original decision by the treating psychiatrist on the basis that it adheres to general and approved practice.[192] Cooney & O'Neill point out that: "it is precisely the general and approved practice of psychiatrists in overriding the decision of detained patients which created the need for reform in the first place."[193]

2. It is submitted that if it is proposed to administer ECT to a person without that person's consent a truly independent review process is required in order to determine that person's competency to consent. Any such process should be interdisciplinary in nature and include lay and legal elements. It should be independent of the treating psychiatrist and detaining authority and afford the patient meaningful access to the body in question together with a fair opportunity to express and defend what s/he perceives to be in his/her best interests.[194]

3. A patient should have the right to nominate a third party to represent his/her interests in relation to any proposal to administer treatment by ECT and to give or refuse consent on the patient's behalf to such treatment.

4. Non-consensual treatment may only be justified where a patient is incapable of making a rational decision concerning proposed treatment and of consenting to it. Proposals which impose treatment upon a person who has the capacity to consent infringe the individual's constitutional right to self determination. In *In re A Ward of Court*,[195] the Supreme Court recognised this essential human right of autonomy or self determination. Hamilton J. referred to the right "to privacy, to bodily integrity and to self determination".[196] O'Flaherty J. specified that there was a constitutional right of self determination (otherwise bodily integrity) which was also regarded as a privacy right.[197] Blayney J. stated that:

> "Where a person who is *compos mentis* has a condition which in the absence of medical intervention will lead to death such a person has in law the right to refuse such intervention."[198]

Denham J. stated:

> "Medical treatment may not be given to an adult person of full capacity without his or her consent. ... The consent which is given by an adult of full capacity is a matter of choice. It is not necessarily a decision based on medical

[192] See *Kritik 1 Psychiatric Detention Civil Commitment in Ireland, op. cit.*, p.263 Commenting on the operation of the second opinion scheme in England Bartlett and Sandland note that the English draft Mental Health Bill 2002 provides for a multidisciplinary scrutiny of treatment plans by a tribunal with a power of veto "in an admission that the Second Opinion Scheme has failed sufficiently to protect the rights of patients." See Bartlett and Sandland, *Mental Health Law, Policy and Practice* (2nd ed., Oxford University Press, 2003), p.348.
[193] *Ibid.*
[194] In this regard it is interesting to note that the English Mental Health Bill 2002 requires a responsible medical officer to apply to a Mental Health Tribunal for permission to administer ECT when the patient does not consent See clause 118.
[195] [1995] I.L.R.M. 401.
[196] *Ibid.*, p.426.
[197] *Ibid.*, p.431.
[198] *Ibid.*, p.442.

considerations. Thus medical treatment may be refused for other than medical reasons. Such reasons may not be viewed as good medical reasons or reasons most citizens would regard as rational but the person of full age and capacity may make the decision for their own reasons".[199]

Accordingly it is clear that the proposal, which permits the administration of ECT to a person who though competent was unreasonably withholding consent, is constitutionally objectionable. There is a clear tension between the provisions of section 59 in this regard and section 4 of the Mental Health Act which provides that in making a decision under this Act concerning the care or treatment of a person due regard shall be given to the need to respect the right of the person to dignity, bodily integrity, privacy and autonomy.

5. It is also ironic that where treatments other than ECT, and the administration of medicine after three months is concerned section 57 requires the consent of the patient to such treatment and the treatment may only be administered involuntarily if the patient is incapable of consent.

It is submitted that any legislative proposals to permit ECT or other treatment of a patient without his consent should be linked to his/her incapacity to give that consent.

Administration of medicine after three months

General

The administration of psychoactive and neuroleptic medication is not without its controversies. Patients in psychiatric hospitals are administered such medication to change their moods, behaviour or thought processes. Many consent to such treatment others do not. Those who refuse such treatment may do so for reasons, which are related to their mental disorder such as paranoia. Other patients may refuse as an expression of their autonomy for reasons related to the efficacy of the drugs and to fear of the adverse effects of the such drugs and some psychoactive drugs do have undesirable side effects. These include increased heart rate, nasal congestion, blurred vision, constipation, drowsiness, fluctuations of temperature or altered skin pigmentation. They can also produce orthostatic or postural hypotension, dizziness, weakness or fainting when the patient stands up. Further they can impact on appetite, sexuality and secretion of certain hormones. The drugs may also cause abnormalities in motor activity. Individuals may develop a syndrome, which seems like Parkinson's disease showing a general slowing of movement, facial or other mobility (akinesia), muscular rigidity and tremor. Akathesia, another effect, involves restlessness. The most serious adverse effect tardive dyskinesia is a neurological syndrome characterised by stereotypical involuntary movements such as sucking or smacking of the lips, lateral jaw movements and dartings of the tongue. It is generally irreversible.

While psychoactive and neuroleptic medications do produce benefits for people with mental illness by controlling symptoms of mental disorder and never drugs with fewer side effects are continually being developed it is important to bear in mind the

---

[199] *Ibid.*, p.454.

intrusiveness of medication into a person's mind and body and the adverse effects inhering in its use must be examined against the backdrop of the right of the competent individual to vindication of his/her constitutional rights of bodily and psychological integrity.

Position under Mental Treatment Act 1945

The Mental Treatment Act 1945 (still in force) contains no provisions in relation to administration of medication after three months. The position in relation to the administration of such medication is the same as that in relation to administration of medication at any other time. It may be administered to voluntary patients and competent detained patients only with their consent and to detained patients who are incompetent to consent to treatment for as long as they remain incompetent where it is in their best interests and accords with accepted medical practice. At common law a patient is competent when s/he has the capacity to understand the nature and effects of the treatment. The decision as to competency is usually made, in the first instance, by the treating doctor.

Position under Mental Health Act 2001

Section 60 of the Mental Health Act 2001 (not yet implemented) is designed to protect patients from the continual administration of drugs if there is no obvious benefit to the patient in so doing. It provides that where medicine has been administered to a patient for the purposes of ameliorating his or her mental disorder for a continuous period of 3 months the administration of that medicine shall not be continued unless either (a) the patient gives his or her consent in writing to the continued administration of that medicine or (b) where the patient is unable or unwilling to give such consent (i) the continued administration of that medicine is approved by the consultant psychiatrist responsible for the care and treatment of the patient, and (ii) the continued administration of that medicine is authorised (in a form specified by the Mental Health Commission) by another consultant psychiatrist following referral of the matter to him by the first mentioned psychiatrist. The consent or as the case may be approval and authorisation will be valid for a period of three months and thereafter for periods of three months, if, in respect of each period the like consent or as the case may be approval and authorisation is obtained.

A similar provision is provided for in section 61 (not yet implemented) where medicine has been administered to a child in respect of whom an order under section 25 is in force for the purposes of ameliorating his or her mental disorder for a continuous period of three months. Section 61 provides that in those circumstances the administration of that medicine shall not be continued unless either (a) the continued administration of that medicine is approved by the consultant psychiatrist responsible for the care and treatment of the child, and (b) the continued administration of that medicine is authorised (in a form specified by the Mental Health Commission) by another consultant psychiatrist, following referral of the matter to him or her by the first mentioned psychiatrist and the consent or, as the case may be, approval and authorisation shall be valid for a period of three months and thereafter for periods of three months, if in respect of each period, the like consent or, as the case may be approval and authorisation is obtained.

Section 2 defines "child" as a person under the age of 18 years other than a person who is or has been married.

What is "medicine" unders section 60 and 61   The question is what amounts to "medicine" under sections 60 and 61. There is very little guidance in the Irish jurisdiction on this. In England the Mental Health Act Commission has taken the view in relation to the similar section 58 in the Mental Health Act 1983,[200] that medicine "will broadly encompass any substance intended to influence the mental disorder".[201] Further in *B v. Croydon Health Authority*,[202] Hoffman L.J. held that "ordinary food in liquid form, such as would be used in tube feeding, is not medicine within the meaning of section 58".[203]

Patients "unable or unwilling" to give consent   Section 60 authorises the administration of medicine after three months to a patient who is either "unable or unwilling to give … consent" where the continued administration of that medicine is approved by the consultant psychiatrist responsible for the care and treatment of the patient and its continued administration is authorised in a form specified by the Commission by another consultant psychiatrist following a referral by the first mentioned psychiatrist. The equivalent provisions of section 58 of the Mental Health Act 1983 have been the subject of litigation in England and the case law which it has generated is of relevance to Ireland both because of the broad similarity of procedures under section 60 of the Mental Health Act 2001 and section 58 of the Mental Health Act 1983 and the fact that the operation of the English provision has been, following the coming into force of the Human Rights Act 1998, examined in the case law for its consistency with the European Convention on Human Rights. With the coming into force of section 2 of the European Convention on Human Rights Act 2003, sections 60 and 61 of the Mental Health Act 2001 will have to be similarly interpreted. An examination of the English case law is therefore pertinent.

In the English case of *R (Wilkinson) v. Broadmoor Special Hospital Authority and others*,[204] W was detained in Broadmoor hospital with a diagnosis of psychopathic disorder. The responsible medical officer was of the view that W was also suffering from an underlying mental illness, namely a psychotic disorder, which might respond to medical treatment. He proposed to treat him with anti-psychotic medication but W refused consent. In the view of the responsible medical officer ("RMO") however, W did not have the capacity to give or refuse consent. Nonetheless the treatment was administered and it was necessary to used force to administer it.

W then sought legal advice to challenge the administration of further doses of the medication. He obtained a report from an independent consultant psychiatrist, Dr G who disputed the RMO's views and another doctor, Dr H who supported the RMO's views in some respects. Dr G first disagreed with the diagnosis that W was suffering

---

[200] S.58 of the Mental Health Act 1983 authorises the continued administration of medication after three months to a patient in a case where a second opinion appointed doctor certifies that (a) the patient is not capable of understanding the nature, purpose and likely effects of the treatment or (b) has not consented to it but that, having regard to the likelihood of its alleviating or preventing a deterioration in the patient's condition the treatment should be given.

[201] DHSS (1984) Circular No. DDL (84) 4, *Mental Health Act Commission: Guidance for Responsible Medical Officers – Consent to Treatment*.

[202] [1995] 1 All E.R. 683.

[203] *Ibid.*, p.687.

[204] [2002] 1 W.L.R. 419.

from a psychotic illness and accordingly with the likelihood that anti-psychotic medicine would benefit him. Secondly, he disagreed that W lacked capacity and thirdly he disagreed with the decision to administer the treatment by force. In relation to this third point his reason for disagreeing was that W had coronary heart disease and was at risk of heart attack and, in fact, had had an angina attack after the first dose of anti-pyschotic medication had been administered. Although the Court of Appeal in the case was delivering judgment on interlocutory appeal against a judges refusal to order that the doctors attend the hearing and so was not required to decide on issues of substance the Court did consider the application of the European Convention on Human Rights for the operation of section 58.

In relation to the application of the Convention it was argued for the claimant that Article 2 of the Convention was in issue because of the risk identified by Dr G of the claimant suffering a fatal heart attack if treatment was imposed without his consent; Article 3 was relevant because the forcible injection of an unwilling claimant constituted degrading treatment and, if the claimant was properly to be regarded as capacitated it clearly violated his fundamental rights to autonomy and bodily inviolability and even if Article 3 was not breached Article 8 was as there was no sufficient justification under Article 8(2) for so fundamental an invasion of the claimant's autonomy and inviolability which were basic ingredients of his right to privacy. Article 6 was invoked on the grounds that the treatment decisions in question profoundly affected the claimant's civil rights and accordingly entitled him to a determination by an independent and impartial tribunal of the lawfulness of the interference with those rights particularly those of autonomy and inviolability. It was also argued that Article 14 was breached because no sufficient reason existed for distinguishing between those capacitated patients who were detained and those who are not. Non-detained capacitated patients could not be treated against their will.

It was argued further that a capacitated patient's refusal of consent could be overridden only in the most tightly circumscribed circumstances. These would include the protection of others from serious harm and perhaps, the safety of the patient himself.

The majority of the Lords Justices were agreed[205] that, following the enactment of the Human Rights Act 1998 section 58 had to be interpreted consistently with Article 3 of the Convention which provides that "No one shall be subjected to inhuman or degrading treatment" In this context reference had to be made to the decision of the European Court of the Human Rights in *Herczegalvy v. Austria*[206] which stated:

> "The court considers that the position of inferiority and powerlessness which is typical of patients confined in psychiatric hospitals calls for increased vigilance in reviewing whether the Convention is being complied with. While it is for the medical authorities to decide, on the basis of the recognisable rules of medical science, on the therapeutic methods to be used, if necessary by force, to preserve the physical and mental health of patients who are entirely incapable of deciding for themselves and for whom they are responsible, such patients nevertheless remain under the protection of Article 3, the requirements of which permit no derogation.

---

[205] See Simon Brown L.J. at para.30, Hale L.J. at paras 77–78.
[206] [1992] 15 E.H.R.R. 437.

The established principles of medicine are admittedly in principle decisive in such cases; as a general rule, a method, which is a therapeutic necessity, cannot be regarded as inhuman or degrading. The court must nevertheless satisfy itself that the medical necessity has been convincingly shown to exist."[207]

Thus to comply with Article 3 the compulsory administration of medical treatment to persons with mental illness who were incapable of consent had to comply with established principles of psychiatry and be a therapeutic necessity. The fact that the administration of medicine was a medical necessity had convincingly to be shown to exist.

The equivalence of the position of capacitated and incapacitated patients under the provisions of section 58 was also addressed by the court. Simon Brown L.J. quoted from a report by the European Committee for the Prevention of Torture and Inhuman or Degrading Treatment or Punishment[208] made in August 2000 as follows:

"Patients should, as a matter of principle, be placed in a position to give their free and informed consent to treatment. The admission of a person to a psychiatric establishment on an involuntary basis should not be construed as authorising treatment without his consent. It follows that every competent patient, whether voluntary or involuntary, should be given the opportunity to refuse treatment or any other medical intervention. Any derogation from this fundamental principle should be based on law and only relate to clearly and strictly defined exceptional circumstances."[209]

He then commented:

"That gives some indication of modern thinking on this sensitive subject. The precise equivalence under section 58(3)(b) between incompetent patients and competent but non-consenting patients seems to me increasingly difficult to justify."[210]

Hale L.J. was hesitant to express a view as to whether the degradation suffered by a patient where forcible measures were inflicted was greater or lesser according to whether or not the patient had capacity.[211] She was also reluctant to accept the view that that the criteria for non-consensual treatment of a capacitated person were distinct from those which applied in the case of an incapacitated person. She stated:

"Whether the criteria for non-consensual treatment of the capacitated should be limited to treatment which is for their own safety (as opposed to their health) is a difficult and complex question. ... There are indeed indications that the issue of capacity is assuming a greater importance in the context of psychiatric treatment. But we have not yet reached the point where it is an accepted norm that detained

---

[207] [1992] 15 E.H.R.R. 437 at 484.
[208] 8th General Report (CPT/Inf (98) 12).
[209] *Ibid.*, para.41.
[210] [2002] 1 W.L.R. 419 at 433.
[211] *Ibid.* at 446.

patients who fulfil the *In re MB*[212] criteria for capacity can only be treated against their will for the protection of others or for their own safety."[213]

Given the disagreement between the Lords Justices on the point and the fact that the case involved an interlocutory application the issue whether the Convention required a distinction to be made between the criteria for administration of psychiatric treatment to the incapacitated patient and the patient who does not consent was in effect left undecided.

As to the application of Article 3 to the situation if the patient had capacity Simon Brown L.J. did express the view that:

> "If in truth this claimant has the capacity to refuse consent to the treatment proposed here, it is difficult to suppose that he should nevertheless be subjected to it ... its impact on the claimant's rights above all to autonomy and bodily inviolability is immense and its prospective benefits (not least given his extreme opposition) appear decidedly speculative."[214]

In essence he appeared to doubt whether on the facts the treatment was a therapeutic necessity such as to justify its imposition in the face of W's refusal. Hale L.J. emphasising that "substantial benefit" would be required for the treatment to be justified as a medical necessity seemed to hint that she also doubted whether it was on the facts.[215] These conclusions on the facts seem to suggest that treatment which is of doubtful benefit, which is adamantly refused by the patient and which will require force in its administration with possible deleterious effects for the general health of the patient will (notwithstanding the application of the "medical necessity" test) by failing that test be in breach of Article 3 of the European Convention on Human Rights

The court also briefly addressed the issue of whether the treatment was in breach of Article 8 of the Convention, by virtue of not being justified by Article 8(2). Simon Brown L.J. pointed out that in *Herczegfalvy* the claim under Article 8 was dismissed because the detained patient who lacked capacity and had been forcibly fed and medicated was unable to disprove the view that his psychiatric illness rendered him "entirely incapable of taking decisions for himself"[216] during the time the treatment was administered to him. This seems to imply that the conclusion as to a breach of Article 8 may have been different if that patient was found to have had capacity and in this regard Simon Brown L.J.'s remarks about the lack of justification for the equivalence of status of incompetent and competent but non-consenting detained patients acquire particular significance. However, as the court was primarily concerned with a procedural matters the substantive issue in this regard remains to be decided in another case.

W also challenged the legality of the second opinion procedure more generally on the basis that it infringed his rights under Article 6 of the Convention. It was argued that the decision to subject him to treatment by force constituted a determination of his civil

---

[212] [1997] 2 F.L.R. 426.
[213] [2002] 1 W.L.R. 419 at 446.
[214] *Ibid.* at 433.
[215] *Ibid.* at 447.
[216] *Ibid.* at 430.

rights and accordingly he was entitled to a "fair and public hearing" by an "independent and impartial tribunal" as stipulated by Article 6(1) and that the second opinion procedure did not afford him such a hearing.

Brown L J. held that if it were the only mode of review of the decision of a RMO[217] the second opinion certification process could hardly be said to involve a fair and public hearing and it would not meet the requirements of Article 6. However, since it was always open to the claimant to bring an action in tort for assault in respect of past treatment and since it was his conclusion in the case that it was always open to the claimant to seek a review of the legality of past or proposed future treatment, the requirements of Article 6(1) were met.[218]

However, qualifying these statements he added that anything less than a full merits review would not satisfy the requirements of Article 6[219] and also he stated that Article 6 "did not entitle a mental patient in every case to challenged a treatment plan before being subjected to it."[220] Hale L.J. stated that "Whatever the position before the Human Rights Act 1998, the decision to impose treatment without consent upon a protesting patient is a potential invasion of his rights under Article 3 or Article 8. ... The claimant is entitled to a proper hearing on the merits of whether the statutory grounds for imposing this treatment upon him against his will are made out"[221] but stated that not every patient was entitled to such a hearing in advance. Her view was that the RMO and the SOAD (second opinion appointed doctor) were "not determining" the patient's civil rights and liabilities "They were merely deciding to impose or authorise treatment in the belief that the statutory grounds for doing so exist."[222]

It is interesting to note that in the course of their judgments the Lords Justices in *Wilkinson* also exhorted that a more rigorous approach be followed in relation to the second opinion certification procedure than had heretofore been followed. Simon Brown L.J. called for "a less deferential approach than appears to be the norm" from the SOAD[223]

---

[217] *i.e.* the responsible medical officer.

[218] [2002] 1 W.L.R. 419 at 434–435.

[219] *Ibid.* at 434.

[220] *Ibid.* at 434.

[221] *Ibid.* at 447.

[222] *Ibid.* at 447. This view appears to be supported by the Scottish decision of the Outer House of Session in the case of *W.M. Petitioner* [2003] S.L.T. 219. In this case the petitioner, a detained patient argued that the administration of anti-psychotic medication against his will breached Art. 6 as it was "a determination of his civil rights and obligations" (i.e. a deprivation of the right to refuse treatment at common law) . In addition he argued that his RMO who made the decision to treat was not "an independent and impartial tribunal". The court held that the Mental Health (Scotland) Act 1984 defined the right of a particular class of persons, namely those detained to object to treatment. Having defined the rights of those within that class the statute then subjected entry to (i.e. detention) and continuing membership of that class to judicial scrutiny by way of appeal to the sheriff. The petitioner did not complain about any inadequacy in the access to judicial review. The complaint related to the substantive consequences of membership. Accordingly the complaint of the petitioner was truly that national law did not confer a *substantive right* on those within the category defined by the legislation. There was therefore no "contestation" or dispute as to the extent of his rights. Therefore the petitioner's invocation Article 6(1) was misplaced. (at para. 17). The clear implication from the courts statements was that Article 6 was relevant at the point of determination of rights *i.e.* the point of initial or continued detention.

[223] *i.e.* the second opinion appointed doctor.

and stated that while it was proper for the SOAD to pay regard to the views of the RMO that did "not relieve him of the responsibility of forming his own independent judgment as to whether or not "the treatment should be given".[224] Brooke L J. agreed that "the SOAD must form his/her own independent opinion as to whether treatment should be given"[225] and Hale L.J. agreed with Simon Brown and Brooke L.JJ. that "the SOAD has to form his own independent opinion upon the existence of the statutory criteria. At the very least his must act in good faith and with reasonable care in forming his judgment".[226]

Following the enactment of section 2 of the European Convention on Human Rights Act 2003 the provisions of sections 60 and 61 of the Mental Health Act 2001 will have to be interpreted in a manner compatible with the State's obligations under the Convention. The *Wilkinson* case suggests that it may be more fruitful to rely on Articles 3 and 8 of the Convention rather than Article 6 or Article 14 when making objections as a matter of law to forced treatment. In this regard it is worth noting the decision of the European Court of Human Rights in *Raninen v. Finland*[227] in which the court held that although Article 3 will not apply until a minimum level of severity is reached "there might be circumstances in which Article 8 could be regarded as affording a protection in relation to conditions during detention which do not attain the level of severity required by Article 3".[228]

In the later case of *Regina (N) v. M and others*[229] it was held by the English Court of Appeal, (on appeal from a refusal of judicial review of a decision of SOAD's decision that the claimant required anti-psychotic medical treatment and could not consent to it), that before a court could give permission for treatment to which the patient *with capacity* did not consent the court, had to be satisfied that the proposed treatment was both in the patient's best interests and "medically necessary" – the standard that applies to incompetent patients - to be consistent with the requirements of Article 3 the European Convention on Human Rights as scheduled to the Human Rights Act 1998. The court followed the decision of the European Court of Human Rights in *Herczegfalvy v. Austria*,[230] in ruling that the standard of proof required was that the court should be satisfied that medical necessity has been "convincingly" shown.

The court held that the answer to the question as to whether the proposed treatment had been convincingly shown to be medically necessary depended on such factors as:

> "(a) how certain is it that the patient does suffer from a treatable mental disorder (b) how serious a disorder is it; (c) how serious a risk is presented to others; (d) how likely is it that if the patient does suffer from such a disorder the proposed treatment will alleviate the condition, (e) how much alleviation is there likely to be, (f) how likely is it that the treatment will have adverse consequences for the patient and (g) how severe may they be?"[231]

---

[224] [2002] 1 W.L.R. 419 at 434.
[225] *Ibid.* at 438.
[226] *Ibid.* at 444.
[227] [1997] 26 E.H.R.R. 563.
[228] Para. 63.
[229] [2003] 1 W.L.R. 562.
[230] [1992] 15 E.H.R.R. 437.
[231] [2003] 1 W.L.R. 562 at 569.

The court also held that treatment could not be in a patient's best interests unless a responsible and competent body of medical opinion agreed with it. – the test set out in *Bolam v. Friern Hospital Management Committee*[232] This was a:

> "necessary but not sufficient condition of treatment in a patient's best interests. If the proposed treatment does not even satisfy the *Bolam* test, the best interests test fails at the first hurdle".[233]

The court suggested that the "best interests" test "embraces issues far wider than the medical."[234] The court stated that it did not follow that the treatment could not be in the patient's best interests or medically necessary merely because there was a responsible body of medical opinion to the effect that treatment was not in the patient's best interests and not medically necessary. Although this latter body of opinion was relevant the court had to decide in the light of all the evidence whether the treatment was necessary.

While some of the criteria promulgated by the Court of Appeal for determining whether treatment is medically necessary are peculiar to section 58 of the Mental Treatment Act 1983, the decision in *Regina (N) v. M* is persuasive in the Irish context in furtherance of the argument that following the enactment of the European Convention on Human Rights Act 2001, the powers in the Mental Health Act 2001 to administer medicine to incapable patients or against the wishes of a patient must be interpreted consistently with the jurisprudence of the European Court regarding Article 3 of the European Convention on Human Rights.

The second opinion

The role of the second opinion appointed doctor ("SOAD") was further at issue in the English case of *R v. Feggetter and the Mental Health Act Commission*,[235] when the question was raised as to whether the decision of a SOAD sanctioning the administration of medical treatment against the wishes of a competent patient with mental illness should be accompanied by reasons. Brooke L.J. held that the common law[236] implied a duty to give reasons for an administrative decision where the subject matter of that decision was an interest so highly regarded in law (for example personal liberty) that fairness required that reasons at least for particular decisions be given as of right.[237] In the light of the judgments of the Court of Appeal in *R (Wilkinson) v. Broadmoor Special Hospital Authority*,[238] a decision to administer medical treatment to a competent non consenting

---

[232] [1957] 1 W.L.R. 582.

[233] [2003] 1 W.L.R. 562 at 572.

[234] *Ibid.*

[235] [2002] E.W.C.A. Civ. 554.

[236] Brooke L J. referred to a trilogy of cases in support of this proposition namely the Court of Appeal decision in *R v. Civil Service Appeal Board ex parte Cunningham* [1991] 4 All E.R. 310, the decision of the House of Lords in *R v. Secretary of State for the Home Department ex parte Doody* [1994] 1 A.C. 531 and the decision of the Divisional Court in *R v. Higher Education Funding Council ex parte Institute of Dental Surgery* [1994] 1 W.L.R. 242.

[237] Para. 24.

[238] [2002] 1 W.L.R. 419.

adult patient fell into this category.[239] Running together the common law principles and European Convention rights he stated that:

> "With the coming into force of the Human Rights Act 1998 the time has come in my judgment for this court to declare that fairness required that a decision by a SOAD which sanctions the violation of autonomy of a competent adult patient should be accompanied by reasons".[240]

The fact that the critical decision was made by a doctor in the exercise of his clinical judgment and not by a tribunal following a more formal process could not be allowed to diminish the significance of the doctor's decision. Brooke L.J. noted the results of a review,[241] which established that in Australia ten years after a fairly wide statutory duty to give reasons, had been introduced a higher quality of decision-making had resulted. The authors of the review had observed that the "cost" of providing statements of reasons had to be balanced against the social justice benefit, which flowed from the fact that aggrieved individuals knew how their cases had been decided.

Sedley L.J. found the duty to give reasons to be based first on existing common law.[242] He stated that: "the impact of the decision is so invasive of physical integrity and moral dignity that it calls without more for disclosure of the reasons for it".[243] Responding to the argument that there was a material difference between an administrative decision relating to incarceration and a medical opinion relating to treatment he said that in the case of both the prisoner and the patient:

> "a person with special qualifications was equipped in the public interest with statutory powers which impact directly on someone's physical and moral autonomy. Any such power carries a heavy burden of responsibility. The SOAD's opinion, while of course it is clinical, has legal and moral dimensions which cannot be marginalized and which are in every sense the SOAD's business and – if necessary – the court's".[244]

Unlike Brooke L.J., Sedley J. was concerned to keep the claimant's common law and Convention rights separate. He noted that the common law set high standards of due process in non-judicial settings to which the European Court of Human Rights declined to apply Article 6. In the instant case he was of the view that the claimant could derive better protection from the common law than from the Convention. Accordingly the "difficult argument about the point at which Article 6 [bit] on the s.58 process [was] only of secondary importance."[245] Nevertheless Sedley L.J. took the view that the effect

---

[239] Para.25.

[240] Para.25.

[241] The court referred to an essay by Sir Patrick Neill QC entitled "The Duty to Give Reasons: the Openness of Decision-making" in Christopher Forsyth and Ivan Hare *The Golden Metwand and the Crooked Cord* (Clarendon, Oxford, 1998), pp.163–164.

[242] He referred to the decision in *R v. Secretary of State for the Home Department ex parte Doody* [1994] 1 A.C. 531.

[243] Para.37.

[244] Para.38.

[245] Para.46.

of section 3 of the Human Rights Act 1998 operating "as a strong canon of construction" of statutes in the light of the European Convention of Human Rights was that section 58 had to be interpreted in the context of Article 8 of the Convention and this led to the conclusion that a patient was entitled "as a matter of right to know in useful form and at a relevant time what the SOAD's reasons [were] for his opinion on the RMO's proposal to override his will".[246]

Potter L.J. was of the view that the claimant could derive the protection to which he was entitled from the duty to give reasons under common law and it was not necessary to resort to any consideration of the effect of Article 8 of the Convention for the purposes of the decision.[247]

As to the nature of the duty imposed on the second opinion appointed doctor, Brooke L.J. stated the law would not requires the second opinion appointed doctor to dot every "i" and cross every "t" when giving reasons for his opinion. So long as he gave his reasons clearly on what he reasonably regarded as the substantive points on which he formed his opinion that would suffice.[248] Sedley L.J. ruled that the reasons should be given "in useful form".[249]

The Lords Justices agreed that in future the SOAD should send a statement of reasons to the RMO or to the hospital and that this should be disclosed to the patient unless the second opinion appointed doctor or the responsible medical officer properly considered that such disclosure would be likely to cause serious harm to the physical or mental health of the patient or any other person.[250] According to Brooke L.J. the reasons should be prepared and disclosed to the patient "as soon as practicable."[251] Sedley L.J. ruled that the patient was entitled to know the doctor's reasons "in a form and at a time which allow the individual to understand and respond to them".[252]

The decision in *Feggetter* constitutes persuasive authority in support of a requirement on common law grounds and (following the enactment of the European Convention on Human Rights Act 2003) on the grounds of the requirement of consistency in interpretation of section 60 and 61 with Article 8 of the Convention that the consultant psychiatrist appointed to give a second opinion under sections 60 and 61 of the Irish Mental Health Act 2001 give reasons for his/her decision if his/her decision is that a patient who after three months of medication refuses medication should be administered medication notwithstanding his/her refusal to consent to it.

Commentary on Irish law relating to administration of medication after three months

International principles Principle 11.6 of the United Nations Principles for the Protections of Persons with Mental Illness and the Improvement of Mental Health Care provides that except as provided in paragraphs 7, 8, 12,[253] 13,[254] 14 [255] and 15[256]

---

[246] Para.49.
[247] Para.50.
[248] Para.29.
[249] Para.49.
[250] Para.32, Sedley L.J. concurred at para. 36 and Potter L.J. concurred at para.50.
[251] Para.33.
[252] Para.37.
[253] Para.12 provides that sterilisation shall never be carried out as a treatment for mental illness.

below a proposed plan of treatment may be given to a patient without a patient's informed consent if the following conditions are satisfied:

(a) the patient is, at the relevant time, held as an involuntary patient;

(b) an independent authority, having in its possession all relevant information, including the information specified in paragraph 2 is satisfied that at the relevant time the patient lacks capacity to give or withhold informed consent to the proposed plan of treatment or if, domestic legislation so provides, that, having regard to the patient's own safety or the safety of others the patient unreasonably withholds such consent; and

(c) the independent authority is satisfied that the proposed plan of treatment is in the best interests of the patient's health needs

The information specified in paragraph 2 is information relating to (a) the diagnostic assessment; (b) the purpose, method, duration and expected benefit of the proposed treatment; (c) alternative modes of treatment including those less intrusive and (d) possible pain or discomfort, risks and side-effects of the proposed treatment.

Paragraph 7 provides:

> "Paragraph 6 above does not apply to a patient with a personal representative empowered by law to consent to treatment for the patient but except as provided in paragraphs 12, 13, 14, and 15 below treatment may be given to such a patient without his or her informed consent if the personal representative having been given the information prescribed in paragraph 2 above consents on the patient's behalf."

Paragraph 8 provides:

> "Except as provided in paragraphs 12, 13, 14, and 15 below treatment may also be given to any patient without the patient's informed consent if a qualified mental health practitioner authorised by law determines that it is urgently necessary in order to prevent immediate or imminent harm to the patient or to other persons. Such treatment shall not be prolonged beyond the period that is strictly necessary for this purpose."

In effect therefore the UN Principles do not regard a second medical opinion as sufficient to authorise the administration of medicine to an involuntary patient. An independent

---

[254] Para.13 provides, *inter alia*, where a patient is unable to give informed consent that a major medical or surgical procedure can be authorised only after independent review.

[255] Para.14 deals with the conditions under which psycho-surgery may be carried out and has been discussed *supra* in this chapter.

[256] Para.15 provides that clinical trials and experimental treatment shall never be carried out on any patient without informed consent except that a patient who is unable to give informed consent may be admitted to a clinical trial or given experimental treatment but only with the approval of a competent, independent, review body specifically constituted for this purpose.

authority must do so unless the patient has a personal representative who has given consent on the patient's behalf or unless an emergency exists.

Conclusions

Like electro-convulsive therapy the administration of medicine to a patient after three months falls into the category of treatment requiring consent or a second opinion. The criticisms of section 60 mirror those of section 59 in some respects.

1. Experience in other jurisdictions has shown that the requirement of a second opinion from a consultant psychiatrist does not necessarily provide a convincing safeguard against unnecessary intrusive treatment by medication.

2. It is submitted that the administration of medication to an involuntary but competent patient where that patient does may amount to a violation of his/her constitutional right to bodily integrity and self determination[257] particularly if the benefits of such administration are not substantially demonstrated. Further it should be noted that there inherent tension between sections 60 and 61 of the 2001 Act and section 4 which provides that in making a decision under the Act concerning the care or treatment of a person due regard shall be given to the need to respect the right of the person to dignity, bodily integrity, privacy and autonomy.

3. It would appear by implication from the judgments of the Court of Appeal in *R(N) v. M* that the criteria which apply in determining whether the forcible administration of medicine to the competent and non-consenting patient amounts to "inhuman and degrading" treatment under Article 3 of the European Convention are similar those which apply in the case of an incompetent patient.

    However, support for the view that the absence of a distinction in the criteria, which apply to both categories of patient, is increasingly difficult to justify may be gleaned from the judgment of Brown L.J. in *Wilkinson*. It is submitted that a patient's competence and his/her refusal to consent to medication are factors which warrant special attention in relation to the matter of whether a treatment is inhuman and degrading and it is submitted that where a competent involuntary patient refuses to give consent to treatment he or she should not be treated against his or her wishes unless the situation invites pressing reasons for overriding such refusal to consent. Such reasons it is submitted would exist where s/he is an imminent danger to himself or herself or others.

4. Where an involuntary patient is unable to give consent to the administration of medicine to him/her it is submitted that the consultant psychiatrist responsible for his or her care and treatment should be permitted to administer the proposed medicine provided its administration has been approved by a Mental Health Tribunal. Before approving the administration of medicine to a patient who is unable to give consent the Mental Health Tribunal should be required to be satisfied that, at the relevant time the patient lacks the capacity to give or withhold informed consent to the proposed treatment and that the proposed plan of treatment is in the best interest of the patient's health needs.

---

[257] See *In re a Ward of Court* [1995] I.L.R.M. 401.

5. Section 61 is premised upon the incapacity of the child both by virtue of mental disorder and age. Where incapacity by virtue of age is concerned "child" is defined by section 2 as a person under 18 years other than a person who is or has been married. It is interesting to note the contrasting provisions of section 23 of the Non-Fatal Offences against the Person Act 1997 which provide in effect that minors who have attained the age of 16 years are as competent to give consent to medical treatment as if they were of full age. The provisions of section 2 of the 2001 Act therefore are clearly inconsistent with section 23 may create a situation where 16-18 year olds may refuse consent generally to medical treatment with the exception of treatment for mental disorder and it is submitted that to remove the anomaly the definition of "child" in the Act should be amended to mean a person under the age of 16 years and section 61 should be amended to provide that medicine may not be administered to a child detained under section 25 after 3 months unless that child being over the age of 16 years gives his or her consent in writing to the continued administration of that medicine.

THE LAW REGULATING CLINICAL TRIALS

Current Irish law

Position under the Control of Clinical Trials Act 1987 as amended

Under the Control of Clinical Trials Act 1987 as amended by the Control of Clinical Trials and Drugs Act 1990 a person who intends to carry out a clinical trial must obtain the permission of the Minister for Health and Children. This permission will only issue if an ethics committee (the membership of which has been approved by the Minister) has approved the trial.

The Act outlines some of the criteria to be considered by the ethics committee in deciding whether to grant permission to conduct a clinical trial. These include the objectives of the trial, the qualifications of the parties involved and the risks to the proposed participants and the procedures proposed for obtain the consent of participants in the trial.[258]

People who are voluntarily admitted to psychiatric hospitals may participate in clinical trials provided they give consent to participation in accordance with section 9 of the 1987 Act. Section 9(2) provides that consent to participation in a clinical trial[259] shall

---

[258] Control of Clinical Trials Act 1987, s.8.

[259] "Conduct a clinical trial "is defined by the Control of Clinical Trials Act 1987, s.6(2) as amended by Control of Clinical Trials and Drugs Act 1990, s.2 as meaning "the conducting of a systematic investigation or series of investigations for the purpose of ascertaining the effects (including kinetic effects) of the administration of one or more substances or preparations on persons where such administration may have a pharmacological or harmful effect but does not include the conducting of such a systematic investigation or series of investigations: (a) where (i) the administration of one or more substances or preparations, as the case may be, is on a patient in the ordinary course of medical practice (in the case of a registered medical practitioner) or of a dental practice (in the case of a registered dentist), and (ii) the principal purpose of that administration is to prevent disease in, or to save the life, restore the health, alleviate the condition or relieve the suffering of the patient, or (b) where the substance or preparation concerned is to be administered to persons

not be valid unless given in writing and signed by the person who is to be the participant[260] in the trial. Section 9(3) states that the person giving the consent must be capable of comprehending the nature, significance and scope of his consent and the consent must be obtained by or on behalf of the person conducting the clinical trial. Significantly section 9(4) provides that the person conducting the trial must ensure that every person shall be made aware of certain matters, before giving his consent in accordance with section 9. The relevant matters are: (a) the objectives of the trial, (b) the manner in which the substance or preparation is to be administered, (c) the risks and any discomfort involved in and the possible side effects of the trial (d) whether or not a pharmacologically inactive substance or preparation (placebo) is to be administered to some persons in respect of each of whom a consent has been given to being a participant in the trial in accordance with section 9; (e) such other matters (if any) as may be (i) prescribed by regulations made by the Minister under the 1987 Act as amended or (ii) specified in the permission granted by the Minister to undertake a clinical trial.

The Irish Medical Council's *Guide to Ethical Conduct and Behaviour*[261] contains similar requirements in relation to obtaining the patient's informed consent to clinical trials or any form of research.[262] In addition it states:

> "Doctors engaged in research have a duty to be truthful to patients about all aspects of the study. Doctors must be truthful about their results …".[263]

It adds:

> "Refusal to participate in research must not influence the care of the patient in any way".[264]

Section 9(5) states that a clinical trial must not be conducted on any person within the period of six days after the day on which the information specified in section 9(4) has been communicated. The only exceptions to this rule are where the permission granted by the Minister or any amendment to that permission agreed to by the Minister provides otherwise.[265]

A person who has given his consent in accordance with section 9 may withdraw it at any time and no contractual liability will be incurred by that person from the withdrawal.[266]

---

undergoing a course of training leading to a qualification which will entitle such a person to be registered as a registered medical practitioner or as a registered dentist or as a registered pharmaceutical chemist and where it is to be administered as part of such a course of training, or (c) for the purpose of examining the nutritional effect of the substance or preparation concerned where that substance or preparation is a normal dietary constituent.

[260] "Participant" is defined in s.1 of the 1987 Act as "a person to whom one or more substances or preparations are administered in the course of the clinical trial".

[261] 6th edition, 2004.

[262] See para.20.1.

[263] See para.4.14.

[264] See para.20.3.

[265] Control of Clinical Trials Act 1987, s.9(5).

[266] *Ibid.*, s.9(6).

Where it is proposed to conduct a clinical trial on any person suffering from an illness, the remedy for or alleviation of which constitutes an objective of the trial then where such person is capable of comprehending the nature, significance and scope of a consent to be given for the purposes of section 9 but is physically unable to give such consent in accordance with section 9(2) it will be sufficient if his consent is clearly given in any other manner where it is so given in the presence of two witnesses present at the same time to a registered medical practitioner who is treating him for that illness and where the consent is expressed in writing and is attested by the signatures of both witnesses.[267] However, in this situation the clinical trial may be conducted only if the substance or preparation under trial is to be administered for the purpose of saving the life of such a person, restoring his health, alleviating his condition or relieving his suffering.[268]

Where a person is incapable of comprehending the nature, significance and scope of a consent to be given for the purpose of a clinical trial (e.g. where a person is a minor or a mentally incapacitated adult not involuntarily admitted to an approved centre under the Mental Health Act 2001) then according to section 9(7)(b) of the 1987 Act that person may be a participant in a clinical trial only if a written and signed consent is given for such participation by a person or persons, independent of the person who applied to undertake or is conducting the trial who in the opinion of the ethics committee[269] is or are competent to give a decision on such participation.[270] Further the clinical trial in question must be of a substance or preparation, which is to be administered for the purpose of saving the life of a person, restoring his health, alleviating his condition or relieving his suffering.[271]

Section 9(8) imposes a prohibition on the offering of inducements or rewards to persons for participating in a clinical trial. It provides that no person shall offer or cause to be offered any inducement or reward (whether monetary or otherwise) to a person for becoming or being a participant in a clinical trial unless provided for by the permission to undertake the clinical trial.

Further the Irish Medical Council's *Guide to Ethical Conduct and Behaviour*[272] provides that doctors should not allow their relationship with commercial forms to influence their attitude towards the design or results of trials.[273]

The Guide also states that research results must always preserve patient anonymity unless permission has been given by the patient to use his or her name.[274]

Failure to obtain consent from a participant in a clinical trial is an offence.[275] The offence is punishable (a) on summary conviction by a fine not exceeding €1,269.74 or

---

[267] Control of Clinical Trials Act 1987, s.9(7)(a).

[268] *Ibid.*, s.9(7).

[269] Where the Minister for Justice is satisfied that a proposed ethics committee is competent to consider the justification for conducting the proposed trial and the circumstances under which it is to be conducted he will give his approval of the proposed committee which thereupon becomes the ethics committee for the proposed clinical trial. Control of Clinical Trails Act 1987, s.8(1).

[270] Control of Clinical Trials Act 1987, s.9(7)(b).

[271] *Ibid.*, s.9(7).

[272] 6th edition, 2004.

[273] See paras 20.1, 4.14.

[274] See para.20.2.

[275] Control of Clinical Trials Act 1987, s.13.

at the discretion of the court by imprisonment for a term not exceeding 12 months or by both, (b) on conviction on indictment by a fine not exceeding €12697.38 or, at the discretion of the court by imprisonment for a term not exceeding three years or by both.[276] It is a good defence to a prosecution for such an offence for a person to show that the offence was committed without his knowledge and that he exercised all due diligence to prevent the commission of the offence as he ought to have exercised having regard to the nature of his position as director, manager, secretary or other officer and to all the circumstances.[277]

In a catch-all provision in its *Guide to Ethical Conduct and Behaviour*[278] the Medical Council indicates its support for the resolutions and draws attention to the Declaration of Helsinki on Ethical Principles for Medical Research involving Human Subjects adopted by the 18th World Medical Assembly and revised by the 48th World Medical Assembly.[279] This declaration sets out basic ethical standards for medical research generally which "promote respect of all human beings and protect their health and their rights"[280] and also sets out additional fundamental ethical standards to be observed in the situation where medical research is combined with medical care.

Position under Mental Health Act 2001

Prior to the Mental Health Act 2001 where it was proposed to conduct a clinical trial of new substances or preparations on a person who was incompetent to consent by reason of mental disorder it was necessary to comply with conditions laid down in section 9(7)(b) of the Control of Clinical Trials Act 1987.

Following the *UN Principles for the Protection of Persons with Mental Illness and the Improvement of Mental Health Care*,[281] the Government White Paper on Mental Health proposed to build on the protections in the Clinical Trials Act 1987 and to provide that participation of patients without consent in clinical trials be approved by the proposed Mental Health Review Board and that the Board be satisfied that there is a reasonable expectation of benefit direct or indirect to the patient's health.

There are a number of ethical objections which may be made to the participation of incompetent patients in therapeutic clinical trials. Firstly, the sample of involuntary patients with a mental disorder in psychiatric hospitals cannot be regarded as representative of the general population with mental disorder. Secondly, in the carrying out of clinical trials on incompetent patients the medical practitioner would fail in his duty to respect the principle of autonomy since s/he would make no attempt to obtain the informed consent of the participants. Thirdly, the medical practitioner administering the drug may find himself/herself in a situation of conflict of interest where the patient

---

[276] Control of Clinical Trials Act 1987, s.15.

[277] *Ibid.*, s.13(2).

[278] 6th edition, 2004.

[279] See para.20.6 of the Guide.

[280] See para.8.

[281] Principle 11.15 of the *UN Principles for the Protection of Persons with Mental Illness and the Improvement of Mental Health Care* provides that clinical trials and experimental treatment shall never be carried out on any patient without informed consent except that a patient who is unable to give informed consent may be admitted to a clinical trial or given experimental treatment but only with the approval of a competent, independent review body specifically constituted for this purpose.

shows adverse reactions to the treatment. S/he has a duty to cater for the patient's best interests. S/he also has a duty to carry out the trial in a scientifically rigorous way. If s/he intervenes s/he may compromise the scientific rigour of the trial and if s/he does not he may find that s/he is compromising his duty to his patient. Finally, a medical practitioner has a duty to choose a drug, which s/he thinks best for the patient. However, the fact that a particular pharmaceutical company is sponsoring the medical practitioner may influence his choice of medication for the patient

Section 70 (which has yet to be brought into force) of the Mental Health Act 2001 goes further than the White Paper and the UN Principles and now provides that notwithstanding section 9(7) of the Control of Clinical Trials Act 1987 a person suffering from a mental disorder who has been admitted to an approved centre under this Act shall not be a participant in a clinical trial. On balance given the ethical objections to the participation of involuntary patients in clinical trials this is a welcome provision.

Commentary

Insofar as the participation of voluntary patients in clinical trials is concerned the Control of Clinical Trials Act 1987 is defective[282] in a number of respects.

1.   The Acts requirements in relation to disclosure are limited. There is no requirement to provide information about the funders of the trial or where the treatment may have therapeutic effects to provide alternatives to the treatment, which is proposed.

2.   By focusing on information disclosure the Act fails to address the issue of patient understanding. In this regard Directive 2001/20/EC on clinical trials[283] is of relevance . This Directive which had to be introduced into Irish law by May 1, 2003 requires that a trial subject have "had the opportunity in a prior interview with the investigator or a member of the investigating team, to understand the objectives, risks and inconveniences of the trial".[284] There is therefore as a minimum a requirement that persons intending to carry out a clinical trial make all reasonable efforts to make the information relating to the trial accessible to the participants. It is submitted that it should also be a requirement that applicants for permission to carry out a clinical trial make a record these efforts in their application for permission.

3.   It is submitted that the legislation should contain a provision prohibiting threats or the exertion of pressure to compel persons to be participants in a clinical trial.

4.   Directive 2001/20/EC requires that minors[285] and persons not able to give informed consent[286] be given information according to their capacity of understanding regarding the trial, the risks and the benefits and that the explicit wish of a minor or

---

[282] See generally Donnelly M., *Consent Bridging the Gap between Doctor and Patient* (Cork University Press, 2002), pp.34–37.

[283] Directive 2001/20/EC of the European Parliament and of the Council of April 4, 2001 on the approximation of the laws, regulations and administrative provisions of the Member states relating to the implementation of good clinical practice in the conduct of clinical trials on medicinal products for human use (2001) O.J. L.121/34 1.5.2001.

[284] Art.3.2(b).

[285] Art.4(b)(c).

[286] Art.5(b)(c).

of a subject who is capable of forming an opinion and assessing this information to refuse participation or to be withdrawn from the clinical trial at any time is considered by the investigator or where appropriate the principal investigator. These requirements have, at the time of writing, yet to be implemented in Irish law.

5. Finally, the Directive provides that a clinical trial may only be carried out if the rights of the subject to physical and mental integrity and to the protection of data concerning him in accordance with Directive 95/46/EC on the protection of individuals with regard to the processing of personal data are safeguarded.[287] The Data Protection (Amendment) Act 2003 implements Directive 95/46/EC in a general context in Irish law and its provisions are generally relevant to data controllers processing personal data and sensitive personal data relating to a data subject who may be a patient, This would include personal data held for the purposes of a clinical trial even though the Act is not made specifically applicable in its terms to that context as yet.[288]

The Legality of Constraints

Within a psychiatric hospital it may be necessary to deprive a patient of liberties in order to protect that patient from harm to himself or others and to preserve a therapeutic environment.[289] Among the forms of restraint used in a psychiatric ward are bodily restraint by one person of another, confinement in a locked ward or room or in the security conditions of a Central Mental Hospital. When used properly for protective reasons such intervention would appear to be constitutional.[290] However, problems arise when powers of restraint are abused for example for the administrative convenience of staff or for reasons of punishment and it is in this regard that the law plays a role in balancing the exercise of powers of restraint with the right to bodily integrity and liberty of the patient.

Current Irish law

Position under Mental Treatment Act 1945

The Mental Treatment Act 1945 (still in force) legislates for two instances of restraint. It provides first that it was unlawful to employ a male person in the personal custody or restraint of a female patient in a psychiatric hospital except where the person in charge of the institution adjudges that the urgency of the situation renders it necessary.[291] In

---

[287] See art.2(c).

[288] See Chap.3, "Access to Medical Records", pp.162 *et seq.* and Data Protection and Confidentiality, pp.214 *et seq.*

[289] See Alty & Mason, *Seclusion and Mental Health* (Chapman & Hall, London, 1994).

[290] See *State (C) v. Frawley* [1976] I.R. 365.

[291] In *Fennelly v. Midland Health Board*, unreported, High Court, Carroll J., December 6, 1996, it was held that s.265 did not preclude a male nurse from being employed in connection with the care, medical or otherwise of a female patient. Carroll J. was of the view that s.265 was discriminatory and once the derogation contained in s.17(2)(d) of the Employment Equality Act 1977 which was permitted by Art.2.2. of Council Directive 76/207/EEC on equal treatment of men and women as

each case where such restraint is exercised, the matter must be reported to the Inspector of Mental Hospitals on his next visit to the institution and an entry made in a book kept for that purpose in the institution.[292]

Secondly, no person may apply mechanical means of bodily restraint to a person of unsound mind unless the restraint was "necessary for the purposes of medical or surgical treatment or to prevent the patient injuring himself or others."[293] Where a person used such means he must proceed in accordance with regulations made by the Minister[294] and enter full details of the application in a book kept for that purpose.[295] Failure to comply with the statutory requirement constitutes an offence punishable on summary conviction by a fine.[296]

These circumstances under which restraints may be used under the Act were wider than those in the Mental Treatment Regulations 1961 which provided that seclusion or bodily restraint could not be used except where it is "essential for the safety of the patient or the safety of others and was certified as essential by a medical officer". Even then it had to be as moderate in duration and extent as is consistent with the safety of the patient and his benefit.[297]

"Seclusion" is defined as "the placing of the patient (except during the hours fixed generally for the patients in the institution to retire for sleep) in any room alone and with the door of exit locked or fastened or held in such a way as to prevent the egress of the patient" and "bodily restraint" is defined as "the application of clothing or other material whereby the movements of the body or any part of the limbs of a patient are restrained or impeded."

Where seclusion or bodily restraint is found to be necessary then the Regulations require details describing the means of seclusion or restraint used and the grounds therefore must be entered in a register[298] kept for that purpose each day while the seclusion or restraint continues and the entry had to be signed by the medical officer who ordered the seclusion or restraint.[299]

Only certain materials[300] may be used for the purpose of restraint and while under

---

regards access to employment (and which provided that the sex of a person shall be taken to be an occupational qualification for a post where either the nature of or the duties attached to a post justify on grounds of privacy or decency the employment of persons of a particular sex) was repealed by S.I. No.302 of 1982 there was no justification for the continuation of s.265 in domestic law. The Directive took precedence over domestic law.

[292] Mental Treatment Act 1945, s.265.

[293] *Ibid.*, s.263.

[294] *Ibid.*, s.263(2).

[295] *Ibid.*, s.264.

[296] *Ibid.*, s.263(3).

[297] See art.6(3).

[298] Art.24 of the 1961 Regulations prescribes the form (Form No. 2) of a "register of seclusion and of bodily restraint".

[299] See art.6(4)(a).

[300] These are set out in the art.6 of the Mental Treatment Regulations 1961 as follows: "(i) a jacket or dress laced or buttoned down the back made of strong linen or similar material, with long outside sleeves fastened to the dress only at the shoulders, and having closed ends to which tapes may be attached for tying behind the back when the arms have been folded across the chest, or (ii) a jacket with blind sleeves; (iii) gloves without fingers, fastened at the wrists and made of strong linen, chamois leather or similar material; (iv) sheets or towels, when tied or fastened to a bed or other object." Certain other forms of restraint are not considered as means of bodily restraint for the

restraint the patient must be kept under special supervision and visited at frequent intervals by the nurse in charge of the department in which the patient is accommodated and by a medical officer at such intervals as the officer considers necessary. While the patient is in seclusion s/he must be visited at least once every fifteen minutes by the nurse in charge of the department and by a medical officer at such intervals as the officer considered necessary.[301]

The *Guidelines on Good Practice and Quality Assurance in Mental Health Services*, issued by the Inspector of Mental Hospitals in 1998, provide that:

> "Seclusion and mechanical restraint have now largely been eliminated from the repertoire of mental health care. However, there are still a very small number of instances when these measures are resorted to but this should happen as a last resort. Where seclusion occurs there should be a clear written seclusion policy incorporating the procedures to be followed when it is utilised, including the definition of seclusion and with extracts from the Mental Treatment Act 1945 and amending legislation. Staff should be fully informed of the need for separate nursing seclusion care plan for the patient including information on events prior to the episode, the actual behaviour, the interventions used prior to seclusion, patient's response to seclusion and the reason for seclusion. Seclusion should only be prescribed in writing by a consultant psychiatrist and should be reviewed on a six hourly basis. The same conditions apply to mechanical restraint although this is virtually never used now.
>
> In every case where seclusion or bodily restraint is applied, particulars describing the means of seclusion or restraint and the grounds therefore, shall be entered in the register as prescribed in Article 24 of the Mental Treatment Regulations and signed in full by the medical officer who ordered such seclusion or restraint. [Article] 6(1) of the Mental Treatment Regulations (S.I. No 261 of 1961) requires a nurse to visit the patient in seclusion at least every 15 minutes. All visits and observations that are made should be fully documented by the nurse."[302]

The White Paper

The Government White Paper on Mental Health entitled "A New Mental Health Act" recommended a redefinition of the permissible methods of seclusion and restraint in regulations made under new legislation following consultation with relevant medical

---

purposes of the Regulations. These are "(i) splints, bandages and other like appliances used in accordance with recognised surgical practice for the operation or the treatment of fractures or other local injuries and so applied as not to interfere with the free movement of the body or limbs more than is necessarily incident to their use for such purpose (ii) gloves if fastened as to be removable by the wearer; (iii) trays or rails fastened to the front of chairs to prevent young persons, cripples or aged or infirm adults from falling, where in the case of an adult it is within the patient's power to undo the fastening; (iv) any restraint which is necessary for the sole purpose of giving electrical or other special treatment to a patient, or for the purpose of feeding a patient."

[301] Art.6(1) of the Mental Treatment Regulations 1961.
[302] Para.4.6.

and health professional representative groups.[303] It was also proposed to remove the prohibition on the employment of a male person in the personal custody and restraint of a female patient in a mental institution on the grounds that the development of modern nursing standards and practice made the retention unnecessary.

Position under Mental Health Act 2001

Section 69 of the Mental Health Act 2001 (which has yet to be implemented) deals in part with the issues of restraint and seclusion by providing that a person shall not place a patient in seclusion or apply mechanical means of bodily restraint to the patient unless such seclusion or restraint is determined in accordance with rules made by the Mental Health Commission to be necessary for the purposes of treatment or to prevent the patient injuring himself or herself or others and unless the seclusion or restraint complies with such rules. A "patient" in this section of the Act includes in addition to an involuntary patient, a child in respect of whom an order under section 25 is in force and a voluntary patient.[304]

A person who contravenes section 69 or a rule made under it shall be guilty of an offence and liable on summary conviction to a fine not exceeding €1,904.61.[305] However, the rules have not yet been made and so we are left with a skeletal provision dealing with the issue of seclusion and restraint.

Section 265 of the Mental Treatment Act 1945 which prohibited except in cases of urgency the employment of a male person in the personal custody or restraint of a female patient in a psychiatric hospital is repealed by the Schedule to the Mental Heath Act 2001.

Common law powers of restraint

Quite apart from the powers under the Mental Health Act 2001 at common law a person may use reasonable force to restrain a person in the act of committing a grave crime or in effecting or assisting the lawful arrest of offenders.[306] Where this power is relied upon by a private person as opposed to a member of the Garda Síochána[307] the person concerned must show that the offence has actually been committed whether by the person arrested or by someone else and if in fact the offence has not been committed it is no defence that there was reasonable and probable cause for believing the person arrested was guilty.

Secondly, reasonable steps may be taken to restrain a breach of the peace. There is a breach of the peace whenever harm is actually done or is likely to be done to a person or in his presence to his property or a person is in fear of being so harmed through an assault, an affray, a riot, unlawful assembly or other such disturbance.[308]

---

[303] Para.10.22.
[304] S.69(4).
[305] S.69(3).
[306] *R v. Mc Kay* [1957] V.R. 560.
[307] *Walters v. WH Smith & Sons* [1914] 1 K.B. 595 It is sufficient for the police officer to show that there was reasonable and probable cause for suspicion even though no offence had in fact been committed. See also *Christie v. Leachinsky* [1947] A.C. 573.
[308] *R v. Chief Constable of Devon* [1981] 3 All E.R. 826 at 832.

Thirdly, a person may use reasonable force in self defence,[309] to defend another person against unlawful force[310] or in order to repossess property, which he owns.[311]

Finally, common law permits a private person to confine a person who is disordered in his mind who seems disposed to do mischief to himself or any other person.[312]

All of these powers are however, subject to a requirement of reasonableness namely the force used must be no more than a reasonable person would consider necessary to accomplish the object intended and the force is not permitted to continue once the need for it has passed.[313] Where a member of staff of a hospital purports to act in self defence or in defence of another in the mistaken belief that harm was intended when none is in fact threatened then for a defence to be established it must be shown that the person making the mistake had reasonable grounds for his belief in the circumstances justifying the application of force. Where the only defence relied upon is that the patient is suffering from a mental disorder then it must be shown that the patient was so suffering and even a reasonable mistake as to this is no defence.[314]

Commentary

Principles and standards relating to restraint and seclusion in International law

Provisions controlling the restraint and seclusion of patients with mental illness are to be found in many international instruments. The guiding principles are to be found in Article 7 of the *International Covenant on Civil and Political Rights* 1966 which provides that "No one shall be subject to torture or to cruel, inhuman or degrading treatment or punishment"[315] and in Article 10 which states that "All persons deprived of their liberty to be treated with humanity and with respect for the inherent dignity of the human person".

In 1971 the United Nations adopted the *Declaration on the Rights of Mentally Retarded Persons*.[316] Among the rights recognised by this Declaration are the right of the mentally retarded person to protection from abuse and degrading treatment.[317]

In 1975, the General Assembly adopted the *Declaration on the Rights of Disabled Persons*, which includes people with mental illness and intellectual disability within its definition of disabled persons.[318] The Declaration also states that disabled persons must be protected against all exploitation, all regulations and all treatment of a discriminatory, abusive or degrading nature.[319]

---

[309] *Dullaghan v. Hillen* [1957] Ir. Jur. Rep. 10.

[310] *People (A.G.) v. Keatley* [1954] I.R. 12.

[311] *Green v. Goddard* 2 Salk 641, 91 E.R. 540.

[312] Bacon's Abridgement cited in Clerk and Lindsell, *Torts* (16th ed., Sweet & Maxwell, London, 1989), para.17.47.

[313] *The People (AG) v. Keatley* [1954] I.R. 12.

[314] *Fletcher v. Fletcher* (1859) 1 El. & El. 420.

[315] In its General Comment 20(44) the UN Human Rights Committee specifically mentions "prolonged solitary confinement" as a practice that may amount to a violation of Article 7."

[316] General Assembly Resolution 2856 (1971).

[317] Art.6.

[318] A "disabled person" is defined as "any person unable to ensure by himself or herself, wholly or partly, the necessities of a normal individual and/or social life, as a result of deficiency either congenital or not, in his or her physical or mental capacities". See Art.1.

[319] Art.10.

The *Body of Principles for the Protection of All Persons under any form of Detention or Imprisonment* adopted by the General Assembly on December 9, 1988 contains a number of provisions relevant to the situation of patients involuntarily admitted to psychiatric hospitals. Among these is the right of all persons under any form of detention or imprisonment to be treated in a humane manner and with respect for the inherent dignity of the human person;[320] and the right not to be subjected to torture or inhuman or degrading treatment or punishment. In this context the term "cruel, inhuman or degrading treatment or punishment" is to be interpreted so as to extend to the widest possible protection against abuses whether physical or mental including the holding of a detained or imprisoned person on conditions which deprive him, temporarily or permanently of the use of any of his natural senses such as sight or hearing or of his awareness of place and the passing of time.[321]

These principles are echoed in the field of mental health by the *UN Principles for the Protection of Persons with Mental Illness and the Improvement of Mental Health Care*[322] in the form of a positive requirement which provides: "All persons with a mental illness or who are being treated as such persons, shall be treated with humanity and respect for the inherent dignity of the human person."[323] The Principles proceed to address the issues of restraint and involuntary seclusion specifically in Principle 11.11 which provides:

> "Physical restraint and involuntary seclusion of a patient shall ... only be employed when it is the only means available to prevent immediate or imminent harm to the patient or others. It shall not be prolonged beyond the period, which is strictly necessary for this purpose. ...
>
> A patient who is restrained or secluded shall be kept under humane conditions and be under the care and close and regular supervision of qualified members of staff. A personal representative, if any and if relevant, shall be given prompt notice of any physical restraint or involuntary seclusion of the patient."

The Principles go further than the skeletal provisions of the Mental Health Act 2001 in that they do not permit restraint or seclusion "where it is necessary for the purposes of treatment." Secondly there is the requirement that restraint or seclusion be "the only means available" to prevent the patient from injuring himself and thirdly there is a requirement that the harm which the restraint is designed to prevent be "immediate or imminent." Finally there are the additional requirements that the patient who is restrained or secluded be kept under humane conditions and be under the care and close and regular supervision of qualified members of staff and that a personal representative if any and if relevant be given prompt notice of any physical restraint or involuntary seclusion of the patient.

Principle 10 of the *UN Principles* addresses the issue of medication being employed in behaviour control. It provides:

---

[320] Principle 1.
[321] Principle 6.
[322] Adopted by the General Assembly, December 17, 1991.
[323] Principle 1.1.

"1. Medication shall meet the best health needs of the patient, shall be given to a patient only for therapeutic or diagnostic purposes and shall never be administered as a punishment or for the convenience of others.

All medication shall be prescribed by a mental health practitioner authorised by law and shall be recorded in the patient's records."

These requirements are absent from the Mental Health Act 2001.

In European law the prohibition on torture and inhuman and degrading treatment and punishment is to be found in Article 3 of the European Convention on Human Rights. Although it has been held that "ill treatment" must attain "a minimum level of severity" to fall within Article 3,[324] it is not inconceivable that given the absence of any other provision in the Convention that could be used to protect persons vulnerable to ill-treatment in detention a more demanding interpretation might be adopted that would not devalue or trivialise Article 3. In *A v. UK*,[325] the applicant complained, *inter alia*, of the conditions in a secure single cell in Broadmoor Hospital in which he had been segregated as a seriously disturbed patient. A friendly settlement was reached whereby the United Kingdom agreed to pay compensation and to make various improvements in the conditions of detention of segregated patients.

Council of Europe Recommendation No. R(83)2 of the Committee of Ministers to Member States concerning the legal protection of persons suffering from mental disorder placed as involuntary patients[326] which recommends that governments of member states should adapt their laws to the rules annexed to the Recommendation provides at Article 5.1 that a patient put under placement has a right to be treated under the same ethical and scientific conditions as any other sick person and under comparable environmental conditions. Article 6 of the Recommendation provides that the restrictions on personal freedom of the patient should be limited only to those, which are necessary because of the state of his health and for the success of the treatment.

Recommendation 1235 (1994) of the Parliamentary Assembly of the Council of Europe on Psychiatry and Human Rights addresses the issues of restraint and seclusion more specifically. In relation to use of restraints it provides that no mechanical restraint should be used and that the use of pharmaceutical means of restraint must be proportionate to the objective sought. It also recommends in relation to pharmaceutical means of restraint that there must be no permanent infringement of the individual's right to procreate.[327] On the matter of seclusion the Parliamentary Assembly recommends that the use of isolation cells be strictly limited.[328] If this Recommendation is adopted by the Council of Ministers then clearly it will be necessary to reconsider the provisions of section 69 of the Mental Health Act 2001, which permits the use of mechanical means of bodily restraint.

---

[324] *Ireland v. UK* [1979–80] 2 E.H.R.R. 25.
[325] [1980] 3 E.H.R.R. 131.
[326] Adopted by the Committee of Ministers on February 22, 1983.
[327] Recommendation iii.c.
[328] Recommendation iii.b.

Principles of restraint and seclusion in comparative law

Restraint and seclusion in English law In England and Wales, while not regulated by legislation, the Mental Health Act *Code of Practice*[329] contains detailed guidelines in relation to restraint and seclusion. Addressing the issue of methods of restraining behaviour the Code of Practice provides:

> "*Physical restraint* should be used as little as possible. Restraint which involves either tying or hooking a patient (whether by means of tape or by using a part of the patient's garments) to some part of the building or to its fixtures or fittings should never be used. Staff must make a balanced judgment between the need to promote an individual's autonomy by allowing him to move around at will and the duty to protect him from likely harm. Where physical restraint is used staff should: record the decision and the reasons for it; state explicitly in a care plan under what circumstances restraint may be used; record what form the restraint may take and how its application will be reviewed.[330]
>
> Restraining aggressive behaviour by physical means should be done only as a last resort and never as a matter of course. It should be used in an emergency when there seems to be a real possibility that significant harm would occur if no intervention is made. Any initial attempt to restrain aggressive behaviour should, as far as the situation will allow, be non-physical. ...[331]
>
> If non-physical methods have failed or immediate action is needed, the person in control of the incident may decide to use physical restraint and should organise a small number of staff members to assist in managing the incident Any restraint used should:
>
> – be reasonable in the circumstances;
>
> – apply the minimum force necessary to prevent harm to the patient or others;
>
> – be used for only as long as is absolutely necessary;
>
> – be sensitive to gender and race issues.[332]

The Code of Practice sets out a complaints procedure which is applicable to any patient who is being subjected to a form of restraint that lasts for more than two hours.[333] The Code of Practice also provides that health providers should have "clear written policies on the use of restraint of which all staff should be aware."[334]

Addressing the issue of seclusion the Code of Practice sets out strict conditions for its use:

> "Seclusion is the supervised confinement of a patient alone in a room which may be locked for the protection of others from significant harm. Its sole aim is to

---

[329] Published March 1999, pursuant to s.118 of the Mental Health Act 1983 by the Department of Health and Welsh Office.

[330] Para.9.10.

[331] Para.19.11.

[332] Para.19.12.

[333] See para.19.13.

[334] Para.19.14.

contain severely disturbed behaviour which is likely to cause harm to others. Seclusion should be used as a last resort; for the shortest possible time. Seclusion should not be used: as a punishment or threat; as part of a treatment programme; because of shortage of staff; where there is any risk of suicide or self harm."[335]

The Code of Practice requires hospitals to have "clear written guidelines" on the use of seclusion which:

"... ensure the safety and well-being of the patient; ensure the patient receives care and support rendered necessary by his or her seclusion both during and after it has taken place; distinguish between seclusion and "time-out"[336]; specify a suitable environment taking account of patient's dignity and physical well-being; set out the responsibilities of staff; set requirements for recording, monitoring, reviewing the use of seclusion and any follow-up action" [337]

The Code of Practice sets out a detailed procedure for seclusion as follows:

"The decision to use seclusion can be made in the first instance by a doctor or the nurse in charge. Where the decision is taken by someone other than a doctor, the RMO[338] or duty doctor should be notified at once and should attend immediately unless the seclusion is only for a very brief period (no more than five minutes)."[339]

"A nurse should be readily available within sight and sound of the seclusion room at all times throughout the period of the patient's seclusion, and present at all times with a patient who has been sedated."[340]

"The aim of the observation is to monitor the seclusion and behaviour of the patient and to identify the time at which seclusion can be terminated. The level should be decided on an individual basis and the patient should be observed continuously. A documented report must be made at least every 15 minutes."[341]

"The need to continue seclusion should be reviewed every two hours by two nurses (one of whom was not involved in the decision to seclude, and every four hours by a doctor. A multidisciplinary review should be completed by a consultant or other senior doctor and other professionals who were not involved in the incident which led to the seclusion if the seclusion continues for more than eight hours consecutively or twelve hours intermittently over a period of 48 hours. If the need

---

[335] Para.19.16.
[336] Time out is a behaviour modification technique which denies a patient for a period of no more than 15 minutes opportunities to participate in an activity or to obtain positive reinforcers immediately following an incident of unacceptable behaviour. The patient is then returned to his or her original environment. See Mental Health Act 1983 *Code of Practice*, para.18.9.
[337] Para.19.17.
[338] The responsible medical officer i.e. the registered medical practitioner in charge of the treatment of the patient in question. See Mental Health Act 1983, s.64 (1).
[339] Para.19.18.
[340] Para.19.19.
[341] Para.19.20.

for seclusion is disputed by any member of the multidisciplinary team the matter should be referred to a senior manager."[342]

The conditions of seclusion are also stipulated in the Code of Practice

"The room used for seclusion should: provide privacy from other patients; enable staff to observe the patient at all times; be safe and secure; not contain anything which could cause harm to the patient or others; be adequately furnished, heated, lit and ventilated; be quiet but not soundproofed and with some means of calling for attention; the means of operation should be explained to the patient.

Staff may decide what a patient may take into the seclusion room but the patient should always be clothed." [343]

The Code also requires that detailed and contemporaneous records be kept in the patient's case notes of any use of seclusion, the reasons for its use and subsequent activity, cross referenced to a special seclusion book r forms which should contain a step by step account of the seclusion procedures in every instance. The principal entry is required to be made by the nurse in charge of the ward and the record is required to be countersigned by the a doctor and a senior nurse. The Hospital Managers are required to monitor and regularly review the use of seclusion.[344]

The Code also addressed the issue of control of behaviour by medication indicating that it "requires careful consideration."[345]

"Medication to reduce excitement and activity may be useful to facilitate other therapeutic interventions. Other than in exceptional circumstances the control of behaviour by medication should only be used after careful consideration and as part of a treatment plan. Medication which is given for therapeutic reasons may become a method of restraint if used routinely for prolonged periods. Before medication is given, the doctor in charge should consider whether it would be lawful and therapeutic in the longer term. Medication should never be used to manage patients in the absence of adequate staffing."[346]

Principles of restraint and seclusion in US law In general US case law provides that restraint and seclusion may be used only when the person with mental illness could harm himself or others and there is no less restrictive alternative available to control this danger.[347] Other common elements in the decisions are that: (1) restraints and seclusion may be imposed only pursuant to written order, (2) such orders must be confined

---

[342] Para.19.21.
[343] Para.19.22.
[344] Para.19.23.
[345] Para.19.15.
[346] Para.19.15.
[347] See *Rogers v. Okin* 478 F. Supp 1342 (D. Mass 1979); *Eckerhart v. Hensley* 475 F. Supp. 908 (W.D.Mo. 1979); *Davis v. Balson* 461 F. Supp. 842 (N.D. Ohio 1978); *Davis v. Watkins* 384 F. Supp. 1196 (N.D.Ohio 1974): *Wyatt v. Stickney* 344 F. Supp. 375 (M.D. Ala. 1973); *Negron v. Ward* 74 Civ. 1480, 1 M.D. L.R. 191 (S.D.N.Y July 13, 1976); *Youngberg v. Romeo* 457 U.S.307 (1982); *New York State Association for Retarded Inc.v. Carey* 393 F. Supp 715 (E.D.NY 1975); *Welsch v. Likins* 373 F. Supp. 487 (D. Minn 1974).

to limited time periods (3) the patient's condition must be charted at regular time intervals,[348] and (4) if orders are extended beyond the initial period the extension must be authorised by a doctor, often with review by the medical director or superintendent required.[349] Many of these requirements are now also found in state statutes.[350]

Restraint and seclusion in Canadian law There is a dearth of Canadian legislation dealing with the issues of restraint and seclusion. In most provinces reliance is placed on the common law defences of necessity and self defence to afford the psychiatric facility authority to use such force as is reasonably necessary to prevent a patient harming himself or others.[351] In the province of Ontario, however, legislation provides that an admission certificate is authority to restrain a patient.[352] However, a person may only be restrained "when necessary to prevent serious bodily harm to the patient or to another person." In addition "minimal use of such force…as is reasonable having regard to the physical and mental condition of the patient" must be employed in placing the patient under control.[353] The Act also provides that nothing in the Act authorises a psychiatric facility to restrain a voluntary patient.[354] Yukon legislation contains similar provisions.

Conclusions

1. It is submitted that if methods of seclusion or restraint are to be permitted the circumstances in which they may be employed should be clearly stipulated in statutory instrument form.

2. Seclusion and restraint interfere with the patient's right to freedom of movement and bodily privacy. It is submitted that the restraints involved should be the least restrictive alternative available. The exercise of the powers should be limited to situations where there is a substantial threat of imminent physical harm to self or others and where the danger which might arise cannot be averted by supervision. The extent of the force which may be employed in restraint should be limited to the minimum as is reasonable having regard to the physical and mental condition of the patient and the restraint and seclusion should not be prolonged beyond the period which is strictly necessary for this purpose. All instances of restraint and seclusion, the reasons for them and their nature and extent should be recorded in the patient's treatment plan. A patient who is restrained or secluded should be kept under humane and comfortable conditions and be under the care and constant supervision and attention of the hospital staff approved for this purpose.

---

[348] See e.g. the decision in *Wyatt v. Stickney* 344 F. Supp 373 (M.D. Alal. 1972) which first set forth the limitations on which other courts have frequently based their rulings.

[349] See *Negron v. Ward* 74 Civ. 1480, 1 M.D.L.R. 191 (S.D.NY July 13, 1976).

[350] See Brakel, *The Mentally Disabled and the Law* (3rd ed., American Bar Foundation, 1985), p.273.

[351] It is implicit from the reasoning in *Brennan v. Director of Mental Health*, unreported, February 18, 1977 No. 83414 (Alta. S.C. Judicial District of Edmonton, Bowen J.) that an orderly was entitled to use reasonable force to restrain a patient.

[352] R.S.O. 1980, c.262, s.14(4).

[353] *Ibid.*, s.1 (t) [am. 1986, c.64, s.33(3)]. On the other hand, however, inconsistently with international trends the Act permits the use of force by "mechanical means or chemicals". See also definition of "detain" in equivalent Yukon provisions R.S.Y.T. 1971, c.M-7, s.2(1) [en. 1984, c.21, s.2].

[354] *Ibid.*, s.8b [en. 1986, c.64, s.33(7)].

3. It is submitted that legislation should prohibit the use of mechanical restraints (e.g. tying a patient by use of clothing, tapes or other material).[355]

4. The use of force to punish or discipline a patient must be expressly prohibited.

5. The Mental Health Regulations 1961 forbid the use of seclusion or bodily restraint "except where it is essential for the safety of the patient or the safety of others and is certified as so essential by a medical officer."[356] Reports of the Inspector of Mental Hospitals revealed practices whereby junior doctors prescribed seclusion,[357] and medical staff pre-signed episodes of seclusion thereby authorising nursing staff to place any patient in seclusion at their discretion.[358] Regulations are required so as to confine the exercise of the power to authorise seclusion to consultant psychiatrists who may exercise the power only after the conditions required for its exercise have arisen.

6. Provision should be made for review at stated intervals of the necessity for continued exercise of the powers of restraint and seclusion.[359] In addition a maximum limit should be placed on the period of seclusion or restraint.

7. Where a patient is placed in seclusion or under restraint the patient should have a right to have his advocate or lawyer, his guardian or another person of his choosing notified of same.

POWERS TO EXTEND THE PERIOD OF DETENTION

Current Irish Law

Position under Mental Treatment Act 1945

Under the Mental Treatment Act 1945 (which is still in force), temporary patients are normally detained for a period of up to six months. However, where the chief medical officer of an approved institution becomes of the opinion that that the patient concerned

---

[355] The use of such restraints has been shown to have distinct clinical and psychological consequences for the patient. Immobility from restraints may cause compromised circulation, decreased vital capacity, contractures, muscle weakness, nerve compression and incontinence. The psychological consequences of humiliation and loss of dignity can lead to depression, a paradoxical increase in agitation and behavioural problems similar to symptoms shown in torture related syndromes. See Moss & La Puma, "The Ethics of Mechanical Restraints", *Hastings Center Report* (January February 1991) 22.

[356] Art. 6(2).

[357] See *Report of Inspector of Mental Hospitals*, December 1995, 67.

[358] *Ibid.*, p.38.

[359] Cooney & O'Neill suggest that the initial authorisation be effective for not more than three hours during which a nurse on the ward maintain and keep a continuing review of the patient's condition and his or her need for seclusion. Where the seclusion is to continue for more than 12 hours the prior written authorisation of the clinical director of the hospital should be required and where it is proposed to extend the seclusion or restraint for more than seventy two hours the prior written authorisation of the mental health review board should be required. It is also suggested that the maximum duration of seclusion or restraint not exceed in all a period of duration of 120 hours. See *Psychiatric Detention Civil Commitment in Ireland* (Baikonur, 1996).

will not have recovered upon the expiration of six months he may extend the period of detention by endorsement on the order by further periods not exceeding six months each and the aggregate of which could not exceed six months in the case of an addict[360] and eighteen months in any other case.[361]

Where the order is endorsed the chief medical officer must give the person to whom the order relates a notice stating the particulars of the endorsement and informing that person of their right and that of the applicant for the reception order to send an objection to the extension of the period of detention to the Inspector of Mental Hospitals.[362] A similar notice must be given to the applicant for the order.

Where the Inspector of Mental Hospitals receives an objection to the extension he is obliged to require the chief medical officer to forward him a full report on the person to whom the order relates.[363] The latter must forward this report immediately and on consideration of the report the Inspector may take such steps as he considered necessary for ascertaining whether or not the detention of the person to whom the order relates should be continued.[364]

Position under Mental Health Act 2001

Section 15 of the Mental Health Act 2001 (not yet implemented) provides that an admission order shall remain in force for a period of 21 days from the making of the order. This order may be extended by a renewal order made by the consultant psychiatrist responsible for the care and treatment of the patient concerned for a further period not exceeding three months.[365] On the expiration of the three month period the order may be further extended by an order of the consultant psychiatrist for a period not exceeding six months and on the expiration of the six month period for periods each of which does not exceed 12 months.[366]

The 21 day period may be not extended unless the consultant psychiatrist concerned has not more than one week before the making of the order concerned examined the patient concerned and certified in a form specified by the Mental Health Commission that the patient continues to suffer from mental disorder.[367]

Where a consultant psychiatrist makes a renewal order s/he must not later than 24 hours thereafter: (a) send a copy of the order to the Mental Health Commission and (b)

---

[360] S.189(1)(a) of the Mental Treatment Act 1945 as substituted by s.18 of the Mental Treatment Act 1961.

[361] Mental Treatment Act 1945, s.18(ii).

[362] *Ibid.*, s.189(1)(b).

[363] *Ibid.*, s.189(1)(b)(ii).

[364] *Ibid.*, s.189(1)(b)(iii).

[365] *Ibid.*, s.15(2).

[366] *Ibid.*, s.15(3).

[367] "Mental disorder" is defined by s.3 as meaning "mental illness, severe dementia or significant mental handicap where: (a) because of the illness, handicap or dementia there is a serious likelihood of the person concerned causing immediate and serious harm to himself or herself or to other persons or (b)(i) because of the severity of the illness, handicap or dementia, the judgment of the person concerned is so impaired that failure to admit the person to an approved centre would be likely to lead to serious deterioration in his or her condition or would prevent the administration of appropriate treatment that could be given only by such admission, and (ii) the reception, detention

give notice in writing of the making of the order to the patient.[368] The notice must include a statement in writing to the effect that the patient, (a) is being detained pursuant to section 15; (b) is entitled to legal representation; (c) will be given a general description of the proposed treatment[369] to be administered to him or her during the period of his or her detention; (d) is entitled to communicate with the Inspector of Mental Health Services; (e) will have his or her detention reviewed by a tribunal in accordance with the provisions of section 18 and (f) is entitled to appeal to the Circuit Court against a decision of a tribunal under section 18 and (g) may be admitted to the approved centre concerned as a voluntary patient[370] if he or she indicates a wish to be so admitted.[371]

Review by a Mental Health Tribunal When the Commission receives a copy of the renewal order it must as soon as possible (a) refer the matter to a Mental Health Tribunal (b) assign a legal representative[372] to represent the patient concerned unless he or she proposes to engage one (c) direct in writing a member of the panel of consultant psychiatrists established under section 33(3)(b)[373] to (i) examine the patient concerned (ii) interview the consultant psychiatrist responsible for the care and treatment of the patient and (iii) review the records relating to the patient in order to determine in the interest of the patient whether the patient is suffering from a mental disorder [374] and to report in writing within 14 days on the results of the examination, interview and review to the tribunal to which the matter has been referred and to provide a copy of the report to the legal representative of the patient.[375]

Where the Commission gives a direction under section 17 (not yet implemented) to a member of the panel of consultant psychiatrists the consultant psychiatrist concerned, must on presentation by him or her of the direction at the approved centre[376] concerned be admitted to the centre and allowed to (a) examine the patient and the records relating to the patient, and interview the consultant psychiatrist responsible for the care and treatment of the patient.[377] A person who obstructs or interferes or fails to co-operate with a consultant psychiatrist in the performance of his or her functions under section 16 is guilty of an offence.[378]

---

and treatment of the person concerned in an approved centre would be likely to benefit or alleviate the condition of that person to a material extent".
[368] S.16(1).
[369] "Treatment" is defined by s.2 as including the administration of physical, psychological and other remedies relating to the care and rehabilitation of a patient under medical supervision, intended for the purposes of ameliorating a mental disorder.
[370] "Voluntary Patient" is defined by s.2 as meaning a person receiving care and treatment in an approved centre who is not the subject of an admission order or a renewal order.
[371] S.16(2).
[372] "Legal representative" is defined by s.2 as meaning a barrister or a solicitor.
[373] The Mental Health Commission is empowered by s.33(3)(b) to establish a panel of consultant psychiatrists to carry out independent medical examinations under s.17.
[374] This is defined by s.3, fn.36.
[375] S.17(1).
[376] A centre which is registered in the Register of Approved Centres is an "approved centre" See ss.2 and 63.
[377] S.17(2).
[378] S.17(4).

If the consultant psychiatrist to whom a direction has been given under section 17 is unable to examine the patient concerned, he or she must notify the Commission in writing and the Commission must give a direction under section 17(1) to another member of the panel of consultant psychiatrists.[379]

Where a renewal order has been referred to a tribunal the tribunal must review the detention of the patient[380] and must (a) if satisfied that the patient is suffering from a mental disorder[381] and (i) that the provisions of sections 15 and 16 have been complied with or (ii) if there has been a failure to comply with any such provision that the failure does not affect the substance of the order and does not cause an injustice, affirm the order. If it is not satisfied that these conditions have been met the tribunal must revoke the order and direct that the patient be discharged.[382] Before making a decision the tribunal must have regard to the consultant psychiatrists report submitted to it under section 17(1)(c) (after examination of the patient, interviewing the consultant psychiatrist responsible for the care and treatment of the patient and reviewing the records relating to the patient).[383]

A decision must be made by a tribunal not later than 21 days after the making of the renewal order concerned.[384] This period may be extended by order by the tribunal concerned either of its own motion or at the request of the patient concerned for a further period of 14 days and thereafter may be further extended by it by order for a period of 14 days on the application of the patient if the tribunal is satisfied that it is in the interest of the patient and the renewal order shall continue in force until the date of the expiration of the order made under this provision.[385]

Notice in writing of a decision under section 17(1) and the reasons therefor must be given to (a) the Mental Health Commission (b) the consultant psychiatrist responsible for the care and treatment of the patient concerned, (c) the patient and his or her legal representative and (d) any other person to whom, in the opinion of the tribunal, such notice should be given. This notice must be given as soon as may be after the decision and within 21 days after the making of the renewal order concerned[386] or, if it be the case that that period is extended by order of the tribunal concerned for a further period of 14 days and thereafter by order of the tribunal further extended for a period of 14 days on the application of the patient, within the period specified in that order.[387]

Right of appeal from decision of Mental Health Tribunal A patient may appeal to the Circuit Court of the circuit in which the approved centre concerned is situate or, at the option of the patient, the circuit in which the patient is ordinarily resident[388] against a decision of a tribunal to affirm a renewal order in respect of him on the grounds that

---

[379] S.17(3).
[380] A patient is defined by ss.2 and 14 as a person to whom an admission order relates.
[381] See s.3 discussed at p.367 *supra*.
[382] S.18(1).
[383] S.18(3).
[384] S.18(2).
[385] S.18(4).
[386] See s.18(6), (2).
[387] Such extensions are permitted under ss.18(4) and 18(6).
[388] S.19(3).

he or she is not suffering from a mental disorder.[389] The appeal must be brought by the patient by notice in writing within 14 days of the receipt by him or her or by his or her legal representative of notice of the tribunal's decision under section 18.[390] Notice of the proceedings must be served[391] by the person bringing the proceedings on (a) the consultant psychiatrist concerned, (b) the Tribunal concerned, (c) the clinical director of the approved centre concerned and (d) any other person specified by the Circuit Court.[392] Before making an order under section 19 the Circuit Court must have regard to any submission made to it in relation to any matter by or on behalf of a party to the proceedings concerned and any other person on whom notice is served under section 19(6) and any other person having an interest in the proceedings.[393] In addition section 19(14) provides that a document purporting to be a report of a member of the panel of consultant psychiatrists under section 17 concerning a patient shall be evidence of the matters stated in the document without further proof and shall, unless the contrary is proved, be deemed to be such a document.

The Circuit Court must affirm the order unless it is shown by the patient to the satisfaction of the Court that he or she is not suffering from a mental disorder. If it is shown by the patient that s/he is not suffering from a mental disorder the Circuit Court must revoke the order.[394] An order by the Circuit Court may contain such consequential or supplementary provisions as the Circuit Court considers appropriate.[395] No appeal lies against the order of the Circuit Court under section 19 other than an appeal on a point of law to the High Court.[396]

Section 19 of the Mental Health Act 2001 (not yet implemented) contains detailed provisions to protect the privacy of the person bringing an appeal to the Circuit Court. Thus under section 19(8) the Circuit Court must exclude from the Court during the hearing of the appeal all persons except officers of the court, persons directly concerned in the hearing, *bona fide* representatives of the Press and such other persons (if any) as the court may in its discretion permit to remain. However, without prejudice to this subsection the Circuit Court may, in any case if satisfied that it is appropriate to do so in the interests of the patient, by order dispense with the prohibitions of that subsection in relation to him or her to such extent as may be specified in the order.[397]

Under section 19(9) no matter likely to lead members of the public to identify a patient who is or has been the subject of proceedings under this section shall be published

---

[389] S.19(1).

[390] S.19(2).

[391] Notice required by s.19(6) to be served on a person may be so served (a) by delivering it to him or her or to his or her solicitor (b) by addressing it to him or her and leaving it at his or her usual or last known residence or place of business or by addressing it to his or her solicitor and leaving it at the solicitor's office and leaving it at the solicitor's office (c) by sending it by registered post to him or her at his or her usual or last known residence or place of business or to his or her solicitor at the solicitor's office, or (d) in the case of a body corporate, by delivering it or sending it by registered post to the secretary or other officer of the body at its registered or principal office. See s.19(15).

[392] S.19(6).

[393] S.19(7).

[394] S.19(4).

[395] S.19(5).

[396] S.19(16).

[397] S.19(10).

in a written publication available to the public or be broadcast. "Written Publication" is defined as including "a film, a sound track and any other record in permanent form (including a record that is not in a legible form but which is capable of being reproduced in a legible form) but does not include an indictment or other document prepared for use in particular legal proceedings."[398] "Broadcast" means "the transmission, relaying or distribution by wireless telegraphy of communications, sounds, signs, visual images or signals, intended for direct reception by the general public whether such communications, sounds, signs, visual images or signals are actually received or not."[399] If any matter is published or broadcast in contravention of this section 19(9) then the following persons shall be guilty of an offence (a) in the case of a publication in a newspaper or periodical, any proprietor, any editor and any publisher or the newspaper or periodical, (b) in the case of any other publication, the person who publishes it and (c) in the case of a broadcast, any person who transmits or provides the programme in which the broadcast is made and any person having functions in relation to the programme corresponding to those of an editor of a newspaper. Nothing in section 19 affects the law as to contempt of court.[400]

Commentary on Irish law relating to the power of extension of detention

Comparative law

Canadian law Section 10 of the Canadian Charter of Rights and Freedoms provides that:

> "Everyone has the right on arrest or detention (a) to be informed promptly of the reasons therefor; and (b) to retain and instruct counsel without delay and to be informed of this right."

Interestingly on the authority of *R v. Jones*[401] it would appear Section 10 requires that each time a renewal certificate is issued the involuntary patient must be informed of the reasons for his continued detention and of his right to retain and instruct counsel without delay since when a renewal certificate issues the legal basis for a patient's detention rests entirely on a new foundation. Under the Mental Health Act 2001 the person detained involuntarily has no right to be informed of the reasons for his continued detention but simply that he is being detained under the section authorising the renewal of the detention order.

Significantly the involuntary patient appears to enjoy a more favourable position in regard to his/her rights in Canada than under Irish law in other respects also. Canadian

---

[398] S.19(13).

[399] S.19(13).

[400] S.19(12).

[401] (1986) 48 Alta. L.R. (2d) 81 (C.A.) In that case it was held that when a person who is already in custody serving a sentence is charged with an additional offence, his detention rests partly on a new foundation of legal authority and thus he must be informed of his rights under s. 10. Without a renewal certificate the legal authority for the patient's detention would come to an end and consequently when one issues the authority for the patient's detention rests not just partly but entirely on a new foundation of legal authority.

legislation authorises detention for periods which are substantially less than those in the Irish context. With two exceptions (British Columbia and the Yukon Territory)[402] initial periods of compulsory confinement subject to renewal range between two weeks and one month.[403] Most psychiatric patients in Canada stay less than one month in hospital and interestingly it appears from national health statistics that provisions authorising long periods of initial detention pose a risk of patients being detained for longer than is necessary.[404]

In most provinces an involuntary patient's confinement may be extended beyond the initial period by means of renewal certificates. This normally takes the form of examination by one physician who then certifies that the patient should remain in the facility. The criteria for issuing a renewal certificate are the same as for admission certificates.

The period of authorised confinement usually increases with each renewal certificate before becoming static. Periods of renewal are nonetheless generally shorter than those prevailing in the Irish jurisdiction. In Ontario, for example the patient's confinement is continued for one month by the first renewal certificate, for another two months by the second certificate, and then for three months at a time by each subsequent certificate.[405]

Saskatchewan limits each renewal period to twenty one days.[406] In other provinces the renewal period eventually increases to either six months or one year.[407] In the Northwest Territories legislation provides for one period of renewal not exceeding twenty one days on the basis of a physician's certificate. Any further renewal must be authorised by the court.[408]

US law In the USA a person may be committed short-term on an emergency basis where the person concerned has posed an immediate danger to self or others or on a temporary basis prior to holding extended commitment proceedings. Extended commitment proceedings involve a formal hearing. Extended commitment itself is usually for a limited duration. Recommitment procedures generally are quite similar if not

---

[402] In British Columbia an involuntary patient may be detained for an initial period of one year. See R.S.B.C. 1979, c.256, s.21(1). In the Yukon admission to a psychiatric facility is by means of a court order, and the patient is detained "until the pleasure of the Commissioner is known or the person is discharged by law." See R.S.Y.T. 1971, c.M-7 s.6(2).

[403] R.S.A. 1980, c.M-13. S.19(1) (1 month); S.S.1984085086, c.M-13.1, s.24(3) (21 days); R.S.M. 1970 c.M110, s.10(1) [am. 1980, c.62, s.38] (21 days); R.S.O 1980, c.262, s.14(4) (2 weeks); R.S.N.B. 1973, c.M-10, s.8(5) {re. en. 1976, c.12, s.1] (1 month); R.S.N.S.1967, c.249, s.36(2) {en. 1977, c.45, s.8] (1 month); R.S.P.E.I 1974, c.M-9, s.10(5) (1 month); S.N. 1971, No. 80, s.7(3) (30 days); R.S.N.W.T 1974, c.M-11, s.4(6) (1 month).

[404] In British Columbia where legislation authorises the detention of an involuntary patient for an initial period of one year has the highest median length of stay of involuntary patients in Canada. The median figures are 28 days for males and 36 days for females. In British Columbia the figures are 68 days and 89 days. See *Mental Health Statistics: 1981–82* (Statistics Canada, 1984), pp.56–57.

[405] R.S.O. 1980, c.262, s.14(4).

[406] S.S.1984–85–86, c.M-13.1, s.24(7).

[407] R.S.A. 1980, c.M-13, s.21(2); R.S.N.B. 1973, c.M-10, s.1393) {am. 1976, c.12, s.2): R.S.N.S.1967, c.249, s.36(3) {en. 1977, c.45, s.8]; R.S.P.E.I 1974, c.M-9, s.15(3); S.N. 1971, No. 80 , s.9(2).

[408] R.S.N.W.T. 1974, c.M-11, s.5(1), (2), (3), (4) {am. 1978 (2nd) c.16 (Sched. B). Under the New Act all renewals must be authorised by the court – see S.N.W.T. 1985 (2nd) c.6. s.24.

identical to the initial commitment proceedings and require a new petition, a new mental health evaluation and a new hearing and the state bears the burden of proof.[409]

Conclusions

1. It is submitted that in addition to certifying that the patient continues to suffer from a mental disorder the consultant psychiatrist authorising the renewal order should be required to state:
    (a) what treatment has been given to the patient and what progress has been made as a result of the provision of treatment;
    (b) why an extended period of detention is necessary;
    (c) rhat there is a substantial probability that the treatment to be provided to the patient will significantly improve his/her mental condition.[410]

2. It is submitted that the patient should have a right to be informed of the reasons for the extension of his detention.

3. The Act appears to provide a measure of discretion to the Tribunal when there has been a failure to comply with the procedures for renewal. In that event the Tribunal is empowered to affirm the order in the circumstances where "the failure does not affect the substance of the order and does not cause an injustice."[411] It is submitted that this could lead to conflict and a negation of the original intention of the Tribunal which is there to ensure procedural and substantive adherence to the law. Indeed in a dissenting judgment in the Supreme Court in *O'Dowd v. North Western Health Board*,[412] Henchy J. stated that there was similarity between the form which must be completed by the registered medical practitioner recommending reception in a psychiatric hospital and a warrant for arrest and stated that the requirements set out in the form had to be strictly accurate.[413]

4. The patient has a right of appeal against a decision of a tribunal to affirm an order made in respect of him or her but the onus is on the patient to show that he or she is not suffering from a mental disorder. This is an impossible burden for someone who for example suffers from chronic mental illness but which is not of such a degree as to require hospitalisation. It is submitted that the burden should be one the detaining authority to show that the patient does have an illness severe enough to require continuing hospitalisation. This would accord more fully with the decision of the European Court of Human Rights in *Winterwerp v. Netherlands*[414] where the onus is placed on the detaining authority to prove the person is in need of continuing detention. In addition, in the English case of *R (H) v. London North and East Region Mental Health Review Tribunal (Secretary of State for Health intervening)*,[415] the

---

[409] See *Fasulo v. Arufeh* 378 A. 2d. 553 (Conn. Sup. Ct. 1977) 2 M.D. .L.R. 171.
[410] See Cooney & O'Neill, *Kritik 1 Psychiatric Detention Civil Commitment in Ireland* (Baikonur, 1996), p. 178.
[411] Mental Health Act 2001, s.17(1)(a)(ii).
[412] [1983] I.L.R. 186.
[413] *Ibid.*, pp.201–202.
[414] [1979] 2 E.H.R.R. 387.
[415] [2001] 3 W.L.R. 512.

Court of Appeal held that placing the burden of proof on the patient to prove that they no longer needed to be detained breached Articles 5(1) and 5(4) of the European Convention on Human Rights.

MAINTAINING HIGH STANDARDS OF CARE THROUGH LAW

The duty of care at common law

The current Irish law

It is well established that for a carer to be held liable in negligence it must be proved on the balance of probability that there was a duty of care owed by the defendant carer; that the duty of care was breached; that the plaintiff suffered actual injury and that the breach of duty was the direct cause of the injury.

The standard of care, which must be observed by the carer, is that which is reasonable in all the circumstances of the case. In *Dunne (infant) v. National Maternity Hospital*,[416] the Supreme Court set out the standards applicable in medical negligence actions. A mental health carer will be liable in negligence if s/he displays such lack of care as no carer of equal specialist or general status or skill display if acting with ordinary care. While deviation from a generally accepted and approved practice will not in itself make a carer liable in negligence the carer will be liable if s/he took a course which no carer of like specialisation and skill would have followed had he or she been taking the ordinary care required from a person of his or her qualifications. Equally a carer cannot escape liability on the ground that s/he followed a generally accepted practice if the plaintiff establishes that the practice: "has inherent defects which ought to be obvious to any person giving the matter due consideration."

Increasingly in recent years the Irish courts have imposed liability on carers in respect of patients who present a risk of suicide where the standard of care offered has failed adequately to take account of this risk.

In *Armstrong v. Eastern Health Board and St Patrick's Hospital*,[417] it was held that a failure by doctors to consult correspondence and notes indicating that the plaintiff was a suicide risk and a failure consequently to admit the plaintiff to hospital following upon which she jumped from a balcony of her home and suffered serious injuries rendered the defendants liable in negligence to the plaintiff.

In *Kelly v. St Laurence's Hospital*,[418] Walsh J. held that the nursing staff of the defendant hospital owed a duty to the plaintiff to take reasonable care to avoid permitting him to be exposed to the risk of injuring himself when due to the nature of his condition that risk was a foreseeable one. In this case the plaintiff who suffered from epilepsy and abnormal behaviour which was possibly psychotic in origin was taken off his anti-psychotic medication on admission to hospital in an effort to ascertain whether his behaviour was a manifestation of a condition of schizophrenia or temporal lobe epilepsy with a view to adjusting his medication accordingly. He left his bed on the ward and

---

[416] [1989] I.R. 91.
[417] Unreported, High Court, Egan J., October 5, 1990.
[418] [1989] I.R. 402.

walked out into the adjoining corridor where he passed two nurses. He proceeded unaccompanied to the toilet area where he climbed out of one of the windows and fell onto the roof of a car parked beneath sustaining serious injuries.

Walsh J. held that in the circumstances it was not merely foreseeable but actually expected that the plaintiff would suffer a further attack of automatism and other psychotic abnormal behaviour. The nurses were fully aware or ought to have been aware of the plaintiff's previous history and of the particular complications, which had been manifested in his epileptic attacks. Accordingly the absence of continued observation of the plaintiff when he left his bed was in the patient's special circumstances an omission, which was unquestionably negligent.

In *Healy v. The North-western Health Board*[419] the duty of care to prevent a patient causing foreseeable injury to himself was extended to patients who present a known suicide risk on discharge. In that case Mr Justice Flood applying the principles laid down by Finlay CJ in *Dunne (an infant) v. National Maternity Hospital* held that a that the defendants had been negligent in not carrying out a pre-discharge assessment for firm remission in relation to a depressed patient who committed suicide four days after discharge.[420]

On the other hand in *C v. North Western Health Board*,[421] the defendant health board was held not liable in negligence for the assault on the plaintiff and his wife caused by a voluntary patient who had suffered an undiagnosed panic attack, escaped from the hospital and forcibly entered the plaintiff's home. Judge White in the Circuit Court held that while the defendant owed a duty of care to the plaintiff following the *Dunne* principles that duty of care had not been breached and it was not reasonably foreseeable that the patient would escape and assault the plaintiff. However, if the plaintiff had been dangerous and this was known "every step possible" would have to be taken to prevent him from doing damage.

In essence examples of cases where a breach of duty of care has been found must represent cases of extreme consequences resulting from a failure to comply with the duty of care. In general however there are few malpractice cases against the psychiatric services in the Irish jurisdiction – a feature shared with other common law jurisdictions.[422] One of the primary reasons for this is the imprecision of diagnosis and treatment of mental and emotional disorders making it difficult to establish a standard of proper care against which to measure unsuccessful treatments. Added to this is the absence of physical

---

[419] High Court (1996) M.L.J.I. 29.

[420] More recently in the case of *Palmer v. Western Health Board and Fahy, Irish Times*, January 29, 2004 a husband of a woman who committed suicide by driving her car off a pier and killing herself and her two daughters sued the head of the psychiatric unit where she had been a patient. The woman had believed she was terminally ill and that the illness would give her a horrible death and that she had infected her two daughters. She was admitted to the psychiatric unit of the health board hospital and kept there for one week. She was then released but no system was put in place for monitoring her condition post discharge nor how she progressed. Her husband was awarded €110,000 and costs in settlement of his action against the former head of the psychiatric unit following a withdrawal of denial of liability by the latter. The case against the health board was struck out with no order.

[421] [1997] Irish Law Log Weekly 133 (Circuit Court Judge White).

[422] See Brakel, *The Mental Disabled and the Law* (American Bar Foundation, 1985), p.582; Robertson, *Mental Disability and the Law in Canada* (2nd ed., Carswell, Toronto, 1994), p.455–458.

injury the problem of proving that the treatment or lack of treatment thereof proximately caused the harm and the difficult task of measuring damages. In addition in Ireland the balance of procedural advantage seems to lie with the defendants in the litigation process. First there is the question of whether statutory immunity applies. This is considered below. Secondly, plaintiffs seeking to sue the psychiatric services in negligence may experience difficulties in obtaining expert witnesses in a small jurisdiction or may not be able to afford such a witness. Thirdly, although the approved litigation practice is for mental health carers to make records of treatment available to suing patients, patients still encounter difficulties in obtaining adequate records of treatment.

Commentary

International principles setting standards of care The *United Nations Principles for the Protection of Persons with Mental Illness and the Improvement of Mental Health Care* contain a number of principles addressing the issue of the standard of care to be afforded to persons with mental illness in psychiatric hospitals. In contrast to the current jurisprudence in the Irish law of tort which appear to suggest that claims of breaches of standards of care can be made successfully only in extreme circumstances where a person harms himself or herself the Principles recognise that issues relating to standards of care arise in the ordinary course of care and treatment of a person with mental illness.

Addressing standards of care Principle 8 provides:

> "1. Every patient shall have the right to receive such health and social care as is appropriate to his or her health needs and is entitled to care and treatment in accordance with the same standards as other ill persons.
>
> 2. Every patient shall be protected from harm, including unjustified medication, abuse by other patients, staff or others or other acts causing mental distress or physical discomfort."

In order to maintain standards of care Principle 14 provides that resources should be provided to ensure:

(a) qualified medical and other appropriate professional staff in sufficient numbers and with adequate space to provide each patient with privacy and a programme of appropriate and active therapy;

(b) diagnostic and therapeutic equipment for the patient;

(c) appropriate professional care; and

(d) adequate, regular and comprehensive treatment including supplies of medication."

Principle 13 addresses rights and conditions in mental health facilities. Among the rights it recognises which are relevant to patient care are the right of every patient in a mental health facility to full respect of his or her privacy and freedom of communication. The Principle further addresses standards of accommodation and provides that:

> "The environment and living conditions in mental health facilities shall be as close as possible to those of the normal life of persons of similar age".

This includes facilities for leisure, education and vocational rehabilitation.

Standards of care in comparative law

Canadian law Where the issue of self-harm is concerned there is comparative authority in Alberta demonstrating that in that province the legislature has treated the issue of protection from self-harm as a significant one. Section 19(2) of the Alberta Mental Health Act 1988[423] imposes a duty on the Board of the mental health facility, (1) to determine what level of security is reasonably required for each patient, (2) to provide that level of security and (3) to review it every three months.

English law Further in the English case of *Walsh v. Gwynedd Health Authority*,[424] the defendant health authority was held liable to the daughter of a voluntary patient for its failure to prevent the suicide of her father. The deceased had on admission to hospital, been recorded as having feelings of guilt, hopelessness, self-blame and depression but had denied feeling suicidal. The registrar who had assessed him formed the view that he did not show any evidence of suicidal risk and accordingly he was placed under nominal observation only. The deceased, unnoticed, left the ward the following morning and his body was found later that day. The coroner entered a verdict of suicide. Having heard evidence from experts on both sides the court concluded that on the information available at the time of his assessment the registrar should have concluded that the deceased presented a suicide risk and should have taken appropriate steps to ensure that the deceased did not harm himself whilst undergoing treatment. Although accepting that even had precautions been taken it could not be guaranteed that the suicide would have been prevented the judge found that the failure to take precautions materially increased the risk of suicide.

Conclusions

1. The *UN Principles for the Protection of Persons with Mental Illness and the Improvement of Mental Health Care* set out standards of care to be observed in psychiatric hospitals and the rights of patients in such hospitals. It is submitted that these standards and rights should be should be specifically stated in domestic legislation conferring on patients a right of action for breach of statutory duty when the standards of care are breached.

2. Where protection of patients from self harm is concerned it is submitted consideration should be given to imposing a duty on the consultant psychiatrist responsible for the care of a patient to determine what level of security is required for each patient, to provide that level of security and review it at regular intervals.

3. It is submitted that records of diagnosis, ongoing treatment and review of patient treatment should be statutorily prescribed and mental health carers should have a statutory duty to keep them.

---

[423] c. M–13.1.
[424] *Health Law* (September 1998), p.8.

Offences created by statute

Ill-treatment and wilful neglect of patients It is an offence under section 253 of the Mental Treatment Act 1945 (still in force) for a person in charge of a mental institution or a person employed in the institution to ill-treat or wilfully to neglect a patient[425] in the institution. It is also an offence for a person who has charge, whether by virtue of a contract, tie of relationship, marriage or otherwise of a person of unsound mind to ill-treat or wilfully to neglect that person. The word "ill-treats" includes striking or otherwise assaulting the person.[426]

The Schedule to the Mental Health Act 2001 (not yet in force) appears to repeal section 253 of the Mental Treatment Act 1945 and no alternative provision to guard against ill treatment or neglect is included in the Act's provisions.

Unlawful sexual acts with a patient

Position under Mental Treatment Act 1945 etc. Section 254 of the Mental Treatment Act 1945 provided that where a person has been convicted on indictment of the offence of unlawful carnal knowledge of a woman or girl "who is an idiot or an imbecile or is feeble minded" under section 4 of the Criminal Law Amendment Act 1935 and the judge was satisfied that at the time when the misdemeanour was committed that the person convicted had the care or charge of the woman or girl in relation to whom the misdemeanour was committed or was the manager, officer or employee in an institution where the victim was a patient or prisoner therein then the range of sentences imposed by section 4 of the Criminal Law (Amendment) Act 1935 was increased and the person convicted could be liable on conviction to imprisonment for a term between three and five years or to imprisonment for a term not exceeding two years. Currently, however, legislation is required to clarify the status of section 254 in the light of the enactment of the Criminal Law (Sexual Offences) Act 1993. The 1993 legislation repeals the 1935 Act but makes no reference to section 254 of the 1945 Act.[427]

Position under Criminal Law (Sexual Offences) Act 1993 Section 5 of the Criminal Law (Sexual Offences) Act 1993[428] provides that it is an offence for a person to have or

---

[425] It is submitted that consideration should be given to extending the scope of the offence of ill-treatment or wilful neglect of patients to outpatients attending the hospital for treatment for mental disorder.

[426] S.253 of the Mental Treatment Act 1945 as amended by s.35 of the Mental Treatment Act 1961. It appears that a single act is sufficient to establish ill-treatment. *R v. Holmes* [1979] Crim. L.R. ruling on comparable s.127(1) of the English Mental Health Act 1983.

[427] S.254 of the Mental Treatment Act 1945.

[428] Prior to the enactment of this provision the proscription of sexual offences against a person with an intellectual disability was governed by s.4 of the Criminal Law (Amendment) Act 1935 and s.254 of the Mental Treatment Act 1945. S.4 of the 1935 Act made it an offence for a person to have sexual intercourse with any female who was "an idiot, imbecile or feeble-minded person." This offence was punishable on conviction on indictment by a maximum of two years imprisonment. S.254 of the 1945 Act increased the penalty to a maximum of five years penal servitude in a case where the accused had care or charge of the victim or was carrying on, or an officer or employee of an institution in which the victim was a patient or prisoner. The provision was limited in the protection it afforded in that it its terms were confined to vaginal sexual intercourse or attempted intercourse and it did not protect mentally handicapped males. The Law Reform Commission in its

attempt to have sexual inter-course[429] or to commit or attempt to commit an act of buggery[430] with a person who is mentally impaired. The complete offence in either case is punishable by a term of imprisonment not exceeding ten years,[431] and the inchoate offence by a term of imprisonment not exceeding three years in the case of a first conviction and by a term not exceeding five years in the case of a second or subsequent conviction.

The Act also provides that it is an offence for a male person to commit or attempt to commit an act of gross indecency with another male person who is mentally impaired. This offence is punishable on conviction on indictment by a term of imprisonment not exceeding two years.[432]

The expression "mentally impaired" is defined as meaning "suffering from a disorder of the mind, whether through mental handicap or mental illness, which is of such a nature and degree as to render a person incapable of living an independent life or of guarding against serious exploitation.[433] The question of whether the complainant was mentally impaired at the time of the offence is one of fact to be decided by the jury.

No offence is committed if the accused is married to the other party or believes with reasonable cause that he is so married.[434] It is also a defence[435] for the accused to show that at the time the alleged offence was committed he did not know and had no reason to suspect that the person in respect of whom he was charged was mentally impaired.[436] In *R v. Hudson*,[437] it was held in relation to an equivalent English provision that the test to be applied in determining the accused's knowledge is a subjective one viz. whether he himself knew or had reason to suspect that the complainant was mentally impaired. The court ruled that the entire circumstances of the case should be put to the jury so that a defendant who had deliberately closed his eyes to the complainant's condition should not escape conviction.

Report, *Sexual Offences Against the Mentally Handicapped* (LRC 33 1990) recommended the repeal of the provisions and its replacement with provisions which reflected contemporary knowledge of mental impairment and the removal of the offensive references to "idiots" and "imbeciles" both of which terms were undefined in the Act.

[429] Criminal Law (Sexual Offences) Act 1993, s.5(1)(a).

[430] *Ibid.*, s.5(1)(b). There is no statutory definition of the offence of buggery but the courts have adopted a well settled definition. According to Stephen's *Digest of the Criminal Law* (9th ed., MacMillan & Co., London, 1877), p.169: "Everyone commits the felony called sodomy who (a) carnally knows an animal; or (b) being a male, carnally knows any man or any woman (per anum)." Expressed in more contemporary language buggery or sodomy consists of anal intercourse between two males or a male and a female, as well as intercourse between a person of either sex with an animal.

[431] The penalty is substantially increased from a maximum of two years imposed by s.4 of the Criminal Law (Amendment) Act 1935.

[432] Criminal Law (Sexual Offences) Act 1993, s.5(2).

[433] *Ibid.*, s.5(5).

[434] *Ibid.*, s.5(1). However, given that the Criminal Law (Rape Amendment) Act 1990 abolishes the so called spousal rape exemption a man could be convicted of rape if he had intercourse with his wife when she was so mentally disabled as to be unable to give consent to sexual intercourse.

[435] Under previous legislation it had to be proved that the accused knew that the woman was an idiot, imbecile or feeble minded although the court was entitled to have regard to all the circumstances in deciding whether this was the case. The 1993 Act partially reverses this onus of proof by providing this defence.

[436] Criminal Law (Sexual Offences) Act 1993, s.5(3).

[437] [1966] 1 Q.B. 448.

The consent of the Director of Public Prosecutions is required to initiate a prosecution under the Act. This, in effect, rules out the possibility of the initiation of private prosecutions. Where a prosecution is initiated section 27 of the Criminal Evidence Act 1992 facilitates the giving of evidence by the victim by providing that the evidence of a person under 14 years or of a person with mental handicap who has reached the age of 14 years may be received "otherwise than on oath or affirmation if the court is satisfied that he is capable of giving an intelligible account of events which are relevant to those proceedings."[438] The time limit, which applied to the initiation of prosecutions under previous legislation, has been removed.[439]

Position under Mental Health Act 2001 The Mental Health Act 2001 repeals most of the provisions of the Mental Treatment Act 1945 including section 254 of the Act (but the repealing provisions have yet to come into force) and makes no provision for an offence similar to that in section 254 in the Act. It therefore appears that when the legislation comes into force there will be no safeguards directed specifically against sexual offences committed by persons having care or charge of a mentally impaired person or by a person who was the manager or an employee of an approved centre in which the person was a patient.

Commentary

In England and Wales it is an offence under section 127(1) of the Mental Health Act 1983 for any person who is a manager or officer on the staff of or otherwise employed in a hospital or mental nursing home to ill-treat or wilfully to neglect on the premises of which the hospital or home forms part an *out-patient* for the time being receiving treatment for mental disorder there.

A person guilty of an offence is liable on summary conviction to imprisonment for a term not exceeding six months or to a fine not exceeding the statutory maximum or to both.[440]

In England and Wales, section 128(2) of the Mental Health Act 1959 as amended provides that it is not an offence of having unlawful sexual intercourse with a woman who is for the time being receiving treatment for mental disorder in a hospital or home if the offender did not know and had no reason to suspect that the woman was a mentally

---

[438] These provisions deal with problems in practice with the prosecution of offences under the Criminal Law (Amendment) Act 1935. In practice the wording of the 1935 Act and the fact that a complainant might be deemed not competent to give evidence proved substantial obstacles to prosecution where there was no other evidence. Ironically also a finding that a complainant was competent to give sworn evidence could raise a question as to her "feeble-mindedness" and consequently as to whether there was a charge to be met. The provisions of Pt III of the Criminal Evidence Act 1992 which allows the videotaping of evidence of children in respect of certain offences and for the evidence of such victims to be given by live television link and, if necessary, through an intermediary, apply also to mentally handicapped complainants of sexual or violent offences. The 1992 Act's reference to "mental handicap" alone suggests that its provisions might not be available to persons impaired through mental illness.

[439] Under the Criminal Law (Amendment) Act 1935 no prosecution could be brought more than 12 months after the date on which the offence was alleged to have been committed. S.4(2).

[440] Mental Health Act 1983, s.127(3).

disordered patient. The burden of proof of this exception lies on the person relying on it.[441]

Conclusions

1.   The proposed repeal of section 254 of the Mental Treatment Act 1945 by the Mental Health Act 2001 must be questioned. The Law Reform Commission had recommended that the offence under section 254 of the Mental Treatment Act 1945 be retained and that the maximum sentence attaching to it be increased from five to ten years' imprisonment. In principle there are cogent grounds for marking out as a distinct crime warranting separate punishment abuse perpetrated on the vulnerable confined to institutions on grounds of infirmity or vulnerability. By virtue of the relative positions of the perpetrator and victim such crimes involve a grave breach of trust as well as the commission of a substantive offence. It is submitted however that a defence be provided that the offender did not know and had no reason to suspect that the victim was a patient.

2.   It is submitted that section 254 of the Mental Treatment Act 1945 should be preserved by legislation amending the Mental Health Act 2001 and consideration be given to extending the scope of the offence of ill-treatment or wilful neglect of patients to outpatients attending the hospital for treatment for mental disorder.

Administrative structures

The Mental Health Act 2001 continues the powers of certain office holders to investigate and remedy abuses occurring within the psychiatric health system.

The Inspector of Mental Hospitals

The role of the Inspector of Mental Hospitals under the Mental Treatment Act 1945

The Mental Treatment Act 1945 contains a number of provisions relating to the appointment and functions of the Inspector of Mental Hospitals. The terms of the Mental Treatment Act 1945 relating to the appointment and functions of the Inspector of Mental Hospitals under the 1945 Act have not yet been expressly repealed although the Mental Health Act 2001 provisions relating to the appointment of the Inspector of Mental Health Services were brought into force on April 5, 2002 and an Inspector of Mental Health Services has been appointed under the 2001 Act. It follows that until such time as the Mental Treatment Act 1945 is expressly repealed the Inspector of Mental Hospitals retains his powers under the terms of 1945 Act.

       Under the terms of the Mental Treatment Act 1945 the Inspector of Mental Hospitals is a medical practitioner appointed by the Minister for Health[442] endowed with wide

---

[441] Mental Health Act 1959, s.128(5).
[442] Mental Treatment Act 1945, s.12.

statutory powers to visit and inspect any mental institution and examine any patient therein at any time and as often as he thinks fit.[443]

He is statutorily obliged to visit and inspect every district mental hospital and every other institution maintained by a mental hospital authority at least once each year and every mental institution not maintained by a mental hospital authority and the Central Mental Hospital at least once in each half year.[444] He may be assisted in the performance of his functions by an assistant inspector of mental hospitals who will have all the powers conferred by law on the Inspector.[445] When making a visit and inspection required by the Mental Treatment Act 1945 the Inspector must inspect every part of the premises included in the institution and ascertain whether or not due regard is being had in the management of the institution to the 1945 Act and Regulations.[446]

The Inspector is particularly obliged to ascertain whether the accommodation provided in the institution is adequate and suitable; whether or not the care and treatment provided for the patients is adequate; whether or not the facilities provided for the occupational and recreational therapy provided for the patients are adequate; whether or not the diet of the patients is adequate and suitable; whether or not the classification of the patients is carried out; whether or not a system of coercion, restraint or seclusion is in operation. He must also enquire as to the staffing arrangements and any other matter which considers should be enquired into.[447] In addition he must see every patient whom he has been requested to examine or the propriety of whose detention he has reason to doubt and where he doubts the propriety of the detention notify the person in charge of the institution that he has such doubts.[448]

Where the patient concerned is detained in a district mental hospital or other institution maintained by a mental hospital authority he must report the matter to the Minister for Health.[449] Having considered the Inspector's report the Minister may require the Inspector to visit the patient to whom the report relates and to make a report on his mental condition to the Minister. After consideration of this report the Minister may if s/he thinks fit direct the discharge of the patient.

Where the person the propriety of whose detention is in issue is detained in a privately maintained hospital the matter must be reported to the Minister for Health by the Inspector of Mental Hospitals. After consideration of this report the Minister for Health may, require the Inspector and the resident medical superintendent of the nearest district mental hospital to visit the patient. These visitors must visit the patient twice the second visit being not less than eighteen days after the first.[450] After the second visit the Inspector must make a report on the patient's mental condition to the Minister for Health who after considering it may direct the discharge of the patient.[451]

---

[443] *Ibid.*, s.235.

[444] *Ibid.*, ss 236 and 248(2).

[445] *Ibid.*, s.13.

[446] *Ibid.*, s.237 as amended by Mental Treatment Act 1961, s.33.

[447] *Ibid.*

[448] *Ibid.*

[449] *Ibid.*, s.239.

[450] *Ibid.*, s.240. 14 days notice of the second visit must be given to the person in charge of the institution where the person is detained and if it is practicable to the person at whose instance the patient is detained. S.240(5), Notice to the person in charge of the mental institution may be given by an appropriate entry in any register of patients kept in the institution. S.240(6).

[451] Mental Treatment Act 1945, s.240(7), (8)

When making a visit and inspection the Inspector must also ascertain whether any extensions of detention have been effected under section 189 and if so give particular attention to the patients concerned.[452] When visiting the Central Mental Hospital he must investigate any complaint in regard the administration of the hospital or the treatment of any inmate thereof.[453]

For the purpose of carrying out his duties the Inspector of Mental Hospitals has power to administer and examine a person on oath,[454] require the production of a list of patients, registers and documents including patient records[455] and must be afforded all facilities reasonably necessary for the inspection. In that regard he must be shown every part of the institution and every patient in it[456] and has power to call on the assistance of an independent medical practitioner residing within a reasonable distance of the institution to assist him in making a visit and may pay him for his services.[457]

It is an offence punishable by a fine and/or at the discretion of the court, imprisonment, for a person to obstruct or interfere with the Inspector of Mental Hospitals while he is exercising any power under the 1945 Act. It is also an offence to fail to give any information which is within a person's knowledge and reasonably required by the Inspector in the course of carrying out his duties.[458]

Having visited the institution and carried out the inspection the Inspector must furnish a report to the Minister for Health and Children.[459] In addition he must make annual report to the Minister on every mental institution and the care of the patients in that institution. He must include in that report a general account relating to the year of the administration of the law relating to mental institutions and care, welfare and treatment of persons of unsound mind. This annual report must be laid before each House of the Oireachtas and a copy of it sent to the President of the High Court.[460]

The role of the Inspector of Mental Health Services under the Mental Health Act 2001
Sections 50 to 55 of the Mental Health Act 2001 (which came into force on April 5, 2002) establishes the office of the Inspector of Mental Health Services[461] to replace that of the Inspector of Mental Hospitals under the 1945 Act (which has yet to be expressly repealed). The Office of Inspector of Mental Health Services has, at the time of writing, been established. The Inspector of Mental Health Services is a consultant psychiatrist appointed by the Mental Health Commission established under the 2001 Act.[462] This contrasts with the position of the former Inspector of Mental Hospitals who was appointed directly by the Minister under the 1945 Act.[463] S/he is paid such remuneration and allowances for expenses as the Commission may, with the consent of the Minister for

---

[452] *Ibid.*, s.237(b) as amended by the Mental Treatment Act 1961, s.33.
[453] *Ibid.*, s.248.
[454] *Ibid.*, s.242.
[455] *Ibid.*, s.244.
[456] *Ibid.*, s.245.
[457] *Ibid.*, s.246.
[458] *Ibid.*, s.279.
[459] *Ibid.*, s.243.
[460] *Ibid.*, ss.247, 248(7), (8).
[461] S.50(1).
[462] S.50(2).
[463] S.12(2).

Health and Children and the Minister for Finance determine,[464] and hold office for such period and upon and subject to such terms and conditions as the Commission may determine.[465]

Under the 1945 Act the Minister for Health may employ registered medical practitioners as Assistant Inspectors of mental institutions under that Act.[466] By virtue of section 54 of the 2001 Act the Mental Health Commission may appoint Assistant Inspectors of Mental Health Services to assist the Inspector of Mental Health Services in the performance of his/her functions.[467] Under the 2001 Act Assistant Inspector is obliged to perform such functions of the Inspector to such extent as the Inspector may determine subject to any directions that may be given to the Inspector by the Commission.[468]

An Assistant Inspector is obliged to perform his functions subject to the general direction of the Inspector and a function of the Inspector performed pursuant to the 2001 Act by an Assistant Inspector shall be deemed for the purposes of the Act to have been performed by the Inspector.[469] An Assistant Inspector is paid such remuneration and such (if any) allowances for expenses as the Commission with the consent of the Minister and the Minister for Finance may from time to time determine.[470] An Assistant Inspector will hold office for such period and upon and subject to such terms and conditions as the Commission may, with the consent of the Minister and the Minister for Finance determine.[471]

Under section 51(1) of the Act the principal functions of the Inspector are:

(a) to visit and inspect every approved centre at least once annually and to visit and inspect any other premises where mental health services are being provided as he or she thinks appropriate; "Mental health services" are defined by section 2 as "services which provide care and treatment to persons suffering from a mental illness or mental disorder under the clinical director of a consultant psychiatrist";

(b) to carry out an annual review of mental health services in the State and to furnish a report in writing to the Mental Health Commission on: (i) the quality of care and treatment given to persons in receipt of mental health services; (ii) what s/he has ascertained pursuant to any inspections carried out by him or her of approved centres or other premises where mental health services are being provided: (iii) the degree and extent of compliance by approved centres with any code of practice prepared by the Mental Health Commission; (iv) such other matters as he or she considers appropriate to report on arising from his or her review.

Under section 51(2) the Inspector is to have all such powers as are necessary or expedient for the performance of his or her functions under the 2001 Act including but, without prejudice to the generality of this statement, the following powers:

---

[464] S.50(3).
[465] S.50(4).
[466] See s.13.
[467] S.54(1).
[468] S.54(2).
[469] S.54(3).
[470] S.54(4).
[471] S.54(5).

(a) to visit and inspect at any time any approved centre or other premises where mental health services are being provided and to be accompanied on such visit by such consultants or advisors as he or she may consider necessary,[472] or expedient for the performance of his or her functions;

(b) to require any person in such an approved centre or other premises to furnish him or her with such information in possession of the person as he or she may reasonably require for the purposes of his or her functions and to make available to the Inspector any record or other document in his or her power or control that in the opinion of the Inspector is relevant to his or her functions;

(c) to examine and take copies of or extracts from, any record or other document made available to him or her or found on the premises;

(d) to require any person who, in the opinion of the Inspector, is in possession of information or has a record in his or her power or control that, in the opinion of the Inspector is relevant to the purposes aforesaid, to furnish to the Inspector any such information or record and where appropriate, require the person to attend before him or her for that purpose;

(e) to examine and take copies in any form of, or of extracts from any record that, in the opinion of the Inspector, is relevant to the review or investigation and for those purposes take possession of any such record, remove it from the premises and retain it in his or her possession for a reasonable period; and

(f) to take evidence on oath and for that purpose to administer oaths.[473]

A person to whom a requirement is addressed under section 51 of the 2001 Act will be entitled to the same immunities and privileges as a witness in court.[474] Subject to this no enactment or rule of law prohibiting or restricting the disclosure or communication of information may preclude a person from furnishing any information or record.[475]

When making an inspection under section 51 the Inspector is obliged to (a) see every resident (within the meaning of Part 5 of the Act)[476] whom he or she has been requested to examine by the resident himself or herself or by any other person (b) see every patient the propriety of whose detention he or she has reason to doubt; (c) ascertain whether or not due regard is being had to the Act and the provisions made thereunder, in the carrying on of an approved centre or other premises where mental health services are being provided; (c) ascertain whether any regulations made under section 66, (regulations in relation to approved centres) any rules made under sections 59 (administration of electro-convulsive therapy) and 69 (bodily restraint and seclusion)

---

[472] In the course of the Dáil Debates the Minister for Health and Children, Mr Martin referred specifically to advisers such as architects or civil engineers to advise on the structure of a building and health and safety experts to advise on necessary precautions See HC 3 No. 3 *Dáil Debates* Col. 145.

[473] S.50(2).

[474] S.50(4).

[475] S.50(5).

[476] S.62 defines "resident" as a person receiving care and treatment in a centre .

and the provisions of Part 4 (Consent to Treatment)[477] are being complied with. The Inspector must make a report in writing to the Mental Health Commission in relation to any of the matters aforesaid as he or she considers appropriate.

A person who (a) obstructs or interferes with the Inspector while he or she is exercising any power conferred by or under the Act or (b) fails to give any information within his or her knowledge reasonably required by the Inspector in the course of carrying out his or her duties shall be guilty of an offence and liable on summary conviction to a fine not exceeding €1904.61 or to imprisonment for a term not exceeding 12 months or both.[478]

The Mental Health Commission is obliged to include the Inspector's report in its annual report to the Minister for Health.[479] The report must be submitted as soon as may be after the end of each year and not later than 6 months thereafter and the Minister is obliged to cause copies of the report to be laid before each House of the Oireachtas within one month after the submission of the report to him.[480]

Section 55 of the Act provides that the Mental Health Commission may and shall if so requested by the Minister for Health and Children cause the Inspector to inquire into (a) the carrying on of any approved centre or other premises in the state where mental health services[481] are provided (b) the care and treatment provided to a specified patient or a specified voluntary patient by the Commission (c) any other matter in respect of which an inquiry is appropriate having regard to the provisions of this Act or any regulations or rules made thereunder or any other enactment.

Where the Inspector carries out such an inquiry he or she must as soon as may be prepare a report in writing of the results of the inquiry and submit the report to the Mental Health Commission.[482] A report so prepared is absolutely privileged wherever and however published.[483]

Section 66 of the Mental Health Act 2001 (which has yet to be brought into force) empowers the Minister for Health and Children after consultation with the Mental Health Commission to make such regulations as he or she thinks appropriate for the purpose of ensuring proper standards in relation to approved centres including adequate and suitable accommodation, food and care for the residents while being maintained in centres and the proper conduct of centres.

Section 66(5) provides that a person who wilfully obstructs or interferes with the Inspector of Mental Health Services in the performance of functions under the regulations or who fails or refuses to comply with a requirement of the Inspector under the regulations shall be guilty of an offence.

---

[477] S.52.
[478] S.53.
[479] S.42(2).
[480] S.42(1).
[481] "Mental Health Services" are defined by s.2 as services, which provide care and treatment to persons suffering from mental illness or mental disorder under the clinical direction of a consultant psychiatrist.
[482] S.55(2).
[483] S.55(3).

Commentary from the perspective of international law

Principles for maintenance of standards of care in International law Principle 14.2 of the UN Principles for the Protection of Persons with Mental Illness and the Improvement of Mental Health Care provides that:

> "every mental health facility shall be inspected by the competent authorities with sufficient frequency to ensure that the conditions, treatment and care of patients comply with these Principles."

The principles remain vague about the level of frequency with which inspections are carried out but it is clear from the terms of Principle 14.2 that the terms of reference of the inspection are wider than those which are currently the responsibility of the Inspector of Mental Health Services and would include ensuring that standards of care are in accordance with the same standards as other ill persons,[484] ensuring that the patient is treated in the least restrictive environment and with the least restrictive or intrusive treatment appropriate to the patient's health needs[485] and is based on an individually prescribed plan, discussed with the patient, reviewed regularly, revised as necessary and provided by qualified professional staff[486] and that the treatment is directed towards preserving and enhancing personal autonomy.[487]

The *Body of Principles for the Protection of All Persons under any form of Detention or Imprisonment* adopted by the General Assembly on 9 December 1988 require that the place of detention be visited regularly by qualified and experienced persons appointed by and responsible to a competent authority distinct from the authority directly in charge of the administration of the place of detention and provide that a detained person should have the right to communicate freely and in full confidentiality with the persons who visit the places of detention subject to reasonable conditions to ensure security and good order in such places.[488]

The Principles also provide for the right of the detained person or his counsel to make a request or complaint regarding his treatment, in particular in case of torture or other cruel, inhuman or degrading treatment to the authorities responsible for the administration of the place of detention and to higher authorities and when necessary to appropriate authorities vested with reviewing or remedial powers. Confidentiality concerning the request or complaint must be maintained if so requested by the complainant. Every request or complaint must be promptly dealt with and replied to without undue delay. If the request or complaint is rejected or in the case of inordinate delay the complainant shall be entitled to bring it before a judicial or other authority. Neither the detained person nor the complainant may suffer prejudice for making a request or complaint.[489]

In addition, *Recommendation 1235 (1994) of the Parliamentary Assembly of the Council of Europe on Psychiatry and Human Rights* proposes that an inspection system

---

[484] Principle 8.1.
[485] Principle 9.1.
[486] Principle 9.2.
[487] Principle 9.4.
[488] Principle 29.
[489] Principle 33.

similar to that of the European Committee for the Prevention of Torture and Inhuman or Degrading Treatment or Punishment be set up to monitor standards of treatment in mental health facilities.[490]

In New South Wales, official visitors comprising a medical practitioner and one suitably qualified or interested person are assigned to each hospital or health care agency with a mandate to inspect the facilities at least once per month.

Conclusions

1. It is arguable that the Inspectorate of Mental Health Services should comprise both a consultant psychiatrist and a legally trained advocate appointed by the President of the High Court. This may go some way towards ensuring the independence of the Inspectorate of Mental Health Services.

2. The Mental Health Act provisions appear to remove some of the powers of the Inspector of Mental Hospitals to review detention. While the Inspector is obliged in the course of his inspections to see every patient the propriety of whose detention he has reason to doubt he is obliged to report on this to the Commission but the Inspector's former power under the Mental Treatment Act 1945 to report the matter to the Minister and the Minister's power to direct the discharge of the patient if appropriate after further visit(s) is removed and what remains is simply a duty to report on the matter to the Commission who make a report to the Minister. It is submitted that the Inspectorate should at least have the power to report on the position of a patient the propriety of whose detention he has reason to doubt to the Mental Health Tribunal and the latter should have a duty to appoint an independent consultant psychiatrist to investigate the matter.

3. The entitlement of a patient to communicate with the Inspector is referred to in section 15 of the Act but no section conferring an express power to that effect is contained in the legislation. It is submitted that an express provision entitling a patient to conduct uncensored communications with the Inspector of Mental Health Services should be included in the Act.

4. The Inspector's powers are limited to inspecting premises where mental health services are being provided. Concern was expressed during the passage of the Mental Health Bill by organisations representing people with intellectual disabilities that approved centres for treatment of people with intellectual disabilities who have a mental disorder may be inspected by the Inspector but not those parts of residential institutions which house people with intellectual disabilities who are not receiving psychiatric care and a real danger that a two tier system may develop in relation to standards of care where for example the approved centre is situated in the grounds of a residential institution.

5. It is recommended that a statutory duty be placed upon the Inspectorate of Mental Health Services to make proposals in relation to the Mental Health Act Code of Practice to be prepared by the Mental Health Commission under the 2001 Act.[491]

---

[490] Para.ii.f.
[491] See s.33(3)(e).

Breaches of the Code should be treated as prima facie evidence of negligence by the party concerned.

6.   In addition to an Inspectorate there should be a team of official visitors assigned to each approved centre in the state with a duty to inspect the facilities at least once per month and to report to the Inspectorate of Mental Health Services.

The President of the High Court

Under the Mental Health Treatment Act 1945 the President of the High Court has power to require and authorise the Inspector of Mental Hospitals to visit and examine any person detained at any place as a person of unsound mind and to the report to the President of the High Court on the condition of that person.[492]

Where he is of the opinion that the assistance of counsel is necessary for the conduct of an investigation under the Act he may appoint a barrister at law of not less that six years standing to assist in such visit or investigation.[493] These powers are expressly preserved in the Mental Health Act 2001.[494]

The Minister for Health

Position under Mental Treatment Act 1945

Under the Mental Treatment Act 1945, (which is still in force in this regard), the Minister for Health retains overall responsibility for the administration of the mental hospital services by the Health Service Executive.[495] As we have seen above, the Inspector of Mental Hospitals is also appointed by him, and he has power to direct the discharge of patients who the Inspector reports to be improperly detained. In addition, matters of serious importance relating to the welfare of the patients must be reported to him,[496] and he is the recipient of annual reports made by the Inspector which must be laid before the Oireachtas. The Minister for Health also has power to cause the Inspector of Mental Hospitals to hold an inquiry into any complaint relating to:

(i)   the administration of any mental institution, or

(ii)   the negligence of any officer or servant employed in a mental institution in the discharge of his duties or the failure by him/her to discharge those duties, or

(iii) the misconduct of any officer or servant employed in a mental institution and in relation to any matter relating to a mental institution in respect of which an inquiry is appropriate in accordance with the provisions of the Mental Treatment Act 1945 or any other enactment.

The Minister also has power to direct the discharge of any person improperly detained

---

[492] Mental Treatment Act 1945, s.241.
[493] *Ibid.*, s.276.
[494] Mental Health Act 2001, s.6 and Schedule.
[495] Health Act 1970, ss.4 and 6.
[496] Mental Treatment Act 1945, s.272.

in a mental institution.[497] To that end any person may apply to the Minister for Health for an order for two registered medical practitioners approved of by the Minister to examine a person detained in a mental institution at the applicant's expense. The Minister, may make such an order if he thinks fit and where he does so, the practitioners must be admitted and allowed to examine the person on presentation of the order at the institution on two occasions at least seven days apart. If as a result of these examinations, the practitioners certify that such person may be discharged without risk of injury to himself or others the Minister may, if he thinks fit, by order direct the discharge of the person concerned.

Position under Mental Health Act 2001

The Mental Health Act 2001, when brought fully into force, will commute the powers of the Minister for Health in light of the fact that Mental Health Tribunals are granted power automatically to review admission and renewal orders under the Act. Thus the Minister will no longer have power to discharge patients who the Inspector of Mental Hospitals reports to be improperly detained. Matters of serious importance to the welfare of the patients (e.g. injuries, assaults or alleged assaults, outbreaks of infectious or epidemic diseases) will no longer to be reported to him. In addition, where application is made to him by a person at whose expense a person is detained in an institution, the Minister no longer will have the power to discharge a private patient on the certificate of two registered medical practitioners that the person may be discharged without risk of injury to himself or others.

In lieu of this the Minister has power to appoint the members of the Mental Health Commission (see below) whose principal functions are "to promote, encourage and foster the establishment and maintenance of high standards and good practices in the delivery of mental health services and to take all reasonable steps to protect the interests of persons detained in approved centres"[498] under the Act. The Minister also has power if he or she so thinks fit by order to confer such additional functions as he or she considers appropriate on the Commission provided they are connected with the functions for the time being of the Commission or the services or activities that the Commission is authorised for the time being to provide or carry on.[499]

Commentary in relation to the power of the Minister

Under the terms of the Mental Health Act 2001 Ministerial power to monitor standards of care in the psychiatric services is to a large degree vested in the Mental Health Commission. Among its duties is an obligation to prepare and review periodically after consultation with such bodies as it considers appropriate a code or codes of practice for the guidance of persons working in the mental health services. It is not clear what status these codes will have as a matter of law. It is submitted that their evidential value should be clarified in legislation.

---

[497] Mental Treatment Act 1945, s.222.
[498] Mental Health Act 2001, s.33.
[499] *Ibid.*, s.34(1)(a).

The Mental Health Commission

Current Irish law

The Mental Health Commission is a body established under sections 31 to 47 of the Mental Health Act 2001, which came into force on April 5, 2002.[500] Its principal functions are "to promote, encourage and foster the establishment and maintenance of high standards and good practices in the delivery of mental health services,[501] and to take all reasonable steps to protect the interests of persons detained in approved centres"[502] under the Act.

Without prejudice to the generality of its principal functions the Commission has a duty (a) to furnish whenever it so thinks fit or is so requested by the Minister advice to the Minister in relation to any matter connected with the functions or activities of the Commission and (b) to prepare and review periodically after consultation with such bodies as it considers appropriate, a code or codes of practice for the guidance of persons working in the mental health services.[503]

Membership of the Commission The Commission comprises 13 members appointed by the Minister for Health. Of the members:

(a) one must be a person who has not less than 10 years experience as a practising barrister or solicitor in the State ending immediately before his or her appointment to the Commission;

(b) three must be representative of registered medical practitioners (of which two are to be consultant psychiatrists) with a special interest or expertise in relation to the provision of mental health services;

(c) two must be representative of registered nurses whose names are entered in the division applicable to psychiatric nurses in the register of nurses maintained by An Bord Altranais under section 27 of the Nurses Act 1985;

(d) one must be representative of social workers with a special interest in or expertise in relation to the provision of mental health services;

(e) one must be representative of psychologists with a special interest in or expertise in relation to the provision of mental health services;

(f) one must be representative of the interest of the general public, and

(g) three must be persons who are representative of voluntary bodies promoting the interest of persons suffering from mental illness (at least two of whom shall be a person who is suffering from or has suffered from mental illness);

---

[500] See the Mental Health 2001 (Sections 1 to 5, 7, 31 to 55) (Commencement) Order 2002 (S.I. No. 90 of 2002). The Mental Health Commission was established on April 5, 2002. See Mental Health Act 2001 (Establishment Day) Order 2002 (S.I. No. 91 of 2002).
[501] "Mental health services" are defined by s.2 as meaning "services which provide care and treatment to persons suffering from mental illness or a mental disorder under the clinical direction of a consultant psychiatrist".
[502] Mental Health Act 2001, s.33(1).
[503] *Ibid.*, s.33(3).

(h) one must be an employee of the Health Service Executive nominated by the Executive and

(i) not less than four must be women and not less than four must be men.[504]

The persons appointed under (b), (c), (d), (e) and (g) will be nominees of organisations as the Minister considers representative of their respective professional interests or in the case of (g) a nominee of such organisation(s) as the Minister considers representative of such voluntary bodies.[505]

A member of the Commission holds office for a period not exceeding 5 years and on such other terms as the Minister for Health and Children determines.[506] Each member of the Commission must be paid such remuneration (if any) and allowances for expenses incurred by him or her (if any) as the Minister for Health and Children may with the consent of the Minister for Finance determine.[507] A member may be removed by the Minister if in the Minister's opinion the member has become incapable of performing his or her functions or has committed stated misbehaviour or his or her removal appears to the Minister to be necessary for the effective performance by the Commission of its functions.[508] A member of the Commission may resign his or her membership by letter addressed to the Minister and the resignation shall take effect from the date specified therein or upon receipt of the letter by the Minister whichever is the later.[509]

A member of the Commission will be disqualified for holding and will cease to hold office if he or she is adjudged bankrupt or makes a composition or arrangement with creditors or is sentenced by a court of competent jurisdiction to a term of imprisonment or penal servitude.[510]

Where a member of the Commission dies, resigns, becomes disqualified or is removed from office the Minister may appoint a person to be a member of the Commission to fill the casual vacancy so occasioned and the person so appointed shall be appointed shall be appointed in the same manner as the member of the Commission who occasioned the casual vacancy. A person appointed to fill a casual vacancy shall hold office for the remainder of the term of office of the member who occasioned the casual vacancy he or she is appointed to fill.[511] A member of the Commission whose period of membership expires by the effluxion of time shall be eligible for re-appointment as a member of the Commission.[512]

The chairperson of the Commission is also appointed by the Minister for Health and Children.[513] The chairperson of the Commission must be paid such remuneration (if any) and such allowances for expenses as the Minister for Health with the consent of the Minister for Finance shall from time to time determine.[514] Where the chairperson of

---

[504] Mental Health Act 2001, s.35(2).
[505] *Ibid.*, s.35(3)–(7).
[506] *Ibid.*, s.36(1).
[507] *Ibid.*, s.36(3).
[508] *Ibid.*, s.36(4).
[509] *Ibid.*, s.36(2).
[510] *Ibid.*, s.36(6).
[511] *Ibid.*, s.36(5).
[512] *Ibid.*, s.36(7).
[513] *Ibid.*, s.37(1).
[514] *Ibid.*, s.37(5).

the Commission ceases to be a member of the Commission he or she shall also thereupon cease to be chairperson of the Commission.[515] The chairperson of the Commission may at any time resign his or her office as chairperson by letter sent to the Minister for Health and Children and the resignation shall, unless previously withdrawn in writing, take effect at the commencement of the meeting of the Commission held next after the Commission has been informed by the Minister for Health and Children of the resignation.[516]

The chairperson of the Commission, holds office until the expiration of his or her period of membership of the Commission unless he or she dies or otherwise ceases to be chairperson as a result of ceasing to be a member of the Commission or as a result of resignation but, if he or she is re-appointed as a member of the Commission, he or she shall be eligible for re-appointment as chairperson of the Commission.[517]

Provision is also made in the Act for the appointment of a chief executive officer of the Commission[518] who is not a member of the Commission,[519] but whose functions are to carry on and manage and control generally the administration and business of the Commission and perform other functions (if any) as may be determined by the Commission.[520] The Chief Executive is obliged to devote the whole of his or her time to his or her duties as Chief Executive and must not hold any other office or position without the consent of the Commission.[521]

Provision is also made for the appointment of members of staff of the Commission with the consent of the Minister for Health and Children and the Minister for Finance.[522] Significantly, the Commission may appoint such staff and such number of staff as it considers necessary to assist the Inspector of Mental Health Services in the performance of his or her functions.[523]

Commission's obligation to submit annual reports to Minister Within six months of the end of each year the Commission is obliged to prepare and submit an annual report to the Minister for Health and Children of its activities during that year and not later than one month after such submission the Minister must cause copies of the report to be laid before each House of the Oireachtas.[524] The Commission's report must include the report of the Inspector under section 51 and other information in such form and regarding such matters as the Minister for Health and Children may direct.[525]

Commission's obligation to furnish information to Minister The Commission must also, whenever so requested by the Minister furnish to the Minister information relating

---

[515] Mental Health Act 2001, s.37(2).
[516] *Ibid.*, s.37(3).
[517] *Ibid.*, s.37(3).
[518] *Ibid.*, s.38(1).
[519] *Ibid.*, s.38(9).
[520] *Ibid.*, s.38(3).
[521] *Ibid.*, s.38(8).
[522] *Ibid.*, s.39(1).
[523] *Ibid.*, s.39(2).
[524] *Ibid.*, s.42(1).
[525] *Ibid.*, s.42(2).

to such matters as he or she may specify concerning or relating to the scope of its activities or in respect of any account prepared by the Commission or any annual report of the Commission specified in section 42(1) or any report specified in section 55.[526]

Power of commission to cause inspection to conduct inquiries Section 55 specifies that the Commission may and must whenever requested by the Minister for Health and Children cause the Inspector of Mental Health Services or such other person as may be specified by the Commission to inquire into: (a) the carrying on of any approved centre or other premises in the State where mental health services are provided, (b) the care and treatment provided to a specified patient or a specified voluntary patient by the Commission, (c) any other matter of which an inquiry is appropriate having regard to the provisions of the Act or any regulations or rules made thereunder or any other enactment. Where a person carries out an inquiry under this section he or she shall as soon as may be prepare a report in writing of the results of the inquiry and submit the report to the Commission.[527]

Obligation of commission to report after 18 months on operation of 2001 Act Further, the Commission must not later than 18 months after the commencement of Part 2 of the Act (Involuntary Admission of Persons to Approved Centres) prepare and submit a report in writing to the Minister on the operation of that Part together with any findings, conclusions or recommendations concerning such operation as it considers appropriate.[528] The Commission may also publish such other reports on matters related to its activities and functions as it may from time to time consider relevant and appropriate.[529]

Commentary

In England and Wales the Mental Health Act Commission takes an active role in reviewing treatments such as electro-convulsive therapy and the administration of medication once the period of three months has elapsed since the first time in that period when the patient was given medication for his mental disorder. Both of these forms of treatment may be given if the conditions of section 58 of the Mental Health Act 1983 are complied with. It appoints independent medical practitioners to give certificates for this treatment.[530] It also receives reports from the responsible medical officer about all treatment, which is carried out without consent but with a second opinion under section 58. The Commission has power to cancel the certificates authorising the treatment by notifying the responsible medical officer. This will usually prevent the treatment taking place.[531]

---

[526] Mental Health Act 2001, s.42(3).
[527] *Ibid.*, s.55(2).
[528] *Ibid.*, s.42(4).
[529] *Ibid.*, s.42(5).
[530] Mental Health Act 1983 (England and Wales), s.121(2)(c); Mental Health Act Commission Regulations 1983, reg.3(2)(c).
[531] Mental Health Act 1983 (England and Wales). s.121(2)(b); Mental Health Act Commission Regulations 1983, reg.(2)(b).

The Mental Health Act Commission in England and Wales must arrange to visit and interview in private detained patients in both hospitals and mental nursing homes.[532]

It must also arrange to investigate complaints.[533] These are of two sorts: (i) complaints about something which has happened while the patient was detained in a hospital or mental nursing home and which he considers has not been properly dealt with by the management. In this instance the Commission may insist that the patient go through the hospital procedures first; and (ii) any other complaint about the exercise of the Act's powers and duties in relation to someone who is or has been detained.

Conclusions

1. The majority of members of the Commission comprise mental health professionals. In order to ensure against the appearance of bias in membership it is submitted the membership should be balanced between medical, legal and lay elements.

2. It is submitted that the functions of the Mental Health Commission should also be expressed to extend to protecting the interests of voluntary patients.

Registration of psychiatric centres

Registration of institutions under the Mental Treatment Act 1945

The Mental Health Act 1945 provides for a system of registration of private institutions, female charitable institutions, the recognition of authorised institutions and the approval by order of institutions ("approved institutions") as a means of monitoring standards of accommodation and care in psychiatric centres. This nature of the system is outlined in Chapter 1.

Registration of approved centres under Mental Health Act 2001

Register of approved centres When the Mental Health Act 2001 comes fully into force the standards in psychiatric hospitals will be monitored by means of the system of registration of approved centres. Provisions of the Mental Health Act 2001, not yet fully implemented, requires that "centres," i.e. hospitals or other in-patient facility for the care and treatment of persons suffering from mental illness or mental disorder[534] be registered as "approved centres." A person may not carry on a centre unless the centre is registered and the person is the registered proprietor thereof.[535]

The Mental Health Commission is obliged to establish and maintain a Register of Approved Centres.[536] The particulars entered on the Register in respect of each centre

---

[532] Mental Health Act 1983 (England and Wales), s.120(1)(a).

[533] *Ibid.*, s.120(1)(b).

[534] See Mental Health Act 2001, s.62.

[535] Mental Health Act 2001, s.63(1) A person who carries on a centre in contravention of this provision is guilty of an offence (s.63(2)) and is liable on summary conviction to a fine not exceeding £1,500 (€1904.61) or to imprisonment for a term not exceeding 12 months or to both, (b) on conviction on indictment to a fine not exceeding £50,000 (€63,486.90)or to imprisonment for a term not exceeding 2 years or to both.(s.68).

[536] Mental Health Act 2001, s.64(1).

are the name of the person by whom it is carried on, the address of the premises in which it is carried on, a statement of the number of patients who can be accommodated in the centre, the date on which the registration is to take effect and other particulars which may be prescribed.[537] The Register must be available for inspection free of charge by members of the public at all reasonable times.[538]

Applications for registration of approved centres An application for registration must be in a form specified by the Commission.[539] The Commission may request an applicant for registration or, as the case may be, a registered proprietor to furnish it with such information as it considers necessary for the purposes of its functions under Part V of the 2001 Act.[540]

When an application is made to it by a person who proposes to carry on an approved centre the Commission has a discretion as to whether to register the centre.[541] Where the centre is registered the period of registration is three years from the date of registration.[542] Where the Commission registers a centre it must issue a certificate of registration to the registered proprietor of the centre.[543]

The Commission has the power to refuse to register,[544] and to remove[545] a centre from the register and to attach conditions to the registration.[546]

Refusal of registration The Commission may not refuse to register a centre in relation to which an application for registration has been duly made.[547] In addition it may not remove a centre from the Register unless:

(i) it is of opinion that—
   (a) the premises to which the application or as the case may be the registration relates does not comply with the regulations, or
   (b) the carrying on of the centre will not be or is not in compliance with the regulations;

(ii) the registered proprietor has been convicted of an offence under Part V[548] of the Act;

(iii) the registered proprietor has failed or refused to furnish the Commission with

---

[537] Mental Health Act 2001, s.64(2)(a).
[538] *Ibid.*, s.64(2)(b).
[539] *Ibid.*, s.64(7).
[540] *Ibid.*, s.64(8)(a) A person who, whether in pursuance of a request or otherwise furnishes information to the Commission for the purposes of Part V of the Act that is false or misleading in a material particular shall be guilty of an offence unless s/he shows that, at the time the information was furnished to the Commission, s/he was not aware that it was false or misleading in a material particular. See Mental Health Act 2001, s.64(8)(b).
[541] Mental Health Act 2001, s.64(3)(a).
[542] *Ibid.*, s.64(3)(b).
[543] *Ibid.*, s.64(3)(c).
[544] *Ibid.*, s.64(5).
[545] *Ibid.*, s.64(4).
[546] *Ibid.*, s.64(6).
[547] *Ibid.*, s.64(5).
[548] *Ibid.*, ss.62–68.

information requested by it pursuant to section 64(8) or has furnished the Commission that is false or misleading in a material particular; or

(iv) the registered proprietor has, not more than one year before the date from which the registration or removal from the register would take effect, contravened a condition imposed by the Commission under section 64(6).[549]

Power to attach conditions to registration The Commission has power (i) at the time of registration or subsequently to attach to registration conditions in relation to the carrying on of the centre concerned and such other matters as it considers appropriate having regard to its functions under Part V of the Act (ii) to attach different conditions to the registration of different centres and (iii) to amend or revoke a condition of registration.[550]

Without prejudice to its general power to impose conditions, conditions attached to the registration of a centre may:

(i)   require the carrying out of essential maintenance or refurbishment of a centre or specified areas within a centre;

(ii) require the closure, temporarily or permanently of a specified area or areas within a centre;

(iii) specify the maximum number of residents[551] who may be accommodated in a centre or in a specified area or areas within a centre;

(iv) specify the minimum number of staff required to be employed in a centre;

(v)   require the introduction or review, as the case may be, of specified policies, protocols and procedures relating to the care and welfare of patients and residents and relating to the ordering, prescribing, storing and administration of medicines;

(vi) specify measures to be taken to ensure that patients and residents are informed of their rights under the Mental Health Act 2001.[552]

Conditions imposed and amendments and revocations of conditions must be notified in writing to the registered proprietor of the centre concerned.[553] Where there is a contravention of a condition of registration in relation to an approved centre the registered proprietor shall be guilty of an offence.[554]

Requirement to notify the applicant or registered proprietor Where the Commission proposes to refuse to register a centre, to remove a centre from the register, to attach a condition to or amend or revoke a condition attached to a registration it must notify the applicant or registered proprietor as the case may be of its proposal and of the reasons

---

[549] Mental Health Act 2001, s.64(5).

[550] *Ibid.*, s.64(6).

[551] "Resident" is defined by s.62 of the Mental Health Act 2001 as a person receiving care and treatment in a centre. The definition clearly encompasses both voluntary and involuntary patients.

[552] Mental Health Act 2001, s.64(6)(b).

[553] *Ibid.*, s.64(6)(c).

[554] *Ibid.*, s.64(13).

for it.[555] A notification of such a proposal must include a statement that the person concerned may make representations to the Commission within 21 days of the receipt by him/her of the notification and a notification of the decision must also include a statement that the person concerned may appeal to the District Court under section 65 against the decision within 21 says from the receipt by him/her of the notification.[556] A person who has been notified of such a proposal may, within 21 days of receipt of the notification make representations in writing to the Commission and the Commission is obliged: (i) before deciding the matter to take into consideration any representations duly made to it under this paragraph in relation to the proposal, and (ii) notify the person in writing of its decision and of the reasons for it.[557]

Appeals against decision of Commission Section 65 of the Act provides that the registered proprietor or, as the case may be, the person intending to be the registered proprietor of an approved centre may appeal to the District Court[558] against a decision of the Commission to refuse to register the centre, to remove the centre from the register or to attach a condition, or to amend or revoke a condition attached to the registration of a centre. The appeal must be brought within 21 days of the receipt by the person of the notification of the decision by the Commission under section 64.[559]

The Mental Health Commission must be given notice of an appeal under section 65 and shall be entitled to appear, be heard and adduce evidence on the hearing of the appeal.[560]

The District Court has a discretion as it thinks proper to confirm the decision or direct the Commission, as may be appropriate, to register or to restore the registration of the centre, to withdraw the condition or the amendment to or revocation of a condition, to attach a specified condition to the registration or to make a specified amendment to a condition of the registration.[561] A decision of the District Court under section 65 on a question of fact shall be final.[562]

Where a notification of a decision is given under section 64 then (with the exception of a decision to refuse to register a centre which was not registered or deemed to be registered at the time of a relevant application for registration) during such period from the notification as the Commission considers reasonable and specifies in the notification and which is not less than 21 days the centre shall be treated as if the decision had not been made and if the decision was to refuse an application for registration under section 64(10)(a) it shall be treated as if it had been registered and the registration had attached to it any conditions attached to the relevant registration that had ceased by virtue of section 64(10)(a)(i).[563]

---

[555] Mental Health Act 2001, s.64(11)(a).
[556] *Ibid.*, s.64(12).
[557] *Ibid.*, s.64(11)(b).
[558] The jurisdiction conferred on the District Court by s.65 must be exercised by the judge of the District Court for the time being assigned to the district court district in which the centre concerned is situated. See Mental Health Act 2001, s.65(2).
[559] Mental Health Act 2001, s.65(1).
[560] *Ibid.*, s.65(5).
[561] *Ibid.*, s.65(1).
[562] *Ibid.*, s.65(3).
[563] *Ibid.*, s.65(4)(a).

If an appeal against the decision of the Commission is brought under section 65 then
(i) during the period from the end of the period mentioned in the previous paragraph
until the determination or withdrawal of the appeal or any appeal therefrom or from any
such appeal and (ii) such further period as the court concerned considers reasonable
and specifies in its decision the centre shall (a) be treated for the purposes of section 64
as if the appeal had been upheld and (b) if the appeal was against a decision of the
Commission to refuse an application for registration under section 64(10)(a) it shall be
treated as if the registration had attached to it any conditions attached to the relevant
registration that had ceased by virtue of section 64(10)(a)(i).[564]

Requirement to register Section 64(10)(a)(i) provides that where an approved centre
commences to be carried on by a person other than the registered proprietor the centre
thereupon ceases to be registered. The person other than the registered proprietor must
apply not later than four weeks after the commencement to the Commission for the
registration of the centre, if he or she has not done so before the commencement.[565] A
person who does not do so commits an offence.[566] If the application for registration is
duly made and is not refused then during the period from the commencement until the
centre is registered the centre shall be deemed, for the purposes of section 63, to be
registered and any conditions attached to the previous registration shall be deemed to
be attached to the registration.[567] If the application is granted the date of registration of
centre shall be the day following the day the centre ceases to be registered under section
64(10)(a)(i).[568]

The registered proprietor of a centre who proposes to carry on a centre immediately
after the expiration of the period of registration of a centre may apply under section
64(3) of the Act to the Commission for registration of the centre not less than two
months before the expiration of the period of registration. If the Commission does not
notify him/her that it proposes to refuse to register the centre before the expiration of
the period of registration then it must register the centre and its date of registration shall
be the day following the day of the expiration of the period of registration.[569]

**Power of Minister for Health and Children to make regulations in relation to
approved centres** Section 66 of the Mental Health Act 2001 (which has yet to be
implemented) empowers the Minister for Health and Children, after consultation with
the Mental Health Commission to make such regulations as he or she thinks appropriate
in relation to such centres for the purpose of ensuring proper standards in relation to
centres including adequate and suitable accommodation, food and care for residents
while being maintained in centres and the proper conduct of centres.[570] Without prejudice
to the generality of this power regulations under section 66 may:

(a) prescribe requirements as to the maintenance, care and welfare of residents,

[564] Mental Health Act 2001, s.65(4)(b).
[565] *Ibid.*, s.64(10)(a)(ii).
[566] *Ibid.*, s.64(10)(b).
[567] *Ibid.*, s.64(10)(a)(iii).
[568] *Ibid.*, s.64(10)(a)(ii).
[569] *Ibid.*, s.64(9).
[570] *Ibid.*, s.66(1).

(b) prescribe requirements as to the staffing including requirements as to the suitability of members of staff of centres,

(c) prescribe requirements as to the design, maintenance, repair, cleaning and cleanliness, ventilation, heating and lighting of centres,

(d) prescribe requirements as to the accommodation provided in centres,

(e) prescribe requirements as to the establishment and maintenance of a register of residents,

(f) prescribe requirements as to the records to be kept in centres and for the examination and copying of any such records or of extracts therefrom by the Inspector,

(g) prescribe requirements as to the drawing up and carrying out by centres, so far as practicable, in consultation with each resident of an individual care plan for that resident including the setting of appropriate goals,

(h) prescribe requirements as to the information to be provided to the Inspector,

(i) provide for the enforcement and execution of regulations by the Mental Health Commission.[571]

Where there is a failure or refusal to comply with the regulations in relation to a centre the registered proprietor shall be guilty of an offence.[572] In addition a person who fails or refuses to comply with the regulations shall be guilty of an offence.[573]

By virtue of section 66(4) where a person is convicted of an offence under section 66 the Circuit Court[574] may, on application of the Commission which is brought not more than six months after the conviction or where there is an appeal against the conviction the final determination of the appeal or of any further appeal (if it is a determination affirming the conviction) or the withdrawal of any such appeal therefrom, by order declare that the person shall be disqualified during such period as may be specified in the order from carrying on the centre to which the conviction related or, at the discretion of the court from carrying on any centre.[575] A person in respect of whom such a disqualifying order is made shall not during the period specified in the order carry on the centre specified in the order or, if the order so specifies, any centre.[576] A person who contravenes this prohibition shall be guilty of an offence.[577] Notice of an application by the Commission under section 66(4) must be given to the person convicted of the offence concerned and he or she shall be entitled to appear, be heard and adduce evidence on the hearing of the application.[578]

A person who wilfully obstructs or interferes with the Inspector of Mental Health

---

[571] Mental Health Act 2001, s.66(2).

[572] *Ibid.*, s.66(3)(a).

[573] *Ibid.*, s.66(3)(b).

[574] The jurisdiction conferred on the Circuit Court by s.66(4) must be exercised by the judge of the Circuit Court for the time being assigned to the circuit in which the premises concerned are situated. See s.66(4)(e).

[575] Mental Health Act 2001, s.66(4)(a).

[576] *Ibid.*, s.66(4)(b).

[577] *Ibid.*, s.66(4)(c).

[578] *Ibid.*, s.66(4)(d).

Services in the performance of functions under the regulations or who fails or refuses to comply with a requirement of the Inspector under such regulations will be guilty of an offence.[579]

A person guilty of an offence under Part V of the Act shall be liable (a) on summary conviction, to a fine not exceeding £1,500 (€1904.61) or to imprisonment for a term not exceeding 12 months or to both or (b) on conviction on indictment to a fine not exceeding £50,000 (€63486.90) or to imprisonment for a term not exceeding two years or to both.[580]

Commentary

The system of registration of approved centres to ensure a minimum standard of service to patients is to be welcomed. However, much of the detail in relation to the standards of accommodation and care is left by section 66 of the 2001 Act to be filled in by Ministerial regulation after consultation with the Mental Health Commission. It remains to be seen whether the regulations when drafted will be such as to secure high standards of accommodation and care in psychiatric hospitals generally which in some instances have had a history of less than acceptable conditions.[581]

The Ombudsman

Current Irish law

Under the terms of the Ombudsman Act 1980 the Ombudsman may investigate any administrative action taken by the Department of Health or the Health Service Executive,[582] where it appears to him after a preliminary examination that:

(a) it has or may have adversely affected a person and that action was or may have been:
    (i)   taken without proper authority,
    (ii) taken on irrelevant grounds,
    (iii) the result of negligence or carelessness,
    (iv) based on erroneous or incomplete information,
    (v) improperly discriminatory,
    (vi) based on an undesirable administrative practice, or
    (vii) otherwise contrary to fair or sound administration.[583]

He may not however investigate actions of persons when acting on behalf of the Health Service Executive and (in the opinion of the Ombudsman) solely in the exercise of clinical judgment in connection with the diagnosis of illness or the care or treatment of a patient, whether formed by the person taking the action or by any other person. Nor

---

[579]Mental Health Act 2001, s.66(5).
[580] *Ibid.*, s.68.
[581] See Reports of Inspector of Mental Hospitals.
[582] Added Ombudsman Act (First Schedule) (Amendment) Order 1984 (S.I. No. 322 of 1984), reg. 2(a).
[583] Ombudsman Act 1980, s.4.

may he investigate actions of the Health Service Executive when acting on the advice of such persons where the actions of the Health Service Executive were in the opinion of the Ombudsman taken solely on that advice.[584]

The Ombudsman may after carrying out a preliminary examination of the matter decide not to carry out an investigation under the Act if the complaint is trivial or vexatious or he becomes of the opinion that the person making he complaint has not taken reasonable steps to seek redress in respect of the subject matter of the complaint or, if he has, has not been refused redress.[585] In addition, a complaint may not be the subject of investigation if the person affected by the action has a right conferred by or under statute of appeal, reference or review to or before a court in the state or if the person affected by the action has a right of appeal reference or review to or before a person other than the Department of Health or the Health Service Executive.[586]

Complaints to the Ombudsman must be made within 12 months of the action having been taken or of the time when the person making the complaint became aware of the action, whichever is the later.[587] Where an Ombudsman, having investigated a matter forms the view that the action has adversely affected a person he may make recommendations to the Department of Health or Health Service Executive: (a) that the matter in question be further considered, (b) that measures be taken to remedy mitigate or alter the adverse effect of the action or (c) that the reason for taking the action be given to the Ombudsman. He may also stipulate that he be notified within a specified time of the Department of Health's or the Health Service Executive's response to the recommendation.[588]

The Ombudsman is also obliged to publish an annual report on the performance of his functions and to lay the same before each House of the Oireachtas.[589]

Commentary

By contrast to the situation in Ireland in Canada most provincial ombudsman statutes confer jurisdiction on the Ombudsman to investigate complaints from patients in hospitals including psychiatric hospitals. The Ombudsman also has power to conduct investigations on his own initiative without a complaint having been received. In practice the Annual Reports of the Ombudsman in a variety of provinces reveal that the Ombudsman has conducted a wide range of investigations in particular such issues as denial of transfer and discharge requests and allegations of improper conditions or treatment. Patients must normally exhaust all statutory remedies before the Ombudsman can investigate a complaint.

While the Ombudsman's powers are limited to issuing recommendations and reports, recommendations in particular tend to be quite influential and are frequently implemented by the hospital authorities.

---

[584] Ombudsman Act (First Schedule) (Amendment) Order 1984 (S.I. No. 322 of 1984), reg. 2(b).
[585] Ombudsman Act 1980, s.4(5).
[586] *Ibid.*, s.5(1).
[587] *Ibid.*, s.5(1)(f).
[588] *Ibid.*, s.5(3).
[589] *Ibid.*, s.6(7).

Conclusions

The Canadian experience reveals that there may be a potential role for an Irish Ombudsman in maintaining standards of care in the psychiatric services. Although this role might seem to conflict with that envisaged for the Inspector of Mental Health Services the requirement of exhaustion of all other remedies should avoid a clash of jurisdictions.

THE PATIENT'S RIGHT OF ACCESS TO THE COURTS

Position under Mental Treatment Act 1945

Section 260(1) of the Mental Treatment Act 1945 (which is still in force) provides that no civil proceedings may be instituted in respect of an act purporting to have been done in pursuance of the Act except with the leave of the High Court and that leave shall not be granted unless the High Court is satisfied that there are substantial grounds for contending that the person against whom such proceedings are to be brought acted in bad faith or without reasonable care.

Section 260(2) provides that notice of an application for leave of the High Court under subsection (1) of this section should be given to the person against whom it is proposed to institute the proceedings and such person should be entitled to be heard against the application.

Section 260(3) provides that where proceedings are, by leave granted in pursuance of subsection (1) of this section instituted in respect of an act purporting to have been done in pursuance of the 1945 Act, the Court should not determine the proceedings in favour of the plaintiff unless it is satisfied that the defendant acted in bad faith or without reasonable care.

Henchy J. (dissenting on the facts but not on the law) in *O'Dowd v. North Western Health Board*,[590] expressed the legislative policy behind section 260 as follows:

> "It is an unfortunate syndrome of certain kinds of mental illness that a patient compulsorily detained in a mental hospital for treatment conceives a deep-seated but quite unjustified conviction that his detention was unnecessary, even malevolent or unlawful, and that what he considers to be victimisation should give him a good cause of action for damages. The undesirability of giving free rein in the courts to such a delusional obsession is recognised by Section 260 of the Mental Treatment Act 1945. It re-enacts a bar to litigation which existed in the law of lunacy in England since the Lunacy Act 1890".[591]

The standard of proof, which had be satisfied by the plaintiff under section 260, has been canvassed in a number of cases. In four cases *O'Dowd v. North Western Health Board*,[592] *Murphy v. Green*,[593] and *O'Reilly v. Moroney and Midwestern Health*

---

[590] [1983] I.L.R.M. 186.
[591] *Ibid.*, p.196.
[592] [1983] I.L.R.M 186.
[593] [1991] 2 I.R. 566.

Board,[594] the Supreme Court refused leave to take civil action due to a failure to satisfy the burden of proof and in one case *Lehaney v. Loftus and the Western Health Board*[595] the High Court reached a similar conclusion.

In *O'Dowd v. North Western Health Board*,[596] the plaintiff alleged first that the Health Board was vicariously liable for the negligence of a psychiatrist who had failed to reply to correspondence from another medical practitioner asking for his advices as to what course of treatment should be followed and seeking a case summary from him, the second medical practitioner being of the opinion that the plaintiff's mental disorder had been an isolated condition. The plaintiff also alleged that the psychiatrist was negligent in making a reception order certifying that the plaintiff was unlikely to recover within a period of six months when in fact he was discharged within six days. The Plaintiff was successful in obtaining leave in the High Court. However, the Supreme Court allowed the Health Board's appeal against the order of the High Court by a majority of 2:1. O'Higgins C.J. said that that section 260 required the applicant for leave to establish:

> "something approaching a *prima facie* case before he could obtain such leave. He is not to be permitted to mount a vexatious or frivolous action or one based on imagined complaints. I think that the section does no more than to require the applicant for leave to sue to discharge the same onus of proof as he would be required to discharge in pursuing a claim for damages outside the Act but to discharge it at an earlier point in time".[597]

Griffin J. also in the majority ruled somewhat inconsistently with O'Higgins C.J.'s view that:

> "The use of the word "satisfied" indicates that the Oireachtas had in mind a somewhat higher standard of proof than that which a plaintiff must ordinarily discharge in a civil case."[598]

So ruling the majority held on the facts that the psychiatrist had not displayed an absence of reasonable care in overlooking writing to or consulting the other medical practitioner since this did not relate to his duties under the Act and the discharge by the same psychiatrist within six days was not inconsistent with the original reception order since he was satisfied that the respondent had sufficiently recovered to permit such a discharge. Henchy J. dissenting on the facts found that substantial grounds existed for holding that the health board was vicariously liable for the negligence of the psychiatrist who had signed the reception order three hours *after* the plaintiff was forcibly detained in hospital and had not examined the plaintiff prior to signing the reception order in respect of the plaintiff. In addition he made no effort to see if the applicant was willing to receive in-patient treatment on a voluntary basis.

---

[594] [1992] 2 I.R. 145.
[595] Unreported, High Court, Ó Caoimh J., July 20, 2001.
[596] [1983] I.L.R.M. 186.
[597] *Ibid.*, p.190.
[598] *Ibid.*, 194.

In *Murphy v. Greene*,[599] the defendant a medical practitioner responded to an emergency call to attend the plaintiff who was not his patient at his residence. On arriving he was informed by the plaintiff's wife that the plaintiff had been drunk, had violently assaulted her and their daughter, had been arrested by the Gardaí for breach of a protection order and was in custody in a Garda station. The defendant visited the plaintiff at the Garda station where the plaintiff appeared drunk and aggressive and refused to submit to physical examination. Having checked the plaintiff's medical history the defendant signed a certificate under the 1945 Act, and the plaintiff was admitted to a psychiatric hospital for treatment. The plaintiff was released by the psychiatric hospital the following day and subsequently sought leave to institute proceedings pursuant to section 260 alleging wrongful detention in the psychiatric hospital and seeking damages for negligence, defamation and false imprisonment. The High Court granted the plaintiff leave to institute proceedings but a unanimous Supreme Court allowed the defendants appeal. In relation to the construction of section 260 it ruled that as section 260 imposed a limitation on the individual's constitutional right of access to the courts it must be strictly construed. Finlay C.J., following O'Higgins C.J. in *O'Dowd*, held that section 260 required an intending plaintiff to prove "as a matter of probability"[600] the existence of facts establishing substantial grounds for contending that the proposed defendant acted in bad faith or without reasonable care, though it was not necessary for the court to try and conclude whether, as a matter of probability the plaintiff was likely to succeed in the proposed action. Declining to follow Griffin J.'s ruling in *O'Dowd* he held that there was no requirement to go beyond the normal civil standard of proof. So ruling it held that a diagnosis of the plaintiff's condition by the defendant that was incorrect did not of itself show a lack of reasonable care on the defendant's part. Accordingly the plaintiff had not established substantial grounds supporting his contention that the defendant had acted without reasonable care and was not entitled to leave to institute proceedings against the defendant.

Given the wide area of discretion afforded to defendants by the general language in which their duties are couched by the 1945 Act the burden of proof of negligence is difficult to discharge.

In *O'Reilly v. Moroney and the Mid Western Health Board*,[601] the Supreme Court held that an unseen observation by a medical practitioner conducted from a position twelve to fifteen yards from an aggressive plaintiff amounted to a sufficient examination for the purposes of making a recommendation for reception under Section 184 of the Act and so holding cited with approval dicta of McCarthy J. in *Murphy v. Greene* that "[t]he standard of reasonable care under the [1945] Act may be quite different from such standard in ordinary medical practice."[602]

In the High Court judgment in *Lehany v. Loftus and the Western Health Board*,[603] the applicant was admitted to a psychiatric hospital based on a certificate signed by the first respondent a registered medical practitioner known to the applicant who had received a report from the applicant's brother that the applicant had engaged in threatening

---

[599] [1990] 2 I.R. 566.
[600] *Ibid.*, p.573.
[601] Unreported, Supreme Court, November 16, 1993.
[602] *Per* Egan J., p.10.
[603] Unreported, High Court, July 20, 2001.

behaviour towards him and a report from the applicant's sister in law that the applicant had attacked her with a pitch fork and threatened to kill pets owned by her children. Apparently there had been a land dispute between the two brothers but this was not known to the first respondent. He was escorted to the hospital by members of the Garda Síochána to the hospital and was detained overnight but thereafter released. He sought leave to issue proceedings on the basis that in giving the certificate the first respondent was not acting in good faith and was negligent in the manner in which he gave the certificate; that there were no justifiable grounds for it and the first respondent made no independent investigation to ascertain the veracity of the background dispute. Ó Caoimh J. held that the evidence disclosed a clear conflict between the applicant and the respondents and in the light of the fact that none of the witnesses who had sworn affidavits on behalf of the respondents had been cross examined on their evidence he was not satisfied that there were substantial grounds for contending that either of the respondents acted in bad faith or without reasonable care.

He held that care was exercised by the officers of the health board concerned in dealing with the applicant and as soon as they had observed him overnight and were satisfied that no risk was present they released him back to the community. Secondly while it was clear that further inquiries might have changed the first respondent's conclusion that the applicant was in need of psychiatric treatment nevertheless the first respondent had acted in the belief that his informants were reliable persons; furthermore he had a medical history showing that that the applicant had suffered depression some years prior to the events in question and thirdly based on his own clinical assessment and judgment of the applicant's condition he believed that there was a genuine and immediate risk to the safety and welfare of the applicant and to the members of his family which required urgent psychiatric assessment and if necessary treatment. While subsequent events cast doubt on the veracity of what was said by the applicant's brother that was not the basis on which the court had to judge matters. In all the circumstances of the case Ó Caoimh J. was not satisfied that the applicant had discharged the relevant onus of proof so as to enable the court to be satisfied that there were substantial grounds for contending that the first respondent acted in bad faith or without reasonable care.[604]

On the other hand in three cases the applicants were successful in obtaining leave from the courts to take civil action in connection with their detention. In the recent case of *Bailey v. Gallagher*,[605] a medical practitioner examined the plaintiff on May 12, 1988 and certified him as in need of treatment under section 184 of the Act. Under section 184(4) the certificate ceased to be valid on May 19, 1988 However, the plaintiff's wife sought to have him removed to the local district hospital May 21, 1988 and to this end the plaintiff was removed from his home and detained in a Garda Station where he consulted his solicitor who immediately contacted the defendant medical practitioner. After it became apparent that a psychiatrist would not be able to carry out an immediate examination of the plaintiff the medical practitioner agreed that he would instruct the Gardaí to release the plaintiff. This was on condition that he would present himself for psychiatric examination to the local district mental hospital the following Monday. The

---

[604] The court also found that even had the respondents acted in bad faith and without reasonable care the action was statute barred under s.11(2)(b) of the Statute of Limitations 1957. The detention occurred on July 18, 1996 and the Plenary Summons had not issued before July 18, 1999.
[605] [1996] 2 I.L.R.M. 433.

plaintiff issued proceedings in negligence, false imprisonment and/or defamation against the medical practitioner who had certified him. The High Court refused him leave to issue proceedings and the plaintiff appealed to the Supreme Court. Keane J. and O'Flaherty J. (Murphy J. concurring) granting the plaintiff leave to issue the proceedings addressed the standard of proof under section 260 as follows:

> "As to the degree of proof which is required before leave can be given it is clear from the judgments of O'Higgins C.J in *O'Dowd* and Finlay CJ in *Murphy v. Greene* that, while the applicant is not to be allowed to mount a vexatious or frivolous action or one based on imagined complaints he is not required to do more than satisfy the court on the balance of probabilities that substantial grounds exist."[606]

In addition Keane J. delivering the Supreme Court judgment and finding that there had been want of reasonable care not in the diagnosis but in the medical practitioner's failure to bring the detention of the plaintiff promptly to an end and granting leave to the plaintiff remarked:

> "It is ... clear that in cases of mental illness, more than perhaps in any others a mistaken diagnosis does not of itself constitute a failure to take reasonable care on the part of a doctor".

However, qualifying this broad statement later in his judgment he stated that where a committal is taking place against a background of marital discord a doctor must proceed: "with even greater caution than the care which the law expects in every case of doctors exercising their far-reaching powers under this legislation" and "should be aware, if only in the most general terms of the strict requirements that must be met before citizens can be deprived of their liberty under the 1945 Act."[607]

More recently in the case of *Melly v. Moran and the North Western Health Board*,[608] the Supreme Court overruling the High Court held that a recommending medical practitioner's failure to examine the plaintiff within 24 hours before the hospital's receipt of the application for admission as required by section 163 of the 1945 Act and his statement on the relevant form that he had examined the plaintiff some three days before admission constituted substantial grounds for contending that the defendant's acted without reasonable care. O'Flaherty J. stated:

> "I believe that [failure to comply with section 163 of the 1945 Act] constitutes substantial grounds for contending that the defendants acted without reasonable care because if the matter had been tested by way of an application under Article 40 section 4 of the Constitution for the release of the plaintiff shortly after his admission to hospital then the document that the hospital would produce justifying his detention would clearly be defective on its face. Any deprivation of liberty can only be justified if done in accordance with law. So I believe that the plaintiff has

---

[606] *Ibid.* at 446.
[607] *Ibid.* at 448.
[608] Unreported, Supreme Court, May 28, 1998.

established substantial grounds for contending that there was a want of reasonable care in the filling out of the form by the doctor and by the hospital authorities in accepting it as sufficient."[609]

Further in the case of *Kiernan v. Harris, Kiernan and the Midland Health Board*[610] O'Higgins J. held that in the light of uncontroverted evidence that the recommending medical practitioner had failed to examine the plaintiff prior to involuntary admission there was a prima facie case that the practitioner had not acted with reasonable care and the plaintiff should be permitted to institute proceedings against him. It was also held that the applicant for the certificate (who was the second named defendant in the action) had failed in his statutory duty under section 5 of the Mental Treatment Act 1953 to inform the person who was the subject of the application of the nature of the medical certificate and of the fact that he could request a second opinion and that this failure amounted to a failure to take reasonable care. Consequently leave to proceed was also granted in respect of the second named defendant.

Position under the Mental Health Act 2001

In the White Paper on Mental Health the Government was of the view that the retention of section 260 of the Mental Treatment Act 1945 was warranted to protect persons engaged in acts undertaken in accordance with the terms of mental health legislation from vexatious legal actions. However, it was proposed to revise the standard of proof that the plaintiff should have to satisfy before being granted leave to institute proceedings that a patient applying to the High Court should have to satisfy the Court that there were "reasonable grounds" for contending that the person against whom the proceedings are to be brought acted in bad faith or without reasonable care.[611] At the report stage of the Mental Health Bill in the Dáil section 73(1) of the Bill was amended to read

> "No civil proceedings shall be instituted in respect of an act purporting to have been done in pursuance of this Act save by leave of the High Court and such leave shall not be refused unless the High Court is satisfied:
>
> (a) that the proceedings are frivolous or vexatious, or
> (b) that there are no reasonable grounds for contending that the person against whom the proceedings are brought acted in bad faith or without reasonable care."

The two other subsections of section 73 re-enact section 260(2) and (3) of the 1945 Act. They provide:

> (2) Notice of an application for leave of the High Court under subsection (1) shall be given to the person against whom it is proposed to institute the proceedings and such person shall be entitled to be heard against the application.

---

[609] *Ibid.*
[610] Unreported, High Court, O'Higgins J., May 12, 1998.
[611] Para.10.38.

(3) Where proceedings are, by leave granted in pursuance of subsection (1) of this section, instituted in respect of an act purporting to have been done in pursuance of this Act, the Court shall not determine the proceedings in favour of the plaintiff unless it is satisfied that the defendant acted in bad faith or without reasonable care.

In contrast to the previous provision under the 1945 Act, section 73 will, when brought into force, place the burden of proof on the defendant in the proceedings to prove (a) that the proceedings were frivolous or vexatious or (b) that there were no reasonable grounds for contending that the person against whom the proceedings were brought acted in bad faith or without reasonable care.

The scope of the section is wide. It covers "any act purporting" to be done under the 1945 Act so that the application of excessive force could come within its ambit. It also applies to "any person" not just medical nursing or other staff under the Act and to acts in respect of voluntary and involuntary patients. However, since the statutory protection under section 73 is expressed to apply to civil proceedings it does not apply to prosecutions for a criminal offence committed under the terms of the 2001 Act.

While section 73 is a welcome development the question is whether it goes far enough in removing the obstacles to litigation for plaintiffs with mental illness.[612]

Commentary

1. Section 260 of the Mental Treatment Act 1945 is based on section 16 of the English Mental Treatment Act 1930 which had its roots in section 12 of the Lunacy Amendment Act 1889. Psychiatrists threatened not to implement the system of civil commitment unless the 1889 Act had such a provision. In *Murphy v. Greene*,[613] it was recognised that the section imposes a limitation upon the constitutional right of access to the courts and had to be strictly construed.

2. The effect of the requirement in section 73 of the Mental Health Act that the plaintiff show reasonable grounds for contending that the person against whom the proceedings are brought acted in bad faith or without reasonable care and that notice of the application for leave to sue be sent to the defendant who is then entitled to a hearing opposing the application for permission to sue is that the plaintiff's case is revealed to the defendant at the beginning. The requirement of leave also increases the cost of litigation and delays justice.

3. Further the application for leave is tried on the basis of affidavits. The resolution of issues of fact is thus carried out on the basis of written evidence so that it is questionable whether they are tested in a genuinely adversary manner since the plaintiff does not have the right to cross examine the defendant or adverse witnesses. The cumulative effect of this is that the plaintiff faces significant obstacles and the

---

[612] Following the decision of Carroll J. in *B. v. Minister for Health and Children*, December 7, 2004, the constitutionality of section 260 of the 1945 Act and section 73 of the 2001 Act are now in question insofar as they limit the applicant's right to challenge acts done under either Act to cases of "bad faith" or "want of reasonable care". See Preface.

[613] [1990] 2 I.R. 566; [1991] I.L.R.M. 404.

question must be asked whether a requirement to seek leave to institute proceedings even in a less onerous form such as section 73 of the Mental Health Act 2001 serves a legitimate and compelling public interest.

4. Section 260 of the Mental Treatment Act 1945 and section 73 of the Mental Health Act are premised on the assumption that psychiatrists, hospital and health authorities need to be protected from vexatious or frivolous or unfounded actions by individuals who have been involuntarily hospitalised. However, neither the courts nor the legislature have examined whether the basis for the policy of the Act is well founded. If the purpose of the section whether in its existing or proposed modified terms is to protect mental health carers against groundless legal actions by patients then it must be demonstrated that people who receive mental health care may be generally likely to harass those concerned with them with groundless charges and litigation. In the absence of such evidence it must be argued that the section is over-inclusive and discriminates unfairly. Hoggett comments in relation to the requirement of leave to bring proceedings stipulated by UK legislation:

> "Only a minority of patients, even of those compulsorily detained are suffering from disorders which make it at all likely that they will harass other people with groundless accusations. Rather more of them are suffering from disorders, which make it likely that they will not complain at all even if they have every reason to do so. There is no evidence that the floodgates would open if section 139 [of the Mental Health Act 1983] were entirely repealed. There is more evidence from a series of reports and investigations that mental patients are in a peculiarly powerless position which merits if anything extra safeguards rather than the removal of those available to everyone else."[614]

No one would argue that those involved in the provision of the psychiatric services have a difficult and sometimes dangerous job to do but if protection similar to section 260 of the Mental Treatment Act 1945 or section 73 of the Mental Health Act 2001 is not afforded to police or prison officers are there any special reasons for retaining it for those involved in the provision of psychiatric care. There is an on-going danger that practical protection from suit will lead to a lowering of standards and indifference to personal rights to the detriment of patients.

---

[614] Haggett B., *Mental Health Law* (Sweet and Maxwell London, 1994), p.250.

CHAPTER FIVE

Departure from Hospital

INTRODUCTION

Departure represents the final stage in the continuum that stretches from admission, treatment, discharge, to a return to the community. As such there is a need to examine whether the patient's rights and interests are adequately taken into account and upheld at this stage. The release itself may be graduated or straightforward.

The law and procedure implicated may well have a bearing upon whether the person with mental illness makes a successful return to community life or not. There are a variety of release mechanisms. A patient may be:

– granted leave from hospital;

– transferred to another hospital;

– abscond or escape;

– be lawfully discharged.

The detained patient may obtain release from an institution via a *habeas corpus* application to the court or judicial review. Each of these departure routes is discussed in turn and an examination made on the efficacy of the law.

THE LAW RELATING TO LEAVE OF ABSENCE

Current Irish law

Position under Mental Act 1945

The provisions of the Mental Treatment Act 1945 (which is still in force)[1] relating to the grant and revocation of leave vest a considerable amount of discretion in the resident medical superintendent of the relevant hospital but are silent in relation to the manner of its exercise and reflect a certain inflexibility in relation to the periods for which leave could be given.

The 1945 provide that the resident medical superintendent of a district mental hospital may permit a person detained in that hospital or any other institution maintained by the Health Service Executive to be absent from the hospital on trial for any period not exceeding thirty days and may extend the period for a further period not exceeding thirty days or for two or more periods not exceeding in the aggregate ninety days.[2] Similar powers are given to the person in charge of a private institution.[3]

---

[1] Note that the repealing provisions of the 2001 Act have yet to be implemented.
[2] Mental Treatment Act 1945, s.203(1) as amended by the Mental Treatment Act 1961, s.22(1).
[3] Mental Treatment Act 1945, s.203(2) as amended by the Mental Treatment Act 1961, s.22(2).

Under the *Guidelines on Good Practice and Quality Assurance in Mental Health Services,* published in 1998, the Inspector of Mental Hospitals recommended as follows:

> "The decision to grant a patient absence on trial or to extend the period should rest with the patient's consultant psychiatrist and, as it can be an important part of a patient's treatment plan, the patient must be fully involved in the decision. Absence on trial should be well planned and involve consultation with relatives and staff in community settings. The patient must be asked to consent to any consultation with relatives or other professional staff thought necessary before the decision to grant absence on trial is made. Decisions relating to absence on trial should be recorded in the patient's file outlining the date absence on trial commenced and the conditions attached. A separate record should be kept of the relevant dates and attached to the reception order. Written policy guidelines relating to absence on trial should be available in each service. The guidelines should give information on the procedures for informing relatives of a patient's absence on trial if appropriate and for informing professionals in the community responsible for patient follow up and for the recording of decisions in the administrative and medical file."[4]

Under the 1945 Act the chief medical officer of a mental institution may permit a person detained in the institution who is not dangerous to himself or others to be absent from the institution on parole for any period not exceeding forty-eight hours.[5]

The Inspector of Mental Hospitals *Guidelines* recommend as follows:

> "Each service should have clearly written absence on parole guidelines to ensure that there can be no confusion about a patient's parole/pass status. All decisions to grant parole/pass should be made by a consultant psychiatrist or a doctor of the service in consultation with a consultant psychiatrist. Decisions to grant parole/pass should be recorded in the patient's file and nursing notes with the precise return time, the signature of the authorising doctor and the conditions attaching to each parole/pass."[6]

The grant of absence on parole is designed to enable a detained person to attend to family and other obligations whereas where absence on trial is granted it is seen as a stepping-stone to discharge.

Where a person is absent on trial,[7] or parole,[8] his permission to be absent may be withdrawn by the person in charge of the institution at any time before the expiration of the period during which he is permitted to be absent, and if the permission is withdrawn the person absent on trial or parole may be retaken within twenty eight days after the withdrawal as if he has escaped from the institution.

---

[4] *Guidelines on Good Practice and Quality Assurance in Mental Health Services* (1998), para.4.7.
[5] Mental Treatment Act 1945, s.204(1).
[6] *Guidelines on Good Practice and Quality Assurance in Mental Health Services* (1998), para.4.7.
[7] Mental Treatment Act 1945, s.203(5) as inserted by the Mental Treatment Act 1961, s.22(3).
[8] Mental Treatment Act 1945, s.204(4) as inserted by the Mental Treatment Act 1961, s.23.

Where a person absent on trial does not return on the expiration of the period or the extended period during which he was permitted to be absent and no medical practitioner has furnished a medical certificate to the person in charge of the institution stating that his detention is no longer necessary the person concerned may be retaken as if he had escaped from the institution.[9] Similar powers applied when a person absent on parole does not return.[10]

Position under the Mental Health Act 2001

Section 26(1) of the Mental Health Act 2001 (not yet brought into force) provides that the consultant psychiatrist responsible for the care and treatment of a patient may grant permission in writing to the patient to be absent from the approved centre concerned for such period as he or she may specify in the permission being a period less that the unexpired period provided for in the relevant admission order,[11] renewal order[12] or order under section 25[13] as the case may be. The permission may be made subject to such conditions as the consultant psychiatrist considers appropriate and so specifies.

Section 26(2) provides that where the patient is absent from an approved centre pursuant to subsection (1), the consultant psychiatrist may, if he or she is opinion that it is in the interests of the patient to do so, withdraw the permission granted under subsection (1) and direct the patient in writing to return to the approved centre.

A "patient" in the context of section 26 is a person to whom an admission order relates and a child in respect of whom an order under section 25 (involuntary admission of children) is in force.[14]

Section 26(1) of the Mental Health Act 2001, which permits a consultant psychiatrist to grant leave for a period less than the unexpired period provided for in the relevant admission order, renewal order or order under section 25 introduces greater flexibility to the system of granting of leave than the 1945 Act.

However, it should be noted that following the enactment of the European Convention on Human Rights Act 2003 the consultant's powers to withdraw the permission to be absent and to direct the patient to return to the approved centre must be exercised consistently with Article 5(1)(e) of the European Convention on Human Rights and following the decision of the European Court of Human Rights in *K v. UK,*[15] except in

---

[9] Mental Treatment Act 1945, s.203(3).

[10] *Ibid.*, s.204(3).

[11] S.14 provides that where a recommendation in relation to a person the subject of an application is received by the clinical director of an approved centre a consultant psychiatrist on the staff of the approved centre shall, as soon as may be, carry out an examination of the person and if he or she is satisfied that the person is suffering from a mental disorder he or she shall make and order known as an involuntary admission order and referred to in this Act as "an admission order" in a form specified by the Commission for the reception, detention and treatment of a person. See Mental Health Act 1945, ss.2 and 14.

[12] An admission order authorises the reception, detention and treatment of the person concerned for a period of 21 days form the date of the making of the order. This period may be extended by order to be known as and referred to in the Act as a "renewal order" made by the consultant psychiatrist responsible for the care and treatment of the patient concerned. See Mental Health Act 2001, ss.2 and 15.

[13] S.25 provides for the making of court orders authorising the involuntary admission of children.

[14] See Mental Health Act 2001, ss.2, 14, 26(3).

[15] (1998) 40 B.M.L.R. 20.

emergency situations, a patient should not be recalled to an approved centre in the absence of "objective medical evidence" that s/he remains mentally disordered.

Proposed power of clinical director of a designated centre to order temporary release of a patient

The proposed power of a clinical director of designated centre to order temporary release of a patient under section 13 of the Criminal Law (Insanity) Bill 2002 is discussed in Chapter 7 on Mental Disability and the Criminal Law.

Commentary

International principles

Interestingly international principles favours measures to facilitate the early return of the person with mental illness to the Community. Principle 7 of the *UN Principles for the Protection of Persons with Mental Illness and the Improvement of Mental Health Care*[16] provides:

> "Where treatment takes place in a mental health facility a patient shall have the right to return to the community as soon as possible."

Comparative law

Leave in England and Wales In England and Wales the responsible medical officer may grant leave of absence to any compulsory patient[17] for a special occasion (such as a wedding) or for a definite period (such as a weekend) or indefinitely. He may also extend leave without bringing the patient back to hospital.[18] This introduces greater flexibility into the system.

In common with his counterpart in Ireland the responsible medical officer may revoke leave at any time if he thinks this is necessary in the interests of the patient's own health or safety or for the protection of other people. However, if leave is revoked notice of revocation and recall must be in writing and addressed either to the patient or to the person in charge of him.[19]

Section 17(5) of the English Mental Health Act 1983 provides expressly that a patient cannot be recalled once the power to detain him/her has lapsed. The power to detain an unrestricted patient lapses automatically once he has been on six months continuous leave.[20]

---

[16] Adopted by the General Assembly on December 17, 1991.

[17] Mental Health Act 1983, s.17(1). If the patient is restricted the permission of the Home Secretary is also required. Mental Health Act 1983, s.41(3)(c) (I); see sch. Pt 11.

[18] Mental Health Act 1983, s.17(2).

[19] *Ibid.*, s.17(4).

[20] The six month's limit does not apply to restricted patients who can be recalled by the Home Secretary (though not after six months by the responsible medical officer) at any time. See Sch.1. Pt 11 nor does it apply to an unrestricted patient who has in the meantime returned to hospital or been transferred to another or who is absent without leave at the end of those six months.

The English Courts have also examined cases of abuse of the leave provisions. In *R v. Hallstrom ex p. W*,[21] it was held that it was unlawful to use prolonged leave of absence as a means of ensuring that patients who did not need to be in hospital could be obliged to go on taking their medication outside. The court also ruled that it was unlawful to recall from leave a patient subject to section 3 solely in order to renew the authority to detain the patient if it was not appropriate and necessary for him to be detained in hospital for treatment

In England and Wales, Mental Health Review Tribunals also have power to recommend that unrestricted patients be given leave although they cannot order that leave be granted.

The English statutory provisions in relation to leave are supplemented by the *Mental Health Act Code of Practice*[22] Paragraph 20 of which sets out the criteria for the grant and revocation of leave:

> "[Leave of absence] can be an important part of a patient's treatment plan. ...[23]
>
> The granting of leave should not be used as an alternative to discharging the patient. ...[24]
>
> Leave of absence should be properly planned, if possible well in advance. Leave may be used to assess an unrestricted patient's suitability for discharge from detention. The patient should be fully involved in the decision to grant leave and should be able to demonstrate to his professional carers that he is likely to cope outside the hospital. Subject to the patient's consent there should be detailed consultation with any appropriate relatives or friends (especially where the patient is to reside with them) and with community services. Leave should not be granted if the patient does not consent to relatives or friends who are to be involved in his or her care being consulted.[25]

> **Recording and information**
> The granting of leave and the conditions attached to it should be recorded in the patient's notes and copies given to the patient, any appropriate relatives or friends and any professionals in the community who need to know. ...[26]

> **Care and treatment while on leave**
> A patient granted leave under section 17 remains "liable to be detained' and the provisions of Part IV of the Act[27] continues to apply. If it becomes necessary to administer treatment in the absence of the patient's consent under Part IV consideration should be given to recalling the patient to hospital. The refusal of

---

[21] [1986] Q.B. 1090.
[22] Published March 1999, pursuant to s.118 of the Mental Health Act 1983 by the English Department of Health and the Welsh Office.
[23] Para.20.1.
[24] Para.20.2.
[25] Para.20.5.
[26] Para.20.6.
[27] Pt IV of the Act deals with the issue of Consent to Treatment.

treatment would not on its own be sufficient grounds for recall. Such a recall direction should be in writing. ...[28]

Recall to hospital

The RMO[29] may revoke a patient's leave at any time if he or she considers this to be necessary in the interests of the patient's health or safety or for the protection of other people. The RMO should consider very seriously the reasons for recalling a patient and the effects that this may have on him or her. For example a refusal to take medication would not on its own be a reason for revocation; the RMO would have to be satisfied that this was necessary in the patient's interests or for the safety of others. The RMO must arrange for a notice in writing revoking the leave to be served on the patient or on the person for the time being in charge of the patient. The reasons for recall must be fully explained to the patient and a record of such explanation placed in the patient's case notes. A restricted patient's leave may be revoked either by his RMO. or the Home Secretary."[30]

Leave in US law Currently in the USA before a patient's leave can be revoked many states require that due process be observed Brakel[31] notes that traditionally the patient's conditional freedom could be revoked upon evidence of generally poor adjustment in the community or upon violation of specific conditions and he could be reinstitutionalised without the need for new commitment proceedings or formal proceedings of any kind. The theory was that even though the patient might be living with relatives or friends in a community home he remained in legal custody of the hospital. However, current law no longer favours such easy revocation and return. Relying on *Morrissey v. Brewer*,[32] in which the United States Supreme Court held that a basic due process must be applied before a prisoner's parole could be revoked (that is, written notice and at least an informal hearing before a neutral decision maker) several state and federal courts have mandated similar protections for patients conditionally discharged from mental facilities whose return is sought.[33] While not requiring full duplication of judicial committal proceedings the cases make clear that summary revocation without notice or a hearing of any kind will not be condoned. The patient must be provided with some forum at which he has a chance to hear and contest the evidence upon which a revocation is sought. Only in emergency situations is summary revocation permitted; the patient is then accorded his due process rights after the emergency passes. In addition at least one of the cases suggests that mere extension of the patient's conditional status (as opposed to return to

---

[28] Para.20.8.

[29] The responsible medical officer i.e. the registered medical practitioner in charge of the treatment of the patient in question. See Mental Health Act 1983 (England and Wales), s.64(1).

[30] Para.20.11.

[31] See *The Mentally Disabled and the Law* (American Bar Foundation, 1985), p.206.

[32] 408 U.S. 471.

[33] *Meisel v. Kremens* 405 F Supp. 1253 (E.D. Pa. 1975): *Lewis v. Donahue* 437 F. Supp. 112 (W.D. Okla 1977); *K.B. v. Sprenger* No. 770292 5 M.D. L.R. 182 (Minn. Dist. Ct., Hennepin County. Sept. 10 1980; *Flick v. Noot.* No. 4–78 Civil 359, 3 MDLR 299 (D.Minn. July 6, 1979): *Hamel v. Brooks* No. 78–115, 4 M.D. L.R. 170 (D.Vt. filed Dec. 16 1979) and *Application of True* 645 P. 2d. 891 (Idaho 1982).

hospital) requires a hearing,[34] and a case from the criminal area involving an insanity acquittee raises the possibility that the mere violation of a release condition may not suffice as a justification for reinstitutionalisation and that a new finding of need of institutionalisation or dangerousness is required.[35]

Clearly if system of absence on trial in Ireland is to work there is a need for community-based support for the patient who through the process of absence on trial is preparing to leave hospital. Deutsch[36] makes the following observation of the effects of lack of community support in the USA, which might equally well, apply to poorly resourced community services in the Irish context.

Unfortunately, there are some states in which the practice of parole is grossly abused and perverted. In several backward states the parole system is nothing more than a mockery and a sham. Patients are "paroled" without any adequate supervision or follow-up care and protection. Little or no effort is made to follow the progress of the patient after removal from the hospital. Lacking continued psychiatric treatment and advice or the helpful guidance of competent social workers in the critical early period of attempted rehabilitation many a patient, who under proper supervision, might have found adjustment in society, fails to do so and has to be returned to the hospital.

Conclusions

1. For the avoidance of doubt it is submitted that specific provision should be made by Irish legislation for extension of leave to be granted without the necessity of a patient's returning to hospital.

2. A Mental Health Tribunal should have power to recommend that leave be granted to a detained patient.

3. Section 26(1) of the Mental Health Act 2001 empowers the consultant psychiatrist responsible for the care and treatment of the patient who grants leave of absence to attach such conditions as he or she considers appropriate to the leave. If such conditions are not to prove anti-therapeutic the consent of the patient should be required in advance to their imposition. In addition as envisaged by the Government White Paper entitled "A New Mental Health Act" the Mental Health Tribunal should have power to review conditions attached to leave.[37]

4. It is submitted that to guard against arbitrary revocation of leave permission for a patient to be absent on trial or parole should not be withdrawn without affording a patient a hearing before a Mental Health Tribunal to contest evidence on which permission is withdrawn. In emergencies such a hearing should be afforded as soon as the emergency has passed.

5. Specific provision should be made by legislation for the power to recall a patient to cease upon his ceasing to be liable to be detained under the Act's provisions.[38]

---

[34] *Flick v. Noot* 3 M.D.L.R. 299 (D. Minn., July 6, 1979).
[35] *Cochenour v. Psychiatric Sec. Review Board* 615 P.2d. 1455 (Or. Ct. App. 1980).
[36] See *The Mentally Ill in America: A History of their Care and Treatment from Colonial Times* 438 (2nd ed., Columbia University Press, New York, 1949).
[37] See para.3.36.
[38] Brakel notes: "The general consensus is that it is neither necessary nor desirable to keep patients

6. Since the issue of the grant of leave to a patient is a discretionary matter the statutory provisions governing this and other issues such as the revocation of leave should be supplemented with a Code of Practice outlining the criteria to be taken into account and consultation procedures to be followed in either event.[39] Since both sides had notice of the criteria to be this would contribute to greater fairness and consistency in decision-making in the practitioner/patient relationship.

7. In the interests of the patient a specific duty should be imposed on the Health Service Executive and the Department of Social Welfare to provide aftercare to patients on leave of absence.

THE LAW RELATING TO TRANSFERS FROM ONE INSTITUTION TO ANOTHER

Transfers between public and private institutions

Position under Mental Treatment Act 1945

The Mental Treatment Act 1945 (which is still in force) provides that where chief executive officer of the Health Service Executive acting on the advice of the resident medical superintendent of the appropriate district mental hospital maintained by the board is of the opinion that it would be for the benefit of the health of a person detained in the district mental hospital or in any other institution maintained by the board, or that it is necessary for the purpose of that persons obtaining special treatment that he should be temporarily transferred to another district mental hospital in which he may be received in pursuance of an arrangement under section 206(1) of the 1945 Act, the chief executive officer may apply to the Minister for Health for an order directing and authorising the transfer and the Minister may if he thinks fit make the order and may at any time thereafter on the request of the chief executive officer acting as aforesaid by order direct and authorise the return of such person to the hospital or other institution from which he was transferred.[40] Subject to these provisions the Health Service Executive may make an arrangement for the purpose of carrying out these provisions.[41]

Under the 1945 Act, the chief executive officer of the Health Service Executive acting on the advice of the resident medical superintendent of the appropriate district mental hospital maintained by the board is empowered to transfer a person detained in such hospital to any other institution maintained by the board and to transfer a patient detained in any other institution (other than that hospital) maintained by the board to that hospital or to any other institution maintained by the board.[42]

Wide powers of transfer are conferred by the section 213 of the Mental Treatment

---

under the threat of reinstitutionalisation for indeterminate periods." See *The Mentally Disabled and the Law* (American Bar Foundation, 1985), p.206.

[39] In his *Guidelines on Good Practice and Quality Assurance in Mental Health Services*, the Inspector of Mental Hospitals provided guidelines for absence on trial and on parole under the 1945 Act.

[40] Mental Treatment Act 1945, s.206(1) as substituted by Mental Treatment Acts (Adaptation) Order 1971 (S.I. No.108 of 1971).

[41] Mental Treatment Act 1945, s.206(2).

[42] Mental Treatment Act 1945, s.205 as substituted by Mental Treatment Acts (Adaptation) Order 1971 (S.I. No.108 of 1971).

Act 1945 upon persons managing private institutions. A person carrying on a private institution may, with the consent of the Minister for Health transfer a person detained in an institution for the benefit of his health to any particular place for any particular period and may from time to time with the consent of the Minister change the place and extend the period.[43] The person carrying on a private institution may also apply to the Minister for an order authorising the transfer to another mental institution.[44] Before the Minister gives consent or makes an order he must obtain the approval in writing of the applicant for the reception order relating to the person whom it is proposed to transfer to the proposed transfer unless for due cause the Minister dispenses with the production of such approval.[45]

Position under Mental Health Act 2001

When the provisions of the Mental Health Act 2001 are brought into force provisions in relation to transfer from one district mental hospital to another; transfer from District Mental Health Hospital to another institution maintained by the Health Service Executive and transfer between private institutions will be replaced by one provision – section 21(1) of the Mental Health Act 2001 (enacted but not yet brought into force) which provides that where the clinical director[46] of an approved centre[47] is of the opinion that it would be for the benefit of a patient detained in that centre that he or she should be transferred to another approved centre the clinical director may arrange for the transfer of the patient to the other centre with the consent of the clinical director of that centre. Section 21(3) provides that where a patient is transferred to an approved centre under section 21 the clinical director of the centre from which he or she has been transferred must, as soon as may be, give notice to the Mental Health Commission. By virtue of section 21(4) the detention of a patient in another approved centre under section 21 will be deemed for the purposes of the Act to be detention in the centre from which he or she was transferred.

Commentary

Principles relating to transfer of patients in International law

Interestingly Principle 7 of the *UN Principles for the Protection of Persons with Mental*

---

[43] Mental Treatment Act 1945, s.213(1).

[44] *Ibid.*, s.213(2).

[45] *Ibid.*, s.213(3).

[46] By virtue of s.2 of the Act: "clinical director" means a person appointed under s.71. S.71 provides that the governing body of each approved centre shall appoint in writing a consultant psychiatrist to be the clinical director of the centre. S.71(2) provides that nothing in s.71 is to be construed as preventing a consultant psychiatrist from being the clinical director of more than one approved centre.

[47] "Approved centre" is defined by ss. 2 and 63. A "centre" means a hospital or other in-patient facility for the care and treatment of persons suffering from mental illness or mental disorder. See s.62 By virtue of s.63 a person may not carry on a centre unless the centre is registered in the Register of Approved Centres and a centre which is so registered is to be known and referred to in the Act as "an approved centre".

Illness and the Improvement of Mental Health Care provides that:

> "Where treatment takes place in a mental health facility a patient shall have the right whenever possible to be treated near his or her home or the home of his or her relatives or friends."[48]

This philosophy of treatment in the community is not reflected in Irish legislation although in practice it is favoured.[49]

Article 7 of Council of Europe Recommendation (83) 2 of the *Committee of Ministers to Member States concerning the Legal Protection of Persons Suffering from Mental Disorders Placed as Involuntary Patients* provides that:

> "A patient should not be transferred from one establishment to another unless his therapeutical interest and as far as possible his wishes are taken into account."

Although Recommendation No. R (83) 2 is cited in the appendix to the Government White Paper as one of the one of the international instruments to which it will have regard in the reform process reference is not made to the issue of transfers (other than transfers under section 207 of the 1945 Act) or to the transfer provisions of Recommendation No.R (83) 2 in the body of the White Paper and Irish legislation does not provide for consideration to be given to the wishes of the patient in the matter of transfers.

Comparative law

Principles relating to transfer of patients in US law The statutes of a majority of states in the United States in addition to specifying the criteria subject to which a transfer may take place provide the patient with an explicit right to object to transfer. The patient's right to object is usually statutorily expressed in the form of a right to a hearing, administrative or judicial or some less elaborate form of review.[50] Notice of the transfer decision is also generally required with the patient's guardian, his relatives or the committing court as the most common recipients of same.[51]

Conclusions

1. Section 21 of the Mental Health Act removes some of the bureaucracy from the process of transfer as the matter becomes one exclusively within the discretion of the clinical director of the relevant hospital without the involvement of the chief executive officer of the Health Service Executive or the Minister but with the requirement that the Commission be notified. However, there is no provision for the wishes of the patient to be taken into account in the matter of transfer; no right of the patient to object or for notice to be given to the important figures in the

---

[48] Adopted by the General Assembly, December 17, 1991.
[49] See Department of Health Report, *Planning for the Future* (1984) Pl 3001.
[50] *Ibid.*, ss.4805, 4700 *et seq.*
[51] See Colorado Rev. Statute Ann. (1973 & Supp. 1981), 27 10. 5–125(2).

patient's life. All these are required if the autonomy of the patient in the matter of transfer is to be respected.

2.   The right of the patient whenever possible to be treated near his or her home or the home of his or her relatives or friends might be built into a Code of Practice relating to the statutory power of transfer.

3.   A patient should also have a right to object to any transfer and a right to a hearing before a Mental Health Tribunal to revoke or modify any proposal to transfer.[52]

Transfer to the Central Mental Hospital

This matter is addressed in Chapter 7 – Mental Disability and the Criminal Law.[53]

Transfer of Patient requiring Treatment not Available Elsewhere to Central Mental Hospital

The transfer of a patient from a psychiatric hospital to the Central Mental Hospital involves a movement from a relatively unrestrictive to a more restrictive regime. As such there is a relative deprivation of liberty for the patient which warrants safeguards being put in place in the procedure for transfer to ensure that the person is not arbitrarily deprived of their relative liberties. The question is whether current law reflects the need to respect the patient's rights in this regard.

Position under Mental Treatment Act 1945

Section 208 of the Mental Treatment Act 1945[54] (which is still in force) provides that where the chief executive officer of the Health Service Executive, acting on the advice of the resident medical superintendent of a district mental hospital maintained by the board, is of the opinion that a person detained in a mental hospital or in any other institution maintained by the board requires treatment including surgical treatment which was not available except pursuant to section 208, the chief executive officer may direct and authorise the removal of the person concerned to any hospital or other place where treatment is obtainable. The person may then be received in that hospital or place in pursuance of an arrangement under the section between the Health Service Executive and the controlling authority of the hospital or other place where treatment is obtainable.[55] Similar powers may be exercised by the medical attendant of a person detained in a mental institution not maintained by the Health Service Executive, however in this event the receiving institution must agree to receive him.[56]

A person removed to a hospital under section 208 may be kept there for so long as

---

[52] See Connecticut General Statute Ann. (West 1975 & Supp. 1981), ss.17–193.

[53] See, *inter alia*, discussion of proposed s.13 of Criminal Law (Insanity) Bill 2002.

[54] as amended by the Mental Treatment Acts (Adaptation) Order 1971 (S.I. No. 108 of 1971), art.5 and Schedule.

[55] Mental Treatment Act, 1945, s.208(2).

[56] *Ibid.*, s.208(3).

[57] *Ibid.*, s.208(5).

was necessary for the purpose of his treatment and then must be taken back to the place from which he was removed unless it is certified by a registered medical practitioner that his detention is no longer necessary.[57]

In *Croke v. Smith*[58] it was held that the Central Mental Hospital was a "hospital" where treatment "not available" could be received and that a person could lawfully be detained there under section 208(5) for a long as was necessary for the purpose of his treatment. Accordingly in that case it was held that in principle it was possible for an authorisation to issue to transfer to the Central Mental Hospital a patient who had stabbed three nurses in an attempt to resist being brought back to a psychiatric hospital from which he had absconded. However it was also held that for the powers under section 208 to be exercised there had to be in existence a valid order authorising the applicant's continued detention. Accordingly where in this case the procedures for the extension of a temporary patient reception order had not been complied with under section 189 and consequently no valid order authorising the detention of the patient was in existence it was held that the patient was entitled to be released.

Position under the Mental Health Act 2001

Section 208 of the Mental Treatment Act 1945 is repealed by section 5 and the Schedule to the Mental Health Act 2001 (which have been enacted but are not yet in force.)

Section 21(2)(a) of the Mental Health Act 2001 (enacted but not yet brought into force) replaces section 208 and provides that where the clinical director of an approved centre (i) is of opinion that it would be for the benefit of a patient detained in that centre, *or that it is necessary for the purpose of obtaining special treatment for such a patient* to transfer him or her to the Central Mental Hospital and (ii) proposes to do so he or she shall notify the Mental Health Commission in writing of the proposal and the Commission shall refer the proposal to a Mental Health Tribunal.

Section 21(2)(b) provides that where a proposal is so referred to a tribunal the tribunal shall review the proposal as soon as may be but not later than 14 days thereafter and shall either (i) if it is satisfied that it is in the best interest of the health of the patient concerned authorise the transfer of the patient concerned and (ii) if it is not so satisfied, refuse to authorise it.

By virtue of Section 21(2)(c) the provisions of section 19 and 49 apply to the referral of a proposal to a tribunal under section 21 as they apply to the referral of an admission order to a tribunal under section 17 with any necessary modifications. Thus a patient has a right of appeal to the Circuit Court against a decision of a tribunal on the grounds that s/he was not suffering from a mental disorder and the powers of mental health tribunals set out in section 49 apply to the review by the tribunal.

Effect will not be given to a decision to which section 21(2)(b) applies before (i) the expiration of the time for the bringing of an appeal to the Circuit Court or (ii) if such an appeal is brought the determination or withdrawal thereof.

Section 21(3) provides that where a patient is transferred to an approved centre under section 21 the clinical director of the centre from which he is transferred shall, as

---

[58] [1994] 3 I.R. 529.

[59] S.62 defines a "centre" as a hospital or other in-patient facility for the care and treatment of persons

soon as may be give notice in writing of the transfer to the Commission. The Central Mental Hospital falls within the definition of "approved centre" in sections 62 and 63[59] of the Act.

Section 21(4) provides that the detention of a patient "in another approved centre" under section 21 shall be deemed for the purposes of the Act to be detention in the centre from which he or she is detained so that the provisions of the 2001 Act relating to renewals and review of detention on renewal of detention apply. Accordingly a patient may be detained for an initial period of 21 days within which time his detention must be reviewed. This initial period of 21 days may be extended by a renewal order made a consultant psychiatrist responsible for the care and treatment of the patient concerned for a further period not exceeding 3 months and on the expiration of that period further extended by the consultant psychiatrist by renewal order for a further period not exceeding 6 months and thereafter further extended by order made by the psychiatrist for periods each of which does not exceed 12 months. Each renewal must be reviewed by a Mental Health Tribunal.[60]

Commentary

In the US case of *Eubanks v. Clarke*[61] it was held that there can be no transfer of an involuntary patient from one mental facility to another that is more restrictive without according the patient a hearing. This requirement has been enacted Pennsylvania statutes[62] as well as those in Ohio[63] and South Carolina.[64]

It is submitted that a detained patient should be entitled to a hearing before the Mental Health Tribunal before a transfer to the more restrictive regime of the Central Mental Hospital is effected on the grounds that special treatment is required.

Power of patient or applicant for reception order to request transfer

Position under Mental Treatment Act 1945

The Mental Treatment Act 1945, which is still in force, provides that where a person who applies for the reception order under which a person is detained in a mental institution applies to the Minister for an order authorising the transfer of the person detained to another mental institution the Minister, if he so thinks fit, may by order authorise the transfer.[65]

The 1945 Act empowers the applicant for the reception order alone to request a transfer.

Position under Mental Health Act 2001

---

suffering from mental illness or mental disorder and s.63 defines an "approved centre" as a centre which is registered in accordance with the 2001 Act.
[60] See Mental Health Act 2001, ss.15–18.
[61] 454 F. Supp. 1022 (F.D. PA 1977).
[62] Pennsylvania Stat. Ann 50 Section 7306.
[63] Ohio Rev. Code Ann. Section 5122.20 (Baldwin 1982).
[64] South Carolina Code Ann Section 44-23 210(4) Law Co-0p 1976.
[65] Mental Treatment Act 1945, s.214.

When the Mental Health Act 2001 is brought fully into force this will be replaced by section 20(1) of the Mental Health Act 2001 (which has yet to come into force) which empowers a person who applied for a recommendation[66] or a patient detained in an approved centre[67] to apply to the clinical director[68] of the approved centre for a transfer of the patient to another approved centre. Where such an application is made the clinical director may, if he or she thinks fit arrange for the transfer of the patient to the centre with the consent of the clinical director of the second mentioned approved centre. Section 20(2) provides that where a patient is transferred to an approved centre under section 20(1) the clinical director of the centre from which he or she has been transferred must, as soon as may be give notice in writing of the transfer to the Commission.

A patient may be detained in an approved centre to which he or she has been transferred under section 20(1) until the date of the expiration of the admission order[69] pursuant to which he or she was detained in the centre from which he or she was transferred.[70] In addition the detention of a patient in another approved centre under the section shall be deemed for the purposes of the Act to be detention in the centre from which he or she was transferred.[71]

Commentary

1. Section 20(1) makes no reference to the criteria which the clinical director should bear in mind when deciding whether to accede to the request for transfer. It is submitted that legislation should make it a condition of any transfer of a patient from one institution to another that such a transfer be in the best interests of the patient. The patient's social and legal interests should be taken into account in addition to his medical interests in determining his best interests. Such interests might include his proximity at the receiving institution to family, friends, his lawyer (if he has one) and the institution's visitation and correspondence rules governing access to them. It is submitted that these concerns should be reflected in a Code of Practice governing transfers.

2. It is submitted that a patient should also have the right to object to any transfer

---

[66] Where a registered medical practitioner is satisfied following an examination of the person the subject of an application that the person is suffering from a mental disorder he or she must make "a recommendation" in a form specified by the Commission that the person be involuntarily admitted to an approved centre (other than the Central Mental Hospital) specified by him or her in the recommendation. See Mental Health Act 2001 ss.2, 10.

[67] "Approved centre" is defined by ss.2 and 63. A "centre" means a hospital or other in-patient facility for the care and treatment of persons suffering from mental illness or mental disorder. See s.62 By virtue of s.63 a person may not carry on a centre unless the centre is registered in the Register of Approved Centres and a centre which is so registered is to be known and referred to in the Act as "an approved centre".

[68] By virtue of s.2 of the Act "clinical director" means a person appointed under s.71. S.71 provides that the governing body of each approved centre shall appoint in writing a consultant psychiatrist to be the clinical director of the centre. S.71(2) provides that nothing in s.71 is to be construed as preventing a consultant psychiatrist from being the clinical director of more than one approved centre.

[69] By virtue of s.20(5) references to an admission order include references to a renewal order.

[70] Mental Health Act 2001, s.19(3).

[71] *Ibid.*, s.19(4).

effected at the request of an applicant for a recommendation and right to a hearing before a Mental Health Review Tribunal to revoke or modify any proposal to transfer.

3.   The patient should also have a right to appeal to a Mental Health Tribunal against a refusal of a transfer.

ABSCONDING AND ESCAPING

Absence without leave

Position under Mental Treatment Act 1945

The 1945 Act (which is still in force) provides that where a person detained in a mental institution escapes from an institution where s/he is being detained those entitled to retake a person who has escaped from the institution are the resident medical superintendent (or where the hospital was a private hospital, the person in charge of the hospital), the medical officers and the other officers and servants of the hospital and where the person was detained under an eligible patient reception order a representative of the Health Service Executive maintaining the relevant district mental hospital.[72] A member of the Garda Síochána may also retake a person detained under a reception order who escaped not later than 28 days after his escape and may bring that person back to the place from which he escaped. However, a person detained as a temporary patient may not be retaken or brought back after the expiry of six months from the date of making of the reception order or where the order was extended after the period of extension of the order under section 189.[73]

The 1945 Act also contains provisions dealing with the situation where a person fails to return when absent on trial or parole. It provides that where a person permitted to be absent from a mental institution on trial does not return on the expiration of the period or extended period during which he is permitted to be absent and no certificate from a registered medical practitioner certifying that his detention is no longer necessary was furnished to the person in charge of the relevant mental institution the person may be retaken at any time within twenty eight days after the expiration of such period or extended period in the same manner as if he had escaped from such institution.[74]

Further under the 1945 Act where a person absent on parole does not return on the expiration of the period during which he was permitted to be absent he may at any time within twenty eight days after the expiration of such period be retaken in like manner as if he had escaped from the institution.[75]

Where a person is absent under these provisions those entitled to apprehend him/her and retake him/her are the medical officers and the other officers and servants of the hospital and any member of the Garda Síochána.

The provisions of the Mental Treatment Act 1945 which thus deals with absconding and escaping from a psychiatric hospital set out the bare powers and formalities to be

---

[72] Mental Treatment Act 1945, ss.172(2), 181(2) and 186(2).

[73] *Ibid.*, s.229(2).

[74] *Ibid.*, s.203.

[75] *Ibid.*, s.204(3).

observed in order to effect the return to hospital of a patient who has absconded or escaped. Little consideration is given to the criteria for the exercise of powers and the fact that the powers are being applied in respect of a person who is ill and not a law breaker *simpliciter.*

Position under Mental Health Act 2001

Section 27 of the Mental Health Act 2001 (which has yet to come into force) provides that where a patient[76] in respect of whom an admission order,[77] a renewal order[78] or an order under section 25 (order of the District Court authorising involuntary admission of child) is in force: (a) leaves an approved centre without permission to be absent granted by a consultant psychiatrist; (b) fails to return to the approved centre in accordance with any direction given under section 26 (absence with leave) or on the expiration of the period for which absence or leave was permitted under that section or (c) fails in the opinion of the consultant psychiatrist responsible for the care and treatment of the patient to comply with any condition specified in section 26 the clinical director of the approved centre concerned may arrange for members of the staff of the centre to bring the patient back to the approved centre or, if they are unable to do so and the clinical director is of the opinion that there is a serious likelihood of the person concerned causing immediate and serious harm to himself or herself or to other persons the clinical director or a consultant psychiatrist acting on his or her behalf may, if necessary, request the Garda Síochána to assist the members of staff of the approved centre in the removal by the staff of the person to that centre and the Garda Síochána shall comply with any such request.

Section 27(2) provides that a member of the Garda Síochána may for the purposes of section 27 (a) enter if need be by force any dwelling or other premises where he or she has reasonable cause to believe that the patient may be and (b) take all reasonable measures necessary for the return of the patient to the approved centre including where necessary the detention and restraint of the patient.

Commentary

In England and Wales, a person who escapes from legal custody can be retaken by the

---

[76] "Patient" is defined by ss.2 and 14 as a person to whom an admission order relates. By virtue of s.27(3) "patient" includes a child in respect of whom an order under s.25 is in force.

[77] "Admission order" is according to s.2 of the Act to be construed in accordance with s.14. S.14 provides that where a recommendation in relation to a person the subject of an application is received by the clinical director of an approved centre a consultant psychiatrist on the staff of the approved centre shall, as soon as may be, carry out an examination of the person and shall thereupon either (a) if he or she is satisfied that the person is suffering from a mental disorder make an order to be known as an involuntary admission order and referred to in this Act as "an admission order" in a form specified by the Commission for the reception, detention and treatment of the person.

[78] According to s.2 "renewal order" is to be construed in accordance with s.15. S.15 provides that an admission order shall authorised the reception, detention and treatment of the patient concerned and shall remain in force for a period of 21 days from the date of making the order. This period may be extended by order (to be known as "a renewal order") made by the consultant psychiatrist responsible for the care and treatment of the patient concerned.

person from whom he escaped or by any police officer or by any approved social worker. If he has already been compulsorily admitted to hospital he can also be retaken by someone on the staff of or authorised by that hospital.[79] Those who take or detain such people have all the "powers, authorities, protection and privileges" of a constable for the purpose.[80] However, the wide remit of such powers is qualified by the fact that even constables must use only such force as is reasonably necessary to achieve their lawful object. In England and Wales, the *Mental Health Act Code of Practice* provides that:

> "it is the responsibility of the Hospital Managers and of the local Social Services Authority where guardianship is concerned to ensure that there is a clear written policy in relation to the action to be taken when a detained patient or a patient subject to a guardianship goes absent without leave. All staff should be familiar with this policy. "[81]

It is recommended that the guidance provided in the policy include the circumstances when the police should be informed and that this should be the subject of agreed local arrangements with the police. Where police assistance is concerned the Code states:

> "The police should be asked to assist in returning a patient to hospital only if necessary, but they should always be informed immediately of the absence without leave of a patient who is considered to be vulnerable dangerous or who is subject to restrictions under Part III of the [1983] Act. There may be other cases where, although the help of the police is not needed, a patient's history makes it desirable to inform them that he or she is absent without leave in the area. Whenever the police are asked for help in returning a patient they must be informed of the time limit for taking him or her into custody."[82]

Conclusions

1. It is submitted that hospitals should have a clear written policy in relation to the action to be taken when a detained patient goes absent without leave or fails to return when absent on leave.

2. Where powers are conferred on medical, nursing and Health Service Executive staff to retake a patient it is desirable that the limits of the powers of such persons in the retaking of a patient should be clearly defined in legislation and should be confined to using such force as is reasonably necessary in retaking a patient absent without leave.

3. In recognition of the fact that they may be dealing with a person who is ill Gardaí should be accompanied by a member of the clinical team responsible for the patient when entering a dwelling or other where s/he has reasonable cause to believe that

---

[79] Mental Health Act 1983, s.138(1).

[80] *Ibid.*, s.137(2).

[81] Para.21.5.

[82] Para.21.6(d).

the patient may be to retake that person. Such a provision was envisaged by the Government White Paper.[83]

Patients unlawfully at large

See the discussion of proposed section 13 of the Criminal Law (Insanity) Bill in Chapter 7 – Mental Disability and the Criminal Law.

Abetting absence without leave

Position under Mental Treatment Act 1945

The Mental Treatment Act 1945 (which is still in force) provides that it is an offence for a person to induce or assist the escape or attempted escape of a patient in mental institution.[84] It is also an offence to induce or assist a patient who is absent on trial or parole from a mental institution to escape or leave the place where he is maintained while absent on trial or parole.[85] It is further an offence to induce or assist a patient who has been removed for treatment or for the benefit of his health from a mental institution or has been boarded out by a mental hospital authority to escape or leave the place where he is under treatment or where he is for the benefit of his health or while boarded out.[86] It is also an offence to harbour or conceal a patient who had so escaped.[87]

Position under Mental Health Act 2001

There are no provisions relating to aiding and abetting escapte in the Mental Health Act 2001. When brought fully into force the Mental Health Act 2001 will repeal the provisions of the 1945 Act relating to aiding and abetting escape.

Commentary

In England and Wales, it is an offence punishable with up to two years imprisonment to "induce or *knowingly* assist" any compulsory patient to absent himself without leave or to escape from legal custody or *knowingly* to harbour one who has escaped *or to give him help in order to prevent or hinder his recapture.*[88]

In *R v. Soul*, it was held that it can also be a conspiracy to commit a common law public nuisance to bring in such things as rope, hacksaw, glass cutters and other tools to help a "homicidal lunatic" escape from Broadmoor.

Conclusions

1. The offence of aiding and abetting the absence without leave of a patient should be

---

[83] Para.3.39.
[84] Mental Treatment Act 1945, s.251(b).
[85] *Ibid.*, s.251(c).
[86] *Ibid.*, s.251(c)(ii), (iii).
[87] *Ibid.*, s.251(d).
[88] *Ibid.*, s.128.

retained as it is in the best interests of a person with mental illness to obtain treatment and not in his/her interests to go without.

2. The defence of lack of knowledge should be available to persons charged with abetting the absence without leave of a patient subject to powers of detention or of concealing such a person.

DISCHARGE

"Voluntary" Patients

Position under Mental Treatment Act 1945

The Mental Treatment Act 1945 (still in force) provides that where a voluntary patient over the age of sixteen years wishes to leave the institution s/he is required to give written notice to the person in charge of the institution that s/he wishes to leave the institution not earlier than seventy two hours from the giving of the notice. Upon the giving of such notice the 1945 Act provides that the patient "shall be entitled and allowed to leave the institution on or at any time after the expiration of the 72 hours."[89] Where the patient is under the age of sixteen the parent or guardian of the person could give 72 hours notice of their wish to remove the patient from the institution.[90]

Where a voluntary patient who is being treated in an approved institution becomes mentally incapable of expressing himself as willing or not willing to remain in the institution he must be discharged into the custody of whatever person the person in charge of the institution approves of not later than twenty eight days after becoming so incapable unless he becomes capable of expressing himself/herself before then or a reception order is obtained in respect of him/her.[91]

Construing section 194 in the light of the of Act as a whole, the Supreme Court in *Gooden v. Waterford Regional Hospital*[92] held that there was an implied power to make a reception order under section 184 detaining a person who sought to leave an institution contrary to his/her own medical interests.

Position under Mental Health Act 2001

The Government White Paper on Mental Health (1995) proposed that the seventy two hour notice rule be removed and that in its place new powers be conferred on nursing and medical staff to refuse to permit voluntary patients to leave where they had been admitted initially with their consent but who became so disturbed as to meet the criteria for detention. Sections 23 and 24 of the Mental Health Act 2001 (enacted but not yet in

---

[89] Mental Treatment Act 1945, s.194. It appears that in practice the seventy two hour notice requirement is not commonly observed. See Cooney, "Psychiatric Detainees and the Human Rights Challenge to Psychiatry and law: Where do we go from here?" in Liz Heffernan (ed.), *Human Rights A European Perspective* (Round Hall Press in association with the Irish Centre for European Law 1994).
[90] Mental Treatment Act 1945, s.194(2).
[91] *Ibid.*, s.195.
[92] Unreported, Supreme Court, February 21, 2001.

force) provide for such powers. Their terms and the Supreme Court's construction of section 194 are discussed in Chapter 3, Primary Care and Admission to Hospital.

Commentary on discharge of voluntary patients

It is submitted that voluntary patients be made aware of their rights including the existence of the holding power before admission to hospital.

On expiry of certificate

Current Irish law

Irish legislation does not provide expressly that authority to detain a patient ceases on the expiry of the certificate authorising his detention. The effect of the absence of such a provision and of any duty on the part of medical personnel to inform the patient of the change in status is that many patients may mistakenly assume that they remain subject to compulsory powers.

Commentary

In some Canadian provinces legislation provides that on the expiry of the certificate detaining him/her the patient is deemed to be a voluntary patient. The province of Alberta is alone in requiring that the patient be informed of this change in status.[93] Without such a requirement it is submitted that it is unreasonable to assume that a patient's continued stay in the facility is voluntary in nature. The patient may be unaware of the expiry of the certificate and of his right to be discharged on request.

Conclusions

It is submitted that Irish legislation should provide expressly that authority to detain a patient ceases on the expiry of the certificate detaining him and for the patient be informed of this change of status at the moment of its expiry.

On direction of person financing care or relative

Position under Mental Treatment Act 1945

The Mental Treatment Act 1945, which is still in force, provides that a person who is detained as a private patient in an institution must be discharged on the written direction of the person by whom the last payment on account of the person detained is made. Where that person is not available the direction as to discharge may be given by a spouse if available or if not by a parent or if a parent is not available by the nearest of

---

[93] R.S.A. 1980 c. M–13 s.14(6). See also Saskatchewan 1984–85–86. C. M–13.1, s.31(1) and Manitoba's Mental Health Act (Act 59, first reading June 5, 1987).

[94] Mental Treatment Act 1945, s.215.

[95] *Ibid.*, s.215(3).

376 Irish Mental Health Law

kin of the person detained.[94] A person who is detained in a district mental hospital or other institution maintained by the Health Service Executive may not be discharged except with the approval of the resident medical superintendent.[95]

Position under Mental Health Act 2001

There is no reference in the Mental Health Act 2001 to the power of person financing the care of a patient or a relative to apply for discharge. Sole power of discharge appears to be vested under section 28 in the consultant psychiatrist responsible for the care and treatment of a patient.

Commentary

In England and Wales the nearest relative of a patient may discharge a patient admitted for treatment or for assessment under civil powers.[96] To effect a discharge the relative must serve an order on the managers.[97] The relative is entitled to instruct an independent doctor to visit the patient at any reasonable time, examine him in private and inspect the records relating to his detention and treatment in order to advise on a possible discharge. This may be advisable because the nearest relative must always give the hospital at least 72 hours prior notice of his intention to seek the patient's discharge. During the period of 72 hours the responsible medical officer is empowered to report to the managers that the patient, if discharged, "would be likely to act in a manner dangerous to other persons or to himself." This prevents the nearest relative from discharging him at that point in time and also for the next six months.[98]

The patient's nearest relative must be informed where the patient is detained for treatment. That relative may then apply to a Mental Health Review Tribunal and has 28 days from the date of detention within which to do so. The tribunal must allow the discharge if they are satisfied that the patient is not dangerous. If the patient is detained for assessment there is nothing a relative can do except wait for it to expire and object to any admission for treatment.

A relative may be replaced by the court if s/he proposes to discharge the patient without due regard for the patient's welfare or the interests of the public.[99]

Conclusions

1. It is submitted that a relative should retain the right to apply for the discharge of a patient subject to the approval of the consultant psychiatrist responsible for the care and treatment of the patient. The relative applying for discharge of a patient should also be entitled to instruct an independent medical practitioner to visit the patient,

---

[96] Mental Health Act 1983, s.23(2).
[97] Mental Health Act (Hospital, Guardianship and Consent to Treatment) Regulations 1983, reg.15(1).
[98] Mental Health Act 1983, s.25(1).
[99] *Ibid.*, s.29(3)(d). This will not be necessary where the responsible medical officer can bar discharge but it may occasionally be useful for patients under guardianship where the responsible medical officer has no such power.

examine him in private and inspect the records relating to his detention and treatment in order to obtain an independent view on a possible discharge.

2. In addition it is in a patient's interests that his/her relative have a right to apply to the Mental Health Tribunal for the discharge of a detained patient.

Where a detained person wishes to be received as a voluntary patient

Position under Mental Treatment Act 1945

Under the Mental Treatment Act 1945 Act (which is still in force) where a person detained under a reception order in an institution maintained by the Health Service Executive becomes capable of and expresses a desire to be received as a voluntary patient in an approved institution,[100] and both the chief executive officer of the Health Service Executive and the resident medical superintendent approve of that course and the necessary steps for adopting it are taken[101] then the person detained must be discharged from institution where s/he is detained for the purpose of being received as a voluntary patient in an approved institution.[102] Similar provisions apply to persons detained in private institutions.[103] However, in that case both the person in charge of the institution and the chief medical officer of the institution[104] must approve of the course being taken.[105]

Position under Mental Health Act 2001

By virtue of section 16 of the Mental Health Act 2001 (which has yet to be brought into force) where a consultant psychiatrist makes an admission order or a renewal order he must not later than 24 hours thereafter, inter alia, give notice in writing of the making of the order to the patient. This notice must include a statement in writing to the effect that the patient may be admitted to the approved centre as a voluntary patient if he or she indicates a wish to be so admitted.[106]

In addition, section 29 provides that: "Nothing in this Act shall be construed as preventing a person who is suffering from a mental disorder … from remaining on in an approved centre after he or she has ceased to be so liable to be detained."

Commentary

It is submitted that in addition to being informed of the option to convert to voluntary status the right of the patient to convert from detained to voluntary status should be

---

[100] Under s.158 of the Act the Minister may by order approve of any institution or premises as an institution or premises for the reception of persons as temporary and/or voluntary patients.

[101] Mental Treatment Act 1945, Pt XV.

[102] *Ibid.*, s.216 (1).

[103] *Ibid.*, s.216(3).

[104] Where the institution consists of one person only the reference to the chief medical officer is to be construed as a reference to the medical attendant of that person. S.216(4).

[105] Mental Treatment Act 1945, s.216(3)(b).

[106] Mental Health Act 2001 s.16(2)(g).

contained in the body of the Act. Conversion to voluntary status means that the patient will share in the decision making process regarding his/her treatment. This has a therapeutic value as it tends by recognition of the person's autonomy to bring a degree of personal commitment on the part of the patient towards achieving a successful treatment outcome which is not present when the patient is coerced into following a course of treatment.[107]

Discharge where consultant psychiatrist responsible for the care and treatment of the patient becomes of opinion that the patient is no longer suffering from a mental disorder

Position under Mental Treatment Act 1945

Under the Mental Treatment Act 1945 discharge at the instigation of the person in charge of the institution depends upon the clinical judgment of that person that the patient has "recovered." Thus where a person in charge of an institution maintained by the Health Service Executive is satisfied that a person detained therein as an eligible patient has recovered he was obliged to give notice to that effect to whichever relative of the person concerned as he thinks proper. Notice could only be given with the approval of the resident medical superintendent[108] and must contain an indication that unless the person detained is removed from the institution before a date after the expiry of seven days of the date on which notice is given he will be discharged. [109] If the person concerned is not removed before that date he had to be discharged. On removal or discharge the authority may, if they think proper, pay him such sum as they consider reasonable towards his travelling expenses on his journey to his home.[110]

Where a person to be discharged pursuant to these provisions has no relatives to whom notice may be given then subject to the approval of the resident medical superintendent he must nevertheless be discharged and the authority may, if they think proper, pay him or in respect of him such sum as they considered reasonable towards his travelling expenses on his journey to his home.[111]

Similar provisions apply to person detained as private patients in institutions maintained by the Health Service Executive,[112] or in private institutions.[113] In the former case notice must be given by the person in charge of the institution[114] and in the latter the chief medical officer of the institution must be satisfied that the person has recovered before the person in charge gives notice.[115] In both cases notice must be given to the person by whom the last payment on account of the person detained was made.[116]

---

[107] See Bandura, *Social Foundations of Thought and Action: A Social Cognitive Theory* (Englewood Cliffs, Prentice Hall, New Jersey, 1986).
[108] Mental Treatment Act 1945, s.218(3) as amended by Mental Treatment Act 1961, s.28.
[109] *Ibid.*, s.218(1).
[110] *Ibid.*, s.218(4).
[111] *Ibid.*, s.219(3).
[112] *Ibid.*, s.217(1)(a) as amended by Mental Treatment Act 1961, s.27.
[113] *Ibid.*, s.217(1)(b) as amended by Mental Treatment Act 1961, s.27.
[114] *Ibid.*, s.217(1)(a) as amended by Mental Treatment Act 1961, s.27.
[115] *Ibid.*, s.217(1)(b) as amended by Mental Treatment Act 1961, s.27.
[116] *Ibid.*, s.217 as amended by Mental Treatment Act 1961, s.27.

In 1996 in the case *Healy v. North Western Health Board*,[117] the High Court in effect found that there is a common law duty of care placed on those taking discharge decisions. In that case Flood J. held the defendants liable in negligence to the daughter of a former patient at a psychiatric hospital operated by the health board who had committed suicide within four days of discharge for failing to carry out a pre discharge mental assessment in relation to the deceased and to ascertain that the deceased was in a firm remission before discharge.

The Inspector of Mental Hospitals' *Guidelines on Good Practice and Quality Assurance in Mental Health Services,* issued in 1998, refer to the importance of good discharge planning and aftercare services in place and it is submitted that insofar as they recommend good practices for discharge:

"It is essential that well planned discharge policies and procedures are in place. Most patients are able to return home with little or no support, while others will require a package of care to support them and some patients with complex care needs may require continuing care from the Community Mental Health Service which may include supported housing accommodation. A clear discharge plan designed for the safe discharge of the patient should be in place. This will include documentation and a pre-discharge checklist to ensure all appropriate information is given and all appropriate services are arranged prior to the patient's actual discharge.

Immediately following discharge, a discharge summary should be sent to the general practitioner and to the members of the psychiatric services providing aftercare, setting out the principal details of the patient's management and treatment while in hospital, including medication on discharge and whether and for how long it is to be continued. The patient too should be supplied with a standard information form giving information on the drugs prescribed, the name of his or her general practitioner and the telephone number of the mental health centre or service where staff can be contacted and a domiciliary visit or other intervention be carried out in case of an emergency. The type of aftercare planned for the patient should be discussed with the patient taking into account the patient's diagnosis, needs, physical and emotional and personal preferences. Arrangements must be made for the first review of the patient post discharge. An aftercare plan for the patient should be recorded in detail in the patient's care file and available to each member of the professional team responsible for the patient. The discharge plan should be drawn up by the patient's treating consultant psychiatrist and should fully consider and provide for the immediate and long term needs of the patient and include an assessment of the risk of the patient harming himself and others. Aftercare should be properly co-ordinated and supervised under the general direction of the patient's treating consultant psychiatrist. A mechanism should be in place to review patients who have been lost to follow up and everything possible done to find out what has happened to the patient and to take appropriate action."[118]

---

[117] Unreported, High Court, January 31, 1996.
[118] Para.4.8.

Position under Mental Health Act 2001

Section 28(1) of the Mental Health Act 2001 (which has yet to come into force) deals exclusively with the situation where it is proposed to discharge a patient who is detained under the terms of the Act and provides by way of a more formal procedure than that under the 1945 Act that where the consultant psychiatrist responsible for the care and treatment of a patient becomes of the opinion that the patient is no longer suffering from a mental disorder he or she shall by order in a form specified by the Mental Health Commission revoke the relevant admission order or renewal order as the case may be and discharge the patient.

Section 28(2) provides that in deciding whether and when to discharge a patient under section 28 the consultant psychiatrist responsible for his or her care and treatment must have regard to the need to ensure (a) that the patient is not inappropriately discharged and (b) that the patient is detained pursuant to an admission order or a renewal order only for so long as is reasonably necessary for his or her proper care and treatment. Section 28(3) provides that on such discharge the consultant psychiatrist must give the patient concerned and his legal representative[119] a notice in a form specified by the Commission to the effect (a) that he or she is being discharged pursuant to section 28; (b) that he or she is entitled to have his or her detention reviewed by a tribunal in accordance with the provisions of section 18 or where such review has commenced, completed in accordance with that section if he or she so indicates by notice in writing addressed to the Commission within 14 days of the date of his or her discharge.[120]

Where the consultant psychiatrist discharges a patient under this section he or she must cause copies of the discharge order made under section 28(1) and the notice to the patient referred to in subsection (2) to be given to the Mental Health Commission and, where appropriate, the the Health Service Executive and housing authority.[121]

Where a patient is discharged under section 28 then (a) if a review under section 18 has then commenced it must be discontinued unless the patient requests by notice in writing addressed to the Commission within 14 days of his or her discharge that it be completed, or (b) if such a review has then not commenced it must not be held unless the patient indicates by notice in writing addressed to the Commission within 14 days of his or her discharge that he or she wishes such a review to be held. If the patient requests that a review under section 18 be completed or held the provisions of sections 17 to 19 shall apply in relation to any review with any necessary modifications. This in effect means that the Mental Health Commission will assign a legal representative to the patient unless he or she proposes to engage one; will direct in writing a member of the panel of psychiatrists to examine the patient, interview the consultant psychiatrist responsible for the care and treatment of the patient and review the records relating to the patient in order to determine in the interest of the patient whether the patient is suffering from a mental disorder. The member of the panel of psychiatrists so appointed must report in writing within 14 days on the results of the examination, interview and review to the tribunal; the tribunal must conduct a review of the admission order or renewal order and the patient has a right of appeal to the Circuit Court against a decision

---

[119] According to s.2 of the Act this means a barrister or a solicitor.
[120] Mental Health Act 2001, s.28(3).
[121] *Ibid.*, s.28(4).

of the tribunal to affirm a renewal order made in respect of him or her on the grounds that he or she is not suffering from a mental disorder.[122]

It should also be noted that following the coming into force of the European Convention on Human Rights Act 2003 the consultant's powers of discharge under both under the 1945 Act and when brought into force under section 28 of the Mental Health Act 2001 must be exercised consistently with the requirements of the European Convention on Human Rights. Following the decision of the European Court of Human Rights in *Winterwerp v. the Netherlands*[123] continued detention of a patient is justified under Article 5(1) of the Convention only so long as the person detained remains of unsound mind. In *Johnson v. UK*,[124] the court held that an unreasonable delay in discharging a person whose mental state no longer warrants detention will breach Article 5(1). The delay will be unreasonable where there is no good reason for it.[125] However, the court held that discharge need not be immediate if time is required, for example, to organise aftercare – thereby accepting that factors other than the patient's soundness of mind are relevant to the discharge decision.

Commentary from the perspective of international and comparative law

International principles favour discharge of patients at the earliest possible opportunity. Thus Principle 7.2 of the *UN Principles for the Protection of Persons with Mental Illness and the Improvement of Mental Health Care* provides that:

> "where treatment takes place in a mental health facility, a patient shall have the right ... to return to the community as soon as possible."

Article 8 of *Council of Europe Recommendation No.R (83)2 of the Committee of Ministers to member states concerning the legal protection of persons suffering from mental disorders placed as involuntary patients*[126] provides that:

> "a placement[127] should be for a limited period or, at least the necessity for placement should be examined at regular intervals...".

In New South Wales the medical superintendent of a hospital is required to medically examine or cause to be medically examined at such intervals as may be prescribed each

---

[122] The onus on the patient to prove that s/he is not suffering from mental disorder in order to secure discharge has been held to infringe the provisions of Art.5(1) and Art.5(4) of the European Convention on Human Rights in *R (H) v. London North and East Region Mental Health Review Tribunal (Secretary of State for Health intervening)* [2002] Q.B. 1 In that case the English Court of Appeal held that Arts 5(1) and 5(4) require the Mental Health Review Tribunal to be positively satisfied that the patient is suffering from a mental disorder (and that the other criteria for detention are satisfied) before refusing a patient's discharge.

[123] [1979] 2 E.H.R.R. 387.

[124] [1997] 29 E.H.R.R. 296.

[125] *Ibid.*, para.71.

[126] Adopted by the Committee of Ministers on February 22, 1983.

[127] "Placement" in this context refers to "involuntary placement." See Art.1.2.

continued treatment patient for the purpose of determining whether or not the patient's continued detention in the hospital is necessary.[128]

Brakel observes that in 1969, US statutes regulating discharge spoke mainly in terms of the patients "recovery, improvement or lack of improvement" but notes that the "modern criteria tend to be more specific and more legalistic."[129] Some refer to the fact of the patient no longer meeting the commitment criteria (21 jurisdictions). Others provide for the criterion of no longer being dangerous to oneself or others (18 jurisdictions); the patient no longer requires treatment (19 states) and is no longer mentally ill (13 states).

Conclusions

1. It is submitted that the treating consultant psychiatrist should have a duty periodically to examine whether a detained patient's continued detention in hospital is warranted.

2. A degree of consistency between admission and discharge criteria is desirable when it comes to setting the criteria for discharge and it is submitted that it should be made clear[130] in legislation that a patient should be entitled to discharge when s/he on objective grounds no longer meets the criteria for commitment.[131] This is consistent with modern trends towards greater specificity in the criteria for discharge and also with international standards which favour discharge at the earliest possible opportunity.

3. The power of the consultant psychiatrist under the Mental Health Act 2001 to discharge without reference to the person in charge of the institution is to be welcomed.

On the application of a relative or friend[132]

Position under the Mental Treatment Act 1945

The Mental Health Act 1945 (which is still in force) provides that any relative or friend of a person detained as a chargeable patient in a district mental hospital or other institution maintained by a mental hospital authority may apply to the person in charge of the institution to allow him to take care of the person detained.[133] Where such an application is made, then, subject to the approval of the resident medical superintendent,[134] the

---

[128] Mental Health Act 1990 (NSW), s.61.

[129] See *The Mentally Disabled and the Law, op. cit.*, p.210.

[130] The definition of "mental disorder" in s.3 of the Mental Health Act 2001 incorporates the criteria for committal. It is submitted that this is unsatisfactory and confusing and the committal criteria should be stipulated separately from the definition of a medical condition.

[131] See discussion of White Paper criteria for involuntary admission in Chap.3.

[132] Historically this ground has its origins in s.10 of 30 & 31 Vic. c.118 which empowered a relative or friend to take out an inmate on entering into a bond 'for his or her peaceable behaviour or safe custody" before two justices.

[133] Mental Treatment Act 1945, s.220(1).

[134] Mental Treatment Act 1945, s.220(2). In *In re O'Reilly* (1894) 29 Irish Law Times Reports 33, the Court of Appeal held that an asylum superintendent had a discretion at common law to decide whether a lunatic on whose behalf a recognisance had been entered into should be discharged or not.

person in charge of the institution may, if he thinks fit and if satisfied that the person detained would be properly taken care of discharge the person detained.[135]

Position under the Mental Health Act 2001

There is no provision in the Mental Health Act 2001 entitling a relative or friend to apply to be allowed to take care of a person obtained. When brought fully into force the Mental Health Act 2001 will repeal the 1945 Act provisions in this regard.

Commentary from a comparative law perspective

In New South Wales a relative or friend of a temporary patient or a continued treatment patient may, at any time, apply orally or in writing to the medical superintendent for the discharge of the patient. On receiving the application the medical superintendent may discharge the patient, (a) if the relative or friend gives the medical superintendent an undertaking in writing that the patient will be properly taken care of and (b) if the medical superintendent is satisfied that adequate measures will, so far as is reasonably practicable, be taken to prevent the patient from causing harm to himself or herself or others.[136]

Conclusions

1. The power of a relative or friend to apply for the discharge of a patient should be retained as a necessary safeguard against continued unwarranted detention. In addition a relative or friend of a patient should be entitled to instruct an independent medical practitioner to visit the patient, examine him in private and inspect the records relating to his detention and treatment in order to obtain an independent view on a possible discharge into their care.

2. In addition it is submitted that it is in the patient's interests that the relative or friend should have a right to apply to a Mental Health Tribunal for the discharge of the detained patient.

The former power of discharge of the Minister for Health and Children and the present powers of the Mental Health Tribunal

Position under the Mental Treatment Act 1945

The Mental Treatment Act 1945 (which is still in force) empowers any person to apply to the Minister for Health and Children for an order for the examination by two medical practitioners of a detained patient and the Minister may, if he or she thinks fit grant such an order.[137] The effect of the order is to permit the practitioners to examine a patient at the institution on at least two occasions at least seven days intervening between the first

---

[135] Mental Treatment Act 1945, s.220(1).
[136] Mental Health Act 1990 (NSW), s.68.
[137] Mental Treatment Act 1945, s.222.

and second occasion.[138] If the practitioners certify that such person may be discharged without risk of injury to himself the Minister could, if he thinks fit direct the discharge of the patient.

Position under the Mental Health Act 2001

When the Mental Health Act 2001 is brought fully into force the power of the Minister for Health and Children to order medical examinations of a detained patient will be repealed and replaced by a system of automatic review by a Mental Health Tribunal. As part of that automatic review a member of a panel of consultant psychiatrists will be instructed by the Mental Health Commission to examine the patient, interview the consultant psychiatrist responsible for the care and treatment of the patient and review the records relating to the patient in order to determine in the interest of the patient whether the patient is suffering from a mental disorder and report in writing on the results of the examination, interview and review to a Mental Health Tribunal. The tribunal, (a) will affirm the admission or renewal order if satisfied that the patient is suffering from a mental disorder and that the provisions of the Act relating to the procedures for detention have been complied with or if there has been a failure to comply with any such provision the failure does not affect the substance of the order and does not cause an injustice or (b) will revoke the admission or renewal order and direct that the patient be discharge from the approved centre concerned if not satisfied in accordance with (a).

Commentary

The efficacy of the system of automatic review under the Mental Health Act 2001 and the answer to the question as to whether it is preferable to a system where a third party instigates a medical examination of a detained patient will depend on the degree of independent judgment brought to bear on the patient's situation. It is therefore important that the composition of the Mental Health Commission and Mental Health Tribunal be shown to be free from the appearance of bias. At present the Minister for Health and Children who is ultimately accountable for the health services is responsible for the appointment of the members of the Commission and the Commission is obliged to appoint members of the mental health tribunal. A system of automatic review which defers to Ministerial patronage may be unlikely to be zealous in upholding patient rights if it means political embarrassment. In such circumstances a system where an independent third party may apply to a tribunal for review of a patient's detention while not dealing directly with the problem in issue may be a useful addition to powers. At least it would mean that an application for judicial review could be made if the tribunal unreasonably refused to act.

---

[138] It is a criminal offence for a person carrying on an institution to contravene whether by act or omission the obligations imposed upon him by s.222(2). See s.249 and sch.5.

Refusal of discharge

Position under the Mental Treatment Act 1945

The Mental Treatment Act 1945 provides that where the resident medical superintendent of an institution maintained by the Health Service Executive or in any other case his medical attendant gives a written certificate containing a statement of the grounds therefor that a person is dangerous or otherwise unfit to be discharged the person detained may not be discharged unless the Minister for Health so directs.[139]

Where a certificate is given notice in writing of objection may be given to the Minister for Health by or on behalf of the person to whom it relates.[140] On receipt of that notice, the Minister may, by notice in writing require the person in charge of the relevant mental institution to give him/her a copy of the certificate which must be provided forthwith.[141] On receipt of the copy of the certificate the Minister may require the Inspector of Mental Hospitals to examine the person concerned.[142] After consideration of the report of the Inspector of Mental Hospitals on his examination and provided no more than fourteen days has elapsed since s/he received the copy certificate the Minister may, if he so thinks fit by order direct the discharge of the person to whom the certificate relates.[143]

Position under the Mental Health Act 2001

When brought fully into force the Mental Health Act 2001 will repeal section 221 of the Mental Treatment Act 1945 and will not replace it with an equivalent provision then the question will arise. Since the enactment of the Mental Health Act the question arises as to what rights of appeal a person will have where the clinical director of a hospital or a consultant psychiatrist refuses to discharge a patient. The question will be doubly vexing since it is not clear in the light of the establishment of Mental Health Tribunals that the Inspector of Mental Health Services will retain his role in examining and reporting upon the condition of detained patients.

Conclusions

1. A person applying for discharge of a detained patient and/or the patient himself/herself should have a right of appeal to an independent Mental Health Tribunal against a refusal of discharge by the clinical director of a psychiatric hospital or a consultant psychiatrist.

2. A person applying for discharge of a patient should be entitled to instruct an independent medical practitioner to visit the patient at any reasonable time, examine him in private and inspect the records relating to his detention and treatment, in order to advise on a possible discharge.

---

[139] Mental Treatment Act 1945, s.221(1).
[140] *Ibid.*, s.221(2)(a).
[141] Mental Treatment Act 1945, s.221(2)(b).
[142] *Ibid.*, s.221(2)(c).
[143] *Ibid.*, s.221(2)(d).

Discharge of patients from Central Mental Hospital

See discussion of section 208 of the Mental Treatment Act 1945 at page 366 above.

REVIEW OF DETENTION

Habeas Corpus

Current Irish law

Where a patient believes himself or herself to be unlawfully detained s/he or another person on his/her behalf [144] may have recourse to the ancient common law writ[145] now embodied in Article 40.4 of the Constitution. This involves making an *ex parte* application to the High Court for a conditional order directing the person causing the detention to justify that detention in writing. The judge to whom the complaint is made is then obliged to enquire immediately into it and has a discretionary power make a conditional order directing the person in whose custody the person is detained to produce the body of that person before the court and to certify in writing the grounds of his detention. On the production of the body on the named day the person or body detaining the person[146] must justify the detention and if s/he or it fails to satisfy the court that the detention is in accordance with law and justify it the conditional order is made absolute and the High Court must order the release of the person from detention.[147]

Where the body of a person alleged to be unlawfully detained is produced before the High Court and the court is satisfied that the person is being detained in accordance with the law but that the law is invalid having regard to the provisions of this constitution then the court must refer the question of the validity of the law to the Supreme Court by way of case stated.[148]

---

[144] Art.40.4.2.

[145] Historically the right was little used in Ireland in the case of lunacy committals. In practice the courts adopted a paternalistic approach to such cases ruling even where a person had been invalidly committed his discharge would be refused if it were shown that he was dangerous at a later date. The courts considered that the detention of a person while dangerous was justified whatever the legal basis for the action. *R v. Riall* (1860) 11 Irish Common Law Reports 279; *In re O'Reilly* (1894) 29 Irish Law Times Reports 33. Where the person had not been committed as dangerous the certifying doctors and the person receiving the alleged lunatic could be liable. Accordingly the Lunatic Asylums (Ireland) Act 1875 was enacted and provided that the committal orders and certificates were a justification for confinement. It also provided that incorrect or defective certificates could be corrected within fourteen days of the committal. See 38 & 39 Vic. c.67, ss.3–5. After the enactment of these provisions actions proceeded on the basis of lack of jurisdiction or conspiracy. In 1882 the discharge of an applicant was directed when it was discovered that the warrant of committal had not shown the circumstances of his removal to another petty sessions district. See *Coughlan v. Woods, Molloy and Hatchell* [1882] 10 Irish Law Reports 29. Allegations of conspiracy were more difficult to prove and less successful. *Hutchinson v. Walsh and Another* (1904) 38 Irish Law Times Reports 133.

[146] A third party does not have a right of hearing at the application nor a right to adduce evidence as to why an applicant should not be released. See *Gallagher v. Director of Central Mental Hospital*, unreported, High Court Geoghegan J., July 9, 1996.

[147] Art.40.4.2.

[148] It is interesting to note that in Canada *habeas corpus* has been used successfully to challenge

The *habeas corpus* procedure has been used in the past to test the sufficiency of documents or proceedings which led to the patient's committal. Thus there would be grounds for application were the prescribed statutory procedures have not been followed,[149] or the statute misconstrued.[150] The procedure is however, confined to making inquiries after detention has taken place and to situations where there has been "such a default of fundamental requirements that the detention may be said to be wanting in due course of law"[151] and complaints regarding conditions of detention and legal errors or improprieties must be brought using other forms of proceedings.[152] One case where an order of *habeas corpus* was made absolute was *In re J*,[153] where the reception order had not been signed as the law then[154] required by "the person in charge" of the hospital. On the other hand in other cases there is considerable evidence of the court's adoption of a paternalistic approach to applications challenging the constitutionality of the Mental Treatment Act provisions. Thus in *In re Philip Clarke*,[155] the applicant called in question the constitutionality of section 165 of the Mental Treatment Act 1945 which empowers a member of the Garda Síochána to take a person believed to be of unsound mind into custody and remove him to a Garda Station where the Garda is of opinion that it is necessary for the public safety or the safety of the person himself that the person be placed forthwith under care and control. Section 165(2) authorises the person to be detained in a psychiatric hospital on the application of the member of the Garda Síochána who took him into custody. The applicant argued that the section was unconstitutional because of the absence of any judicial intervention or determination between the arrest of the person alleged to be of unsound mind and his subsequent detention under a reception order.

In upholding the constitutionality of the section O'Byrne J. referred to the legislation as being of a "paternal character" and continued:

"The existence of mental infirmity is too widespread to be overlooked, and was, no doubt, present to the minds of the draughtsmen when it was proclaimed in

under the Charter of Rights and Freedoms the adequacy of provincial mental health legislation which failed to prescribe any objective criteria for involuntary committals for treatment. See *Thwaites v. Health Sciences Centre Psychiatric Facility* (1988) 48 D.L.R. 338.

[149] *In re R v. Pinder, Greenwood* (1855) 24 L.J. Q.B. 148.

[150] *In re Steneult* (1894) 29 L. Jo.

[151] *State (Mc Donagh) v. Frawley* [1978] I.R. 131.

[152] *Rock v. Governor of St Patrick's Institution*, unreported, Supreme Court, March 22, 1993. In *In re Philip Clarke* [1950] I.R. 235 it was held that the requirement to fill in particulars in the Statement of Particulars to accompany an application for a Recommendation for Reception under the Act was directory only and not obligatory. Accordingly the failure of the Garda to fill in details of the applicant's medical history on the form did not render the detention of the applicant unlawful. The Garda had a duty to make the application for recommendation *forthwith* and consequently would not be in a position to retain the person in custody while he was making enquiries. The particulars themselves were mainly intended for the assistance of the medical officer whose duty it was to examine the patient when the latter was brought before him. (*Ibid.*, p.250).

[153] 88 I.L.T.R. 120.

[154] Subsequently the Mental Treatment Act 1953 provided that a power or duty of the resident medical superintendent, the chief medical officer or the person in charge of a district mental hospital could be exercised or performed by any other medical officer of the institution authorised in that behalf by the mental hospital authority maintaining the institution. See s.3(1).

[155] [1950] I.R. 235.

Article 40.1 of the Constitution that, though all citizens, as human beings, are to be held equal before the law, the State may, nevertheless, in its enactments have due regard to differences of capacity, physical and moral and of social function. We do not see how the common good would be promoted or the dignity and freedom of the individual assured by allowing persons, alleged to be suffering from such infirmity to remain at large to the possible danger of themselves and others.

The section is carefully drafted so as to ensure that the person alleged to be of unsound mind, shall be brought before, and examined by, responsible medical officers with the least possible delay. This seems to us to satisfy every reasonable requirement and we have not been satisfied and do not consider that the Constitution requires that there should be a judicial enquiry or determination before such a person can be placed and detained in a mental hospital.

The section cannot, in our opinion, be construed as an attack on the personal rights of the citizen. On the contrary it seems to us to be designed for the protection of the citizen and for the promotion of the common good."[156]

On the other hand in later cases there has been some evidence of a departure from this approach. In *O'Dowd v. North Western Health Board*,[157] the defendants appealed against a High Court decision granting the plaintiff leave to institute proceedings for false imprisonment. The Supreme Court was divided two to one against permitting the plaintiff to proceed. In his dissenting judgment Henchy J. referred to what he perceived to be want of reasonable care on the part of the defendants. First the authorised medical officer who purported to make the reception order failed to examine the applicant forthwith on his arrival at the hospital as required by section 165(3) of the Act; secondly the medical officer who examined the patient did not make the reception order but detained and drugged the applicant without legal authority; thirdly the applicant was not informed that he could obtain in-patient treatment on a voluntary basis and fourthly the authorised medical officer who had not examined the patient purported to complete a reception order in which he stated that he had examined the patient that day. Henchy J. stated:

"I venture to think that if what happened in this case had happened in Clarke's case, *habeas corpus* would not have been refused. Article 40.3.1. of the Constitution provides that 'The State guarantees in its laws to respect and, as far as practicable, by its laws to defend and vindicate the personal rights of the citizen.' Article 40.3.2. provides further that 'The State shall, in particular, by its laws protect as best it may from unjust attack and, in the case of injustice done, vindicate the life, person, good name and property rights of every citizen'.

It was the implementation of those constitutional guarantees that caused the Legislature to hedge round the making of a chargeable patient reception order with the formalities mandated by the Act and the regulations made under it. As *Clarke's* case shows some of those formalities are only formalities but others are clearly obligatory, designed to implement the constitutional guarantees I have

---

[156] *Ibid.*, pp 247–248.
[157] [1983] I.L.R.M. 186.

quoted, and in particular to ensure that, not even for a short period will a citizen be unnecessarily deprived of his liberty and condemned to the tragic and degrading status of a compulsory inmate of a mental hospital, with the dire social consequences that such a fate is likely to have on his future and that of his relations."

The High Court has expressed its reluctance to enumerate an established or finite catalogue of factors which will render a detention unlawful [158] and these later dicta are consistent with its general view statutes restrictive of personal liberty should be strictly construed. [159]

Case law has also demonstrated that the purpose of the *habeas corpus* remedy is to provide a speedy and effective remedy in cases whereby the lawfulness of a person's detention may be determined so that a hearing may not be adjourned while other proceedings are contemplated. In *In re D*, [160] Hamilton P. adjourned an application under Article 40.4.2 to enable a health board to bring a wardship petition in respect of a person with an intellectual disability who was under their care. The Supreme Court held on appeal that an adjournment was inappropriate. Finlay C.J. remarked:

"The High Court on hearing an application [under Article 40.4.4] must reach a single decision, namely whether the detention of the person is or is not in accordance with law. Such a procedure does not ... admit of any supervision or monitoring of the interests of the person concerned, even allowing for a condition of mental retardation or other want of capacity."

Also in *Sheehan v. O'Reilly*, [161] the Supreme Court held that the fact that the Constitution places a duty on the judge to enquire "forthwith" into the complaint received emphasised the importance of speed and urgency in the proceedings and meant that he had a

"jurisdiction and discretion ... even prior to reaching a conclusion that a sufficient doubt as to the legality of the detention of the applicant has been raised to warrant calling upon the jailor or detainer to show cause, to make inquiries of a speedy and, if necessary, informal nature to try and ascertain the facts."

However, the practicalities of the availability of *habeas corpus* as a speedy and effective remedy to patients detained in a psychiatric hospital was canvassed by Budd J. in *Croke v. Smith*[162] as follows:

---

[158] In *State (Boyle) v. Kelly* [1974] I.R. 259 Henchy J. commenting upon the phrase "in accordance with law" stated: "The expression is a compendious one and is designed to cover these basic legal principles and procedures which are so essential for the preservation of personal liberty under our Constitution that departure from them renders a detention unjustifiable in the eyes of the law. To enumerate them in advance would not be feasible and, in any case, an attempt to do so would only tend to diminish the constitutional guarantee".

[159] In *Attorney General v. Mc Bride* [1928] I.R. 451, Hanna J. said: "It is the first duty of the courts to show the greatest solicitude in protecting the liberty of the subject from anything but a strict application of a statute of this nature even though this statute be essential to the public safety".

[160] [1987] I.R. 449.

[161] [1993] 3 I.L.R.M. 427.

[162] Unreported, High Court, July 31, 1995.

"It is undoubtedly a speedy and efficacious remedy. However, the situation of a mental patient who is illiterate, harmless and without kith and kin to initiate such an inquiry on his behalf by way of *habeas corpus* perhaps poses the problem in stark form. Such a patient may not be aware of his or her rights to seek *habeas corpus* and may be incapable of the necessary written or verbal communication to trigger such an inquiry."[163]

Article 40.4.2 makes it clear that where there is a finding that the detention is not in accordance with law the release of the applicant must be ordered. This order is unconditional and cannot be combined with an order that the applicant be retaken.[164] It does not however, preclude a fresh detention on lawful grounds.[165]

At common law it was the general view that appeals to the Supreme Court in relation to *habeas corpus* existed only for the benefit of an unsuccessful applicant and not an unsuccessful respondent.[166] This rule was confirmed by the former Supreme Court in *State (Burke) v. Lennon*,[167] but in *State (Browne) v. Feran*,[168] the present Supreme Court held that unless such an appeal was expressly excluded by statute law an appeal to the Supreme Court enured for the benefit of both parties under Article 34.4.3. of the Constitution.

In a recent statistical study of *habeas corpus* applications made to challenge the lawfulness of detention under the Mental Treatment Acts Mary Keys concluded that *habeas corpus* applications were infrequently used by persons in local psychiatric hospitals and there was slightly more use of the procedure by patients detained in the high security conditions of the Central Mental Hospitals. The infrequency of applications was explained partly by the fact that there was no obligation under the 1945 Act to inform persons detained under the Act of the right to apply and the absence of legal aid (apart from the limited right to legal representation under the non-statutory Attorney General's scheme). She concluded:

"*Habeas corpus* is the only form of independent review of continuing detention in Irish law [prior to the coming into force of the 2001 Act]. Yet a total of 111 applications by, or on behalf of psychiatric patients over an 85 year period hardly suggests an effective and accessible means of review of psychiatric detention This is especially so when one considers that this figure was exceeded in a two year period in 1998–1999 by 113 prisoner[169] applications"[170]

The establishment of Mental Health Tribunals and the patients right to automatic review of detention after 21 days under the Mental Health Act 2001 may herald a slight diversion away form away from the use of *habeas corpus* applications in the context of challenging

---

[163] *Ibid.*, p.18.

[164] *State (Mc Donagh) v. Frawley* [1978] I.R. 131.

[165] *In re Singer (No. 2)* (1964) 98 I.L.T.R. 112.

[166] *Cox v. Hakes* 15 App. Cas 506.

[167] [1940] I.R. 136.

[168] [1967] I.R. 147.

[169] i.e., prisoners transferred from prisons to the Central Mental Hospital.

[170] M. Keys, "Challenging the Lawfulness of Psychiatric Detention under Habeas Corpus in Ireland" (2002) 24 *Dublin University Law Journal* 26 at 36–37.

the lawfulness of detention of by reason of mental disorder. The proposal for review under the 2001 Act and the provisions Article 5 of the European Convention on Human Rights with which the 2001 Act must be interpreted in a consistent manner cover much the same ground as *habeas corpus*.

However, prisoners detained in designated centres pursuant to orders of the criminal courts under the Criminal Law (Insanity) Bill 2002 will not enjoy an equivalence of safeguards with those detained under the Mental Health Act 2001, so the efficacy of review afforded by the proposed Mental Health Review Boards under the Bill may be called into question. Further, while in *X v. United Kingdom*,[171] the European Court of Human Rights held that *habeas corpus* proceedings were not enough to enable a person detained as a person of unsound mind to avail of his entitlement under Article 5(4) of the European Convention on Human Rights to take proceedings at reasonable intervals before a court to test the lawfulness of his detention and the *habeas corpus* proceedings could not provide a full assessment of the merits the court did acknowledge that *habeas corpus* could be used as an effective check against arbitrary detention in short-term emergency situations.

Commentary

Comparative law: Canada Section 10(c) of the Canadian Charter of Rights and Freedoms embodies the right to *habeas corpus* and provides that on detention everyone has the right "to have the validity of the detention determined by way of *habeas corpus* and to be released if the detention is not lawful."

In a series of decisions delivered under section 10(c), the Canadian Courts have illustrated a range of circumstances in which the writ of *habeas corpus* might be employed to assist a person with mental disability who is unlawfully detained.

Thus in *In re A.B*,[172] it was held that the validity of the application for *habeas corpus* could not be challenged on the basis of the applicant's mental incapacity to bring the application or to instruct counsel.

Also in a number of recent decisions,[173] the Supreme Court of Canada has held that a prisoner has a right not to be deprived unlawfully of the residual liberty enjoyed by the general inmate population of the institution and that any significant deprivation of that liberty (such as placement in a special handling unit) may be challenged on a writ of *habeas corpus*. These authorities might equally well apply to patients in a psychiatric facility, which would open up the possibility of challenging practices such as physical restraints and seclusion by means of a writ of *habeas corpus*. In the USA Brakel *et al* observed:

> "The function of the mental hospital when it was first established as an institution separate and apart from jails was basically custodial. Few patients were discharged as cured or improved; death accounted for most 'terminations'. This fact, together

---

[171] [1981] 4 E.H.R.R. 181.

[172] (1905) C.C.C. 390 (Que. K.B.).

[173] *R v. Miller* [1985] 2 S.C.R. 613; *Cardinal v. Director of Kent Institution* [1985] 2 S.C.R. 643 and *Morin v. National Special Handling Unit Review Committee* [1985] 2 S.C.R. 662.

with the spectre of 'railroading' stimulated the use of the writ of *habeas corpus* as a major method of separation from the mental hospital."[174]

All but a couple of states explicitly include within their discharge statutes the right of the patient to seek a writ of *habeas corpus* as a means of securing his release if he believes he is being improperly detained. Even in the jurisdictions without such provisions the right exists by common law, as this writ has traditionally been available in Anglo-American jurisprudence to any person, including a mentally disabled individual to contest the legality of detention.

Some courts[175] have however, expanded the scope of the writ to permit inquiry into the mental condition of a petitioner who was legally committed at the outset but who later recovered or improved and who may be entitled to release under existing institutional standards and 11 states explicitly provide for *habeas corpus* release based on the patient's current medical condition.[176] Under these statutes the mental condition of the patient at the time of the *habeas corpus* proceedings and not the validity of his initial institutionalisation serves as the basic criterion for retention and discharge.

Recently the writ of *habeas corpus* has been used successfully to challenge the continued detention of an involuntary patient who was not being provided treatment[177] and to secure the release of a patient from the hospital into the community or his transfer to a community treatment facility under "the least restrictive alternative" doctrine.[178]

Conclusions

1. It is submitted that since the legality of a patients continued detention is based upon the criteria for detention continuing to exist, the writ of *habeas corpus* should lie to test the legality of detention of a patient who was legally committed at the outset but who may be entitled to release on the basis that the grounds for continued detention no longer exist.

2. Since in principle *habeas corpus* is available to contest the lawfulness of any significant deprivation of liberty it is submitted that it must be available to contest the lawfulness of the placement of a psychiatric patient in seclusion or indeed in a secure unit.

3. Existing case law and in particular the cases of *In re Philip Clarke*,[179] and *O'Dowd v. North Western Health Board*,[180] fails to make a clear distinction between mandatory and directory obligations in committal procedures. The making of such a distinction

---

[174] Brakel et al., *The Mentally Disabled and the Law* (3rd ed., American Bar Foundation, Chicago, Illinois, 1985).
[175] See *Hiatt v. Soucek* 240 Iowa 300, 36 N.W. 2d. 432 (1949).
[176] California, Delaware, Iowa., New York, Ohio, Oklahoma, Rhode Island, South. Dakota., Tennessee, Virginia, Wisconsin.
[177] *Rouse v. Cameron* 375 F 2d 451 (D.C. Cir. 1966).
[178] *Lake v. Cameron* 364 F. 2d. 657 (D.C. Cir. 1966) *Covington v. Harris* 419 F 2d. 617 (D.C. Cir. 1969) In the latter case the court stated that *habeas corpus* was available to challenge the place as well as the period of confinement.
[179] [1950] I.R. 235.
[180] [1983] I.L.R.M. 186.

in the context of committal procedures is essential if some element of certainty is to be introduced into the law in this area and so that the constitutional right to liberty of the person with mental disability in the context of committal procedures is given some real meaning.

Judicial review

Following the introduction of judicial review procedure by Order 84 of the Rules of the Superior Courts 1986, a practice developed whereby applications for release under Article 40 of the Constitution where frequently treated by the High Court as applications for judicial review and leave to apply for judicial review was often granted instead of an inquiry under Article 40. This occurred in the case of *Sheehan v. Reilly*[181] and the practice was held to be wrong by the Supreme Court. Finlay C.J. stated:

> "Applications which clearly, in fact, raise an issue as to the legality of the detention of a person must be treated as an application under Article 40, no matter how they are described."

AFTER-CARE

Position under the Mental Treatment Act 1945

Under the Mental Treatment Act 1945 the Health Service Executive has power subject to the sanction of the Minister for Health to arrange for the provision of preventive or after care services for any chargeable patient ordinarily resident in their area.[182]

In the recent case of *Healy v. The North Western Health Board*,[183] it was held that the medical staff of a psychiatric hospital had a duty to assess the risk of suicide before discharging a patient suffering from depression and that failure to carry out a proper assessment in that regard with the ensuing suicide of the plaintiff amounted to negligence. Flood J., noted that the experts were agreed:

> "that depression has an inherent risk of suicide and that it is vital that a patient be monitored as he is a risk to himself and could be a risk to others. Monitoring in that sense, may be either formal or informal but it must be done and the result of the monitoring must be assessed by the medical staff in conjunction with the nursing staff."[184]

---

[181] [1993] 2 I.R. 81, [1993] I.L.R.M. 927.

[182] Mental Treatment Act 1945, s.222A as inserted by s.31 of the Mental Treatment Act 1961.

[183] Unreported, High Court, January 31, 1996.

[184] *Ibid.*, p.19 In the English case of *Thorne v. Northern Group Hospital Management* [1964] 108 S.J. 484 in holding the defendants not liable in damages for the failure adequately to supervise a woman who had walked out of the hospital, gone home and committed suicide Lord Justice Edmund Davies ruled that the degree of care and supervision required of hospital staff in relation to a patient with known or, perhaps, even suspected suicidal tendencies was greater than that called for in relation to patients generally. In contrast in *Selfe v. Ilford and District Hospital Management Committee* [1970] 114 S.J. 935, the court held the defendants were liable where the plaintiff, aged 17 (who was admitted to hospital following an attempted suicide by an overdose of sleeping tablets)

In the light of the judgment it appears that hospitals may need to review their practice regarding discharge of patients into the community and give special consideration to maintaining contact with recently discharged patients on an out-patient basis. Commenting on the case, Cooney and O'Neill state:

> "The fear of legal liability for rare, unpredictable violence may have an adverse effect on the rights of detained patients and the willingness of doctors to respect the autonomy of patients."[185]

In his *Guidelines on Good Practice and Quality Assurance in Mental Health Services* published in 1998, the Inspector of Mental Hospitals highlights the need to co-ordinate aftercare services:

> "Immediately following discharge, a discharge summary should be sent to the general practitioner and to the members of the psychiatric services providing aftercare, setting out the principal details of the patient's management and treatment while in hospital, including medication on discharge and whether and for how long it is to be continued. The patient too should be supplied with a standard information form giving information on the drugs prescribed, the name of his or her general practitioner and the telephone number of the mental health centre or service where staff can be contacted and a domiciliary visit or other intervention be carried out in case of an emergency. The type of aftercare planned for the patient should be discussed with the patient taking into account the patient's diagnosis, needs, physical and emotional and personal preferences. Arrangements must be made for the first review of the patient post discharge. An aftercare plan for the patient should be recorded in detail in the patient's care file and available to each member of the professional team responsible for the patient. The discharge plan should be drawn up by the patient's treating consultant psychiatrist and should fully consider and provide for the immediate and long term needs of the patient and include an assessment of the risk of the patient harming himself and others. Aftercare should be properly co-ordinated and supervised under the general direction of the patient's treating consultant psychiatrist. A mechanism should be in place to review patients who have bee lost to follow up and everything possible done to find out what has happened to the patient and to take appropriate action."[186]

Conclusions

1. It is submitted that an element of certainty is required in the law relating to discharge a hospital or medical practitioner should only be liable for wrongful discharge only if they have exercised what is their statutory administrative discretion to discharge

---

climbed out of a window and jumped off a roof resulting in serious injuries. In this case in view of the greater degree of risk the defendants owed a greater degree of care. The risk of suicide had not been diagnosed and it was held that there was a breakdown of proper nursing supervision which had caused the accident.

[185] See Cooney & O'Neill, *Kritik 1 Psychiatric Detention Civil Commitment in Ireland*, p.164.
[186] Para.4.8.

illegally, irrationally or unreasonably in the sense of reaching a decision in which no reasonable medical practitioner or hospital could have reached in the circumstances.[187]

2. It has been argued[188] that there is a need to afford people who have been detained in a psychiatric hospital a right to an integrated aftercare package. It has been stated that unless effective methods of after-care are developed for persons who experience serious mental illness "their relapses and readmissions are inevitable."[189] If the right to treatment is to be effective it should include the preparation of an individualised after-care plan which will provide at least the possibility of a productive and good quality of life in the community after institutional care. The patient's right to be free from harm must also require the provision of a therapeutic plan following upon discharge from hospital as if s/he is simply discharged to the setting which made his or her admission inevitable then s/he might simply be exposed to more harm. The principle of the least restrictive alternative also makes the provision of an after-care plan necessary. In practice the principle operates thus – when at a periodic review of treatment a determination is made that further detention would no longer be conducive to proper treatment the least restrictive principle obliges the hospital either to discharge the patient unconditionally or release him/her to a less restrictive setting for adequate transitional treatment and after care.

Consequently a patient should have a statutory right to an individualised after care plan to facilitate his effective return to the community and the avoidance of circumstances which contributed to his hospitalisation in the first place.

---

[187] See *Associated Provincial Picture Houses Ltd v. Wednesbury Corporation* [1948] 1 K.B. 223.

[188] See Cooney & O'Neill, *Kritik I Psychiatric Detention Civil Commitment in Ireland*, p.p345–347.

[189] Raskin & Dyson, "Treatment Problems Leading to Readmissions of Schizophrenic Patients" (1968) 19 *Archives Gen Psychiatry* 356 at 359.

CHAPTER SIX

Mental Health Tribunals

INTRODUCTION

Central to the due process model of rights for people with mental illness in hospital are structures designed to ensure that patients are given a fair hearing in relation to their detention and aspects of their treatment, which may be restrictive or hazardous. This Chapter examines the administrative machinery under the Mental Health Act 2001, with a view to ascertaining whether the constitution and powers of the Mental Health Tribunals will ensure that they will deliver on their professed aims of protecting the interests of patients with mental illness[1] and in particular those of patients detained in psychiatric hospitals.

Prior to the enactment of the Mental Health Act 2001, and apart from *habeas corpus* there has been no provision under existing Irish law for automatic independent judicial review of the propriety of detentions. The principal safeguards against the unlawful detention of a person under the Mental Treatment Act 1945 (still in force) are as follows:

Under section 220 of the 1945 Act any relative or friend of a person detained as a chargeable patient in a district mental hospital or other institution maintained by the Health Service Executive may apply to the person in charge of the institution to allow him to take care of the person detained. When such an application is made, the person in charge of the institution may, if he so thinks fit and if satisfied that the person detained will be properly taken care of, discharge the person concerned. The discharge must, however, meet with the approval of the resident medical superintendent.[2] Where the resident medical superintendent is of the view that the detained person is dangerous or otherwise unfit to be discharged and issues a certificate to this effect stating the grounds for this view the detained person may not be discharged.[3]

Appeal against this view lies to the Minister for Health and Children. In order to make the appeal the person to whom the certificate relates or someone on his behalf must give notice in writing of objection to the certificate to the Minister. On receipt of the notice the Minister may require the person in charge of the institution to give him a copy of the certificate and that person must comply immediately with that request. Upon receipt of that certificate the Minister may require the Inspector of Mental Hospitals to examine the person to whom the certificate relates. After considering the report of the Inspector the Minister may direct the discharge of the person to whom the certificate relates, if he thinks fit and provided no more than fourteen days have elapsed since he received the copy certificate.[4]

---

[1] See paras 5.2 and 10.1, White Paper: A Mental Health Act (Department of Health 1995), para.1824.
[2] Mental Treatment Act 1945, s.220 as amended by the Mental Treatment Act 1961, s.30.
[3] *Ibid.*, s.221(1).
[4] *Ibid.*, s.221(2).

Section 222 of the 1945 Act empowers any person to apply to the Minister for Health and Children for an order for the examination by two medical practitioners of a detained patient and the Minister may, if he or she thinks fit grant such an order. The effect of the order is to permit the practitioners to examine a patient at the institution on at least two occasions at least seven days intervening between the first and second occasion.[5] If the practitioners certify that such person may be discharged without risk of injury to himself the Minister may, if he thinks fit direct the discharge of the patient.

The 1945 Act obliges the Inspector of Mental Hospitals to see every patient the propriety of whose detention he has reason to doubt during the course of his inspections of a psychiatric hospital and to notify the person in charge of the institution that he has doubts as to the propriety of such patient's detention.[6] Where the Inspector becomes of the opinion that the propriety of the detention of a patient detained in a district mental hospital or other institution maintained by the Health Service Executive requires further consideration he is obliged to report the matter to the Minister for Health and Children. After consideration of the Inspector's report the Minister may, if he so thinks fit require him to visit the patient to whom the report relates and to make a report on his mental condition to the Minister. After consideration of this second report the Minister may, if he so thinks fit by order direct the discharge of the patient to whom the report relates.[7] In the case of patient detained in a private institution the Minister may require the Inspector and the resident medical superintendent of the district mental hospital nearest to the institution to visit the patient. These visitors are obliged to make two visits to the patient the second visit being not less than eighteen days after the first and a report must be made to the Minister after the second visit.[8] After consideration of the report the Minister may if he so thinks fit by order direct the discharge of the patient to whom the report relates.[9]

Every patient in an institution has the right under section 266 of the 1945 Act to have a letter forwarded unopened to the Minister for Health, the President of the High Court, the Registrar of Wards of Court, the Health Service Executive or the Inspector of Mental Hospitals. Notices setting forth this right must, if the Minister so directs, be kept posted in prominent positions in a mental institution and if the Inspector of Mental Hospitals indicates the positions in which they are to be kept posted, must be kept posted in those positions.[10]

The President of the High Court may also by order require the Inspector of Mental Hospitals to visit and examine any person detained at any place as a person of unsound mind and report to him on the condition of such person.[11]

---

[5] It was a criminal offence for a person carrying on an institution to contravene whether by act or omission the obligations imposed upon him by s.222(2). See Mental Treatment Act 1945, s.249 and Sch.5.

[6] Mental Treatment Act 1945, s.237 as amended by Mental Treatment Act 1961, s.33.

[7] *Ibid.*, s.239.

[8] *Ibid.*, s.240.

[9] *Ibid.*, s.240(8).

[10] *Ibid.*, s.267.

[11] *Ibid.*, s.241. Historically it appears the exercise of these powers were dominated by medical criteria. See Finnane, *Insanity and the Insane in Post Famine Ireland* (Croom Helen, London, 1981), p.118.

Section 189 of the 1945 Act[12] obliges the chief medical officer of an approved institution when he or she extends the period of detention of a temporary patient give notice to the person detained and the applicant for the original reception order which states particulars of the extension as endorsed on the original order and also states that the person detained or the applicant may send an objection to the extension of the period of detention to the Inspector of Mental Hospitals.

On receipt of the objection the Inspector must require the chief medical officer to give him a full report on the person to whom the order relates. This report must be furnished forthwith and on consideration of the report the Inspector of Mental Hospitals must take such steps, as he considers necessary for ascertaining whether or not the detention of the person concerned should continue.

Section 250 of the 1945 Act provides that it is a criminal offence for a person to receive and detain or to undertake for payment the care and control of a person who is or is alleged to be of unsound mind other than in accordance with the provisions of the 1945 Act. The offence is punishable on summary conviction by a fine not exceeding one hundred pounds or at the discretion of the court to imprisonment for a term not exceeding six months imprisonment or to both fine and imprisonment. On conviction on indictment the offence is punishable by a fine not exceeding two hundred pounds or at the discretion of the court to imprisonment for a term not exceeding two years or to both fine and imprisonment.[13]

Sections 217[14] and 218 of the 1945 Act obliges the person in charge of a psychiatric hospital, on the recovery of a person detained there, to give notice of recovery to the person paying for his treatment in the case of a private patient or such relative as he thinks proper in the case of a chargeable patient respectively. The notice must be given with the approval of the resident medical superintendent and contain a statement that unless the person detained is removed before a specified date not earlier than seven days after the date on which the notice is given he will be discharged. If the person is not removed before the date specified in the notice he must be discharged forthwith. Failure to give this notice is a criminal offence punishable by a fine not exceeding fifty pounds and a further fine not exceeding one pound for each day the offence continued.[15]

The above powers have been cited by the Supreme Court in *SC v. Smith*,[16] as evidence of the fact that the patients constitutional right to liberty are sufficiently protected by the provisions of the Mental Treatment Act 1945. However, in the White Paper it was acknowledged that they do not satisfy Ireland's obligations under the *European Convention for the Protection of Human Rights and Fundamental Freedoms* (1950).[17]

Article 5.4 of the Convention requires that "Everyone who is deprived of his liberty by arrest or detention shall be entitled to take proceedings whereby the lawfulness of his detention shall be decided speedily by a court and his release ordered if the detention is not lawful."

---

[12] As substituted by Mental Treatment Act 1961, s.18.
[13] Mental Treatment Act 1945, s.250
[14] As amended by Mental Treatment Act 1961, s.27.
[15] Mental Treatment Act 1945, s.249 and sch.5.
[16] Unreported, Supreme Court, July 31, 1996.
[17] See para.5.3.

In *X v. United Kingdom*,[18] the European Court of Human Rights decided that all people who were detained because they were of "unsound mind" even those originally admitted from the criminal courts were entitled to periodic judicial consideration of the merits of their continued detention. *Habeas corpus* proceedings were not enough because they could not provide a full assessment on the merits.

When section 6 of the Mental Health Act 2001 comes fully into force it will repeal the statutory powers in the Mental Treatment Act 1945 (with the exception of section 241 the power of the President of the High Court to require the Inspector of Hospitals to examine a patient and report to him on the patient's condition) and seek to comply with Article 5.4 of the European Convention by assigning the role of automatic review of detention to a Mental Health Tribunal.

Membership of the Mental Health Tribunal

Current law

Under section 48 of the Mental Health Act 2001 (which came into force on April 5, 2002) Mental Health Tribunals consist of three members appointed by the Mental Health Commission. These members are:

(a) a consultant psychiatrist. "Consultant psychiatrist" is defined by section 2 of the Act as a consultant psychiatrist who is employed by the Health Service Executive or by an approved centre or a person whose name is entered on the division of psychiatry or the division of child and adolescent psychiatry of the Register of Medical Specialists maintained by the Medical Council in Ireland.

By virtue of section 48(12), a "consultant psychiatrist" includes a person who was employed as a consultant psychiatrist by the Health Service Executive or an approved centre not more than 7 years before his or her appointment.

(b) a practising barrister or solicitor who has had not less than seven years experience as a practising barrister or solicitor who is to be the Chairperson of the Tribunal and

(c) a person other than a person referred to in paragraphs (a) or (b) or a registered medical practitioner or a registered nurse.[19]

At a sitting of a tribunal each member of the tribunal will have a vote and every question shall be determined by a majority of the votes of the members.[20]

By virtue of section 48(5), a member of the Mental Health Commission shall be disqualified for membership of a tribunal. Section 48(6) provides that a member will hold office for a period not exceeding three years and on such other terms and conditions as the Commission may determine when appointing him/her. A member of a tribunal whose period of membership expires by the effluxion of time is eligible for re-appointment as a member of a tribunal.[21] By virtue of section 48(8), each member of

---

[18] [1981] 4 E.H.R.R. 181.
[19] Mental Health Act 2001, s.48(3).
[20] *Ibid.*, s.48(5).
[21] *Ibid.*, s.48(11).

the tribunal shall be paid such remuneration (if any) and allowances for expenses incurred by him or her (if any) as the Mental Health Commission may with the consent of the Minister and the Minister for Finance determine.

Section 48(9) states that a member of the tribunal may at any time be removed from membership of the tribunal by the Mental Health Commission if, in the Commission's opinion the member has become incapable through ill health of performing his or her functions or has committed stated misbehaviour or his or her removal appears to the Commission to be necessary for the effective performance by the tribunal of its functions. A member of a tribunal will be disqualified for holding and will cease to hold office if he or she is adjudged bankrupt or makes a composition or arrangement with creditors or is sentenced by a court of competent jurisdiction to a term of imprisonment or penal servitude.[22]

Commentary from international and comparative law perspective

Principle 17 of the *United Nations Principles for the Protection of Persons with Mental Illness and the Improvement of Mental Health Care* provides that the review body "shall be a judicial or other independent and impartial body established by domestic law."

The European Court of Human Rights has ruled that Article 5.4 of the European Convention for the Protection of Human Rights and Fundamental Freedoms provides in effect that the detained person must have access to a body that has a "judicial character" and to be of a judicial character a body must be "independent both of the executive and the parties to the case."[23] Questions must therefore be asked whether the institutions set up by Irish legislation are independent in their structures and membership.

In England and Wales the composition of panels reflects a balance between legal, medical and lay membership. Each panel has three types of member (a) legal members appointed by the Lord Chancellor who have such legal experience, as he considers suitable. Usually these are senior practitioners, but in some cases academics have been appointed (b) medical members appointed by the Lord Chancellor after consultation with the Department of Health. These are usually consultant psychiatrists but other doctors with psychiatric experience including community physicians may be appointed, and (c) lay members also appointed by the Lord Chancellor after consultation with the Department of Health who have " such experience in administration, such knowledge of social services or such other qualifications or experience as the Lord Chancellor considers suitable".[24]

In practice some are magistrates or members of local or health authorities. Others have relevant professional experience for example in social and community work. The suggestion that there should always be a social worker on the tribunal was not adopted.

The regional chairman of the tribunal is a lawyer. Technically it is his function to nominate the members for a particular hearing or class of hearings.[25] He may exercise the tribunal's powers on preliminary and incidental matters at any time up to the hearing.[26]

---

[22] Mental Health Act 2001, s.48(10).

[23] *Winterwerp v. The Netherlands* A 33 para 64 (1979).

[24] Mental Health Act 1983, sch.2.

[25] *Ibid.*, and Mental Health Review Tribunal Rules 1983 (S.I. No. 942 of 1983), r.8.

[26] Mental Health Review Tribunal Rules 1983 (S.I. 1983 No. 942), r.5.

A further function of the regional chairman is to organise conferences and training for members.

Cases concerning restricted patients may only be heard by specially approved members who are Circuit Judges or Recorders with experience of trying serious criminal cases.[27]

English legislation contains provisions to guard against bias. Tribunal members must be independent. They must not be members or officers of the "responsible authority,"[28] or of the registration authority for a mental nursing home or of an authority that maintains the patient in a mental nursing home. They must not have a close knowledge of or connection with the patient but a legal member may preside over more than one hearing about the same patient and other members could probably could do so too provided that there was no reason to question their independence.[29] Finally a member must not have recently treated the patient in a professional capacity.

In Canada, the Mental Health Act, in most jurisdictions, establishes a special Review Board or Panel to which involuntary patients can apply for review of their confinement.[30] The Board is normally comprised of three to five members including a psychiatrist, a lawyer and a layperson. The legislation usually contains provisions against perceived bias such a disqualifying psychiatrists and physicians from sitting as Board members on applications involving the facility of which they are a member of staff.

Conclusions

In order to avoid any appearance of or actual bias it is submitted that there should be a requirement that tribunal members not be members or officers of the approved centre. In addition they should not have a close knowledge of or connection with the patient nor should they have recently treated the patient in a professional capacity.

It is not clear from the legislation what qualifications the third non-medical, non-legal, member of the tribunal should possess.

POWERS OF THE MENTAL HEALTH TRIBUNAL

Automatic reviews of admission or renewal orders by the Mental Health Tribunal

Current Irish Law

Section 48(1) of the Mental Health Act 2001 (which came into force on April 5, 2002) provides that the Mental Health Commission shall from time to time appoint one or more tribunals which or each of which shall be known as a Mental Health Tribunal to

---

[27] Mental Health Act 1983, s.78(4); Mental Health Review Tribunal Rules 1983 (S.I. No. 942 of 1983), r.8(3).

[28] Mental Health Review Tribunal Rules 1983 (S.I. No. 942 of 1983), r.8(2).

[29] *R v. Oxford Regional Mental Health Review Tribunal ex p. Mackman, The Times,* June 2, 1986.

[30] R.S.B.C. 1979 c. 256 s.21(4) [re-en 1985, c.12 s.7]; R.S.A. 1980, c. M-13, s.25; S.S. 1984-85-86, c. M-13.1, S. 34; R.S.O. 1980 c. 262 s. 31 {am. 1986, c.64, s.33(30), (31); R.S.N.B. 1973 c. M-10, s.31; R.S.N.S. 1967 c. 249 s.57 [en. 1977, c. 45, s.8]; R.S. P.E.I 1974 c. M-9, s.26; S.N. 1971, No. 80, s.17; R.S.Y.T. 1971, c. M-7, s.6.3 {en. 1984, c.21, s.5].

determine such matter or matters as may be referred to it by the Commission under section 17. Section 17 (which is not yet in force) first obliges the Commission where it has received copies of admission orders or renewal orders to refer the matter to a tribunal. Secondly, it must assign a legal representative to represent the patient concerned unless he or she proposes to engage one. Thirdly, it must direct in writing a member of the panel of consultant psychiatrists established under section 33(3)(b) of the Act to (i) examine the patient concerned (ii) interview the consultant psychiatrist responsible for the care and treatment of the patient and (iii) review the records relating to the patient in order to determine in the interest of the patient whether the patient is suffering from a mental disorder. The consultant psychiatrist so appointed must also report in writing within 14 days on the results of the examination, interview and review to the tribunal to which the matter has been referred and to provide a copy of the report to the legal representative of the patient.

Section 18(1) of the 2001 Act (which is not yet in force) provides that where an admission order or a renewal order has been referred to a tribunal under section 17 the tribunal shall review the detention of the patient concerned and shall either:

(a) if satisfied that the patient is suffering from a mental disorder and (i) that the provisions of sections 9,10, 12, 14, 15, and 16 where applicable have been complied with or (ii) if there has been a failure to comply with any such provision, that the failure does not affect the substance of the order and does not cause an injustice, affirm the order

(b) if not so satisfied, revoke the order and direct that the patient be discharged from the approved centre concerned.

Before making a decision under section 18(1) the Tribunal must have regard to the consultant's report furnished under section 17(1)(c).[31]

Section 18(2) provides that a decision under section 18(1) shall be made as soon as may be but not later than 21 days after the making of the admission order or renewal order concerned. By section 18(4) this period may be extended by order of the tribunal (either of its own motion or at the request of the patient concerned) for a further period of 14 days and thereafter may be further extended by it by order for a period of 14 days on the application of the patient if the tribunal is satisfied that it is in the interest of the patient and the relevant admission or renewal order shall continue in force until the date of the expiration of the order made under section 18(4).

Following the coming into force section 3 of the European Convention on Human Rights Act 2003 the Mental Health Tribunal must perform its functions in a manner compatible with the State's obligations under the *European Convention for the Protection of Human Rights and Fundamental Freedoms on Human Rights (1950)*. Article 5.4 provides that everyone who is deprived of his liberty by detention shall be entitled to take proceedings by which a court shall decide the lawfulness of his detention speedily and his release ordered if the detention is not lawful.

The Article 5(4) remedy requires that the decision on detention be taken "speedily." In this regard it is worth noting the decision of the European Court of Human Rights in

---

[31] Mental Health Act 2001, s.18(3).

Bezicheri v. Italy,[32] which held that alleged constraints on resources could not be used to justify delay in a given case as it was the responsibility of the Contracting State sufficiently to resource its tribunal system so as to enable Convention compliance.

Article 5(4) of the Convention also permits the detained person to challenge the "lawfulness" of his detention. In this connection the detained person must have the opportunity to question whether his detention is consistent both with the applicable municipal law and with the Convention provisions and is not arbitrary.[33] Following the decision in *Winterwerp v. Netherlands*[34] before a detention can be said to be justified under Article 5(1)(e) of the Convention it must be demonstrated (a) by reference to objective medical evidence that the detained person is suffering from "unsound mind"; (b) that the disorder is of a kind or degree as to warrant compulsory confinement. The validity of the continuing confinement depends on the persistence of the mental disorder. It is submitted that Article 5(4) in conjunction with the *Winterwerp* requirements oblige the Tribunal to weigh up medical evidence from both sides in the case before coming to a decision as to whether the patient is suffering from unsound mind and secondly the requirement that the disorder be of a kind or degree as to warrant compulsory confinement imports an obligation on the Tribunal to be satisfied that least restrictive alternatives to compulsory confinement have been considered before the decision to involuntary admit the patient to an approved centre be taken.

Following the decision in *X v. UK*,[35] Article 5(4) requires that the detained person be provided with a continuing remedy at reasonable intervals either by way of "automatic periodic review of a judicial character" or by opportunity for the person alleged to be of unsound mind to "take proceedings at reasonable intervals before a court" to challenge the lawfulness of his continued detention.[36] The Mental Health Act 2001 provides for automatic review of detention each time it is proposed to renew an admission order but does not enable a detained person to take the initiative to instigate the review.

Commentary from a comparative law perspective

In the Canadian provinces of Ontario, and Yukon the Review Board must hear the application within seven days of receipt.[37] In Saskatchewan the chair of the Review Panel must carry out an investigation "immediately" and the Panel must render its decision within three days of receiving the application.[38]

Conclusions

1. It is submitted that there should be a requirement that the consultant carrying out the examination, interview and review be independent of the approved centre.

---

[32] [1989] 12 E.H.R.R. 210.
[33] *Van Droogenbroeck v. Belgium* A 50 para.48 (1982).
[34] [1979] 2 E.H.R.R. 387.
[35] [1981] 4 E.H.R.R. 181.
[36] See *X v. UK* A 46 (1981).
[37] R.S.O 1990 c. M.7, ss. 44(2), 45(1) [rep. 1992, c. 32, s.20]; re-en as 1992, c. 31, ss. 39(2), (3); S.Y.T. 1989-90,c.28, s.31(3).
[38] S.S. 1984-85,c. M-13.1, ss. 34(6), (9).

2. It is submitted that the patient should have the right to have a psychiatrist of his own choosing independently to examine and present a report to the tribunal on his condition.

3. Section 18(1) of the Act allows the tribunal an element of discretion. It may confirm a detention order or renewal order even if medical practitioners have failed to adhere to relevant procedural criteria. It can do so if the failure "does not affect the substance of the order and does not cause an injustice to the person." It is submitted that any breach of procedure is *ipso facto* an injustice. It is the patient's liberty that is at stake and this right must be properly safeguarded. The element of discretion introduced under section 18(1) may effectively defeat the purpose of the Act, which is to guarantee the rights of persons suffering from mental disorder. It is submitted that this discretionary power should be removed from the legislation.

4. The time period of not later than 21 days after the making of the admission order or renewals order specified in section 18(2) may render the patient's right to review by the Tribunal illusory. In reality the detention a person may be objecting to might be nearly ended before it is reviewed. It is submitted that a person's detention should be reviewed within seven days of admission to hospital.

    During the course of the Dáil Debates on the Mental Health Bill the Minister for Health and Children argued that the timescale for review was dictated to a large extent by the volume of cases the personnel associated with Mental Health Tribunal could process and the Minister promised to revisit the issue of the timescale for reviews and change the Act if necessary if it was discovered that the volume of cases was lower than anticipated or the administrative process was quicker and more efficient. The Mental Health Commission is required by section 42(4) of the 2001 Act to review Part 2 of the Act within 18 months and to report in writing to the Minister on the operation of the process together with any findings, conclusions or recommendations concerning the operation that it considers appropriate. It was envisaged that this report would include recommendations to reduce the 21-day timescale.[39]

5. If the proposed revised criteria for commitment specified in Chapter 2 on Primary Care and Admission to Hospital are adopted it is submitted:
    (i)   There should be a requirement that the Mental Health Tribunal satisfy itself that the conditions of detention or the detention itself meets the requirements of the principle of the least restrictive alternative. This is also necessary if the right to self-determination of the patient is to be recognised.
    (ii) It should also be a requirement if the right to treatment is to be upheld that the Mental Health Tribunal satisfy itself that the psychiatric centre to which the person has been involuntarily admitted provides appropriate treatment.
    (iii) The Tribunal should be required to examine the competence of the patient to make his or her own health care decisions if it is to avoid infringing the right of self determination of the competent patient bearing in mind that a patient may be incompetent when admitted to hospital but acquire

---

[39] 536 *Dáil Debates* Cols 1439–1440.

competence to make his own decisions with treatment and the passage of time.

6. In the interests of natural justice where an extension of detention has taken place the Tribunal should require the treating psychiatrist to state in an adversary hearing the reasons why treatment is taking so long to work and the prognosis in fact for the future.

7. It is submitted that the Mental Health Tribunal should have a range of powers on a review. This should include power to make orders for conditional discharge and reclassification of patients; recommendations for leave of absence and transfer to other institutions with a view to discharge at a future date.

Review of conditions which may be attached to the temporary release of a detained patient by the Mental Health Tribunal

In section 26 of the Mental Health Act 2001 (which is not yet in force), the consultant psychiatrist responsible for the care and treatment of a patient may when granting leave of absence to a detained patient to attach such conditions as he or she considers appropriate to the leave. It was proposed in the White Paper, that any conditions so imposed be subject to review by the Mental Health Review Board.[40] Although desirable from the point of view of protection of the patient from imposition of unreasonable or arbitrary conditions, the Mental Health Act does not confer such a power of review on Mental Health Tribunals.

Authorisation of psycho-surgery by the Mental Health Tribunal

Current Irish law

Section 58(1) of the Mental Health Act 2001 (which is not yet in force) provides that psychosurgery shall not be performed on a patient unless (a) the patient gives his or her consent to the psychosurgery and (b) the psychosurgery is authorised by a tribunal. Psychosurgery is defined as "any surgical operation that destroys brain tissue or the functioning of brain tissue and which is performed for the purposes of ameliorating a mental disorder.[41]

Section 58(2) provides that where it is proposed to perform psychosurgery on a patient and the consent of the patient has been obtained, the consultant psychiatrist responsible for the care and treatment of the patient shall notify the Commission in writing of the proposal and the Commission shall refer the matter to a tribunal.

Section 58(3) provides that where such a proposal is referred to a tribunal under section 58 the tribunal shall review the proposal and shall either:

(a) if it is satisfied that it is in the best interests of the health of the patient concerned authorise the performance of the psycho-surgery, or

(b) if it is not so satisfied, refuse to authorise it.

---

[40] See *White Paper*, para.3.36.
[41] Mental Health Act 2001, s.58(6).

By virtue of section 58(4) the provisions of sections 19 and 49 are to apply to the referral of a matter to a tribunal under section 58(4) as they apply to the referral of an admission order or a renewal order to a tribunal under section 17 with any necessary modifications. In effect therefore a patient may appeal to the Circuit Court against a decision of a tribunal in relation to psychosurgery on the grounds that he or she is not suffering from a mental disorder and a tribunal shall have all the powers mentioned in section 49 for the purposes of its functions. These include power to direct the attendance of patient before the tribunal; power to make provision for examination and cross-examination of witnesses before the tribunal and the taking of evidence on oath.[42]

Effect is not to be given to a decision of the tribunal to which section 58 applies before the expiration of the time for bringing an appeal to the Circuit Court[43] or if such an appeal is brought the determination or withdrawal thereof.

Commentary from an international law perspective

Principle 11, paragraph 14 of the *UN Principles for the Protection of Persons with Mental Illness and the Improvement of Mental Health Care.* provides:

> "Psycho-surgery and other intrusive and irreversible treatments for mental illness shall never be carried out on a patient who is an involuntary patient in a mental health facility and to the extent that domestic law permits them to be carried out they may be carried out on any other patient only where the patient has given informed consent and *an independent external body has satisfied itself that there is a genuine informed consent and* that the treatment best serves the health needs of the patient" (emphasis added.)

At European level *Recommendation 1235 (1994) of the Parliamentary Assembly of the Council of Europe on Psychiatry and Human Rights* provides that lobotomies may not be performed unless informed written consent has been given by a patient or a person, counsellor or guardian chosen by the patient as his or her representative and unless the decision has been confirmed *by a select committee not composed exclusively of psychiatric experts.*[44]

Conclusions

1. It is submitted that the Tribunal to which the proposal to perform psycho-surgery is to be referred should be satisfied that valid informed consent has been given in addition to the requirement that the surgery be in the best interests of the health of the patient before authorising the performance of psycho-surgery.

2. In addition to making it a requirement that the tribunal be satisfied that the patient's consent is genuine and informed the *UN Principles* highlight the need for Mental

---

[42] See below pp.410 *et seq.*

[43] S.19(2) provides that an appeal must be brought within 14 days of the receipt by the patient or his/her legal representative of notice of the tribunals decision.

[44] See para.ii.b.

Health Tribunals to be composed of persons who are independent of the applicant consultant psychiatrist and the patient.

Arrangement for the provision of second opinions in relation to consent to treatment

The Government White Paper proposed that where it was proposed to administer ECT to a detained patient who was unwilling or unable to give consent a consultant psychiatrist approved by the proposed Mental Health Review Board and acting on its behalf would be required to give second medical opinion.[45] This proposal is not followed through by the Mental Health Act 2002 and under the terms of the Act where the patient is unable or unwilling to give consent the programme of therapy is to be authorised by a second consultant psychiatrist (in a form specified by the Commission) following referral of the matter to him or her by the first mentioned psychiatrist.[46]

Commentary from a comparative law perspective

In New South Wales, under the Mental Health Act 1990, application must be made to a Mental Health Tribunal to approve the administration of ECT to an involuntary patient. At least two medical practitioners one of whom is a psychiatrist must certify in writing that ECT is a reasonable and proper treatment and necessary and desirable for the safety and welfare of the patient.[47] The Tribunal must then hold an inquiry to determine whether the patient is capable of genuine informed consent to the treatment, whether that consent has been given and whether, in the absence of informed consent the treatment is reasonable and proper and is necessary or desirable for the patient's safety or welfare. The views of the patient as well as the medical evidence must be taken into account by the Tribunal.[48]

Conclusions

If it is proposed to administer ECT to a person without a person's consent a truly independent review process is required to determine that person's competency to consent. Evidence of practice in other jurisdictions shows that where a second opinion is required it routines supports the original decision by the treating psychiatrist on the basis that it adheres to general and approved practice.[49]

The criteria for an independent review process would be satisfied by a hearing before a Mental Health Tribunal which is independent of the treating psychiatrist and detaining authority and at which the patient had a fair opportunity to express and defend what s/he perceives to be in his/her best interests.

---

[45] See para.6.12(ii).
[46] Mental Health Act 1990 (NSW), s.188.
[47] Mental Health Act 2001, s.59 (which is not yet in force).
[48] Mental Health Act 1990 (NSW), s.193.
[49] See Cooney T. and O'Neill O., *Psychiatric Detention Civil Commitment in Ireland* (Baikonur 1996), p.63.

Review of decisions to transfer patient to the Central Mental Hospital or other special psychiatric centres by the Mental Health Tribunal

Current Irish law

Section 21(2)(a) of the Mental Health Act 2001 (which is not yet in force) provides that where the clinical director of an approved centre (i) is of opinion that it would be for the benefit of a patient detained in that centre or that it is necessary for the purpose of obtaining special treatment for such a patient to transfer him or her to the Central Mental Hospital, and (ii) proposes to do so, he or must notify the Mental Health Commission in writing of the proposal and the Commission must refer the proposal to a Tribunal.

Section 21(2)(b) provides that where a proposal is referred to a tribunal under section 21 the tribunal must review the proposal as soon as may be but not later than 14 days thereafter and shall either (i) if it is satisfied that it is in the best interest of the health of the patient concerned authorise the transfer of the patient concerned, or (ii) if it is not so satisfied, refuse to authorise it.

By virtue of section 21(2)(c), the patient may appeal to the Circuit Court against a decision of the tribunal on the grounds that he or she is not[50] suffering from a mental disorder and the tribunal has all the procedural powers afforded it by section 49[51] to conduct proceedings.

Effect will not be given to a decision of a tribunal under section 21(2)(b) before the expiration of the time for bringing of an appeal to the Circuit Court,[52] or (ii) if such an appeal is brought the determination or withdrawal thereof.[53]

Commentary

In Chapter 5 reference was made to the US case of *Eubanks v. Clarke*,[54] in which it was held that there could be no transfer of an involuntary patient from one mental facility to another that is more restrictive without according a patient a hearing.

Conclusions

It is not clear from the terms of section 21 whether the patient will be afforded a hearing before the tribunal before a decision is taken to transfer him to the Central Mental Hospital or whether the review will take place on the basis of written evidence only. It is submitted that there should be no transfer of patients to the more restrictive conditions of the Central Mental Hospital without affording the patient the opportunity of a hearing before a Mental Health Tribunal.

---

[50] This burden of proof is likely to infringe both Art.5(1) and Art.5(4) of the European Convention on Human Rights. See *R(H) v. London North and East Region Mental Health Review Tribunal* [2002] Q.B. 1 in which it was held that Arts 5(1) and 5(4) require a tribunal to be *positively* satisfied that all the criteria justifying the patient's detention in hospital for treatment continue to exist before refusing a patient's discharge.

[51] See below, p.411.

[52] S.19(2) provides that an appeal to the Circuit Court must be brought by the patient within 14 days of the receipt by him or her or by his or her legal representative of notice of the tribunal's decision.

[53] Mental Health Act 2001, s.21(2)(d).

[54] 454 F. Supp 1022 (F.D. PA 1977).

Review of appropriacy of continuation of child treatment order if the child has been the subject of an order for longer than one year

Under the terms of the Government White Paper entitled "A New Mental Health Act" it was proposed to empower the District Court to make an order ("a treatment order") for the admission of a child with a mental disorder to an approved centre specialising in the care of children where the parent or guardian cannot or will not consent to treatment or where the child objects to admission for treatment.[55] The treatment order was to apply for an initial period of twenty-eight days and may be extended by three months, by a further period of six months and by periods of one year.[56]

The view was expressed in the White Paper that "in view of the court's involvement in the decision to admit a child to an approved centre for treatment, it was not necessary to involve the Mental Health Review Board in the review of the order or its extension."[57] However, it was proposed that the Mental Health Review Board would review by panel the appropriacy of the continuation of the child treatment order where it is proposed to extend it for one year. Where such a review is carried out the Board would be obliged to make its recommendation known to the court. This recommendation is not followed through in the Mental Health Act 2001.

Under section 25 of the Mental Health Act 2001 (which has yet to come into force), the District Court has power to make an order admitting and detaining a child in a specified approved centre for a period not exceeding 21 days where it is satisfied that the child is suffering from a mental disorder as defined in the Act,[58] and requires treatment which s/he is unlikely to receive unless such an order is made. The court also has power to extend the period of detention for an initial period of three months and on the expiration of that period for successive periods not exceeding six months.[59]

Commentary and conclusions

Where an adult is admitted as an involuntary patient to an approved centre his/her detention is automatically reviewable by a Mental Health Tribunal within 21 days. This right of automatic review is not a afforded to children who been involuntarily admitted to an approved centre by order of the District Court for 21 days under section 25. Although the District Court has power to renew the order after 21 days and in order to renew the order must be satisfied that the child is still suffering from a mental disorder[60] the absence of review of the initial order may amount to a breach of Article 5.4 of the European Convention on Human Rights and discriminatory.

Additional powers?

It is submitted that the Minister for Health and Minister for Justice Equality and Law Reform should have power to refer the case of a patient detained under the Act to the

---

[55] See *White Paper*, para.3.28.
[56] *Ibid.*, para.3.29.
[57] *Ibid.*, para.3.30.
[58] See Mental Health Act 2001, s.3.
[59] *Ibid.*, s.25(9), (10).
[60] *Ibid.*, s.25(11).

Tribunal at any time. This power would be particularly useful where the patient's situation has changed substantially and the automatic review does not arise for some time.

THE HEARING

Procedure for automatic review of admission orders and renewal orders by the Mental Health Tribunal

Current Irish Law

The Mental Health Act 2001 provides a broad outline of the nature of the automatic review of admission and renewal orders by the Mental Health Review Tribunals but leaves many questions unanswered about the procedure aspects of the review. It envisages the hearing of the automatic review of an admission order and renewal order would take place in two stages.

First stage

The first stage would take place when the Mental Health Commission directed a member of the panel of consultant psychiatrists in writing to (i) examine the patient concerned, (ii) interview the consultant psychiatrist responsible for the care and treatment of the patient, and (iii) review the records relating to the patient in order to determine in the interest of the patient whether the patient is suffering from a mental disorder and to report in writing within 14 days on the results of the examination, interview and review to the tribunal and provide a copy of the report to the legal representative of the patient.[61]

Second stage

At the second stage, the Act states that "the tribunal shall review the detention of the patient concerned" and shall either (a) if satisfied that the patient is suffering from a mental disorder and that (i) that the provisions of sections 9,10, 12, 14, 15 and 16 where applicable have been complied with or (ii) if there has been a failure to comply with any such provision, that the failure does not affect the substance of the order and does not cause and injustice, affirm the order or (b) if not so satisfied, revoke the order and direct that the patient be discharged from the approved centre concerned.[62] Before making a decision the tribunal must have regard to the report of the consultant psychiatrist furnished under section 17(1)(c).[63]

A decision of the tribunal at the second stage must be made as soon as may be but not later than 21 days after the making of the admission order or renewal order concerned.[64] This period may be extended by order of the tribunal for a further period of 14 days and thereafter may be further extended by it by order for a period of 14 days

---

[61] Mental Health Act 2001, s.17(1)(c).
[62] *Ibid.*, s.18(1).
[63] *Ibid.*, s.18(2).
[64] *Ibid.*, s.18(2).

on the application of the patient if the tribunal is satisfied that it is in the interest of the patient. In the case of extension by order of the tribunal the relevant admission and renewal orders continue in force until the expiration of the order.[65]

Powers of Tribunal in connection wtih review hearing

Under section 49, which came into force on April 5, 2002, of the Act the tribunal is conferred with a number of powers in connection with a review. First under section 49(2)(a) it may direct in writing the consultant psychiatrist responsible for the care and treatment of a patient the subject of the review concerned to arrange for the patient to attend before the tribunal on a date and at a time and place specified in the direction. This is subject to section 49(11) which states that a patient shall not be required to attend before a tribunal under section 49 if in the opinion of the tribunal such attendance might be prejudicial to his or her mental health, well-being or emotional condition.

Under section 49(2)(b) the Tribunal may also direct in writing any person whose evidence is required by the tribunal to attend before the tribunal on a date and at a time and place specified in the direction and to give evidence and to produce any document or thing in his or her possession or power specified in the direction.

Further under section 49(2)(c), the Tribunal may direct any person in attendance before the tribunal to produce to the tribunal any document or thing in his or her possession or power specified in the direction. Under section 49(2)(d) it may also direct in writing any person to send to the tribunal any document or thing in his or her possession or power specified in the direction and under section 49(2)(e) give any other directions for the purposes of the proceedings concerned that appear to the Tribunal to be reasonable and just.

Consequences of failure to co-operate with Tribunal

Failure to co-operate with the requirements of the tribunal will result in an offence. Thus an offence will be committed where a person who having been directed under section 49(2) to attend before a tribunal without just cause or excuse disobeys the direction. An offence will also be committed where a person directed under section 49(2)(b) (direction to attend and give evidence) and having had tendered to him or her any sum in respect of the expenses of his or her attendance which a witness summoned to attend before the High Court would be entitled to have tendered to him or her without just cause or excuse disobeys the direction.[66]

An offence will also be committed where a person attends before a tribunal pursuant to a direction under section 49(2)(b) but refuses to take the oath on being required by the tribunal to do so or refuses to answer any question to which the tribunal may legally require an answer or to produce any document or thing in his or her possession or power legally required by the tribunal to be produced by the person.[67]

A person who fails or refuses to send to the tribunal any document or thing legally

---

[65] Mental Health Act 2001, s.18(4).
[66] *Ibid.*, s.49(4)(a).
[67] *Ibid.*, s.49(4)(b).

required by the tribunal under section 49(2)(d) to be sent to it by the person or without just cause or excuse disobeys a direction under section 49(2)(c), (d), or (e) will also be guilty of an offence.[68]

Further a person who does any other thing in relation to the proceedings before the tribunal, which if done in relation to proceedings before a court by a witness in the court would be contempt of court, will be guilty of an offence.[69] In all of the above cases the offence is punishable on summary conviction by a fine not exceeding €1904.61 or imprisonment not exceeding 12 months or both.

If a person gives false evidence before a tribunal in such circumstances that if he or she had given the evidence before a court he or she would be guilty of perjury he or she will be guilty of that offence.[70]

Tribunal procedure

Section 49 also addresses in general terms the procedural aspects of tribunal hearings. Thus section 49(6) provides that the procedure of a tribunal in relation to a review by it under the Act shall, subject to the provisions of the Act be determined by the tribunal and the tribunal must, without prejudice to the generality of its power to determine procedures make provision for:

(a) notifying the consultant psychiatrist responsible for the care and treatment of the patient the subject of the review and the patient or his or her legal representatives of the date, time and place of the relevant sitting of the tribunal;

(b) giving the patient the subject of the review or his or her legal representative a copy of any report furnished to the tribunal under section 17 and an indication in writing of the nature and source of any information relating to the matter which has come to notice in the course of the review;

(c) subject to section 49(11) enabling the patient the subject of the review and his or her legal representative to be present at the relevant sitting of the tribunal and enabling the patient the subject of the review to present his or her case to the tribunal in person or through a legal representative. Section 49(11) provides that a patient shall not be required to attend before a tribunal under section 49 if, in the opinion of the tribunal such attendance might be prejudicial to his or her mental health, well being or emotional condition;

(d) enabling written statements to be admissible as evidence by the tribunal with the consent of the patient the subject of the review or his or her legal representative;

(e) enabling any signature appearing on a document produced before the tribunal to be taken in the absence of evidence to the contrary to be that of the person whose signature it purports to be;

(f) the examination by or on behalf of the tribunal and the cross-examination by or on behalf of the patient the subject of the review concerned (on oath or otherwise as it may determine) of witnesses before the tribunal called by it;

---

[68] Mental Health Act 2001, s.49(4)(c).
[69] *Ibid.*, s.49(4)(d).
[70] *Ibid.*, s.49(5).

(g) the examination by or on behalf of the patient the subject of the review and the cross examination by or on behalf of the tribunal (on oath or otherwise as it may determine) of witnesses before the tribunal called by the patient the subject of the review;

(h) the determination by the tribunal whether evidence at the tribunal should be give on oath;

(i) the administration by the tribunal of the oath to witnesses before the tribunal; and

(j) the making of a sufficient record of the proceedings of the tribunal.

Witnesses whose evidence has been, is being or is to be given before the tribunal in proceedings under the Mental Health Act are to be entitled to the same privileges and immunities as a witness in a court.[71] A legal representative appearing before the tribunal in proceedings under the Mental Health Act shall be entitled to the same privileges and immunities as a legal representative in a court.[72]

Sittings of the tribunal for the purposes of an investigation by it under the Mental Health Act must be held in private.[73] Documents of the tribunal and documents of its members connected with the tribunal or its functions wherever published, reports of the tribunal wherever published and statements made in any form at meetings or sittings of the tribunal by its members or officials and such statements wherever published subsequently all are absolutely privileged.[74]

Implications of the European Convention on Human Rights Act 2003

With the coming into force of section 3 the European Convention on Human Rights Act 2003 the tribunal will be obliged to perform its functions in a manner compatible with the State's obligations under the provisions of the European Convention on Human Rights. In this regard Article 5.4 of the Convention is particularly pertinent. It provides that "Everyone who is deprived of his liberty …by detention shall be entitled to take proceedings by which the lawfulness of his detention shall be decided speedily by a court and his release ordered if the detention is not lawful." In *Winterwerp v. the Netherlands*,[75] the European Court of Human Rights interpreted Article 5(4) to mean that where a person who is being detained as being of "unsound mind" under Article 5(1)(e) s/he must, *inter alia*, be allowed "to be heard either in person or where necessary[76] through some form of representation."

Commentary and conclusions

In the absence of the procedural rules for reviews it is difficult to determine whether the

---

[71] Mental Health Act 2001, s.49(7).

[72] *Ibid.*, s.49(8).

[73] *Ibid.*, s.49(9).

[74] *Ibid.*, s.49(10).

[75] A 33 para.60 (1979).

[76] In *Winterwerp* the court indicated that legal representation would be vital where a "person of unsound mind" does not understand what is happening.

review as provided for in the 2001 Act will be a mere rubber stamping exercise or will comprise a full hearing of the patient's case. If due process does not feature as a fundamental feature of the rules then they may be "little more than legalised case conferences applying an odd mixture of investigative and adversarial approaches".[77]

It is submitted that in the interests of ensuring that the principles of natural justice are observed in the proceedings when published the procedural rules for reviews should confer on the patient a right to be present at the review subject to the discretion of the tribunal to exclude him/her if attendance would be *seriously* prejudicial to his/her mental health, well-being or emotional condition. This would establish that the rules contemplate that the attendance of the patient would be the general rule subject to limited exceptions and make for greater due process in procedures.

Under the Mental Health Act the review of admission and renewal orders will take place a post-commitment and possibly may not be afforded until 20 days after the person objects to his or her committal. The Act allows for initial detention for a period of 21 days, which may then be extended. In reality the initial detention subject to review might be nearly ended before the review takes place. Except in emergencies a person it is submitted that a patient should have a right to a review within seven days of initial detention.

At the review of a renewal order it is submitted that the treating psychiatrist should be required to state in full adversary hearing why treatment is taking so long to work and what the prospects of treatment working are in fact.

The onus and standard of proof before Mental Health Tribunals

The Mental Health Act requires the tribunal to be "satisfied" before affirming an admission order or renewal order that the patient is suffering from mental disorder; that the procedural provisions relating to recommendations, admission and renewal orders have been complied with or if there has been a failure to comply with any such provision that the failure does not affect the substance of the order and does not cause an injustice

It would appear that the onus is on the person seeking to detain to satisfy the tribunal that the conditions for detention have been met. However, the standard of proof is unclear. Is it "on the balance of probabilities" or "by clear and convincing evidence"?

The Tribunal will rely considerably upon the report of the member of the panel of consultant psychiatrists in reaching its conclusions. The content of his report will therefore be of significance and it is submitted that the use of summary diagnostic labels should be discouraged in such reports as it may unduly influence the Tribunal.

Commentary from a comparative law perspective

In Canada a number of cases have held[78] that in review proceedings the onus of proof

---

[77] See Eastman N., "Mental Health Law: Civil liberties and the principle of Reciprocity" (1994) Vol.308 *British Medical Journal* 43.

[78] *M v. Alberta* (1985) 63 A.R. 14 (Q.B.); *In re Hoskins and Hislop* (1981) 121 D.L.R. (3d) 337 (B.C.S.C.); *Azhar v. Anderson*, unreported, June 28, 1985, No. 609/85, 33 A.C.W.S. (2d) 521 (Ont. Dist. Ct. Toronto Judge H.R. Locke): *G.G. v. Swamy* unreported, April 4, 1986, No. 1179/86, 36 A.C.W.S. (2d) 247 (Ont. Dist. Ct., Thunder Bay, Judge S.R. Kurisko).

rests with the hospital to establish that the statutory criteria for the patients involuntary confinement are satisfied. The standard of proof in review proceedings is the ordinary civil one namely on the balance of probabilities.[79]

However, in a number of decisions unrelated to mental health law the Supreme Court of Canada has endorsed the principle that the cogency of evidence necessary to satisfy the civil standard of proof is directly related to the nature and gravity of the issue in question.[80] This has been applied in several cases involving review proceedings under the Mental Health Act in which the court has stressed that it must have regard to the grave nature of the proceedings in deciding whether the evidence satisfies the standard of proof.[81] In the USA a middle ground standard of clear and convincing evidence is used.[82]

Conclusions

1. It is submitted that where the fundamental right to liberty is in question the party seeking to detain should bear the burden of proving justification for the detention by clear and convincing evidence.

2. To avoid summary labelling the law should require psychiatrists giving evidence to prove the factual descriptions of behaviour and mental or emotional condition with reference to the statutory criteria for committal and without using psychiatric diagnostic labelling. Psychiatrists should be required to substantiate findings of dangerousness by reference to empirical research and to reveal the chances of mistaken prediction in the case.

3. With regard to competence the psychiatrist should not be permitted to offer a conclusive judgment on the matter but to offer evidence of what decision the person facing commitment was confronted with, what information the psychiatrist gave the person, what efforts he or she took to make the information understandable and what responses the person made to all of this. The question of competence being both a legal and social matter should be left to the mental health tribunal to adjudicate upon.

---

[79] *In re Robinson and Hislop* (1980) 114 D.L.R. (3d) 620 (B.C.S.C.); *In re Hoskins and Hislop* (1981) 121 D.L.R. (3d) 337 (B.C.S.C.); *Azhar v. Anderson*, unreported, June 28, 1985, No. 609/85, 33 A.C.W.S. (2d) 521; *G.G. v. Swamy*, unreported, April 4, 1986, No. 1179/86, 36 A.C.W.S. (2d) 247 (Ont. Dist. Ct. Thunder Bay, Judge S.R.Kurisko); *Reference re Procedures and the Mental Health Act* (1984) 5 D.L.R. (4th) 577 (P.E.I.C.A.).

[80] See *R v. Oakes* (1986) 26 D.L.R. (4th) 200 at 226 (S.C.C.); *Continental Insurance Co v. Dalton Cartage Co.* [1982] 1 S.C.R. 164.

[81] *In re Robinson and Hislop* (1980) 114 D.L.R. (3d) 620 (B.C.S.C.); *In re Hoskins and Hislop* (1981) 121 D.L.R. (3d) 337 (B.C.S.C.); *G.G. v. Swamy*, unreported, April 4, 1986, No. 1179/86, 36 ACWS (2d) 247 (Ont. Dist. Ct. Thunder Bay, Judge S.R. Kurisko) but see *M v. Alberta* (1985) 63 A.R. 14 (Q.B.).

[82] See *Addington v. Texas* 441 U.S. 418 (1979).

THE DETERMINATION OF THE MENTAL HEALTH TRIBUNAL AND APPEALS

Determination of Tribunal Where the Tribunal is satisfied that the patient is suffering from a mental disorder or that the procedural provisions relating to recommendations, admission and renewal orders have been complied with or if there has been a failure to comply with any procedural provision that the failure does not affect the substance of the order or cause an injustice, it must affirm the order. If it is not so satisfied it must revoke the order and direct that the patient be discharged from the approved centre concerned.[83]

Where the Mental Health Tribunal has made a decision notice in writing of the decision and the reasons therefor must be given to (a) the Commission, (b) the consultant psychiatrist responsible for the care and treatment of the patient concerned, (c) the patient and his or her legal representative, and (d) any other person to whom, in the opinion of the tribunal such notice should be given.[84] Notice must be given as soon as may be after the decision and within 21 days after the making of the admission order or renewal order concerned or if it be the case that the period has been extended by order of the tribunal for a further period of 14 days and further extended by order for a period of 14 days under section 18(4), within that period.[85]

It is interesting to note that in England it was held in the case of *Bone v. Mental Health Review Tribunal*[86] that a Mental Health Review Tribunal in giving its reasons must do more than simply state that the statutory grounds are met or not met. In that case Nolan J relied on a line of precedents to find that "proper, adequate, reasons must be given"[87] which are sufficient to "enable [the parties to the hearing] to know that the tribunal has made no error of law".[88]

The patient's right of appeal The Mental Health Act 2001, which has yet to come fully into force, provides that the patient has a right of appeal against a decision of a tribunal to affirm an order made in respect of him or her on the limited grounds that he or she is not suffering from a mental disorder.[89] The right of appeal is to the Circuit Court not the High Court as envisaged by the White Paper.[90]

The appellate jurisdiction of the Circuit Court under section 19 (which has yet to come into force) may be exercised by the judge of the circuit in which the approved centre concerned is situated or, at the option of the patient, in which the patient is ordinarily resident.[91] The appeal must be brought by the patient by notice in writing within 14 days of the receipt by him or his or her legal representative or notice under section 18 of the decision concerned.[92] Notice of proceedings must be served by the

---

[83] Mental Health Act 2001, s.18(1).
[84] *Ibid.*, s.18(5).
[85] *Ibid.*, s.18(6).
[86] [1985] 3 All E.R. 330.
[87] *Per* Megaw J. in *In re Poyser and Mills Arbitration* [1963] 1 All E.R. 612 at 616.
[88] *Per* Donaldson P. in *Alexander Machinery (Dudley Ltd) v. Crabtree* [1974] I.C.R. 120 at 122.
[89] Mental Health Act 2001, s.19(1).
[90] See para.5.17.
[91] Mental Health Act 2001, s.19(3).
[92] *Ibid.*, s.19(2).

person bringing the proceedings on: (a) the consultant psychiatrist concerned, (b) the tribunal concerned, (c) the clinical director of the approved centre concerned and (d) any other person specified by the Circuit Court.[93] Before making an order under section 19 the Circuit Court shall have regard to any submission made to it in relation to any matter by or on behalf of a party to the proceedings concerned or any other person on whom notice is served under section 19(6) or any other person having an interest in the proceedings.[94]

The *in camera* rule applies to appeals to the Circuit Court and section 19(8) provides that the Circuit Court shall exclude from the court during the hearing of an appeal under section 19 all persons except officers of the court, persons directly concerned in the hearing, bona fide representatives of the press and such other persons (if any) as the court may in its discretion permit to remain.

Reporting restrictions also apply and section 19(9) provides that no matter likely to lead members of the public to identify a patient who is or has been the subject of proceedings under this section shall be published in a written publication available to the public or be broadcast.

The Circuit Court may however, in any case if satisfied that it is appropriate to do so in the interests of the patient, by order dispense with the prohibitions of that subsection in relation to him or her to such an extent as may be specified in the order.[95]

If a matter is published or broadcast in contravention of the prohibition then the following will be guilty of an offence (a) in the case of publication in a newspaper or periodical any proprietor, any editor and any publisher of the newspaper or periodical; (b) in the case of any other publication,[96] the person who publishes it, and (c) in the case of a broadcast,[97] any person who transmits or provides the programme in which the broadcast is made and any person having functions in relation to the programme corresponding to those of an editor of a newspaper.[98] Nothing in section 19 affects the law as to contempt of court.[99]

In any proceedings under section 19 a document purporting to be a report of a consultant psychiatrist under section 17 concerning a patient shall be evidence of the

---

[93] *Ibid.*, s.19(6). Such a notice may be served on a person by (a) delivering it to him or her or to his or her solicitor (b) by addressing it to him or her and leaving it at his or her usual or last known residence or place of business or by addressing it to his or her solicitor and leaving it at the solicitor's office, (c) by sending it by registered post to him or her at his or her usual or last known residence or place of business or to his or her solicitor at the solicitor's office or (d) in the case of a body corporate by delivering it or sending it by registered post to the secretary or other officer of the body at its registered or principal office. See s.19(15).

[94] Mental Health Act 2001, s.19(7).

[95] *Ibid.*, s.19(10).

[96] "Written publication" is defined by s.19(13) of the Act to include "a film, a sound track and any other record in permanent form (including a record that is not in legible form but which is capable of being reproduced in a legible form) but does not include an indictment or other document prepared for use in particular legal proceedings.

[97] "Broadcast" is defined by s.19(13) as "the transmission, relaying or distribution by wireless telegraphy of communications, sounds, signs, visual images or signals, intended for direct reception by the general public whether such communications, sounds, signs, visual images or signals are actually received or not."

[98] Mental Health Act 2001, s.19(11).

[99] *Ibid.*, s.19(12).

matters stated in the document without further proof and shall, unless the contrary is proved, be deemed to be such a document.[100]

On appeal to it the Circuit Court shall (a) unless it is shown by the patient to the satisfaction of the court that he or she is not suffering from mental disorder by order affirm the order, or (b) if it is so shown as aforesaid revoke the order.[101] No appeal lies against an order of the Circuit Court under section 19 other than an appeal on a point of law to the High Court.[102]

Following the coming into force of section 2 of the European Convention on Human Rights Act 2003 which requires a court to interpret and apply any statutory provision in a manner compatible with the State's obligations under the European Court of Human Rights it appears that the burden of proof imposed by section 19(1) on the patient to prove that s/he no longer suffers from a mental disorder may be open to challenge on the basis of incompatibility with the Convention provisions.

In the English case of *R (H) v. London North and East Region Mental Health Review Tribunal (Secretary of State for Health intervening)*,[103] the Court of Appeal held that placing the burden of proof on the patient to prove that the criteria justifying their detention no longer existed breached articles 5(1) and 5(4) of the European Convention on Human Rights. This accords with the decision of the European Court of Human Rights in *Winterwerp v. Netherlands*,[104] where the onus is placed on the detaining authority to prove the person is in need of continuing detention.

The right of application for judicial review

Both the patient and the detaining authority have a right to apply for judicial review of the tribunal's decision. However in the case of the patient the court has a discretion to require the applicant to exhaust the alternative remedy of appeal to the Circuit Court first.[105] The remedy sought would be typically that of *certiorari* – an order quashing the decision of the Tribunal on stated substantive grounds but in addition the remedies of *mandamus*, prohibition, declaration, and damages may be available in appropriate cases.[106]

Procedurally the applicant for judicial review would be obliged to obtain the leave of the court to institute proceedings.[107] Application must be made within six months from the date when the grounds of the application arose.[108] To obtain leave it would be necessary to establish a stateable ground on the facts for the relief sought and an arguable

---

[100] Mental Health Act 2001, s.19(14).

[101] Mental Health Act 2001, s.19(4).

[102] *Ibid.*, s.19(16).

[103] [2001] 3 W.L.R. 512.

[104] [1979] 2 E.H.R.R. 387.

[105] *State (Roche) v. Delap* [1980] I.R. 170, *State (Litzouw) v. Johnson* [1981] I.L.R.M. 273 *per* Garrnon J. at 279. See M. De Blacam, *Judicial Review* (Butterworths, 2001), pp.233–236.

[106] As to the nature of these remedies see generally M. De Blacam, *Judicial Review* (Butterworths, 2001).

[107] Rules of the Superior Courts, O.84, r.20.

[108] *Ibid.*, O.84, r.21(1).

case in law on those facts. It would also be necessary to show that the only effective remedy on the facts would be an order for judicial review.[109]

As a matter of substantive law a decision of a Mental Health Tribunal may be judicially reviewed on the basis of illegality, irrationality (or unreasonableness), procedural impropriety and more recently in human rights cases,[110] on the grounds of the principle of proportionality.

When it is alleged that the decision of a Tribunal is illegal the assertion is essentially that it does not have the legal authority to make the decision for example by reason of the Tribunal members not having the required qualifications.

When the argument of irrationality or unreasonableness is advanced the assertion in essence is that the Tribunal has used a power given for one purpose for another or has considered irrelevant information or has failed to consider relevant information or has made a decision which is so unreasonable that no other Tribunal in a similar situation could make it.[111]

If procedural impropriety is claimed the argument being advanced is usually that the statutory procedures were not followed and/or that the decision does not accord with the principles of natural or constitutional justice, such as the right to a hearing, the right to impartiality and freedom from bias in decision making and a right to know reasons for a decision.

Where application for judicial review of a Mental Health Tribunal decision is made by an applicant on the grounds of the principle of proportionality what is essentially claimed is that in the making of the decision the Tribunal did not strike an appropriate balance between the means and ends adopted by the legislation i.e. that in the circumstances the limitation of the patient's right was necessary in a democratic society and the interference with the right was proportionate to the legitimate aim being pursued.[112]

In addition to judicial review there is some English authority that suggests that in certain circumstances application could be made by the treating authority to readmit the patient as an involuntary patient. In the English High Court decision in *R v. South Western*

---

[109] See *G v. DPP* [1994] 1 I.R. 374.

[110] Note the decision of the European Court of Human Rights in *Smith and Grady v. UK* [1999] 20 E.H.R.R. 493 in which it held that the system of judicial review in the England and Wales was in breach of Article 13 of the European Convention on Human Rights which guarantees that national courts will provide an effective remedy for breach of substantive Convention rights. This was because the irrationality test did not allow the courts to consider whether the human rights of the applicant had been breached and if so whether for good cause and in an appropriate manner. Following that decision the House of Lords in *R v. Secretary of State for Home Department ex parte Daly* [2001] 2 A.C. 532 held that courts hearing judicial review cases must form a judgment as to whether a Convention Right has been breached and so far as was permissible under the Human Rights Act 1998 grant an effective remedy. This decision in effect means that English courts are obliged to examine whether: (a) an applicant's Convention rights have been breached; (b) if so, whether the reason for the breach is permitted by the Convention and, most significantly, (c) whether the infringement is proportionate to the harm it seeks to avoid. These cases are of particular interest as possible indicators of the approach of the courts in the Irish jurisdiction following the coming into force of the European Convention on Human Rights Act 2003.

[111] See *State(Keegan) v. Stardust Victims Compensation Tribunal* [1987] I.L.R.M. 202.

[112] See *Heaney v. Ireland* [1994] 3 I.R. 593 See *also R. v. Secretary of State for the Home Department, ex p. Daly* [2001] 2 A.C. 532.

Hospital Managers and another, ex parte M,[113] it was held that an application could be made to re-admit the patient as an involuntary patient notwithstanding the tribunal's decision to discharge provided the application was made in good faith. This was the case even if there had been no change in the patient's condition.

Nevertheless in the later decision of *R v. Oxfordshire Mental Healthcare NHS Trust, ex p. H,*[114] while endorsing the decision in *Ex parte M* to the extent that it decided that it was the duty of those making application for involuntary admission following a tribunal decision to discharge to act *bona fide* and objectively the Court of Appeal circumscribed the conditions which had to exist before such an application could be made. Phillips L.J. emphasised that the admission team must have some basis on which to disagree with the tribunal's decision. He stated that usually this would be based on the discharged patient's "reaction to life in the community".[115] Sedley L.J. stated that an order of a tribunal for discharge would always be a relevant fact which the subsequent decision maker would be obliged to take into account and a failure to do so would vitiate a subsequent decision to seek admission.[116]

The circumstances which must exist before an application for re-admission could validly be made were further qualified in *R v. Ashworth Hospital Authority, ex parte H,*[117] where the Court of Appeal following the decision in *R (Von Brandenburg) v. East London and the City Mental Health NHS Trust*[118] held that the effect of that decision was that it was open to professionals to resection a patient only where "material circumstances" existed "of which the tribunal [was] not aware when it [ordered] discharge" or the tribunal's decision has been quashed by a court.[119] Thus it would be appropriate to make an application for re-admission only where new facts existed justifying that application.

Notwithstanding the above decisions it should be noted that after a readmission a patient's detention is again reviewable by a tribunal.

Commentary from an international law perspective

In contrast to the right of appeal in section 19(1) of the Mental Health Act 2001 which is vested in the patient alone Principle 17 of the *United Nations Principles for the Protection of Persons with Mental Illness and the Improvement of Mental Health Care* with which standards it was proposed that the new legislation should comply[120] provides that in addition to the patient, his personal representative or any interested person shall have the right to appeal to a higher court against a decision that the patient be admitted to or be retained in a mental health facility.[121]

---

[113] [1994] 1 All E.R. 161.
[114] [2002] E.W.H.C. 465.
[115] Para.30.
[116] Para.41.
[117] [2002] E.W.C.A. Civ. 923.
[118] [2002] Q.B. 235.
[119] Para.56.
[120] See White Paper, *A New Mental Health Act*, July 1995, Pn.1824, para.1.13.
[121] Principle 17.7.

Conclusions

1. Section 19 of the Mental Health Act 2001 provides that patient may appeal to the Circuit Court against a decision of a tribunal to affirm an order made in respect of him or her on the grounds that s/he is not suffering from a mental disorder. This burden of proof has been shown to contravene Articles 5(1) and 5(4) of the European Convention on Human Rights.[122] Where there is an appeal the onus must be on the detaining authority to show that a patient is suffering from a mental disorder if the detention is to continue.

2. Confining the appeal to cases where the patient must show that s/he does not suffer from mental disorder also means that the patient cannot appeal on the ground that the tribunal has used its discretion unreasonably (although the remedy of judicial review may be available after the avenue of appeal has been exhausted). This is a flaw in the Act. In the past case law has been concerned with adherence to procedural criteria such as time limits and the nature of an examination.[123] It is submitted that the Act should provide a comprehensive right of appeal and expressly state that the appeal covers all aspects of the detention process both substantive and procedural.

3. The right of appeal should be afforded to the patient's personal representative and any interested person wishing to challenge the determination of the court to detain the person with mental illness.

CONCLUSIONS

On examination the provisions of the Mental Health Act 2001 relating to the establishment of Mental Health Tribunals are incomplete, in part inconsistent with the White Paper they were designed to implement and reveal flaws, which are prejudicial to the interests of a patient who may wish to apply to them to vindicate his rights.

There are insufficient protections against bias built into the composition of the tribunal; the hearing may take place just before the patient is discharged so that the vindication of his right to liberty may be academic; the tribunal is given no powers to review conditions attached to the temporary release of a detained patient; it has no power to review whether a patient's informed consent to psycho-surgery is genuine and it is not clear whether a patient will be afforded a hearing before a tribunal before being transferred to the Central Mental Hospital. In addition it has no power to review an initial child treatment order.

The right of the patient to be present at a hearing is not stipulated nor is the onus and standard of proof. Finally the grounds of appeal contravene Articles 5(1) and 5(4) of the European Convention on Human Rights. Subject to what may appear in Regulations regarding procedures what one sees in the Mental Health Act 2001 suggests that Mental Health Tribunals may offer something less than desired in the matter of vindication of the rights of patients with mental illness.

---

[122] *R(H) v. London North and East Region Mental Health Review Tribunal* [2002] Q.B. 1.
[123] See *Bailey v. Gallagher* [1996] 2 I.L.R.M. 433 and *O'Reilly v. Moroney*, unreported, Supreme Court, November 16, 1993.

CHAPTER SEVEN

Mental Disability and the Criminal Law

INTRODUCTION

If a person accused of committing a criminal offence is suffering from mental illness the usual procedures of the law may be affected or distorted in a number of ways. At issue are the myriad substantive and procedural protections allowed to a defendant under the rule of law in the criminal process. Naturally some variation of these protections is necessitated due to the condition of the accused person but the real issue is the extent to which due process protections can or should be extended to meet the particular characteristics of the person involved.

The range of issues are quite broad and include consideration of the following. First, the person concerned may never be reported to the Garda Síochána if the view is taken that s/he is not morally responsible for his/her acts. Secondly, the prosecuting authorities in exercise of their discretion may decide not to prosecute. Thirdly, if a prosecution proceeds the accused person may transferred to a psychiatric hospital for treatment when on remand and/or be found unfit to plead. Fourthly, mental disorder may provide a defence to a criminal charge. Fifthly, a limited range of options exist under the law with respect to the disposition of the accused person with a mental disorder. The Government White Paper on Mental Health proposes to extend the range of options available to the courts when addressing the issue of sentencing an offender who is mentally ill.

This Chapter examines the current and proposed law as it affects or (as the case may be) may affect the offender with mental disability.

This chapter is divided as follows. Part A deals with general police powers and the accused person with mental disability. Part B addresses pre-trial procedures and the mentally disordered accused. Part C discusses procedural issues connected with the trial. Part D examines the insanity defence to a criminal charge. Part E discusses the special case of infanticide. Part F discusses the power of the courts to make orders for the treatment of offenders with mental illness generally. Part G addresses the situation of the prisoner with mental disability and Part H draws conclusions from the aforementioned discussions.

PART A: GENERAL POLICE POWERS AND THE PERSON WITH MENTAL DISABILITY

Irish Police Powers Generally and the Person with Mental Disability

Current Irish Law

The current law regarding treatment of persons with mental disability in Garda custody is contained in the Criminal Justice Act 1984 (Treatment of Persons in Custody in Garda Síochána Stations) Regulations 1987. The general rule with regard to treatment of persons in Garda custody is postulated in Regulation 3(1) which states that in carrying out their functions under the Regulations members of the Garda Síochána shall act with due respect for the personal rights of persons in custody and their dignity as human persons and shall have regard for the special needs of any of them who may be under a physical or mental disability while complying with the obligation to prevent escapes from custody and continuing to act with diligence and determination in the investigation of crime and the protection and vindication of the personal rights of other persons.

Where persons with mental illness are concerned Regulation 21(1) of the Regulations provides that if a person in custody appears to the member in charge[1] to be suffering from a mental illness the member in charge must summon a doctor or cause him to be summoned unless the person's condition appears to the member in charge to be such as to necessitate immediate removal to a hospital or other suitable place. The member in charge must also ensure that any instructions given by a doctor in relation to the medical care of a person in custody are complied with.[2]

Regulation 21(2) provides that notwithstanding that Regulation 21(1) may not apply medical advice shall be sought if the person in custody claims to need medication relating to, *inter alia*, diabetes, epilepsy or other potentially serious condition or the member in charge considers it necessary because the person has in his possession such medication.

Under the Regulations if a person in custody asks to be examined by a doctor of his choice at his own expense the member in charge shall if, and as soon as practicable make arrangements accordingly.[3] This shall not preclude his examination by another doctor summoned by the member in charge provided that the person in custody consents to the examination.[4]

They also provide that where a person in custody has been removed to a hospital or other suitable place an immediate relative and any other person required to be notified under Regulation 9[5] of the person's detention shall be so informed as soon as practicable.[6]

---

[1] The "member in charge" is defined by Reg.4(1) as meaning the member [of the Garda Síochána] who is in charge of a station at a time when the member in charge of a station is required to do anything or causing anything to be done pursuant to these Regulations.

[2] Reg.21(3) provides that the removal of a person in custody to a hospital or other suitable place and the time of removal must be recorded. Any instructions given by a doctor regarding the medical care of a person in custody and the steps taken to comply with them shall also be recorded.

[3] Reg.21(4).

[4] Reg.21(5) provides that a record must be made of any medical examination sought by the member in charge or person in custody the time the examination was sought and the time it was carried out. If it is not practicable to accede to a request by a person in custody for medical examination by the doctor of his choice at his own expense the relevant circumstances must also be recorded.

[5] The persons who must be informed of the person's detention are (i) in the case of a person under the age of seventeen years the parent or guardian of the person or if the member in charge is unable

Where persons with intellectual disability are concerned Regulation 22(1) provides that the provisions of the Regulations relating to persons under the age of seventeen apply in addition to any other applicable provisions in relation to a person in custody not below that age whom the member in charge knows or suspects to be "mentally handicapped".

In effect therefore where the person arrested is "mentally handicapped" he must without delay be informed or caused to be informed that a parent or guardian is being given the information required by Regulation 9(1)(a)(i) and is being requested to attend at the station without delay.

Regulation 9(1)(a) as applied by Regulation 22(1) provides that where the arrested person is "mentally handicapped" the member in charge must as soon as practicable inform or cause to be informed a parent or guardian of the person (I) of his being in custody in the station; (II) in ordinary language of the offence or other matter in respect of which he has been arrested and (III) of his entitlement to consult a solicitor and must request the parent or guardian to attend at the station without delay.

If the member in charge is unable to communicate with a parent or guardian he must inform the arrested person or cause him to be informed without delay of that fact and of his entitlement to have notification of his being in custody in the station sent to another person reasonably named by him.[7]

If the arrested person is married the person's spouse is the person who must be notified and requested to attend at the station.[8]

Where a parent, guardian or spouse of an mentally handicapped arrested person or an adult who is present during the questioning of the arrested person in accordance with Regulation 13(2)(b) or (c) (see below) has asked for a solicitor or has asked that a person reasonably named by him should be notified of the mentally handicapped person's being in custody (i) the member in charge must notify or cause the solicitor or that person to be notified as soon as practicable (ii) if the solicitor or the named person cannot be contacted within a reasonable time or if the solicitor is unable or unwilling to attend at the station the parent, guardian, spouse or adult present during questioning must be given an opportunity to ask for another solicitor or that another person reasonably named by him should be notified and if the relevant person exercises this opportunity

---

to communicate with a parent or guardian another person reasonably named by the arrested person. Where the arrested person is under seventeen and is married the person who must be notified is the person's spouse. (ii) Where the arrested person is over the age of seventeen and has asked for a solicitor or has asked that a person reasonably named by him should be notified of his being in custody the person who should be notified is that solicitor or that person as soon as practicable. If the solicitor or the named person cannot be contacted within a reasonable time or if the solicitor is unable or unwilling to attend at the station the person must be given an opportunity to ask that another solicitor or that another person reasonably named by him should be notified and the member in charge must notify or cause to be notified that other solicitor or person accordingly as soon as practicable. (iii) If the arrested person is under the age of seventeen (ii) above applies in relation to a request for a solicitor by a parent of his or his guardian or spouse or by an adult who is present during the questioning of the arrested person in accordance with Reg.13(2), (b) or (c).

[6] Reg.21(6).
[7] Criminal Justice Act 1984 (Treatment of Persons in Custody in Garda Síochána Stations) Regulations 1987 (S.I. No. 119 of 1987) Reg.9(1)(b).
[8] *Ibid.*, Reg.9(1)(c).

the member in charge must notify or cause to be notified that other solicitor or person as soon as practicable.[9]

Regulation 13(1) as modified by Regulation 22(1) provides that except with the authority of the member in charge an arrested person who is "mentally handicapped" may not be questioned in relation to an offence or asked to make a written statement unless a parent or guardian or if married to an adult his/her spouse is present. Authority may be given by the member in charge for an arrested person who is "mentally handicapped" to be questioned without a parent or guardian or spouse present where (a) it has not been possible to communicate with a parent or guardian or spouse in accordance with Regulation 9(1)(a); (b) no parent or guardian or spouse has attended at the station concerned within a reasonable time of being informed that the person was in custody and of being requested so to attend (c) it is not practicable for a parent or guardian or spouse to attend within a reasonable time (d) the member in charge has reasonable grounds for believing that to delay questioning the person would involve a risk of injury to persons or serious loss of or damage to property destruction of or interference with evidence or escape of accomplices.

A parent or guardian or spouse may be excluded from the questioning on the authority of the member in charge where (i) the parent or guardian or spouse concerned is the victim of or has been arrested in respect of the offence being investigated, (ii) the member in charge has reasonable grounds (a) for suspecting him of complicity in the offence, or (b) for believing that he would, if present during the questioning be likely to obstruct the course of justice or (c) while so present his conduct has been such as to amount to an obstruction of the course of justice.[10]

Regulation 13(2) as modified by Regulation 22(1) provides that where an arrested person who is "mentally handicapped" is to be questioned in relation to an offence in the absence of a parent or guardian (or if married his/her adult spouse) the member in charge must unless it is not practicable to do so arrange for the presence during questioning of (a) the other parent or another guardian (or in the case of a spouse a parent or guardian) ; (b) if the other parent or another guardian (or in the case of a spouse a parent or guardian) is not readily available or his presence having regard to the Regulation 13(1) is not appropriate an adult relative; (c) if the other parent or another guardian (or in the case of a spouse a parent or guardian) or an adult relative is not readily available or the presence of the other parent or another guardian (or in the case of a spouse a parent or guardian) [11] is, having regard to Regulation 13(1) not appropriate some other responsible adult other than a member.[12]

Regulation 22(2) provides that in the application of Regulation 13(2)(c) to such a person the responsible adult referred to in that provision shall, where practicable be a person who has experience in dealing with the "mentally handicapped".

---

[9] *Ibid.*, Reg.9(2)(a) as modified by Reg.9(2)(b) and Reg.22(1).

[10] *Ibid.*, Reg.13(1) as modified by Reg.22(1).

[11] *Ibid.*, Reg. 13(5)(b).

[12] Where an authority is given to a member to question an arrested person in the absence of a parent or guardian or to exclude a parent, guardian or other person form the questioning pursuant to Reg.13(1) or (2) the fact that the authority was given, the name and rank of the member giving it, the reasons for doing so and the action taken in compliance with Reg.13(2) must be recorded. See Reg.13(4).

Regulation 13(3) provides in effect that where a request for the attendance of a solicitor is made during questioning by the parent or guardian, spouse, adult relative or other adult present the arrested person with a mental handicap must not be asked to make a written statement in relation to an offence until a reasonable time for the attendance of the solicitor has elapsed.

The rights in Regulation 13 as applied by Regulation 22(1) to persons with "mental handicap" are without prejudice to the general rights an arrested person has in relation to interviews which are set out in Regulation 12.[13]

---

[13] These require: (1) that before an arrested person is interviewed the member conducting the interview must identify himself and any other member present by name and rank to the arrested person; (2) that the interview must be conducted in a fair and humane manner; (3) that no more than two members may question the arrested person at any one time and not more than four members may be present at any one time during the interview; (4) that if an interview has lasted for four hours it shall be terminated or adjourned for a reasonable time; (5) that as far as practicable interviews shall take place in rooms set aside for that purpose; (6) that except with the authority of the member in charge an arrested person shall not be questioned between midnight and 8 a.m. in relation to an offence. Authority may however be given for questioning between those hours were the arrested person: (i) has been taken to the station during that period (provided that he shall be allowed such reasonable time for rest as is necessary) (ii) in the case of a person detained under s.4 of the Criminal Justice Act 1984 he has not consented in writing to the suspension of questioning in accordance with subs.(6) of that section or (iii) the member in charge has reasonable grounds for believing that to delay questioning the person would involve risk of injury to persons, serious loss of or damage to property, destruction of or interference with evidence or escape of accomplices; (7) where an arrested person is deaf or there is doubt about his hearing ability he shall not be questioned in relation to an offence in the absence of an interpreter, if one is reasonably available, without his written consent (and where he is under the age of seventeen years or mentally handicapped) the written consent of an appropriate adult or in the circumstances specified in (6)(iii) above. The consent must be signed by the arrested person and be recorded in the custody record or a separate document. Where an arrested person has requested the presence of an interpreter and one is not reasonably available any questions must be put to him in writing; (8) that an arrested person who is under the influence of intoxicating liquor or drugs to the extent that he is unable to appreciate the significance of questions put to him or his answers must not be questioned in relation to an offence while he is in that condition except with the authority of the member in charge which authority shall not be given except in the circumstances specified in (6)(iii) above; (9) that if while being interviewed an arrested person makes a complaint to a member in relation to his treatment while in custody the member must bring it to the attention of the member in charge, if he is not present at the interview and record it or cause it to be recorded in the record of the interview; (10) that a record must be made of each interview either by the member conducting it or by another member who is present. It must include particulars of the time the interview began and ended, any breaks in it, the place of the interview, and the names and ranks of the members present. Where an interview is not recorded by electronic or other similar means the record must: (i) be made in the notebook of the member concerned or in a separate document and shall be as complete as practicable (ii) if it is practicable to do so and the member concerned is of opinion that it will not interfere with the conduct of the interview, be made while the interview is in progress or otherwise as soon as practicable afterwards and (iii) be signed by the member making it and include the date and time of signature; (11) that: (a) a record shall be made of the times during which an arrested person is interviewed and the members present at each interview (b) where authority is given pursuant to Regulation 12, the fact that it was given, the name and rank of the member giving the authority and the reasons for doing so must be recorded; (c) the fact that an arrested person has consented in writing under s.4(6) of the Criminal Justice Act 1984 to the suspension of questioning between midnight and 8 a.m. shall be recorded and the consent shall be attached to and form part of the custody record and (d) the particulars specified in s.4(6)(d) of the Criminal Justice Act 1984 must be recorded.

Significantly, however, section 7(3) of the Criminal Justice Act 1984 provides that a failure on the part of any member of the Garda Síochána to observe any provision of the regulations shall not of itself render that person liable to any criminal or civil proceedings or of itself affect the lawfulness of the custody of the detained person or the admissibility in evidence of any statement made by him.

Commentary

1. The 1987 Regulations require that a parent, guardian, spouse, relative or other responsible person be contacted when a person with "a mental handicap" is arrested. The person with mental illness is also a vulnerable person when in police custody and equally deserving of the support of another person who could be a relative, guardian or other person responsible for the care or custody of the person with mental illness, a person of their choice or failing such choice a mental health professional.

2. The 1987 Regulations provide for the presence of the support person but do not set out the qualifications of or role for such a person. If the support person is to play any meaningful part in the process the powers and duties of the support person should also be outlined in a statutory instrument. The role of the support person might include (in general terms) advising the person being interviewed and observing the fairness of the interview and facilitating communication with the interviewee.

3. As a matter of meaningful enforcement there must be a sanction for breach of the regulations. In this regard it is submitted that a judge should be given express legislative discretion to exclude evidence obtained in breach of the Criminal Justice Act 1984 (Treatment of Persons in Custody in Garda Stations) Regulations 1987.

4. In general terms at the stage of arrest of a person with mental illness or intellectual disability regulations should require a member of the Garda Síochána to address such issues as (1) whether the nature of the apparent disorder is so serious as to warrant taking the individual into custody; (2) whether the nature of the offence and the surrounding circumstances are not so serious as to warrant charging; (3) whether there exists in the community the necessary facilities for dealing with the individual; (4) whether the impact of the arrest and charging on the accused person and his family would be excessive having regard to the harm done.[14]

5. In the light of the fact that the Garda Síochána are at the interface between people with mental illness and intellectual disability and the criminal justice system it is imperative that the Gardai receive adequate training in how to identify and deal appropriately and sensitively with people with mental illness and intellectual disability. In 2002 the Report of the Inspector of Mental Hospitals stated that:

> "Gardaí had no formal training in principles of mental health or on service availability or contactability".

---

[14] See Law Reform Commission of Canada's *Report on Mental Disorder in the Criminal Process*, March 1976, pp.10–11.

It noted however that:

> "following discussions between the Department of Health and Children and An Garda Síochána, a mental health module will be introduced into the student Garda training programme in 2003. Thereafter, it is to be hoped that there will be improved communication and mutuality between the mental health services and the Gardai to replace the former distrust between the two. This is all the more important in the light of the proposed further development of forensic psychiatric services".

Commenting on the expertise of the Irish Gardaí in relation to mental health issues Amnesty International has observed that other jurisdictions[15] have employed specially trained police officers to supply on-scene expertise, determine whether mental illness is a factor in a criminal incident and ensure the safety of all involved parties and has advocated that such schemes should be considered in Ireland.[16]

PART B: PRE-TRIAL PROCEDURES AND ACCUSED WITH MENTAL DISABILITY

At the pre-trial stage the role of the Garda Síochána in relation to the mentally disordered accused is two-fold (i) to exercise police powers in relation to the person in custody and gather evidence for the trial and (ii) to adopt a protective role in relation to the mental illness of the accused person. A balance must be maintained between these two roles which at first glance appear incompatible and the rights of the accused person as a person with mental disability. The question is to what extent that balance is effectively maintained in Irish law.

Removal of Prisoner on Remand to Psychiatric Hospital

The powers to remove a prisoner on remand to a psychiatric hospital are seen as the law's response to the needs of a prisoner who is mentally ill. They are by and large contained in nineteenth century statutes which provide summarily a power of removal to a hospital but give little consideration to the issues which impinge on the effective treatment of the accused person or his rights in relation to the removal process.

---

[15] It notes that the Memphis Police Department adopts a Crisis Intervention Team approach whereby uniformed officers specially trained in mental health issues act as primary or secondary responders in every call involving people with mental illnesses. Such an approach is also adopted in Albuquerque, New Mexico, Police Department; The Roanoke, Virginia Police Department and the Houston, Texas, Police Department. A Comprehensive Advanced Approach involving every officer attending advanced 40 hour crisis intervention training to be able to respond appropriately to calls for service involving people with mental illness has been adopted by the Athens-Clarke County Police Department. A system involving mental health professionals who respond has been adopted by the Birmingham Police Department. Under this system a Community Service Officer Unit is attached to each Patrol Division. The unit is composed of social workers who respond directly to an incident location when requested by an officer. They service a variety of populations including people with mental illness.

[16] See *Mental Illness The Neglected Quarter: Marginalised Groups* Report November 2003 at p.58.

Current Irish Law

Section 3 of the Criminal Lunatics (Ireland) Act 1838[17] as amended and adapted by section 8 of the Criminal Justice Act 1960[18] provides that if it is certified to the Minister for Justice by two medical practitioners that any person committed to prison for trial for any offence is or has become insane or is an idiot the Minister for Justice may at his/her discretion order that such person be removed to the district mental hospital for the area in which the person is in custody, the Central Mental Hospital or any district mental hospital and be detained in that hospital unless in the meantime admitted to bail until the hearing at which such person should be brought to trial or indicted according to due course law and the person should then be remitted to the prison from which he was first removed so that he may be indicted and tried for the offence or otherwise disposed of according to law provided always that every such person while detained in the psychiatric hospital shall have the same liberty and privilege of seeing his or her friends and legal advisers at all reasonable times which he or she would have had in the prison from which s/he may have been removed.

Section 13 of the Lunatic Asylums (Ireland) Act 1875[19] as amended and adapted by section 8 of the Criminal Justice Act 1960[20] provides that the Minister for Justice may at his discretion order that any person who had been remanded by a justice for further examination and who had been certified by two medical practitioners during the period of such remand to be of unsound mind may be removed to the district mental hospital for the area in which the person is confined, the Central Mental Hospital or to any district mental hospital. The section further authorises the confinement of such person in the local district mental hospital, the Central Mental Hospital or the district mental hospital until it shall be certified that such person has become of sound mind whereupon the Minister for Justice is authorised to direct that such person be remitted to the prison from which he was first removed and be brought before the justices before whom he was ordered in the warrant of remand to be brought for further examination.

Section 8(2) of the Criminal Justice Act 1960 provides that where a person is detained under section is detained under section 3 of the 1838 Act or section 13 of the 1875 Act the Minister may at his discretion by order direct the transfer of the person (a) if he is detained in the Central Mental Hospital to a district mental hospital and (b) if he is detained in a district mental hospital to the Central Mental Hospital or to another district mental hospital and where a person is transferred under section 8(2) to the Central Mental Hospital or to a district mental hospital references in section 3 of the 1838 Act or section 13 of the 1875 Act to a hospital shall be construed as references to the Central Mental Hospital or to the district mental hospital to which he is transferred, as the case

---

[17] 1 Vict. c. 27.
[18] S.284 of the Mental Treatment Act 1945 saves the powers under s.3 of the Criminal Lunatics (Ireland) Act 1838. S. 284 of the 1945 Act is, in turn, saved by s.6 and the Schedule to the Mental Health Act 2001.
[19] 38 & 39 Vict., c.67.
[20] S.284 of the Mental Treatment Act 1945 specifically saves the powers under s.13 of the 1875 Act. S.284 is preserved by s.6 and the Schedule to the Mental Health Act 2001. If the Criminal Law (Insanity) Bill 2002 is enacted s.13 of the 1875 Act will be repealed. See s.19 and Schedule to the Bill.

may be, and section 3 of the 1838 Act and section 13 of the 1875 Act shall have effect accordingly.

In *State (C) v. Minister for Justice*[21] the Supreme Court held that the provisions Section 13 which authorised the Minister to detain the accused person in a psychiatric hospital beyond the return date of his remand by the District Court were unconstitutional as a legislative interference with the judicial power to administer justice. In effect, therefore, an accused person on remand may only be detained in a district mental hospital until the date ordered in the warrant of remand.

Commentary

Current law responds to the mental illness of the accused person by providing for a power to remove him to a psychiatric hospital and his containment there. No consideration is given to the fact that he might have rights in relation to that process and it is in this light that proposals for reform are made:

1. References in section 3 of the Criminal Lunatics Act 1838 to a person being an "idiot" are anachronistic. Although regarded as such at the time of the passing of the Act intellectual disability of itself is not a mental illness and a finding that a person is intellectually disabled should not be a ground for admission to a psychiatric hospital. Admission to hospital is not in the interests of an offender unless it can be shown that the hospital is in a position to provide appropriate treatment for his condition.

2. Section 3 makes no provision for a right to treatment but merely provides for the offender to be "detained" in the local psychiatric hospital. A right to treatment must be *a sine qua non* of the exercise of the *parens patriae* process of removal from imprisonment to the psychiatric services

3. Neither the 1838 Act nor the 1975 Act makes any provision for due process and to guard against bias of the medical practitioners certifying the accused person. Provision should be made requiring them to be independent of each other and of the institution to which the prisoner is to be removed.

4. There is no express requirement in either the 1838 or the 1875 Act that the medical practitioners certifying the accused person have an expertise in psychiatry. This is a fundamental requirement of due process in the committal procedure.

5. Provision is made in the 1838 and 1875 for an order to be made transferring the accused person to a psychiatric hospital on the basis that he is "insane" in the case of the former Act or of "unsound mind" in the case of the latter Act. This terms are not defined and afford a great deal of discretion to medical practitioners concerned in making decisions as to who should be transferred for psychiatric treatment. In the current climate where places in the Central Mental Hospital are few facilities inadequate and the numbers of prisoners who require psychiatric treatment far exceeds the places available in practice these terms may be interpreted to facilitate only seriously mentally ill patients to hospital. The *UN Principles for the Protection*

---

[21] [1967] I.R. 106.

of Persons with Mental Illness and the Improvement of Mental Health Care[22] comprise a detailed code of standards regarding the diagnosis and treatment of all people with mental illness and require that the grounds for involuntary admission in legislation be more precisely defined.

Principle 16 outlines the criteria for involuntary admission. Admission is permissible if, and only if, a qualified mental health practitioner authorised by law for that purpose determines in accordance with Principle 4[23] that a person has a mental illness and considers (a) that because of that mental illness there is a serious likelihood of immediate or imminent harm to that person or to other persons; or (b) that, in the case of a person whose mental illness is severe and whose judgment is impaired, failure to admit or retain that person is likely to lead to a serious deterioration in his or her condition or will prevent the giving of appropriate treatment that can only be given by admission to a mental health facility in accordance with the principle of the least restrictive alternative.

Principle 16.1 continues that in the case referred to in subparagraph (b) a second such mental health practitioner, independent of the first should be consulted wherever possible. If such consultation takes place, the involuntary admission ... may not take place unless the second mental health practitioner concurs.

Principle 20.3 provides that domestic law may authorise a court or other competent authority acting on the basis of competent and independent medical advice to order that persons who are detained in the course of criminal proceedings or investigations against them and who are determined to have a mental illness or who it is believed may have such an illness to be admitted to a mental health facility.

Given the scarcity of psychiatric facilities for treatment of prisoners with mental illness in practice it is submitted that in practice these criteria may be interpreted facilitatively in the Irish context (i.e as affording positive grounds for facilitating the transfer of a prisoner to a psychiatric hospital) rather than restrictively.

Principle 16.2 provides that involuntary admission ... shall initially be for a short period as specified by domestic law for observation and preliminary treatment pending review of the admission ... by the review body. The grounds for the admission shall be communicated to the patient without delay and the fact of the admission and the grounds for it shall also be communicated promptly and in detail to the review body, to the patient's personal representative, if any, and, unless the patient objects, to the patient's family.

Principle 20.2 of the *UN Principles for the Protection of Persons with Mental*

---

[22] Adopted by the General Assembly on December 17, 1991.

[23] Principle 4.1 provides that a determination that a person has a mental illness shall be made in accordance with internationally accepted medical standards. Principle 4.2 states that a determination of mental illness shall never be made on the basis of political, economic or social status, or membership of a cultural, racial or religious group, or any other reason not directly relevant to mental health status. Principle 4.3 provides that family or professional conflict or non conformity with moral, social, cultural or political values or religious beliefs prevailing in a person's community shall never be a determining factor in diagnosing mental illness. Principle 4.4 states that a background of past treatment or hospitalisation as a patient shall not of itself justify any present or future determination or mental illness. Principle 4.5 provides that no person or authority shall classify a person as having, or otherwise indicate that a person has a mental illness except for purposes directly relating to mental illness or the consequences of mental illness.

Illness and the Improvement of Mental Health Care[24] applies the UN Principles to persons who are detained in the course of criminal proceedings or investigations against them and who are determined to have a mental illness or who it is believed may have such an illness to the fullest extent possible with only such limited modifications and exceptions as are necessary in the circumstances. No such modifications and exceptions are to prejudice the person's rights under the Declaration of Human Rights, the International Covenant on Economic, Social and Cultural Rights, the International Covenant on Civil and Political Rights, the Declaration on the Rights of Disabled Persons and the Body of Principles for the Protection of All Persons under any form of Detention or Imprisonment.

Principle 20.2 provides that all such persons should receive the best available mental health care in accordance with Principle 1.

Principle 8 provides that every patient shall have the right to receive such health and social care as is appropriate to his or her health needs and is entitled to care and treatment in accordance with the same standards as other ill persons.

Principle 20.4 provides that treatment of persons determined to have a mental illness shall in all circumstances be consistent with Principle 11. Principle 11 provides that no treatment shall be given to a patient without his or her informed consent subject to the exceptions outlined in paragraphs 6, 7, 8, 13 and 15 of that paragraph. The issue of consent is dealt with in Chapter 4.

6. The 1838 Act does not make provision for review of the detention of prisoners subject to transfer powers in the psychiatric hospital. A section providing for review is also absent from the provisions of section 13 of the Lunatic Asylums (Ireland) Act 1875. This is undoubtedly a breach of Article 5(4) of the European Convention on Human Rights and requirements for review of detention specified in *X v. United Kingdom.*[25]

7. Where a prisoner is removed under either the 1838 or 1875 Acts either the prisoner or the psychiatric hospital should be entitled to request the return of the prisoner to prison subject to review by a Mental Health Tribunal.

8. Prisoners removed to hospital under the 1838 and 1875 Acts should have the right to apply to a Mental Health Tribunal or transfer to another hospital if they are not receiving appropriate treatment at the hospital to which they have been transferred.

9. Legislation should be enacted indicating the circumstances in which remands for psychiatric examination are appropriate, their purpose and to whom reports of such examinations should be sent. Further in cases where psychiatric examination is proposed the consent of the accused person to such examination should be obtained.

Scope of Reforms Proposed by Criminal Law (Insanity) Bill 2002

Section 19 and Schedule 1 of the 2002 Bill repeal the provisions of section 13 of the Lunatic Asylums (Ireland) Act 1875 which provided for the removal of a prisoner on

[24] Adopted by the General Assembly on December 17, 1991.
[25] (1981) 4 E.H.R.R. 188.

remand to a district psychiatric hospital or the Central Mental Hospital but puts no provision in its place. Further it makes no provision for review of detention of persons (whether prisoners on remand or convicted offenders) transferred from prison to a psychiatric hospital or the Central Mental Hospital. Keys makes the point that based on recent figures this may be 48% of those in the Central Mental Hospital. She states that unless amendments are made to the Bill this group will remain outside the protections available to others in detention and will necessitate further legislation to comply with the European Convention on Human Rights requirements.[26]

Transfer of Patient charged with Indictable Offence to Central Mental Hospital

The power to transfer a person charged but not convicted of an indictable offence to the restrictive conditions of the Central Mental Hospital has been the subject of much controversy not least because of the questionable constitutionality of the procedures laid down in the 1945 Act.

Position under Mental Treatment Act 1945

Section 207(1) of the Mental Treatment Act 1945 (which is still in force) permits the transfer of a person from a district mental hospital to the Central Mental Hospital where a person detained in a district mental hospital or other institution maintained by a mental hospital authority is charged with an indictable offence before a justice of the District Court sitting in such district mental hospital or other institution and evidence is given which in the opinion of the justice constitutes prima facie evidence that such person has committed the offence and that he would, if placed on trial, be unfit to plead.[27] In that event the justice is obliged by order certify that that person is suitable for transfer to the Central Mental Hospital and to send copies of the order to the Minister and to the person in charge of the district mental hospital or other institution.

Where such an order is made the person concerned must be retained in the district mental hospital or other institution and his detention therein must be continued subject to any order which may have been made under section 207(2). The Minister for Health is obliged to require the Inspector of Mental Hospitals to visit the person and report on his mental condition to the Minister. After consideration of the report the Minister is obliged, if he so thinks fit, to make an order directing and authorising the transfer of that person to the Central Mental Hospital. On transfer the person may, notwithstanding any other provision of the Act, be detained there until he is sent to a district mental hospital or other institution or discharged or his death.[28]

If the Minister decides not to make the order he must give notice to the person in charge of the district mental hospital or other institution.[29] If the Minister gives such

---

[26] See "Challenging the Lawfulness of Psychiatric Detention under Habeas Corpus in Ireland", 24 *Dublin University Law Journal* p.26 at p.52.

[27] In *State (O) v. Daly* [1977] I.R. 312 it was held that the provisions of s.2 of the Criminal Justice (Legal Aid) Act 1962 do not apply to an enquiry held pursuant to s.207(1) of the 1945 Act so that a person is not entitled to free legal aid in relation to the proceedings held under the section.

[28] Mental Treatment Act 1945, s.207(2)(d) inserted by Mental Treatment Act 1961, s.25(1).

[29] *Ibid.*, s.207(2)(e) inserted by Mental Treatment Act 1961, s.25(1).

notice the person then if the person is a person who is ordinarily resident in an area served by another district mental hospital he may (notwithstanding the power to retain him in the district mental hospital in which he is presently detained) be sent at any time to the district mental hospital for the area in which he is ordinarily resident.[30] The detention of the person (i) who is retained pursuant to section 207(2)(a) in the original district mental hospital or other institution after the district justice has made an order for transfer to the Central Mental Hospital or (ii) who is sent to the district mental hospital for the area in which he is ordinarily resident after the Minister has decided not to make an order for transfer to the Central Mental Hospital is to be regarded as detention under an eligible patient reception order or a private patient reception order (as may be appropriate).[31]

Under section 207(3) the Minister retains power to direct that the person transferred under an order made under section 207(2) be sent back to the district mental hospital or other institution from which he was transferred or if he is ordinarily resident in an area served by another district mental hospital to direct that the person be sent back to the district mental hospital for that area The detention of the person after he is sent back to the hospital or institution from which he was transferred or after he is sent back to the district mental hospital for the area in which he is ordinarily resident is to be regarded as detention under an eligible patient reception order or a private patient reception order (as may be appropriate.)[32] Where the resident governor and physician of the Central Mental Hospital and the Inspector of Mental Hospitals agree and certify that a person transferred under an order made under section 207(2) has ceased to be of unsound mind, the governor and physician is obliged to discharge the person and where necessary pay him the expenses of travelling home.[33]

The procedure for transfer of detained patients to the Central Mental Hospital under Section 207 have been criticised[34] on a number of grounds. First the section permits the detention of a person in the Central Mental Hospital without their having had the benefit of a full trial either for the offence concerned or in relation to the issue of fitness to plead. Secondly the justice has no discretion in the matter of transfer. Once he is satisfied that there is prima facie evidence that the person has committed the offence he is obliged to grant the certificate. Thirdly the criteria upon which the Minister for Health should exercise his discretion to transfer the person concerned are not clear. Fourthly there are no time limits set on the length of the detention of a person in the Central Mental Hospital nor provision for automatic review. Fifthly the effect of the issue of the certificate on the charge is not clear.

The constitutionality of the section was challenged in *RT v. Director of the Central Mental Hospital*[35] where Costello P. made a number of further observations about the

---

[30] Mental Treatment Act 1945, s.207(2)(f) inserted by Mental Treatment Act 1961, s.25(1) as adapted by Mental Treatment Acts (Adaptation) Order 1971 (S.I. No. 108 of 1971) Schedule.

[31] *Ibid.*, s.207(2)(g) inserted by Mental Treatment Act 1961, s.25(1).

[32] *Ibid.*, s.207(3) as amended by Mental Treatment Act 1961, s.25(2).

[33] *Ibid.*, s.207(4) as adapted by Mental Treatment Acts (Adaptation) Order 1971 (S.I. No. 108 of 1971) Schedule.

[34] See Department of Health's Green Paper (para.23.13) cited by Costello P. in *RT v. Central Mental Hospital* [1995] 2 I.L.R.M. 354.

[35] [1995] 2 I.L.R.M. 367.

section. First, he stated that the section could be operated in relation to offences allegedly committed by patients after the reception order was made and therefore enabled a patient to be prosecuted for an offence who because of mental illness could have lacked the *mens rea* required to support a conviction. He commented that in those circumstances to prosecute may well amount to an abuse of the criminal process. Secondly, he noted that if the hospital authorities believed that a disruptive patient could not be the subject of a transfer under section 208 then section 207 could be used by the hospital authorities solely for purpose of obtaining a transfer of the patient to the Central Mental Hospital and not for the purpose of making him amenable to the criminal law. This also would be an abuse of the criminal process. Thirdly, he commented that the procedures are based on a illogicality as it did not follow that because a patient may be unfit to plead if placed on trial that he is suitable for transfer to the Central Mental Hospital and that the district judge was required by statute to certify something which may be quite untrue and fourthly he noted that there were no safeguards to protect the patient against a possible error in the operation of the section. There were no procedures for the review of the opinion of the Inspector as to the suitability of the patient for transfer to the Central Mental Hospital. Finally he noted that there were serious defects in the provision which enabled indefinite detention in the Central Mental Hospital since there was no practical way in which a transferred patient could procure his re-transfer or his liberty or have his continued detention reviewed. He concluded:

> "The defects in the section are such that there are not adequate safeguards against abuse or error both in the making of the transfer order, and in the continuance of the indefinite detention which is permitted by the section. These defects not only mean that the section falls far short of internationally accepted standards but, in my opinion, render the section unconstitutional because they mean that the State has failed adequately to protect the right to liberty of temporary patients."[36]

Accordingly he referred the question as to whether section 207 is invalid having regard to Article 40.4.1 of the Constitution to the Supreme Court. However the case never came on for hearing before the Supreme Court as the applicant was released from the Central Mental Hospital having spent sixteen years in the Hospital.

In addition to its possible unconstitutionality the provisions of section 207 also probably breaches Ireland's obligations under the European Convention on Human Rights. By providing for indeterminate detention in the Central Mental Hospital without the benefit of a trial on either criminal liability or fitness to plead section 207 may infringe the right to a fair trial guaranteed by Article 6(1) of the Convention which provides that in the determination of any criminal charge against him everyone is entitled to a fair and public hearing within a reasonable time by an independent and impartial tribunal established by law.

In addition there may have be an infringement of Article 5(4) of the Convention whereby a person is entitled to take proceedings at reasonable intervals before a court to test the lawfulness of his detention. In *X v. United Kingdom*[37] it was held that the

---

[36] [1995] 2 I.L.R.M. 367 at 368.
[37] (1981) 4 E.H.R.R. 181.

habeas corpus provisions of English law were not wide enough to satisfy the requirements of Article 5(4). What was required was an automatic periodic review of the detention of a judicial character.[38]

The White Paper

Under the terms of the White Paper entitled *A New Mental Health Act*[39] it was proposed to replace section 207 in new legislation by more appropriate procedures for transfers form approved centres to the specialist services available in the Central Mental Hospital. Accordingly the White Paper reported that the Government had decided that the transfer of detained patients from approved centres to specialist psychiatric centres such as the Central Mental Hospital on the application of the chief executive officer of a health board who *would require the agreement of two consultant psychiatrists – consultant in clinical charge of the patient and the clinical director of the forensic psychiatric service at the Central Mental Hospital or other specialist psychiatric centre.*

It was proposed that the grounds for transfer should be that the patient *for his or her own safety or the safety of others requires psychiatric care in a secure environment.* The decision to transfer was to be subject to review by the Mental Health Review Board with an appeal to the High Court. The transfer would be for a limited period of three months which could be renewed for further periods. It was also proposed that the Board would automatically review the continued detention of any person who has been transferred from another hospital and who had been detained in Dundrum for a year or two yearly intervals thereafter.[40]

Where there was disagreement between the consultant in charge of the patient and the clinical director of the Central Mental Hospital about the need to transfer a patient to or from Dundrum, the proposed Mental Health Review Board was to adjudicate on the matter. It was also proposed to provide for some safeguards for transfers to other special psychiatric centres.[41]

Position under Mental Health Act 2001

Section 6 and the Schedule to the Mental Health Act 2001 (enacted but not yet in force) repeal section 207 of the Mental Treatment Act 2001.

Section 21(2)(a) of the Mental Health Act 2001 (enacted but not yet in force) appears to be the provision which replaces section 207 of the 1945 Act but does not require the assent of two consultant psychiatrists nor confine itself to the limited grounds outlined in the White Paper for transfer of a patient to the Central Mental Hopsital.

Section 21(2)(a) provides that where the clinical director of an approved centre (i) is of opinion that it would be for the benefit of a patient detained in that centre, or that it is necessary for the purpose of obtaining special treatment for such a patient to transfer him or her to the Central Mental Hospital and (ii) proposes to do so he or she shall

---

[38] (1981) 4 E.H.R.R. 181 at 207.
[39] Pn.1824 July 1995.
[40] Para.7.34.
[41] Para.7.34.

notify the Mental Health Commission in writing of the proposal and the Commission shall refer the proposal to a Mental Health Tribunal.

Section 21(2)(b) provides that where a proposal is so referred to a tribunal the tribunal shall review the proposal as soon as may be but not later than 14 days thereafter and shall either (i) if it is satisfied that it is in the best interest of the health of the patient concerned authorise the transfer of the patient concerned and (ii) if it is not so satisfied, refuse to authorise it.

By virtue of section 21(2)(c) the provisions of sections 19 and 49 apply to the referral of a proposal to a tribunal under section 21 as they apply to the referral of an admission order to a tribunal under section 17 with any necessary modifications.

Section 19 (which has been to be brought into force) provides that a patient has a right of appeal to the Circuit Court against a decision of a tribunal on the grounds that s/he was not suffering from a mental disorder. Section 19 also provides for the exercise of the right of appeal by the patient by notice in writing within 14 days of the receipt by him or her or by his or her legal representative of notice of the decision concerned and sets out the procedures and powers of the Circuit Court on appeal.[42]

Section 49 (which came into force on April 5, 2002)[43] outlines the powers of tribunals when it holds sittings for the purpose of review under the Act.[44]

Section 21(2)(d) provides that effect will not be given to a decision to which section 21(2)(b) of the 2001 Act applies before (i) the expiration of the time for the bringing of an appeal to the Circuit Court or (ii) if such an appeal is brought the determination or withdrawal thereof.

Section 21(3) provides that where a patient is transferred to an approved centre under section 21 the clinical director of the centre from which he is transferred shall, as soon as may be give notice in writing of the transfer to the Commission. The Central Mental Hospital falls within the definition of "approved centre" in sections 62 and 63[45] of the Act.

Section 21(4) provides that the detention of a patient "in another approved centre" under section 21 shall be deemed for the purposes of the Act to be detention in the centre from which he or she is detained so that the provisions of the 2001 Act relating to renewals and review of detention on renewal of detention apply. Accordingly a patient may be detained for an initial period of 21 days within which time his detention must be reviewed. This initial period of 21 days may be extended by a renewal order made a consultant psychiatrist responsible for the care and treatment of the patient concerned for a further period not exceeding 3 months and on the expiration of that period further extended by the consultant psychiatrist by renewal order for a further period not exceeding 6 months and thereafter further extended by order made by the psychiatrist for periods each of which does not exceed 12 months. Each renewal must be reviewed by a Mental Health Tribunal.[46]

---

[42] See Chap.2.

[43] See Mental Health Act 2001 (Sections 1 to 5, 7, 31 to 55) (Commencement) Order 2002 (S.I. No. 90 of 2002) (S.I. No. 90 of 2002).

[44] See Chap.6.

[45] S.62 defines a "centre" as a hospital or other in-patient facility for the care and treatment of persons suffering from mental illness or mental disorder and s.63 defines an "approved centre" as a centre which is registered in accordance with the 2001 Act.

[46] See Mental Health Act 2001, ss.15–18.

Commentary

1   The Mental Health Act's provisions for transfer of patients to the Central Mental Hospital do not go far enough in the matter of protecting the constitutional right of the patient to due process. It is submitted that before a transfer is effected it should be proved that the person in question (i) engaged in an overtly dangerous act; (ii) lacks insight into his/her dangerous behaviour, (iii) that no less restrictive alternative is available and (iv) that his or her condition can be treated in the hospital to which he or she is transferred.[47]

2.   By contrast to current Irish law in the US case of *Eubanks v. Clarke*[48] it was held that there can be no transfer of an involuntary patient from one mental facility to another that is more restrictive without according the patient a hearing – a requirement that has since found its way into the Pennsylvania statutes[49] as well as those of Ohio[50] and South Carolina.[51] In *Klein v. Califano*[52] medicaid patients of a New Jersey nursing home were held to be entitled to similar protections before they could be transferred It is submitted that persons subject to the transfer provisions of section 21(2) should be entitled to a hearing before a Mental Health Tribunal before a transfer is effected to the Central Mental Hospital.

3.   Where a patient appeals to the Circuit Court against a decision of a tribunal the onus should be on the detaining authorities to show that he is suffering from a mental disorder. The patient should not have to bear the onus of proving that he or she is not suffering from a mental disorder as provided for in the Act. This would be inconsistent with the ruling of the European Court of Human Rights in the case of *Winterwerp v. the Netherlands*.[53]

Part C: Issues Connected with the Trial

At the trial stage a number of issues arise for consideration when the accused person is a person with mental illness or intellectual disability. The accused person may be so mentally disordered as to be unfit to stand trial. In this section the tests and procedures which determine fitness to plead are examined and the question asked whether due process is really served by the present law. Secondly the accused person's mental illness may have precipitated his commission of the offence to the extent that the question must be asked whether he should bear criminal responsibility for his actions at the time. In this section the question is asked whether current law provides a reliable test for determining that the accused person was so mentally ill at the time of the commission of the offence that he ought not be held criminally responsible for his actions.

---

[47] See Cooney & O'Neill, *Psychiatric Detention Civil Commitment in Ireland*, p.84.
[48] 454 F. Supp. 1022 (F.D. PA. 1977).
[49] Pennsylvania. Stat. Ann. 50 Section 7306.
[50] Ohio Rev. Code Ann. Section 5122.20 (Baldwin 1982).
[51] South Carolina Code Ann. Section 44-23 210(4) Law Co-op 1976.
[52] 586 F. 2d 250 (3d Cir. 1978).
[53] (1979) 2 E.H.R.R. 387.

Fitness to Plead at Trial[54]

Current Irish Law

Criteria for establishing Fitness to Plead At common law every person who is above the age of reason is, unless proven to the contrary, presumed to be sane and to be accountable for his actions.[55] An accused person may, however, be unfit to plead at his trial due to mental illness, disability or injury. In cases where mental illness is raised as a plea in bar of trial the issue is whether the accused person is insane at the time of the trial.[56] The classic statement of criteria for deciding whether an accused person is fit to plead laid down by Alderson B in *R v. Pritchard*[57] as follows:

> "There are three points to be inquired into: First, whether the prisoner is mute of malice or not; secondly whether he can plead to the indictment or not; thirdly, whether he is of sufficient intellect to comprehend the course of the proceedings on the trial, so as to make a proper defence – to know that he might challenge any of you to whom he may object – and to comprehend the details of the evidence, which in a case of this nature must constitute a minute investigation."[58]

This test is well established. Once the court is satisfied that the accused person is not "mute in malice" the accused person's fitness is assessed. If the accused person is found "mute in malice" a plea of not guilty is entered.[59] The test in *Pritchard* has been taken to comprise five separate components:

> "The first is the ability to plead to the indictment, the second is the ability to understand the course of the proceedings, the third the capacity to instruct a lawyer, the fourth the ability to challenge a juror and fifth an ability to understand the evidence."[60]

Inability to meet any one of these demands is would be sufficient for a finding of unfitness[61] and the same basic test applies to both summary proceedings and proceedings on indictment.[62] In the context of Irish Law the test was set out Ó Dálaigh C.J. in *State (C) v. Minister for Justice* where he stated:

---

[54] See generally McAuley F., *Insanity, Psychiatry and Criminal Responsibility* (Round Hall Press, 1993), Chap.7.

[55] *R v. Layton* 4 Cox 149.

[56] *R v. Padola* [1960] 1 Q.B. 325 Foote suggests that the rule is a "by-product of the ban against trials in absentia, the mentally incompetent defendant, although physically present in the courtroom, is in reality afforded no opportunity to defend himself". See "A Comment on Pre-Trial Commitment of Criminal Defendants" (1960) U. Pa. L. Rev. 832.

[57] *R v. Pritchard* (1836) 7 C. & P. 303.

[58] (1836) 7 C. & P. 303 at 304.

[59] Juries Act 1976, s.28.

[60] Mackay, "The Decline of Disability in Relation to the Trial" [1991] *Crim L.R.* pp.91–92.

[61] P.J. Richardson, *Archbold – Pleading, Evidence and Practice in Criminal Cases* (1993) para.4–161.

[62] See *State (C) v. Minister for Justice* [1967] I.R. 106 and *Leonard v. Garavan and the DPP* unreported, High Court (McKechnie J.), April 30, 2002

"Stated in general terms the test to be applied is, has the prisoner sufficient intellect to comprehend the course of the proceedings of the trial so as to make a proper defence, to challenge a juror to whom he may wish to object and to understand the details of the evidence."[63]

This test, propounded obiter in the *State (C)* (as the case mainly concerned the question whether the disposition or custody of the an accused person found unfit to plead was an issue for the courts or for the executive and not the criteria for establishing fitness to plead) was approved in *O'C v. Judges of the Metropolitan District Court*[64] and the *DPP (at the suit of Garda Eugene Murphy) v. P.T.*[65] although it must be said that the approval was again obiter as the *O'C* case dealt with the issue of whether fitness to plead could be determined in the cases to be tried on indictment as the stage of the preliminary examination (before the Criminal Justice Act 1999 abolished the preliminary examination) and in the case of *P.T.* the central determination by McGuinness J in the High Court was that a District Judge could raise the issue of fitness to plead of his or her own motion.

The value underpinning the fitness to plead criteria appears to be fairness to the accused person and that is certainly the aim emphasised by the Irish courts[66] Conway points out that other rationales put forward include ensuring the accuracy of court proceedings, protecting the dignity of the court and maximising the efficacy of punishment by ensuring the accused person full appreciates what is taking place.[67]

However the basic test laid down in *Pritchard* is largely cognitively based. Grubin argues that this arises as a result of an historical anachronism where two distinctive tests one applicable to the "mentally defective" defendant and the other applicable to the "insane" defendant were in the 1830s emasculated and commuted into one test.[68]

Juries try the issue of fitness to plead under the form of an oath which formulates the question as one of insanity. Each member of the jury takes an oath that s/he "will well and diligently inquire whether (stating the name of the accused person) the prisoner at the bar be insane or not and a true verdict give according to the best of my understanding."[69] However insanity in the sense used in section 2 of the Criminal Lunatics Act 1800 as applied to Ireland by section 17 of the Lunacy (Ireland) Act 1821 which deals with fitness to plead is not limited to medical definitions or the McNaghten rules and includes any condition whether mental or physical which prevents the accused person from meeting the criteria for fitness to plead. Curiously a person who is "mute by visitation of God" may raise the plea if his incapacity renders him unable to understand the proceedings or the evidence or incapable of communicating may be able to raise the

---

[63] [1967] I.R. 106.

[64] [1994] 3 I.R. 246.

[65] [1999] 3 I.R. 254.

[66] See for example *O'C v. Judges of Metropolitan District* [1994] 3 I.R. 246 at 251–252; *Leonard v. District Judge John Garavan and the DPP*, unreported, High Court (McKechnie J.), April 30, 2002, paras 35, 37.

[67] See "Fitness to Plead in the Light of the Criminal Law (Insanity) Bill 2002" *Irish Criminal Law Journal* Vol.13 No.4 p.2 citing Grubin, "What Constitutes Fitness to Plead?" [1993] Crim.L.R. 753 and "Incompetency to Stand Trial" 81 *Harvard Law Review* [1967] 454 at 457–458.

[68] This happened in the cases of *R v. Dyson* (1831) 7 C& P 305 and *R v. Pritchard* (1836) 7 C& P 303 Grubin, "What Constitutes Fitness to Plead?" [1993] Crim. L.R.. 753.

[69] Juries Act 1976, s.19(2).

plea.[70] However the jury determining the issue of fitness to plead even in that case will be asked to decide "whether the prisoner at the bar be insane or not."[71] On the other hand the fact that the accused person is "highly abnormal"[72] or that he was not capable of doing things which were in his own best interests[73] or that s/he is suffering from hysterical amnesia with respect to the relevant events is not sufficient to raise the plea if s/he is otherwise capable of following the proceedings.[74]

Procedural Issues The issue is usually raised by the prosecution or the defence before the accused person is arraigned. However it may be raised by either side or by the judge at any time during the trial.[75] Where the prosecution pleads the accused person's fitness to stand trial the burden of proof is on them to prove it beyond reasonable doubt.[76] Where the defence asserts it they must prove the accused person's fitness on the balance of probabilities.[77] The issue must be tried as soon as it arises.[78] Typically psychiatric evidence is adduced at the time the plea is raised to support the contention of unfitness.[79] The inquiry as to the accused person's insanity may be had before a jury empanelled specifically for the purpose. This is usually the case when the issue arises on arraignment. Ryan and Magee state that in the event that the plea arises during a trial on indictment, rather than at the arraignment the appropriate procedure is to discharge the jury and re-arraign the accused for a new jury to consider the issue in the usual way.[80] However there is authority for the plea to be tried before the jury before whom the general issue is to be tried.[81]

If an accused person becomes unfit to follow the proceedings *during* the course of the trial there is some authority to the effect that the proper course for the judge to take is to discharge the jury and have the accused person re-arraigned before a jury specially empanelled for the purpose of determining his fitness to plead.[82]

---

[70] See Scottish case of *HM Advocate v. Wilson* [1942] J.C. 75. However in the case of an accused person who is deaf or dumb another form of communication such as sign language may be used if it is sufficient for him to understand and follow the proceedings. If this is done a finding of unfitness may be avoided. See *R v. Jones* (1773) 1 Leach 102; *R v. Steel* (1787) 1 Leach 451; *R v. McEntyre* (1840) 1 Craw & D. 402.

[71] Juries Act 1976, s.19(2).

[72] *R v. Berry* (1977) 66 Cr. App. Rep. 157 In *Berry's* case expert evidence was given that the accused person was in fact suffering from paranoid schizophrenia. His own evidence demonstrated that he was under a delusion that he was being persecuted but the judge failed to the direct the jury as to the principles to be applied when deciding whether an accused person was unfit to plead.

[73] *R v. Robertson* [1968] 1 W.L.R. 1767.

[74] See *Russell v. HM Advocate* [1946] J.C. 37.

[75] *R v. Podola* [1960] 1 Q.B. at 325.

[76] *R v. Robertson* [1968] 1 W.L.R. 1767.

[77] See *R v. Podola* [1960] 1 Q.B. 325.

[78] See *State (Coughlan) v. Minister for Justice and another* (1968) I.L.T.R. 177 at 186.

[79] If psychiatric evidence at the time points to fitness to plead a court on appeal will be cautious about accepting expert psychiatric evidence adduced after conviction which supports the contention that the accused person was unfit at the time of trial. However, if such evidence is persuasive the court may accept it See *R v. Johnson* [2002] E.W.C.A. Crim. 1900.

[80] See *The Irish Criminal Process* (Dublin 1983), p.269. See also *People(AG) v. Messitt* [1972] I.R. 204 and the authorities cited by Kenny J. at pp.210–211.

[81] *R v. Podola* [1960] 1 Q.B. 325.

[82] *People v. Messitt* [1972] I.R. 204; *R v. Streek* (1826) 2 C. & P. 413.

Where an accused person is found fit to plead he will be arraigned in the usual manner and a fresh jury will be empanelled to try the case. Where an accused person is found unfit to plead he may be held in the Central Mental Hospital pending his/her recovery[83] at which point he might be re-arraigned and tried for the offence.[84] It has been argued[85] that the use of the words "it shall be lawful" in section 2 of the Criminal Lunatics Act 1800[86] effectively confers a residual discretion on judges not to make such an order in cases where it would be unnecessary or inappropriate. However in practice section 2[87] has been interpreted as being mandatory in nature. There is no right of appeal against the decision to the Court of Criminal Appeal.

Dwyer observes that in the Irish jurisdiction persons found unfit to plead have spent substantial periods of time in the Central Mental Hospital[88] as a result yet there is not even an enquiry conducted as to the strength of the evidence against the accused person in relation to the actual offence charged against him before he is dispatched to the Central Mental Hospital.[89] Walsh comments in the same vein that an accused person has little to gain and perhaps much to lose in being found unfit to plead at the arraignment. It may be that if the case went to full trial he would have been acquitted and equally it might be that a submission of no case to answer would have succeeded at the close of the case for the prosecution.[90]

---

[83] Criminal Lunatics Act 1800, s.2; Lunacy (Ireland) Act 1821 s.17; Central Criminal Lunatic Asylum (Ireland) Act 1845, s.8; Mental Treatment Act 1961 s.39.

[84] In *Murray v. DPP*, unreported, High Court, May 13, 1992 the court adjourned the proceedings to allow the accused person suffering from chronic paranoid schizophrenia to receive medical treatment for up to 12 months so that after receiving that treatment a decision could be made as to whether he would be permanently ill and so not triable or not. An application for an injunction to restrain the prosecution on the basis that the accused person was permanently unfit to be tried was deemed premature at the time of application.

[85] See McAuley, *Insanity, Psychiatry and Criminal Responsibility* (1993), p.144.

[86] As applied to Ireland by s.17 of the Lunacy (Ireland) Act 1821.

[87] As applied to Ireland by s.17 of the Lunacy (Irealand) Act 1821.

[88] The mean length of stay has been calculated at 14.3 years. See Gibbons P., Mulryan N., McAleer A. and O'Connor A., "Criminal Responsibility and Mental Illness in Ireland 1850–1995: fitness to plead" 1999 *Irish Journal of Psychological Medicine* Vol.16(2), p.51–56.

[89] He refers to McAuley *Insanity Psychiatry and Criminal Responsibility* Roundhall (1993) at p.145 where he refers to the comments made by the Director of the Central Mental Hospital in an article written in the Sunday Tribune. The Director reounted how one detainee had a twenty one year charge of murdering his mother withdrawn in 1990 subsequent to which he was transferred to St Patrick's hospital. In another case he states that two patients accused of sexual offences had, at the time of the interview, spent seven years in the hospital. See"The Law of Insanity in Ireland", *Bar Review*, June 1996, p.10, n.15.

[90] See Walsh D., *Criminal Procedure* (Thomson Roundhall Dublin 2002), p.781. Gibbons P., Mulryan N., McAleer and O'Connor, *A comment*: "Given the lack of any trial of the facts or the establishment of guilty in these cases [where the accused person is found unfit to plead] detention appears to serve either as a proxy form of punishment on a presumption of guilt or as a form of preventive detention on a presumption of potential dangerousness. In contrast, people actually convicted of serious violent crime appear to be treated more sympathetically by the legal system, given that the average length of time served by people convicted of murder is 12 years [as opposed to an average 14.3 years detention in the Central Mental Hospital when there is a finding of unfitness to plead], the corresponding figure for manslaughter being six years." See "Criminal Responsibility and Mental Illness in Ireland 1850–1995: Fitness to Plead" (1999) *Irish Journal of Psychological Medicine* Vol 16(2), pp.51–56 at p.54.

McAuley notes that findings of unfitness for trial are now relatively rare and rarely exceed five per annum and attributes this at least in part to the development of tranquillisers in the treatment of schizophrenia in the early 1950s and to the fact that regardless of the crime charged they lead to automatic indeterminate detention in the Central Mental Hospital.[91]

Gibbons et al comment that because of the fact that a plea of unfitness leads to the undesirable consequence of indeterminate detention alternative methods of dealing with an accused person with a mental disability are currently being employed in practice:

> "The reality for mentally ill defendants currently appearing before the Irish courts may not be as bleak as was previously the case. In current practice the authors' experience suggest that the courts are willing to remand defendant's in custody for psychiatric assessment and treatment on the recommendation of the attending psychiatrist for periods of six to eight weeks, without any formal hearing on the issue of fitness to plead. Furthermore in cases involving minor charges, the courts often grant a *nolle prosequi,* allowing the charges to be dropped and providing an informal mechanism for diverting the mentally ill from the judicial system to the healthcare service. However, in cases involving serious or violent crime where a *nolle prosequi* is unacceptable to the court, the defendant has an unenviable choice between proceeding with a trial in which he is not able to participate fully or pleading unfitness, with the attending risk of indefinite detention at the Central Mental Hospital. No data is available at this time as to the prevalence of use of the *nolle prosequi* mechanism."[92]

Fitness to Plead in the District Court The test regarding fitness to plead set out in *R v. Pritchard*[93] applies to an accused person before the District Court whether on a summary charge or where a decision is being made whether to send the accused person forward for trial on indictment. If the court is satisfied that the accused person is not fit to plead then an accused person cannot consent either to the continuation of the proceedings or to the summary trial of an indictable offence and a question is raised as to whether or not the accused person is in a condition to enter into a recognisance for the purposes of being admitted to bail. In this regard Walsh J in the case of *State (C) v. Minister for Justice*[94] was of the view that if a District Justice decided that the person was unfit for trial the Justice would have no alternative but to remand the person in custody as he or she would not be able to enter into a recognisance.[95] However in the light of *People (Attorney General) v. O'Callaghan*[96] and *Ryan v. DPP*[97] a constitutional challenge to such a practice could be mounted.

As to the issue of disposition of the case where the issue of unfitness to plead is raised in a court of summary jurisdiction such as the District Court. A District court

---

[91] *Insanity Psychiatry and Criminal Responsibility (1993),* p.141.

[92] See "Criminal Responsibility and mental illness in Ireland 1850–1995: fitness to plead" 1999 *Irish Journal of Psychological Medicine* Vol.16(2), pp.51–56.

[93] (1836) 7 C. & P. 303.

[94] [1967] I.R. 106.

[95] *Ibid.* at 126.

[96] [1966] I.R. 501.

[97] [1989] I.R. 399.

judge can remand an accused person in custody without requiring him to be brought before the court on each remand date if he is satisfied that through illness he is unable to attend.[98] However, at the making of such a remand the court would have to be "judicially satisfied of the continued "unfitness to plead" of the accused person.[99]

In *State (Caseley) v. Daly and another*[100] the accused person charged with arson was remanded in custody by the District Court for further examination with consent to bail if forthcoming. During the period in custody he was transferred to the Central Mental Hospital by order of the Minister for Justice under section 13 of the Lunatic Asylums (Ireland) Act 1875. At the following remand date the accused person did not attend court and medical evidence was given in his absence of his inability to attend due to illness. The District Justice made a series of further orders of remand until the accused person was well enough to attend court. The accused person challenged the making of the orders by way of certiorari. Gannon J in the High Court held that although a person remanded for further examination might legitimately be transferred to a psychiatric hospital for the duration of the remand unless so extended:

> "An order made pursuant to section 24(4) of the Criminal Procedure Act 1967 could … [be] a proper order … for the period specified if on the evidence it could reasonably … [be] expected that the [accused] might sufficiently recover from his illness to permit the matter pending before the court to proceed. But if the evidence offered … suggest[s] a continuing capacity of indefinite duration the District Justice should [take] steps to deal with the matter … pending under the provisions of the Mental Treatment Act 1945."[101]

Where the accused person's incapacity continues it was suggested in *State (C) v. Minister for Justice* that the alternative to further remands was to withdraw the charges or to offer no further evidence so that the proceedings would be discontinued but leaving the way open for a renewal of charges at a future date, if the accused person's condition was sufficiently recovered.[102] In such event the accused person is released and might receive appropriate treatment under the Mental Treatment Act 1945.

Where the substantive issue of guilt or innocence of the accused person is concerned the Supreme Court in *O'Connor v. Judges of the Dublin Metropolitan District*[103] held that if the District Court found an accused person unfit to plead then the constitution demanded that it:

> "should make no order of any description with regard to the further attendance of the accused person or with regard to his custody."

Accordingly an accused person who is found unfit to plead in summary proceedings, pending legislative reform will have no order made against him in the District Court

---

[98] See District Court Rules 1948, Criminal Procedure Act 1967, s.24(4).
[99] *State (C) v. Minister for Justice* [1967] I.R. 106 at 124, *per* Walsh J.
[100] Unreported, High Court (Gannon J.), February 19, 1979.
[101] *Ibid.* at 11–12.
[102] [1967] I.R. 106 at 116, *per* O'Dalaigh C.J. and at 124, *per* Walsh J.
[103] [1994] 3 I.R. 246, *per* Finlay C.J. for the court affirming the High Court (O'Hanlon J.) reported at [1992] I.R. 387.

even if the prosecution does not elect to discontinue proceedings. Accordingly it appears he must go free. Also according to Gannon J. in the *State (Caseley) v. Daly*[104] the District Court has no power to order or direct committal to a psychiatric hospital or that s/he undergo the requisite treatment. Thus in the absence of legislation on the subject there is a significant issue as to the custodial disposition of an accused person who meets the criteria for unfitness to plead by reason of mental disorder short of fulfilling the criteria for involuntary civil committal in the District Court. Gannon J in *Caseley* however suggested an approach whereby a person removed to a psychiatric hospital under section 13 of the Lunatic Asylums (Ireland) Act 1875 might be transferred to the Central Mental Hospital under section 207 of the Mental Treatment Act 1945. However given that in *RT v. Director of the Central Mental Hospital*[105] Costello J found the provisions of section 207 unconstitutional such an approach must be regarded as constitutionally unfeasible.

In addition while section 9 of the Criminal Justice Act 1999[106] which inserts section 4A(1)(c) into the Criminal Procedure Act 1967 provides that the District Court shall send an accused person forward for trial unless, inter alia, it finds the accused person is unfit to plead it fails to outline the consequences of such a finding. Section 19 and Schedule 2 of the Criminal Law (Insanity) Bill 2002 propose to repeal section 4A(1)(c) of the Criminal Justice Act 1967. The 2002 Bill provides new powers of disposition where an accused person is found unfit to be tried by the District Court

Commentary on the Law currently in force

The law relating to fitness to plead is rooted both in criteria and procedure in nineteenth century philosophy and practice both of which require more precise delineation and greater flexibility so as ensure that an accused person is not prejudiced in relation to trial and receives the most appropriate form of treatment for his condition where that is warranted. With these considerations in mind the following proposals are made.

1. The criteria for a finding of "unfitness to stand trial" require reform in that:
    (a) present criteria for fitness to plead give rise to a risk of confusion between the defence of insanity and unfitness to plead. Further to avoid the situation where an accused person with another disability may be labelled mentally disordered on a finding of unfitness the criteria should embrace any "disability" that prevents an accused person from participating in his trial.[107]
    (b) present criteria set out in *R v. Pritchard* regarding fitness represent a concentration on cognitive criteria to the exclusion of other tests of rationality.[108]

---

[104] Unreported, High Court (Gannon J.), February 19, 1979, p.10.

[105] [1995] 2 I.L.R.M. 354.

[106] S.9 of the 1999 Act was brought into force on October 1, 2001 by the Criminal Justice Act 1999 (Part III) Commencement Order 2001 (S.I. No. 193 of 2001).

[107] The Canadian case of *R v. Schupe* (1987) 59 C.R. (3d) 329 is illustrative. In that case sexual assault charges against a deaf mute person who had not learned sign language were stayed. The court held that treating a deaf mute person as an insane person subject to indefinite commitment violated the accused person's rights under ss.7, 14 and 15 of the Canadian Charter of Rights and Freedoms and the infringements could not be demonstrably justified under s.1.

[108] See "The Fitness to Plead Procedure – an adequate protection?", N.L.J. 2002 152 (7024), pp.439–

This is a further argument for extending the criteria to include any disability that prevents an accused person from participating in his/her trial.

(c) the fitness legislation should distinguish clearly between mental disorder and intellectual disability in order to avoid perpetuating confusion between the two conditions.[109] Indeed there may be an argument for different dispositions depending upon whether an accused person is a person with an intellectual disability or is a person with mental illness. Grubin argues:

> "[P]rior to *Dyson*[110] and *Pritchard*[111] a clear distinction was made between defendants who were mentally defective and those who were insane in respect of their fitness to plead. Neither was in a position to have a fair trial; in the former case trial should not take place as the accused person did not have the faculty to understand what was going on, while in the latter trial should be postponed, not cancelled, because the accused person was temporarily unable to use whatever faculties he did have to defend himself adequately. This critical distinction, established by Hale[112] and Kenyon,[113] was lost in *Dyson* and *Pritchard* and has yet to be recovered."

It is submitted that "mental disorder" should not be defined to include "intellectual disability" and the latter term should be defined clearly in legislation.[114] Further it is submitted that a judge should be able to choose between a range of disposition options and tailor them to the disability presented by the accused person. These matters are not adequately dealt with in the Criminal Law (Insanity) Bill 2002. See pages 453 *et seq.*

(d) the use of the term "insanity" as a description of the state of mind of the unfit accused may lead to confusion with the substantive defence. The term "mental disorder" is preferable both on this basis and as being more consistent with current medical practice. This matter is addressed by the Criminal Law (Insanity) Bill 2002. See pages 453 *et seq.*[115]

---

440 In Pritchard the accused person was not mentally ill. He was simply unable to speak or hear. Consequently his case concentrated on cognitive criteria to the exclusion of others.

[109] See Grubin D., "What Constitutes Fitness to Plead?" [1993] *Crim. Law Review* 748 at 751.

[110] *R v. Dyson* (1831) 7 C. & P. 305.

[111] *R v. Pritchard* (1836) 7 C. & P. 303.

[112] M. Hale, *The History of the Pleas of the Crown Vol. 1* (reprinted by Professional Books Ltd., London 1971), p.34.

[113] The reference is to dicta of Lord Chief Justice Lord Kenyon in *Proceedings in the Case of John Frith for High Treason at Justice Hall in the Old Bailey on Saturday, April 17: 30 George III* (1790) Howell's State Trials, Vol.22 (1783–1794), p.308.

[114] The Law Reform Commission of New South Wales in its Report No.80 on *People with an Intellectual Disability in the Criminal Justice System* expresses the belief that any definition in a criminal law context should be "as unambiguous as possible bearing in mind the punitive consequences involved." Within these parameters it defines intellectual disability as "significantly below average intellectual functioning existing concurrently with two or more deficits in adaptive behaviour" – a definition that is "brief and limited in application" and consistent with internationally recognised (World Health Organisation, American Association on Mental Retardation and American Psychiatric Association) definitions.

[115] However the wide definition given to the term "mental disorder" in the Bill itself gives rise to confusion.

2. Where pre-trial remands of an accused person for psychiatric examination are concerned it is submitted that:
   (a) where the issue of fitness is raised before trial legislation should be enacted setting out grounds and procedures for pre-trial remand of an accused person for psychiatric examination. That legislation should empower the judge to make a wide range of possible orders including such orders as would entail a minimum of restraint on individual liberty. Provision should be made for examination without detention if the crime charged is one for which bail would normally be granted and the accused person will be of no danger to society.
   (b) Since the issue of unfitness does not necessarily involve dangerousness, remand for psychiatric examination as to fitness to plead should entail no more restriction of the accused person's freedom that if no examination were required. Where examination in detention is considered necessary as a preventive measure or for therapeutic reasons it should be justified by the person or authority alleging its necessity.
   (c) procedures for remand for psychiatric examination should require that the accused person be returned to court or where it would be detrimental for the accused person's mental health to be sent back to court provide that the issue of fitness may be decided by the court.

      Procedures relating to psychiatric examination as to whether an accused is fit to be tried are not expressly built in to the Criminal Law (Insanity) Bill 2002. Procedures for examination to determine whether an accused is in need of inpatient care or treatment in a designated centre after the issue of fitness has been determined are however, outlined in the Bill.

3. Where the format of psychiatric reports is concerned it is submitted:
   (a) both pre-trial remands and remands during trial for psychiatric examination should be tailored to their purpose and that purpose communicated in the remand provisions to the examining psychiatrist. Pre-trial examinations should focus on the two principal issues relevant at that time i.e. fitness to plead and the possibility of diversion from the criminal process and should not, when these issues are under consideration, contain information prejudicial to the accused person such as the psychiatric likelihood of the accused person committing an offence similar to that charged. In essence information contained in reports should avoid creating the risk of convicting the accused person for what he might do rather than for what he actually did.[116]
   (b) where there is a remand for psychiatric examination during the trial the psychiatric report should avoid creating confusion between the concepts relevant to fitness to plead and the insanity defence by dealing with these matters as separate issues in separate sections of the report.
   (c) to avoid the dangers of summary psychiatric evidence conclusive of the issues to be determined being adopted without question by the court legislation should both require psychiatric reports to be made and provide in detail for their form,

---

[116] The Law Reform Commission of Canada in its *Report to Parliament on Mental Disorder in the Criminal Process* March 1976 expresses similar concerns. See p.33.

content and disposition.[117] It should also make it clear that the psychiatrist's role is to provide information regarding how the accused person's mental disorder prevents him from participating at trial to assist the court in making its decision and that the psychiatrist is not required to apply legal criteria in his reports or testimony.

Requirements relating to the content of psychiatric reports set out in (b), (c) and (d) could be outlined in a statutory instrument made under powers outlined in reforming legislation such as the Criminal Law (Insanity) Bill 2002. These matters are not addressed in the Bill.

4.   As to the trial of the issue as to whether an accused person is fit to plead:
   (a) it should not be an adversary proceeding but a detailed inquiry into the accused person's status. An adversarial approach is particularly inappropriate where there is little dispute about a person's unfitness or where a person has a permanent condition and has been found unfit in relation to previous charges. The relevant procedures should be clearly articulated in legislation.[118]
   (b) the issue of fitness should continue to be capable of being raised by both the prosecution and the accused person. The issue is not simply a defence but a determination which is vital to the trial process. This matter is addressed by section 3(1) the Criminal Law (Insanity) Bill 2002 which permits the matter to

---

[117] The Law Reform Commission of Canada's proposals for draft legislation in its study paper on *Fitness to Stand Trial* (May 1973) are of interest in this regard. They require the psychiatrist's report to contain: (a) a description of the nature of the examination; (b) a diagnosis of the mental health of the accused person; (c) any additional information the examining psychiatrist considers pertinent to the court. They also require the examining medical practitioner to state his opinion and the reasons therefor of the extent if any to which the mental disorder of the accused person prevents him from (a) appreciating the nature of the charge; (b) appreciating the consequences of conviction; (c) understanding the importance of telling the truth in a trial proceeding; (d) communicating with counsel and (e) understanding the evidence given at trial. Where the medical practitioner is of the opinion that the accused person suffers from a mental disorder he is required by the proposals to indicate: (a) the likelihood of recovery; (b) the period of time necessary for treatment; (c) the kind of treatment which the accused person should be given; (d) whether the accused person should be kept in custody for reasons other than the commission of the offence and (e) the length of detention in order to assure the security either of himself or of others. See pp.39–41. In its Report on *Mental Disorder in the Criminal Process* (March 1976) the Commission recommended that the preparation of detailed report forms should be worked out and continuously reviewed by psychiatrists, lawyers and judges in various communities and jurisdictions in order to allow the adjustment of reports to changing scientific developments and local court and psychiatric facilities and to foster communication and understanding between psychiatry and law. See p.35 Gibbons et al. note that: "In North America, standardised instruments such as the Competency Assessment Instrument and the Fitness Interview Test have been developed to improve the reliability of evidence provided by clinicians at fitness to plead hearings." They recommend "The development of a similar instrument adapted to the specific requirements of Irish law would be useful in facilitating research of the concept of legal competence and also in raising the credibility of the evidence provided by psychiatrists in court". See "Criminal Responsibility and Mental Illness in Ireland 1850–1995 fitness to plead" (1999) *Irish Journal of Psychological Medicine*, Vol 16(2), pp.51–56 at p.55. See also Lowenstein L.F., "Competence to Stand Trial", Vol.164, Justice of the Peace, September 2, 2000 p.700 where the author puts forward a list of competence assessment techniques and questions to be applied to persons whose competence to stand trial is in issue.

[118] See similar recommendations made by the Law Reform Commission of Canada in its *Report on Mental Disorder in the Criminal Process* (March 1976), p.19.

be raised at the instance of the defence, the prosecution or the court. See page 454.

(c) because of its technical nature[119] and because there is no consideration of the accused person's culpability the issue of fitness should be tried by the judge.[120] A hearing before a judge alone may also be quicker, less formal and less confusing or stressful for the accused person particularly if experts for both sides agree that the accused person is clearly unfit to be tried. This recommendation is followed in section 3 of the Criminal Law (Insanity) Bill 2002. See pages 454 *et seq.*

(d) in principle evidence of findings at a fitness hearing and in particular statements made by a defendant to an expert about the events relating to the offence should not be received as evidence of the facts against the defendant in the main proceedings. In the words of one commentator:

> "legislation specifically excluding reliance by the Crown upon facts gathered about the accused person or his case in the course of the fitness inquiry would ensure fairness. The court's power to request reports may allow the Crown an advantage which it is denied in the ordinary course of criminal proceedings."[121]

The Criminal Law (Insanity) Bill 2002 does not expressly address this matter.

(e) under the present law the issue of unfitness to plead must be tried as soon as it arises. This does not make allowance for the accused person who, although perhaps unfit has grounds for attacking the criminal charge on its merits. This may arise in a number of situations as where the prosecution may be barred as a matter of law because of lack of jurisdiction. Secondly the charge may be defective as a matter of law because, for example, of a defect in the indictment or lack of evidence of an essential element of the offence charged. To cater for these situations the judge should have power to postpone the issue to the end of the prosecution's case to allow the defence to present legal objections to the charge and to require the prosecution to establish a prima facie case.[122] This matter is addressed by section 3(7) of the Criminal Law (Insanity) Bill 2002. See page 460.

(f) present Irish law does not allow a defence to a charge to be heard after the issue of fitness has arisen. This may give rise to injustice in cases where counsel may

---

[119] The Law Reform Commission of Canada in its study paper on *Fitness to Stand Trial* (May 1973) notes the tendency of juries to confuse the issues of fitness, insanity at the time of the alleged offence, insanity not amounting to fitness and the guilt of the accused person. See p.23.

[120] See also Grubin D., "What Constitutes Fitness to Plead?" [1993] *Crim. Law. Review*, p.748 at 756–758.

[121] See S.C. Hayes and G. Craddock, "Simply Criminal" (2nd Federation Press, Sydney, 1992) at 103. Section 4.09 of the American Law Institute's Model Penal Code provides that a statement made by defendants in the course of psychiatric examinations for the purpose of ascertaining fitness to proceed are not admissible in evidence against him in any criminal proceeding on any issue other than his mental condition. However it is admissible upon that issue whether or not it would otherwise be deemed a privileged communication unless the statement constitutes an admission of guilt of the crime charged.

[122] See for example Criminal Procedure (Insanity) Act 1964, s.4 (UK).

be able to establish a defence through testimony of third parties without the participation of the accused person. The delay occasioned by remand in the Central Mental Hospital may also result in adverse consequences arising from passage of time for an accused person who alleges that he will not be convicted on the merits. It is submitted that where an accused person is found unfit to be tried and makes an application to the court to allow evidence to be adduced as to whether or not the accused person committed the act alleged a jury should be empowered to decide whether or not they are satisfied that the accused person did the act or made the omission charged (i.e committed the *actus reus*) and if they are not they should acquit the accused person in the normal way. In this regard the jury should examine the evidence already given together with any further evidence adduced by the prosecution or defence. If they find that the accused person did the act or made the omission charged the jury should be required to enter a finding accordingly. In this event the court should have a range of options such as: (a) admitting the accused person to hospital, (b) making a form of guardianship order, (c) making an order for treatment or (d) making an order of absolute discharge.[123] Section 3(8) of the Criminal Law (Insanity) Bill 2002 permits the court to make such a determination but only provides for the making of an order for discharge if there is a reasonable doubt as to whether the accused committed the act alleged. See p.461 below.

(g) consideration might be given to empowering a judge to decide not to conduct a fitness inquiry but instead to dismiss the charge and order that a person be released in cases where s/he is of the opinion that it is inappropriate having regard to the trivial nature of the charge or offence, the nature of the person's disability, the periods of custody or detention in respect of the offence or any other matter which the court thinks proper to consider to inflict any punishment or to inflict any punishment other than a nominal punishment. Such a provision may have the effect in appropriate cases of avoiding lengthy and futile fitness proceedings.[124] This flexibility in disposition is not contained in the Criminal Law (Insanity) Bill 2002.

4. When an accused person has been found unfit to plead a number of issues arise:
    (a) The constitutionality and compatibility of the power of indefinite detention in section 2 of the Trial of Lunatics Act 1800 with the provisions of the European Convention on Human Rights is open to question.

    In the case of R.T v. *Director of Central Mental Hospital*[125] section 207 of the Mental Treatment Act 1945[126] which provides for a procedure whereby a person on being charged with an offence in a district mental hospital and found unfit to plead by a District Judge might be transferred to and detained in the Central Mental Hospital was declared unconstitutional by the High Court because there were no safeguards against abuse or error in the making of the

---

[123] See for example s.4A(2) Criminal Procedure (Insanity) Act 1964 (UK).

[124] The Law Reform Commission of New South Wales Report No. 80 on *People with an Intellectual Disability and the Criminal Justice System* December 1996 contains similar recommendations. See p.175.

[125] [1995] 2 I.L.R.M 367.

[126] See above p.433 *et seq.*

transfer order and no safeguards in determining the length of time for which a person could be detained in that hospital. Further Costello P noting that the section enabled a person to be charge with a criminal offence who, because of a mental illness, lacked the *mens rea* for the offence commented that "[i]n such circumstances to prosecute might well amount to an abuse of the criminal process."[127] If section 207 was found to be unconstitutional for these reasons there must surely be some doubt about the constitutionality of the judicial power found in section 2 of the Trial of Lunatics Act 1800 to direct the indefinite detention of an individual in the Central Mental Hospital solely on the basis that s/he is accused of a criminal offence and is found mentally incapable of pleading to the offence and presenting a defence.

It is also entirely probable that the power of indefinite detention without adequate review procedures is not compatible with the terms of Article 5(4) of the European Convention on Human Rights which provides that

> "Everyone who is deprived of his liberty by arrest or detention shall be entitled to take proceedings by which the lawfulness of the detention shall be decided speedily by a court and his release ordered if the detention is not lawful" given interpretative force in Irish domestic law by the European Convention on Human Rights Act 2003."

Further any detention continuing after the accused person has recovered his mental health is likely to be unconstitutional as a form of preventative detention[128] and a breach of Article 5(1)(e) of the European Convention on Human Rights which permits the detention of "persons of unsound mind" but which has been held by the European Court in Human Rights in *Winterwerp v. the Netherlands*[129] to require the persistence of a mental disorder if continuing detention is to be justified.

On both constitutional and Convention grounds therefore it may be argued that the individual's right to liberty requires that there be a determination that the person posed a threat to himself and/or others on account of his mental illness justifying detention[130] These matters are addressed in sections 3 and 12 of the Criminal Law (Insanity) Bill 2002. See below pages 454 and 464 *et seq*.

(b) because of the fact that section 2 of the Criminal Lunatics Act 1800 is interpreted as mandatory in effect the unfit accused may be held in the Central Mental Hospital even where this is not in his/her interests.[131] Detention is justifiable in

---

[127] Costello P. stated a case for the opinion of the Supreme Court pursuant to Art.40.4 of the Constitution as to whether he was correct in law in his ruling but the matter was never decided as the applicant was released from the Central Mental Hospital prior to the case coming on for hearing before the Supreme Court. Dwyer notes that at that stage the applicant had spent sixteen years in the Central Mental Hospital. See "The Law of Insanity in Ireland", *Bar Review*, June 1996, p.9.

[128] See *Application of Gallagher (No.2)* at 18–19 (Geoghegan J.) and 34 (Laffoy J.). See also *Foucha v. Louisiana* 504 U.S. 71, 112 S.Ct. 1780 (1992).

[129] (1979) 2 E.H.R.R. 387.

[130] See Walsh D., *Criminal Procedure* (Thomson Roundhall Dublin 2002), p.781.

[131] This may arise in cases where an accused person is a person with an intellectual disability and is incurably unfit. The consequence for the accused person in such a case is that s/he may never be released from custody.

two circumstances (1) if treatment within the institution is likely to help the accused person become fit and no similar treatment not involving detention is available and (2) if the offence charged is one for which pre-trial detention is normally required. If there is little likelihood the committal will promote recovery or if an alternative treatment is more likely to be more beneficial then other options are preferable. There is clearly a need for a broader range and more flexible disposition options. These might include discharge on condition that an accused person receives out-patient treatment at a psychiatric hospital in cases where an unfit accused is not a danger to himself or others and who can be effectively treated without being institutionalised and absolute discharge in cases where the accused person is neither dangerous to himself nor society and unlikely to benefit from treatment.

The recent Government White Paper entitled "A New Mental Health Act" proposed that when a finding of unfitness is made the court will be empowered to arrange for a medical report by a consultant psychiatrist attached to a service in the area in which the person ordinarily resides or in special circumstances where the person currently resides. This report will indicate the most appropriate way of treating the accused person. The range of options are to include treatment on a voluntary basis as an out-patient or an in-patient; involuntary treatment in an approved centre and involuntary treatment in a special psychiatric centre.

The Criminal Law (Insanity) Bill empowers the court to make an order for commitment of the person found unfit to plead to a designated centre where it is satisfied that the accused is suffering from a mental disorder within the Mental Health Act 2001 and is in need of in-patient care or treatment in a designated centre, but does not specify any other disposition options for the court.

(c) commitment is intended to assist the accused person regain fitness so that he may be returned to trial. Section 2 of the Criminal Lunatics Act 1800 only refers to the accused person's being "kept in strict custody" in the Central Mental Hospital pending his recovery. There is, at present, no method by which the committed accused may ensure that he will receive appropriate treatment. Provision should be made in legislation for the accused person's right to treatment upon commitment. This right might be implied from the terms of section 3 of the Criminal Law (Insanity) Bill 2002 which permits commitment of a person found unfit to be tried on the grounds that the person is suffering from a mental disorder and is "in need of in-patient care or treatment in a designated centre" but no express right is contained in the Bill's provisions.

(d) the present fitness hearing procedure may be abused by the prosecution as a means of avoiding the defence of insanity. It is quicker and easier to have an accused person committed as unfit than to proceed with the issue of criminal responsibility. While originally a finding of unfitness was intended temporarily to delay proceedings until the accused person recovered under the present law it may result in the accused person's being detained indefinitely in a mental institution with no assurance that he will be returned to trial. There is at present no method by which an accused person may ensure that he will be returned to trial if he becomes fit. In effect this may result in the fitness hearing becoming a disposition instead of a deferral of the trial. This fact may be abused by the prosecution as a means of securing some form of detention. This is a further argument for more flexible treatment options. This issue is addressed by section 12 of the Criminal Law (Insanity) Bill 2002. See pages 464 *et seq.*

(e) present Irish law justifies the indeterminate detention of an unfit accused. Detention should be linked only to the length of time it takes the accused person to recover. If the period spent in detention exceeds the term of imprisonment any court might have imposed that should be taken into consideration in making a decision as to whether the accused person on recovering fitness should be returned to court for trial. Where the period spent in detention exceeds the term of imprisonment any further psychiatric treatment should be justified exclusively by reference to the accused person's mental illness and not by reference to the criminal charge. If further detention is required it should proceed under civil commitment legislation. This matter is not addressed by the Criminal Law (Insanity) Bill 2002.

(f) The District Court should have power to direct that an accused person undergo appropriate treatment where the issue of unfitness to plead is established before it. The range of treatment options should include in-patient and out-patient treatment and it should have power to make such a direction without making a determination as to the guilt or innocence of the accused person. Section 3(3) of the Criminal Law (Insanity) Bill 2002 gives the District Court a discretion to commit an accused to a designated centre where it determines that an accused person is unfit to be tried and where having considered the evidence of an approved medical officer and any other evidence that may be adduced before it, it is satisfied that the accused is suffering from a mental disorder and is in need of in-patient care or treatment in a designated centre. There is no express power in the Bill to direct out-patient treatment.

(g) The requirement that an accused person before the District Court enter into a recognisance for bail to be granted might be abolished in cases where the accused person is mentally unfit to enter into them. In this regard it is interesting to note the proposal of the Henchy Committee[132] that adjournments of up to six months be granted if a person was unable by reason of mental disorder to enter into a recognisance and when the reason for the adjournment no longer exists that the person be brought before the court to be dealt with in accordance with law. This matter is not addressed by the Criminal Law (Insanity) Bill 2002

The effect of the Criminal Law (Insanity) Bill 2002 on plea of fitness to be tried

The Criminal Law (Insanity) Bill 2002 introduced to the Seanad on December 10, 2002 and which passed the second stage in the Seanad on February 19, 2003 addresses some but not all of the concerns outlined in the commentary above.

Proposed New Description of the Plea The Bill replaces the term "fitness to plead" with the term "fitness to be tried." This is to be welcomed because as Conway points out "fitness to participate in the proceedings encompasses more than merely a capacity

---

[132] See *Third Interim Report of the Interdepartmental Committee on Mentally Ill and Maladjusted Persons: Treatment and Care of Persons Suffering from Mental Disorder who appear before Courts on Criminal Charges* Prl. 8275, J 85/1, Draft Bill, s.37.

to enter a plea thought the latter is obviously a necessary prerequisite to proceeding with a trial".[133]

Proposed New Criteria to Establish Fitness The Bill replaces the common law criteria for fitness to plead with statutory provisions. Section 3(1) of the Bill provides that where in the course of proceedings against an accused person the question arises at the instance of the defence, the prosecution or the court as to whether or not the person is fit to be tried the following subsections of section 3 are to have effect.

The phrase "in the course of the proceedings" suggests that the plea may be raised at any stage in the proceedings. What is not clear however is whether the plea may be raised more than once so that an initial finding of unfitness would not prevent the issue being raised again if circumstances change.[134]

Further section 3(1) makes it clear that the judge or the prosecution may raise the issue of fitness of its own initiative but does not impose an obligation to do so. This appears to run contrary to the recent High Court decision in *Leonard v. Garavan and the DPP*[135] in which McKechnie J. held in judicial review proceedings that even where the defence does not raise the issue of fitness to plead there is a duty on the court to raise the matter itself where there is evidence from the behaviour of the accused person that suggests that the accused person may not in fact be fit to plead. Once it becomes apparent that the issue of fitness to plead was relevant McKechnie J. held that it should have been considered and the trial halted if necessary. This accorded with the accused person's constitutional right to a fair trial and one in due course of law. Accordingly despite the absence of an obligation on the judge or the prosecution to raise the issue of fitness in the 2002 Bill it is submitted the decision in *Leonard* regarding the duty of the court to raise the issue of fitness is likely to remain authoritative on the context of the general constitutional rights of the accused and the duty of the judge and prosecution to ensure and fair and just trial.

Section 3(2) provides that an accused person shall be deemed unfit to be tried if he or she is unable by reason of mental disorder to understand the nature or course of the proceedings so as to (a) plead to the charge, (b) instruct a legal representative, (c) make a proper defence, (d) in the case of a trial by jury, challenge a juror to whom he or she might wish to object, or (e) understand the evidence.[136]

The criterion of capacity "to make a proper defence" is a broad one and arguably a catchall criterion which could be availed of by an accused person with a disability who failed technically to meet the other cognitively oriented criteria.[137] It might include an

---

[133] Conway G., "Fitness to Plead in Light of the Criminal Law (Insanity) Bill 2002" (2003) Vol.13(4) *Irish Criminal Law Journal* 2 at 3.

[134] See Conway, "Fitness to Plead in Light of the Criminal Law (Insanity) Bill 2002", (2003) Vol.13(4), *Irish Criminal Law Journal* 2 at 6.

[135] Unreported, High Court, April 30, 2002.

[136] At Committee Stage in the Seanad the Minister for Justice, Equality and Law Reform indicated that he was thinking of bringing forward a further ground for unfitness namely a person's inability to elect for trail by jury in the case of an indictable offence. See 176 *Seanad Debates* Col. 382.

[137] See Conway, "Fitness to Plead in Light of the Criminal Law (Insanity) Bill 2002" (2003) Vol.13(4) *Irish Criminal Law Journal* 2 at 3 It appears to approach the concept of "effective participation" which envisaged by Art.6 of the European Convention on Human Rights.

accused person who could not act in his own best interests[138] or an accused person who on account of a psychiatric disorder is unwilling to defend him or herself or falsely confesses to a crime.[139] It could also encompass an accused person who as in the case of *JO'C v. DPP*[140] had developed Alzheimer's disease which affected his ability to "recollect effectively" and "marshal his thoughts and arguments"[141] giving rise to a real and substantial risk of prejudice to a fair trial. In that case Peart J was of the view that a plea of unfitness was "inappropriate"[142] and he granted relief in judicial review pro-ceedings restraining the prosecution on the grounds that by reason of lapse of time between the subject matter of the trial and the actual trial itself and the accused person's condition there was a real and substantial risk of an unfair trial. Had Peart J. been of the view that the plea of unfitness was available as an adequate alternative remedy relief in the judicial review proceedings it must be supposed that the relief would have been refused.

The statutory tests in the 2002 Bill otherwise set out the traditional common law criteria for "fitness to plead" and attract the criticisms of the common law test that it focuses exclusively on intellectual and cognitive functioning and excludes other types of mental disabilities.[143]

"Mental disorder" is defined by section 1(1) of the Bill to include mental illness, mental handicap or any disease of the mind, but does not include intoxication. The Bill accordingly does not appear to afford other persons with disabilities other than mental illness or intellectual disability (e.g. people with hearing or speaking disabilities) which might affect their fitness to be tried a statutory right to plead and it must be assumed that the common law continues to apply in their situations. It would be preferable however if the Bill made it clear that physical disabilities (such as muteness) are covered and the full extent of the common law plea incorporated into the statute. To achieve this the misleading description of the conditions which form the basis of the plea viz. "mental disorder" would need to be changed to "disability" and the definition revised accordingly.[144]

---

[138] In *R v. Robertson* [1968] 3 All E.R. 557 an accused person who could comprehend the proceedings but it was unable to act in his own best interests because of delusions and persecution mania was held by the Court of Appeal not to meet the traditional fitness to plead criteria set out in *R v. Pritchard* [1836] 7 C. & P. 303.

[139] This situation is mentioned Casey and Craven., *Psychiatry and the Law* (Oaktree Press, Dublin 1999), p.431 as an instance to which the traditional criteria would not apply. Such cases would fall within the category of what has been described as "decisional incompetence" i.e. cases where an accused cannot make true choices in relation to decisions about the trial process. See Mackay J., "Some Thoughts on Reforming the Law of Insanity and Diminished Responsibility in England" (2003) *Juridical Review*, 1, 57–80 at p.61–64.

[140] Unreported, High Court, October 8, 2002.

[141] At p.9.

[142] Although the matter was not referred to in Peart J.'s judgment "hysterical amnesia" giving rise to an inability of an accused person to remember events relating to the commission of the offence has been held not to be sufficient basis to assert unfitness to plead. See *R v. Podola* [1960] 1 Q.B. 325. However Conway argues that the "medically verifiable physical condition affecting memory in general as well as the ability to marshal one's thoughts" might have fallen within the traditional criteria. See "Fitness to Plead in Light of the Criminal Law (Insanity) Bill 2002" (2003) Vol.13(4) *Irish Criminal Law Journal* p.2 at p.4.

[143] See Grubin, "What Constitutes Fitness to Plead?" [1993] *Crim. L.R.* 753 at 754.

[144] The Scottish Law Commission in its *Discussion Paper No. 122 on Insanity and Diminished Responsibility* published in January 2003 favours renaming the plea "disability in bar of trial".

The 2002 Bill does not address the issue of the burden of proof in relation to the issue of fitness to be tried. As a consequence it must be presumed that the common law authorities apply establishing that the accused must satisfy the test of unfitness on the balance of probabilities[145] and the prosecution challenging it must show beyond a reasonable doubt that the accused person is fit to plead[146] apply.

There are no procedures set out in the Bill regarding the psychiatric examination to be conducted to determine whether an accused is fit to be tried. Procedures for examination to determine whether an accused is in need of inpatient care or treatment in a designated centre after the issue of fitness has been determined are however, outlined in the Bill.

It is submitted that the legislation should contain a provision empowering the Minister for Justice, Equality and Law Reform to stipulate specific requirements which psychiatric reports on fitness to be tried should meet in order to avoid confusion with the defence of insanity and to maintain the psychiatrists role as an expert witness.

It is submitted that the 2002 Bill should specifically preclude the prosecution from relying on facts gathered about the accused person or his case in the course of the determination of whether an accused person is fit to be tried as the court's power to request reports may allow the prosecution an advantage which is denied in the course of ordinary proceedings.

Proposed New Procedures in the District and Higher Trial Courts for determining whether accused person is unfit to be tried and powers of disposition where the accused person is so found

The Criminal Law (Insanity) Bill proposes to establish a unified approach to the issue of fitness to plead or be tried in indictable and summary cases by putting the issue of fitness to plead or be tried - which was a statutory plea[147] in cases where the accused person was to be tried on indictment but a common law plea in summary cases – on a statutory basis in the case of both types of trial. It also confers statutory powers on the District Court in relation to the disposition of an accused found unfit to plead or be tried which are lacking under the current law.

It provides that where the accused person is charged with a summary offence or with an indictable offence which is to be tried summarily before the District Court section 3(3)(a) of the Bill provides that "any question whether or not the accused person is fit to be tried shall be determined by the Court." If the court determines that the accused person is unfit to be tried the court must adjourn the proceedings until further order and may, if is satisfied having considered the evidence of an approved medical officer and any other evidence that may be adduced before it that the accused person is suffering from a mental disorder within the meaning of the Mental Health Act 2001 and is in need of in-patient care or treatment in a designated centre commit him or her to a specified designated centre until an order is made by the Mental Health Review Board under section 12.

---

[145] *R v. Podola* [1960] 1 Q.B. 325.
[146] *R v. Robertson* [1968] 1 W.L.R. 1767.
[147] See Criminal Lunatics Act 1800, s.2.

An "approved medical officer" is defined by section 1(1) as a consultant psychiatrist within the meaning of the Mental Health Act 2001.[148] A "designated centre" is described in section 2 of the Bill as a psychiatric centre or a prison or section of a prison that has been designated by the Minister for Health and Children or in the case of a prison by the Minister for Health and Children with the consent of the Minister for Justice Equality and Law Reform as a centre for the reception, detention and, where appropriate, treatment of persons or classes of persons committed thereto under the provisions of the Bill. A "psychiatric centre" is defined by section 2(4) as "a hospital or other institution in which care or treatment is provided for persons suffering from a mental disorder" and a "prison" is defined as "a place of custody administered by the Minister for Justice, Equality and Law Reform." If the accused person is found fit to be tried then the proceedings continue.[149]

Section 3(4) provides that where the accused person is before the District Court charged with an offence other than summary offence or an indictable offence that is to be tried summarily then the question of fitness is not to decided by the District Court. In that case the accused person is to be sent forward to the court in which the matter would be tried if the accused person were fit to be tried. The question of whether the accused person is fit to be tried is then to be determined by the judge sitting alone in that court.

If the accused person is found fit to be tried before a court to which he has been sent forward by the District Court then section 3(4)(c) provides that the provisions of the Criminal Procedure Act 1967 will apply as if the accused person had, on the date when he was sent forward for consideration of the question of fitness to be tried, been the subject of an order returning him to be tried under section 4A of the Criminal Justice Act 1967 as inserted by section 9 of the Criminal Justice Act 1999.

Section 3(4)(e) provides that where the court of trial subsequently determines (*i.e.* during the course of its own proceedings) that the person is fit to be tried the provisions of the Criminal Procedure Act 1967 will apply as if an order returning the person for trial had been made by the District court on the date the determination was made

Section 3(4)(d) provides that if the court to which the accused person has been sent forward for trial by the District Court judge finds that a person is unfit to be tried the provisions of section 3(5) which set out the criteria and powers of committal of a court following a finding of unfitness to be tried shall apply.

Section 3(5)(b) provides that where the accused person is before a court other than the District Court charged with an offence the following provisions apply.

First the question of fitness to be tried is also to be decided by a judge sitting alone. (section 3(5)(b)).

Secondly section 3(5)(c) provides that subject to section 3(7) (power to defer consideration of question of fitness to be tried) and 3(8) (power of court to determine whether the accused person committed the act alleged notwithstanding finding of fitness to be tried) if the judge of a court other than the District Court before which the accused person is charged with an offence determines that the accused person is unfit to be tried

---

[148] "Consultant psychiatrist" is defined by s.2(1) of the Mental Health Act 2001 to mean "a consultant psychiatrist who is employed by the Health Service Executive or by an approved centre or a person whose name is entered on the division of psychiatry or the division of child and adolescent psychiatry of the Register of Medical Specialists maintained by the Medical Council in Ireland".

[149] Criminal Law (Insanity) Bill 2002, s.3(3)(c).

the judge must adjourn the proceedings until further order and may, if s/he is satisfied having considered the evidence the evidence of an approved medical officer adduced pursuant to section 3(6) (following medical examination) and any other evidence that may be adduced to determine that the accused person is suffering from a mental disorder within the meaning of the Mental Health Act 2001 and is in need of an in-patient care or treatment in a designated centre commit him to a specified designated centre until an order relating to his detention had been made by the Mental Health Review Board under section 12.

Thirdly where the court determines that the accused person is fit to be tried the proceedings shall continue (section 3(5)(d)).

Section 3(6) provides that for the purpose of determining where or not to exercise a power of committal under section 3(3), (4) or (5) the court may commit the accused person to a designated centre for a period of not more than 28 days and must direct that the accused person be examined by an approved medical officer at that centre. The approved medical officer must then report back to the court within the 28 days on whether in his or her opinion the accused person is suffering from a mental disorder within the meaning of the Mental Health Act 2001 and is in need of in-patient care or treatment in a designated centre.

It is also clear from the terms of the Bill that there is no power of detention on the ground of dangerousness alone absent a finding of mental disorder. It is also worth noting that if an accused person is not suffering from a mental disorder within the meaning of the Mental Health Act 2001 the court has no statutory power of committal albeit that the accused person may be suffering from a mental disorder within the wider meaning of the Criminal Law (Insanity) Bill 2002.[150]

A power to remand a person on bail to attend for assessment on an outpatient basis is also absent from the Bill.[151] The inclusion of such a power would be in line with international best practice in mental health care and treatment.[152] It would also accord with the recommendations of the Henchy Report[153] which states in the Introduction that "the powers of the courts shall be such that, having regard to the expert opinion that may be called on, out-patient treatment and community care will be the primary consideration, so that only those whose condition so requires will be detained in a designated centre".

In addition there are no powers of management of persons who do not need treatment but are unlikely to regain fitness to plead for example because of intellectual disability or other disabilities. Options such as guardianship and community supervision available under the law of other jurisdictions might be appropriately employed in the Irish

---

[150] See Mills S., "Criminal Law (Insanity) Bill 2002. Putting the sanity back into insanity?", *Bar Review*, June 2003, p.101.

[151] See comments in 171 *Seanad Debates* Col. 775 (Senator Terry).

[152] The United Nations Principles for the Protection of Persons with Mental Illness and the Improvement of Mental Health Care adopted by the General Assembly, December 17, 1991 provide: "Every patient shall have the right to be treated and cared for, as far as possible, in the community in which he or she lives." (Principle 7.1) They also provide "Every patient shall have the right to be treated in the least restrictive environment and with the least restrictive or intrusive treatment appropriate to the patient's health needs and the need to protect the physical safety of others" (Principle 9.1).

[153] *Third Report of the Interdepartmental Committee on Mentally Ill and Maladjusted Persons* (1978).

jurisdiction although the resource implications for the probation and community care services would need to be addressed.[154]

Further prior to exercising the power of committal for 28 days the court need not conduct any prior medical assessment. This is likely to be in breach of the provisions of Article 5(1)(e) of the European Convention on Human Rights and the criteria for detention as a person of unsound mind set out in *Winterwerp v. the Netherlands*.[155]

The designation of a "prison" as a centre for the care and treatment of persons with mental illness does not accord with international best practice.[156] This point was raised by Senator Henry in the course of the Committee Stage Debates in the Seanad. The Minister for Justice, Equality and Law Reform replied:

> "We cannot rule out the possibility that at some stage the requirements of public safety might override other considerations and that a person may have to be detained within the confines of the most secure facility available".[157]

He indicated that he was "talking about a rare phenomenon or possibility" and referred to the fictional character "Hannibal Lecter" as the "kind of situation – where it would be necessary for somebody to be kept in the most secure accommodation possible."[158]

Further the definition of "designated centre" in the Bill does not appear to address the need to provide for separate facilities for persons under the age of 18 who could be committed under its terms.

Commenting on the practical implications of the new procedures for referring persons found unfit to plead or not guilty by reason of insanity to "designated centres" under the Bill Amnesty International in a report in 2003 stated:

> "[T]he Bill speaks of referring defendants to 'designated centres' for their assessment and detention. Where exactly these centres are to be however, does not seem to have been considered. ... [C]ivil psychiatric hospitals and units do not currently accept patients from the criminal justice system. Even if they are forced to change this policy, the majority of in-patient facilities are already overburdened. There are no specialist forensic units other than the Central Mental Hospital which is under impossible strain at all times, and its physical conditions are widely condemned. There are no in-patient psychiatric facilities within the prison system. There are no stated plans in the Bill to create new specialist units for these referrals, nor to increase the number of places in the mainstream services. Neither is there provision in the Bill for increased resources for this new regime."[159]

---

[154] See Gibbons *et al.*, "Criminal Responsibility and Mental Illness in Ireland 1850–1995: fitness to plead" (1999) *Irish Journal of Psychological Medicine*, Vol.16(2), p.51–56 at p.55.

[155] [1979] 2 E.H.R.R. 387.

[156] See United Nations Principles for the Protection of Persons with Mental Illness and the Improvement of Mental Health Care Adopted by the General Assembly, 17 December 17, 1991, Principle 1.1: "All persons have the right to the best available mental health care, which shall be part of the health and social care system". See also UN Standard Minimum Rules for the Treatment of Prisoners which state that: "Prisoners found insane shall not be detained in prisons and shall be removed to mental institutions as soon as possible".

[157] 176 *Seanad Debates* Col.372.

[158] 176 *Seanad Debates* Col.372.

[159] See "Mental Illness: The Neglected Quarter: Marginalised Groups", November 2003, p.57.

It is submitted that the Bill's aspirations and the requirements to comply with international standards will not be met unless substantial resources are committed to the development of the forensic psychiatric system.

In addition the accused person committed under the provisions of section 3 does not appear to have a right to information and there is duty to devise a care plan in respect of that patient yet these rights are afforded to patients detained under the Mental Health Act 2001 who, it appears will be cared for side by side with those detained under the Criminal Law (Insanity) Bill 2002.

Proposed Powers to Defer Hearing of the Plea Section 3(7) of the Bill proposes that all courts should have power, before exercising their power to make an order regarding the disposition of the accused person, to defer consideration of whether the accused person is fit to be tried until any time before the opening of the case for the defence where the court considers that it is expedient and in the interests of the accused person to do so. If following this procedure and before the question of fitness falls to be determined, the jury by the direction of the court or the court as the case may be return a verdict in favour of the accused person or find the accused person not guilty as the case may be on the count(s) on which the accused person is being tried the question of fitness must not be determined and the accused person must be acquitted.

The provision is designed to address the situation where the accused may have no case to answer. However Conway points out[160] that the provision may be open to constitutional challenge in the light of the decision in *O'C v. Judges of the Metropolitan District*[161] which appears to be authority for the proposition that fitness to plead must be dealt with as a matter of constitutional law when it arises before any significant aspects of the trial are conducted. In that case consideration of the issue of fitness to plead could not be postponed until after the preliminary examination stage (before the latter was abolished) on the basis of constitutional fairness to the accused. As a consequence it could be argued that it would be constitutionally impermissible to postpone it until any time before the opening of the defence as section 3(8) of the 2002 Bill does. Conway develops the point:

> "It could theoretically arise, for example, that material highly prejudicial to the accused would be adduced in open court, but the accused might then, immediately before the defence had opened its case, be found unfit to be tried, in effect without having the opportunity to respond to the prosecution case. The provision in s.3(8) is intended to allow for the entry of a not guilty verdict at this point, but it is always possible that an acquittal would not be warranted by that point of the proceedings, thereby leaving open the possibility that the accused could be found unfit to be tried at that point, without having the opportunity to respond to the prosecution case".[162]

---

[160] Conway G., "Fitness to Plead in Light of the Criminal Law (Insanity) Bill 2002" (2003), Vol.13(4) *Irish Criminal Law Journal* 2 at 6.
[161] [1994] 3 I.R. 246 at 251–252.
[162] Conway G., "Fitness to Plead in Light of the Criminal Law (Insanity) Bill 2002" (2003), Vol.13(4) *Irish Criminal Law Journal* 2 at 6.

Proposed Power to Determine whether Accused Committed the Act Alleged Notwithstanding Finding of Unfitness Section 3(8) of the Bill proposes that all courts should have a discretion where a determination has been made by them that an accused person is unfit to plead to allow evidence to be adduced before them (where an application in that regard has been made to them) as to whether or not the accused person committed the act alleged and if the court is satisfied that there is a reasonable doubt as to whether the accused person committed the act alleged it must order the accused person to be discharged. This power must be exercised before the court exercises its powers in relation to the disposition of the accused person.

This power will address the situation under the current law whereby a person may be the subject of indefinite detention following a finding of unfitness to plead where no determination of guilt or innocence has been made and where there is no possibility of automatic review by a court or tribunal of the detention. If an accused person is acquitted pursuant to this provision the Minister for Justice Equality and Law Reform indicated that it would be open the relevant authorities under the civil law i.e. the Mental Health Act 2001 to take whatever measures they may deem necessary in relation to the person concerned.[163]

It is interesting to note that the House of Lords in the case of *R v. H*[164] the appellant person argued that a determination that the accused person committed the *actus reus* of the offence was a "determination" of a criminal charge which attracted the guarantees of Article 6 of the European Convention on Human Rights which afforded him certain rights to facilitate a fair trial and his full participation in it.[165] He argued that these guarantees had not been met as, *ex hypothesi,* he was unfit to plead, to give instructions and thereby participate fully in his own defence. The House of Lords however disagreed and dismissed the appeal. It noted that the purpose and function of the English legislation providing for the determination was not to decide whether the accused person had committed a criminal offence but to protect those with a disability. The procedure could result in a final acquittal but it could not result in a conviction and could not result in punishment. Even an adverse finding could lead to an absolute discharge. Further a finding that the accused did the act or made the omission charged was not conclusive and did not preclude a full trial of the accused if he became fit to be tried.

The European Court of Human Rights reached a similar conclusion in *Antoine v. United Kingdom.*[166]

---

[163] 171 *Seanad Debates* Col. 771.

[164] [2003] 1 W.L.R. 411.

[165] Art.6(1) provides that in the determination of any criminal charge against him, everyone is entitled to a fair and public hearing within a reasonable time by an independent and impartial tribunal established by law. Art.6(2) provides that everyone charged with a criminal offence shall be presumed innocent until proved guilty according to law and in particular Art.6(3) provides that everyone charged with a criminal offence has the following minimum rights: (a) to be informed promptly, in a language which he understands and in detail, of the nature and cause of the accusation against him; (b) to have adequate time and facilities for the preparation of his defence; (c) to defend himself in person or through legal assistance of his own choosing or, if he has not sufficient means to pay for legal assistance, to be given it free when the interests of justice so require; (d) to examine or have examined witnesses against him and to obtain the attendance and examination of witnesses on his behalf under the same conditions as witnesses against him; (e) to have the free assistance of an interpreter if he cannot understand or speak the language used in court.

[166] Application No. 62960/00, May 13, 2003, (2003) *European Human Rights Law Review* 547.

Procedural Measures The Bill also removes the necessity for fitness to be tried to be tried by a jury and instead in all courts the determination falls to be made by a judge sitting alone and hearing medical evidence.

New Power to Appeal the Finding of Unfitness Under section 6(1) of the 2002 Bill an appeal lies to the Circuit Court from a determination of the District Court that an accused person is unfit to be tried. According to section 6(2) the Circuit Court if it allows the appeal must order that the appellant be tried or retried by the District Court as the case may be for the offence alleged. However if the District Court exercised its power to postpone consideration of the question of the accused person fitness to be tried and the Circuit Court is of opinion that the appellant ought to have been found not guilty before the question as to the fitness to be tried was considered then the Circuit Court must order that the appellant be acquitted.

If a decision on fitness to be tried is made by the Circuit Court, the Central Criminal Court or the Special Criminal Court then according to section 6(3) an appeal lies to the Court of Criminal Appeal. The Court of Criminal Appeal has the same options open to it where it allows an appeal from a finding of unfitness as the Circuit Court has in similar circumstances on appeal from the District Court. Thus it must order that the appellant be tried or retried for the offence alleged and where there has been postponement of the issue of fitness to be tried and the Court of Criminal Appeal is of opinion that the appellant ought to have been found not guilty before the question of fitness to be tried was considered the court must order that the appellant be acquitted.

According to section 6(5) there is no appeal permitted to the Supreme Court from a determination by a court that an accused person is unfit to be tried.

A notable absence from the appeal provision is a right to appeal a finding of "fitness to be tried."[167]

Further Conway points out that one potentially anomalous aspect of the appeal procedure is that on appeal to the Court of Criminal Appeal an acquittal may be ordered even though the jury would not have reached a determination on the issue of guilt or innocence and this might not be consistent with the provisions of Article 38.5 of the Constitution which requires that a criminal charge of a non-minor offence be tried by a jury. However on the other hand he points out that given that the Court of Criminal Appeal cannot enter a guilty verdict on appeal this aspect of the appeal process could also be regarded as an admissibility type hearing comparable to the former preliminary examination of indictable offences rather than a trial within Article 38.5 and on this analysis the problem would not arise.[168]

Section 8(3) provides that all ancillary and procedural provisions contained in a statute or an instrument made under statute relating to appeals against convictions including provisions relating to leave to appeal shall apply with the necessary modifications to appeals under section 6.

Section 8(4) extends the powers of the appellate courts and provides that the powers of an appellate court in an appeal under section 6 shall include the power to make any

---

[167] See 171 *Seanad Debates* Col.775 (Senator Terry).

[168] Conway G., "Fitness to Plead in the Light of the Criminal Law (Insanity) Bill 2002" (2003) Vol.13(4) *Irish Criminal Law Journal* 2 at 8.

such order as may be necessary for the purpose of doing justice in accordance with the provisions of the Criminal Law (Insanity) Bill 2002

Disposition following appeal on grounds accused ought to have been found unfit to be tried Section 8(2) provides that where the Circuit Court or the Court of Criminal Appeal allows an appeal against a conviction or against a verdict of not guilty by reason of insanity on the ground that the appellant ought to have been found unfit to be tried it shall have the same powers to deal with the appellant as the court of trial would have had under section 3 if it had come to the same conclusion.

Power to Appeal Order for Committal made pursuant to statutory criteria subsequent to finding of unfitness to be tried By virtue of section 8(1) of the Criminal Law (Insanity) Bill the defence or the prosecution has a right of appeal against a decision of the court of trial (but not a decision by an appellate court) to make or not to make an order for committal under sections 3(3)(b) (power of District Court to order committal if certain criteria satisfied after finding by it that accused charged with summary offence or indictable offence triable summarily is unfit to be tried), 3(4)(d) (power of court of trial to which accused charged with indictable offence has been sent forward to direct committal following a finding by the trial judge that the accused person is unfit to be tried and certain criteria for committal are met), 3(5)(c) (power of court of trial to direct committal of accused if question arises during trial and there is finding that s/he is unfit to be tried and certain other criteria for committal are met), or 3(6)(a) (power of courts outlined to direct committal of accused for up to 28 days to determine whether or not to exercise longer term power of committal). The right of appeal is to the Circuit Court or the Court of Criminal Appeal as may be appropriate. The court hearing the appeal may, having considered the evidence or any new evidence relating to the mental condition of the accused person given by a consultant psychiatrist, make any order which it was open to the court of trial to make, as it considers appropriate. This power is without prejudice to the powers of the Mental Health Review Board to review detentions under section 12 of the Bill. No further appeals lies from the order of the Circuit Court or the Court of Criminal Appeal under section 8(1).

Section 8(3) provides that all ancillary and procedural provisions contained in a statute or an instrument made under statute relating to appeals against convictions including provisions relating to leave to appeal shall apply with the necessary modifications to appeals under section 8(1)

Section 8(4) provides that the powers of an appellate court in an appeal under section 8(1) shall include the power to make any such order as may be necessary for the purpose of doing justice in accordance with the provisions of the Criminal Law (Insanity) Bill 2002.

Where the matter of appeals against detention are concerned the decision of the European Court of Human Rights in *Hutchinson Reid v. TheUnited Kingdom*[169] makes it clear that legislation placing the burden of proof on an applicant in an appeal to establish that his continued detention did not satisfy the conditions of lawfulness amounted to a breach of Article 5(4) of the Convention. The Irish case of *The People*

---

[169] Application No. 5072/99, February 20, 2003 at paras 72–73.

(D.P.P.) v. Conroy[170] establishes that the position regarding the burden of proof under Article 40.4 of the Irish Constitution is similar to that under the Convention. In that case the Supreme Court ruled that it was for the State to establish the lawfulness of the detention under Article 40.4.1 and there was no *prima facie* burden on the detainee to do so.

New Powers of Proposed Mental Health Review Board to Review Detention of Person found unfit to be tried, suffering from a mental disorder and in need of in-patient care and treatment in a designated centre   Section 10(1) of the Bill provides for the establishment of a Mental Health Review Board to review independently and speedily the detention, *inter alia*, of a person found unfit to be tried and detained as suffering from a mental disorder within the meaning of the Mental Health Act 2001 and being in need of in-patient care or treatment in a designated centre. By virtue of section 10(2) the Review Board must be "independent in the exercise of its functions under [the] Act and shall have regard to the welfare and safety of the person whose detention it reviews under [the] Act and to the public interest"

By virtue of section 11(1) the Review Board is obliged to hold sittings for the purpose of a review by it under the Act and at the sittings may receive submissions and such evidence as it thinks fit. It must also take account of the court record (if any) of the proceedings of the court to whose decision the request for the review relates and where such a record exists the court must make it available to the Board. The Review Board must also assign a legal representative to a patient the subject of the review unless he or she proposes to engage one.

The Review Board has powers set out in section 11(2) to 11(4),[171] *inter alia*, to summon witness and direct the production of documents and other items of evidence. Failure to comply with a direction without just cause or excuse and anything that would amount to contempt of a court is an offence under the Bill. The Review Board also has power with the consent of the Minister for Justice Equality and Law Reform to determine its own procedures.[172]

By virtue of section 12(2) the Review Board is obliged to ensure that the detention of a "patient" is reviewed at intervals of not more than six months as it considers appropriate and the clinical director of a designated centre is obliged to comply with any request by the Review Board in connection with the review. Section 12(1)(a) in effect defines a "patient" as any person detained in a designated centre as unfit to be tried or found not guilty by reason of insanity.

Review on application of Clinical Director of Designated Centre or Governor of Prison
Section 12(3)(a) provides that where the clinical director of a designated centre (or the governor of a prison[173] in the case of a prison being the designated centre), forms the opinion that a patient detained as unfit to be tried is not longer unfit to be tried for an indictable offence he must immediately notify the court that committed the patient to

---

[170] [1986] I.R. 460.
[171] See in more detail p.468 below.
[172] See in more detail p.469 below.
[173] The governor must obtain the advice of the approved medical officer when exercising the duties or powers under ss.12 and 13. See s.12(1)(b).

the designated centre of this opinion and the court must order that the patient be brought before it to be dealt with as the court thinks proper. However the reason for confining this power to indictable cases is not explained.

Section 12(4) provides that where the clinical director of a designated centre forms the opinion in relation to a patient detained as unfit to be tried and in need of in-patient care or treatment in a designated centre under section 3 that the patient although still unfit to be tried is no longer in need of in-patient treatment or care at a designated centre he or she must immediately notify the Review Board of this opinion. Section 12(5) provides that where the Review Board receives such a notification it must order that the patient be brought before it "as soon as may be", and shall, having heard evidence relating to the mental condition of the patient given by the consultant psychiatrist responsible for his or her care and treatment, determine the question whether or not the treatment referred to in section 12(4) is still required in the same manner as if that question were being determined pursuant to section 3 of the Act and must make such order as it thinks proper for the patient's disposal. The disposal options available to the Review Board are further detention, care or treatment in a designated centre, or discharge whether unconditionally or subject to conditions for outpatient treatment or supervision or both.

On application by Patient Under section 12(8) any patient detained as unfit to be tried and in need of in-patient care or treatment in a designated centre pursuant to section 3 of the Bill may also apply to the Mental Health Review Board for a review of his detention which the Board is obliged to carry out unless satisfied that such a review is not necessary because of any review already undertaken.

Where the patient applies the Board in these circumstances it must order that the patient be brought before it "as soon as may be" and if, having heard evidence relating to the mental condition of the patient given by the consultant psychiatrist responsible for his or her care and treatment, the Review Board determines that he or she is no longer unfit to be tried by reason of mental disorder or to participate in proceedings referred to in section 3 it must order that the patient be brought before the court which committed him or her to the designated centre to be dealt with as that court thinks proper. If the Review Board determines that the patient, although still unfit to be tried is no longer in need of in-patient treatment or care at a designated centre, the Review Board may make such order as it thinks proper for the patient's disposal. In this regard it may order further detention, care or treatment at a designated centre or his or her discharge whether unconditionally or subject to conditions for out-patient treatment or supervision or both.

Review by the Review Board on its own Initiative The Review Board may on it own initiative review the detention of a patient detained as unfit to be tried or following a special verdict and section 12(8) and 12(9) are deemed to apply to the review as if the patient himself/herself had applied for the review under those subsections.

The wording of section 12 of the Bill appears to require the Board to review the detention of a patient using the same criteria as the court does in ordering the initial detention *i.e.* whether or not the patient is suffering from a mental disorder within the meaning of the Mental Health Act 2001 and is in need of in-patient care and treatment.

The possibility of independent review after at most six monthly intervals and the facilitation of applications by patients will bring about an element of consistency between Irish law and the requirements of Article 5(4) of the European Convention on Human Rights. Conway makes the point that it may also "increase the frequency with which the plea [of unfitness] is made, given that the existing consequence of a successful plea – indeterminate detention – may have inhibited the defence from raising it to date".[174] However in practical terms it must be said that it is difficult to see how this automatic review will be triggered. How will the Review Board learn of the detention?

Under the terms of section 12 the court which committed the person found unfit to be tried has a wide discretion to deal with that person returned to it for trial on his/her recovery as it "thinks proper." It is submitted that it should be specifically entitled to take into consideration the fact that a period spent by a person found unfit to be tried in detention exceeds the term of imprisonment any court might have imposed in making a decision as to whether the accused person on recovering fitness should be returned to it for trial.

Application of Act to Existing Detentions Section 15(1) of the Bill provides that the Act shall apply to a person detained under section 17 of the Lunacy (Ireland) Act 1821 as if he or she were a person detained pursuant to an order under section 3 and accordingly such a person shall be entitled to the benefit of the provisions of the Act. According an accused person found unfit to plead under the 1821 Act has the right, (assuming he is within time) to appeal the finding of unfitness and to have his/her detention reviewed by a Mental Health Review Board.

Persons governed by the Defence Act 1954 Section 16 of the Criminal Law (Insanity) Bill 2002 substitutes a new section 202 for the existing provision in the Defence Act 1954[175] to provide for a new plea of mental disorder at the time of trial which may be availed of by a person charged with an offence before a court martial who is by reason of mental disorder unfit to take his trial. The court martial has powers (similar to a court under section 3 if the Bill) to commit the person specially found unfit to take his trial to a designated centre where it is satisfied that the person so found is suffering from a mental disorder within the meaning of the Mental Health Act 2001 and is in need of in-patient treatment or care in a designated centre.

Section 12 of the Bill imposes a duty on the Mental Health Review Board to review the detention of a person specially found by a court martial to be unfit to take his trial and committed to a designated centre as suffering from a mental disorder and in need of in-patient treatment or care in a designated centre. A duty to notify the Review Board that the patient is either (a) still unfit to take his trial or (b) still unfit to be tried but no longer in need of in-patient treatment or care at a designated centre is placed on the clinical director of the designated centre or governor of a prison on the advice of an approved medical officer. The patient detained may also apply for review and the Review Board may on its own initiative review the detention of patient detained pursuant to section 202.

---

[174] Conway G., "Fitness to Plead in the Light of the Criminal Law (Insanity) Bill 2002" (2003), Vol.13(4) *Irish Criminal Law Journal* 2 at 5.

[175] As amended by Courts-Martial Appeals Act 1983, s.5.

A full treatment of the issues relating to persons found unfit to take trial as a matter of military law is beyond the remit of a general text on civilian law such as this.

The Constitution and Procedures of the New Mental Health Review Board to be established under powers in the Criminal Law (Insanity) 2002

Section 10(1) of the Criminal Law (Insanity) Bill 2002 provides for the establishment of a Mental Health Review Board to review independently and speedily the propriety of any involuntary detention. By virtue of section 10(2) the Review Board:

> "shall be independent in the exercise of its functions under this Act and shall have regard to the welfare and safety of the person whose detention it reviews under this Act and to the public interest".

The Mental Health Review Board will replace the current *ad hoc* committees which advise the Minister for Justice Equality and Law Reform on the matter of discharge from the Central Mental Hospital and, according to the Minister for Justice, Equality and Law Reform speaking in the Seanad, it is envisaged that in order to comply with the State's obligations under the European Convention on Human Rights the Mental Health Review Board, "will act independently of the Executive, in this case the Minister for Justice, Equality and Law Reform or the Government".[176]

It is difficult to understand however why the Mental Health Review Board should be established as an entity which is different from Mental Health Tribunals which perform similar functions.

Constitution of Review Board By virtue of section 10(3) and Schedule 1 the Review Board is to consist of a chairperson who has not less than 10 years experience as a practising barrister or practising solicitor ending immediately before his appointment or a judge or former judge of the Circuit Court, High or Supreme Court and such number of members as the Minister for Justice Equality and Law Reform after consultation with the Minister for Health and Children, may appoint from time to time. It must comprise at least one consultant psychiatrist as an ordinary member.

This provision outlining the membership of the Board is quite vague and could allow for variation in terms of numbers and levels of expertise at each sitting of the Board. It is desirable that the required numbers of the Board and the qualifications of its members be specifically delineated.[177]

Terms of Office of the Members of the Review Board By virtue of paragraph 3 of Schedule 1 the members of the Review Board hold office subject to the provision of the Schedule upon such terms and conditions as the Minister may determine. Paragraph 4 stipulates that the term of office of a member of the Review Board shall be five years and subject to the provisions of the Schedule he or she shall be eligible for re-appointment as such member. Paragraph 5 states that a member of the Review Board may at any time resign his or her office by letter addressed to the Minister and the resignation shall take

---

[176] 171 *Seanad Debates* Col. 772.
[177] See Mental Health Commission Response to Criminal Law (Insanity) Bill 2002 (March 2003).

effect on and from the date of receipt of the letter. By virtue of paragraph 6 a member of the Review Board may be removed from office by the Minister after consultation with the Minister for Health and Children for stated reasons. Paragraph 7 states that the chairperson other than a chairperson who is a serving judge and each member of the Review Board shall be paid, out of monies provided by the Oireachtas, such remuneration (if any) and such allowances or expenses as the Minister for Justice, quality and Law Reform may, with the consent of the Minister for Finance determine. Paragraph 8 provides that if a member of the Review Board dies, resigns, becomes disqualified or is removed from office, the Minister may appoint another person to be a member of the Review Board to fill the casual vacancy so occasioned and the person so appointed shall be appointed in the same manner as the member of the Review Board who occasioned the vacancy and shall hold office for the remainder of the term of office for which his or her predecessor was appointed.

Members of Staff of the Review Board   Paragraph 9 of Schedule 1 provides that the Minister for Justice Equality and Law Reform may appoint such and so many persons to be members of staff of the Review Board as he or she considers necessary to assist the Review Board in the performance of its functions and such members of staff of the Review Board shall hold their offices or employment on such terms and subject to such conditions and receive such remuneration as the Minister may, with the consent of the Minister for Finance, determine. Paragraph 10 states that Members of staff of the Review Board shall be civil servants within the meaning of the Civil Service Regulation Act 1956.

Sittings of the Review Board   Paragraph 11 of Schedule 1 provides that the Review Board shall hold such sittings as may be necessary for the performance of its functions under the Act.

By virtue of section 11(8) of the Bill sittings of the Review Board for the purposes of an investigation by it under the Act are to be held in private.

The Bill does not specify what the quorum of the Board is to be.

Decisions of the Review Board   Schedule 1 paragraph 12 provides that every question at a sitting of the Review Board must be determined by a majority of the votes of the members voting on the question and, in the case of an equal division of votes the chairperson will have a casting vote.

Preliminary Duties of the Review Board   Under section 11(1) the Review Board is obliged to hold sitting to review the detention of patients committed to designated centres under the Bill. It must take account of the court record (if any) of the proceedings of the court to whose decision the request for review relates and, where such a record exists, the court must make it available to the Board. The Board must also assign a legal representative to a patient the subject of the review unless he or she proposes to engage one.

Powers of the Review Board   The Review Board has a number of powers which it may exercise for the purposes of its functions which are set out in section 11(2). It may direct the consultant psychiatrist responsible for the care and treatment of the patient to arrange for the patient to attend before the Review Board;[178] direct the attendance of witnesses and the giving of evidence and production of documents by them; direct the production of documents and items of evidence generally and give any other directions for the purpose of the proceedings concerned that appear to the Review Board to be reasonable and just. The reasonable expenses of witnesses directed to attend before the Board must be paid by the Board. Failure to comply with the directions without just cause or excuse or the doing of any other thing in relation to the proceedings before the Review Board which, if done in relation to proceedings before a court by a witness in the court would amount to contempt of the court is an offence under the Act which is punishable on summary conviction by a fine not exceeding €3,000 or to imprisonment for a term not exceeding 12 months or both.

Procedure for Hearings by the Board   Section 11(6) provides that the procedure of the Review Board in relation to a review is to be determined by the Review Board with the consent of the Minister for Justice Equality and Law Reform and must make provision for:

(a) for the purpose of section 11(1)(c) the making with the consent of the Minister for Justice, Equality and Law Reform and the Minister for Finance of a scheme or schemes for the granting by the Board of legal aid to patients,

(b) notifying the consultant psychiatrist responsible for the care and treatment of the patient the subject of the review and the patient or his or her legal representative of the date, time and place of the relevant sitting of the Review Board,

(c) giving the patient the subject of the review or his or her legal representative a copy of any document furnished to the Review Board and an indication in writing of the nature and source of any information relating to the matter which has come to the notice in the course of the review,

(d) subject to section 11(10) enabling the patient the subject of the review and his or her legal representative to be present at the relevant sitting of the Review Board and enabling the patient the subject of the review to present his or her case to the Review Board in person or through a legal representative, Section 11(10) provides that a patient shall not be required to attend before the Review Board under section 11 if, in the opinion of the Review Board such attendance might be prejudicial to his or her mental health, well-being or emotional condition,

(e) enabling the Minister for Justice, Equality and Law Reform, the Director of Public Prosecutions and, where appropriate, the Minister for Defence to be heard or represented at sitting of the Review Board,

(f) enabling written statements to be admissible as evidence by the Review Board with the consent of the patient the subject of the review or his or her legal representative,

(g) enabling any signature appearing on a document produced before the Review Board

---

[178] This is subject to s.11(10) which states that a patient shall not be required to attend before the Review Board under s.11 if, in the opinion of the Review Board such attendance might be prejudicial to his or her mental health, well-being or emotional condition.

to be taken, in the absence of evidence to the contrary, to be that of the person whose signature it purports to be,

(h) the examination by or on behalf of the Review Board and the cross examination by or on behalf of the patient the subject of the review concerned on oath or otherwise as it may determine of witnesses before the Review Board called by it,

(i) the examination by or on behalf of the patient the subject of the review and the cross examination by or on behalf of the Review Board (on oath or otherwise as the Review Board may determine) of witnesses before the Review Board called by the patient the subject of the review;

(j) the determination by the Review Board whether evidence at the Review Board should be given on oath,

(k) the administration by the Review Board of the oath to witnesses before the Review Board, and

(l) the making of a sufficient record of the proceedings of the Review Board.

Otherwise section 10 and Schedule 1 paragraph 13 of the Bill provide that subject to the provisions of the Schedule the Review Board shall establish its own rules of procedure.

Evidence before the Review Board   Section 11(7) provides that a witness whose evidence has been, is being or is to be given before the Review Board in proceedings under the Act shall be entitled to the same privileges and immunities as a witness in court.

Section 11(9) of the Bill outlines three categories of information which shall be absolutely privileged. These are: (a) documents of the Review Board and documents of its members connected with the Review Board or its functions wherever published, (b) reports of the Review Board wherever published and (c) statements made in any form at meetings or sittings of the Review Board by its members or officials and such statements wherever published subsequently

Section 11(5) provides that if a person gives false evidence before a Review Board in such circumstances that, if he or she had given the evidence before a court he or she would be guilty of perjury he or she shall be guilty of that offence.

There appears to be no provision for appeal from a decision of a Review Board specified in the legislation. Robinson notes that significant funding will be required for the establishment and running of the Mental Health Review Boards and expresses the hope that they will not be delayed to the same extent as their counterparts in civil law.[179]

In the course of Debates at Committee Stage in the Seanad the Minister for Justice, Equality and Law Reform alluded to the political considerations involved in providing for a Mental Health Review Board. He stated:

> "The purpose of the Board is to advise and come to conclusions about whether a person should continue to be detained. ..."[180]

---

[179] See "Crazy Situation", *Law Society Gazette*, Jan./Feb. 2003, p.12 at p.17.
[180] 176 *Seanad Debates* Col.271.

"[I]t is somewhat undesirable that it should fall to a political officeholder such as myself simply to operate on the basis of a very unstructured process in which the fate of a person who has been found not guilty, despite the wording of the verdict [viz."guilty but insane"], lies in the Minister's hands."[181]

In the course of Debates at Committee Stage in the Seanad Senator Mary Henry raised the point that people covered by the Criminal Law (Insanity) Bill 2002 did not have "half the protections given under the Mental Health Act" and questioned why this was so. She also questioned the distinction being made between Mental Health Tribunals established to review detentions under the Mental Health Act 2001 and the Mental Health Review Boards under the 2002 Bill.[182] The Minister for Justice, Equality and Law Reform replied:

"I do not see why the tribunals established to decide whether mentally ill people have been appropriately committed and properly detained in the context of the civil law governing mental health and should be brought into play in this particular measure What is needed is a body that will deal specifically with the decisions that must be made concerning people who have been acquitted of serious crimes on the ground of mental incapacity. It is important that a dedicated body that specialises in that function should be established. I see no advantage in marrying the Bill to the Mental Health Act."[183]

Indeed it appears that political considerations rather than issues of patients' rights underly the distinction. The Minister continued:

"Until now it has been my unhappy chalice to make a decision as to whether an individual should go free from the Central Mental Hospital on the basis that he is cured. When he signs his decision on the file, the Minister for Justice, Equality and Law Reform knows in the back of his mind that he will not be easily forgiven by the public, the relatives of the deceased and possibly the relatives of a second victim if he makes a mistake and his decision turns out to have been wrong. It is a matter of huge gravity. If we remove that power from the Minister, as a member of the Executive and confer it on another body, we must do so very solemnly. We must retain public confidence in decisions. ...

Senator Henry knows ... what will happen if the body makes an incorrect decision if a repeat offence takes place as it has on previous occasions or if people are released in circumstances that give rise to controversy. One can imagine the reactions of the relatives of the victims of the first and second offences, just as one can imagine what the media would make of it all. Such thoughts enter my head form time to time when I sign one of these orders. I wonder if I am getting it right, if I can be sure and if I will be willing a day later to stand over the decision as absolutely right.

---

[181] 176 *Seanad Debates* Col.272.
[182] 176 *Seanad Debates* Cols 363–364.
[183] 176 *Seanad Debates* Col.364.

A specialised board is being established with the solemnity and formality that attaches to it to deal with such decisions. That is not quite the same as somebody complaining that they have been wrongly committed to a mental institution on flimsy or inadequate grounds, that psychiatrists have made the wrong decision about them and that they are entitled to go free. It is a question of public perception. Regardless of the individual ingredients of the decision, the people's confidence in the system will have to be maintained."[184]

At a later stage in the Dáil Debates the Minister stated:

"The tribunal will at least be regarded as separate from the political process, and it will be expected to act without regard to media sensitivities. I trust however that it will have to take into account the fact that public confidence in its decisions must be upheld."[185]

PART D: THE INSANITY DEFENCE TO A CRIMINAL CHARGE[186]

If an accused person is found fit to plead he may raise the defence of insanity at the time of trial. Whereas in the preliminary stages the issue in question is the accused person's sanity at the time of the inquiry where the defence of insanity is raised at trial the issue is the accused person's state of mind at the time when s/he committed the act in question. If this defence is successfully raised he may be detained in the Central Mental Hospita.[187]

1. The Nature of the Current Insanity Defence

Irish Law currently in force

The McNaghten Rules Where an accused person raises the defence of insanity the fact that he may be shown to be suffering from a psychiatric illness in the medical sense will not necessarily afford him/her a defence. To raise the defence of insanity successfully he must satisfy the legal criteria for establishing it. The difficulty is that there is no comprehensive definition of insanity in Irish law. The McNaghten Rules formulated by the judges in the House of Lords in 1843 do promulgate a set of criteria but have come to be regarded in Irish law as being confined to the facts on which they were based i.e. cases of insane delusion.[188] The facts of the McNaghten case were as follows: McNaghten was charged with murdering the English Prime Minister's secretary Edward Drummond whom he mistook for the Prime Minister, Robert Peel. It was proved at his trial that he acted in the insane belief that he was being persecuted by the Tory Party and

---

[184] 176 *Seanad Debates* Col.365.

[185] 176 *Seanad Debates* Col.397.

[186] See generally McAuley F., *Insanity, Psychiatry and Criminal Responsibility* (Roundhall Press 1993).

[187] See Criminal Lunatics Act 1800, s.1; Lunacy (Ireland) Act 1821, ss.16–18; Central Criminal Lunatic Asylum (Ireland) Act 1845, s.8; Mental Treatment Act 1961, s.39.

[188] See *Doyle v. Wicklow County Council* [1974] I.R. 55 at 70. Contrast this with the English position where the rules are regarded as being of general application. See *R v. Windle* [1952] 2 Q.B. 826; [1952] 2 ALL E.R. 1.

that his life had been endangered as a result. He was acquitted. However his acquittal aroused such controversy that the House of Lords in its legislative capacity put a series of questions to the judges regarding the proper ambit of the insanity defence and the answers to the questions became known as the McNaghten rules. In essence they provide first, that everyone is to be presumed sane until the contrary is proved and secondly, that it is a defence to a criminal prosecution for the accused person to show that he was labouring under such a defect of reason due to a disease of the mind as either not to know the nature and quality of his act or if he did know this, not to know that what he was doing was wrong.[189]

In cases of insanity not involving insane delusion the Irish courts in practice[190] have require an accused person to satisfy broader criteria specified in the definition of insanity adopted by Sir James Fitzjames Stephen in his *Digest of Criminal Law*. These provide:

> "No act is a crime if the person who does it, at the time when it is done, is prevented either by defective mental power or by any disease affecting his mind (a) from knowing the nature and quality of his act or (b) from knowing that the act is wrong, or (c) from controlling his own conduct, unless the absence of the power of control has been produced by his own default".[191]

These criteria reflect the courts dissatisfaction with the narrow criteria of the Mc Naghten rules and indicate clearly that irresistible impulse may be raised under the rubric of the insanity defence in Ireland.[192] This criterion was not included in the McNaghten rules.

Should the McNaghten Rules be abolished? The question has been raised as to whether the McNaghten rules should be abolished or retained with modifications.[193] Proponents of the abolition of the rules have argued that the law should be concerned with issues of criminal intent and not with moral responsibility and that the moral test that the defendant knew the wrongness of his or her act is too vague to be a true test of moral responsibility. It has also been argued that the issue of the defendant's mental state is one which is only relevant at the stage of sentencing.[194] Further it has been contended that the various formulations of the defence of insanity only serve to confuse juries and that the distinction between external causes which may give rise to a defence of non-insane automatism and internal factors which can only give rise to a defence of insanity is artificial. Finally the argument has been advanced that it is not possible validly to distinguish between normal and abnormal behaviour.[195]

---

[189] See Appendix 2 for fuller text.

[190] See *People (AG) v. Coughlan*, unreported, June 28, 1968, *The Irish Times*.

[191] See Digest (1894) Ed Article 28.

[192] See *People (AG) v. Hayes* [1985] I.R. 517.

[193] See O'Leary, "Reforming the Insanity Defence in Criminal Law – A Comparative View" *Dli*, Winter 1992, p.54.

[194] See Wootton, *Crime and the Criminal Law* (1963), pp.52–53. Also H.L.A. Hart, *Punishment and Responsibility* (1968) who advocates the abolition of the defence of insanity but that the notion of *mens rea* should otherwise be allowed.

[195] This argument is based on the anti-psychiatry view that mental illnesses cannot adequately be distinguished. See Thomas Szasz, *The Myth of Mental Illness* (1961); *Law Liberty and Psychiatry* (1963); and *The Manufacture of Madness* (1970).

On the other hand those favouring the retention of the rules have argued that the defences available at common law are not limited to negations of intent. There are a range of situations where punishable intentional conduct is excused or justified by way of a recognised defence and it would thus be inconsistent to abolish the insanity defence. Furthermore they argue that the legitimacy of the criminal law depends on its justice. If a defendant is seriously mentally ill and unable to distinguish between right or wrong the requisite *mens rea* is absent and it would be unjust if the law did not make provision for this state of mind. As a consequence the issue of insanity is not adequately dealt with as a matter of sentencing.

While the case for abolition of the McNaghten rules is not without merit the argument that a person should not be held responsible where s/he is seriously mentally ill or unable to distinguish between right and wrong and as a consequence lacks a vital ingredient of the offence namely *mens rea* is more persuasive. Accordingly it is submitted that the defence be retained and improved.

Commentary

It is submitted that the term "insanity" should be abolished as a description of the defence on the basis that it is anachronistic and does not reflect the terminology used in modern medical practice. The terms "mental disorder," "mental illness" or "mental impairment" should be substituted and the rule amended by legislation to reflect the change.

The McNaghten rules were framed solely by reference to insane delusions. Their extension in *R v. Windle*[196] to cover all cases of insanity and not just delusions has been most controversial.[197]

Proposed New Definition of "Insanity" under the Criminal Law (Insanity) Bill 2002

Section 4(1) of the Criminal Law Insanity Bill 2002 provides that where an accused person is tried for an offence and, in the case of the District Court or Special Criminal Court, the court or in any other case the jury finds that the accused person committed the act alleged against him or her and, having heard evidence relating to the mental condition of the accused person given by a consultant psychiatrist finds that: (a) the accused person was suffering at the time from a mental disorder; and (b) the mental disorder was such that the accused person ought not to be held responsible for the act alleged by reason of the fact that he or she: (i) did not know the nature and quality of the act, or (ii) did not know what he or she was doing was wrong or (iii) was unable to refrain from committing the act the court or jury as the case may be shall return a special verdict to the effect that the accused person is not guilty "by reason of insanity."

"Mental disorder" is defined by section 1(1) as including "mental illness, mental handicap or any disease of the mind, but does not include intoxication"

The perpetuation of the use of the anachronistic term "insanity" to describe the mental state of the accused person who has successfully raised a defence of mental disorder in the 2002 Bill must be questioned. Indeed it was the source of some controversy

---

[196] [1952] 2 All E.R. 1.
[197] See S. Glueck, *Mental Disorder and the Criminal Law* (Boston, 1925), pp.168, 180 and 426.

during the course of the debates at Committee Stage of the Bill in the Seanad. In the course of the debates Senator Mary Henry proposed that the term "mental disorder" rather than "insanity" be used in the title of the Bill on the basis that the former term could be described as stigmatising whereas mental disorder is the term used in current medical textbooks[198] The Minister for Justice, Equality and Law Reform, however, defended the use of the term on the grounds that the word "insanity" "denoted a category of disorder which was far from trivial, minor or incidental. ... It [was] a threshold which [had] a degree of seriousness attached to it. ..."[199]

He continued:

> "Language is always imprecise and doubtless in 20, 30 or 40 years time someone will look back at this debate with mirth and say that my defence of the term "insanity" was a piece of early 21st century. To change the word "insanity" to "mental disorder" would send a signal that thresholds were being significantly lowered."[200]

Senator Henry replied:

> "The Bill asks professional people to go before the courts to use vague forms of wording and definitions they do not believe are suitable. I object to the term "mental handicap" being used because it went out with buttoned boots. The definition is pitched too low. The Minister claims people want it pitched high enough. Its use does not means it is high enough. ... [M]odern psychiatric terminology should be used in a Bill concerning mentally ill people. Psychiatrists coming before the courts to give professional opinions in cases must believe they are doing so within the parameters of psychiatric disease."[201]

One must surely add that the description "serious mental disorder" appropriately defined would be immeasurably preferable to the use of nineteenth century terminology and would serve to send the correct "signals" to a jury that a conviction should not be returned for a mental disorder which had an insignificant effect on the accused's mental functioning.

Persons subject to the Defence Act 1954   Section 16 of the Criminal Law (Insanity) Bill 2002 substitutes a new section 203 for the existing provision of the Defence Act 1954[202] to provide for a new defence of mental disorder at the time of commission of the offence and a new special finding by the court martial of not guilty by reason of insanity. The precise effect of the amendments as a matter of military law are beyond the scope of a general text on civilian law such as this.

---

[198] 176 *Seanad Debates* Col. 253.
[199] 176 *Seanad Debates* Col. 263.
[200] *Ibid.*
[201] 176 *Seanad Debates* Col. 264.
[202] As amended by Courts-Martial Appeals Act 1983, s.6.

2. Key Elements of the Insanity Defence under the McNaghten Rules

When the defence of insane delusion is raised under the McNaghten rules the accused person has two possible lines of defence. First it is open to him to show that because of a disease of the mind he did not know the nature and quality of his act and secondly even if he did know the nature and quality of his act he may show that because of a disease of the mind he did not know that it was "wrong".

The Meaning of "Disease of the Mind"

Current Irish Law

Under either branch of the McNaghten Rules it must be shown that the defendant was suffering from "a defect of reason from a disease[203] of the mind." In cases where an accused person is unaware of the nature and quality of his act for a reason not related to a disease of the mind he will lack the necessary *mens rea* to commit the crime and is usually entitled to a simple acquittal. If an accused person was unaware that his act was "wrong" for a reason other than a disease of the mind he will generally have no defence since neither ignorance of the law nor good motive may be raised as a plea in this regard.

The question of what amounts to a disease of the mind is a legal and not a psychiatric one. By mind is meant "the mental faculties of reason memory and understanding."[204] The issue is whether these faculties were impaired by illness not whether a person is suffering from a psychiatric illness. Any disease which impairs the mind is regarded as a disease of the mind. This would include arteriosclerosis,[205] epilepsy[206] and diabetes.[207] Any physical disease may amount in law to a disease of the mind if it results in the relevant impairment and it need not be classified medically as a mental disorder. There is no requirement that the disease be a disease of the brain.[208] However a malfunctioning of the mind is not regarded as a disease of the mind if it is caused by some external factor such a blow to the head, alcohol,[209] drugs[210] or the administration of an anaesthetic. Thus in *R v. Quick*[211] where an accused person's condition of hypoglycaemia was caused by the use of insulin prescribed by a doctor and not by his diabetes it was held that the defence of automatism and not insanity should have been left to the jury. Also

---

[203] The use of the terms "disease" and "illness" in connection with mental matters has been criticised as illogical by Szasz. In his view the concept of disease imports the existence of a set of observable symptoms which can be correlated with an identifiable organic state which is their underlying cause and is inappropriate when these criteria cannot be satisfied. See *Law Liberty and Psychiatry* (2nd ed., New York, 1989), p.12.

[204] See House of Lords in *R v. Sullivan* [1983] 2 All E.R. 673.

[205] *R v. Kemp* [1957] 1 Q.B. 399.

[206] See *Bratty v. AG of Northern Ireland* [1963] A.C. 386, *R v. Sullivan* [1984] A.C. 156.

[207] *R v. Hennessy* [1989] 2 All E.R. 9.

[208] See Devlin J. in *R v. Kemp* [1957] 1 Q.B. 399 at 407.

[209] Interestingly in Canada delirium tremens resulting from habitual misuse of alcohol has been held to be a disease of the mind See *R v. Malcolm* (1989) 71 C.R. (3d) 238.

[210] In the Canadian case of *R v. Mailloux* (1986) 25 C.C.C. (3d) 71 moreover cocaine toxic psychosis was held to be a disease of the mind.

[211] [1973] QB 910.

"drunkenness, conditions of intense passion and other transient states attributable either to the fault or to the nature of man"[212] are excluded.

Where a disease of the mind is established it matters not whether the condition is curable or incurable transitory or permanent.[213]

There is Canadian authority which suggests that a dissociative state resulting from a psychological blow may form the basis for a plea of insanity. In *R v. Rabey*[214] an accused person who had become infatuated with a fellow student, discovered that she did not regard him particularly highly and he reacted by hitting her on the head with a rock which he had taken from a geology laboratory. The Supreme Court of Canada upholding the judgment of the Court of Appeal judge overruling the trial judge held that the sociological blow of his rejection did not amount to an external cause giving rise to the defence of automatism. Quoting the judgment of Martin J. the Supreme Court took the view "the ordinary stresses and disappointments of life which are the common lot of mankind do not constitute an external cause."[215] and that the exceptional effect which this ordinary event had on the accused person "must be considered as having its source primarily in the [accused's] sociological or emotional make-up." Once so categorised as a potential insanity defence the defence bears the onus of proving on the balance of probabilities that the defendant was an dissociative state.

Commentary on the Current Law

1. The concept of "disease of the mind" raises problems of definition. The use of the terms "disease" and "illness" in relation to mental phenomena has been criticised as illogical by Szasz.[216] In addition McAuley points out that the distinction between pathological and non-pathological states is sometimes difficult to draw.[217]
   Mills comments:

   > "as understanding of medical or psychiatric conditions has advanced so also have certain conceptions become outmoded. Can depression or schizophrenia truly be categorised nebulously and unthinkingly as "diseases of the mind" as contemporary research demonstrates that biochemical or structural changes underpin many conditions that we regard as psychiatric."[218]

   Accordingly it is submitted that the nature of mental disabilities which may ground the defence should be redefined in order to facilitate consistency with current recognised descriptions and categories of mental illness and the admission of testimony on the latest medical expertise in the relevant fields.
   In *Winterwerp v. Netherlands*[219] the European Court of Human Rights held that

---

[212] See Sir Owen Dixon, *A Legacy of Hadfield, McNaghten and Maclean* (1957–58) 31 A.L.J. 255 at 260.

[213] See Devlin J. in *R v. Kemp* [1957] 1 Q.B. 399 at407.

[214] (1977) 37 C.C.C. (2d) 461.

[215] [1980] 54 C.C. (2b) at p.7.

[216] See *Law, Liberty and Psychiatry* (2nd ed., New York, 1989), p.12.

[217] See *Insanity, Psychiatry and Criminal Responsibility* (The Round Hall Press, 1993), p.73.

[218] See Mills S., "Criminal Law (Insanity) Bill 2002: Putting the Sanity Back into Insanity", *Bar Review*, June 2003, p.101.

[219] (1979) E.H.R.R 387.

there must be "objective medical expertise" supporting the fact that a person is of unsound mind. The way the courts have interpreted disease of the mind to include diabetic hyperglycaemia[220] and epilepsy[221] which are not recognised psychiatric conditions run counter to this requirement.[222]

The law of most jurisdictions demonstrates a move away from reliance on a general pathologically based concept represented by the expression "disease of the mind." In most cases the description of the mental state is in general terms but defined more specifically than the traditional description. Section 7.3 of the Australian Commonwealth Criminal Code provides for a wide defence of "mental impairment" and defines it as including "senility, intellectual disability, mental illness, brain damage and severe personality disorder".

The reference to mental illness in section 7.3(8) is defined as a:

"reference to an underlying pathological infirmity of the mind, whether of long or short duration and whether permanent or temporary but does not include a condition that results from the reaction of a healthy mind to extraordinary external stimuli. However such a condition may be evidence of mental illness if it involves some abnormality and is prone to recur."

The Explanatory Memorandum to the Bill commented that:

"[a] broad definition of mental impairment allows the jury to hear psychiatric testimony based on the latest expertise while properly leaving the ultimate question of responsibility to the jury."[223]

In England and Wales the Butler Committee in 1975 proposed by contrast to limit the defence to those who could show "severe mental illness" or "severe mental handicap." Severe mental illness was defined in detail as:

"mental illness which has one or more of the following characteristics: (a) lasting impairment of intellectual functions shown by failure of memory, orientation, comprehension and learning capacity; (b) lasting alteration of mood of such a degree as to give rise to delusional appraisal of the defendant's situation, his past or his future or that of others or lack of any appraisal; (c) delusional beliefs, persecutory jealous or grandiose; (d) abnormal perceptions associated with delusional misinterpretation of events; (e) thinking so disordered as to prevent reasonable appraisal of the defendant's situation or reasonable communication with others."

Severe mental handicap is defined as:

"a state of arrested or incomplete development of mind which includes severe impairment of intelligence and social functioning"

In the USA the courts have striven for a definition which both permits up to date

---

[220] *R v. Hennessy* [1989] 2 All E.R. 9.

[221] *R v. Sullivan* [1984] A.C. 156.

[222] See *Attorney General v. Jason Prior*, unreported judgment at www.jerseyinfo.co.uk/judgments/judgment/judgment.htm.

[223] Explanatory Memorandum to the Criminal Code Bill 1994 (Cth) at 18.

medical testimony to be admitted on the matter of mental state but leaves the ultimate test of criminal responsibility to the jury. Thus in *Durham v. United States*[224] the United States Court of Appeals for the District Court of Columbia proposed that a defendant would not be criminally responsible if his or her unlawful act was "the product of a mental disease or mental defect." Judge Bazelon delivering judgment added:

> "We use disease in the sense of a condition which is considered capable of either improving or deteriorating. We use "defect" in the sense of a condition which is not considered capable of either improving or deteriorating and which may be either congenital or the result of injury or the residual effect of a physical or mental disease."[225]

The court considered that the questions of fact laid down by the test were capable of determination by a jury. The decision led to a mountain of criticism. Its major deficiency was perceived to be the fact that it laid down no legal standard. Psychiatrists rather than jurors held sway. This was dramatically illustrated in the case of *Blocker v. US*[226] in which a hospital staff's reclassification of psychopathy as a mental disease meant that the accused person previously held responsible now had to be acquitted.

One year after the *Durham* decision the American Law Institute in its Model Penal Code made the following proposal:

(i) A person is not responsible for criminal conduct if at the time of such conduct *as a result of mental disease or defect* he lacks *substantial capacity* either to appreciate the criminality [wrongfulness] of his conduct or to conform his conduct to the requirements of law

(ii) As used in this Article, the terms 'mental disease or defect" do not include an abnormality manifested only by repeated criminal or otherwise anti-social conduct." [227]

The Model Penal Code test is a compromise which leaves a significant role for psychiatrists to testify within the limits of their experience while at the same time proposing tests of legal responsibility to be decided by a jury. It recognises partial incapacity. The Explanatory note to the proposal states that the terms "mental disease or defect" are not defined "those terms being left open to accommodate developing medical understanding."[228]

Subsection (2) however has been criticised as too rigid both by those who deny the existence of psychopathy as a syndrome and hence the ability to make the exclusion and by those who claim that the syndrome is not synonomous with repeated anti-social conduct not necessarily associated with other mental disorder.[229]

By 1984 all circuits of the Federal Court of Appeals, 24 of the 50 states and the

---

[224] 214 F. 2d. 862.

[225] *Ibid.* at 874–875.

[226] (1961) 288 F. 2d. 853 (1961 U.S. C.A.D.C.).

[227] S.4.01.

[228] See p.62.

[229] G.H. Morris, *The Insanity Defence: A Blueprint for Legislative Reform* (1975) pp.18, 31.

District of Columbia had adopted the Model Penal Code formulation with minor modifications in most jurisdictions. However following the acquittal of John Hinckley on account of unsoundness of mind in attempting to assassinate President Reagan Federal law was altered statutorily to limit the defence to defendants who "as a result of severe mental disease or defect was unable to appreciate the nature and quality or the wrongfulness of his acts." It added "mental disease or defect does not otherwise constitute a defense".[230]

2.   It has been suggested[231] that since "imbecility" was medically regarded as a form of insanity in 1843 when *McNaghten's* case was decided (or at least could not be differentiated from it) it was intended to be included in the legal definition of insanity. This anomaly has been perpetuated by the failure of the law to keep pace with the recognition of the distinct nature of intellectual disability.[232] It is submitted that the legislation should be enacted so that intellectual disability does not continue to be defined as an illness for the purposes of defences to criminal charges. In the words of one commentator:

> "Quite apart from the questions of principle involved, it is ludicrous that during the trial a jury will hear from the experts that intellectual disability is not an illness and then be directed by the trial judge that they must consider it as such for the purposes of determining whether to return a special verdict."[233]

Proposed Changes in the Criminal Law (Insanity) Bill 2002

Section 4 of the Criminal Law (Insanity) Bill codifies with some new additional elements the defence of insanity. The defence may be accepted where the accused person is tried for an offence and in the case of the District Court or Special Criminal Court the court or, in any other case, the jury, finds that the accused person committed the act alleged against him or her and, having heard evidence relating to the mental condition of the accused person given by a consultant psychiatrist finds that: (a) the accused person was suffering at the time from a *mental disorder* and (b) *the mental disorder was such* that the accused person ought not to be held responsible for the act alleged by reason of the fact that s/he: (i) did not know the nature and quality of the act or (ii) did not know that what s/he was doing was wrong or (iii) was unable to refrain from committing the act. In the event that the defence is made out the court or the jury as the case may be must return a special verdict of "not guilty by reason of insanity".

"Mental disorder" is defined by section (1) the Criminal Law Insanity Bill 2002 as including "mental illness, mental handicap or any *disease of the mind*" but it does "not include intoxication".

---

[230] (USA) Insanity Defense Reform Act 1984, 18 USC 20.

[231] See Williams G., *Criminal Law* (The General Part, 2nd ed., Stevens and Sons, London, 1961) at 447.

[232] See Williams G., *Criminal Law* (The General Part, 2nd ed., Stevens and Sons, London, 1961) at 447; Hayes S.C. and Craddock G., *Simply Criminal* (2nd ed., Federation Press, Sydney, 1992) at 140–141: J.H. McClemens and J.M. Bennett, "Historical Notes on the Law of Mental Illness in New South Wales" (1962–1964) 4 *Sydney Law Review* 49.

[233] See Hayes and Craddock at 141.

The requirement that evidence of mental disorder be given by a consultant psychiatrist is to be welcomed in that it facilitates the admission of up to date developments in the understanding of mental disorder.

The new definition of "mental disorder" is clearly wider than the older description – "disease of the mind" in the McNaghten rules although the wisdom of the perpetuation of the use of the phrase "disease of the mind" as an element of the new definition of "mental disorder" in the light of the fact that it embodies a possible mistaken conception of mental states must be doubted . The situation is not assisted by the fact that there is no attempt to define a "disease of the mind" and it would appear that although it falls within a very general definition of "mental disorder" it is not confined to psychiatric disorders. Further the problems associated with including "mental handicap" (intellectual disability) within a general definition of "mental disorder" and the resulting confusion arising from the fact that the finding if the medical evidence is accepted is one of "insanity" remain.

Moreover the definition of "mental disorder" in the context of the criminal defence differs markedly from the definition contained in the Mental Health Act 2001.

"Mental disorder" is defined in section 3 of the Mental Health Act 2001 as:

> "mental illness, severe dementia or significant intellectual disability where. ..."

[and the 2001 Act in effect then continues to set out the criteria for detention]:

(a) because of the illness, disability or dementia, there is a serious likelihood of the person concerned causing immediate and serious harm to himself or herself or to other persons, or

(b) (i) because of the severity of the illness, disability or dementia, the judgment of the person concerned is so impaired that failure to admit the person to an approved centre would be likely to lead to a serious deterioration in his or her condition or would prevent the administration of appropriate treatment that could be given only by such admission, and

   (ii) the reception, detention and treatment of the person concerned in an approved centre would be likely to benefit or alleviate the condition of that person to a material extent.

"Mental illness" is defined as:

> "a state of mind of a person which affects the person's thinking, perceiving, emotion or judgment and which seriously impairs the mental function of the person to the extent that he or she requires care or medical treatment in his or her own interest or in the interest of other persons".

"Severe dementia" is defined as meaning:

> "a deterioration of the brain of a person which significantly impairs the intellectual function of the person thereby affecting thought, comprehension and memory and which includes severe psychiatric or behavioural symptoms such as physical aggression".

"Significant intellectual disability" means:

> "a state of arrested or incomplete development of mind of a person which includes significant impairment of intelligence and social functioning and abnormally aggressive or seriously irresponsible conduct on the part of the person".

Clearly the definition of mental disorder in the Mental Health Act 2001 is crafted with object of involuntary treatment of persons with serious mental illness in mind. While the Criminal Law (Insanity) Bill 2002 definition is concerned with procedural fairness at trial and criminal responsibility but the imposition of two definitions use of two definitions within one Act is unhelpful. Under the Criminal Law (Insanity) Bill the courts have to make initial findings of "unfitness to be tried" and "not guilty by reason of insanity" using the definition of mental disorder in the 2002 Bill and then are called upon to decide whether to make orders of committal to designated centres based on the Mental Health Act 2001 definition of "mental disorder" which is considerably different. This is likely to generate not insignificant confusion.

Further the vexed issue of how the courts should deal with persons with personality disorders who commit crimes is left unaddressed. There appears to be a prevalent view among psychiatrists that anti-social personality disorder which is the disorder most linked to criminal conduct should not be equated with mental illness.[234] It does not appear in any of the medical classifications of mental disorder. Schopp has pointed out that the problem of defining personality disorder is one of circularity. Any attempted definition merely restates the pattern of conduct which gave rise to the charges or convictions.[235] As such personality disorder appears to be a set of behavioural characteristics rather than an illness. Accordingly it would appear to fall outside the criteria for establishing the defence of insanity.[236] Accordingly for the sake of clarity personality disorder should be specifically excluded from the conditions giving rise to the defence.

The Requirement that the accused person suffer from a "Defect of Reason" so as not to "Know the Nature and Quality of the Act"

Current Law

The disease of the mind must have given rise to a defect of reason. It must be shown that there has been a deprivation of reasoning power. A mere failure to use the powers of reasoning which one possess does not afford the accused person the defence of insanity. Thus in *R v. Clarke*[237] the defence was not available to an accused person who claimed that absentmindedness resulting from depression led her to take articles from a supermarket without paying for them. The court held that even if she was suffering from a disease of the mind she was simply denying that she had *mens rea* and not raising the insanity defence.

---

[234] See McSherry B., "Mental Impairment and Criminal Responsibility: Recent Australian Legislative Reforms" (1999) 23 *Crim. L.J.* 135.
[235] Schopp R., *Competence Condemnation and Commitment* (2001), p.25.
[236] See Robinson D., "Crazy Situation", *Law Society Gazette*, Jan./Feb. 2003, p.12 at 13.
[237] [1972] 1 All E.R. 219.

The words "nature and quality of his act" referred to the physical nature and quality of the act and not the moral or legal quality.[238] The jury must be satisfied that the accused person did not know what he was doing *or* did not appreciate the probable consequences of his conduct or did not realise the circumstances in which he was acting. To illustrate the point Stephen[239] refers to the case where A kills B when under a insane delusion that he is breaking a jar. The same principle would apply in a case where a person cut a sleeper's head off because "it would be great fun to see him looking for it when he woke up."[240] Where insane delusions arise from a disease of the mind the accused person may plead insanity and will be liable to be indefinitely detained in the Central Mental Hospital. Where however they arise from some other cause the accused person will be entitled to an acquittal on the grounds that he lacks the necessary *mens rea*.

Where a person's acts are involuntary because he is unconscious it will be held that he does not know "the nature and quality of his act."[241]

Commentary

1. It is submitted that the McNaghten rules are based on an obsolete theory of psychology that the functions of the mind – understanding, willing and feeling can be compartmentalised whereas the human personality functions as an integrated unit. Serious mental illness impairs not only the cognitive function of the mind but also the will and the emotions.[242]

2. In Canada the requirement of "appreciation" of the nature and quality of an act rather than "knowledge" prevails. Article 16(2) of the Canadian Criminal Code provides that:

   > "a person is insane when the person is in a state of natural imbecility or has a disease of the mind to an extent that renders a person incapable of *appreciating* the nature and quality of an act or omission or of knowing that the act or omission is wrong. ..."

   In the McRuer Report the Royal Commission on the Law of Insanity as a Defence in Criminal Cases[243] contrasted the broader Canadian criterion of "appreciation" to the initial formulation of the McNaghten Rules:

   > "[M]ere knowledge of the nature of the nature and quality of the act ...is not the true test to be applied. The true test necessary is ... was the accused

---

[238] See *R v. Codere* (1916) 12 Cr. App. Rep. 21.

[239] See *Digest* (8th ed.) 6.

[240] See Stephen, *History of the Criminal Law* Vol 11 166.

[241] See *R v. Sullivan* [1983] 2 All E.R. 673, 678.

[242] Phipson states that the "defect of reason" requirement is the "central notion in the rules even though it is not the concept around which most case law turns. It is the basic reason why irresistible impulse and other emotional or volitional defects or disorders are not within the rules, since they are not defects of reason. Rationality is the litmus test of criminal responsibility and defects of will are regarded either as non-existent or as irrelevant". See *Phipson on Evidence* (14th ed., London, Sweet & Maxwell, London) at p.42.

[243] (1956).

person by reason of disease of the mind, deprived of the mental capacity to foresee and measure the consequences of the act."

In *R v. Cooper*[244] Mr Justice Dickson endorsing the McRuer Report held that the test of appreciation embraces "emotional as well as intellectual, awareness of the significance of the conduct." Endorsing the view of Mr Justice Martin in *R v. Simpson*[245] he held that there had to be "real understanding of the nature, character and consequences of the act at the time of its commission." In other words he continued there had to be "an ability to perceive the consequences, impact and results of the physical act."

In *R v. Barnier*[246] Mr Justice Estey held that appreciating would include "knowing" but that the converse was not necessarily true:

> "The verb "know" has a positive connotation requiring a bare awareness, the act of receiving information without more. The act of appreciating, on the other hand, is a second stage in the mental process requiring the analysis of knowledge or experience in one matter or another."[247]

The application of the criterion of "appreciation" may be illustrated by reference to two cases where the defence of insanity succeeded under the Mc Ruer criteria. In the case of *R v. O*[248] a woman charged with the murder of her three children had admitted to a neighbour that she had hung them but later showed no appreciation of what she had done and wanted to return to look after them. Similarly in *R v. Adamcik*[249] a person with schizophrenia suffering from delusions that he was in direct contact with God and was the "reincarnation of a Czechoslovakian Robin Hood who had lived in Europe some 400 years ago" used a toy gun to rob a bank to obtain money to buy a crucifix. It was for sale in a shop in what he considered was a blasphemous fashion.

In *R v. Simpson*[250] however Mr Justice Martin limited the operation of the appreciating test in the case of psychopathic offenders:

> "I do not think the exemption provided by ... section [16] extends to one who has the necessary understanding of the nature, character and consequences of the act but merely lacks appropriate feelings for the victim or lacks feelings of remorse or guilt for what he has done, even though such lack of feeling stems from a "disease of the mind". Appreciation of the nature and quality of the act does not import a requirement that the act be accompanied by appropriate feeling about the effect of the act on other people. No doubt the absence of such feelings is a common characteristic of many persons who engage in repeated and serious criminal conduct."[251]

---

[244] (1980) 51 C.C.C. (2d) 129.
[245] (1977) 35 C.C.C. (2d) 337.
[246] (1980) 51 C.C.C. (2d) 193.
[247] *Ibid.* at 203.
[248] (1959) 3 C.L.Q. 151.
[249] (1977) 33 C.C.C.(2d) 11.
[250] (1977) 35 C.C.C. (2d) 337.
[251] *Ibid.* at 355.

Mr Justice Martin's qualification was adopted by McIntyre J for the Supreme Court in *R v. Kjeldsen.*[252] Social policy arguments in favour of this qualification point to the controversy surrounding the existence or at least the identification of the psychopathic syndrome and the difficulty of treatment or prognosis. There is no adequate indication that for such persons a hospital setting is superior to a prison setting.

In *R v. Swain*[253] it was confirmed that one who understands the physical character of an act but lacks the normal emotional response appreciates the nature and quality of the act. In *R v. Kirkby*[254] Martin J.A. guarded against holding that all cases of knowledge that an act will be fatal will necessarily mean that the accused person is capable of appreciating the nature and quality of the act. He gave as examples a killing where the accused person is under the delusion that he is an absolute monarch executing for high treason or where the accused person had a delusion that his neighbour was filling him and his family with "thought waves." In *R v. Abbey*[255] Mr Justice Dickson held that an inability to appreciate the penal consequences of an act did not go to *mens rea* since punishment was not an element of the offence itself.

It is submitted that the Canadian criterion of "appreciation" of the nature and quality of an act more closely reflects current medical understanding of the effects of mental disorder and should be considered as a legislative alternative to "knowledge" of the nature and quality of the relevant act.[256]

3.   The McNaghten rules fail to recognise degrees of incapacity. The choice is simply between mental disorder resulting in knowledge or no knowledge. This denies the modern understanding which warns against absolutes and categorises the effects of mental disorders as shading into one another. A mental disorder could prevent an accused person from knowing certain matters but may not affect his knowledge of others. It is submitted that a requirement that mental disorder result in the "substantial incapacity" of the accused person to appreciate the nature and quality of his act would more accurately accord with modern understanding of the effects of mental disorder.[257]

Proposed Changes in the Criminal Law (Insanity) Bill 2002

The 2002 Act abolishes the requirement that the accused person be labouring under "a defect of reason" which was a requirement under the McNaghten rules and which arose mainly from the fact that the House of Lords in that case were dealing with a an accused person who was under an insane delusion. The requirement under the codified defence is that the accused person's "mental disorder was such" that he or she:

---

[252] (1981) 24 C.R. (2d) 289 at 299 (S.C.C.).

[253] (1986) 50 C.R. (3d) 97 at 128.

[254] (1985) 21 C.C.C. (3d) 31 at 56–57.

[255] (1982) 29 C.R. (3d) 193 at 204 (S.C.C.).

[256] The Scottish Law Commission in its Discussion Paper No. 122 on Insanity and Diminished Responsibility published in January 2003 also favours the concept of "appreciation of the nature of conduct".

[257] See Yeo S., "Rethinking the Incapacities of Insanity" (2001) 36 *Irish Jurist* 275–287.

"ought not to be held responsible for the act alleged by reason of the fact that he or she (i) did not know the nature and quality of the act. ...""

The requirement of "knowledge" perpetuates the cognitive emphasis of the rules. For the reasons given above a requirement of "appreciation" more fully reflects the integrated nature of the mental process incorporating both intellectual and emotional awareness of the nature and quality and consequences of the act. Further a requirement that the mental disorder of the accused person "substantially impair his capacity" to appreciate the nature and quality of his act would more closely reflect modern understanding of the effects of mental disorder.

The Requirement that the accused person knows that the Act is Wrong

Current Irish Law

The requirement that the accused person know that the act is wrong does not involve an examination as to whether he is able to distinguish between right and wrong in general but whether he was able to appreciate the wrongness of a particular act he was doing at the particular time. It is settled law that if the accused person knew that his act was contrary to law then he will be held to know that the act was wrong.[258] An accused person will be also liable even if he did not know that his act was contrary to law if he knew that it was wrong "according to the ordinary standard adopted by reasonable men."[259] The fact that the accused person thought his act was right was irrelevant and if he knew that people generally considered it wrong. This view is supported by the McNaghten Rules.[260] While the English Court of Appeal in *R v. Windle*[261] ruled that the sole test is whether the accused person knew the act was contrary to law in *Stapleton v. R*[262] the High Court of Australia refused to follow *Windle* and after a detailed examination of English law held that if a defendant believed his act to be right according to the ordinary standard of reasonable men he is entitled to be acquitted even if he knew it to be legally wrong. The Irish Supreme Court in *Doyle v. Wicklow County Council* has noted the authority of *Stapleton v. R* but it has been pointed out that the decision in *Stapleton* appears to extend the scope of the defence potentially beyond the scope of the rules themselves.[263] In practice however Irish juries are told where the issue arises that wrong in the context of the McNaghten Rules means morally wrong.[264]

---

[258] See *McNaghten's Case* 10 Cl. & F. at 209.

[259] See *R v. Codere* [1916] 12 Cr. App. Rep. 21 at 27, *Doyle v. Wicklow County Council* [1974] I.R. 55 at 67 following *Stapleton v. R* (1952) 86 C.L.R. 358. See Archbold, *Pleading, Evidence and Practice in Criminal Cases* (1992) para.17–131.

[260] See 10 Cl. & F. at 210.

[261] [1952] 2 Q.B. 826 at 833–834.

[262] (1952) 86 C.L.R. 358.

[263] See Smith and Hogan, *Criminal Law* (7th ed., 1992), p.203.

[264] See Direction of Lavan J. in the *O'Donnell* case, unreported, Central Criminal Court, January–April 1996.

Commentary

1. The test of whether an accused person "knew" that an act is wrong is unduly restrictive and vague. Knowledge implies mere intellectual awareness that conduct is wrong whereas an accused person may be intellectually aware that conduct is wrongful but fail to understand and perceive the implications of that. The substitution of the term "appreciate" rather than "know" reflects more clearly the integrated nature of understanding which is required which is more than intellectual awareness and does not rely solely on cognitive elements of the personality.

2. The requirement of "substantial" rather than total impairment of capacity to appreciate would accord more closely with modern understanding of the effects of mental disorder. It would indicate that any incapacity is not sufficient to avoid criminal responsibility but that total incapacity is also unnecessary.[265]

3   The use of the terms "wrongfulness of his conduct" in legislation would also convey more clearly the sense that what is intended to be addressed by the criterion is conduct which is wrong according to the ordinary standards adopted by reasonable men.[266] Alternatively a formulation similar to that adopted in New Zealand requiring the accused person who raises the defence of insanity to show that he was "incapable of knowing that the act or omission was morally wrong, having regard to the commonly accepted standards of right and wrong"[267] might prove an effective solution to the issues.

Proposed Criminal Law (Insanity) Bill 2002

The Criminal Law (Insanity) Bill retains the test of knowledge that the act was wrong. It provides at section 4(1) that to raise the defence of "insanity" the mental disorder of the accused person must be such that:

> "the accused person ought not to be held responsible for the act alleged by reason of the fact that he or she ... (ii) did not know what he or she was doing was wrong"

The problems associated with the exclusively cognitive test of "knowledge" which existed under the common law remain. Further there is no clarity as to what test should be adopted in determining whether an act is "wrong." The difficulties associated with the common law test remain.

---

[265] See, for example, s.4.01 of the American Law Institute Model Penal Code which states "A person is not responsible for criminal conduct if at the time of such conduct as a result of mental disease or defect he lacks *substantial capacity* either to *appreciate* the *wrongfulness* of his conduct or to conform his conduct to the requirements of the law." The adoption of this test was proposed by the US Court of Appeals in New York in *US v. Freeman* 357 2d 606 (1966) .

[266] *Ibid.*

[267] Crimes Consolidation Act 1961, s.23(2).

The Situation Pertaining to "Insane Delusions"

Current Irish Law

In their advice in McNaghten's case the judges were asked whether a person who commits an offence as a consequence of an insane delusion would thereby be excused. In their reply they indicated that where a man commits a criminal act under an insane delusion he is under the same degree of responsibility as he would have been if the facts had been as he imagined them to be. They added:

> "For example, if under the influence of his delusion the accused person supposes another man to be in the act of attempting to take away his life, and he kills that man, as he supposes, in self defence, he would be exempt from punishment. If his delusion was that the deceased had inflicted serious injury to his character and fortune, and he killed him in revenge for such supposed injury, he would be liable to punishment."[268]

This test is not regarded as adding anything to the previous answers since these insane delusions would prevent the accused person in any event from knowing the nature and quality of his act or knowing it is wrong.

The rule that the insane person "must be considered in the same situation as to responsibility as if the facts of the respect of which the delusion exists were real" is defective in that in the case where an accused person kills his spouse under the insane delusion that he is killing a wild beast it would permit the conviction of the accused person for the offence in relation to the beast. However this is clearly wrong as there is no *actus reus* in relation to the beast. The effect of the rule seems to be to emphasise that delusions which do not prevent the accused person from having *mens rea* will afford a defence.

In *Attorney v. O'Brien*[269] Kennedy CJ noted that the questions which the judges were asked in the *McNaghten* case related to crimes committed by persons "afflicted with insane delusions in respected of one or more particular subject or questions" and held that the opinions given by them should be read with the "like specific limitation." In *Doyle v. Wicklow Co. Council*[270] Griffin J. agreed with this view.

Commentary

It is submitted the McNaghten Rules in relation to insane delusions should be codified and where a person is affected by an insane delusion he should be held criminally responsible to the same extent as if the real state of things had been such as he was induced by the delusion to believe to exist.[271]

---

[268] (1843) 10 Cl. & Fin. 200 at 211.
[269] [1936] I.R. 263.
[270] [1974] I.R. 55.
[271] In a number of jurisdictions the legislatures have codified the law relating to insane delusions. Thus s.27 of the Criminal Code of Western Australia and Queensland provides that "A person whose mind, at the time of doing or omitting to do an act is affected by delusions on some specific matter or matters … is criminally responsible for act or omission to the same extent as if the real state of things had been such as he was induced by the delusion to believe to exist." S.16(3) of the

Proposed Criminal Law (Insanity) Bill 2002

The Criminal Law (Insanity) Bill 2002 does not specifically address the situation where an accused person is suffering from an insane delusion. It assumes that such an accused person should fall to be dealt with under the general tests for establishing the "insanity" defence.

The Situation pertaining to "Irresistible Impulse"

Current Irish Law

Psychiatrists recognise that a man may know the nature and quality of his act or may even know that it was wrong but yet perform it under an impulse that it almost or quite uncontrollable. While this defence is not available under the McNaghten Rules in Ireland judges in three cases[272] prior to 1967 in the Court of Criminal Appeal indicated that they might be prepared to entertain of plea of irresistible impulse under a test outside the Rules in a suitable case where it was not caused by the accused person's own fault.

Finally in the *People (Attorney General) v. Hayes*[273] Henchy J. made the definitive statement:

> "Certain serious mental diseases such as paranoia, schizophrenia, in certain cases unable a man to understand the morality or immorality of his act or the legality or illegality of it or the nature and quality of it, that nevertheless preventing him from exercising a free volition as to whether he should or should not do the act. In the present case the medical witnesses are unanimous in saying that the accused person man was in medical terms, insane at the time of the act. However, legal insanity does not necessarily coincide with what medical men would call insanity but if it is open to the jury to say, as say they must, on the evidence, that this man understood the nature and quality of his act, and understood its wrongfulness morally and legally, but that nevertheless he was debarred from refraining from assaulting his wife fatally from a defect of reason, due to his mental illness, it seems to me that it would be unjust, in the circumstances of this case, not to allow the jury to consider the case in these grounds."

This was accepted as a correct statement by the law by the Supreme Court in *Doyle v. Wicklow County Council*.[274] Further in the recent case of *People (DPP) v. Courtney*[275]

Canadian Criminal Code provides: "A person who has specific delusions but is in other respects sane shall not be acquitted on the ground of insanity unless the delusions caused that person to believe in the existence of a state of things that, if it existed would have justified or excused the act or omission of that person." In England and Wales the Law Commission recommended that if a mental disorder alone or combined with intoxication had caused the defendant to act believing in the existence of a circumstance affording a defence and this was the only reason for acquittal the defendant should be found not guilty on evidence of mental disorder. The onus disproving belief in an exempting circumstance would be on the prosecution.

[272] See *O'Brien* [1936] I.R. 263; *Boylan* [1937] I.R. 449; McGrath, An unreported decision of 1960 cited by O'Hanlon in "Not Guilty by Reason of Insanity" (1968) 3 *Ir. Jur. (n.s.)* 61 at 71.

[273] Unreported, Central Criminal Court, November 13, 1967.

[274] [1974] I.R. 55 at 71.

[275] Unreported, Court of Criminal Appeal, July 21, 1994.

the following direction of the trial judge to the jury was approved:

> "There is a limited form of insanity recognised by our law, commonly called irresistible impulse. That means in this case an irresistible impulse caused by a defect of reason due to mental illness. Merely because an impulse is not in fact resisted does not mean that it is an irresistible impulse. If so, no one could ever be convicted of a crime- they would only have to say, I found the impulse irresistible. It must be an irresistible impulse not an unresisted impulse to constitute that form of insanity. Diminished self control or weakened resistance to impulse is not necessarily the same as irresistible impulse. Diminished self control makes the resistance to an impulse more difficult but does not necessarily make it irresistible. This must arise from a defect of reason due to mental illness...."

Since the decision in Doyle reliance has been placed on a wide variety of mental disorders as constituting evidence of insanity. Thus in *DPP v. McCourtney*[276] the defendant claimed he was suffering from post-traumatic stress disorder and in *DPP v. O'Mahony*[277] the Supreme Court indicated that a condition of psychopathy could constitute insanity.

Commentary

On balance it may be said that the McNaghten rules focus on the cognitive element of mental illness but cannot be stretched to deal with incapacity primarily relating to the aspect of will. It is arguable that a test of irresistible impulse is necessary to supplement the McNaghten rules if recognition is to be given to the fact that mental illness may affect a person's will and emotions as well as his cognitive or intellectual capacity.[278]

---

[276] *Irish Times*, January 22, 1993.

[277] [1986] I.L.R.M. 91.

[278] The laws of other jurisdictions are divided on the matter of recognition of irresistible impulse as a defence. S.27 of the Criminal Code of Western Australia provides a defence based on the Mc Naghten rules and includes irresistible impulse. "A person is not criminally responsible for an act or omission if at the time of doing the act or making the omission he is in such a state of mental disease or natural mental infirmity as to deprive him of ... capacity to control his actions.".

S.7.3(1)(c) of the Commonwealth Criminal Code provides that: "A person is not criminally responsible for an offence if, at the time of carrying out the conduct constituting the offence the person was suffering from a mental impairment that had the effect that the person was unable to control the conduct." The Canadian courts have refused to recognise that irresistible impulse can of itself afford a legal defence of insanity. However it has been recognised that evidence of irresistible impulse might be relevant to establishing that there was a disease of the mind and that there was the necessary incapacity as a result. In *R v. Borg* [1969] 4 C.C.C. 262 (S.C.C.) and *R v. Simpson* (1977) 35 C.C.C. (2d) 337 at 354–355 (Ont C.A.) approval was given to the remarks of Lord Tucker in *Attorney General for the State of South Australia v. Brown* [1960] A.C. 432: "Their Lordships must not, of course be understood to suggest that in a case where evidence has been given (and it is difficult to imagine a case where such evidence would be other than medical evidence) that irresistible impulse is a symptom of the particular disease of the mind from which a prisoner is said to be suffering and as to its effects on his ability to know the nature and quality of his act of that his act is wrong it would not be the duty of the judge to deal with the matter in the same way as any other relevant evidence given at the trial." The introduction even in this limited manner of the defence has not proved popular and has attracted two sorts of criticism. First that it does not go far enough since by requiring total volitional incapacity it is confined to sudden

The real question is what degree of impairment of volitional capacity should be sufficient to ground the defence. It is submitted that total impairment of volitional capacity should not be required as the caption "irresistible impulse" would tend to suggest since its effect would be to limit the defence to sudden unplanned action. In essence the defence is concerned with lack of control and it is submitted that a planned act accompanied by a substantial impairment of capacity or control should suffice to ground it.[279]

Proposed Criminal Law (Insanity) Bill 2002

The Criminal Law (Insanity) Bill 2002 includes the defence of irresistible impulse as a component element of the defence of insanity as contemplated in *Doyle v. Wicklow County Council*. Section 4(1) provides specifically that the defence of insanity may be raised if the accused person's "mental disorder was such" that:

> "the accused person ought not to be held responsible for the act alleged by reason of the fact that he or she ... (iii) was unable to refrain from committing the act"

It leaves unanswered the vexing question posed by the common law as to what degree of volitional incapacity should ground the defence.

---

explosive actions and excludes all acts of cool premeditation.However Goldstein points out that jurisdictions using the text do not in fact apply this restriction and simply require lack of control. See *The Insanity Defence* (1967), pp.69–75 Secondly it goes too far since it is questionable whether it is possible to distinguish between irresistible impulse and impulses which are not resisted. See H.R.S. Ryan "Mental Abnormality and the Criminal Law" (1967) 17 *U.N.B.L.J.* 1 at14, Williams *Textbook of Criminal Law*, p.659 In England the judges have opposed the admissibility of such a defence on the grounds of the impossibility of distinguishing between an impulse which proved irresistible because of insanity and one which is irresistible because of ordinary motives of greed, jealousy or revenge. The view has also been expressed that the harder an impulse is to resist the greater for the need for a deterrent.See *R v. Creighton* (1909) 39 C.C.C. 349. Proposals for legislative reform have also met with little acceptance. As early as 1923 a committee under the chairmanship of Lord Atkin recommended that a defendant should not be held responsible "when the act is committed under an impulse which the prisoner was by mental disease in substance deprived of any power to resist" (Cmnd 2005). This recommendation was not implemented. Further as an alternative to the abolition of the McNaghten Rules the Royal Commission on Capital Punishment in 1953 recommended that the third limb be added to the rules that the accused person "was incapable of preventing himself from committing it" (Cmnd 8932). In the USA in the case of *US v. Currens* the US Court of Appeals proposed that a defendant have a defence where "at the time of the prohibited act...as a result of mental disease or defect, [the defendant] lacked substantial capacity to conform his conduct to the requirements of the law which he is alleged to have violated." The American Law Institute's Model Penal Code (1962) provides, *inter alia*, that "a person is not responsible for criminal conduct if at the time of such conduct as a result of mental disease or defect he lacks substantial capacity ...to conform his conduct to the requirements of the law." This part of the Institute's standard explicitly reaches volitional incapacities. It does not require a total lack of capacity but only that the capacity be substantial.

[279] Morris notes that major criticism of the irresistible impulse test comes from those who favour broadening McNaghten to take into account the volitional element but who regard the irresistible impulse test as inadequate in that it requires a total impairment of volitional capacity. See Wechsler, "The Criteria of Criminal Responsibility" 22 *U. Chicago Law Review* 367, 375 (1955); British Royal Commission on Capital Punishment 1949–1953 Report No. 80 (London, HMSO, 1953); *The Insanity Defense: A Blueprint for Legislative Reform* (Lexington Books, Massachusetts, 1975).

3. TECHNICAL ELEMENTS OF THE INSANITY DEFENCE

The Burden of Proof with Respect to the Insanity Defence

Under current law the burden of proof of insanity is regarded as one of the exceptions to the current law rule that the prosecution must prove the guilt of the accused person for it requires the accused person to prove insanity arguably on the balance of probabilities. Questions arise as to whether the accused person alone should be entitled to raise the defence of insanity and the extent of the reverse onus.

Current Irish Law

The accused person bears the burden of proving insanity and he must prove clearly that at the time of committing the act he was insane.[280] Insanity is thus regarded as the one exception to the common law rule which requires the prosecution to prove the guilt of the accused person in all particulars.[281] However the accused person need only prove he was insane on the balance of probabilities, the standard of proof in a civil action and is entitled to a verdict in his favour if the jury finds that it is more likely than not that he was insane.[282] However in *AG v. Fennell*[283] the Court of Criminal Appeal held that it was not a misdirection for judge to tell a jury that the accused person had to prove the matter "beyond all reasonable doubt." This would appear to suggest that the accused person bears a heavier burden of proof in Irish law. However the decision has been criticised[284] as having mistaken an argument of counsel for the appellant as a direction of the trial judge in *Sodeman v. R*.[285]

An accused person who seeks to prove insanity need not adduce psychiatric evidence.[286] However there appear to be no contemporary cases where the defence of insanity has been raised successfully without such evidence.[287] Where it is not pleaded the words and actions of the accused person whether prior to or contemporary with the alleged offence may be sufficient to discharge the burden of proof [288] and arguably

---

[280] *People (DPP) v. O'Mahony* [1985] I.R. 517 at 522.
[281] See *Woolmington v. DPP* [1935] A.C. 462.
[282] See *Sodeman v. R* [1936] 2 All E.R. 1138. To discharge the burden of proof the defence should call any witness whose evidence is directed to that issue and it is the duty of the prosecution to supply the defence with a copy of any report or statement of any prison medical officer who can give evidence on that issue and to make that person available to the defence. *R v. Casey* (1947) 32 Cr. App. R. 91.
[283] [1940] I.R. 445.
[284] See *R v. Carr Briant* [1943] 2 All E.R. 156 at 158.
[285] [1936] 2 All E.R. 1138.
[286] The value of psychiatric evidence may be quite limited for as McAuley points out psychiatrists testifying on the issue of the insanity defence are being asked to offer an opinion on the accused person's state of mind at some time in the past. Correct evaluation may be difficult since the expert must only have faded or distorted memories of the participants in the event on which to base his conclusions and he may be asked to reconstruct psychological states that typically existed under conditions of haste and pressure. See *Insanity, Psychiatry and Criminal Responsibility* (1993), p.6.
[287] See McAuley, *Insanity Psychiatry and Criminal Responsibility* (1993), p.97.
[288] See *Attorney General for South Australia v. Brown* (1960) Cr. App. Rep. 100, 112–113.

words and actions subsequent to the date.[289] Psychiatric evidence itself is only admissible in cases where the mental functioning of the accused person is outside the normal scope of experience and knowledge of the jury and therefore requires expert explanation. In *R v. Turner*[290] the English Court of Appeal upheld the refusal of a trial judge to allow an accused person to call a psychiatrist to prove that prior to the offence of murder with which the accused person was charged he had not shown known signs of mental illness and had not required psychiatric treatment and that, in support of the defence of provocation, he had a deep emotional tie with the deceased which was likely to have caused an explosive outburst of rage after a confession of infidelity and that he had shown profound grief after the crime. The court held that this absence of a previous history of mental illness was irrelevant and that the other factors were within the ordinary scope of experience upon which the jury did not require expert assistance.

In cases where psychiatric evidence is admitted it is the duty of the prosecution to probe the soundness of the evidence relating to an accused person's state of mind.[291]

Normally medical evidence of insanity may only be given by medical practitioners who have clinically examined the accused person.[292] However the McNaghten Rules provided that an exception to this rule may arise where the facts are not in dispute and the question "is one of science only" and in this case evidence may be given by medical practitioners who have simply observed the accused person in the course of the trial.

Where the defence raises evidence to establish insanity the prosecution may call rebutting evidence.[293] A trial judge is entitled to comment adversely on the failure of defence to allow a psychiatrist nominated by the state to examine the accused person who is presented as being insane through psychiatric testimony led by the defence.[294]

In *People (Attorney General) v. Messitt*[295] it was held that while the onus of establishing insanity rests with the accused person it is the duty of the prosecution to give such evidence if the accused person or his legal advisers are not prepared to do so. The court said in such circumstances:

> "the duty of putting such evidence as is available on the topic before the jury rests with the People, if the Attorney General is of opinion that the evidence is such that the jury might reasonably conclude that the accused person was insane."[296]

This is the only Irish authority on the subject of whether the prosecution is entitled to raise evidence of insanity. The court did not quote any earlier authorities in support of what it framed as the "duty" of the prosecution and the factual context was rather unusual. The appellant who had been charged with serious assault offences had dismissed his legal team after the trial began and had to be removed from the court on account of his

---

[289] See *R v. Dart* (1878) 14 Cox 143; *R v. Rivett* (1950) 34 Cr. App. Rep. 87. See Archbold, *Pleading, Evidence and Practice in Criminal Cases* (1992) para.17–132.
[290] See *R v. Turner* [1975] Q.B. 834; [1975] 1 All E.R. 70.
[291] See *DPP v. Buckley, Irish Times*, November 24, 1989.
[292] *R v. Frances* [1849] 4 Cox C.C. 57.
[293] See *R v. Gilbert Smith* (1912) 8 Cr. App. Rep. 72.
[294] See *R v. Malcolm* (1989) 50 C.C.C. (3d) 172.
[295] [1972] I.R. 204.
[296] [1972] I.R. 204 at 213.

disruptive behaviour. Most of the trial proceeded in his absence a procedure which is only permitted in the most exceptional circumstances. Given the particular circumstances the rule is therefore very far reaching and it is to be hoped that the issue of the role of the prosecution will be addressed more fully in a future case.

Commentary

The requirement that an accused person must "prove" that he or she is insane on the balance of probabilities could be challenged on the basis that it infringes the constitutional right to the presumption of innocence[297] and Article 6(3) of the European Convention of Human Rights which provides that "Everyone charged with a criminal offence shall be presumed innocent until proven guilty according to law." On the other hand the decision of the House of Lords in *R v. Lambert*[298] would seem to suggest that the accused person raising the insanity defence bears no more than an evidential burden. It is submitted that the nature of the accused person's burden should be made clear in amending legislation.

Secondly in the interests of justice it is submitted both the defendant and limited circumstances the prosecution should be permitted to lead evidence of mental illness and that the standard of proof should be on the balance of probabilities. It would be unjust for the prosecution to stand idly by and allow a person who is legally innocent to be convicted simply because a pertinent issue was not raised. Secondly it would be wrong to allow a person who may be a danger to the public to walk free without any psychiatric examination, treatment or confinement as would happen if the defendant were acquitted or given a non custodial sentence. On the other hand it could be argued that the civil powers of commitment are available in the latter situation and since a rule that the prosecution could leave evidence of insanity would infringe the principle that an accused person should be treated as an autonomous agent who in accordance with the adversarial nature of the justice system should be entitled to determine the arguments to be advanced in his defence[299] it is submitted that the leave of the court should be required before the prosecution can raise such an issue. This leave should only be granted after the defendant's own defence has in the view of the trial judge put the defendant's capacity for criminal intent in issue.[300]

Changes Proposed by the Criminal Law (Insanity) Bill 2002

Section 14 of the Bill provides that no evidence relating to the mental state of the accused person shall be adduced by the defence as to the mental condition of the accused person

---

[297] *O'Leary v. A.G.* [1993] 1 I.R. 102.

[298] [2001] 3 W.L.R. 206.

[299] See *R v. Swain* (1991) 63 C.C.C. (3d.) 481; 5 C.R. (4th) 253.

[300] The English Law Commission in its draft Criminal Code for England and Wales recommended that the existence of the illness should be proved either by the prosecution or the defence on the balance of probabilities but that the prosecution should be prevented from adducing evidence of mental disorder until the accused person had raised an issue which justified this course. It also recommended that the fact that the offence was not attributable to the illness or incapacity should be proved by the prosecution beyond a reasonable doubt. See s.35(2) Law Comm. No. 177.

unless notice of intention to do so is given to the prosecution in such form and within such period as rules of court shall provide.

The Bill appears to confine the right to raise the issue of the accused person's mental condition to the defence.

The Role of the Judge

In current Irish law the technical question of whether the accused person has raised the defence of insanity as a matter of law is one for the judge. The question is whether the judge should continue to make this determination or whether it should be left to the jury to decide the matter.

Current Irish Law

Where the defendant puts his state of mind in issue the question as to whether he has raised the defence of insanity one of law for the judge.[301] While medical experts may testify as to the fact and nature of the condition the judge to must decide whether as a matter of law that amounts to evidence of "a defect of reason from disease of the mind."

If the judge concludes that there is medical evidence in support of all the elements of the defence of insanity he may of his own volition rule that the accused person is raising the defence of insanity and leave it to the jury to decide whether the criteria are met. However the circumstances in which he will do this will be "exceptional and very rare"[302] Where the judge makes a decision to leave the defence of insanity to the jury he must give counsel on both sides the opportunity to call evidence on the point before he does so even if that means adjourning the trial.[303]

Commentary

The technical question whether evidence is evidence of mental illness going to the issue of criminal responsibility should remain a question of law. As such it is the judge who is best equipped in terms of expertise to determine the issue. However it is submitted that the nature of psychiatric testimony particularly recent developments in understanding of psychiatric illness admitted in evidence should not be restricted on the basis of strict legal definitions and that the admission of evidence such recent developments having a bearing on the accused person's responsibility should be permitted by statute.[304]

Position under the Criminal Law (Insanity) Bill 2002

Where the defendant puts his state of mind in issue the question of whether s/he has raised the defence of insanity remains a question of law for the judge. In this regard the Act does not affect the common law position.

---

[301] *R v. Kemp* [1957] 1 Q.B. 399 [1956] 3 All E.R. 249; *Bratty v. AG for Northern Ireland* [1963] A.C. 386 at 411–412; *R v. Dickie* [1984] 3 All E.R. 173.

[302] *R v. Dickie* [1984] 3 All E.R. at 178; *R v. Thomas (Sharon)* [1995] Crim. L.R. 314.

[303] *R v. Dickie* [1984] 3 All E.R. at 178.

[304] See O'Leary J., "Reforming the Insanity Defence in Criminal Law – A Comparative View", *Dli*, Winter 1992, p.54.

The Function of the Jury

Current Law

It is for the jury, after proper direction from the judge, to determine the issue of insanity.[305] Where medical evidence wholly supports a special verdict of guilty but insane and there is nothing on the facts which could lead to a contrary conclusion then a verdict of guilty will be set aside[306] but if there are facts which justify the jury in coming to a conclusion different from that of the experts their verdict will be upheld.

Position under Criminal Law (Insanity) Bill 2002

Section 4 of the Bill provides that where an accused is tried for an offence in the District Court or the Special Criminal Court it is for the judge to decide whether the accused committed the act alleged against him or her and having heard evidence relating to the mental condition of the accused given by a consultant psychiatrist: (a) whether the accused person was suffering from a mental disorder at the time of the commission of the offence and (b) whether the mental disorder was such that the accused person ought not to be held responsible for the act alleged by reason of the fact that he or she (i) did not know the nature and quality of the act or (ii) did not know that what he or she was doing was wrong, or (iii) was unable to refrain from committing the act. In all other cases it is for the jury to decide these issues.

The Bill therefore allows the possibility of the defence of insanity being raised in a summary trial and in a non-jury trial in the Special Criminal Court.

4. Relationship Between Insanity Defence and other Defences

Automatism and the Insanity Defence

Current Irish Law

In general terms an accused person will have a defence if he can show that the act, omission or event with which he is charged was involuntary[307] in the sense that his mind did not function at all[308] when he committed the offence.[309]

In *Bratty v. AG for Northern Ireland*[310] Lord Denning stated:

---

[305] *R v. Rivett* (1950) 34 Cr. App. Rep. 87 at 94.

[306] *R v. Matheson* [1958] 2 All E.R. 87. See also *R v. Rotana* (1995) 12 C.R.N.Z. 650. It has been argued that in cases where the medical evidence is uncontroverted the jury should nevertheless be directed that psychiatric evidence should be considered in the light of the evidence as a whole and that their attention should be drawn to the fact that psychiatric evidence relating to the accused person's state of mind does not strictly speaking have the value of a diagnosis since medical diagnosis is normally based on the more or less contemporaneous examination of the patient. See McAuley, *Insanity, Psychiatry and Criminal Responsibility* (1993), p.6.

[307] See Edwards, *Automatism and Criminal Responsibility* (1958) 21 M.L.R. 375; Hart *Punishment and Responsibility*, p.90.

[308] As opposed to a malfunctioning of the mind which may entitle him to avail of the insanity defence.

[309] See Archbold, "Pleading, Evidence and Practice in Criminal Cases" (1992) para.17–128.

[310] [1963] A.C. 386 at 409.

"No act is punishable if it is done involuntarily; and an involuntary act in this context – some people nowadays prefer to speak of it as automatism - means an act done by the muscles without any control by the mind such as a spasm, a reflex action or a convulsion or an act done by a person who is not conscious of what he is doing, such as an act done while suffering from concussion or while sleepwalking."

For the defence of automatism to be left to the jury a proper foundation for it must have been laid. Whether there is evidence of automatism is a matter of law. Once a foundation is laid it is for the prosecution to negative it by proving beyond a reasonable doubt that the defendant's acts were voluntary in the sense that they were committed when he was fully conscious.[311]

It is sometimes difficult to distinguish the insanity defence from that of automatism. In Ireland this is particularly so since the definition of insanity in Irish law is itself uncertain. The English courts have taken the view that as the McNaghten Rules require the accused person to be suffering from a disease of the mind and that transient states caused by external factors[312] are more properly described as automatism.[313] Transient abnormalities or disorders of the mind caused by an internal factor, which manifest themselves in violence and are prone to recur are considered in England to be insanity.[314] In *R v. Quick*[315] it was held that self administered insulin injections were an external factor which resulted in the issue of automatism being left to the jury. In *R v. Hennessy*[316] however the English Court of Appeal held that the underlying condition of hyperglycaemia amounted to "McNaghten Insanity." The distinction between the two cases was that the external factor in *R v. Quick i.e.* the lowering of the blood sugar level might have been the insulin injection administered earlier in the day whereas the high blood sugar level in the cases of hyperglycaemia was caused by an inherent defect which, when not corrected by insulin, was a disease.

Moreover automatism must be distinguished from acts done under irresistible impulse. The latter are not regarded as "involuntary acts" because although the person concerned may not be able to control the impulse to do the act the physical performance of it is not beyond his effective control.[317] Winn J in *Watmore v. Jenkins*[318] described automatism as being limited to "involuntary movement of the body or limbs of a person."

Automatism cannot be pleaded where the accused person's involuntary state was caused by voluntary intoxication.[319]

In *R v. Burgess*[320] the Court of Appeal described the task of judge as involving a

---

[311] See *Bratty v. AG for Northern Ireland* (1961) 46 Cr. App. Rep. 1.
[312] The ordinary stresses and disappointments of life are not regarded as external factors for the purpose of the defence of automatism. *R v. Rabey* [1977] 37 C.C.C. (2d) 461. However a rape which precipitates post traumatic stress disorder may be. See *R v. T* [1990] Crim. L.R. 257.
[313] See *R v. Quick* [1973] Q.B. 910.
[314] *R v. Kemp* [1957] 1 Q.B. 399; See *Bratty v. AG for Northern Ireland* [1963] A.C. 386.
[315] [1973] Q.B. 910.
[316] [1989] 2 All E.R. 9.
[317] See *Bratty v. AG for Northern Ireland* [1963] A.C. 386 at 409.
[318] [1962] 2 Q.B. 572 at 586.
[319] See *R v. Lipman* [1970] 1 Q.B. 152.
[320] [1991] 2 Q.B. 92, [1991] 2 All E.R. 769.

498 *Irish Mental Health Law*

decision on two issues before the defence of automatism[321] could properly be left to the jury. First he had to decide whether a proper evidential basis for the defence of automatism had been laid and secondly whether the evidence showed the case to be one of insane automatism or of non-insane automatism. If the medical evidence before the court indicates that the alleged automatism arose from a disease of the mind the judge may determine that the defence be treated as one of insanity.[322]

Where the defence raised is one of automatism the accused person bears the burden of adducing evidence [323] and once the foundation is laid the burden of disproving it is on the prosecution in accordance with the principles laid down in *Woolmington v. DPP.* [324] Where the defence of insane automatism is raised the accused person bears the burden of proof as well as the burden of adducing evidence.[325]

Where the defence of automatism is raised successfully the accused person is entitled to a complete acquittal whereas if the case is one that the accused person was suffering from a defect of reason due to a disease of the mind the accused person is liable to be detained in the Central Mental Hospital pending a decision by the executive that he has recovered.[326]

Automatism should be also be distinguished from a defence based on a plea that the accused person did not act within intent. Intent is only relevant where the mental element of a crime requires that the accused person act with the purpose causing the external element.

Commentary

In order to facilitate the making of a distinction between cases of insanity and automatism consideration might be given to limiting the defence of insane automatism to cases of involuntary action due to illness involving a risk of recurrence.

The Partial Defence of Diminished Responsibility

Current Irish Law

Since the full defence of insanity is available in the Irish jurisdiction only when a person is suffering from severe mental illness the question has been raised as to whether diminished responsibility should be introduced as a partial defence to supplement it. Traditionally the insanity defence in Irish law has been concerned with the accused person's ability to act rationally. Where mental illness does not undermine an accused person's ability to perceive reality or grasp the distinction between right and wrong s/he has no defence. This is despite several attempts in cases to persuade the courts to declare

---

[321] Together with a direction on the relevant law and burden of proof.

[322] See *R v. Kemp* [1957] 1 Q.B. 399; *R v. Hennessy* [1989] 2 All E.R. 9.

[323] *Bratty v. AG for Northern Ireland* [1963] A.C. 386 at 414.

[324] *Woolmington v. DPP* [1935] A.C. 462. The English courts have held that the accused person's evidence will rarely be sufficient to support the defence of automatism unless it is supported by medical evidence. See *R v. Dervish* [1968] Crim. L.R. 37; *Cook v. Atchison* [1968] Crim. L.R. 266 D.C.; *R v. Stripp* (1978) 69 Cr. App. Rep. 318; *R v. Pullen* [1991] Crim. L.R. 457.

[325] See *People (DPP) v. O'Mahony* [1985] I.R. 517 at 522.

[326] See *DPP v. Gallagher* [1991] I.L.R.M. 339.

a defence of diminished responsibility on the grounds of mental illness part of the Irish common law.[327] Accordingly in 1978 the Henchy Report[328] recommended the introduction of the defence of diminished responsibility into the Irish legal system on the basis that many people appearing before the criminal courts were suffering from mental disorders which substantially diminished their responsibility for their crimes

Comparative Law

The English defence of diminished responsibility is to be found in section 2 of the Homicide Act 1957. Section 2 provides that:

> "Where a person kills or is a party to the killing of another, he shall not be convicted of murder if he was suffering from such abnormality of mind (whether arising from a condition of arrested or retarded development of mind or any inherent causes or induced by disease or injury) as substantially impaired his mental responsibility for his acts and omissions in doing or being a party to the killing."

Under English law it is generally[329] only the accused person who can raise evidence of diminished responsibility and when raised s/he has the burden of proving the three elements required to establish the defence on the balance of probabilities. First it must be shown that the accused person was suffering from "abnormality of mind" at the material time. In *R v. Byrne*[330] it was held that "abnormality of mind" meant "a state of mind so different from that of an ordinary person that the reasonable man would term it abnormal."[331] Lord Parker C.J. stated that the description was:

> "wide enough to cover the mind's activities in all its aspects not only the perception of physical acts and matters and the ability to form a rational judgment as to whether an act is right or wrong but also the ability to exercise will-power to control physical acts in accordance with that rational judgment."

Secondly it must be proved that the abnormality of mind resulted from a condition of arrested or retarded development of mind or any inherent causes or be induced by disease or injury. Accordingly an abnormality of mind which resulted from hate, jealousy or self induced intoxication[332] is outside the scope of the defence.[333]

---

[327] *AG v. O'Shea* [1931] I.R. 728; *People (AG) v. Manning* [1955] 89 I.L.T.R. 155; *D.P.P. v. O'Mahony* [1986] I.L.R.M. 244.

[328] *Treatment and Care of Persons Suffering from Mental Disorder who Appear before the Court on Criminal Charges* (3rd Interim Report of the Inter-Departmental Committee on Mentally Ill and Maladjusted Persons) at p.5, para.9.

[329] See *R v. Campbell* (1986) 84 Cr. App. Rep. 255. However under s.6 of the Criminal Procedure (Insanity) Act 1964 where on a charge of murder the accused person contends that was insane under the McNaghten rules the prosecution may adduce or elicit evidence that he was suffering from diminished responsibility. In this case the prosecution must prove diminished responsibility beyond a reasonable doubt.

[330] [1960] 2 Q.B. 396.

[331] *Ibid.* at 403, *per* Lord Parker C.J.

[332] Intoxication resulting in brain injury giving rise to gross impairment of judgment and emotional response or involuntary intoxication such that the accused person was unable to control an impulse

Thirdly it must be shown that the abnormality of mind substantially impaired the accused person's mental responsibility for his acts and omissions in doing or being a party to the killing. Substantial impairment in this regard means something more than trivial or minimal but need not be total.[334] Where an accused person who has experienced difficulty in controlling his conduct raises the defence he could avail of the defence where his difficulty is substantially greater than would have been experienced by an ordinary person without mental abnormality in the circumstances even if it did not amount to total inability to exercise will power.[335]

The defence cannot be left to the jury unless there is medical evidence to supports its three elements.[336] If the elements are made out the issue of whether the accused person is suffering from such an abnormality of mind as substantially to impair his mental responsibility is one for the jury who are required to approach the issues in a broad commonsense way taking into account all the evidence including the accused person's acts or statements and his demeanour.[337] The jury is only bound to accept medical evidence if it is unanimous, and unchallenged.[338] Where there is other evidence which justifies the jury in departing from and outweighs the medical evidence the jury is not bound to follow it.[339]

In cases where there is clear and undisputed medical evidence of diminished responsibility the court, with the prosecution's consent, may accept a plea of guilty of manslaughter on grounds of diminished responsibility.[340] In this event a verdict from the jury is not required.

Changes proposed by the Criminal Law (Insanity) Bill 2002

The Criminal Law (Insanity) Bill adopts an approach which is quite similar to that in England and Wales in introducing a statutory defence of diminished responsibility into Irish law. The effect of the introduction of a defence of diminished responsibility is to afford an accused person charged with murder who does not come within the criteria for establishing the insanity defence a mitigating factor which if successfully pleaded would result in a conviction for manslaughter. In effect this means that instead of a sentence of life imprisonment for murder the court would have a discretion in the matter of punishment which in the case of manslaughter may vary from imprisonment for life to an absolute discharge.

---

to drink may be held to be an abnormality of mind due to a specified cause ("disease or injury"). See *R v. Tandy*, *The Times*, December 23, 1987.

[333] See *R v. Fenton* (1975) 61 Cr. App. Rep. 261. However the Scottish Law Commission in its Discussion Paper No. 122 on Insanity and Diminished Responsibility published in January 2003 argues that chronic intoxication resulting from an underlying condition of alcoholism or intoxication should found a plea of diminished responsibility. It describes chronic intoxication as referring to those accused who are habitual users and suffer from an underlying condition and addiction which explains their intoxication at the time of the act in question.

[334] See *R v. Lloyd* [1967] 1 Q.B. 175.

[335] See *R v. Simcox* [1964] Crim. L.R. 402.

[336] See *R v. Dix* (1982) 74 Cr. App. Rep. 306.

[337] See *R v. Simcox* [1964] Crim. L.R. 402.

[338] *R v. Matheson* [1958] 2 All E.R. 87.

[339] *R v. Byrne* [1960] 2 Q.B. 396; *Walton v. R* [1978] A.C. 788.

[340] *R v. Cox* (1968) 52 Cr. App. R. 130.

Section 5 of the Criminal Law (Insanity) Bill provides that the defence applies only where a person is tried for murder and where:

"the jury, or as the case may be the Special Criminal Court finds that the person–

> (a) committed the act alleged,
> (b) was at the time suffering from a mental disorder and
> (c) the mental disorder was not such as to justify finding him or her not guilty by reason of insanity, but was such as to diminish substantially his or her responsibility for the act

the jury or court, as the case may be, shall find the person not guilty of that offence but guilty of manslaughter on the ground of diminished responsibility."

The term "mental disorder" is preferred in the Irish legislation to "abnormality of mind "in its English counterpart which has given rise to some confusion in interpretation amongst the English judiciary.[341] "Mental disorder" is defined by section 2 of the Act to mean "mental illness, mental handicap, dementia or any disease of the mind but does not include intoxication"

The burden is on the defence to establish that the person is, by virtue of the statutory provision not liable to be convicted of the offence.

Section 4(4) of the Bill provides that where on a trial for murder the accused person contends either: (a) that at the time of the alleged offence he or she was suffering from a mental disorder such that he or she ought to be found not guilty by reason of insanity or (b) that at the time of the offence he or she was suffering from a mental disorder giving rise to a defence of diminished responsibility the court shall allow the prosecution to adduce evidence tending to prove the alternative of the contention made by the accused person and may give directions as to the stage of the proceedings the evidence may be adduced

Persons subject to the Defence Act 1954 Section 16 of the Criminal Law (Insanity) Bill 2002 substitutes a new section 203A for the existing provision of the Defence Act 1954. The effect of that provision is to apply section 5 of the Criminal Law (Insanity) Bill 2002 (which sets out the criteria for establishing a defence of diminished responsibility) with any necessary modifications to a person subject to military law who is tried by court-martial for murder as it applies to a person who is tried under the criminal law for murder.

Commentary

1. In the Seanad the Minister for Justice indicated that the defence of diminished responsibility was being introduced in the case of murder only as it carried a mandatory sentence of life imprisonment and if a defence of diminished responsibility was successfully pleaded a conviction for manslaughter would be recorded affording

---

[341] See Mackay R.D., "The Abnormality of Mind Factor in Diminished Responsibility" [1999] *Criminal Law Review* p.117.

the court a discretion in the matter of sentencing. The Minister indicated that there was no need to apply the concept of diminished responsibility in respect of other crimes where there was no mandatory sentence as in the case of conviction in those instances the judge could take the mental condition of the convicted person into account when considering what sentence to impose.[342]

2.   The definition of "mental disorder" in section 2 of the Bill (which condition grounds the defence of diminished responsibility) gives rise to difficulties of interpretation which have been discussed in the context of the use of the same term in the context of the defence of insanity.

3.   Under the new defence of diminished responsibility it appears that psychiatrists may be asked to give evidence as to whether the mental disorder "was such as to diminish substantially the accused person's responsibility for the act". This may give rise to a situation which encourages role confusion between being expert witness and fact finder as the medical evidence will go to the ultimate issue to be decided namely whether liability should be diminished to the level of manslaughter.[343]

4.   The Government White Paper on Mental Health issued in 1995[344] indicated that it was proposed that the Minister for Health would designate special psychiatric centres in which persons who are the subject of such a verdict guilty of manslaughter on the ground of diminished responsibility would be detained. In 1995 it was noted that the only suitable special centre was the Central Mental Hospital but it stated that "in future there may be other secure units which could be designated as special psychiatric centres for this purpose".[345] The Criminal Law (Insanity) Bill 2002 confers no express powers on the court to direct the treatment of a person found guilty of manslaughter on the ground of diminished responsibility where that person is still suffering from a "mental disorder" at the time of trial.

5   Further the Bill does not provide for any appeal from a finding of manslaughter on the ground of diminished responsibility.

5. The Special Verdict

(a) The Special Verdict of 'Guilty but Insane' and the Right of Appeal

Current Law

Prior to 1800 the verdict in cases of insanity was "not guilty" and the accused person was entitled to a simple acquittal and the accused person was released into the community. It was the attempt on the life of George III by Hadfield[346] and his subsequent acquittal on the grounds of insanity that prompted the enactment of the Criminal Lunatics Act

---

[342] 171 *Seanad Debates* Col. 772.

[343] See Mackay R.D., "Some Thoughts on Reforming the Law of Insanity and Diminished Responsibility in England", (2003) *Juridical Review*, p.1 p.57 at pp.77–78.

[344] See "A New Mental Health Act" Pn. 1824 July 1995.

[345] See para.7.27.

[346] [1800] 27 St. Tr.1281.

1800, which empowered the court to detain the defendant accused of a felony and found insane until his Majesty's pleasure was known and provided that the jury should declare that the accused person was not guilty on the grounds of insanity. This legislation was extended to Ireland when the Lunacy (Ireland) Act was passed in 1821.[347] In 1850 the Central Criminal Lunatic Asylum (now the Central Mental Hospital) was built in Dundrum specifically to detain the criminally insane pursuant to the Lunacy (Ireland) Act 1845. The Trial of Lunatics Act 1883 extended the Criminal Lunatics Act 1800 to misdemeanours and also provided that in cases tried with a jury the verdict should be "guilty of the act or omission charged against him but was insane at the time when he did the act or made the omission."[348] This was subsequently commuted to "guilty but insane."[349] The verdict has been criticised as illogical since where a defendant is found not to be responsible in law for his actions the correct finding should be one of not guilty.[350] On the other hand it has been pointed out that since in cases where the defence is successfully raised the accused person is kept in custody and since the usual consequence of a finding of not guilty is liberation the verdict is consistent with the form of disposition.[351]

Despite the form of the verdict it was generally accepted[352] that it was tantamount to an acquittal and no appeal lay from a finding either of guilty of doing the act charged or of insanity.[353] In England, however, a right of appeal is now available by section 12 of the Criminal Appeal Act 1968 and the Henchy Report[354] has recommended that a right of appeal be available in Ireland.

The fact that the verdict is an acquittal has the consequence that the courts have no role in the detention of the person concerned. The fact that the accused person is not insane when the verdict of returned or recovers his sanity during detention in the Central Mental Hospital has no bearing on the validity and effect of the court order directing his detention there. By virtue of the terms of section 2(2) of the Trial of Lunatics Act 1883 the continuance of the detention and its length becomes one entirely for the Government[355] In practice where a detainee wishes his/her detention to be reviewed s/he must make an application to the government and a hearing is held before a special committee set up by the Minister for Justice following the *Gallagher* case. The committee comprises a senior counsel as chairperson, a consultant psychiatrist and a general practitioner. The committee then "advise[s] the Minister for Justice as to whether the

---

[347] 1& 2 Geo. IV. c.33, ss.16–18.

[348] Trial of Lunatics Act 1883, s.2. Apparently this change was effected at the behest of Queen Victoria who was distressed on finding that a certain McLean who fired a pistol at her was "not guilty" on account of his insanity.

[349] S.1 of the Criminal Procedure (Insanity) Act 1964 in England now provides that the verdict shall be one of "not guilty by reason of insanity.".

[350] *Report of the Committee on Insanity and Crime* (1924) Cmd 2005 *per* Sir Herbert Stephen; Cross and Jones, and Card, *Introduction to Criminal Law* p.132; Mcauley, *Insanity Psychiatry and Criminal Responsibility* (1993), p.110.

[351] Walker, *Crime and Insanity in England* (Edinburgh) 1968.

[352] See *In the application of Gallagher* [1991] I.R. 31.

[353] See *Felstead v. R* [1914] A.C. 254; *R v. Duke* [1963] 1 Q.B. 120; [1961] 3 All E.R. 737.

[354] Third Interim Report of the Interdepartmental Committee on Mentally Ill and Maladjusted Persons. *Treatment and Care of Persons Suffering from Mental Disorder who Appear before the Courts on Criminal Charges* (Dublin 1978).

[355] This view was confirmed in *DPP v. Gallagher* [1991] I.L.R.M. 339.

applicant is suffering from any mental disorder warranting his continued detention in the public and private interests (including the question of whether he would be a potential danger to any member of the public if released)."[356] The government must use fair and constitutional procedures in hearing the case[357] but the advisory committee's findings are not binding and the government is not obliged to hold any automatic review of detention where the detainee has not requested a review.[358]

The practical result of the verdict and of the mandatory sentence of indefinite detention in the Central Mental Hospital which follows it is that since the abolition of the death penalty[359] those accused of murder are unwilling to rely on the defence of insanity and prefer to run the risk of conviction and sentence rather than to be labelled insane and face indefinite detention.[360] Indeed some cases where the court has ruled that the evidence amounts to a plea of insanity and not non-insane automatism defendants who pleaded not guilty of the offence have preferred to plead guilty.[361] For their part juries may be reluctant to return insanity verdicts because of a perception that a detainee may have an "easier" time in a hospital than in a prison. Further many jurors may undoubtedly be aware that a person found not guilty by reason of insanity could be released into the community at any time after the verdict is returned.[362]

Commentary

There are several undesirable effects of the special verdict which follows the insanity defence which require reform to reflect the fact that the accused person is a person who primarily requires treatment for the illness which prompted the offence.

1. Where the defence is accepted on the basis that the defendant did not know that what he was doing was wrong a verdict of not guilty is logically demanded and on this basis it is submitted the verdict should be changed to "not guilty on the grounds of. ..."[363] If this verdict is then to preserve its quality as a true acquittal it should be subject only to a post-verdict hearing to determine whether the individual should be detained on account of his mental illness. This matter is addressed by the Criminal Law (Insanity) Bill 2002 (see below page 507).

2. In the recent case of *Varbanov v. Bulgaria*[364] the European Court of Human Rights ruled that in a case dealing with the lawfulness of detention under Article 5(1)(e) that:

---

[356] See *Irish Times*, February 13, 1991.

[357] The inquiry may be subject to judicial review to ensure compliance with such procedures. See *Application of Gallagher* [1991] 1 I.R. 31 at 37.

[358] See McAuley, *Insanity, Psychiatry and Criminal Responsibility* (1993), pp.115 *et seq.*

[359] The death penalty was abolished in Ireland by the Criminal Justice Act 1964.

[360] Since 1947 the defence has been successfully raised on indictment on a total of 118 occasions. See Report on Crime 1947–87.

[361] See Smith and Hogan, *Criminal Law* (1992), p.196.

[362] See Dwyer P., "The Law of Insanity in Ireland", *Bar Review* 1996, p.9 at 19.

[363] The *Third Interim Report of the Interdepartmental Committee on Mentally Ill and Maladjusted Persons* known as the Henchy Report Prl.8275 (Dublin 1978) known as the Henchy Report recommended in similar terms that the verdict should be "not guilty by reason of mental disorder".

[364] October 5, 2000. Application No. 00031365/96.

"the medical assessment must be based on the actual state of mental health of the person concerned and not solely on past events. A medical opinion cannot be seen as sufficient to justify deprivation of liberty if a significant period of time has elapsed."

The defence of insanity relates to the accused person state of mind at the time of the commission of the offence. It is possible that by the time of the trial the accused person is mentally well and does not require in-patient treatment. The mandatory confinement of accused in the Central Mental Hospital following a finding of insanity is likely therefore to be contrary to the European Convention of Human Rights.

In Canada the Supreme Court held in *R v. Swain*[365] that the mandatory detention of an insane acquittee without any chance of a judicial hearing offended the principles of fundamental justice contrary to section 7 of the Canadian Charter of Rights and Freedoms and that detention without criteria constituted arbitrary detention under section 9.

McAuley points out that the assumption exists that all people found guilty by the court are dangerous and that there is no evidence that persons who have been diagnosed as mentally ill are more prone to violence than the mentally healthy or that those acquitted on the grounds of insanity are more prone to violence than other violent killers or other offenders convicted of crimes other than homicide.[366] Other arguments adduced to this end include the fact that an accused person's insane beliefs or attitudes which led him to kill on one occasion does not necessarily mean that he is likely to kill for the same or similar reasons in future; that the presumption of dangerousness is inconsistent with the finding that the accused person was fit to plead which in itself raises a presumption that he is no longer insane and consequently no longer dangerous. The presumption of dangerousness is also inappropriate when applied to defendants acquitted on grounds of insanity on foot of the psychological effects of an isolated bout of physical illness or a chronic physical illness that has been brought under control by medication. Finally there is the possibility that the automatic detention of defendants in respect of whom the special verdict has been delivered may amount to a breach of Article 5 of the European Convention on Human Rights since the necessity for committal is not established by objective medical expertise which is a mandatory requirement following the decision of the European Court of Human Rights in *Winterwerp v. The Netherlands*.[367]

The matter of automatic indeterminate detention of the accused following the

---

[365] (1991) 5 C.R. (4th) 253.

[366] See McAuley, *Insanity Psychiatry and Criminal Responsibility* (1993), p.115 citing Rabkin, "Criminal Behaviour of Discharged Mental Patients: A Critical Appraisal of the Research" (1979) 86 *Psychological Bulletin* 1–27 and generally, Thornberry and Jacoby, *The Criminally Insane: A Community Follow-up of the Mentally Ill Offenders* (Chicago, 1979): Steadman and Cocozza, *Careers of the Criminally Insane: Excessiv.e Social Control of Dev.iance,* (Boston, 1974).

[367] [1979] 2 E.H.R.R. 387. Prl. 8275 (Dublin) 1978. In Australia the New South Wales Mental Health (Criminal Procedure) Act 1990 provides that a special verdict of "not guilty by reason of mental illness" should be returned where a person is found to have committed the relevant offence but at the relevant time was "mentally ill, so as not to be responsible according to law."

special verdict is addressed in part by section 4 of the Criminal Law (Insanity) Bill 2002. This requires the court to obtain a report from an approved medical officer as to the accused person's state of mind at the time of trial. However the range of disposition options expressly available to the court appear to be limited to detention in a designated centre in the event that an accused is found to be suffering from a mental disorder within the meaning of the Mental Health Act 2001 and is in need of in patient care and treatment. It is not clear what is to happen if the accused at the time of trial is found not to be suffering from a mental disorder.

3. Present law provides that where a special verdict is returned an order providing for the person to be "kept in custody" as a criminal lunatic be made. Provision should also be made for a right to appropriate treatment. The fact that treatment will be provided is assumed in the terms of the Criminal Law (Insanity) Bill 2002 empowering the court to make an order for commitment to a designated centre of a person found not guilty by reason of insanity where that person is established to be in "need of in-patient care or treatment" but no right to treatment is expressly provided for.

4. Following the recommendations in the Henchy Report[368] it is submitted that hospital facilities other than the Central Mental Hospital in Dundrum should be designated for the detention of persons subject to the special verdict and special units should be designated for persons suffering from violent personality disorders. Section 2 Criminal Law (Insanity) Bill 2002 which provides for the designation of centres for the reception, detention and where appropriate care or treatment of persons committed under the Bill's provisions attempts to address the Henchy Reports recommendations but as has been mentioned above see page 459 (re Amnesty International's Report) the practical implications of finding centres for designated have yet to be addressed.

5. A system of automatic review of detention of those in respect of whom a special verdict has been delivered should be introduced to avoid the risk of persons subject to the special verdict being subject to indeterminate detention. The Criminal Law (Insanity) Bill 2002 addresses this need and proposes of system of automatic review of detention at six monthly intervals by the Mental Health Review Board.

6. In the United States of America there has also been some judicial discussion as to whether the term that the person subject to the special verdict spends in a psychiatric should reflect the maximum term of imprisonment for the offence. In *Jones v. U.S.*[369] the U.S. Supreme Court has held that a person may constitutionally be confined to a psychiatric institution until such time as he has regained his sanity or is no longer a danger to himself and society. A majority of the court held that there was no constitutional prohibition on an insanity acquittee being detained for longer than he would have been imprisoned if convicted. On the other hand in *Jackson v. Indiana*[370] the court has held that the due process of the Constitution "requires that the nature

---

[368] Prl. 8275 (Dublin) 1978.
[369] 463 U.S. 354 (1983).
[370] 406 U.S. 715 at 738 (1972).

and duration of commitment bear some reasonable relation to the purpose for which the individual was committed". The court has also held in *Foucha v. Louisiana*[371] that once an insanity acquittee is no longer mentally ill he must be released despite a finding of dangerousness.

Californian law provides that special commitment may last only as long as the acquittee could have been imprisoned if convicted. At the expiration of the maximum term the acquittee must be released and civilly committed under the state's commitment law or held on a state commitment (renewable every two years) pursuant to the state showing that the acquittee remains particularly dangerous. At the expiration of the maximum term the burden shifts to the state to justify further confinement. The matter has yet to be litigated before the Irish Courts under the current law.

Under the terms of the Criminal Law (Insanity) Bill 2002 the period of detention is directly related to the time taken for the accused to recover and in the powers of review of detention conferred on the Mental Health Review by section 12 no mention is made of whether the Board may give consideration to the length of sentence which would have been imposed had s/he been sentenced to a term of imprisonment.

Changes Proposed by Criminal Law (Insanity) Bill 2002

The New Special Verdict   Section 4(1) of the Criminal Law (Insanity) Bill proposes that where a defence of "insanity" is successfully raised on the criteria set out in the Bill a special verdict of "not guilty by reason of insanity" should be returned.

New Powers of Disposition   If the court considers that an accused person found not guilty by reason of insanity is suffering from a mental disorder within the meaning of the Mental Health Act 2001 and may be in need of in-patient care or treatment in a designated centre[372] then for the purposes of determining its ultimate disposition the court may pursuant to section 4(3) commit that person to a specified designated centre for a period of not more than 28 days and direct that during that period he or she be examined by an approved medical officer at that centre. This period of committal directed by the court may be extended by the court if it considers it appropriate to do so for a period or, in aggregate, periods of up to six months on the application to the court by any party. Within the authorised period of committal the approved medical officer[373] concerned must report to the court on whether in his or her opinion the accused person so committed is suffering from a mental disorder within the meaning of the Mental Health Act 2001 and is in need of in-patient care or treatment in a designated centre.

---

[371] 112 S. Ct 1780 (1992).

[372] S.2(1) of the Bill provides that the Minister for Health and Children may by order designate a psychiatric centre or with the consent of the Minister for Justice, Equality and Law Reform, a prison or any part thereof as a centre for the reception, detention and where appropriate care or treatment of persons or classes of persons committed thereto under the provisions of the Bill. S.2(4) defines a "psychiatric centre" as a "hospital or other institution in which care or treatment is provided for persons suffering from a mental disorder".

[373] An "approved medical officer" is defined by s.1(1) as "a consultant psychiatrist within the meaning of the Mental Health Act 2001".

Section 4(2) provides that if the court having considered any report submitted to it in this regard and such other evidence as may be adduced before it, is satisfied that the accused person is suffering from a mental disorder within the meaning of the Mental Health Act 2001 and is in need of in-patient care or treatment in a designated centre the court must commit that person to a specified designated centre where his mental state will be reviewed by the Mental Health Review Board under section 12.

The disposition options available to the court following a finding or not guilty by reason of insanity appear to be limited. Only one is clearly specified that of committal to a designated centre where the accused person is found to be still suffering from a conventional psychiatric illness. It is not clear whether the court has a power to discharge an accused person who is not in need of psychiatric treatment. This would however seem to be warranted by the verdict of not guilty. There appears to be no power vested in the court to order discharge with conditions as to out-patient treatment. Further it is not clear what is to happen to an accused person who falls within the Bill's definition of mental disorder giving rise to the defence of insanity such as an accused person with epilepsy or arteriosclerosis but who does not fall within the definition of mental disorder within the meaning of the Mental Health Act 2001.

Whereas a power to remand a person in custody for assessment is the first appearance in Irish criminal law of a power to remand a person to hospital for assessment is to be welcomed there are flaws in the procedure as the person can be committed to the designated centre for assessment without any medical examination beforehand. This is a clear breach of Article 5(1)(e) of the European Convention on Human Rights and the criteria for detention of a person as a person of unsound mind as outlined by the European Court of Human Rights in *Winterwerp v. The Netherlands.*[374] Further the detained person has no right of information whether s/he is detained for assessment or on a more long-term basis and there is no duty to draw up a care plan. Both of these rights are accorded to a person detained in accordance with the terms of the Mental Health Act 2001. Further there appears to be no power to remand a person on bail for assessment in the 2002 Bill.

New Rights of Appeal of Accused Found Not Guilty By Reason of Insanity Section 7 of the Bill grants a new right of appeal to accused person's found not guilty by reason of insanity. A finding of the District Court that a person is not guilty by reason of insanity may be appealed to the Circuit Court on all or any of the following grounds:

(a) that it was not proved that he or she had committed the act in question. If this ground is made out the Circuit Court must acquit the appellant; (section 7(2)).

(b) that at the time when the act was committed he or she was not suffering from a mental disorder of the nature referred to in section 4(1)(b) of the Bill; If this ground is made out on the evidence of a consultant psychiatrist the court must substitute a verdict of guilty of the offence charged or of any other offence of which it is satisfied that the person could (by virtue of the charge) and ought to have been convicted and the Circuit Court can then exercise such powers of punishing or other disposition as the District Court would have had in the circumstances (section 4(3)).

---

[374] [1979] 2 E.H.R.R. 387.

(c) that the District Court ought to have made a determination in respect of the person that he or she was unfit to be tried. If this ground is made out the Circuit Court must make such a finding and substitute it for the verdict (section 4(4)).

Section 7(5) provides that if on appeal to the Circuit Court the court is satisfied having considered the evidence or any new evidence relating to the mental condition of the appellant that he or she was at the time that the offence alleged was committed suffering from a mental disorder of the nature referred to in section 4(1)(b) and that but for that disorder the appellant would have been found guilty of the offence charged or of another offence of which the person could have been found guilty by virtue of the charge the court must dismiss the appeal.

Section 7(6)–7(9) provides that a verdict of not guilty by reason of insanity that is delivered following trial on indictment in the Circuit Court, the Central Criminal Court or the Special Criminal Court may be appealed to the Court of Criminal Appeal on all or any of the grounds set out above in relation to appeals from the District Court and similar powers are available to the Court of Criminal Appeal in respect of circumstances where those grounds of appeal are upheld.

A right of appeal against the delivery of a special verdict is to be welcomed . However a problem exists with regard to ground (b) above. It is submitted that the onus should be on the prosecution to prove that the accused person was suffering from a mental disorder and it should not be on the accused person to prove that s/he was not. Such a requirement is likely to contravene the provisions of Article 6(1) of the European Convention on Human Rights. *(Develop this)*

Appeal against an order by a court to commit a person pursuant to statutory criteria following a finding of not guilty by reason of insanity By virtue of section 8 of the Criminal Law (Insanity) Bill 2002 the defence or the prosecution may appeal against a decision by a court of trial (but not a decision of an appellate court) to make or not to make an order of committal under section 4(2) (power to commit a person found not guilty by reason of insanity to a designated centre if certain criteria are met) or 4(3) (power to commit a person found not guilty by reason of insanity to a designated centre for 28 days for the purposes of determining whether an order should be made under section 4(2)) of the 2002 Act. The appeal lies to the Circuit Court or the Court of Criminal Appeal as appropriate. The court hearing the appeal may, having considered the evidence or any new evidence relating to the mental condition of the accused person given by a consultant psychiatrist, make such order, being an order that it was open to the court of trial to make, as it considers appropriate. This is without prejudice to the powers of the Mental Health Review Board to review detention. No further appeal lies from an order of the Circuit Court or the Court of Criminal Appeal on appeal under section 8(1).

Section 8(3) provides that all ancillary and procedural provisions contained in a statute or an instrument made under statute relating to appeals against convictions, including provisions relating to leave to appeal, shall apply with the necessary modifications to appeals under section 8(1).

Section 8(4) provides that the powers of an appellate court in an appeal under section 8(1) shall include the wide power to make any such order as may be necessary for the purpose of doing justice in accordance with the provisions of the Criminal Law (Insanity) Bill 2002.

Powers of Disposition where appeal against conviction on ground accused ought to have been found not guilty by reason of insanity   Section 8(2) provides that where the Circuit Court or the Court of Criminal Appeal allows an appeal against a conviction on the grounds that the appellant ought to have been found not guilty by reason of insanity, the appellate court shall have the same powers to deal with the appellant as the court of trial would have had under section 4 if it had come to the same conclusion.

The Procedure for Review by Mental Health Review Board of Detention following a verdict of not guilty by reason of insanity and a subsequent order made pursuant to statutory criteria to commit accused to a designated centre   By virtue of section 12(2) the Review Board is obliged to ensure that the detention of a "patient" is reviewed at intervals of not more than six months as it considers appropriate. Section 12(1)(a) in effect defines a "patient" as any person detained in a designated centre as unfit to be tried or found not guilty by reason of insanity. Section 12(2) also provides that the clinical director of the relevant designated centre (or where the designated centre is a prison the governor of the prison on the advice of an approved medical officer[375]) is obliged to comply with any request of the Review Board.

On application of Clinical Director of Designated Centre or Governor of Prison Section 12(6) provides that where the clinical director of a designated centre (or the governor of a prison[376] in the case of a prison being the designated centre), forms the opinion in relation to a patient detained pursuant to section 4 (having been found not guilty by reason of insanity but suffering from a mental disorder within the meaning of the Mental Health Act 2001 and in need of in-patient care or treatment in a designated centre) that he or she is no longer in need of in-patient treatment or care at a designated centre he or she must immediately notify the Review Board of this opinion.

Where the Review Board receives such a notification it must according to section 12(7) order that the patient be brought before it, as soon as may be, and must, having heard evidence relating to the mental condition of the patient given by the consultant psychiatrist responsible for his or her care and treatment, determine the question whether the treatment referred to in section 12(6) is still required and must make such order as it thinks proper for the patient's disposal. The options available to the Review Board are an order for further detention, care or treatment in a designated centre or for his or her discharge whether unconditionally or subject to conditions for out-patient treatment or supervision or both.

On application by Patient By virtue of section 12(9) a patient detained under section 4 (by virtue of being found not guilty by reason of insanity but suffering from a mental disorder within the meaning of the Mental Health Act 2001 and in need of care or treatment in a designated centre) may apply to the Review Board for a review of his or her detention and the Review Board must unless satisfied that such a review is not necessary because of any review taken in accordance with section 12 order that the patient be brought before it, as soon as may be. Having heard the evidence relating to the mental condition of the patient given by the consultant psychiatrist responsible for

---

[375] See s.12(1)(b).

[376] The governor must obtain the advice of the approved medical officer when exercising the duties or powers under ss.12 and 13. See s.12(1)(b).

his or her care and treatment it must determine the question of whether or not the patient is still in need of in-patient treatment in a designated centre and must make such order as it thinks proper for the patient's disposal. In this regard it may order further detention, care or treatment in a designated centre or his or her discharge whether unconditionally or subject to conditions for out-patient treatment or supervision or both.

By the Review Board on its own Initiative Under section 12(10) the Review Board may on it own initiative[377] review the detention of a patient detained pursuant to section 4 (i.e following a special verdict and a finding that the patient was suffering from a mental disorder within the meaning of the Mental Health Act 2001 and was in need of in-patient care and treatment) and section 12(9) is deemed to apply to the review as if the patient himself/herself had applied for the review under that subsection.

Under the terms of section 12 the Mental Health Review Board may make "such order as it thinks proper for the patient's disposal". Presumably once the need for treatment has ceased the Board will order early discharge so as to comply with the requirements of the European Convention on Human Rights given effect in domestic law by the European Convention on Human Rights Act 2003.[378]

If Mental Health Review Boards are to be empowered to review the detention of persons detained pursuant to the special verdict it is desirable that such persons have a right of appeal on questions of law from the Board's decisions to the Supreme Court.[379]

Application of Act to Existing Detentions   Section 15(2) provides that the Criminal Law (Insanity) Bill 2002 shall apply to a person found guilty but insane and detained under section 2 of the Trial of Lunatics Act 1883 as if s/he were a person detained pursuant to an order of the court under section 4 and accordingly such a person shall be entitled to the benefit of the provisions of the Act. Accordingly the person has the right to appeal the previous finding of guilty but insane as if it were a finding of not guilty by reason of insanity under the 2002 Act. A person so found may also appeal on the ground that he ought have been found unfit to be tried. S/he may appeal the order mandating his detention and is entitled to have his/her detention reviewed by a Mental Health Review Tribunal.

Patients detained under section 203 of the Defence Act 1954   The provisions relating to review of detention set out above in sections 12(6), 12(9) and 12(10) are equally applicable to patients detained pursuant to a finding by a court-martial that a person charged with an offence is not guilty by reason of insanity but is suffering from a mental disorder within the meaning of the Mental Health Act 2001 and is in need of in-patient treatment or care in a designated centre.

---

[377] Quite how this review is to be triggered in practice is not clear.

[378] In this regard see *Winterwerp v. Netherlands* (1979) 2 E.H.R.R. 387.

[379] Similar recommendations are to be found in the Law Reform Commission of New South Wales *Report No. 80 on Intellectual Disability and the Criminal Justice System*, December 1996. See pp.193–194.

Transfer of Patients between Hospitals after Detention for Treatment

New Transfer Provisions proposed by the Criminal Law (Insanity) Bill 2002

Section 13(2) of the Criminal Law (Insanity) Bill 2002 provides that the clinical director of a designated centre may by the consent of the Minister for Justice, Equality and Law Reform and the Minister for Health and Children, direct the transfer to another designated centre of a patient on such conditions and for such period(s) as the clinical director deems appropriate with the consent of the clinical director of the centre.

"Patient" is defined by section 12(1)(a) as "person detained in a designated centre pursuant to the Criminal Law (Insanity) Bill 2002". Accordingly the transfer provisions apply to a person detained pursuant to a determination that s/he requires in-patient care or treatment for mental disorder as defined in the Mental Health Act 2001 after a finding of unfitness to plead or not guilty by reason of insanity.

"Clinical director" is defined by section 1 to have the meaning assigned to it by the Mental Health Act 2001 i.e.a consultant psychiatrist appointed by the governing body of an approved centre to be the clinical director. Section 1 of the 2002 Bill goes on to provide that where an approved medical officer is duly authorised by a clinical director to perform his or her functions under the Criminal Law (Insanity) Bill 2002 Act the officer shall, in relation to those functions, be deemed for the purposes of the Act to be a clinical director. An "approved medical officer" is defined by section 1 of the 2002 Bill as a consultant psychiatrist within the meaning of the Mental Health Act 2001 *i.e.* a person who is employed by the Health Service Executive or by an approved medical centre or a person whose name is entered on the division of psychiatry or the division of child and adolescent psychiatry of the Register of Medical Specialists maintained by the Medical Council in Ireland.

Section 11(1)(b) of the 2002 Bill provides that where a person is detained in a designated centre which is a prison the duties and powers conferred by section 13 on a clinical director shall be carried out by the governor of the prison on the advice of an approved medical officer. Thus a governor of a prison may direct the transfer of a patient on the advice of an approved medical officer. A "designated centre" is by virtue of section 2 any psychiatric centre[380] or with the consent of the Minister for Justice, Equality and Law Reform a prison[381] or any part thereof designated by the Minister for Health and Children for the reception, detention and where appropriate, care or treatment of persons or classes of persons committed thereto under the 2002 Bill.

Section 13(3) provides that where the transfer of the patient is made subject to conditions the conditions must be communicated to the patient by notice in writing at the time of his or her release or transfer and by virtue of section 13(4) a patient whose transfer is directed under section 13 must comply with any conditions to which his or her release is made subject.

It appears the clinical director has absolute discretion in the matter of transfer and no grounds need be specified. There is no provision for the views of the patient to be

---

[380] "Psychiatric centre" is defined by s.2(4) as meaning "a hospital or other institution in which care r treatment is provided for persons suffering from mental disorder".

[381] "Prison" is defined by s.2(4) as "a place of custody administered by the Minister for Justice, Equality and Law Reform".

taken into account in the matter of the transfer. The patient may have legitimate interests to protect such as the proximity of the receiving centre to family, friends, his lawyer (if s/he has one) and the institution's visitation and correspondence rules governing access to them. Further the patient has no right to object to the transfer.

It is submitted that the patient should have a right to a hearing before the Mental Health Review Board and a right to seek revocation or modification of the proposal to transfer.

The provision also makes it clear that the consent of the patient need not be sought in relation to any conditions which might be imposed. Best therapeutic practice would dictate that the consent of the patient be sought and conditions agreed between psychiatrist and patient before the transfer.

Further the designation of a "prison" as a designated centre for the care and treatment of people with mental illness to which a person may be transferred[382] may be a contravention of the *UN Principles for the Protection of Persons with Mental Illness and the Improvement of Mental Health Care*[383] which represents best practice internationally in the field of mental health care and *the Standard Minimum Rules for the Treatment of Prisoners*.[384] It is also likely to attract international criticism.[385]

By virtue of section 13(8) a patient may be removed from a designated centre to a hospital in order to receive medical attention not available in the designated centre and while detained in that hospital he or she shall be in lawful custody. Where a patient is so removed the clinical director must within 48 hours of such removal forward a report of the circumstances regarding the removal to the Minister for Justice, Equality and Law Reform.

Section 13(9) confers on the Minister for Justice Equality and Law Reform power to direct that a patient be removed from a designated centre to a specified place where s/he is satisfied that it is in the interests of justice to do so and during such authorised absence the patient shall be deemed to remain in lawful custody of the designated centre.

This is a very wide discretion to move a patient to an undefined "specified place" where it is in "the interests of justice to do so." It would cover removal to a prison which is not a designated centre and presumably for a short period to a Garda Station or court holding cells. It is submitted that acknowledging that the person being transferred is a person with mental illness the person should be accompanied by or observed by a member of staff of the designated centre. It is also submitted that the removal of a person suffering from a mental illness to a more restrictive regime of a prison where s/he might not

---

[382] Or committed. See ss3(3)(b), 3(5)(c), 3(6)(b) , 4(2), 4(3) of the Bill *(Cross reference)*.

[383] Adopted by the General Assembly, December 17, 1991, Principle 1.1 states: "All Persons have the right to the best available mental health care, which shall be part of the health and social care system.".

[384] Adopted by the First United Nations Congress on the Prevention of Crime and the Treatment of Offenders, held at Geneva in 1955 and approved by the Economic and Social Council by its resolution 663C (XXIV) of July 31, 1957 and 2076 (LX11) of May 13, 1977. They provide that "Prisoners found insane shall not be detained in prisons and shall be removed to mental institutions as soon as possible".

[385] The European Committee for the Prevention of Torture following its visit in 1998 to Irish places of detention recommended "that the provision of prison psychiatric services be reorganised as a matter of urgency. The aim should be to ensure that it is always possible to transfer mentally ill inmates to an appropriate psychiatric facility without delay."

receive the same level of psychiatric care should be subject to review by the Mental Health Review Board.[386]

Temporary Release of Patients after Detention for Treatment

New Legislative Powers to Direct Temporary Release proposed by the Criminal Law (Insanity) Bill 2002

Section 13(1) of the Criminal Law (Insanity) Bill 2002 empowers the clinical director of a designated centre or the governor of a prison on the advice of an approved medical officer (where a prison is a designated centre),[387] with the consent of the Minister for Justice Equality and Law Reform,[388] to direct the temporary release of a patient on such conditions and for such period(s) as the clinical director or the governor deems appropriate.

Section 13(3) provides that where the release of a patient under subsection (1) is made subject to conditions, the conditions shall be communicated to the patient by notice in writing at the time of his or her release. By virtue of section 13(4) a patient whose temporary release or directed must comply with any conditions to which his or her release is made subject.

The clinical director and the governor on the advice of the approved medical officer have an absolute discretion in the matter of temporary release. Therapeutically the involvement of the patient in the planning of his release and his consent to any conditions proposed are desirable. It is submitted that the making of a Code of Practice supplementing the Bill's provisions and incorporating these elements of the planning and implementation of temporary release would be desirable. In addition it is desirable that the Mental Health Review Board should have power to review conditions attached to temporary release.

Section 13(5) states that a patient who, by reason of having been temporarily released from a designated centre, is at large shall be deemed to be unlawfully at large if (a) the period for which he or she was temporarily released has expired or (b) a condition to which his or her release was made subject has been broken.

Section 13(7) provides that without prejudice to any other power conferred by law, a member of the Garda Síochána or an officer or servant of the designated centre may arrest without warrant any person who s/he suspects to be unlawfully at large while subject to an order for his or her detention in a designated centre under the Act and bring him or her back to such centre.

Section 13(6) states that where, by reason of the breach of the condition to which his or her release was made subject, a patient is deemed to be unlawfully at large and is arrested under section 13(7) or otherwise or returns voluntarily the period for which he or she was temporarily released shall thereupon be deemed to have expired.

It is submitted that designated centres should have a clear policy outlined in a Code

---

[386] See *Eubanks v. Clarke* 454 F.Supp. 1022 (F.D. PA 1977).

[387] See Criminal Law (Insanity) Bill 2002, s.12(1)(b).

[388] The requirement that the consent of the Minister for Justice, Equality and Law Reform be obtained was designed "to ensure the public interest is safeguarded". See comments of Minister for Justice, Equality and Law Reform: 171 *Seanad Debates* Col. 773.

of Practice indicating the action which should be taken when a patient is "unlawfully at large."

It is submitted that constitutional due proces[389] requires that before a patient's leave is revoked s/he should at least be given written notice, be given an opportunity to make representations and except in emergencies have the right to a hearing before a Mental Health Review Board to contest the evidence upon which the temporary release is withdrawn. In emergencies the patient should have a right to a hearing when the emergency has passed.

It is submitted that provision should also be made by legislation for the extension of temporary release to be granted without the necessity of the patient's returning to hospital.

Part E: The Special Case of Infanticide

Current Law

Section 1(3) of the Infanticide Act 1949 provides that a woman is guilty of infanticide if by any wilful act or omission she causes the death of her child being a child under the age of twelve months, the circumstances are such that the act or omission would have amounted to murder but for the provisions of section 1 and at the time of the act or omission the balance of the woman's mind was disturbed by reason of her not having fully recovered from the effect of giving birth to the child or by reason of the effect of lactation consequent upon the birth of the child. Where these elements are established the accused person may be tried and punished as if for manslaughter.

The offence evolved from the practice of commuting the sentence of murder (which carried a death sentence up to 1964) to manslaughter in cases where a mother in distressed circumstances killed a child shortly after birth. In effect the creation of the offence amounted to acknowledgement that the physical effect of childbirth, hormonal changes, the weight of the responsibility of caring for a new life and in earlier years the stigma of illegitimacy could combine to create intolerable mental stresses for a new mother such that she ought not to be held to be punishable for the crime of murder.

Section 1(1) of the 1949 Act empowers the District Justice, on a preliminary investigation of a charge against a woman for the murder of her child under twelve months, to alter the charge to one of infanticide, if he thinks it proper, and send the accused person forward for trial on that charge. Where at the trial the jury are satisfied that the accused person is guilty of infanticide they may return a verdict accordingly. It is also possible for the offence of infanticide to be charged at the outset. Indeed this may be the most appropriate course where the Garda investigation reveals that the offence concerned falls squarely within the provisions of the Act.

In contrast to insanity where infanticide is raised as a defence the accused person bears no persuasive burden rather the burden is on the prosecution to disprove the evidence supporting infanticide beyond a reasonable doubt.[390] The question in issue being whether the balance of the accused person's "mind was disturbed by reason of

---

[389] See *Morrissey v. Brewer* 408 U.S. 471. In that case the US Supreme Court held that basic due process had to be applied before a prisoner's parole could be revoked.

[390] See *People (AG) v. Quinn* [1965] I.R. 366.

her not having fully recovered from the effect of giving birth." It has also been argued[391] that the wording of the section would encompass social stresses (such as inadequate housing, drain on meagre resources, failure to bond as a result of the mother being ill,) consequent upon birth which may have an effect on the mother. While undoubtedly a more enlightened and compassionate view it is respectfully submitted that the current wording of the section does have to be stretched somewhat to encompass it. For example the use of the word "recovered" does appear to suggest a return to a state which existed prior to the birth and the use of the word "effect" in the singular linked to the words "giving birth" does appear to suggest that what is in issue is the consequence of the physical act rather than the sociological consequences of the presence of another life. On the other hand if the interpretation of the section is to be limited to encompass the physical effects of birth such as exhaustion or hormonal changes it is likely that it is practical use is limited for it has been pointed out that mental illness is not now considered to be a significant cause of infanticide and that the relationship of incomplete recovery from the effects of childbirth such as physical exhaustion or hormonal changes or lactation to the child killing remote[392] from which one may conclude that the section may indeed be the product of the assumptions of undeveloped psychiatric medicine of an earlier era.[393]

Commentary

The view of the Royal College of Psychiatrists in England is that the effect of giving birth was joined as a factor in child killings by sociological stresses such as: (1) overwhelming stress from the social environment being highlighted by the birth of the baby, with the emphasis on the unsuitability of the accommodation etc; (2) overwhelming stress from an additional member to a household struggling with poverty; (3) psychological injury and pressures and stress from a husband or other member of a family from the mother's incapacity to arrange the demands of the extra member of the family; (4) failure of bonding between the mother and child through illness or disability which impairs the development of the mother's capacity to care for the infant"

In the light of these findings the Criminal Law Reform Committee in England recommended extending the definition of the offence to the balance of the mother's mind being disturbed by the effect of giving birth to the child or "circumstances consequent upon the birth".[394] On the other hand it has been argued that the intolerable pressure of environmental circumstances do not enter into the equation where other offenders are charged with murder and are unprovoked by their victims.[395]

It may be that the introduction of a defence of diminished responsibility wide enough to cover the circumstances of infanticide may result in the section 1 of the Infanticide

---

[391] See Charleton, *Offences against the Person*, p.190.

[392] *Butler Commitee Report* Cmnd 6244 at paras.19.23–19.24.

[393] The English Criminal Law Revision Committee was presented with evidence indicating that a syndrome known as lactation insanity was recognised in the early part of the century but that there was little or no evidence to support the existence of such an illness. See Criminal Law Revision Committee "Offences against the Person Report", para.107.

[394] Offences against the Person Report, para.106.

[395] See Hoggett, *Mental Health Law* (3rd ed.), p.172.

Act 1949 falling into relative disuse. On the other hand the Criminal Law Revision Committee has pointed out that one of the benefits of retention of the section is that it avoids the necessity of charging a mother with murder.[396]

Position under Criminal Law (Insanity) Bill 2002

The offence of infanticide is not addressed in the 2002 Bill.

PART F: THE POWER OF COURTS TO ORDER THE TREATMENT OF OFFENDERS WITH MENTAL ILLNESS GENERALLY

Present Law

Under the present law where an accused person during the trial or prior to sentencing appears to be suffering from mental disorder the judge may postpone sentence remanding him/her on bail on the understanding that s/he seeks assessment and/or treatment. The Probation and Welfare Service facilitates such assessment and treatment by liaising with the person's local psychiatric service or with the forensic psychiatric service.

The court may also remand a person convicted of a criminal offence to custody with a recommendation that s/he be psychiatrically assessed prior to sentencing. Where the accused person consents remand is for twenty one days. Where s/he does not the accused person is remanded for seven days. Another option available is for the court to annex a recommendation for psychiatric treatment to a sentence which the prison service must then arrange. The accused person is either treated in prison or in severe cases by the transfer of the prisoner to the Central Mental Hospital. In the recent case of *People (DPP) v. MC*[397] the court suspended four years of a six year prison sentence on condition that the offender give an undertaking to abide in a treatment programme prescribed for him.

Under the current law the courts however, have no power to remand a person to a psychiatric hospital for assessment or treatment. Where courts have requested a psychiatric opinion the assessment more often than not takes place in prison albeit the person undergoing assessment may be transferred to the Central Mental Hospital at the request of a psychiatrist. Further the courts have no power to order that a convicted person be sent directly to a psychiatric hospital for treatment. The most that a judge can do is, as pointed out above, to annex a recommendation for psychiatric treatment to a sentence of imprisonment. As long ago as 1978 the Interdepartmental Committee on Mentally Ill and Maladjusted Persons (The Henchy Committee)[398] observed that "the inability or restricted ability of the courts to order that convicted persons receive appropriate treatment is a grave defect in the present state of the criminal law."

---

[396] See Criminal Law Revision Committee, Offences against the Person, Working Paper 26.
[397] Unreported, High Court, June 16, 1995.
[398] Third Interim Report of the Interdepartmental Committee of Mentally Ill and Maladjusted Persons (1978).

Current Proposals for Reform

The Government White Paper on Mental Health addresses this issue[399] by proposing that where in the course of proceedings before a court the defence or the judge raised the issue of mental disorder the court should arrange for the Probation and Welfare Service to carry out a report on the accused person or convicted person. If that report recommends that a medical report is necessary the court will be empowered to order that a medical examination be carried out and a report be made by a consultant psychiatrist in a service in the area in which the accused person or convicted person normally resides to establish whether s/he is suffering from a mental disorder, if so, the seriousness of that disorder. Mental disorder in this regard will be defined as including mental illness, mental handicap and dementia. The psychiatrist will also be required to make recommendations as to the most appropriate form of care. Where the medical report indicates that the person concerned is suffering from a mental disorder which is not severe and the person is willing to accept treatment either as an outpatient or inpatient s/he will be required to enter into a recognisance that s/he will accept treatment in the service in which the consultant psychiatrist is employed and the case will be adjourned until the treatment is completed.

Where the medical report indicates that the mental disorder is of such severity that the criteria for involuntary detention are met[400] and the person is not willing to accept treatment on a voluntary basis the consultant psychiatrist will be empowered to detain that person. In that event the psychiatrist would be obliged to inform the court of the order and the judge would be required to adjourn the case until the person had recovered sufficiently to continue the trial or to face sentence. The accused person or convicted person would be detained in an approved centre in which the consultant psychiatrist who made the medical report was attached initially for twenty eight days, with provision for extensions for a further three months followed by a further period of six months and by periods of one year thereafter. In each case the extension would be reviewed by the Mental Health Review Board. Following treatment the accused person would return to court for completion of the trial or sentencing.

Where the medical report indicates that the accused person or convicted person is suffering from a mental disorder that is so serious that he or she meets the criteria for involuntary admission, is unwilling to accept treatment on a voluntary basis and that his or her behaviour is so disturbed that s/he requires psychiatric care in the secure environment of a special psychiatric centre and the clinical director of the special psychiatric centre confirms the need for such treatment then the consultant psychiatrist may detain the person and arrange for his or her transfer to the special psychiatric centre. This decision to transfer will be subject to review by the Mental Health Review Board. Detention will be for an initial period of twenty eight days with the possibility of extension for three months followed by a further period of six months and thereafter for

---

[399] See paras 7.1–7.21.

[400] *viz.* because of a mental disorder there is a serious likelihood of the person causing immediate or imminent harm to him or herself or to other persons or where the mental disorder is severe and the persons judgment is impaired failure to admit or detain that person is likely to lead to a serious deterioration in his or her condition or will prevent the giving of appropriate treatment that can only be given by admission to an approved centre. See para.2.35.

a year. The Mental Health Review Board will be empowered to review the decision to detain for a year and subsequently at two yearly intervals thereafter.

The White Paper also proposes that power be conferred on the courts to remand an accused person or convicted person to custody for treatment for example in cases where bail is refused and a medical report indicates that the person concerned requires treatment for a mental disorder. In this case it is envisaged that treatment may be provided in prison or in severe cases by transferring a person from prison to a special psychiatric centre.

Commentary

The White Paper proposals are deficient and give rise to concern in a number of respects.

1. The White Paper proposes to empower the court to direct that a psychiatric report be carried out. If such examination is to be meaningful it is desirable that the consent of the accused person where competent be sought to the order being made.

2. Any proposed legislation should provide in detail for the form and content of psychiatric reports. The proposed form and content should be designed to encourage the understandable presentation of psychiatric evidence and discourage psychiatrists from testifying in legally conclusive terms.

3. Before an accused person or convicted person is required to enter into a recognisance to receive psychiatric treatment the relevant consultant psychiatrist should be required to demonstrate that the service in which he is employed has the facilities to assist the accused person and that better facilities are not available elsewhere. The court should also be satisfied that the accused person understands the nature of the treatment proposed and has consented to it before accepting his/her recognisance in relation to treatment.

4. The case of the accused person whose mental disorder is not severe and who is unwilling to accept treatment is not addressed in the White Paper proposals. There is a danger that the accused person's unwillingness to accept treatment may be cited as evidence that his/her mental disorder is more severe than is actually the case and compulsory powers employed in unjustifiable circumstances.

5. It is undesirable that a consultant psychiatrist be empowered to detain an accused person referred to him for psychiatric examination. The role of the psychiatrist is to assist the court in making decisions regarding the most appropriate form of treatment not to assume to himself/herself its decisionmaking powers. In order to ensure that the accused person or convicted person continues to benefit from the safeguards of the criminal law in relation to trial and/or sentence, decisions relating to the detention of an accused person or convicted person should be made by the judge after consideration of the psychiatrists report.[401]

---

[401] The necessity for such a course to be taken is further emphasised by the fact that the White Paper does not specify precisely how mental disorder will be defined beyond indicating that it will include the subjectively and vaguely defined categories of mental illness, mental handicap and dementia which form the basis for the exercise of the powers of civil commitment and that it will be wider

6. Counsel for the prosecution and defence should be empowered to make representations in relation to the medical report presented to the court and on treatment options before an order remanding an accused person or convicted person in custody for treatment is made.

7. The White Paper recommends that the court have power to remand an accused person or convicted person in custody for treatment. The treatment of an offender without his/her consent may amount to an unwarranted interference with his/her constitutional right to bodily integrity.[402] Before making the order the court should be satisfied that the accused person or convicted person understands the nature of any treatment proposed by the remand order and has consented to it. An order for treatment of an accused person without his consent should not be made unless it is clearly shown that the accused person lacks the capacity to consent to same or there is a need for emergency treatment.

8. Before an order remanding an accused person or convicted person to custody is made the court should be satisfied that any treatment proposed is for the individual's benefit and recognised as likely to be effective for the condition diagnosed. It should also be demonstrated that the proposed treatment does not unreasonably subject the individual to danger to life, limb or mental impairment. Further it is submitted that it be a condition precedent to the making of an order remanding an accused person or convicted person in custody for treatment that the prison[403] or psychiatric hospital demonstrate that they have the facilities to assist the offender and have agreed to accept the offender for treatment.[404]

9. It is submitted that the judge should have power to direct that a term of imprisonment be spent in whole or in part in a psychiatric hospital.[405]

---

and more comprehensive than this (see para.7.16). In addition the fact that the consultant psychiatrist who makes the report as to the necessity for detention for treatment is attached to the approved centre in which the accused person is to receive treatment (see para.7.18) must give rise to concern. In a case of civil commitment such a connection would disqualify a medical practitioner from making a recommendation. Moreover the nature of the "disturbed" behaviour which gives rises to necessity for detention in a secure unit is not specified (see para.7.19). Moreover the conferring of power on a consultant psychiatrist to detain a person and transfer him/her to a secure unit without the possibility of review by an independent authority for nine months and twenty eight days is a development which must give rise to concern and is likely to be a breach of Art.5(4) of the European Convention.

[402] While some may feel that society is justified in imposing any treatment on offenders if it will reduce the possibility of further criminality the assumption that psychiatric treatment has a pronounced effect on criminality is an assumption not always borne out by the facts.

[403] Prisons in particular are not presently seen as institutions of treatment with custody taking priority over treatment and punishment over rehabilitation.

[404] The Law Reform Commission of Canada makes similar recommendations in its *Report to Parliament on Mental Disorder in the Criminal Process* (March 1976). It notes: "The requirement of consent and full consultation should avoid over burdening already overtaxed psychiatric services with individuals they may not be able to help because of inadequate and non-existent services or lack of co-operation, p.24.

[405] In its Report on *Mental Disorder in the Criminal Process* (March 1976) the Law Reform Commission of Canada favoured the making of hospital orders in this regard. Under the terms of the proposed scheme where the offender has been convicted the accused person, prosecution or presiding judge would be empowered to raise the question as to whether a hospital order would be appropriate.

10. In general the White Paper Proposals for Reform tend to be concerned with issues relating to expedient disposition of mentally ill offenders and do not consider with sufficient particularity the wide range of options which could be available to a judge considering a sentence. Sentencing options elsewhere serve to highlight the need for a more thorough investigation of alternatives in that regard.[406]

PART E: THE PRISONER WITH MENTAL DISABILITY[407]

Introduction

The European Committee for the Prevention of Torture and Inhuman and Degrading Treatment or Punishment in its report on Ireland issued in 1998 stated that "in comparison with the rest of the population, there is a high incidence of psychiatric symptoms among

Before making the order the judge would be obliged to remand the offender to a psychiatric institution for examination to determine whether the accused person is suffering from a psychiatric disorder that is susceptible to treatment and whether the institution to which he has been remanded or another institution would be able and willing to provide a program of treatment. Having considered the psychiatric report and the representations of both defence counsel and the prosecution the presiding judge would have a discretion to make the order with the consent of the accused person and the agreement of the appropriate psychiatric institution. The Commission recommended that release procedures generally should be governed by the same principles and criteria as ordinary prison sentences and be under the general supervision of the Sentencing Supervision Board or in appropriate circumstances the sentencing court. An offender who had consented to the hospital order would be empowered to request the Sentence Supervision Board or the sentencing court to order that the balance of his sentence be served in prison even if he could still benefit for further treatment in hospital. He could also apply to the Board to be transferred to another hospital if he is not receiving the anticipated treatment. The hospital administration would be empowered to request the Sentence Supervision Board or the sentencing court to transfer the offender back to prison at any time before the expiration of the hospital order. Before the transfer would be made, however, the offender would be informed in writing of the reason for the discharge and have the right to apply to the Sentence Review Board for transfer to another hospital. An offender sentenced to a hospital order would be entitled to parole. The hospital authorities would also have power to recommend for psychiatric reasons that the offender be released on parole rather than returned to prison. The offender serving his sentence under a hospital order would be deemed to be serving his sentence in prison for the purposes of escapes and being at large without lawful excuse. Other rights and privileges such a recreation, visiting, correspondence or temporary absences would be governed by the rules and regulations of the psychiatric institution and such criteria as fairness and decency as would be prescribed by law. The judges decision to impose or not to impose a hospital order could be appealed in the same manner as any other sentence of the court.

[406] In England and Wales for instance the courts have a considerable range of powers at their disposal when dealing with an offender with a mental illness at the sentencing stage. In 1948 express power was given to the English judiciary to insert conditions relating to psychiatric treatment in probation and (in the case of offenders under the age of 17 years) supervision orders. See Powers of Criminal Courts Act 1973 s.3(1), Children and Young Persons Act 1969, s.7(7)(b) and Children Act 1989, Sch.3, para.5(1) The courts also have powers in specified circumstances to make: (i) a hospital order directing the detention of an offender in a named hospital, (ii) an interim hospital order authorising detention in hospital for a period not exceeding 12 weeks renewable for up to six months, (iii) a restriction order where it is necessary to protect the public from serious harm or (iv) an order placing the offender under the guardianship of a local social services authority or private individual. See Mental Health Act 1983, ss.37, 38, 40, 41, 42, 43.

[407] See generally McDermott P., *Prison Law* (Round Hall Ltd, Dublin, 2000), Amnesty International *Mental Illness The Neglected Quarter Marginalised Groups*, November 2003.

prisoners".[408] In a General Healthcare Study of the Irish Prisoner Population commissioned by the Minister for Justice Equality and Law Reform[409] in 2000 it was found that all the mental health indicators were much worse for prisoners than the general population. In his first report the newly appointed Inspector of Prisons and Places of Detention observed in 2003 that "[t]he prison has become a dumping ground for many of the psychiatrically ill amongst us. This issue has been raised in [the Prison Chaplains'] annual report for years".[410]

There is also a high level of intellectual disability in the Irish prisoner population. In a "Survey of the Level of Learning Disability among the Prison Population in Ireland" carried out in 1999 on behalf of the Irish Government[411] 254 prisoners representing about 10 per cent of prisoners in Irish prisons were randomly selected and were given an intelligence test. 28.8 per cent scored so low as to suggest a significant degree of intellectual disability. It was also indicated that there was a strong possibility of the dual conditions of mental illness and intellectual disability in this group.

Despite these established facts it is widely acknowledged that the treatment and care afforded to prisoners with mental illness and intellectual disability in the prison system is extremely unsatisfactory and falls far short of international standards.[412] The question therefore is to what extent can the law be called in aid by the prisoner with mental illness or intellectual disability to secure appropriate treatment and/or care.

Current Law

Psychiatric Treatment in Prison

The State has a constitutional duty to protect the health of persons whom it imprisons.[413] This duty arises from the prisoner's unenumerated personal constitutional right to bodily integrity.[414] The duty extends to a prisoner's psychiatric and mental health.[414] However the standard of care which must be provided does not appear to be equivalent with standards of care available outside of prison. In the US case of *Harris v. Thigpen*[416] Fay J. stated:

> "Unfortunately, as with all medical care provided to prisoners, it is not constitutionally required that mental health care be "perfect, the best obtainable of even very good".

---

[408] Report to the Irish Government on the visit to Ireland carried out by the European Committee for the Prevention of Torture and Inhuman or Degrading Treatment or Punishment from August 31 to September 9, 1998 CPT/ Inf (99) 15 (EN) Publication date December 17, 1998.

[409] The report was produced by the Centre for Health Promotion Studies, Department of Health Promotion, National University of Ireland, Galway.

[410] First Annual Report of the Inspector of Prisons and Places of Detention" Department of Justice, Equality and Law Reform (2003).

[411] Murphy M., Harrold Dr M., Carey Dr S. and Mulrooney M., Department of Justice, Equality and Law Reform, August 6, 1999.

[412] See *Mental Illness The Neglected Quarter, Marginalised Groups* Report by Amnesty International November 2003.

[413] *State (Richardson) v. Governor of Mountjoy Prison* [1980] I.L.R.M. 82.

[414] See *State (C) v. Frawley* [1976] I.R. 365.

[415] *Harris v. Thigpen* 941 F. 2d 1495 (1991).

[416] (1991) 941 F. 2d 1495.

Further in the Irish case of *State (C) v. Frawley*[417] the court refused to intervene in relation to the standard of psychiatric care available in a prison to a prisoner suffering from a sociopathic personality disturbance who was at the time of application being treated by being kept in solitary confinement in prison and occasionally detained in the Central Mental Hospital, where his treatment consisted solely of sedation and custodial care. The court refused to order the building of a specialised psychiatric unit equipped with specially trained staff where the applicant could be involuntarily detained which on the unchallenged evidence was the only long term psychiatric treatment which would have had a reasonable chance of benefiting the applicant. It also refused to order the applicant's release.

In the English case of *Knight v. The Home Office*[418] the English High Court also made it clear that the standard of care provided for a prisoner with mental health difficulties was not required to be as high as the standard of care provided in a psychiatric hospital outside prison. In that case the deceased prisoner was known to have suicidal tendencies. He was subject to the prison's special watch procedure where he was observed at intervals of not less than 15 minutes. Because he was also violent he deemed not suitable for accommodation in the prison's hospital wing where he would have been subject to a continuous watch. He was instead placed in a cell and subjected to the special watch procedure. On one occasion between 15 minute intervals he committed suicide by hanging. His personal representatives sued in negligence. Pill J. held that the standard of care provided for a mentally ill prisoner detained in a prison hospital was not required to be as high as the standard of care provided in a psychiatric hospital outside of prison. Psychiatric hospitals and prison hospitals performed different functions and the duty of care in respect of each type of hospital had to be tailored to act and function to be performed. Consequently Pill J. held that there had been no negligence on the part of the hospital wing of the prison in failing to provide the same patient/staff ratio which existed in psychiatric hospitals. Applying the accepted practice text for determining the standard of care in medical negligence cases he held that the prison staff had not been negligent in failing to keep the deceased under continuous observation since their decision to observe him at 15 minute intervals was a decision which ordinarily skilled medical staff in their position could have made.

Livingstone and Owen point out that the decision in *Knight* is open to challenge on the basis that when a prison keeps physically or mentally ill people in prison instead of transferring them to a hospital the standard against which the standard of care should be measured should be the standard that applies to the institutions the prisoners would have gone to had they not been detained.[419]

There is a dearth of authority on the issue of whether the duty to safeguard the psychiatric health of a prisoner would extend to the provision of counselling, psychotherapy and mental health education. Such authority as exists tends towards a narrow view that the constitutional duty does not extend this far.[420] Further the existing authority appears to suggest that there is no constitutional duty owed by the prison authorities to help prisoners cope with the ordinary mental stresses of detention such as

---

[417] [1976] I.R. 365.
[418] [1990] 3 All E.R. 237.
[419] *Prison Law* (2nd ed., 1999), p.201–202.
[420] *Harris v. Thigpen* (1991) 941 F. 2d 1495.

psychological depression.[421] In *State (Smith) v. Governor of Curragh Military Detention Barracks*[422] the applicant sought an order of *habeas corpus* on the basis that he was unable to cope with his position as a prisoner. Medical evidence was adduced to support this contention and established that he had attempted to kill himself on a number of occasions. Barrington J came to the conclusion that the applicant was suffering from reactive depression and found it difficult to endure prison conditions. He also found that he had suffered more deeply from his confinement than prisoners normally do or than a court would normally contemplate in imposing a sentence of imprisonment. While he was of the opinion that these factors were matters which the Minister for Justice, Equality and Law Reform might take into consideration in deciding whether to remit a portion of the prosecutor's sentence or to release him on parole they did not make his detention illegal and accordingly an order of *habeas corpus* could not issue.

Consent to Treatment

The legal principles regarding consent to and refusal of medical treatment which apply to prisoners of full capacity are similar to those which apply to persons outside prison.[423]

Transfer to Central Mental Hospital

Transfer to the Central Mental Hospital is effected by means of a number of anachronistic nineteenth century and early twentieth century pieces of legislation.

The most commonly used provision under which prisoners are transferred is section 8 of the Lunatic Asylums (Ireland) Act 1845 which empowers the Minister for Justice Equality and Law Reform to order and direct that "criminal lunatics" who are in custody in prison to be removed without delay to the Central Mental Hospital and be kept there so long as the "criminal lunatic" shall be detained in custody.

If section 19 and the Schedule to the Criminal Law (Insanity) Bill is enacted this provision will be repealed.

Where a prisoner is suffering from mental disorder he may be transferred to a district mental hospital or the Central Mental Hospital for treatment under section 2 of the Criminal Lunatics (Ireland) Act 1838. Section 2 of the 1838 Act as amended and adapted by section 8 of the Criminal Justice Act 1960[424] provides specifically that the Minister for Justice, Equality and Law Reform may, at his discretion, direct that any person in jail under sentence of imprisonment who is certified by two medical practitioners to be insane to be removed to the district mental hospital for the area in which the person is in custody, the Central Mental Hospital or to any district mental hospital and shall be detained in that hospital until it shall be duly certified to the Minister by two medical practitioners that the person has become of sound mind whereupon the Minister may direct the remittal of the person to the prison from which he was taken if the person is

[421] *Harris v. Thigpen* (1991) 941 F. 2d 1495.
[422] [1980] I.L.R.M. 208.
[423] *Freeman v. The Home Office* [1984] 1 All E.R. 1036.
[424] S.2 of the 1838 Act is expressly preserved by s.284 of the Mental Treatment Act 1945 and s.284 is in turn preserved by s.6 and the Schedule to the Mental Health Act 2001.

still subject to custody. If the period of imprisonment or custody of the person shall have expired then the person must be discharged.

Section 8(2) of the 1960 Act extends the Minister for Justice, Equality and Law Reform's powers and provides that where a person is detained under section 2 the Minister may, at his discretion by order direct the transfer of the person: (a) if he is detained in the Central Mental Hospital to a district mental hospital and (b) if he is detained in a district mental hospital to the Central Mental Hospital or to another district mental hospital and where a person is so transferred under section 8(2) references to an "asylum" in section 2 of the 1838 Act are to be construed as references to the Central Mental Hospital or to the district mental hospital to which the person is transferred as the case may be and section 2 is to have effect accordingly.

The section assumes that a certification by two medical practitioners that the prisoner is "insane" means that the prisoner lacks capacity to give consent to psychiatric treatment and may consequently be treated in his best interests.

Section 2 of the 1838 Act remains in force despite the enactment of the Mental Health Act 2001 and its repeal is not envisaged by the Criminal Law (Insanity) Bill 2002.

There is no specially equipped psychiatric facility for prisoners within the Irish prison system. As a result prisoners requiring hospitalisation are frequently transferred to the Central Mental Hospital under the above provision. The Committee for Prevention of Torture and Inhuman and Degrading Treatment was informed in 1993 that it could take "some time" to arrange such transfers and periods of up to two weeks were not uncommon.[425] During this time it has not been uncommon in practice for prisoners to be held for not inconsiderable periods in isolation in padded cells a practice which may be in breach of Article 3 of the European Convention on Human Rights as constituting inhuman and degrading treatment. The practice has however been recently addressed by the Minister for Justice, Equality and Law Reform who has directed the Director General of the Prison Service "to replace them with safety observation cells which, while soft surfaced so as to protect the prisoner from self-harm will fully meet the needs and respect the dignity of the prisoner in every way consistent with his or her safety".[426]

Section 12 of the Central Criminal Lunatic Asylum (Ireland) Act 1845[427] provides that it shall be lawful for the Minister for Justice, Equality and Law Reform to direct by warrant that any person sentenced to imprisonment or in any district mental hospital and in respect of whom two registered medical practitioners have certified that that person has become "insane" shall be removed to the Central Mental Hospital. Every

---

[425] Report to Irish Government on the visit to Ireland carried out by the European Committee for the Prevention of Torture and Inhuman and Degrading Treatment or Punishment (CPT) from September 26 to October 5, 1993 CPT/ Inf (95) 14 para. 134.

[426] Letter to the Irish Penal Reform Trust dated December 11, 2002 In a follow-up report on padded cells the Irish Penal Reform Trust noted that the new cells would bring with them physical improvements on the old padded cells. The new cells would have fixed beds on plinths at normal bed height; all walls would be soft surfaced so as to protect the prisoner from self harm; there would be a call button in every cell; toilets would exist in or adjacent to each observation cell and a gown would be provided to prisoners who would no longer be naked. See Bresnihan V., "To be or not to be, in observation cells? A discussion paper on the introduction of observation cells for mentally ill and suicidal prisoners? IPRT (2003).

[427] 8 & 9 Vict. c.107.

person so removed shall remain in detention in that hospital so long as the person shall remain subject to custody or until it is certified to the Minister for Justice, Equality and Law Reform by two registered medical practitioners that the person has become of sound mind. In these events if the person remains subject to be continued in custody, the Minister for Justice, Equality and Law Reform is authorised to issue a warrant to the person in charge of the Central Mental Hospital directing that the person shall be remitted to the prison or the place of confinement from which s/he shall have been taken or if the person is entitled to discharge to direct the discharge accordingly.

Section 8(2) of the Criminal Justice Act 1960 provides that where a person is detained under section 12 of the Central Criminal Lunatic Asylum (Ireland) Act 1845 the Minister at his discretion may, at his discretion, by order under section 8 (2) direct the transfer of the person (a) if he is detained in the Central Mental Hospital, to a district mental hospital, and (b) if he is detained in a district mental hospital, to the Central Mental Hospital to another district mental hospital.

The Criminal Law (Insanity) Bill 2002 does not envisage the repeal of section 12 of the 1845 Act.

A further provision which is frequently called in aid to facilitate the transfer of the prisoners to hospital is section 17(6) of the Criminal Justice Administration Act 1914. In effect it provides that the Minister for Justice, Equality and Law Reform on being satisfied that a prisoner is suffering from a disease and cannot be properly treated in the prison, or that he should undergo or desires to undergo a surgical operation which cannot properly be performed in the prison may order that the prisoner be taken to a hospital or other suitable place for the purpose of treatment or the operation and while absent from the prison in pursuance of such an order the prisoner shall be deemed to be in legal custody.

However this provision is limited to situations where a prisoner is suffering from a "disease" and it must be questioned whether in the light of modern knowledge of psychiatry it applies to prisoners suffering from mental illness. This provision is however expressly preserved by section 284 of the Mental Treatment Act 1945 and there are no proposals to repeal in the Criminal Law (Insanity) Bill 2002.

The Prison Rules

The Rules for the Government of Prisons 1947 contain detailed provisions regarding day to day attendance to the health needs of prisoners. They set out the day to day duties of medical officers, prison officers and governors of prisons regarding the health including the mental health of prisoners.[428] In practice however, the rules, insofar as they relate to health care have come to be regarded as obsolete, "outmoded and impractical" in light of modern prison conditions and have been ignored by the authorities.[429] In *Brennan v. Governor of Portlaoise Prison*[430] Budd J highlighting the need for reform of the rules in the light of this situation pointed to the unfairness and oppression and deprivation of

---

[428] See generally McDermott P.A., *Prison Law* (Round Hall Press, Dublin, 2000), pp.290–298.
[429] See *Brennan v. Governor of Portlaoise Prison* [1999] 1 I.L.R..M. 190 at 194.
[430] [1999] 1 I.L.R.M. 190.

basic rights which may result from such a situation of "divergence between the rules and practice".[431]

The European Convention on Human Rights

It is clear from the decision of the European Court of Human Rights in *Keenan v. United Kingdom*[432] that the lack of appropriate medical treatment can amount "inhuman and degrading" treatment contrary to Article 3 of the European Convention on Human Rights which provides that:

> "No one shall be subjected to torture or to inhuman or degrading treatment or punishment."

In that case the applicant's son had been diagnosed as suffering from paranoid schizophrenia and had a history of threatening to kill himself. He was initially admitted to the prison health care centre. Various attempts had been made to transfer him to the ordinary prison but were unsuccessful because his condition deteriorated whenever he was transferred. On one occasion after the question of being transferred to the main prison was raised with him he assaulted two hospital officers, one seriously. He was placed the same day in a segregation unit of the prison punishment block. He was subsequently found guilty of assault and his overall prison sentence (of four months for assault) was increased by 28 days including seven extra days in segregation in the punishment block. On the day after sentence he was discovered hanging from the bars of his cell.

The court held that the lack of adequate specialist medical supervision before the death of the prisoner who was a known suicide risk combined with additional internal disciplinary punishment on him amounted to the subjection of a prisoner to inhuman and degrading treatment by the prison authorities.

In the course of its judgment the court stated that the that ill treatment had to attain a minimum level of severity if it was to fall within the scope of Article 3. The assessment of that minimum was relative and depended on the circumstances of the case such as the duration of the treatment, its physical and mental effects and the state of health of the victim. Treatment could be described as degrading when it was such as to arouse feelings of fear, anguish and inferiority capable of humiliating or debasing the victim and possibly breaking their physical or moral resistance or as driving the victim to act against his will or conscience.

The court held that it was relevant to note that the authorities were under an obligation to protect the health of persons deprived of their liberty. The lack of appropriate treatment could amount to treatment contrary to article 3. The assessment of whether the treatment or punishment concerned was incompatible with the standards of Article 3 had, in the case of persons with mental illness to take into consideration their vulnerability and their inability in some cases to complain coherently or at all about how they are being affected by any particular treatment.

---

[431] [1999] 1 I.L.R.M. 190 at 210.
[432] (2001) 33 E.H.R.R. 38; *The Times*, April 18, 2001.

The court was struck by the fact that there was a lack of medical notes concerning the prisoner who was an identifiable suicide risk and undergoing the additional stresses that could be foreseen from segregation and later, disciplinary punishment. The inadequate concern to maintain full and detailed records where there were a number of prison doctors involved in caring for him undermined the effectiveness of any monitoring or supervision process.

Although the prisoner asked the prison doctor to point out to the governor at the adjudication that the assault occurred after a change in medication there was no reference to a psychiatrist for advice either as to his future treatment or his fitness for adjudication and punishment.

The court found the lack of effective monitoring of the prisoner's condition and the lack of informed psychiatric input into his assessment and treatment disclosed significant defects in the medical care provided to a mentally ill person known to be a suicide risk. The belated imposition on him in those circumstances of a serious disciplinary punishment which might well have threatened is physical and moral resistance was not compatible with the standard of treatment required in respect of a mentally ill person. Accordingly the court found by a majority[433] that Article 3 had been breached.

However the court held that the prisoner's right to life guaranteed by Article 2 of the Convention had not been breached because although the variability of the prisoner's mental state required that he be monitored carefully, the prison authorities did all that was reasonably expected of them placing him in hospital care and under watch, and they had not omitted any step which should reasonably have been taken.

Since sections 2 and 4 of the European Convention on Human Rights Act 2003 came into force on 31 December 2003 courts are obliged to interpret Irish rules of law including rules of common law in a manner with the state's obligations under the European Convention on Human Rights and to take judicial notice of the Convention provisions and decisions of the European Court of Human Rights and when interpreting and applying the Convention provisions it must take due account of the principles laid down in its decisions.

European "Soft Law" Standards

There have been a variety of initiatives taken at European level to set standards of international best practice in the field of mental health care in prisons. These initiatives are significant in they bring international pressure to bear on governments to frame their legislation and practice so as to conform with the stated internationally accepted standards and the initiatives also form part of the development of customary international law in the mental health field

European Committee for the Prevention of Torture Reports
At the European Regional level the European Committee for the Prevention of Torture and Inhuman or Degrading Treatment or Punishment (CPT) established under the European Convention for the Prevention of Torture and Inhuman and Degrading Treatment or Punishment 1987 has been involved in monitoring activities under the

---

[433] Judges Fuhrmann and Kuris dissenting.

provisions of Convention examining the treatment of persons deprived of their liberty and particular their health care with a view to strengthening the protection of such persons from torture and from inhuman or degrading treatment or punishment.[434]

In its Third General Report on its activities covering the period January 1 to December 31, 1992[435] the European Committee for the Prevention of Torture and Inhuman or Degrading Treatment or Punishment (CPT) specifically addressed the issue of health care in prisons and stated that an inadequate level of health care afforded to persons deprived of their liberty "can lead rapidly to situations falling within the scope of the term "inhuman and degrading treatment.""[436] It made it clear in its report that it attached particular importance to the general principle that "prisoners are entitled to the same level of medical care as persons living in the community at large". It stated:

"This principle is inherent in the fundamental rights of the individual."[437]

One of the considerations which guided the CPT during its visits to prisons was the matter of equivalence of care. In relation to the provision of psychiatric care the CPT noted that in comparison with the general population there was a high incidence of psychiatric symptoms among prisoners. As a consequences it was of the view that a doctor qualified in psychiatry should be attached to the health care service of each prison and some of the nurses employed there should have training in this field.[438] It added that the provision of medical and nursing staff, as well as the layout of prisons should be such as to enable regular pharmacological, psychotherapeutic and occupational therapy programmes to be carried out.[439] It stated that prison management had a role to play in the early detection of prisoners suffering from psychiatric ailment such as depression or reactive state with a view to enabling the appropriate adjustments to be made to their environment. This activity could be encouraged by the provision of appropriate health training for certain members of the custodial staff.[440]

In its first report investigating standards in Irish prisons in 1993 the CPT[441] emphasised that mentally ill prisoners should be kept and cared for in a hospital facility which is adequately equipped and possesses appropriately trained staff. That facility should be a civil mental hospital or a specially equipped psychiatric facility within the prison system. Whichever course was chosen the accommodation capacity of such a facility should be sufficient to avoid prolonged waiting periods before necessary transfers are effected. The Committee also recommended that the highest priority should be given to the transfer of prisoners with mental illness to an appropriate psychiatric facility.

Following its visit to Ireland in 1998 the Committee recommended that the provision of prison psychiatric services in Ireland be reorganised "as a matter of urgency" and that the aim should be to ensure that it is always possible to transfer mentally ill inmates

---

[434] See European Convention for the Prevention of Torture and Inhuman and Degrading Treatment or Punishment (1987), Art.1.

[435] CPT/Inf (93) 12 [EN] Publication Date: June 4, 1993.

[436] Para.30.

[437] Para.31.

[438] Para.41.

[439] Para.41.

[440] Para.42.

[441] C.P.T./Inf (95) 14 para.136.

to an appropriate psychiatric facility without delay.[442] Elaborating on the matter on in-patient care in prisons it stated:

> "A mentally ill prisoner should be kept and cared for in a hospital facility which is adequately equipped and possesses appropriately trained staff. That facility should be a civil mental hospital or a specially equipped psychiatric facility within the prison system. Whichever course is chosen, the accommodation capacity of the psychiatric facility in question should be sufficient to avoid prolonged waiting periods before necessary transfers are effected."

Following its visit to Ireland in 2002[443] the Committee noted that psychological support in the prisons it visited was very limited and recommended that the psychological services of the prisons visited be developed. In its response the Government referred to the difficulties in recruitment of psychologists to the prison Psychology Service and the fact that a steering group to oversee the development of the service was established in 2002.[444]

Council of Europe recommendation on European Prison Rules

The Council of Europe has also been involved in promulgating standards for prison rules. In its *Recommendation R(87) 3 of the Committee of Ministers to Member States on the European Prison Rules* the Committee of Ministers emphasised "the precepts of human dignity, the commitment of prison administrations to humane and positive treatment".[445]

Part 1 of the rules outlines a number of basic principles with underpin the operation of the rules. Among these are requirements that:

> "1. The deprivation of liberty shall be effected in material and moral conditions which ensure respect for human dignity and are in conformity with these rules.
> ..."

> "3. The purposes of the treatment of persons in custody shall be such as to sustain their health and self-respect and, so far as the length of sentence permits, to develop their sense of responsibility and encourage those attitudes and skills that will assist them to return to society with the best chance of leading law-abiding and self-supporting lives after their release.

> 4. There shall be regular inspections of penal institutions and services by qualified and experienced inspectors appointed by a competent authority. Their task

---

[442] Report to the Irish Government on the visit to Ireland carried out by the European Committee for the Prevention of Torture and Inhuman or Degrading Treatment or Punishment (CPT) from August 31 to September 9, 1998 CPT/Inf (99) 15, para.76.

[443] Report to the Government of Ireland on the visit to Ireland carried out by the European Committee for the Prevention of Torture and Inhuman and Degrading Treatment or Punishment (CPT) from May 20–28, 2002 CPT/Inf (2003) 36.

[444] CPT/Inf (2003) 37.

[445] Preamble.

shall be, in particular, to monitor whether and to what extent these institutions are administered in accordance with existing laws and regulations, the objectives of the prison services and the requirements of these rules".

The rules state at Rule 26(1):

"At every institution there shall be available the services of at least one qualified general practitioner. *The medical services should be organised in close relation with the health administration of the community or nation.* They shall include psychiatric service for the diagnosis and, in proper cases, the treatment of states of mental abnormality".

The recommendation for integrated health administration would clearly suggest that healthcare in prison should fall within the remit of the Department of Health and not be exclusively within the remit of the Department of Justice, Equality and Law Reform as is currently the case.

Rule 26 continues:

"Sick prisoners who require specialist treatment shall be transferred to specialist institutions or to civil hospitals. Where hospital facilities are provided in an institution, their equipment, furnishings and pharmaceutical supplies shall be suitable for the medical care and treatment of sick prisoners and there shall be a staff of suitably trained officers".[446]

Rule 29 recommends that an obligation be placed on a medical officer to conduct a mental and physical examination of prisoner on admission.

"The medical officer shall see and examine every prisoner as soon as possible after admission and thereafter as necessary, with a particular view to the discovery of physical or mental illness and the taking of all measures necessary for medical treatment ... the noting of physical or mental defects which might impede resettlement after release and the determination of the fitness of every prisoner to work."

Rule 30.2 acknowledges that prison may have an impact on a prisoner's mental health and imposes an obligation on the medical officer to be vigilant in this regard. It states:

"The medical officer shall report to the director whenever it is considered that a prisoner's physical or mental health has been or will be adversely affected by continued imprisonment or by any condition of imprisonment."

Rule 32 indicates a role for medical care and treatment in rehabilitation of prisoners. It states:

"The medical services of the institution shall seek to detect and shall treat any

---

[446] Rule 26.2.

physical or mental illnesses or defects which may impede a prisoner's resettlement after release. All necessary medical, surgical and psychiatric services including those available in the community shall be provided to the prisoner to that end."

Rule 42 provides that prisoners should have the opportunity to make requests or complaints to the director of the institution, to an inspector of prisons, central prison administration, the judicial authority or other proper authorities. The recognition of an effective right of complaint is in addition to the obligation of the state authorities to inspect prisons a means of enforcing and ensuring compliance with the rules.

Rule 100 specifically addresses the situation of prisoners with mental illness or impairment. It points specifically to the need for the provision of prompt treatment of and specialised facilities for the treatment of prisoners with mental illness and the desirability of the provision of psychiatric aftercare upon release from prison.:

> "1. Prisoners who are found to be insane should *not* be detained in prisons and arrangements shall be made to remove them to appropriate establishments for the mentally ill *as soon as possible.*
> 2. Specialised institutions or sections under medical management should be available for the observation and treatment of prisoners suffering gravely from any other mental disease or abnormality.
> 3. The medical or psychiatric service of the penal institutions shall provide for the psychiatric treatment of all prisoners who are in need of such treatment.
> 4. Action should be taken with the appropriate community agencies to ensure where necessary the continuation of psychiatric treatment after release and the provision of social psychiatric aftercare

Council of Europe recommendation concerning ethical and organisational aspects of health care in prisons

In addition to bodies monitoring standards of treatment under European Conventions the Council of Europe has been engaged in recommending standards to be adopted by governments by way of legislative and other measures in relation to the provision of psychiatric care throughout Europe. *Council of Europe Recommendation No. R(98)7 of the Committee of Ministers to Member States concerning the ethical and organisational aspects of health care in prison* addresses a number of the deficiencies relating to psychiatric care in prison and recommends that governments take the principles and recommendations in the Appendix to the Recommendation into account when reviewing their legislation and in their practice in the area of health care

Under the heading of main characteristics of the right to health in prison the Appendix to the Recommendation advises that on admission to prison:

> "[s]pecial emphasis should be put on the screening of mental disorder, of psychological adaptation to prison, of withdrawal symptoms resulting from use of drugs, medication or alcohol and of ... chronic conditions".[447]

---

[447] Appendix I A. 1.

It also recommends that:

> "5. An access to psychiatric consultation and counselling should be secured. There should be a psychiatric team in larger penal institutions. If this is not available as in the smaller institutions consultations should be assured by a psychiatrist, practising in hospital or in private."

The Appendix to the Recommendation specifically addresses the matter of equivalence of care between care in prison and that in the wider community and provides:

> "10. Health policy in custody should be integrated into, and compatible with national health policy. A prison health care service should be able to provide medical, [and] psychiatric ... treatment in conditions comparable to those enjoyed by the general public ...
> 11. The prison health care service should have a sufficient number of qualified medical, nursing and technical staff as well as appropriate premises, installations and equipment of a quality comparable if not identical to those which exist in the outside environment.
> 12. The role of the ministry responsible for health should be strengthened in the domain of quality assessment of hygiene, health care and organisation of health services in custody, in accordance with national legislation. A clear division of responsibilities and authority should be established between the ministry responsible for health or other competent ministries, which should co-operate in implementing a integrated health policy in prison."

It provides further under the rubric of "Professional Independence":

> "19. Doctors who work in prison should provide the individual inmate with the same standards of health care as are being provided to patients in the community"

At a later point addressing the professional training of prison health care staff the Appendix states:

> "34. Prison doctors should be well versed in both general medical and psychiatric disorders."

The Appendix to the Recommendation also addresses the need for the prisoner to have information about seeking help if necessary and advises that:

> "26. On admission to prison, each person should receive information on rights and obligations, the internal regulations of the establishment as well as guidelines as to how and where to get help and advice. This information should be understood by the inmate. Special instruction should be given to the illiterate."

Addressing specifically the issues raised by "psychiatric symptoms, mental disturbance and major personality disorders, and risk of suicide" The Appendix makes the following significant suggestions for reform of law and practice:

"52. The prison administration and the ministry responsible for mental health should co-operate in organising psychiatric services for prisoners.

53. Mental health services and social services attached to prisons should aim to provide help and advice for inmates and to strengthen their coping and adaptation skills....

55. Prisoners suffering from serious mental disturbance should be kept and cared for in a hospital facility which is adequately equipped and possesses appropriately trained staff....

56. In those cases where the use of close confinement of mental patients cannot be avoided, it should be reduced to an absolute minimum and be replaced with one to one continuous nursing care as soon as possible....

58. The risk of suicide should be constantly assessed both by medical and custodial staff. Physical methods designed to avoid self-harm, close and constant observation, dialogue and reassurance, as appropriate should be used in moments of crisis.

59. Follow up treatment for released inmates should be provided for at outside specialised services."

International Standards

At international level the United Nations has taken a number of initiatives to set standards applicable internationally for psychiatric practice in prisons.

The First UN Congress on the Prevention of Crime and the Treatment of Offenders in 1955 adopted *Standard Minimum Rules for the Treatment of Prisoners.*[448] These rules provided the model upon which the European Prison Rules are based and the European Prison Rules largely reiterate their provisions.

In 1990 the United Nations adopted *Basic Principles for the Treatment of Prisoners* Principle 5 of which states:

"Except for those limitations that are demonstrably necessitated by the fact of incarceration, all prisoners shall retain the human rights and fundamental freedoms set out in the Universal Declaration of Human Rights and the International Covenant on Economic, Social and Cultural Rights and the International Covenant on Civil and Political Rights, as well as such other rights as are set out in other United Nations covenants."

It follows from this that prisoners, at the very least are entitled to an equivalence of mental health care with the rest of the population a right which derive from the requirement of non-discrimination in Article 2(2) of the *International Covenant on Economic, Social and Cultural Rights.* Further authority for equivalence of mental health care may be found in Principle 9 of the *Basic Principles for the Treatment of Prisoners* which states:

---

[448] The Congress was held at Geneva in 1955 and the rules approved by the Economic and Social Council by its resolution 663C (XXIV) by July 31, 1957 and 2076 (LXII) of May 13, 1977.

"Prisoners shall have access to the health services available in the country without discrimination on the grounds of their legal situation"

The *United Nations Principles for the Protection of Persons with Mental Illness and the Improvement of Mental Health Care*[449] apply to persons serving sentences of imprisonment for criminal offences or who are otherwise detained in the course of criminal proceedings against them and who are determined to have a mental illness or who it is believed may have such an illness. By virtue of Principle 20.2 they are expressed to apply to such persons "to the fullest extent possible, with only such limited modifications and exceptions as are necessary in the circumstances." No such modifications and exceptions may prejudice the person's rights under the instruments noted in paragraph 5 of Principle 1 (the right of mentally ill person to exercise all human rights under certain international instruments).[450]

Accordingly Principle 8.1 potentially applies to the situation of prisoners with mental illness. It sets out a standard of equivalence of care and provides that every patient shall have the right to receive such health and social care as is appropriate to his or her health needs and is entitled to care and treatment in accordance with the same standards as other ill persons.

Principle 9.1 is also of particular relevance to the situation of persons with mental illness who are dealing with conditions of detention. It provides that every patient shall have the right to be treated in the least restrictive environment and with the least restrictive or intrusive treatment appropriate to the patient's health needs and the need to protect the physical safety of others.

Principle 14 is of particular relevance in the context of management of facilities providing care to prisoners with mental illness. It states that a mental health facility shall have access to the same level of resources as any other health establishment. The Principle goes further and states that such facilities should in particular have: (a) qualified medical and other appropriate professional staff in sufficient numbers and with adequate space to provide each patient with privacy and a programme of appropriate and active therapy; (b) diagnostic and therapeutic equipment for the patient; (c) appropriate professional care; and (d) adequate, regular and comprehensive treatment, including supplies of medication.

Principle 20.3 provides that domestic law may authorise a court or other competent authority acting on the basis of competent and independent medical advice to order that such persons be admitted to a mental health facility.

The World Health Organisation has recently begun a "Health in Prison" project in order to identify and promote good practice in prison health care. It starts from the basic premise that:

"it is important both for the rights of the prisoner and for the public health of all

---

[449] Adopted by the General Assembly, December 17, 1991.

[450] Para.5 of Principle 1 provides that every person with a mental illness shall have the right to exercise all civil, political, economic, social and cultural rights as recognised in the Universal Declaration of Human Rights, the International Covenant on Economic, Social and Cultural Rights, the International Covenant on Civil and Political Rights and in other relevant instruments, such as the Declaration of Rights of Disabled Persons and the Body of Principles for the Protection of All Persons under Any Form of Detention or Imprisonment.

countries that time spent in custody is used positively for the prevention of disease and the promotion of health and that negative effects of custody on health are reduced to a minimum".[451]

With this aim in mind it is in the process of developing some practical schemes for mental health promotion in prisons. These include "listener" and "befriending" schemes to help vulnerable prisoners, telephone helplines, counselling and therapy, psychiatric and psychological services, monitoring of prisoners considered at risk of suicide and self-harm and schemes to reduced their vulnerability, schemes to reduce bullying of vulnerable prisoners and courses to improve prisoners' coping, social and parenting skills including anger management therapy.

Commentary

Commenting on the Irish mental health services Kennedy has highlighted the need for attention to be directed to the provision of adequate mental health care in general for those at risk of offending and particularly in prisons:

> "Severe mental illness, such as schizophrenia, bipolar affective disorder and delusional disorder, is about four times more common in prisoners than in the general population. ... It follows that the mentally ill in prisons are there because of the consequences of their illness, and this amounts to a systematic discrimination against the severely mentally ill at the institutional level. In the case of the mentally ill, it is the lack of access to appropriate resources in the community which leads by default to the use of the prisons as a form of haven for those incapable of living independently and as a means of control for those who ought instead to be receiving treatment."[452]

1. Given the prevalence of mental illness among the prisoner population there is clearly a need for adequate mental health care. For the individual this may be secured by establishing a right to care for his mental health. It is submitted that the following general principles should be embodied in legislation as statutory rights:
   (a) A prisoners should be entitled to mental health care which is equivalent to the right to mental health care of any other mentally ill person outside of prison.
   (b) There are prisoners within the prison system who may be people with an intellectual disability and also be suffering from a mental illness. It is submitted that prison rules should provide for an initial examination to detect the presence of such dual disabilities and prisoners with a dual diagnosis should have the right to appropriate treatment and rehabilitative therapy. The need for detention and appropriate intervention has been

---

[451] www.hipp-europe.org/background/0020.
[452] See Kennedy H.G., "Human Rights Standards and Mental Health in Prisons", Vol.8(2) *Medico-Legal Journal of Ireland* 58 at 64.

highlighted by the Irish College of Psychiatrists:

"Given the dual disabilities of intellectual disability and the high prevalence of mental health needs in the population, increasingly their vulnerability within the Criminal Justice System is being identified. The treatment of people with an intellectual disability within the criminal justice system depends on the extent to which their disability is recognised by those coming into contact with them as this is a factor which will often determine their course through the system. For those already within the system access to appropriate multi-professional evaluation to assess the needs of the this group particularly those with a dual diagnosis and plan appropriate rehabilitative and therapeutic interventions." [453]

(c) The oppressive psychological pressures which detention brings with it may just be the environmental stressor which trigger a state of ill health in a person with a predisposition to mental illness. It is submitted that the right to health care in prison should include a right to psychological counselling to deal with the pressures of incarceration in an appropriate case.

(d) Prisoners with mental illness should have a right to independent psychiatric assessment in any case in which it is proposed to impose punishment or disciplinary measures upon them.

(e) The matter of transfer of prisoners requiring treatment for mental illness from custody to a psychiatric hospital and the Central Mental Hospital which is currently governed by antiquated legislation should be amended to include safeguards against arbitrary committal and indefinite detention in the relevant psychiatric institution. The Mental Treatment Act 1945 expressly preserved this legislation and accordingly none of its safeguards applied to its operation.[454] The Mental Health Act 2001 does not address it and the Criminal Law (Insanity) Bill 2002 proposes to repeal some of these provisions but fails to put any provision in their place. It is submitted that prisoners removed to a psychiatric facility under any amending legislation should as a minimum have the protections of the Mental Health Act 2001 afforded to them.

(f) In order to address the present delays in referring prisoners to the Central Mental Hospital for treatment repealing provisions in mental health legislation should provide for the transfer of prisoners to designated centres which would include but not be confined to the Central Mental Hospital. In this regard it has been suggested that prisoners could be transferred to regional psychiatric intensive care units with effective but discreet security systems staffed by multidisciplinary teams with training and expertise in forensic psychiatry. [455] This would undoubtedly involve a necessary but considerable deployment of resources. Further while prisoners are awaiting

---

[453] Response to the Prison Health Care Review Group cited in *Mental Illness The Neglected Quarter Marginalised Groups op. cit.*, p.54.
[454] Mental Treatment Act 1945, s.284.
[455] See Mental Health Commission response to Criminal Law (Insanity) Bill 2002, March 2003, p.4.

transfers to such centres resources are needed to ensure that the patients in observation cells are properly cared for and their rights respected.[456] International law dictates that resources be deployed as a matter of priority to provision of appropriate mental health care in prisons. The need for the development of a system in Ireland to address promptly the mental health needs of prisoners has been raised by international monitoring bodies[457] and in the light of the state's obligations to provide adequate health care under the European Convention on Human Rights is now in view of the European Convention on Human Rights Act 2003 a matter of pressing domestic concern for the state.

(g) Prisoners rights to appropriate medical treatment should be underpinned by (i)an obligation on state authorities to inspect mental health care conditions in prisons (ii) the right of access by a prisoner to effective complaint mechanisms (iii) sanctions for professional misconduct and/or violation of patients rights whether by way of disciplinary proceedings by professional bodies or proceedings before the courts Such mechanisms are recommended by Principle 22 of the *United Nations Principles for the Protection of Persons with Mental Illness and the Improvement of Mental Health Care* and as having application to all facilities caring for people with mental health difficulties.

Further where prisoners' rights to make complaints is concerned the European Health Committee of the Council of Europe in its report in 1998 on "The Organisation of Health Care Services in the prisons in European Member States" has also recommended in specific terms that:

"prisoners should have direct free and direct access to a judicial body, a specific committee for complaints [regarding the arrangement and provision of medical care], an ombudsman or any other sort of authority that has the legal competence to deal with such complaints and the power to make binding decisions."

At domestic level in Ireland some steps have been taken to put in place inspection and complaints mechanisms within the prison service. However while an Inspector of Prisons and Places of Detention was appointed in Ireland in April 2002 attention has been drawn to the fact that the office lacks statutory powers and sufficient resources.[458] Further the Irish Government has promised inclusion of provisions in relation to a Prison Inspectorate and Visiting Committees in the Prison Service Bill but the publication of this piece of legislation is still awaited

(h) Prisoners who are receiving mental health care before entering prison should have a right to continuation of that care in prison and prisoners receiving

---

[456] See Bresnihan V., "To be or not to be, in observation cells? A Discussion Paper on the introduction of observation cells for mentally ill and suicidal prisoners", Irish Penal Reform Trust 2003.

[457] See above Reports of Committee on the Prevention of Torture and Inhuman and Degrading Treatment or Punishment, pp.528 *et seq.*

[458] *Ibid.*, p.55.

mental health care in prison should have the right to follow up treatment outside of prison.

(i)   It is submitted that the 1947 Prison Rules should be reformed and a new set of rules promulgated which clearly set out the day to day entitlements of prisoners to health care and the nature and extent of the duties of prison and medical staff to provide for prisoner's health care.

2.   In order to encourage equivalence of treatment of prisoners with mental illness or care of prisoners intellectual disability with the rest of the populations the provision of prison health services should be the subject of an arrangement between the Department of Health and the relevant prison authorities.[459]

3.   As has been demonstrated above international best practice dictate that prisoners are entitled to a therapeutic environment and at least an equivalence of care with the rest of the community. The European Committee for the Prevention of Torture in report to the Irish state in 1998 commented on the unacceptable physical conditions in the Central Mental Hospital including lack of in-cell sanitation and in the older buildings limited access to light, the absence of chairs in the rooms, lack of privacy afforded by sanitary facilities for use by prisoners during the day and poor heating. It is submitted that while there are plans for the refurbishment of the hospital international standards including the article 3 of the European Convention on Human Rights dictate that exchequer funding be applied to a refurbishment project without delay.[460]

4.   It is submitted that prison rules should require that prisoners placed in new observation cells pending transfer to a psychiatric hospital should be supervised at stated intervals and a detailed record of the reasons for, and use of the observation cells be kept.[461]

H. General Conclusions

It is without doubt that the criminal law as it applies to persons with mental disability requires re-evaluation mainly to take account of the fact that the persons to whom it applies may not only be offenders but are also people with a disability whose disability requirements need to be addressed as early as possible in their interaction with the criminal justice system if any form of meaningful rehabilitation is to be achieved. The

---

[459] See Report of the Group to Review the Structure and Organisation of the Prison Health Care Services (2001) See also Bresnihan V., "The Politics of Prison Medicine", Irish Penal Reform Trust (2002) which outlines the view of the Irish Penal Reform Trust that healthcare in prisons should be delivered through a formal partnership between the health services and the prison service. It advocates that the prison service should remain financially and managerially responsible the primary care delivered in prisons and the health service should be responsible for secondary and tertiary care even within prisons and that an inter-ministerial agreement is required.

[460] See *Mental Illness The Neglected Quarter Marginalised Groups* Report of Amnesty International November 2003.

[461] See Amnesty International *Mental Illness The Neglected Quarter Marginalised Groups*, November 2003, p.50.

practical effect of such an approach would be divert the person away from the criminal justice system for treatment as a priority at the earliest possible stage in the trial process with the accused person returning to court to face trial only on recovery. This must accord with the public interest in having a fair and effective criminal justice system. Where the accused is fit to be tried, pleads a defence putting his mental condition in issue at trial which defence is accepted the outcome must be one which achieves the delicate balance between the accused's present need for treatment (if any) and protecting society against crime preferably without the traditional assumption in the case of the latter concern that detention of the person who was mentally ill at the time of the offence is the only appropriate deterrent for the future.

CHAPTER EIGHT

Issues of Legal Capacity in Private Law

INTRODUCTION

The image of personhood of the person with mental disability can be directly affected by the laws determination of his/her capacity to exercise ordinary legal rights. Even when a person is not in the hospital environment the exercise of many ordinary legal rights can be affected by his/her condition. As a matter of common law there are certain general principles which apply in relation to establishment of a person's legal capacity such as the principles that: (a) adults are presumed to have legal capacity unless the contrary is proved,[1] and (b) the onus of proving that a person does not have legal capacity rests on the person asserting this,[2] but in most cases the capacity required of an individual by law is capacity in relation to the transaction which is to be effected, that is, it is issue specific and legal position turns on the determination of individual's capacity to perform the particular function in question. It is important therefore to ask whether the law's measure of a person's capacity accurately reflects the capability of the person to perform the function in question. If it underestimates that capability the law may be said unfairly to discriminate against the individual in question and to adversely affect the image of personhood of the person with mental disability. This in an age when knowledge of the aetiology of mental illness is expanding all the time is increasingly unacceptable. If it overestimates that capability then it may be failing to protect the person against the difficulties presented by his/her condition. This is also an outcome to be guarded against. In this and the two chapters which follow the law relating to capacity to exercise various types of legal rights is examined, compared with the laws in jurisdictions similar to our own, and where appropriate proposals for reform made. First however, an examination is made of the capacity of the person with mental disability to exercise rights in private law.

CAPACITY TO CONTRACT

Capacity to enter contractual relations under Irish law

The position at common law

The criterion for determining whether a person with mental illness has capacity to enter into a contract other than a contract for necessaries at common law is whether or not the

---

[1] *Masterman-Lister v. Brutton & Co.* [2002] E.W.C.A. Civ. 1889.
[2] *ibid.*

person concerned was capable of understanding the nature of the contract and also that the other party was aware of this incapacity.[3] Where these two criteria are satisfied the contract is voidable at the option of the person with mental illness.[4] The law in this regard represents a compromise between two principles, first that a person should not be held liable in contract if s/he is incapable of giving meaningful consent and the secondly that it might operate to the prejudice of an unsuspecting contracting party to permit the other party to "stultify[5] himself"[6] by relying on his mental incapacity in order to avoid contractual liability.

The degree of capacity required to enter a contract will vary according to the nature of the specific contract in question,[7] *i.e.* buying a bus ticket or selling a house will require wholly different degrees of understanding.[8] What is required in essence is that the party in question have an understanding of the general nature of what he is doing.[9] Thus in *Manches v. Trimborn*,[10] an action on a cheque was unsuccessful where the drawer was capable of understanding the act of drawing a cheque but not the transactions of which it formed a part.

Where a party has capacity at the time of contracting evidence of prior or subsequent mental disorder is irrelevant.[11] In cases where contractual capacity is doubtful, such evidence may create a suspicion that he was mentally disordered at the time of making the contract.[12]

The presence of a delusion in the mind of a contracting party does not amount to conclusive evidence that he did not understand the transaction even if the delusion is connected with the subject matter of the contract. The delusion must be such as to render the affected party incapable of understanding.[13]

Evidence that a person was being treated for mental disorder under the terms of the Mental Treatment Act 1945 (still in force) or the Mental Health Act 2001 (most of which in large part has yet to come into force) or has been found by the President of the High Court exercising the wardship jurisdiction to be incapable of managing his property

---

[3] See *Boughton v. Knight* (1873) L.R. P&D 64 at 72; *Jenkins v. Morris* (1880) 14 Ch. D 674 at 681, *Rhodes v. Rhodes* (1890) 44 Ch.D. 94 at 105.

[4] The original common law rule was that a contract with a person of unsound mind was void since consensus ad idem was impossible. Later the rule became qualified to one that a person could not plead his own unsoundness of mind to avoid a contract he had made. From this the present rule evolved that a person could plead his own mental incapacity if it were shown that the other party knew of it.

[5] Early common law followed the view in civil law jurisdictions and permitted a person to raise mental disability in order to avoid contractual obligations that occurred while the disability subsisted. Despite its attractions this approach soon fell victim to the technicalities of early English pleading in the form of the rule in *Beverley's Case* (1603) 4 Co. Rep. 123b whereby parties were not permitted to stultify themselves by relying on their own mental incapacity in order to avoid contractual liability.

[6] See Treitel, *The Law of Contract* (6th ed., 1983), pp.434–435.

[7] *Gibbons v. Wright* (1954) 91 C.L.R. 423.

[8] See *Manches v. Trimborn* (1946) 174 LT 344.

[9] *In the estate of Park* [1954] P. 112, *Gibbons v. Wright* [1954] 91 D.L.R. 423 and *Moore v. Confederation Life Association* [1918] 25 B.C.R. 465.

[10] (1946) 174 L.T. 344.

[11] *Hall v. Warren* (1804) 9 Ves. Jun 605.

[12] See *McAdam v. Walker* (1813) 1 Dow 148 at 177.

[13] See *Jenkins v. Morris* (1880) 14 Ch. D. 674. See also *Weller v. Copeland* 120 N.E. (Illinois. 1918).

and affairs would amount to *prima facie* evidence of mental disorder required to establish incapacity. Where a person with mental illness seeks to avoid a contract s/he bears the burden of proving his/her own incapacity *and* that the other contracting party knew of the incapacity at the time[14] or knew such facts and circumstances that he must be taken to have known of the incapacity. In *York Glass Co. v. Jubb*[15] Warrington L.J. stated:

> "If circumstances are proved which are such that any reasonable man would have inferred from those circumstances that the man was insane, than the man who contracts with him ... will be taken to know that the man was of unsound mind."[16]

Evidence that a person was well known to be mentally disordered in the neighbourhood will not suffice.[17] Where knowledge of the mental disorder is not proved the validity of the contract will be judged as if the person with mental incapacity was fully capable of entering into the contract.

A contract made by a person who at the time lacks capacity renders it voidable but not void. Thus the person concerned may be bound by the contract if he subsequently ratifies it upon recovery or during a lucid interval.[18]

There is some dispute as to whether a contract can be avoided if it is unfair. It has been suggested that the sane party can only sue if he did not know of the other party's disability and the contract was fair,[19] and conversely that the sane party can sue if the contract was fair even though he did know of the other's disability.[20] Following the decision of the Privy Council in *Hart v. O'Connor*[21] it appears that the transaction can only be avoided by the person with mental illness on the grounds of unfairness where that unfairness amounts to unconscionability or equitable fraud of such a degree that would have enabled the complaining party to avoid the contract even if he had been

---

[14] *Imperial Loan Company v. Stone* [1892] 1 Q.B. 199; *York Glass Co., v. Jubb* (1925) 134 LT 36; *Baxter v. Earl of Portsmouth* (1826) 5 B&C 170; *Brown v. Jodrell* (1827) 3 C&P 30; *Price v. Berrington* (1851) 3 Mac &G 486; *Elliot v. Ince* (1857) 7 De G M & G 475 at 487.

[15] (1925) 134 L.T. 36 at 41.

[16] The Newfoundland case of *Lingard v. Thomas* (1984) 46 Newfoundland and Prince Edward Island Reports 245 (Nfld T.D.) provides a striking example of the principle that knowledge will be imputed in circumstances where one party ought to have known of the other's mental incapacity or ought to have been sufficiently suspicious as to warrant making further inquiries. In this case the plaintiff aged seventy six and suffering from a serious mental impairment owned a cottage, which the defendant was interested in purchasing. The defendant made a verbal offer of $3,000 prefacing it with the remark: "you may laugh at this offer". Instead of reacting as anticipated, the plaintiff told the defendant that he could have the property for $2,500. The court held that the defendant must be deemed to know of the plaintiff's mental incapacity. The plaintiff's reaction to the defendant's offer and opening remark was so unusual that it ought to have alerted the defendant and raised questions in his mind as to the plaintiff's mental condition.

[17] *Greenslade v. Dare* (1855) 20 Beav. 284 at 290.

[18] *Matthews v. Baxter* (1873) L.R. 8 Ex. 132.

[19] See Treitel, *The Law of Contract* (6th ed.), p.435 citing *Molton v. Camroux* (1848) 2 Ex. 487, 503 affirmed 4 Ex. 17. In *Baxter v. Portsmouth* (1826) 5 B&C 169, 108 E.R. 63 it was held that if the purchaser's incapacity is not known to the seller and if the contract was fair he could recover the contract price.

[20] *Dane v. Kirkwall* (1838) 8 C&P 679.

[21] [1985] 2 All E.R. 880.

sane.[22] Further there must be "procedural unfairness" in the sense of pressure, victimisation and the like as well as "substantive unfairness" or contractual imbalance.[23] However, in *Hassard v. Smith*[24] the Irish Courts appeared to take a less restrictive approach. In that case the court upheld the validity of a lease granted by a lessor of unsound mind on the grounds that the lessee believed the lessor to be of sound mind. In the course of his judgment, however, Chatterton VC remarked that for a contract with a plaintiff who lacked capacity to be upheld in equity the lessee would have to show it was "fair and *bona fide*."[25] He also appears to have accepted that a disparity between the price paid and the market value may afford proof of that the transaction is not honest, that the buyer may know that the purchase is not a fair exchange and that the seller has been taken advantage of. On the facts of the case however, the defendant did not know that the lessor was of unsound mind and the plaintiffs had failed to prove that the lease was at an undervalue.

Indeed the Irish courts have gone beyond their English counterparts in holding that persons with diminished intellectual capacity should be protected from entering into improvident bargains even if there is not proof of unfair dealings by the other party to the contract. Thus in *Grealish v. Murphy*,[26] the court relying on the jurisdiction of the courts of equity to intervene where the parties to a contract do not meet on equal terms[27] set aside an improvident transaction entered by an elderly farmer with a mental disability whereby he surrendered his life interest in a farm to a farm worker in consideration of personal covenants supported with no adequate sanctions. In doing so Gavan Duffy J. held that the plaintiff did not have a complete explanation of the nature and effect of the transaction he was entering into from an independent advisor and thus was not afforded the protection necessary to put him on an equal footing with his co-contractor.[28] In *Rooney v. Conway*[29] concerned an action by a beneficiary of lands under a will against the defendant purchaser of the lands from the previous owner (the testator) during his lifetime. In that case Hutton J. set aside the transfer of land by the previous owner to the purchaser on the grounds that the transfer was at a grave under-value. In addition the testator at the time of the transfer was in a weak mental condition and had inadequate independent legal advice. Accordingly following dicta of Stuart VC in *Longmate v. Ledger*,[30] it was unconscionable for the defendant to retain the lands.

---

[22] [1985] A.C. 1000 There seems to be something of a deceptive simplicity in the rule that a person whose mental illness is not suspected should comply with the standards applicable to sane persons and only released from liability if s/he can show equitable fraud. Given that a relatively serious degree of mental illness must be shown if incapacity is to be established the effect of the rule is to place a contracting party with mental illness at a disadvantage relative to their sane co-contractors. Raising the plea of incapacity is likely to have the effect of making it correspondingly difficult as a matter of credible evidence for the party concerned to fix the other party with knowledge of that incapacity. See A.H Hudson, "Mental Incapacity Revisited" *The Conveyancer* (1986 May–June) 178.

[23] [1985] 2 All E.R. 880 at 887.

[24] (1872) I.R. 6 E.Q. 429.

[25] *Ibid.*, p.433.

[26] [1946] I.R. 35; See also *Rooney v. Conway*, N.I. March 8, 1982.

[27] See Lord Hatherley's dissenting judgment in *O'Rorke v. Bolingbroke* 2 A.C. 814 at 823.

[28] [1946] I.R. 35 at 50–51.

[29] N.I. March 1982.

[30] [1860] 2 Giff 157, 66 E.R. 67.

At common law whenever necessaries are supplied to a person with mental disability s/he has an implied obligation to pay a fair price for them provided it can be shown that they are supplied with the intention of claiming payment.[31] This common law obligation arises not from contract but quasi contract[32] and was converted into a statutory duty in relation to the sale of goods by the Sale of Goods Act 1893.

The legislative position in relation to contracts for necessaries

Section 2 of the Sale of Goods Act 1893 provides:

> "Where necessaries are sold and delivered[33] to … a person who by reason of mental incapacity or drunkenness is incompetent to contract, he must pay a reasonable price therefor."

The obligation therefore in relation to the supply of goods is to pay a "reasonable price" and it appears that it arises whether or not the seller knew of the incapacity. A reasonable price need not be the same as the sale price. "Necessaries" are defined by section 2 of the Act as " goods suitable to the condition in life of the person and to his actual requirements at the time of sale and delivery" [34] The reference to goods being suitable to his condition in life means his or her place in society rather than any mental or physical condition. Goods will not be necessaries if the person's existing supply is sufficient. Thus a person with mental health difficulties who buys a pair of shoes would probably be bound to pay for them but if the same person purchased a dozen pairs the contract might be voidable at the option of the patient.[35] The burden of proving that the items are necessaries and if they are, that the person with mental illness was not adequately supplied with such goods is on the person supplying the goods.[36]

Although the Sale of Goods Act 1893 does not apply to the provision of necessary services, a reasonable price for such services is recoverable at common law provided the person supplying such services intended at the time that he should be repaid.[37] It also appears that the cumulative effect of the 1893 Act and the common law is that the obligation to pay a reasonable price also applies to the supply of money to purchase goods and services.[38]

---

[31] *In re Rhodes, Rhodes v. Rhodes* (1890) 44 Ch. D. 94; *Nash v. Inman* [1908] 2 K.B. 1 at 8.

[32] *Ibid.*

[33] An executory contract for the sale of necessaries to a mentally incompetent purchaser is unenforceable.

[34] Sale of Goods Act 1893, s.2.

[35] See *Assessment of Mental Capacity –Guidance for Doctors and Lawyers* A Report of the British Medical Association and the Law Society (British Medical Association December 1995).

[36] It is a matter of law whether on the evidence an item is capable of being a necessary and a matter of fact whether, having regard to the actual requirements of the buyer it is a necessary in the actual circumstances of the case. See *Ryder v. Wombwell* (1868) L.R. 4 Ex. 32.

[37] It appears that this may include expenditure on professional services necessary to preserve the property of a person who lacks mental capacity but it is not clear whether it would apply to measures taken to enhance its value. See Ashton and Ward, *Mental Handicap and the Law* (1992), p.23.

[38] *In re Beavan, Davies, Banks & Co. v. Beavan* [1912] 1 Ch. 196 it was held that necessaries can include interest on mortgages, repairs, insurance and rent audit expenses.

Where a person's property and affairs have become subject to the wardship jurisdiction any transaction which a ward enters into during this time is void irrespective of whether or not he has the capacity to enter into it,[39] since to hold otherwise would interfere with the court's control over the property.[40] It seems that the same principle applies regardless of whether the ward as contracting party knew that his affairs were under the court's control. However, the court may elect to adopt and validate *ab initio* a contract made by a mentally incapacitated person before his affairs become subject to its jurisdiction.[41]

Commentary from a comparative law perspective

A particularly interesting discussion on the meaning of mental incapacity in the context of contractual relations is to be found in the judgment of Nicholson J. in the Canadian case of *Bank of Nova Scotia v. Kelly*.[42] This case establishes that mental capacity involves an ability to understand not only the nature of the contract but also its effect on the party's interests. The cases concerned an action by a bank to enforce a number of promissory notes executed by a defendant with a long history of mental illness. In discussing whether the defendant lacked the necessary mental capacity at the date of the contract, Nicholson J. observed that:

> " Assuming he could be said to be capable of understanding the terms of the contract as being a promise to pay the amount of the note on demand, he having borrowed the money from the plaintiff does it follow that he understood the consequences of not paying the notes? The consequences are that the plaintiff could take an action against him and if successful a judgment entered against him having the effect of encumbering his land and the possible sale of his property to satisfy the judgment. I am not satisfied that the defendant is capable of understanding this very real consequence of not paying the notes. The defendant has a property registered in his name in Charlottetown. This is probably one of his main interests in life and I doubt if one in his state of mind is able to grasp the effect of non-payment of the notes would have on him and his property interests. It is in my opinion that failure of the defendant to fully understand the consequences of his failure to meet his obligations under the promissory notes is a circumstance, which must be taken into account. I find that the defendant was probably able to understand the terms and conditions of the notes and his obligation to pay the notes but that he was incapable because of his mental incompetence of forming a rational judgment of their effect on his interests. I therefore find that by reason of

---

[39] In *In re Walker* [1905] 1 Ch. 160 in which it was held that a deed executed by a person found lunatic by inquisition even during a lucid interval was held to be null and void. In *In re Marshall, Marshall v. Whateley*, it was held that an equitable charge executed after appointment of a receiver was null and void.

[40] It would be quite inconvenient to require a committee to go to court each time a transaction was entered into by the ward.

[41] *Baldwyn v. Smyth* [1900] 1 Ch. 588.

[42] [1973] 41 D.L.R. (3d) 273.

mental incompetence the defendant was not capable of understanding the terms of the notes *and of forming a rational judgment of their effect on his interests.*"[43]

The fact that the court considered the defendant's ability to understand not only the nature of the contract but also its effect is consistent with the spirit if not with the actual wording of the actual authorities. However, what makes the case significant is the way in which the term "the effect of the contract" was interpreted. The court construed it as meaning the effect on this particular defendant in his particular circumstances rather than merely the legal effect of the contract generally.

In England in its *Report No. 231 on Mental Incapacity*,[44] the Law Commission recommended that the "necessaries" rule be codified and that a single statutory provision cover the supply of goods and services to a person who is without capacity to contract.[45] The Commission also noted that the "necessaries" rule simply establishes that the person without capacity must pay. Where that person lacks the capacity to arrange for such payment to be made the person who has arranged for the goods or services may also have to arrange settlement of the bill. The legal position of such a person is at present obscure in English law. Accordingly the Commission recommended that where reasonable actions for the personal welfare or health care of the person lacking capacity involve expenditure it should be lawful for the person who is taking action (i) to pledge to the other's credit for that purpose, or (ii) to apply money in the possession of the person concerned for meeting the expenditure and if the person taking the action bears the expenditure then he or she is entitled to be reimbursed or otherwise indemnified from the money of the person concerned.[46] Similar observations and recommendations might be made under the law in Ireland.

It is submitted that the scope of the rule that all contracts made with a ward of court are void may be little too wide. It is not clear for example whether it is intended to apply to contracts, which impose an obligation on a ward to refrain from carrying out a particular activity. It is possible it does not.[47] Moreover, if the Committee's authority is restricted to part only of a ward's estate contracts affecting property outside the committee's control would presumably not be void. It is submitted that the scope of the rule should be restricted so as to render void only those contracts, which in fact interfere with the effective management of the estate by the committee.

AGENCY RELATIONSHIPS

As a general rule for a valid contract of agency to exist both principal and agent must be capable of acting as such. The nature of the mental capacity, which is required to appoint an agent, is unclear. However, it certainly should involve an ability on the part of the principal to understand the nature and effect of appointment *i.e.* capacity to understand that it confers authority on the agent to act on the principal's behalf and to impose

---

[43] *Ibid.*, p.284.

[44] Law Com. No. 231 (1995).

[45] *Ibid.*, para.4.9.

[46] *Ibid.*, para.4.10.

[47] See Treitel, *The Law of Contract* (6th ed., Stevens, London, 1983), p.435.

contractual liability. It may also require an ability to understand the nature and effects of the contracts, which an agent is authorised to make. This would follow since it would be difficult to understand how valid authority can be granted to an agent to enter into a contract the nature and effect of which the principal is incapable of understanding.

Where mental disability renders a person incapable of acting on his own behalf s/he is automatically rendered incapable of appointing an agent.[48] In *Elliot v. Ince*,[49] it was held that a power of attorney granted by a person found to be of unsound mind by inquisition at the date of execution was invalid. However, it appears that acts done by a person who would otherwise lack mental capacity during a lucid interval are valid.[50]

If a person becomes mentally ill to such a degree as to lack capacity at a time after s/he has appointed an agent and while the contract is operative its effect is to terminate the agency.[51] For mental illness to revoke the authority of the agent it must, however, be of a pronounced character and "mere weakness of mind or partial derangement" is insufficient.[52] It is clear that the agent's authority is revoked if the principal becomes incapable of understanding the nature of the contract of agency. It has been suggested however, that if the principal becomes incapable of understanding the nature of certain of the contracts which the agent is authorised to make the agent's authority is not completely revoked but merely restricted.

Where a principal who lacks capacity holds out another as his/her agent, the principal may be liable to a third party dealing with him/her who has no knowledge of the supervening mental illness.[53] Thus in *Drew v. Nunn*,[54] a husband gave his wife authority to act on his behalf and held her out as his agent and then became mentally ill. His wife continued to order goods from the plaintiff who was unaware of the husband's mental incapacity. The husband was held liable for the price of the goods when he recovered.

If the third party has constructive knowledge or a knowledge of such circumstances as would put a reasonable man on his inquiry as to the mental incapacity of the principal he will be deemed to have had notice that the contract of agency had been determined and that the authority of the agent had been revoked. Thus in the Canadian decision of *In re Parks, Canada Permanent Trust Co. v. Parks*,[55] the New Brunswick Supreme Court held that a power of attorney given by a medical practitioner for the purpose of making specific payments in relation to her maintenance was held to have been determined when the medical practitioner became mentally ill. However, it was also held that since the payees knew of the mental disorder or were aware of sufficient facts from which that mental disorder would or should properly have been inferred or at least investigated further, the payments had been made improperly and had to be reimbursed by the payee to the estate of deceased medical practitioner. It should be noted that in Ireland the Powers of Attorney Act 1996, now provides for the creation of an enduring power of attorney, which will survive the subsequent mental incapacity of the donor.

---

[48] *Grove v. Johnston* (1889) 24 L.R. I.R.; *Daily Telegraph Newspaper Co. v. McLaughlin* [1904] A.C. 776.
[49] (1857) 7 De G M & G 475.
[50] *Elliot v. Ince* (1857) 7 De GM & G 475; See also *Drew v. Nunn* (1879) 4 Q.B.D 661.
[51] See *Drew v. Nunn* (1879) Q.B.D 661 at 666 *per* Brett L.J.
[52] *Ibid., per* Cotton L.J. at 669 and 670.
[53] *Ibid.* 667 to 669.
[54] (1879) 4 Q.B.D. 661.
[55] [1957] 8 D.L.R. (2d) 155.

In *Yonge v. Toynbee*,[56] it was held that where a principal lacks mental capacity a representation by his/her agent that he is authorised to act as agent may render the agent liable in breach of warranty of authority even if the agent was unaware of his/her principal's mental incapacity. This is a difficult situation in practice since it may be difficult for an agent to determine the precise moment at which a principal's authority is revoked in a situation where the principal's mental condition is gradually deteriorating. However, where an agent is held to be in breach of warranty of authority and is unaware of a principal's incapacity he should be able to claim reimbursement from his principal.

Where an agent becomes mentally ill to such a degree as to lack capacity to manage his own affairs he is incompetent to bind his principal even where he is acting under commission.[57] Where however, the circumstances give rise to constructive or implied agency an act which would have been binding on the incapacitated agent in his individual capacity would be binding on his principal where the act is done by the person concerned as agent.[58] Where the acts are purely formal or ministerial, they may be completed notwithstanding the incapacity of the agent.[59] Acts falling into this category would include the signing of receipts for rent received or the surrender of a bond for cancellation after a condition has been fulfilled by the obligor.[60]

Commentary from a comparative law perspective

Legislation in every common law province of Canada has expressly overruled the decision in *Yonge v. Toynbee* in the context of powers of attorney.[61] It is submitted that the rule is of doubtful validity. The rights of a third party who is unaware of the principal's incapacity are unaffected so why is it necessary to impose personal liability on the agent? Conversely if the third party is aware of the incapacity the agent could not be taken to warrant the truth of something that the third party knew to be false. The rule is manifestly unfair and should be repealed by legislation.

ENDURING POWERS OF ATTORNEY

Irish law on the enduring power of attorney

At common law a power of attorney terminates automatically when the donor of the power loses the mental capacity to handle his/her affairs.[62] An enduring power of attorney

---

[56] [1910] 1 K.B. 215.

[57] GW Abraham, *The Law and Practice of Lunacy in Ireland* (E. Ponsonby, Dublin, 1886), p.335.

[58] *Ibid.*

[59] See Abraham, *op. cit.*, p.335.

[60] *Ibid.*

[61] Powers of Attorney Act, S.A. 1991, c P-13.5, s.14 (1); Powers of Attorney Act R.S.B.C. 1979, c.334, s.3 [re-en. 1987, c. 42, s.90]; Powers of Attorney Act R.S.M. 1987 c. P97, s.2(2); Property Act, R.S.N.B. 1973, c. P19, s.58(1) [re-en 1989, c.31, s.1]; Conveyancing Act S.N. 1970, c.63, s.13: Enduring Powers of Attorney Act, R.S.N. 1990, c. E-11, s.7; Powers of Attorney Act, R.S.N.S.1989, c. 352, s.3(1); Powers of Attorney Act R.S.O. 1990, c. P20, s.3; Substitute Decisions Act S.O. 1992, c. 30 S.13(1); Powers of Attorney Act R.S.P.E.I. 1988, c. P-16, s.3(1); Powers of Attorney Act, S.S.1982–83, c. P-20.1, s.2(2).

[62] See *Yonge v. Toynbee* [1910] 1 K.B. 215.

on the other hand is one, which is capable of continuing in force after the donor becomes mentally incapable of handling his/her affairs.

In 1989, the Law Reform Commission recommended that a system of enduring powers of attorney be introduced into Ireland.[63] The Powers of Attorney Act 1996, which came into force on August 1, 1996,[64] puts in place structures and procedures to enable a person to grant an enduring power of attorney in relation to their property and affairs and to empower a person to take decisions on their behalf in the event that s/he becomes mentally incapable of doing so.

The scope of an enduring power of attorney[65]

The enduring power of attorney may confer general authority on an attorney to act on behalf of the donor in relation to all or part of the donor's property, financial and business affairs and personal care decisions of the donor or specific authority in relation to certain matters such as in relation to property and business affairs only or in relatin to personal care decisions only. Where the instrument confers general authority on the attorney it operates to confer on the attorney authority to do anything which the donor can lawfully do subject to certain restrictions regarding the making of gifts contained in section 6(5) and any conditions or restrictions contained in the instrument.[66]

An attorney under an enduring power is empowered to execute or exercise any of the powers or discretions vested in the donor as tenant for life within the meaning of the Settled Land Act 1882 unless the power expressly restricts the attorney's power to do so.[67]

An attorney under an enduring power may act in relation to his own benefit,[68] or that of any other person if the donor might be expected to provide for those needs and may do whatever the donor might be expected to do to meet those needs subject to any conditions or restrictions contained in the instrument.[69] So for example, the attorney may make provision for the donor's dependants.

If specific provision is made to that effect in the instrument the attorney may, subject to any conditions or restrictions contained in the instrument make gifts of a seasonal nature or at a time or on an anniversary of a birth or marriage, to persons (including the attorney) who are related to or connected with the donor and gifts to any charity to which the donor made or might be expected to make gifts provided the value of each gift is not unreasonable having regard to all the circumstances and in particular the extent of the donor's assets.[70]

An enduring power of attorney may confer authority on the attorney to make specified

---

[63] See *Report on Land Law and Conveyancing Law (2) Enduring Powers of Attorney* L.R.C. 21–1989.
[64] See Powers of Attorney Act 1996 (Commencement) Order 1996 (S.I. No.195 of 1996).
[65] The Law Society has issued Guidelines for Solicitors when drafting provisions regarding the scope of the enduring power. See "Enduring Powers of Attorney: Guidelines for Solicitors", para.1.6.
[66] Powers of Attorney Act 1996, s.6(2).
[67] *Ibid.*, s.6(3).
[68] It is possible for the instrument itself to make provision for the remuneration of the attorney. See Enduring Powers of Attorney Regulations 1996 (S.I. 196 of 1996), reg.6.
[69] Powers of Attorney Act 1996, s.6(4).
[70] *Ibid.*, s.6(5).

personal care decision(s) on the donor's behalf.[71] "Personal care decision" is defined by section 4 to mean a decision on any one or more of the following matters in relation to the donor of an enduring power:

> "(a) where the donor should live,
> (b) with whom the donor should live,
> (c) whom the donor should see and should not see,
> (d) what training or rehabilitation the donor should get,
> (e) the donor's diet and dress,
> (f) inspection of the donor's personal papers,
> (g) housing, social welfare and other benefits for the donor:"

Personal care decisions involving exclusions of powers do not include consent to medical treatment.

The attorney conferred with this power is obliged to make any personal care decision in the donor's best interests. In deciding what is in the donor's best interests the attorney must have regard (i) as far as ascertainable to the past and present wishes and feelings of the donor and the factors which the donor would consider if he or she were able to do so, and (ii) the need to permit and encourage the donor to participate or to improve the donor's ability to participate as fully as possible in any decision affecting the donor. The attorney must also have regard (so far as is practicable and appropriate to consult them) to the views of any person named by the donor as someone to be consulted in relation to the matters on which a decision is to be made and to the views of anyone engaged in caring for the donor or interested in the donor's welfare on the matter of the donor's wishes and feelings and as to what would be in the donor's best interests. The attorney must also have regard to the question of whether the purpose for which any decision is required can be as effectively achieved in a manner less restrictive of the donor's freedom of action.[72]

Where an attorney makes a personal care decision on the donor's behalf it will be a sufficient compliance with these criteria if the attorney reasonably believes that what he or she decides is in the best interests of the donor.[73] Section 17(10) of the 1996 Act provides that no disclaimer whether by deed or otherwise of an enduring power which has not been registered under section 10 shall be valid unless and until the attorney gives notice of it to the donor.

Executing an enduring power of attorney

To create a valid enduring power it is necessary for the donor to comply with the terms of section 5 of the 1996 Act and any regulations relating to form and execution and content prescribed by the Minister for Equality and Law Reform thereunder. The instrument must also contain a statement by the donor to the effect that the donor intends the instrument to be effective during any subsequent mental incapacity of the donor.[74]

---

[71] Powers of Attorney Act 1996, s.6(6).
[72] *Ibid.*, s.6(7).
[73] *Ibid.*, s.6(7)(c).
[74] *Ibid.*, s.5(1).

The Enduring Power of Attorney Regulations 1996,[75] made by the Minister for Equality and Law Reform set out rules regarding, among other things, the form of instruments creating enduring powers of attorney, their execution and the requirement to notify specified people.

They also prescribe certain safeguards, which must be observed in the execution process. They require a solicitor, *inter alia*, to state in the document that s/he is satisfied that the donor understood the effect of creating the enduring power and has no reason to believe that the document is being executed as a result of fraud or undue influence.[76] They also require that a medical practitioner state that at the time the document was executed the donor had the mental capacity with the assistance of such explanations as may have been given to him/her to understand the creation of the power.[77] In addition they require that the instruments contain certain explanatory information set out in Part A of the prescribed forms for the instruments set out in the Regulations.[78] Further, they require that enduring power must contain a statement that the donor has read the information as to the effect of creating the power or that such information has been read to him or her.

They also require that the instrument contain a statement by the attorney that the attorney understands the duties and obligations of an attorney and the requirement of registration.

Regulation 4 of the Enduring Powers of Attorney Regulations,[79] provides that an instrument creating an enduring power of attorney must be executed by the donor and the attorney (who shall execute the instrument after the donor but not necessarily on the same date) each in the presence of a witness, but not necessarily the same witness, who shall give his or her full name and address. The donor must not witness the signature of the attorney nor the attorney witness the signature of the donor or of another attorney.

Section 15 of the 1996 Act provides that where any instrument creating a power of attorney is signed by the direction of the donor it must be signed in the presence of the donor and of another person who shall attest the instrument as witness. Section 15 also states that a power of attorney is not required to be made under seal. Section 15 is expressed to be without prejudice to any requirement in or under any other enactment as to the witnessing of powers of attorney or as to the execution of instruments by bodies corporate.

---

[75] S.I. No.196 of 1996.

[76] The Law Society's Guidelines for Solicitors in rleation to Enduring Powers of Attorney expand on the duties of solicitors in this regard. They advise that a solicitor should ensure that instructions are taken directly from the intending donor of the enduring power, that the donor is fully and independently advised without regard to the interests of any third party and that instructions are given freely by the donor client. See "Enduring Powers of Attorney: Guidelines for Solicitors" issued by the Probate, Administration and Taxation Committee of the Law Society, April 2004, para.1.1.

[77] The Law Society's Guidelines advise that the statement of capacity by a medical prectitioner (who should indicate his/her medical qualifications) and the certificate of the solicitor should ideally be completed within 30 days of the signing of the donor (see "Enduring Powers of Attorney: Guidelines for Solicitors", para.1.9).

[78] S.I. No.196 of 1996, reg.3.

[79] *Ibid.*, reg.4.

The Requirement to give notice of execution

Notice of the execution of the enduring power by the donor must be given by or on behalf of the donor to at least two persons named by the donor in the enduring power. At least one of those persons must be (i) the donor's spouse if s/he is living with the donor, or if (i) does not apply, (ii) a child of the donor, or if (i) and (ii) do not apply a relative (if any) of the donor. In this context "relative" means a parent, brother or sister, stepbrother or stepsister or grandchild of the donor, the widow or widower of a child of the donor or a child of the donor's brother or sister or stepbrother or stepsister.[80] The notice must take the form set out in the Third Schedule to the Enduring Powers of Attorney Regulations 1996.[81] There is no period of notice prescribed by the legislation but the Law Society's Guidelines advise that the notice should be served by registered or recorded post as soon as practicable (preferably within 30 days) of the execution of the enduring power.[82]

Who may be appointed?[83]

The attorney may be an individual (or more than one may be appointed) or a trust-corporation within the meaning of section 30 of the Succession Act 1965.[84] The attorney cannot be a person aged under 18 at the time the enduring power was executed or a person who has been adjudicated bankrupt or convicted of an offence involving fraud or dishonesty or an offence against the person or property of the donor of the power. In addition the attorney cannot be a person in respect of whom a declaration has been made under section 150 of the Companies Act 1990,[85] or a person who is or was subject or deemed subject to a disqualification order by virtue of Part VII of that Act.

---

[80] Enduring Powers of Attorney Regulations 1996 (S.I. No.196 of 1996).

[81] S.I. No.196 of 1996, reg.8.

[82] "Enduring Powers of Attorney: Guidelines for Solicitors", para.1.5.

[83] Powers of Attorney s.30(4) defines "trust corporation" as: (a) a corporation appointed by the High Court in any particular case to be a trustee; (b) a corporation empowered by its constitution to undertake trust business and having a place of business in the State or Northern Ireland and being– (i) a company established by Act or charter; (ii) an Associated Bank under the Central Bank Act 1942; (iii) a company (whether registered with or without limited liability) within the definition contained in the Companies Act 1963, or within the meaning of the corresponding law of Northern Ireland having a capital being issued of not less than £250,000 of which not less than £100,000 has been paid up in cash, or (iv) a company (registered without limited liability) within the definition contained in Companies Act 1963 or within the corresponding law of Northern Ireland, one of the members of which is a corporation within any of the previous provisions of this paragraph; or (c) a corporation which satisfies the President of the High Court that it undertakes the administration of any charitable, ecclesiastical or public trust without remuneration or that by its constitution it is required to apply the whole of its net income for charitable, ecclesiastical or public purposes and is prohibited from distributing, directly or indirectly any part thereof by way of profits and is authorised by the President of the High Court to act in relation to such trusts as a trust corporation.

[84] The Law Society has issued Guidelines to Solicitors when advising clients regarding choice of attorney. They point to the advidability for the attorney to be trustworthy and the need to advise clients that a conflict of interest may arise for an attorney where the attorney is also a potential beneficiary in the donor's estate (see "Enduring Powers of Attorney: Guidelines for Solicitors", para.1.4).

[85] S.150 empowers the court, unless it is satisfied that certain defence specified in s.150(2) are made out, to make a declaration that a person to whom Chapter 1 of Part VII of the Companies Act 1990

The owner of a nursing home (whether or not it is a nursing home within the meaning of the Health (Nursing Homes) Act 1990) in which the donor resides or a person residing with or an employee or agent of the owner cannot be an attorney under an enduring power unless the attorney is a spouse, parent, child or sibling of the donor. "Owner" includes a person managing a nursing home or a director or a shadow director within the meaning of section 27 of the Companies Act, 1990 of, or a shareholder in, a company, which owns or manages such a home.[86] These criteria must be applied at the time of executing the power.[87] A power of attorney, which gives the attorney a right to appoint a substitute or a successor, cannot be an enduring power.[88]

Subject to sections 5(8), 14(3) and 14(5), section 5(6) provides that an enduring power is invalidated or as the case may be, ceases to be in force, on the adjudication in bankruptcy of the attorney or if the attorney is a body corporate by its winding up or dissolution or on the attorney being convicted of an offence involving fraud or dishonesty or an offence against the person or property of the donor or becoming a person in respect of whom a declaration has been made under section 150 of the Companies Act 1990, or a person who is or was subject or deemed subject to a disqualification order by virtue of Part VII of that Act, or becoming the owner of a nursing home in which the donor resides or a person residing with or an employee or agent of the owner (unless the attorney is a spouse, parent, child or sibling of the donor). An enduring power is not invalidated or does not cease to be in force, if the attorney is an attorney appointed by the power and the donor of the enduring power has in the document creating the power appointed one or more specified persons, being persons who are not disqualified to act as attorney if an attorney appointed is unable to act or declines too act or is disqualified from acting.

Section 5(8) provides that section 5(6) does not apply (and an enduring power shall not be invalidated or as the case may be cease to be in force) where an enduring power authorises or to the extent that it authorises an attorney to make personal care decisions on behalf of the donor unless the attorney has been convicted of an offence against the person of the donor or has become a person who would be disqualified from acting as attorney by virtue of the fact that the attorney is the owner of a nursing home in which the donor resides or a person residing with or an employee or agent of the owner.

Section 5(7) provides that an enduring power in favour of a spouse shall, unless the power provides otherwise, be invalidated or cease to be in force if subsequently:

(a) the marriage is annulled or dissolved under the law of the State or is annulled or dissolved under the law of another state and is, by reason of that annulment or divorce, not or no longer a subsisting valid marriage under the law of the State;[89]

(b) either a decree of judicial separation is granted to either spouse by a court in the

---

(disqualifications and restrictions: directors and other officers) applies shall not for a period of five years be appointed or act in any way whether directly or indirectly as a director or secretary or be concerned or take part in the promotion or formation of a company unless it meets certain requirements specified in s.150(3).

[86] Powers of Attorney Act 1996, s.5(11).
[87] Powers of Attorney Act 1996, s.5(4).
[88] *Ibid.*, s.5(5).
[89] As Amended by the Family Law (Divorce) Act 1996, s.50.

State or any decree is so granted by a court outside the State and is recognised in the State as having the like effect;

(c) a written agreement to separate is entered into between the spouses, or

(d) a protection order, interim barring order, barring order or safety order is made against the attorney on the application of the donor or vice versa.

Section 5(9) provides that an enduring power shall be invalidated or as the case may be shall cease to be in force on the exercise by the court of any of its wardship powers under the Lunacy Regulation (Ireland) Act 1871 if the court so directs.

Revocation of an enduring power of attorney

Until an application has been made to register an enduring power the donor has power to revoke or destroy the power at any time. If the donor does so but the attorney believes that s/he lacks the capacity to revoke the power the attorney can apply for registration of the power. The donor may then object to the registration on the basis that the power is no longer valid.[90] The court must decide whether this ground is valid. Once registered the enduring power may not be revoked by the donor unless and until the court confirms the revocation.[91]

Whether the power is revoked before or after registration the English courts in determining whether there has been an effective revocation apply the principles applicable to revocation of wills set out in *In re Sabatini*,[92] that donors must have the same degree of capacity when revoking or destroying an enduring power as they had when they made it. In the absence of any Irish authority on the point it is possible but not certain that the Irish courts may follow this approach.

The Law Society's Guidelines advise that as a matter of prudence and in order to avoid difficulties at a later stage, the formalities that apply for the exclusion of enduring power should be complied with on revocation, *i.e.* notice should be served on the notice parties and a solicitor's certificate should confirm that the donor understands the effect of revocation and a medical practitioner should certify that the donor had the mental capacity to understand the effect of revocation.[93]

In practice in England, where the donor of a registered enduring power wishes to revoke it the attorney often disclaims *i.e.* gives notice to the court that he or she wishes to cease acting as attorney. In Ireland the effect of such a disclaimer would be that the court must decide whether to consent to it[94] and whether the donor has capacity to resume management of his or her own affairs so that the registration may be cancelled or whether the donor should be made a ward of court.[95]

---

[90] Powers of Attorney Act 1996, s.10(3)(b).
[91] *Ibid.*, s.11(1)(a).
[92] (1969) 114 Sol. Jo. 35 (Probate Division).
[93] See "Enduring Powers of Attorney: Guidelines for Solicitors", para.1.10.
[94] Powers of Attorney Act 1996, s.11(1)(b).
[95] *Ibid.*, s.12(4).

Attorney's Power to Execute Instruments

Section 17(1) provides that the donee of a power of attorney may (a) execute any instrument with his or her signature and where sealing is required with his or her own seal, and (b) do any other thing in his or her own name by the authority of the donor of the power and any instrument executed or thing done in that manner will be as effective as if executed or done by the donee with the signature and seal or, as the case may be, in the name of the donor of the power.

Section 17(2) provides that a person who is authorised under a power of attorney to convey any estate or interest in property in the name or on behalf of a corporation sole or aggregate may either execute the conveyance as provided in section 17(1) or as donee of the power execute the conveyance by signing his or her name as acting in the name or on behalf of the corporation in the presence of at least one witness and, in the case of a deed, by affixing his or her own seal and such execution takes effect and is valid in like manner as if the corporation had executed the conveyance.

Section 17(3) states that where a corporation aggregate is authorised under a power of attorney to convey any interest in property in the name or on behalf of any other person, a person appointed by that purpose by the corporation may execute the deed or other instrument in the name of such other person and where an instrument appears to be executed by a person so appointed then in favour of a purchaser the instrument is deemed to have been executed by that person unless the contrary is shown. "Purchaser" in this context means a purchaser in good faith for valuable consideration and includes a lessee, mortgagee or other person who, for valuable consideration, acquires an interest in any property and includes also an intending purchaser.[96] Section 17 applies whenever the power of attorney was created.[97]

Duties of an attorney under an enduring power

The 1996 Act does not specify in any great detail the duties imposed on an attorney under an enduring power. However, the Enduring Powers of Attorney Regulations 1996 provide that an attorney who is appointed to act on the donor's behalf in relation to the property and affairs of the donor shall keep adequate accounts[98] of the management thereof and, in particular, of any expenditure to meet the needs of persons other than the donor or to make any gifts authorised by the enduring power.[99] The Law Society's Guidelines indicate that a solicitor for the donor of the power has a duty to advise the attorney of his obligations to the donor both prior to and on registration of the power. The Law Society's Guidelines indicate specifically that the attorney should be advised, *inter alia*, of the requirements: (i) to keep the donor's property separate from the attorney(s)'s property; (ii) not to profit from the position of attorney and the fact that the attorney is in a fiduciary relationship with the donor and that the attorney must use proper care in exercising the authority under the enduring power. These duties arise from the position

---

[96] Powers of Attorney Act 1996, s.17(4), s.18(6).

[97] *Ibid.*, s.17(5).

[98] However, no detailed guidance is given to attorneys as to the meaning of "adequate accounts." See Law Reform Commission Consultation Paper on the Law and the Elderly L.R.C. CP23–2003, p.77.

[99] Reg.5.

of trust occupied by the attorney and are common law duties additional to those imposed on the attorney by the 1996 legislation.[100]

Remuneration of Attorney

The Enduring Powers of Attorney regulations also provide that the enduring power "may make provision in relation to the remuneration of an attorney".[101] If no such provision is made then the attorney can only recover out of pocket expenses. The Law Society's Guidelines advise that where a donor wishes an attorney to be remunerated he should issue clear instructions as to the circumstances in which remuneration should be paid. They also advise that a solicitor should discuss with the client/donor whether it is necessary to provide for the payment of remuneration at all. They provide further that where a professional advisor is being appointed a charging clause should be included as the attorney is acting in a fiduciary capacity and would otherwise be unable to charge.[102]

Powers of court prior to registration

Where the court has reason to believe that the donor of an enduring power may be or may be becoming mentally incapable and the court is of the opinion that it is necessary to exercise any power with respect to the power of attorney, or the attorney[103] appointed to act under it before the instrument creating the power is registered then the court may on application to it by any interested party exercise any power under section 8 which would become exercisable on registration and may do so whether or not the attorney has made an application to the court for the registration of the instrument. Application in this regard could, for example, be made where an attorney has not taken steps to register the enduring power in appropriate circumstances. The procedure for application is set out in Order 129 of the Rules of the Superior Courts.[104]

Another power exercisable by the court prior to registration is the power to determine the validity of the enduring power of attorney on application to it by the attorney.[105]

Registration of the enduring power of attorney

Subject to section 7(2) (power of attorney to take action under power when application has been made for registration) and section 8 (functions of the court prior to registration), an enduring power of attorney comes into force when registered in the Wards of Court Office of the High Court and is not revoked by the donor's subsequent mental incapacity.[106] An attorney is obliged make an application for registration of the power as soon as practicable where s/he has reason to believe that the donor is or is becoming

---

[100] See "Enduring Powers of Attorney: Guidelines for Solicitors", para.3.1.
[101] Enduring Powers of Attorney Regulations 1996 (S.I. No.196 of 1996), reg.6.
[102] See "Enduring Powers of Attorney: Guidelines for Solicitors", para.1.7.
[103] This applies to any attorney under the power. Powers of Attorney Act 1996, s.14(2), sch.2, Pt 1.
[104] As inserted by the Rules of the Superior Courts (No.1) (Powers of Attorney Act 1996) 2000 (S.I. No. 66 of 2000).
[105] See Powers of Attorney Act 1996, s.9(3).
[106] Powers of Attorney Act 1996, s.7(1).

mentally incapable.[107] Mental incapacity in this context means an individual's incapacity by reason of a mental condition to manage and administer his or her own property and affairs.[108] The application must be made to the Registrar of Wards of Court.[109] The attorney must produce evidence of the donor's declining capacity. In this regard a certificate to the effect that the donor is or is becoming incapable by reason of a mental condition of managing and administering his or her own property and affairs and purporting to be signed by a registered medical practitioner may be accepted as evidence of such matters contained in it.[110] To safeguard against abuse of the procedure the 1996 Act provides that any person, who in an application for registration makes a statement which he or she knows to be false in a material particular shall be liable (a) on conviction on indictment to imprisonment for a term not exceeding two years or to a fine not exceeding £10,000 (€1,269.74) or both, and (b) on summary conviction to imprisonment for a term not exceeding six months or to a fine not exceeding £1,000 (€1,269.74) or both.[111]

The requirement to give Notice of Intention to Register Power of Attorney   Before making the application the attorney must give notice in writing[112] of his intention to do so to the donor and simultaneously to the Registrar of Wards of Court.[113] However, on application by the attorney the court may make an order dispensing with the requirement to give notice to the donor if it is satisfied that it would be undesirable or impracticable for the attorney to give such notice or that no useful purpose is likely to be served by giving it.[114]

Written notice must also be given to those persons entitled to receive notice of the execution of the enduring power.[115] Where any of those persons is dead or mentally incapable or his or her whereabouts cannot reasonably be ascertained notice must be

---

[107] Powers of Attorney Act 1996, s.9(1). A solicitor on receiving instructions to register an enduring power is under a duty to satisfy himself/herself personally that the donor is or is becoming incapable of managing his/her affairs. See "Enduring Powers of Attorney: Guidelines for Solicitors", para.3.2.

[108] *Ibid.*, s.4(1).

[109] *Ibid.*, s.9(6).

[110] Powers of Attorney Act 1996, s.9(4) It is an offence for a person to make a statement which he or she knows to be false in a material particular in an application for registration. The offence is punishable on conviction on indictment by imprisonment for a term not exceeding two years or a fine not exceeding £10,000 or both and on summary conviction to imprisonment for a term not exceeding six months or a fine not exceeding £1,000 or both. S.9(5).

[111] Powers of Attorney Act 1996, s.9(5).

[112] For the purpose of the First Schedule notice given by post may be sent by prepaid registered post to the usual or last known place of residence of the person to whom it is to be given and is to be regarded as given on the day on which it was posted. Powers of Attorney Act 1996, s.9(2), sch.1, para.9.

[113] Powers of Attorney Act 1996, s.9(2), sch.1, para.2(2).

[114] *Ibid.*, s.9(2), sch.1, para.1(2).

[115] *Ibid.*, s.9(2), sch.1, para.2. For persons entitled to receive notice of execution of power see Enduring Powers of Attorney Regulations 1996 (S.I. No.196 of 1996), art.7. If any of those persons is dead or mentally incapable of his or her whereabouts cannot reasonably be ascertained notice should be given to the other person(s). S.9(2), sch.1, para.2(1)(b) It is interesting to note that the Law Reform Commission in its Consultation Paper on the Law and the Elderly recommends that the donor should have power to exclude a named individual from the notice provisions and that the notice parties should include a "qualifying cohabitee." See L.R.C. CP23 –2003 p.74–75.

given to certain persons (if any) entitled to receive notice by virtue of paragraph 3 of the First Schedule.[116] These are:

(a) the donor's husband or wife;

(b) the donor's children;

(c) the donor's parents;

(d) the donor's brothers and sisters, stepbrothers and stepsisters;

(e) the widow or widower of a child of the donor;

(f) the donor's grandchildren;

(g) the children of the donor's brothers, sisters, stepbrothers and stepsisters.

No more than three persons in these categories are entitled to receive notice and in determining who is entitled to receive notice the categories are accorded priority in the order in which they are ranked.[117] Notwithstanding this limit where there is more than one person entitled to receive notice in each of the categories then all the persons in that category are entitled to receive notice.[118] Where the name of a person who falls into any of these categories is not known to and cannot reasonably be ascertained by the attorney that person is not entitled to receive notice.[119] In addition an attorney may before applying for registration make an application to court to be dispensed from the requirement to give a person notice and the court may grant that application if it is satisfied that it would be undesirable or impracticable for the attorney to give such notice or that no useful purpose is likely to be served by giving it.[120]

Where notice is given the notice to the donor must be in the form prescribed by the Fourth Schedule to the Enduring Powers of Attorney Regulations 1996.[121] It must state that the attorney proposes to make an application to the court for the registration of the instrument creating the enduring power and inform the donor that whilst the instrument remains registered any revocation of the power by the donor will be ineffective unless and until the revocation is confirmed by the court.[122]

Notice to other persons should also be in the form prescribed by the Fourth Schedule to the 1996 Regulations,[123] contain the statement that the attorney proposes to make an application to court for the registration of the instrument creating the power and inform

---

[116] Where the attorney applying for registration or any other attorney joining in making the application is one of these people s/he will not be required to give notice to himself or herself or to the other attorney by virtue of being one of the persons specified in paragraph 3. See sch.1, para.4(1).

[117] So persons falling into category (a) are preferred to those in category (b) and those in category (b) are preferred to those in category (c). See Powers of Attorney Act 1996, s.9(2), sch.1, para.3(3).

[118] Powers of Attorney Act 1996, s.9(2), sch.1, para.3(4).

[119] *Ibid.*, s.9(2), sch.1, para.3(2).

[120] *Ibid.*, s.9(2), sch.1, para.4(2). The procedure for making such an application is set out in O.129 of the Rules of the Superior Courts as inserted by Rules of the Superior Courts (No.1) (Powers of Attorney Act, 1996), 2000 (S.I. No.66 of 2000).

[121] S.I. No.196 of 1996, art.9.

[122] Powers of Attorney Act 1996, s.9(2), sch.1, para.5.

[123] S.I. No.196 of 1996, reg. 9.

the person to whom it is given that that person may object to the proposed registration by notice in writing to the Registrar of Wards of Court within a period of five weeks from the date on which notice was given. The notice must also specify the grounds upon which an objection to registration may be made.[124] The procedure to be followed in making an application for registration is laid down in Order 129 of the Rules of the Superior Courts.[125]

The application for registration must be served personally on the donor and on all other parties who either have or should have received notice of an intention to apply for registration.[126] The court or where appropriate the Registrar may require such proof of service of the notice of the applicant's intention to seek the registration or of any other notice sent or purportedly sent to any person in any case in which it appears necessary to do so and may adjourn such application until such service or notification has been proved to the satisfaction of the court or the Registrar as the case may be.[127]

Registration of the Enduring Power of Attorney   Where the attorney makes an application for registration the Registrar of Wards of Court is bound to register the instrument. However, in certain circumstances outlined in section 10(2) of the Act the court is obliged to defer registration until it has made such enquiries or caused such enquiries to be made as it thinks appropriate in the circumstances of the case. These circumstances are (a) where it has received a valid notice of objection to the registration from a person other than the donor to whom notice of the application for registration has been given pursuant to paragraph 2(1) of the First Schedule and that notice of objection has been received by the court within five weeks of the date on which the notice was given; (b) it appears from the application that there is no one other than the donor to whom notice has been given pursuant to paragraph 2 of the First Schedule; (c) there is reason to believe that appropriate enquiries might bring to light evidence on which the court could be satisfied that a valid ground of objection could be established.

Objections to Registration   A ground of objection is valid if it is made on the grounds (a) that the power purported to have been created by the instrument was not valid; (b) that the power created by the instrument is no longer a valid and subsisting power; (c) that the donor is not or is not becoming mentally incapable; (d) that, having regard to all the circumstances the attorney is unsuitable to be the donor's attorney;[128] and (e) that fraud or undue pressure was used to induce the donor to create the power.[129] The court may refuse to register the instrument on any of these grounds.[130]

---

[124] Powers of Attorney Act 1996, s.10(3).

[125] See Rules of the Superior Court (No.1) (Powers of Attorney Act 1996) 2000 (S.I. No.66 of 2000) inserting O.129 into the Rules of the Superior Courts.

[126] Except for service on the donor such service may be effected by pre-paid post to the usual or last known place of residence of the person to whom it is given or by personal service or in such other substituted manner as the court may allow as being appropriate in the circumstances on an ex parte application for that purpose. See O.129, r.3(3).

[127] O.129, r.3(5).

[128] This applies to any attorney under the power. See s.14(2), sch.2, Pt 1.

[129] S.10(3).

[130] S.10(4).

In *In re Hamilton's Application*,[131] Morris P. was presented with an objection to the registration of a power on the ground that the proposed attorneys were not suitable persons under section 10(3)(d) to be the donor's because of the manner in which it was alleged they had mismanaged the donor's affairs up to the date of the execution of the power. Morris P. held that the complaints of mismanagement were misdirected because at the time of the matters complained of the donor was capable of and was managing her affairs. Moreover, Morris P. held that lack of business skill was not a valid objection to the registration under section 10. He stated:

> "It would, in my view, be an improper exercise of the discretion vested in the court to refuse to register an instrument simply because the chosen attorney did not possess management and business skills to a high degree."[132]

In his view the grounds of objection set out in section 10 were fundamental in nature and in order to constitute a ground for registering the power the criticism of the attorney "must far exceed the corresponding test applied by the courts in applications for removal of a trustee".[133]

In the English case of *In re W (Power of Attorney)*,[134] it was held that hostility towards the attorney on the part of other interested parties (in this case the attorney's siblings) did not mean that the attorney was unsuitable. However, it was held such hostility could render the attorney unsuitable if it would impact adversely on the administration of the estate.

Failure to comply with prescribed form   Where an instrument differs in an immaterial respect in form or mode of expression from the form of an enduring power of attorney specified by regulations the instrument will be treated a sufficient in point of form or expression. In addition the court may, notwithstanding that an instrument may not comply with the provisions of section 5 or regulations made thereunder, register an instrument as an enduring power if it is satisfied (i) that the donor intended the power to be effective during any mental incapacity of the donor; (ii) that the power was not executed as a result of any fraud or undue pressure; (iii) that the attorney is suitable to be the donor's attorney and (iv) that it is desirable in the interests of justice to register the instrument.[135] There have been instances where enduring powers of attorney executed under the legislation of England and Wales have been admitted for registration under this power.[136]

If at the time of application for registration there is already in force an order made in wardship proceedings under the Lunacy Regulation (Ireland) Act 1871 appointing a committee of the estate and the enduring power created by the instrument has not also been revoked the court may make such order as seems proper in the circumstances including if appropriate an order revoking the order made under the Act.[137]

---

[131] [1999] 2 I.L.R.M 509.
[132] *Ibid.* at 512.
[133] *Ibid.* at 512–513.
[134] [2000] 1 All E.R. 175.
[135] Powers of Attorney Act 1996, s.10(5).
[136] See "Enduring Powers of Attorney: Guidelines for Solicitors", para.2.5.
[137] Powers of Attorney Act 1996, s.10(6).

Actions pending Registration   Once the attorney makes an application for registration and pending the determination of the application an attorney may take action under the power (a) to maintain the donor or prevent loss to the donor's estate, (b) to maintain the attorney or other persons if the donor might be expected to provide for his/he or that person's needs respectively and may do whatever the donor might be expected to do to meet those needs,[138] or (c) to make a personal care decision which cannot reasonably be deferred until the application has been determined.[139] Where an attorney purports to act in pursuance of these powers in a transaction with a third party who deals with the attorney without knowledge that the attorney is acting otherwise then in favour of that third party, the transaction between them shall be as valid as if the attorney were acting in accordance with those powers.[140]

Effect and proof of registration

Once the instrument creating the power is registered the donor may not validly revoke the power[141] unless the court confirms the revocation.[142] In addition a disclaimer of the power will be invalid unless notice of it has been given to the donor and the consent of the court has been obtained to the disclaimer.[143] Further, the donor may not extend or restrict the scope of authority conferred by the instrument and no consent or instruction given by the donor after registration will have any effect either in relation to the attorney or other persons.[144] These effects continue for as long as the instrument is registered whether or not the donor is for the time being mentally incapable.[145]

Section 11 provides that on registration of an enduring power, the Registrar of Wards of Court must supply an attested copy of the enduring power to the donor and any persons who were given notice under paragraph 2 of the First Schedule to the 1996 Act of the application for registration.[146] Section 11(5) provides that a document purporting to be a copy attested by an officer of the Office of Wards of Court of an instrument registered under the 1996 Act shall be evidence of the contents of the instrument and of the fact that it has been so registered.[147]

---

[138] Powers of Attorney Act 1996, s.7(2)(b) and s.6(4).

[139] *Ibid.*, s.7(2).

[140] *Ibid.*, s.7(3).

[141] At present legislation does not provide for any procedures for the formal revocation of an enduring power of attorney prior to registration. Thus is not clear what amounts to revocation in this regard.

[142] See below. The court has power to confirm the revocation under s.12(3) where it is satisfied that the donor has done whatever is necessary in law to effect an express revocation of the power and was mentally capable of revoking a power of attorney at the time of the purported revocation.

[143] S.11(1)(b). By virtue of O.129, r.4 an application to disclaim a power must be made by notice of motion to the court and be lodged in the Office of Wards of Court. Such motion must as far as practicable be in the Form No.2 set out in the Appendix to O.129 and be grounded upon the affidavit of the moving party. The affidavit must fully set forth the facts and circumstances giving rise to the making of the application. The provisions of r.3(2) to 3(9) (which apply to applications for registration (see above)) apply also to applications to disclaim a power.

[144] Powers of Attorney Act 1996, s.11(1).

[145] *Ibid.*, s.11(2).

[146] *Ibid.*, s.11(3).

[147] Note s.21 provides an alternative method of proving an instrument creating a power of attorney. It provides that a power of attorney may be proved by production of the original copy or of a copy

Notification to the Registrar of Wards of Court after Registration

The Law Society's Guidelines advise that attorneys should be advised that the Registrar of Wards of Court be notified if any of the following events occur after the registration of the enduring power:

(a) change of address of attorney;

(b) change of address of donor;

(c) death of donor;

(d) where the attorney becomes mentally incapable (in this event their committee/ attorney should notify the Registrar);

(e) where the attorney dies (in this event the attorney's personal representative should notify the Registrar);

(f) any other event which would terminate or invalidate the enduring power (e.g. if the donor recovers capacity or if the attorney is adjudicated a bankrupt).[148]

Functions of the court in relation to a registered power

Once the enduring power has been registered the court also has certain powers that may be exercised under section 12 of the Act on application[149] to it by the donor, the attorney or any other interested party to deal with certain matters arising in the course of the

---

which: (a) is certified by the donor of the power or by a solicitor or member firm (within the meaning of the Stock Exchange Act, 1995) or in such other manner as the court approves to be a true copy of the original, or (b) where the instrument has been deposited in the Central Office of the High Court pursuant to s.22 is attested in accordance with that section. S.22(1) provides that an instrument creating a power of attorney, its execution being verified by affidavit, statutory declaration or other sufficient evidence, may with the affidavit or declaration, if any, be deposited in the Central Office of the High Court. S.22(3) provides that a copy of an instrument so deposited may be presented at the Central Office and may be stamped or marked as an attested copy and when so stamped or marked shall become an attested copy. S.22(4) states that an attested copy of an instrument so deposited shall without further proof be sufficient evidence of the contents of the instrument and of the deposit thereof in the Central Office. S.22(5) provides that ss.22(2)–22(4) apply to instruments deposited in the Central Office before the commencement of this section. By virtue of s.22(6), s.22 applies to instruments creating powers of attorney whenever executed.

S.21(2) provides that it is immaterial for the purposes of s.21(1) how many removes there are between copy and original or by what means (which may include facsimile transmission) the copy produced or any intermediary copy was made. S.21(3) provides that s.21 is without prejudice to any other method of proof authorised by law. Accordingly, s.21 is not excluded from applying to enduring powers. However, it would seem preferable to rely on s.11(5) in relation to the proof of an enduring power and the fact that it has been registered.

[148] See "Enduring Powers of Attorney: Guidelines for Solicitors", para.3.3.

[149] Where an application is made to the court to exercise any power conferred on it by ss.12(2)–12(6) of the 1996 Act. O.129, r.4 provides that it must be made by notice of motion to the court and be lodged in the Office of Wards of Court. The motion must as far as practicable be in the Form No.2 to the Appendix to O.129 and be grounded upon the affidavit of the moving party. The affidavit must fully set forth the facts and circumstances giving rise to the making of the application. The provisions of O.129, rr 3(2) to 3(9) (which apply to applications for registration (see above)) apply to applications to the court for the exercise of powers by it under ss.12(2)–12(6) inclusive.

management of the donor's affairs during the period of registration. First, it may determine any question as to the meaning and effect of the instrument. Secondly, it may give directions in relation to certain matters regarding the management of the donor's affairs. These are:

(i)   the management or disposal by the attorney[150] of the property and affairs of the donor;

(ii) the rendering of accounts by the attorney and the production of the records kept by the attorney for that purpose;

(iii) the remuneration or expenses of the attorney whether or not in default of or in accordance with any provision made by the instrument including directions for the repayment of excessive remuneration or the payment of additional remuneration;

(iv) a personal care decision made or to be made by the attorney.[151]

The court may also require the attorney to furnish information or produce documents or things in his or her possession as attorney or give any consent or authorisation to act which the attorney would have to obtain from a mentally capable donor. It may authorise the attorney to act for the attorney's own benefit or that of persons other than the donor otherwise than in accordance with section 6(4) (qualified power to provide for needs) and section 6(5) (restrictions on the making of gifts). It may also, where appropriate relieve the attorney wholly or partly from any liability incurred or which may have been incurred on account of a breach of duty as attorney.

The court may confirm a revocation of a power on application to it by or on behalf of a donor with notice having been given to the attorney if it is satisfied that the donor has done whatever is necessary in law to effect an express revocation of the power, and was mentally capable of revoking a power of attorney at the time of the purported revocation.[152]

Cancellation of Registration of Enduring Power

The court may cancel the registration of an instrument where it confirms the revocation of a power on the application of a donor under section 12(3),[153] or consents to the disclaimer of the power on notice to the donor under section 11(1)(b), or when it gives

---

[150] The powers of the court under this section are exercisable in the case where more than one attorney has been appointed in relation to any attorney appointed under the power. See S.14(2) Second Schedule Part 1.

[151] Powers of Attorney Act 1996, s.12(2) The procedure for application to the court is set out in O.129 of the Rules of the Superior Courts as inserted by the Rules of the Superior Court (No.1) (Powers of Attorney Act 1996) 2000 (S.I. No.66 of 2000). Application must be made by notice of motion to the court and be lodged in the Office of Wards of Court. Such motion must so far as practicable be in Form No.2 of the Appendix to O.129 and must be grounded upon the affidavit of the moving party which must set forth fully the facts and circumstances giving rise to the application. The provisions of O.129, rr 3(2)–3(9) apply to such an application. See O.129, r.4.

[152] S.12(3).

[153] See preceding paragraph.

a direction revoking the power on the exercise by it of any of its powers of wardship under the Lunacy Regulation (Ireland) Act 1871.

It may also cancel the registration on being satisfied that the donor is and is likely to remain mentally capable and in certain other circumstances. These include where it is satisfied that the power has ceased to be in force by the death or adjudication in bankruptcy of the donor or by virtue of the lapse of the power under section 5(7) (invalidation of power in favour of spouse on dissolution of marriage, separation or making of protection or barring order) or its cessation in force under section 5(9) on the direction of the court on exercise by it of its wardship jurisdiction under the Lunacy Regulation (Ireland) Act 1871, or by the death or mental incapacity of the attorney or by his disqualification under the terms of section 5(6).[154]

The powers of cancellation also extend to the circumstances where it is satisfied that the power was not a valid and subsisting enduring power when registration was effected. In the circumstances where it is satisfied having regard to all the circumstances that the attorney was unsuitable to be the donor's attorney,[155] or that fraud or undue pressure was used to induce the donor to create the power it has power to cancel the registration and if it does so it must also by order revoke the instrument.[156] Finally, it has a residual discretionary power to cancel the registration for any other good and sufficient reason.[157]

Where it cancels the registration of an instrument in any of the above circumstances other than where it is satisfied that the donor is and is likely to remain mentally capable the instrument must be delivered up to be cancelled unless the court otherwise directs.[158] An enduring power ceases to be in force, *inter alia*, on the exercise by the court of its wardship jurisdiction under the Lunacy Regulations (Ireland) Act 1871 if the court so directs.[159]

Protection of attorney and third person where registered power is invalid or not in force

Section 13(2) of the 1996 Act provides that an attorney who acts in pursuance of an enduring power which is not or is no longer a valid power of which has ceased to be in force will not thereby incur any liability (either to the donor or to any other person) unless at the time of acting the attorney knows (a) that the instrument did not create a valid enduring power, or (b) that an event has occurred which, if the instrument had recreated a valid enduring power, would have invalidated the power or caused it to cease to be in force, or (c) that the instrument has been cancelled. Section 13(3) states that any transaction between the attorney and another person shall, in favour of that person, be as valid as if the power had then been in evidence, unless at the time of the

---

[154] See above circumstances in which an enduring power ceases to be in force. Where there is more than one attorney appointed under the power this provision is applicable to any attorney under the power subject to the power of the remaining attorney(s) to continue to act unless the instrument creating the power expressly provides to the contrary. Powers of Attorney Act 1996, s.14(2), (3).

[155] This applies to any attorney where more than one is appointed. See Powers of Attorney Act 1996, s.14 (2).

[156] Powers of Attorney Act 1996, s.12(4), (5).

[157] *Ibid.*, s.12(4).

[158] *Ibid.*, s.12(6).

[159] *Ibid.*, s.5(9).

transaction that person has knowledge of any of the matters mentioned in section 13(2). Sections 13(2) and (3) apply where an instrument, which did not create a valid enduring power, has been registered, whether or not the registration has been cancelled at the time of the act or transaction in question.

Where the interest of a purchaser depends on whether a transaction between the attorney and another person was valid by virtue of section 13(3), section 13(4) provides that if (a) the transaction between that person and the attorney was completed within twelve months of the date on which the instrument was registered, or (b) that person makes a statutory declaration[160] before or within three months after completion of the purchase, it shall be presumed in favour of the purchaser (unless the contrary is shown that the transaction was valid) that he or she had no reason at the time of the transaction to doubt that the attorney had authority to dispose of the property which was the subject of the transaction. "Purchaser" means a purchaser in good faith for valuable consideration and includes a lessee, mortgagee or other person who, for valuable consideration, acquires an interest in any property and also includes an intending purchaser.[161]

Protection of attorney and other persons where an enduring power attorney is revoked

Section 18(1) of the Act provides that a donee of a power of attorney who acts in pursuance of the power at a time when it has been revoked shall not, by reason of the revocation, incur any liability (either to the donor or to any other person) if at that time the donee did not know that the power had been revoked. Section 18(2) provides protection to third parties who deal with the donee when a power of attorney has been revoked and states that where a power of attorney has been revoked and a person, without knowledge of the revocation deals with the donee of the power, the transaction between them shall in favour of that person be as valid as if the power had then been in force.

Section 18(4) provides that where the interest of a purchaser depends on whether a transaction between the donee of a power of attorney and another person was valid by virtue of section 18(2) it shall be presumed in favour of the purchaser, unless the contrary is shown, that that person did not at the material time know of the revocation of the power if (a) the transaction between the person and the donee was completed within twelve months of the date on which the power came into operation, or (b) that person makes a statutory declaration[162] before or within three months after the completion of the purchase, that that person did not at the material time know of the revocation of the power. "Purchaser" means a purchaser in good faith for valuable consideration and includes a lessee, mortgagee or other person who, for valuable consideration, acquires an interest in any property and includes also an intending purchaser.[163]

For the purposes of section 18 knowledge of the revocation of the power of attorney

---

[160] Powers of Attorney Act 1996, s.3 provides that where for any purpose of the 1996 Act a statutory declaration is to be made by a person being a corporation aggregate it may be made on behalf of the corporation by a person authorised by the corporation to act on its behalf.

[161] Powers of Attorney Act 1996, s.13(6), s.18(6).

[162] S.3 of the 1996 Act provides that where, for any purpose under the 1996 Act a statutory declaration is to be made by a person being a corporation aggregate it may be made on behalf of the corporation by a person authorised by the corporation to act on its behalf.

[163] Powers of Attorney Act 1996, s.18(6).

includes knowledge of the occurrence of any event (such as the death of the donor), which has the effect of revoking the power.[164] Where section 18 applies to an enduring power the revocation of which by the donor is, by virtue of section 11(1)(a) invalid unless and until confirmed by the court under section 12(3), knowledge of the confirmation of the revocation is knowledge of the revocation but knowledge of the unconfirmed revocation is not.[165] Section 18 applies to a power of attorney whenever created but only to acts and transactions after the commencement of the section.[166]

Protection of transferee under a stock exchange transaction

Section 19 provides that without prejudice to section 18 where (a) the donee of a power of attorney executes as transferor an instrument transferring registered securities, and (b) the instrument is executed for the purposes of a stock exchange transaction it shall be presumed in favour of the transferee unless the contrary is shown that the power had not been revoked at the date of the instrument if a statutory declaration[167] to that effect is made by the donee of the power on or within three months after that date. In section 19, "registered securities" and "stock exchange transaction" have the same meanings as under the Stock Transfer Act 1963. Section 1 of the 1963 Act defines "securities" as including shares, stock, debentures, debenture stock, loan stock and bonds and "registered securities" as securities the holders of which are entered in a register. "Stock exchange transaction" is defined as meaning a sale and purchase of securities in which each of the parties is a member of a stock exchange acting in the ordinary course of his business as such or is acting through the agency of such a member.

Joint and several attorneys

A donor of an enduring power may appoint one or more than one attorney to manage the donor's affairs. The Law Society's Guidelines point out that the advantage of appointing more than one attorney is that the opportunities for abuse of power by an attorney acting alone are limited.[168] Section 14 of the Act provides that an instrument, which appoints more than one person to be an attorney, may specify that the attorneys are appointed to act either jointly (*i.e.* act together when making decisions) or jointly and severally. In default of specification the attorneys shall be deemed to have been appointed to act jointly. The 1996 Act in its application to joint attorneys applies to them collectively as it applies to a single attorney. This is subject to the modifications specified in section 14(3) and Part 1 of the Second Schedule.

---

[164] Powers of Attorney Act 1996, s.18(5).

[165] *Ibid.*, s.13(5) An enduring power cannot be revoked after registration without the confirmation of the court See s.12(3) and s.12(4)(a). An enduring power may be revoked prior to registration but this revocation will be of no significance to donees or purchasers because an enduring power cannot come into force until it has been registered under s.10.

[166] The Act came into force on August 1, 1996. See Powers of Attorney Act 1996 (Commencement) Order 1996 (S.I. No.195 of 1996).

[167] S.3 of the 1996 Act provides that where, for any purposes of the 1996 Act a statutory declaration is to be made by a person being a corporation aggregate it may be made on behalf of the corporation by a person authorised by the corporation to act on its behalf.

[168] See "Enduring Powers of Attorney: Guidelines for Solicitors", para.1.4.

Section 14(3) provides that where two or more persons are appointed or are deemed to have been appointed to act jointly then, in the case of the death, incapacity or disqualification of any one or more of them, the remaining attorney or attorneys may continue to act, whether solely or jointly as the case may be *unless the instrument creating the power expressly provides to the contrary.*

The Law Society's Guidelines point out these provisions indicate that it is possible to appoint substitute attorneys but that provision for substitute attorneys must be made at the time of the execution of the enduring power.[169]

Part 1 of the Second Schedule provides that in section 5(4) the reference to the time when the attorney executes the instrument shall be read as a reference to the time when the second or last attorney executed the instrument. Paragraph 2 of Part 1 of the Second Schedule provides that in sections 5(5) (a power of attorney which gives an attorney a right to appoint a substitute or successor cannot be an enduring power), 8 (functions of the court prior to registration), 10(3) (validity of notices of objection), 12(2) (powers of court in relation to registered power) and 12(4) (power of court to cancel registration) references to the attorney shall be read as including references to any attorney under the power and in the case of 12(4)(d)[170] references to the attorney shall be read subject to section 14(3) (see above, para.10–49). Paragraph 2A of Second Schedule, Part 1,[171] provides that the expiry of an enduring power of attorney in the circumstances mentioned in section 5(7) (expiry on annulment or dissolution of marriage) shall apply only so far as it relates to an attorney who is the spouse of the donor.

The Act in its application to joint and several attorneys applies with the modifications specified in sections 14(5) to 14(8) and in Part II of the Second Schedule. Section 14(5) provides that a failure as respects any other attorney to comply with the provisions of section 5 and regulations made thereunder shall prevent the instrument applying in that attorney's case without However, affecting its efficacy as respects the other or others.

Section 14(6) provides that where one or more but not both or all of the attorneys makes or joins in making an application for registration of the instrument then (a) an attorney who is not an applicant as well as one who is may act pending the determination of the application as provided in section 7(2) or under section 8; (b) notice of the application shall also be given under the First Schedule to the other attorney or attorneys; and (c) objection may validly be taken to the registration on a ground relating to an attorney or to the power of attorney who is not an applicant as well as to one or the power of one who is an applicant.

---

[169] See Powers of Attorney Act 1996, s.5(3) and (5). See also "Enduring Powers of Attorney: Guidelines for Solicitors", para.1.4.

[170] S.12(4)(d) refers to the power of the court to cancel registration on being satisfied that the power has ceased to be in force by the death or adjudication in bankruptcy of the donor or by virtue of s.5(7) (circumstances in which power in favour of spouse invalidated or ceases to be in force) or by virtue of s.5(9) (on the exercise by the court of any of its powers under the Lunacy Regulations Act 1871 if the court so directs) or by the death or by virtue of mental incapacity of the attorney or by virtue of s.5(6) (invalidation of enduring power or cessation in force by virtue of the adjudication in bankruptcy of the attorney or if the attorney is a body corporate on it winding up or dissolution or on the attorney being convicted of certain offences or becoming a person in respect of whom a declaration is made under s.150 of the Companies Act 1990 or a person who is or was subject to a disqualification order by virtue of Part VII of that Act or becoming the owner of a nursing home in which the donor resides or a person residing with or an employee or agent of the owner.

[171] As amended by Family Law (Divorce) Act 1996, s.50.

Section 14(7) states that the court shall not refuse under section 10(4) to register an instrument because a ground of objection to an attorney or a power is established if an enduring power subsists as respects an attorney who is not affected thereby but the court shall give effect to it by the prescribed[172] qualification of the registration.

Section 14(8) provides that the court shall not cancel the registration of an instrument under section 12(4) in any of the circumstances specified in that subsection if an enduring power subsists as respects an attorney who is not affected thereby but shall give effect to it by the prescribed[173] qualification of the registration.

Part II of the Second Schedule provides that the expiry of an enduring power effected in the circumstances mentioned in section 5(7) (on annulment or dissolution of marriage, judicial separation, separation agreement, protection order etc.) shall apply only so far as it relates to an attorney who is the spouse of the donor. If a person does not wish to create an enduring power of attorney, then it is possible to take such measures as transferring bank accounts into joint names or the creation of an inter vivos trust particularly if the assets involved are substantial but in this case the tax implications should be considered.

Commentary

1. The Irish enduring power of attorney may confer authority only in relation to the donor's financial affairs and certain personal care decisions. It may not confer authority in relation to healthcare decisions. When the Powers of Attorney Bill 1995 was being debated in the Oireachtas, an amendment was proposed by the opposition to enable a power of attorney to be granted in respect of health care. The Government rejected the amendment. The Minister for Justice Equality and Law Reform stated that:

   "the extension of the powers of attorney to such matters would involve issues of the greatest sensitivity and that it would be wrong to amend the Bill before the matter had been researched thoroughly and there had been extensive consultations".[174]

   The Minister also stated that health care:

   "can involve difficult operations, such as putting people on and taking them off life support machines … it would have to be approached with a good deal of care and research".[175]

   The Irish Law Reform Commission in its *Consultation Paper on the Law and the Elderly*,[176] recommends that attorneys under enduring powers of attorney should

---

[172] "Prescribed" is stated to mean prescribed by rules of court. See s.14(9) and O.129, r.4(8) of the Rules of the Superior Courts (S.I. No.66 of 2000).

[173] "Prescribed" means prescribed by rules of court. See 1996 Act, s.14(9) and O.129, r.4(8) of the Rules of the Superior Courts (S.I. No.66 of 2000).

[174] *Dáil Debates* Vol.465, May 15, 1996, Col.1126.

[175] *Ibid.*, Col.1132.

[176] L.R.C. CP 23–2003.

be empowered to take minor or emergency health care decisions on behalf of the donor if the specific authority to do so is contained in the enduring power of attorney.[177]

Health care matters for both physical and mental conditions are perhaps among those most frequently addressed during a donor's incapacity, and it is appropriate that they should be considered for inclusion within the enduring power of attorney scheme.

2. While the Powers of Attorney Act 1996 in Ireland is to be welcomed as a less cumbersome alternative to wardship it has been criticised on the basis that its usefulness is limited to those cases where people have the foresight to put the procedure in place as a donor must be shown to be mentally competent to create the power.[178] In addition does leave a number of matters unaddressed.

    (a) It does not specify directly the degree of capacity required to create the power. However, in the English decision of *In re K*,[179] it was held that the degree of capacity required for the donor to create a general power was an understanding that the attorney can assume control over all his affairs, can do anything the donor can do, can continue in power even if the donor becomes incapable and the power cannot then be revoked without the confirmation of the court. The judge in that case also commented that if the donor was capable of signing an enduring power of attorney but incapable of managing and administering his or her property and affairs the attorney has an obligation to register the power right away. The British Medical Association/Law Society of England and Wales Report on *Assessment of Mental Capacity*,[180] notes that nearly half of the applications received by the Court of Protection involve enduring powers which have been created less than three months before application was made and suggests that arguably the attorney has a moral duty in such cases to forewarn the donor that registration is not merely possible but is intended immediately. This highlights the need for a well-defined test of capacity. It notes that the test in *In re K*, for assessing capacity has been criticised as imposing too simple a test of capacity to create an enduring power and states that it may be inferred from the decision in *In re Beaney*,[181] that in assessing capacity under the test closed questions inviting a "Yes" or "No" answer are inadequate for assessing capacity.[182]

    (b) In practice by the time the power has to be registered it may be too late to object to it on the grounds that it was not valid, that it was induced by fraud or undue pressure or that in all the circumstances the attorney is unsuitable. A right to object at the time of creation may be a better safeguard.

---

[177] L.R.C. CP 23–2003, p.67.

[178] See Patricia Rickard Clarke, "Critical Issues in Disability Law Reform: Legal Capacity: Proposals for Reform" (Paper delivered to Conference Global Trends in Disability Law Reform Law Society September 2003) 4.

[179] [1988] Ch. 310.

[180] British Medical Association, December 1995, p.24.

[181] [1978] 2 All E.R. 595.

[182] Assessment of Mental Capacity: Guidance for Doctors and Lawyers (British Medical Association December 1995) 24.

(c) At present legislation does not specify how an enduring power of attorney may be revoked prior to its registration. The Law Reform Commission in its *Consultation Paper on the Law and the Elderly*,[183] has pointed out that donors may consider that a power has been revoked simply by stating this to the relevant people or by destroying the instrument and that while in the absence of legislation this may constitute a revocation the situation as a matter of law is not clear. The Commission therefore recommended that prior to its registration the revocation of the enduring power of attorney should be governed by the same formal requirements as its execution and that solicitors be obliged to inform clients of their right to revoke at the time of execution.

(d) Once a power is registered the Irish legislation does not provide adequate supervision of the system to ensure that attorneys appointed under the legislation carry out their functions in an appropriate manner.[184] It is submitted that clearly specified duties to act should be placed by the legislation upon attorneys appointed under an enduring power with clear guidelines as to how the attorney should exercise his/her powers.

(e) The present legislation contains inadequate provisions for accountability of attorneys. There is no independent monitoring of the acts of the attorneys and no requirement to file accounts. To address this situation the Law Reform Commission in its *Consultation Paper relating to the Law and the Elderly*,[185] has recommended that attorneys be required to prepare and maintain a list of property and rights over which they have taken control and a list of transactions involving the donor's property and rights. In addition, it recommends that the donor of the enduring power of attorney should be empowered by regulations to nominate another person to receive the accounts and the attorney should be required to submit accounts at intervals for inspection, and that a proposed Office of the Public Guardian should have power to call for accounts if doubts have been cast on the attorneys activities.[186]

Further, it is submitted that the court should have explicit power to revoke an enduring power of attorney where the donee is behaving or proposes to behave in such a way that: (1) contravenes of would contravene the authority in an enduring power of attorney, or (2) is not or would not be in the donor's best interests.

3. It is submitted that would add flexibility to the scheme if the court had express power to modify or extend the attorney's capacity to act unless the instrument creating the power provided otherwise. The court could have such power to act where the donor is without capacity to act and the court thinks it desirable to do so.

---

[183] L.R.C. CP23–2003, p.72.
[184] See P. Rickard-Clarke, *op. cit.*
[185] L.R.C. CP23–2003.
[186] *Ibid.*, p.78.

INCAPACITY OF PARTNERS

Current law

"Unsoundness of mind" does not of itself bar a person from becoming a partner unless the unsoundness of mind is such as to deprive the person concerned of the capacity to enter into the contract of partnership. Where a person lacks such capacity but purports to enter into a partnership contract he may still, on normal contractual principles be bound as a partner if the other partner acts *bona fide* and had no knowledge of the incapacity.[187] The other partner may also be liable to third parties with whom s/he deals if he holds him/herself out or allows him/herself to be held out as the partner of the person who lacked the relevant capacity to enter into partnership.[188]

Where a person has capacity at the time of entering into the partnership contract, his subsequent incapacity will not disentitle him to the share of the profits made at a later date by his co-partners[189] nor relieve him of responsibility for their misconduct[190] nor will it automatically bring the partnership to an end,[191] but it is a ground for applying to the court for a dissolution of the partnership.[192]

Section 35(a) of the Partnership Act 1890 provides that the High Court has jurisdiction to decree dissolution of partnership, whenever a partner is found lunatic by inquisition or is shown to the satisfaction of the court to be permanently of unsound mind. Application may be made by the committee or next friend of the partner concerned or another partner. In deciding whether to order a dissolution the court will take into consideration the need to protect the ward or partner with mental illness[193] and the need to relieve co-partners of the difficult position in which the mental disorder of the partner places them.[194] There must be confirmed evidence of permanent mental illness before the court will act[195] and it will not order a dissolution if the partner alleged to be of unsound mind is only temporarily ill[196] or recovers before the hearing[197] or on the grounds of a partners former unsoundness of mind.[198]

The court also has power to grant relief pending dissolution for the preservation of

---

[187] See *Imperial Loan Co. v. Stone* [1892] 1 Q.B. 599; *Drew v. Nunn* (1879) 4 Q.B.D 661; *Moulton v. Camroux* (1849) 2 Ex. 487 and 4 Ex. 17; *Beavan v. McDonnell* (1854) 9 Ex. 309 and 10 Ex. 184; *Baxter v. The Earl of Portsmouth* (1826) 5 B & C 170; *Brown v. Jodrell* (1827) 3 C&P 30.

[188] Partnership Act 1890, s.14 (1).

[189] *Joy v. Noy* (1833) 3 M& K 125.

[190] *Sadler v. Lee* (1843) 6 Beav 324.

[191] Twomey suggests that the effect is to render an incapacitated partner a dormant partner. See Twomey M., *Partnership Law* (Butterworths, 2000), p591.

[192] *Sayer v. Bennet* (1784) 1 Cox Eq. Cas. 107 cited in *Jones v. Lloyd* (1874) L.R. 18 Eq. 265 at 273–274.

[193] *Jones v. Lloyd* (1874) 18 Eq. 265.

[194] *Sayer v. Bennet* (1784) 1 Cox 107; *Wrexham v. Hudleston*(1734) 1 Sw 514; *James v. Noy* (1833) 2 M & K 125; *Sadler v. Lee* (1843) 6 Beav. 324; *Leaf v. Coles* (1851) 1 De GM & G 171; *Anon* (1856) 2 K& J. 441 and Lord Eldon's observations in *Waters v. Taylor* (1813) 2 V& B 299 at 303.

[195] *Sadler v. Lee* (1843) 6 Beav 324; *Waters v. Taylor* (1807) 2 V & B 299.

[196] *Leaf v. Coles* (1851) 1 De GM & G 171.

[197] *Whitwell v. Arthur* 35 Beav. 140.

[198] *In re Anon*, 2 K&J. 765. A partner who previously was a person of unsound mind and has recovered may be entitled to an injunction restraining the other partners from excluding him from the business on that ground.

the partnership interest of the mentally disorder partner if that is needed.[199] In an appropriate case an injunction may be granted restraining a mentally disordered partner from interfering in the conduct of the partnership affairs.[200]

Where the court orders a dissolution on the grounds of mental incapacity, it will declare the partnership dissolved as of the date of judgment and not from any date prior to that.[201] Where a dissolution takes place pursuant to a power of dissolution in the articles, the dissolution will date from the time when the partnership was dissolved in accordance with the articles and not from the date of the judgment.[202] In cases where the partnership is at will and notice to dissolve had been given, the dissolution would be ordered as from the date fixed by the notice.[203] Where the court orders a dissolution on grounds of mental disorder, it will direct the costs to be paid out of partnership assets.[204]

Where a partner becomes of unsound mind, application to the court may also be made under section 35(b) of the Partnership Act 1890 on the grounds that the partner has become permanently incapable of performing his part of the partnership contract. This indeed is usually the principle upon which the court will order a dissolution where it is established that one partner is of unsound mind but it is generally agreed that the scope of section 35(b) is wider than section 35 (a) and covers situation and covers any form of incapacity which would render a partner permanently incapable of performing his/her part of the partnership contract.

Finally, the court has a wide discretion under section 35(e) to order a dissolution whenever in any case circumstances have arisen which in the opinion of the court render it just and equitable that the partnership be dissolved. The court's discretion in this regard is not limited to situations *eiusdem generis* to those in the previous subsections and extends to any case in which it is no longer reasonably practicable to attain the object of the partnership agreement or to carry out the partnership contract according to its terms.[205] This provision would enable the court to declare a dissolution where a partner suffers from such mental illness as would render dissolution just.

Section 35 of the 1890 Act also applies to the dissolution of a limited partnership. Section 35(a) which provides for the dissolution of a partnership when a partner becomes of unsound mind is however, subject to section 6(2) of the Limited Partnership Act 1907 which provides that "[t]he lunacy of a limited partner shall not be a ground for dissolution of the partnership by the court unless the lunatic's share cannot be otherwise ascertained or realised." Accordingly the dissolution of limited partnership can be avoided in such circumstances where the continuing partners arrange to purchase the share of the incapacitated partner.[206]

---

[199] *Jones v. Lloyd* (1874) L.R. 18 Eq. 265.

[200] See *J. v. S* [1894] 3 Ch.72.

[201] *Besch v. Frolich* (1842) 1 Ph. 172.

[202] See *Robertson v. Lockie* (1846) 15 Sim. 285; *Bagshaw v. Parker* (1847) 10 Beav. 532.

[203] *Mellersh v. Keen* (1859) 27 Beav. 236 and Partnership Act 1890, s.32.

[204] *Jones v. Welch* (1855) 1 K & J. 765.

[205] *Harrison v. Tennant* (1856) 21 Beav. 482; *Electric Telegraph Co. of Ireland* (1856) 22 Beav. 471 and *Baring v. Dix* (1786) 1 Cox 213.

[206] Twomey, however, remarks that "realising a partner's share is not the easiest of matters since it is not an interest in a specific piece of partnership property but is an identical and equal right with the other partners in all the partnership assets." See *Partnership Law, op. cit.*, para.28.49. Thus if the incapacitated limited partner cannot dispose of his share in the firm it will be necessary to dissolve the partnership.

Where a partner has been taken into wardship, application also may be made by the committee, another partner or such other person as the President thinks entitled may apply for an order under section 73 of the Lunacy Regulation (Ireland) Act 1871 that the partnership be dissolved. Where such an application is made, the ensuing proceedings are indemnified against impeachment or repudiation by the ward in the event that s/he recovers.[207] If the President makes an order that the partnership be dissolved the court may make consequential orders under the 1871 Act. Thus after the order is made the committee in the name and on behalf of the ward may join with the other parties concerned in conveying the property and generally winding up the affairs of the partnership and must apply the ward's share of the assets in the manner directed by the President.[208] The costs of dissolution are payable out of the partnership assets.[209]

It is also worth mentioning that the Powers of Attorney Act 1996 would enable a partner to grant an enduring power of attorney over his partnership interest and if s/he becomes incapacitated the continuing partners would be able to deal with the donee of the power. This may avoid the need for a dissolution of the partnership. However, where a partner is by virtue of incapacity unable to undertake his obligations under a partnership agreement an application for court dissolution may still be considered necessary. However, the court is less likely to grant such an application where the partner is dormant because the impact his incapacity has on the firm is likely to be limited.

Capacity to Make Valid Deeds

Current law

If a person with mental illness is capable of understanding the nature and effect of the deed and what s/he does by executing the deed in question then s/he is deemed capable of executing the deed.[210] A person may also execute a valid deed during a lucid interval,[211] or before mental disorder and consequent incapacity supervenes.[212]

The degree or extent of understanding required in relation to a deed depends on the nature of the transaction to which the deed is to give effect. If the subject matter and the value of the gift are trivial or small when compared with the donor's other property then a low degree of understanding will suffice but if the deed, in effect disposes of the donor's only valuable asset and to all intents and purposes pre-empts the devolution of his estate then the degree of understanding required will be as high as that required for making a valid will and the donor must understand the claims of all donees and the extent of the property disposed of.[213]

---

[207] See Lunacy Regulation (Ireland) Act 1871, s.93.
[208] *Ibid.*, s.93.
[209] See *Jones v. Welch* 1 K& J. 765.
[210] See *Ball v. Mannin* (1829) 3 Bli NS 1 at 22, *Beverley's Case* (1603) 4 Co. Rep. 123b; *Yates v. Boen* (1738) 2 Stra. 1104; *Faulder v. Silk* (1811) 3 Camp 126; *Daily Telegraph Newspaper Co. Ltd v. McLaughlin* (1904) A.C. 776; *Price v. Berrington* (1849) 7 Hare 394 at 402; *Howard v. Earl of Digby* (1834) 2 Cl & Fin 634 at 663.
[211] *Towart v. Sellars* (1817) 5 Dow. 231; *Beverley's Case* (1603) 4 Co. Rep 123b; *Hall v. Warren* (1804) 9 Ves. 605; *Selby v. Jackson* (1844) 6 Beav. 192.
[212] See *Affleck v. Affleck* (1857) 3 Sm & G 394.
[213] *In re Beaney* [1978] 2 All E.R. 595; [1978] 1 W.L.R. 770 In that case an elderly woman suffering

A deed executed by a person who lacks mental capacity is void.[214] However, in deciding whether to set aside such a deed the courts of equity will consider the circumstances of the case and will grant rescission unless it is inequitable to do so.[215] While the court has powers extend to setting aside a voluntary disposition even as against subsequent purchasers for value without notice,[216] in *Towart v. Sellars*[217] rescission was refused on the grounds of delay where application was made 20 or 30 years after the disposition and the parties best acquainted with the circumstances were dead. In cases where the transaction was prudent and rescission would be inequitable the courts may also decline to grant it. [218]

The British Medical Association and the Law Society of England and Wales in their Report on *Assessment of Mental Capacity*[219] has devised a checklist of questions which may need to be asked to establish whether someone has the capacity to make a lifetime gift of a substantial asset. These include detailed questions in relation to donor's understanding of the nature and purpose of the transaction;[220] the effect of the

---

from senile dementia made a gift of her house to one of her daughters and the court on the evidence arrived at the conclusion that the donor lacked capacity to make the gift. A similar conclusion was reached in the case of *Special Trustees of Great Ormond Street Hospital for Children v. Rushin*, unreported High Court, Chancery Division April 19, 2000 where a testator found to have been suffering from Alzheimer's disease disposed of a house valued at between £200,000 and £300,000 comprising the major asset of her estate, during her lifetime, for a consideration of £50 and a promise by the donee, her housekeeper, to care for her at the house for life. It was found that the primary motivation for the transactions was the testator's desire to prevent her family's selling the home and putting her in a nursing home – a consideration which would not have entered her mind had she been in complete control of her faculties. It was also found that the disposition was unnecessary to secure her continued care at home for as long as she was fit enough to live there. Rimer J., applying the dicta in *In re Beaney* held that the requisite degree of understanding required for the testator to validly effect the agreement to sell the house was as high as that required for a will and that at the time of the transaction the testator did not have an understanding of the true effect and implications of the transaction sufficient to endow her with the capacity to make it. In the alternative, having found that the testator was suffering from a material degree of dementia occasioned by Alzheimer's disease, Rimer J. held, that the burden of proving that she had the requisite degree of capacity shifted to the donees which they had not discharged. See also the Canadian case of *Mathieu v. Saint Michel* [1956] S.C.R. 477 at 487.

[214] See *Ball v. Mannin* (1829) 3 Bli Ns 1 at 22.
[215] See *Neill v. Morley* (1804) 9 Ves 478, *Campbell v. Hooper* (1855) 3 Sm & G 153 at 158 and *Price v. Berrington* (1849) 7 Hare 394 at 402; on appeal (1851) 3 Mac & G 486.
[216] See *Clerk v. Clerk* (1700) 2 Vern 412; *Elliot v. Ince* (1857) 7 De G M & G 275; *Sentance v. Poole* (1827) 3 CNP; *Manning v. Gill* (1872) L.R. 13 Eq. 485.
[217] (1817) 5 Dow 231 at 236–237.
[218] See *Selby v. Jackson* (1844) 6 Beav. 192, *Niell v. Morley* (1804) 9 Ves 478, *Campbell v. Hooper* (1855) 3 Sm & G 153 at 158 cited by Sargant L.J. in *York Glass Co. Ltd v. Jubb* (1925) 124 L.T .36 at 44.
[219] British Medical Association December 1995, p.42–43.
[220] The Checklist states that the person making the gift should understand (i) that it is a gift rather that say a loan or mortgage advance or the acquisition of a stake or share in the recipient's business or property; (ii) whether he or she expects to receive anything in return; (iii) whether he or she intends the gift to take effect immediately or at some later date – perhaps on death (iv) who the recipient is (v) whether he or she has already made substantial gifts to the recipient or others; (vi) whether the gift is an one–off or part of a larger transaction or series of transactions; (vii) the fact that, if the gift is outright, he or she will not be able to ask for the asset to be returned to them; (viii) the underlying purpose of the transaction.

transaction;[221] the extent of the property particularly in the context of his other assets[222] and the claims to which the giver ought to give effect.[223]

Most of the existing authorities regarding capacity to execute deeds, predate the later cases on capacity to execute contracts and it may be that where deeds are made for valuable consideration the criteria applicable to capacity to contract apply and that different criteria apply to voluntary dispositions.[224] A deed of disposition executed by a person who is property or affairs are under the wardship jurisdiction of the President of the High Court is void.[225]

Commentary

The Law Reform Commission in its Consultation Paper on *Law and the Elderly* provisionally recommended that a number of protective measures be taken when elderly clients propose to make gifts of property. In particular it recommends that detailed guidelines should be considered to assist solicitors and other professionals in dealing with financial and property transactions including gifts of property for vulnerable elderly people. These guidelines should be so designed as to assist solicitors in detecting and dealing appropriately with suspected cases of undue influence and in advising elderly clients as to the consequences of their actions in respect of their own future care. The Commission recommended that the guidelines be formulated and updated by the relevant professional bodies and with the proposed Office of the Public Guardian.[226]

The guidelines should address the issues of (i) who is the client? – advising the solicitors to avoid conflict of interest situations where s/he is acting for both the donor and recipient of the gift unless each party agrees separately to this scenario; (ii) is the gift appropriate in the client's circumstances? – and in this regard examine the motivation for the gift and whether the result may be achieved by other means; (iii) alternative measures – whether a will or an enduring power of attorney would equally well give effect to the client's intentions.

---

[221] The Checklist states that the person making the gift should understand (i) the effect that making the gift will have on his or her own standard of living in the future, having regard to all the circumstances including his or her age, life expectancy, income, financial resources, financial responsibilities and financial needs; and (ii) the effect making the gift may have on the recipient.

[222] The Checklist states that the person making the gift should understand (i) that the subject matter of the gift belongs to him or her, and that he or she is entitled to dispose of it; and (ii) the extent (and possibly the value) of the property comprised in the gift in relation to all the circumstances and, in particular, in the context of his or her other assets.

[223] The Checklist states that the person making the gift should be able to comprehend and appreciate the claims of the potential beneficiaries under his or her will or intestacy. For instance (i) the effect the gift could have on other beneficiaries; (ii) why the recipient is more deserving than others. For example the recipient may be less well-off financially, have devoted more time and attention to caring for the person in need of greater assistance because of age, gender or physical or mental disabilities; (iii) whether it is necessary to compensate others, perhaps by making a new will; (iv) did the person show any bias or favouritism towards the recipient before making the gift.

[224] In *In re Beaney* [1978] 2 All E.R. 595, [1978] 1 W.L.R. 770 the English Court declined to express a view on the matter.

[225] See *In re Walker* [1905] 1 Ch. 160; *In re Marshall, Marshall v. Whateley* [1920] 1 Ch. 284.

[226] This office is to be set up following the abolition of the wards of court jurisdiction of the High Court proposed by the Consultation Paper.

The Commission recommends that the Guidelines should also require that the solicitor keep a record of the advice and set a written note to the client of the advice, explaining the nature and effect of the proposed transaction. The Commission further recommends that the Guidelines require the solicitor make an assessment of the legal capacity of the client to enter the proposed transaction and if in doubt arrange for a medical assessment. Finally the Commission recommends that the guidelines require the solicitor to advise the client about the existence of and the services to be provided by the proposed Office of the Public Guardian.[227]

TESTAMENTARY CAPACITY

Capacity to make a valid will

Section 77 of the Succession Act 1965 provides that if a will is to be valid it must be made, *inter alia*, by a person who is of sound disposing mind. The term "sound disposing mind" is not defined in the statute, but in the case of *In re Glynn (Deceased)*,[228] McCarthy J. stated that the term was:

> "a judicial term of art requiring that the testator should know and approve the contents of the will and, at the time of execution of the will be of sound mind, memory and understanding."

There is a presumption that a testator has capacity to make a will and where a duly executed will is rational on its face a presumption of capacity will arise.[229] Provided a testator has testamentary capacity at the time of making the will he may make whatever dispositions he chooses however, unwise or unkind. This is in accordance with the principle of testamentary freedom. Thus in *Bird v. Luckie*[230] Wigram V.C. stated:

> "No man is bound to make a will in such a manner as to deserve approbation from the prudent, the wise or the good. A testator is permitted to be capricious and improvident, and is moreover at liberty to conceal the circumstances and the motives by which he has been actuated in his disposition."

Role of medical witnesses

Where, however, testamentary capacity is contested the determination as to whether or not a person has testamentary capacity is ultimately a decision for a court. Medical witnesses and other witnesses have a crucial role to play in providing the evidence that is considered in that determination. A medical witness who attended a testator may give

---

[227] L.R.C. CP23–2003, pp.146–148.
[228] [1990] 2 I.R. 326.
[229] *Wellesly v. Vere* (1841) 2 Curt 917; *Symes v. Green* (1859) 1 Sw & Tr 401; *Sutton v. Sadler* (1857) 3 C.B. (n.s.) 87, 98. See *Arbery v. Ashe* (1828) 1 Hagg. Ecc. 214; *Austen v. Graham* (1854) 8 Moo. P.C. 493 regarding wills which appear irrational on their face.
[230] (1850) S. Hare 301 at 306.

evidence, as a witness of fact, of facts, which s/he has personally observed. An expert medical witness who did not see or examine the testator may express an opinion on facts otherwise proved in evidence. An expert witness owes a duty to the court as well as to the person who capacity has been assessed. Notwithstanding the evidence of expert medical witnesses evidence of other eyewitnesses who observed and knew the putative testator has been preferred in some cases.[231]

The elements of Testamentary Capacity

The key legal criteria, which are applied to establish whether capacity exists, are those of understanding, memory and awareness of moral obligations. The classic statement of the law is to be found in the case of *Banks v. Goodfellow*.[232] In that case Cockburn C.J. stated that if a testator is to make a valid will:

> "It is essential ... that [s/he] shall understand the nature of the act and its effects; shall understand the extent of the property of which he is disposing; shall be able to comprehend and appreciate the claims to which he ought to give effect. ..."

In order to establish that a testator understands "the nature of the act and its effects" it is not necessary to show that s/he understood the precise legal effect of the will but will be necessary to establish that s/he comprehended the effect of his/her wishes being carried out at his/her death, the fact that the will would not take effect until death and could be revoked until then.

The test to establish that a testator understands "the extent of the property of which he is disposing" is a relative one. The law does not expect a testator with a wide variety of property interests to carry in his mind a detailed inventory of them,[233] but it would require one modest means to recall his assets and record information relating to them in the will.

Sound mind, memory and understanding

The testator must also be able to "comprehend and appreciate the claims to which he ought to give effect."[234] While there is nothing to prevent a testator from disinheriting people who may have a moral claim on his property he must at least be aware of their existence. Thus in *Harwood v. Bake*,[235] where a testator executed a will on his deathbed bequeathing all his property to his wife the will was held to be invalid because the testator was, as a result of his illness, unable to understand and balance the claims of his relatives upon him and to form an intelligent decision to exclude them from a share in his property.

---

[231] See Casey and Craven, *Psychiatry and the Law* (Oak Tree Press, Dublin, 1999), p.321.
[232] (1870) L.R. 5 Q.B. 549, 565.
[233] *Waters v. Waters* (1848) 2 De G & Sm 591, 621 where the requirement was stated to be that the testator have a recollection "generally of the state of his property and what it consists of".
[234] *Per* Sir J. Hannen in *Boughton v. Knight* (1873) L.R. 3 P. & D. 64, 65–66.
[235] (1840) 3 Moo P.C. 282.

Proving Testamentary Capacity

The person who propounds the will bears the onus of proving testamentary capacity.[236] It will be judged in the first instance from the terms of the will. Where it is rational on its face a presumption of testamentary capacity arises so that the evidential burden shifts to the person contesting the will to rebut this presumption by evidence to the contrary. Where the will is irrational on its face there is a presumption that the testator lacked the necessary testamentary capacity so that the person propounding the will must satisfy the court as to the testator's capacity at the time it is made.[237] The court will permit the admission of extrinsic evidence in this regard so that the testator's remarks before, at the time of and after execution of the will be admitted in evidence as will the manner and nature of his instructions, letters in relation to the will and a variety of other matters.[238]

Further, if the circumstances surrounding the execution of the will are such as to excite the suspicion of the court the onus is once again on the person propounding the will to prove that the testator had the requisite testamentary capacity. Such circumstance may arise where the person who stands to benefit from the will prepares it and when they arise the party propounding the will must "satisfy the conscience of the court that the instrument ... propounded is the last will of a free and capable testator".[239] Since the crucial time for proving testamentary capacity is the date of the execution of the will,[240] it may be possible to show that a testator with mental illness made a will during a lucid interval,[241] or that the testator has recovered enough to have the required capacity but relapsed again.[242] The burden of proof on the person propounding the will in this context is quite onerous since there is a presumption that a person who was suffering from mental illness and who lacked testamentary capacity prior to the execution of the will continued to do so up to and including the time of execution.[243] In discharging the burden the propounder may need to adduce "firm evidence from a doctor in a position to assess the testator's mental capacity" [244] and may also point to the rationality of the document itself as the "strongest and best proof."[245] Provided that the testator can be shown to have executed the will during a lucid interval there is no need to show the length of that interval or that the testator made a final recovery.[246] In *In re the Estate of Andrew O'Donnell (deceased)*,[247] it was held that a testator who suffered from paranoid schizophrenia which was under control through the use of medication at the time of

---

[236] *Cleare v. Foster & Cleare* (1869) L.R. 1 P&D 655.

[237] See *Harwood v. Baker* (1840) 3 Moo. P.C. 282 at 291.

[238] *Levey v. Linde* 3 Mer 81; *Filmer v. Gott* 3 Br. P.C. 230.

[239] See *In re Goods of Corboy, Deceased: Leahy v. Corboy* [1969] I.R. 148 at 156.

[240] See *Bellinghurst v. Vickers* 1 Phill. Eccl. R. 187, 191; *Wood v. Wood* ib. 357;.

[241] *Cartwright v. Cartwright* (1793) 1 Phill. 90; *Chambers and Yatman v. Queen's Proctor* (1840) 2 Curt. 415; *In the Estate of Walker* (1912) 28 T.L.R. 466.

[242] *Ex. parte Holyland* (1805) 11 Ves Jun 10; *Cartwright v. Cartwright* (1793) 1 Phill Ecc 90, *Banks v. Goodfellow* (1870) Lr 5 Q.B. 549.

[243] See *Barry v. Butlin* (1838) 2 Moo. P.C. 480; *Cleare v. Cleare* (1869) L.R. 1 P&D 655.

[244] *In re the Goods of Corboy* [1969] I.R. 148 at 167.

[245] See GW Abraham, *op cit.*, p.280 citing decision of Sir William Wynne.

[246] *Ex p Holyland* (1805) 11 Ves 10 at 11; *Creagh v. Blood* (1845) 8 1 Eq. R 434 at 439; *Prinsep and East India Co. v. Dyce Sombre* (1856) 10 Moo. P.C. 232.

[247] (1999) *Conveyancing and Property Law Journal*, Vol.4, No.2, p.43.

making the will and who did not exhibit signs of suffering from the disorder did not lack testamentary capacity.

Generally, testamentary capacity must be established at the time the testator executed the will. However, where a testator's mental condition deteriorates after giving instructions for a will and before he executes it, the propounder of the will may rely on the rule in *Parker v. Felgate*[248] to establish testamentary capacity at the time of execution. This rule provides that where a testator has testamentary capacity at the time when s/he gives instructions to a solicitor for the preparation of the will then provided (i) that the will is prepared in accordance with those instructions and (ii) that at the time of execution the testator is capable of understanding and does understand that he is executing a will for which he has given instructions he will be presumed to have testamentary capacity at the time of execution.[249] In *Parker v. Felgate*, a testatrix drifted into a partial coma after giving instructions for a will and executed it at a time when she had been temporarily roused from it. She understood at that time that she was executing a will for which she had given instructions and the will was upheld. It was held to be irrelevant that at the time of execution she was unable to remember her instructions and incapable of understanding the clauses in the will. In the subsequent case of *Battan Singh v. Armirchand*,[250] the Judicial Committee of the Privy Council advised that because of the possibility of error, misunderstanding and deception, the principle in *Parker v. Felgate* should be applied with the greatest caution in cases where the testator gave instructions to a lay intermediary to be transmitted to the testator's solicitor.[251]

Where a testator experiences a delusion which influences or is capable of influencing the provisions of his will he may be found to lack testamentary capacity.[252] A testator is deemed to suffer from a delusion if he holds a belief on any subject that no rational person could hold and which cannot be permanently eradicated from his mind by reasoning with him.[253] Where however, it can be shown that the particular delusion could not have had any influence upon the testator in making his will he will not be deprived of testamentary capacity.[254] In *Banks v. Goodfellow*,[255] Cockburn C.J. stated that:[256]

> "A degree or form of unsoundness which neither disturbs the exercise of the faculties necessary for such an act, nor is capable of influencing the result ought not to take away the power of making a will. ..."

---

[248] (1883) 8 P.D. 171.

[249] See *Parker v. Felgate* (1883) 8 PD 171 and *Perera v. Perera* [1901] A.C. 354 at 361–362.

[250] [1948] A.C. 161 at 169.

[251] Taking the Privy Council decision in *Battan Singh v. Amirchand* further in *In re Fergusons Will* (1981) 43 N.S.R. (2d) 89 (C.A.) and *In re Griffin's Estate* (1978) 21 Nfld and P.E.I.R. 21 at 39 (P.E.I.S.C.) the Canadian courts have suggested that the rule in *Parker v. Felgate* cannot be applied in circumstances when the testator does not himself give instructions to the solicitor who draws the will but to a lay intermediary who repeats them to the solicitor.

[252] See *Dew v. Clark* (1826) 3 Add. 79, 5 Russ 163; *Smee v. Smee* (1879) 5 P.D. 84.

[253] *Dew v. Clark* (1826) L.R. 3 Add. 79 at 90.

[254] *Jenkins v. Morris* (1880) 14 Ch. D 674; *Frere v. Peacocke* (1846) 1 Rob Eccl. 442; *Smith v. Tebbit* (1867) L.R. 1 P.&D. 398; *Boughton v. Knight* (1873) L.R. 3 P.&D. 64; *Smee v. Smee* (1879) 5 PD 84; *Murfett v. Smith* (1887) 12 P.D. 116.

[255] (1870) L.R. 3 P.& D. 64 at 68.

[256] (1870) L.R. 5 Q.B. 549 at 566.

In *Banks v. Goodfellow*[257] the testator was suffering from a delusion that he was being pursued by a man who was already dead and by evil spirits that he claimed he could see. Despite this evidence the court held that he was capable of making a will since it was satisfied that the delusions under which he laboured were not capable of influencing the provisions of his will. Also it appears from the case of *In re the estate of Bohrmann*,[258] that if a delusion impairs testamentary capacity in relation only to a part of will the remainder of the will may be will may be admitted to probate[259] by analogy with the court's practice of excluding from probate matters which are not within the knowledge and approval of the testator. However the validity of this principle has been questioned.[260] In practice it may be difficult to distinguish between serious misjudgment and delusions. While the principle of freedom of testation dictates that mere caprice or eccentricity will not render a testator incapable of making a will,[261] where capricious harsh and unreasonable views are established to stem from irrational aversions amounting to delusions[262] the testator's capacity may be in issue. In *Mudway v. Croft*,[263] it was stated that in order to decide whether a testator is merely eccentric or suffering from a mental disorder the eccentricity should be tested against the whole life and habits of the testator. Moreover, while confusion or forgetfulness do not have the effect of making a testator incapable provided the testator had the ability to concentrate at the time, where these characteristics induced the testator to make the will then they may give rise to a finding of incapacity.[264]

The elements of Testamentary Capacity: Knowledge and approval of contents of the will

A testator must know and approve the contents of his will at the time he executes it.[265] He need not however know its legal effect.[266] Alternatively on an application of the principle in *Parker v. Felgate* mentioned above it is sufficient if the testator knows and approves of the contents of instructions which he gives to his solicitor for the preparation of a will if (i) the will is prepared in accordance with his instructions, and (ii) at the time of execution he is capable of understanding and does understand that he is executing a will for which he has given instructions.[267]

The burden of proof is on the person propounding the will to satisfy the court that it is the last will of "a free and capable testator."[268] Where it is proved that the testator

---

[257] (1870) L.R. 5 Q.B. 549.
[258] [1938] 1 All E.R. 271.
[259] See also *Trimlestown v. Dalton* 1 Dow & C 85.
[260] See C.A. Wright (1938) 16 Can. Bar Rev. 405, 410–411; R.F Cross (1950) 24 A.L.J. 12.
[261] See *Bird v. Luckie* (1850) S. Hare 301 at 306; *In re James's Will Trusts* [1962] Ch. 226 at 234 (*per* Buckley J.).
[262] *Boulton v. Knight* (1873) L.R. 3 P.&D. 64.
[263] (1843) 3 Curt 671.
[264] See *Benyon v. Benyon* (1844) 2 L.T. 477; *Singh v. Armirchand* [1948] A.C. 161.
[265] *Hastilow v. Stobie* (1865) L.R. 1 P.&D. 64; *Guardhouse v. Blackburn* (1866) L.R. 1 P.&D. 109 at 116.
[266] *In the Estate of Beech* [1923] P. 46 at 53; *Collins v. Elstone* [1893] P. 198.
[267] See *In re the Estate of Wallace* [1952] 2 T.L.R. 925.
[268] *Barry v. Butlin* (1838) 2 Moo. P.C. 480 at 482; *Cleare v. Cleare* (1869) L.R. 1 P.&D. 655.

duly executed the will, then in ordinary circumstances a rebuttable presumption arises that the testator was of sound disposing mind. If a testator of sound disposing mind has a will read over to him then there is a further presumption that he knew and approved of the contents of the will at the time of execution.[269] Then the evidential burden of proof passes to the person contesting the will to rebut these presumptions. If person contesting the will, succeeds in rebutting the presumption of knowledge and approval, or if the presumption of knowledge and approval is not applicable the propounder of the will must produce affirmative proof of the testator's knowledge to discharge the legal burden of proof.

Where the presumption of knowledge and approval is rebutted the person propounding the will may adduce affirmative proof that the testator read over the will or had it read over to him at the time he executed it. It may not be sufficient for a testator merely to cast his eye over the will.[270] In addition where a will is read over to a testator it must be done in such a way as to ensure that the testator hears and understands what is read.[271] While this is no longer conclusive proof of knowledge and approval it will be given the weight appropriate to the circumstances of the case.[272] Alternatively the propounder of the will may adduce affirmative proof that the testator gave instructions for his will and that the will was drafted in accordance with those instructions.[273] The greater the degree of suspicion surrounding the execution of the will the stronger the affirmative proof required to remove it.[274]

The presumption of knowledge and approval does not apply to testators who by reason of mental disability are incapable of reading or writing. In such cases knowledge and approval must be established by evidence that the will was read over to the testator before being executed.[275] The presumption is also inapplicable in suspicious circumstances where for example a person writes, prepares or is active in obtaining a will (e.g. by making suggestions as to its terms and choosing the testator's solicitor) under which s/he takes a substantial benefit.[276]

Signature

Where a testator is by reason of mental disability unable to form a signature s/he may in the alternative make a mark such as a cross, which may be witnessed by or acknowledged to the persons who sign as witnesses.[277] Alternatively another person may sign on behalf of the testator provided that this is in the testator's presence and by his direction,[278] and

---

[269] See *Blackall v Blackall*, unreported, Supreme Court, April 1, 1998, *Barry v. Butlin, op. cit.*, p.484, *Cleare v. Cleare, op. cit.*, p.658.

[270] *In re Morris* [1971] P. 62.

[271] See *Garnett Botfield v. Garnett Botfield* [1901] P. 335.

[272] *Per* Sachs J. in *Cerar v. Cerar* (1956) 106 L.J. 694.

[273] *Fincham v. Edwards* (1842) 3 Curt 63, 4 Moo. P.C. 198.

[274] See *Wintle v. Nye* [1959] 1 W.L.R. 284 at 291.

[275] *Fincham v. Edwards* (1842) 3 Curt 63, 4 Moo. P.C. 198.

[276] See *Barry v. Butlin* (1838) 2 Moo P.C. 480 at 481.

[277] *In re the Goods of Gannon* (1931) 65 I.L.T.R. 113; *In re the Goods of Kieran* [1933] I.R. 222; *In re the Estate of Holtam* (1913) 108 L.T. 732.

[278] Succession Act 1965, s.78.

the testator confirms this to the witnesses. The signature should be at the foot or end of the will.[279]

Wards of Court and will-making

A person may make a will even though he is a ward of court and deemed incapable of managing his property and affairs and a receiver has been appointed in relation to his property.[280] This is because of the general principle that the court only has jurisdiction over the patient's estate while he is alive.[281] While there is no presumption that a person with an alcohol or drug addiction problem lacks testamentary capacity at the time the will was made a person contesting the will may prove that at the time the will was made the testator was under the influence of drink or drugs and where this is done the court will require evidence that notwithstanding the inebriation the testator had the necessary capacity.[282]

Practice when testamentary capacity is in doubt

Where a person's mental incapacity is in doubt, it is wise[283] to arrange for an experienced medical practitioner[284] to be present so that s/he may examine the testator's state of mind at the time of executing the will,[285] and if he is satisfied of the testator's testamentary capacity that he may witness the will.[286] Indeed where it is asserted that the will was made during a "lucid interval" or will is made or the testator dies in a psychiatric hospital or in a residential care unit for people with mental disabilities the practice of the Probate Office is to request the submission of an affidavit as to the testamentary capacity of the

---

[279] Succession Act 1965, s.78.

[280] *In re Walker* [1905] 1 Ch. 160 at 172.

[281] *In re Bennett* (1913) 2 Ch. 318.

[282] See *Ayrey v. Hill* (1824) 2 Add 206; *Handley v. Stacey* (1858) 1 F.&F. 574; *Wheeler and |Batsford v. Alderson* (1831) Hag Ecc. 574; *Brunt v. Brunt* (1873) L.R. 3 P.&D. 37.

[283] In the Canadian case of *Murphy v. Lamphier* (1914) 31 O.L.R. 287 Chancellor Boyd emphasised the solicitor's duty to "satisfy himself" that his client had testamentary capacity. It is clear however that the duty goes further and that the solicitor must be in a position to satisfy the court that the testator had capacity, *i.e.* that the steps the solicitor took were sufficient to warrant his satisfaction.

[284] In some cases it may be advisable for a specialist such as a psycho-geriatrician to witness the will so as to put the matter of capacity beyond doubt.

[285] The medical practitioner should record his examination and findings. See *Kenward v. James, The Times* November 29, 1975; *In re Simpson* (1977) 121 S.J. 224.

[286] In 1995 the British Medical Association and the Law Society of England produced a joint publication entitled "Assessment of Medical Capacity – Guidance for Doctors and Lawyers" (BMA Professional Division Publications 1995). This provides "that a solicitor when drawing up a will for an elderly person or someone who is seriously ill, should ensure that the will is witnessed and approved by a medical practitioner. The medical practitioner should record his or her examination and where there is an earlier will, it should be examined and any proposed alterations should be discussed with the testator or testatrix" at pp.35–36. See also *Kenward v Adams, The Times*, November 29, 1975. The English Law Society further recommends that, where there is any doubt about the patient's capacity, the doctor should not witness the patient's signature on a document unless: (a) the doctor has formally assessed his capacity; (b) he is satisfied, on the balance of probabilities, that the patient has the requisite capacity to enter into the transaction effected by the document; and (c) makes a formal record of his examination and findings.

testator from the medical practitioner then attending him. If that is not available the Office will require reliable evidence from the solicitor attending the testator before the will is admitted to probate.[287]

In 1995 the British Medical Association and the English Law Society in a joint report provided guidance for legal and medical practitioners as to the meaning of "testamentary capacity." A checklist was drawn up although it was pointed out that it was not intended to be either authoritative or exhaustive. The checklist stated that people making a will should be able to understand:

> "(i) that they will die: (ii) that the will will come into operation on their death but not before; (iii) that they can change or revoke the will at any time before their death, provided they have the capacity to do so; (iv) who the executor is or who the executors are (and perhaps why they should be appointed as executors); (v) who gets what under the will; (vi) whether a beneficiary's gift is outright or conditional; (vii) that if they spend their money or give away or sell their property during their lifetime the beneficiaries might lose out; (viii) that a beneficiary might die before them; (ix) whether they have already made a will and, if so, how and why the new will differs from the old one ... (x) the extent of all the property owned solely by them; (xi) the fact that certain types of jointly-owned property might automatically pass to the other joint owner, regardless of anything that is said in the will; (xii) whether there are any benefits payable on their death which might be unaffected by the terms of their will ... (xiii) that the extent of their property could change during their lifetime."[288]

It was stated that testators should also be able to comprehend and appreciate the claims of possible beneficiaries and understand the legitimate reasons why they might choose to prefer some beneficiaries and exclude others, for example where they had already made adequate provision for particular people or where some of the potential beneficiaries were in greater need than others.[289]

The British Medical Association and Law Society of England and Wales report

---

[287] Mongey, *Probate Practice in a Nutshell* (Dublin, 1980), p.24 The extent of the precautions which a solicitor should take to satisfy himself or herself as to the testator's mental capacity depend largely on the degree of suspicion surrounding the client's capacity. If the testator's mental health is in doubt a mental status examination is advisable. Similarly if the testator is receiving drug medication inquiries should be made of the attending medical practitioner as to the possible effect of the medication on the testator's mind and memory. In every case solicitors should record in writing what steps they have taken to satisfy themselves of the client's capacity and these notes should be retained even after the will has been admitted to probate. In two reported cases in Canada the solicitors took the precaution of tape recording the interview with their clients; the recordings were played in court and were influential in the courts' conclusion that testamentary capacity was present. See *In re Eastland Estate: Shuttleworth v. Watts* (1977) 9 A.R. 504 (T.D.): *In re Wright Estate: Carleton v. Goldstone* (1981) 13 Sask. R 297 (S. Ct). The practice of video-recording adopted in the Germany is an even greater precaution (1984) 58 Aust. L.J. 246.

[288] A Report of the British Medical Association and the Law Society *Assessment of Mental Capacity – Guidance for Doctors and Lawyers* (BMA Professional Division Publications 1995), pp.36–37. See also Lyttleton, "Of sound mind? (2003) N.L.J. 153 (7086), pp.986, 988.

[289] *Ibid.*

states that it is not clear how far a solicitor or doctor can assist in enhancing the capacity of someone who is making a will. It suggests:[290]

"An explanation in broad terms and simple language of relevant basic information about the nature and effect of the will is probably in order. Within reason, the person making the will could also be reminded of the extent of his or her assets. But the final test, being able to comprehend and appreciate the claims to which he or she ought to give effect, is one that the testator or testatrix must pass unaided. There is a substantial body of judicial authority, which insists that "unquestionably, there must be a complete and absolute proof that the party who had so formed the will did it without any assistance. ..."[291]

Position where a person with an intellectual disability wishes to make a will

Where a person is a person with an intellectual disability as opposed to being a person with mental illness it should not be assumed that s/he is incapable of making a will and where s/he expresses a clear wish as to how his/her property should be disposed of after his/her death and satisfies the test of capacity s/he should be facilitated to record his/her intentions in the will notwithstanding the fact that his/her mental abilities may be limited.

Generally the rules of intestacy are not affected by the mental incapacity of the intestate.

Capacity to revoke a will

A testator must have testamentary capacity in order to revoke a will.[292] Section 85(2) of the Succession Act 1965 provides that a will may be revoked in whole or in part by "some writing declaring an intention to revoke it and executed in the manner in which a will is required to be executed." The same section also provides that a will is revoked by the burning, tearing or destruction of it by the testator or by someone in his presence and by his direction with the intention of revoking it. It is clear therefore that the destruction of a will results in revocation only if it is accompanied by an intention to revoke, which in turn requires capacity to form that intention.

In the English case of *In re Sabatini*,[293] it was held that the test for assessing to capacity to revoke a will is whether the individual has the same standard of mind and memory and the same degree of understanding in revoking a will as when making a will, *i.e.* she must have testamentary capacity. Specifically the person who intends to revoke his or her will must be capable of (i) understanding the nature of the act of revoking the will; (ii) understanding the effect of revoking the will; (iii) understanding the extent of his or her property; and (iv) comprehending and appreciating the claims to which he or she ought to give effect.

The logic of requiring the equivalent of testamentary capacity to effect a valid

---

[290] Report on *Assessment of Mental Capacity Guidance for Doctors and Lawyers* (British Medical Association December 1995), p.34.
[291] *Cartwright v. Cartwright* (1793) 1 Phill. 90.
[292] *In re the Goods of Brassington* [1902] P. 1, *In re the goods of Hine* [1893] P. 282.
[293] (1969) 114 Sol. Jo. 35 (Probate Division).

revocation is sound. If a testator's insane delusions about his son (the major beneficiary under his will) cause him to destroy the will, he may well be capable of understanding the effect of the revocation yet his lack of testamentary capacity must render the revocation ineffective. It would be illogical for the law to permit a testator to do by destruction what he is legally incapable of doing by express writing. It would follow that if a testator executes a valid will and then suffers a permanent loss of testamentary capacity, the will may become irrevocable.[294] It may be otherwise if the testator's subsequent unsoundness of mind was not incurable but a presumption will arise that a testator's mental incapacity persisted at the time of the purported revocation and such presumption will only be rebutted by the clearest evidence.[295]

Commentary from a comparative law perspective

In England the Mental Health Act 1983 empowers the Court of Protection to make a statutory will where it has reason to believe that the patient is incapable of making a valid will for himself.[296] Those with an interest can ask the Court of Protection to consider the patient's presumed wishes and authorise a new will if appropriate. This will can do anything the patient could have done if he were not mentally disordered and has the same effect as if the patient had made it and was capable of doing so.

The Court is not expressly required to apply a "substituted judgment' test to determine what the patient himself would have wanted. The only statutory guidance given is in court's general power to do whatever is "necessary and expedient" for the maintenance or other benefit of the patient or members of his family, for providing for other people or purposes for which the patient might be expected to provide if he were not mentally disordered, or otherwise for administering his affairs.[297]

In *In re D(J)*,[298] Megarry V.C. set out five principles to be considered when the court makes a will for the patient:

(a) that it is to be assumed that the patient is having a brief lucid interval at the time the will is made;

(b) that during that brief lucid interval the patient has a full knowledge of the past and a full realisation that as soon as the will is executed he or she will relapse into the actual mental state that previously existed;

(c) that it is the actual patient "whose views while still of sound disposing mind might be idiosyncratic and far from impartial" who has to be considered and not the hypothetical patient on the Clapham omnibus;

(d) that during the hypothetical lucid interval the patient is to be envisaged as being advised by competent solicitors;

---

[294] An exception to this may be revocation by subsequent marriage, given that a person who lacks testamentary capacity may still have capacity to marry. *In re McElroy* (1978) 93 D.L.R. (3d) 522 (Ont. Surr. Ct.) *In re Park* [1954] P. 112.

[295] *Banks v. Goodfellow* (1870) L.R. 5 Q.B 549, 570.

[296] Mental Health Act 1983 (UK), s.96(i)(e) and (4)(b).

[297] *Ibid.*, s.95(1).

[298] [1982] Ch. 237.

(e) that in all normal cases "the patient is to be envisaged as taking a broad brush to the claims on his bounty rather than an accountants pen".

The English courts have evolved further propositions to assist in cases where the patient has been incapable for so long there is little or no evidence of the patient's personality and circumstances, which might influence his likely wishes. In such cases the court may assume that the patient would have been a normal decent person acting in accordance with contemporary standards of morality.

Where the patient is intestate there is a presumption that the patient while he had testamentary capacity would have been satisfied to allow his estate to pass under the intestacy rules. The court must be satisfied that the patient would wish to depart from the results of an intestacy. Where the patient's wishes were ascertained clearly at a particular time prior to the onset of the incapacity then there is a presumption that the patient would not want to alter those wishes.

Applications are made in the first instance to the Court of Protection (although the High Court exercises the same jurisdiction as "the judge" under the Mental Health Act 1983). The Official Solicitor will usually be made a party to the application to represent the patient and anyone adversely affected by the application will need to be notified. The parties involved make written submissions and may be heard at an oral hearing. The court's role is effectively an inquisitorial one. A party who feels that his or her case has been inadequately aired may appeal to the High Court within 14 days of the order authorising the statutory will to be drawn up and entered.

The circumstances in which a statutory will might be made are illustrated by *In re Davey (Deceased)*.[299] In that case an elderly spinster with a reasonably large estate moved into a nursing home in June. In July, she made a will dividing her property between her relations. In September she was married to a middle-aged employee at the nursing home. This automatically revoked the will. The fact of the marriage came to light in December during the process of placing her affairs under the jurisdiction of the Court of Protection. Her receiver at the instance of the court immediately applied for a statutory will in the same terms as the one, which she herself had made in July. The court granted this without giving notice to her husband or to the proposed beneficiaries. She died six days after it was executed. The husband's appeal was dismissed. However it remained possible for him to apply for reasonable provision under the Inheritance (Provision for Family and Dependants Act 1975 whereas the other beneficiaries could not have done if the statutory will had not been made.

The New South Wales Law Reform Commission in its report *Wills for Persons Lacking Will-making Capacity*[300] recommended the enactment of a similar power for four categories of person (1) persons suffering from a development disorder or disability; (2) persons diagnosed as suffering from a mental illness or disorder including both organic and non-organic psychological conditions; (3) persons lacking capacity by reason of disease or accident including the diseases and incapacities associated with old age and brain damage affecting capacity such as results from a stroke or accident; and (4) persons who may have testamentary capacity but through severe physical disabilities or injury are completely unable to communicate.

---

[299] [1981] 1 W.L.R. 164.
[300] L.R.C. 68, February 1992.

The enactment of a power to make statutory wills in the Irish jurisdiction might prevent injustices arising on an intestacy as a result of a person's lacking testamentary capacity. In any event where it is established that a person lacks mental capacity a right conferred on interested parties to make application to the court to consider the client's presumed wishes and make a statutory will if appropriate would certainly be preferable to more expensive and contentious probate proceedings after the person's death.

The Law Reform Commission recommended that its proposed Guardianship Tribunal should have the power to execute a statutory will on behalf of a Protected Adult where the intention of an existing will cannot be put into effect but not where there is no will as this would have the effect of ousting the statutory rules on intestacy. It acknowledged that the application of the intestacy rules in some cases could work an injustice – as where the testator's child was a person with a disability whose capacity to earn a living was limited and a just and prudent parent would have made particular provision for the child. However, it could not recommend that the Tribunal have power to change those rules.[301] The Law Reform Commission's objection appears to hedge around vesting such a power in a Tribunal (as opposed to a court), and so the merits of the arguments in favour of the making of such a will by the High Court exercising its inherent jurisdiction remain.

Further the Law Reform Commission in its *Consultation Paper on Law and the Elderly* has made a number of practical recommendations for practice when testamentary capacity is in issue. First, it recommended that a medical practitioner should execute a contemporaneous certificate of capacity as a prudent precaution in cases of doubtful capacity and where a later challenge to a will appears likely. Secondly, it recommended that guidelines should be drawn up by the Law Society and the Medical Council on the assessment of testamentary capacity for the assistance or both solicitors and medical practitioners. Thirdly, it recommended that Guidelines for Solicitors should advise that contemporaneous notes be made by solicitors regarding details of the meeting with the client when the issue of testamentary capacity is an issue.[302]

CAPACITY AND LIABILITY IN TORT

The old common law rule was that a person with mental illness was liable in tort unless it could be shown that s/he did not know the nature and quality of his/her act.[303] If s/he did so s/he was liable and could not raise the defence that s/he did not know what s/he is doing is wrong.[304] Nowadays the rule has been modified and the principles vary somewhat depending on the mental ingredient, which must be proved to establish the tort in question. Where torts of strict liability are concerned a person lacking the mental

---

[301] L.R.C. CP 23–2003, pp.189–190.

[302] *Ibid.*, pp.58–59.

[303] *Hanbury v. Hanbury* (1892) 8 T.L.R. 559 at 569 *cf. Mordaunt v. Mordaunt* (1870) L.R. 2 P&D 103, 142 *per* Kelly C.B.

[304] See *Weaver v. Ward* (1616) Hob 134; *Haycraft v. Creasy* (1801) 2 East 92 at 104 *per* Lord Kenyon C.J.; *Mordaunt v. Mordaunt, Cole and Johnson* (1870) L.R. 2 P &D 103 at 142; *Morris v. Marsden* [1952] 1 All E.R. 925; *Hanbury v. Hanbury* (1892) 8 T.L.R. 559 at 560 *per* Lord Esher MR and *Emmens v. Pottle* (1885) 16 Q.B.D. 354 at 356.

capacity to be regarded as acting voluntarily will not be held responsible for his conduct e.g. where s/he was in a state of complete automatism. Where the tort in question is one such as malicious prosecution or libel in circumstances where the defence of qualified privilege may be raised and that tort requires a specific mental element such as malice to be proved there is New Zealand authority that the defendant will not be liable where his mental condition prevents him from having that necessary mental element.[305]

Liability in trespass to the person, goods or land

Where the tort in question is that of trespass to the person, goods or land it seems that where the defendant acted voluntarily he will be liable if he is aware of the nature and quality of his act even though he does not know that what he is doing is wrong. In *Morris v. Marsden*,[306] a person with catatonic schizophrenia who struck the manager of a hotel in which he was staying as a guest on the head with a blunt instrument was held liable in battery as he "knew the nature and quality of his act notwithstanding his "incapacity of reason arising from the disease of his mind was of so grave a character that he did not know what he was doing was wrong".[307] However, Stable J. indicated that had his disease been so severe that his act was not a voluntary one at all and had been executed in a state of complete automatism then he would not have been liable.[308] In the Irish Circuit Court decision of *Donohue v. Coyle*[309] Sheehy J. in a short judgment felt compelled to follow the English decision of *Morris v. Marsden* and found person with mental illness liable in battery.[310]

Liability in negligence

It is not clear whether a mentally ill person can be held liable in negligence or contributory negligence. In *Kingston v. Kingston*[311] Walsh J. held that "it is sufficient to say that the question of the standard of care required of a plaintiff who is mentally infirm is still open. ..." In other common law jurisdictions the courts are divided on the matter.[312] It

---

[305] *Donaghy v. Brennan* (1900) 19 N.Z.L.R. 289 *per* Connolly J. at 294 and the Court of Appeal at 299.

[306] [1952] 1 All E.R. 925.

[307] *Ibid.*, pp.926–927.

[308] *Ibid.*, p.927.

[309] [1953–54] I.R. Jur. Rep. 30.

[310] The judgment has been criticised for the absence of a ratio decidendi. See Mc Mahon & Binchy, *Irish Law of Torts* (2nd ed., Butterworths, Dublin, 1990).

[311] 102 I.L.T.R. 65 at 67.

[312] The Australian decision of *Adamson v. Motor Vehicle Trust* 50 W.A.L.R. at 56 makes no concession to mental illness; On the other had the Canadian decisions of *Slattery v. Hailey* [1923] 3 D.L.R. 156 at 160 and *Buckley v. Smith Transport* [1946] 4 D.L.R. 721 recognise that mental illness may prevent a defendant from appreciating the duty to take care. The US decision of *American Family Insurance Co.* 45 W.S. 2 D 526, 173 N.W. 2D 619 (1970) provides that a defendant is not liable where there is a sudden onset of insanity. Other cases such as *Sforza v. Green Bus Lines* 150 Misc. 108, 268 NYS 446 (1934) and *Turner v. Caldwell* 36 Conn. Supp. 350 at 421 A 2d 876 (1980) as well as the Second Restatement of the Law of Torts s.283 require all defendants regardless of mental incapacity to comply with an objective standard.

has been suggested[313] that the liability of a person with mental illness is similar to that of a minor in the same circumstances, *i.e.* it is a question of fact for the court to determine in each case whether the defendant was sufficiently self possessed to be capable of taking reasonable care in the circumstances. However it does appear that in road traffic cases the courts are reluctant to take into account factors tending to show mental incapacity and to depart from a pure objective standard. Thus in the English case of *Roberts v. Ramsbottom*,[314] the defendant who had suffered from stroke just before getting into his car negligently injured the plaintiff on his way into town. It was held that in deciding whether he had fallen below the standard of care required of a motorist his impaired mental capacity should be disregarded.

The adoption of an objective test of liability, which prevents a person with mental disability from invoking their disability in their defence, is objectionable both on grounds of policy and principle. If persons who are not affected by mental illness can raise temporary loss of consciousness in their defence and if physical disability is a factor determining the standard of care to be applied to a physically disabled person then mental illness should be admissible as a factor having a bearing on the liability of a person with mental illness in tort.

The position regarding the liability of intellectually disabled adult in negligence is also uncertain. In the absence of Irish authority, we turn to the United States where the courts have adopted a range of views ranging from the narrow and restrictive to the generous in cases relating to contributory negligence. Thus in some cases they have refused to take the plaintiff's condition into consideration,[315] in others they have adopted a middle ground where allowance will be made for the plaintiff's condition if it "prevented him from comprehending the danger and from taking action to avoid it but not otherwise"[316] and in yet others they have adopted a more accommodating approach which makes allowance for the plaintiff's inability to exercise the judgement of a reasonable person.[317] In England, there is some indication that a lower standard of care applies to infants and it has been suggested that this should applied to people with intellectual disability.[318] Where cases of serious intellectual disability are concerned the argument for the adoption of a subjective test on humanitarian grounds is compelling.

Commentary

In its report on the *Liability in Tort of Mentally Disabled Persons* the Irish Law Reform Commission made detailed proposals for reform of the law. First they were of the view that the term "mental disability" should include mental illness, mental retardation and other disabling mental conditions.

Where the torts of trespass to the person to goods and to land are concerned the Commission recommended that where it is shown (a) that the defendant was so affected

---

[313] See Charlesworth & Percy, *Negligence* (8th ed., Sweet & Maxwell, London, 1990), para.2–203.

[314] [1980] 1 W.L.R. 823.

[315] *Second Restatement of the Law of Torts* s.464, Comment g.

[316] Prosser Wade and Schwartz, *Cases and materials on Torts* (7th ed., Foundation Press, New York, 1982), p.184.

[317] See *Lynch v. Rosenthal* 396 SW 2d 272.

[318] Ashton and Ward, *Mental Handicap and the Law* (Sweet & Maxwell, London, 1992), p.59.

by mental disability as substantially to lack the capacity to act freely, and (b) as a result of this substantial lack of capacity the defendant did the act complained of, the defendant should be relieved of liability for a trespass on the ground that his/her act was not voluntary. It also recommended that notwithstanding that a defendant's conduct might be voluntary, he should nonetheless be relieved of liability if his mental disability was "such as to prevent (him) from acting with the purpose of bringing about the effect in question".[319]

The Commission also considered that where the present law relieves a defendant from liability for trespass and other torts on grounds of reasonable mistake it should also be a valid defence for the defendant to show that he did the act complained of as a result of a mistake brought about by mental disability. It further recommended that the changes proposed in relation to trespass should also apply to other torts in which questions of voluntariness and intention can arise.

The Commission recommended that where a tort required proof of a specific intention on the part of the defendant if a defendant suffers from a mental disability which is such as to prevent him or her from acting with the specific purpose of bringing about the effect in question the defendant should be relieved from liability. Where the tort requires some other specific state of mind the defendant should escape liability if he or she suffers from a mental disability, which is such as to prevent him or her from having that state of mind.

The Commission also recommended that the law should apply an objective test when determining a person's negligence or contributory negligence unless that person established (a) at the time of the act in question he/she was suffering from a serious mental disability which affected him/her in performance of the act, and (b) that this disability made him/her unable to behave according to the standard of care appropriate to the reasonable person. If these elements are established the person should be held not to have been guilty of negligence or contributory negligence.

However, it is to be noted that the objective test can only be dispensed with under these recommendations in cases of serious mental disability where it was of such a degree as to render the affected person unable to behave according to the objective test.

Moreover, the Commission was not prepared to apply a subjective test of this nature in cases where the mentally disabled person caused injury to others or themselves when driving a motor vehicle. In these cases it recommended that the objective test should remain and be qualified only by the Commission's recommendations regarding voluntariness, which it considered would "afford sufficient flexibility to deal with cases involving the sudden onset of insanity." The Commission further recommended that in cases where a defendant was not liable in tort by virtue of his/her mental disability an employer or principal who would otherwise be vicariously liable should continue to be so. However, before the employer should be made liable the general principle that the tort should have been committed in the course of the employee's employment should be complied with.

---

[319] *Ibid.*, p.59.

CAPACITY AND DOMICILE

It would appear from the early authority of *Bempde v. Johnstone*[320] that from the moment a person becomes of unsound mind his domicile is immutable and cannot be changed either by his own act or by a person having charge of him since s/he is regarded as incapable of forming an intention. In accordance with the general principle applicable to children the domicile of a child of unsound mind is dependent upon that of his father during his childhood. In *Sharpe v. Crispin*,[321] Sir J.P. Wilde held that if a person is continuously insane both during childhood and after the age of 18 his domicile will continue to be dependent on that of his father. Where, however, a person becomes mentally ill after s/he reaches full age then his/her domicile may not be changed. The basis for this somewhat tenuous distinction is apparently that if the power of changing domicile were vested in the father in the case of his adult offspring "the interests of others" might be endangered. The approach has been criticised as inconsistent and irrational[322] as the interests of others are equally in issue whether the person lacking capacity be a minor or adult. Nevertheless the approach has generally been followed in subsequent decisions.[323]

Commentary

The New Zealand Supreme Court in its decision in *In re G*,[324] appears to have embarked on the task of clarifying the issues. While following the principle in *Sharpe v. Crispin* that where insanity occurs during minority the father's domicile will dominate after majority, it ruled following English authority[325] that where the mother's domicile was in issue she could, in changing her own domicile, decide not to change the domicile of her child if it is in the child's interests.

The matter of a person's capacity to change domicile is not the only vexing issue in this area. The position of persons whose domicile is dependent upon parents who are mentally incapacitated and the effect of a parental change of domicile upon them is not clear. Moreover there is considerable uncertainty as to what type or degree of mental incapacity renders a person incapable of acquiring a domicile of choice. Most of the English authorities involve either persons "found lunatic by inquisition",[326] save one where there was a clear admission of legal incapacity.[327] A blanket status based approach whereby a person suffering from mental disorder regardless of a kind or degree is incapable of forming an intention to acquire a domicile of choice is out of step with current developments in approaches to mental disability and it is likely that the courts will examine as a matter of fact in each case whether the person was capable of forming

---

[320] 3 Ves Jun 198, 30 E.R. 967.

[321] L.R. 1 P&D 611 (1869).

[322] See Binchy, *Irish Conflicts of Law* (Butterworths, Dublin, 1988), p.94 Cheshire and North, *Private International Law* (10th ed., Butterworths, London, 1979), p.181.

[323] *In the estate of S* [1928] N.I. 46; *In re Joyce; Corbet v. Fagan* [1946] I.R. 277.

[324] [1966] N.Z.L.R. 1028.

[325] *In re Beaumont*, [1893] 3 Ch. 490.

[326] See Morris, *The Conflict of Laws* (4th ed., Sweet & Maxwell, London, 1993), p.29.

[327] See *In re Bariatenski* 13 L.J. Ch. 69 where the person was "admitted to be a declared lunatic.".

the necessary intention to acquire or lose a domicile of choice.[328] In the United States, the courts have held that the test of domiciliary capacity differs from and is less demanding than that of capacity to execute a deed or will.[329]

Proposals for reform have been made in both the English and the Irish jurisdictions. The English and Scottish Law Commissions in the Report on the Law of Domicile[330] have recommended new statutory rules for "adults under disability". Under the proposed rules an adult lacking the capacity to form the intention necessary to acquiring a domicile would be domiciled in the country with which he was for the time being most closely connected. When that capacity was restored to him he would retain the capacity he had immediately before it was restored but, of course, could then acquire a new domicile under the rules applying to adults generally.

The Irish Law Reform Commission in its Working Paper on *Domicile and Habitual Residence as Connecting Factors in the Conflict of Laws*[331] formed the view that present law which freezes the domicile at what it was before the onset of illness afforded 'a rather blunt and uncompromising solution.'[332] It recommended that a degree of flexibility be introduced whereby the court would be enabled on the application of an interested party[333] to change the domicile of a mentally ill person where it appeared to it to "be in the interest of the person and having regard to the interests of other persons, proper to do so."[334] The Commission was also of the view that rule that the domicile of a mentally ill child after majority should still depend on that of his parents for the rest of his or her life or until he or she gets well should not be retained as it involved "too great an assumption of a continuing close association of interests between parent and child."[335] Instead tentatively suggested that it would be better to let the child retain the domicile s/he had before reaching majority, permitting the court to change it in an appropriate case. They also recommended that there be power to apply to the courts on behalf of child whose domicile was dependent upon that of a mentally ill person for a change of domicile.[336]

---

[328] See Morris, *op. cit.*, p.29.

[329] See *The Power to Change the Domicile of Infants and of persons Non Compos Mentis* 30 Colum. Law Rev. 703 at 713 (1930) *Degree of Mental Capacity Required to Change Domicile* 3 Calif. Law Review 491.

[330] Law Com No. 168 Pt VI.

[331] WP No. 10 1981.

[332] *Ibid.*, p.81.

[333] Where one had been appointed the Committee of a mentally ill person's estate was considered to be the appropriate applicant.

[334] WP No. 10 1981, p.81.

[335] *Ibid.*, p.82.

[336] Note the Law Commission's subsequent view that domicile be replaced by a concept of habitual residence.

CAPACITY TO CONSENT TO MEDICAL TREATMENT GENERALLY

Current law relating to capacity to consent and to refuse consent to non-psychiatric medical treatment

To give valid consent to medical treatment a person must have (a) capacity to give consent; (b) must be given appropriate information prior to consent; (c) consent to the particular treatment given and (d) give consent voluntarily. These concepts have been examined in the specific context of consent to psychiatric treatment in Chapter 4. In this chapter the principles applicable to the capacity to consent of a person with mental disability who requires treatment unrelated to the amelioration of his mental condition are examined.

A person with mental illness or intellectual disability may be said to have capacity to give consent to medical treatment if s/he understands in broad terms the nature and effect of the treatment proposed and has capacity to communicate that decision.[337] The precise criteria for determining whether a person has capacity in a given case have never been set out in an Irish court but have been addressed in England in the case of *In re C. (Adult: Refusal of Treatment)*,[338] in the context of the refusal by a person of treatment unrelated to his mental condition. In this case Thorpe J. held that a person does not have the capacity to consent if there is impairment or disturbance of mental functioning, which renders the patient unable to make a decision. This inability to make a decision may be established where (a) the patient is unable to understand and retain the information which is material to the decision especially as to the likely consequences of having or not having the treatment in question; (b) the patient unable to believe it and (c) the patient is unable to use the information and weigh it in the balance as part of the process of making the decision. Thorpe J. also indicated that the capacity to consent to medical treatment would be commensurate with the gravity of the decision.

Assessment of capacity as a matter of medical practice

Applying these criteria to the practical assessment of capacity to consent to medical treatment the British Medical Association and Law Society of England and Wales report on the *Assessment of Mental Capacity Guidance for Doctors and Lawyers*,[339] states that to demonstrate capacity individuals should be able to:

---

[337] According to Exner clinical competency addresses: "the extent to which cognitive functioning is 'minimally adequate' in areas of word knowledge, recent and remote memory, perceptual accuracy or reality testing abstraction and judgment as it is applied to both the personal and social spheres". Competency criteria from this psychological point of view "imply some specific basis from which the content of a stimulus field are received and processed fairly accurately and that processing is, in turn translated in such a way as to make decision making actions commensurate with the purpose and nature of the legal procedure." See Exner, "Diagnosis versus Description in Competency Issues", 347 *Annals N.Y. Acad. Sci.* 20 (1980). Applying these criteria a person with mental illness may be clinically incompetent but because of the "temporary" nature of their disability may improve to the point that they can make rational decisions. A person who is permanently mentally incapacitated on the other hand may never become clinically competent.

[338] [1994] 1 W.L.R. 290.

[339] British Medical Association, December 1995.

(i) understand in simple language what the medical treatment is, its purpose and nature and why it is being proposed;

(ii) understand its principal benefits, risks and alternatives;

(iii) understand in broad terms what will be the consequences of not receiving the proposed treatment;

(iv) retain the information for long enough to make an effective decision;

(v) make a free choice (*i.e.* free from pressure).[340]

As an indication of accepted practice in dealing with patients whose capacity to consent is in issue the Irish Medical Council's *Guide to Ethical Conduct and Behaviour*[341] provides:

> "It is accepted that consent is implied in many circumstances by the very fact that the patient has come to the doctor for medical care. There are however situations where verbal and if appropriate written consent is necessary for investigation and treatment. Informed consent can only be obtained by a doctor who has sufficient training and experience to be able to explain the intervention, the risks and the benefits and the alternatives.
>
> In obtaining consent the doctor must satisfy him/herself that the patient understands what is involved by explaining in appropriate terminology. A record of this discussion should be made in the patient's notes.
>
> A competent adult patient has the right to refuse treatment. While the decision must be respected the assessment of competence and the decision on consent should be carried out in conjunction with a senior colleague.[342]
>
> *Special Situations and Consent*
>
> *The Violent Patient* A doctor asked to examine or treat a violent patient is under no obligation to put him/herself or other healthcare staff in danger but should attempt to persuade the patient concerned to permit an assessment as to whether any therapy is required.[343]
>
> *Psychiatric Illness* Most patients with psychiatric illness are competent to provide consent …".[344]

The assessment of a person's ability to consent will usually be based upon a medical

---

[340] Report on *Assessment of Mental Capacity Guidance to Doctors and Lawyers* (British Medical Association December 1995), p.66.

[341] 6th ed., 2004.

[342] Para. 17.1.

[343] Para. 18.1.

[344] Para 18.2 The remainder of this paragraph refers to the fact that that Mental Health Act 2001 may provide a process for giving consent where a patient with psychiatric illness is not competent to give consent. However the processes provided for in the Mental Health Act 2001 apply only to consent to psychiatric treatment not consent to medical treatment for conditions unrelated to the psychiatric illness. See definition of "treatment" in s.2 of the 2001 Act.

practitioner's judgment of the patient's understanding of the particular treatment concerned and the information provided by the medical practitioner. In essence the question of capacity will be one of fact in each case. Capacity to consent will vary depending upon the nature of the decision. The more serious the decision the greater the capacity that will be required.[345] In addition a medical practitioner should assess capacity on each occasion and continually re-assess this capacity with each particular treatment and at each stage of treatment.

It is important to note that while in practice doctors frequently consult with parents, guardians and relatives where a doctor has doubts about a patient's capacity to consent this process of decision making has no legal basis and it appears that the Irish courts may be obliged to rely on persuasive English authority to determine as a matter of law when medical treatment may be given to a patient who cannot give a personal consent.[346]

It is important to emphasise that while on involuntary admission to a psychiatric hospital a person with mental illness may lack the competence to make decisions concerning the treatment of their mental illness patients who may have presented a danger to themselves or others at the time of involuntary admission to hospital may regain their capacity to make their own decisions.

Further, people with intellectual disabilities present with particular problems concerning capacity. It should be noted that often the patient with intellectual disability may be unused to making decisions but attuned to acquiescence in the decisions of other. Shevin and Kline have pointed out "professionals and advocates are at risk of mistaking lack of protest for informed consent, habitual behaviour for active choice and resignation to one's lot as contentment with that lot."[347] Psychiatrists who are clinically disinterested in the decision and who are trained in the assessment of capacity of people with intellectual disability should make the assessment in such cases and should aim to enhance the capacity of the person to exercise capacity to make a decision in the case.[348]

Assessment of Capacity to refuse medical treatment

The question then arises as to whether an adult with mental disability can validly refuse medical treatment. In the Irish case of *In re A Ward of Court*,[349] the Supreme Court discussed the right of the mentally insentient person to refuse consent to medical treatment when the issue arose as to whether on the application of her family and the committee of the ward who had been in an almost persistent vegetative state for 20 years artificial nutrition and hydration should be withdrawn from her and she be permitted to die a

---

[345] See *In re T (Adult: Refusal of Medical Treatment)* [1992] 4 All E.R. 749.

[346] The English courts have held that a medical practitioner who treats a patient without consent is not acting unlawfully provided that the treatment in question is in the best interests of the patient as determined by the medical practitioner. *In re F (Mental Patient Sterilisation)* [1990] 2 A.C. 1. See *Treatment without consent where a patient is incapable of giving consent, infra* pp. 605 *et seq.*

[347] The importance of choice making skills for students with severe disabilities: 1984 Vol. 9(3) *J. Assoc Persons with Severe Handicaps* 159–166.

[348] See J. Hillery, "Consent to Treatment and People with Learning Disabilities" (1998) Vol. 15(4) *Irish Journal of Psychological Medicine* 117–118. Longer term, Hillery *et al* argue that proactive theoretical and experiential training in decision making should become part of the life plan for every person with an intellectual disability.

[349] [1995] 2 I.L.R.M. 428.

natural death. In the course of their judgments, Hamilton C.J. and Denham J. held that the unenumerated constitutional right to privacy recognised by Article 40.3 included a right of a competent adult if terminally ill to forego or discontinue treatment and that the loss by an individual of his or her mental capacity does not result in any diminution of his or her personal rights recognised by the Constitution including the right to bodily integrity, the right to privacy including self-determination and the right to refuse medical care or treatment.[350]

O' Flaherty J. held that there is an absolute right in a competent person to refuse medical treatment even if it leads to death. He stated that he could not find any constitutional or other rationale for make a finding that by virtue of mental incapacity a person loses these rights but that on the contrary such a finding would operate as an invidious discrimination between the well and the infirm.[351] Denham J. citing *In re Quinlan*,[352] stated that "the individual's right to privacy grows as the degree of bodily invasion increases." A constituent of the right to privacy was the right to die naturally with dignity and with minimum suffering. This right was not lost to a person if they became incapacitated or insentient.[353] Accordingly the majority of the Supreme Court ruled that that it was in the best interests of the ward who was almost in a persistent vegetative state for the court to direct that invasive life sustaining treatment be discontinued.[354]

The broad principles for determining the circumstances in which a refusal of medical treatment was valid were also discussed in some detail in the English case of *In re T, (Adult; Refusal of Treatment)*.[355] In that case the patient who was 34 weeks pregnant was injured in a road traffic accident. The patient had been brought up by her mother who was a Jehovah's Witness but she herself was not a member of that sect. On admission to hospital the patient refused a blood transfusion after having spent a period of time alone with her mother. She gave birth to a stillborn child and afterwards her condition became critical. Her father and boyfriend had applied for a court declaration that it would not be unlawful to administer a transfusion without her consent. The Court of Appeal held that a competent adult patient had the right to refuse treatment so long as he or she has been properly informed of the implications and could make a free choice. In a situation where the refusal is contested for a refusal to be valid the medical practitioner had to be satisfied that the patient's capacity to decide had not been diminished by illness, medication, false assumptions or misinformation or that the patients will had not been overborne by another's influence. In the instant case the court found on the facts that the effect of patient's condition, together with misinformation and the influence of her mother rendered her refusal ineffective. Nevertheless the case is significant for its affirmation of the competent patient's absolute right to refuse treatment. Butler-Sloss L.J. stated:

"A man or woman of full age and sound understanding may choose to reject medical

---

[350] [1995] 2 I.L.R.M. 428.

[351] Citing *O'Brien v. Keogh* [1972] I.R. 144; [1995] 2 I.L.R.M. 431.

[352] (1976) N.J. 10 at 41.

[353] [1995] 2 I.L.R.M. at 460.

[354] Hamilton C.J., O'Flaherty, Blayney and Denham JJ. (Egan J. dissenting).

[355] [1992] 4 All E.R. 649.

advice and medical or surgical treatment either partially or in its entirety. A decision to refuse medical treatment by a patient capable of making the decision does not have to be sensible, rational or well considered. ..."[356]

However, where a patients capacity is in issue the Lord Donaldson M.R. stated:

> "Doctors faced with a refusal of consent have to give very careful and detailed consideration to the patient's capacity to decide at the time when the decision was made. It may not be the simple case of the patient having no capacity because, for example, at that time he had hallucinations. It may be the more difficult case of temporarily reduced capacity at the time when his decision is made. What matters is that the doctors should consider whether at that time he had a capacity which was commensurate with the gravity of the decision which he purported to make. The more serious the decision the greater the capacity required. If the patient had the required capacity, they are bound by his decision. If not, they are free to treat him in what they believe to be his best interests."[357]

In cases of doubt the Master of the Rolls recommended that judges seek a declaration from the courts as to the lawfulness of the action.

As has been mentioned above[358] the precise criteria for determining whether an individual had capacity to refuse consent to medical treatment and in particular the right of a person with mental illness to refuse medical treatment unrelated to his mental disorder were set out in more detail in English decision of *In re C Adult (Refusal of Treatment)*,[359] In that case, Thorpe J. stated that an adult patient has the right and capacity to decide whether or not to accept medical treatment although that presumption of capacity was rebuttable. On the facts of the case it was held C a person with paranoid schizophrenia had capacity to refuse consent to the amputation of a gangrenous leg on the grounds that notwithstanding his illness C understood the nature purpose and effects of the treatment and was capable of refusing treatment. Thorpe J. found it helpful to approach the determination of capacity in three stages *i.e.* first, whether the patient had the capacity to comprehend and retain information relevant to the decision in question, secondly whether the patient could believe it and thirdly whether the patient could weigh it in the balance to arrive at a decision Thorpe J. however stated that where "an adult patient did not have the capacity to decide at the time of the purported refusal and still does not have that capacity it is the duty of the doctors to treat him in whatever way they consider in the exercise of clinical judgment to be in his best interests."

In some cases it may not be clear whether an issue of capacity arises when an individual refuses treatment however the British Medical Association and Law Society of England report on *Assessment of Mental Capacity Guidance for Doctors and Lawyers* states that if an individual appears to be choosing an option which is "not only contradictory to what most people would choose but also appears to contradict the

---

[356] *Ibid.*, p.665.
[357] [1992] 4 All E.R. 649 at 661.
[358] See para.10–106.
[359] [1994] 1 W.L.R. 290.

individuals previously expressed attitudes" health professionals would be justified in questioning in greater detail the individual's capacity to make a valid refusal in order to eliminate the possibility of a depressive. illness or a delusional state and a specialist psychiatric opinion may be required.[360]

In a decision subsequent to *In re C*, Butler Sloss L.J., delivering the judgment of the English Court of Appeal later decision of *In re MB, (Medical Treatment)*,[361] followed the test applied to determine capacity in *In re C* in ruling that a woman who was 40 weeks pregnant who had refused to consent to a necessary caesarean operation because of needle phobia was temporarily incompetent to give consent to the operation. Butler Sloss L.J. found that the woman's fear of needles dominated to such an extent that she was unable to make a decision at all and therefore she was temporarily incompetent.[362] Accordingly Butler Sloss L.J. ruled that the operation could be carried out without her consent in her best interests. However, best interests in this respect were held not to be limited to her best medical interests and in determining her best interests Ms MB's wishes that the child should be born alive and healthy and the fact that she was in favour of the operation subject only to her needle phobia were relevant considerations.

Subsequently, in the case of *St George's Healthcare NHS Trust v. S; R v. Collins and others ex parte S*[363] a woman was diagnosed by her general practitioner as suffering from pre-eclampsia late in her pregnancy which she was advised risked the health and life both of herself and her child. She nevertheless was adamant in refusing treatment. Her general practitioner considered her to be depressed as did doctors involved in later stages. On the application of a social worker under section 2 of the Mental Health Act 1983 the woman was admitted to hospital against her will, detained there and subsequently admitted to another hospital. She took legal advice and reiterated her refusal of treatment. Unbeknown to the woman or her solicitors the hospital authority sought and obtained an *ex parte* declaration from the trial judge that treatment including Caesarean section was in her best interests and therefore lawful. The judge had been told that incorrectly that labour had commenced. Following the birth of a daughter by Caesarean section the woman discharged herself. She later sought to appeal the declaration and to obtain judicial review of her admission detention and treatment. The Court of Appeal held that at common law a competent adult was entitled to refuse

---

[360] Report on Assessment of Mental Capacity Guidance to Doctors and Lawyers (British Medical Association December 1995), p.68. Pt IV of the Report sets out the Practical Guidance for Doctors in assessing capacity including interestingly the doctor's duty to enhance capacity before making a determination.

[361] [1997] 2 F.L.R. 427.

[362] A similar decision was reached in the case of *Bolton Hospitals NHS Trust v. O* [2003] Fam. Law 319 where the patients fear and anxiety about having a caesarian section arising from difficulties following a previous caesarian section caused her to consent to the operation in the hospital and then refuse it in the operating theatre on four separate occasions. The patient recognised she had a psychological problem but that she needed the operation. Dame Butler Sloss in the High Court granted the hospital's application for a declaration that the patient suffered from temporary incapacity to consent. It was held that the patient was temporarily without capacity to consent due to her overwhelming fear and anxiety when she went to the operating theatre. Consequently she did not have capacity in the operating theatre to consent or to refuse the surgery proposed or to refuse the anaesthesia which was an essential prerequisite to the surgery. Accordingly the caesarian section operation was lawful notwithstanding her inability to consent.

[363] [1998] Fam. Law 526.

medical treatment even where her own life is thereby placed at risk. The mother's right to refuse treatment was not diminished because her right to exercise it posed a risk to the unborn child and a battery had therefore been committed on S. The woman's admission, detention and treatment under the Mental Health Act 1983 were unlawful. The professionals failed to distinguish between S's need for treatment arising from her pregnancy and the essential question under section 2(2)(a) of the Act which was whether her mental disorder was of such a nature and degree as to warrant detention in hospital for assessment or assessment and treatment. At no stage was she offered treatment for depression *i.e.* for mental disorder. The court also pointed out that even where a patient was lawfully admitted under the Act any treatment unconnected with his or her mental condition was subject to the requirements of competence and consent. Accordingly the woman was entitled to have the declaration of Hogg J. set aside *ex debito justitiae*. The court also ruled that a declaration *ex parte* was ineffective to determine rights and should not have been made.

After giving judgment the Court of Appeal received further written submissions from counsel who had taken soundings from the midwives, nursing and medical professions and from patient's organisations and following upon those issued in *In re MB* issued new guidelines to be followed in cases where a patient refuses consent. The guidelines are of interest in that they emphasise the considerations to be borne in mind in cases where issues of capacity to refuse arise. They state, *inter alia*:

(1) In principle a patient may remain competent notwithstanding detention under the Mental Health Act 1983.

(2) If a patient is competent and refuses consent to treatment an application to the High Court for a declaration was pointless. In such a situation the advice given to the patient should be recorded and the hospital authorities should seek unequivocal assurances from the patient recorded in writing that the refusal represents an informed decision *i.e.* that she understands the nature and reasons for the proposed treatment and the risks and likely prognosis involved in the decision to refuse or accept it. If the patient is unwilling to sign a written indication of this refusal this should be recorded in writing. Such a written indication is merely a record for evidential purposes and is not to be regarded as a disclaimer.

(3) If the patient is incapable of giving or refusing consent either in the long term or temporarily (for example due to unconsciousness) the patient must be cared for according to the authority's judgment of the patient's best interests. Where the patient has given an advance directive before becoming incapable treatment and care should normally be subject to the advance directive but if there is reason to doubt its reliability (for example because it may sensibly be thought not to apply to the circumstances which have arisen) then an application for a declaration should be sought.

(4) The authority should identify as soon as possible whether there is concern about a patient's competence to consent to or to refuse treatment.

(5) If the patient's capacity is seriously in doubt it should be assessed as a matter of priority. In serious or complex cases the issue should be examined by an independent psychiatrist ideally one approved under section 12(2) of the Mental Health Act

1983.[364] If there remains doubt and the seriousness and complexity of the issues in the case may require the involvement of the court the psychiatrist should consider whether the patient is incapable by reason of mental disorder of managing her property or affairs. If so, she may be unable to instruct a solicitor and will require a guardian *ad litem* in any court proceedings. The authority should seek legal advice as soon as possible and if a declaration is sought should inform the patient's solicitors immediately, who should, if practicable have a proper opportunity to take instructions and apply for legal aid where necessary. ...

(6) If the patient is unable to instruct solicitors or is believed to be incapable of doing so the authority or its legal advisers must notify the Official Solicitor and invite him to act as guardian ad litem.

(7) The hearing before the judge should be *inter partes.* ...[365]

In the later decision of *In re B (Adult; Refusal of Medical Treatment)*,[366] Dame Butler Sloss President of the Family Division of the English High Court was called upon to decide whether the applicant who, as a result of an intramedullary cervical spine cavernoma became completely paralysed from the neck down, had mental capacity such that effect could be given to her wishes for artificial ventilation to be removed. Such a removal would almost inevitably lead to her death. In granting Ms B's application for, inter alia, a declaration that she had mental capacity to choose whether to accept, or refuse medical treatment Butler Sloss laid down guidelines to be followed in similar cases as follows:

(i) There is a presumption that a patient has the mental capacity to make decisions whether to consent to or refuse medical treatment offered to him/her.

(ii) If mental capacity is not in issue and the patient, having been given the relevant information and offered the available options, chooses to refuse the treatment, that decision should be respected by the doctors. Considerations that the best interests of the patient would indicate that the decision should be to consent to treatment are irrelevant.

(iii) If there is concern or doubt about the mental capacity of the patient, that doubt should be resolved as soon as possible by doctors within the hospital or NHS trust or by other normal medical procedures.

(iv) In the meantime, while the question of capacity is being resolved the patient must, of course, be cared for in accordance with the judgment of the doctors as to the patient's best interests.

(v) If there are difficulties in deciding whether the patient has sufficient mental capacity, particularly if refusal may have grave consequences for the patient, it is most important that those considering the issue should not confuse the question

---

[364] *i.e.* one approved by the Secretary of State as having special experience in the diagnosis and treatment of mental disorder.
[365] The remainder of the Guidelines relate to procedures before the court.
[366] [2002] 2 All E.R. 449.

of mental capacity with the nature of the decision made by the patient, however grave the consequences. The view of the patient may reflect a difference in values rather than an absence of competence and the assessment of capacity should be approached with this firmly in mind. The doctors must not allow their emotional reaction to or strong disagreement with the decision of the patient to cloud their judgment in answering the primary question whether the patient has the mental capacity to make the decision.

(vi) In the rare case where disagreement still exists about competence it is of the utmost importance that the patient is fully informed of the steps being taken and made a part of the process. If the option of enlisting independent outside expertise is being considered, the doctor should discuss this with the patient so that any referral to a doctor outside the hospital would be, if possible, on a joint basis with the aim of helping both sides to resolve the disagreement. It may be crucial to the prospects of a good outcome that the patient is involved before the referral is made and feels equally engaged in the process.

(vii) If the hospital is faced with a dilemma, which the doctors do not know how to resolve, it must be recognised and further steps taken as a matter of priority. Those in charge must not allow a situation of deadlock or drift to occur.

(viii) If there is no disagreement about competence but the doctors are for any reason unable to carry out the wishes of the patient their duty is to find other doctors who will do so.

(ix) If all appropriate steps to seek independent assistance from medical experts outside the hospital have failed, the [hospital authorities] should not hesitate to make application to the High Court or seek the advice of the Official Solicitor.

(x) The treating clinicians and the hospital should always have in mind that a seriously physically disabled patient who is mentally competent has the same right to personal autonomy and to make decisions as any other person with mental capacity."

Commentary

1. The English Law Commission in its *Report No. 231 on Mental Incapacity*,[367] has examined the issue of the criteria to determine whether a person has capacity as a matter of law.[368] Its template is of comparative interest. It recommends:

    (i) that there should be a presumption against lack of capacity and that any question whether a person lacks capacity to be decided on the balance of probabilities.

    (ii) The expression "mental disability" should mean any disability or disorder of the mind or the brain whether permanent or temporary which results in an impairment or disturbance of mental functioning.

---

[367] London: HMSO, February 28, 1995.
[368] Paras 3.2 to 3.22.

(iii) a person is to be regarded as without capacity if at the material time he or she (i) is unable by reason of mental disability to make a decision on the matter in question or (2) is unable to communicate a decision on that matter because he or she is unconscious or for any other reason.

(iv) A person should be regarded as unable to make a decision by reason of mental disability if the disability is such that, at the time when the decision needs to be made, he or she is unable to understand or retain the information relevant to the decision including information about the reasonably foreseeable consequences of deciding one way or another or failing to make the decision.

 (v) A person should be regarded as unable to make a decision by reason of mental disability if the disability is such that, at the time when the decision needs to be made, he or she is unable to make a decision based on the information relevant to the decision, including information about the reasonably foreseeable consequences of deciding one way or another or failing to make the decision.

(vi) A person should not be regarded as unable to understand the information relevant to a decision if he is able to understand an explanation of that information in broad terms and simple language.

(vii) A person is not to be regarded as unable to make a decision by reason of mental disability merely because he makes a decision, which would not be made by a person of ordinary prudence.

(viii) A person is not be regarded as unable to communicate his decision unless all practicable steps to enable him to do so have been taken without success.[369]

Whatever the template adopted it is misleading to think in terms of global or total legal incapacity arising from mental disability and it is imperative that a functional approach be adopted in determining whether a person lacks the requisite legal capacity to perform a particular act such as consenting to medical treatment. In this approach the assessor asks whether an individual is able at the time when the decision has to be made to understand its nature and effects.[370] This will enable both partial and fluctuating capacity to be recognised.

It is submitted that legislation should be enacted in the Irish jurisdiction providing for a statutory test of mental capacity in the field of health care and the grounds upon which such health care may be given without consent. The recommendations of the English Law Commission provide a useful guideline in this regard. As a matter of practice to ensure that accusations against bias in decision making can be refuted psychiatrists clinically disinterested in the relevant case and trained in assessment of capacity should make the assessment of capacity of a person of mental disability (whether mental illness or intellectual disability) to consent to medical treatment.

---

[369] Paras 11.5 to 11.12.

[370] This contrasts with the "status" and "outcome" approaches. Under the "status" approach the status for example of being a ward of court would deprive a person of contractual capacity. Under the "outcome" approach the focus is on the final content of an individual's decision. Any decision which is inconsistent with conventional values or with which the assessor disagrees may be classified as incompetent.

2. In *In re A Ward of Court*,[371] O'Flaherty J. alluded to the possibility that advance refusals of medical treatment may become more common.[372] In *In re C (Adult Refusal of Treatment)*,[373] it was common ground that a refusal of treatment can take the form of a declaration of intention never to consent to that treatment in future or never to consent in some future circumstances. In *In re AK, (Medical Treatment: Consent)*,[374] it was held that the refusal of an adult of full capacity to consent to treatment or care must in law be observed and to this extent an advance indication of the wishes of a patient of full capacity is effective. However it was added that care should be taken to ensure that such anticipatory declarations of wishes still represent the wishes of the patient. It is submitted that the principle of individual autonomy should be copper fastened in legislation. In what may be a useful template for consideration the *Report of English Law Commission on Mental Incapacity*,[375] suggests that statute should provide:

    (i)   that a person aged 18 or over may make an advance refusal of consent of any medical, surgical or dental treatment or other procedure to be carried out at any future time when he or she may be without capacity to give or refuse consent if that person has the capacity to do so;

    (ii)   that the advance refusal of consent shall not apply in circumstances where those having the care of the person who made it consider that the refusal (a) endangers that person's life or (b) if that person is a woman who is pregnant the life of the foetus;

    (iii) no person should incur liability (1) for the consequences of withholding any treatment or procedure if he or she has reasonable grounds for believing that an advance refusal of treatment applies or (2) for carrying out any treatment or procedure to which an advance refusal applies unless he or she knows or has reasonable grounds for believing that an advance refusal applies;

    (iv)   in the absence of any indication to the contrary it should be presumed that an advance refusal was validly made if it is in writing, signed and witnessed;

    (v)   the advance refusal of treatment should be capable of being withdrawn or altered by the person who made it if he or she has capacity to do so;

    (vi)   an advance refusal should not preclude the provision of " basic care" namely care to maintain bodily cleanliness and to alleviate severe pain as well as the provision of direct oral nutrition and hydration;

    (vii) an advance refusal of treatment should not preclude the taking of any action to prevent the death of the maker or a serious deterioration in his or her condition pending a decision of the court or the validity or applicability of an advance refusal or on the question whether it has been withdrawn or altered;

---

[371] [1995] 2 I.L.R.M. 401 at 434.

[372] In the United States, statutes regulate advance directives in 48 out of 50 states (except New Jersey and Massachusetts). In addition, the Patient Self Determination Act 1990 obliges institutions in receipt of federal funding to inform patients about the possibility of making advance directives.

[373] [1994] 1 W.L.R. 290 at 294.

[374] [2001] 1 F.L.R. 129.

[375] No. 231 (1995) paras 5.16–5.38.

(viii) the court should have power to make a declaration regarding the validity of the applicability of an advance refusal of treatment.

Treatment without Consent where a person is mentally incapable and treatment is in the patient's best interests

Treatment without consent where a patient is incapable of giving consent

Where a person with mental disability is incapable of giving consent to medical treatment not relating to a psychiatric illness) that treatment may be given to such person where it is in that person's best interests.[376] In *In re F*,[377] Lord Brandon stated that an operation or other treatment will be in the best interests of patients who are incapable of consenting "if, but only if, it is carried out in order either to save their life or to ensure improvement of their physical or mental health." And if "otherwise [the patients concerned] would be deprived of medical care which they need and to which they are entitled." It was further stated in *In re F*:

> "Action properly taken to preserve the life health or well being of the assisted person may well transcend such measures as surgical operations or substantial medical treatment and may extend to include such humdrum matters as routine medical or dental treatment even simple care such as dressing and undressing and putting to bed".

Thus, the right to act in the patient's best interests is not confined to emergency situations. Further the doctor not only has the right but also has the common law duty to act in the patient's best interests where the patient is incapacitated but only where this is necessary to ensure improvement in health. If a person is incapacitated at the time of the decision whether to treat but is known to have objections to some or all of the treatment there is some English authority which suggests that medical practitioners may not be entitled to proceed even in an emergency.[378] Further, it was stressed in *In re F*, that the court cannot give consent in the place of a person but merely clarifies whether or not certain actions are in the person's best interests and therefore lawful.

In cases where it is necessary to treat an adult patient who is not capable of consenting there is what has been described as a "limited and woefully inadequate facility"[379] to enable consent to be given on behalf of the patient. Application may be made under the Lunacy Regulation (Ireland) Act 1871 for that person to be taken into wardship. A representative of the ward known as a committee is then appointed and in some circumstances the committee of the person may give proxy consent on behalf of the ward. Where more serious or controversial procedures are concerned application must be made to the President of the High Court for a declaration that the proposed treatment

---

[376] See *In re Ward of Court* [1995] 2 I.L.R.M. 401.

[377] [1989] 2 All E.R. 545.

[378] In *In re T (Adult Refusal of Treatment)* [1992] 3 W.L.R. 782 it was held that an advance refusal of treatment by an adult would be legally binding if it is: (a) clearly established; (b) applicable to the current circumstances; and (c) made without undue pressure from other people.

[379] M. Donnelly, *Consent: Bridging the Gap between Doctor and Patient* (Cork University Press, 2002), p.59.

is not unlawful. In this regard, the President will exercise the *parens patriae* jurisdiction of the court – a jurisdiction which emanates from the power of the king in feudal times to make decisions for those of his subjects who were incapable of taking control of their own affairs and which subsequently passed to the courts.[380] In making his decision, the President must act in the best interests of the ward. In determining whether the proposed operation is in the best interests of the patient the court will apply the established test of what would be accepted by a reasonable body of medical opinion skilled in that particular form of treatment.[381]

The fact that a person is mentally ill does not however inevitably mean that s/he is incapable of giving consent. This applies equally to patients detained under the provisions of the Mental Treatment Act 1945. Skegg comments:

> "the fact that a person is suffering from a mental disorder...does not of itself preclude that person from giving legally effective consent. Whether the person is capable of doing so depends on whether that person can understand and come to a decision upon what is involved. Most patients in mental hospitals are capable of giving a legally effective consent, including many who are compulsorily detained. Doctors are sometimes free to proceed without consent but even then a patient will sometimes have the capacity to give a legally effective consent which would, of itself, prevent the doctor's conduct from amounting to the tort of crime or battery."[382]

In *In re C (Adult Refusal of Treatment)*,[383] Thorpe J. stated that the relevant question in each case was whether it had been established that the patient's capacity is so reduced by his mental illness that s/he does not sufficiently understand the nature, purpose and effects of the treatment.[384] A similar test should be applied in any case in which the capacity of a person with intellectual disability is in issue.

In the later case of *In re B*,[385] Thorpe J. ruled that feeding 24 year old patient with mental illness against her will, although permitted under the Mental Health Act 1983

---

[380] Courts (Supplemental Provisions) Act 1961 s.9(1). See question as to survival of *parens patriae* prerogative in section on wardship, p.647 below.

[381] See House of Lords decision in *In re F* [1989]'2 All E.R. 545. The decision in *In re F*, has been criticised on the grounds that it appears to suggest that acting in a person's best interests amounts to no more than not being negligent. Accordingly the English Law Commission has proposed that in deciding what is in a person's best interests regard should be had to: (1) the ascertainable past and present wishes and feelings of the person concerned and the factors that a person would consider if able to do so, (2) the need to permit and encourage the person to participate or to improve his or her ability to participate as fully as possible in anything done for and any decision affecting him or her, (3) the views of other people whom it is appropriate and practicable to consult about the person's wishes and feelings and what would be in his or her best interests, (4) whether the purpose for which any action or decision is required can be as effectively achieved in a manner less restrictive of the person's freedom of action. See Report No. 231 *Mental Incapacity*, paras 3.26 to 3.37).

[382] P.D.G. Skegg, *Law Ethics and Medicine* (Clarendon Press, Oxford, 1984), pp.56–57.

[383] [1994] 1 W.L.R. 29.

[384] Although decided in the context of the Mental Health Act 1983, Thorpe J. applied common law principles in reaching his conclusion.

[385] *The Guardian*, July 26, 1994.

would not be in her best interests "unless and until her physical state was so debilitated as to threaten her survival." In the course of his judgment Thorpe J. remarked that it was disquieting that the 1983 Act legalised what common law would not permit that is the treatment of a competent patient against her will.

In *In re MB (Medical Treatment)*[386] the English Court of Appeal found that a panic fear of needles completely prevented a pregnant woman from coming to a decision to have a necessary caesarian operation such that she was temporarily incompetent and consequently could be treated without her consent in her best interests. In coming to its decisions the court considered the following criteria as necessary to establish whether the patient lacked the capacity to consent to treatment:

> "A person lacks capacity if some impairment or disturbance of mental functioning renders the person unable to make a decision whether to consent to or refuse treatment. That inability to make a decision will occur when:
> (a) the patient is unable to comprehend and retain information which is material to the decision, especially as to the likely consequences of having or not having the treatment in question;
> (b) the patient is unable to use the information and weigh it in the balance as part of the process of arriving at the decision. If as Thorpe J. observed in *In re C*, a compulsive disorder or phobia from which the patient suffers stifles belief in the information presented to her, then the decision may not be a true one. As Lord Cockburn put it in *Banks v. Goodfellow* (1870) L.R. 5 Q.B. 549 at 569:
>
> > "one object may be so forced upon the attention of the invalid as to shut out all others that might require consideration".
>
> ... The temporary factors mentioned by Lord Donaldson in *In re T* (confusion, shock, fatigue, pain or drugs) may completely erode capacity but those concerned must be satisfied that such factors are operating to such a degree that the ability to decide is absent.
>
> ... Another such influence may be panic induced by fear. Again careful scrutiny of the evidence is necessary because fear of an operation may be a rational reason for refusal to undergo it. Fear may also, however, paralyse the will and thus destroy the capacity to make a decision."[387]

In *Norfolk and Norwich Healthcare (NHS) Trust v. W,*[388] Johnson J. held that where a patient lacks capacity at common law within the threefold test laid down by Thorpe J. in *In re C (Refusal of Medical Treatment)* to decide on his/her treatment then reasonable force may be used to carry out treatment which is deemed to be in the patient's best interests. So ruling he granted a declaration authorising W's pregnancy to be brought to an end by either forceps delivery or by Caesarian section having found that W lacked the capacity to decide upon treatment. In addition there was a risk that the foetus might

---

[386] [1997] 2 F.L.R. 427.
[387] *Ibid.* at 437.
[388] [1997] Fam. Law 17.

suffocate unless delivery were speeded up and a risk that W's old Caesarean scar might reopen with risk to both foetus and patient.

In *St Georges Healthcare NHS Trust v. S; R v. Collins and others ex parte S*,[389] the Court confirmed that even where a patient is lawfully admitted under the Mental Health Act 1983 any treatment unconnected with his or her mental condition is subject to the requirements of competence and consent. In promulgating guidelines in relation to cases where a patients capacity to consent is in issue the court advised that in serious and complex cases the issue of the patient's capacity to consent should be examined by an independent psychiatrist ideally one approved under section 12(2) of the Mental Health Act 1983. If there remains doubt then application should be made to the court.

In its *Report on Assessment of Mental Capacity Guidelines for Doctors and Lawyers* the British Medical Association and the Law Society offers some practical guidelines in relation to the approach to treatment of incapacitated patients. According to the report, treatment decisions can be divided into two categories (a) low-level decisions, and (b) serious treatment decisions.

Where low level decisions are concerned there should generally be agreement between health professionals, people close to the patient and the incapacitated person insofar as s/he can express a view as to treatment. Simple treatment or diagnostic options such as the taking of blood samples for monitoring of lithium levels or the provision of antibiotics for an infection in an otherwise fit person are uncontroversial and the Report advises that they can be taken by the clinician, the patient and people providing care. Serious treatments such as non-therapeutic sterilisation and withdrawal of artificial hydration and nutrition from patients in a persistent vegetative state must following specific case law on the point[390] be brought before the courts for independent review. Other cases involving such treatments as tissue donation are likely also to require court authorisation.

The British Medical Association/Law Society Report also recommends that a number of general principles be taken into account when considering the medical treatment of patient lacking capacity. They state:

A patient has a right to:

(i)   be free from discrimination and should not be treated differently solely because of the condition that gives rise to the incapacity;

(ii) privacy: The patient should be free from any medical procedures unless there are good therapeutic reasons for them; For example questions are sometimes raised about subjecting non-sexually active incapacitated women to cervical cytology;

(iii) confidentiality of personal health information;

(iv) liberty: Patients should be free from interventions that inhibit the liberty or the capacity to enjoy life unless such intervention is necessary to prevent a greater harm to the patient or to others. Appropriate justification must be shown for the use of restraints and it is inappropriate for restrictive measures to be used as an alternative to adequate staffing levels;

---

[389] [1998] Fam. Law 526.
[390] *In re F (Mental Patient: Sterilisation)* [1990] 2 AC 1; *Airedale NHS Trust v Bland* [1993] A.C. 789.

(v) dignity: The patient's social and cultural values should also be respected;

(vi) have his or her view taken into account even where they are considered legally incapable of determining what happens."[391]

The BMA/Law Society of England and Wales Report notes that assessing capacity to consent to medical treatment is somewhat different to other capacity assessments since the assessor may be the person proposing the treatment. Clearly with this in mind it advises that as a matter of good practice a second opinion from another doctor should be obtained where a complex decision is contemplated. It states that this can both assure the doctor proposing to treat the patient that the patient does lack capacity to consent and that the treatment is in the patient's best interests. Where a serious procedure is contemplated it advises that doctors follow a series of basic steps including:

(a) considering whether there are alternative ways of treating the patient, particularly measures which might be less invasive;

(b) discussing the treatment with the health care team;

(c) discussing the treatment with the patient insofar as this is possible;

(d) considering the anticipatory statement of the patient's views;

(e) consulting other appropriate professionals involved with the patient's care in the hospital or community;

(f) consulting relatives[392] and/or carers;

(g) obtaining a second opinion form a doctor skilled in the proposed treatment; and

(h) ensuring that a record is made of the discussions.[393]

Commentary on treating the incompetent patient from a comparative law perspective

US Decisions

In the US where life-threatening decisions are concerned the US courts determine whether the patient is in fact incompetent and if so, whether the patient has provided or can provide any indications about his or her feelings about the treatment in question. If so, under the substituted judgment standard it has been held that the surrogate decision maker must make the decision the incompetent patient would make, if he were able to choose himself. In the case of *Superintendent of Belchertown v. Saikewicz*,[394] the Supreme Judicial Court of Massachusetts directed that chemotherapy be withheld from

---

[391] *Report on Assessment of Mental Capacity Guidance for Doctors and Lawyers* (British Medical Association, December 1995), pp.70–71.

[392] Relatives may be in a position to provide an indication of what the patient would have chosen if in a position to do so. See *In re T: Refusal of Treatment* [1992] 3 W.L.R. 782. Their consent to treatment of an incapacitated adult is however of no legal effect.

[393] *Ibid.*, pp.71–72.

[394] 370 N.E. 2d. 417 (Mass. 1977).

a 67-year-old profoundly intellectually disabled resident of state institution who was suffering from leukaemia. In the court's view the right to privacy outweighed the need for medical treatment. The limited extension of life, possible if chemotherapy was used was less persuasive than the fact that the patient had an incurable illness, would suffer substantial side effects and discomfort and might experience considerable fear because of his lack of understanding about what was happening. The court ruled that in order to decline the treatment the substituted consent had to be based on the patient's actual interests and preferences not on the basis of his best interests. It was held that substituted judgment should be made by the judiciary and not by an ethics committee or some "other group purporting to represent the "morality and conscience of our society.""[395]

The US courts are hesitant to order elective surgery unless the person is incompetent and the surgery is consistent with what the person would want if competent to decide. In *In re Schiller*,[396] a New Jersey Court appointed a special guardian to approve the amputation of an incompetent man's foot because even though the man's surgery was considered elective his life would soon be in danger if surgery were not performed. By contrast in *In re Nemser*,[397] a New York court refused to appoint a guardian to approve amputation where there was a genuine dispute about the operation's medical necessity and the man expressed an unwillingness to go ahead with the surgery. In *In re Weberlist*,[398] yet another New York court approved cosmetic surgery for an intellectually disabled adult in order to enhance his opportunity for human development. The procedure was approved because the ward's appearance kept him from fulfilling his social and educational potential. He was a person with hydrocephalus and had a cleft palate and webbed fingers. In arriving at its decision the court ruled that in the absence of parents to provide consent, the court "must decide what its ward would choose, if he were in a position to make a sound judgment."[399]

A new Best Interests Standard?

However, there is an element of artificiality in adopting a substituted judgment standard in cases where the patient has never been competent to express a preference and it is submitted that Irish legislation should provide that where a person is without capacity to consent to medical treatment it should not be administered unless it is necessary in that persons best interests. However, a best interests test without any criteria to support it has been criticised as allowing "too much room for medical manoeuvre"[400] and it is submitted that the decision as to the best interests should be based on a broader set of factors than persuasive case law has heretofore considered. In deciding whether a course of action is in a person's best interests regard might be had to (1) the ascertainable past

---

[395] *Ibid.*, p.435. Three years later the same court in *In re Spring* 405 N.E. 2d 115 (Mass. 1980) qualified its view that there was an absolute requirement that the court review such matters. The court noted that while in general it was undesirable to shift the ultimate responsibility from the judiciary doctors could end life-prolonging treatment but would be subject to liability if they were wrong.

[396] 372 A.2d. 360 (N.J. Super. Ct. Ch. Div. 1977).

[397] 273 N.Y.S. 2d 624 (1966).

[398] 360 N.Y.S. 2d. 783 (Sup. Ct. N.Y. County 1974).

[399] *Ibid.*, p.787.

[400] See J. Hillery *et al*, "Consent to Treatment and People with Learning Disabilities", *Irish Journal of Psychological Medicine* (1998) Vol. 15(4) 117.

and present wishes and feelings of the person concerned and the factors that a person would consider if able to do so, (2) the need to permit and encourage a person to participate or to improve his or her ability to participate as fully as possible in anything done for and any decision affecting him or her, (3) the views of other people[401] whom it is appropriate and practicable to consult about the person's wishes and feelings and what would be in his or her best interests, (4) whether the purpose for which any action or decision is required can be as effectively achieved in a manner less restrictive of the person's freedom of action.[402]

Proposal that Treatment Decisions be made through Guardianship System

It is noteworthy that the Irish Law Reform Commission in its Consultation Paper on *Law and the Elderly*,[403] provisionally proposes to abolish the wards of court system and to replace it by a system of Guardianship. This system would facilitate the making of substitute decisions by statutory substitute decision makers for people who lacked the capacity to make health care decisions. A decision as to whether a person lacked such capacity would be made by a Guardianship Tribunal. The decision would be based, *inter alia*, on an assessment of need made by the Health Service Executive or a certificate of a registered medical practitioner with the person alleged to be in need of protection being given due process rights including the right to have a second expert medical assessment considered by the Tribunal.[404] Where a person was found to lack legal capacity a Guardianship Order would be made. Once the Guardianship Order was made the system of substitute decision making (if provided for in the order) would come into play. Henceforth decisions in relation to health care would be made for the "protected adult" by the Personal Guardian, the Public Guardian the Guardianship Tribunal and the Court respectively in ascending order of seriousness. Decisions made at each level would be appealable to the next level. It is envisaged that the Personal Guardian would be entitled to give consent to emergency and minor or routine decisions,[405] and the definition of what constitutes minor or routine decisions would be the subject of an agreement between the Irish Medical Council and the Office of the Public Guardian.[406] The Personal Guardian would also be empowered to override a refusal of consent by the protected adult (who would by virtue of the guardianship order be deemed incapable of consenting and therefore refusing consent).[407] The Office of the Public Guardian would supervise the Personal Guardian,[408] and have the power to approve certain (undefined but it must be assumed, more serious) health care decisions.[409] Major health

---

[401] Such people would be: (1) any person named in advance by the person who is without capacity; (2) a person (for example a spouse, relative or friend) engaged in caring for the person or who is interested in the person's welfare.

[402] This template is adopted by the English Law Commission in its *Report No. 231 on Incapacity*, para.3.28.

[403] L.R.C. CP 23–2003.

[404] Paras 6.50–6.54.

[405] Para.6.62.

[406] Para.6.64.

[407] Para.6.66.

[408] Para.6.43.

[409] Para.6.41.

care decisions would be specifically reserved to the President of the High Court or a judge appointed by him such as turning off a life-support machine or organ donations.[410]

In making any decision about health care it is envisaged that the Personal Guardian, the Public Guardian or the Court/Tribunal would be obliged to take account of the protected person's best interests. In doing so the report provisionally recommends that consideration should be given "among other matters" to the (i) the wishes of the protected person, so far as they can be ascertained; (ii) what would happen if the proposed procedure were not carried out; (iii) what alternative treatments are available; and (iv) whether it can be postponed because better treatments may become available.[411]

The creation of a system whereby a statutorily appointed person may give consent to medical treatment on behalf of an adult who lacks capacity without recourse to the court is to be welcomed as a practical solution to the practical difficulties encountered under the current law when an adult is incapable of consenting to treatment. However, the total abolition of the wardship system in order to bring this about it is submitted is a disproportionate means to achieving a desired end and there is no reason why the existing powers and duties of the committee of the person could not be extended to bring about effectively the same result. However, the duty imposed on the substitute decision maker to act in the incapacitated adults best interests is to be welcomed and indeed the Law reform Commission's report reflects the need for more detailed criteria for determining the "best interests" of an adult without capacity to consent to medical treatment. More detailed and final proposals are awaited in the Law Reform Commissions Report.

TREATMENT OF MINORS WITH MENTAL DISABILITY

Current law

A parent may give legally effective consent to treatment of a minor where the procedure is in the best interests of the minor and the minor is incapable of consenting on his/her behalf. A minor may be incompetent to consent to medical treatment by reason of immaturity, *i.e.* where notwithstanding normal development and function of his/her mental faculties his/her level of maturity is such that s/he is as yet unable to understand the nature and effects of the medical treatment. Secondly, a minor may be capable of consenting by virtue of maturity but may be incompetent to consent to medical treatment by reason of mental disability. Thirdly, a minor may be incapable of consenting by reason of immaturity and mental disability. In any of these three sets of circumstances the test of capacity employed by the courts is the same *viz.* a minor will be incompetent if, first s/he is unable to comprehend and retain the information which is material to the decision, secondly, whether s/he is capable of believing it and thirdly whether s/he is unable to use the information and weigh it in the balance to arrive at a choice.[412]

For the purposes of the analysis of the competence of a minor by virtue of maturity to consent to medical treatment, section 23 of the Non-Fatal Offences against the Person Act 1997 is significant. It provides that the consent of a minor who has attained the age

---

[410] Para.6.58.
[411] Para.6.65.
[412] See *In re C, op. cit.*

of 16 years to any surgical, medical or dental treatment which in the absence of consent would constitute a trespass to his or her person shall be effective as it would be if he or she were of full age and where a minor by virtue of section 23 has given an effective consent to any treatment it shall not be necessary to obtain any consent for it from his or her parent or guardian. Thus clearly the consent of a minor aged 16 to medical treatment is valid. However, the section does not specifically prohibit minors aged less than 16 years from giving a legal consent to treatment. It remains to be seen whether the courts will interpret the section as being facilitative (giving an automatic power to consent to all minors over the age of 16 but not preventing all minors under the age of 16 from giving consent) or restrictive (preventing all minors aged less than 16 from giving a valid consent).

What is clear, however, is that a parent may consent to treatment, which is in the best interests of a minor under the age of 16 years. In addition there is a common law principle that beneficial contracts for services (of which a contract for medical treatment is one) which are entered into by a minor [413] are voidable in the sense that unless the minor affirms them they are not binding. Accordingly where a minor under the age of 16 meets the test of competence it is advisable to seek the consent of that minor to any proposed medical treatment.

Further support for the argument that a minor under the age of 16 has capacity in some circumstances to consent to medical treatment might be gleaned from English authority in this area. In *Gillick v. West Norfolk and Wisbech Area Health Authority*,[414] a majority of the House of Lords held that minors under the age of 16 years may also give valid consent without the requirement of parental consent if they achieve a "sufficient understanding and intelligence to enable [them] to understand fully" the nature and consequences of the proposed treatment. The matter of a whether a child seeking advice has sufficient understanding of what is involved to give a consent valid in law is a question of fact in each case. Lord Scarman added:

> "Until a child achieves the capacity to consent, the parental right to make the decision continues save only in exceptional circumstances. Emergency, parental neglect, abandonment of the child or inability to find the parent are examples of exceptional situations justifying the doctor proceeding to treat the child without parental consent."[415]

Following *Gillick*, as a matter of practice the British Medical Association and Law Society of England and Wales *Report on the Assessment of Mental Capacity Guidance for Doctors and Lawyers* offered the following advice when assessing a minor's maturity for the purpose of consenting to medical treatment:

> "From the viewpoint of good practice, assessment of capacity should include consideration of the young person's:

---

[413] *i.e.* any person under the age of 18 years. Age of Majority Act 1985, s.2(1), but the argument is, since the enactment of s.23 of the Non Fatal Offences against the Person Act 1997, only really relevant to the case of a person under the age of 16 years.

[414] [1985] 3 All E.R. 402.

[415] *Ibid.* at 424.

(i)   ability to understand that there is a choice and that choices have consequences;

(ii) willingness and ability to make a choice (including the option of choosing that someone else makes treatment decisions);

(iii) understanding of the nature and purpose of the proposed procedure;

(iv) understanding of the proposed procedure's risks and side effects;

(v)   understanding of the alternatives to the proposed procedure and the risks attached to them and the consequences of no treatment; and freedom from pressure."[416]

Subsequently, in *In re R (A Minor) (Wardship: Consent to Treatment,*[417] Lord Donaldson limited the ambit of the dicta in Gillick. In that case R was 15 years old and was mentally ill to the extent that she was paranoid, aggressive and hallucinatory. She had been placed in an adolescent psychiatric unit following an application under section 2 of the Mental Health Act 1983 (admission for assessment) where she was sedated form time to time with her consent. The unit wishes to treat her with anti-psychotic drugs and sought permission to do so from the local authority that had obtained the initial place of safety and interim care orders. R was refusing to consent to the medication and the local authority was unwilling to impose treatment on her. In the light of R's deteriorating condition the authority instituted wardship proceedings. R's refusal of the proposed medication took place during a period when she appeared to be lucid and rational but the medical opinion was that, without the treatment she would return to a psychotic state and would, inter alia, be seriously suicidal. Her competence was accordingly found to be fluctuating in nature. Waite J. held that a wardship judge would not override the decision of a *Gillick* competent ward but that, on the facts, R was not competent. The Court of Appeal agreed with the finding that R was not competent but went on to say that in any event a *Gillick competent* child's refusal of treatment could be overridden by the court or, according to Lord Donaldson M.R. by those having parental rights or responsibilities. This conclusion was based on the analysis that the achieving of *Gillick* competence while conferring a right on the child to consent does not thereby extinguish the concurrent rights of the parents or courts. The effect of the analysis is that both minors and parents have powers to consent. The agreement of either is legally sufficient for treatment but only the refusal of both parent and minor constitutes a veto in relation to proposed medical treatment.

In the case of *In re W (A Minor) (Medical Treatment),*[418] the English courts went further to restrict the autonomy of a minor over the age of 16 in relation to making decisions relating to medical treatment. In that case W was in a specialist adolescent residential unit being treated for anorexia nervosa. She had been the subject of a care order since being orphaned at the age of 8, although her aunt had concurrent parental responsibility. Her condition deteriorated to such an extent that the local authority decided that it might become necessary to treat her without her consent. No particular treatment was contemplated but it was thought possible that W might refuse consent "because

---

[416] *Report on Assessment of Mental Capacity Guidance for Doctors and Lawyers* (British Medical Association December 1995), p.73.

[417] [1991] 4 All E.R. 177.

[418] [1992] 4 All E.R. 627.

one of the symptoms of anorexia nervosa is a desire by the sufferer to "be in control" and such a refusal would be an obvious way of demonstrating this."[419] The authority applied to the High Court for leave to move W to another treatment centre without her consent and for leave to give her medical treatment without her consent. Thorpe J. gave leave in both respects. He held that although W had sufficient understanding to make an informed decision, he had inherent jurisdiction to make the order sought. W appealed. Before the hearing of the appeal her condition deteriorated to such an extent that at the hearing of the appeal the Court of Appeal made an emergency order that she be removed to hospital for treatment. At the hearing the Court of Appeal upheld the decision of Thorpe J. and expanded on the views expressed in *In re R.*

Since W was 16 she came within section 8 of the Family Law Reform Act 1969 which provided that the consent of a minor who had attained the age of 16 years to, inter alia, any medical treatment was to be "as effective as it would be if he were of full age." The question arose as to whether such a minor had an exclusive right to consent to such treatment and therefore an absolute right to refuse medical treatment because no one else would be in a position to consent. Lord Donaldson M.R. held that the consent of a 16-year-old minor to which section 8 applied could not be overridden by those with parental responsibility. It could however be overridden by the court. A minor of any age who is "*Gillick* competent" in the context of particular treatment had a right to consent to that treatment, which again could not be overridden by those with parental but could be overridden by the court. However, no minor of whatever age had power by refusing consent to treatment to override consent to treatment by someone who had parental responsibility for the minor and a fortiori a consent by the court.

Nevertheless, such a refusal was a very important consideration in making clinical judgments and for parents and the court in deciding whether themselves to give consent. Its importance increased with the age and maturity of the minor. According to Balcombe L.J. the court exercising its unlimited jurisdiction over minors could in a child's best interests, objectively considered, override the wishes of a child who had sufficient understanding and intelligence to make an informed decision and who sought to refuse medical treatment in circumstances which would in all probability lead to the death of the child or to severe permanent injury. However, before exercising its jurisdiction the court should approach its decision with a strong predilection to give effect to the child's wishes. Balcombe L.J. further held that the purpose of the section 8 was simply to make clear that a minor aged 16 or over may give a valid consent to medical treatment which in the absence of consent by the child or his/her parents would constitute a trespass to the person and the section had no application to whether such a minor had an absolute right to refuse medical treatment. On the facts given the deterioration in W's condition W's wishes had to be overridden.

On the issue of W's capacity it is interesting to note that Lord Donaldson M.R. and Balcombe L.J. found that it was " a feature of anorexia nervosa that it is capable of destroying the ability to make an informed choice".[420] Lord Donaldson M.R. stated further:

"[Anorexia nervosa] creates a compulsion to refuse treatment or only to accept

---

[419] [1992] 4 All E.R. 627 at 631.
[420] *Ibid.* at 637.

treatment which is likely to be ineffective. This attitude is part and parcel of the disease and the more advanced the illness, the more compelling it may become. Where the wishes of the minor are themselves something which the doctors reasonably consider need to be treated in the minors own best interests, those wishes clearly have a much reduced significance."[421]

Morris comments:

"Both R and W were troubled individuals whose states of mind properly raised questions about their ability to understand and make informed choices. In each case however there seems to have been an assumption that the very fact that they did not (or more accurately *might not*) agree with the view of the medical profession as to what was in their best interests was in itself an indication of their lack of understanding."[422]

In the later case of *In re C (Detention: Medical Treatment)*,[423] Wall J. following the authority of *In re W* ruled that he had the power exercising the inherent jurisdiction of the court to authorise the detention of a 16 year old girl with anorexia nervosa in a clinic (which was not a hospital with powers of detention under the Mental Health Act) for the purposes of treatment and to override C's objections to an order being made. He regarded C's capacity to give or refuse consent as relevant to the weight, which should be given to her wishes, but it would not be determinative of the court's decision. Applying the criteria set out by Thorpe J. in *In re C (Adult: Refusal of Treatment*,[424] in the event C was found to lack the capacity to weigh information in the balance to arrive at a choice.

Notwithstanding the decisions in *In re R Minor*, and *In re W*, the British Medical Association and the Law Society of England and Wales in their report on *The Assessment of Mental Capacity: Guidance for Doctors and Lawyers* advise that:

"Children and young people should be kept as fully informed as possible about their care and treatment. The individual's overall welfare should be the paramount consideration and listening to the minor's views is conducive to promoting their welfare in the widest sense. They should be encouraged to take decisions in collaboration with parents. If a minor refuses necessary treatment however, parents or people with parental responsibility or the courts may legally authorise it."[425]

This advice would seem to apply whether the child is *Gillick* competent or not.

In Ireland, it is arguable that Article 41.1.1 of the Constitution which accords special status to the rights of the family within society and provides that "[t]he state recognises the family as the natural, primary and fundamental unit group of society and as a moral

---

[421] [1992] 4 All E.R. 627 at 637.

[422] See "Treating children properly: law ethics and practice", *Professional Negligence* Vol.15 No. 4 (1999) 249.

[423] [1997] 2 F.L.R. 180.

[424] [1994] I W.L.R. 290.

[425] Report on the *Assessment of Mental Capacity Guidance for Doctors and Lawyers*, *op. cit.*, p.75.

institution possessing inalienable and imprescriptible rights antecedent and superior to all positive law" and Article 42 which guarantees the inalienable right and duty of parents to provide for the "religious and moral, intellectual, physical and social education of their children" may provide a barrier to a decision similar to that in *Gillick* in the Irish jurisdiction. In addition judicial dicta of the Supreme Court in *G v. An Bord Uchtála*,[426] would appear to suggest that a child may not achieve full autonomy until s/he reaches 16. Thus O'Higgins J. states:

> "[t]he child also has natural rights. Normally these will be safe under the care and protection of the mother. Having been born the child has the right to be fed and to live, to be reared and educated and to have the opportunity of working and of realising his or her full personality and dignity as a human being. These rights of the child and others which I have not enumerated must equally be protected by the state".

The *Gillick* competence concept may not fully accord with this perception of the autonomy of the child. Neither indeed would it seem to accord to the precedence given to parental authority in the recent case of *North Western Health Board v. W.*[427] In that case the defendants were the parents of a 14-month-old infant, (called "Paul" for the purposes of the proceedings). The health board wished to conduct a PKU screening test on Paul. The PKU test enables medical practitioners to ascertain whether a child who may look healthy and well is suffering from certain biochemical,[428] or metabolic disorders[429] that can be extremely serious but are treatable if identified at an early age. The test involved taking a small blood sample from Paul's heel. The defendants refused to allow the test to be carried out as they considered it overly intrusive. Instead they offered the health board a urine or hair sample from Paul in order that the test could be carried out. However hair and urine are less reliable detectors than blood samples. The health board claimed that the defendants refusal to consent to carrying out the PKU test represented a failure to vindicate Paul's personal rights and they sought, *inter alia*, a mandatory injunction requiring the defendants to furnish their consent to the PKU test The health board contended that the rights of Paul were paramount and that Paul's welfare had to be the first and primary consideration. The rights of the parents could not be exercised in such a manner as to derogate from the Paul's rights. The relevant test was whether the carrying out of the heel test was in the best interests of Paul. The defendant's contended that no legislation made either the test in question compulsory. The rights of the family and, therefore, in the case of a young infant, the parents, must take precedence under the Constitution over the rights of the child unless there was an exceptional case where the parents, for physical or moral reasons, had failed in their duty to their children. This was not such a case. It was generally the right of the parent to determine what, if any, medical treatment would be given to his child. (It was acknowledged that the court might intervene in exceptional circumstances such as to order a blood transfusion in a life saving situation).

---

[426] [1980] I.R. 32.
[427] [2001] 3 I.R. 622.
[428] Phenylketonuria, and homocystinuria.
[429] Hypothyroidism.

The defence pointed out that parents were not bound to act in accordance with generally accepted principles or generally accepted medical opinion.

McCracken J. in the High Court ruled that the decision of the parents did not amount to an exceptional case permitting the state to interfere with the parents decision pursuant to Article 42.5 of the Constitution and the provisions of the Child Care Act 1991. The spirit and word of the Constitution would be contravened if the State were entitled to intervene to override the decision of parents where professional opinion differed from that of the parent's concerned. It was for the Oireachtas to provide for the making of such tests compulsory. It was not the function of the Courts to make such decisions. Any legislation thus passed by the Oireachtas could then be tested in the courts for its constitutionality. The plaintiffs appealed to the Supreme Court.

By a 4:1 majority the Supreme Court upheld the High Court decision.

Murphy J. admitted that he was impatient with the attitude of the defendants and was alarmed by the real possibility that the young boy may be a victim of one of the metabolic conditions, which the PKU test could so easily detect. Nevertheless he did not accept that a particular ill advised decision made by parents (whose care and devotion generally to their child was not disputed) could properly be categorised as such a default by parents of their moral and constitutional duty so as to bring into operation the supportive role of the state. He continued:

> "If the State had an obligation in the present case to substitute its judgment for that of the parents numerous applications would be made to the courts to overrule decisions made by caring but misguided parents. Such a jurisprudence and particular decisions made under it would tend to damage the long term interests of the child by eroding the interest and dedication of the parents in the performance of their duties. In my view the subsidiary and supplemental powers of the State in relation to the welfare of children arises only where either the general conduct of the parents is such as to constitute a virtual abdication of their responsibilities or alternatively the disastrous consequences of a particular parental decision are so immediate and inevitable as to demand intervention and perhaps call into question either the basic competence or devotion of the parents."[430]

At an earlier point in his judgment he stated:

> "The failure of the parental duty which would justify and compel intervention by the State must be exceptional indeed. It is possible to envisage misbehaviour or other activity on the part of parents which involves such a degree of neglect as to constitute abandonment of the child and all rights in respect of it."[431]

Denham J. reasoned that the defendants had exercised their parental responsibility and duty to the child and that it had not been established that the parents had failed in their duty to the child nor had it been shown that the child's constitutional rights had been infringed. However Denham J. did emphasise:

---

[430] [2001] 3 I.R. 622 at 733.
[431] *Ibid.* at 733.

"In seeking the balance to be achieved between the child's rights within and to his family and the family (as an institution) rights, and the parent's rights to exercise their responsibility for the child, and the child's personal constitutional rights, the threshold will depend on the circumstances of the case. Thus, if the child's life is in immediate danger (e.g. needing an operation) then there is a heavy weight to be put on the child's personal rights superseding family and parental considerations"[432]

and further,

"The State (which includes the legislative, the executive and the courts) should not intervene so as to weaken or threaten [family] bonds unless there are exceptional circumstances. Exceptional circumstances will depend on the facts of a case; they include an immediate threat to the health or life of the child."[433]

Murray J. noted that decisions, which are sometimes taken by parents concerning their children, may be a source of discomfort or even distress to the rational and objective bystander. Nevertheless there had to be something exceptional arising from a failure of duty before the state could intervene in the interest of the individual child. He added:

"It would be impossible and undesirable to seek to define in one neat rule or formula all the circumstances in which the State might intervene in the interests of the child against the express wishes of the parent. It seems however to me that there must immediate and fundamental threat to the capacity of the child to continue to function as a human person, physically morally or socially, deriving from an exceptional dereliction of duty on the part of the parents to justify such an intervention."[434]

He continued that unwise and disturbing as the decision of the parents may have been in the instant case it was a decision which they had the liberty to take and that it was not a case in which there had been such an abdication of responsibility, moral or otherwise as would justify the State's view being substituted for that of the parents.

Hardiman J. stated that he did not view a conscientious disagreement with the public health authorities as constituting either a failure in duty or an exceptional case justifying State intervention. He added that the Constitution plainly accords a primacy to the parent and this primacy gives rise to a presumption that the welfare of the child is to be found in the family exercising its authority as such. This, he believed, reflects the rights of both parents and children to have the family protected from State interference. He concluded that in the instant case he did not consider the presumption described to have been rebutted or the conditions for displacement of parental authority to have been met.

Keane C.J. dissenting did not accept that the Irish courts were obliged to allow the wishes of the parents, however irrational they may be to prevail over the best interests of Paul. Far from giving effect to the values enshrined in Article 42 of the Constitution

---

[432] [2001] 3 I.R. 622 at 722–723.
[433] *Ibid.* at 725.
[434] *Ibid.* at 741.

such an approach would gravely endanger Paul's right to a happy and healthy life. Keane C.J. considered that the defendant's refusal to allow the test to be carried out amounted to a failure on their part to vindicate the constitutional right of Paul to be guarded against unnecessary and avoidable dangers to his health and welfare.

On the matter of a child's capacity to consent The Irish Medical Council's *Guide to Ethical Conduct and Behaviour*[435] advises doctors as a matter of practice that:

> "if the doctor feels that a child will understand a proposed medical procedure, information or advice, this should be explained fully to the child. Where the consent of parent's or guardians is normally required in respect of a child for whom they are responsible due regard must be had to the wishes of the child. The doctor must never assume that it is safe to ignore the parental/guardian interest."[436]

This suggests that as a matter of practice in Ireland while the wishes of a child under 16 will be taken into account by doctors seeking consent in regard to medical treatment parental wishes will take precedence.

Conflicts between the interests of parent and child where the child has a mental disability and the condition of the child is life threatening have also been presented to the English courts for decision. In the absence of Irish authority on the subject these decisions are of persuasive authority in the Irish jurisdiction. Thus in the English case of *In re B (A Minor) (Wardship: Medical Treatment)*,[437] B was a baby with Down's Syndrome suffering from an intestinal blockage and surgery had been proposed. Without this surgery B would die within a few days. Her parents did not consent to the surgery and argued that " nature had made its own arrangements to terminate a life which would not be fruitful and nature should not be interfered with." The child was made a ward of court . Application was made to decide whether the operation should go ahead giving the child a possibility of 20 or 30 years life. The Court of Appeal held that the child must live and that the duty of the court was to decide this on the basis of the child's interest.

In the later case of *In re C (A Minor) (Wardship: Medical Treatment)*,[438] C had been born with a severe form of hydrocephalus resulting in extensive and irreparable brain damage and was terminally ill. C had been made a ward of court shortly after her birth because the local authority's social services department were of the view that her parents would have great difficulty looking after her. After she had been made a ward of court the question arose as to the appropriate treatment for C, the extent to which the medical staff looking after her should seek to prolong her life and whether the child should receive treatment appropriate to a child without a disability or treatment appropriate to her condition. The Official Solicitor, as C's guardian ad litem, obtained a specialist's report, which stated that the aim of treatment of the baby should be to ease her suffering rather than achieve a short prolongation of her life. The trial judge directed that leave be given to the hospital authorities to treat the ward in such a way that she ended her life peacefully with the least pain, suffering and distress and that the hospital authorities

---

[435] Sixth edition, 2004.
[436] Para.18.3.
[437] [1990] 3 All E.R. 927.
[438] [1989] 2 All E.R. 782 CA.

were not required to treat any serious infection which the baby contracted or to set up any intravenous feeding system for her. The Official Solicitor appealed against the terms of the order contending that the judge had been wrong to direct that treatment of serious infections and intravenous feeding were not necessary. The Court of Appeal determined that C should receive treatment "appropriate to her condition" and that it would authorise treatment which would relieve the ward's suffering during the remainder of his or her life but rather than give directions as to specific treatment of a terminally ill child it would accept the opinions of the medical staff in charge of the ward if they decided that the aim of the care should be to ease suffering rather than achieve a short prolongation of the child's life. The Official Solicitor's appeal was allowed to the extent that the judge's direction that treatment of serious infections and intravenous feeding were not necessary were deleted.

Then in *In re J (a minor) (Wardship: Medical Treatment)*,[439] the Court of Appeal considered the case of a child with profound intellectual and physical disabilities whose life expectancy was uncertain and who would on occasions require painful ventilation treatment to survive. It held that although the court would never sanction positive steps to terminate life where disabilities were so grave that life would be so intolerable for the individual that he would choose to die if able to make a judgment then the court could direct that treatment to prolong life need not be given. The court had to perform a balancing exercise in the best interests of the child looked at from his point of view.[440]

In the subsequent case of *In re J (a minor) (Child in Care: Medical Treatment)*,[441] J had sustained serious head injuries as a result of a fall when he was one month old and had been rendered severely mentally and physically disabled as a result. He was blind, was a child with cerebral palsy and epilepsy and needed to be fed by a nasogastric tube. He had been resuscitated on a number of occasions due to his frequent convulsions but his consultant paediatrician had concluded that ventilation should not be carried out if J were to have an attack in the future. J's mother disagreed with the views of the consultant, and at first instance Waite J. held that ventilation should be provided if this became necessary. The local authority appealed to the Court of Appeal, which reversed the

---

[439] [1990] 3 All E.R. 930 CA.

[440] In 1984 the US Congress specifically addressed the obligations of physicians and the states in preventing the withholding of treatments from infants born with mental or physical impairments. Only in three exceptional circumstances may a treating physician withhold "medically indicated treatment." These are embodied in exclusions from the definition of the latter phrase as follows. The term "withholding of medically indicated treatment" means the failure to respond to the infant's life threatening conditions by providing treatment (including appropriate nutrition, hydration, and medication) which in the treating physician's or physician's reasonable judgment will be most likely to be effective in ameliorating or correcting all such conditions." The term does not however include "the failure to provide treatment (other than appropriate nutrition, hydration or medication) to an infant when, in the treating physician or physician's reasonable medical judgment (a) the infant is chronically and irreversibly comatose (b) the provision of such treatment would (i) merely prolong dying (ii) not be effective in ameliorating or correcting all of the infant's life threatening conditions or (iii) otherwise be futile in terms of the survival of the infant or (c) the provision of such treatment would be virtually futile in terms of the survival of the infant and the treatment itself under such circumstances would be inhumane." Each state's child protection agency is obliged to develop a system to handle reports of medical negligence in relation to these infants including legal remedies where the law is violated. 42 U.S.C. Section 5101.

[441] [1992] 3 W.L.R. 507.

decision at first instance. Lord Donaldson held that no doctor can be required by a court or by a patient's parents to treat a child in a way, which the doctors feel is medically contra-indicated.

A similar approach was taken in the case of *In re C.*[442] In that case the President of the Family Division of the High Court authorised the withdrawal of ventilation from a three-month-old child who had sustained profound brain damage following meningitis. The child suffered from convulsions and required to be fed by a nasogastric tube. She also had a breathing tube in her windpipe and required fluid to be drawn from her brain each day. Her prognosis was poor in that she was likely to be deaf and blind. The judge described C's condition as "almost a living death" and authorised the removal of the child from the ventilator and the administration of morphine. He declined to lay down guidelines for future cases stating that each case had to be considered on its merits.

A recent case which demonstrates the approach of the English courts where disagreement arises between the medical team and the family of the patient who is a child and incompetent is that of *R v. Portsmouth Hospital NHS Trust ex parte Glass.*[443] In that case the mother and other relatives of David Glass refused to accept the advice of the medical team caring for David that he should be allowed "to die with dignity". David was 12 years old and had been brain damaged from birth. He was blind and was a person with spastic quadriplegia although the evidence for his general practitioner and from a specialist was that he was basically a happy child in a loving family. In October 1998 he was admitted to hospital with pneumonia where doctors apparently decided that there was nothing that could be done and that it would be better to let nature take its course. They therefore withdrew treatment and administered diamorphine which would depress respiratory function. This was done against the mother's wishes on the authority of the chief executive of the hospital. The family physically and forcibly intervened and resuscitated David and effectively prevented him from dying. That night an unqualified "Do Not Resuscitate" order had been placed on David's notes without consulting his mother. David returned home and was successfully treated by his general practitioner. As a result of these incidents David's mother applied for a declaration that the hospital should neither treat not withdraw treatment in future without her consent. The High Court and subsequently the Court of Appeal refused to grant such a declaration. Scott Baker J. stated that the case had involved the inter-relationship of the boundaries of a number of principles namely the sanctity of life; the non-interference by courts in areas of clinical judgment in the treatment of patients; the refusal of the courts to dictate appropriate treatment to a medical practitioner; that treatment without consent was a trespass to the person; and that the courts would interfere to protect the interests of a child or person under a disability. In such circumstances application for judicial review was inappropriate. Both Scott Baker J. and the Court of Appeal took the view that the best course of action was that, should there be a disagreement the particular case should be brought to court so that the court could decide what was in the best interests of the child.

The converse of the *Glass* case is demonstrated in *In re T (a minor),*[444] which concerned a baby suffering from biliary artresia for whom the prognosis was that without

---

[442] *The Times*, April 4, 1996.
[443] [1999] 3 F.C.R. 145.
[444] [1997] 8 Med. L.R. 166.

a liver transplant he would not live beyond 2 to 2½ years. The doctors wished to operate but the parents were opposed not least because previous major surgery when he was 3½ weeks old had appeared to cause severe pain and distress and had not proved successful. The trial judge concluded that the mother's refusal to accept the advice of the doctors was not the conduct of a reasonable parent. The Court of Appeal took a different view. It reiterated the principle that when an application was made to the court under its inherent jurisdiction the welfare of the child was of paramount importance and although a parent's consent or refusal of consent was an important consideration to weigh in the balance it was for the court to decide the matter and in doing so it pointed out that it might override the decision of a reasonable parent. However, Butler Sloss L.J. held that the trial judge had concentrated on the clinical assessment of the likely success of treatment and did not weigh the wider issues including the effect of coercing the mother into playing a crucial and irreversible part in the aftermath of major invasive surgery. The mother had focused on the present peaceful life of the child. She wished the child to spend the rest of his short life without the pain, stress and upset of intrusive surgery. The mother and child were one for the purposes of this unusual case and the welfare of the child depended on the mother. While there was a strong presumption in favour of a course of action, which would prolong life, that was not the sole objective of the court and "to require it at the expense of other considerations might not be in the child's best interests".[445] Morris comments that the *In re T* case was unusual in that: " the courts for once overrode the clinical judgment of the doctors." However, she adds that this was done:

> "by effectively subsuming the interests of the child within the interests of the mother – it was not a case in which one can discern much attention being devoted to the "rights" of the child."[446]

When it comes to the withholding or withdrawal of treatment in the case of incompetent children both the British Medical Association[447] and the Royal College of Paediatrics and Child Health.[448] Guidelines emphasise that any such decisions must be taken on the basis that to initiate or to continue to treat would not be in the best interests of the patient either because to do so would be futile or because it would impose a burden on the patient which was not outweighed by any possible benefits. The British Medical Association advises that such decisions must be taken on an individual case-by-case basis and that the factors to be taken into account in assessing whether the provision life prolonging treatment would provide an overall benefit to the patient include:

(a) the patient's own wishes and values where these can be ascertained;

(b) clinical judgment about the effectiveness of the proposed treatment;

(c) the likelihood of the patient experiencing severe unmanageable pain or suffering;

---

[445] [1997] 8 Med. L.R. 166, 171.

[446] "Treating children properly: law, ethics and practice", *Professional Negligence*, Vol.15, No.4 (1999) 261.

[447] *Withholding and Withdrawing Life Prolonging Medical Treatment* (BMJ London 1999).

[448] *Withholding or Withdrawing Life Saving Treatment in Children: A Framework for Practice*, RCPCH 1997.

(d) the level of awareness the individual has of his or her existence and surroundings as demonstrated by, for example:
   (i) ability to interact with others, however expressed;
   (ii) capacity for self directed action or ability to take control of any aspect of his or her life;

(e) likelihood and extent of any degree of improvement in the patient's condition if treatment is provided;

(f) whether the invasiveness of treatment is justified in the circumstances;

(g) the views of the parents where the patient is a child;

(h) the views of people close to the patient especially close relatives, partners and carers about what the patient is likely to see as beneficial.

The Guidance also states that where there is genuine uncertainty about which treatment option would be of most clinical benefit parents are usually best placed and equipped to weigh the evidence and apply it to their children.[449]

In the recent decision of *In re A (Children) (Conjoined Twins: Surgical Separation)*,[450] the Court of Appeal was called upon to decide upon the lawfulness of an operation to separate conjoined twins which would inevitably result in the death of one in the light of the objection of the parents to the operation. The twin girls, Jodie and Mary, were born in Manchester on August 8, 2000. They were joined at the pelvis and each had her own brain, heart and lungs and other vital organs and her own arms and legs. The medical evidence showed that Jodie, the stronger twin supported the life of Mary, the weaker twin by circulating oxygenated blood through a common artery and that Mary's heart and lungs were too deficient to oxygenate and pump blood through her own body. The unanimous medical evidence was that if they were not separated Jodie's heart would eventually fail and they would both die within a few months of their birth.

However, if they were separated the medical evidence was that Jodie would have a life that was worthwhile but Mary would die within minutes. The twin's parents were adamant that they should not be divided and that both their children should be allowed to die. It was accepted that although Mary had a severely impaired brain, heart and lungs she was alive and that the twins were two separate persons. However, as Robert Walker put it: "The fact that she [Mary] is alive as a distinct personality but is not viable as a separate human being is the awful paradox at the centre of this case." The hospital sought a declaration from the High Court that it could lawfully carry out the separation surgery. Johnson J. held that in any matter relating to the future of a child the interest of that individual child was to be paramount. In considering the consequences for Mary the court had to focus only on her interests. These were not limited to her medical interests but encompassed medical, emotional and all other welfare issues. The evidence showed that Mary's state would never improve during the few months she would have to live and that those few months would not simply be worth nothing to her they were hurtful. To prolong Mary's life would be seriously to her disadvantage and therefore the proposed separation represented her best interests. The proposed operation was not a

---

[449] Para.15.1.
[450] [2001] 2 W.L.R. 480.

positive act but rather by analogy with the situation where a court authorised the withholding of food and hydration represented the withdrawal of Mary's blood supply and therefore the operation could be lawfully performed. Johnson J. also held that while the court had to give due weight to the views of devoted and responsible parents it was the court's duty to give effect to its own independent and objective judgment. On appeal the Court of Appeal granted the hospital's application to carry out the surgery and dismissed the parents' appeal.

The Court of Appeal held that notwithstanding the conflict of duties owed by the doctors to each twin in respect of her right to life and the impossibility of undertaking any relevant surgery on one without affecting the other, the proposed operation was an act of necessity to avoid inevitable and irreparable evil. The purpose of the operation was to preserve the life of Jodie and not to cause the death of Mary. No more would be done than was reasonably necessary for this purpose to be achieved and the evil inflicted would not be disproportionate to the evil avoided. It was, therefore, inappropriate in the unique circumstances of the case to characterise foresight of Mary's accelerated death as amounting to criminal intent.

Their Lordships considered article 2 of the European Convention on Human Rights briefly. Article 2 protects the right to life and prohibits the intentional deprivation of life. Their Lordships concluded that no different conclusion would be reached by the court in Strasbourg. In particular, Mary's death, while foreseen as an inevitable consequence of an operation which was intended and was necessary to save Jodie's life would not be the purpose or intention of the surgery. She would die because her body on its own was not and never would be viable. Her death therefore would not be intentional within the meaning of the article. Ward L.J. was of the view that in essence there was no difference between resort to legitimate self-defence and the doctors coming to J's defence and removing the threat of fatal harm to her presented by Mary's draining her lifeblood. Accordingly the operation could be lawfully performed.

Dissenting from Johnson J.'s analysis, Ward and Brooke L.JJ. held that the proposed operation was a positive act of invasive surgery and not a withdrawal of treatment or an omission and although clearly in Jodie's best interests could not be in the interests of Mary since it could not effect any other improvement in her condition and would bring her life to an end before its natural span and deny her inherent right to life. Given the conflict of duty the court faced in considering the best interests of each twin its task was to strike a balance between each and do what was best for each by considering the worthwhileness of the proposed treatment, having regard to the actual condition of each twin and the advantages and disadvantages which flowed from the performance or non-performance of that treatment. The question was always whether the treatment would be worthwhile not whether the patient's life would be worthwhile. The court was not prepared to balance the potential of each life of each in the sense of considering the worth of one life compared with the other, as that would offend the principle of the sanctity of life and was unlawful.

However, it was legitimate, Ward L.J. held to bear in mind the actual quality of life each child enjoys and may be able to enjoy. The prospect of a normal expectation of relatively normal life for Jodie was counterbalanced by an acceleration of certain death for Mary so that in the unique circumstances of the case the court was obliged to consider the manner in which each twin was individually able to exercise her right to life. The balance was heavily in favour of Jodie since the best interests of the twins was to give the chance of life to the twin whose actual bodily condition was capable of accepting the chance to her advantage even if that had to be at the cost of the sacrifice of life which was so unnaturally supported. Therefore, the least detrimental choice, balancing the interests of Jodie against Mary and Mary against Jodie was to permit the operation to be performed. Walker L.J. stated that there was a strong presumption that the proposed operation would be in the best interests of each twin since its purpose would be to give Jodie a reasonably good prospect of a long and reasonably normal life and, although Mary's death would be its inevitable consequence, she would obtain even in death bodily integrity and human dignity which was her right. Her death was not the purpose of the operation. She would die because her own body could not sustain her life. Her continued life whether short or long conferred no benefit on her except possible pain and discomfort and was to her disadvantage.

Commentary

If the Irish courts take the view that a mature minor under the age of 16 cannot, for constitutional reasons, give valid consent to medical treatment in his or her own right they may find that they are in breach of Article 12 of the UN Convention on the Rights of the Child 1989 which was been ratified by the State on 28 September 1992 and which provides:

> "States parties shall assure to the child who is capable of forming his or her own views the right to express those views freely in all matters affecting the child, the views of the child being given due weight in accordance with the age and maturity of the child."

There is a need in cases where parents views conflict with those of medical practitioners regarding the treatment of minors with mental disabilities to give meaning to the concept of the best interests of the child and formulate acceptable guidelines by which decisions in those best interests can be taken.

SPECIFIC TYPES OF TREATMENT PROCEDURES

Withdrawal of life support treatment from an adult incompetent to consent

In its judgment in *In re Ward of Court*,[451] the Irish Supreme Court was called upon to decide whether it was lawful for invasive life support treatment to be withdrawn from a woman who had been insentient for 23 years. In April 1972, when the ward was 22 years of age she underwent a minor gynaecological operation under general anaesthetic in the course of which she suffered three cardiac arrests, resulting in serious brain damage.

---

[451] [1995] 2 I.L.R.M. 401. See commentary "Right to Life", *Annual Review of Irish Law 1995*, p.156; D. Cusack, "*Re A Ward of Court*: Medical Law and Medical Ethics Diverge, a Medico-Legal Analysis", Vol.1(2) *M.L.J.I.* 43; Tomkin and McAuley, "*Re A Ward of Court*; Legal Analysis", Vol.1(2) *M.L.J.I.* 45; Iglesias, "Ethics, Brain-Death and the Medical Concept of the Human Being", Vol.1(2) *M.L.J.I.* 51; Kearon, "*Re A Ward of Court*: Ethical Comment", Vol.1(2) *M.L.J.I.* 56.

Although there was some initial improvement in her condition, this did not continue. The ward's jaw's were clenched, she could not swallow and was incontinent. Her heart and lungs functioned normally and for 20 years she received nutrition and hydration through a nasogastric tube but in later years she seemed to find this distressing and in April 1992 it was replaced by a gastrostomy tube. This became detached in December 1993. A new tube was inserted which came out the next day and had to be reinserted under general anaesthetic. The ward was unable to speak or communicate. There was evidence that she appeared to recognise members of the nursing staff and that she reacted to strangers by showing distress.

In 1974, she was made a ward of court. Her father who was appointed as committee of her person and estate died in 1988. Her sister was then appointed as her committee. She retired in 1994 and her mother was appointed as committee in her place. On March 7, 1995, the committee and family of the ward sought an order that all artificial nutrition and hydration of the ward should cease. On March 10, 1995 Lynch J. appointed the General Solicitor for Wards of Court as guardian ad litem for the Ward. The application was opposed by the General Solicitor and by the institution in which the ward was cared for and the Attorney General.

The existence of a permanent vegetative state

Lynch J. accepted that the ward was "nearly but not quite" in a persistent vegetative state. The Supreme Court, following Lynch J., accepted the definition of the condition of persistent or permanent vegetative state given by Sir Thomas Bingham in the Court of Appeal in the *Bland* case as:

> "A medical condition quite distinct from other conditions sometimes known as 'irreversible coma', 'the Guillain-Barre syndrome', 'the locked in syndrome' and "brain death'. Its distinguishing characteristics are that the brain stem remains alive and functioning while the cortex of the brain loses its function and activity. Thus the PVS patient continues to breathe unaided and his digestion continues to function. But although his eyes are open he cannot see. He cannot hear. Although capable of reflex movement particularly in response to painful stimuli, the patient is incapable of voluntary movement and can feel no pain. He cannot taste or smell. He cannot speak or communicate in any way. He has no cognitive function and can thus feel no emotion, whether pleasure or distress."[452]

The High Court judge found that "while the ward was not in a fully persistent or permanent vegetative state she was nearly so and such cognitive capacity as she possessed was extremely minimal".[453]

---

[452] [1993] A.C. 789 at 806; Cusack *et al*, "Near PVS: A New Medico-Legal Syndrome?", Vol.40(2), (2000) *Med. Sci. Law* 133.
[453] *Per* Lynch J. at p.5 of the High Court judgment.

Whether the ward was terminally ill

In the course of the judgments the issue arose as to whether the patient was chronically or terminally ill. Lynch J. in the High Court held that the ward was not terminally ill in the sense of having an illness, which would reach a fatal outcome within a period of months. So long as the ward's condition was stabilised she could live for years or decades even. In the Supreme Court, Hamilton C.J. disagreeing with Lynch J. held that the ward was "terminally ill" since she was kept alive by artificial means which, if withdrawn, would result in her death. Denham J. regarded this distinction as immaterial. She was of the view that the decision to withhold or continue treatment would have to be made irrespective of the classification of the illness.

Mr Justice Egan, in his dissenting judgment accepted Lynch J.'s finding that the ward was in a near permanent vegetative state and said that in this case the ward had "some" cognitive function. By implication she was not in a permanent vegetative state. Having asserted that were the ward in a permanent vegetative state it would be legitimate to withdraw artificial treatment he questioned where the line should be drawn:

> "Cognition in a human being is something which is either present or absent, and should in my opinion, be recognised and treated. Any effort to measure its value would be dangerous".[454]

Whether medical treatment was in issue

For 20 years the ward had been fed and hydrated through a naso-gastric tube, which she did not tolerate well. This was eventually replaced under general anaesthetic by a gastrostomy tube. Lynch J. in the High Court that the intubation and gastrostomy constituted medical treatment and indicated that it was the manner of the administration of hydration and nutrition, which constituted medical treatment. Each of the Supreme Court judges agreed that hydration and nutrition in this case constituted medical treatment.

The elements of the ward's "best interests"

Lynch J. in the High Court adopted a hybrid test of "best interests" plus "substituted judgment" in finding that such a withdrawal was lawful. Lynch J regarded the "best interests" part of the hybrid as "the acid test". The question was whether the ward's life should be prolonged by the abnormal methods of life prolongation or whether she should be allowed to die. In order to apply this test he ruled the court should approach the matter from the standpoint of a "prudent, good and loving parent". In his approach, he appears to balance the benefits on the one hand (prolonged life) and the burdens (severely restricted existence) on the other but does not specify the factors to be considered in the "best interests" test or indicate how the test is to be applied.

Lynch J. also held that he could take account of what would be the ward's own wishes could she be granted a momentary lucid and articulate period in which to express them. Lynch J. found that the evidence was "clear and convincing" that the ward would refuse the continuation of the present treatment.

---

[454] [1995] 2 I.L.R.M. 401 at 437.

A majority of Supreme Court applying an unmodified "best interests" test as to whether it was in the ward's best interests "that her life should be prolonged by continuance of the particular medical treatment which she was receiving"[455] declared that it was lawful for the withdrawal to take place. However, Denham J.'s version of the best interests test was wider than that of the other judges in the majority. It extended to the best interest of the ward "within constitutional parameters' taking into account fifteen specific factors as follows:

"(1) The wards condition.

(2) The current medical treatment and care of the ward.

(3) The degree of bodily invasion of the ward the medical treatment requires.

(4) The legal and constitutional process to be carried through in order that medical treatment be given and received.

(5) The ward's life history, including whether there has been adequate time to achieve an accurate diagnosis.

(6) The prognosis on medical treatment.

(7) Any previous views that were expressed by the ward that are relevant and proved as a matter of fact on the balance of probabilities.

(8) The family's view.

(9) The medical options.

(10) The view of any relevant carer.

(11) The spiritual aspect.

(12) The ward's constitutional right to:
  (a) Life.
  (b) Privacy.
  (c) Bodily Integrity.
  (d) Autonomy.
  (e) Dignity in life.
  (f) Dignity in death.

(13) The constitutional requirement that the ward's life be (a) respected (b) vindicated and (c) protected.

(14) The constitutional requirement that life be protected for the common good. The case commences with a constitutional presumption that the ward's life be protected.

(15) The burden of proof is on the applicants to establish their application on the balance of probabilities, taking into consideration that this Court will not draw its conclusions lightly or without due regard to all the relevant circumstances."[456]

In qualifying the "best interests" test by these several constitutional factors Denham J. emphasises that the court's decision is not a medical but a wider philosophical one. In his judgment O' Flaherty J. commenting on the alternative to the best interests test stated:

---

[455] *Per* Lynch J. approved by Hamilton J. as "the proper test" at p.429.
[456] [1995] 2 I.L.R.M. 401 at 463.

"For myself, I find it impossible to adapt the idea of 'substituted judgment' to the circumstances of this case and, it may be, that it is only appropriate where the person has had the foresight to provide for future even-tualities."[457]

The appropriate standard of proof

The judges disagreed as to the standard of proof required to establish that withdrawal of treatment would be in the ward's best interests. Lynch J. held that the onus of proof lay on the family who wished to change the status quo and that clear and convincing evidence was required that the medical treatment should be discontinued. While Hamilton C.J. expressly endorsed this approach, O'Flaherty J. expressed no opinion but upheld the trial judges findings while Denham J. was of the view that the standard was on the balance of probabilities. Mr Justice Blayney appeared to favour an inquisitorial approach in wardship cases over the adversarial approach where it was necessary to determine the burden and standard of proof and stated that though Lynch J. was not obliged to deal with the standard and burden of proof as he did, since this was not a *lis inter partes*, his doing so did not affect the propriety of the High Court decision. Both the High Court and the Supreme Court also addressed a number of constitutional issues in reaching their decision.

The relevant constitutional rights of the incompetent patient

The rights of the family The first constitutional issue concerned the position of the family. It was argued that the family's decision should be binding on the court by virtue of the family's inalienable and imprescriptible rights, antecedent and superior to all positive law under Article 41.1 of the Constitution. Lynch J. rejected any contention to this end. He held that Article 41.1 referred to the rights of the family as an entity. It did not refer too the rights of individual members of the family. Other constitutional articles could be used to reinforce the individual and personal rights of the person concerned. The fact that the patient was a ward weighed more with the court than any family related Constitutional argument.

In the Supreme Court, Hamilton C.J. held that as the family had instituted proceedings to make the patient a ward of court and that as this jurisdiction provides that decisions are made by the court taking into consideration (but not being bound by) the wishes of the family, the family could not argue that their rights were being infringed.

The right to equality The majority of the Supreme Court also factored in constitutional guarantees of equality in reaching their decision. Addressing the issue of whether a person would lose their right to consent or refuse consent to treatment because of their mental condition, O'Flaherty J. stated that no such authority could be found, but relying on the decision *O'Brien v. Keogh*[458] came to the conclusion that to so hold would constituted an arbitrary and invidious discrimination between the well and the infirm. Denham J. was of the view that the constitutional guarantee of equality raised the issue of how persons of different capacity could be treated equally before the law. In the

---

[457] [1995] 2 I.L.R.M. 401 at 434.
[458] [1972] I.R. 144.

instant case the difficulty related to how the ward because of her impaired capacity could have her rights exercised on her behalf. Denham J. held that the function of the court was to acknowledge the principle of equality and discover how in this instance the ward's acknowledged rights could be implemented and exercised.

Hamilton C.J. held that arising from Article 40 the ward must have the right to bodily integrity, the right to privacy including self determination and the right to refuse medical care and treatment respected and vindicated from unjust attack. These rights were in no way lessened by reason of her incapacity.

The right to life Addressing the constitutional rights to life, to self determination and the common good, Lynch J. in the High Court reasoned that a person's right to life is enshrined in Article 40.3.1. The right to die in accordance with nature is part of the right to life. The right to life may consequently include a rejection of medical treatment and accordingly a person may have the right to determine his or her own fate. The right to life will be protected and vindicated by the State under Article 40.3.2. However, the citizen has a choice whether or not to institute the State processes of protection and vindication of his or her rights. He or she is not obliged to institute proceedings in every case. This choice is an example of the right to self-determination. The exercise of the right to self-determination is limited by considerations of "the common good, public order and morality." Such considerations must inhibit the exercise of individual autonomy or the right to self-determination. Consequently there are limits to autonomy of choice in connection with the exercise of the right to life or the right to die. Nevertheless the right to refuse medical treatment at life's end is a valid example of the right to life.

In the Supreme Court Denham J. held that in the hierarchy of rights the right to life is supreme. Nevertheless she held that the right to refuse treatment is absolute and in order to justify treatment withdrawal it would be necessary to show that on the balance of probabilities the life of the ward is best respected by the withdrawal of treatment. She held further that neither the pre-eminence of the right to life nor the sanctity of life is affected by the withdrawal of treatment at life's end. Essentially such treatment is designed to respect life by easing the transition from life (thus maximising respect for it) into death.

Hamilton C.J. argued that there was a constitutional obligation to preserve and respect the life of the ward but this obligation may be suspended in certain exceptional circumstances. Such an exceptional circumstance would be where "abnormal artificial means" may be or are used to sustain life.

This distinction between natural and artificial prolongation of life fitted with the Supreme Court's employment of the distinction between acts and omissions and its consequent rejection of any constitutional right to active euthanasia. In his dissenting judgment Egan J. stated:

> "[t]he removal of the tube would result in death in a short time. It matters not how euphemistically it is worded. The inevitable result of removal would be to kill a human being."[459]

---

[459] [1995] 1 I.L.R.M. 401 at 437.

By contrast, the majority of judges in the Supreme Court held that the removal of treatment would not, in fact, be the cause of the ward's death. The medical procedures applied to the ward since her initial operation simply had the effect of postponing her death. The natural course of events would be restored by the permitted withdrawal of treatment. The true cause of death would be the traumatic events of 1972. There was, on this analysis, no question of active euthanasia.

The right to privacy The constitutional right to privacy was also a major feature in the ultimate decision of the Supreme Court. Denham J. held that the giving or refusing of consent to medical treatment was part of the right to privacy. However it had to be balanced against other rights particularly the right of the State to defend and vindicate life. A constituent of the right to privacy is the right to die naturally, with dignity and with minimum suffering and like all other rights is granted equally to the incapacitated as well as those with capacity. Denham J. went on to state that there is an unenumerated substantive and independent "right to be treated with dignity" which is breached in medical treatment is afforded without consent. The more invasive the treatment the more the dignity of the person is infringed.

Accordingly the Supreme Court dismissed the appeal from Lynch J.'s judgment and concluded that it was lawful and consistent with the ward's constitutional rights and in her best interests for treatment to be withdrawn and she be allowed to die a natural death.

The aftermath of the decision in In re Ward of Court

Following upon the case of *In re Ward of Court*, the Medical Council issued a statement on August 4, 1995 in which it repeated what it had stated in its *Guide to Ethical Conduct and Behaviour and to Fitness to Practice.* In that text it emphasised the obligation upon doctors to do their best to preserve life and never to act to the detriment of their patient. It stated:

> "access to nutrition and hydration is one of the basic needs of human beings. This remains even so when, from time to time, this need can only be fulfilled by means of long established methods such as naso gastric and gastrostomy tube feeding".

In the 6th edition of the Guide (2004), the Medical Council states:

> "Access to nutrition and hydration remain one of the basic needs of human beings and all reasonable and practical efforts should be made to maintain both".[460]

An Bord Altranais issued a statement on August 18 reaffirming the principle laid out in the *Code of Professional Conduct for Each Nurse and Midwife* that:

> "The nurse must at all times maintain the principle that every effort should be

---

[460] See para.22.1.

made to preserve human life, both born and unborn. When death is imminent care should be taken to ensure that the patient dies with dignity.

This ethical principle requires that so long as there remains a means of nutrition and hydration of this patient it is the duty of the nurse to act in accordance with the Code and to provide nutrition and hydration. In this specific case, a nurse may not participate in the withdrawal and termination of the means of nutrition and hydration by tube. In the event of the withdrawal and termination of the means of nutrition and hydration by tube the nurse's role will be to provide all nursing care."

It indeed appears that Supreme Court's decision in Ireland on the withdrawal of nutrition from patients do not have the support of medical ethics as stated by the relevant medical and nursing bodies.

The approach of the English Courts

In England the courts in their earlier decisions have tended towards the unmodified best interests test and a more restricted analysis confined to medical issues[461] in relation to the withdrawal of life prolonging treatment incompetent patients. This approach involves the surrogate decision maker coming to a decision based on what he considers the benefits or otherwise of continued treatment. Thus such factors as the present condition of the patient, the degree of pain, the loss of dignity, the prognosis and the benefits and risks of the various treatments available will be of relevance. In *Airedale NHS Trust v. Bland*,[462] Tony Bland suffered brain damage as a result of having been involved in the Hillsborough football disaster in 1989, which left him in a persistent vegetative state. The issue before the court was whether it was in the best interests of Mr Bland to continue feeding him artificially. It was held that the duty of care imposed on the doctor will not extend to keeping a patient, with no possibility of ever regaining sentience alive. In the words of Browne Wilkinson L.J.:

"if there comes a stage where the responsible doctor comes to the reasonable conclusion (which accords with the views of a responsible body of medical opinion) that further continuance of an intrusive life support system is not in the best interests of the patient, he can no longer lawfully continue that life support system; to do so would constitute the crime of battery and the tort of trespass to the person. Therefore he cannot be in breach of any duty to maintain the patient's life. Therefore he is not guilty of murder by omission."[463]

The decision in *Bland* has not been without its critics. Indeed Laurie and Mason argue that "the courts have medicalised the problem of the patient in PVS and have, thus, handed over responsibility to the medical profession"[464] Nevertheless best interests

---

[461] See Doyle and Carroll, "The Slippery Slope" (1996) *N.L.J.* 146 (6745) 759–761.
[462] [1993] 2 W.L.R. 316.
[463] *Ibid.*, p.385.
[464] G.T. Laurie and J.K. Mason, "Negative treatment of Vulnerable Patients: Euthanasia by Any Other Name?" [2000] *Juridical Review* 159 at 167.

tests and the adoption of an approach which accords with the views of a responsible body of medical opinion have been applied in subsequent cases.

In *Frenchay Healthcare NHS Trust v. S*[465] S was suffering from severe brain damage as a result of a drug overdose. Like Tony Bland he was in a persistent vegetative state and was fed by means of a gastronomy tube that was inserted through his stomach wall. The question before the court was whether it would be lawful for a medical practitioners not to re-insert a gastronomy tube into the stomach of the patient, which had become accidentally dislodged. The surgeon in charge of S's case was of the view that it was in S's best interests to refrain from intervening and to allow him to die naturally. Reserving to the court the ultimate power and duty to review the doctor's decision in the light of all the facts the Court of Appeal upheld a decision of the High Court to the effect that it would be lawful for doctors not to re-insert the tube.

Following upon the *Bland* and *S* cases, a *Practice Note* was issued in the UK by the Official Solicitor in March 1994 which laid down the procedures to be followed in relation to the termination of the artificial feeding and hydration of patients in a persistent vegetative state. The Practice Note provides that the termination of artificial feeding and hydration will in virtually all cases require the prior sanction of a High Court judge. In diagnosing persistent vegetative state doctors should observe the guidelines issued by the British Medical Association in July 1993. According to the BMA current methods of diagnosing PVS cannot be regarded as infallible. Such a diagnosis should not be considered confirmed until the patient has been insentient for at least twelve months. Before then, as soon as the patient's condition has stabilised, rehabilitative measures such as coma arousal programmes should be instituted. The appropriate forum for the hearing of applications is the Family Division of the High Court. In addition the court should consider any previously expressed views of the patient, on the issue of continuing life-sustaining treatment in the event of his entering a persistent vegetative state. It is clear form this document that provided the guidelines are adhered to the withdrawal of artificial means of nutrition and hydration from a PVS patient would not be contrary to ethical standards of the profession. This contrasts with the statements issued by the Irish professional bodies who were strongly of the opinion that nutrition and hydration were a basic human need and remained so even when artificial means were the only option available for providing such sustenance.

In *In re T (Adult: Refusal of Medical Treatment)*,[466] Lord Donaldson MR was of the view that anticipatory refusals of medical treatment will be binding provided that (i) when the patient made such a declaration he was competent to consent to or to refuse treatment; (ii) that the declaration was applicable in the circumstances under review and (iii) the declaration did not come about as a result of undue influence.

In the later decision of *In re D (Medical Treatment)*,[467] D was a patient who was nearly but not quite in an irreversible vegetative state. One paragraph of the Royal College of Physicians' guidelines for determining the existence of a persistent vegetative state was not fulfilled namely the requirement that there should not be nystagmus in response to ice water caloric testing and that the patient should not be able to track

[465] [1994] 2 All E.R. 403.
[466] [1992] 3 W.L.R. 782.
[467] [1998] F.L.R 411.

moving objects with the eyes or show "a menace" response. Application was made to the Family Division of the High Court by the hospital trust with the concurrence of all the expert witnesses and the plaintiff's mother that it would be in the best interests of D to allow the withdrawal of artificial nutrition and hydration. Sir Stephen Brown P quoted the judgment of Lord Goff in the *Bland* case:

> "For my part I cannot see that medical treatment is appropriate or requisite simply to prolong a patient's life when such treatment has no therapeutic purpose of any kind, as where it is futile because the patient is unconscious and there is no prospect of any improvement in his condition. It is reasonable also that account should be taken of the invasiveness of the treatment and of the indignity to which, as the present case shows, a person has to be subjected if his life is to be prolonged by artificial means, which must cause considerable distress to his family – distress which reflects not only their own feelings but their perception of their relative who is being kept alive. But in the end, in a case such as the present, it is the futility of the treatment which justifies its termination. I do not consider that, in circumstances such as these, a doctor is required to initiate, or to continue, life-prolonging treatment or care in the interests of his patient. It follows that no such duty rests upon the respondents or upon Dr Howe, in the case of Anthony Bland, whose condition is in reality no more than a living death and for whom such treatment or care would be futile."[468]

Having cited this passage Sir Stephen Brown P. found, accepting the evidence of the three expert witnesses, that "for all practical purposes" the patient was in fact in a permanent vegetative state. He found that she was, in the words of Lord Goff suffering, what he described, as a "living death." There was no evidence of "any meaningful life whatsoever" The learned judge did not therefore believe that if a declaration were to be granted it would be extending the range of cases in which a declaration might properly be considered and accordingly on the totality of the evidence including the evidence of the patient's mother that it was not in the patient's best interests to keep her body alive the declaration sought should be granted. Taken in conjunction with the case of *In re A Ward of Court*, this case raises the question as to what level of cognitive impairment in fact would in fact lead a court to refuse an application in cases of "near" permanent vegetative state.

More recently in the joined cases of *NHS Trust A v. M and NHS Trust B v. H*,[469] the English courts have been obliged by the Human Rights Act 1998 to extend their analysis beyond medical issues to grapple with the question of whether the discontinuance of nutrition and hydration in the case of two patients in a permanent vegetative would contravene the right to life in Article 2 of the European Convention for the Protection of Human Rights and Fundamental Freedoms 1950. In particular in the instant cases the court was asked to determine whether such discontinuance constituted an intentional deprivation of life within the meaning of article 2 and, if not, whether in the circumstances, that article imposed a positive obligation to provide life sustaining treatment. The court

---

[468] [1993] 1 F.L.R. 1036 at 1040.
[469] [2001] 1 All E.R. 801.

was further presented with the question as to whether the prohibition on inhuman and degrading treatment in article 3 of the Convention would be breached during the period between the withdrawal of treatment and the patients' deaths or whether that article could be invoked to ensure protection of the right of a patient in a permanent vegetative state to die with dignity.

Dame Butler Sloss P. cited the speeches in the House of Lords in the *Bland* case that the duty of the doctor is to treat the patient as long as it is in his best interests to have that treatment. If, however it is no longer in the patient's best interests to have that treatment, it is not the duty of the medical team to continue it. She continued:

> "Although the intention in withdrawing artificial nutrition and hydration in PVS cases is to hasten death, in my judgment the phrase deprivation of life must import a deliberate act, as opposed to an omission, by someone acting on behalf of the state, which results in death. A responsible decision by a medical team not to provide treatment at the initial stage could not amount to intentional deprivation of life by the state. Such a decision based on clinical judgment is an omission to act. The death of the patient is the result of the illness or injury from which he suffered and that cannot be described as a deprivation. It may be relevant to look at the reasons for the clinical decision in the light of the positive obligation of the state to safeguard life, but in my judgment it cannot be regarded as falling within the negative obligation to refrain from taking life intentionally. I cannot see the difference between that situation and a decision to discontinue treatment which is no longer in the best interests of the patient and would therefore be a violation of his autonomy, even though that discontinuance will have the effect of shortening the life of the patient.
>
> The analysis of these issues by the House of Lords in *Bland's* case is entirely in accordance with the convention case law on Article 2 and is applicable to the distinction between negative and positive obligations. An omission to provide treatment by the medical team will, in my judgment, only be incompatible with Article 2 where the circumstances are such as to impose a positive obligation on the state to prolong a patient's life."[470]

As to whether Article 2 imposed a positive obligation to provide life sustaining treatment Dame Butler Sloss P. held that the standard applied by the European Court in the case of *Osman v. UK*,[471] bore a close resemblance to the standard adopted in the domestic law of negligence and approximated to the obligation recognised by the English courts in the *Bolam* test. Accordingly:

> "Article 2 … imposes a positive obligation to give life sustaining treatment in circumstances where, according to respectable medical opinion, such treatment is in the best interests of the patient but does not impose an absolute obligation to treat if such treatment would be futile."[472]

---

[470] [2001] 1 All E.R. 801 at 809–810.
[471] [1998] 5 B.H.R.C. 293.
[472] [2001] 1 All E.R. 801 at 811.

Regarding the question of whether article 3 was breached during the period of withdrawal of treatment and the patient's deaths Dame Butler Sloss P. held:

> "I am satisfied that the proposed withdrawal of treatment from these two patients has been thoroughly and anxiously considered by a number of experts in the field of PVS patients and is in accordance with the practice of a responsible body of medical opinion. The withdrawal is for a benign purpose in accordance with the best interests of the not to continue life-saving treatment. It is legitimate and appropriate that the residual treatment be continued until death. I am, moreover satisfied that Article 3 requires the victim to be aware of the inhuman and degrading treatment which he or she is experiencing or at least to be in a state of physical or mental suffering. An insensate patient suffering from permanent vegetative state has no feelings and no comprehension of the treatment accorded to him or her. Article 3 does not in my judgment apply to these two cases."[473]

In the case of *In re G (Adult incompetent: Withdrawal of Treatment)*,[474] the court considered the case of a patient who following minor surgery inhaled some of her own vomit which blocked her trachea and which caused serious anoxic brain damage As a result she was in an insensate but not a persistent vegetative state. On the medical evidence presented the court was convinced that there was no prospect of recovery. There was also unanimous support from G's family for her to be allowed to die in peace with dignity and not to be sustained in her continuing twilight limbo. G was also said to have expressed the strong view that were she to be found in the situation in which she was when the matter came to court that she would not wish to be kept alive regardless. Dame Butler Sloss, following her decision in *NHS Trust A v M, NHS Trust B v H* and the decision of the House of Lords in the *Bland* case, held that it was not inconsistent with the right to life as guaranteed under the Human Rights Act 1998 to permit G to die with dignity and in peace by withdrawing that which kept her artificially alive.

The law in the United States

In the United States, the dilemma presented by withdrawal of life support has been judicially described as follows:

> "Since medical science has created a new state of human existence "minimal human life sustained by man-made life supports ... [society] ... must now devise and fashion rules and parameters for that existence."[475]

In the United States the court have adopted two standards in relation to withdrawal of life-prolonging treatment from incompetent patients. These are the tests are of: (i) substituted judgment and (ii) best interests. In relation to the former it has been held that the surrogate decision maker must make the decision the incompetent patient would

---

[473] [2001]1 All E.R. 801 at 814.
[474] 65 B.M.L.R. 6.
[475] See *Leach v. Akron Gen. Medical Center* 426 N.E. 2d. 809 (Ohio. Ct. Com. Pl. 1980).

make, if he were able to choose himself. This will involve examining evidence of the patient's attitude to life-sustaining treatment when that patient was in a position to express that attitude. The best interests test involves the surrogate decision-maker coming to a decision based on what he considers to be the benefits or otherwise of continued treatment. Thus such factors as the present condition of the patient, the degree of pain, the loss of dignity, the prognosis and the benefits and risks of the various treatments available will be of relevance.

The substituted judgment standard was applied in *In re Quinlan*.[476] In this case Karen Ann Quinlan had become permanently comatose after ingesting drugs and was supported by a mechanical respirator. The Supreme Court of New Jersey held that a father should be authorised to give substituted consent for his daughter in order to withdraw extraordinary life sustaining treatment. The court's reasoning was that if competent the patient would have had a constitutional right under notions of privacy to decline medical treatment even if death would result. Since she was unable to make that decision for herself her guardian could substitute his decision for hers by consulting with responsible physicians and then attempting to divine his daughter's preference.

However, the standard was somewhat elusive. The court seemed to be less concerned with what the daughter would have done than reflecting a consensus of responsible physicians that there was no "reasonable possibility" that she would become conscious again and of the recommendation by both the treating physicians and the guardian to discontinue the life-supporting apparatus. Significantly the physicians who made up the ethics committee disagreed with the treating physicians about the ultimate decision. In part, the outcome was a battle of experts and the decision was not made on the basis of clear facts. Even after the issue was legally resolved Karen Ann Quinlan survived for eight years without mechanical assistance. Tomkin & Hanafin however assert:

> "It is submitted that the substituted judgment doctrine is entirely inappropriate in the case of a patient in a permanently unconscious state who has never expressed a preference in relation to treatment withdrawal, as the surrogate cannot really base his decision on the presumed preferences of such a patient."[477]

Nonetheless the substituted judgment standard has been adopted in judicial decision-making on behalf of the incompetent person. In the Massachusetts case of *Superintendent of Belchertown State School v. Saikewicz*,[478] the patient who was a sixty seven year old person with a profound intellectual disability was suffering from leukaemia and required chemotherapy. He had never been competent and therefore never in a position to express his wishes in relation to the termination of life prolonging medical treatment. Nevertheless the Supreme Court of Massachusetts applied the substituted judgment standard, ruling that any such treatment should be based on the decision the incompetent patient would make if s/he "were competent, but taking into account the present and future

---

[476] 700 N.J. 10, 355 A.2d 7647.
[477] See Medical Treatment at Life's End: The Need for Legislation, *Medico-Legal Journal of Ireland*, Vol.1 No.1.
[478] 373 Mass. 728, 370 NE 2d 417 (1977).

incompetency of the individual as one of the factors which would necessarily enter into the decision making process of the competent person."[479]

In the Delaware case of *Severn v. Wilmington Medical Center Inc.*,[480] the Supreme Court determined that even without specific legislative direction a Chancery court applying the principles of equity could appoint a guardian for a comatose patient who would then be allowed to recommend termination of life sustaining medical treatment. Granting a petition to cease extraordinary care the court relied upon statements made by the patient before her car accident which indicated that she wished to die with dignity if she were ever unable to care for herself and reached its decision after reviewing the evidence in a full hearing.

In Ohio, prior expressions as related in testimony by friends and relatives that a comatose patient had often stated that she did not want to be placed on a life support system convinced the court in *Leach v. Akron Gen. Medical Center*,[481] to allow the woman's husband to carry out her wishes. Elsewhere a federal court in the California case of *Foster v. Tourtellotte*,[482] determined that a terminally ill war veteran who had lapsed into a coma retained his right to die where he had recently requested while he was competent to do so that his artificial respirator be detached from his body. The fact that his wife and child opposed the disconnection of the respirator did not outweigh the clear, previous expression of the patient's right to privacy.

In the joined cases of *Storar (Eichner), re*,[483] and *Westchester County Medical Center (O'Connor), re*,[484] the New York Court of Appeals adopting the substituted judgment approach in the case of withdrawal of a respirator from a PVS patient and for the discontinuance of blood transfusions from a patient with cancer of the bladder and required evidence of prior statements of the patient which expressed a "firm and settled commitment" to the withdrawal of life-prolonging treatment ruling that the statements must be more than immediate reactions to the unsettling experience of seeing or hearing another's unnecessarily prolonged death.[485]

The Florida Supreme Court went a step further in *John F. Kennedy Memorial Hospital v. Bludworth*,[486] and held that persons who are involved in the execution of a living will on behalf of a comatose patient-guardians, consenting family members, physicians and hospital personnel should be absolved from all civil and criminal liability if they in good faith terminate extraordinary life support systems for the patient even without obtaining prior court approval. *Bona fides* is demonstrated if three physicians certify that the patient is in a permanent vegetative state there is no reasonable prospect that the patient will regain cognitive brain function and he is being sustained only through extraordinary life-sustaining measures. The court departed from the decision in *Quinlan* by dismissing the necessity even of a hospital ethics committee reviewing the decision. The court also ruled that only where there is disagreement among the primary parties or

---

[479] *Id.* 752–753 and p.431.

[480] 421 A.2d. 1334 (Del. 1980).

[481] 426 N.E. 2d 809 (Ohio Ct. Com. Pl. 1980).

[482] No. Civ. 81–51046–RMT (AAX) 6 M.D.L.R. 15 (C.D. Cal. Nov. 16 1981).

[483] 52 NY 2d 363, 420 NE 2d 64, 438 NYS 2d 266, cert. denied, 454 US 858 (1981).

[484] 72 NY 2d 517, 531, NE 2d 607, 534 NYS 2d 886 (1988).

[485] On the other hand in *Eichner v. Dillon* 426 N.Y.S. 2d 517 (App. Div. 1980) a friend's hearsay testimony was admitted in the furtherance of justice as evidence of the patient's previous decision.

[486] 452 So. 2d. 921 (Fla. 1984).

evidence of wrongdoing or malpractice is judicial intervention warranted following the initiation of a proper petition.

However, US law in relation to the standard to be adopted in cases where the withdrawal of life support treatment is neither certain nor uniform. In *Dockery v. Dockery*,[487] a Tennessee Court ruled that further treatment for an unconscious woman in a vegetative state would not be authorised without the consent of her family. It reasoned similarly to the court in *Quinlan*, that at certain point the patient's right to bodily privacy would overcome the state's interest in preserving her life artificially. However the court based its ruling on an evaluation of the patient's best interests rather than upon an assessment of what the patient's preference might have been in the situation. It also pointed out that the withdrawal of extraordinary life support systems, which do not benefit the patient, involved a negative act (as opposed to the positive act involved in euthanasia) with no criminal or civil liability implications.

In the California Court of Appeal decision in *In re Conservatorship of Drabnik*,[488] it was held that a statutorily appointed conservator should decide the issue of treatment withdrawal on the basis of the best interests standard in the case of an incompetent patient who had not made a formal advance directive.

In the case of *In re Conroy*,[489] the court required that cessation of treatment under the best interests standard would only be countenanced where "recurring, unavoidable and severe pain" would make the treatment inhumane. In this case the court adopted a three-stage test, which combined the elements of the substituted judgment, and best interests tests. The court stated the subjective judgment test should be the first test used by the surrogate decision maker. This equates broadly with the substituted judgment test adopted by other courts. However if there was not enough evidence of the patient's wishes in this regard then the surrogate should proceed to decide upon the best interests test. The surrogate could choose one of two versions of the best interests or objective test. First one could decide on the basis of the limited objective test, which could be used in the situation where there is some evidence of the patient's past wishes but not enough to satisfy the substituted judgment or subjective test. Secondly one could decide on the basis of the pure objective test where there is no evidence whatsoever of the patient's desires in this area. However, the court in *Conroy* limited the decision in the case to patients who were in a similar fact situation to Ms Conroy:

> "An elderly nursing home resident ... who is suffering form serious mental and physical impairments, who will probably die within approximately one year even with the treatment and who, though formerly competent is now incompetent to make decisions about her life-sustaining treatment and is unlikely to regain such competence."[490]

The court was in addition was influenced by the recommendations of the Report of the

---

[487] No. 51439 1 M.D.L.R. 453.

[488] 109 S.Ct. 399 (1988).

[489] 98 NJ 321, 486 A.2d 1209 (1985).

[490] 486 A.2d 1209 (1985) at 1219. See *In re Peter* 529 A.2d. 419 (1987) and *In re Jobes* 529 A.2d. 424 (1987) at 448 in which the Conroy standard was held not applicable to patients in a persistent vegetative state.

President's Commission for the Study of Ethical Problems in Medicine and Biomedical and Behavioural Research on *Deciding to Forego Life-Sustaining Treatment*.[491] The Commission recommended a two-tiered test in relation to decision making which was similar to the *Conroy* standard but without the limited best interests test. The Commission proposed that when possible the substituted judgment standard should be used but when that was not possible then the surrogate should have recourse to the best interests test and in so doing "choose a course that will promote the patient's well-being as it would probably be conceived by a reasonable person in the patient's circumstances."[492]

Commentary

There is at present no legislation or case law relating to advance directives in Ireland. Legislation should be introduced placing the law in relation to advance directives on a statutory footing. This would enable people who are competent to create a document, which would set out their wishes in relation to medical treatment if they were ever to enter a state of incapacity. It would also facilitate the ascertainment of those wishes. In the absence of any indication to the contrary it should be presumed that an advance directive was validly made if it is in writing, signed and witnessed. To deal with questions, which might arise as to, whether the patient had capacity to make the refusal and whether the refusal applies to the treatment proposed and in given circumstances a Code of Practice should be prepared in relation to advance directives.[493]

Secondly, in addition to providing by statute for the making of advance directives it is submitted that the enduring power of attorney provided for under the Powers of Attorney Act 1996 should be extended to allow an individual (donor) to give legal authority to a person of his choosing (attorney) to make and implement health care decisions on behalf of the donor when the donor is no longer capable of making such decisions.

Thirdly, in determining whether life-sustaining treatment should be withdrawn from a patient in a persistent vegetative state it is submitted that neither the substitute judgment nor an exclusively objective best interests test applied individually is satisfactory. The

---

[491] See Deciding to Forego Life Sustaining Treatment: A Report on the Ethical Medical and Legal Issues in Treatment Decisions, (1983).

[492] At p.136.

[493] The English Law Commission Report No. 231 on *Mental Incapacity* (1995) HMSO paras 5.16–5.38 recommended that the common law principles in relation to advance directives set out in *In re T (Adult; Refusal of Treatment)* [1992] 2 W.L.R. 782 ; *Airedale NHS Trust v. Bland* [1993] 2 W.L.R. 316 and *In re C (Adult Refusal of Treatment)* [1994] 1 W.L.R. 290 be put on a statutory footing. It recommended that an "advance refusal of treatment" be defined as "a refusal made by a person aged eighteen or over with the necessary capacity of any medical surgical or dental treatment or other procedure and intended to have effect at any subsequent time when he or she may be without capacity to give or refuse consent" see para.5.16. In Canada, the Alberta Law Reform Institute in its *Report on Advance Directives and Substitute Decision-Making in Personal Health Care* No.11, November 1991 makes the recommendation that legislation be introduced to enable individuals to execute a health care directive in which they can appoint someone as their health care agent who will have authority to make health care decisions on their behalf in the event of their becoming incapable of making these decisions personally and/or identify anyone whom they do not wish to act as their health care proxy and/or provide instructions and information concerning future health care decisions.

substituted judgment test alone may lead to the court's allocating presumed preferences to a person who was never competent to hold such preferences. In addition the application of a high standard of proof to evidence of expression of preferences may lead to a situation where many incompetent patients are forced to endure intrusive, unbeneficial treatment that a similarly situated competent patient would not choose or be obliged to endure. An exclusively objective best interests test applied without considering a patient's choice may deprive the patient of the element of autonomy in relation to his treatment. It is submitted that a broad test be adopted taking into account both the wishes and feelings of the patient and the factors which s/he would consider if s/he were able to do so and other relevant objective factors to arrive at a conclusion as to his/her best interests in the circumstances. The English Law Commission *Report on Mental Incapacity* suggests one such template:[494]

> "In deciding what is in the patient's best interests in this context regard should be had:
>
> (a) so far as ascertainable to his past and present wishes and feelings and the factors which he would consider if he were able to do so,
> (b) if it is practicable and appropriate to consult them the views as to that person's wishes and as to what would be in his best interests of:
>   (i)   any person named by him as someone to be consulted on those matters;
>   (ii) anyone (whether his spouse, a relative, friend or other person) engaged in caring for him or interested in his welfare;
>   (iii) the donee of any enduring power of attorney granted by him;
>   (iv) any committee appointed for him by the court; and
>   (v)   whether the purpose for which any action or decision is required can be as effectively achieved in a manner less restrictive of his freedom of action."[495]

Fourthly, statute should clarify what degree of impaired cognitive function is required to justify an order such as that in the *In re A Ward of Court* case.[496]

Fifthly, in view of the discordance which exists between the decision in *In re A Ward of Court*, and the statements of the Irish professional bodies in this regard statute should clarify and regulate the distinction between medical treatment, withdrawal of hydration and nutrition and the palliative administration of drugs such as morphine and valium which together may result in death

Organ or tissue donation

There is an absence of Irish case law on the issue of organ or tissue donation by a mentally incapable person. However the issue arose for consideration in the English

---

[494] English Law Commission Report on Mental Incapacity No. 231 (1995) HMSO, paras 6.16.–6.22, 3.26–3.28.

[495] See Clause 3(2) of Commission's Draft Bill.

[496] See John A. Harrington, "Constitutional Law – Withdrawal of Treatment from an Incompetent Patient" (1995) 17 *D.U.L.J.* (1995) 120–135.

case of *In re Y (Mental Incapacity: Bone Marrow Transplant).*[497] In that case Y, a 35-year-old woman was severely intellectually disabled and had been so since birth. She was a person with hydrocephalaus and had a cardiac arrest early in life, which may have damaged her brain further. Since she was 17 years old she lived in a community home. Y's sister the plaintiff, aged 36 had pre-leukaemic bone marrow disorder for which she had undergone extensive chemotherapy. There was a strong likelihood that her situation would progress to acute myeloid leukaemia within three months. A bone marrow transplant from a healthy compatible donor offered the best chance of recovery. A donation from a blood relative held a 40 per cent chance of recovery for 18 months whereas a donation from an unrelated donor lowered that chance to, at best 30 per cent. The plaintiff applied for a declaration that two preliminary blood tests and a bone marrow removal under general anaesthetic could lawfully be taken from Y despite the fact that she could not consent.

Connell J. granting the application held that despite the fact that Y was incompetent to consent to or refuse the application the harvesting of the bone marrow was in Y's best interests. Without transplantation the plaintiff's prospects were poor; if the plaintiff died this would adversely affect the health of Y's mother such that the mother's ability to visit Y would be handicapped significantly and Y would be harmed by the reduction in or loss of contact with her mother. It was to Y's emotional, psychological and social benefit that the transplantation take place. Connell J. also found that the transplantation would also improve Y's relationship with her mother who wanted it to take place and with the plaintiff who would be "eternally grateful" to her.

The court found that the disadvantages of the harvesting to Y would be "very small". She had experienced a general anaesthetic on many occasions including for a hysterectomy without any apparent adverse effects. The bone marrow to be removed would be speedily regenerated. Removal of two pints of blood from a healthy individual would have no long-term consequences. The court granted the declaration subject to further tests to be taken and examination of Y by an independent anaesthetist. The judge gave liberty to apply if those tests revealed further concerns. The court also concluded per curiam that if on any future occasion a bone marrow harvesting procedure on a mentally incapacitated adult were sought it would be "appropriate for the matter to first be ventilated in court" before the procedures took place.

Commentary

Article 20 of the Council of Europe Convention on Human Rights and Biomedicine[498] provides that

> "Exceptionally and under the protective conditions prescribed by law the removal of regenerative tissue from a person who does not have the capacity to consent may be authorised provided the following conditions are met:
>
> i.   there is no compatible donor available who has the capacity to consent,

---

[497] [1996] 2 F.L.R. 787.
[498] Oviedo 4.4.1997.

    ii.   the recipient is a brother or sister of the donor,

    iii. the donation must have the potential to be life saving for the recipient

    iv. the authorisation provided for under paragraphs 2 and 3 of Article 6[499] has been given specifically and in writing in accordance with the law and with the approval of the competent body,

    v.   the potential donor concerned does not object."

In the US case of *Strunk v. Strunk*,[500] the donor was incapable of giving consent since he was an adult with an intellectual disability and a mental age of six. The procedure in question was the donation of a kidney by the donor to his brother. The court permitted the transplant to proceed principally on the basis that the donor would derive substantial psychological benefits from helping a loved one, *i.e.* that it would be in the "best interests" of the donor due to the close relationship between the donor and his brother. Parry comments that despite the careful judicial analysis it would seem likely that the donation was approved based on a consensus that the sibling without a kidney needed the kidney more that the mentally disabled child. Strictly from the viewpoint of the donor's health the donor's best interests would be served better by retaining the kidney.[501]

    It is submitted that Irish legislation should provide that any treatment or procedure to facilitate the donation of non-regenerative tissue or bone marrow by a person who is unable to give consent to same should require court authorisation.[502] The court should be obliged to consider: (a) the risk to the donor, (b) the risk of the failure of the donated tissue, (c) whether the life of the proposed recipient would be in danger without the donation, (d) any other compatible donor is reasonably available, (e) there is or has been a close personal relationship between the proposed donor and the proposed recipient (e) the donor objects to the procedures.[503] It is submitted the Minister for Health and Children should have power to prescribe further treatments of a person with mental disability, which require court authorisation.

---

[499] Art.6.2 provides that where, according to law, a minor does not have the capacity to consent to an intervention the intervention may only be carried out with the authorisation of his or her representative or an authority or a person or body provided for by law. The opinion of a minor shall be taken into consideration as an increasingly determining factor in proportion to his or her age and degree of maturity.

    Art.6.3 provides that where, according to law, an adult does not have the capacity to consent to an intervention because of a mental disability, a disease or for similar reasons the intervention may only be carried out with the authorisation of his or her representative or an authority or a person or body provided for by law. The individual concerned shall as far as possible take part in the authorisation procedure.

[500] 445 S.W. 2d. 145 (Kentucky Court of Appeal).

[501] See *The Mentally Disabled and the Law* (1985), p.456.

[502] See Report of English Law Commission on Mental Incapacity No. 231, para.6.5.

[503] Assisted and Substituted Decisions Report No. 49 Queensland Law Reform Commission June 1996 in which the Commission recommends that such decisions be subject to special consent procedures before an independent tribunal appointed by Governor in Council. See Vol.111 (xlvii).

THE WARDS OF COURT SYSTEM[504]

When a person becomes so mentally incapacitated that s/he is unable to manage his/her person or property application may be made to the High Court or Circuit Court for a person to be brought into the wardship of the court. If a person is, following an inquiry, brought into wardship a representative called a "committee" or (in the case of temporary ward or a person taken into the wardship of the Circuit Court) a "guardian" may be appointed to or care for his/her person and/or manage his/her property and affairs for the duration of the incapacity.

The administration of the wardship system

Responsibility for the operation of the wards of court system in the High Court now rests with the President of the High Court and the system is administered by the Registrar of Wards of Court and the Office of Wards of Court. Judges of the Circuit Court also have power to entertain wardship applications.

In certain cases the General Solicitor for Minors and Wards of Court also has a role in the operation of the system. The General Solicitor is appointed by the President of the High Court and in appropriate cases may be asked:

(a) to issue wardship proceedings in respect of a particular individual;

(b) to act as Committee for a particular ward;

(c) to act as solicitor and committee in matters involving wards for example by instituting or defending proceedings on behalf of a ward or by dealing with conveyancing matters in relation to a ward's property;

(d) to act as opponent before the Taxing Master where a solicitor seeks to have the costs of bringing an individual into wardship measured by the Taxing Master; or

(e) to act as *amicus curiae* (or friend of the court) in representing a particular interest in court proceedings which involve a particular ward or issues concerning wardship.

The Accountant of the Courts of Justice also performs a role in the administration of the wards of court system. The Accountant's office facilitates the opening of a separate account in the name of the committee and all income of the ward is lodged to this account. The Accountant also invests the funds of the ward as instructed by the President of the High Court and the Registrar of Wards of Court and makes funds available for the ward's maintenance and benefit.

The origins of the wardship jurisdiction

The origins of the wardship system lie in the *parens patriae* prerogative of the English

---

[504] For a detailed outline and discussion of the law and procedure in wardship see A.M. O'Neill, "Wards of Court in Ireland" (First Law, 2004). See also N.D. Doherty and J. Costello, "Wards of Court" Law Society Continuing Legal Education Series, January 15, 2003; See also Law Reform Commission *Consultation Paper on the Law and the Elderly* LRC CP 23–2003, Chap.4.

Monarchs whose power and duty it was to look after the property of "lunatics and idiots." This prerogative was recognised in the fourteenth century statute *De Praerogativa Regis* of Edward II.[505] In time the practice evolved where, by sign manual, the monarch delegated authority to administer the jurisdiction to successive Lords Chancellor and in relation to Ireland by the Lord Chancellor of Ireland.[506] Sign manual issued to each successive Lord Chancellor by the Monarch's Letter in Lunacy.[507] The Lunacy Regulation (Ireland) Act 1871[508] as the title of the statute suggests regulated this authority[509] and conferred further statutory powers on the Lord Chancellor in relation to the administration of the estates of persons of unsound mind who were not found lunatic by inquisition and in relation to the estates of criminal lunatics. The powers of the under the Lunacy Regulation (Ireland) Act 1871 exercisable by the Lord Chancellor entrusted by Sign-manual with the care of persons and property of persons of unsound mind were, after a series of enactments to take account of the 1922 constitutional changes made exercisable by the Chief Justice of the Irish Free State. The enactments in question were as follows. By section 4 of the Lunacy (Ireland) Act 1901 the powers, authorities and duties to be had, exercised and performed under the Lunacy (Regulation) Ireland Act 1871 by the Lord Chancellor for the time being "intrusted by virtue of the King's Sign Manual with the care and commitment of the persons and estates of persons found idiot, lunatic or of unsound mind" (*i.e.* only the statutory powers) were made also exercisable by such Judges of the Supreme Court "as may for the time being be intrusted as aforesaid" Section 38 of the Government of Ireland Act 1920 abolished the Supreme Court of Judicature in Ireland and established a Supreme Court of Judicature in Southern Ireland and a Supreme Court of Judicature in Northern Ireland. Under the powers vested in him by virtue of section 69 of the 1920 Act the King made the Supreme Court of Judicature (Southern Ireland) Order 1921 (No. 1803 of 1921). Section 5(2) of that Order provided that references in any enactment to the Lord Chancellor of Ireland intrusted for the time being by virtue of sign manual with special jurisdiction in lunacy should from and after the establishment [of the Supreme Court of Judicature in Southern Ireland,] be construed as references to the Lord Chief Justice of Ireland "for the time being intrusted in the like manner with the like jurisdiction in lunacy in Southern Ireland." Following the adoption of the 1922 Constitution section 19(1) of the Courts of Justice Act 1924 the jurisdiction formerly exercisable by the Lord Chancellor of Ireland in lunacy and minor matters and at the time of the passing of the 1924 Act exercised by the Lord Chief Justice of Ireland was transferred to and made exercisable by the Chief Justice of the Irish Free State from whom appeal lay to the Supreme Court. This was followed by section 3 of the Courts of

---

[505] 17 Edw. St. 1 cc.9 and 10. See *Ruffhead's Statutes* (ed. Runnington, 1786).

[506] *In re Earl of Lanesborough* (1826) Beat 638; *In re McDermott* (1843) 3 Dr. & War. 480; *In re Singleton* (1958) 8 Ir. Ch. R. 263

[507] The terms of one Letter in Lunacy were quoted in *In re Birch* (1892) 29 L.R. Ir. 274 at 275 It read "Whereas it belongeth to us in right of our royal prerogative to have the custody of idiots and lunatics and their estates in that part of the United Kingdom called Ireland... we therefore have thought fit to entrust you with the care and commitment of the custody of the idiots and lunatics and their estates."

[508] In particular ss 68, 70 and 103.

[509] See Law Reform Commission *Consultation Paper on the Law and the Elderly* LRC CP23–2003, p.92.

Justice Act 1928 providing that references in the Lunacy Regulation (Ireland) Act 1871 and the Acts amending it and any rules and orders made under those Acts to "the Lord Chancellor entrusted as aforesaid" should be construed and have effect as references to the Chief Justice of the Irish Free State and should be deemed to have effect from the commencement of Part 1 of the Courts of Justice Act 1924 (which transferred the jurisdiction to the Chief Justice of the Irish Free State) .

Thereafter, section 9(1) of the Courts of Justice Act 1936 provided that the jurisdiction in lunacy and minor matters which was transferred to and vested in the Chief Justice by section 19(1) of the Courts Act 1924 should become and be transferred to the High Court and be exercisable by the President of the High Court from the appointed day or if and whenever the President of the High Court so directed by an ordinary judge assigned in that behalf by the President. Following the adoption of the 1937 Constitution section 2(2)(a) of the Courts (Establishment and Constitution) Act 1961 established formally the office of the President of the High Court in accordance with Article 34 of the Constitution. Eventually, under section 9(1) of the Courts (Supplemental Provisions) Act 1961 jurisdiction in lunacy and minor matters formerly exercised by the Lord Chancellor of Ireland and his successors was formally vested in the High Court and made exercisable by the President of the High Court who also is empowered to assign an ordinary judge of the High Court to exercise the jurisdiction for the time being.[510]

The question however remains, absent specific legislation transferring it to the new state, whether the Crown's parens patriae prerogative itself survived the constitutional changes in 1922 it having been argued that the legislation passing on the power to administer the jurisdiction merely changed the official responsible for exercising the prerogative but did not address the survival of the prerogative itself.[511] Harris writing in 1930 endorsed this view:[512]

> "It should be observed that neither the delegation of its administration to the Lords Chancellor nor the enactments regulating that administration diminished or affected in any way the prerogative of the ... Crown to the control and management of ... the estates of lunatics, within the jurisdiction during their lifetime and lunacy[513] for the sign manual did not confer any original jurisdiction on the Lord Chancellor whatsoever, but merely endowed him during the life of the reigning monarch[514] with the powers of administration which it was inconvenient for the monarch to personally exercise and this prerogative would seem still to vest in the ... Crown".[515]

Accordingly in the absence of a Constitutional article and/or specific statute transferring

---

[510] Courts (Supplemental Provisions) Act 1961, s.9(2).

[511] See Tomkin and McAuley, "*Re A Ward of Court*: Legal Analysis" (1995) 1 M.L.J.I. 45.

[512] *A Treatise on the Law and Practice in Lunacy in Ireland* (Dublin 1930), p.2.

[513] Harris cites as authority for this assertion De Praerogativa Regis 17 Edw.11; *Abraham on The Law and Practice of Lunacy in Ireland*, p.3; *I.G. Collinson on Lunacy* (1812), pp.86–95; Pope *Law and Practice of Lunacy* (2nd ed., 1890), p.27.

[514] Harris notes that on the death of the Monarch a new sign manual was necessary to vest the authority of the new Monarch and cites H.S. Theobald, *The Law relating to Lunacy* (Stevens and Sons, London, 1924), p.15. See *A Treatise on the Law and Practice in Lunacy in Ireland* (Dublin, 1930), p.2 fn (k) .

[515] See Harris, *A Treatise on the Law and Practice in Lunacy in Ireland* (Dublin, 1930) p.2.

the *parens patriae* jurisdiction from the Crown to the courts of the Irish Free State and from those courts to the courts established under the 1937 Constitution it may be argued that the *parens patriae* jurisdiction has lapsed.[516] However, in the alternative it might be argued that the President's authority in wardship might be grounded in the inherent jurisdiction of the court to protect an individual's personal rights under Article 40.3 of the Constitution.[517]

The current legislative basis of the wardship jurisdiction

Where a person is of unsound mind and incapable of managing his/her person and/or property

The criteria for admitting a person to wardship and the procedure for admitting a person to wardship in the High Court are set out in the Lunacy Regulation (Ireland) Act 1871[518] and Orders 65 and 67 of the Rules of the Superior Courts 1986.[519] The powers of the Circuit Court to admit a person to wardship are set out in the section 22(2) of the Courts (Supplemental Provisions) Act 1961 as amended[520] and Order 47 of the Circuit Court Rules 2001.[521]

Where the person is a minor

The High Court also has power to admit minors to wardship[522] and the procedure for such applications is set out in Order 65 of the Rules of the Superior Courts. The Circuit Court also has jurisdiction to admit infants to wardship where the value of their personal property does not exceed (£5,000[523]) €6348.69 or the rateable value of their real property does not exceed (£200[52]) €253.95. [525] Its rules however do not set out the procedure for having the minor taken into the wardship of the Circuit Court. In the absence of Circuit Court Rules of Procedure the High Court practice and procedure governs the issue.[526]

---

[516] See "*Re A Ward of Court*: Legal Analysis" [1995] *Medico-Legal Journal of Ireland* 45 at pp.46–47. This was the view taken in *Byrne v. Ireland* [1972] I.R. 241.

[517] See dicta of Finlay C.J. in *In re D* [1987] I.R. 449 where he referred to Art.40.3.2. as a possible source of jurisdiction.

[518] The Act is entitled "An Act to amend the Law in Ireland relating to Commissions of Lunacy and the proceeding under the same, and the management of the Estates of Lunatics and to provide for the visiting and the protection of the Property of Lunatics in Ireland: and for other purposes." It came into force on May 25, 1871.

[519] S.I. No.15 of 1986.

[520] The monetary limits of the jurisdiction were raised by Courts Act 1971, s.4.

[521] S.I. No.510 of 2001.

[522] Courts (Supplemental Provisions) Act 1961, s.9(1), (2).

[523] *Ibid.*, s.22(1) (a) and Sch. 3, para.24 as amended by the Courts Act 1971, s.2(1)(a).

[524] Courts Supplemental Provisions Act 1961, s.22(1) (a), sch.3 para. 24 as amended by the Courts Act 1971, s.2(1)(d) and re-amended by the Courts Act 1981, s.2(1)(d).

[525] Euro equivalent as specified by Council Regulations (EC) 974/98 of May 3, 1998 on the introduction of the Euro. See Arts 1, 14.

[526] O.47, r.20, Circuit Court Rules 2001 and O.67, r.16, Rules of the Superior Courts.

Criteria for admitting a person to wardship

In order to be brought in to wardship under the Lunacy Regulation (Ireland) Act 1871 a person must be declared to be of unsound mind and incapable of managing his/her person and/or property. Each of the criteria must be met. Consequently in the case *In the matter of Catherine Keogh*,[527] a jury found that the person it was sought to have admitted to wardship was not of unsound mind but that she was incapable of managing her person and her property. Finnegan P. accordingly ruled that the person could not be made a ward of court.

Even if the person meets each of the criteria it seems that the court has discretion as to whether or not wardship is the appropriate course of action to take. The Registrar of Wards of Court has indicated that in addition to meeting the statutory criteria the court must be satisfied that the person or the property of the respondent is in need of protection or that there is some benefit to the respondent being taken in to wardship.[528] These additional discretionary criteria appear to have their roots in the "parens patriae" origins of the jurisdiction of the court.[529]

In general when lack of capacity is alleged the onus of proof is on the person asserting it and the standard of proof is proof of incapacity on the balance of probabilities. The Lunacy Regulation (Ireland) Act 1871 requires that an inquiry be carried out as to the capacity of the person to manage his/her person or property. Accordingly the hearings in wardship matters are of an inquisitorial rather than an adversarial nature and the rules of evidence are relaxed.[530]

The procedures for taking a person into wardship

General

The Lunacy Regulation (Ireland) Act 1871 provides the basis for a number of different procedures for taking a person into wardship. Section 15 of the Act provides for a standard procedure; section 12 of the Act makes provision for emergency applications; section 68 provides a procedure for taking people with limited amounts of property into wardship; section 70 empowers the court to take a person found "guilty but insane" under the criminal law into wardship and section 103 provides for temporary wardship. There is also a jurisdiction, which derives from the "inherent jurisdiction" of the court to take into wardship a person whose person alone requires protection and who has no property.

Certain features are common to all the procedures. If it is considered that a person needs to be admitted to the wardship of the court application is made to the President of the High Court. The applicant is usually called the petitioner and the person whom it is sought to admit to wardship, the respondent. Any person may present the petition but in practice it is usually the next of kin or a family member and the procedure envisages that a solicitor be instructed in the matter. Where no one is willing to act as petitioner

---

[527] Unreported, High Court, Finnegan P., October 15, 2002.
[528] See N. Doherty (Registrar of Wards of Court), "Wards of Court", Law Society of Ireland Continuing Legal Education Lectures, January 15, 2003.
[529] As to the survival of which see pp.645 *et seq.*
[530] See *Eastern Health Board v. MK and MK* [1999] 2 I.R. 99

the Registrar of Wards of Court may initiate proceedings under section 12 of the Act. The forms to be used in the procedure are set out in Appendix K to the Rules of the Superior Courts 1986 or in the case of the Circuit Court Schedule B Form 2F of the Circuit Court Rules 2001.

The President of the High Court usually rules on applications but he has power under section 9(2) of the Courts (Supplemental Provisions) Act 1961 to assign another judge to deal with cases.

When a person is found to be of unsound mind and incapable of managing his/her person or property a declaration order is made admitting him/her to wardship; a committee or (in the case of a temporary ward) a guardian is appointed to take over such management subject to the supervision of the court which has powers to make orders concerning the management of the ward's property and the care of the ward's person.

Procedure by petition under section 15 of the 1871 Act

Application by way of petition under section 15 of the 1871 Act is the standard procedure used in the majority of cases. The stages in the procedure are set out in Order 67 of the Rules of the Superior Courts and the forms to be used are contained in Appendix K to the Rules. In effect under this procedure the petitioner applies to the court for an inquiry to be carried out as to whether or not the respondent is of unsound mind and capable or incapable of managing their person and property. In practice the petition may include a Statement of Facts (a detailed statement of the ward's circumstances which is required by the rules to be filed after the respondent is admitted to wardship) but it must include the following particulars

(a) The name, religion, age, description and marital status of the respondent;

(b) The names, religion, descriptions and residences of his next-of-kin, and of the person(s) in whose house or under whose care he is, or has been during the preceding 12 months, or with whom he resides;

(c) The nature and amount of his property and his debts;

(d) The name, religion, address and description of the petitioner and his authority for presenting the petition; and

(e) An undertaking by the petitioner that in the event that the petition is dismissed or does not proceed he will pay the costs or expenses relating to any "visitation" of the respondent or otherwise arising in relation to the inquiry before the court.[531]

The petitioner must swear a verifying affidavit and this affidavit must be attested by his solicitor.[532] The petition must be accompanied by the supporting affidavits of two registered medical practitioners.[533] The medical practitioners need not be specialists but the opinion of a specialist may carry greater weight. The Wards of Court Office advise that the medical affidavits should contain the following information:

---

[531] O.67, r.4(1), Rules of the Superior Courts. The form of the petition is set out in Form No. 2 of Appendix K to the Superior Court Rules

[532] O.67, r.4(3), Rules of the Superior Courts. The affidavit of the Petitioner is set in Form No. 3 of the Appendix K to the Superior Court Rules.

[533] O.67, r.4(3).

   (a) The date on which and the place at which the examination of the respondent took place; (the examination should have been carried out within a maximum of one month prior to the statement);

   (b) A description of the response of the respondent to the examination, including where relevant, references to symptoms, demeanour and answers to mental tests;

   (c) A diagnosis of the respondent's mental condition, where applicable;

   (d) Any other observations relevant to the issue of the respondent's mental capacity or incapacity;

   (e) The opinion of the medical practitioner as to whether or not the respondent is of unsound mind and incapable of managing his/her affairs.

Order 67 of the Rules of the Superior Courts provides for the originating petition together with the two supporting medical affidavits to be lodged in the Wards of Court Office and requires the Registrar of Wards of Court to submit them to the President of the High Court.[534] If the President is satisfied by the medical evidence he proceeds to make an "inquiry order".[535] If not so satisfied the matter proceeds no further. In an inquiry order is made one of the medical visitors of the President of the High Court (a panel of consultant psychiatrists) examines the respondent and reports to the President of the High Court. This report is confidential to the court and is not shown to the respondent unless the court so directs.

    The Office of Wards of Court then writes to the solicitor who initiated the proceedings and directs that notice of the petition be served on the respondent and to such other persons as the Judge may direct.[536] This notice must be served in all cases even if the respondent is unconscious or otherwise unable to acknowledge its receipt. In the latter case where personal service would be impracticable or inexpedient substituted service may be effected by delivering notice to the person for the time being in charge of the psychiatric hospital or other institution in which the respondent is resident or (where the respondent is not a patient in a psychiatric hospital) by delivering it to some person aged twenty one or over who is resident at the ward's dwelling house or usual or last known place of abode within the jurisdiction.[537]

    The notice informs the respondent that there are seven days in which to object to the wardship proceedings and, if the respondent so wishes, to seek a hearing before a jury.[538] After service has been effected an affidavit must be completed by the person who served the petition,[539] and details of service must be endorsed on the back of the petition. The attested petition and the affidavit of service must be filed in the Office of Wards of Court. If a notice of objection is not filed within the seven-day period the case is listed for hearing.

    Where a respondent wishes to object s/he must sign the notice of objection and this

---

[534] O.67, r.5.

[535] O.67, r.6.

[536] O.67, r.7.

[537] O.67, r.94(2).

[538] The notice must take the form set out in Appendix K, Form No. 4 of the Rule of the Superior Courts.

[539] This must take the form set out in Appendix K, Form No. 15. See O.67, r.95.

must be witnessed by a solicitor.[540] He must forward the notice of objection to the Registrar of Wards of Court within seven days of the being served with the notice of the inquiry.[541] A hearing must then take place. The hearing may be before judge or before a judge and jury. However, a hearing before a judge and jury must be requested by the respondent[542] within seven days[543] and the judge has a discretion whether to grant the request. Initially the respondent may be asked to appear before the judge for a personal examination. The Judge may then order that an inquiry should be held before a jury and issues any necessary directions in relation to the conduct of the inquiry. Alternatively the judge may hold an inquiry without a jury. The Judge is empowered to do so when satisfied that the respondent is not mentally competent to "form and express a wish in that behalf"[544] (in relation to a jury trial) or when it appears to him from a consideration of the evidence and the surrounding circumstances that a jury inquiry is "unnecessary or inexpedient".[545]

The jury or the judge then make the decision as to whether or not the respondent is of unsound mind and capable of managing his/her person or property and if the person is found to be of unsound mind and incapable of managing his/her person or property a Declaration Order is made accordingly. If the person is not so found the petition is dismissed

Procedure under section 12 of the 1871 Act

Application may be made under section 12 of the 1871 Act, where it is not feasible to use the section 15 procedure for example in a case of urgency or where a person whether it be a family member or another person considers that a person needs to be taken into wardship but does not wish to institute the proceedings themselves.

In this event, the case is brought to the attention of the Registrar of Wards of Court who treats this as the commencement of the procedure. The Registrar then directs one of the medical visitors to examine the proposed ward.[546] If it appears from the report that the respondent is of unsound mind and incapable of managing his person and affairs then the President may direct that the report of the medical visitor stand and be proceeded upon as a petition for an inquiry.[547] A single further independent medical report forms the basis for the application and the process continues as described under section 15.

The principal difference between the section 12 and section 15 procedure is that there is no petition and the two medical affidavits are not supplied.

Procedure under section 68 of the 1871 Act

Section 68 of the 1871 Act provides for simpler proceedings in cases where a person's

---

[540] The notice of objection must take the form set out in Appendix K, Form No. 6.
[541] O.67, r.18, Rules of the Superior Courts.
[542] The respondent should use Appendix K, Form No. 6 indicating that he is not objecting to the inquiry but demanding that it be had before a jury.
[543] O.67, r.11, Rules of the Superior Courts.
[544] Lunacy Regulation (Ireland) Act 1871 s.14.
[545] *Ibid.*, s.15.
[546] *Ibid.*, s.11 and O.67, r.83.
[547] *Ibid.*, s.12.

property is valued at less than €6348.69 or where the income from the property is less than €380.92 per annum.[548] There are two distinctive types of procedure under section 68. One is commenced by the Registrar of Wards of Court and the procedure relating thereto set out in Order 67, Rule 30. The second is commenced a third party and the procedure governed by Order 67, Rule 21.

(i) Applications by the Registrar; Order 67, rule 30 The Registrar has a discretion as to the manner of initiating applications under Order 67, rule 30.[549] However, as a first step s/he usually obtains a report from a Medical Visitor as to the respondent's state of mind.[550] If it is established from the report that the respondent is of unsound mind and incapable of managing his affairs the Registrar must give carriage of the proceedings to the General Solicitor for Minors and Wards of Court or such other solicitor as s/he may think fit.[551] The Registrar must then direct that an originating notice of the application and report in the Form No. 11 of Appendix K be served on the respondent.[552]

This notice, informs the respondent of the medical report, the Registrar's application and the possibility of an order being made on the grounds that he is of unsound mind and incapable of managing his affairs for the purpose of rendering his property or the income thereof available for the maintenance of himself/herself and his/her family or for carrying on his/her trade or business. The notice will also inform the respondent of his right to object to the proceedings. To exercise this right the notice of objection should be signed by him and attested by his solicitor and sent to the Registrar of Wards of Court within seven days of service of the originating notice upon him.[553]

As soon as practicable after the expiry of seven days from the service of the originating notice on the respondent the Registrar must submit the Medical Visitors report, the evidence regarding the respondent and his property and affairs, the affidavit of service of the originating notice upon him and the notice of objection (if any) to the President.[554]

After considering the documents submitted to him the President may make an order pursuant to section 68 without the attendance of counsel, solicitors or parties. Alternatively he may direct that the application be set down for hearing or refer the matter to the Registrar to make a particular inquiry.[555]

(ii) Applications by external third parties: Order 67, rule 21 Where applications are made by external third parties proceedings are commenced by the filing of a petition together with one medical certificate /affidavit in the Office of Wards of Court.

Notice of the application must be served on the respondent[556] and the latter may within seven days make an objection to the application.[557] Where an objection to the petition is made by the respondent or any other person notified of it the Registrar must

---

[548] Courts Act 1971, s.4.
[549] O.67, r.30(a).
[550] O.67, r.30(b).
[551] O.67, r.30(c).
[552] Lunacy Regulation (Ireland) Act 1871, s.68 and O.67, r.30(c), Rules of the Superior Courts.
[553] To this end he may use Form No. 14 of Appendix K, O.67, r.30(d), Rules of the Superior Courts
[554] O.67, r.30(e).
[555] O.67, r.30 (f).
[556] The notice must take the form set out in Appendix K, Form No. 10, and O.67, r.24.
[557] The notice of objection may be in Form No. 14 of Appendix K. See O.67, r.24.

obtain a report from one of the medical visitors in respect of the respondent.[558] The Registrar may also seek such a report where s/he considers that the evidence in support of a section 68 petition was inconclusive or otherwise unsatisfactory.[559] The judge may then make an order without any further inquiry.[560]

Proceedings under section 70 where a person is found not guilty by reason of insanity

The President is empowered by section 70 to apply the property of a person tried on indictment and acquitted by reason of insanity or found to be insane for that persons benefit.

The procedure is initiated by petition,[561] which must be signed by the petitioner and attested by his/her solicitor[562] In addition to the matters set out in that form the petition must contain a statement of the verdict or finding of insanity of the respondent and as to his still being in confinement.[563] The petition must also be supported by an affidavit or certificate of a registered medical practitioner as to the respondent's continued insanity.[564]

The respondent must be served personally with notice of the petition[565] This notice, inter alia, informs the respondent of his/her right of objection. To exercise this right a notice of objection,[566] and must be signed by him should be transmitted by the respondent or his solicitor to the Registrar of Wards of Court within seven days of the service upon him of the notice endorsed on the attested petition.[567]

Where the Registrar receives the notice of objection or where the prayer of the petition is opposed by any person having notice of it then as in cases proceeding by petition under section 68 it becomes his/her duty, in cases where he has not already obtained a report to direct one of the Medical Visitors to visit the respondent and report as under section 11 of the Act.[568]

As in cases, which proceed by petition under section 68, the President may after considering the petition and other documents submitted to him make an order without the attendance of counsel, solicitor or parties. To this end he may make any order with respect to the property of a person and its application thereof for his maintenance or benefit for that of his family or for carrying on his trade of business mentioned in sections 68[569] and 69.[570]

Alternatively he may direct that the petition be set down for hearing or refer the

---

[558] O.67, r.26.

[559] O.67, r.25.

[560] O.67, rr 28, 29.

[561] The petition must be in the form set out in Appendix K, Form No.9. See O.67, r.22.

[562] O.67, r.3.

[563] O.67, r.22.

[564] O.67, r.22.

[565] O.67, r.23. The Notice must take the form indicated in Appendix K, Form No.10.

[566] The notice may in the form set out in Appendix K, Form No.14.

[567] O.67, r.24.

[568] O.67, r.26.

[569] S.68 empowers him to make any order he may consider expedient for the purpose of rendering the ward's property available for his maintenance or benefit or for carrying on his trade or business.

[570] S. 70. See above, p.646.

matter to the Registrar to make a particular inquiry regarding any matter to which the petition relates.[571]

While the President's powers to make an order under section 70 are wide, he cannot of course appoint a Committee of the person since he can have no control over the person of the ward.

Procedure under section 103 – Temporary wardship

Application for a person to be admitted to wardship as a temporary ward may be made under section 103 if it can be shown that the person is "of weak mind and temporarily incapable of managing his affairs." Given modern developments in the medical treatment of mental illness which, when a person becomes mentally ill facilitate a speedier return to health, this procedure is rarely used in practice.

However, if sought to be used application is way of petition[572] similar to that which applies under section 15, but the supporting medical certificates need not be in affidavit form. The certificates should state that the respondent is "of weak mind and temporarily incapable of managing his affairs". The certificate should state the nature of, and the reason for such incapacity and its probable duration. Notice of the petition must also be served on the respondent.[573]

The Registrar of Wards of Court arranges for an examination by a medical visitor.[574] The visitor is required to inform the respondent that notice must be given within four days if there is to be an objection.[575]

After the expiration of six clear days from the receipt of the Visitor's report, the Registrar must submit the petition, the notice of the petition served upon the respondent, the affidavit of service, the medical certificates, the notice of objection (if any), the visitor's report and any evidence that might be available as to the respondent or his affairs to the President for his consideration. [576]

The Judge may make "such order under the provisions of section 103 of the Act as he may consider expedient" direct the petition to be set down for an in camera hearing or refer the matter back to the Registrar for further inquiry.[577] Orders made following a section 103 application may involve the appointment of a "guardian" to act during a finite period. This may not exceed six months and cannot be renewed more than once.

Application to have a person who has no property a ward of court

In the 1987 case of *In the Application by the Midland Health Board to Initiate Proceedings to make a person a Ward of Court*,[578] Finlay C.J. ruled:[579]

---

[571] O.67, r.28.
[572] O.67, r.32.
[573] O.67, r.35. The Notice must take the form set out in Appendix K, Form No. 13.
[574] O.67, r.37.
[575] *Ibid.* The respondent may use Form No. 14 of Appendix K to serve notice of objection.
[576] O.67, r.38 (1).
[577] O.67, r.38(2).
[578] [1988] I.L.R.M. 251.
[579] *Ibid.*, p.256

> "there is vested in the High Court a jurisdiction where necessary and appropriate to take into its wardship a person of unsound mind whose person requires protection and management but who is not entitled to any property which requires protection and management"

This jurisdiction is discretionary in nature and exists, not by virtue of the 1871 Act but as part of the general protective jurisdiction over persons of unsound mind, the exercise of which was vested in successive Lords Chancellor by the Crown[580] and inherited by the President of the High Court.[581]

In the *Midland Health Board* case a 20-year-old woman was detained by the Health Board in a residential institution on the grounds that her welfare was at risk if she continued to reside at home. Her parents had brought an application for *habeas corpus* and for an order under Article 40.4.2 of the Constitution directing the Health Board to produce her before the court and to certify in writing the grounds of her detention and the Health Board applied for an order to enable it to file a petition praying for an inquiry as to the soundness of mind of the respondent. While the court expressed no opinion on whether the ward actually required protection in the case the decision does open up the possibility that an institution detaining a mentally ill or disabled person might apply to have a person made a ward of court as a mechanism to justify the detention on the grounds that the person required protection from others and possibly even from him/herself.

Finlay C.J. stated that the exercise of the prerogative jurisdiction did not involve the procedures and regulations provided for in the 1871 Act or the Rules of the Superior Courts consequent upon the Act. He stated:

> "If the Learned President decides to take the respondent into his wardship the procedures to be followed are entirely at his discretion and ... would clearly not include compliance with many of the provisions of the Act of 1871 or with the Rules and Forms contained in the Rules of the Superior Courts relevant to that Act."[582]

However, he stated further that it was

> "desirable that consideration be given to the introduction of Rules of Court appropriate to simple and practical procedures for dealing with persons alleged to be of unsound mind whose person alone requires protection."[583]

While the learned judge did not describe the type of procedure that might be used he did appear to envisage the holding of an inquiry in such cases,[584] which assumes that application, should be made by petition and a procedure similar to that under section 15 adopted.

---

[580] Finlay C.J. cited Lord Ashbourne's interpretation of the letter in lunacy vesting jurisdiction in the Lord Chancellor in *In re Birch* (1892) 29 L.R. Ir. 274 and *In re Godfrey* (1892) 29 L.R. Ir. 278 in support of the existence of this jurisdiction.

[581] See p.2, n.10

[582] [1988] I.L.R.M. 251 at 258.

[583] *Ibid.*

[584] *Ibid.*

The recent decision in *In re M ex parte*[585] provides a further illustration of the exercise by the court of this inherent jurisdiction. In this case the question was whether a woman should be taken into wardship in order that consent be given to a life saving medical procedure. The woman had given her consent and then withdrawn it. Finnegan P. held that because of the urgency of the issue arising it was not practical to use the procedures set out in the 1871 legislation. Accordingly he applied the *parens patriae* principle and taking the woman into wardship ruled that "jurisdiction in this matter has not been circumscribed by the Lunacy Regulation Act,"[586] but provided no further detail of the basis for the jurisdiction.

Procedure following the making of a declaration order

The statement of facts Where an order is made declaring a person to be of unsound mind and incapable of managing his/her person or property the judge will usually order that a statement of facts be lodged in the Office of Wards of Court. This is the case if one has not been already included in the original petition. The Statement of Facts must be sworn by the petitioner or the solicitor and contain the following information:

(a) The ward's situation;
(b) The nature of his mental illness;
(c) Who should be appointed committee of his person and of his estate;
(d) His property and the net amount or estimated value thereof;
(e) The amount of his gross income;
(f) The amount of his clear net income;
(g) In what manner and at what expense and by whom and where he has been maintained; what should be allowed for his past maintenance; whether anything, and if so, what is due and to whom in respect thereof, and to whom and out of what fund it should be paid;
(h) What should be allowed for his future maintenance, from what time allowance should commence and out of what fund it should be paid;
(i) Whether any, and if so what costs are payable out of the ward's estate, and to whom and out of what fund they should be paid;
(j) Whether any, and if so what debts are due by the ward and whether any special circumstances exist as to any of them;
(k) Whether a receiver should be appointed over the ward's estate;
(l) Whether the ward is known to have made any will, and if so who has custody of it.[587]

The Registrar may then summon the solicitors to a hearing of the statement of facts on the basis of which a report is drawn up which forms the basis of an order of the President or a Judge assigned by him.[588]

---

[585] Unreported, Finnegan P., October 24, 2002.
[586] *Ibid.*, p.2.
[587] O.67, r.40.
[588] O.67, r.47(2), (3).

Costs

Section 94 of the 1871 Act provides for the costs of wardship proceedings[589] to be paid out of the Ward's estate and this is the usual practice. The costs are usually paid when all of the ward's assets are brought under the control of the court. After a ward has been made a ward of court further issues may arise and further costs incurred. To meet such costs there is a levy paid on all ward's incomes known as a court percentage which is paid to the State.[590]

While an originating petition does contain an undertaking on the part of the petitioner to pay the costs or expenses relating to any visitation of the respondent or otherwise arising in relation to the inquiry before the court in the event that the petition is dismissed or does not proceed the petitioner may not always have to bear the costs of the application. Thus in the case of *In the Matter of Catherine Keogh*,[591] it would appear that the petitioner should have been liable for the costs as the petition was dismissed. However, Finnegan P. held that while section 94 of the 1871 Act allowed the Lord Chancellor to direct costs to be paid out of the estate it did not confer "an express power of ordering costs and enforcing payment against persons who may have presented a petition for inquiry improperly". The practice of the courts since 1871 has been not to make the petitioner liable for the costs where the petition is presented bona fide *i.e.* where there are reasonable grounds for alleging mental capacity and where the petition is brought for the benefit of the proposed ward.

Management of ward's affairs after admission to wardship

When a declaration order is made and a person is consequently made a ward of court "the court is vested with jurisdiction over all matters relating to the person and the estate of the ward."[592] Accordingly when a declaration order is made wards of court essentially lose the right to make decisions about their person and their property and may not enter into binding contracts, defend legal proceedings and may not sell or buy property or have a bank account.

Appointment of the Committee or Guardian

When the President makes a declaration order he will also usually make an order appointing a "committee" to manage the affairs of the ward. Both a Committee of the Person and a Committee of the Estate may be appointed and the usual practice is to appoint the same person to both roles. The Committee may not be the proprietor , the keeper, and the medical superintendent of the hospital or care facility where the ward lives nor a person residing with or an employee of any of the above.[593]

The powers of the Committee are set out in the order and are limited by the precise

---

[589] In its *Consultation Paper on The Law and the Elderly*, LRC CP 23–2003, the Law Reform Commission reported that the staff of the Wards of Court Office estimate that the average cost of bringing a person into wardship in recent times is about €4,500. pp.104–105.
[590] See Supreme Court and High Court (Fees) (No.2) Order 2001 (S.I. No. 488 of 2001).
[591] Unreported, High Court, October 15, 2002.
[592] *In the matter of a Ward of Court (Withholding Medical Treatment) (No.2)* [1996] 2 I.R. 79.
[593] O.67, r.58.

terms of the order. The Committee is empowered to make decisions on behalf of the ward in so far as those are authorised by the court orders. The Judge may appoint replacement Committee if the person appointed dies or becomes unwilling or unable to act.

Where matters arise that are not dealt with in the court's order the Committee can obtain guidance from the Office of Wards of Court and directions may be obtained from the judge if necessary.

The Committee may be authorised to receive money and make payments on behalf of the ward. This money must be kept in a separate specific account and the Committee must account for these monies annually or as directed by the Registrar.[594]

A Committee who is in receipt of the Ward's income may be required to give security.[595] This is to provide security against the possible failure of the Committee to account for the ward's monies. In practice there appear to be difficulties in obtaining such bonds from insurance companies.[596]

The costs of the Committee in dealing with the ward's assets may be recovered from those assets. Prior to 2002 remuneration would only be paid if there were special circumstances or for a special cause. An amendment to the rule of court in that year now allows the judge to award remuneration on such terms and conditions as may be determined from time to time.[597] In practice the Committee may be allowed remuneration by reference to a scale of commissions on the various sources of income of the ward received by the committee.[598]

Care of the ward's person

The Committee of the Person monitors the personal welfare of the ward from day to day. The Registrar of Wards of Court is entitled to require the committee of the person to report at intervals on such matters as the ward's "residence, physical and mental condition, maintenance, comfort and such other matters in relation to the ward as he may wish to be informed of"[599] The Committee of the Person may not change the ward's residence "except with the leave of the Judge or the Registrar".[600]

Frequently when a person who is brought into wardship is living in a psychiatric hospital or care facility an order is made that the person should be detained there until further order.

Sections 57 and 58 of the 1871 Act provide for medical and legal visitors to visit wards from time to time and report to the President of the High Court on the state of mind, bodily health and general condition and care and treatment. Order 67, rule 50

---

[594] O.67, r.63.

[595] O.67, r.62.

[596] See Law Reform Commission *Consultation Paper on the Law and the Elderly*, LRC CP 23–2003, p.107.

[597] See Rules of the Superior Courts (No.1) (Remuneration of Committees of Wards of Court) (S.I. No.208 of 2002) which amends O.67, r.65.

[598] See Law Reform Commission *Consultation Paper on the Law and the Elderly*, LRC CP 23–2003, p.107.

[599] O.67, r.59.

[600] O.67, r.60.

provides that the President may order the registrar to make such visits but such orders are not made in practice.

It seems that in Ireland the High Court has exclusive jurisdiction to grant or withhold consent to the treatment of a ward of court,[601] subject to the principle that, in the case of an emergency a medical practitioner is entitled to take urgent action, which is considered necessary to preserve the life and health of the patient. In practice, a request for consent to the carrying out of an elective surgical procedure or the administration of an anaesthetic is normally made by the clinical director of the hospital or the surgeon concerned to the Office of Wards of Court. In practice the Registrar of Wards of Court is authorised by the President of the High Court to issue consents to the carrying out of non-controversial procedures in the name of the President of the High Court. Procedures considered non controversial include routine investigative procedures or the treatment of fractures or other procedures.

Procedures considered "controversial" are considered personally by the President of the High Court. These include non-routine procedures or those, which carry a more substantial risk to the patient. These might include procedures involving the insertion of gastrostomy tubes or the amputation of limbs. Controversial procedures may also include procedures to which the ward, if capable of indicating agreement did not agree or to which the next of kin did not agree, if the ward himself/herself was not capable of indicating agreement. In controversial cases the President of the High Court seeks the advice of one of the members of his panel of Medical Visitors as to whether it would be appropriate to give the consent of the court to the treatment. In exercising the jurisdiction the court's prime consideration is the best interests of the ward and while the views of the committee and family of the ward should be heeded and give careful consideration they will not and prevail over the court's view of the ward's best interests.[602]

The role of guardians

In the case of temporary wardship under section 103, a Guardian is appointed rather than a Committee. The functions of a Guardian are similar to those of a Committee. Guardians are subject to the control of the President and have and may exercise in relation to the ward's estate only such powers as are expressly conferred in the order of appointment.[603]

In some respects the duties of the Guardian mirror those of the Committee. Thus Guardians may not change the ward's residence unless they have the leave of the President or the Registrar;[604] they must give security immediately upon appointment;[605] they must account annually or at such other intervals as the Registrar may determine;[606] they must lodge all moneys received on behalf of the ward's estate forthwith in a separate bank account;[607] and make annual returns as required by the Registrar of Wards of Court.[608]

---

[601] *In re a Ward of Court (Withholding Medical Treatment) (No.2)* [1996] 2 I.R. 79 (*per* Denham J. at p.156).

[602] *Ibid., per* Hamilton C.J. at p.106.

[603] O.67, r.78.

[604] O.67, rr.60, 71.

[605] O.67, rr.61, 62, 71.

[606] O.67, rr.63, 71.

[607] O.67, rr.66 and 71.

In addition to these duties and in accordance with section 105[609] of the Act, the Guardian of every temporary ward, must file in the Office of Wards of Court a monthly account of all moneys or other property received, sold, conveyed, assigned or otherwise disposed of by the ward, setting out the mode in which the same or the proceeds thereof have been applied by him[610] and every act, deed and thing done by him as Guardian in relation to the person or property of the temporary ward.[611] This must be accompanied by a statement of the moneys or other property of the ward then in the Guardian's possession power or control and by a statement signed by the Guardian of the the then physical and mental condition of the ward and the probable duration of his incapacity.[612] All these accounts must be verified by affidavit and taken by the Registrar.[613]

The Registrar must make a special report to the President of the High Court in any case where he is of the opinion that an account submitted by the Guardian is unsatisfactory or that the temporary ward's affairs require special investigation or that there is any other matter or question which should be dealt with by order of the President.[614] Where he reports any matter arising the account or in relation to ward's person or property under this provision the matter must be considered and disposed of by the President *in camera*.[615] A Guardian may be made personally liable for the balance of any moneys due as if he were a Receiver.[616]

Guardians may not be allowed at the expense of the ward's estate any costs or expenses for any work proper to be done by them personally and not requiring professional assistance.[617] They may however be allowed remuneration on such terms and subject to such conditions (if any) as the judge may from time to time determine.[618]

The Guardian may appoint a solicitor to assist him in the performance of his duties in the same manner as a Committee. A solicitor so instructed may charge and be allowed such fees and expenses for professional services rendered in relation to wardship matters as would be allowed generally in relation to High Court proceedings.[619]

---

[608] O.67, rr.68 and 71.

[609] The reference in the rules to s.103 appears to be a misprint

[610] O.67, r.75.

[611] See Lunacy Regulation (Ireland) Act 1871, s.105

[612] O.67, r.75.

[613] Lunacy Regulation (Ireland) Act 1871, s.105 and O.67, r.76. Applications by a Guardian to vouch accounts are made in the same manner as those by a Committee except that the date of the hearing is fixed by letter, no summons is issued and the hearing is in camera. See Lunacy Regulation (Ireland) Act 1871, s.106.

[614] O.67, rr.71 and 64.

[615] The Registrar must give notice by post of the date and time of such consideration to the solicitors named in the petition or any other solicitors permitted to appear in the matter. These notices must be sent by post to their registered places of business. O.67, r.77.

[616] Lunacy Regulation (Ireland) Act 1871, s.105.

[617] O.67, r.101.

[618] O.67, r.71 and O.67, r.65 as substituted by Rules of the Superior Courts (No.1) (Remuneration of Committees of Wards of Court) 2002 (S.I. No.208 of 2002).

[619] O.67, r.97 Rules of the Superior Courts

Management of the ward's property

The ward's funds

When bringing a person into wardship the judge may order that all the Ward's funds, which are in bank accounts or in other financial institutions, be lodged into the Accountant's Office in the Four Courts.[620] The Office provides forms of privity, which are forms that may be used to order the relevant financial institutions to transfer the funds to the Accountants Office. The Accountant's Office then invests the funds as directed by the Wards of Court Office. Existing stocks and shares may be kept but usually they are reinvested as directed by the Registrar of Wards of Court. When the ward's money is taken into the Accountant's Office it must be lodged in Trustee Authorised Investments.

The Wards of Court Office is obliged by law and by its role of guardian to take a "conservative" approach to management of a wards money. This approach has been criticised on the basis that "some estates under the administration of the wards of court office involve large sums of money and require sophisticated investment techniques."[621] More recently a more active and sophisticated approach has been taken. The range of trustee-authorised investments has been expanded by the Trustee (Authorised Investments) Order 1998.[622]

In November 2001 a firm of investment consultants was appointed to review funds management and funds accounting in the Courts Service and to advise on best practice. They recommended the establishment of an investment committee, which came into being in April 2002. The committee is chaired by the President of the High Court and includes the Director of Finance of the Courts Service and the Accountant of the High Court (both positions being currently combined), the Registrar of Wards of Court, an Assistant Registrar of Wards of Court, a Judge of the Circuit Court, a County Registrar, a Judge of the District Court, the Chief Clerk of the Dublin Metropolitan District Court and a representative form the National Treasury Management Agency. The Committee acts in an advisory capacity. Its functions include the view of investment strategies, the setting of best practice guidelines for court officers and offering advice on the appointment of investment managers and advisors

Accordingly new investment strategies have been specifically designed to meet the needs of a range of beneficiaries and two leading financial institutions appointed to manage the funds. As fund managers these institutions report to the Courts Service Investment Committee. Whereas in the past investments were made principally in cash deposits with authorised banks, in Government Gilts and in bank stock, it was recognised that deposit type investments are no longer likely to meet the long term needs of some beneficiaries due to low interest rates and high levels of inflation and it was necessary to diversify. Under the new investment arrangements beneficiary funds are invested in unitised funds comprising a mix of equities,[623] bonds[624] and cash deposits. The unitised funds are pooled. Accordingly the beneficiary holds units in a large pool of assets rather

---

[620] Lunacy Regulation (Ireland) Act 1871, s.30.

[621] S. Ní Chúlacháin, "Wardship: Time for Reform?" (2000) *Bar Review* 239 at p.240

[622] S.I. No. 28 of 1998.

[623] Shares in large established companies.

[624] These are issued by Governments and Government backed entities.

than holding a small amount of the individual assets themselves. One of the benefits of pooling is perceived to be a significant reduction in investment manager fees. Four strategies have been devised to meet the needs of different groups of beneficiaries.

> Strategy 1 is a low risk strategy aimed primarily at maintaining the invested capital. In accordance with this strategy 25% of the beneficiary's fund is invested in bonds and 75% in cash deposits

> Strategy 2 aims to ensure the stability of the capital sum and to provide a moderate level of income for the beneficiary. Accordingly 30% of the beneficiary's fund is invested in equities, 30% in bonds and 40% in cash deposits.

> Strategy 3 is designed to achieve a combination of reasonable income and sound capital growth. In accordance with this strategy 48% of the beneficiary's fund is invested in equities, 32% in bonds and 20% in cash deposits.

> Finally, Strategy 4 aims to achieve a stronger level of capital growth in order to provide for expenditure over the lifetime of the beneficiary. Consequently 65% of the beneficiary's fund is invested in equities and 35% in bonds.

The firm of investment consultants appointed to advise on the arrangements has created a projection tool for the Courts Service to facilitate the allocation of each beneficiary's funds to one of the above strategies, based on the beneficiary's circumstances. The strategy will be chosen based on criteria relating to the age of the beneficiary, the sum to be invested and the level of anticipated annual expenditure.[625] Each case is periodically reviewed and if the beneficiary's circumstances change the strategy may be varied accordingly.

Order 47, rule 12 of the Circuit Court Rules 2001 gives the Circuit Court Judge a discretion at any time to direct the investment of any fund the property of the person of unsound mind in such securities and subject to such conditions as may seem proper

The ward's maintenance

The Court's orders will usually give the Committee power to collect the ward's income and use it for the maintenance of the ward and of the ward's dependants and to deal with the ward's property.

Power of the court to order payment of the ward's debts

When a respondent becomes a ward of court all of his/her outstanding property must be collected and accounted for.[626] The usual direction is that cash and moneys on deposit be lodged in court for investment. Stocks, shares and securities[627] are also usually lodged

---

[625] See *A Guide to the New Investment Policy* (Courts Service Information Office November 2003).
[626] Third parties having dealings with the ward's estate must account for them. Personal representatives may be called upon to furnish and vouch an account of a ward's unascertained share in a deceased's estate.
[627] Except bank or other shares subject to liabilities which are usually realised.

in court in specie and the dividends paid to the Committee as they accrue.[628] Alternatively the order may Jewellery and scrip may also be lodged. Wasting property is sold while the tools of the ward's trade or profession and household effects may be retained by the ward. Moneys to which a ward is entitled by way of annuities, pensions, compensation, and remuneration or otherwise from a trading or business concern are also collected and applied for his benefit.[629]

Where a creditor of the ward seeks payment out of the ward's property which is in the care of the court, the court has a discretion as to whether to direct payment,[630] and will only do so if there is already ample provision made for the maintenance of the ward[631] (even where the estate is insolvent) and if it would be beneficial to the estate.

Payment is usually made out of cash in the hands of the Committee, Receiver or the Accountant General or by a sale, mortgage or charge of the property.[632]

A judgment creditor of a person found to be of unsound mind by inquisition may apply for a charging order against stock held in court.[633] However, he must obtain the leave of the President of the High Court to raise the charge and this will only be granted if the estate will be able to bear it and if a sufficient amount of capital remains for the maintenance of the ward.[634]

The judgment creditor is also entitled to execute judgment against the estate of a person of unsound mind who is not a ward of court even after he has had notice of the petition of inquiry unless an order has been made in the matter by the President of the High Court[635] and even after a declaration order has been made at the conclusion of the inquiry in respect of property not taken under the President's wardship jurisdiction.[636]

Claims in respect of the past maintenance of the ward are treated as ordinary debts.[637] However, reasonable advances for maintenance prior to the wardship matter may be treated as well charged on the property.[638] Statute barred debts incurred prior to the wardship are not considered.[639] Where a ward dies and his estate is insolvent debts and costs incurred in connection with the wardship proceedings take priority over those not incurred.[640]

Claims in relation to costs are dealt with and paid in the same way as other claims. Costs must usually be taxed or measured under order. However, Order 67, rule 99(1) of

---

[628] Alternatively the Declaration Order may contain authority for the Committee to sell the shares and lodge the proceeds of sale in court. This however is not usual because of the current charge to Capital Gains Tax on the encashment of equity holdings.

[629] In practice the terms of the Declaration Order may direct that these monies be lodged in court and may authorise the Committee or (if relevant) the Proprietor of a nursing home where the ward is resident to give a valid receipt for a pension and apply same for the maintenance and benefit and in discharge of the debts of the ward.

[630] *Ex parte Hastings* 14 Ves. 182 *ex parte* Dikes 8 Ves. 79.

[631] *In re Winkle* [1894] 2 Ch. 519.

[632] Lunacy Regulation (Ireland) Act 1871, s.63.

[633] *Horne v. Pountain* 23 Q.B.D. 264.

[634] *In re Plenderleith* [1893] 3 Ch. 336.

[635] *In re Clarke* [1898] 1 Ch 336.

[636] *Ibid.*

[637] *In re Weaver* 21 Ch D 615; *In re Newbegin* 36 Ch. D. 477; *In re Harris* 49 L.J. Ch. 327.

[638] *In re O'Grady's Estate* 15 Ir. L.T.R. 45.

[639] *In re Kenrick* [1907] 1 I.R. 480.

[640] *In re JJH*, Order of Chief Justice, June 23, 1928. See Harris, *op. cit.*, p.51.

the Superior Court Rules provides that the Registrar of Wards of Court may measure a sum for costs where the President of the High Court directs, where the parties consent or where the Registrar considers that the amount which would be allowed on taxation would not exceed £1,000 (€1269.74) Where the Registrar measures costs under this rule the Accountant may pay the amount measured notwithstanding that the order under which the costs are payable directs payment upon production of a certificate of taxation.[641]

Payment of costs may be effected out of cash, by sale of the property or by mortgage[642] and is usually made subject to a provision as to maintenance.

In certain cases, section 117 of the 1871 Act empowered the President of the High Court to direct that costs incident to the Wards of Court office be treated as expenses of the Office of Wards of Court and paid out of the fees of the Wards of Court Office. It was argued in the case of *In the Matter of Catherine Keogh*[643] that the court should make an order directing that the unsuccessful petitioners costs be borne by the State. Finnegan P. considered that section 117 provided the only possible statutory basis for such an order. However, he pointed out that section 55 of the Court Officers Act 1926 provided for the Lunacy Fund (into which the fees of the Ward of Court Office were paid) to be wound up and for the expenses which were payable by same to be defrayed either out of monies provided by the Oireachtas or by deduction from court percentages. He further stated that section 55 was repealed by the Courts Supplemental Provisions Act 1961[644] so that there was no longer a power to deduct from court percentages. Accordingly the petitioner's costs could not be imposed on the state.

Section 117 also authorises the President of the High Court to direct that the remuneration due to the Medical Visitor, and General Solicitor for Minors and Wards of Court and any expenditure connected with the management of the estate of any ward be paid out of and borne by the estate.[645]

Voluntary allowances may be made out of the surplus income of the estate or, in exceptional circumstances, the capital where it can afford it but they cannot be sued for mortgaged,[646] alienated nor anticipated.[647] The appropriate person to make application for the allowances is the Committee. Voluntary allowances have been made for the benefit of the ward's children,[648] his spouse from whom he has been judicially separated,[649] and for relatives,[650] servants,[651] and church or educational purposes[652] where in the circumstances the ward would probably have made the allowances himself.

---

[641] O.67, r.99(2).
[642] The payment of costs out of mortgage is not favoured by the court. See Colles, *op. cit.*, p.84.
[643] Unreported, High Court, Finnegan P., October 15, 2002
[644] See s.3 and sch.1.
[645] Lunacy Regulation (Ireland) Act 1871, s.117.
[646] *In re Weld* 20 Ch. D. 451.
[647] *In re Robinson* 27 Ch. D. 160.
[648] *In re Jones, ex parte Haydock* 5 Russ 154; *Bradshaw v. Bradshaw* 1 J. &W. 647.
[649] *In re Robinson* 27 Ch. D. 160.
[650] *In re Thomas* 2 Phill. 169.
[651] *In re Carysfort* 1 Cr. & Ph. 78.
[652] *In re Strickland* 19 W.R. 515.

Sale or mortgaging of the ward's property

While the ward retains ownership of property and money these may be dealt with or used in accordance with orders made by the court. Section 63 of the Lunacy Regulation (Ireland) Act 1871 provides for the circumstances in which a ward's property may be sold. It provides that where it appears to the court to be just and reasonable or for the benefit of the ward an order may be made for the sale or mortgaging of land or stock. The sale or mortgage must be:

> "for the purpose of raising money to be applied... for or towards all or any of the purposes following:
>
> 1. The payment of the [ward's] debts or engagements;
> 2. The discharge of any incumbrances on his estates;
> 3. The payment of any debt or expenditure incurred or made after inquisition....for the [ward's] maintenance or otherwise for his benefit;
> 4. The payment of or provision for the expenses of his future maintenance;
> 5. The payment of the costs of applying for, obtaining and executing the inquiry and of opposing the same;
> 6. The payment of the costs of any proceeding under or consequent on the inquisition, or incurred under order of [the Judge]; and
> 7. The payment of the costs of any such sale, mortgage, charge or other disposition as his hereby authorised to be made."

While a restrictive interpretation of the section would suggest that the court may order a sale only where the object of the sale is to fund expenditure in practice the section has been interpreted widely or the court has taken the view that its jurisdiction is not fettered by its provisions. Accordingly the court has authorised sales to provide for nursing home expenses and to prevent a property being vandalised.[653] It has also ordered sales of dilapidated property and the purchase of new property in the ward's name preserving the rights of residence of a cohabitee of a ward in the property.[654]

The procedure for making application to the court to sell or mortgage the property of the ward is set out in Order 67, rule 81 and Order 67, rule 82 respectively.

The court's powers to authorise the making of leases[655]

Where the ward is a lessor Where a ward is entitled to land or leaseholds for an absolute interest the President of the High Court may, if for his benefit, direct the Committee to make a lease or under-lease to encourage the erection or repair or improvement of buildings on the land or for farming or other purposes subject to such rents and covenants as the President may specify in the order.[656]

Where a ward is entitled to land in fee or in tail and the President of the High Court

---

[653] See *Wards of Court – An Information Booklet* (Department of Justice, Equality and Law Reform, 1988), p.10.

[654] *In the matter of JR A Ward of Court* [1993] I.L.R.M. 657.

[655] This power is exercised rarely in practice.

[656] Lunacy Regulation (Ireland) Act 1871, s.78.

is of the opinion that it is for the benefit of the ward that a mine or quarry which is already opened in upon or under the land should be worked he may empower the Committee by order to make a lease of mines and quarries concerned with or without the surface or other land convenient to be held with them subject to the rents and covenants contained in the order.[657]

Where it is necessary for the maintenance of the ward or his immediate family or expedient in the due course of management of the ward's estate that a mine or quarry in on or under land to which he is seised or possessed in fee or in tail should be opened and worked, the Committee of the Estate under order of the President of the High Court, may make a lease of the unopened mines or quarries with or without the surface and any land convenient to be held with same subject to the rents and covenants specified in the President's order.[658]

The moneys arising such a lease must be applied in or towards the maintenance of the ward and his/her immediate family and the surplus not so applied must be carried to a separate account to be applied in the payment off of debts and incumbrances or in any other manner for the ward's benefit that the President directs. On the ward's death any moneys remaining to the credit of the account must be treated for the purposes of succession as real estate.[659]

If a ward is entitled to a limited estate in land only but has a power of leasing then the Committee of the Estate may, under an order from the President of the High Court execute power of leasing and after deduction of all necessary incidental charges and expenses must apply all fines or other moneys for the ward's benefit as the President orders. Upon the ward's death any surplus remaining must be treated for the purposes of succession as realty unless the ward is a tenant for life in which case it is treated as personalty.[660]

When the ward is entitled to renew a lease and it would be for his benefit to do so or he might, if not under a disability be compelled to renew the President the High Court may, by order, empower the Committee to accept a surrender in the name of the ward and authorise him to execute a new lease for the term of the surrendered lease or otherwise as ordered by the President. However, the renewed lease may not be executed unless any fine or sum of money payable on renewal has been paid and all covenants by the lessee and tenant paid and performed and a counterpart duly executed by the lessee.[661]

As in cases where the Committee exercises a power of leasing under Section 83 all sums received upon renewal must, after deduction of all necessary incidental charges and expenses be applied for the ward's benefit as the President of the High Court directs and on the ward's death any portion remaining unexpended must considered for the purposes of succession as real estate unless the patient was a tenant for life in which case it is considered as personalty.[662]

Leases made by the Committee under the powers conferred by the 1871 Act are as valid and binding as if made by the ward when sane.[663] Leases of entailed land are as

---

[657] Lunacy Regulation (Ireland) Act 1871, s.79.
[658] *Ibid.*, s.80.
[659] *Ibid.*, s.82.
[660] *Ibid.*, ss.83 and 85.
[661] *Ibid.*, s.84.
[662] *Ibid.*, s.85.
[663] *Ibid.*, s.89.

binding against the ward, his heir and the remainderman, if any, and their successors, including the State as if the ward held the estate in fee simple. However, the reversioner entitled upon the ward's death has the same remedies and advantages against the lessee as the ward or Committee might have had.[664]

Powers of leasing may also be granted by the President exercising his jurisdiction in wardship under section 63 of the Settled Land Acts 1882–1890

The procedure for making application to the court to authorise the making or renewal of a lease of underlease of the ward's property is set out in Order 67, rule 80 of the Rules of the Superior Courts.

Where the ward is a lessee[665] Where a ward is a lessee of a lease the Committee of the Estate may be empowered by an order of the President of the High Court to surrender the lease and accept a new lease of the premises comprised in the surrendered lease for the same term[666] and subject to the same encumbrances and conditions[667] as the surrendered lease. In that case every fine, premium or income upon renewal and all reasonable charges incidental to it may be paid out of the estate or be charged upon the leasehold premises as directed by the President of the High Court.

Where the ward is entitled to a lease or underlease and it appears to the President of the High Court that it is desirable and for the benefit of the ward or his estate that it be disposed of the Committee of the Estate may under order of the President surrender, assign or otherwise dispose of it upon the terms and in the manner directed by the President.[668]

Court's powers to authorise exchanges and partitions of land[669]

Where a ward is entitled to land the President of the High Court may, if it is for his benefit and expedient direct the Committee to effect an exchange of that land for other land to be held subject to the same trusts powers and provisions.[670]

In cases where the ward is entitled to an undivided share of land and it is for his benefit and expedient the President of the High Court may direct the Committee to join with the co-owners and do all things necessary to effect a partition on the terms directed by the President of the High Court.[671] Moneys received by the Committee from the sale or partition must be applied for the ward's benefit as the President of the High Court orders and on the ward's death any sum remaining unapplied for his benefit must be considered real estate for the purposes of succession unless the ward is a tenant for life in which case it must be considered as personal estate.[672]

Where a person contracts to make a partition or exchange of land prior to becoming

---

[664] *Ibid.*, s.81.
[665] Applications by a ward as lessee are rare in practice.
[666] Lunacy Regulation (Ireland) Act 1871, s.60.
[667] *Ibid.*, s.62.
[668] *Ibid.*, s.72.
[669] These powers are rarely used in practice.
[670] Lunacy Regulation (Ireland) Act 1871, s.74.
[671] *Ibid.*
[672] Lunacy Regulation (Ireland) Act 1871, ss.74 and 85.

a ward[673] of court and either a decree for specific performance is granted or the contract is not disputed the President of the High Court, if he thinks it ought to be performed,[674] may on the application of any plaintiff in the suit or party claiming the benefit of the contract, authorise the Committee to carry it out.[675]

Termination of wardship

Traverse of inquiry

Where a person has been declared to be of unsound mind and incapable of managing his affairs by inquisition[676] a petition to traverse the inquiry may be presented to dispute the finding in question on the grounds (a) that it runs contrary to the weight of the evidence, or (b) that illegal evidence has been admitted or (c) that the jury has been misdirected at hearing by Commission.

The ward himself or a third party showing how the finding adversely affects him are entitled to present the petition. In the latter case the third party must give sufficient security for all parties proceeding to trial, if required by the President of the High Court and provide it within three weeks of the date of the order.[677]

The petition must be presented within three months of the day of return of the inquisition. In his order granting the traverse the President must set a trial date for a time not exceeding six months from the date of the order. Where the petition is not presented within the prescribed time or the petitioner fails to give the required security or does not proceed to trial within the prescribed six months then his/her right to traverse and the right of all claiming through him/her is absolutely barred unless the President of the High Court in the special circumstances of a case makes an order[678] permitting to traverse to be heard out of time.[679]

At the hearing of the traverse the Committee must uphold the finding of the inquisition.[680] If a petitioner succeeds at the trial of the traverse he should then present a petition to have the inquisition and proceedings superseded. Where a inquisition has been successfully superseded any Medical Visitors reports will be destroyed unless the President of the High Court directs otherwise.[681] If the President of the High Court is dissatisfied with the verdict returned upon a traverse, he may order one or more new trials.[682]

Where a petition to traverse or for a new trial is filed the jurisdiction of the President of the High Court, the power to levy fees and percentages and the authority of the

---

[673] Contracts made when a person was of unsound mind but not a ward may be confirmed by order of the President of the High Court. See *Baldwyn v. Smith* [1900] 1 Ch. 588.

[674] The order will not be made if it is prejudicial to the ward. See Abraham, *op. cit.*, p.209.

[675] Lunacy Regulation (Ireland) Act 1871, s.72.

[676] A person is not permitted to traverse more than once. See Lunacy Regulation (Ireland) Act 1871, s.99.

[677] Lunacy Regulation (Ireland) Act 1871, s.97.

[678] Application must be made by petition for an extension.

[679] Lunacy Regulation (Ireland) Act 1871, s.98.

[680] See Abraham, *op. cit.*, p.412.

[681] Lunacy Regulation (Ireland) Act 1871, s.59.

[682] *Ibid.*, s.99.

Committee of the Person and the estate to act on the ward's behalf are unaffected.[683] In addition the solicitor for the ward is entitled to his costs of the traverse out of the estate unless the proceedings are shown to have been frivolous or vexatious.[684]

Petition for a new trial

In cases where the issue of whether a person is of unsound mind is ordered to be heard before a jury and under the powers contained in section 16 the President sends the issue to be tried by the common law courts a petition to traverse may not be presented. Instead a petition for a new trial of the inquisition in the Circuit or High Court should be presented. It is however usually based on the same grounds as a petition for a traverse.[685] It must be filed within three months of the date of trial of the issue and unlike the limits on the presentation of the petition to traverse there is no limit on the number of times a petition for a new trial may be presented.[686]

As in the case of the trial on a traverse the duty of the Committee on the hearing of a petition for a new trial is to uphold the finding of the inquisition and he is entitled to his costs of doing so.[687] If the petitioner for a new trial is successful then s/he should proceed by petition to supersede the inquisition and proceedings. Again the filing of a petition of new trial does not interfere with the jurisdiction of the President of the High Court, the power to levy fees and percentages and the authority of the Committee[688] and the solicitor for the ward is allowed his costs of the proceedings out of the estate unless the proceedings are shown to be frivolous or vexatious.[689]

Petition for a supersedeas

A petition for a supersedeas may be presented in cases where there has been an irregularity in the course of the proceedings. In practice however this procedure is obsolete as the result was always the issue of a new petition.

Dismissal from wardship on death of a ward

Where a ward dies the Committee of the Person or of the estate should immediately inform the Registrar of Wards of Court. The Registrar, may then open and read any will[690] of the deceased ward, to ascertain the identity of the executor, and also what direction, if any, there is regarding the ward's funeral or place of interment. The Registrar must then transmit the will to be dealt with by the Probate Officer,[691] and must certify the death and the opening and delivering out of the will accordingly.[692]

---

[683] *Ibid.,* s.100.

[684] *Wentworth v. Tubb* 2 Y and Ch. Cas. 537.

[685] See Harris, *op. cit.,* p.29.

[686] Lunacy Regulation (Ireland) Act 1871, s.101.

[687] See Abraham, *op. cit.,* p.412.

[688] Lunacy Regulation (Ireland) Act 1871, s.100.

[689] See *Wentworth v. Tubb, op. cit.*

[690] The language of the statute is wide and covers any paper writing purporting or alleged to be the ward's will. See O.67, r.88, Rules of the Superior Courts.

[691] The ward's estate will, of course, be distributed in accordance with the terms of his will. Where

The Registrar must also destroy all Medical Visitors reports relating to the ward and direct the Accountant to suspend all periodic payments from the funds in court.

While the powers of the President of the High Court continue after the ward's death,[693] the Committee's authority to act on behalf of the ward is terminated,[694] and it becomes the duty of the personal representative to administer the ward's estate and the only remaining duty of the Committee is to have the ward dismissed from wardship.

To effect a dismissal the Committee[695] should lodge[696] a statement of facts in the Office of Wards of Court. It should contain the following particulars[697]:

(i)   the date of the death of the ward;
(ii) whether the ward died testate or intestate;
(iii) the claims and demands against his estate for costs, maintenance or otherwise;
(iv) who are the heirs or next of kin;
(v)   the name and address of the executor (if applicable) or proposed administrator (if ascertained), trustees under the will and devisees of his real estate.

When a statement of facts has been lodged the Registrar must make a report for the submission to the President of the High Court reciting the details in the statement of facts and stating what proceedings (if any) the Registrar recommends should be brought to wind up the matter. This report must be settled by the Registrar in the presence of and on notice to any person(s) he directs.[698]

The Committee of the Estate must or any other party interested in the confirmation of the report may apply[699] to the President for its confirmation.[700] Upon hearing this application the President may confirm the report with or without variation and make any other orders as he considers just.[701] If the application is successful a dismissal order

---

s/he dies intestate the estate will be distributed according to the rules of intestate succession. The estate of a ward does not revert to the State on his death. The latter is a common but mistaken assumption. See N. McLoughlin, "Wardship: A Legal and Medical Perspective" (1998) *Medico Legal Journal of Ireland* 61 at p.62.

[692] Lunacy Regulation (Ireland) Act 1871, s.53 and O.67, r.88, Rules of the Superior Courts.
[693] Lunacy Regulation (Ireland) Act 1871, s.51.
[694] He cannot sue on covenants made by him during the ward's lifetime nor in respect of rents even if continued in office for that purpose. See *Foot v. Leslie* 16 Lr. (Ir.) 411 nor can he enter into new agreements regarding the estate unless he has obtained the permission of the personal representatives of the ward or the devisee.
[695] If the Committee is dead then the statement of facts should be lodged by the solicitor for the late Committee, or failing him by the personal representative of the late Committee or failing him by the original petitioner in the matter or such other person as the Registrar may authorise. Where the ward dies before the appointment of any Committee of his estate the statement of facts should be lodged by the original petitioner or any other person authorised by the Registrar. See O.67, r.89, Rules of the Superior Courts.
[696] The Registrar has power to dispense with the lodgment of a statement of facts in any case in which s/he thinks fit to do so. O.67, r.89, Rules of the Superior Courts.
[697] Lunacy Regulation (Ireland) Act 1871, s.52 and O.67, r.89 of the Rules of the Superior Courts.
[698] Lunacy Regulation (Ireland) Act 1871 s.52 and O.67, r.90 of the Rules of the Superior Courts.
[699] Application is by motion supported (where necessary) by affidavit. See O.67, r.3(2).
[700] Lunacy Regulation (Ireland) Act 1871, s.54 and O.67, r.91(1).
[701] O.67, r.91(1).

will issue referring to any claims in the matter, discharging the Committee, vacating the bond where appropriate and directing the dismissal and termination of the matter generally.

The Registrar is empowered in any case in which he thinks fit[702] to dispense with the lodgment of the statement of facts[703] and with the report.[704] Where s/he has dispensed with either he may submit the minutes of the order necessary to terminate the matter to the President with any necessary evidence (if any) in support of same. The President, having considered the matter may without the attendance of counsel, solicitor or parties make an order in the terms of such minutes with or without variation.[705]

The terms of a dismissal order will generally make provision for the payment of claims in the matter, the vouching of final accounts,[706] the discharge of the Committee[707] and Receiver,[708] the vacating of their bonds and where the matter is not being sent to the High Court for administration[709] for the transfer of property to the executors, administrators or beneficiaries and will direct the dismissal and termination of the matter generally. [710]

All proven debts, measured or taxed costs incurred in the course of the proceedings and funeral expenses of the ward are payable either out of the funds of the court or funds held by the Committee or Receiver or by a sale of the ward's real property. The general order of priority for payment of claims is as follows:

(1) funeral expenses,
(2) costs of the solicitor having carriage of the matter and the Committee's fees (if any) and costs of dismissing[711] the matter out of wardship.
(3) past maintenance;[712]

---

[702] He may do so in cases where the estate is very small.

[703] O.67, r.89.

[704] O.67, r.90.

[705] O.67, r.91(2).

[706] The Committee or Receiver (whoever is responsible for accounting) will be directed to lodge, vouch and pass a final account.

[707] The Committee may be directed to apply balance of the ward's moneys in his hands in a certain way and to produce a certificate to the Registrar that all ascertained claims have been paid and upon the performance of these duties to be discharged and have his security vacated.

[708] The court will direct the Receiver to pass a final account, and on the due application of the balance of the ward's funds in his hands to be discharged. Occasionally where his continuance in office is required to receive the rents of the real estate he may be directed to remain on until a further order discharges him or a certificate pursuant to the President's order issues from the Registrar to the effect that the purposes for which he was kept on in office have been accomplished and ended. See Lunacy Regulation (Ireland) Act 1871, s.55(1).

[709] The order will normally direct that upon the carrying out of the administration or fulfilment of a special order, e.g. the ascertainment of the next of kin that the matter be returned to the President of the High Court for dismissal.

[710] Where a grant of probate or administration have not issued at the time of the dismissal order it operation may be made subject to the production of same to the Registrar. See Lunacy Regulation (Ireland) Act 1871, s.55(4).

[711] The costs of the argument on the hearing of the petition for dismissal have been preferred to maintenance *In re Maguire* [1923] 1 I.R. 108.

[712] The costs of past maintenance have been preferred over the costs of the Committee in a case where the ward was received into a private psychiatric institution at an approved rate of maintenance

(4) Costs of the parties in the wardship matter;

(5) Other claims in the wardship matter;

(6) Other claims including mortgage debts not connected with the wardship matter.

Where no representation has been raised to the estate of a ward who has died intestate and the ward's total assets appear to the President of the High Court not to exceed (£5,000) €6,500[713] in value then any funds to which the ward was or his personal representatives would be entitled may by direction of the President be paid, transferred or delivered to the person who would be entitled to obtain letters of administration of his estate under the Succession Act 1965 when that person makes and files a declaration in the Appendix K Form 18 with the Registrar.[714]

The schedule to the dismissal order will direct that the residue of the estate be paid to the personal representative. The residue which is usually made up of funds in court will be released to the personal representative when the final account has been passed, the costs of the solicitor having carriage have been measured or taxed and a grant of probate or letters of administration are produced to the Accountant.

Discharge of ward on his/her recovery

Where a ward recovers he may apply informally[715] to the President of the High Court to be remitted to the management of his own affairs.[716] To this end he should submit a medical report to the Registrar indicating that he has recovered[717] and the Registrar will place the matter before the President in chambers. Where there are any doubts as to the ward's recovery the President will direct a Medical Visitor to examine the ward and report to the court as to his present condition.

If the President is satisfied[718] that the ward is capable of managing his person, property and affairs, generally he will make such order as the circumstances require[719] and discharge the matter out of lunacy.[720]

The terms of the order will typically restore the ward to full possession and

---

pursuant to an order of the Judge in Lunacy. See *In re P* [1926] I.R. 422 but not where the ward was maintained in a public hospital. See Harris, *op. cit.*, p.37.

[713] Convenient euro equivalent specified by Rules of the Superior Courts (No.4) (Euro Changeover) 2001 (S.I. No.585 of 2001), art.5.

[714] O.67, r.92.

[715] Formerly there were two methods of dismissing a matter out of wardship. A petition for a writ of supersedeas being required where a ward had been declared to be of unsound mind by inquisition and application upon a Medical Visitors report being made in cases where a person was so found by summary order. In time the cumbersome procedure by supersedeas fell into disuse and is nowadays practically obsolete being required only in cases where a transcript of the record of the inquisition has been transmitted to the Court of Protection in England. For details of the procedure. See Harris, *op. cit.*, p.32.

[716] O.67, r.93.

[717] The level of mental health needed to succeed in this application is superior to that which would be required to prevent a finding of unsoundness of mind. See *AG v. Parnther* 3 Bro. CC. 440.

[718] The President may require the personal attendance of the ward to satisfy himself.

[719] The terms of the order will generally be settled beforehand between the Registrar and the solicitors for the parties.

[720] O.67, r.93.

management of his property on the Committee's paying the costs and debts in the matter and filing and passing a final account in the Office of Wards of Court. It will also direct the discharge of the Receiver and the Committee on the passing of their final account. Alternatively the order may restore the ward to part of his/her property or as to income only until such time as s/he is fit to take full charge of it at which time a further order will be made dismissing the matter out of wardship.

On the dismissal of the matter all Medical Visitors reports are destroyed.[721] The costs of the application are payable out of the ward's estate unless the application is found by the President of the High Court to be fraudulent in which case the promoters of the action must bear their own costs.[722]

The Circuit Court's jurisdiction

Judges of the Circuit Court also have jurisdiction in relation to wardship matters but only where they concern persons alleged to be of unsound mind not the other categories of wards.[723] By virtue of section 22(2) of the Courts (Supplemental Provisions) Act 1961, as amended,[724] the Circuit Court has, jurisdiction in cases where the property of the person alleged to be of unsound mind and incapable of managing his affairs does not exceed (£5.000) €6,348.69 in value, or[725] the income therefrom does not exceed (£300) €380.92 [726] per annum.[727] The jurisdiction is concurrent with that of the High Court and is exercisable by the Circuit Court for the county where the person of or alleged to be of unsound mind ordinarily resides.[728] In practice, however, few applications are made in the Circuit Court as application may be made more expeditiously in the High Court.[729]

Procedure for admitting a person to wardship of the Circuit Court

Procedure to be followed in the Circuit Court when applying to have somebody made a ward of that court is governed by Order 47 of the Circuit Court Rules 2001[730] and in the absence of a provision of these rules dealing with a particular aspect of procedure, by the High Court rules and practice.[731]

---

[721] Lunacy Regulation (Ireland) Act 1871, s.59.

[722] See Abraham, *op. cit.*, p.412.

[723] The origins of the jurisdiction lie in the County Court Jurisdiction in Lunacy (Ireland) Act 1880 which conferred limited jurisdiction in wardship matters upon all Civil Bill Courts. By virtue of s.51 of the Courts of Justice Act 1924, this jurisdiction became exercisable by the Circuit Court.

[724] See Courts Act 1971, s.2(3).

[725] Note the monetary jurisdiction is stated in the alternative. Thus property of less than €6, 500 in value or income of less than €375 may ground the jurisdiction.

[726] Euro equivalent as specified by Council Regulation (EC) No. 974/98 of May 3, 1998 on the introduction of the Euro. See Arts 1 and 14.

[727] The jurisdiction of the President of High Court in this regard is to be found in s.68 of the 1871 Act. S.22(2) of the 1961 Act confers concurrent jurisdiction under s.68 of the 1871 on the Circuit Court. The current monetary limits were fixed by s.2(3) of the Courts Act 1971.

[728] O.2(d), Circuit Court Rules 2001.

[729] Particularly those under ss 68 and 103 of the 1871 Act.

[730] S.I. No. 510 of 2001.

[731] O.47, r.20.

Proceedings in the Circuit Court are commenced by the petitioner or his solicitor filing of a Civil Bill as to Capacity[732] with the County Registrar[733] of the Circuit Court of the county where the person of or alleged to be of unsound mind resides.[734] The Civil Bill as to Capacity should be in Form No 2F of Schedule B to the Circuit Court Rules and be signed by the applicant and his solicitor (if any). The Civil Bill should set out:

(a)   the name, address and religion of the next of kin and of the persons in whose house and under whose care the person alleged to be of unsound mind is for the time being residing;

(b)   the amount and nature of his property and debts;

(c)   the names and ages of the members of his family who are dependent upon him;

(d)   that his property does not exceed (£5,000) €6348.69 in value or that the income therefrom does not exceed (£300) €380.92 per annum.

Prior to the issue[735] of the Civil Bill two affidavits should also be filed, one sworn by a person interested in the well-being of the person alleged to be of unsound mind and the second by a medical practitioner.[736]

The affidavit[737] of the person interested in the well-being of the respondent[738] must attest to the name and residence of the person alleged to be of unsound mind and of his next of kin (in so far as the details are known to the deponent). It must also set out evidence, within the deponent's personal knowledge, of the alleged unsoundness of mind of the respondent and must give details of the property required to be protected and to be applied for the respondent's advantage.[739]

The affidavit of the medical practitioner[740] must set out "distinctly and particularly" the nature of the respondent's alleged unsoundness of mind and the evidence as to the

---

[732] *Ibid.*, O.47, r.1.

[733] "County Registrar" is defined by the 2001 Rules as including any deputy County Registrar and any person appointed to act as such Registrar. See Interpretation of Terms, para.5.

[734] O.2(d).

[735] A Civil Bill is deemed to be issued when it is presented to the Circuit Court Office in a county having jurisdiction according to the Circuit Court Rules, sealed, marked with the record number by the proper officer subject to the provisions of s.7(6)(a)(ii) of the Courts Act 1964. See O.11, r.3, Circuit Court Rules 2001. S.7(6)(a)(ii) of the 1964 Act provides that where service of a document on a person is effected by sending a copy by prepaid post in an envelope pursuant to s.7(3) the document shall be deemed to be issued at the time the envelope is posted.

[736] O.47, r.1.

[737] As to the form which affidavits must generally take. See O.25.

[738] Any relation of the person alleged to be of unsound mind having an interest in the well-being of the person may institute proceedings. Where a person not related to such person institutes proceedings they should set out their connection with the person and their special grounds of interest in the well-being of the person in an affidavit and in the Civil Bill as to capacity.

[739] O.47, r.2.

[740] The affidavit should be grounded on a medical report from the medical practitioner. It should be exhibited in the affidavit. The report should specify the date of the examination, the nature of the symptoms suffered by the patient, the psychiatric condition from which the patient is suffering and whether this is likely to continue on a long term basis.

respondent's demeanour, conversation, acts and physical causes upon which the medical practitioner's opinion is founded.[741]

The applicant or his solicitor must cause the civil bill together with notice of filing of the affidavits to be served[742] on the respondent and the person with whom he resides or under whose care s/he is, as soon as shall be practicable after the civil bill is issued.[743]

If the respondent wishes to contest the proceedings he should send an appearance in the prescribed form to the County Registrar within ten days of service [744] of the civil bill upon him (exclusive of the day of service) and lodge or send a copy of the appearance with or to the applicant or his solicitor.[745]

Where the respondent fails to lodge an appearance the applicant must, before proceeding further, apply to the Circuit Court Office under Order 19 of the Circuit Court Rules for an order that a guardian *ad litem* be appointed for the respondent.[746]

Within 10 days of the entry of the appearance[747] the respondent should give or send a copy of the defence by post to the applicant or his solicitor and lodge with or send the original to the County Registrar.[748] The defence should state clearly the grounds upon which the defendant disputes the plaintiff's claim.[749] The defence should be carefully drafted as amendments are subject to the discretion of the court or County Registrar to permit amendments.[750] No defence will be admitted to defeat the claim unless, in the opinion of the judge, it could fairly have been inferred from the particulars contained in the written document.[751]

Where the time for entry of an appearance has expired or, in cases where an appearance has been entered, on the expiry of the time for the lodgment of a defence, the applicant or his solicitor may serve notice of trial upon all persons served with notice of the civil bill and any other persons who may have entered an appearance to the civil bill.[752] Where the petitioner or his solicitor does not serve notice of trial then the person alleged to be of unsound mind and any person who has entered an appearance on his behalf may do so in accordance with Order 33, rules 4 and 5 of the Circuit Court Rules 2001,[753] or may apply to the court by motion on notice to the applicant to have the civil bill dismissed for want of prosecution.[754]

---

[741] O.47, r.3.

[742] Service is effected by the Summons Servers appointed by the County Registrar, O.10, r.5.

[743] O.47, r.4.

[744] O.47, r.5 and O.15, r.2. No appearance may be lodged out of time without the leave of the Circuit Court judge or by agreement between the parties. O.15, r.2.

[745] O.47, r.5 and O.15.

[746] O.47, r.5 and O.15, r.3.

[747] A defence may not be entered out of time without the leave of the County Registrar or by agreement between the parties See O.15, rr.4 and 17.

[748] O.47, r.5, O.15, r.4 .

[749] O.47, r.5, O.15, r.5.

[750] *Ibid.*

[751] *Ibid.*

[752] O.47, r.6.

[753] O.33, r.4 provides, in effect, that where the applicant has failed to serve notice of trial within ten days after the delivery of the defence the respondent may do so and may file the same in accordance with the 2001 Rules. R.5 provides in effect that if the applicant does not within ten days after the delivery of the defence serve notice of trial, the respondent may, in lieu of serving notice of trial in accordance with r.4, apply to court to dismiss the action for want of prosecution and on the hearing

At the hearing the Circuit Court judge will consider the evidence in support of the application and if he considers it insufficient he may require such other evidence as he considers necessary and expedient. S/he may direct a medical practitioner other than the practitioner upon whose affidavit the Civil Bill was grounded to make a confidential report to him on the circumstances of the case. He may also adjourn the hearing until such a report has been received.[755]

The medical practitioner visiting and reporting under the direction of the court is entitled to such fee as the Judge may think proper. Although the Judge may direct that the allowance be paid in the first instance by the petitioner or the solicitor having carriage of the proceedings it must be dealt with by the judge as part of the expenses of the proceedings.[756]

If the judge is of the opinion on the hearing of the Civil Bill that the respondent is of unsound mind and incapable of managing his person or property and that the property requires to be protected and applied for his advantage, he may declare that such person is of unsound mind and incapable of managing his person or property and that such property requires to be protected and applied for his advantage. In that event the Judge must appoint or give directions for the appointment of a guardian of the person and the property of the respondent and may commit to the guardian the care of the person and the management of his property. In any case in which the Judge may think proper he may appoint different persons guardians of the person and of the property.

Where the respondent is married the judge will usually appoint their spouse as guardian of the person and property of the respondent spouse.[757] Where the respondent is unmarried or where a spouse is unavailable to act the person who is next of kin may be appointed.[758] However, where the judge considers that a spouse or next of kin would be incapable of acting as guardian s/he may appoint a stranger if that would better serve the interests of the patient.[759] The preferences and wishes of the respondent may be taken into account by the judge in appointing a guardian where the respondent is capable of understanding the nature of the application.[760]

Whether the Judge makes a declaration order or dismisses the civil bill he must make such order as to the costs and expenses of and incidental to the proceedings as seems right to him.[761] Every application to the court subsequent to the declaration order must be made by motion on affidavit setting forth the facts relevant to the application.[762]

Where an order is made directing the appointment of such a guardian or guardians the person to be appointed unless otherwise ordered must give security to be approved

---

of such application the judge may order the action to be dismissed accordingly and may make such other order and on such terms as to him may seem just.

[754] O.47, r.7.

[755] O.47, r.8.

[756] O.47, r.11.

[757] *In re Davey* [1892] 3 Ch. 38.

[758] *In re Booth* 15 L.T. 429.

[759] See *Gaffney v. Gaffney* (1896) 31 I.L.T.R. 11.

[760] *Ex parte Fletcher* (1801) 6 Ves. 427.

[761] O.47, r.10. Where the application which is brought to the court is *bona fide* in the interests of the person alleged to be of unsound mind and for his benefit exclusively then even if the application is unsuccessful the costs of the application may be allowed out of the estate of the person alleged to be of unsound mind. See *In re M.J.* [1929] I.R. 509.

[762] O.47, r.19.

by the Judge for the faithful discharge of his duties. The guardian must duly account for what he receives as such guardian and must pay the same as the Judge directs.[763]

The Powers and Duties of a Guardian appointed by the Circuit Court

The nature and extent of the powers to be exercised by the guardian of the person or property will be specified by the Circuit Court Judge.

The Circuit Court Judge is empowered to direct the investment of any fund of the ward in securities and subject to such conditions as may seem proper.[764] He is also empowered to direct the Guardian of the property to pass such accounts as he shall think necessary at such time and in such manner as he shall appoint. All such accounts must by taken by the County Registrar and be filed in the Circuit Court Office.[765]

The Guardian must notify the County Registrar in the event that the value of the property of the person of unsound mind increases and if it is enlarged by such increase beyond the jurisdiction of the Circuit Court the County Registrar must notify this fact to the Circuit Court and to Registrar of Wards of Court.[766] Subsequently application may be made by the Guardian to the Circuit Court Judge to transfer the matter to the High Court.[767]

When any judgment or order has been made by the Circuit Court declaring any person to be of unsound mind and incapable of managing his person or property, the County Registrar must forthwith send notice of such judgment or order with a sealed copy of same to the Registrar of Wards of Court and the notice must set out the then known amount of such property and the net income arising from it.[768]

The Guardian of a person of unsound mind must also make annual returns to the County Registrar setting out the particulars which Committees of High Court wards are obliged to furnish to the Registrar of Wards of Court under Order 67, rule 68 and which are set out in Appendix K Form No. 16 of the Rules of the Superior Court.[769]

Where a person of unsound mind resides in a psychiatric institution or hospital under order of the court one of the Inspectors of Mental Hospitals must forward an annual report as to the care, treatment and general condition of the person to the County Registrar for the information of the court.[770]

Discharge from wardship of Circuit Court

Where a person found to be of unsound mind in the Circuit Court dies his/her Guardian must file a certificate or other evidence of the death with the County Registrar. S/he must also file a verified statement setting out the circumstances of the person's property

---

[763] O.47, r.9.

[764] Under proposed new investment arrangements it is suggested that responsibility for investment be transferred to a new Funds Accounting Office.

[765] O.47, r.12.

[766] O.47, r.13.

[767] *In re E McD* [1929] I.R. 523.

[768] O.47, r.14.

[769] O.47, r.16.

[770] O.47, r.15.

and the claims (if any) in respect of the costs, maintenance[771] or otherwise in the matter of the wardship.

If the Circuit Court judge is satisfied that that all claims have been duly discharged and if s/he requires that probate or letters of administration be exhibited to the County Registrar, when that requirement is met he will direct the matter to be dismissed out of the jurisdiction of the court.[772]

A person found to be of unsound mind who wishes to be discharged from wardship of the Circuit Court should apply on medical evidence of his recovery for an order discharging his Guardian.[773] The Circuit Court may make an order for discharge if, after personal examination,[774] the Circuit Court Judge is satisfied that the person concerned has been restored to sound mind and to the capacity for managing his property.[775]

Proposals for reform of the wardship system

In its *Consultation Paper on the Law and the Elderly*[776] the Law Reform Commission provisionally recommended that legislation should be enacted to deal with "adults who may be in need of protection" and if a person is in need of protection that person should become a "Protected Adult". It proposes that an adult may be in need of protection even if legally capable. The Commission provisionally proposes that there be two strands to the new system:

(a) A substitute decision making system called Guardianship. This would provide for the making of Guardianship orders in the case of people who do not have legal capacity and who are in need of guardianship and is envisaged to apply to people with a decision making disability. It would provide for the appointment of Personal Guardians who would make some of the required decisions

(b) an intervention and personal protection system which would provide for the making of specific orders – services orders, intervention orders and adult care orders. These would be available to be made in respect of two broad categories of person; (i) a person who has legal capacity but who needs protection and is unable to obtain this for himself/herself or (ii) a person who does not have legal capacity but who does not need guardianship (probably because there is no need for a substitute decision maker because no decisions need to be made.)

The system would be supervised by the new independent Office of the Public Guardian

---

[771] A guardian's claims for maintenance take priority over the payment of a debt, even where a creditor has obtained a standing order. See *In re Plenderleith* (1893) 3 Ch. 332. Maintenance in a public hospital is categorised as an ordinary debt. See *GrangeGorman Mental Hospital v. Waters* (1926).

[772] O.47, r.18 Circuit Court Rules 2001.

[773] See *Blyth v. Green* (1876) W.N. 214. The application must be brought by way of motion on notice grounded on an affidavit setting out the medical evidence that supports the application.

[774] This is a requirement in all applications for discharge. See O.47, r.17.

[775] O.47, r.17.

[776] LRC CP23–2003.

with specific decision making powers, the power to require the provision of certain services and an overall supervisory role over Personal Guardians. The Public Guardian would be subject to the Tribunal and protected adults would always have the right to appeal to the Tribunal against all substitute decisions. There would be a right of appeal to the Circuit Court against decisions of the Tribunal. Certain major health care decisions such as the turning off of a life support machine or organ donation would be specifically reserved to the President of the High Court.

CHAPTER NINE

Legal Capacity in the Context of Personal and Family Relationships

INTRODUCTION

Issues of capacity are raised by legislation and jurisprudence in the context of the personal and family relationships of the person with mental disability. To what extent should that person be protected from sexual exploitation and how does this weigh in the balance with freedom of sexual expression? How does the law address the issue of control of the capacity to procreate of the person with mental disability and what standards should be adopted in the Irish jurisdiction? What degree of capacity is required to enter a contract of marriage and what degree of incapacity should nullify a marriage? How does the mental disability of a spouse impact in the context of judicial separation and divorce? To what extent does and should the law intervene in the relationship between a parent with a mental disability and his/her child? How does and should the law address mental disability of the natural mother and adopters in the adoption process? Behind all of these questions lies the power of the law to affect society's view of the personhood of the person with mental disability. It is proposed in this section to examine the questions posed in turn, to look at comparative legislation and case law where applicable and to propose changes to the law where appropriate.

CAPACITY AND PERSONAL RELATIONSHIPS

Legal Capacity to Engage in Sexual Relations in Ireland

Article 41 of the Irish Constitution guarantees a range of family rights to the family. These rights are however, guaranteed to the family based on marriage. A number of provisions of the European Convention on Human Rights support the right of an adult to enter personal relationships. Article 8 of the Convention provides that "Everyone has the right to respect for his private and family life, his home and his correspondence." Article 12 provides that "Men and women of marriageable age have the right to marry and to found family according to the national laws governing the exercise of this right."

In Ireland, sexual relationships between people aged 17 or over are lawful provided they are consenting relationships.[1] Where people with intellectual disability or with serious mental health difficulties are concerned, the question may arise as to whether they had the capacity to consent to a sexual relationship. In this regard a dilemma presents itself in that has been expressed as follows:

---

[1] Criminal Law (Amendment) Act 1935, ss.1 and 2, Criminal Law (Sexual Offences) Act 1993, s.3.

"a balance must be maintained between respecting individual rights to sexual relationships, marriage and parenthood and the duty of society (parents, carers and others) to protect vulnerable people and people with disabilities. In this context judgments about capacity are extremely important and must be made with the aim of enabling people to make their own decisions wherever possible."[2] The common law test of capacity to consent to sexual relations requires that a person (a) must be capable of understanding what is proposed and its implications; and (b) must be able to exercise choice. In relation to (b) it will be important to consider whether one party is in a position of power, which will influence the ability of the other party to consent."[3]

Where people with intellectual disability are concerned it has been noted that relatives and/or carers may attempt to stop the relationship because of concerns about pregnancy, the existence of a sexual relationship and risks of infection ad also about possible future marriage and parenthood. The British Medical Association and Law Society of England and Wales in their report on the *Assessment of Mental Capacity Guidance for Doctors and Lawyers* advises that where a medical practitioner who is asked to give a view about the appropriateness of two people embarking on a close relationship has concerns about the capacity of one or both parties to enter the relationship s/he should see the person privately to assess and advise on capacity.[4]

Where the right of people with mental disability to enter sexual relationships is concerned, what has to be questioned is whether the correct balance is struck by the current law between them from potentially exploitative relationships and respecting their right to appropriate and satisfying relationships. The criminal law in relation to sexual offences is particularly relevant in this context and it is to its provisions that we now turn.

A person who has sexual intercourse with a woman who is incapable of understanding the situation and exercising free choice and who is aware of this defect[5] is guilty of rape.[6] The same principle holds in respect of an offence contrary to section 4 of the Criminal Law (Rape) (Amendment) Act 1990 which may be committed against a male or a female. In *D.P.P v. Morgan*,[7] it was held that to prove absence of consent the prosecution must show that the victim did not have sufficient knowledge and understanding to comprehen:

(a) that what was proposed to be done was the physical act of penetration of her body by the male organ or, if that is not proved,

---

2   See British Medical Association and Law Society of England and Wales report on the Assessment of Mental Capacity Guidance for Doctors and Lawyers (British Medical Association) December 1995, p.56.

3   *DPP v. Morgan* [1970] V.R. 337.

4   See *Report on Assessment of Mental Capacity Guidance for Doctors and Lawyers* (British Medical Association, December, 1995), p.59 In Pt IV the report offers Practical Guidelines to Doctors in assessing capacity and indicates that the doctor has a duty to enhance capacity before making a final assessment.

5   See Criminal Law (Rape) Act 1981, s.2.

6   See *R v. Barratt* (1873) L.R. 2 C.C.R. 81.

7   [1970] V.R. 337.

(b) that the act of penetration proposed was one of sexual connection as distinct from an act of a totally different character. In practice this is difficult to prove and consequently a statutory offence has been created proscribing sexual intercourse with a mentally defective girl or woman.

Section 4(1) of the Criminal Law (Amendment) Act 1935, made it an misdemeanour punishable by imprisonment for a term of up to two years for a person to have unlawful and carnal knowledge of any woman or girl who was an "idiot", or an "imbecile", or was "feeble minded" or to attempt to have same if the circumstances prove that the person knew at the time that the woman or girl was an "idiot", or an "imbecile", or "feeble minded". Prosecutions for an offence under this section had to be commenced within twelve months of the date on which the offence is alleged to have been committed.[8]

Section 254 of the Mental Treatment Act 1945 (which is still in force) makes it an aggravated offence for a person to commit a misdemeanour under section 4 of the Criminal Law (Amendment) Act 1935 when at the time of committing it s/he either: (1) had the care or charge of the woman or girl in relation to whom the misdemeanour was committed, or (2) was carrying on a mental institution and the woman or girl concerned was a patient therein, (3) was employed as an officer or servant in a mental institution or an institution for the detention of persons of unsound mind and the woman or girl was a patient or prisoner therein. If convicted under this provision the accused faces a sentence of penal servitude for a term of between three and five years or imprisonment for a term of up to two years. Section 4 of the 1935 Act is, however, repealed by the Criminal Law Sexual Offences Act 1993 so that the status of section 254 is uncertain. However, when section 6 of the Mental Health Act 2001 comes into force, section 254 will be repealed and the aggravated offence will cease to exist.

The deficiencies of the statutory offence created by section 4 of the Criminal Law (Amendment) Act 1935 were many. First, it was limited to acts of sexual intercourse and afforded no protection against other sexually exploitative conduct. Secondly, for an offence under the section to be committed it had to be shown that the girl consented to intercourse. If such consent could not be proved beyond a reasonable doubt then the accused had to be acquitted. This led to the situation where the commission of the crime of rape may have been a defence to the charge[9] Thirdly, the terms "idiot," "imbecile," and "feeble minded", were anachronistic and did not reflect modern classifications of mental disability, which proceed by defining intellectual disability as falling into the mild, moderate, severe and profound categories based on recognised intelligence quotient assessments.[10] Further the terms were not defined in the legislation. The categories appear to be borrowed from earlier legislation, which did not apply to Ireland.[11]

---

[8] Criminal Law (Amendment) Act 1935, s.4(2).

[9] See Charleton, *Offences against the Person* (Butterworths Dublin, 1999), p.314.

[10] A mental disability is classified as mild where it is IQ range 50–70, moderate where it is within the 35–49 range, severe where it is within IQ range 20–34 and profound where it is an IQ range below 20.

[11] Mental Deficiency Act 1913, s.1, defined the categories as follows: "Idiots": persons who are so deeply defective in mind from birth or from an early age as to be unable to guard themselves against common physical dangers; "Imbeciles": persons in whose case there exists from birth or from an early age mental defectiveness not amounting to idiocy yet so pronounced that they are incapable of managing themselves or their affairs or in the case of children, of being taught to do so; "Feeble

Moreover, it appears that they were mutually exclusive and it was a defence to a charge of unlawful carnal knowledge within one category that the victim fell within another.

Fourthly, given the nature of the offence the primary evidence against the accused would usually be that of the victim. It is a cruel irony that if the accused was shown to be competent to take the oath and give evidence this might be evidence that she did not fit within the categories of mental disability set out in section 4 while, if on the other hand she was adjudged incompetent because of her mental state the prosecution case would collapse at the outset.[12]

In its *Report on Sexual Offences against the Mentally Handicapped*[13] the Law Reform Commission, *inter alia*, recommended that the offence under section 4 be replaced by an offence of having unlawful sexual intercourse with another person who was at the time of the offence mentally handicapped or suffering from mental illness which in either case was of such a nature or degree that the person was incapable of guarding himself or herself against exploitation. Section 5 of the Criminal Law (Sexual Offences) Act 1993 implements most of the Law Reform Commissions regarding sexual offences against the mentally handicapped and creates three categories of offences against mentally impaired persons (a) sexual intercourse or attempted sexual intercourse with a mentally impaired person, (b) buggery[14] or attempted buggery of a mentally impaired person; (c) the commission or attempted commission of an act of gross indecency[15] by a male with another male who is mentally impaired.

In the case of (a) the relevant offence is punishable with ten years imprisonment for the completed offence, three years for attempt in the case of a first conviction, five years for attempt in the case of a second or subsequent conviction; In the case of (b) the relevant maximum sentences are the same as for sexual intercourse and attempted sexual intercourse, and in the case of (c) the maximum sentence is 10 years imprisonment.

Section 5 defines "mentally impaired" as "suffering from a disorder of the mind whether through mental handicap or mental illness, which is of such a nature or degree as to render a person incapable of living an independent life or of guarding against

---

minded persons": persons in whose case there exists from birth or from an early age mental defectiveness not amounting to imbeciles yet so pronounced that they require care, supervision and control for their own protection or for the protection of others, or, in the case of children, that they by reason of such defectiveness appear to be permanently incapable of receiving proper benefit from the instruction in ordinary schools.

[12] This was the result in two cases before the Circuit Court in 1973, *DPP v. JS* and *DPP v. MW*. See Charleton, "*Criminal Law – Protecting the Mentally Subnormal against Sexual Exploitation*" (1984) six D.U.L.J. NS 165.

[13] LRC 33–1990.

[14] There is no statutory definition of buggery (also known as sodomy) but the established definition is that of Stephen propounded in his Digest of the Criminal Law (9th ed., Macmillan & Co., London, 1877), p.169: "Everyone commits the felony called sodomy who (a) carnally knows any animal or (b) being a male, carnally knows any man or any woman (per annum)".

[15] There is no statutory definition of gross indecency. In general the courts have adopted general definitions. In the Canadian case of *Quesnel v. Quesnel* (1979) 51 C.C.C. (2d) 270, 280 the Ontario Court of Appeal held that it may be defined as a "marked departure from the decent conduct expected from the average Canadian in the circumstances that existed." In *Norris v. Attorney General* [1984] I.R. 36 McWilliam J. stated that the classification of behaviour as grossly indecent may depend upon whether it is committed in public or private.

serious exploitation." The question of whether the complainant was mentally impaired at the time of the offence is one of fact to be decided by the jury in a trial on indictment.[16]

The accused will not be guilty of an offence involving sexual intercourse or buggery if he is married to or believes with reasonable cause that he is married to the mentally impaired person. However, following the removal of the spousal rape exemption by the Criminal Law Rape Amendment Act 1990 a man could be convicted of rape if he had intercourse with his wife when she was so mentally disabled as to be incapable of giving consent to it.[17]

To secure a conviction under section 5 the prosecution must prove that the accused knew or was reckless as to the mental impairment of the victim. Recklessness, *i.e.* the taking of a serious advertent risk as to the victim being mentally impaired is a sufficient mental element. Section 5(3) of the Act partly reverses the onus of proof by providing that "it shall be a defence for the accused that at the time of the alleged commission of the offence he did not know and had no reason to suspect that the person in respect of whom he is charged was mentally impaired." Accordingly it would appear that it is for the defence to prove the absence of a mental element on the balance of probabilities.[18]

The latter criterion of having no reason to suspect is not necessarily an objective one. In *R v. Hudson*,[19] it was held that the equivalent English provision required a subjective test to be employed. Thus the question to be asked was whether the defendant himself knew or had reason to suspect that the complainant was mentally impaired. In *Hudson*, it was also held that the entire circumstances of the case had to be put to the jury so that a defendant who had deliberately closed his eyes to the complainant's condition would not escape conviction. The offence created by section 5 is intended to deal with those who have sexual intercourse or other sexual contact with persons who do not fall within the category of low intellectual ability contemplated by the rule in *D.P.P. v. Morgan*.[20] The offence will be one of less gravity than rape because the complainant will in some sense have consented.

Commentary

It is interesting to note that section 128(1)(a) of the English Mental Health Act 1959, as amended and remains in force, creates an offence for a man who is a manager or an officer on the staff of or otherwise employed in a hospital or mental nursing home to have unlawful sexual intercourse with a woman who receiving treatment in that hospital or home as an outpatient on the premises of which the hospital or home forms a part. However, it is not an offence if he did not know and had no reason to suspect the woman to be a mentally disordered patient.[21] The maximum penalty is two years

---

[16] See *R v. Rivett* (1950) 34 Cr. App. R. 87 at 94 in which Lord Goddard C.J. stated "it is for the jury and not for medical men of whatever eminence to determine the issue. Unless and until Parliament ordains that this question is to be determined by a panel of medical men, it is to a jury, after a proper direction by a judge that by the law of this country a decision is to be entrusted".

[17] *D.P.P. v. Morgan* [1970] V.R. 337.

[18] See analysis of s.29(2) of the Misuse of Drugs Act 1977 by the Court of Appeal in *The People (DPP) v. Byrne, Healy and Kelleher* [1998] 2 I.R. 417.

[19] [1966] 1 Q.B. 448.

[20] [1970] V.R. 337.

[21] Mental Health Act 1959 (UK), s.128(2).

imprisonment.[22] The offence is also applied[23] to homosexual acts with a man who is suffering from severe mental handicap. It is submitted that consideration might be given to creating (in the light of the imminent repeal of section 254) of an aggravated offence under section 5 of the Criminal Law (Sexual Offences) Act 1993 where the perpetrator is the manager or employee of an approved centre and the mentally impaired person is a patient or an outpatient receiving treatment at that centre.

Secondly, as mentioned above the status of section 254 of the Mental Treatment Act 1954 is unclear in view of the fact that the Criminal Law (Sexual Offences) Act 1993 repeals section 4 of the Criminal Law (Amendment) Act 1935 but makes no reference to section 254 of the 1945 Act in its provisions. However, when section 6 of the Mental Health Act 2001 comes into force section 254 will be repealed. The Law Reform Commission has recommended the retention of the provision and the increase of the maximum sentence for an offence under it to 10 years. Thomas O'Malley comments the because of the additional grave breach of trust involved there is much to be said on grounds of social policy for marking out institutional abuse by an increase in penalty as more heinous than crimes arising from relationships formed in the community.[24]

Thirdly, commenting on the social attitudes and policy adopted by section 5 of the 1993 Act, he states:

> "While there are many aspects of the section to be welcomed, notably the range of offences covered and their gender based application, it reflects certain ancient biases against mentally disabled persons being unable to make personal decisions and the more insidious prejudice against mentally disabled women who were traditionally deemed 'uncontrollable' so long as they were fertile."[25]

Thomas O'Malley also notes that even allowing the assumption that prosecutorial discretion will diminish the incidence of "hard cases" the section fails to reflect the right of persons who are mentally impaired, to have a sexual life.[26] He urges that in applying this section the criminal courts be vigilant to interpret it in accordance with fundamental rights guaranteed expressly or implicitly by the Constitution including the right to marry,[27] the right to privacy,[28] and the right to beget children.[29] It is submitted

---

[22] *Ibid.*, s.128(3).

[23] *Ibid.*, s.1(4).

[24] See *Sexual Offences Law Policy and Punishment* (1996), p.131.

[25] *Ibid.*, p.134.

[26] The right to establish and develop relationships with other human beings is recognised by Art.8 of the European Convention on Human Rights. Interestingly while the *United Nations Declaration on the Rights of Mentally Retarded Persons* (1971) recognises the persons right to live with his own family. It says nothing about his right to develop sexual and family relationships for himself. Brenda Hoggett comments "There are obvious risks of degradation and exploitation against which some people may need protection but that protection need not be given at the cost of denying to mentally handicapped people the opportunity to form warm and satisfying relationships". See Mental Health Law (Sweet & Maxwell, London, 1990), p.334.

[27] *Ryan v. Attorney General* [1965] I.R. 294.

[28] *Kennedy v. Ireland* [1987] I.L.R.M. 587.

[29] *Murray v. Ireland* [1991] I.L.R.M. 465 (S.C.). See O'Malley, *Sexual Offences Law Policy and Punishment* (Round Hall Sweet & Maxwell, 1996), p.133. The right to establish and develop relationships with other human beings is protected by Article 8 of the European Convention on Human Rights to which Ireland is a signatory.

that the adoption of such an approach is to be welcomed if the fundamental rights of persons with mental disability are to be preserved and are consistent with the intention of the legislation. Indeed when introducing the 1993 legislation to the Dáil, the then Minister for Justice stated:

> "Mental impairment is sometimes, particularly in a case of mild mental impairment, a difficult concept to quantify in the context of offences committed against such persons. A very mildly mentally handicapped person may be able to give consent to sexual intercourse and I do not wish anything in this Bill to do anything that might be seen as unduly restrictive in relation to such persons"[30]

Further, in a Discussion Paper in 1998, the Department of Justice Equality and Law Reform expressed the view that the objective of the criminal law is "to achieve a satisfactory balance between protecting mentally impaired persons from sexual abuse and ensuring their right to engage in loving including sexual relationships where circumstances allow." It continued however, in a qualified vein to state that it "is doubtful if the criminal law can be expressed with the type of sensitivity that would achieve this balance"[31]

The National Association for the Intellectually Disabled of Ireland (NAMHI) has pointed out that the Law Reform Commission in its report argued that it should not be a criminal offence for a mentally impaired person to engage in sexual activity with another mentally impaired person but this freedom was not incorporated into the 1993 legislation.[32] This would suggest that the criminal law's ambit is in fact over inclusive and discriminatory and may in fact be impeding the ability of persons with intellectually disability to enter relationships. It is interesting to note that mental impairment under the 1993 legislation is defined in terms of the victim's ability to guard against serious exploitation but it is not clear what the outcome would be if the accused was also seriously mentally impaired within that definition.

Fourthly, as to whether the legislation meets its protective aims the point must be made that it does not apply to indecent conduct beyond sexual intercourse or buggery, and attempts at same except in the case of gross indecency in males. Accordingly sexual acts between a man and a woman, which fall short of intercourse or buggery or attempts at same where the subject of the charge is mentally impaired, are not unlawful. This loophole needs to be addressed if the legislation is to live up to its aim of protecting people with mental impairment against serious sexual exploitation.

Fifthly, it must be conceded that it is open to question whether the creation of a criminal offence will in fact protect persons with mental disability against exploitation. It is acknowledged that convictions in relation to sexual offences are in general difficult to secure because the evidence in most cases is uncorroborated. In cases where a complainant is a person with a mental disability a judge may well exercise his discretion to warn against conviction on the uncorroborated evidence of the complainant and in

---

[30] *Dáil Debates*, Vol.432, June 23, 1993.
[31] *The Law on Sexual Offences A Discussion Paper*, Department of Justice, Equality and Law Reform (1998), Chap.9.
[32] See *"Who Decides and How? People with Intellectual Disabilities and Decision Making A Discussion Document"*, NAMHI, October 2003.

some cases the court may decide that the complainant is not competent to give evidence. On the other hand, it has been argued that notwithstanding the difficulties of prosecuting an sexual offence involving a mentally impaired person it may be possible to provide support and advice to enable person who is mentally impaired to give reliable evidence and the opinion of a medical practitioner or other professional may assist the court in reaching a decision as to whether the person then has the capacity to take the oath and give evidence. Further, professionals with knowledge of intellectual disability may be in a position to assist the court by giving evidence on the level of understanding of a particular witness with an intellectual disability.[33]

MARITAL CAPACITY

The law regarding capacity to enter marriage in Ireland

The Marriage of Lunatics Act 1811 provides, *inter alia*, that where a person has been found to be lunatic "by Inquisition" or where as a "Lunatic or Person under a Phrenzy" his/her person or estate has been committed to the care or custody of trustees and any such person marries before being declared sane that marriage is null and void to all intents and purposes.[34] It appears that the provisions of this Act may apply even where a marriage has been contracted during a lucid interval.[35]

    At common law, a person with mental disability may be capable of giving a valid consent to marriage where s/he understands the nature of the marriage contract and its resulting obligations and duties.[36] Since this is a relatively simple matter the degree of understanding required may not be as great as it is for the purpose of making a valid will.[37] If a party is capable of understanding the legal consequences and responsibilities which form an essential part of the concept of marriage, *i.e.* that the relationship of marriage is monogamous, interminable except by death or divorce and involves mutual support and encouragement, capacity is present.

Nullity of marriage – Grounds

Absence of consent

Where a party, at the time of the marriage is unable due to mental or psychological incapacity to give "full free and informed consent" to the marriage a marriage will be void *ab initio*. A number of factors may render a party incapable of giving consent. They may be transitory such as temporary intoxication or more long term such as chronic mental illness. It is recognised that intoxication which is of such a degree as to induce

---

[33] See British Medical Association/Law Society of England and Wales Report on the *Assessment of Mental Capacity Guidance for Doctors and Lawyers* (British Medical Association December 1995), p.63.

[34] 51 Geo 111 C 37 which extended the provisions of 15 Geo 11 to Ireland.

[35] *Turner v. Meyers* (1808) 1 Hag. Con. 414 at 417.

[36] *Durham v. Durham* (1885) 10 P.D. 80; *Hunter v. Edney* (1885) 10 P.D. 93. *In re Park's Estate, Park v. Park* [1953] 2 All E.R. 1411 at 1430.

[37] *In re Park's Estate, Park v. Park* [1954] P. 89.

"a want of reason or volition amounting to incapacity to consent" may render a marriage invalid.[38] Where one party petitions for a decree of nullity on the grounds of the other's incapacity to contract the issue is whether the party's mind "was in so unsound a state as to incapacitate him from giving consent to the contract."[39] In *Legeyt v. O'Brien*,[40] it was held that the onus of proof lay on the party alleging unsoundness of mind and that they should make their case by proving that the person in question of unsound mind at some time prior to the act in question. This would raise a presumption that the mental illness continued up to and including the act in question. It then fell to the other party to rebut the presumption by proving clearly that the mental illness had either ceased or the person concerned was in a lucid interval.[41]

In practice, it has been rare for a decree of nullity to be granted on the grounds of incapacity to consent. The ground is normally pleaded in addition to one alleging that one party lacks the capacity to form and sustain a normal marital relationship. Nonetheless, in *M.E. v. A.E.*,[42] O'Hanlon J. granted a decree based in part on the basis that the respondent was suffering from paranoid schizophrenia at the time of the marriage and this psychiatric illness prevented him from giving a full, free and informed consent to the marriage. Also in *D v. E*[43] Barr J. granted a decree on the grounds that the respondent wife's gross immaturity prevented her from giving full, free or informed consent to the marriage. It has been noted that from the emphasis upon the information element in these decisions it does seem that the courts are going beyond the requirement of basic understanding and opening up the possibility of a grant of a decree of nullity on the grounds that a party did not fully appreciate all the implications of the marriage contract.[44] Indeed in *G.F. v. J.B. (orse J.F.)*,[45] the petitioner decided to get married after the respondent became pregnant and wishing not to disturb his mother he decided to present marriage as a solution to the problem. Medical evidence was given to the effect that the petitioner's was grossly immature and his decision to marry depended on his attitude towards his parents and his inordinate need to please not on his own need and his decisions were made on a more proximate need and not on any long-term basis. He was immature and not able to consent. He also did not have an adequate emotional capacity to enter into or sustain a normal marital relationship with the respondent. Murphy J. concluded that the Petitioner was not fully free in his mind or fully informed to consent to the marriage ceremony with the respondent.

Inability to enter and sustain a normal marital relationship

An expansion of the grounds of nullity has also taken place in another respect. In recent years Irish Judges in nullity actions have gone beyond simply enquiring as to whether a

---

[38] *Legeyt v. O'Brien* (1834) Milward Reports 325.

[39] *Ibid.*, p.334.

[40] *Ibid.*, p.325.

[41] *Ibid.*, p.334.

[42] Unreported, High Court, May 8, 1987.

[43] Unreported, High Court, March 1, 1989.

[44] Also in *N (orse K) v. K* [1986] I.L.R.M. 75 McCarthy J. emphasised the need for the parties to a marriage to have a "full appreciation of what that contract entails". See Duncan and Scully, *Marriage Breakdown in Ireland, Law and Practice* (Butterworths, Dublin, 1990), para.2.072.

[45] Unreported, High Court, Murphy J., March 29, 2000.

person understood the nature of marriage and have examined the capacity of the party to maintain an emotional and psychological relationship. This has been described as "a largely homespun ground with nebulous origins."[46] Nevertheless, a party's inability to enter and sustain a normal marital relationship renders a marriage voidable which means that the marriage remains valid until a competent tribunal declares otherwise. A decree of nullity in respect of a voidable marriage retrospectively invalidates the marriage.

Psychiatric illness existing at time of marriage   In *RSJ v. JSJ*,[47] Barrington J. recognised that inability or lack of capacity to form a caring or considerate marital relationship due to illness existing at the time of the marriage could found a ground for nullity. He acknowledged that section 13 of the Matrimonial Causes and Marriage (Ireland) Amendment Act 1870 required that relief be granted on the basis of "principles and rules which in the opinion of the court, shall be as nearly as may be conformable to the principles and rules" of the ecclesiastical courts but expressed agreement with Kenny J. in *S v. S*,[48] that the section did not have the effect of fossilising the law in its state in 1870. He was also emphasised that where parties had capacity to enter into a contract of marriage then an illness which was known to both of the parties prior to their entering into the marriage was incapable of rendering that marriage void. To hold otherwise would be, "an unwarranted interference with the right to marry."[49] He remarked that people have entered into marriage for all sorts of reasons and their motives have not always been of the highest. The motive for marriage might have been policy, convenience or self-interest. In those circumstances one could not say that a marriage was void because one party did not love or had not the capacity to love the other. While accepting that the petitioner both before and after his marriage suffered from some form of personality defect or illness similar to schizophrenia which made it difficult for him to have a successful marriage Barrington J. was not satisfied that on the date of his wedding the petitioner was so incapacitated as to render the marriage a nullity and even if had lacked the capacity he would not have granted the decree because the respondent had not repudiated the marriage.

In *D v. C*[50] the petitioner relying on this new ground of nullity successfully argued that the respondent suffered from manic depression both before and at the time of his marriage and this disorder was so serious as to incapacitate him from entering into and sustaining a viable marital relationship. Costello J. held that while this illness was not such as to prevent the respondent from understanding the nature of the marriage contract an "incapacitating psychiatric illness" which exists at the time when the parties marry and is such as to render a party "unable to enter into and sustain the normal inter-personal relationship which marriage ... requires"[51] has the effect of making the marriage voidable. In reaching his conclusion, Costello J. adopted the reasoning of Wilde L.J. in *A v. B*,[52] who held that impotence renders a marriage voidable. It should be noted that

---

[46] See *Nullity of Marriage: The Case for Reform* (A Report of the Law Society's Law Reform Committee, October 2001), p.34.

[47] [1982] I.L.R.M. 263.

[48] [1976] I.L.R.M. 156 at 163.

[49] [1982] I.L.R.M. 263 at 264.

[50] [1984] I.L.R.M. 173.

[51] *Ibid*. at 189.

[52] (1868) L.R. 1 P.&D. 559.

while impotence must be incurable if a petition in nullity is to succeed no mention was made in Costello J.'s judgment as to whether the psychiatric illness must also be incurable.

In the subsequent cases of *R v. R*,[53] and *WK v. MC*,[54] decrees of nullity were granted. In both of these cases the court was satisfied that at the date of the ceremony of marriage one of the parties was diagnosed as suffering from paranoid schizophrenia rendering such party incapable of entering into and sustaining a normal interspousal relationship with the petitioner. In *R v. R*, the psychiatric evidence which was given regarding psychiatric treatment received by the parties prior to the marriage and this evidence was found to be "very persuasive" in leading to the conclusion that the particular respondent in the case was suffering from a psychiatric illness at the date of his marriage and as a result was unable to enter into and sustain a normal marital relationship with the particular petitioner. While granting the decree in that case Costello J. was careful to point out that "it did not follow" from his ruling that "every unfortunate sufferer from paranoid schizophrenia is as a matter of law incapable of entering into a valid ceremony of marriage."[55] In the case of *WK v. MC*, the fact that the petitioner was unaware of the respondent's condition seem to carry significant weight with Lavan J. in granting the decree of nullity.

Accordingly it would appear that that the mental incapacity required to support a petition for nullity is a matter of degree and relative to the particular petitioner concerned. This leaves open to possibility that even though his/her marriage to a particular petitioner may be declared a nullity a person with mental illness may have capacity to contract a marriage with another party in the future.

In *DC v. DW*,[56] Blayney J. held, by analogy with the case of impotence, the petitioner in nullity could successfully rely on her own incapacity stemming from an illness (in this case paranoid schizophrenia) existing at the time of the ceremony of marriage where this rendered her incapable of entering into a meaningful marital relationship with the respondent and the respondent had repudiated the marriage. In this case he held that the respondent had repudiated the marriage at the time when the petitioner sought and was granted an ecclesiastical annulment and the fact that the petitioner was subsequently able to establish a stable relationship with another man was held not to undermine her case for a decree of nullity.

In *ME v. AE*,[57] a decree of nullity was granted to the petitioner who had married the respondent, an unlaicised catholic priest in a registry office. According to the medical evidence the respondent probably suffered from paranoid schizophrenia at the time of the marriage. His condition was, it appears, brought about by a succession very distressing events which the respondent had witnessed within a short period of time. From the respondent's evidence, it appeared that he had always regarded himself as a priest even after the marriage and that for him marriage was a temporary arrangement, which he hoped would bring him back to stable mental health. O'Hanlon J. concluded that the respondent suffered from psychiatric disorder which prevented him from giving a full, free and informed consent to the marriage. He also held that it rendered him incapable

---

[53] Unreported, High Court, December 21, 1984.
[54] Unreported, High Court, July 31, 1992.
[55] See p.5 of judgment.
[56] [1987] I.L.R.M. 58.
[57] Unreported, High Court, May 8, 1987.

of entering into and sustaining a normal marriage relationship with the petitioner. In O'Hanlon J.'s view, this lack of capacity to consent meant that the marriage was void and a declaration would be granted on the grounds that one party lacked the mental capacity to understand the nature of the contract of marriage and not on a new ground of nullity.

In *GM (orse G) v. TG*,[58] psychiatric evidence indicated that prior the marriage the respondent had received treatment for "a severe psychotic endogynous depression but did not continue with that treatment." The parties separated fifteen months after the marriage. Lavan J. reached the conclusion on the evidence that "on and immediately before" the day of the wedding the respondent was suffering from severe depression such that "the respondent was incapable of entering into and sustaining a normal marriage relationship with the petitioner".[59]

Finally, in *SC v. PD (orse C)*,[60] it was held that the mental illness relied upon to form the basis for a nullity decree must exist at the date of marriage. In that case a distinction was made between an actual and a latent mental illness. In the High Court, McCracken J. came to the conclusion that the respondent after marriage suffered from a manic depressive illness. On the evidence he found that the illness was congenital in nature caused by a chemical imbalance. However, at the time of the marriage the illness had not manifested itself and it was found not to have affected the ability of the respondent to have a normal relationship within marriage "unless triggered by some event." Some time after the marriage ceremony the illness was triggered by the pregnancy of the respondent spouse. McCracken J. came to the conclusion that the respondent suffered from a latent illness at the time of the marriage, but that this illness did not render her incapable of forming and sustaining a normal lifelong marital relationship and consequently he declined to grant a nullity decree.

Psychological incapacity   In *W v. P*,[61] Barrington J. accepting Costello J.'s analysis of the law in *D v. C* granted the petitioner a decree of nullity on the ground that the respondent was at the time of the marriage "suffering from such psychological or emotional disability or incapacity as made it impossible for him to enter into and sustain a normal marriage relationship with the petitioner".[62] The medical evidence which was before the court showed that the respondent was of such a degree of immaturity and underdevelopment as to impair markedly his capacity to sustain a normal and viable interpersonal relationship but did not appear to suggest that the respondent suffered from any mental illness. The marriage had been entered into only after the respondent had threatened to commit suicide on two occasions. Following the marriage, the respondent's behaviour had become childish and dependent. He threw tantrums and would bang his head against the wall. On one occasion he hit himself with a poker and on another he put his head over a gas ring. He would sometimes lock himself in a bedroom and cry. The wife also discovered that the respondent's mother with whom he had a strangely intense relationship had written love letters on his behalf prior to the

---

[58] Unreported, High Court, November 22, 1991.
[59] See pp.2 and 7 of judgment.
[60] Unreported, High Court, March 14, 1996.
[61] Unreported, High Court, June 7, 1984.
[62] *Ibid.*, pp.23–24.

marriage. The wife left the respondent after two years following a double suicide attempt by him. Accordingly the effect of the decision appears to be to broaden the grounds on which a decree of nullity may be obtained to include inability to enter into a normal marriage relationship.

In *BD v. MC (orse M.D.)*,[63] Barrington J. held that a decree of nullity could be granted on foot of proof of a psychological disorder and held that proof of illness was not essential to the grant of the decree. In that case the petitioner alleged that his wife was emotionally immature. Barrington J. granted the decree on the basis that the petitioner and the respondent were unable to enter into and sustain a normal marital relationship because of the incapacity of the respondent resulting from emotional immaturity and because of the respective states of mind and mental conditions of the petitioner and respondent. He remarked:

> "I do not know if M's condition can be described as an illness. It is apparently a 'disorder' which requires and may be susceptible to psychotherapy. But whether it is an illness or a disorder, it is equally incapacitating so far as the formation of a marital relationship is concerned."[64]

Barrington J.'s decision in *B.D. v. M.C (orse M.D.)* was followed. O'Hanlon J. in *P.C. v. V.C.*,[65] who granted a decree of nullity on the grounds that both parties "were unable to enter into and sustain a normal marital relationship with each other by reason of incapacity deriving from lack of emotional maturity and psychological weakness and disturbance affecting both parties to a greater of lesser degree." Evidence was given that the principle source of friction between the parties was the wife's deep attachment to her parents and grandmother which resulted in the husband's feeling excluded and developing an "obsessive pre-occupation with his own place in his wife's affections contrasted with that of her original family and particularly her mother." This coupled with the inability of both parties to compromise and adjust to the emotional needs of the other partner meant that the circumstance went beyond temperamental incompatibility and fell in the category of cases where want of capacity was in issue.

In *UF (orse C) v. JC*,[66] Finlay C.J. in the Supreme Court, delivering the court's main judgment, upheld the view that proof that a person at the date of marriage lacked the capacity to enter into and sustain a proper or normal marital relationship was a valid basis for decree of nullity. He stated that such incapacity could arise not only

> "from psychiatric or mental illness so recognised or defined but also in cases where it arose from some inherent quality or characteristic of an individual's nature or personality which could not be said to be voluntary or self induced."[67]

Thus it appears strict proof of actual mental illness is not required to secure relief.[68]

---

[63] Unreported, High Court, March 27, 1987.
[64] *Ibid.*, p.34.
[65] July 7, 1989.
[66] [1991] 2 I.R. 330.
[67] *Ibid.* at 356.
[68] See particularly [1991] I.L.R.M. 65 at 85 *per* Egan J.

These dicta received approval in *O'R v. B*[69] in which Kinlen J. granted a decree of nullity ruling that if both parties enter a marriage unaware that by reason of factors connected with the personal or psychological profile or one or other of them that it is impossible for them to sustain a normal marital relationship a petitioner should not be denied a decree of nullity because a respondent wished to hold him to the marriage bond. In this case psychiatric evidence was given the petitioner at the time of entering the marriage was so emotionally immature that he was unable to enter into and sustain a normal marital relationship. The respondent who resisted the claim of incapacity had also contributed with a 'baggage of traumas" to an immature relationship.

The dicta of Finlay CJ in *U.F. (orse U.C.) v. J.C.* were also followed in *MOC v. MOC*,[70] a case in which Finlay Geoghegan J. hearing a case on appeal from a Circuit Court order granted a declaration of nullity on the grounds that the respondent's personality disorder, which fell short of mental illness but which was characterised by a "limited capacity to form and sustain an intimate relationship and an inability to take "responsibility within a relationship,"[71] established that the respondent lacked the capacity to enter into and sustain a proper or normal marital relationship. In this case Finlay Geoghegan J. concluded that the evidence of the parties and of two clinical psychologists giving evidence independently of each other established the ground for nullity according to the requisite standard of proof viz, on the balance of probabilities.

In *DK v. TH (orse T.K)*[72] the High Court held that the evidence of the cumulative effects of the psychological and emotional history of the petitioner justified the conclusion that he lacked the capacity to enter into a long-term marital relationship at the date of the marriage ceremony. O'Higgins J. was of the view that psychiatric evidence in relation to the sexual abuse of the petitioner by a priest for a protracted period when he was about 12 years old; the death of his father when he was 14 years year old and considerable friction between the petitioner and his stepfather whom his mother married one year after his father's death; the damage done to the petitioner's state of mind by substance abuse during his teenage years was such as to satisfy the court that the petitioner was not capable of understanding the nature and consequence of a long-term marriage relationship and further that the petitioner did not have the capacity to enter such a relationship at the relevant date.

In *DMcC v. EC*,[73] McCracken J. found that the applicant for a decree of nullity was extremely immature when it came to entering into close relationships with other people. He had never know or been in a home with a proper marriage relationship at all as his father had sexually abused him and physically abused his mother for years. He was an alcoholic and got engaged within a year of having stopped drinking while the accepted psychiatric evidence given in the case was that an alcoholic ought not to make serious decisions or commitments for the first year or two after he had stopped drinking. The respondent had not repudiated the marriage but following the judgment of the Supreme Court of *PC v. VC*,[74] this was not a bar to the granting of a decree of nullity. McCracken

---

[69] [1995] I.L.R.M. 57.
[70] Unreported, High Court on Circuit, July 10, 2003.
[71] *Ibid.*, p.7.
[72] [1998] 2 I.J.F.L 23.
[73] Unreported, High Court, July 6, 1998.
[74] [1990] 2 I.R. 91 at 107.

J. concluded that the applicant did not understand the nature of a proper marriage and was incapable of entering into or sustaining a normal marital relationship with the respondent and accordingly granted a decree that the marriage entered into between the parties was null and void.

Powers of medical inspectors in nullity proceedings   The Master of the High Court has the power under Order 70, rule 32 of the Rules of the Superior Courts,[75] where incapacity is alleged to appoint two medical inspectors "to examine the parties and report to the court the result of such examination." In the absence of such an order being made the court itself has jurisdiction to order an examination and power in this regard includes a power to order a psychiatric examination.[76] A social report can also be obtained in nullity cases under section 47 of the Family Law Act 1997.In the case of *PMcG v. A.F (falsely called McG)*,[77] the High Court was called upon to rule upon the powers of medical inspectors in nullity proceedings where it is alleged that petitioner or respondent lacked the capacity to enter into and/or sustain a normal life-long relationship by reason of his or her state of mind at the state of the marriage. In this case, the medical inspector was appointed by Order of the Master of the High Court to carry out a psychiatric examination of the parties. A motion was brought to the High Court to seek directions as to whether the inspector could interview third parties regarding the relationship between the parties, and whether he could have access to the respondents diary for 1993 which the petitioner had in his possession. Budd J. in the High Court, giving directions held that the contents of the diary could be discoverable and arguments as to the admissibility of the diary were best dealt with in an application for discovery. The medical inspector should not be given sight of the diary. Secondly he held that statutory provisions governing the application for nullity and the Rules of Court made thereunder contained no provision for interviewing any party other than the parties to the action. Confining the report to interviews with the parties lessened its chances of being tainted by the use of hearsay or other inadmissible evidence. If a third party had relevant evidence he or she could be called as a witness. Notwithstanding the general rule if both parties agree the court in the particular circumstances of the case might sanction such an interview.

Canon law   It is interesting to note that prior to Barrington J.'s recognition in *RSJ* of inability through illness to form a caring, considerate marital relationship church annulments were being granted on the basis of psychological incapacity which rendered a person incapable of assuming the essential obligations of marriage,[78] thus if a couple were couple were incapable of achieving an intimate sharing of life and love by reason of psychological defects inherent in their personalities at the time of marital consent the marriage could be declared null.[79] The guiding principle in the development of this

---

[75] S.I. No.15 of 1986.

[76] See *J.S. v. C.S. (orse C.T.)* [1997] I F.L.R. 140.

[77] [2000] 2 I.J.F.L 32.

[78] See Corriden, Green and Heintschel, *The Code of Canon Law: A Text and Commentary* (Paulist Press, New York, 1985), pp.775–779.

[79] See McCandlish, "Psychological Factors Involved in Ecclesiastical Annulments", 29 *Catholic Lawyer* 266 (1984) at p.267.

area of canon law was the consideration that a marital obligation should not be imposed upon a person who by reason of his incapacity would find it impossible to fulfil it.[80]

Canon law appears also to go beyond the confines of ability to consent in determining whether a person is capable of contracting marriage. Thus Canon 1095 of the Revised Code of Canon Law[81] provides:

> "They are incapable of contracting marriage—
> (1) Who lack the sufficient use of reason;
> (2) Who suffer from a grave lack of discretion of judgment concerning essential matrimonial rights and duties which are to be mutually given and accepted;
> (3) Who are not capable of assuming the emotional obligations of matrimony due to causes of psychotic nature."[82]

Costello J.'s decision in *RSJ* appears to be consonant with (3) above. Also Barrington J's decision in *W v. P* to grant a decree of nullity on the grounds of emotional immaturity appears to coincide with the concept previously recognised by canon lawyers who described it as a "psychological condition which affects the ability to make judgments to control ones actions and to relate to another" and as being "not a temporary condition but a permanent one."[83]

Bars to decree of nullity

There are four potential bars to relief on a claim of nullity. These are: (i) failure to repudiate the marriage; (ii) approbation of the Marriage; (iii) long delay in the institution of the proceedings for relief, and (iv) collusion.

(i) If a marriage was potentially voidable it was formerly thought that a petitioner could rely on his own incapacity only where the respondent had repudiated the validity of the marriage.[84] However, in more recent times the courts have not insisted that the respondent have acted in this way before granting a petitioner a decree based on his own incapacity.[85]

(ii) A party may however, lose the right to a decree if s/he has approbated the marriage, *i.e.* with knowledge of his right to avoid the marriage the party has acted in such a way from which it may reasonably be inferred that he affirmed the existence of the marriage. The classic definition of approbation was delivered in *G v. M*,[86] by Lord Selborne who stated that approbation included:

---

[80] See Reinhardt and Arella, "Essential Incompatibility as Grounds for Nullity of Marriage" *16 Catholic Lawyer* 173 (1970) at pp.174–175.

[81] (1983).

[82] See Mendonca, "The Incapacity to Contract Marriage; Canon 1095" 19 Stud. Can. 259 (1985).

[83] See Corriden Green & Hentschel, *The Code of Canon Law: A Text and Commentary* (Paulist Press, New York, 1985), p.778. See also generally O'Connor, *Key Issues in Irish Family Law* (The Round Hall Press, Dublin, 1988).

[84] See *R.S.J v. J.S.J.* [1982] I.L.R.M. 263.

[85] See *P.V v. V.C* [1990] 2 I.R. 91, *O'R v. B* [1995] 2 I.L.R.M. 57 at 72.

[86] (1885) 10 A.C. 171 at 186.

"any act from which the inference ought to be drawn that during the antecedent time the party has, with knowledge of the facts and of the law, approbated the marriage which she or he afterwards seeks to get rid of, or has taken advantages or derived benefits from the matrimonial relationship which it would be unfair and inequitable to permit him or her, after having received them to treat as if no such relation existed."

In effect the law relating to approbation operates like an estoppel *i.e.* one party to the marriage has by his apparent representation of the validity of the marriage induced another party to act to his or detriment in reliance on it so that it would be inequitable to allow the representing party to rely on his strict legal rights to terminate the marriage contract.

(iii) Where a long delay precedes the institution of proceedings a court may decline to grant a decree on the basis that delay may imply an intention on the part of the petitioner to forego their rights. In *M.O'D v. C.O'D*,[87] a serious delay of some 20 years disqualified the petitioner from relief. However, where the delay is explicable on some ground such as lack of financial resources to institute proceedings[88] or ignorance of the right to obtain a decree of nullity,[89] delay may not be fatal to the application.

(iv) Collusion occurs where parties improperly combine with a view to obtaining a decree of nullity. In these circumstances the court has a discretion to deny relief. Where collusion is suspected the onus is on the petitioner to prove that there are in fact no reasonable ground for thinking that the true case was not presented to the court.[90] The Law Society has pointed out that owing to the potential for collusion and improper co-operation in nullity cases some judges have suggested the possibility of appointing "a defender of the bond" in undefended petitions to argue in favour of the validity of the marriage and note that in *O'R v. B*,[91] Kinlen J. recommended that a *legitimus contradictor* or *amicus curiae* should be appointed in such cases.[92]

Consequences of decree of nullity

A decree of nullity means that a marriage, which was presumed to exist in fact, does not and the parties' status is changed from being apparently married to being single again. In the case of a void marriage e.g. where there was no consent to the marriage the decree recognises that the marriage never existed so that an legal consequences flowing from the supposed marriage were based on a mistake of fact. In the case of a voidable marriage, *i.e.* where the party pleads inability to sustain the marital relationship the effect of the decree is to render the marriage void *ab initio* with the same practical

---

[87] Unreported, High Court, O'Hanlon J., August 5, 1992.
[88] *W.v.P.*, unreported, High Court, Barrington J., June 7, 1984.
[89] *N.F. v. M.T.* [1982] I.L.R.M 545.
[90] *E.P. v. M.C.* [1985] I.L.R.M. 34.
[91] [1995] 2 I.L.R.M. 57.
[92] See *Nullity of Marriage: The Case for Reform* (A Report by the Law Society's Law Reform Committee October 2001), p.39.

effects. These are that the children cease to be the children of a marriage and become children born outside marriage. (The obligation of both parents to maintain their children however, continues after the decree.[93]) There is no jurisdiction in the courts to make "ancillary orders" relating to financial matters and property between the parties so that the practice has evolved of agreeing financial settlements in nullity cases prior to the hearing of the case so that the court may be told that a settlement has been reached and provision made by the financially weaker party.[94] Once a marriage is annulled the parties have no claim to each other's estates on death and are not entitled to any legal share on intestacy. The former "spouse" with no proprietary interest in the family home loses the right to reside in it once of decree of nullity is granted. When a decree of nullity is pronounced the former "spouse" is eligible only for the lesser remedies available to a co-habitee or co-resident under the Domestic Violence Act 1976.

Frequency of decrees of nullity

Kieron Wood,[95] observes that since the introduction of divorce there have been relatively few reported High Court decisions relating to nullity. He suggests that one reason for this, may be that section 39(1) of the Family Law Act 1995 now gives the Circuit Court power decide applications for nullity if one of the following requirements is satisfied:

"(a) either of the spouses concerned was domiciled in the State on the date of the institution of the proceedings concerned.
 (b) either of the spouses was ordinarily resident in the State throughout the period of one year ending on that date.
 (c) either of the spouses died before that date and –
    (i) was at the time of death domiciled in the State
    or
    (ii) had been ordinarily resident in the State throughout the period of one year ending on that date."

He also notes that since the introduction of divorce the number of nullity applications plummeted from 84 in 1995 to just 20 after the introduction of divorce and concludes that many family practitioners had predicted that with the introduction of divorce a number of those who might earlier have sought a decree of nullity would opt for divorce instead and the figures seem to prove them right.[96]

Alternatives to a decree of nullity

This trend away from granting decrees of nullity may also have been facilitated by powers vested in the courts in under the Family Law Act 1995 and the Family Law

---

[93] See Status of Children Act 1987, s.3 and Family Law (Maintenance of Spouses and Children) Act 1976 as amended.
[94] See *Nullity of Marriage The Case for Reform* (A Report by the Law Society's Law Reform Committee October 2001), p.45.
[95] "Nullity and Divorce – The New Alternatives?" [1999] 2 I J.F.L. 12 at 17.
[96] *Ibid.* at 12.

Divorce Act 1996 to entertain alternative applications for decrees of judicial separation and divorce when application is made for a decree of nullity and *vice versa*. In this regard, section 39(2) of the Family Law Act 1995 provides:

"Where proceedings are pending in a court in respect of an application for the grant of a decree of nullity or in respect of an appeal from the determination of such an application and the court has or had, by virtue of [section 39(1)] jurisdiction to determine the application, the court, notwithstanding section 31(4) of the [Judicial Separation and Family Law Reform Act 1989][97] shall have jurisdiction to determine an application for the grant of a decree of judicial separation in respect of the marriage concerned."

Section 39(3) of the Family Law (Divorce) Act 1996 provides that:

"Where proceedings are pending in a court in respect of a an application for the grant of a decree of nullity or in respect of an appeal from the determination of such an application and the court has or had, by virtue of section 39 of the Act of 1995 jurisdiction to determine the application the court shall notwithstanding [section 39(1) of the 1996 Act][98] have jurisdiction to determine an application for the grant of a decree of divorce in respect of the marriage concerned."

A similar but converse jurisdiction is granted by section 39(2) of the Family Law (Divorce) Act 1996 which provides:

"Where proceedings are pending in a court in respect of an application for the grant of a decree of divorce ... the court shall ... have jurisdiction to determine an application for a the grant of a decree of judicial separation or a decree of nullity in respect of the marriage concerned"

Wood concludes that:

"More and more spouses are likely to avail of the divorce remedy. And, while nullity still remains a real option for parties who genuinely believe that their marriage never existed and for parties on whom it might confer some financial advantage, it may be predicted that, with the availability of a practical alternative remedy for spouses wishing to remarry the judicial development of the doctrine of nullity is likely to become less adventurous in the foreseeable future".[99]

---

[97] Such jurisdiction is not conferred by s.31(4) of the Judicial Separation and Family Law Reform Act 1989.

[98] S.39(1) of the 1996 Act provides that the court may grant a decree of divorce if, but only if, one of the following requirements is satisfied – (a) either of the spouses concerned was domiciled in the State on the date of the institution of the proceedings concerned, (b) either of the spouses was ordinarily resident in the State throughout the period of one year ending on that date.

[99] K. Woods, "Nullity and Divorce – The New Alternatives?" [1999] 2 I.J.F.L. 12 at 18.

Commentary

11–38 A comparative piece of legislation of interest is the UK Marriage Act 1983, which permits patients who are detained under the long term powers in the Mental Health Act to be married in hospital.[100] It is also interesting to note that under section 12 of the UK Matrimonial Causes Act 1973 the marriage of a mentally ill person may be annulled on the grounds (1) that s/he did not consent to it on the grounds of unsoundness of mind, or (2) although able to give a valid consent s/he was suffering (whether continuously or intermittently) from mental disorder within the meaning of the Mental Health Act but this must be "of such a kind or to such an extent as to be unfitted for marriage."[101] These grounds render the marriage voidable rather than void. This permits the parties themselves to decide whether they wish to continue it or not. Even after the decree is granted the marriage is treated as if it had existed up until that time.[102]

The Law Reform Commission in its *Report on Nullity of Marriage* was of the view that the Marriage of Lunatics Act 1811 should be repealed on the grounds that it rendered void a marriage, which would be valid if judged by the common law test of insanity. It is difficult to disagree with the Law Reform Commission's recommendation that the Marriage of Lunatics Act be repealed. Capacity to marry is different to the capacity to make other decisions and the Act does not address the capacity to enter the marriage relationship (as opposed to capacity to manage one's financial affairs) with a sufficient degree of precision. In addition it is over inclusive in that some persons who may fall within its provisions may satisfy the criteria for capacity to marry. Other criticisms may also be made notably the fact that the 1811 Act renders the marriage void would also inevitably raise questions about the spouses right to property and the legitimacy of the children to the marriage which are not addressed in the legislation. Secondly, it has been established above at common law a marriage is invalid on the ground of mental incapacity where, at the time of the marriage either spouse was unable to understand the nature of the marriage and its duties and responsibilities.[103] In some cases of mental incapacity the marriage may be advantageous to a spouse with a disability in other cases it may be exploitative of the incapacitated person.[104] In the latter case the person may want to sever the relationship but may require assistance in doing so. To assist in such cases there is much merit in the Law Reform Committee of the Law Society's recommendation that a court should be enabled to appoint a relative, friend or statutory body on that person's or body's application to protect the legal interests of a person with an incapacity by challenging the validity of a marriage to which the incapacitated person is a party.[105]

---

[100] See s.1 and Sch.1 and DHSS Circular No. HC(84) 12.

[101] In *Bennett v. Bennett* [1969] 1 W.L.R. 430 Ormrod J. decided that it was not enough that the wife was difficult to live with because of her disorder and should probably not have got married. She had to be incapable of living in the married state and carrying out the ordinary duties and obligations of the marriage and this she was not.

[102] Matrimonial Causes Act 1973 (U.K), s.16.

[103] *Turner v. Meyers* 1808 1 Hag. Con. 414 at 417, 161 E.R. 600 at 601, *per* Sir William Scott.

[104] See *In the matter of BEW* [1994] N.Z.L.R. 730 an situation of the exploitation of a person with an intellectual disability.

[105] See *Nullity of Marriage: The case for reform* (A Report by the Law Society's Law Reform Committee October 2001), pp.72–73.

Thirdly, the concept of the voidable marriage which have been regarded *de facto* as existing valid marriages for a time and then on application for a decree of nullity declared void ab initio gives rise to difficulties in practice and the grounds for obtaining a decree of nullity on the basis of inability to enter and sustain a normal marital relationship are not clear. It might be argued that the grounds should be clarified and codified in legislation relating to the law of nullity.[106] However, Law Reform Committee of the Law Society in its report *Nullity of Marriage: The case for reform*,[107] goes further and recommends on practical grounds that the concept of a voidable marriage should be abolished and the grounds which make a marriage voidable including the inability to enter and sustain a normal marital relationship should be abolished and cases which could be pleaded on those grounds should instead be pleaded under the divorce jurisdiction. In making its case the Law Society Law Reform Committee considered the arguments for and against the concept of a voidable marriage. It stated first that there is no disadvantage in recognising marriages as voidable where personal and not policy issues are at stake. Matters of consent and emotional capacity are very personal and specific to the parties whereas the formalities of the marriage are policy matters in which the general public has a valid interest. Where protection of individuals involved in a marriage are concerned it argues that it ought to be left up to the individuals to take steps to affirm or avoid the marriage. Against the concept of the nullity of a voidable marriage the Law Reform Committee argues that the respondent spouse in both short and long marriages often has the most to lose by being stigmatised as somehow inadequate (for example, unable to enter and sustain a normal marital relationship). This can be very hurtful. It also goes against the current ethos of no-fault separation and divorce legislation to have one party being identified as the one to blame.

Another problem the Law Reform Committee argues is that uncertainty as to the status of a voidable marriage, which normally requires expensive court proceedings to remove. In particular, the ground of "inability to enter and sustain a normal marital relationship" has been expanded considerably over the past twenty years and has led to situations in which legal advisors cannot advise with certainty as to whether the client is validly married or not. Further, it can be very difficult to disentangle arrangements, which were made on the basis that a marriage existed. On this basis the Law Reform Committee argues for the abolition of the concept of the voidable marriage and the introduction of legislation to provide for "clean break" divorce.[108] It notes that voidable marriages as a concept have been abolished in Australia,[109] and New Zealand[110] for over 20 years and in both these jurisdictions final divorce settlements are possible.

The Law Reform Commission in its *Report on Nullity of Marriage*,[111] dealing with the want of mental capacity recommended that legislation be enacted providing, *inter alia*, that a marriage should be invalid where a spouse enters a marriage when, at the

---

[106] The Law Reform Committee of the Law Society in its report makes the general recommendation that the law of nullity (with the exception of that relating to voidable marriages) should be codified. See *Nullity of Marriage: The Case for Reform* (A Report by the Law Society's Law Reform Committee October 2001), p.94.

[107] October 2001.

[108] pp. 65–67.

[109] Family Law Act 1975, s.51.

[110] Family Proceedings Act 1980 (N.Z), ss.29–31.

[111] At p.104.

time of marriage, on account of his or her want of mental capacity he or she is unable to discharge the essential obligations of marriage. They were of the view that this definition would afford the courts the appropriate degree of flexibility in deciding cases where want of mental capacity is alleged to have invalidated a marriage. The Law Reform Committee of the Law Society's *Report on Nullity of Marriage: The Case for Reform*, however, illustrates the difficulties encountered by the judges in determining whether the ground of "inability to enter and sustain a normal marital relationship" was made out. Where the ground of emotional immaturity was alleged it was required to be "abnormal" or "gross" and judges experienced difficulties in deciding where to draw the line between "faults and weaknesses of character,"[112] and immaturity, irresponsibility or incompatibility of such a degree as would warrant a decree.[113] In many cases also in the absence of psychiatric evidence judges experienced difficulties in determining whether a marriage should be annulled or whether it had merely broken down in the ordinary way. The Law Reform Committee is of the view that it would be desirable to introduce greater certainty into the law and that the abolition of the "inability to enter and sustain a normal marital relationship" ground would achieve this. Cases based on this ground, which would previously have come within the nullity jurisdiction, could be dealt with under the divorce jurisdiction. In this regard, section 5 of the Family Law (Divorce) Act 1996 enables a court to grant a divorce decree simply on the basis that the parties have lived apart for four out of the previous five years; that there is no prospect of reconciliation between them and that proper provision exists or will be made for the spouses and dependent members of the family. According to the Law Reform Committee there was every advantage in maintaining the simplicity of such a no fault divorce for parties who would have considered the "inability to enter and sustain a normal marital relationship" ground in nullity and no basis for importing this as a ground into the divorce legislation.[114] A further advantage of this proposal is that the parties could avail of ancillary relief on divorce and children would not lose their status of being members of a family protected by Article 41 of the Constitution. The Law Reform Committee also argues that following the abolition of the voidable marriage concept and the nullity ground of "inability to enter and sustain a normal marital relationship" legislation should be introduced to allow for a "clean break" divorce *i.e.* the judge should have a discretion to make a determination of a once and for all final financial settlement in cases where a marriage has been brief and has effectively been "doomed" from the start.[115]

Fourthly, the effects of a decree declaring a marriage void *ab initio* under the current law are quite extreme. To ameliorate the effects of a declaration that a marriage never existed the Law Reform Committee in its report on *Nullity of Marriage; The Case for Reform*[116] makes a number of sensible suggestions. First financial ancillary relief should be available on an equitable basis as part of nullity decrees[117] A court should have a

---

[112] *MJ O'D v. CD O'D*, unreported, High Court, O'Hanlon J., May 8, 1992.
[113] For example see the contrasting decisions made by O'Hanlon J. in *PC v. VC* [1990] 2 I.R. 91 and Lardner J. in *RT v. VP (orse VT)* [1990] I.R. 545.
[114] pp. 69–70.
[115] p.84.
[116] A report by the Law Society's Law Reform Committee, October 2001.
[117] *Ibid.*, p.74.

discretion to permit a previous party to a void marriage to continue in residence in the family home until property adjustment or other financial orders are carried into effect and their consequences realised, for example by partition of the property and sale[118] and the definition of "spouse" in the Domestic Violence Act 1996 should be amended to include a party to a void or annulled marriage.[119]

Fifthly, the Law Reform Committee of the Law Society in its report on *Nullity of Marriage; The Case for Reform*,[120] has identified a number of needed changes, which could be made to the procedural aspects of application for a decree of nullity in the interests of justice. First the court should be empowered to make a discretionary award of maintenance pending suit to either party to a potentially voidable marriage. (Currently only the "wife" is entitled to claim maintenance pending suit);[121] In nullity cases where children are involved their interests should be represented by a *Guardian ad litem*[122] The courts should also be empowered to appoint the Attorney General in the role of a *legitimus contradictor* to argue in support of the validity of a marriage where the constitution imperative to protect the institution of marriage requires it or an uncontested nullity is sought.[123]

Finally, the case of *PMcG v. A.F. (falsely called McG*,[124] illustrates the fact that the law of nullity has surpassed procedures in such cases. The appointment of a medical inspector to report on the reproductive abilities of the parties was appropriate when the sole ground for rendering a marriage voidable was impotence. The new ground of inability to enter or sustain a normal marriage relationship is not catered for in the prescribed role of the medical inspector although there is a practice of appointing a consultant psychiatrist and adapting the court forms for this purpose. It is submitted that it is time that the rules of court provided for this new role.

JUDICIAL SEPARATION

Mental illness, which manifests itself after the ceremony of marriage, may present difficulties for a party with mental illness in sustaining the marital relationship and sometimes contribute to the breakdown of a marriage. Where an existing marriage has broken down either spouse may apply for (a) a decree of judicial separation, or (b) a divorce under Irish law

The current law regarding judicial separation

Under section 2 of the Judicial Separation and Family Law Reform Act 1989 a spouse may apply for a decree of separation on one or more of the following grounds:

(a) that the respondent has committed adultery;

---

[118] *Ibid.*, p.77.
[119] *Ibid.*, p.80.
[120] October 2001.
[121] *Ibid.*, p.80.
[122] *Ibid.*, p.87.
[123] *Ibid.*, p.91.
[124] [2000] 2 I.J.F.L. 32.

(b) that the respondent has behaved in such a way that the applicant cannot reasonably be expected to live with the respondent;

(c) that there has been desertion by the respondent of the applicant for a continuous period of at least one year immediately preceding the date of the application;

(d) that the spouses have lived apart from one another for a continuous period of at least one year immediately preceding the date of the application and the respondent consents to a decree being granted;

(e) that the spouses have lived apart from one another for a continuous period of at least three years immediately preceding the date of the application;

(f) that the marriage has broken down to the extent that the court is satisfied in all the circumstances that a normal marital relationship has not existed between the spouses for a period of at least one year immediately preceding the date of the application.

Each of these grounds must be proved to the court's satisfaction on the balance of probabilities,[125] if a decree is to be granted. In addition where there are dependent children of the family a decree cannot be granted unless the court: (i) is satisfied that such provision exists or has been made, or (ii) intends by order upon the granting of the decree to make such provision for the welfare of the children as is proper in the circumstances.[126]

A decree of judicial separation merely extinguishes the legal duty of spouses to cohabit – a duty which since 1988[127] is no longer enforceable. However, the significance of the decree lies more in the fact that on the granting of the decree the court may make extensive ancillary orders relating to children, support payments, capital payments, pension rights, the family home and other property to enable separated spouses make arrangements to live permanently apart.

Section 5 of the 1989 Act imposes a duty on the solicitor acting for the applicant to discuss with the applicant the possibility of reconciliation with the respondent prior to the commencement of proceedings. The solicitor is also required to discuss with the applicant the possibility of engaging in mediation to help both parties to effect a separation on an agreed basis. The solicitor must provide the applicant with the names and addresses of people qualified to help with such a reconciliation or mediation respectively. The applicant's solicitor must also discuss the possibility of effecting a separation by negotiation with the respondent, concluding with the drafting and signing of a separation agreement. The applicant's solicitor is required to certify his compliance with these requirements when instituting proceedings. If the applicant's solicitor fails to comply with the above requirements the court may adjourn proceedings to allow the solicitor to discuss these matters with the applicant. Section 6 of the 1989 Act places similar obligations on the solicitor for the respondent. Section 7 of the Act provides that where separation is possible the court may at any time adjourn the proceedings to allow the parties if they both so wish to consider reconciliation. The court may also adjourn the

---

[125] Judicial Separation and Family Law Reform Act 1989, s.3(1).

[126] *Ibid.*, s.3(2)(a),(b).

[127] See the Family Law Act 1988 which abolished the action for restitution of conjugal rights.

proceedings under section 7 to allow the spouses the opportunity to agree on the terms of the separation in so far as is possible.

Adultery

Adultery can be relied upon by the applicant spouse as a ground for obtaining a decree of separation provided the applicant and the respondent have not "lived with each other for more than one year after it became known to the applicant that the respondent had committed adultery."[128] Where this proviso is not satisfied adultery may be one of the factors used by the applicant together with other matters to obtain a decree based on the respondents conduct.[129] In order to be guilty of adultery a person must have consented to sexual intercourse. A spouse who is mentally ill may be held to be incapable of giving the requisite consent.[130]

Behaviour

A decree of judicial separation may be granted if a respondent spouse "has behaved in such a way that the applicant cannot reasonably be expected to live with the respondent."[131] Where a couple have continued to live together for a period or periods which do not exceed six months after the "occurrence of the final incident relied upon by the applicant" such cohabitation must be disregarded by the court in determining whether it is reasonable to expect the applicant to continue to live with the respondent. Where the couple have lived together for "a period or periods" exceeding six months after the final such incident the court retains the power to grant the decree but must have regard to the length of time co-habitation has continued and the reason for the couple's continued co-habitation when making its decision.

The central issue, which the court must determine when making a decree on the behaviour ground, is whether it is reasonable to expect this particular applicant to continue to live with this particular respondent. In other words the test is subjective and not objective. Accordingly conduct, which a stronger spouse might disregard or not take seriously, may nevertheless result in a decree being granted to a more vulnerable and sensitive spouse on the ground that it is reasonable to expect him/her to wish to discontinue cohabitation.[132] On the other hand, the subjective test will not result in such a conclusion where the behaviour is innocuous or only mildly annoying or offensive and the applicant is abnormally sensitive. In such cases the court may take the view that it is reasonable for cohabitation to continue as the applicant's reaction is out of proportion to the behaviour disliked by the applicant.

An example of the behaviour which may result in the grant of a decree of judicial separation under section 2(1)(b) is provided by *McA v. McA*,[133] a case in which the wife

---

[128] Judicial Separation and Family Law Reform Act 1989, s.2(1)(a) and s.4(1)(a).

[129] *Ibid.*, s.4(1).

[130] *Long v. Long and Johnson* (1890) 15 P.D. 218; *Yarrow v. Yarrow* [1892] P. 92; *Hanbury v. Hanbury* (1892) 8 T.L.R. 559.

[131] Judicial Separation and Family Law Reform Act, s.2(1)(b).

[132] *Gollins v. Gollins* [1964] A.C. 644.

[133] [1981] 1 I.L.R.M. 361.

was granted a decree of divorce *a mensa et thoro* on the grounds of her husband's mental cruelty. The evidence showed that the husband had refused to communicate with his wife except through their three year old daughter or by means of notes; that he had "deliberately withdrawn himself emotionally from her"[134] seeking "protection from the strain of the family home in the practice of transcendental meditation;"[135] that there had been no sexual intercourse between the couple for over three years, the husband no longer slept with his wife and had refused to co-operate with his wife in seeking to find a solution to their marital problems. In addition there was evidence that the wife suffered anxiety and depression as a result of her husband's behaviour and had been taking anti-depressant medication for over two and a half years. Costello J. granted the wife's application for a decree of judicial separation.

Further, it appears that the behaviour of a mentally ill spouse may give rise to grounds to seek a decree of judicial separation even where the mental illness is the underlying cause for the behaviour. In *MK v. AK*,[136] psychiatric evidence showed that the wife suffered from a "morbid jealousy syndrome" which resulted in her taunting her husband with allegations of homosexuality, accusing him of transmitting venereal disease to her despite medical advice that he had not done so, accusing him of having numerous adulterous affairs, insulting his parents and constantly haranguing and verbally abusing him. The syndrome, which according to the psychiatric evidence, results in the spouse becoming suspicious of and looking for evidence to substantiate their suspicions against their marital partner and being incapable of accepting that their suspicions are wrong, effectively turned a "happy home into a hell on earth."[137] Mackenzie J. granted the husband's cross-petition for a decree of divorce *a mensa et thoro* on the grounds of his wife's cruelty. It is important to note that the mere fact that one spouse suffers from a mental illness will not be a sufficient basis for a decree on the behaviour ground. In this regard the court may have regard to duty of the complaining spouse to care for the sick spouse bearing in mind their obligation to care for one another "in sickness and in health." However, in a given case the court may have to weigh this obligation in the balance against the difficulties, which a spouse is obliged to bear, and which derive from the other spouse's illness whether it be physical or mental.

Desertion

The court may grant a decree of judicial separation on the grounds of desertion by a respondent spouse "for a continuous period of one year immediately preceding the date of the application"[138] In reaching a determination as to whether the period for which it is alleged that the respondent has deserted the applicant is continuous "any one period (not exceeding six months)" or "any 2 or more periods(not exceeding six months in all)" during which the spouses resumed living with each other must be disregarded by the court. However, such period(s) cannot count as part of the period of desertion.[139] In

---

[134] [1981] 1 I.L.R.M. 361 at 363.
[135] *Ibid.*
[136] Unreported, High Court, May 13, 1988.
[137] *Ibid.*, p.19.
[138] Judicial Separation and Family Law Reform Act 1989, s.2(1)(c).
[139] *Ibid.*, s.2(2).

addition a decree of separation cannot be granted if the spouses are living with each other at the time of the application.[140] To establish the ground of desertion an applicant spouse must prove four elements (a) that the spouses are factually living separate and apart; (b) the absence of consent to live apart; (c) intention to desert; (d) absence of just cause for leaving.

Whether a spouse with mental illness can form the requisite intention to desert is a question of fact in each case. Where a spouse leaves the other spouse while under an insane delusion that that other spouse is going to kill her that spouse has been held not to be in desertion.[141] Further supervening mental illness may terminate the desertion of a spouse.[142] Further, "grave and weighty" conduct by one spouse will justify the other spouse in separating and afford that spouse a defence against separation. However, to afford a spouse such a defence the conduct complained of must be of "such a kind as, in effect, makes the continuance of life together impossible."[143] In the English case of *G v. G*,[144] a husband developed a mental illness that led him to frighten his children and the court held that the wife was entitled to remain apart from him for as long as was necessary for the sake of the children.

Further, if a spouse behaves in such a way as to force the other spouse to leave the court may find that the former spouse is in constructive desertion.[145] Under the Judicial Separation and Family Law Reform Act 1989, desertion includes "conduct on the part of one spouse that results in the other spouse with just cause, leaving and living apart from that other spouse."[146] In order for a spouse to prove constructive desertion (or indeed desertion) an intention to bring the cohabitation to an end must be proved against the spouse alleged to have deserted. The conduct of the spouse and its natural and probable consequences can give rise to a rebuttable presumption in favour of the existence of such intention. The more serious the conduct of the spouse the more difficult it is to rebut the presumption.

In the case of *K v. K* (referred to above in the context of separation on the grounds that a spouse's behaviour makes it unreasonable to expect the other spouse to live with him/her,), the husband obtained a decree of divorce *a mensa et thoro* on the grounds of the wife's cruelty and subsequently the High Court refused to make a maintenance order in the wife's favour under the Family Law (Maintenance of Spouses and Children) Act 1976 ruling that the wife was in constructive desertion of her husband by reason of her conduct arising from a mental condition described as "morbid jealousy syndrome." This condition led her to have groundless illusions of misconduct by her husband and to behave towards him with such mental and physical cruelty that he had just cause to leave the family home. On appeal, the Supreme Court rejected the wife's contention that the wife's condition of "morbid jealousy should be equated with a person of unsound mind unable to administer or look after her own affairs" and that she deserved "special protection from the courts" and could not be held in constructive desertion. The Supreme

---

[140] *Ibid.*
[141] *Perry v. Perry* [1963] 3 All E.R. 766 and *Brannan v. Brannan* [1973] Fam. 20.
[142] *Crowther v. Crowther* [1951] A.C. 723.
[143] *Yeatman v. Yeatman* (1868) L.R. 1 P&D 489; *Oldroyd v. Oldroyd* [1896] P. 175.
[144] [1964] P. 133; [1964] 1 All E.R. 129.
[145] *Graves v. Graves* [1864] 3 Sw. & Tr.
[146] Judicial Separation and Family Law Reform Act 1989, s.2(3)(d).

Court found on the evidence, that her ability to look after her own affairs was unimpaired and that she was capable of forming the necessary intention and of understanding the natural and probable consequences of her conduct.

Living apart for one year

A decree of separation may be granted where "spouses have lived apart from one another for a continuous period of at least one year immediately preceding the date of the application and the respondent consents to the decree."[147] For the purpose of computing the period of continuous separation no account is taken of any one period (not exceeding six months) or of any two or more periods (not exceeding six months in all) during which the spouses resumed living together provided that no such period of cohabitation is counted as part of the period during which they were living apart. Also the spouses must not be living together at the time the application is made.[148] While the 1989 Act does not require anything more than proof of the physical fact of separation other jurisdictions have required intention as an additional element to be proved. Thus there is no separation where a spouse is forced by ill health to be hospitalised unless it can be shown that at some point one of the spouses regarded cohabitation as having ended. Separation will be deemed to have commenced at that point in time.

The respondent's consent is also required for a decree to be granted on this ground. This requires the respondent to have the mental capacity to consent. In the English case of *Mason v. Mason*,[149] it was held, in the context of an application for divorce on the grounds of two years separation and the respondent's consent, that the test of capacity consent to the divorce was the same as capacity to consent to a marriage. The respondent must be able to understand the nature, effect and consequences of his consent and to express his consent.

Living apart continuously for three years

Where the spouses have lived apart for a continuous period of at least three years immediately preceding the date of the application a decree of judicial separation can be obtained.[150] The consent of the respondent is not required for the decree to be granted and no evidence of fault or matrimonial misbehaviour is required. Cohabitation for a period or periods not exceeding six months does not break the continuity of the three-year period but those periods of cohabitation do not, of course, count in determining the period of separation. If after spouses have been living apart for some time they cohabit for a period longer than six months, the earlier period during which they were living apart cannot be taken into account in computing the continuous three year period of separation.

---

[147] Judicial Separation and Family Law Reform Act 1989, s.2(3)(a).
[148] *Ibid.*, s.2(1).
[149] [1972] Fam. 302.
[150] Judicial Separation and Family Law Reform Act 1989, s.2(1)(e).

Normal marital relationship non existent

Where a "marriage has broken down to the extent that the court is satisfied in all the circumstances that a normal marital relationship has not existed between the spouses for a period of one year immediately preceding the date of the application" the court may grant a decree of separation.[151] In *TF v. Ireland*,[152] the High Court held that in determining whether to grant a decree under this provision it was not necessary for the court to determine how or when or for what reason the marriage broke down but simply that the marriage has broken down in fact. Proof of "the loss of an essential ingredient of the marriage" is essential. The court may not make a finding of fault against either party and so it follows that the party who was responsible for the breakdown in the relationship could rely on this ground and seek a decree against the other spouse.

A decree of nullity may be granted if a spouse at the time of the marriage lacks the capacity to enter into and sustain a normal marital relationship. Where there is a deterioration in the spouses' relationship some time after marriage which results in their interacting as a normal married couple for at least one year a decree of judicial separation can be obtained. There may also be an overlap between the grounds on which a decree of judicial separation is sought. For example where a spouse is mentally cruel to the other spouse this misbehaviour may provide grounds for an application under section 2(1)(b) ("the behaviour ground"). The effect of such behaviour on the spouses' relationship over a continuous period of at least one year may ground a decree under section 2(1)(f). Further where a spouse (i) has been deserted for a period of one year or (ii) spouses have lived apart for a period of one year and consent to a separation decree or (iii) have lived apart for three years a decree of judicial separation may be granted under sections 2(1)(c), 2(1)(d) or 2(1)(e) respectively. The fact that the spouses have not cohabited for at least one year either because one of the spouses does not wish to live with the other or because there has been a joint agreement to cease living together may form the basis for a decree under section 2(1)(f).

Finally, where the court is considering what financial provision to make for each of the spouses by way of ancillary order consequent upon a decree of judicial separation the court is obliged to take into account "any physical or mental disability of either of the spouses".[153] Where one or other of the parties to the proceedings is a person with a mental or physical disability the court may regard that disability as a burden of that spouse which requires grater financial provision.

DIVORCE

The existing law regarding divorce

The law relating to the grant of decrees of divorce in Ireland and the making of orders for preliminary and ancillary relief in divorce proceedings is governed by Article 41.3.2 of the Constitution and the Family Law (Divorce) Act 1996. Section 5 of the Family Law (Divorce) Act 1996 provides:

---

[151] Judicial Separation and Family Law Reform Act 1989, s.2(1)(f).
[152] [1995] 1 I.R. 321.
[153] Family Law Act 1995, s.16(2)(c).

(1) Subject to the provisions of this Act, where, on application to it in that behalf by either of the spouses concerned, the court is satisfied that:

    (a) at the date of the institution of proceedings, the spouses have lived apart from one another for a period of, or periods amounting to, at least four years during the previous five years,

    (b) there is no reasonable prospect of a reconciliation between the spouses; and

    (c) such provision as the court considers proper having regard to the circumstances exist or will be made for the spouses and any dependent members of the family

the court may, in exercise of the jurisdiction conferred by Article 41.3.2 of the Constitution grant a decree of divorce in respect of the marriage concerned.

Sections 6 and 7 of the Family Law (Divorce) Act 1996 prescribe certain safeguards to ensure that both parties to divorce proceedings are made aware by their solicitors of alternatives to divorce proceedings and that these are discussed. These alternatives are the availability of marriage counselling to effect a reconciliation; the existence of mediation serves to assist in effecting a separation or a divorce on an agreed basis and the possibility of effecting a separation by way of an separation agreement. Solicitors acting for the applicant and the respondent in divorce proceedings must certify that the obligations imposed by these sections have been complied with. Where such certification is absent the court may adjourn the proceedings for such period as it considers reasonable so that these issues may be discussed by the relevant solicitor(s) with the applicant and/ or the respondent. Section 8 of the 1996 Act also provides for the adjournment by the court of divorce proceedings where the parties wish it to enable the spouses to reconcile or agree on some or all of the divorce terms.

Four years separation

Proof of the fact of living apart for the prescribed number of years at the date of the institution of proceedings is all that is required to ground a divorce decree. Neither party is required to prove that the fault lies with the other for or has caused the spouses to live apart. Where a spouse has been hospitalised for an extended period of time a question arises as to whether the period from the commencement of that hospitalisation to be regarded as forming part of the period of living apart which can form a basis for an application for divorce or would the extent to which the other spouse visited and interacted with the spouse in hospital and the length of time spent by the visiting spouse with the ill spouse be taken into consideration? This is a question yet to be answered by the court and as it is not clear whether some mental element or intention to end cohabitation is required.

    If spouses separate for three years and then reconcile and resume cohabitation for no more than twelve months then separate again after a further year's separation either can make application for a divorce. If, however, spouses, continuously cohabit for one day more than twelve months after an earlier period of separation the earlier period must be disregarded and cannot count as a portion of the prescribed period of living apart which is required to ground an application for divorce.

No reasonable prospect of reconciliation

The court can refuse to grant a decree of divorce where it is satisfied that the spouses have lived apart for the prescribed period where it concludes that there is a reasonable prospect of reconciliation. This conclusion must be reached on the basis of evidence before the court. Where the court reaches such a conclusion it may, if both spouses so wish, instead of dismissing the proceedings, adjourn them to enable the spouses to attempt a reconciliation. However, if one spouse does not agree to such an adjournment the court cannot order that spouse to effect a reconciliation and insist on the adjournment. However, there is nothing in Article 41.3.2 preventing the court simply adjourning the proceedings where the trial judge concludes that there is a reasonable prospect of reconciliation. However, one spouse's opposition to the adjournment may be sufficient evidence that no reasonable prospect exists. Where such an adjournment is granted either spouse may subsequently request that proceedings "be resumed as soon as may be" and the court is obliged under the 1996 Act to resume the proceedings.

Proper provision for spouses and children

The 1996 Act provides that the court, at the time of considering the divorce application, must be satisfied that proper provision exists or will be made for the spouses and "any dependent members of the family". Under the 1996 Act dependent members of the family are natural born or adopted children of either or both spouses or children in relation to whom either or both spouses are *in loco parentis*. A person ceases to be a "child" under the 1996 Act, upon reaching the age of 18 years or, if the child has reached that age, upon reaching the age of 23 years or upon ceasing to receive full-time education or instruction in any university, college, school or other educational establishment whichever is the earlier. However, provision may be made for a child over the age of 18 years who has completed his or her education or a child over 23 years where such child has "a mental or physical disability to such an extent that it is not reasonably possible for the child to maintain himself or herself fully".[154]

It is interesting to note that Article 41.3.2. does not refer to: "dependent members of the family" but to "any children of either or both of them (the spouses) and any other person prescribed by law." It remains to be seen what provision, if any, need be made for adult children who do not fall within the definition of "dependent members of the family" under the 1996 Act and whether section 5(1)(c) might be held to be invalid as an unconstitutional delimitation of the obligation imposed by Article 41.3.2. The effect of a decree of divorce is to dissolve the divorced spouses' marriage so that each party is free in civil law to marry again. While a person's legal status as spouse is ended that person's status as guardian of a child under section 6 of the Guardianship of Infants Act 1964 is not. However, the court may declare either of the parties unfit to have custody of any minor child and should it do so the party concerned is not entitled as of right to have custody of the minor on the death of the other party.[155]

Where a decree of divorce is granted the court's jurisdiction to grant ancillary relief under Part III of the Family Law (Divorce) Act 1996 is activated and the parties may

---

[154] See Family Law (Divorce) Act 1996, s.2(1).
[155] *Ibid.*, s.41.

address issues relating to finances, property and succession that require resolution. Disputes over the guardianship, custody and upbringing of minor children may also be addressed by way of ancillary order. In addition the court may, on its own initiative, give directions regarding the welfare, custody and access to children even where the parties are not in dispute.[156] Sections 20(2)(a)–(l) of the Family Law (Divorce) Act 1996 contains a list of factors to which the court is obliged to pay particular regard when making adequate and reasonable provision for the spouses and any dependent member of the family. Among these factors is "any physical or mental disability of either of the spouses"[157] – a factor, which the court may view as necessitating greater provision for the spouse with the disability.

THE LEGAL CAPACITY TO BEAR OR NOT TO BEAR CHILDREN

The legal right to bear or not to bear children in Ireland

The right to freedom of procreative choice was acknowledged in *McGee v. Attorney General*, and while sterilisation in general is not regulated by statute in Ireland, it is acknowledged[158] that in practice operations are available on a limited basis in the country. There is an absence of developed jurisprudence in relation the currently contentious issue of sterilisation of persons with intellectual disability. However, Irish courts have an inherent *parens patriae* jurisdiction to order sterilisation of persons with intellectual disability since under Article 34 of the Constitution the High Court has full jurisdiction on all matters of law and fact. In *In re an application by the Midland Health Board*,[159] it was held by the Supreme Court that a person of unsound mind could be made a ward of court even though such a person had no property. Finlay CJ held that such jurisdiction sprang from the court's duty to protect individual rights under Article 40.3 of the Constitution. Tom Cooney argues that the same protective principle would appear to cover applications to authorise non-voluntary sterilisation of incompetent mentally handicapped persons.[160] As far as the issues are concerned the Law Reform Commission of Canada in its *Working Paper on Sterilisation*[161] has summarised them as follows:

"Sterilisation [has been] justified on the basis that mentally retarded and mentally ill persons make poor parents, that poor parents tend to produce children prone to crime and other social problems, and that to prohibit procreation by these individuals is an act of protection against this eventuality by not placing the responsibility of parenthood upon those unable to cope with it. This argument presumes a state interest in ensuring that children receive sufficient care and attention to develop normally. This concern is both moral and economic."

---

[156] Family Law (Divorce) Act 1996, s.5(2).
[157] *Ibid.*, s.20(2)(e).
[158] See Tomkin and Hanafin, *Irish Medical Law* (Round Hall Press, Dublin, 1995), p.191.
[159] [1988] I.L.R.M. 251.
[160] "Sterilisation and the Mentally Handicapped" (1989) 11 D.U.L.J. 56.
[161] (No. 24, 1979) 32.

The position in English law

The leading English decisions have focused on the "best interests" of the person in respect of whom application is made.[162]

The issue was first raised significantly in *In re D (A Minor) (Wardship: Sterilisation)*.[163] In this case unlike later decisions Heilbron J. ruled against the sterilisation of an eleven year old girl with Soto's syndrome,[164] who was unable to give valid consent on the basis that the evidence showed that her mental and physical condition and attainments had already improved and that the likelihood was in future that she would be able to make her own choice. In arriving at her conclusion Heilbron J. drew a distinction between therapeutic and non-therapeutic sterilisations and indicated that the intervention of the law was necessary to decide upon the validity of the latter procedure.

In the later case *In re B (A Minor)(Wardship: Sterilisation)*,[165] House of Lords held that it was in the "best interests" of a 17-year-old girl with an intellectual disability who was the subject of a wardship application by the local authority to undergo a sterilisation operation. The child's mother was in favour of such a course of action. Drawing a distinction with *In re D*, in which Heilbron J. had stated that the sterilisation operation in that case would amount to a deprivation of a basic human right Lord Hailsham stated:

> "to talk of the 'basic right' to reproduce of an individual who is not capable of knowing the causal connection between intercourse and childbirth, the nature of pregnancy, what is involved in delivery, unable to form maternal instincts or to care for a child appears to me wholly to part company with reality".

The case has been criticised as an *apotheosis* of judicial paternalism for its conclusion that a basic human right did not inhere a person who was unable to appreciate the existence and significance of such a right and that in those circumstances a court was acting in the best interests of a person by authorising a sterilisation procedure.[166] Arguing that the model of analysis in *In re B*, would knock the intellectually disabled persons right to reproduce "off its pedestal by a goal of special urgency," Michael Freeman acknowledges that rights may conflict with one another but postulates a "preferred solution" as "one which maximises the fulfilment of rights and minimises their violations."[167]

In *F v. West Berkshire Health Authority and other (Mental Health Act Commission intervening)*,[168] the House of Lords upheld the validity of an order for the sterilisation of an adult with an intellectual disability who was thirty six years of age but who had the verbal capacity of a child of two and the mental capacity of a child of four to five on the basis that it was in the adult's best interests to do so. F had developed a relationship

---

[162] *In re B (A Minor) (Wardship: Sterilisation)* [1988] A.C. 199; [1987] 2 All E.R. 296 *and In re F (Mental Patient: Sterilisation)* [1989] 2 W.L.R. 1025.

[163] [1976] 1 All E.R. 326.

[164] This syndrome manifested itself in personality dysfunction, epileptic fits and intellectual dysfunction.

[165] [1987] 2 All E.R. 206.

[166] See Tomkin and Hanafin, *op. cit.*, p.197.

[167] M.D.A. Freeman, "Sterilising the Mentally Handicapped" in M.D.A. Freeman (eds.), *Medicine Ethics and the Law* (Current Legal Problems, Stevens, London, 1988).

[168] [1989] 2 All E.R. 545.

with a male patient at the hospital at which she was an in-patient and the hospital authorities were concerned about the consequences of a sexual relationship between F and the other patient. Lord Goff upheld the decision by reference to the doctrine of necessity, which provides a defence to a medical practitioner who operates on a person who is incapable of giving consent if it can be demonstrated that the operation is in the best interests of the patient. However, critics[169] have pointed out that the doctrine of necessity would apply in cases of genuine medical necessity and it is doubtful whether one could place a non-therapeutic sterilisation in this category. This view is substantiated by dicta in the Canadian decision of *In re Eve*, in which La Forest J. quoting a Law Reform Commission of Canada Working Paper on Sterilisation[170] states:

> "[s]terilisation as a medical procedure is distinct, because except in rare cases, if the operation is not performed the physical health of the person involved is not in danger, necessity or emergency not normally being factors in the decision to undertake the procedure."

On a jurisdictional issue the court ruled that since the enactment of the Mental Health Act 1959 it no longer had *parens patriae* jurisdiction to govern the affairs of a mentally incompetent adult but it had an inherent jurisdiction to make a declaration in relation to the sterilisation of such a person. It also stated that in practice, while not strictly necessary to make such a procedure lawful application should be made to the court before such treatment was undertaken as it would establish by judicial process whether the operation was in the individual's best interests and therefore lawful.

In the case of *In re E (A Minor)*,[171] it was established that a sterilisation proposed on the basis of therapeutic reasons (*i.e.* medical need) can be carried out without an application to the High Court for a declaration. In this case parents were able to give consent to a hysterectomy to be performed for therapeutic reasons on their 17-year-old daughter with an intellectual disability without the necessity for a declaration notwithstanding that the incidental result would be sterilisation. A similar decision was reached in the case of a 29-year-old woman with an intellectual disability in *F v. F*.[172]

In *In re GF (Medical Treatment)*,[173] it was held that no application for leave to carry out a hysterectomy on a 29 year old woman with an intellectual disability was necessary where two medical practitioners were satisfied that the operation was:

(1) necessary for therapeutic purposes;

(2) in the best interests of the patient; and

(3) that there was no practicable less intrusive means of treating the condition.

In this case the woman who was largely confined to a wheelchair and had a mental age of a five year old suffered from excessively heavy menstrual periods, which she was unable to deal with. Her medical practitioner and two consultant gynaecologists advised

---

[169] See Tomkin & Hanafin, *op. cit.*, p.200.
[170] The Law Reform Commission of Canada, *Sterilisation*, Working Paper 24 (Ottawa, Canada, 1979).
[171] T.L.R. February 22, 1991.
[172] April 29, 1991.
[173] [1992] Family Law 22, p.63.

a hysterectomy as the only practicable method of treating her condition. The operation would have the incidental effect of sterilisation but its object was essentially therapeutic.

In *In re W (Mental Patient) (Sterilisation)*,[174] Hollis J. made a declaration in favour of a sterilisation operation of a 20 year old intellectually disabled woman who suffered from severe epilepsy and a minor degree of cerebral palsy for contraceptive reasons since she would be unable to cope with any pregnancy and there would be a significant risk of the epilepsy worsening during pregnancy. A responsible body of medical opinion skilled in the particular field of diagnosis and treatment was also in favour of the sterilisation notwithstanding that there was only a small risk of W becoming pregnant. In the light of that fact and the circumstances it was held that it would be in the patient's best interests for the operation to be performed. In this case it appears that a future risk of pregnancy and not an existing one was sufficient to ground a declaration that the operation was in the patient's best interests. Considerable weight was also attached to the fact that "a responsible body of medical opinion skilled in the particular field of diagnosis and treatment" was also in favour of the operation. The Official Solicitor has made practice directions relating to the procedure to be adopted in applications for adults who lack capacity in the light of the developing jurisprudence in this area.[175]

In *In re LC (Medical Treatment: Sterilisation)*,[176] Thorpe J. held that in considering whether a severely intellectually disabled person should be subjected to non-consensual invasive surgery for contraceptive reasons the court must consider not only factors directly affecting the individual concerned but also society's interests and values. Whilst considerations were finely balanced in this case involving an intellectually disabled woman aged 21 with an intellectual age of 31/2 who had been sexually assaulted by a member of staff in a unit in which she had been living, the evidence established that the level of care and supervision (by way of protection from invasive sexual assault) which the woman was receiving in the small residential home to which she had been moved was of such exceptionally high quality that it would not be in her best interests to impose upon her a surgical procedure which was not without risks and painful consequences. This case is interesting in that Thorpe J. held that the balancing exercise in determining best interests in the context of sterilisation extended beyond narrowly personal factors to encompass some consideration of the values held by society. Thorpe J. did not elaborate explicitly on what those values might be although by implication he perhaps identified the need to protect the incompetent person from invasive surgery. It is significant however, that the judgment makes no reference to the person's right to reproduce. It is also clear from his judgment that in assessing the likelihood of pregnancy in relation to a young woman who has no interest in human relationships with any sexual ingredient a high level of supervision appears to be regarded as an appropriate protection.

In *In re S (Medical Treatment: Adult Sterilisation)*,[177] Johnson J. following *In re LC* refused to make a declaration that it would be lawful to have a sterilisation operation performed on a 22 year old woman who was intellectually disabled with no understanding of sexuality. He found on the facts that the risk of her sexual exploitation was merely speculative and not identifiable and in the circumstances sterilisation was not in S's

---

[174] *Ibid.*, p.208.
[175] The latest practice direction is reported at (2001) 31 Family Law 551.
[176] [1997] Family Law 27, pp.604–605.
[177] [1998] Family Law 28, p.325.

best interests. By contrast in *In re X (An Adult Patient)*,[178] Holman J. found on the evidence that there was a risk that X, a 31 year old intellectually disabled woman with an intellectual age of between four and six years, could become pregnant as she had for several years had a relationship with a male user of the centre which she attended regularly. He considered that sterilisation would be in X's best interests as despite the fact that she had expressed the wish to have a baby the process of pregnancy, birth and the inevitable removal of the baby would be frightening and bewildering to X. In addition there were found to be no viable alternatives to sterilisation in X's case, though these had been carefully considered. Sterilisation would allow also X to have the present restrictions on her freedom caused by her carer's fear that she might become pregnant removed.

In the *X* case, there was only one matter which caused Mr Justice Holman to hesitate and that was the fact that X had been able to understand the connection between sexual intercourse and babies and that she had expressed the wish to have a baby. He was concerned that to deny her this might seem to be a gross infringement of her right to bodily integrity and her right to reproduce. However, he found that the process of pregnancy, birth and the inevitable removal of the baby – the doctor's considering that she would be incapable of caring for a child - would be frightening and bewildering to X. In granting the order sought he also made it clear that the theoretical risk that she might give birth to a baby, which had impaired physical or intellectual capacity, played no part in the decision.

In *In re ZM and OS (Sterilisation: Patient's Best Interests)*,[179] the mother and litigation friend of a 19 year old woman with Down's syndrome sought a declaration that her daughter undergo surgery as it was in her best interests that (1) her menstrual periods cease altogether, and (2) that all risks of pregnancy be avoided. The menstrual periods caused significant distress and disturbance to the young woman and the consequences of pregnancy would result in substantial trauma and psychological damage to her. The Official Solicitor opposed the mother's application for a declaration in relation to subtotal hysterectomy arguing that an intra-uterine device would lessen the heaviness of periods, provide an appropriate form of contraception and did not involve a major surgical procedure. The young woman lacked the capacity to decide whether or not to have the sterilisation operation and was unlikely ever to develop that capacity. Bennett J. in the Family Division adopting the best interests approach favoured in *In re F, (Sterilisation Mental Patient)*,[180] granted the declaration sought. He held that the very low risk associated with laparascopic subtotal hysterectomy was worth running in that the young woman would achieve a dramatic improvement in her quality of life by eliminating her periods entirely and providing total protection from pregnancy. The likelihood that the mother would not always be around to protect her daughter but would be replaced by residential carers led Bennett J. to conclude that the small risk of conception associated with the intra-uterine device was best eliminated altogether and that surgery was in her best interests. Once again in this case a future as opposed to present risk of pregnancy was sufficient to ground a declaration that sterilisation was in the woman's best interests.

---

[178] *Medical Law Monitor* (1998) 5(11) 5–6.
[179] [2000] Fam. Law 321.
[180] [1989] 2 F.L.R. 376.

In *In re A (Male Patient: Sterilisation)*[181] a 28 year old man with Down's Syndrome who lived primarily with his 63 year old mother had a significant to severe impairment of intelligence. He was vulnerable and easily led and enjoyed the company of women. His mother provided a high degree of care and supervision and was on her guard against any inappropriate behaviour. Because her health was not good was believed that she would not be able to continue this into the future and feared that when her son moved to local authority care he might form a sexual relationship resulting in making a woman pregnant. Consequently she sought a declaration from the High Court that in his best interests her son should be sterilised by way of vasectomy. Sumner J. refused the application on the grounds that the advantages of vasectomy were unclear, the operation was not essential to the patient's future well-being and a declaration was therefore not in the patient's best interests. As it was the first case to have sought the court's approval for sterilisation of a male patient Sumner J. gave leave to appeal. The Court of Appeal dismissed the appeal and held that the best interests of the patient were not limited to best medical interests but encompassed medical, emotional and all other welfare issues. An operation to sterilise had to be demonstrated to be in the best interests of the person unable to consent and had to be proved following a balancing of all the relevant factors on the individual facts of the case. An application for sterilisation on behalf of a man was not the equivalent of an application in respect of a woman due to obvious biological differences. The refusal to approve the operation would not diminish the mother's care of the patient and nor would he be aware that she was upset. In addition approving the operation would not allow the patient to enjoy a more relaxed lifestyle. In essence the lack of crucial evidence in relation to the positive aspects of sterilisation left the argument incomplete.

Interestingly in this case, a speculative risk of A's engaging in sexual intercourse resulting in the pregnancy of a woman was held not to be sufficient to warrant a declaration that the sterilisation of a man was lawful whereas in the case of a woman such as *In re ZM and OS*, a future risk of pregnancy was sufficient to ground a declaration. Interestingly in the *A Case*, Thorpe J. held that the failure of the appeal did not preclude a fresh application in the future on fresh evidence; the crucial missing piece of evidence in the case was that post-vasectomy A would be permitted greater freedom including the opportunity to develop sexual experience and intimacy.

In *In re S (Sterilisation: Patient's Best Interests)*,[182] S a very attractive young woman of 29 had been born with severe learning difficulties and lived with her mother. Recognising that she could not always care for her daughter the mother sought a declaration that her daughter be sterilised in her best interests despite her inability to consent to the procedure. Wall J. in the High Court granted the declaration for therapeutic purposes and gave permission to appeal. The mother's application was prompted by two reasons one social and one therapeutic. First, S was very attractive looking and closely supervised by her mother. If she entered local authority accommodation she might move in mixed circles unsupervised and might form a close emotional attachment or become the victim of a sexual assault. Secondly, S suffered from heavy menstrual bleeding which caused her distress and with which she had difficulty coping. The Official

---

[181] [2000] 1 F.L.R. 549.
[182] [2000] Fam. Law 711.

Solicitor appealed on behalf of S and argued first, that the judges decision was contrary to expert medical evidence and did not have regard to the principle of *primum non nocere* and that he erred in law in his application of *In re F (Mental Patient: Sterilisation)*[183] and his approach to the *Bolam* test.

The Court of Appeal in allowing the appeal held first in accepting the evidence of family and friends in preference to the expert evidence to the contrary the judge failed to give appropriate weight to the medical view that a less intrusive method of contraceptive and therapeutic treatment should be tried first. The remedy proposed by the judge was out of proportion to the problem to be solved. The judge was in error in his application of the *Bolam* test to his decision making process. In determining the welfare of the patient the *Bolam* test is applied only at the outset to ensure that the treatment proposed is recognised as proper by a responsible body of medical opinion skilled in delivering that particular treatment. Once the judge is satisfied that this is so, it is his decision as to whether he particular treatment is in the best interests of the patient taking into account the broader ethical social moral and welfare considerations.

In the light of the above cases the trend in England appears to be generally in favour of both therapeutic and non-therapeutic sterilisations except in the latter case where it is demonstrably not in the best interests of the patient. However, it must be said that the definition of best interests is wide and varying and it seems that a case by case approach is being adopted.

The position in Canadian law

As far as the Canadian position is concerned the Canadian Supreme Court in *In re Eve*,[184] held that the court's *parens patriae* jurisdiction did not extend to authorising sterilisation for non-therapeutic purposes. La Forest J. delivering judgment for the court stated:

> "[t]he grave intrusion on a person's rights and the certain physical damage that ensues from non therapeutic sterilisation without consent when compared to the highly questionable advantages that can result from it, have persuaded me that it can never safely be determined that such a procedure is for the benefit of that person. Accordingly, procedure should never be authorised for non-therapeutic purposes under the *parens patriae* jurisdiction."[185]

The Supreme Court went on to state that the proper forum to rule on this was the legislature and not the courts. He referred to the lack of knowledge of the judiciary of the concept of mental illness and the fact that the legislature was in a position to inform itself and was attuned to the feelings of the public in this sensitive area.[186] Outlining the basis for its decision the court stated:

> "[T]he importance of maintaining the physical integrity of a human being ranks

---

[183] [1990] 2 A.C. 1.
[184] (1986) 31 D.L.R. (4th) 1.
[185] *Ibid.*, p.32.
[186] *Ibid.*, p.33.

high in our scale of values, particularly as it affects the privilege of giving life. I cannot agree that a court can deprive a woman of that privilege for purely social or other non-therapeutic purposes without her consent. The fact that others may suffer inconvenience or hardship from failure to do so cannot be taken into account."[187]

La Forest J. was also of the opinion that the sterilisation of those who are not capable of giving consent may only be carried out if it is required for *bona fide* medical treatment and because of the importance of the right protected such treatment must be necessary in dealing with a serious condition.

The position in Australian law

In Australia, in the case of *Secretary Department of Health and Community Services v. JWB and SMB (Marion's* Case),[188] the parents of an intellectually disabled girl who was 14 years old had applied to the Family Court of Australia for an order authorising the performance of a hysterectomy and an ovariectomy upon their daughter who was found to be incapable by reason of intellectual disability of giving valid informed consent to medical treatment. On appeal from the Full Court of the Family Court, the High Court was asked to determine whether court approval was necessary before the proposed procedures could lawfully be performed. The majority of the High Court (Mason C.J., Dawson, Toohey and Gaudron JJ. and Deane J.) held that a non-therapeutic sterilisation on a child could only be performed with the permission of the court. Parents had no power to authorise such a procedure. Only therapeutic procedures could be carried out on the basis of parental consent alone. For the majority of the court sterilisation was therapeutic only if it was "a by-product of surgery appropriately carried out to treat some malfunction or disease." Therefore all procedures performed or carried out for the benefit of an intellectually disabled girl but solely intended to result in sterilisation required the approval of the court. Court authorisation was required because of the significant risk of making a wrong decision either as to the child's present or future capacity to consent or about what were the best interests of the child who could not consent and because the consequences of a wrong decision were particularly grave. The function of the court when asked to authorise sterilisation was to decide whether in the circumstances of the case that was in the best interest of the girl.

The court would not approve sterilisations where the intention was eugenic or entirely for the convenience of others such as those caring for her. Sterilisation performed solely for contraceptive purposes could be lawful if it were demonstrated to be necessary for the girl's general welfare and was a step of last resort. The majority further held: "In the context of medical management, "step of last resort" is a convenient was of saying that alternative and less invasive procedures have all failed or that it is certain that no other procedure or treatment will work."[189] The court would give authorisation, not on account of the convenience of sterilisation as a contraceptive measure, but because it was necessary to enable the girl to lead a life in keeping with her needs and capacities.

---

[187] *Ibid.*, p.33.
[188] (1992) 175 C.L.R. 218.
[189] (1992) F.L.C. 92–293, 79, 185.

Deane J. agreed with the majority that the authority of parents did not, in the absence of special statutory provisions, extend to authorising surgery involving the sterilisation of a profoundly intellectually disabled child for purely contraceptive purposes. However, he held parents could authorise the carrying out of surgery involving the irreversible sterilisation of an incapable child where it was obviously necessary for the welfare of the child. To be so obviously necessary for the child's welfare the surgery had to fall within either of two categories. First the surgery had to be immediately necessary to conventional medical purposes, *i.e.* the preservation of life or the treatment or prevention of grave physical illness. For surgery to fall within the second category a number of conditions had to be satisfied.

First, the child had to be so profoundly intellectually disabled that she was not and never would be capable of being a party to a mature human relationship involving informed sexual intercourse, of responsible procreation or of caring for an infant. Secondly, the surgery had to be necessary to avoid grave and unusual problems and suffering which were or would be involved in menstruation, which had either commenced, or which was virtually certain to commence in the near future. These problems could arise from inability to comprehend or cope with pain; a phobic aversion to blood; a complete inability to cope with problems of hygiene with psychiatric or psychological consequences or any of a variety of other possible complications. The pain or suffering which would result from menstruation had to be such that it was plain that, according to general community standards it would be quite unfair for the child and ultimate adult to bear the additional burden of them. Thirdly, the surgery had to be a treatment of last resort in the sense that no alternative and less drastic treatment would be appropriate and effective. Fourthly, there had to be competent medical advice from a multidisciplinary team acting on the basis of appropriate paediatric, social and domestic reports that the previous conditions were satisfied. When parents had received such multidisciplinary advice they would have discharged the obligation of due inquiry and adequate consideration and would be justified in authorising the particular surgery.

Deane J. also agreed with the majority that a sterilisation for purely contraceptive purposes could be lawful but only with the court's approval. In making its determination, Deane J. was of the view that the court should consider a number of factors but in particular identify the child's level of functioning and development and consider whether there is any real likelihood of a significant increase in the child's capabilities in the future.

McHugh J. held that parents could give lawful consent to the sterilisation of an intellectually disabled child if the procedure was necessary for the protection of the health of the child or to alleviate pain, fear or discomfort of such severity and duration or regularity that it is not reasonable to expect the child to bear it. They could also give lawful consent, if the procedure was required to eliminate a real risk of the child becoming pregnant if she did not, and never would have any real understanding of sexual relationships or pregnancy. In addition, parents could give consent if sterilisation was required for any purpose analogous to the foregoing purposes. The parents had no authority to consent to such an operation, however, if the harm could reasonably be avoided by means less drastic than sterilisation. If, for any reason, such as a conflict of interest, the parents are not able to give consent the Family Court of Australia could give its consent in substitution for the parents. Accordingly, subject to the aforementioned conditions, McHugh J. accepted the legality of sterilisation procedures. However, for him, except in the case of a conflict of interests, these procedures could be consented to by the parents.

Brennan J. dissenting considered that all non-therapeutic procedures intended to sterilise the girl were unlawful. Hence for him purely contraceptive sterilisations would never be lawful. His view of what amounted to a non-therapeutic sterilisation was, however, somewhat narrower than the majority of the court. He defined non-therapeutic treatment as "treatment which is inappropriate or disproportionate having regard to the cosmetic deformity, pathological condition or psychiatric disorder for which the treatment is administered and ... treatment which is administered for other purposes" Brennan J. considered that the procedure could be lawful and could be consented to by the parents,[190] where the procedure was carried out for the chief purpose of preventing, removing or ameliorating a cosmetic deformity, a pathological condition or a psychiatric disorder provided the treatment is appropriate for and proportionate to the purpose for which it was administered.

In *L and G.M. v. M.M.: The Director General Department of Family Services and Aboriginal and Islander Affairs*,[191] Warnick J. in the Family Court of Australia addressed the case of Sarah, a 17 year old physically and intellectually disabled young woman whose parents applied for authorisation to consent to her undergoing an abdominal hysterectomy to help maintain hygiene, to control her epilepsy and to prevent pregnancy. Sarah who was not able to communicate or walk was dependent on health care providers for her daily needs including hygiene, bathing, dressing, feeding and toileting. She lived in a hospital and attended a special school. There was a possibility that she would be moved from the hospital to live in accommodation shared with other disabled people with a supervising carer. Her parents argued that it was in Sarah's best interests to undergo the procedure.

Warnick J. held, following the decision in *Secretary Department of Health and Community Services v. JWB and SMB*, that the authorisation of the court was required before the procedure could be carried out. Whether the operation was lawful or not depended upon the guiding principle of the child's best interests. The "best interests of the child" was the perspective from which all other facts and values had to be viewed. He held that the majority's views in *JWB* were not to be taken as elevating the parent's views (who were in favour of the hysterectomy) to the level of a competing principle, far less a presumption as to what best interests might mean. He cited with approval Brennan J.'s observation that "the best interests approach offers no hierarchy of values." Parental views therefore were no more nor less than part of the "factual material" or background to be evaluated along with all the other factors in reaching a view on best interests.

Warnick J. held that when non consensual, non-therapeutic sterilisation was under consideration a fundamental right was at stake and only convincing, indeed compelling evidence would persuade the court to authorise it. He held that the proposed procedure would not with any certainty (subject to the risk of removal of pregnancy) increase

---

[190] Hence the Canadian case of *In re K and the Public Trustee* (1985) 19 D.L.R. (4th) 225 (B.C.C.A.) where the girl had a phobic aversion to blood and the New Zealand case of *In re X* [1991] 2 N.Z.L.R. 365 where menstruation would have had disastrous psychological consequences were cases in which the performance of a hysterectomy was justified on therapeutic grounds.
[191] (1994) F.L.C. 668, *Medical Law Review* (1995) 3(1) 94–97.

Sarah's [the name given to the young woman in the case] capacity to enjoy life or meet a presently unmet need. Sterilisation would not improve Sarah's health. It was unnecessary to enable Sarah to move to residential style accommodation. It would not demonstrably improve the attitude towards Sarah of her carers. Whether the parents' wishes were met or not, would not affect Sarah. Sterilisation would not prevent sexual abuse and may arguably increase the risk thereof. Warnick J. also examined the argument that sterilisation was justified because of the fear that the young woman would otherwise become pregnant and that, if pregnant, a further series of damaging consequences would follow. To Warnick J. the horror at the risk of pregnancy was in fact best understood as an extension of the horror of sexual abuse. He relied on Brennan J.'s judgment in *JWB* that:

> "[t]hose who are charged with the responsibility for the care and control of an intellectually disabled girl ... have a duty to ensure that the girl is not sexually exploited or abused. If her disability inclines her to sexual promiscuity they have a duty to restrain her from exposing herself to exploitation. It is unacceptable that an authority can be given for the girl's sterilisation to lighten that burden of that duty much less to allow for its neglect."

Warnick J. found that the young woman's "pregnancy is a number of steps removed from probability." The risk of pregnancy did not and should not therefore serve as a basis for the proposed sterilisation. That risk was not enough to justify sterilisation for another reason. If it were enough justification this "would be virtually equivalent to establishing a policy that all females, with profound disabilities resembling those afflicting Sarah should be sterilised. There is nothing substantial about the risk nor clearly detrimental to Sarah about pregnancy which justifies the interference with personal inviolability unless it be that where there is any risk (as there must always be) sterilisation should occur." Such an approach, he found, would violate the young woman's fundamental rights in particular the right to personal inviolability

The Australian approach thus differs from the English approach, but is consistent with that in Canada in that it is prepared to use the language of rights to refuse to authorise a non-therapeutic sterilisation. It, however, differs from the Canadian approach (below) in that in *JWB* the court acknowledged that in certain circumstances sterilisation although non-therapeutic could be lawful.

The position in US law

In the past in the USA, persons with mental disabilities were sterilised unnecessarily, frequently without their consent. Today however, substantial due process is required before someone may decide to sterilise a person who is incompetent.

In *In re Haye*,[192] the Washington Supreme court concluded that only in: "the rare and unusual case" is sterilisation "in the best interests of the retarded person" and due process safeguards exist. The safeguards include the following: disinterested guardian ad litem must represent the incompetent person; courts must receive independent advice

---

[192] 608 P. 2d 635 (Wash. Sup.Ct 1980).

based on a comprehensive medical, psychological and social evaluation of the person and consider that persons views. The trial court must find by clear, cogent and convincing evidence that the individual cannot make an informed decision about sterilisation and is unlikely to be able to do so in the foreseeable future. Secondly the court must find that clear and convincing evidence indicates the need for sterilisation because the individual is physically capable of procreation and likely to engage in sexual activity and the person's disability renders her permanently incapable of caring for a child. Finally the court also must find that no reasonable alternative to sterilisation exists because a less restrictive alternative form of contraception is unavailable and the current state of scientific and medical knowledge does not suggest that a less drastic contraceptive method or a treatment of disability will be available shortly.

In *Chasse v. Mazerolle*,[193] Maine's highest court found no basis for dismissing a wrongful sterilisation case brought by a patient with an intellectual disability. The medical practitioner had violated a state statute by failing to consult both a physician and a surgeon to determine whether the patient was competent to give consent and that the procedure was needed for therapeutic reasons. Further, in *McKinney v. McKinney*,[194] the Arkansas Supreme Court struck down provisions of a state law that permitted the administration of involuntary sterilisation of persons with mental disabilities but failed to provide for judicial oversight and the rights to notice, counsel and a hearing. However, in *In re the estate of C.W.*,[195] based on clear and convincing evidence that no less restrictive methods were workable, the Pennsylvania courts granted and the US Supreme Court left standing a decision to grant a mother authority to consent to the sterilisation of her twenty one year old daughter with an intellectual disability, epilepsy and an intellectual age of someone three to five years old.

Commentary

It is difficult to resist the conclusion that case law surrounding the procedure of sterilisation in other jurisdictions reflects a divergence of approach between respecting the reproductive autonomy of persons with intellectual disability in the sense of their right to be free from unwanted and unnecessary sterilisation ("the autonomy approach") as exemplified in *In re Eve*, in Canada, and authorising sterilisation in their best interests ("the best interests approach") an approach which particularly in some of the English cases such as *In re B*, appears to mean guarding against future risks of pregnancy and upholding the views of the medical profession. The decision of Warnick J. in *L and G.M v. MM* in the Australian Family Court represents a hybrid of those approaches. Within a framework of respect for the human rights of the incapable person and the responsibility of the capable for the incapable he adopted a best interests test, which translated into a close examination the evidence for and against non-therapeutic sterilisation.

The issue of non-therapeutic sterilisation of persons with intellectual disabilities has not yet come before the Irish courts nor has any legislation been passed in respect of it.

---

[193] 580 A 2d. 155 (Me. Sup. Jud. Ct. 1990) 15 M.P.D.L.R. 57.
[194] 805 S.W. 2d. 66 (Ark. Sup. Ct. 1991) 15 M.P.D.L.R. 374.
[195] No. 2970. (Pa. Super. Ct. March 17, 1993) 17 M.P.D.L.R. 258, 640 A. 2d. 427 (Pa. Super. Ct. 1994) 18 M.P.D.L.R. 515 cert denied 115 S.Ct. 1175 (1995).

However, if a case ever arose for determination it is submitted that given the varied interpretations of the best interests test which tend in some cases to overlook the reproductive rights of the person with intellectual disability and the opposing position taken in *In re Eve*, which recognises the right to reproductive autonomy of the person with intellectual disability but perhaps does not give sufficient weight to the welfare interests of the person it is submitted that a hybrid approach be adopted and that both the rights to reproductive autonomy and the welfare of the incapacitated person be weighed in the balance to arrive at a decision.

There is considerable controversy as to whether legislation should govern the situation. Mason & McCall Smith resist such a move, on the basis that it would lead to "generalisation in the area where the individual is paramount" and would prefer that decisions continue to be made on a "case to case" basis.[196] Hoggett on the other hand while agreeing that "these decisions require the most sensitive, individualised attention" adds: "It must be questioned whether the High Court is best equipped for the task, particularly as long as it relies upon any "responsible body of medical opinion" however, controversial as a test of the woman's best interests."[197] Ian Kennedy has argued that the best interests test adopted at common law is not in fact a "test" but rather a "crude conclusion of social policy" which allows the courts to believe that they are applying a principled approach while avoiding any detailed analysis of what the best interests are and what weight should be given to them.[198] Michael Bryan appears to agree with this view. He describes the welfare principle as a "smokescreen, which conceals either an absence of coherent decision making or the pursuit by the courts of a hidden agenda."[199] On balance it is submitted that decisions of this nature should not be left in the realms of medical discretion to be decided by varying criteria and that legislation which respects the right to reproductive autonomy of the person with mental disability but would permit sterilisation operations for the treatment of serious conditions and with court approval for contraceptive purposes, subject to the satisfaction of comprehensive and precise criteria, should be considered.

An interesting example of the criteria, which might be adopted, may be found in the Guidelines,[200] published by the Victoria Guardianship Board.[201] Section 42 of the Victorian Guardianship and Administration Board Act 1986 provides that the Guardianship Board may consent to a "major medical procedure" which includes a sterilisation operation if it is satisfied that the "major medical procedure" is in the person's "best interests." Section 4 of the Act provides that it is the intention of Parliament that the provisions of the Act be interpreted and that every function, power, authority, discretion, jurisdiction and duty conferred or imposed by the Act is to be exercised or performed so that the means which is least restrictive of a person's freedom of decision and action as is possible in the circumstances is adopted. The Guidelines outline the

---

[196] *Law and Medical Ethics* (5th ed., Butterworths, London, 1999), p.105.
[197] *Mental Health Law* (4th ed., Sweet & Maxwell, London, 1996), p.233.
[198] See "Patients, doctors and human rights" in Blackburn and Taylor (eds.), 1 *Human Rights for the 1990s*, p.90.
[199] See M. Bryan, "Two cheers for welfare, the Marion case and sterilisation in Australia", 5 *Journal of Child Law* 40.
[200] Powers of the Board with Respect to Medical Procedures issued six August 1990.
[201] See Blackwood, "Sterilisation of the Intellectually Disabled: The Need for Legislative Reform", 5 *Australian Journal of Family Law* 138.

matters, which the Board should consider in determining whether it should consent to an application for medical treatment (including sterilisation). They read in part:

(1) The expressed wishes of the woman who is the subject of the application should be obtained and seriously considered.

(2) A woman with a disability has the right to the same treatment as other women of her age.

(3) The need for evidence that the woman is being given maximum opportunity to develop and receive education which would enable her to participate maximally in decisions which affect her life such as sterilisation.

(4) The age of a woman needs consideration insofar as her future fertility and sexual development is concerned and the need not to make a premature decision affecting this part of her life.

(5) The need for evidence of alternatives less restrictive of a woman's personal growth and freedom being thoroughly explored.[202]

The Board also considered that certain judicial criteria,[203] issued in relation to sterilisation operations were useful guides and should be given weight appropriate to the particular circumstances of the case. The criteria are:

(1) Independent medical and psychological evaluations by qualified professionals should be observed.

(2) The Board must be persuaded by clear and convincing proof that sterilisation is in the best interests of the person and in determining this issue should consider at least:
    (a) the possibility that the person can become pregnant;
    (b) the possibility of trauma or psychological damage arising from pregnancy or birth (or conversely from the sterilisation operation);
    (c) the likelihood that the individual will voluntarily engage in sexual activity or be exposed to a situation where sexual intercourse is imposed upon her;
    (d) the inability of the person to understand reproduction or contraception and the likely permanence of that inability;
    (e) the feasibility and medical advisability of less drastic means of contraception both at the present time and the foreseeable future (e.g. particular hormonal treatments);
    (f) the advisability of sterilisation at the time of application rather than in the future;
    (g) the ability of the person to care for a child and the possibility that the individual may at some future date be able to marry and, with a partner, care for a child;
    (h) evidence of scientific or medical advances which may occur within the foreseeable future and make possible either an improvement of the individual's condition or alternative and less drastic sterilisation procedures;

---

[202] *Ibid.*, pp.35–36.

[203] In particular the criteria of Nicholson C.J. in *In re Jane* (1988) 12 Fam. L.R. 662. In that case it was decided that the court's consent was necessary before a sterilisation operation could be performed.

(i)   a demonstration that the proponents of the sterilisation are seeking it in good
      faith and that their primary concern is for the best interest of the incompetent
      person rather than their own or the public's convenience (e.g. menstrual
      management).[204]

Finally, the Guidelines indicate that the Guardianship Board will consider five key
questions in determining whether the proposed operation is the least restrictive of the
person's freedom of decision and action and therefore ultimately in her best interests.
These questions are:

(1)   Who has the problem? Is it the person? Is it the person's caregivers or parents?

(2)   What is the problem?

(3)   What would be recommended for solving the problem for an intellectually competent
      person of the same age and gender?[205]

(4)   Is the proposed solution proportionate to the problem identified?

(5)   What if we consent or do not consent? *i.e.* what are the immediate and long term
      effects of our decision one way or the other?[206]

Further in November 1994, the Australian Family Law Council published its
recommendations relating to the *"Sterilisation and other Medical Procedures on
Children"* and advocated that a uniform approach be adopted across Australian states
and territories in relation to the sterilisation of mentally incapacitated minors. As an
outline of the major considerations, which might apply in this field, it is worthy of note.
Briefly it recommended a new division in the Family Law Act 1975 to regulate the
sterilisation of young people so that any sterilisation of a child under 18, which is carried
out other than in the prescribed circumstances, would be unlawful. A three stage decision
making process was proposed:
      The first stage addresses four situations where sterilisation could never be authorised
namely (a) for eugenic reasons; (b) purely for contraceptive purposes and (c) in order to
conceal or avoid the consequences of sexual abuse and (d) before the commencement
of menstruation.
      The second stage states that there can only be sterilisation of a person under the age
of 18 if the procedure is necessary to save life or to prevent serious damage to the
person's physical or psychological health.
      The third stage outlines the factors to be considered in the context of the criteria
outlined at the second stage and provides that when deciding whether there is serious
damage to a person's physical or psychological health the decision-maker must consider
(a) the feasibility of less permanent means of contraception if this is relevant; (b) the
person's response to training in menstrual management if this is the problem. If the
decision maker is inclined to approve the application at the third stage s/he must only

---

[204] Powers of the Board with Respect to Medical Procedures at p.36.
[205] The Board suggests that this question is useful to identify latent, unthinking or hidden discriminatory
      attitudes which may be present.
[206] Powers of the Board with Respect to Medical Procedures, pp.36–37.

do so if the procedure would be held to be in the child's best interests. The Council acknowledged in its report that the welfare test is relevant but in its present form was too unstructured. It preferred specific criteria to be provided in legislation and while these are not detailed in the report it advocated that Guidelines such as those outlined by Nicholson C J. in *In re Jane*[207] should be taken into account. These included considerations that the individual could in fact become pregnant, the possibility of suffering trauma or psychological damage in the event of pregnancy and the likelihood that the woman or girl would voluntarily become involved in sexual activity. Also included was the consideration that the woman or girl might be exposed to situations where sexual intercourse is imposed upon her. Less drastic means of contraception were also to be considered taking into account possible future medical advances.

The Council recommended that the Family Court of Australia should hear applications for the proposed sterilisation of minors preferring this option to that of Tribunals having jurisdiction. It recommended that only specially trained judges should hear the applications and that there should only be one court hearing after all other options had failed to produce a satisfactory outcome. Specialist counselling and advisory services were also to be provided for applicants and children regarding sterilisation treatments and alternatives using specially trained officers. It was also recommended that the expensive costs of applications to the Family Court would be met by the Commonwealth government.

CAPACITY IN THE CONTEXT OF GUARDIANSHIP OF CHILDREN

In general relationships between mentally disordered parents and their children are the most vulnerable to state intervention. This intervention is usually justified by reference to the best interests of the child which is the "first and paramount consideration" under the Guardianship of Infants Act 1964[208] and the Child Care Act 1991.[209]

The impact of mental disability in determination of guardianship and custody of children

"Welfare" in the context of guardianship and custody disputes arising under the Guardianship of Infants Act 1964 is said to comprise the "religious and moral, intellectual, physical and social welfare".[210] A parents capacity to provide for any aspect of the child's welfare may be taken into account in deciding custody disputes. In *MacD v. MacD*,[211] Finlay P. held that a child's physical welfare is concerned with the health, bodily comfort, nourishment and hygiene of children with the qualification that their health may be affected by emotional or psychiatric disturbances. The concept of

---

[207] (1988) 94 Australian F.L.R. 1.
[208] See 1964 Act, s.3 as amended by the Age of Majority Act 1985, s.2 and Pt.11 of the Status of Children Act 1987.
[209] S.24.
[210] Guardianship of Infants Act 1964, s.2 as substituted by the Status of Children Act 1987, s.9.
[211] Unreported, High Court, February 19, 1979. Although the decision of the High Court was reversed on appeal the Supreme Court did not disagree with the High Court's determination of the factors comprised in the concept of welfare.

intellectual welfare is primarily concerned with the emotional security, settled affections and psychiatric stability of children and with plans for their education and intellectual development. In *EM v. AM*,[212] Flood J. held that the stability of surroundings in which the child will be brought up and the probable effect on the child of the extended family of which the parent seeking custody forms part is relevant in this regard. Social welfare has been said to mean, "the type of welfare which is judged by what is best calculated to make them (the children) better members of the society in which they live."[213] Social welfare is concerned with enabling the children to grow up to be "good citizens"[214] and well-integrated members of society.[215] It focuses upon ensuring the child is imbued with "correct values" and with a "proper" outlook on life. Moral welfare is concerned with the moral example given by a parent to his child, with the influence that the parent's behaviour may have on the child's development and the manner in which the parent's conduct is likely to affect the child's religious, intellectual and social welfare.[216]

While it is usual for custody of children under 12 years to be given a mother,[217] where her mental illness is such to affect her ability to love and care for her children it may be given to the father or to the Health Service Executive. The marital conduct of the parents has been regarded as relevant only insofar as it relates to an estranged spouses parenting capacity, impacts on a child's development and affects the relationship between parent and child.[218] In determining disputes as to access the welfare of the child is again the first and paramount consideration. In general the court is reluctant to refuse a parent access but will do so if a child's welfare demands it.[219]

Section 8(6) of the Children Act 1997 amends section 11 of the Guardianship of Infants Act 1964 so as to empower the court to make an order for the maintenance of person with mental or physical disability who has attained the age of 18 years where his/her mental disability makes it not reasonably possible for him/her to maintain himself or herself fully. The order may be made on application to the court for its direction on any question affecting the welfare of such person and the terms of the order may direct the father or mother to pay such weekly or periodical sum towards the maintenance of the person with the disability as the court having regard to the means of the father or mother the court considers reasonable.[220] In determining disputes between parents and third parties a child's welfare is again the first and paramount consideration.

Sections 14 to 16 of the 1964 Act are also of relevance. Section 14 of the Act confers a discretion on the court to decline to make an order for custody of an infant in favour of an applicant where a parent[221] of an infant applies for an order for the production of an

---

[212] Unreported, High Court, June 16, 1992.

[213] *MB O'S v. PO O'S* [1974] 110 I.L.T.R. 57, *per* Walsh J. at p.61.

[214] *EK v. MK*, unreported, High Court, Kenny J., May 23, 1974.

[215] *MB O'S v. PO O'S* [1974] 110 I.L.T.R. 57, *per* Henchy J.

[216] See Finlay P. in *MacD v. MacD* , unreported, High Court, February 1979.

[217] See *JJW v. BMW* (1971) I.L.T.R. 45, 49 at 52.

[218] See *MM v. CM*, unreported, High Court, July 26, 1993.

[219] In *O'D v. O'D & Ors* [1994] 3 Fam L.J. 81, Geoghegan J. held that a parent's access can be curtailed where there was a real possibility that the parent had misconducted himself towards his child.

[220] Guardianship of Infants Act 1964, s.11(2)(b).

[221] Under Pt III "Parent" includes a guardian of the person and any person at law liable to maintain an infant or entitled to his custody – see Guardianship of Infants Act 1964, s.13.

infant and the court is of opinion that that parent has abandoned or deserted the infant or that he has otherwise so conducted himself that the court should refuse to enforce his right to the custody of the infant.

Section 15 confers a discretion on the court where application for the production of the infant has been made to it by a parent and it orders that the infant be given up to a parent to make a further order that a parent pay to the person or the Health Service Executive the whole of the costs properly incurred by either in bringing up or providing assistance for an infant or such portion of the costs as the court considers reasonable having regard to all the circumstances of the case including in particular the means of the parent where the court finds (a) that the infant is being brought up at the expense of another person, or (b) that at any time assistance has been provided for the infant by a health authority under section 55 of the Health Act 1953 or that at any time the infant has been maintained in the care of a health board under section 4 of the Child Care Act 1991 at any time before the amendment of that provision by the Health Act 2004 or (c) the child has been maintained by in the care of the Health Service Executive under section 4 of the 1991 Act at any time after the amendment of that provision by the Health Act 2004

Section 16 provides that in circumstances where a parent has (a) abandoned or deserted an infant, or (b) allowed an infant to be brought up by another person at that person's expense, or to be provided with assistance by a health authority under section 55 of the Health Act 1953 or to be maintained in the care of a health board or the Health Service Executive for such a length of time and under such circumstances as to satisfy the court that the parent was unmindful of his parental duties, the court shall not make an order for the delivery of the infant to the parent unless the parent has satisfied the court that he is a fit person to have the custody of the infant.

A parent found to have misbehaved in a manner described in section 16 must satisfy the court that he is "a fit person" to have custody before an order for custody can be made in his favour. However, even where he so satisfied the court, the court may by virtue of the discretion conferred on it by section 14 refuse to grant custody to the parent if the court when having regard to the child's welfare concludes that it is in the interests of the child's welfare that a different order as to custody be made.[222] In *S v. Eastern Health Board and ors*,[223] Finlay P. held that the finding that a parent was a "fit person":

> "constitutes a finding only that there is nothing [the parent's] make-up arising from [his or] her personality or from any physical, emotional or psychiatric abnormality which would prevent her from being capable of caring for a young infant."

In *State (Kavanagh) v. O'Sullivan*,[224] the court reinforced the principle that a parent whose wife was mentally ill and confined in a psychiatric institution and who was forced by economic circumstances to give custody of his children to third parties was not guilty of abandonment or unmindful of his duties.

---

[222] See *S v. The Eastern Health Board & Ors*, unreported, High Court, February 28, 1979.
[223] Unreported, High Court, February 28, 1979.
[224] [1933] I.R. 68.

On the other hand in the later case of *PW v. AW & Ors*,[225] the court was called upon to rule upon the custody of a 5½ year old girl one of a family of four children who had been placed in the custody of her aunt since she was a few weeks old. The child's mother, AW, had suffered from ill health, primarily due to psychiatric illness and had required both in-patient and out-patient hospital treatment. Shortly after the child's birth (AW's fourth child) due to AW's inability to cope the child went to live with her aunt, M. Originally this was a temporary arrangement and the intention was that the child would return to reside with AW when she had sufficiently recovered her health. However, she continued to be unwell and when the child was a few months old the evidence was that she "gave" the child to M permanently. The child then continued to reside with M, but after *PW* and *AW* separated in 1976 her natural mother was granted access. Ellis J. in holding that the child's welfare required that she remained in the custody of M took into account both the fact that no mother and child relationship existed in the true sense between AW and child and the fact that the child "would be exposed to and endangered by physical and emotional risks and potential if not actual present domestic conflicts"[226] if she were returned to AW. Ellis J. also held that insofar as it was the duty of AW as a parent to provide for the requirements of A specified in Article 42.1 of the Constitution (viz to provide for the religious and moral, intellectual, physical and social education of their children) AW had failed for physical reasons under Article 42.5 "which would include reasons of health … which ..combined to prevent and render her (AW) unfit or unable to carry out her required duty or duties towards (the child)."

However, Ellis J's dicta leave open the question as to whether parental inadequacy as opposed to total failure constitutes "physical or moral" failure by parents "in their duty towards their children" on the basis of which the parent can be deprived of custody in the absence of deliberate fault or misconduct. It is also interesting that the psychiatric evidence in the case was uncertain. First, A.W's condition was described by one psychiatrist as "a disease of mood with depression, the delusions being of a persecutory type from which she could or could not in time recover" and by another as a "schizo-affective disorder." The psychiatrists giving evidence also expressed some uncertainty as to the prognosis:

> "There was a risk of recurrence of her condition under stress, and in relation to the return of [A] [the psychiatrist] could only say from [A]'s point of view that it was a case of trial and error with a doubt about the future about which she could not predict."[227]

> "[The psychiatrist] felt there was a risk of recurrence of A.W's illness through worry and problems and that for her children if this happened "it would be like close to an emotional storm manifested by disorganisation in A.W's thinking; in her reality precepts, and in her feeling – very bothered and worked up- impulsive, arbitrary and angry. He felt *if* [italics added] such an occurrence occurred the monitoring person would have to act quickly to have [A] returned to M or that serious psychological damage could result."[228]

---

[225] Unreported, High Court, April 21, 1980.
[226] *Ibid.*, p.43.
[227] *Ibid.*, pp.34–35.
[228] *Ibid.*, p.7.

On foot of this evidence Ellis J. concluded:

> "All the medical evidence leads me to the view that to restore [A] now to the custody of her mother would be to take an undue risk for the general welfare of Annette and that such a return *could* [italics added] lead to a recurrence of A.W's illness with potential danger to [A]'s psychological and physical health and well-being."[229]

In the case of *D, L v. D, T*,[230] Murphy J. delivering the judgment of the Supreme Court held that a psychiatrist making an assessment of parties for the purposes of custody proceedings had no duty to "put" the "evidence" given by one party to another party so that the other party could give evidence in relation thereto. The psychiatrist was not determining matters of fact nor were the procedures adopted by him comparable to a court of law or subject to review by reference to criteria appropriate to those procedures. Cases could arise where the conclusions of a medical expert would be invalidated for the reason that he was misled or had misled himself on a fundamental matter of fact or where the facts were insufficient to enable him to reach the conclusion he reached but in the absence of such situations his conclusions could not be challenged.

The Irish law regarding state intervention in the parent/child relationship

The Child Care Act 1991 prescribes the circumstances in which the Health Service Executive and the courts may intervene in the parent/child relationship to provide for the care and protection of children. Section 3 of the Child Care Act 1991[231] provides that the Health Service Executive has a general duty "to promote the welfare of children who are not receiving adequate care and protection." In performing it function in this regard it is required to "take such steps as it considers requisite to identify children who are not receiving adequate care and protection" and to "co-ordinate information from all relevant sources relating to children in its area." In doing so it is obliged to (i) regard the welfare of the child as the first and paramount consideration, and (ii) insofar as is practicable, give due consideration, having regard to his age and understanding to wishes of the child.[232] However, the Act emphasises that in the application of (i) and (ii) the Health Service Executive "must have regard to the rights and duties of parents whether under the Constitution or otherwise"[233] and to the principle that 'it is generally in the interests of a child to be brought up in his own family".[234]

As a consequence where the Health Service Executive deems it necessary to intervene

---

[229] *Ibid.*, p.38.
[230] Unreported, Supreme Court, November 9, 1998.
[231] Until October 31, 1995 the Children Act 1908 as amended governed the circumstances under which children could be placed in care by the courts. It contained provisions for the making of emergency care orders where children were in immediate and serious risk and for placing children in long term residential or foster care. Many of its provisions were however irrelevant or inadequate to provide the multi-dimensional framework required to respond to the needs of children who were the victims of or at risk of abuse or neglect.
[232] Child Care Act 1991, s.3(2)(b).
[233] *Ibid.*, s.3(2)(b).
[234] *Ibid.*, s.3(2)(c).

consideration must first be given by the Health Service Executive to determining whether a child "not receiving adequate care and protection" is likely to receive such care if the child continues to reside in the family home, if help is provided by the Health Service Executive to the child's parents and family. The Health Service Executive is obliged to provide not only "child care" but also "family support services" and the section's emphasis is on providing the support and assistance required to enable children to remain at home, where possible.

Voluntary care

The Health Service Executive has a variety of powers to intervene in the parent/child relationship where a child requires care and protection. In the first place it may take a child into voluntary care. The Health Service Executive has a duty to take a child into voluntary care if it appears to the Executive "that a child requires care or protection that he is unlikely to receive unless he is taken into its care" [235] However, the child may not be taken into care under this section against the wishes of the parent and may not maintain the child in care if the parent wishes to resume care of the child.

Care orders

The Health Service Executive may further make an application to the District Court for a care order. Section 18(1) of the 1991 Act provides that before making a care order the District Court must be satisfied that (a) the child has been or is being assaulted, ill-treated, neglected or sexually abused, or (b) the child's health, development or welfare has been or is being avoidably impaired or neglected or (c) the child's health, development or welfare is likely to be avoidably impaired or neglected and that the child requires care or protection which he is unlikely to receive unless the court makes an order. If the court is so satisfied it may make a care order placing a child in the care of the Health Service Executive "for as long as he remains a child" or for a shorter period. In making orders for the care and protection of children under Parts III, IV and VI of the Child Care Act 1991 the District court is obliged by section 24 of the 1991 Act "having regard to the rights and duties of parents whether under the Constitution or otherwise" to (a) regard the welfare of the child as the first and paramount consideration, and (b) in so far as is practicable [to] give due consideration to the wishes of the child having regard to his age and understanding."

Where a care order is in force the Health Service Executive has "the like control over the child as if it were his parent" and must do "what is reasonable in all the circumstances of the case for the purpose of safeguarding or promoting the child's health, development or welfare". In particular the Health Service Executive has authority "to give consent to any necessary medical or psychiatric examination, treatment or assessment with respect to the child" [236] and any such consent is "sufficient authority for the carrying out of a medical or psychiatric examination or assessment" and "the provision of medical or psychiatric treatment" as the case may be.[237] In essence therefore

---

[235] Child Care Act 1991, s.4(1).
[236] *Ibid.*, s.18(3).
[237] *Ibid.*, s.18(4).

care orders could be used to provide psychiatric treatment for a child who needs it without parental consent.

Interim care orders

The District Court also has power to make interim care orders. It may do so when it is satisfied that (a) an application for a care order has been or is about to be made and (b) there is reasonable cause to believe that any of the circumstances mentioned at paragraph (a), (b) or (c) of section 18(1) exists or has existed with respect to the child and that it is necessary for the protection of the child's health or welfare that he be placed or maintained in the care of the Health Service Executive pending the determination of the application of the care order.[238] A child cannot be retained in care for more than 28[239] days under an interim care order without parental consent or the consent of a person acting *in loco parentis*. However, if the judge is satisfied that the grounds for the making of an interim care order still exist further 28[240] days extensions can be permitted.[241] An application for an interim care order or for an extension of such an order must be made on notice to a parent having custody of the child or to a person acting *in loco parentis* except where, having regard to the interests of justice or the welfare of the child the judge otherwise directs.[242] Where an interim care order is made the judge may give directions as he thinks proper inter alia in relation to the medical or psychiatric examination, treatment or assessment of the child.[243]

Emergency care orders

The 1991 Act also makes provision for the making of emergency care orders. Section 12 authorises a member of the Garda Síochána "accompanied by such persons as may be necessary" without warrant to enter any house or other place and remove a child to safety where the member has reasonable grounds for believing (a) that there is an immediate and serious risk to the health or welfare of a child, and (b) it would not be sufficient for the protection of the child from such immediate and serious risk to await the making of an application for an emergency care order by the Health Service Executive under section 13. "As soon as possible" after being removed to safety the child must be delivered into the custody of the Health Service Executive which, if it does not return the child to the custodial parent or parents or a person acting in loco parentis must then "make application for an emergency care order at the next sitting of the District Court. An emergency care order under section 13 will only be made if the District Justice concludes that there is reasonable cause to believe (a) that there is an immediate and serious risk to the health or welfare of a child which necessitates his being placed in the

---

[238] Child Care Act 1991, s.17(1).
[239] *Ibid.*, s.17(2) as amended by Children Act 2001, s.267, which came into force on May 1, 2002 by virtue of Children Act 2001 (Commencement) Order 2002 (S.I. No.151 of 2002).
[240] *Ibid.*
[241] *Ibid.*, s.17(2) as amended by Children Act 2001, s.267 which came into force on May 1, 2002 by virtue of the Children Act 2001 (Commencement) Order 2002 (S.I. No.151 of 2002).
[242] Child Care Act 1991, s.17(3).
[243] *Ibid.*, s.17(4).

care of the Health Service Executive, or (b) there is likely to be such risk if the child is removed from the place where he is for the time being.[244]

Supervision orders

The court has the power to make supervision orders as an alternative to care orders. These will be made where it is desirable that a child should be visited periodically by or on behalf of the Health Service Executive. It is assumed that a supervision order will be made where a care order is not deemed necessary. The supervision order authorises the Health Service Executive to arrange periodic visits to the child "in order to satisfy itself as to the welfare of the child" and to give "necessary advice as to the care of the child." If a parent is dissatisfied with the approach of the Health Service Executive following the making of a supervision order application may be made to the court to give directions to the Executive.[245] When a supervision order is made the court may also give directions relating to the care of the child and require him to attend for medical or psychiatric examination, treatment or assessment.[246]

Care orders in custody access proceedings

Finally, a court asked to determine guardianship custody or access also has power to make a care order in the course of those proceedings. Where as a result of evidence heard in the course of such proceedings, a trial judge is concerned that the welfare of a child may be at risk if placed in the custody of either parent section 20 of the Child Care Act provides a mechanism whereby the court, pending the Health Service Executive investigating matters, may temporarily place a child in care or provide for Health Service Executive supervision of the child in the home of the parent with whom the child is residing pending the completion of the investigation sought. The Health Service Executive is required to consider whether it should (a) apply for a care order or for a supervision order with respect to the child, (b) provide services or assistance for the child or his family, or (c) take any other action with respect to the child.

The Children Act 2001 – Proposals for the making of special care orders

The Children Act 2001[247] re-enacts and up-date provisions in the Children Act 1908, which create criminal offences and prescribe criminal penalties for the mistreatment of a child by a person who has custody, charge or care of a child. Part III of the Act also provides a statutory mechanism to ensure that children who require it receive special care and protection. Section 16 of the 2001 Act amends the Child Care Act 1991 by inserting a new Part IVA after section 23 of the 1991 Act.[248]

---

[244] See Child Care Act 1991, s.13(1).
[245] Child Care Act 1991, s.19(3).
[246] *Ibid.*, s.19(4).
[247] The Act was passed on July 8, 2001.
[248] See Preface

Special care orders

Section 23A provides that where it appears to the Health Service Executive –the statutory body with responsibility for promoting the welfare of children at risk- that a child requires special care and protection which he or she is unlikely to receive unless the court makes a special care order or an interim special care order it shall be the duty of the Health Service Executive to apply for whichever order is appropriate in the circumstances. The word "child" has been defined to mean "person under the age of 18 years."[249]

Grounds for making special care order

The court may make such an order if it is satisfied that (a) the behaviour of the child is such that it poses a real and substantial risk to his or her health, safety, development or welfare, and (b) the child requires special care or protection which he or she is unlikely to receive unless the court makes such an order.[250] The concept of special care orders is adopted from New Zealand and is designed to maximise the use of a child's social and family support networks at a time of crisis in his life. The special care order is designed to fill a gap in the Child Care Act 1991 which was widely criticised for failing to make provision for secure placements for disturbed children in need of care.[251] However, the grounds for making the special care order under the 1991 Act as amended by the 2001 Act, *i.e.* the concepts of "substantial risk", "health," "safety," "development" or "welfare" are not defined nor is the requirement that the child needs "special care or protection" (albeit the latter appears to tied up with the behaviour of the child himself/herself). It would appear therefore that in the absence of statutory definition these concepts will have to be defined by the courts on an *ad hoc* basis.

Proposed requirements to convene a family welfare conference The philosophy of the Act envisages that the special care order should be used only as a last resort. Accordingly before applying for an order the Health Service Executive must arrange for the convening of a family welfare conference within the meaning of the Children Act 2001 in respect of the child. The family welfare conference provides a framework by which the child, his/her family and the relevant professionals and agencies can find solutions to the difficulties that led to the child becoming a risk to himself/herself. The purpose of a conference is to produce a plan for the future care, protection and development of the child. The emphasis is on consensus and partnership. Children are entitled to be present at the conference and according to the Minister for Justice, Equality and Law Reform speaking during the passage of the Bill through the Dáil the core principles underlying any family conference are that the child's interests are paramount and that insofar as is possible, the child is best looked after within its own family.[252]

A family welfare conference is convened by a co-ordinator appointed by the Health

---

[249] Children Act 2001, s.3(1).

[250] *Ibid.*, s.16 inserting new s.23B(1) into the Child Care Act 1991.

[251] The High Court had partly filled the gap by using its inherent jurisdiction over children to secure detention. See *F.N v. Minister for Health* [1995] 1 I.R. 409; *D.B. v. Minister for Justice* [1999] 1 I.R. 29 and *T.D. v. Minister for Education, Ireland, the Attorney General, the Eastern Health Board and the Minister for Health and Children*, High Court, Kelly J., February 25, 2000.

[252] See Dáil Éireann Debates No. 517 Col.95.

Service Executive.[253] The co-ordinator acts as chairperson of the family welfare conference. Since the basic purpose of the conference is to produce a plan for the future care, protection and development of the child that family must take responsibility for the child and come up with proposals for the plan with the assistance of professionals attending the conference. A family conference is obliged to decide whether a child is in need of special care and protection, which he is unlikely to receive unless a special care order is made. If it decides that the child is in need of a special care order it must recommend to the Health Service Executive that it seek such an order. If it does not so decide it must make such recommendations to the Health Service Executive in relation to the care or protection of the child as it considers necessary including, where appropriate, (but not limited to) a recommendation that the Health Service Executive should apply for a care order or supervision order under the Child Care Act 1991.[254] It may also recommend the provision of services or assistance to the child and his family.[255] The family welfare conference is designed to ensure that children who require special care and protection will only be sent to a special care unit as a last resort.

In convening a family conference the co-ordinator should discuss with all the parties the persons he believes should be permitted to participate in the conference. The guiding consideration is the welfare of the child. A variety of different people are entitled to attend the conference. They include (a) the child, (b) the child's parents or guardian, (c) any guardian *ad litem* appointed for the child; (d) other relatives ad determined by the co-ordinator following consultation with the child and his/her parents and guardians; (e) an officer or officers of the Health Service Executive.[256] Under section 9(f) of the 2001 Act the co-ordinator can permit certain other persons to attend. Those persons are persons who "in the opinion of the co-ordinator, after consultation with the child and his or her parents or guardian, would make a positive contribution to the conference because of the person's knowledge of the child or the child's family or because of his or her particular expertise." This provision could facilitate the presence of a social worker, teacher or solicitor at the conference. The co-ordinator has a discretion to exclude a person from participation or further participation in the conference if, before or during the conference the coordinator is of opinion that the presence or continued presence of any person is not in the best interests of the conference or the child.[257]

A family welfare conference may set out its own procedure in whatever manner it thinks fit.[258] Section 11 of the Act requires the Health Service Executive to provide such administrative services as are necessary to enable the conference to discharge its functions. Section 12 of the Act obliges the co-ordinator to notify the recommendations of the conference to the participants, the Health Service Executive, a body, which referred the child to the Health Service Executive, and any other body or persons the co-ordinator deems appropriate. Section 13 of the Act sets out the range of possible actions, which may be taken by the Health Service Executive on receipt of the recommendation of the family welfare conference. It may either apply for a special care order, a care order or a

---

[253] Children Act 2001, s.7.
[254] Children Act 2001, s.8.
[255] See Dáil Éireann Debates No. 517 Col.115.
[256] Children Act 2001, s.9.
[257] *Ibid.*, s.9(2).
[258] *Ibid.*, s.10. See Preface for recent developments in prescription of procedures.

supervision order or provide any service or assistance for the child or his or her family as it considers appropriate having regard to the recommendations of the conference. Section 14 provides that no evidence shall be admissible in court of any information, statement or admission disclosed or made in the course of a family welfare conference. While there is no formal requirement to inform the attendees of a conference of the privilege attaching to the proceedings it would appear to be useful and necessary to do so as this privilege would promote an informal atmosphere at the conference and permit its participants to speak without fear of legal repercussions. In particular any admission by the child and/or other parties to the conference will not be admissible as evidence in court proceedings. Section 14(2), of necessity, renders admissible a record of a decision or recommendations of a family welfare conference. Where on the conclusion of the conference proceedings the Health Service Executive proposes to apply for a special care order in respect of the child, it must also seek the views of the Special Residential Services Board[259] on the proposal.[260] A parent may request the Health Service Executive to apply for a special care order in respect of his or her child. If the Health Service Executive decides following such a request not to apply for such an order the Executive must notify the parent in writing of its reasons for so deciding.[261]

A court may, having taken into account the views of the Special Residential Services Board, make a special care order on the application of the Health Service Executive if it is satisfied that (a) the behaviour of the child is such that it poses a real and substantial risk to his or her health, safety, development or welfare, and (b) the child requires special care or protection which he or she is unlikely to receive unless the court makes such an order.[262]

Effect of making special care order

The effect of the order is commit the child to the care of the Health Service Executive for as long as the order remains in force and to authorise it to provide appropriate care, education and treatment for the child and for that purpose to place and detain the child in a special care unit provided by or on behalf of the Health Service Executive.[263] The special care order also authorises the Health Service Executive to take such steps as are reasonably necessary to prevent the child: (a) causing injury to himself or herself or to other persons in the unit, or (b) absconding from the unit.[264] A special care order shall

---

[259] The functions of the Special Residential Services Board are, *inter alia*, to advise the Minister for Health and Children on policy relating to the remand and detention of children and ensure the efficient, effective and coordinated delivery of services to children in respect of whom children detention orders or special care orders are made. See Children Act 2001, s.227. See Children Act 2001 (Pt II) (Commencement) Order 2003 (S.I. No.527 of 2003) which appointed November 7, 2003 as the day on which Part II of the 2001 Act (which establishes the Special Residential Services Board on a statutory basis) should come into operation.
[260] Children Act 2001, s.16 inserting new s.23A(2) into the Child Care Act 1991.
[261] *Ibid.*, s.16 inserting new s.23A(3) into the Child Care Act 1991.
[262] *Ibid.*, s.16 inserting new s.23B(1) into the Child Care Act 1991.
[263] *Ibid.*, s.16 inserting new s.23B(2) into the Child Care Act 1991. However Part 3 of the Children Act 2001 which empowers the court to make special care orders does not deprive the High Court of the inherent constitutional jurisdiction it has developed to order the detention of a child. See *FN v. Minister for Health* [1995] 1 I.R. 409. Both jurisdictions will operate concurrently.
[264] Where the issue of recovery of a child who absconds from a special care unit s.46 of the 1991 Act

generally remain in force for a period specified in the order which is not less than three months or more than six months.[265] The court may on the application of the Health Service Executive extend the period of validity of a special care order if and so often as the court is satisfied that the grounds for making the order continue to exist with respect to the child concerned.[266]

While in *DG v. Ireland*,[267] the European Court of Human Rights held that the placement of a non offending disturbed child in a penal institution as opposed to a safe , suitable therapeutic unit was a breach of Article 5.1 of the Convention and found specifically that the penal institution in which the child was placed was not "an interim custody measure for the purpose of an educational supervisory regime which was followed speedily by a the application of such a regime" this ruling is unlikely to affect the placement of children in special care units under the 2001 Act because of the wide interpretation afforded by the European Court to the term "educational supervision"

---

applies. See Child Care Act 1991, s.23L inserted by Children Act 2001, s.16. Thus the Health Service Executive may request the Garda Síochána to search for the child and deliver him to the custody of the Executive and the Garda Síochána must take all reasonable measures to comply with such a request (s.46(2)). A justice of the District Court may, if satisfied by information on oath that there are reasonable grounds for believing that a person specified in the information can produce the child named in the application, make an order directing that person to deliver up the child to the custody of the Executive (s.46(3)). Without prejudice to the law as to contempt of court where the District Court has made an order under s.46(3) directing that a child be delivered up to the care of the Health Service Executive any person having the actual custody of the child who, having been given or shown a copy of the order and having been required, by or on behalf of the Health Service Executive, to give up the child to the Executive, fails or refuses to comply with the requirement, shall be guilty of an offence and shall be liable on summary conviction to a fine not exceeding €634.87 or, at the discretion of the court, to imprisonment for a term not exceeding 6 months or both such fine and such imprisonment (s.46(4)). For the purposes of s.46 a person shall be deemed to have been given or shown a copy of an order made by a justice of the District Court under s.46(3) if that person was present at the sitting of the court at which such an order was made. A justice of the District Court may, if satisfied by information on oath that there are reasonable grounds for believing that the child named in the application is in any house or other place (including any building or part of a building, tent, caravan or other temporary or moveable structure, vehicle, vessel, aircraft or hovercraft) specified in the information, issue a warrant authorising a member of the Garda Síochána, accompanied by such other members of the Garda Síochána or such other persons as may be necessary, to enter (if need be by force) and to search the house or other place for the child; and if the child is found he shall be returned to the custody of the Health Service Executive (s.46(6)). An application for an order under s.46(3) may, if the justice is satisfied that the urgency of the matter so requires, be made *ex parte*. (s.46(7)). An application for an order under s.46(3) or for a warrant under s.46(6) may, if the justice is satisfied that the urgency of the matter so requires be heard and an order made thereon elsewhere than at a public sitting of the District Court (s.46(8)). Without prejudice to s.28 of the 1991 Act (proceedings under Pt IV may be brought heard and determined before and by a justice of the District Court for the time being assigned to the district court district where the child resides or is for the time being): (a) an order under s.46(3) may be made by a justice of the District Court for the time being assigned to the District Court district where the person specified in the information resides or is for the time being, and (b) a warrant under s.46(6) may be issued by a justice for the time being assigned to the District Court where the house or other place specified in the information is situated and, in either case, where such justice is not immediately available the order may be made, or the warrant issued, by any justice of the District Court (s.46(9)).

[265] Children Act 2001 s.16 inserting new s.23B(4) into Child Care Act 1991.
[266] *Ibid.*, inserting new s.23B(4)(b) into the Child Care Act 1991.
[267] [1998] 1 I.L.R.M. 241.

which justifies detention of a minor in Article 5(1)(d) of the Convention. In particular the European Court in *Koniarska v. U.K*,[268] has held that placing a child in secure accommodation was not contrary to the Convention as it amounted to "educational supervision" within the meaning of Article 5 of the Convention.

Returning to the provisions of the 2001 Act. The Health Service Executive must as soon as practicable apply to the court for the discharge of the order if it appears to the Executive that the circumstances which led to the making of the order no longer exist.[269] A special care order will cease to have effect when the person to whom it relates reaches 18 years of age.[270] The special care unit is the ultimate level of care provided for the child and the Act provides that where a special care order is in force the Health Service Executive may also as part of its programme for the care education and treatment of the child place the child on a temporary basis with a foster parent, in residential care, or make such other suitable arrangements (which may include placing the child with a relative) as the Health Service Executive thinks proper. The Health Service Executive also retains power to send a child subject to a special care order to any hospital or institution, which provides nursing, or care for children suffering from physical or mental disability.[271] In addition while the special care order in force the Health Service Executive may arrange for the temporary release of the child from the unit on health or compassionate grounds. Any placement or arrangement by the Health Service Executive will be subject to its control and supervision.[272]

Where a special care order is in force the Health Service Executive has authority to give consent to any necessary medical or psychiatric examination treatment or assessment with respect to the child and any consent given by a health authority will be sufficient authority for the carrying out of a medical or psychiatric examination or assessment and the provision of medical or psychiatric treatment.[273]

Interim special care order

An interim special care order may be made where a judge of the Children's Court (established under the Act) is satisfied that the Health Service Executive is complying with the requirements of section 23A(2) in relation to the making of an application for a special care order in respect of a child (*viz.* the convening of a family welfare conference and seeking the views of the Special Residential Services Board) and that there is reasonable cause to believe that (i) the behaviour of the child is such that it poses a real and substantial risk to his or her health, safety development or welfare, and (ii) it is necessary in the interests of the child pending determination of the application for a special care order that he or she be placed and detained in a special care unit.[274] An interim care order will require that the child named in the order be placed and detained in a special care unit: (a) for a period not exceeding twenty eight days, or (b) where the

---

[268] European Convention on Human Rights, October 12, 2000.
[269] Children Act 2001 s.16 inserting new s.23B(5) into the Child Care Act 1991.
[270] *Ibid.*, s.16 inserting new s.23B(6) into the Child Care Act 1991.
[271] *Ibid.*, s.16 inserting new s.23B(7) into the Child Care Act 1991.
[272] *Ibid.*, s.16 inserting new s.23B(7) into the Child Care Act 1991.
[273] *Ibid.*, s.16 inserting new s.23B(8) into the Child Care Act 1991.
[274] *Ibid.*, s.16 inserting new s.23C into the Child Care Act 1991.

Health Service Executive and the parent having custody of the child or a person acting *in loco parentis* consent for a period exceeding twenty eight days. The judge concerned may by order extend any such period on the application of any of the persons specified in (b) above. He may extend the period for a period exceeding 28 days with the consent of those persons if he or she is satisfied that the grounds for making the interim special care order continue to exist with respect to the child.[275]

An application for an interim special care order or for an extension of a period of an interim order must be made on notice to a parent having custody of the child or a person acting *in loco parentis* or where appropriate to the Health Service Executive except where having regard to the interests of justice or the welfare of the child the judge otherwise directs.[276]

Section 13(3) and (7) of the Child Care Act 1991 apply in relation to an interim special care order as they apply in relation to an emergency care order with any necessary modifications. Thus were a justice makes an interim special care order he may for the purposes of executing that order issue a warrant authorising a member of the Garda Síochána, accompanied by such other members of the Garda Síochána or such other persons as may be necessary to enter (if need be by force) any house or other place specified in the warrant[277] where the child is or where there are reasonable grounds for believing that he is and to deliver the child into the custody of the Health Service Executive.[278]

The interim special care order must be made by the justice for the district in which the child resides or is for the time being. If such a justice is not immediately available an order may be made by any justice of the District Court. An application for such an order may, if the justice is satisfied that the urgency of the matter so requires be made *ex parte*. An application for an interim special care order may, if the justice is satisfied that the urgency of the matter so requires, be heard and an order made elsewhere that at a public sitting of the District Court.[279] An appeal from an interim special care order will not stay the operation of the order.[280] It is not necessary to name the child in an application or order if the name of the child is not known.[281]

Where a justice makes an interim special care order he may, of his own motion or on the application of any person give such directions (if any) as he thinks proper in relation to (i) whether the address or location of the place at which the child is being kept is to be withheld form a parent or both parents of the child, a person acting *in loco parentis* or any other person; (ii) the access, if any, which is to be permitted between the child and any named person and the conditions under which the access is to take place; (iii) the medical or psychiatric examination, treatment or assessment of the child. A direction may be given at any time during the currency of the order and may be varied or discharged on the application of any person.[282]

---

[275] *Ibid.*, s.16 inserting new s.23C(2) into the Child Care Act 1991.

[276] *Ibid.*, s.16 inserting new s.23C(3) into the Child Care Act 1991.

[277] This includes any building or part of a building, tent, caravan or other temporary or moveable structure, vehicle, vessel, aircraft or hovercraft. See s.13(3) Child Care Act 1991.

[278] Child Care Act 1991 s.13(3).

[279] *Ibid.*, s.13(4).

[280] *Ibid.*, s.13(5).

[281] *Ibid.*, s.13(6).

[282] *Ibid.*, s.13(7).

Emergency Special Care Order

Section 23D of the Child Care Act 1991[283] outlines specific powers of the Garda Síochána where a child needs special care or protection and an emergency special care order is required.[284] It provides that where a member of the Garda Síochána has reasonable grounds for believing that (a) the behaviour of a child is such that it poses a real and substantial risk to the child's health, safety, development or welfare; (b) the child is not receiving adequate care or protection; and (c) it would not be sufficient for the protection of the child from such risk to await the making of an application for an interim special care order by the Health Service Executive the member of the Garda Síochána must endeavour to deliver or arrange for the child to be delivered to the custody of the Health Service Executive and shall inform the Executive of the circumstances in which the child came to the notice of the Garda Síochána. Where a child is delivered to the custody of the Health Service Executive or comes to its notice in the circumstances described in this paragraph, and it appears to the Health Service Executive that the child requires care or protection which he or she is unlikely to receive unless the court makes an order under Part IV in respect of the child the Health Service Executive must make an application for a special care order or an interim special care order as appropriate in the particular circumstances.[285]

Parents to be informed of placing of child in special care unit pursuant to interim special care order

Where a child is placed in a special care unit pursuant to an interim special care order the Health Service Executive must as soon as possible inform or cause to be informed of the placement a parent having custody of the child or a person acting *in loco parentis* unless the parent or person is missing and cannot be found.[286]

Discharge of special care order

Without prejudice to section 23B(5)[287] the court has power of its own motion or on the application of any person to vary or discharge a special care order. In discharging a special care order the court may, of its own motion or on the application of the Health Service Executive either: (a) make a supervision order in respect of the child, or (b) if the court is of opinion that: (i) the child requires care and protection which he or she is unlikely to receive unless he or she remains in the care of the Health Service Executive,

---

[283] As inserted by Children Act 2001, s.16.

[284] The new s.23 of the 1991 Act is to be brought into force at the end of 2003 with the exception of s.23D.

[285] Children Act 2001, s.16 inserting new s.23D into the Child Care Act 1991.

[286] Children Act 2001, s.16 inserting new s.23E into the Child Care Act 1991. For the purposes of the section a person shall be deemed to have been informed of the placing of a child in a special care unit if the person is given or shown a copy of the interim special care order or if the person was present at the sitting of the court at which the order was made. See s.23E(2).

[287] S.23B(5) provides that if while a special care order is in force in respect of a child, it appears to the Health Service Executive concerned that the circumstances which led to the making of the order no longer exist with respect to the child the Executive must as soon as practicable apply to the court which made the order to have the order discharged.

or (ii) the delivery or return of the child to a parent or any other person would not be in the best interests of the child make a care order in respect of the child.[288]

Appeals

Section 21 of the Child Care Act 1991 applies to an appeal from an interim special care order or a special care order as it applies to an appeal from an order under Part IV of the Child Care Act 1991.[289] Thus an appeal from an order shall if the court that made the order or the court to which the appeal is brought so determines (but not otherwise) stay the operation of the order on such terms (if any) as may be imposed by the court making the determination.

Powers of Court where special care order is invalid

Section 23 of the Child Care Act 1991 applies to a special care order as it applies to a care order with the modification that the court may as an alternative to making a special care order make a care order in respect of the child.[290] Thus where a court finds or declares in any proceedings that a special care order for whatever reason is invalid, that court may of its own motion or on the application of any person refuse to exercise any power to order the delivery or return of the child to a parent or any other person if the court is of opinion that such delivery or return would not be in the best interests of the child . In any such case the court, of its own motion or on the application of any person may (a) make a valid special care order as if it were a court to which an application had been made by the Health Service Executive; (b) make an order remitting the matter to a justice of the District Court for the time being assigned to the District Court district where the child resides or is for the time being or was residing or was at the time that the invalid order was made or the application therefor was made. Where the matter is so remitted the Health Service Executive shall be deemed to have made an application for a special care order; (c) direct that any order under (a) shall, if necessary be deemed for the purpose of the Child Care Act 1991 to have been made by a justice of the District Court for the time being assigned to a district court district specified by the court or (d) where it makes an order under (b) it may make a temporary order under (a) pending the making of an order by the court to which the matter or question has been remitted.

Court procedures on making special care orders

The new section 23I of the Child Care Act 1991 applies Part V of the 1991 Act to proceedings relating to an application for an interim special care order or a special care order.[291]

---

[288] Children Act 2001, s.16 inserting new s.23F into the Child Care Act 1991.

[289] *Ibid.*, s.16 inserting new s.23G into the Child Care Act 1991.

[290] *Ibid.*, s.16 inserting new s.23H into the Child Care Act 1991.

[291] See also Children Act 2001, s.267(2) which provides that references in Pt V (Jurisdiction and Procedure) of the Act of 1991 to Pt IV of that Act shall be construed as including references to Pt IVA (Children in Need of Special Care and Protection) and IVB (Private Foster Care) inserted by s.16 of the Children Act 2001. However s.267(2) has yet to be commenced.

The new section 23J of the Child Care Act 1991[292] provides that sections 37, 42, 45 and 47 of the Child Care Act 1991 shall apply to a child who is committed to the care of the Health Service Executive pursuant to an interim special care order or a special care order.

Access when special care order is made

Section 37(1) of the 1991 Act provides for access to children in care and provides that where a child is in the care of the Health Service Executive the Executive shall, subject to the provisions of the 1991 Act facilitate reasonable access to the child by his parents, any person acting *in loco parentis* or any other person, who, in the opinion of the Executive, has a bona fide interest in the child and such access may include allowing the child to reside temporarily with any such person.

Section 37(2) provides that any person who is dissatisfied with arrangements made by the Health Service Executive under section 37(1) may apply to the court and the court may (a) make such order as it thinks proper regarding access to the child by that person, and (b) vary or discharge that order on the application of any person. On the other hand by virtue of section 37(3) the court, on the application of the Health Service Executive, and if it considers that it is necessary to do so in order to safeguard or promote the child's welfare, may (a) make an order authorising the Executive to refuse to allow a named person access to a child in its care, and (b) vary or discharge that order on the application of any person.

Section 37(4) provides that section 37 is to operate without prejudice to section 4(2) of the 1991 Act which concerns the maintenance of children placed voluntarily in care by parents or a person acting *in loco parentis*. Section 4(2) provides that without prejudice to the provisions of Parts III, IV and V (which include the powers to make special care orders and interim special care orders),[293] nothing in section 4 shall authorise the Health Service Executive to take a child into its care against the wishes of a parent having custody of him or of any person acting *in loco parentis* or to maintain him in its care under section 4 (voluntary care) if that parent or any such person wishes to resume care of him. In effect persons to whom section 4 applies may not have their rights to access interfered with and should the Health Service Executive wish to curtail access the appropriate procedures of obtaining the necessary care order and other orders must first be complied with

Review of case of child

Section 42 obliges the Minister for Health and Children to make regulations requiring the case of each child in the care of the Health Service Executive to be reviewed in accordance with the provisions of the regulations. Regulations under this section may make provision (a) as to the manner in which each case is to be reviewed, (b) as to the frequency of reviews, and (c) requiring the Executive to consider whether it would be in the best interests of the child to be given into the custody of his parents.[294]

---

[292] Inserted by Children Act 2001, s.6.
[293] See Child Care Act 1991, s.23M of Child Care Act 1991 inserted by Children Act 2001, s.16.
[294] See Preface.

Aftercare

Section 45 of the 1991 Act deals with the subject of aftercare and section 45(1)(a) provides that where a child leaves the care of the Health Service Executive the Executive may in accordance with section 45(2) assist him for so long as the Executive is satisfied as to his need for assistance and subject to section 45(1)(b) he has not attained the age of 21 years. Section 45(1)(b) provides that where the Health Service Executive is assisting a person in accordance with section 45(2)(b)(*i.e.* arranging for the completion of his education) and that person attains the age of 21 years the Executive may continue to provide such assistance until the completion of the course of education in which he is engaged.

Section 45(2) outlines the ways in which the Health Service Executive may assist a person under section 45. They are (a) by causing him to be visited or assisted; (b) by arranging for the completion of his education and by contributing towards his maintenance while he is completing his education; (c) by placing him in a suitable trade, calling or business and paying such fee or sum as may be requisite for that purpose; (d) by arranging hostel or other forms of accommodation for him; (e) by co-operating with housing authorities in planning accommodation for children leaving care on reaching the age of 18 years. By section 45(4) the Health Service Executive in providing assistance under section 45 is obliged to comply with any general directions given by the Minister.

Court directions

The final section of the of the Child Care Act 1991 which is expressed by section 23J of the 1991 Act[295] to apply to a child who is committed to the care of the Health Service Executive pursuant to an interim special care order or a special care order is section 47. It provides that where a child is in the care of the Health Service Executive the District Court may, of its own motion or on the application of any person, give such directions and make such order on any question affecting the welfare of the child as it thinks proper and may vary or discharge any such direction or order.[296]

Proposed special care units

The new section 23K(1) of the 1991 Act[297] provides that the Health Service Executive may with the approval of the Minister for the purposes of sections 23B and 23C (a) provide and maintain a special care unit or (b) make arrangements with a voluntary body or any other person for the provision and operation of such a unit by that body or person on behalf of the Executive. Section 10 of the Child Care Act is expressed to

---

[295] Inserted by the Children Act 2001, s.16.

[296] An application for directions must, under r.32(1) of the District Court (Child Care) Rules 1995 be made on notice to each of the parties or any other person affected by the direction. Two days notice of the hearing of the application must be given to the respondent and the notice must be served. An order making a direction may be varied or discharged and an application to do so must, under r.32(2) of the District Court (Child Care) Rules 1995 be made on notice and served in accordance with the rule. Where an order is made varying or discharging a direction it must be served upon the parties and any other person affected by the order.

[297] Inserted by the Children Act 2001, s.16.

apply to the arrangements made under 23K(1)(b).[298] Thus the Health Service Executive may, subject to any general directions given by the Minister and on such terms or conditions it thinks fit, assist a voluntary body or any other person who provides or proposes to provide a child care or family support service similar or ancillary to a service which the Health Service Executive may provide under the 1991 Act by (a) by a periodic contribution to funds of the body or person; (b) by a grant; (c) by a contribution in kind (whether by way of materials or labour or any other service). However, the Health Service Executive may not delegate the power to apply for an order under section 23B or 23C to a voluntary body or any other person.[299]

Where a child is detained in a special care unit provided under section 23K(1)(b) the provisions of section 23B(3) apply in relation to the voluntary body or other person providing or operating the unit. Thus the voluntary body or other person providing or operating the unit may take steps as are reasonably necessary to prevent the child from (a) causing injury to himself or herself or to other persons in the unit, or (b) absconding from the unit.[300] However nothing in section 23K may authorise the placing of a child in a special care unit otherwise than in accordance with an interim special care order or a special care order.[301]

Provision is also made by section 23K for the Minister for Health and Children to approve the provision of a special care unit if (a) having caused the unit to be inspected by a person authorised in that behalf by the Minister for Health and Children and having considered a report in writing of the inspection he or she is satisfied that the requirements of regulations under section 23K will be complied with by the Health Service Executive, voluntary body or other person, as the case may be, in relation to the unit.[302] The duration of an approval of a special care unit by the Minister is 3 years from the date of approval. The approval may be renewed for a further period or periods of a similar duration.[303] On approving a special care unit, the Minister must cause a certificate to be issued to the Health Service Executive and the certificate shall without further proof, unless the contrary is shown be admissible in any proceedings as evidence that the unit has been approved of by the Minister for the purposes of section 23B and 23C.[304] The Minister may cancel such a certificate if he or she is of opinion that the special care unit concerned is no longer suitable for use as such a unit or is no longer required for that purpose.[305]

Under section 23K(6) the Minister must make regulations with respect to the operation of special care units provided by or on behalf of the Health Service Executive under section 23K and for securing the welfare of children detained there.[306] Without prejudice to the generality of section 23K(6) regulations under section 23K may prescribe requirements as to: (a) the maintenance, care and welfare of children while being detained in special care units, (b) the staffing of those units, (c) the physical standards in those

---

[298] Child Care Act 1991, s.23K(8) inserted by the Children Act 2001, s.16.
[299] *Ibid.*, s.23K(9) inserted by the Children Act 2001, s.16.
[300] *Ibid.*, s.23K(10) inserted by the Children Act 2001, s.16.
[301] *Ibid.*, s.23K(11) inserted by the Children Act 2001, s.16.
[302] *Ibid.*, s.23K(2) inserted by the Children Act 2001, s.16.
[303] *Ibid.*, s.23K(3) inserted by the Children Act 2001, s.16.
[304] *Ibid.*, s.23K(4) inserted by the Children Act 2001, s.16.
[305] *Ibid.*, s.23K(5) inserted by the Children Act 2001, s.16.
[306] See Preface.

units, including the provision of adequate and suitable accommodation and facilities, (d) the periodical review of the cases of children in those units and the matters to be considered in such reviews, (d) the records to be kept in those units and the examination and copying of any such records or of extracts therefrom by persons authorised in that behalf by the Minister, and (f) the periodical inspection of those units by persons authorised in that behalf by, (i) the Health Service Executive in the case where the units were provided under section 23K(1)(b) by arrangement with a voluntary body or any other person and by (ii) the Minister for Health and Children in any other case in accordance with section 69 of the Child Care Act 1991.[307] No regulations have yet been made and concern has been expressed by some commentators,[308] that there is as yet insufficient provision regarding rules and inspection of units to ensure that children in special care units will receive the proper care and protection they need.

The Social Services Inspectorate set up in 1999 has drawn up national standards for special care units which provide the basis on which their inspectors form judgments about the quality of care provided in the units and it is to be hoped that these standards together with regulations when made will ensure maintenance of high standards of care in the units. Where a child has been found guilty of an offence that child may not be ordered to be placed or detained in a special care unit.[309]

Commentary

Following the enactment and coming into force of section 2 the European Convention on Human Rights Act 2003 the Irish legislation and common law in relation to custody and guardianship of children and in relation to the making of care orders must be interpreted in a manner compatible with the State's obligations under the European Convention on Human Rights. In the context of the rights of parents with mental illness or with intellectual disability to the custody of their children Article 8 of the Convention and the jurisprudence of the European Court of Human Rights in relation to the Article are particularly relevant. The relevant provisions of Article 8 state:

1. Everyone has the right to respect for his private and family life, his home and his correspondence.

2. There shall be no interference by a public authority with the exercise of this right except such as is in accordance with the law and is necessary in a democratic society ... for the protection of health or morals, or for the protection of the rights and freedoms of others.

---

[307] *Ibid.*, s.23K(7) inserted by the Children Act 2001, s.16. S.69 of the 1991 Act empowers a person authorised by the Minister to inspect any service provided or premises maintained by the Health Service Executive. To that end the authorised person may: (a) enter any premises maintained by the Health Service Executive under the 1991 Act and make such examination into the state and management of the premises and the treatment of children therein as he thinks fit and (b) examine such records and interview such members of the staff of the Executive as he thinks fit.

[308] See G. Shannon, *Paper on Children Act 2001* delivered to Children Act Conference, November 7, 2002, p.11.

[309] Children Act 2001, s.16 inserting s.23N into Child Care Act 1991.

In the case of *Kutzner v. Germany*,[310] two parents with intellectual disability alleged (i) that the withdrawal of their parental responsibility for their two daughters by a German Guardianship Court on the grounds that they did not have the intellectual capacity to bring up their children and their failure to co-operate with social services; (ii) the placement of the children in unidentified foster homes in the interests of promoting the children's emotional and physical development and (iii) their restricted right of access to their children (initially one hour per month) infringed their right respect for their family life as guaranteed by Article 8 of the Convention. The European Court of Human Rights stated at the outset of its judgment that the mutual enjoyment by parent and child of each other's company constituted a fundamental element of family life,[311] and that the children continued placement in foster homes and the restrictions imposed on contact between the applicants and their children amounted to an interference with the applicants' rights to respect for their family life.[312]

While the interference was in accordance with German domestic law the question which had to be decided was whether it was "necessary in a democratic society". The court held that the notion of necessity implied that the interference corresponded to a pressing social need and in particular that it was proportionate to the legitimate aim pursued.[313] Among the positive obligations imposed on the State by Article 8 was the duty of the State to act in a manner calculated to enable a tie to be developed where the existence of a family tie had been established and to take measures to enable the parent and child to be reunited.[314] In determining whether state reasons for intervention were relevant and sufficient it held that the court had to have regard for the fact that perceptions of the appropriateness of intervention by public authorities in the care of children varied among Member States. However consideration of what was in child's best interests was of crucial importance. National authorities had the benefit of direct contact with all the persons concerned and the task of the court was not to substitute itself for the domestic authorities in the exercise of their responsibilities for the regulation of the public care of children and the rights of parents whose children had been taken into care but rather to review under the Convention the decisions that the authorities had taken in exercise of their power under the margin of appreciation afforded to them in assessing the necessity of taking a child into care.[315] However, the court stated

> "a stricter scrutiny is called for both of any further limitations, such as restrictions placed by those authorities on parental rights and access and of any legal safeguards designed to secure an effective protection of the rights of parents and of children to respect for their family life. Such further limitations entail the danger that family relations between the parents and a young child are effectively curtailed."[316]

---

[310] Application No. 46544/69. Judgment February 26, 2002.
[311] Para.58.
[312] Para.59.
[313] Para.60.
[314] Para.61.
[315] Paras 66–67.
[316] Para.68.

The court's starting point in assessing whether the interference with the parent's rights to the company of the child was justified was to note that:

> "the fact that the child could be placed in a more beneficial environment for his or her upbringing would not on its own justify a compulsory measure of removal from the care of the biological parents; there must exist other circumstances pointing to the "necessity" for such an interference with the parent's right under Article 8 of the Convention to enjoy a family life with their child."[317]

Also it had the outset of its judgment stated that while Article 8 contains no explicit requirements the decision making process leading to interference with "private and family" rights must be fair as such as to afford due respect to the interests safeguarded by Article 8.[318]

The court recognised that the authorities might have had legitimate concerns about the late development of the children noted by the various social services departments and psychologists but the care order itself and the manner in which it was implemented were unsatisfactory. The facts were that the children had benefited from an early age and at their parents' request from education support and the situation had only become acrimonious as a result of conflict between the parents and a social worker who submitted a very negative report to the local Youth Office. The opinions given by psychologists during the proceedings were contradictory if not in their conclusions then at least as regards the reasons relied on. It held that the opinions of the psychologists adduced on behalf of the applicants, which stated that the parents were entirely fit to bring up their children emotionally and intellectually and that the children should be given additional educational support should have been taken into full consideration, and could not be disregarded simply because they were acting on behalf of one of the parties to the proceedings. Further there had been no allegations that the children were neglected or ill-treated by their parents. Coming to the core of its decision the court stated that although educational support measures taken initially subsequently proved to be inadequate

> "it was questionable whether the domestic administrative and judicial authorities had given sufficient consideration to additional measures of support as an alternative to what is by far the most extreme measure namely separating the children from their parents".[319]

In effect, this dicta of the European Court of Human Rights imposes on authorities responsible for the welfare of children in Contracting states the obligation under Article 8 to consider additional measures to support parents with intellectual disability in the upbringing of their children before resorting to the drastic measure of a care order. Even if this last resort measure is adopted, the court stated that a care order should "in principle be regarded as a temporary measure, to be discontinued as soon as circumstances permit, and that any measures implementing temporary care should be consistent with the ultimate

---

[317] Para.69.
[318] Para.56.
[319] Para.75.

aim of reuniting the natural parents and the child."[320] It stated further that the positive duty to facilitate family reunification as soon as reasonably feasible would begin "to weigh on the responsible authorities with progressively increasing force as from the commencement of the period of care, subject always to its being balanced against the duty to consider the best interests of the child"[321] The court noted, further, that having regard to the fact that the children were very young severing contact with their parents and the imposition of severe restrictions on parent's visiting rights could lead to the child's "alienation" from their parents and from each other.[322]

Having regard to all these considerations, the court found that although the reasons relied on by the domestic authorities and courts were relevant they were insufficient to justify such a serious interference in the applicant's family life. Notwithstanding the domestic authorities' margin of appreciation the interference was "not proportionate" to the legitimate aims pursued,[323] and consequently there was a violation of Article 8. The court awarded €15,000 in non-pecuniary damages jointly to the applicants in respect of the injury to their physical and psychological health as a result of their separation from their children and the restrictions on their visiting rights.[324]

The *Kutzner* case may be regarded as a vindication of the right of parents with intellectual disability to custody of his/her child and a clear message to authorities in contracting states under the European Convention to consider that there primary obligation is to provide support to parents with mental disabilities in raising their children.

Further, the Canadian case of *Children's Aid Society of Kingston v. Reeves*[325] may provide useful guidance on the approach to be adopted, when it is alleged that a child of parents with intellectual disabilities is in need of protection. In that case Thomson J. stated:

> "It is my opinion that the court should take the following approach when faced with cases such as the one now before me. First of all, the fact of low parental intelligence should not be taken as determinative in itself of the child's need for protection. Rather, the question should be one of deciding whether, in the light of their individual capabilities, these parents are able to meet their parental responsibilities. If the answer to this question is no, then the judge should decide whether, given the proper assistance and intervention, the parents can be provided with the tools necessary to care adequately for their child. This issue should not be resolved by simply noting the difficulties involved in securing the needed help when the child remains within the home. The actions of person involved in this case show that, with a co-ordinated effort, extensive assistance can be given to parents such as the Reeves. Only if it is felt that the risk to the child is too great even with outside help should the court remove the child from the home."

In America criticism has been directed at the courts tendency to attach considerable

---

[320] Para.76.
[321] Para.76.
[322] Para.79.
[323] Para.81.
[324] Paras 85, 87.
[325] (1975) 23 R.F.L. 391 at 394.

importance to the parent's IQ in assessing their ability to care for their children.[326] A number of American authors have expressed concern, that parental rights of persons with intellectual disabilities are too readily terminated simply on the ground of low intelligence.[327] Vitello and Soskin comment:

> "[w]hatever gains have been made in the rights of mentally retarded persons to marry and bear children, these gains may be offset by judicial decisions terminating their parental rights to keep and raise their children."[328]

There are many reported cases in Canada in which children have been held to be in need of protection due to their parent's inability to provide proper care and protection because of mental illness. In a number of cases the court found the parent to be capable of caring adequately for the child's physical needs but incapable of providing for the child's emotional and developmental needs. In *Minister of Social Services v. V.S.*[329] is a case which provides an interesting illustration of the approach of the Canadian courts. The case involved a mother who suffered from chronic paranoid schizophrenia the court granted a committal order terminating parental rights on the ground that:

> "Although [the mother] ... provided for all of the physical needs of her son she had a hard time grasping the relationship she should have with her child; the inter-relationship a baby has with its mother; the developmental milestones to be promoted and expected in a child; and the need for a child to be parted from its mother from time to time. She trusted no one to look after the child. She behaved irrationally in front of the child including assaulting a child welfare worker while the worker was holding the baby in her arms. In a phrase she was unable to provide to her son the emotional stability, consistency and environment needed for the child to survive."

Again in Canada the fact that the child is mentally or physically disabled may be relevant in determining whether the parents are capable of providing the care which the child requires. In *In re Eccles*,[330] the child, a 17 year old girl developed a mental illness which resulted in her having an irrational and inexplicable fear of her parents. Her reaction to her parents was so severe that she was diagnosed as potentially suicidal. The British Columbia Court of Appeal held (Esson J.A. dissenting) held that notwithstanding that the parents were loving and caring, they were unable to provide necessary care for their daughter because of her mental illness. Accordingly the girl was committed to the temporary custody of the Superintendent of Family and Child Service.

In the USA states statutory law of custody uniformly defers to the best interests of the child. Where it is modelled after the Uniform Marriage and Divorce Act the law

---

[326] See Haavik & Meninger, *Sexuality, Law and the Developmentally Disabled Person* (1981), p.91.
[327] *Ibid.*, pp.90–92: Vitello and Soskin *Mental Retardation: Its Social and Legal Context* (Prentice Hall, New Jersey, 1985), pp.93–95; Sales et al *Disabled Persons and the Law* (1982), pp.25–26; Kindred *et al.*, *The Mentally Retarded Citizen and the Law* (Free Press, New York, 1976), pp.14–15.
[328] See Mental Retardation Its Social and Legal Context (1985), p.93.
[329] (1985) 69 N.S.R. (2d) 435 (Fam. Ct.).
[330] (1986) 24 D.L.R. (4th) 413 (B.C.C.A.).

provides that a determination of this interest shall include consideration of "the mental and physical health of all individuals concerned."[331] The content of the standards may be illustrated by reference to two contrasting cases. In *Price v. Price*,[332] a husband separating from his disabled spouse claimed custody of the children. The court held that the wife's mental illness and formal legal incompetency for general purposes did not suffice as a matter of law to deprive her of the right to custody of the children. Incompetence to rear children was a specific issue which had to be specifically alleged and proved in a custody case. It could not be inferred from the fact of general or even legal incapacity.

By contrast in *In re CLM*,[333] the court approved a decision giving custody to the state on the mere basis of evidence of the mother's incapacity to provide necessary and proper care. The court stated that the custody change could properly be construed as a preventative measure and that actual harm to the child or actual neglect need not be shown as this adverse potential was implicit in the mother's general incapacity. By contrast in *In re Calkins*[334] it was held that parental unfitness to retain custody must be proved by clear and convincing evidence.

Where support obligations are concerned in the majority of Canadian provinces the parental obligation to support ceases once the child reaches the age of majority. The justification being that the responsibility for maintaining adults who are unable to support themselves should lie with the State rather than with the parents. In Nova Scotia[335] and Manitoba[336] the court has power to require a parent to support a child beyond the age of majority if the child is unable by reason of illness disability or other cause to withdraw from the charge of his parents or to provide himself with reasonable needs. In Alberta and the Northwest Territories the obligation exists even if there is no court ordered support. In these two jurisdictions legislation obliges the parents of an "old, blind, lame, mentally deficient or impotent person or any other destitute person who is not able to work" to provide him with reasonable maintenance if he is unable to maintain himself.[337] The Irish Oireachtas is moving in the direction of a parental maintenance obligation with section 8(6) of the Children Act 1997 but the scope of the obligation is as yet confined to Guardianship of Infants matters. Section 197 of the Canadian Criminal Code goes further and imposes a duty on a person to provide the necessaries of life to a person under one's charge if that person is unable by reason of detention, age, illness, insanity or other cause to withdraw himself from that charge and is unable to provide himself with the necessaries of life. Failure to perform this duty without lawful excuse is a criminal offence if it endangers the life of the person to whom the duty is owed or

---

[331] See for example Illinois Ann. Stat. Ch 40 Section 602. The commentary to this statute cites s.402 of the Uniform Marriage and Divorce Act (9 U.L.A.) as the source from which this language derives.

[332] 255 S.E. 2d 652 (N.C. Ct. App. 1979).

[333] 625 S.E. 2d. 613 (Mo. 1981).

[334] 96 Ill. App. 3d 74, 420 N.E. 2d 861 (1981).

[335] Nova Scotia Family Maintenance Act Section 2(c),9 [am. 1983, c.64, s.3]. See also *In re Nowe and Nowe* (1986) 25 D.L.R. (4th) 105 (N.S.C.A.) leave to appeal to S.C.C. refused 73 N.S.R. (2d) 270n: *Kings County v. Cogswell* (1985) 46 R.F.L. (2d) 148 (N.S. Fam.Ct.).

[336] Manitoba Family Maintenance Act s.12(5) [en. 1982–83–84, c.54, s.18].

[337] In *In re F* (1976) 27 R.F.L. 372 (Alberta Juvenile Court) the term "destitute person who is not able to work" was interpreted as not being restricted to mental or physical incapacity.

causes (or is likely to cause) permanent injury to his health.[338] However, the duty imposed by the Criminal Code does not give rise to civil liability for maintenance.

In all Canadian jurisdictions children may be required to provide reasonable support for parents who are unable to maintain themselves.[339] In some jurisdictions, this obligation arises only if the parent's inability to support themselves is due to factors such as destitution, age, infirmity or illness.[340] In others the scope of the jurisdiction is wider and imposes a duty on children to support parents in accordance with their need to the extent that the child is capable of doing so.[341]

The responsibility of parents to provide for financial support of a disabled child once that child reaches majority has been addressed by the courts in the USA. In *Wilkinson v. Wilkinson*[342] and *Kamp v. Kamp*,[343] it was held that the current judicial view was that parental responsibility in that regard was a continuing one at least when the disabled person continues to reside at home. By contrast where an institutionalised child reaches majority the legal trend appears to be towards extinguishing financial liability for him/her.[344]

By contrast to that, in Ireland the general trend in other jurisdictions tends towards a more precise determination of parental mental capacity to retain custody of children. The prevailing analysis in the Canadian and US jurisdictions is functional viz whether the parents' difficulties de facto impact on his/her ability to rear children as opposed to status based. It is submitted that this functional approach might be more closely followed in the Irish courts in custody disputes. Secondly, the legislatures of other jurisdictions have also grappled with the issue of family provision of maintenance for family members with mental disabilities who are unable to support themselves financially. Such an option might be considered by our legislature to assist those who find themselves having to depend solely upon the state system for financial support.

CAPACITY IN THE CONTEXT OF ADOPTION

Capacity to consent to adoption and to adopt under Irish law

Section 14(1) of the Adoption Act 1952 provides that an adoption order shall not be made without the consent of every person being the child's mother or guardian or having

---

[338] If the duty is owed to a child under the age of sixteen failure to perform the duty is a criminal offence if the child is in destitute or necessitous circumstances.

[339] This obligation applies only to children over the age of majority except in Alberta, Saskatchewan, Manitoba, Newfoundland and the Northwest territories. In some jurisdictions "parent" ncludes[i] grandparent.

[340] Family Relations Act R.S.B.C. 1979 c.121 s.58; Maintenance Order Act R.S.A. 1980, c.m–1 s.2(1); Parents Maintenance Act R.S.m. 1970 c.P10; Family Maintenance Act S.N.S. 1980, c.6 s.2(d), 15 [am. 1983, c.64, s.8]; Maintenance Act R.S.N. 1970, c.223 s.2(c), 3; Maintenance Act R.S.N.W.T. 1974, c.M–2 s.3(1) [re-en 1985 (3rd) c.10, s.85].

[341] Parent's Maintenance Act R.S.S. 1978, c.P–1, s.2: Family Law S.O. 1986, c.4 s.32; Family Services Act S.N.B. 1980, c.F–2.2 s.114; Family Law Reform Act S.P.E.I. 1978 c.6 s.18; Matrimonial Property and Family Support Act S.Y.T. 1979 (2nd) c.11 s.30.4 [en. 1980 (2nd) c.15 s.7(1)].

[342] 585 P. 2d. 599 (Colo. Ct. App 1978).

[343] No. 5514 6 M.D.L.R. 171 (Wyo. Sup. Ct. Jan 28, 1982).

[344] See *The Mentally Disabled and the Law, op. cit.*, p.516.

charge of or control over the child. However evidence of mental illness may be relevant to the question of whether a parent has given valid consent. Finlay P., in the course of his judgment in *S v. the EHB and others*,[345] indicated that:

> "the test which I must apply to each of the separate alleged agreements to place for adoption are that they have been made freely with full knowledge of their consequences and under circumstances when neither the advice of persons engaged in the transaction nor the surrounding circumstances deprived the mother of the capacity to make a full informed free decision."

In *JM & GM v. An Bord Uchtála*,[346] the Supreme Court on appeal from a finding that the mother had not given full and free consent held in the circumstances that the mother was not so uncertain and distressed before and after the signing of the consent form as to render her consent invalid. Gannon J. commenting on the state of mind which might render parental consent invalid stated:

> "I would exclude a decision made impetuously thoughtlessly, grasped out of panic or unreasonable anxiety or when the ability to make a rational decision might be so emotionally disturbed as to render unreliable the consideration of the information upon which it purports to be based."[347]

Section 14(2) provides that the Adoption Board is empowered to dispense with the consent of a person if satisfied that that person in incapable by reason of mental infirmity of giving consent. However the consent of a ward of court may not be dispensed with except with the sanction of the court.[348] Kerry O'Halloran notes that the ground of mental infirmity may be satisfied by evidence that a parent lacks the capacity to give a proper consent due either to profound intellectual disability or to severe mental illness.[349]

Under section 3(1) of the Adoption (Amendment) Act 1974 in any case where a person has applied for an adoption order relating to a child and any person whose consent to the making of an adoption order relating to the child is necessary and who has agreed to the placing of the child for adoption either (a) fails or refuses to give consent, or (b) withdraws a consent already given the applicant for the adoption order may apply to the High Court for an order, *inter alia*, dispensing with the consent of person concerned and the making of an adoption order in favour of the applicant. The High Court, may make such an order if it is satisfied that it is in *the best interests of the child* so to do. The consent of a ward of court shall not be dispensed with by virtue of a High Court order under section 3(3) except with the sanction of the Court.

In *G v. An Bord Uchtála*,[350] Finlay P. indicated that the court might dispense with the consent of the mother under section 3 if she "failed to establish to the court that she is a fit and proper person to have custody of the child."

---

[345] Unreported, High Court, February 28, 1979.

[346] [1987] I.R. 510 (Supreme Court).

[347] [1987] I.R. 510 (Supreme Court). This passage was later quoted by Lavan J. in *JP & SP v. An Bord Uchtála*, unreported High Court, November 9, 1990.

[348] Adoption Act 1952, s.14(3).

[349] O'Halloran, *Adoption Law and Practice* (Butterworths Ireland, 1992) p.865.

[350] [1980] I.R. 32.

In *NB & TB v. An Bord Uchtála and others*,[351] the mother indicated that she had placed her son for adoption as she had been violent towards him, had rejected him and had been unable to cope with him. Finding that if the child was returned to the mother there was "nothing to suggest that she will be able to cope with him any better than she did in the past." Barron J. went on to consider the evidence of psychiatrists that the best interests of the child would be served by his remaining with the adopters and made an order dispensing with the mother's consent to the adoption.

In *MM v. An Bord Uchtála*,[352] the adopters failed to disclose to the Adoption Board that the adoptive father had suffered from depression and mood swings and had required medical treatment. It was also suggested during the course of the court hearings that there was a degree of marital disharmony in the adopter's home. The trial judge found on the evidence that the adoptive parents enjoyed a stable happy marriage and that the adoptive father's illness had been stabilised by medication. Accepting evidence that if the child were moved from her present environment should would probably suffer psychological injury, Lynch J. found in favour of the adopters and dispensed with the mother's consent.

Since July 26, 1988, the adoption of any child, whether or not born to married parents, has been permitted in specifically defined circumstances where it is first established in court proceedings that the parents of the child have "for physical or moral reasons … failed in their duty towards the child."[353] In these circumstances the Adoption Act 1988 provides for the adoption of the child without parental consent. Section 3(1)(I) of the 1988 Act requires a number of factors to be shown to the satisfaction of the court.

(A) For a continuous period of not less than 12 months immediately preceding the making of the application the sole parent or each of the parents "for physical or moral reasons have failed in their duty towards the child"

(B) It is likely that such failure will continue without interruption until the child attains the age of 18 years.

(C) Such failure constitutes an abandonment on the part of parents of all parental rights whether under the Constitution or otherwise with respect to the child

(D) By reason of such failure the state as guardian of the common good should supply the place of parents

In *In re Adoption (No.2) Bill 1987*,[354] the Supreme Court held that the failure in duty must be "total in character". In addition it must arise for physical or moral reasons and not from external circumstances such as poverty. Thus in *Southern Health Board v. An Bord Uchtála*,[355] where a child of eight years had been physically abused over an extended period Costello P held that the parents had failed to discharge their duty "to act as his guardians and loving parents to further his welfare" and had by their actions caused their child to be placed in the health board's care under a Fit Person Order pursuant to the Children Act 1908.

---

[351] Unreported, High Court, February 18, 1983 .
[352] Unreported, High Court, Lynch J., May 11, 1984.
[353] See Adoption Act 1988, ss.2 and 3.
[354] [1989] I.R. 656.
[355] [1996] I F.L.R. 47 (HC), [1995] 2 I.L.R.M. 369.

In determining whether the failure will continue without interruption until the child attains the age of 18 years, the court will examine in detail the conduct of the parents towards the child up to the date of the court hearing and make its determination as to the course of future events on the balance of probabilities.[356]

The determination of whether there has been an abandonment of parental rights is quite separate and distinct from the finding of failure of parental duty and there may be a failure without abandonment. Statements by parents do not amount to conclusive evidence of abandonment. In *Southern Health Board v. An Bord Uchtála*,[357] mentioned above however Costello P. held that the conduct of the parents was "so egregious and so reprehensible that it constituted an abandonment of their rights."[358] The Supreme Court has also emphasised that "the necessity for proof of abandonment indicates a special regard for the constitutionally protected parental rights."[359] In *The Western Health Board v. An Bord Uchtála*[360] this "special regard' for parental rights was pivotal to the determination of Lardner J. not to free a child for adoption. Factors favouring the making of an adoption order were the fact that her natural mother had abandoned her and favoured the making of an adoption order and her father had failed in his duty towards her for the first four years of her life never having contributed to her support and never meeting her. Other factors however weighed against a finding of abandonment. Six months after a DNA test establishing he was the father her father had told a social worker that he wished the adopters to return his daughter. Subsequently in July 1992, he brought District Court proceedings under the Guardianship of Infants Act 1964 seeking her custody. Lardner J. held that having considered the father's:

> "conduct from 1988 to 1992 ... of delay and procrastination, his expressed reluctance to give up the child and his expressed claim to recover her and having heard his explanation of this in evidence, I am unable to conclude that the proper inference is that all the conduct constituting failure by (the father) to perform his duty as a parent amounts to a total and final abandonment of his rights as a parent"[361]

In the case of *Northern Area Health Board v. An Bord Uchtála and PO'D (Notice Party)*,[362] the question arose as to whether a natural parent, P., who had a mild intellectual disability and suffered from chronic schizo-affective psychosis and who was satisfied to leave her child J. – a child with cerebral palsy – in permanent long term foster care while visiting her from time to time, had abandoned her child. J was less than one year old at the time of the placement and almost 14 years old at the date of the proceedings. The Supreme Court found that on account of her mental disability P had been unable to fulfil her parental role for the entire of J's life. Accordingly for 'physical reasons" she had failed in her duty towards her child. It was also likely that such failure would continue

---

[356] *In re Adoption (No.2) Bill 1987* [1989] I.R. 656 at 664.
[357] [1996] I F.L.R 47.
[358] [1995] 3 I.R. at p.58.
[359] *In re Adoption (No. 2) Bill 1987, op. cit.*
[360] Unreported, High Court, July 5, 1994.
[361] [1995] 3 I.R. 186. In November 1995, an appeal against the decision of Lardner J. was dismissed by the Supreme Court.
[362] Unreported, Supreme Court, December 17, 2002.

without interruption until the child attained the age of eighteen since P could scarcely care for herself and would be unable to care for J. McGuinness J., delivering the judgment of the Supreme Court, considered the meaning of "abandonment" which had been discussed by Denham J. in *Southern Health Board v. An Bord Uchtála*.[363] In that case, Denham J. held that in section 3 (1)(I)(C) the word "abandonment" is used as a special legal term. The section did not require that there be an intention to abandon. Denham J. held:

> "The legal term "abandon" can be used also where, by their actions, parents have
> failed in their duty so as to enable a court to deem that their failure constitutes an
> abandonment of parental rights."[364]

McGuinness J. held that while failure of parental duty does not necessarily or invariably amount to abandonment the requirement of abandonment was not to be considered in isolation separate from the failure of duty. The statute stated that "such failure" could constitute an abandonment. In the present case P agreed to the continuing care of J by the applicants for adoption over virtually J's entire life. She was happy that this situation could continue. She had allowed and willingly continued to allow J to become in a practical sense a member of the prospective adopters family. She had left and continued to leave to them the crucial decisions regarding J's health and education and the carrying into effect of those decisions together with the by no means insubstantial costs that arose from them. This situation amounted in a real and objective sense to abandonment of her rights as parent. The infrequent visits by P to her daughter, largely initiated by others were not inconsistent with the reality of her abandonment of her position as a parent and her opposition to adoption did not of itself contradict the fact of abandonment. The test of abandonment had to be an objective one. Accordingly, McGuinness J. made an order authorising An Bord Uchtála to make an adoption order in relation to J in favour of the prospective adopters.[365]

In addition to the factors outlined in (a) to (d) above, it must be shown to the satisfaction of the court that the child is, at the time of making the application in the custody of the applicants and has a home with them and for a continuous period of not less than 12 months immediately preceding the making of the application has been in the continuous custody of and has had a home with the prospective adopters[366] The court must also be satisfied that "the adoption of the child by the applicants is an appropriate means by which to supply the place of the parents."[367]

---

[363] [2000] 1 I.R. 165.

[364] *Ibid.*, p.177.

[365] In making the order, McGuinness J. noted that J. had expressed clear and reasoned views in favour of her adoption by the prospective adopters and the prospective adopters had indicated that they were happy for P to visit J, from time to time and there was no reason to believe that they would not continue these visiting arrangements. Mc Guinness J. remarked:
> "Adoption practice in general has become more open in recent years. The old insistence on secrecy and a complete exclusion of the natural mother has virtually gone and it is not uncommon for adopted children to continue to meet their birth parents from time to time" (at p.138 of Judgment).

[366] Adoption Act 1988, s.3(1)(II).

[367] *Ibid.*, s.3(1)(III). *In re Adoption (No. 2) Bill 1987, op. cit.*

In making its overall decision under section 3 of the 1988 Act the court is obliged to have "due regard for the rights, whether under the Constitution or otherwise, of the persons concerned (including the natural and imprescriptible rights of the child)" and if it then reaches the conclusion that "it would be in the best interests of the child" to do so it may authorise the Adoption Board to make an adoption order in favour of the applicants.[368] In *In re Adoption (No.2) Bill 1987*,[369] the Supreme Court ruled that the "persons concerned" means "all persons who in the opinion of the High Court judge have an interest in or are likely to be affected by the application."

Before making an order the court must also in so far as is practicable give due consideration having regard to his age and understanding to the wishes of the child concerned.[370] Before making an order the court must hear the parents of the child "and any other persons, who, in the opinion of the court ought to be heard by it."[371] However, where a child's parent or parents "fail or refuse" to give evidence, having been requested to do so, the court is not prevented from making an order authorising the adoption of a child.[372] Moreover the court may dispense with the need for parental evidence inter alia where one or both parents are "incapable by reason of mental infirmity of giving reliable evidence to the court."[373]

Commentary

Significantly however legislation in the USA relating to the substantive standard which must be met before parental rights may be terminated have clearly established that a mere finding of mental disorder is not enough. There must be specific evidence that the disorder renders the parent unfit to rear children and statutes failing to require this have been struck down.[374] Another dominant thread running through the case law is a requirement that the untenable parent-child relationship must persist for the foreseeable future.[375]

Where procedural rights are concerned in *South Carolina Dept of Social Services v. McDow*,[376] it was held that the state cannot terminate the parental rights of alleged incompetent parents without appointing a *guardian ad litem* even where the parents did have appointed legal counsel. The case emphasised the special trust relationship that exists between a *guardian ad litem* and a disabled parent which was different to the one between legal counsel and client. Further, in *In re Guardianship of Daniel Aaron D*,[377] the court mandated the presence of the parent where no showing of the need to exclude him or her is made. The case also supports the allegedly disabled parent's entitlement to a recent psychiatric examination.

---

[368] *Ibid.*, s.3(1)(III).
[369] [1989] I.R. 656 at p.665.
[370] Adoption Act 1988, s.3(2).
[371] Adoption Act 1988, s.4(1).
[372] *Ibid.*, s.4(2) and (3).
[373] *Ibid.*, s.4(4).
[374] See *Helvey v. Rednour* 86 Ill App. 3d 154, 408 N.E. 2d. 17 (1980).
[375] E.g. *In re Young* 600 P. 2d. 1312 (Wash Ct. App 1979); *In re Brendenick* 74 Ill. App. 3d. 946, 393 N.E. 2d. 675 (1979).
[376] 280 S.E. 2d 208 (1981).
[377] 403 N.E. 2d 451 (N.Y. 1980).

Authorising adoption without the consent of the mentally disabled parent and even more so termination against parental wishes is a very difficult decision to make involving a delicate problem of balancing interests as between parent and child.

Brakel describes the situation in the USA thus:

> "The requisite scientific knowledge about mental disability – its nature, duration, curability – as well as the sociological knowledge about what ultimately is best for parents or children which would give decision makers confidence in the substantive correctness of their decisions is wanting. As a result perhaps there has been heavy emphasis on decision-making procedure not merely to minimise the chance of error but to legitimise as it were decisions that are based on inadequate knowledge of what is really right or best."[378]

While this may be the case in the USA similar concerns must affect those concerned with adoptions against the wishes of a mentally disabled person in the Irish context and while not wishing to put due process correctness in place as a substitute for substantive requirements Irish law can draw from the US experience. The situations in which a parent's consent to adoption is dispensed with on the basis that by virtue of mental infirmity the person lacks the capacity to give proper consent should be confined to cases where there is specific evidence that the disorder renders the person incapable of understanding the nature and effects of consenting to adoption. It must be in very rare circumstances that the nature of a mental illness or intellectual disability would render a person incapable of giving consent to the adoption of their child by another. It is submitted that in such circumstances the need for constitutional due process is obvious to guard against abuse of parental rights. The person concerned should have the right to representation by a *guardian ad litem*, a solicitor and counsel and be entitled to the benefit of a recent psychiatric examination in this regard and to an oral hearing on the issue of his/her capacity to consent where there is no demonstration of the need to exclude him or her.

In other circumstances where the court proposes to dispense with parental consent on the grounds that the best interests of the child require it under section 3(1) of the Adoption (Amendment) Act 1974 on grounds of mental disability then as a minimum it should be clearly established that there is parental unfitness in the sense of inability to care for the children, harm to the children (or at least the potential for it) if they remain with the parent and the probability that the unfitness to provide care and support will persist for the foreseeable future.

---

[378] See *The Mentally Disabled and the Law, op. cit.*, p.517.

CHAPTER TEN

Legal Capacity under Public Law

INTRODUCTION

The impact of mental incapacity on the exercise of public rights is a matter of crucial importance to a person with mental disability. It is essential that his/her incapacity not adversely affect these rights disproportionately to the degree of incapacity he or she experiences for to do so amounts to an unfairly discriminatory deprivation of rights some of which are central to citizenship in Ireland such as the right to influence the parliamentary process and the right to access to the courts and others which can influence a persons life considerably such as having permission to drive a motor vehicle. The Chapter sets out to examine the impact of mental incapacity as a matter of law in these areas.

POLITICAL AND CIVIL RIGHTS

The impact of incapacity on political rights – the right to vote

The right to vote is essential, if persons with mental disability are to be in a position to voice their concerns and participate in a democratic political process. Discrimination in relation to this right in effect means a section of the population are deprived of the ability to determine who is to represent their interests and influence legislation, which can have a major impact on their lives.

Legal incapacity to vote was defined in the case of *Stowe v. Joliffe*[1] as "some quality inherent in a person, which either at common law or by statute deprives him of the status of an elector." The common law rules provide that the name of an "idiot" (now regarded as a person with a severe intellectual disability) could not appear on the electoral register and hence such a person could not vote.[2] At common law, persons of unsound mind are also disqualified from voting or standing in parliamentary and local elections.[3] However, a person of unsound mind can vote during a lucid moment.[4] In practical terms the test of legal capacity in this regard will probably be whether at the time of voting the individual can understand in broad terms what he is doing and the effects of it and has the ability to make a choice between candidates.

In order to exercise their franchise electors with capacity must first be registered to

---

[1] (1874) L.R. CP 446.

[2] See *Bedford County Case, Burgess' Case* (1785) 2 Lud. E.C. 381.

[3] See *Halsbury's, Laws of England* Vol.15, para.315, n.9 citing Heywood's County Elections 259–261 and *Bedford County Case, Burgess' Case* (1785) 2 Lud. E.C. 381 at 567.

[4] *Oakhampton Case, Robins'Case* (1791) 1 Fras. 69 at 162; *Bridgewater Case, Tucker's Case* (1803) 1 Peck 101 at 108.

vote in a constituency in which they were ordinarily resident on the qualifying date.[5] The voters' registration form does not enquire as to whether a person suffers from a mental illness or disability and so the relevant persons name may be included on it. Section 11(6) of the Electoral Act 1992 however provides that where a person is a patient or inmate in any hospital or home for persons suffering from mental disability or similar institution s/he is deemed to be ordinarily resident in the place where he would have been residing but for his having been such a patient where this can be ascertained by the registration authority and where it cannot he is deemed to be resident in the place where he last resided before becoming such a patient or inmate.[6]

Where a person's name is on the electoral register the question of capacity will be one of fact for the officer presiding at the polling station. In the usual course of events, voters are only asked whether they are the same person as the person whose name appears as AB on the register of Dáil electors now in force for the constituency of (the constituency which the polling station serves), whether they have already voted at the election and whether they are over eighteen years of age,[7] and will be permitted to vote if they are capable of answering – the result being unlikely to be challenged. In essence therefore test of capacity in practise is largely dependent upon the intending voter's capacity to communicate rather than upon more comprehensive test of his/her mental capacity. In cases where a Dáil elector applying for a ballot paper satisfies the presiding officer that he is unable to read or write to such an extent that he is unable to vote without assistance and if required by the presiding officer takes an oath or makes an affirmation to this effect s/he may request that his ballot paper shall be marked for him by a companion or alternatively have it marked for him by the presiding officer.[8]

Commentary

Interestingly as far back as 1977, the Council of Europe in its *Recommendation 818 (1977)*[9] *on the situation of the mentally ill*, recommended that the Committee of Ministers invite the governments of the member states to implement the right to vote for those mental patients able to understand the meaning of the vote by taking the necessary steps with a view to facilitating the exercise of it, by ensuring that information on public affairs is made available, by informing the patients about the procedures, deadlines and registration etc. and by offering material assistance to those who are physically handicapped. The Council further recommended that the Committee invite governments to afford the possibility of appeal to mental patients declared unfit to vote.[10]

In a further recommendation, *Council of Europe Recommendation (83)2 of the Committee of Ministers to member states concerning the legal protection of persons*

---

[5] Electoral Act 1992, s.7–9.
[6] *Ibid.*, s.11(6).
[7] *Ibid.*, s.111(2)(c) as amended by the Electoral (Amendment) Act 2001, s.27(a); See also Electoral Act 1992 (Section 165) Regulations 1994 (S.I. No.132 of 1994), reg.14(g), Electoral Act 1992 (Section 165) Regulations 1999 (S.I. No.153 of 1999), reg.19(f). In the case of European Parliament elections a person may also be asked whether they are a citizen of Ireland and/or a national of a Member State of the European Union other than Ireland.
[8] Electoral Act 1992, s.103.
[9] Adopted by Parliamentary Assembly of the Council of Europe on October 8, 1977.
[10] Para. 13. I. v.

suffering from mental disorders placed as involuntary patients, the Council provided that "placement [in a psychiatric hospital], by itself, cannot constitute, by operation of law, a reason for the restriction of the legal capacity of the patient".[11]

In Alberta, patients in hospitals including psychiatric hospitals are deemed to be ordinarily resident in the electoral division in which the hospital is located but their names do not appear on the published voters lists.[12] In addition the Election Acts of Alberta,[13] Saskatchewan,[14] Ontario,[15] and New Brunswick[16] expressly require polling stations to be established inside hospitals (including psychiatric hospitals) at the times of provincial elections.

The effect of section 11(6) of the Electoral Act may mean people resident in a psychiatric hospital whose place of residence is some distance away from the hospital may be unable to vote. A solution may be to deem patients ordinarily resident in the electoral division in which the hospital is located. Although a possible objection to the latter approach might be that it would result in the hospital's constituency having a disproportionate number of people whose interests and concerns might not necessarily be related to the local community.

Legal incapacity and public representation – membership of the Dáil

By virtue of section 41 of the Electoral Act 1992,[17] a person of unsound mind is ineligible for membership of the Dáil. Section 42 of the same Act provides that a member of the Dáil who becomes of unsound mind thereupon ceases to be a member and that a vacancy shall exist accordingly in the membership of the Dáil.

Commentary

The description "person of unsound mind" is not defined in the Electoral Act 1992 and there appears to be no requirement that the person concerned be incapable of managing his/her property and affairs before this disqualification bites.

The impact of incapacity on civic duties – jury service

The right of a person to be judged by a jury of his peers is a fundamental part of the trial process. Under Article 38.5 of the Constitution the jury is intended to represent a genuine cross-section of the community so that the hallmark of its verdict will be the fairness and acceptability that comes with a decision that represents the views of a broad spectrum of the community. The right of a person with mental disability to serve on that jury provided his mental disability does not affect his ability to adjudicate on the facts therefore must also be fundamental.

---

[11] See Art.9.
[12] See Election Act R.S.A., 1980 c. E-2 s.25(4), 118.
[13] S.117.
[14] S.91(1).
[15] S.14.
[16] S.83.1.
[17] Ss 41 and 42 were brought into force on December 11, 1992 by the Electoral Act 1992 (Commencement) (No. 3) Order 1992 (S.I. No. 386), para. 3(1)(d).

The effect of section 7 and Part I of the First Schedule to the Juries Act 1976 is that a person who suffers or has suffered from mental disorder or mental disability and on account of that condition either is resident in a hospital or other similar institution or regularly attends for treatment by a medical practitioner is ineligible for jury service.[18]

Commentary

In most provinces in Canada the Jury Act disqualifies persons who have a "mental infirmity incompatible with the discharge of the duties of a juror."[19] In the USA, 22 states disqualify jurors who are "incapable of rendering satisfactory service due to mental disability" or a closely similar formulation. It is submitted that Irish provision rendering ineligible for jury service a person who suffers or who has suffered from mental illness or mental disability, and on account of that condition regularly attends for treatment by a medical practitioner is anachronistic and discriminatory, as there seems to be no logical reason for excluding a person who has suffered from mental illness in the past but has now recovered from jury service nor does there appear to be any good reason for excluding a person whose illness is properly controlled. Finally, the provision seems to act as a disincentive to people with mental illness to seek medical assistance, since it discriminates against those who do and leaves open the possibility that the undiagnosed and those who do not keep in touch with their medical practitioner may be eligible for service. It is submitted that a functional approach should be adopted to a person's ability to serve as a juror, such that a person with mental illness or disability should not be disqualified from serving on a jury unless that disability is incompatible with the discharge of the duties of a juror.

Legal capacity and the professions

Solicitors – the current law

Law Society's powers in relation to issue of practising certiifcates in case of mental incapacity of solicitor   Under section 49 of the Solicitors Act 1954,[20] where a solicitor makes an application to the Law Society of Ireland for a practising certificate and: (i) he is a person in respect of whose person or property any of the powers of the Lunacy Regulation (Ireland) Act 1871, or any act amended or extending that Act relating to management and administration apply (*i.e.* he is in effect a ward of court);[21] (ii) he has failed to satisfy the Society that he fit to carry on the practise of a solicitor, having regard to the state of his physical or mental health;[22] (iii) he has failed to satisfy the

---

[18] Juries Act 1976, s.7, sch.1, Pt 1: That person is also ineligible to serve on a coroner's jury. See Juries Act 1976, s.31.

[19] R.S.B.C. c. 210 s.3(1)(n); S.A. 1982, c. J-2.1 s.5(1)(e); S.M. 1982-83-84 c. 69 (also C.C.S.M. C. J30), S 3(o); R.S.O. 1980 c.226, s.4(1); S.N.B. 1980, C. J-3.1, s.2(1)(c) [re-en. 1981, c.38 ,s.1; renumbered 1983 c.4, S. 12(1) (A); R S.P.E.I 1974, c. J-5, s.4(k) [re-en 1980, c.30, s.2]; S.N. 1980, c. 41 s.5(M); R.S.N.W.T. 1974, c. J-2, s.6(b) [re-en 1985 (3rd), c. 10, s.68].

[20] As substituted by the Solicitors (Amendment) Act 1994, s.61.

[21] Solicitor Act 1954, s.49(1)(c) as substituted by the Solicitors (Amendment) Act 1994, s.61 This is a rare occurrence in practise.

[22] Solicitors Act 1954, s.49(1)(p) as substituted by the Solicitors (Amendment) Act 1994, s.61.

Society that he or she should be issued with a practising certificate or a practising certificate not subject to conditions having regard to all the circumstances including where appropriate: (i) the financial state of his practise, (ii) the number and nature of complaints made to the Society either alleging misconduct by the solicitor or under section 8[23] or 9[24] of the Solicitors (Amendment) Act 1994 within the preceding two practise years, or (iii) the need adequately to protect or secure the interests of the solicitor's clients,[25] the Law Society must as soon as practicable consider the application and any submissions as may be made by or on behalf of the applicant and thereafter may direct the registrar of solicitors to do one of three things. First, it may direct the Registrar of Solicitors to issue a practising certificate unconditionally;[26] secondly it may direct the Registrar to issue a practising certificate subject to such specified conditions as the Society think fit. These conditions may include conditions requiring the solicitor concerned to take any steps that the Society consider necessary for his carrying on an efficient practise as a solicitor notwithstanding that any such specified steps may result in expenditure being incurred by the solicitor concerned;[27] thirdly the Law Society may direct the Registrar of Solicitors to refuse to issue a certificate.[28]

Solicitor's right of appeal   If the Law Society directs the Registrar either to refuse to issue a practising certificate or to issue it subject to specified conditions the solicitor concerned must as soon as possible be notified in writing by the Law Society of the direction and the grounds on which it was given.[29] In the event that a direction is issued by the Law Society to the Registrar that the practising certificate be refused or be issued subject to specified conditions the solicitor has under section 49(3) of the Solicitors Act 1954,[30] a right of appeal to the President of the High Court. The right of appeal must be exercised within 21 days of receipt by the solicitor of the notification in writing of such direction and the appeal may be against the direction to refuse or against any or all of the specified conditions as the case may be.[31]

Notwithstanding that the solicitor appeals to the President of the High Court under section 49(3) of the Solicitors Act 1954, the direction by the Law Society to the Registrar to refuse to issue the certificate or to issue it subject to conditions shall have effect up to the determination of the appeal. The only exception to this rule is where the solicitor makes an application to the President of the High Court and the President orders otherwise under section 49(4) of the Act pending the determination of the appeal.[32] In this regard the President of the High Court may on such an application, make an order directing the Registrar to issue a practising solicitor either unconditionally or subject to specified

---

[23] S.8 empowers the Law Society to impose sanctions for inadequate services.
[24] S.9 empowers the Law Society to impose sanctions for charging excessive fees.
[25] Solicitors Act 1954 s.49(1)(q) as substituted by the Solicitors (Amendment) Act 1994, s.61 and amended by the Solicitors (Amendment) Act 2002, s.2.
[26] Solicitors Act 1954 s.49 (2)(a)(i) as substituted by the Solicitors (Amendment) Act 1994, s.61.
[27] *Ibid.*, s.49(2)(a)(ii) as substituted by the Solicitors (Amendment) Act 1994, s.61.
[28] *Ibid.*, s.49 (2)(a)(iii) as substituted by the Solicitors (Amendment) Act 1994, s.61.
[29] *Ibid.*, s.49(2)(b) as substituted by the Solicitors (Amendment) Act 1994, s.61.
[30] As substituted by the Solicitors (Amendment) Act 1994, s.61.
[31] Solicitors Act 1954, s.49(3) as substituted by the Solicitors (Amendment) Act 1994, s.61.
[32] *Ibid.*, s.49(4) as substituted by the Solicitors (Amendment) Act 1994, s.61.

conditions to that solicitor pending the hearing of the appeal.[33] Where such an order is made, the Law Society may under section 49(5) of the Act make an application to the President of the High Court having given notice to the solicitor to (presumably although this is not specified in the Act) set aside the order under section 49(4) and for a confirmation of its direction to the Registrar, and the President of the High Court may dismiss the appeal and confirm the direction of the Law Society to the registrar to refuse to issue the practising certificate or to issue it subject to conditions if the President is satisfied that the solicitor concerned has delayed unduly in proceeding with the appeal and the President may for that purpose revoke any order which he has made under section 49(4).[34]

Powers of President of the High Court on appeal   On hearing the appeal under section 49(3) against a direction by the Law Society to the registrar of solicitors to refuse to issue the certificate to the solicitor concerned the President of the High Court may by order (i) confirm the direction to refuse and revoke any practising certificate already issued pursuant to an order of the President of the High Court pending the determination of the appeal under section 49(4); (ii) rescind the direction to refuse and direct that any practising certificate already issued pursuant to an order of the President pending the determination of the appeal under section 49(4) or any practising certificate to be issued by the registrar be issued unconditionally or (iii) rescind the direction to refuse and direct that any practising certificate already issued pursuant to an order of the President pending the determination of the appeal under section 49(4) or any practising certificate to be issued by the registrar be issued subject to such specified conditions as the President of the High Court thinks fit.[35]

Where the appeal is against a direction by the Law Society to the registrar to issue a practising certificate subject to specified conditions the President of the High Court may by order:

(i)   confirm the direction,

(ii) rescind the direction, or

(iii) vary any or all of the specified conditions.[36]

The registrar must cause particulars of a direction by the Society to the registrar to issue a certificate subject to specified conditions or to refuse to issue a certificate or an order of the President of the High Court made on the determination of the appeal to be entered in the register of solicitors in relation to the solicitor concerned.[37]

Law Society's powers where practising certificate in force and solicitor in suffering from mental incapacity

In addition to the Law Society's powers on application to it for a practising certificate,

---

[33] This is implicit in Solicitors Act 1954, s.49(5) as substituted by the Solicitors (Amendment) Act 1994, s.61.

[34] Solicitors Act 1954, s.49(5) as substituted by the Solicitors (Amendment) Act 1994, s.61.

[35] *Ibid.*, s.49(6)(a) as substituted by the Solicitors (Amendment) Act 1994, s.61.

[36] *Ibid.*, s.49(6)(b) as substituted by the Solicitors (Amendment) Act 1994, s.61.

[37] *Ibid.*, s.49(7) as substituted by the Solicitors (Amendment) Act 1994, s.61.

the Law Society has power under section 59(1) of the Solicitors (Amendment) Act 1994 to give a direction that the practising certificate issued to a solicitor and for the time being in force shall have effect subject to such specified conditions as the Society may think fit. In particular the Society may give a direction. Where, had an application for a practising certificate been made by the solicitor concerned at the time the direction was given, one or more of the circumstances set out in section 49(1)(c) to (p) would have applied to the solicitor, i.e this would include the circumstances where he is a person in respect of whose person or property any of the powers and provisions of the Lunacy Regulation (Ireland) Act 1871 or any Act amending or extending that Act relating to management and administration of property apply (section 49(1)(c)) or he has failed to satisfy the Society that he is fit to carry on the practise of a solicitor having regard to the state of his physical or mental health (section 49(1)(p)). The solicitor has a right of appeal against the giving of such a direction to the President of the High Court and this right must be exercised within 21 days of the receipt by him of notification in writing of the giving of the direction.[38] On hearing the appeal the President of the High Court may:

(a) confirm the direction given by the Society;

(b) direct that the current practising certificate of that solicitor shall have effect subject to such conditions as the President of the High Court thinks fit;

(c) direct that any subsequent practising certificate shall have effect subject to such conditions as the President of the High Court thinks fit;

(d) revoke any direction given by the Society;

(e) direct as the President of the High Court otherwise thinks fit;

(f) revoke or vary any order he has made under section 59(5) (order by President that the direction should not have effect pending the appeal).[39]

Where there is no appeal against the Law Society's direction or the conditions specified in a direction by the Law Society are upheld on appeal and the solicitor fails to comply with the conditions and the Society is of opinion that the failure is serious the Society may on notice to the Solicitor apply to the President of the High Court and the President of the High Court after hearing such evidence and receiving such submissions form the Society, the solicitor concerned and such other person(s) as the President of the High Court thinks fit may by order:

(a) suspend the current practising certificate of the solicitor for such period as the President of the High Court thinks fit up to and including the end of the current practise year;

(b) direct the Society not to issue to the solicitor a practising certificate during any subsequent practise year until such time as the President of the High Court thinks fit;

---

[38] Solicitors (Amendment) Act 1994, s.59(4).
[39] *Ibid.*, s.59(5).

(c) direct the solicitor to take such action as the President of the High Court thinks fit to remedy any consequences of his failure to comply with such conditions;

(d) direct the solicitor to take such action as the President of the High Court thinks fit to ensure that the solicitor does not in the future so fail to comply with such conditions;

(e) adjourn the application and direct that further enquiries be made by the Society in regard to the matter or require the Society to furnish further information to the court;

(f) adjourn the application for such period as the President of the High Court thinks fit to enable the solicitor to comply with any direction(s) of the President of the High Court under (c) and/or (d);

(g) dismiss the Society's application.[40]

The Law Society is obliged unless otherwise directed by the President of the High Court to arrange to publish the terms of any order made by the President of the High Court under (a) or (b) in the *Iris Óifigiúil* and in the Law Society Gazette and in an manner as the Society may think fit as soon as possible after the order is made.[41]

Law Society's powers to intervene in practice of sole practitioner in cases of incapacity Section 61(2) of the Solicitors Act 1954[42] empowers the Law Society to intervene in the practice of sole practitioner in cases of incapacity. Specifically it provides that where a solicitor who is a sole practitioner becomes of unsound mind or becomes otherwise incapacitated by illness or accident to such an extent that he is, in the opinion of the Society, incapable (whether permanently or temporarily) of managing his own affairs or the affairs of the practise, the Society or the committee of the estate of the incapacitated solicitor on notice to the solicitor may apply to High Court for an order directing the appointment of another solicitor to carry on the practise of that incapacitated solicitor for such period and on such terms as the Court thinks fit. The solicitor so appointed may, in addition to being authorised to carry on the practise, be authorised to operate any client account either solely or jointly with another person nominated by the Society and approved of by the Court. The High Court may also require the production and delivery to the appointed solicitor of all documents of the practise in the possession or control or within the procurement of the incapacitated solicitor or any clerk or servant or former clerk or servant of the incapacitated solicitor. The Law Society has similar powers to apply to the High Court for an order directing the appointment of another solicitor to carry on the practise where the solicitor has abandoned the practise.[43]

Alternatively, where a solicitor who is a sole practitioner has effectively abandoned his practice, and adequate arrangements have not been made for making available to the clients of the solicitor files and documents held in the possession or in the control or within the procurement of that solicitor on behalf of the clients, the Society may move

---

[40] *Ibid.*, s.59(1).
[41] *Ibid.*, s.58(2).
[42] As substituted by Solicitors (Amendment) Act 1994, s.31.
[43] Solicitors (Amendment) Act 1994, s.61(4) as substituted by the Solicitors (Amendment) Act 1994, s.31.

under section 19(1)(b) of the Solicitors (Amendment) Act 1960[44] for production of the files. It has power take possession of the files, distribute them to the appropriate persons and close the practise.

In practise, matters relating to the incapacity of a solicitor frequently come to the Law Society's attention because of a succession of complaints made to the Law Society's Complaints department about the solicitor's dealings with clients which are then referred to the Registrar's Committee for resolution. Alternatively where a complaint of misconduct is made this is referred to the Disciplinary Tribunal which is independent of the Law Society. At the consideration of the complaint by the Registrar's Committee or the Disciplinary Tribunal, the solicitor may plead ill health. In such circumstances the Law Society frequently requires the solicitor to obtain a medical report from an appropriate specialist dealing with the issue of his capacity to practise. If the report specifies that the practitioner does not have the capacity to carry on the practice for a period of time another solicitor may be appointed to carry on the practice under section 61 of the Solicitors Act 1954[45] for a period of time. The Law Society may also impose a condition on the solicitor's practising certificate either under section 49 or under section 59(1). The most usual condition is that the solicitor not be permitted to practise, except in the employment and under the supervision of a solicitor of at least 10 years standing to be approved by the Law Society.

Pharmacists – the current law

If a registered chemist becomes of unsound mind his committee may keep open his shop for the dispensing or compounding of medical prescriptions provided it is personally supervised by an authorised person.[46]

Medical practitioners – the current law

Section 27(3) of the Medical Practitioners Act 1978 reserves the right to the Medical Council to refuse to register the name of any person who is otherwise entitled to be registered on the grounds of the unfitness of that person to engage in the practise of

---

[44] As substituted by the Solicitors (Amendment) Act 1994, s.27.

[45] As substituted by the Solicitors (Amendment) Act 1994, s.31.

[46] Pharmacy Act 1962, s.2(1)(b)(ii): "Authorised person" is defined by s.2(3) as "a registered pharmaceutical chemist, a registered pharmaceutical chemist, a registered dispensing chemist and druggist, a licentiate of Apothecaries Hall, or a registered medical practitioner who, before the commencement of the section began a course of study to be gone through for the purpose of obtaining a qualifying diploma within the meaning of the Medical Practitioners Acts 1927 to 1961 or a corresponding qualification awarded outside the state and who has passed or passes an examination in pharmacy in order to qualify for the grant of the qualifying diploma or the award of the corresponding qualification outside the state." An "authorised person" does not include a person registered by virtue of s.22 of the Pharmacy Act (Ireland) 1875 acting in respect of a shop for the dispensing or compounding of medical prescriptions or for the sale of poisons where such shop has been in operation for less than three years. See s.2(3A) of the Pharmacy Act 1962 as inserted by art.4 of the European Communities (Recognition of Qualifications in Pharmacy) Regulations 1987 (S.I. No.239 of 1987) and as substituted by art.4 of the European Communities (Recognition of Qualifications in Pharmacy) Regulations 1991 (S.I. No.330 of 1991).

medicine.[47] Under section 45 of the same Act, the Medical Council or any person may apply to the Fitness to Practise Committee established by the Council for an inquiry into the conduct of a registered medical practitioner on the grounds of his fitness to engage in the practise of medicine by reason, *inter alia*, of his mental disability and the Fitness to Practise Committee is obliged to consider it and if there is a prima facie case to hold an inquiry.[48]

As a matter of practice the Irish Medical Council's *Guide to Ethical Conduct and Behaviour*[49] provides that doctors have a responsibility to protect the interests of the public when they become aware that a physical or psychological disorder or the ageing process appear seriously to affect a doctor's professional competence in such circumstances the code advises:

> "they should express their anxiety directly to the colleague concerned and adise that expert professional help be attained or that a colleague be referred to the Medical Council's Health Committee. If such approaches fail or where the interests of patients are or may be at risk, the facts must be given promptly to the Fitness to Practice Committee. Any dereliction of the doctor's responsibility in this regard will be viewed seriously".[50]

The Code states further:

> "Doctors should be aware that they too can suffer ill health. Doctors should ask advice and help from another doctor rather than treating themselves. Doctors are advised that they should have a general practitioner of their own".[51]

The Health Committee of the Medical Council In December 1999, the Medical Council decided to separate the misconduct and health related functions of the Council into separate structures and to establish a Health Committee. The reasons for this decision, set out in a Discussion Document on Health Procedures, were that medical practitioners affected by health problems were not accused of misconduct and it was believed should not be dealt with in a fashion that implied that they may be guilty of misconduct. Secondly, the perceived disciplinary structures covering health problems acted as a barrier for medical practitioners to report their own problems or those of their colleagues. Thirdly, the adversarial nature of the disciplinary procedures and the strict legal procedures which guided them were unnecessary in the majority of health matters and fourthly the ethos of any disciplinary or health procedure had to be to protect members of the public

---

[47] Medical Practitioners Act 1978, s.27(3). Where it makes a decision in this regard the person concerned has the right to apply to the High Court within two months of the date of the decision for its cancellation and if that person so applies the High Court may either declare that it was proper for the Council to make the decision or cancel it and direct the Council to register the name of the person making the application. See s.27(5). A similar right of refusal to register is reserved to the Medical Council in relation to registration of persons in the Register of Medical Specialists under s.31(3) of the Medical Practitioners Act 1978.

[48] Medical Practitioners Act 1978, s.45(3).

[49] 6th ed., 2004

[50] See paras 5.1 and 5.2.

[51] See para.5.4.

from dysfunctional medical practitioners. However a committee addressing, health problems could have the additional aim of enabling medical practitioners to return to normal work as soon as possible.

Membership of the Health Committee The Members of the Health Committee are health practitioners who practise in specialities relevant to the practise of the medical practitioners referred and to the problems they present. A lay member of the Medical Council represents the public interest on the Committee. A member of the Medical Council chairs the Committee and acts as liaison between the Health Committee and the Medical Council. The other members of the Committee are not members of the Council and comprise two psychiatrists, two general practitioners and one consultant physician.

Terms of reference of the Health Committee The terms of reference of the Health Committee envisaged by the Discussion Document were deemed to be (i) to deal with complaints against medical practitioners which have a health component and where no allegations of patient harm were included; (ii) to carry out appropriate investigation into suggestions of ill-health of medical practitioners by gathering information, obtaining expert reports and meeting with the medical practitioner concerned and others, if necessary; (iii) to make recommendations to the medical practitioner on the management of his/her professional responsibilities, compliance with medical advice and monitoring of progress; (iv) to co-operate in a non-adversarial fashion, inviting the co-operation of a medical practitioner with relevant inquiries and recom-mendations; (v) to monitor compliance with its recommendations and (vi) to report to the Fitness to Practise Committee on medical practitioners (a) who do not comply with its recommendations and (b) who are initially dealt with in relation to a health complaint but who later raise concerns in relation to misconduct.

When set up, its specific role and functions were stated to be to act as a monitor of therapy in order to (a) assess whether a health problem exists and its severity; (b) assess the adequacy of the proposed treatment and of planned professional safeguards; (c) ensure appropriate paths to recovery are being followed; (d) motivate adherence to therapy; (e) advise on and monitor capacity to work; and (f) advise the Medical Council in relation to the medical practitioner's situation at any time.

Health Committee procedures The Health Committee's detailed procedures are available on the Medical Council's website.[52] Briefly, the Committee contacts the medical practitioner who has been the subject of correspondence or other communication and offers him access to the health procedures and provides him with details of the Health Committee's procedures. The medical practitioner will be asked to give his consent, to enable the Health Committee to obtain and receive all relevant medical reports and he will be asked to confirm that he will attend a specialist medical practitioner for assessment. If the Health Committee's offer is accepted by the medical practitioner, the Committee will review all the information it has received. If the Committee concludes that the Health Procedures are relevant to the medical practitioner, at least two members of the

---

[52] www.medicalcouncil.ie.

Health Committee will meet with the medical practitioner to discuss the problem and the therapeutic options. These may initially include a period of sick lease with no patient contact. The consequences of non-compliance with the procedures will be explained, and the medical practitioner will be informed that the procedures are without prejudice to the provisions of Part V of the Medical Practitioners Act 1978. In the event that the Health Committee is satisfied that a therapeutic approach is possible, the relevant members of the Committee will meet with the medical practitioner to discuss the plan for treatment and recovery. The plan will be in written form and if agreed with by the Health Committee given to the medical practitioner for formal acceptance.

Where the attention of the Medical Council is drawn by a person or a body to a health problem of a medical practitioner members of the Health Committee may meet with that person or body and give them information about the Health Committee's procedures and such general information about the medical practitioner's progress as is deemed appropriate.

The Health Committee will, having received all medical reports, make a decision as to whether it is possible to continue monitoring of the practitioner and/or is other steps are required. The medical practitioner may be monitored during treatment and at work by the Health Committee. The outcome of the monitoring procedure is reported to the Medical Council.

If at any stage in the procedure it appears that the public interest is at risk the Health Committee will immediately inform the President of the Medical Council to enable appropriate steps to be taken under the Medical Practitioner's Act 1978.[53]

It is envisaged that all Health Committee inquiries and recommendations would be carried out with the voluntary co-operation of the medical practitioner and without the need for legal procedure. If a medical practitioner fails to co-operate, produces false information or did not comply with the recom-mendations then a complaint could be made to the Fitness to Practise Committee. If a complaint included both health and disciplinary elements the medical practitioner involved should have the option to bring the health matters to the attention of the Health Committee.

Procedure on reference to Fitness to Practise Committee If a matter is referred to the Fitness to Practise Committee because of a failure to comply with a recommendation of the Health Committee or because of a misconduct complaint the Fitness to Practise Committee carries out an investigation. The procedure when a complaint is made is set out in detail on the Medical Council's website but briefly in practise the procedure is as follows. When a complaint is made by a person to the Council the complaint is sent to the medical practitioner concerned with a request to provide his/her observations and comments. When these are received a copy may be sent to the complainant so that s/he can comment or reply if that is wished. Once that material is received the correspondence and documents are put before the Fitness to Practise Committee. It may request further information but if it considers that it has sufficient information and there is a *prima facie* case the Fitness to Practise Committee instigates an Inquiry. At the inquiry the lawyers instructed by the Registrar presents the complainants case to the Fitness to

---

[53] The procedures were established by the Medical Council at its meeting on December 9 and 10, 1999.

Practise Committee. The medical practitioner and/or his legal representative will attend the Inquiry and present his case to the Committee. Witnesses will be called for the complainant and they may be cross-examined by the medical practitioner's legal representative. The members of the Committee may also put questions to the witnesses. The medical practitioner can then call his/her witnesses to give evidence and they in turn may be cross-examined. At the conclusion of the inquiry the Committee must decide whether the evidence amounts to professional misconduct or the medical practitioner is unfit to practise medicine and is obliged to report its findings to the Medical Council. The Medical Council considers the findings of the Committee. Where the Committee has reported that the practitioner is unfit to practise because of mental disability the Medical Council has power to decide that the name of that person be erased from the register or from the Register of Medical Specialists or that the registration of his name in the register should not have effect during a specified period.[54] It can also attach conditions to the retention of the practitioner's name on the register and/or issue a censure, admonishment or advice. The person to whom the decision relates may apply to the High Court for cancellation of the decision.[55]

The appeal takes the form of a complete re-hearing of the case and witnesses are required to give evidence at the hearing just as in the Inquiry. The High Court has power to cancel the decision or to declare that it was properly made.[56] Where no such application is made within 21 days of the date of the decision the Council may apply *ex parte* to the High Court for its confirmation. In this event the High Court must make a declaration confirming the decision unless it sees good reason to the contrary and it must either direct the Council to erase the name of the person concerned from the register or direct that during a specified period registration of the person's name shall not have effect.[57] The decision of the High Court in this regard is final except where leave is granted either by the High Court or the Supreme Court to appeal to the Supreme Court on a point of law.[58]

Section 33(4) of the Act reserves the right to the Council to refuse to restore to the register the name of any person who is otherwise entitled to be registered on the grounds of unfitness of that person to engage in the practise of medicine.

Legal capacity and other positions

Legal capacity and directorships

There is no general statutory provision or common law rule disqualifying persons from holding the position of director of a company on the grounds of mental incapacity. It is, however, open to a company registered under the Companies Acts to insert a provision in their articles to this effect. Older forms of articles of association frequently contained a provision providing for the automatic vacation of the office of director in the event that "he is found lunatic or becomes of unsound mind". More modern equivalents provide

---

[54] Medical Practitioners Act 1978, s.46(1).
[55] *Ibid.*, s.46(3).
[56] *Ibid.*, s.46(3)(a).
[57] *Ibid.*, s.46(4).
[58] *Ibid.*, s.46(5).

that a disqualification should takes effect only when the director in question is admitted to a psychiatric hospital under the provisions of the Mental Treatment Act 1945 or where s/he is taken into wardship before such disqualification takes effect. Where the director's behaviour is inappropriate but neither of these additional events occurs then it is possible for the other directors[59] or the shareholders in general meeting to move for his removal using their other powers under the Companies Acts.[60]

Where the company is one limited by guarantee formed to carry out activities in the area of mental illness or disability and it is desired that membership of the board should include people with mental illness or disability then consideration should be given to an appropriately tailored form of words. This might provide for the vacation of the office of director on grounds of mental disorder unless the other directors are satisfied that his disorder is not such as will affect the discharge by the person concerned of his duties as director.[61]

Legal capacity and trustees

While mental illness does not in theory disqualify a person from being a trustee it may be a ground for his removal from office and the appointment of new trustees in his place. Where a trustee is unfit [62] or incapable of acting as such then the person or persons nominated for appointing new trustees in the trust instrument (other than the incapacitated trustee) may appoint a new trustee out of court in place of the incapacitated trustee.[63] If there is no person in whom the power of appointment is vested or no such person able and willing to act, then by virtue of section 10(1) of the Trustee Act 1893 the surviving or continuing trustees, or trustee, or the personal representatives of the last surviving or continuing trustee, may, in writing, appoint a new trustee in place of the trustee who is incapable. This is the case unless the statutory power is expressly negatived or modified.[64]

The President of the High Court, exercising his jurisdiction in wardship, has power under the Trustee Acts 1850–1852 to appoint one or more new trustees in place of a trustee who is of full age and of unsound mind whether s/he is a ward of court or not or of any trustee who is an infant and is found lunatic by inquisition.[65] He may also vest in the new trustees all trust property within the jurisdiction, which stands in the name of a deceased person, or standing in the name of a deceased person whose personal representative(s) is or are of unsound mind.[66] In the alternative he may vest the right to

---

[59] The regulations of some companies empower the directors to remove any of their number from the board.

[60] S.182 of the Companies Act 1963 provides that shareholders may remove a member of the board by ordinary resolution. At least 28 days extended notice must be given of a resolution to remove a director under that section. See Companies Act 1963, s.142.

[61] See Ashton and Ward, *Mental Handicap and the Law* (Sweet & Maxwell, London, 1992), p.31.

[62] *In re Blake* [1887] W.N. 173; *In re Lemann's Trusts* (1883) 22 Ch.D. 633; *In re Weston's Trusts* [1898] W.N. 151.

[63] See Harris, *A Treatise on the Law and Practise of Lunacy in Ireland* (Corrigan & Wilson Ltd, Dublin, 1930), p.84.

[64] *Cecil v. Langdon* 28 Ch.D. 1; *In re Wheeler and de Rochow* [1896] 1 Ch. 315.

[65] Trustee Act 1852, ss10.

[66] Trustee Act 1850, ss.3–6.

convey or transfer property in an unconnected third party.[67] Acting in his capacity as a judge of the High Court, the President of the High Court also has jurisdiction under section 25 of the Trustee Act 1893 to appoint a new trustee whenever it is found inexpedient, difficult or impracticable to do so without the assistance of the High Court.

Legal capacity of executors and administrators

A person who suffers from a mental disability, which impairs his ability to manage his property and affairs, will be unable to act as executor while the disability continues.[68] It has been suggested that such mental disability will also render him incapable of determining whether or not to assume the office. If an executor becomes unfit after a grant of probate has been made to him the grant may be revoked.[69] Where the executor is taken into wardship, the usual procedure is for the committee to apply pursuant to an order of the President to the High Court for the issue of a new grant to himself in the name and on behalf of the patient which is limited to the duration of the wardship matter, and reserves the right of the ward to apply in the event of his/her recovery for a fresh grant to himself.[70] Order 79, rule 26 of the, rules of the Superior Court provides that a grant of administration may be made to the committee of a person of unsound mind for such person's use and benefit. Where a person of unsound mind does not have a committee appointed by the court a grant may issue to such person as the Probate Officer may, by order, assign with the consent of the Registrar of Wards of Court.[71]

However, the, rules also provide that unless the court or Probate Officer otherwise directs a grant of probate should be given to a person not under a legal disability in preference to the committee or guardian of a person under a legal disability who is equally entitled provided that where application is made by the committee of a person under a legal disability the court or Probate officer must, before a grant is given, consult the Registrar of Wards of Court.[72]

Where a person, before being taken into wardship has obtained a grant of administration the usual procedure is for the grant not to be revoked but impounded and re-delivered to the ward on his/her recovery[73] and for a fresh grant limited during the wardship matter to be made to the committee. However if the grant is made to two or more administrators it will be revoked and a special grant issued to the remaining administrators.[74]

Where a ward is the sole personal representative of a deceased person and no grant of probate or administration has been issued in respect of the estate of the deceased then

---

[67] *Ibid.*, s.20.

[68] See *Evans v. Tyler* (1849) 2 Rob. 128.

[69] See *In re the goods of Ryan* [1927] I.R. 174; *In re the goods of Galbraith* [1951] P. 422.

[70] *In re Marshall*, 1 Curt. 297.

[71] Applications for such orders must be grounded on an affidavit of the applicant setting out the amount of the assets, the age and residence of the person of unsound mind and his relationship to the applicant together with an affidavit of a medical practitioner detailing the incapacity of the person concerned. See O.79, r.27.

[72] See O.79, r.5(1)(m).

[73] *In re Bincke*, 1 Curt. 286.

[74] *In re Newton*, 3 Curt. 428.

the President will either make a vesting order under the Trustee Acts,[75] or more usually direct the Committee to apply for a grant of limited administration with or without the will annexed for the benefit of the ward during the wardship and authorising the committee to seek to have the security dispensed with. Where a ward is named as executor jointly with another leave will usually be given to the other executor to apply for a grant of probate alone.

Commentary

In Canada where joint executors or administrators have been appointed and one becomes mentally incapable of discharging the duties of the office, the others can apply to the court to have the grant revoked and a new one issued in their favour. The new grant can reserve a right to the incompetent person to join in the administration on recovery.[76] The making of a rule of court in the Irish jurisdiction similar to that which applies in Canada would be a constructive development.

THE IMPACT OF INCAPACITY ON THE JUDICIAL PROCESS

The right of the citizen to have access to the courts to vindicate their rights is a fundamental one and in no case more so than in the case of vulnerable groups such as groups with disability in society which who may be subject to abuse and exploitation on account of their disability. A person's mental disability may affect their capacity to exercise judgment in relation to matters, which affect them. The question must then be asked as to the extent to which in a procedural sense the judicial process accommodates the incapacity of the person with mental disability.

Pre-trial incapacity and the retainer of a solicitor

The relationship between solicitor and client is one of agency and thus if a person is incapable of appointing an agent he cannot validly authorise a solicitor to act on his behalf. The mental capacity necessary to appoint an agent involves an ability to understand the nature and effect of the appointment. If the person is found to be of unsound mind and incapable of managing his property and affairs,[77] and has a committee of estate appointed on his behalf it is clear that s/he lacks the necessary capacity to retain counsel and institute litigation. However, in other cases the test of capacity must be related to the particular transaction or legal relationship in issue. The fact that a person is an involuntary patient in a psychiatric hospital does not necessarily mean that he is incapable of managing his own affairs, or incapable of instructing counsel.

  Since the authority of an agent is revoked by the supervening incapacity of the principal even if the client has the required capacity when first instructing the solicitor

---

[75] Trustee Act 1850, s.6.

[76] See I. MacDonnell, T. Sheard and M. Hull, *Probate Practice* (3rd ed., Carswell 1981), pp. 27–28.

[77] In the English case of *In re F (Mental Patient: Sterilisation)* [1990] 2 A.C. 1 at 59 Lord Brandon stated that the expression "property and affairs" was limited to "business matters, legal transactions or other dealings of a similar kind.".

the latter's authority will be terminated if the client subsequently becomes incapacitated and the solicitor cannot proceed on the basis of instructions given before the incapacity.[78]

The Law Society of Ireland has published in the form of a Practise Note guidelines for solicitors in relation to *"Clients of Unsound Mind"* which is worth quoting at length as an indication of the profession's approach in practise to the issue of mental incapacity of clients:

> "As with any other contract, if a client is of unsound mind, he or she does not have the legal capacity to enter into a contractual relationship with a solicitor.
>
> If the solicitor's instructions predate the mental illness, the retainer of the solicitor is determined by law when the client becomes mentally ill. The solicitor cannot proceed on the basis of instructions given before the mental illness.
>
> The solicitor is a layman and not a medical practitioner and can only make a judgment of the client's mental health on that basis. Indications of illness would include incidents of forgetfulness, confusion or erratic or abnormal behaviour. Even if the client subsequently presents normally, the solicitor should treat the previous incidents as significant.
>
> The mental illness may be irreversible. On the other hand, it may be merely an episode of mental illness from which the client will recover after treatment. This is clearly a delicate matter for a solicitor when dealing with a client. Whether the matter is discussed with the client or not can only be decided on a case-by-case basis.
>
> In marginal cases the solicitor may consider discussing his or her concerns with the client and advising the client that, in order to avoid possible queries from family or third parties in relation to the validity of instructions at a later date, the client should obtain a medical certificate confirming mental health.
>
> If an issue arises with regard to a client's mental health, the solicitor should ensure that detailed and accurate attendances of all meetings or conversations with the client are made.
>
> The solicitor should take reasonable steps to ensure that the client's interests are protected. This may involve contact with relatives, medical practitioners or with the Wards of Court Office. In these circumstances, the professional duty of absolute confidentiality is lessened in the client's own interest, to the extent necessary. Having contacted the appropriate parties, the solicitor's professional obligations are at an end.
>
> If the solicitor is on record in a litigation matter, the solicitor should, as a matter of courtesy, inform the court that he or she considers any instructions given to have been terminated."

While these instructions touch on the issue of a solicitor's obligations in the event that a client becomes of unsound mind, they do not directly address the central issue namely the degree of mental illness which renders a client incapable of giving instructions and

---

[78] See *Yonge v. Toynbee* [1910] 1 K.B. 215 (C.A.). See "A Guide to Professional Conduct of Solicitors in Ireland" (2nd ed.), p.12 Also "Clients of Unsound Mind" Practice Note *Gazette* (December 1998) 33.

tend to assume that all types of mental illness render a client incapable of giving instructions which is clearly not the case. The degree of mental illness, which renders a client incapable of giving instructions, is that which renders the client incapable of understanding the nature and effect of the appointment of the solicitor and/or the legal transaction in question. Clearly if a person is found by a court to be of unsound mind and incapable of managing his property and affairs and has a committee appointed, that client will be incapable of giving instructions. However, to assume that all types of mental illness render a client incapable of giving instructions is clearly discriminatory. Indeed under the terms of the Mental Health Act 2001, it is quite rightly assumed as a matter of law that clients involuntarily detained in an approved centre may retain the capacity to instruct a legal representative in relation to the matter of the lawfulness of their detention.[79]

If the agreement to retain a solicitor is invalid because of the client's mental incapacity the solicitor may still be able to recover reasonable remuneration for services provided to the client by virtue of the common law rule that a reasonable price is provided for necessary services provided to a mentally incompetent client. In the English case of *Stedman v. Hart*[80] it was held that legal services come within the ambit of this rule.

Since solicitors impliedly warrant that they have valid authority to act on behalf of their client they can be held personally liable for costs for breach of this warranty. In *Yonge v. Toynbee*,[81] it was held that the authority of solicitors acting for a defendant in litigation was revoked by the supervening incapacity of their client. The solicitors being unaware of this, continued to act and were held personally liable for the plaintiff's costs since they had impliedly warranted an authority, which they did not have.

The prospect of personal liability must mean that solicitors must ensure that they have been granted valid authority to act. Where a client has a committee of estate an agreement to retain a solicitor should be signed by and instructions obtained from the committee on behalf of a client. If the client does not have a committee of an estate but is mentally incapable of retaining a solicitor then the solicitor should obtain instructions from someone who is willing to act as next friend or guardian *ad litem* and ensure that the latter has no conflict of interest. If no suitable person can be found then the solicitor should consider contacting the Office of the General Solicitor for Minors and Wards of Court to ascertain whether the General Solicitor would be willing to act as guardian *ad litem* or to bring proceedings for the appointment of a committee of the estate.

If there is no person who is willing to act as next friend or guardian *ad litem* and the General Solicitor is not willing to intervene it is submitted that it is arguable that the solicitor as an officer of the court has an ethical duty to institute proceedings notwithstanding the absence of a valid retainer and to raise the issue of competency in court so that a next friend could be appointed. It is submitted that the action would not be a nullity but merely irregular in form and capable of amendment by the addition of a next friend.[82]

A ward of court cannot retain a solicitor in his own right. This is because s/he lacks

---

[79] Mental Health Act 2001, s.16.
[80] (1854) Kay, 607, 69 E.R. 258.
[81] [1910] 1 K.B. 215 (C.A.).
[82] See Baker, "Representing the Handicapped Client" in Canadian Bar Association (Ontario) *Law and the Handicapped* (1983) 2.

contractual capacity and also because control over litigation vests in the committee. However exceptions to this rule do exist. Thus an application for *habeas corpus* cannot be challenged on the grounds of the applicant's disability. It is also possible that other exceptions exist such as proceedings to have a committee removed or to have the applicant declared no longer incapable of managing his affairs.

Commentary

Abella in her report to the Attorney General of Ontario entitled *Access to Legal Services by the Disabled*,[83] advocates that the rule that a solicitor who continues to act for a mentally disabled client may be held personally liable in damages for breach of warranty of authority creates a decided disincentive to lawyers to act for mentally disabled clients and should be abolished. It is submitted that the rule that a solicitor who continues to act for a mentally disabled client may be held personally liable in damages for breach of warranty of authority should be abolished. As has been pointed out above where there is no person willing to act as next friend or guardian *ad litem* it is submitted that the solicitor as an officer of the court has an ethical duty to institute proceedings notwithstanding the absence of a valid retainer and raise the issue of competency so that a next friend can be appointed. The irregularity in form of the proceedings could then be capable of amendment by the addition of the next friend.

Pre-trial incapacity and the running of time limitations for the institution of legal proceedings

In general where a person is under a disability the Statute of Limitations 1957 provides that the limitation period within which an action must be instituted will not run until such time as that person ceases to be under a disability.

Section 49(1) of the Statute of Limitations 1957 extends the period of limitation where a person is "under a disability" which is defined[84] to include a person of "unsound mind." Thus if on the date of accrual of a cause of action for which a period of limitation is prescribed by statute the person to whom it accrued was of "unsound mind" the action may be brought at any time before the expiration of six years (three years in personal injuries cases) from the date when the person ceased to be of unsound mind or died whichever event occurred first notwithstanding that the period of limitation has expired.[85]

The Act does not define "of unsound mind" but section 48(2) provides that a person is conclusively presumed to be of unsound mind while he is detained in pursuance of any enactment authorising the detention of persons of unsound mind or criminal lunatics. Also in *Kirby v. Leather*,[86] the English Court of Appeal held that a person was of "unsound mind" when he was by reason of mental illness incapable of managing or administering his property and affairs in a manner that a reasonable person would. In

---

[83] 1983.

[84] Statute of Limitations 1957, s.48(1).

[85] *Ibid.*, s.49(1)(a).

[86] [1965] 2 Q.B. 367 applied in *Kotulski v. Attard* [1981] 1 N.S.W.L.R. 115 and *King v. Coupland* [1981] Qd. R. 121.

that case the plaintiff a skilled craftsman suffered, *inter alia*, grave mental damage in the course of a road accident. He instituted proceedings eighteen months after the limitation period had expired. The defendants claimed, *inter alia*, that the action was statute barred. The Court of Appeal held that from the moment of the accident the plaintiff became incapable of managing or administering his property and affairs. He had no insight at all into his own mental state, he was not able to appreciate the nature or extent of any claim he might have, he was not capable of instructing a solicitor properly, and he was not capable of exercising any reasonable judgment upon a possible settlement. It was held that he was consequently under a disability at the time the cause of action accrued so that his action was not statute barred. The court also stated that the period of limitation could not be suspended in cases where a person was merely unconscious or ill.

This test of "ability to manage his own affairs" was applied by Barron J. in *Rohan v. Bord na Mona*,[87] in the case of a person who as a result of an accident also sustained severe mental damage leaving him intellectually impaired. In the course of his judgment the judge rejected the argument that Section 48 of the Limitation Act 1957 only applied to in cases where the disability predated the date of accrual of the action and held that it also applied in cases where the disability was the immediate result of the action.

Brady and Kerr,[88] also comment that the wording of section 48 and this judgment leave open the question as to whether the section applies to cases where the disability supervenes on a date subsequent to the date of the accident or accrual of the action. There are exceptions to the rule postponing the right of action of a person with a disability to a time when that person ceases to be under a disability. First where the right of action accrued to some person not under a disability through whom the person under a disability claims no extension will be permitted.[89] Presumably the legislature considered that an inherited claim is in the nature of a windfall and that the person under a disability should not therefore be permitted to impose his condition, so to speak on a defendant with whom he had no direct contact. Secondly, where a right of action, which has accrued to a person under a disability, accrues on his death while still under a disability to another person under a disability no further extension of time is allowed by reason of the disability of the second person.[90] In both of these cases the defendant's interests are treated as outweighing those of the person who inherits the right of action.

The Law Reform Commission in its *Report on the Statutes of Limitations: Claims in Contract and Tort in respect of Latent Damage (other than personal injury)*,[91] has recommended that the term "disability" in section 49 should be replaced by the term "legal incapacity" which would encompass both minority and mental incapacity.[92] It was also of the view that the term "unsoundness of mind" was too narrow a concept as it excluded categories of people who, though not suffering the necessary mental illness should come within section 48, as they are incapable of managing their own affairs. Examples included those who were unconscious or in a coma. Accordingly adopting a

---

[87] [1990] 2 I.R. 425.
[88] See Brady and Kerr, *The Limitation of Actions* (2nd ed., Butterworths, Dublin, 1994), p.32.
[89] Statute of Limitations 1957, s.49(1)(b).
[90] *Ibid.*, s.49(1)(c).
[91] LRC 64–2001.
[92] Para. 7.07.

Canadian model,[93] it recommended that section 48(1)(b) which formerly stated that a person is treated as being under a disability if "he is of unsound mind" should be amended to read that a person is treated as being under a "legal incapacity" "where a person is incapable of the management of his affairs because of disease or impairment of physical or mental condition."[94] It also recommended that legislation should be changed to allow supervening legal incapacity to suspend the accrual period,[95] and the discoverability limitation period [96] recommended in its report,[97] until the incapacity ceases or the plaintiff dies and where either is suspended there should be a 30 year long-stop for claims in respect of physical damage.[98]

The impact of incapacity on limitation periods in personal injury cases The law in relation to latent personal injuries was amended by the Statute of Limitations (Amendment) Act 1991. Section 3 of the Act provides that the three-year limitation period[99] in personal injury actions will run from the date of accrual of the cause of action or from the date of knowledge if this is later. Section 2(1) of the Act provides that references to a person's "date of knowledge" are references to:

"the date on which he first had knowledge of the following facts:

(a) that the person alleged to have been injured had been injured,
(b) that the injury in question was significant;
(c) that the injury was attributable in whole or in part to the act or omission which is alleged to constitute negligence, nuisance or breach of duty;
(d) the identity of the defendant;
(e) if it alleged that the act or omission was that of a person other than the defendant the identity of that person and additional facts supporting the bringing of an action against the defendant;

and knowledge that any acts or omissions did or did not, as a matter of law, involve negligence, nuisance or breach of duty is irrelevant."

Section 2(2) of the Act clarifies that knowledge also includes knowledge, which an individual might reasonably be expected to acquire from facts observable or ascertainable by him or from facts ascertainable by him with the help of medical or other appropriate expert advice, which it is reasonable for him to seek. Section 3 provides that the limitation

---

[93] See Canadian Uniform Limitation of Actions Act 1931.

[94] Para.7.13.

[95] The accrual period is six years from the date on which the cause of action accrued. See Appendix 1.

[96] The discoverability limitation period that is recommended in the report is three years from the date on which the person first knew or in the circumstances ought reasonably to have known: (i) the loss for which the person seeks a remedy had occurred; (ii) that the damage was attributable to the conduct of the defendant; and (iii) that the loss, assuming liability on the part of the defendant, warrants bringing proceedings. See Clause 3 Draft Statute of Limitations (Amendment) Act, Appendix 1.

[97] Para.7.20.

[98] Para.7.24.

[99] S.7 of the Civil Liability and Courts Act 2004 proposes to change the relevant limiitation period to two years but the section has not yet been brought into force.

period in relation to cases in respect of personal injuries caused by negligence, nuisance or breach of duty is three years from the date on which the cause of action accrued[100] or the date of knowledge if later.[101]

Section 5(1) of the 1991 Act provides that if in an action claiming damages in respect of personal injuries, or in an action under section 48(1) of the Civil Liability Act 1961 (being an action where death is caused by wrongful act, neglect or default), the person having the right to bring the action was under a disability either at the time the right accrued to him or at the date of his knowledge (as defined in section 2 of the 1991 Act), the action may be brought at any time before the expiration of three years[102] from the date he ceased to be under a disability or died whichever event first occurred notwithstanding that the period specified in section 3 of the 1991 Act has expired. Section 5(2) provides that section 5(1) will not affect any case where a right of action first accrued to some person (not under a disability) through whom the person under a disability claims.

Capacity with respect to actions for damages under the Sale of Goods and Supply of Services Act 1980 In the case of an action claiming damages under section 13(7) of the Sale of Goods and Supply of Services Act 1980 where the person to whom it accrued was under a disability the action may be brought at any time before the expiration of two years from the date when the person ceased to be under a disability or died, whichever event first occurred notwithstanding that the period of limitation has expired.

The impact of incapacity on limitation periods in succession cases Section 127 of the Succession Act 1965 provides that section 49 of the Statute of Limitations 1957:

> "which extends the periods of limitation fixed by that Act where the person to whom the right of action accrued was under a disability shall have effect in relation to an action in respect of a claim to the estate of a deceased person or to any share in such estate whether under a will or intestacy or as a legal right as if the period of three years were substituted for the period of six years mentioned in subsection(1) of that section."

Claims by children of a testator under section 117 of the Succession Act that the deceased has failed to make proper provision of a claimant child in accordance with his means, are not included in section 127. Section 117(6) of the Act, as amended by section 46 of the Family Law (Divorce) Act 1996 of the Act, requires a child to make an application for reasonable provision under section 117 within six months of the first taking out of representation to the deceased's estate. In *MPD v. MD*,[103] Carroll J. reluctantly held

---

[100] In *McGuinness v. Armstrong Patents Ltd* [1980] I.R. 289 it was held that in calculating the last date on which a summons may be issued the day on which the cause of action accrues is to be included in computing the limitation period.

[101] In *Boylan v. Motor Distributors Ltd* [1994] 1 I.L.R.M. 115, Lynch J. held that the words "if later" meant later than the date on which the cause of action accrued rather than later than three years from the date on which the cause of action accrued.

[102] S.7 of the Civil Liability and Courts Act 2004 proposes to amend s.5(1) by changing "three years" to "two years". S.7 of the 2004 Act has not yet been brought into force.

[103] [1981] I.L.R.M. 179.

that section 127 did not apply to applications under section 117 instancing cases such as a conflict of interest between stepmother and child where injustice may arise as a consequence of the fact that the disability of infancy under section 117 is not within the scope of section 127.

Commentary

In British Columbia, Saskatchewan and Manitoba legislation has been amended to provide for suspension of the limitation period when a person comes under a disability after his cause of action has arisen,[104] whereas in Nova Scotia the plaintiff's supervening disability is a factor which the court must take into consideration in deciding whether to exercise its discretion to allow an action to be commenced outside the limitation period.[105]

The underlying policy of the provisions postponing the limitation period until a person is no longer under a disability is that it would be unfair for the limitation period to run if the plaintiff is mentally incapable of making reasonable judgments and decisions as to whether the seek legal advice and pursue his cause of action and it is submitted that this policy justification should be reflected in interpreting terms such as person of unsound mind in section 48(1) of the Statute of Limitations 1957. Indeed is submitted that the expression "person of unsound mind" in section 48(1) should be amended to the description "person under a legal incapacity" and the expression defined to mean "a person incapable of managing his affairs because of a disease or impairment of physical or mental condition".

Secondly, in *In re Martin's Trusts*[106] Lord Justice Cotton held that a person could not be considered as "of unsound mind within the Act if his incapacity was a temporary one arising from an accident, as for instance, concussion of the brain or from illness of a temporary character but he is to be so considered where he is subject to a permanent incapacity of mind rendering him incapable of attending to business." If the expression person of unsound mind is changed to the description "person under a legal incapacity" then a temporary mental incapacity e.g. an action that renders a person unconscious for a day could be taken into account in computing the limitation period.

Thirdly, at present the disability provisions in the limitations legislation apply only where the person is under a disability on the date of accrual of the cause of action and not when it arises subsequently. In the latter case it is likely that the plaintiff's disability will prevent him making prompt and reasonable judgments with respect to the claim arising before his disability. It is submitted that the limitation should either be suspended during such period of disability or the court should be empowered to take such a factor into account in deciding whether to permit an action to be commenced outside the limitation period.[107]

Finally, it is submitted that in accordance with the recommendations of the Law Reform Commission, section 117(6) of the Succession Act 1965 be amended so as to

---

[104] See R.S.B.C. 1979, c. 236. S 7(3), (4), R.S.S 1978 c. L-15 s.6 [re-en 1983 c. 80, s.13]; R.S.M. 1970 c. L150 S.9(2) [en. 1980, c. 28, s.2].

[105] R.S.N.S. 1967 c. 168, s.2A(4)(e) [en. 1982, c. 33. s.2].

[106] (1887) 34 Ch.D. 618 at 622–623.

[107] See The Alberta Institute of Law Reform in its Discussion report on Limitations, No.4 1986, p.293.

give a discretion to the court to extend the six month time limit within which applications may be made.[108]

The appointment of guardian and/or next friend

A person of unsound mind may sue as plaintiff by his committee or next friend and may defend by his committee or guardian appointed for that purpose.[109] Before the name of a person is used as next friend that person must sign a written authority to the solicitor for that purpose and the authority must be filed in the proper court office.[110] An application for the appointment of a guardian *ad litem* should be made *ex parte* to the Master of the High Court.[111] The application should be grounded on an affidavit containing sufficient detail of the defendant's state of mind,[112] and demonstrating that the proposed guardian is a fit and proper person to act as such.[113] The affidavit must also aver to the fact that there is no conflict of interest between the guardian and the person of unsound mind.[114]

If a person becomes of unsound mind during the course of proceedings an application for the appointment of a guardian *ad litem* may be made at that point in time.[115]

The guardian's role is to conduct the action in the interests of the person of unsound mind and anything, which in the ordinary conduct of proceedings is required or authorised, to be done by a party to the proceedings may be done by his next friend or guardian *ad litem*.[116]

Where a person of unsound mind not so found by inquisition fails to enter an appearance to a summons then, before taking any further step in the proceedings the plaintiff must apply to the Master for an order that a proper person be assigned as his/her guardian [117] by whom s/he may appear and defend the proceedings.[118] The costs of the appointment of a guardian must be paid by the plaintiff, but may ultimately be

---

[108] See *Report on Land Law and Conveyancing Law* (1) General Proposals (LRC 30–1989) para.47.
[109] Rules of Superior Courts (1986), O.15, r.17 A guardian ad litem may be appointed for the purpose of defending proceedings upon application to the Master of the High Court. See O.63, r.1(3). The person appointed as guardian is usually a relative or close friend but that need not necessarily be the case See *Earl of Normanston v. Brennan* 12 I.L.T. 73; *Biddalph v. Lord Camoys* 9 Beav. 548.
[110] Rules of Superior Courts (1986), O.15, r.20.
[111] O.63, r.1(3).
[112] *Watson v. Knilans* (1874) 8 I.L.T.R. 157.
[113] *Gaffney v. Gaffney* (1896) 31 I.L.T.R. 11.
[114] *Dobbin v. Belling* (1872) I.R. 6 Eq. 623.
[115] *Wolfe v. Wolfe* (1875) I.R. 9 Eq. 392.
[116] See *Fryer v. Wiseman* (1876) 45 L.J. Ch. 199; *Piggott v. Toogood* (1904) 48 Sol. Jo. 573; *Knatchbull v. Fowle* (1876) 1 Ch. D. 604, *Jones v. Lloyd* (1874) L.R. 18 Eq. 265.
[117] The plaintiff may himself/herself nominate a person to act as guardian ad litem. See *O'Connor v. Fetherstone* 13 I.L.T.R. 75.
[118] Rules of the Superior Courts, O.13, r.1. No such order may be made unless it appears at the hearing of the application that the summons was duly served and that notice of the application was served upon or left at the dwellinghouse of the person with whom or under whose care the defendant was at the time of serving the summons. Notice of the application must be served after the expiration of the time allowed for appearance and at least six clear days before the day stated in the notice as the date for hearing the application. In the case of a plenary or summary summons the time allowed for an appearance is eight days exclusive of the day of service. See O.12, r.2. One counsel only is permitted to make such an application. See O.52, r.17(6).

recovered against the defendant.[119] Where a plaintiff is not a ward of court he may apply to have the action dismissed and the next friend ordered to pay costs.[120] In this regard the court may direct an inquiry as to whether the plaintiff is mentally disordered and whether the action is for his benefit.[121] Where it is shown that it is not, the court will stay the action.[122]

Procedural matters

Service of documemts on a person with mental disability

Order 9, rule 6 of the Superior Court rules provides where a lunatic or person of unsound mind not so found by inquisition is a defendant in any proceedings, service on the committee of the lunatic or on the person with whom the person of unsound mind resides or under whose care he is, shall unless the Court otherwise orders be deemed good service on such defendant.

Consent by person with mental disability

A consent as to the mode of taking evidence or as to any other procedure given with the consent of the court by the next friend, guardian, committee or other person acting on behalf of the person under disability has the same force and effect as if the party on whose behalf it was given were under no disability and had given the consent. However the committee of a person of unsound mind cannot give a valid consent unless s/he obtains the sanction of the President of the High Court to such consent.[123]

Setting down a case in which a person with mental disability is a party

No special case in any proceedings to which a person of unsound mind not so found by inquisition is a party may be set down for argument without the leave of the court. An application[124] in this regard must be supported by sufficient evidence that the statements contained in the special case are true insofar as they affect the interest of such person of unsound mind.[125]

Settlement of action in which person with mental disability is a party

In any proceedings in the High Court in which money or damages are claimed either by or on behalf of a person of unsound mind suing either alone or in conjunction with other

---

[119] See *Woods v. McCann and Neely* 35 I.L.T.R. 210; *Scott v. Brown* 2 N.I.J.R. 113.

[120] See *Palmer v. Walesby* (1868) 3 Ch. App. 732; *Didisheim v. London & Westminster Bank* [1900] 2 Ch. 15.

[121] See *Howell v. Lewis* (1891) 65 L.T. 672.

[122] See *Didisheim v. London & Westminster Bank* (1900) 2 Ch. 15, *New York Security and Trust Co. v. Keyser* [1901] 1 Ch. 666 at 670; *Beall v. Smith* (1873) 9 Ch. App. 85; *Porter v. Porter* (1888) 37 Ch. D. 420; *Waterhouse v. Worsnop* (1888) 59 L.T. 140.

[123] Rules of Superior Courts (1986), O.15, r.21.

[124] An application should be made by way of motion under O.52.

[125] O.34, r.4.

parties no settlement, compromise or payment and no acceptance of money paid into court is valid insofar as the person of unsound mind is concerned without the approval of the court.[126]

Awards to person with mental disability

No money (including damages) recovered, adjudged, awarded or agreed to be paid in respect of the claims of a person of unsound mind whether by verdict or settlement or compromise, payment into court or otherwise before, at or after the trial may be paid to the plaintiff, his/her next friend or solicitor unless the court directs.[127] All money so recovered, adjudged, ordered, awarded or agreed to be paid must be dealt with as the court directs and the money or any part thereof may be directed (a) to be paid into the High Court and to be invested or otherwise dealt with there; or (b) to be paid or transferred to the Circuit Court of the district in which the plaintiff resides or such other Circuit Court as the court may think fit.[128]

The courts' directions may include any general or special directions that the court may think fit to give. Without prejudice to the generality of the provisions of Order 22, rule 10 these directions may include directions as to how the money is to be applied or dealt with and as to any payment to be made, either directly or out of the amount paid into court, and (in the case of transfer to the Circuit Court) either before or after it is transferred to the Circuit Court, to the plaintiff or to the next friend in respect of moneys paid or expenses incurred or for maintenance or otherwise for or on behalf of or for the benefit of the person of unsound mind or otherwise or to the plaintiff's solicitor in respect of costs.[129]

Money paid into or transferred to the Circuit Court under Order 22, rule 10 must (subject to any order or direction that may be given in the judgment or order for payment or transfer thereof) be held, invested, applied or otherwise dealt with for the benefit of such plaintiff in such manner as the Circuit Court in its discretion thinks fit and in accordance with the Circuit Court rules for the time being in force.[130] Nothing in Order 22, rule 10 is to prejudice the lien of a solicitor for costs.[131]

Subject to any order which may be made by the Court (whether on consent or otherwise) as to the costs of the plaintiff(s) in any such cause or matter or as to the amount of such costs of the mode of payment of costs (i) the costs of the plaintiff(s) in any such cause or matter or incident to the claims in such cause or matter or consequent on such cause or matter must, (as regards costs ordered to be paid to such plaintiff(s) by the defendants or any other party to the cause or matter) be taxed by the Taxing Master

---

[126] O.22, r.10(1). Until such time as approval issues the monies do not vest in the plaintiff. See *Carey v. Ryan* [1982] IR 179. The next friend has the right to withdraw from any agreement to settle the claim which has yet to be approved. *Duffy v. McLavan* [1985] N.I. 285. Applications for approval should be made by way of motion under O.52.

[127] O.22, r.10(2). Applications for payment may be made to the Master of the High Court under O.63, r.1(18).

[128] O.22, r.10(3). The forms Nos. 9 and 10 in Appendix E to the, Rules of the Superior Courts may be used in cases to which they are applicable.

[129] O.22, r.10(4)(i).

[130] O.22, r.10(6).

[131] O.22, r.10(7).

as between party and party;[132] (ii) the costs (if any) of the plaintiff(s) not ordered to be paid by or recoverable from any other party must be taxed as between solicitor and client[133] on notice to the General Solicitor for Wards of Court. If any portion of those costs are payable by any adult party to the cause or matter who is *sui juris* the Taxing Master must certify the amount of such portion and the portions payable by such person of unsound mind; and no costs other than those so certified shall be payable to the solicitor for any plaintiff in the cause or matter.[134]

Order 22, rule 10 applies *mutatis mutandis* to (a) money recovered on a counterclaim; (b) money recovered by a person of unsound mind whether so found by inquisition or not so found.[135]

Money paid into court or investments made under the provisions of Order 22, rule 10 and the dividends or interest thereon, shall be sold, transferred or paid out to the party entitled thereto pursuant to the order of the Court.[136] These rules also applies to sums in respect of which a person of unsound mind not so found by inquisition obtains an order under section 76 of the Road Traffic Act 1976 as if the claimant had recovered the sum in an action against a vehicle insurer or vehicle guarantor.[137]

The impact of incapacity on the giving of evidence

At common law

Insanity in early common law was regarded as an absolute bar to a person testifying as a witness in legal proceedings.[138] By the mid nineteenth century, this rule had been relaxed and it was accepted that mental disorder did not necessarily render a person incompetent to testify as a witness.[139] If the individual was capable of being sworn and of giving rational testimony then he was competent as a witness. Today, it is sufficient if it is shown the witness appreciates that an oath involves a moral obligation to tell the truth.[140] In *R v. Hill*,[141] a person suffering from a single delusion that he had a number of spirits about him, which were continually talking to him, was permitted to give evidence on the ground that he understood the nature of an oath. In that case Lord Campbell C.J.

---

[132] On a taxation on a party and party basis there are allowed such costs as were necessary or proper for the attainment of justice or for enforcing or defending the rights of the party whose costs are being taxed. See O.99, r.10(2), Rules of the Superior Courts. Party and party costs include costs to which the person has been put by the acts of the adverse party but do not extend to unusual costs or costs which might have been avoided. See *Irish Trust Bank v. Central Bank of Ireland* [1976–7] I.L.R.M. 50 at 58.

[133] On a taxation as between solicitor and client all costs are allowed except in so far as they are of an unreasonable amount or have been unreasonably incurred. See O.99, r.11.

[134] O.22, r.10(8).

[135] O.22, r.10(9).

[136] O.22, r.11.

[137] O.91, r.4.

[138] See Holdsworth, *A History of English Law*, Vol.9 (3rd ed., 1944) 188; *Wigmore on Evidence*, Vol.11 (Chadbourn rev., 1979), para.492.

[139] See *R v. Hill* (1851) 5 Cox C.C. 259.

[140] See Gochnauer, "Swearing Telling the Truth and Moral Obligation" (1983) 9 *Queens Law Journal* 199.

[141] (1851) 2 Den C.C. 254 90 R.R. 822.

described the procedural position regarding the determination of the witness's capacity as follows:

> "If there be a delusion in the mind of the party tendered as a witness, it is for the judge to see whether the party has a sense of religion and understands the nature and sanction of an oath; and then if the judge admits him as a witness, it is for the jury to say what degree of credit is to be given to his testimony".[142]

Where the witness is a person with an intellectual disability the person must equally understand that there is moral obligation involved in taking an oath.[143] The level of understanding required is similar to that required of children viz. the person must have a sufficient appreciation of the solemnity of the occasion and the added responsibility involved in taking an oath over and above the responsibility to tell the truth in the context of normal social conduct. There is, however, no need for the person to believe in the existence of a God or to have an awareness of the divine sanction of an oath to satisfy this test.[144]

A witness must meet certain minimum requirements with regard to capacity for communication, observation and recollection. In regard to his/her capacity for communication the witness not only must be able to understand and answer simple question, but must also have sufficient intelligence to understand reasonable questions put in cross examination.[145] In *R v. Hill*[146] the witness's evidence was allowed because not only had he a clear apprehension of the obligation of an oath but he was also:

> "capable of giving a trustworthy account of any transaction which took place before his eyes, and he was perfectly rational upon all subjects except with respects of his particular delusion".[147]

It is rare to find reported cases in which a witness has been judged incompetent on the grounds of lack of capacity to communicate, observe and recollect, presumably because a person who clearly lacks capacity in this respect is unlikely to be tendered as a witness.[148] However difficulties of verbal communication resulting from mental disability can sometimes be overcome through interpreters and alternative forms of communication.[149]

---

[142] 90 R.R. 822 at 828.

[143] *R v. Bannerman* (1966) 48 C.R. 110.

[144] *R v. Hayes* [1977] 2 All E.R. 288. It being acknowledged by Bridge L.J. in *Hayes* that "in the present state of society, amongst the adult population the divine sanction of an oath is probably not generally recognised" (at p.291).

[145] *R v. Hill* (1851) 5 Cox. C.C. 259.

[146] (1851) 2 Den. C.C.254 90 R.R. 822.

[147] 90 R. R. 822 at 828.

[148] However, one such is the Canadian case of *R v. Harburg* [1979] 2 W.W.R. 105 (Sask. Q.B.) in which a mentally ill witness who gave "confused and repetitive and incoherent testimony" was held to be incompetent as a witness.

[149] In the Canadian case of *Clark v. Clark* (1982)) O.R. (2d) 383 a witness's difficulties in communication was circumvented by the witness's giving evidence through two interpreters by means of a combination of words, sign language and blissymbols.

Wigmore[150] has emphasised the importance of avoiding the pro-mulgation of detailed rules for determining whether a prospective witness has the necessary capacity for observation and recollection. Each case must be assessed on its own facts having regard to the witness's mental capacity both at the date of the trial and at the time the events took place. The overriding consideration is whether the witness's mental disability affects his powers of observation and recollection to such an extent as to make his testimony substantially untrustworthy.

The requirement that a witness be mentally competent to testify possibly does not apply where the witness mental condition is one of the issues before the court. Although a witness's mental disorder may render his testimony completely untrustworthy and unreliable it may be important for the court to receive the evidence for the purpose of assessing the witness's mental condition. This may be illustrated by reference to the Canadian case of *M v. Alberta*.[151] In this case, the court was called upon to determine whether the applicant should continue to be detained as an involuntary patient under the Mental Health Act. Although the appellant's testimony was described by the judge as "fantasy and untrue," it was held that it would be improper to exclude it in this type of case since it may assist the court in determining the witness' mental condition. Although the requirement of competence to give evidence might be relaxed in such a situation, presumably the witness must still be capable of understanding the nature of an oath otherwise his evidence cannot be admitted.

Evidence relating to the witness' mental capacity is admissible on the issue of his competence to testify.[152] Even where the competence of a witness is not challenged factors such as demeanour and conduct and perhaps even the fact that the witness is a patient is a psychiatric hospital may lead the trial judge to decide to examine the witness to determine whether he is competent to be sworn and to testify.[153] Where a witness's incompetence to testify becomes apparent only after he has been sworn and begun to give evidence the procedure to follow depends upon the circumstances of the case and the nature of the evidence given. Early authorities suggest that the trial judge should stand the witness down and instruct the jury to ignore the witness's testimony.[154] Even if the complainant is competent to give evidence, the judge in the circumstances of a given case may be obliged to be given a warning to a jury to be careful about accepting such evidence where it is uncorroborated. This is illustrated by the English case of *R v. Spencer*,[155] which involved allegations against Rampton staff for abusing patients it was held that although the full corroboration warning given in sex cases was not required, juries had to be warned in clear terms of the dangers of convicting on the unsupported evidence of special hospital patients who were of bad character, mentally unstable and might have a common grudge against the staff. Also in *R v. Neshet*,[156] a case which involved an allegation of dishonesty by the matron of an old people's home the judge

---

[150] *Wigmore on Evidence*, Vol.11, para.496.

[151] (1985) 63 A.R. 14 (Q.B.).

[152] See *Toohey v. Metropolitan Police Commissioner* [1965] A.C. 595 (H.L.); *R v. Hill* (1851) 5 Cox. C.C. 259 (C.A.); *R v. Dunning* [1965] Crim. L. Rev. 372 (C.A.).

[153] See *Wigmore on Evidence*, Vol. 11, para.497.

[154] *R v. Whitehead* (1866) 10 Cox C.C. 234.

[155] [1987] A.C. 128.

[156] *Ibid.*

allowed statements given by two residents to be read in court because the witnesses were unfit to attend. It was held that he should not have done so as the evidence itself was too unreliable having regard to the witness's ages and physical condition.

Civil proceedings – Statutory provisions

Unsworn and unofficial evidence by person with a mental disability

Section 28(1) of the Children Act 1997 provides for the giving of unsworn and unaffirmed evidence by a child under the age of 14 years and a person with a mental disability who has attained that age and stipulates that notwithstanding any rule of law in all civil proceedings,[157] the evidence of child under the age of 14 years and a person with mental disability who has attained that age may be received otherwise than on oath or affirmation if the court is satisfied that the child or the person with mental disability concerned is capable of giving an intelligible account of events which are relevant to the proceedings. In this regard the person's maturity and understanding will be relevant. Unsworn evidence received by virtue of the section may corroborate evidence (sworn or unsworn) given by another person.[158]

Where a child or a person with a mental disability makes an unsworn or unaffirmed statement pursuant to section 28(1) which is material in the proceedings concerned and the maker knows it to be false or does not believe it to be true the Act provides that that person shall be guilty of an offence and on conviction will be liable to be dealt with as if guilty of perjury.[159]

Evidence by video link in cases concerning welfare of person with mental incapacity

Part III of the Children Act 1997 makes special provision for the giving of evidence by a child[160] in civil proceedings concerning the welfare of a child, and by a person with a mental disability in civil proceedings concerning the welfare of that person when that person is of full age but has a mental disability to such an extent that it is not reasonably possible for him/her to live independently.[161] Section 20 provides specifically that Part III of the Act applies to civil proceedings concerning the welfare of the person of full age with such a mental disability before any court commenced after 1 January 1999[162] "with the necessary modifications, in the same manner as it applies to a child".[163]

Accordingly, section 21 of the 1997 Act provides for a child and arguably[164] a person

---

[157] The section is not confined to proceedings concerning the welfare of the person.

[158] Children Act 1997, s.28(4). Cannon & Neligan note that the insertion of subs.(4) may have been a mistake since corroboration requirements do not normally apply in civil proceedings. See Cannon and Nelligan, *Evidence* (Thomson Round Hall Ltd, Dublin, 2002), p.72, n.26.

[159] Children Act 1997, s.28(2).

[160] Child is defined as a person who is not of full age. See s.19(1).

[161] Children Act 1997, s.20.

[162] Commencement date for Part III set by Children Act 1997 (Commencement) Order 1998 (S.I. No. 433 of 1998).

[163] Children Act 1997, s.20(b).

[164] Cannon & Neligan point out that s.21 (in contrast to s.28) applies on the face of it only to children. See *Evidence, op. cit*, p.74. However, s.20 makes the whole of Part III (of which s.21 is one provision) applicable "with the necessary modifications, *in the same manner as it applies to a*

who is of full age but has a mental disability to such an extent that it is not reasonably possible for the person to live independently to give evidence with the leave of the court[165] through a live television link either from within or outside the State in civil proceedings before any court commenced after January 1, 1999[166] concerning the welfare of that person.[167] The evidence must be video-recorded.[168] The giving of evidence by live television link, whether direct or in cross-examination, is subject to the normal rules governing evidence with one exception. Where evidence is given by a child or a person with a mental disability who is of full age under section 21(1) that any person was known to him or her before the date of commencement of the proceedings the person giving evidence will not be required to identify the person during the course of those proceedings unless the court directs otherwise.[169]

Because section 21 marks such a departure from the normal giving of evidence, section 21(3) makes it an offence for a child or person with mental disability who is of full age when giving evidence under section 21(1) from outside the State to make a statement material in the proceedings which the child or person with mental disability who is of full age knows to be false or does not believe to be true and section 21(3) provides that such child or person with mental disability shall be guilty of perjury or if section 28 applies (evidence given otherwise than on oath or affirmation) shall be guilty of an offence and on conviction shall be liable to be dealt with as if guilty of perjury under section 28(2). Proceedings for an offence under section 28(3) may be taken and the offence may, for the purposes of the jurisdiction of the court, be treated as having been committed in any place in the State.[170]

Question put through an intermediary

Section 22(1) provides that where evidence is being given or is to be given through a live television link the court may direct that any question be put to child or the person with the mental disability who is of full age through an intermediary if having regard to the age or mental condition of the child or the age or mental condition of the person with mental disability who is of full age the court is satisfied that any questions should be so put. The court may make such a direction of its own motion or on the application of a party to the proceedings.[171]

---

child to civil proceedings before any court concerning the welfare of a person who is of full age but who has a mental disability to such an extent that it is not reasonably possible for the person to live independently". If a purposive construction of s.21 is adopted the section does permit persons with a mental disability to avail of video link provisions in civil proceedings relating to their welfare.

[165] The Act does not provide criteria regarding when such leave may be granted.

[166] See Children Act 1997 (Commencement) Order 1998 (S.I. No. 433 of 1998).

[167] A person with mental disability who makes a statement material in the proceedings which s/he knows to be false or does not believe to be true in giving evidence under s.21(1) from outside the State will be guilty of perjury. See s.21(3). If s.28 applies (i.e. the person gives unsworn or unaffirmed evidence) the person will be guilty of the offence of perjury under s.28(2). See s.21(3).

[168] Children Act 1997, s.21(2).

[169] *Ibid.*, s.21(5).

[170] *Ibid.*, s.21(4).

[171] *Ibid.*, s.22.

Questions put to a person with a mental disability through an intermediary under section 22(1) must be either in the words used by the questions or in words that convey to the person with mental disability in a way that is appropriate, *inter alia*, to his or her mental condition the meaning of the question being asked.[172] This intermediary must be appointed by the court and must be a person who, in its opinion is competent to act as such.[173]

Inadmissibilty of statements

Section 23(1) provides that a statement made by a child or by person with mental disability who is of full age in accordance with these provisions is admissible as evidence of any fact of which direct oral evidence would be admissible in any Part III proceedings notwithstanding the hearsay rule[174] but only where the court considers that the child is

---

[172] Children Act 1997, s.22(2).

[173] *Ibid.*, s.22(3).

[174] The issue of the admissibility of hearsay evidence of children at common law was addressed in the *Southern Health Board v. CH* [1996] 1 I.R. 219. The evidence in issue was a video recording of an interview held by a social worker with a child as well as the social worker's opinion as to the validity of the allegations of child sexual abuse. The respondent in the case objected to the admission of evidence of the video tape on the grounds that it was hearsay. The Supreme Court held that the proceedings in question were in essence an inquiry as to what was best to be done for the child in the particular circumstances and were similar to proceedings where a court was exercising its wardship jurisdiction. The focus of the inquiry had to be on the welfare and best interests of the child. It was held that the key evidence was that of the social worker which should be regarded as expert testimony and was subject to cross examination. The video recording of the interview with the child was not to be admitted as the independent evidence of the child, but rather as a portion of the material on which the expert evidence of the social worker would be based. It was held that the District Judge would be justified in admitting evidence of the video recording if he was satisfied having heard such expert evidence as he thought right: (a) that the child was incompetent to give evidence or alternatively, (b) that the trauma the child would suffer would make it undesirable that she should give *viva voce* evidence in court. In the subsequent case of *Eastern Health Board v. MK and MK* [1999] 2 I.R. 99 (which was heard before the Children Act 1997 came into force) the applicant sought to have the children of the respondents made wards of court. During the wardship proceedings, it was alleged that the second respondent had sexually abused his child, S.K. who was a child with a hearing disability, a serious speech impediment and whose behaviour had in the past been very disturbed to the extent that he was expelled from a school for children with hearing disabilities and for a year prior to the proceedings was not attending any school. The allegation was based on (a) the evidence of a speech therapist as to what S.K. had said to her on two occasions and (b) the evidence of a senior social worker of what S.K said and did at an interview he had with him, a video of which was made and seen by the High Court and Supreme Court on appeal. The High Court admitted the evidence on a *de bene esse* basis notwithstanding the objections of the respondents and made it clear that if the hearsay evidence had been excluded the other evidence would not have justified the order making the children wards of court. The respondents appealed to the Supreme Court which, allowing the appeal, held that wardship proceedings were inquisitorial in nature and the welfare of the child was paramount. Hearsay evidence was admissible at the discretion of the judge in such proceedings as the nature of the jurisdiction justified a departure from such proceedings. A majority of the Supreme Court (Denham, Barrington, Keane and Lynch JJ.) held that hearsay evidence regarding statements of a child alleging sexual abuse by its parents could not be received in the context of assessing the risks to the welfare of the child, but it did not follow automatically that it was also capable of proving the truth of its contents. Barron J. held that the hearsay evidence of statements made by S.K to the speech therapist would have been admissible to support the opinion of an expert but the speech therapist was not such an expert. Therefore the

unable to give evidence by reason of age or , that the giving of oral evidence by the child or the person with mental disability who is of full age either in person or under section 21 would not be in the interest of the welfare of the child or the person with mental disability who is of full age.[175] Further, a statement (or part statement) referred to under section 23(1) will not be admitted in evidence if the court is of the opinion that, in the interests of justice, the statement (or part statement) ought not to be admitted.[176] In considering whether the statement (or part statement) ought to be admitted the court must have regard to all the circumstances[177] including any risk that the admission will result in unfairness to any of the parties to the proceedings.[178]

---

statements should not have been admitted. The Supreme Court held that the essential test was not whether the alleged abuse had occurred but whether there were unacceptable risks to the welfare of the child if the child was not taken into wardship. Denham and Lynch JJ. were of the view that the court must carry out a separate inquiry as to whether the child should give evidence, and if so in what circumstances. In this regard the age of the child and the potential trauma of giving evidence in court were relevant factors. The judge also had to assess the reliability and weight of the evidence. The trial judge failed to carry out a separate inquiry as to whether it was necessary to adduce hearsay evidence and if so, in what circumstances. He also heard evidence *de bene esse* which was an unfair process. That process did not have the explicit fair procedures necessary to vindicate rights in determining such an important matter.In the course of his judgment, Keane J. was of the view that there had to be an inquiry as to whether the child was competent to give evidence and if so whether the trauma the child would suffer would make it undesirable that he or she should give evidence. There was no inquiry as to whether S.K. was competent to give evidence in the case, and on that ground alone the decision of the trial judge to take the children into wardship had to be set aside. In the course of their judgments Keane, Lynch and Barrington JJ., raised the question whether evidence adduced by way of a video recordings could properly be described as hearsay evidence as the court could see and hear an exact electronic recording of the statement as it was actually made and for all practical purposes the court was in as good a position to assess the credibility of the maker of the statement as if he or she were giving evidence in court subject to the qualifications that the maker of the statement was not subjected to cross-examination; the evidence is unsworn; the questioning was conducted by a non-lawyer and there were no lawyers present on behalf of the parties to object to any questions or answers. Keane J. was of the view that given the significantly different nature of video evidence treating its admissibility in certain circumstances and subject to safeguards as a proper exception to the rule against hearsay would be a reasonable development by the courts of the law on this topic.

[175] Children Act 1997, s.23(1). In *Southern Health Board v. C.H* [1996] 2 I.L.R.M. 142 at 151, O'Flaherty J. stated "if [the judge] receives evidence that the child is incompetent to give evidence, or, as a distinct condition, he finds that the trauma that she would suffer would make undesirable that she should come to give evidence, then he will be justified in allowing in the evidence of the video-recordings. In this regard, it is well to point out that a courtroom, is, in general, an unsuitable environment for a child of such tender years as this child". The child in question was five years and four months at the time of the hearing in question.

[176] Children Act 1997, s.23(2)(a).

[177] Note the decision of Carney J. in *Eastern Health Board v. Mooney*, unreported, High Court, March 20, 1998 where it was held that hearsay evidence is admissible in proceedings under the Child Care Act 1991 and went on to state that where witnesses were competent, compellable and available to give evidence it may not be necessary or appropriate to receive hearsay evidence. In the *Mooney* case foster parents were available as witnesses who could be compelled by the court of its own motion.

[178] Children Act 1997, s.23(2)(b). Note the dictum of Ward L.J. in the English Court of Appeal decision in *In re N.* [1997] 1 W.L.R. 153 at 165 citing Neill L.J. in *In re W. (Minors) (Wardship: Evidence)* [1990] 1 F.L.R. 203 at 208 to the effect that "the court will be very slow indeed to make a finding of fact adverse to a parent if the only material before it has been untested by cross-examination".

Requirement of notice

A party proposing to adduce evidence pursuant to section 23(1) must give the other
party or parties to the proceedings (a) such notice, if any, of that fact, and (b) such
particulars of or relating to the evidence as is reasonable and practicable in the
circumstances for the purpose of enabling such party or parties to deal with any matter
arising from its being hearsay.[179] A fundamental requirement where hearsay evidence
is contained in a video recording or a report is to give a copy of the relevant document
to the other parties in sufficient time to allow them to assess the hearsay evidence and
arrange for the evidence to be rebutted by their own witness.[180] The statutory requirement
as to notice will not apply where the parties concerned agree that it should not apply.[181]

Weight attached to statements

In estimating the weight, if any, to be attached to any statement admitted in evidence
pursuant to section 23 the court must have regard to all the circumstances from which
any inference could reasonably be drawn as to its accuracy or otherwise.[182] In assessing
the weight to be attached to the statement the court may in particular have regard as to
whether (a) the original statement was made contemporaneously with the occurrence or
existence of the matters stated, (b) the evidence involves multiple hearsay,[183] (c) any
person involved has any motive to conceal or misrepresent matters, (d) the original
statement was an edited account or was made in collaboration with another for a particular
purpose, and (e) the circumstances in which the evidence is adduced as hearsay are
such as to suggest an attempt to prevent proper evaluation of its weight.

Evidence regarding credibility of person with mental disability as a witness admissible

Where information is given in a statement admitted in evidence under section 23 certain
evidence relevant to the credibility of the child or the person with a mental disability
who is of full age who originally supplied the information is admissible under the terms
of section 25. Thus any evidence, which would have been admissible as relevant to his/
her credibility as a witness if s/he had been called as a witness, will be admissible for
that purpose.[184] Evidence may be given with the leave of the court of any matter which
could have been put to him/her in cross examination if s/he had been called as a witness
as relevant to his or her credibility as a witness but of which evidence could not have
been adduced by the cross-examining party.[185] Accordingly, a cross examining party

---

[179] Children Act 1997, s.23(3).
[180] See Costello P. in *In re M., S. & W. (Infants)* [1996] 1 I.L.R.M. 370 at 371.
[181] Children Act 1997, s.23(4).
[182] *Ibid.*, s.24(1).
[183] For example an expert witness testifying to the veracity of a person's statement that the expert
repeats.
[184] This may take the form of the opinion of a person interviewing or assessing a child or a person
with mental disability and their belief as to whether the child in recounting facts to be admitted as
hearsay evidence is true or otherwise. See *In re M., S. & W. (Infants)* [1996] 1 I.L.R.M. 370 where
reliance was placed on the evidence of speech therapist and a senior social worker as to the veracity
of the child's evidence regarding sexual abuse.
[185] Children Act 1997, s.25(b).

may adduce evidence relevant to credibility[186] that could have been elicited from the child or person with mental disability who is of full age had the child or the person with mental disability given evidence. Evidence tending to prove that the child or the person with a mental disability who is of full age, whether before or after supplying the information, made (whether orally or not) a statement which is inconsistent with it will, if not already admissible, be admissible for the purpose of showing that the witness has contradicted himself or herself. [187]

Position regarding documented evidence

Where information contained in a document is admissible in evidence in proceedings to which Part III applies the information may be given in evidence by producing a copy of the document or of the material part of it authenticated in a manner approved by the court whether or not the document is still in existence.[188] In this context "document" includes a sound recording and video recording.[189] It is immaterial in this context how many removes there are between the copy and the original, or by what means[190] (which may include facsimile transmission) the copy was produced or any intermediate copy was made.[191]

Possibility of transfer to Court where video link facilities are available

Where the court is of the opinion that it is desirable that evidence be taken by live television link or by means of a video-recording and facilities for doing so are not available the has power to transfer proceedings to a court where those facilities are available.[192] Where such an order is made the jurisdiction of the court to which the proceedings have been transferred may be exercised (a) by a circuit court judge of the circuit concerned, or (b) in the case of the District Court by a judge of that court for the time being assigned to the district court district concerned.[193]

Criminal Proceedings – Statutory Provisions

Part III of the Criminal Evidence Act 1992 permits particular arrangements to be made for persons with mental handicap to give evidence in respect of certain offences. Part III applies where the offence concerned is a sexual offence;[194] an offence involving violence

---

[186] In proceedings relevant to the welfare of the child or the person with mental disability who is of full age evidence of hostility in relationships with parents/carers which might colour the evidence of the witness may be relevant in this regard.

[187] Children Act 1997, s.25(c).

[188] *Ibid.,* s.26(1).

[189] *Ibid.,* s.26(3).

[190] It appears that electronic methods of producing copies of documents would be covered by the section for example reports sent by e-mail and photocopies and digital methods of recording pictures and sound.

[191] Children Act 1997, s.26(2).

[192] *Ibid.,* s.27.

[193] *Ibid.,* s.27.

[194] The term sexual offence is defined by s.2 of the 1992 Act. It includes the offences of rape, buggery, of a person under the age of 17 years (under s.3 of the Criminal Law (Sexual Offences) Act 1993),

or the threat of violence to a person, an offence consisting of attempting or conspiring to commit or of aiding, abetting, counselling, procuring or inciting the commission of such offences or an offence under section 3 (child trafficking and taking, detaining, restricting the personal liberty of or using a child for sexual exploitation), 4 (allowing a child to be used for the production of child pornography), 5 (producing, distributing, printing, publishing, knowingly importing, exporting, selling or showing, or advertising child pornography or encouraging or knowingly causing or facilitating such activity relating to child pornography or knowingly possessing child pornography for the purpose of distributing, publishing, exporting, selling or showing it) or 6 (knowingly possessing child pornography) of the Child Trafficking and Pornography Act 1998.[195]

Person with intellectual disability may give evidence through live television link

In proceedings to which Part III applies a person under 18[196] years of age, and a person with a mental handicap irrespective of age may give evidence[197] through a live television link from either within or outside the state: (a) if the person is under 17 years of age unless the court sees good reason to the contrary, and (b) in any other case with the leave of the court.[198] The proceedings to which Part III applies include proceedings under section 4E (pre-trial dismissal) or 4F (deposition proceedings) of the Criminal Procedure Act 1967.[199] This evidence must be video-recorded.[200] While such evidence

---

sexual assault (within the meaning of s.2 of the Criminal Law (Rape) (Amendment) Act 1990, aggravated sexual assault (within the meaning of s.3 of the Act), rape under s.4 of the 1990 Act or an offence under s.3 of the Criminal Law (Amendment) Act 1885 (as amended by s.8 of the Criminal Law (Amendment) Act 1935) (procuring unlawful sexual intercourse with a woman by threats, fraud or administering alcoholic or other intoxicants or drugs), an offence under s.6 of the Criminal Law (Amendment) Act 1885 (as amended by s.9 of the Criminal Law Amendment Act 1935) (owner or occupier of premises permitting unlawful sexual intercourse with young girls on his premises), an offence under s.4 of the Criminal Law (Sexual Offences) Act 1993 (male person committing or attempting to commit acts of gross indecency with another male person under the age of 17), an offence under s.1 or 2 of the Punishment of Incest Act 1908 (s.1 is amended by s.12 of the Criminal Justice Act 1993 and s.5 of the Criminal Law (Incest) Proceedings Act 1995. S.2 is amended by s.12 of the Criminal Law (Amendment) Act 1935) (incest by males, or females over seventeen), an offence under s.17 of the Children Act 1908 as amended by s.11 of the Criminal Law (Amendment) 1935 (person causing, encouraging or favouring seduction or prostitution of young girl) or an offence under s.1, (unlawful sexual intercourse with girl under fifteen years of age) 2, (unlawful sexual intercourse with girl between 15 and 17 years of age) of the Criminal Law Amendment Act 1935 or an offence under s.5 of the Criminal Law (Sexual Offences) Act 1993 (sexual intercourse or buggery with a person who is mentally impaired, commission of an act of gross indecency with another male person who is mentally impaired) but not attempts to commit any of these offences.

[195] Criminal Evidence Act 1992, s.12 as amended by the Child Trafficking and Pornography Act 1998 s.10.

[196] *Ibid.*, Pt III as amended by Children Act 2001, s.257(3) which came into force on May 1, 2002. See Children Act 2001 (Commencement) Order 2002 (S.I. No. 151 of 2002).

[197] See Criminal Evidence Act 1992, ss.13 and 19.

[198] In *O'Sullivan v. Hamill* [1999] 2 I.R. 9 it was held that since s.13(1)(b) provided that evidence could be given by way of a live television link in all cases with the leave of the court the jurisdiction of the court to allow evidence to be given by way of television link was not based on a prior finding that the person involved had a mental handicap.

[199] Criminal Evidence Act 1992, s.13(1) as amended by Criminal Justice Act 1999, s.18(3).

[200] See Criminal Evidence Act 1992, s.13(2). "Video-recording" is defined by s.2 as meaning "any

is being given by live television link the judge, or the barrister or solicitor concerned in the examination of the witness are obliged not to wear a wig and gown.[201]

The question as to whether a judge should hold an inquiry into a person's intellectual disability prior to granting leave to a person to give evidence by video link was raised in *O'Sullivan v. Hamill*.[202] In that case the applicant was charged with having sexual intercourse with a person who was mentally impaired contrary to section 5(1) of the Sexual Offences Act 1993. The applicant wished the person with the mental impairment to give evidence and at first instance the trial judge ruled that she should be permitted to give evidence by live television link under the Criminal Evidence Act 1992. However, prior to making the order to this effect the judge did not hold any inquiry.

The applicant argued that the judge should have heard evidence to the effect that the victim had an intellectual disability prior to making the order. O'Higgins J. held that an inquiry to establish intellectual disability was necessary for unsworn evidence to be given since section 27(1) of the 1992 Act required the court to be satisfied that the person was "capable of giving an intelligible account of events which [were] relevant to the proceedings" However, the jurisdiction of the court to allow evidence to be given by video-link was not based on a prior finding that the person involved had an intellectual disability. The trial judge had the right to grant leave to give video link evidence not just in respect of mentally impaired witnesses but in any case where he felt there was good reason to do so. In this case good reason had been shown to exist.

Questions may be put through intermediary

Where a person is accused of an offence to which Part III applies and a person under the age of 18[203] years, or a person with mental handicap irrespective of age is giving, or is to give evidence through a live television link application may be made to the court by either the prosecution or the accused for questions to be put to the accused through an intermediary. The court may direct that the questions be so put, if it is satisfied that having regard to the age or mental condition of the witness the interests of justice require it.[204] The intermediary must be appointed by the court and must be a person who, in its opinion, is competent to act as such.[205] The questions put to a witness through the appointed intermediary, must be either in the words used by the questioner or so as to convey to the witness in a way, which is appropriate to his age and mental condition the meaning of the questions being asked.[206]

Requirement of notice of intention to adduce video evidence

Section 15 of the 1992 Act provides that where the prosecutor consents to the sending

---

recording, on any medium, from which a moving image may by any means be produced and includes the accompanying soundtrack (if any).".

[201] See Criminal Evidence Act 1992, ss.13(3) and 19. This requirement applies unless the evidence is being given through an intermediary pursuant to s.14(1).

[202] Unreported, High Court, February 25, 1998.

[203] Criminal Evidence Act 1992, Pt III as amended by the Children Act 2001 s.257(3).

[204] See Criminal Evidence Act 1992, s.14(1).

[205] *Ibid.*, s.14(3).

[206] *Ibid.*, s.14(2).

forward for trial of an accused person who is charged with an offence to which Part III applies under Part 1A of the Criminal Procedure Act 1967 and the person in respect of whom the offence is alleged to have been committed is under the age of 18[207] years, or is a person with mental handicap irrespective of age on the date consent is given to the accused being sent forward for trial and it is proposed that a video recording of a statement made by a person under the age of 18 years,[208] or a person with mental handicap irrespective age during an interview with a member of the Garda Síochána, or any other person who is competent for that purpose shall be given in evidence pursuant to section 16, the prosecutor must in addition to causing the documents specified in section 4B (1) of the Criminal Procedure Act 1967[209] to be served on the accused (i) notify the accused that it is proposed to give evidence of a video recording of the statement made during the interview and (ii) give the accused an opportunity of seeing the video recording of the interview.

Section 15(2) of the 1992 Act provides that if the person in respect of whom the offence is alleged to have been committed is available for cross examination at the hearing of an application under section 4E of the Criminal Procedure Act 1967 (application by accused for dismissal of a charge) the judge hearing the application may consider any statement made in relation to that offence by that person on a video recording mentioned in section 16(1)(b) of the 1992 Act.

Section 15(3) states that if the accused consents, an edited version of the video recording of an interview of a person under the age of 14 years or a person with mental handicap irrespective of age with a member of the Garda Síochána or any other person who is competent for that purpose under section 16(1)(b) of the 1992 Act may, with the leave of the judge hearing an application for dismissal of a charge under section 4E of the Criminal Procedure Act 1967, be shown at the hearing of the application and in that event, section 15(2) of the 1992 Act and section 16(1) (b) of the 1992 Act shall apply in relation to that version as it applies in relation to the original video recording.[210]

Admissibility of video evidence

Section 16(1) provides for the admissibility at the trial of an offence of (a) a video-recording of any evidence given by a person under 18[211] years, and a person with mental handicap irrespective of age through a live television link in proceedings under Part 1A of the Criminal Procedure Act 1967[212] in relation to an offence to which Part III of the

---

[207] *Ibid.*, Pt III as amended by Children Act 2001, s.257(3).
[208] *Ibid.*
[209] Where the prosecutor consents to the accused being sent forward for trial the prosecutor must, within 42 days after the accused first appears in the District Court charged with the indictable offence or with any extension of that period cause certain documents to be served on the accused or his solicitor if any. These are: (a) a statement of any charges against the accused; (b) a copy of any sworn information in writing upon which the proceedings were initiated; (c) a list of the witnesses the prosecutor proposed to call at the trial; (d) a statement of the evidence that is expected to be given by each of them; (e) a copy of any document containing information which it is proposed to give in evidence by virtue of Part II of the Criminal Evidence Act 1992; (f) where appropriate, a copy of a certificate under s.6(1) of that Act; (g) a list of the exhibits (if any).
[210] Criminal Evidence Act 1992 s.15 as amended by Criminal Justice Act 1999, s.19.
[211] *Ibid.*, Pt III as amended by Children Act 2001, s.257(3).
[212] *Ibid.*, s.16(1)(a) as amended by the Criminal Justice Act 1999, s.20(a). Pt 1A of the Criminal

1992 Act applies, and (b) a video-recording of any statement made by a person under 14 years of age, and a person with mental handicap irrespective of age during an interview with a member of the Garda Síochána or any other person who is competent[213] for such a purpose, where the person under the age of 14 years and the person with mental handicap irrespective of age is the person in respect of whom an offence to which Part III applies is alleged to have been committed. This video-recorded evidence is to be admissible at the trial as evidence of any fact stated therein of which direct oral evidence by the person concerned would be admissible.

Where the video recording is of a statement made by a person under the age of 14 years or a person with mental handicap irrespective of age during an interview with a member of the Garda Síochána or any other person who is competent for the purpose under (b) in the previous paragraph the person whose statement was video-recorded must be available for cross-examination at the trial.[214]

The video-recording or any part of same may not be admitted in evidence at the trial under section 16, if the court is of the opinion that in the interests of justice the video-recording or any part ought not to be admitted. In considering whether in the interests of justice the video-recording or part ought not to be admitted the court must have regard to all the circumstances including any risk that its admission will result in unfairness to the accused or any co-accused.[215]

In estimating the weight, if any, to be attached to any statement contained in such a video-recording the court must have regard to all the circumstances from which any inference can reasonably be drawn as to its accuracy or otherwise.[216] In this regard, "statement" includes any representation of fact, whether in words or otherwise.[217]

Transfer of proceedings to District or Circuit Court with necessary technical facilities

Section 17 enables the Circuit or District Court to transfer proceedings to which Part III of the Act applies to Circuit or District Court district which has the necessary technical facilities to allow evidence to be given through a live television link or by video-recording. It provides that in any proceedings for an offence to which Part III applies in any Circuit or District Court district in relation to which any of the provisions of sections 13 to 16 or section 29 (evidence through television link by persons outside the State) is not in operation the court concerned may, by order transfer the proceedings to a circuit or district court district in relation to which those provisions are in operation if in its opinion it is desirable that evidence be given in the proceedings through a live television link or by means of a video recording. Where such an order is made the jurisdiction of the court to which proceedings have been transferred may be exercised (a) in the case of the Circuit Court by the judge of the circuit concerned, and (b) in the case of the District

---

Evidence Act 1947 as inserted by s.9 of the Criminal Justice Act 1999 details the procedure to be followed in proceedings relating to indictable offences.

[213] No definition of the term competent is provided but it probably includes videos of interviews at assessment units where the possibility of abuse is investigated.

[214] Criminal Evidence Act 1992, s.16 as amended by the Criminal Justice Act 1999, s.20(b).

[215] *Ibid.*, s.16(2).

[216] *Ibid.*, s.16(3).

[217] *Ibid.*, s.16(4).

Court by the judge of that court for the time being assigned to the district court district concerned.

No need for victim to identify known accused

Section 18 of the Act relieves the alleged victim of an offence to which Part III of the 1992 Act applies who has given evidence through a live television link pursuant to section 13 of the Act of the necessity of identifying the accused in court in certain circumstances.

If evidence is given that the accused was known to the witness before the date on which the offence was alleged to have been committed the witness will not be required to identify the accused at the trial unless the court in the interests of justice directs otherwise. However, if the accused is not known to the accused the victim will have to identify the accused in court. Section 18(b (ii) provides by way of exception to the hearsay rule that where evidence is given by a person other than the witness that the witness identified the accused at an identification parade as being the offender that evidence is admissible as evidence that the accused was so identified.

Giving of evidence otherwise than on oath

Section 27 of the 1992 Act provides that notwithstanding any other enactments the evidence of a person under the age of 14 years and a person with mental handicap irrespective of age may be received in any criminal proceedings otherwise than on oath or affirmation if the court is satisfied that the person concerned is capable of giving an intelligible account of events which are relevant to those proceedings. It is the court's duty to decide whether the person has a mental handicap and whether the person with mental handicap is capable of giving an intelligent account of events relevant to the proceedings.[218] Section 27(2) provides that if any person whose evidence is received in this way makes a statement material in the proceedings concerned which he knows to be false or does not believe to be true that person shall be guilty of an offence and on conviction shall be liable to be dealt with as if he had been guilty of perjury.

Commentary

At common law a person with mental disability may only give evidence if s/he understands not only the duty to tell the truth but also the extra obligation and sanction involved in the oath or affirmation. However, a person may be quite capable of giving an accurate account of what happened even if s/he understands neither of these concepts.

Secondly, the Criminal Evidence Act 1992 applies to persons with "mental handicap." It would appear therefore that its provisions would not be available to persons who are impaired through mental illness. However since there no settled definition of handicap the issue is complicated. The United Nations Standard, rules of the Equalisation of Opportunities for Persons with Disabilities, describe "handicap" as in terms of the relationship between the disabled person and his/her environment. It is a loss or limitation

---

[218] *O'Sullivan v. Hamill* [1999] 2 I.R. 9.

of opportunities to take part in community life at an equal level with others. The Law Reform Commission in its report *Sexual Offences Against the Mentally Handicapped*[219] on the other hand had defined handicap in terms of IQ following a World Health Organisation classification. According to the WHO classification, there a four categories of handicap on a continuum from mild (IQ range 50 to 70) to profound (IQ range less than 20). The Law Reform Commission noted that this classification extends to those whose mental condition may be affected by mental illness. The Commission's report was presented to the Government in 1990. It may be that the Government intended the word "handicap" to include mental illness but the issue is not clear.

Thirdly, despite legislative reforms a plaintiff with mental disability may not be able to persuade a lawyer to file suit on his/her behalf where the plaintiff's credibility on the stand will be an important factor in the case. There may also be instances where the prosecution will not go ahead if a witness is mentally disabled and lacks credibility on the stand. It is submitted that in such cases expert witnesses could play a greater role in explaining the precise nature of the plaintiff's or prosecution witness's mental disability to the lawyer or prosecuting authority so as to maintain the credibility of the person with mental disability.

Enforcement against a person with mental disability

A stay of execution may be granted in cases where judgment is obtained against a defendant who is under a mental disability.[220] This is to enable the receiver of the income to make an application to a judge exercising the wards of court jurisdiction for leave to pay the amount of the judgment debt out of the ward's estate.[221] Where judgment creditor obtains a charging order against the property of a person with mental disorder under the general enactments relating to execution the court has no power to make an order providing that the amount to be charged shall be determined by a judge exercising the wards of court jurisdiction as the judgment creditor is entitled to an unconditional order.[222]

Mental incapacity is not a bar to being made bankrupt nor in itself to the to the granting of an injunction or the enforcing of an order. However if a person against whom an injunction is being sought is incapable of understanding what he is doing or that it is wrong there is English authority to the effect that an injunction ought not to be granted against him because he would not be capable of complying with it and it would have no deterrent effect. Furthermore any breach by him would not be subject to effective enforcement proceedings since he would have a clear defence to an application for committal for contempt.[223] It has been suggested that the appropriate way of restraining unsocial behaviour by a person who is under a disability by reason of mental incapacity, is the use of mental health legislation powers under but that a limited interlocutory injunction might be appropriate while the mental condition of the person concerned is being investigated.[224]

---

[219] LRC 33–1990 para.23.

[220] See *Burt v. Blackburn* (1887) 3 T.L.R. 356.

[221] See *Ames v. Parkinson* (1847) 2 Ph .388.

[222] See *Horne v. Pountain* (1889) 23 Q.B.D. 264.

[223] *Wookey v. Wookey, In re S (A Minor)* [1991] Fam. 121; [1991] 3 All E.R .365.

[224] *Wookey v. Wookey, In re S (A Minor)* [1991] 3 All E.R. 365 at 371–372.

Miscellaneous Public Law Impacts

Legal capacity and personal mobility – driving

It is an offence to drive a motor vehicle on the road unless the driver holds a licence authorising him to drive a vehicle of the class so driven.[225] However, a licensing authority may refuse to issue a licence to a person who suffers from a relevant disability.[226] Vehicles are divided into categories and sub categories for driver licensing purposes. The categories are based primarily on the type and degree of driving skills and experience, which a driver requires. For the purpose of assessing the medical fitness of drivers, however, vehicles are divided into two broad groups, which are based on the mental and physical demands placed on the driver of the vehicle and on the potential danger in the event of loss of control of by the driver. The grouping is as follows:

Group 1 comprising the licensing categories A, AI, B, EB, M and W[227] – which are (generally) motorcycles, cars and tractors (with or without trailers).

Group 2 comprising the licensing categories C, C1, D, D1, EC, EC1, ED, OR ED1[228] – which are (generally) trucks and buses (with or without a trailer).[229]

The vehicles in Group 2 are regarded as higher risk vehicles, which require a higher standard of physical and mental fitness on the part of the driver.

---

[225] Road Traffic Act 1961, s.38.

[226] *Ibid.*, ss 23 and 32.

[227] Category A are motorcycles. Category A1 are motor vehicles with an engine capacity not exceeding 125 cubic centimetres and with a power rating not exceeding 11 kilowatts. Category B are vehicles (other than motorcycles, mopeds, work vehicles or land tractors) having a design gross vehicle weight not exceeding 3,500 kg., and having passenger accommodation for not more than 8 persons and where the design gross vehicle weight of the trailer is not greater than 750 kg. Category EB are vehicles in category B with a trailer attached where the design gross vehicle weight of the trailer is not greater than 750 kg. Category M are mopeds and Category W are work vehicles and land tractors. See Road Traffic (Licensing of Drivers) Regulations 1999 (S.I. No. 352 of 1999), art.5 as amended by Road Traffic Licensing of Drivers) (Amendment) Regulations 2004 (S.I. No. 705 of 2004), art.3(b). See Preface.

[228] Category C are vehicles other than work vehicles or land tractors having a design gross vehicle weight exceeding 3,500 kg and having passenger accommodation for not more than 8 persons and where the design gross vehicle weight of the trailer is not greater than 750 kg. Category C1 are vehicles in category C having a design gross vehicles weight not exceeding 7,500kg where the design gross vehicle weight of the trailer is not greater than 750 kg. Category D are vehicles having passenger accommodation for more than 8 persons and where the design gross vehicle weight of the trailer is not greater than 750 kg. Category D1 are vehicles in Category D having passenger accommodation for not more than 16 persons. Category EC are vehicles in category C with a trailer attached. Category EC1 are vehicles in category C1 with a trailer attached having a combined gross weight not exceeding 12,000 kg Category ED are vehicles in category D with a trailer attached and where the design gross vehicle weight of the trailer is not greater than 750 kg. Category ED1 are vehicles in category D1 with a trailer attached having a combined design gross vehicle weight not exceeding 12,000 kg and where the design gross vehicle weight of the trailer is not greater than 750 kg. See Road Traffic (Licensing of Drivers) Regulations 1999 (S.I. No. 352 of 1999), art.5 as amended by Road Traffic Licensing of Drivers) (Amendment) Regulations 2004 (S.I. No. 705 of 2004), art.3(b). See Preface.

[229] See *Medical Aspects of Driver Licensing: A Guide for Registered Medical Practitioners* (Department of the Environment and Local Government November 1999), p.3.

The distinction between the two groups in practical medical terms is that a person seeking a Group 1 licence generally merely needs to undergo an eyesight test, conducted by an optician or physician whereas a person seeking a Group 2 licence must undergo a full medical examination conducted and recorded by a registered medical practitioner. However where a person is over 70 years of age or suffers from any of the disabilities requiring a medical report s/he must undergo a medical examination and an eyesight test even if s/he is only applying for a Group 1 licence.[230]

Section 32 of the Road Traffic Act 1961 prohibits a person who is suffering from a physical or mental disease or disability as defined by the Minister from holding a driving licence for the period of the disability. This provision applies also to provisional driving licences.[231] Regulation 9 of Road Traffic (Licensing of Drivers) Regulations 1999,[232] and the Second Schedule to the statutory instrument prescribe dependence on or regular abuse of psychotropic substances[233] as a disease or disability that completely disqualify a person from holding a licence.

An applicant for a driving licence must declare that to the best of his knowledge and belief he is not suffering from any of the diseases specified in the Second and Third Schedules to Road Traffic (Licensing of Drivers) Regulations 1999;[234] that he has not suffered in the past from epilepsy or alcoholism and that he is not taking on a regular basis drugs or medicaments which would be likely to cause the driving of a vehicle by him in a public place to be a source of danger to the public.[235] The Second Schedule to the Statutory Instrument specifies dependence on or regular abuse of psychotropic substances as a disqualifying disease or disability. The Third Schedule to the Statutory Instrument specifies a number of diseases or disabilities where a medical report is required. These include alcoholism, any illness which requires the regular use of psychotropic substances; any illness or disease which requires the regular use of medications likely to affect ability to drive safely; epilepsy; encephalitis, multiple sclerosis, myasthenia gravis or hereditary diseases of the nervous system associated with progressive muscular atrophy and congenital-myotonic disorders; diseases of the peripheral nervous system; trauma of the central or peripheral nervous system; cerbrovascular diseases; mental disturbance due to disease or trauma of or operation upon the central nervous system; severe mental retardation, psychosis, and psychoneurosis or personality disorders.

---

[230] *Ibid.*, p.6.

[231] Road Traffic Act 1994, s.29 and the Road Traffic (Licensing of Drivers) Regulations 1999 (S.I. No. 352 of 1999), art.19.

[232] S.I. No.352 of 1999.

[233] Psychotropic substances are any substances which affect the functioning of the mind through chemical action on the central nervous system.

[234] S.I. No.352 of 1999.

[235] *Ibid.*, art.15(1). In *Devon CC v. Hawkins* [1967] 2 K.B. 26, it was held that a person who had successfully controlled his epileptic fits with drugs for two years was still suffering from epilepsy and was obliged to make disclosure. However, in *Balmer v. Hayes* (1950) S.C. 947, it was held that where a bus driver failed to disclose epilepsy lost consciousness and caused injury, his failure to disclose the illness in itself did not confer a right of action in damages to a third party. Finally in *Swift v. Norfolk CC* [1955] Crim. L.R. it was held that a person who is subject to periodic attacks of unconsciousness is not fit to hold a driving licence.

Requirement for a medical report

Where an application form for a provisional licence or licence does not contain the required declaration mentioned above then the applicant for a driving licence concerned will be required to submit a medical report with his/her application for a licence.[236] This medical report is also required where the applicant is suffering from any of the diseases mentioned in the Third Schedule of the Road Traffic (Licensing of Drivers) Regulations 1999,[237] or where the applicant has suffered in the past from epilepsy or alcoholism, or takes on a regular basis drugs or medicaments which would be likely to cause the driving of a vehicle by him in a public place to be a source of danger to the public. A medical report is further required where the application is for a provisional licence for Group 2 category vehicles unless the licensing authority is satisfied that a medical report previously submitted by the applicant is still applicable. A medical report is also required where the application is an application for a driving licence for any of the aforementioned categories unless the licensing authority is satisfied that the applicant has either previously submitted a medical report (i) in connection with a driving licence application in respect of any of the above mentioned categories, or (ii) within the preceding year in connection with a provisional licence application in respect of any of the said categories.[238] The medical report to accompany an application for a provisional licence or a driving licence must be provided by a medical practitioner and be dated not more than one month prior to the application. It must indicate that in the opinion of the registered medical practitioner (a) that the applicant meets the minimum standards of physical and mental fitness specified in Schedule 6 to the 1999 Regulations and is fit to drive vehicles of the category to which the application relates and (b) that the applicant does not appear to requires medical review during the period in respect of which the licence is sought.[239] A certificate of fitness may be provided by an applicant in lieu of a medical report for the purposes of article 42 of the 1999 Regulations and references in the 1999 Regulations to a medical report are to be so construed with the appropriate modifications.[240]

    The minimum standards of fitness with which the applicant must comply are specified in the Sixth Schedule to the Road Traffic (Licensing of Drivers) Regulations 1999.[241]

---

[236] Road Traffic (Licensing of Drivers) Regulations 1999 (S.I. No. 352 of 1999), art.42.

[237] There are 20 of these: (1) alcoholism; (2) any physical disablement which is likely to affect ability to drive safely; (3) any illness which requires the regular use of psychotropic substances; (4) any illness or disease which requires the regular use of medications likely to affect ability to drive safely; (5) cardiovascular disease; (6) diplopia, defective binocular vision or loss of visual field; (7) serious hearing deficiency; (8) diabetes; (9) epilepsy; (10) encephalitis, multiple sclerosis, myasthenia gravis or hereditary diseases of the nervous system associated with progressive muscular atrophy and congenital myotonic disorders; (11) diseases of the peripheral nervous system; (12) trauma of the central or peripheral nervous system (13) cerebrovascular diseases; (14) lesion with damage to spinal cord and resultant paraplegia; (15) mental disturbance due to disease or trauma of or operation upon the central nervous system, (16) severe mental retardation; (17) psychosis; (18) psycho neurosis or personality disorders, (19) serious disease of the blood; (20) any disease of the genito-urinary system (including renal disorder) which is likely to affect ability to drive safely.

[238] Road Traffic (Licensing of Drivers) Regulations 1999 (S.I. No.352 of 1999), art.42(1).

[239] *Ibid.*, art.42(2).

[240] *Ibid.*, art.42(4).

[241] S.I No. 352 of 1999. An explanatory leaflet entitled "Guide for Registered Medical Practitioners"

The preamble to Part 2 of the Sixth Schedule is instructive as to the general approach to be taken to physical and mental fitness to drive. It states that driving is more comfortable and safe if all medical conditions are under optimal control. Specialist opinion may be helpful in cases of doubt, not only to help decision-making when driving may no longer be safe but also to ensure a maximisation of health status and the provision of relevant compensatory measures such as spectacles, car choice, vehicle adaptation and physiotherapy.

General health issues which the medical practitioner must take into account

In paragraph 1 of Part 2 of the Sixth Schedule – a general provision – it is stated that in the case of an applicant for a licence to drive a vehicle of any category the medical examination shall take account of, *inter alia*,[242] the condition of the applicant's nervous system and the condition of his/her mental system insofar as any condition or abnormality in any one or more of these aspects of the applicant's condition would affect the applicant's fitness to drive safely vehicles of the category specified in the application having regard to: (a) the ability of the person concerned, physically and mentally to operate efficiently and safely the controls of the vehicle and to continue so to operate the controls over a reasonable period; (b) the susceptibility of the person concerned to sudden incapacity such as loss of consciousness, fainting or giddiness, which might affect such person's ability to operate the controls of the vehicle so as to bring the vehicle to a stop safely and (c) the susceptibility of the person concerned to fatigue such that that person's ability to operate the controls of the vehicle might be seriously impaired.[243] Fitness to drive must not be certified in the case of an applicant to drive a vehicle of any category who suffers from any condition or abnormality, *inter alia*, of the nervous or mental system to such an extent that the driving by the applicant of the vehicles of the category to which the application relates would be a danger to the applicant or other road users.[244] The Regulations, however, do not offer specific guidelines as to the general physical and mental conditions would render an applicant for a driving licence a danger to himself or herself or to other road users and this may pose a problem for medical practitioner relying on these provisions to assess a person's capacity to drive.[245]

---

which details the standards of fitness with which drivers must comply has been issued to members of the profession by the Department of the Environment in 1999.

[242] The other aspects of the applicant's physical and mental condition to be taken into account at the medical examination are: ear conditions (vertigo and labyrinthine conditions), general physique and physical disabilities, conditions of the cardio-vascular system, condition of the haemopoietic system, condition of the endocrine system, condition of the respiratory system, condition of the gastro-intestinal system, and condition of the genito-urinary system. See Road Traffic (Licensing of Drivers) Regulations 1999 (S.I. No.352 of 1999), sch.6, Pt 2, para.1(1).

[243] Road Traffic (Licensing of Drivers) Regulations 1999 (S.I No. 352 of 1999), sch.6, Pt 2, para.1(1).

[244] Road Traffic (Licensing of Drivers) Regulations 1999 (S.I No. 352 of 1999), sch.6, Pt 2, para.1(2).

[245] See S. Mills, *Clinical Practise and the Law* (Butterworths Dublin, 2002), p.389 In contrast Mills points out that the UK Driver and Vehicle Licensing Authority Regulations are a valuable resource which may be consulted by medical practitioners except where they conflict with the Irish Regulations as they do in the case of epilepsy.

Relevant of diseases of the nervous system

In the case of an applicant for a licence to drive a vehicle of any category who suffers from (a) encephalitis, multiple sclerosis, myasthenia gravis or hereditary diseases of the nervous system associated with progressive muscular atrophy and congenital myotonic disorders, (b) diseases of the peripheral nervous system, or (c) trauma of the central or nervous system fitness to drive may only be certified for a limited period so as to ensure that the applicant remains under medical supervision. Neurological disturbances associated with diseases or surgical intervention affecting the central or peripheral nervous system, which lead to sensory or motor deficiencies and affect balance and co-ordination, must be taken into account in relation to their functional effects and the risks of progression. In such cases and in the event of risk of deterioration, fitness to drive may be certified for a limited period only.[246]

With effect from November 15, 2004 where an applicant to drive a Group 1 vehicle, suffers or has suffered in the past from epilepsy, fitness to drive may be certified for a limited period where the applicant: (i) has not suffered any epileptic attack during the 12 months preceding the date of the medical examination; (ii) has only nocturnal seizures over a period of two years preceding the date of medical examination and certification is by a consultant neurologist; (iii) has only had a single provoked seizure and such seizure was prior to the six month period preceding the date of the medical examination and certification is by a consultant neurologist or (iv) has only simple partial seizures where awareness is fully maintained at all times and certification is by a consultant neurologist. Fitness to drive may not be certified in relation to Group 3 vehicles.[247]

Where an applicant for a licence to drive Group 1 vehicles suffers from a cerebro-vascular disease, fitness to drive may be certified (a) provided that where necessary, the controls of the vehicle to be driven are suitably rearranged or modified or a suitable special type of vehicle is used, and (b) for a limited period only so as to ensure that the applicant remains under medical supervision.[248]

Relevance of mental disorders

Where a person suffers from a mental disorder no standard is specified and no psychiatric conditions is expressly listed as being a bar to certification of fitness to drive. Instead in the case of an applicant to drive Group 1 vehicles the medical practitioner in conducting a medical examination must take due account of: (a) severe mental disturbance whether congenital or due to disease, trauma or neurosurgical operation on the central nervous system; (b) severe mental retardation, (c) psychosis, which in particular has caused general paralysis or (d) severe behavioural problems due to dementia, psychoneurosis or personality defects or disorders leading to seriously impaired judgement, behaviour or adaptability If necessary certification must be for a limited period only when deemed necessary to permit regular review.[249] In the case of an applicant for a licence to drive

---

[246] Road Traffic (Licensing of Drivers) Regulations 1999 (S.I. No. 352 of 1999), sch.6, Pt 2, para.6.

[247] Road Traffic (Licensing of Drivers) Regulations 1999 (S.I. No. 352 of 1999), sch.6, Pt 2, para.6 as amended by Road Traffic (Licensing of Drivers) (Amendment) Regulations 2004 (S.I. No. 705 of 2004), art.3(o).

[248] *Ibid.*, sch.6, Pt 2, para.6(3).

[249] *Ibid.*, sch.6, Pt 2, para.7(1).

Group 2 vehicles who suffers from any of the above disorders, the medical examination shall take due account of the additional risks and dangers involved in the driving of such vehicles.

Relevance of consumption of alcohol

In the case where an applicant who applies for a licence to drive vehicles of any category suffers from or has suffered in the past from alcoholism, fitness to drive may be certified for a limited period only, so as to ensure that the applicant remains under medical supervision.[250]

Relevance of taking drugs and medications

The 1999 Regulations also addresses the issue of drugs (prescription and illicit) and medications. The regulations first deal with the abuse of psyschotropic substances, and state that where an applicant who applies for a licence to drive vehicles of any category, fitness to drive cannot be certified if the applicant concerned is dependent on psychotropic substances or, if the person is no dependent on such substances, regularly abuses them.[251] The regulations then address regular use of psychotropic substances and state that in the case of an applicant for a licence to drive Group 1 vehicles fitness to drive will not be certified if the person concerned regularly uses psychotropic substances, in whatever form, which can hamper the ability to drive safely where the quantities absorbed are such as to have an adverse effect on driving. This applies also to all other medications or combination of medications, which affect the ability to drive.[252] In the case of an applicant for a licence to drive Group 2 vehicles who regularly uses psychotropic substances or medications the medical examination must take due account of the additional risks and dangers involved in the driving of such vehicles.[253]

One of the difficulties with this provision is that "psychotropic" is not defined. It is not clear if it includes prescribed medications such as anti-depressants, short acting sleeping tablets or anti-psychotic medication by way of depot injection. Mills points out that the UK DVLA Medical Guidelines provide that "the prescribed use of [benzo-diazepines] at therapeutic doses without evidence of impairment does not amount to misuse/dependency for licensing purposes." He suggests that "it would probably follow in Ireland that prescribed psychoactive medications at therapeutic doses without any evidence of impairment of concentration or reaction are not "psychotropic" drugs for the purposes of the regulations."[254]

Other instances where a medical report is required

A medical report is also required where the applicant is a person in respect of whom a certificate of competency is deferred pending production of a certificate of fitness.[255]

---

[250] *Ibid.*, sch.6, Pt 2, para.8.
[251] *Ibid.*, sch.6, Pt 2, para.9(1).
[252] *Ibid.*, sch.6, Pt 2, para.9(2)(a).
[253] *Ibid.*, sch.6, Pt 2, para 9(2)(b).
[254] See S. Mills, *op. cit.*, p.393.
[255] Road Traffic Act 1961, s.33(4).

The latter circumstance may arise where a driver tester forms the opinion in the course of a driving test that an applicant may be suffering from some disability which may affect his ability to drive safely and may defer a decision on the application for certificate of competency until that person produces a certificate of fitness. A certificate of fitness may also be required where a person is disqualified from holding a licence pending a certificate of fitness.[256] Where a person is disqualified under section 32 of the 1961 Act from holding a licence s/he may not apply for a certificate of fitness under section 34.[257]

Outcome of medical assessment

A medical practitioner has a number of options where s/he has completed an assessment of fitness to drive. S/he may refuse to certify fitness where the patient would be a danger on the road. S/he may indicate that the applicant's fitness to drive does not need further review in the foreseeable future based on the information available to him/her and the clinical findings at the time of assessment or s/he may certify fitness for a limited period only. The available options are one, three or ten year periods.

The certificate of fitness

An application for a Certificate of Fitness is made to the Minister[258] on a specified form,[259] with the medical report[260] from a registered medical practitioner stating that s/he has examined the applicant as to the relevant aspects of the physical and mental condition.[261] The certificate of fitness must certify that the person as being fit to drive for an unlimited period or for a limited period of not less than one year from the date of issue.[262] The certificate must be submitted to the licensing authority within six months of the date of issue.[263]

An application for a certificate of fitness based on a medical report may be granted, refused or deferred pending production of a certificate of competency.[264] If the grant of the certificate is refused no subsequent application may be made for a further six months unless the applicant makes a successful appeal to the District Court.[265] A decision to defer the grant of a certificate of fitness pending production of a certificate of competency may also be appealed. On appeal the District Court Judge may either refuse the

---

[256] Road Traffic Act 1961, s.34(2).

[257] *Ibid.*, s.34(2). S.34 applies to provisional driving licences as it applies to driving licences. See Road Traffic Act 1994, s.29, Road Traffic (Licensing of Drivers) Regulations 1999 (S.I. No. 352 of 1999), art.19.

[258] The form is sent to the Drivers Fitness Section, Department of the Environment, O'Connell Bridge House Dublin 2.

[259] Form D502.

[260] Form D501.

[261] See s.34(3) of the Road Traffic Act 1961. The relevant aspects of his physical and mental condition which are to be considered in the case of an application for a certificate of fitness are specified in the Road Traffic (Licensing of Drivers) Regulations 1999 (S.I. No. 352 of 1999), art. 34, 42(4) and the Sixth Schedule thereto.

[262] Road Traffic (Licensing of Drivers) Regulations 1999 (S.I. No.352 of 1999), art.37(2).

[263] *Ibid.*, art.37(3).

[264] Road Traffic Act 1961, s.34(4).

[265] Road Traffic (Licensing of Drivers) Regulations 1999 (S.I. No.352 of 1999), art.40(2).

appeal or give such direction to the Minister as s/he considers just and the Minister must comply with that direction.[266] The decision of the District Judge is final and unappealable.[267]

In the English case of *Devon County Council v. Hawkins*,[268] the applicant had suffered from epilepsy but his last fit had occurred two years prior to his application. He claimed that the risk of his having another attack was practically eliminated so long as he continued to take the necessary drugs. The court upheld the licensing authority's refusal to grant a licence as for so long as drugs were necessary to prevent the manifestation of the disease, the disease remained. However, by contrast, in *In re Leddington's Application*,[269] on appeal from a licensing authority's refusal of a licence magistrates in similar circumstances considered whether given the fact that the appellant had received treatment and was taking drugs to prevent the repetition of fits the appellant still "suffered" from epilepsy within the meaning of section 5 of the English Road Traffic Act 1930. The Magistrates allowed the appeal.[270]

Disqualifications

When an officer of the Garda Síochána or the appropriate licensing authority has reasonable grounds[271] for believing that a licensed driver is unfit to drive by reason of disease or physical or mental disability, s/he or the licensing authority may apply to the District Court where the person ordinarily resides for a special disqualification order disqualifying that person from holding a driving licence[272] or a provisional licence.[273] Ten days written notice must be given to the driver.[274] If the District Justice is satisfied that the allegation of unfitness by reason of disease or physical or mental disability is proved he may declare the person is disqualified from holding a driving licence until he produces a certificate of fitness to the appropriate licensing authority.[275] The disqualification may be general or relate to such class or classes of vehicle covered by the application.[276] Appeal lies to the Circuit Court.[277] Details of the special disqualification must also be endorsed on the licence.[278] On the making of the disqualification order, a driving licence held by the applicant at the date of the order is suspended.[279]

---

[266] Road Traffic Act 1961, s.34(5)(a).

[267] *Ibid.*, s.34(5)(b).

[268] [1967] 1 All E.R. 235.

[269] [1958] Crim L.R. 550.

[270] Although their reasoning is not clear from the report presumably they decided that L was not suffering from epilepsy.

[271] What amounts to reasonable grounds is a matter of fact for the court.

[272] Road Traffic Act 1961, s.28(1).

[273] See Road Traffic Act 1994, s.29, Road Traffic (Licensing of Drivers) Regulations 1999 (S.I. No. 352 of 1999) which apply Road Traffic Act, ss 28(1), (3), (4), (5) to provisional licences.

[274] Road Traffic Act 1961, s.28(3).

[275] *Ibid.*, s.28(1).

[276] *Ibid.*, s.28(1).

[277] *Ibid.*, s.28(4). The appeal is by way of full rehearing and the Court may annul, vary or confirm the order. By virtue of s.124 of the Road Traffic Act 1961 special disqualification orders may not remitted by the Minister for Justice in exercise of his powers under s.23 of the Criminal Justice Act 1951.

[278] See Road Traffic Act 1961, s.36(4).

[279] Road Traffic Act 1961, s.30(1).

Commentary

In England and Wales the only prescribed disabilities are severe mental handicap as a result of which the patient is under guardianship or receiving local authority care and epilepsy unless the patient has been free from attacks for two years or had had attacks only while asleep for the previous three years.[280] An applicant for a driving licence must disclose any prescribed disability as must a licence holder if he acquires one or it gets worse.[281] On learning of such a disability the Department must refuse or revoke a licence.

It has been argued that the Irish regulations are too oppressive of those who suffer from epilepsy.[282] As has been pointed out in the previous paragraph greater latitude is afforded in England and Wales to persons who suffer only from night-time seizures and a person who has attacks only while asleep during the three years prior to apply for a licence may obtain a Group 1 licence. In addition applicants are not absolutely excluded (as they are in Ireland) from obtaining a Group 2 licence solely because they have suffered from epilepsy at some time in the past. Instead a person who has been free from fits for ten years or more without medication may apply for a Group 2 licence. This approach appears to achieve a better balance between upholding the disabled persons rights and guarding against dangers on the road than the Irish blanket and (it appears) status based exclusion.

In the USA the capriciousness of state systems which allow individuals who have repeatedly had accidents while under the influence to drive but deny the privilege to persons with controlled epilepsy who have near perfect driving records[283] has been criticised. It has been pointed out that this situation prevails even where there are not reliable data linking any known disease or condition except alcoholism to increased accidents.[284] In the USA the American Bar Association's Commission for the Mentally Disabled have identified three elements, which should be included in a good piece of legislation relating to driver licensing. First licensing should be based on a functional ability to drive and not a determination of whether a person belongs to a particular category of people. Secondly determinations should be made individually according to established procedures and thirdly each person should have a meaningful opportunity to challenge adverse determinations in administrative hearings.[285] The highlighting of such substantive elements in Irish licensing procedures would be a welcome development.

---

[280] Motor Vehicle (Driving Licence) Regulations 1987, reg.24 amended by S.I. No.373 of 1989, reg.24.
[281] Road Traffic Act 1988, s.92.
[282] See Mills, *op. cit.*, p.391.
[283] See *Ormond v. Garrett* 175 S.E. 2d 371 (North Carolina Court of Appeal 1970); *Geen v. Foschio* No. Civ. 82-83B (c) 6 M.D.L.R. 253 (W.D.N.Y May 4 1982); *Rodriguez v. Miera* No. 78 P. 2 M.D.L.R. 565 (D.N.M. April 11, 1978) (consent judgment).
[284] See R.C. Allen, E.Z. Ferster and H. Weihofen, *Mental Impairment and Legal Incompetency* 345 (Prentice Hall, New Jersey, 1968).
[285] See Sales Powell Van Duizend and Associates, *Disabled Persons and the Law* (Plenum, New York, London, 1982).

Legal capacity and the right to bear arms

Section 8 of the Firearms Act 1925[286] provides that a person of unsound is disentitled to hold a firearm certificate or permit in relation to any firearm or ammunition.

Legal capacity and passports

Where a person by virtue of his/her mental disability is unable to sign a passport application form a declaration signed by a parent, medical practitioner or social worker who is responsible for his/her welfare may be accepted.[287] The signatory should explain in a separate letter that the applicant is mentally disabled and that the signatory has signed on the applicant's behalf.

---

[286] As amended by Firearms Act 1964, s.17.

[287] See s.7 of Form PAS 1 issued by the Department of Foreign Affairs.

Appendices

European Convention for the Protection of Human Rights and Fundamental Freedoms and Protocols

thereto as contained in the Schedules to the European Convention on Human Rights Act 2003

SCHEDULE 1

CONVENTION FOR THE PROTECTION OF HUMAN RIGHTS AND
FUNDAMENTAL FREEDOMS
Rome, 4.XI.1950

THE GOVERNMENTS SIGNATORY HERETO, being members of the Council of Europe,

Considering the Universal Declaration of Human Rights proclaimed by the General Assembly of the United Nations on 10th December 1948;

Considering that this Declaration aims at securing the universal and effective recognition and observance of the Rights therein declared;

Considering that the aim of the Council of Europe is the achievement of greater unity between its members and that one of the methods by which that aim is to be pursued is the maintenance and further realisation of human rights and fundamental freedoms;

Reaffirming their profound belief in those fundamental freedoms which are the foundation of justice and peace in the world and are best maintained on the one hand by an effective political democracy and on the other by a common understanding and observance of the human rights upon which they depend;

Being resolved, as the governments of European countries which are like-minded and have a common heritage of political traditions, ideals, freedom and the rule of law, to take the first steps for the collective enforcement of certain of the rights stated in the Universal Declaration,

Have agreed as follows:

Article 1[1] **Obligation to respect human rights**

The High Contracting Parties shall secure to everyone within their jurisdiction the rights and freedoms defined in Section I of this Convention.

SECTION I:[2] RIGHTS AND FREEDOMS

Article 2[3] **Right to life**

1. Everyone's right to life shall be protected by law. No one shall be deprived of his life intentionally save in the execution of a sentence of a court following his conviction of a crime for which this penalty is provided by law.

2. Deprivation of life shall not be regarded as inflicted in contravention of this article when it results from the use of force which is no more than absolutely necessary:

    a. in defence of any person from unlawful violence;

    b. in order to effect a lawful arrest or to prevent the escape of a person lawfully detained;

    c. in action lawfully taken for the purpose of quelling a riot or insurrection.

Article 3[4] **Prohibition of torture**

No one shall be subjected to torture or to inhuman or degrading treatment or punishment.

Article 4[5] **Prohibition of slavery and forced labour**

1. No one shall be held in slavery or servitude.

2. No one shall be required to perform forced or compulsory labour.

3. For the purpose of this article the term "forced or compulsory labour" shall not include:

    a. any work required to be done in the ordinary course of detention imposed according to the provisions of Article 5 of this Convention or during conditional release from such detention;

    b. any service of a military character or, in case of conscientious objectors in countries where they are recognised, service exacted instead of compulsory military service;

    c. any service exacted in case of an emergency or calamity threatening the life or well-being of the community;

    d. any work or service which forms part of normal civic obligations.

---

[1] Heading added according to the provisions of Protocol No.11(ETS No.155).
[2] *Ibid.*
[3] *Ibid.*
[4] *Ibid.*
[5] *Ibid.*

Article 5[6] **Right to liberty and security**

1. Everyone has the right to liberty and security of person. No one shall be deprived of his liberty save in the following cases and in accordance with a procedure prescribed by law:

    a. the lawful detention of a person after conviction by a competent court;

    b. the lawful arrest or detention of a person for non-compliance with the lawful order of a court or in order to secure the fulfilment of any obligation prescribed by law;

    c. the lawful arrest or detention of a person effected for the purpose of bringing him before the competent legal authority on reasonable suspicion of having committed an offence or when it is reasonably considered necessary to prevent his committing an offence or fleeing after having done so;

    d. the detention of a minor by lawful order for the purpose of educational supervision or his lawful detention for the purpose of bringing him before the competent legal authority;

    e. the lawful detention of persons for the prevention of the spreading of infectious diseases, of persons of unsound mind, alcoholics or drug addicts or vagrants;

    f. the lawful arrest or detention of a person to prevent his effecting an unauthorised entry into the country or of a person against whom action is being taken with a view to deportation or extradition.

2. Everyone who is arrested shall be informed promptly, in a language which he understands, of the reasons for his arrest and of any charge against him.

3. Everyone arrested or detained in accordance with the provisions of paragraph 1.c of this article shall be brought promptly before a judge or other officer authorised by law to exercise judicial power and shall be entitled to trial within a reasonable time or to release pending trial. Release may be conditioned by guarantees to appear for trial.

4. Everyone who is deprived of his liberty by arrest or detention shall be entitled to take proceedings by which the lawfulness of his detention shall be decided speedily by a court and his release ordered if the detention is not lawful.

5. Everyone who has been the victim of arrest or detention in contravention of the provisions of this article shall have an enforceable right to compensation.

Article 6[7] **Right to a fair trial**

1. In the determination of his civil rights and obligations or of any criminal charge against him, everyone is entitled to a fair and public hearing within a reasonable time by an independent and impartial tribunal established by law. Judgment shall be pronounced publicly but the press and public may be excluded from all or part of the trial in the interests of morals, public order or national security in a democratic

---

[6] *Ibid.*

[7] *Ibid.*

society, where the interests of juveniles or the protection of the private life of the parties so require, or to the extent strictly necessary in the opinion of the court in special circumstances where publicity would prejudice the interests of justice.

2. Everyone charged with a criminal offence shall be presumed innocent until proved guilty according to law.

3. Everyone charged with a criminal offence has the following minimum rights:

    a. to be informed promptly, in a language which he understands and in detail, of the nature and cause of the accusation against him;

    b. to have adequate time and facilities for the preparation of his defence;

    c. to defend himself in person or through legal assistance of his own choosing or, if he has not sufficient means to pay for legal assistance, to be given it free when the interests of justice so require;

    d. to examine or have examined witnesses against him and to obtain the attendance and examination of witnesses on his behalf under the same conditions as witnesses against him;

    e. to have the free assistance of an interpreter if he cannot understand or speak the language used in court.

Article 7[8] No punishment without law

1. No one shall be held guilty of any criminal offence on account of any act or omission which did not constitute a criminal offence under national or international law at the time when it was committed. Nor shall a heavier penalty be imposed than the one that was applicable at the time the criminal offence was committed.

2. This article shall not prejudice the trial and punishment of any person for any act or omission which, at the time when it was committed, was criminal according to the general principles of law recognised by civilised nations.

Article 8[9] Right to respect for private and family life

1. Everyone has the right to respect for his private and family life, his home and his correspondence.

2. There shall be no interference by a public authority with the exercise of this right except such as is in accordance with the law and is necessary in a democratic society in the interests of national security, public safety or the economic well-being of the country, for the prevention of disorder or crime, for the protection of health or morals, or for the protection of the rights and freedoms of others.

Article 9[10] Freedom of thought, conscience and religion

1. Everyone has the right to freedom of thought, conscience and religion; this right

---

[8] *Ibid.*
[9] *Ibid.*
[10] *Ibid.*

includes freedom to change his religion or belief and freedom, either alone or in community with others and in public or private, to manifest his religion or belief, in worship, teaching, practice and observance.

2. Freedom to manifest one's religion or beliefs shall be subject only to such limitations as are prescribed by law and are necessary in a democratic society in the interests of public safety, for the protection of public order, health or morals, or for the protection of the rights and freedoms of others.

Article 10[11] Freedom of expression

1. Everyone has the right to freedom of expression. This right shall include freedom to hold opinions and to receive and impart information and ideas without interference by public authority and regardless of frontiers. This article shall not prevent States from requiring the licensing of broadcasting, television or cinema enterprises.

2. The exercise of these freedoms, since it carries with it duties and responsibilities, may be subject to such formalities, conditions, restrictions or penalties as are prescribed by law and are necessary in a democratic society, in the interests of national security, territorial integrity or public safety, for the prevention of disorder or crime, for the protection of health or morals, for the protection of the reputation or rights of others, for preventing the disclosure of information received in confidence, or for maintaining the authority and impartiality of the judiciary.

Article 11[12] Freedom of assembly and association

1. Everyone has the right to freedom of peaceful assembly and to freedom of association with others, including the right to form and to join trade unions for the protection of his interests.

2. No restrictions shall be placed on the exercise of these rights other than such as are prescribed by law and are necessary in a democratic society in the interests of national security or public safety, for the prevention of disorder or crime, for the protection of health or morals or for the protection of the rights and freedoms of others. This article shall not prevent the imposition of lawful restrictions on the exercise of these rights by members of the armed forces, of the police or of the administration of the State.

Article 12[13] Right to marry

Men and women of marriageable age have the right to marry and to found a family, according to the national laws governing the exercise of this right.

---

[11] *Ibid.*
[12] *Ibid.*
[13] *Ibid.*

Article 13[14] Right to an effective remedy

Everyone whose rights and freedoms as set forth in this Convention are violated shall have an effective remedy before a national authority notwithstanding that the violation has been committed by persons acting in an official capacity.

Article 14[15] Prohibition of discrimination

The enjoyment of the rights and freedoms set forth in this Convention shall be secured without discrimination on any ground such as sex, race, colour, language, religion, political or other opinion, national or social origin, association with a national minority, property, birth or other status.

Article 15[16] Derogation in time of emergency

1. In time of war or other public emergency threatening the life of the nation any High Contracting Party may take measures derogating from its obligations under this Convention to the extent strictly required by the exigencies of the situation, provided that such measures are not inconsistent with its other obligations under international law.

2. No derogation from Article 2, except in respect of deaths resulting from lawful acts of war, or from Articles 3, 4 (paragraph 1) and 7 shall be made under this provision.

3. Any High Contracting Party availing itself of this right of derogation shall keep the Secretary General of the Council of Europe fully informed of the measures which it has taken and the reasons therefor. It shall also inform the Secretary General of the Council of Europe when such measures have ceased to operate and the provisions of the Convention are again being fully executed.

Article 16[17] Restrictions on political activity of aliens

Nothing in Articles 10, 11 and 14 shall be regarded as preventing the High Contracting Parties from imposing restrictions on the political activity of aliens.

Article 17[18] Prohibition of abuse of rights

Nothing in this Convention may be interpreted as implying for any State, group or person any right to engage in any activity or perform any act aimed at the destruction of any of the rights and freedoms set forth herein or at their limitation to a greater extent than is provided for in the Convention.

---

[14] *Ibid.*
[15] *Ibid.*
[16] *Ibid.*
[17] *Ibid.*
[18] *Ibid.*

Article 18[19] Limitation on use of restrictions on rights

The restrictions permitted under this Convention to the said rights and freedoms shall not be applied for any purpose other than those for which they have been prescribed.

SECTION II[20] EUROPEAN COURT OF HUMAN RIGHTS

Article 19 Establishment of the Court

To ensure the observance of the engagements undertaken by the High Contracting Parties in the Convention and the Protocols thereto, there shall be set up a European Court of Human Rights, hereinafter referred to as "the Court". It shall function on a permanent basis.

Article 20 Number of judges

The Court shall consist of a number of judges equal to that of the High Contracting Parties.

Article 21 Criteria for office

1. The judges shall be of high moral character and must either possess the qualifications required for appointment to high judicial office or be jurisconsults of recognised competence.

2. The judges shall sit on the Court in their individual capacity.

3. During their term of office the judges shall not engage in any activity which is incompatible with their independence, impartiality or with the demands of a full-time office; all questions arising from the application of this paragraph shall be decided by the Court.

Article 22 Election of judges

The judges shall be elected by the Parliamentary Assembly with respect to each High Contracting Party by a majority of votes cast from a list of three candidates nominated by the High Contracting Party.

  The same procedure shall be followed to complete the Court in the event of the accession of new High Contracting Parties and in filling casual vacancies.

Article 23 Terms of office

1. The judges shall be elected for a period of six years. They may be re-elected. However, the terms of office of one-half of the judges elected at the first election shall expire at the end of three years.

---

[19] *Ibid.*
[20] *Ibid.*

2. The judges whose terms of office are to expire at the end of the initial period of three years shall be chosen by lot by the Secretary General of the Council of Europe immediately after their election.

3. In order to ensure that, as far as possible, the terms of office of one-half of the judges are renewed every three years, the Parliamentary Assembly may decide, before proceeding to any subsequent election, that the term or terms of office of one or more judges to be elected shall be for a period other than six years but not more than nine and not less than three years.

4. In cases where more than one term of office is involved and where the Parliamentary Assembly applies the preceding paragraph, the allocation of the terms of office shall be effected by a drawing of lots by the Secretary General of the Council of Europe immediately after the election.

5. A judge elected to replace a judge whose term of office has not expired shall hold office for the remainder of his predecessor's term.

6. The terms of office of judges shall expire when they reach the age of 70.

7. The judges shall hold office until replaced. They shall, however, continue to deal with such cases as they already have under consideration.

Article 24 Dismissal

No judge may be dismissed from his office unless the other judges decide by a majority of two-thirds that he has ceased to fulfil the required conditions.

Article 25 Registry and legal secretaries

The Court shall have a registry, the functions and organisation of which shall be laid down in the rules of the Court. The Court shall be assisted by legal secretaries.

Article 26 Plenary Court

The plenary Court shall:

  a. elect its President and one or two Vice-Presidents for a period of three years; they may be re-elected;
  b. set up Chambers, constituted for a fixed period of time;
  c. elect the Presidents of the Chambers of the Court; they may be re-elected;
  d. adopt the rules of the Court, and
  e. elect the Registrar and one or more Deputy Registrars.

Article 27 Committees, Chambers and Grand Chamber

1. To consider cases brought before it, the Court shall sit in committees of three judges, in Chambers of seven judges and in a Grand Chamber of seventeen judges. The Court's Chambers shall set up committees for a fixed period of time.

2. There shall sit as an *ex officio* member of the Chamber and the Grand Chamber the judge elected in respect of the State Party concerned or, if there is none or if he is unable to sit, a person of its choice who shall sit in the capacity of judge.

3. The Grand Chamber shall also include the President of the Court, the Vice-Presidents, the Presidents of the Chambers and other judges chosen in accordance with the rules of the Court. When a case is referred to the Grand Chamber under Article 43, no judge from the Chamber which rendered the judgment shall sit in the Grand Chamber, with the exception of the President of the Chamber and the judge who sat in respect of the State Party concerned.

Article 28 Declarations of inadmissibility by committees

A committee may, by a unanimous vote, declare inadmissible or strike out of its list of cases an application submitted under Article 34 where such a decision can be taken without further examination. The decision shall be final.

Article 29 Decisions by Chambers on admissibility and merits

1. If no decision is taken under Article 28, a Chamber shall decide on the admissibility and merits of individual applications submitted under Article 34.

2. A Chamber shall decide on the admissibility and merits of inter- State applications submitted under Article 33.

3. The decision on admissibility shall be taken separately unless the Court, in exceptional cases, decides otherwise.

Article 30 Relinquishment of jurisdiction to the Grand Chamber

Where a case pending before a Chamber raises a serious question affecting the interpretation of the Convention or the protocols thereto, or where the resolution of a question before the Chamber might have a result inconsistent with a judgment previously delivered by the Court, the Chamber may, at any time before it has rendered its judgment, relinquish jurisdiction in favour of the Grand Chamber, unless one of the parties to the case objects.

Article 31 Powers of the Grand Chamber

The Grand Chamber shall:

   a. determine applications submitted either under Article 33 or Article 34 when a Chamber has relinquished jurisdiction under Article 30 or when the case has been referred to it under Article 43; and

   b. consider requests for advisory opinions submitted under Article 47.

Article 32 Jurisdiction of the Court

1. The jurisdiction of the Court shall extend to all matters concerning the interpretation and application of the Convention and the protocols thereto, which are referred to it

as provided in Articles 33, 34 and 47.

2. In the event of dispute as to whether the Court has jurisdiction, the Court shall decide.

Article 33 Inter-State cases

Any High Contracting Party may refer to the Court any alleged breach of the provisions of the Convention and the protocols thereto by another High Contracting Party.

Article 34 Individual applications

The Court may receive applications from any person, non-governmental organisation or group of individuals claiming to be the victim of a violation by one of the High Contracting Parties of the rights set forth in the Convention or the protocols thereto. The High Contracting Parties undertake not to hinder in any way the effective exercise of this right.

Article 35 Admissibility criteria

1. The Court may only deal with the matter after all domestic remedies have been exhausted, according to the generally recognised rules of international law, and within a period of six months from the date on which the final decision was taken.

2. The Court shall not deal with any application submitted under Article 34 that

    a. is anonymous; or

    b. is substantially the same as a matter that has already been examined by the Court or has already been submitted to another procedure of international investigation or settlement and contains no relevant new information.

3. The Court shall declare inadmissible any individual application submitted under Article 34 which it considers incompatible with the provisions of the Convention or the protocols thereto, manifestly ill-founded, or an abuse of the right of application.

4. The Court shall reject any application, which it considers inadmissible under this Article. It may do so at any stage of the proceedings.

Article 36 Third party intervention

1. In all cases before a Chamber of the Grand Chamber, a High Contracting Party one of whose nationals is an applicant shall have the right to submit written comments and to take part in hearings.

2. The President of the Court may, in the interest of the proper administration of justice, invite any High Contracting Party which is not a party to the proceedings or any person concerned who is not the applicant to submit written comments or take part in hearings.

Article 37 Striking out applications

1. The Court may at any stage of the proceedings decide to strike an application out of its list of cases where the circumstances lead to the conclusion that

   a. the applicant does not intend to pursue his application; or

   b. the matter has been resolved; or

   c. for any other reason established by the Court, it is no longer justified to continue the examination of the application.

   However, the Court shall continue the examination of the application if respect for human rights as defined in the Convention and the protocols thereto so requires.

2. The Court may decide to restore an application to its list of cases if it considers that the circumstances justify such a course.

Article 38 Examination of the case and friendly settlement proceedings

1. If the Court declares the application admissible, it shall:

   a. pursue the examination of the case, together with the representatives of the parties, and if need be, undertake an investigation, for the effective conduct of which the States concerned shall furnish all necessary facilities;

   b. place itself at the disposal of the parties concerned with a view to securing a friendly settlement of the matter on the basis of respect for human rights as defined in the Convention and the protocols thereto.

2. Proceedings conducted under paragraph 1.b shall be confidential.

Article 39 Finding of a friendly settlement

If a friendly settlement is effected, the Court shall strike the case out of its list by means of a decision which shall be confined to a brief statement of the facts and of the solution reached.

Article 40 Public hearings and access to documents

1. Hearings shall be in public unless the Court in exceptional circumstances decides otherwise.

2. Documents deposited with the Registrar shall be accessible to the public unless the President of the Court decides otherwise.

Article 41 Just satisfaction

If the Court finds that there has been a violation of the Convention or the protocols thereto, and if the internal law of the High Contracting Party concerned allows only partial reparation to be made, the Court shall, if necessary, afford just satisfaction to the injured party.

Article 42 Judgments of Chambers

Judgments of Chambers shall become final in accordance with the provisions of Article 44, paragraph 2.

Article 43 Referral to the Grand Chamber

1. Within a period of three months from the date of the judgment of the Chamber, any party to the case may, in exceptional cases, request that the case be referred to the Grand Chamber.

2. A panel of five judges of the Grand Chamber shall accept the request if the case raises a serious question affecting the interpretation or application of the Convention or the protocols thereto, or a serious issue of general importance.

3. If the panel accepts the request, the Grand Chamber shall decide the case by means of a judgment.

Article 44 Final judgments

1. The judgment of the Grand Chamber shall be final.

2. The judgment of a Chamber shall become final:
    a. when the parties declare that they will not request that the case be referred to the Grand Chamber; or
    b. three months after the date of the judgment, if reference of the case to the Grand Chamber has not been requested; or
    c. when the panel of the Grand Chamber rejects the request to refer under Article 43.

3. The final judgment shall be published.

Article 45 Reasons for judgments and decisions

1. Reasons shall be given for judgments as well as for decisions declaring applications admissible or inadmissible.

2. If a judgment does not represent, in whole or in part, the unanimous opinion of the judges, any judge shall be entitled to deliver a separate opinion.

Article 46 Binding force and execution of judgments

1. The High Contracting Parties undertake to abide by the final judgment of the Court in any case to which they are parties.

2. The final judgment of the Court shall be transmitted to the Committee of Ministers, which shall supervise its execution.

Article 47 Advisory opinions

1. The Court may, at the request of the Committee of Ministers, give advisory opinions on legal questions concerning the interpretation of the Convention and the protocols thereto.

1. Such opinions shall not deal with any question relating to the content or scope of the rights or freedoms defined in Section I of the Convention and the protocols thereto, or with any other question which the Court or the Committee of Ministers might have to consider in consequence of any such proceedings as could be instituted in accordance with the Convention.

1. Decisions of the Committee of Ministers to request an advisory opinion of the Court shall require a majority vote of the representatives entitled to sit on the Committee.

Article 48 Advisory jurisdiction of the Court

The Court shall decide whether a request for an advisory opinion submitted by the Committee of Ministers is within its competence as defined in Article 47.

Article 49 Reasons for advisory opinions

1. Reasons shall be given for advisory opinions of the Court.

2. If the advisory opinion does not represent, in whole or in part, the unanimous opinion of the judges, any judge shall be entitled to deliver a separate opinion.

3. Advisory opinions of the Court shall be communicated to the Committee of Ministers.

Article 50 Expenditure on the Court

The expenditure on the Court shall be borne by the Council of Europe.

Article 51 Privileges and immunities of judges

The judges shall be entitled, during the exercise of their functions, to the privileges and immunities provided for in Article 40 of the Statute of the Council of Europe and in the agreements made thereunder.

Section III[21] [22]

Miscellaneous Provisions

Article 52[23] Inquiries by the Secretary General

On receipt of a request from the Secretary General of the Council of Europe any High Contracting Party shall furnish an explanation of the manner in which its internal law ensures the effective implementation of any of the provisions of the Convention.

Article 53[24] Safeguard for existing human rights

Nothing in this Convention shall be construed as limiting or derogating from any of the human rights and fundamental freedoms which may be ensured under the laws of any High Contracting Party or under any other agreement to which it is a Party.

Article 54[25] Powers of the Committee of Ministers

Nothing in this Convention shall prejudice the powers conferred on the Committee of Ministers by the Statute of the Council of Europe.

Article 55[26] Exclusion of other means of dispute settlement

The High Contracting Parties agree that, except by special agreement, they will not avail themselves of treaties, conventions or declarations in force between them for the purpose of submitting, by way of petition, a dispute arising out of the interpretation or application of this Convention to a means of settlement other than those provided for in this Convention.

Article 56[27] Territorial application

1. Any State may at the time of its ratification or at any time thereafter declare by notification addressed to the Secretary General of the Council of Europe that the present Convention shall, subject to paragraph 4 of this Article, extend to all or any of the territories for whose international relations it is responsible.

2. The Convention shall extend to the territory or territories named in the notification as from the thirtieth day after the receipt of this notification by the Secretary General of the Council of Europe.

---

[21] Heading added according to the provisions of Protocol No.11 (ETS No.155).
[22] The articles of this section are renumbered according to the Provisions of Protocol No.11 (ETS No.155).
[23] Heading added according to the provisions of Protocol No.11 (ETS No.155).
[24] *Ibid.*
[25] *Ibid.*
[26] *Ibid.*
[27] *Ibid.*

3.   The provisions of this Convention shall be applied in such territories with due regard, however, to local requirements.

4.   Any State which has made a declaration in accordance with paragraph 1 of this article may at any time thereafter declare on behalf of one or more of the territories to which the declaration relates that it accepts the competence of the Court to receive applications from individuals, non-governmental organisations or groups of individuals as provided by Article 34 of the Convention.

Article 57[28] **Reservations**

1.   Any State may, when signing this Convention or when depositing its instrument of ratification, make a reservation in respect of any particular provision of the Convention to the extent that any law then in force in its territory is not in conformity with the provision. Reservations of a general character shall not be permitted under this article.

2.   Any reservation made under this article shall contain a brief statement of the law concerned.

Article 58[29] **Denunciation**

1.   A High Contracting Party may denounce the present Convention only after the expiry of five years from the date on which it became a party to it and after six months' notice contained in a notification addressed to the Secretary General of the Council of Europe, who shall inform the other High Contracting Parties.

2.   Such a denunciation shall not have the effect of releasing the High Contracting Party concerned from its obligations under this Convention in respect of any act which, being capable of constituting a violation of such obligations, may have been performed by it before the date at which the denunciation became effective.

3.   Any High Contracting Party which shall cease to be a member of the Council of Europe shall cease to be a Party to this Convention under the same conditions.

4.   The Convention may be denounced in accordance with the provisions of the preceding paragraphs in respect of any territory to which it has been declared to extend under the terms of Article 56.[30]

Article 59[31] **Signature and ratification**

1.   This Convention shall be open to the signature of the members of the Council of Europe. It shall be ratified. Ratifications shall be deposited with the Secretary General of the Council of Europe.

---

[28] *Ibid.*

[29] *Ibid.*

[30] Text amended according to the provisions of Protocol No.11 (ETS No.155).

[31] Heading added according to the Provisions of Protocol No.11 (ETS No.155).

2. The present Convention shall come into force after the deposit of ten instruments of ratification.

3. As regards any signatory ratifying subsequently, the Convention shall come into force at the date of the deposit of its instrument of ratification.

4. The Secretary General of the Council of Europe shall notify all the members of the Council of Europe of the entry into force of the Convention, the names of the High Contracting Parties who have ratified it, and the deposit of all instruments of ratification which may be effected subsequently.

Done at Rome this 4th day of November 1950, in English and French, both texts being equally authentic, in a single copy which shall remain deposited in the archives of the Council of Europe. The Secretary General shall transmit certified copies to each of the signatories.

SCHEDULE 2

PROTOCOL TO THE CONVENTION FOR THE PROTECTION OF HUMAN RIGHTS AND FUNDAMENTAL FREEDOMS[32]

Paris, 20.III.1952

THE GOVERNMENTS SIGNATORY HERETO, being members of the Council of Europe,

Being resolved to take steps to ensure the collective enforcement of certain rights and freedoms other than those already included in Section I of the Convention for the Protection of Human Rights and Fundamental Freedoms signed at Rome on 4 November 1950 (hereinafter referred to as "the Convention"),

Have agreed as follows:

Article 1 Protection of property

Every natural or legal person is entitled to the peaceful enjoyment of his possessions. No one shall be deprived of his possessions except in the public interest and subject to the conditions provided for by law and by the general principles of international law.

The preceding provisions shall not, however, in any way impair the right of a State to enforce such laws as it deems necessary to control the use of property in accordance with the general interest or to secure the payment of taxes or other contributions or penalties.

Article 2 Right to education

No person shall be denied the right to education. In the exercise of any functions which it assumes in relation to education and to teaching, the State shall respect the right of parents to ensure such education and teaching in conformity with their own religious and philosophical convictions.

Article 3 Right to free elections

The High Contracting Parties undertake to hold free elections at reasonable intervals by secret ballot, under conditions which will ensure the free expression of the opinion of the people in the choice of the legislature.

Article 4[33] Territorial application

Any High Contracting Party may at the time of signature or ratification or at any time

---

[32] Headings of articles added and text amended according to the provisions of Protocol No.11(ETS No.155).

[33] Text amended according to the provisions of Protocol No.11(ETS No.155).

thereafter communicate to the Secretary General of the Council of Europe a declaration stating the extent to which it undertakes that the provisions of the present Protocol shall apply to such of the territories for the international relations of which it is responsible as are named therein.

Any High Contracting Party which has communicated a declaration in virtue of the preceding paragraph may from time to time communicate a further declaration modifying the terms of any former declaration or terminating the application of the provisions of this Protocol in respect of any territory.

A declaration made in accordance with this article shall be deemed to have been made in accordance with paragraph 1 of Article 56 of the Convention.

Article 5 Relationship to the Convention

As between the High Contracting Parties the provisions of Articles 1, 2, 3 and 4 of this Protocol shall be regarded as additional articles to the Convention and all the provisions of the Convention shall apply accordingly.

Article 6 Signature and ratification

This Protocol shall be open for signature by the members of the Council of Europe, who are the signatories of the Convention; it shall be ratified at the same time as or after the ratification of the Convention. It shall enter into force after the deposit of ten instruments of ratification. As regards any signatory ratifying subsequently, the Protocol shall enter into force at the date of the deposit of its instrument of ratification.

The instruments of ratification shall be deposited with the Secretary General of the Council of Europe, who will notify all members of the names of those who have ratified.

Done at Paris on the 20th day of March 1952, in English and French, both texts being equally authentic, in a single copy which shall remain deposited in the archives of the Council of Europe. The Secretary General shall transmit certified copies to each of the signatory governments.

PROTOCOL NO. 4 TO THE CONVENTION FOR THE PROTECTION OF HUMAN RIGHTS AND FUNDAMENTAL FREEDOMS SECURING CERTAIN RIGHTS AND FREEDOMS OTHER THAN THOSE ALREADY INCLUDED IN THE CONVENTION AND IN THE FIRST PROTOCOL THERETO[34]

Strasbourg, 16.IX.1963

THE GOVERNMENTS SIGNATORY HERETO, being members of the Council of Europe,

Being resolved to take steps to ensure the collective enforcement of certain rights and freedoms other than those already included in Section 1 of the Convention for the Protection of Human Rights and Fundamental Freedoms signed at Rome on 4th November 1950 (hereinafter referred to as the "Convention") and in Articles 1 to 3 of the First Protocol to the Convention signed at Paris on 20th March 1952,

Have agreed as follows:

Article 1 Prohibition of imprisonment for debt

No one shall be deprived of his liberty merely on the ground of inability to fulfil a contractual obligation.

Article 2 Freedom of movement

1. Everyone lawfully within the territory of a State shall, within that territory, have the right to liberty of movement and freedom to choose his residence.

2. Everyone shall be free to leave any country, including his own.

3. No restrictions shall be placed on the exercise of these rights other than such as are in accordance with law and are necessary in a democratic society in the interests of national security or public safety, for the maintenance of *ordre public*, for the prevention of crime, for the protection of health or morals, or for the protection of the rights and freedoms of others.

4. The rights set forth in paragraph 1 may also be subject, in particular areas, to restrictions imposed in accordance with law and justified by the public interest in a democratic society.

---

[34] Headings of articles added and text amended according to the provisions of Protocol No.11 (ETS No.155).

Article 3 Prohibition of expulsion of nationals

1. No one shall be expelled, by means either of an individual or of a collective measure, from the territory of the State of which he is a national.

2. No one shall be deprived of the right to enter the territory of the state of which he is a national.

Article 4 Prohibition of collective expulsion of aliens

Collective expulsion of aliens is prohibited.

Article 5 Territorial application

1. Any High Contracting Party may, at the time of signature or ratification of this Protocol, or at any time thereafter, communicate to the Secretary General of the Council of Europe a declaration stating the extent to which it undertakes that the provisions of this Protocol shall apply to such of the territories for the international relations of which it is responsible as are named therein.

2. Any High Contracting Party which has communicated a declaration in virtue of the preceding paragraph may, from time to time, communicate a further declaration modifying the terms of any former declaration or terminating the application of the provisions of this Protocol in respect of any territory.

3. A declaration made in accordance with this article shall be deemed to have been made in accordance with paragraph 1 of Article 56 of the Convention.[35]

4. The territory of any State to which this Protocol applies by virtue of ratification or acceptance by that State, and each territory to which this Protocol is applied by virtue of a declaration by that State under this article, shall be treated as separate territories for the purpose of the references in Articles 2 and 3 to the territory of a State.

5. Any State which has made a declaration in accordance with paragraph 1 or 2 of this Article may at any time thereafter declare on behalf of one or more of the territories to which the declaration relates that it accepts the competence of the Court to receive applications from individuals, non-governmental organisations or groups of individuals as provided in Article 34 of the Convention in respect of all or any of Articles 1 to 4 of this Protocol.[36]

Article 6[37] Relationship to the Convention

As between the High Contracting Parties the provisions of Articles 1 to 5 of this Protocol shall be regarded as additional articles to the Convention, and all the provisions of the Convention shall apply accordingly.

---

[35] Text amended according to the provisions of Protocol No.11 (ETS N0. 155).
[36] Text added according to the provisions of Protocol No.11 (ETS No.155).
[37] *Ibid.*

Article 7 Signature and ratification

1. This Protocol shall be open for signature by the members of the Council of Europe who are the signatories of the Convention; it shall be ratified at the same time as or after the ratification of the Convention. It shall enter into force after the deposit of five instruments of ratification. As regards any signatory ratifying subsequently, the Protocol shall enter into force at the date of the deposit of its instrument of ratification.

2. The instruments of ratification shall be deposited with the Secretary General of the Council of Europe, who will notify all members of the names of those who have ratified.

In witness whereof the undersigned, being duly authorised thereto, have signed this Protocol.

Done at Strasbourg, this 16th day of September 1963, in English and in French, both texts being equally authoritative, in a single copy which shall remain deposited in the archives of the Council of Europe. The Secretary General shall transmit certified copies to each of the signatory states.

SCHEDULE 4

PROTOCOL NO. 6 TO THE CONVENTION FOR THE PROTECTION OF HUMAN RIGHTS AND FUNDAMENTAL FREEDOMS CONCERNING THE ABOLITION OF THE DEATH PENALTY[38]

Strasbourg, 28.IV.1983

THE MEMBER STATES OF THE COUNCIL OF EUROPE, signatory to this Protocol to the Convention for the Protection of Human Rights and Fundamental Freedoms, signed at Rome on 4 November 1950 (hereinafter referred to as "the Convention"),

Considering that the evolution that has occurred in several member States of the Council of Europe expresses a general tendency in favour of abolition of the death penalty;

Have agreed as follows:

Article 1 Abolition of the death penalty

The death penalty shall be abolished. No one shall be condemned to such penalty or executed.

Article 2 Death penalty in time of war

A State may make provision in its law for the death penalty in respect of acts committed in time of war or of imminent threat of war; such penalty shall be applied only in the instances laid down in the law and in accordance with its provisions. The State shall communicate to the Secretary General of the Council of Europe the relevant provisions of that law.

Article 3 Prohibition of derogations

No derogation from the provisions of this Protocol shall be made under Article 15 of the Convention.

Article 4[39] Prohibition of reservations

No reservation may be made under Article 57 of the Convention in respect of the provisions of this Protocol.

Article 5 Territorial application

1.   Any State may at the time of signature or when depositing its instrument of

---

[38] Headings of articles added and text amended according to the provisions of Protocol No.11 (ETS No.155).

[39] Text amended according to the provisions of Protocol No.11 (ETS No.155).

ratification, acceptance or approval, specify the territory or territories to which this Protocol shall apply.

2. Any State may at any later date, by a declaration addressed to the Secretary General of the Council of Europe, extend the application of this Protocol to any other territory specified in the declaration. In respect of such territory the Protocol shall enter into force on the first day of the month following the date of receipt of such declaration by the Secretary General.

3. Any declaration made under the two preceding paragraphs may, in respect of any territory specified in such declaration, be withdrawn by a notification addressed to the Secretary General. The withdrawal shall become effective on the first day of the month following the date of receipt of such notification by the Secretary General.

Article 6 Relationship to the Convention

As between the States Parties the provisions of Articles 1 and 5 of this Protocol shall be regarded as additional articles to the Convention and all the provisions of the Convention shall apply accordingly.

Article 7 Signature and ratification

The Protocol shall be open for signature by the member States of the Council of Europe, signatories to the Convention. It shall be subject to ratification, acceptance or approval. A member State of the Council of Europe may not ratify, accept or approve this Protocol unless it has, simultaneously or previously, ratified the Convention. Instruments of ratification, acceptance or approval shall be deposited with the Secretary General of the Council of Europe.

Article 8 Entry into force

1. This Protocol shall enter into force on the first day of the month following the date on which five member States of the Council of Europe have expressed their consent to be bound by the Protocol in accordance with the provisions of Article 7.

2. In respect of any member State which subsequently expresses its consent to be bound by it, the Protocol shall enter into force on the first day of the month following the date of the deposit of the instrument of ratification, acceptance or approval.

Article 9 Depositary functions

The Secretary General of the Council of Europe shall notify the member States of the Council of:

a. any signature;

b. the deposit of any instrument of ratification, acceptance or approval;

c. any date of entry into force of this Protocol in accordance with Articles 5 and 8;

d. any other act, notification or communication relating to this Protocol.

In witness whereof the undersigned, being duly authorised thereto, have signed this Protocol.

Done at Strasbourg, this 28th day of April 1983, in English and in French, both texts being equally authentic, in a single copy which shall be deposited in the archives of the Council of Europe. The Secretary General of the Council of Europe shall transmit certified copies to each member State of the Council of Europe.

PROTOCOL NO. 7 TO THE CONVENTION FOR THE PROTECTION OF HUMAN RIGHTS AND FUNDAMENTAL FREEDOMS[40]

Strasbourg, 22.XI.1984

The member States of the Council of Europe signatory hereto,

Being resolved to take further steps to ensure the collective enforcement of certain rights and freedoms by means of the Convention for the Protection of Human Rights and Fundamental Freedoms signed at Rome on 4 November 1950 (hereinafter referred to as "the Convention"),

Have agreed as follows:

Article 1 Procedural safeguards relating to expulsion of aliens

An alien lawfully resident in the territory of a State shall not be expelled therefrom except in pursuance of a decision reached in accordance with law and shall be allowed:

    a. to submit reasons against his expulsion,

    b. to have his case reviewed, and

    c. to be represented for these purposes before the competent authority or a person or persons designated by that authority.

An alien may be expelled before the exercise of his rights under paragraph 1.a, b and c of this Article, when such expulsion is necessary in the interests of public order or is grounded on reasons of national security.

Article 2 Right of appeal in criminal matters

1. Everyone convicted of a criminal offence by a tribunal shall have the right to have his conviction or sentence reviewed by a higher tribunal. The exercise of this right, including the grounds on which it may be exercised, shall be governed by law.

2. This right may be subject to exceptions in regard to offences of a minor character, as prescribed by law, or in cases in which the person concerned was tried in the first instance by the highest tribunal or was convicted following an appeal against acquittal.

Article 3 Compensation for wrongful conviction

When a person has by a final decision been convicted of a criminal offence and when subsequently his conviction has been reversed, or he has been pardoned, on the ground

---

[40] Headings of articles added and text amended according to the provisions of Protocol No.11 (ETS No.155).

that a new or newly discovered fact shows conclusively that there has been a miscarriage of justice, the person who has suffered punishment as a result of such conviction shall be compensated according to the law or the practice of the State concerned, unless it is proved that the non-disclosure of the unknown fact in time is wholly or partly attributable to him.

Article 4 Right not to be tried or punished twice

1. No one shall be liable to be tried or punished again in criminal proceedings under the jurisdiction of the same State for an offence for which he has already been finally acquitted or convicted in accordance with the law and penal procedure of that State.

2. The provisions of the preceding paragraph shall not prevent the reopening of the case in accordance with the law and penal procedure of the State concerned, if there is evidence of new or newly discovered facts, or if there has been a fundamental defect in the previous proceedings, which could affect the outcome of the case.

3. No derogation from this Article shall be made under Article 15 of the Convention.

Article 5 Equality between spouses

Spouses shall enjoy equality of rights and responsibilities of a private law character between them, and in their relations with their children, as to marriage, during marriage and in the event of its dissolution. This Article shall not prevent States from taking such measures as are necessary in the interests of the children.

Article 6 Territorial application

1. Any State may at the time of signature or when depositing its instrument of ratification, acceptance or approval, specify the territory or territories to which the Protocol shall apply and state the extent to which it undertakes that the provisions of this Protocol shall apply to such territory or territories.

2. Any State may at any later date, by a declaration addressed to the Secretary General of the Council of Europe, extend the application of this Protocol to any other territory specified in the declaration. In respect of such territory the Protocol shall enter into force on the first day of the month following the expiration of a period of two months after the date of receipt by the Secretary General of such declaration.

3. Any declaration made under the two preceding paragraphs may, in respect of any territory specified in such declaration, be withdrawn or modified by a notification addressed to the Secretary General. The withdrawal or modification shall become effective on the first day of the month following the expiration of a period of two months after the date of receipt of such notification by the Secretary General.

4. A declaration made in accordance with this Article shall be deemed to have been made in accordance with paragraph 1 of Article 56 of the Convention.[41]

---

[41] Text amended according to provisions of Protocol No.11 (ETS No.155).

5. The territory of any State to which this Protocol applies by virtue of ratification, acceptance or approval by that State, and each territory to which this Protocol is applied by virtue of a declaration by that State under this Article, may be treated as separate territories for the purpose of the reference in Article 1 to the territory of a State.

6. Any State which has made a declaration in accordance with paragraph 1 or 2 of this Article may at any time thereafter declare on behalf of one or more of the territories to which the declaration relates that it accepts the competence of the Court to receive applications from individuals, non-governmental organisations or groups of individuals as provided in Article 34 of the Convention in respect of Articles 1 to 5 of this Protocol.[42]

Article 7[43] Relationship to the Convention

As between the States Parties, the provisions of Articles 1 to 6 of this Protocol shall be regarded as additional Articles to the Convention, and all the provisions of the Convention shall apply accordingly.

Article 8 Signature and ratification

This Protocol shall be open for signature by member States of the Council of Europe which have signed the Convention. It is subject to ratification, acceptance or approval. A member State of the Council of Europe may not ratify, accept or approve this Protocol without previously or simultaneously ratifying the Convention. Instruments of ratification, acceptance or approval shall be deposited with the Secretary General of the Council of Europe.

Article 9 Entry into force

1. This Protocol shall enter into force on the first day of the month following the expiration of a period of two months after the date on which seven member States of the Council of Europe have expressed their consent to be bound by the Protocol in accordance with the provisions of Article 8.

2. In respect of any member State which subsequently expresses its consent to be bound by it, the Protocol shall enter into force on the first day of the month following the expiration of a period of two months after the date of the deposit of the instrument of ratification, acceptance or approval.

Article 10 Depositary functions

The Secretary General of the Council of Europe shall notify all the member States of the Council of Europe of:

   a. any signature;

---

[42] Text added according to provisions of Protocol N. 11 (ETS No.155).
[43] *Ibid.*

b. the deposit of any instrument of ratification, acceptance or approval;

c. any date of entry into force of this Protocol in accordance with Articles 6 and 9;

d. any other act, notification or declaration relating to this Protocol.

In witness whereof the undersigned, being duly authorised thereto, have signed this Protocol.

Done at Strasbourg, this 22nd day of November 1984, in English and French, both texts being equally authentic, in a single copy which shall be deposited in the archives of the Council of Europe. The Secretary General of the Council of Europe shall transmit certified copies to each member State of the Council of Europe.

The McNaghten Rules

The pertinent parts of the McNaghten Rules are as follows:

Rule 1

Persons who labour under partial delusions only, and are not in other respects insane, and who act under the influence of an insane delusion, of redressing or revenging some supposed grievance or injury or producing some public benefit are nevertheless punishable if they knew at the time of committing the crime that they were acting contrary to the law of the land.[1]

Rule 2

Every man is presumed to be sane and to possess a sufficient degree of reason to be responsible for his crimes until the contrary be proved.

Rule 3

To establish a defence on the ground of insanity it must be clearly proved that, at the time of committing the act, the party accused was labouring under such a defect of reason from a disease of the mind, as not to know the nature and quality of the act he was doing, or, if he did know it, that he did not know he was doing what was wrong. [With respect to the latter part of this rule], if the accused was conscious that the act was one that he ought not to do, and if that act was at the same time contrary to the law of the land, he is punishable.[2]

Rule 4

A person labouring under a partial delusion only and not in other respects insane must be considered in the same situation as to responsibility as if the facts with respect to which the delusion exist were real. For example, if under the influence of his delusion he supposes another man to be in the act of attempting to take away his life and he kills that man as he supposes in self defence, he would be exempt from punishment. If his delusion was that the deceased had inflicted a serious injury to his character and fortune and he killed him in revenge for such supposed injury he would be liable for punishment.[3]

---

[1] 4 St. Tr. (n.s.) 930.
[2] *Ibid.*, p.931.
[3] *Ibid.*, p.932.

Bibliography

A & L Goodbody, *A Practical Guide to Data Protection Law in Ireland* (Round Hall, Dublin, 2003).

Abraham G.W., *The Law and Practice of Lunacy in Ireland* E. Ponsonby Dublin (1886).

American Bar Association Commission on the Mentally Disabled and Commission on Legal Problems of the Elderly, *Guardianship An Agenda for Reform* (1989).

American Psychiatric Association, "Model Law on Confidentiality of Health and Social Service Records" *American Journal of Psychiatry* [1979] Vol. 136 137.

Amnesty International, *Mental Illness the Neglected Quarter: Children* (Amnesty International, September 2003).

Amnesty International, *Mental Illness the Neglected Quarter: Homelessness* (Amnesty International, May 2003).

Amnesty International, *Mental Illness the Neglected Quarter: Marginalised Groups* (Amnesty International, November 2003).

Anand R., "Involuntary Civil Commitment in Ontario: The Need to Curtail the Abuses of Psychiatry" [1979] Vol XVII *La Revue du Barreau Canadien* 250.

Andalman E. and Chambers D.L., "Effective Counsel for Persons facing Civil Commitment: A Survey, A Polemic and a Proposal" [1974] Vol. 45 *Mississippi Law Journal* 43.

Appelbaum P.S., "Almost a Revolution An International Perspective on the Law of Involuntary Commitment" (1997) Vol. 25 (2) *Journal of the American Academy of Psychiatry and Law* 135.

Appelbaum P.S., *Almost a Revolution Mental Health Law and the Limits of Change* (Oxford University Press, New York, 1994).

Archbold, *Pleading Evidence and Practice in Criminal Cases* Sweet & Maxwell London (1992).

Arthur R., "Medical Treatment: The Welfare of the Child v. The Wishes of the Parents" [2002] 1 *Irish Journal of Family Law* 20.

Arthur R., "North Western Health Board v H.W and C.W. – Reformulating Irish Family Law" (2002) No. 3 *Irish Law Times* 39.

Ashton G., "Acting for Persons who lack Mental Capacity" *The Law Society's Gazette* December 5, 1990.

Ashton G., "Must mental disability be a legal handicap" *The Law Society's Gazette* November 4, 1992.

Ashton G., *Elderly People and the Law* (Butterworths London, 1995).

Ashton G.R., "Mental Incapacity and Civil Justice" *Law Society's Gazette* (April 28, 1993) 18, (May 12, 1993) 245, (January 19, 1994) 30.

Ashton G.R. and Ward A.D., *Mental Handicap and the Law* (Sweet & Maxwell London, 1992).

Ball D. and Chakrabarti M., *Mental Health and the Law in Scotland* (Jordanhill College of Education).

Barlett P. and Sandford R., *Mental Health Law Policy and Practice* (2nd ed., Oxford University Press, 2003).

Barrington R., *Health, Medicine and Politics in Ireland 1900–1970*, Institute of Public Administration Dublin (1987).

Bell S. and Brookbanks W.J., *Mental Health Law in New Zealand* (Brookers Ltd, Wellington, New Zealand, 1998).

Binchy W., *Irish Conflicts of Law* (Butterworths (Ireland) Ltd, Dublin, 1988).

Bingley W., "Achieving Human Rights for People who Lack Capacity", February 2000 *Journal of Mental Health Law* 83.

Bissett Johnson A. and Ferguson P., "Striving to Keep Alive? Care and Treatment Decisions Affecting Severely Handicapped Patients in Britain" (1997) Vol. 4 *European Journal of Health Law* 321.

Blackwood J., "Sterilisation of the Intellectually Disabled – The Need for Legislative Reform", Vol. 5 *Australian Journal of Family Law* 138.

Boland F., "Compulsory Detention and the General Practitioner in Irish Mental Health Law: Armour or Weapon in Wrongful Committals?" Vol. 52 (2) *Northern Ireland Legal Quarterly* 205.

Boland F., "Diminished Responsibility as a Defence in Irish Law" [1996] *Irish Criminal Law Journal* Vol. 6 19.

Boland F., "Insanity, the Irish Constitution and the European Convention on Human Rights", Autumn 1996 *Northern Ireland Legal Quarterly* 260.

Boland F., *Anglo-American Insanity Defence Reform The War between Law and Medicine* (Ashgate Dartmouth, 1999).

Bonnie R.J. and Monahan J., *Mental Disorder, Work Disability and the Law* (The University of Chicago Press, Chicago, 1997).

Borovoy A., "Guardianship and Civil Liberties", 3 *Health Law in Canada* 51.

Bourke J., "Mental Illness Discrimination in Employment and the Disability Discrimination Act 1992", Vol. 3 May 1996 *Journal of Law and Medicine* 318.

Bradbury Little G., "Comparing German and English Law on Non-Consensual Sterilisation; A Difference in Approach" [1997] *Medical Law Review* 269.

Brady J.C. and Kerr A., *The Limitation of Actions* (Incorporated Law Society of Ireland, Dublin, 1994).

Brady J.C., *Succession Law in Ireland* (Butterworths (Ireland) Ltd Dublin., 1989).

Brakel S.J. et al., *The Mentally Disabled and the Law* (3rd ed., American Bar Foundation Chicago, Illinois, 1985).

Brennan C., "The Right to Die" 16 July 1993 *New Law Journal* 1041.

Bridge C., "Adolescents and Mental Disorder: Who Consents to Treatment?" (1997) Vol. 3 *Medical Law International*, 51.

British Medical Association and Law Society of England and Wales *Assessment of Mental Capacity Guidance for Doctors and Lawyers A Report* British Medical Association London (December 1995).

Brody B.A. and Engelhardt H.T. Jr. (eds), *Mental Illness: Law and Public Policy* D.Reidel Publishing Company (1980).

Brookbanks W., "Insanity in the Criminal Law; Reform in Australia and New Zealand" 2003 *Juridical Review* 81.

Browne C., Daly A, and Walsh D., *Activities of Irish Psychiatric Services 1998*, Health Research Board (April 2000).

Browning Hoffman P. and Foust L.L., "Least Restrictive Treatment of the Mentally Ill: A Doctrine in Search of its Senses", Vol. 14 *San Diego Law Review* 1100.

Brownlie I., *Principles of Public International Law* (4th ed., Clarendon Press, Oxford, 1990).

Butler S., "The Psychiatric Services Planning for the Future: A Critique", Vol. 35(1) *Administration* 47.

Butler T., *Mental Health, Social Policy and the Law* (Macmillan England, 1985).

Butterworths Tax Guide 2002 (Butterworths (Ireland) Ltd, Dublin, 2002).

Campbell T. et al., *Human Rights From Rhetoric to Reality* (Basil Blackwell, Oxford, 1986).

Cannon R., *Evidence* (Thomson Roundhall Ltd, Dublin, 2002).

Carey T.G. et al., "Involuntary Admissions to a district mental health service – implications for a new mental treatment act" 1993 Vol. 10(3) *Irish Journal of Psychological Medicine* 139.

Casey P. and Craven C., *Psychiatry and the Law* (Oak Tree Press Dublin, 1999).

Caulfield E., *The Organisation of the Health Services in Ireland – A General Practitioner's Perspective*, Irish College of General Practitioners Dublin (2001).

Cavadino W., *Mental Health Law in Context Doctor's Orders?* (Dartmouth Publishing Co. England, 1989).

Chalmers J., "Reforming the Pleas of Insanity and Diminished Responsibility: Some Asepcts of the Scottish Law Commission's Working Paper", 2003 Vol. 8(2) *Scottish Law and Practice Quarterly* 79.

Charleton P., "Criminal Law – Protecting the Mentally Subnormal against Sexual Exploitation" (1984–1985) *Dublin University Law Journal* 165.

Charleton P. and McDermott P.A., *Criminal Law* (Butterworths Ireland Ltd, Dublin, 1999).

Charleton P., *Offences against the Person* (The Round Hall Press, Dublin, 1992).

Chitty on Contracts (26th ed., Sweet & Maxwell, London, 1989).

Christie J., "Guardianship: The Alberta Experience: A Model for Change", 3 *Health Law in Canada* 58.

Clark R., *Annotated Guide to Social Welfare Law* (Sweet & Maxwell London, 1995).

Clark R., *Contract Law in Ireland* Third Edition (Sweet & Maxwell London, 1992).

Clements L. et al., *European Human Rights: Taking a Case under the Convention* (2nd ed., Sweet & Maxwell London, 1999).

Cohen F., "The Function of the Attorney and the Commitment of the Mentally Ill" [1966] Vol. 44 *Texas Law Review* 426.

Colles J.M., *The Lunacy Act and Orders* (William McGee Dublin, 1895).

Collins M., "Solicitors' Negligence and Wills" October 15 1999 *New Law Journal* 1510.

Comhairle, *Entitlements for People with Disabilities* (Comhairle, July 2003).

Commission of Inquiry on Mental Handicap, *Report of Commission of Inquiry on Mental Handicap* Pr. 8234 (1965).

Commission of Inquiry on Mental Illness, *Report of the Commission of Inquiry on Mental Illness* Pr. 9181 Dublin, Government Stationery Office (1966).

Commission on the Status of People with Disabilities, *A Strategy for Equality* Cahill Printers (November 1996).

Connolly M., "Equal Access to Goods and Services – The Equal Status Act 2000", 2001 December *Commercial Law Practitioner* 275 .

Constitution Review Group, *Report of the Constitution Review Group*, Government Stationery Office Dublin Pn. 2632 May 1996.

Conway G., " Fitness to Plead in Light of the Criminal Law (Insanity) Bill 2002" 2003 Vol. 13 (4) *Irish Criminal Law Journal* 2.

Cooney T., "Psychiatric Detainees and the Human Rights Challenge to Psychiatry and Law Where do we go from here?" in Liz Heffernan (ed.), *Human Rights A European Perspective* (The Round Hall Press Dublin, 1994).

Cooney T. and O'Neill O., *Kritik 1 Psychiatric Detention Civil Commitment in Ireland* (Baikonur Wicklow, 1996).

Costello C. and Barry E. (eds), *Equality in Diversity – The New Equality Directives* (Irish Centre for European Law, 2003).

Costello J., "The Enduring Problem of Powers of Attorney" (1998) Vol. 3(2) *Conveyancing and Property Law Journal* 35.

Cousins M., "The Health (Nursing Homes) Act 1990" January/February 1994 *Law Society Gazette* 15.

Cousins M., *Social Welfare Law* Second Edition Thomson Roundhall, Dublin (2002).

Craven C., "Litigation against Psychiatrists 1997–1999" (1999) *Medico Legal Journal of Ireland* 70.

Creaby M. et al., "Section 207 of the Mental Treatment Act 1945 A Critical Review of its Use 1955–1994" (1995) *Medico-Legal Journal of Ireland* 11.

Cretney S., "The Enduring Power of Attorney – could it be improved?" February 1993 *Trusts and Estates* 39.

Cross, Jones and Card, *Introduction to Criminal Law* (11th ed., Butterworths, London, 1988).

Crowley-Smith L., "Intellectual Disability and Mental Illness A Call for Unambiguous and Uniform Statutory Definitions" Vol. 3 November 1995 *Journal of Law and Medicine*.

Curran W.J., "Comparative Analysis of Mental Health Legislation in Forty-Three Countries: A Discussion of Historical Trends" [1978] Vol. 1 *International Journal of Law and Psychiatry* 79.

Curran W.J. and Harding T.W., *The Law and Mental Health: Harmonising Objectives* (World Health Organisation Geneva, 1978).

Curry J., *Irish Social Services* (3rd ed., Institute of Public Administration, Dublin, 1998).

Cusack D., Sheikh A., Hyslop-Westrup, "Near PVS: A New Medico-Legal Syndrome" (2000) Vol. 40(2) *Medicine Science and Law* 133.

Daly A. and Walsh D., *Activities of Irish Psychiatric Services 2001* (Health Research Board, January 2003).

Daly A. and Walsh D., *Activities of Irish Psychiatric Services 2002* (Health Research Board, December 2003).

De Blacam M., "Children, Constitutional Rights and the Separation of Powers" (2002) *Irish Jurist* 113.

De Vries U., "The New Mental Health Bill – Failing to be Progressive" (1999) *Medico Legal Journal of Ireland* 19.

Degener T. and Koster Dreese (eds), *Human Rights and Disabled Persons Essays and Relevant Human Rights Instruments* (Martinus Nijhoff Publishers, Dordrecht, The Netherlands, 1995).

Dell S., "Wanted: An Insanity Defence that Can be Used" [1983] *Criminal Law Review*.

Department of Health (England) and Welsh Office, *Mental Health Act 1983 Code of Practice* TSO London (March 1999).

Department of Health and Children, *Quality and Fairness: A Health System for You: Health Strategy* Government Stationery Office (2001).

Department of Health and Children, *Report of the Inspector of Mental Hospitals for the Year Ending December 1998* Government Stationery Officer Pn. 7706 (1999).

Department of Health and Children, *Report of the Inspector of Mental Hospitals for the Year Ending December 1999* Government Stationery Office Pn. 8606 (2000).

Department of Health and Children, *Report of the Inspector of Mental Hospitals for the Year Ending December 2000* Government Stationery Office Pn.10218 (2001).

Department of Health and Children, *Report of the Inspector of Mental Hospitals for the Year Ending December 2001* Government Stationery Office Pn. 11872 (2002).

Department of Health and Children, Report of the Inspector of Mental Hospitals for the Year Ending December 2002 Government Stationery Office Prn. 287 (2003).

Department of Health and Children, *Second Report of Working Group on Child and Adolescent Psychiatric Services* (June 2003).

Department of Health, *Green Paper on Mental Health* June (1992) Pl.8918.

Department of Health Report of a Study Group on the Development of the Psychiatric Services, *The Psychiatric Services Planning for the Future* PL3001 (December 1984).

Department of Health, *White Paper A New Mental Health Act*, Pn. 1824 (July 1995).

Doherty K. et al., "Services for Autism in Ireland" (2000) 21 *Irish Journal of Psychology* 51–69.

Doherty N. and Costello J., *Wards of Court* Law Society Continuing Legal Education Lecture (January 2003).

Donnelly M., *Consent; Bridging the Gap between Doctor and Patient* (Cork University Press, Cork, 2002).

Doolan B., *Constitutional Law and Constitutional Rights in Ireland* (3rd ed., Gill and MacMillan, Dublin, 1994).

Doran K., "The Confidentiality of Computerised Medical Records: Legal Protection in the United States of America " (2000) *Medico-Legal Journal of Ireland* 83.

Doran K., "The Legislative Position Governing Patient Access to Medical Records" 1998 Vol. 91(1) *Irish Medical Journal* 27.

Doran K., "Freedom of Information Act 1997 A Legal Cul de Sac?" (1997) 9 *Law Society Gazette*.

Doran K., "Patient Access to Medical Records" 1998 Vol. 91 (5) *Irish Medical Journal* 179.

Doran K., "The Defence of Consent to the Tort of Battery" 1998 Vol. 91(3) *Irish Medical Journal* 98.

Doran K., "The Legal Position Governing Access to Medical Records" (1997) *Medico-Legal Journal of Ireland* 50.

Doran K. and Cusack D., "Access to Medical Records: The Effect of the Freedom of Information Act 1997" (1997) *Medico-Legal Journal of Ireland* 106.

Dowling M., "Disability Discrimination" December 1996 *Bar Review* 121.

Downie A., "A Metropolitan Borough Council v DB and Re C (Detention: Medical Treatment) Extra-statutory confinement -detention and treatment under the inherent jurisdiction" Vol. 10 No. 1 *Child and Family Law Quarterly* 101.

Doyle B.J., *Disability Discrimination Law and Practice* (3rd ed., Jordans, 2000).

Doyle C. and Carroll A., "The Slippery Slope" 24 May 1995 *New Law Journal* 759.

Duff, "Fitness to Plead and Fair Trials: 1 A Challenge" [1994] *Criminal Law Review* 419.

Duncan W.R. and Scully P.E., *Marriage Breakdown in Ireland* (Butterworths (Ireland) Ltd, Dublin, 1990).

Dutertre G., *Key Case Law Extracts European Court of Human Rights* (Council of Europe Publishing, 2003).

Dworkin G., *The Theory and Practice of Autonomy* (Cambridge University Press USA, 1988).

Dwyer P., "The Law of Insanity in Ireland", 1996 June, *Bar Review* 9.

Eastman N., "Bournewood; An Indefensible Gap in Mental Health Law", 1998 Vol. 317, *British Medical Journal* 94.

Eastman N., "Mental Health Law; Civil Liberties and Reciprocity" ,1994 Vol. 308, *British Medical Journal* 43.

Edwards M.H., "The ADA and the Employment of Individuals with Mental Disabilities" 1992/93 Vol. 18(3) Winter *Employee Relations Law Journal* 347.

Eldergill A., *Mental Health Review Tribunals Law and Practice* (Sweet & Maxwell, London, 1997).

Ellis J.W., "The Consequences of the Insanity Defense: Proposals to Reform Post-acquittal Commitment Laws" [1986] Vol. 35 *Catholic University Law Review* 961.

Enderby P., "The Testamentary Capacity of Dysphasic Patients" Vol. 62(2) *Medico-Legal Journal* 70.

Evans M.D. (ed.), *Blackstone's International Law Documents* (2nd ed., Blackstone Press Ltd (Great Britain), 1994).

Farry M., *Education and the Constitution* (Roundhall Sweet & Maxwell, Dublin, 1996).

Feinberg J., *Harm to Self The Moral Limits of the Criminal Law* (Oxford University Press Inc New York, 1986).

Fellowes, "Australia's Recommendations for the Sterilisation of the Mentally Incapacitated Minor – A More Rigorous Approach?" 2000 *Web Journal of Current Legal Issues* 1.

Fennell C., *The Law of Evidence in Ireland* (2nd ed., Butterworths (Ireland) Ltd, Dublin, 2003).

Finucane M., *Insanity and the Insane in Post-Famine Ireland* (Croom Helm, London, 1981).

Forde M., *Company Law in Ireland* (The Mercier Press Cork and Dublin, 1985).

Forde M., *The Constitutional Law of Ireland* (The Mercier Press Cork and Dublin, 1987).

Fridman G.H.L., *The Law of Agency* (6th ed., Butterworths, London, 1990).

Frolik L., "A Plenary Guardianship: An Analysis, a Critique and a Proposal for Reform" [1981] Vol. 23 *Arizona Law Review* 599.

Gallagher B., *Powers of Attorney Act 1996* (2nd ed., 2001).

Gendreau C., "The Rights of Psychiatric Patients in the Light of the Principles Announced by the United Nations", 1997 Vol. 20(2) *International Journal of Law and Psychiatry* 259.

George B.J., "The American Bar Association's Mental Health Standards: An Overview" [1985] *The George Washington Law Review* 338.

Gibbons P., "Committal Law in Ireland" (1993) Vol. 10(2) *Irish Journal of Psychological Medicine* 104–109.

Gibbons P., "Criminal Responsibility and Mental Illness in Ireland 1850–1995: Fitness to Plead" 1999 Vol. 16(2) *Irish Journal of Psychological Medicine* 51.

Gibbons P. Walshe D.G, and Dillon J., "Committal Procedures in Ireland" 1992 Vol. 85 (3) *Irish Medical Journal* 91.

Glendenning D., *Education and the Law* (Butterworths (Ireland) Ltd, Dublin, 1999).

Gordon R., "Legal Services for Mental Health Patients: Some Observations on Canadian and Australian Developments" [1983] 6 *Canadian Community Law Journal* 17.

Gordon R. and Verdun Jones S.N., "The Right to Refuse Treatment: Commonwealth Development and Issues" [1983] 6 *International Journal of Law and Psychiatry* 57.

Gostin L., "Contemporary Social Historical Perspectives on Mental Health Reform", Summer 1983 Vol. 10(1) *Journal of Law and Society* 47.

Gostin L.O., *A Human Condition* The Mental Health Act from 1959 to 1975 Observations, Analysis and Proposals for Reform. MIND London (1975).

Gostin L.O., "Human Rights of Persons with Mental Disabilities: The European Convention on Human Rights", 2000 Vol. 23 (2) *International Journal of Law and Psychiatry* 125.

Gostin L.O., "Human Rights, Judicial Review and the Mentally Disordered Offender" [1982] *Criminal Law Review* 779.

Gostin L.O., *A Human Condition Vol. 11 The Law relating to Mentally Abnormal Offenders: Observations, Analysis and proposals for Reform* MIND London (1977).

Gostin L.O., *The Court of Protection* A Legal and Policy Analysis of the Guardianship of the Estate MIND London (1983).

Gostin L.O., *The Mental Health Act 1959 Is it fair?*, MIND London (March 1978).

Grainger, "Mental Incapacity: the Medical or Legal View", *The Law Society Gazette* 29 May 1991 17.

Gregory R.L. (ed.), *The Oxford Companion to the Mind* (Oxford University Press, Oxford, 1987).

Grubin D., "What Constitutes Fitness to Plead" [1993] *Criminal Law Review* 748.

Halsbury's *Laws of England* (Vol. 30, Butterworths, London, 1992).

Harris L.G.E., *A Treatise on the Law and Practice in Lunacy in Ireland* (Corrigan and Wilson Ltd, Dublin, 1930).

Hart Edwards M., "The ADA and the Employment of Individuals with Mental Disabilities", Vol. 18 (3) Winter 1992–1993 *Employee Relations Law Journal* 347.

Havers P. and Hyam J., "Capacity Consent and Human Rights" [1998] *Juridical Review* 205.

Henchy Report, *Third Interim Report of the Interdepartmental Committee on Mentally Ill and Maladjusted Persons: Treatment and Care of Persons suffering from Mental Disorder who appear before the Courts on Criminal Charges* Prl. 8275 (November 1978).

Hensey B.. *The Health Services of Ireland* (Institute of Public Administration, Dublin, 1979).

Herr S.S., Aarons S. and Wallace R.E., *Legal Rights and Mental Health* (Care Gower Publishing Co. Ltd., 1983).

Hewitt P., "Assessing Testamentary Capacity" Summer 2000 *Charities Management* 12.

Hockton A., *The Law of Consent to Medical Treatment* (Sweet & Maxwell, London, 2002).

Hodson K.J., "The American Bar Association Standards for Criminal Justice: Their Development Evolution and Future" [1981] Vol. 59 *Denver Law Journal* 3.

Hoggett B., *Mental Health Law* (4th ed., Sweet & Maxwell, London, 1996).

Institute of Public Administration, *Administration Yearbook and Diary* IPA Dublin (2004).

Interdepartmental Committee on Mentally Ill and Maladjusted Persons, *Treatment and Care of Persons suffering from Mental Disorder who appear before the Courts on Criminal Charges*, Third Interim Report Prl. 8275 (Dublin 1978).

Jones K., "The Limitations of the Legal Approach to Mental Health" [1980] Vol. 3 *International Journal of Law and Psychiatry* 1.

Jones Michael A., *Medical Negligence* (Sweet & Maxwell, London, 1991).

Keane R., *Equity and the Law of Trusts in the Republic of Ireland* (Butterworths London, 1988).

Kelleher D., "FOI Reloaded" 2003 Aug/Sept *Law Society Gazette* 22.

Kelly J.M., *The Irish Constitution* (4th ed., Lexis Nexis Butterworths Dublin, 2003).

Kemp & Kemp, *The Quantum of Damages in Personal Injury and Fatal Accident Claims* (Vol. 2, Sweet & Maxwell, London, 1996).

Kennedy H.G., "Human Rights Standards and Mental Health in Prisons" Vol. 8(2) *Medico-Legal Journal of Ireland* 58.

Kennedy I. and Grubb A., *Medical Law Text with Materials* Second Edition Butterworths, London (1994).

Keogh F. and Walsh D., *Activities of Irish Psychiatric Hospitals and Units 1994* Health Research Board (December 1995).

Keys M., "Challenging the Lawfulness of Psychiatric Detention under *Habeas Corpus* Law in Ireland" [2002] Vol. 24 *Dublin University Law Journal* 26.

Keys M., "Council of Europe Proposals on Protecting the Mentally Ill", 2000 June *Law Society Gazette* 45.

Keys M., "Guarded Welcome for Mental Health Bill 1999" (2000) *Medico-Legal Journal of Ireland* 28.

Keys M., "Issues for the New Mental Health Act" (1997) *Medico Legal Journal of Ireland* 97.

Keys M., "Mental Treatment Legislation: Are the White Paper Proposals Adequate?" 1996 Summer *Dli* 51.

Keys M., *Mental Health Act 2001* (Roundhall, Sweet and Maxwell, Dublin, 2002).

Keys M., "Mental Treatment Legislation Are the White Paper Proposals Adequate?" *Dli* Summer 1998 51.

Kimber C., "Equality and Disability Part 1" September 2001 *Bar Review* 494.

Kimber C., "Equality and Disability Part II" December 2001 *Bar Review* 66.

Kirkpatrick T.P.C., *A Note on the History of the Care of the Insane in Ireland up to the end of the nineteenth century* (University Press Ponsonby and Gibbs, Dublin, 1931).

La Fond J.Q. and Durham M.L., "Cognitive Dissonance: Have Insanity Defense and Civil Commitment Reforms Made a Difference?" [1994] Vo. 39 *Villanova Law Review* 1.

Law Commission (England) Report No. 231, *Mental Incapacity* London HMSO (1995).

Law Reform Commission (Ireland), *Consultation Paper on the Law and the Elderly* (LRC CP 23–2003) Law Reform Commission, Ireland (2003).

Law Reform Commission (Ireland), *Report on Land Law and Conveyancing Law (2) Enduring Powers of Attorney* (LRC 31 1989) Law Reform Commission, Ireland (1989).

Law Reform Commission (Ireland), *Report on Nullity of Marriage* (LRC 9 1984) The Law Reform Commission, Ireland (1984).

Law Reform Commission (Ireland), *Report on Sexual Offences against the Mentally Handicapped* (LRC 33–1990) The Law Reform Commission, Ireland (1990).

Law Reform Commission (Ireland), *Report on the Statutes of Limitations: Claims in Contract and Tort in respect of Latent Damage (other than Personal Injury)*(LRC 64–2001) The Law Reform Commission, Ireland (2001).

Law Reform Commission (Ireland), *Working Paper on Domicile and Habitual Residence as Connecting Factors in the Conflict of Laws* (No. 10 1981) Law Reform Commission, Ireland (1981).

Law Reform Commission of Alberta, *Advance Directives and Substitute Decision-Making in Personal Health Care*, Report No. 11 (November 1991).

Law Reform Commission of Canada, *A Report to Parliament on Mental Disorder in the Criminal Process* (March 1976).

Law Reform Commission of Manitoba, *Emergency Apprehension, Admissions and Rights of Patients under the Mental Health Act*, Report No. 29 (February 12 1979).

Law Reform Commission of New South Wales, *Partial Defences to Murder: Diminished Responsibility* Report No. 82 (May 1997).

Law Reform Commission of New South Wales, *People with an Intellectual Disability and the Criminal Justice System*, Report No. 80 (December 1996).

Law Reform Commission of Nova Scotia, *Final Report on Reform of the Laws Dealing with Adult Guardianship and Personal Health Care Decisions,* (November 1995).

Law Reform Commission of Ontario, *A Study Paper on Fitness to Stand Trial* (May 1973).

Law Reform Commission of Queensland, *Assisted and Substituted Decision Making for People with a Decision Making Disability*, Working Paper No. 43 (1996).

Law Reform Commission of Saskatchewan, *Proposals for a Compulsory Mental Health Care Act* (March 1985).

Law Reform Commission of Saskatchewan, *Proposals for a Guardianship Act Part 1 Personal Guardianship*, Report to the Attorney General (January 1983).

Law Society of Ireland Law Reform Committee, Report of, *Nullity of Marriage The Case for Reform* (October 2001).

Leenen H.J.J. et al., *The Rights of Patients in Europe A Comparative Study* (Deventer Kluwer Law and Taxation Publishers, 1993).

Lindley on the *Law of Partnership* (15th ed., Sweet & Maxwel, London, 1984).

Lowenstein L.F., "Competence to Stand Trial", 2000 Vol. 164 *Justice of the Peace* 700.

Lyttleton T., "Of Sound Mind", 27 June 2003 *New Law Journal* 986.

Macdonald R.P., "Medical, Ethical and Legal Considerations of Electroconvulsive Therapy" [1984] Vol. 22(4) *Osgoode Hall Law Journal* 683.

Machado S.M. and DeLorenzo, *European Disability Law* (Escuela Libre Editorial, Madrid, 1997).

Mackay R.D., "The Abnormality of the Mind Factor in Diminished Responsibility" [1999] *Criminal Law Review* 117.

Mackay R.D. and Gearty C.A., "On being Insane in Jersey – the Case of *Attorney General v Jason Prior*" [2001] *Criminal Law Review* 560.

Mackay R.D.. "Fact and Fiction about the Insanity Defence" [1990] *Criminal Law Review* 247.

Mackay R.D.. "Some thoughts on Reforming the Law of Insanity and Diminished Responsibility in England" (2003) *Juridical Review* p 57.

Mackay R.D. and Kearns G., "The Trial of the Facts and Unfitness to Plead" [1997] *Criminal Law Review* 644.

Madden D., *Medicine Ethics and the Law* (Butterworths, Dublin, 2002).

Mangan S.P., *Mental Health Care in the European Community* (Croom Helm, London, 1985).

Marshland C & Brown N., "Mental Incapacity" (2003) *Solicitors Journal* 254.

Mason JK and McCall Smith R.A., *Law and Medical Ethics* (6th ed., Butterworths, London, 2002).

McGrath S.D., "Schizophrenia and the Law" *Incorporated Law Society of Ireland Gazette*, October 1990, November 1990.

McAuley F., *Criminal Liability A Grammar* (Roundhall Press, Dublin, 2000).

McAuley F., *Insanity Psychiatry and Criminal Responsibility* (Round Hall Press, Dublin, 1993).

McDermott P.A., *Contract Law* (Butterworths (Ireland) Ltd, 2001).

McDermott P.A., *Prison Law* (Roundhall Press, Dublin, 2000).

McDermott P.A. and Robinson T., *The Children Act 2001* (Thomson Roundhall, Dublin, 2003).

McDonagh M., *Freedom of Information Law in Ireland* (Roundhall Sweet and Maxwell, Dublin, 1998).

McDowell M., "Arresting and Detaining the Mentally Disordered: An analysis of the Statutory Powers" [1994] *New Zealand Recent Law Review* 297.

McHale J. et al., *Health Care Law: Text, Cases and Materials* (Sweet & Maxwell, London, 1997.

McIntyre O., "Mental Health: The Case for Reform" (1999) *Medico Legal Journal of Ireland* 53.

McLoughlin N., "Wardship: A Legal and Medical Perspective" (1998) *Medico-Legal Journal of Ireland* 61.

McMahon B.M.E. and Binchy W., *Law of Torts* (3rd ed., Butterworths (Ireland) Ltd, Dublin, 2000).

Melton G.B., *No Place to Go The Civil Commitment of Minors* (University of Nebraska Press, USA, 1998).

Mills S., "Criminal Law (Insanity) Bill 2002: Putting the Sanity Back into Insanity?", 2003 June *Bar Review* 101.

Mills S., "The Mental Health Act 2001: Involuntary Psychiatric Treatment and Detention", 2003 February *Bar Review* 42.

Mills S., *Clinical Practice and the Law* (Butterworths (Ireland) Ltd, Dublin, 2002).

Mongey E.G., *Probate Practice in a Nutshell* (The Author, Dublin, 1980).

Montgomery J., *Health Care Law* (Oxford University Press, 1997).

Morris A.E., "Treating children properly: law, ethics and practice" (1999) Vol. 15(4) *Professional Negligence* 249.

Morris G.H. *The Insanity Defense: A Blueprint for Legislative Reform* (Lexington Books, Massachusetts, 1975).

Morris J.H.C., *The Conflict of Laws* (4th ed., Sweet & Maxwell, London, 1993).

Moss R.J. and La Puma J., "The Ethics of Mechanical Restraints", January–February 1991 *Hastings Center Report* 22.

Mullins M., "The New Mental Disorder Tribunal", 2000 February *Journal of Mental Health Law* 28.

Murphy R., "The Incorporation of the ECHR into Irish Domestic Law" [2001] Issue 6. *European Human Rights Law Review* 640.

Murphy R. and Wills S., "The European Convention on Human Rights and Irish Incorporation – Adopting a Minimalist Approach", Part 1, 2001 September *Bar Review* 541.

Murphy R. and Wills S., "The European Convention on Human Rights and Irish Incorporation – Adopting a Minimalist Approach", Part 2, 2001 October/November *Bar Review* 41.

National Association for the Intellectually Disabled of Ireland (NAMHI), *Who Decides and How? People with Intellectual Disabilities – Legal Capacity and Decision Making A Discussion Document* (October 2003).

National Association of Principals and Deputy Principals, *Irish Education Manual* (Roundhall Sweet & Maxwell, Dublin, 2001).

National Council on Ageing and Older People, *The Law and Older People A Handbook for Service Providers*, Report No. 51 National Council on Ageing and Older People, Dublin (1998).

National Disability Authority, *Towards Best Practice in Provision of Health Services for People with Disabilities in Ireland* (National Disability Authority, Dublin, November 2003).

National Disability Authority, *Towards Best Practice in the Provision of Further Education, Employment and Training Services for People with Disabilities in Ireland* (National Disability Authority, 2003).

National Rehabilitation Board, *Equal Status –a blueprint for action*, Submission to the Commission on the Status of People with Disabilities NRB, Dublin (October 1994).

Ni Chulachain S., "Wardship: Time for Reform", 2000 March *Bar Review* 239.

Ni Raifeartaigh U., "Reversing the Burden of Proof in a Criminal Trial: Canadian and Irish Perspectives on the Presumption of Innocence" (1995) *Irish Criminal Law Journal* 135.

Norton W.W., "Ombudsman in Mental Health", 1985 Vol. 33 *Canada's Mental Health* 17.

Nurcombe B. and Partlett D.F., *Child Mental Health and the Law* (The Free Press, New York, 1994).

O'Connell D., *Equality Now The SIPTU Guide to the Employment Equality Act 1998* (Equality Unit and the Publications Department of SIPTU, 1999).

O'Connor P.A. & McCarthy N., *Key Issues in Irish Family Law* (The Roundhall Press, Dublin, 1988).

O'Flaherty M. and Heffernan L., *The International Covenant on Civil and Political Rights: International Human Rights Law in Ireland* (Brehon Publishing, Dublin, 1995).

O'Halloran K., *Adoption Law and Practice* (Butterworth Ireland Ltd, Dublin, 1992).

O'Leary J., "Reforming the Insanity Defence in Criminal Law A Comparative View", Winter 1992 *Dli* 54.

O'Mahony C., "Education, Remedies and the Separation of Powers" (2002) 24 *Dublin University Law Journal* 57.

O'Malley T., *Sentencing Law and Practice* (Roundhall Sweet and Maxwell, Dublin, 2000).

O'Malley T., *Sexual Offences: Law Policy and Punishment* (Roundhall Sweet and Maxwell, Dublin, 1996).

O'Neill A.M., "Matters of Discretion – The Parameters of Doctor/Patient Confidentiality", 1995 Vol. 1(3) *Medico-Legal Journal of Ireland* 94.

O'Neill A.M., "Mental Committal Law leaves Individual almost Powerless", *Irish Times* April 3, 1992.

O'Neill A.M., "O'Reilly v Moroney and the Mid-Western Health Board: Highlighting the Case for Mental Health Law Reform", *Irish Law Times* (September 1994), 211.

O'Neill Nick, "Mental Incapacity and Guardianship" *Lawyers Practice Manual* (New South Wales, 1998).

O'Shea N., "Some thoughts on the Law relating to the Admission Procedures to Psychiatric Hospitals in the Republic of Ireland today", 1993 Winter *Dli* 77.

Parry J., "Involuntary Civil Commitment in the 90s: A Constitutional Perspective", Vol. 18 (3) *Mental and Physical Disability Law Reporter* 320.

Parry J. and Philips Gilliam P., *Handbook on Mental Disability Law* (American Bar Association Commission on Mental and Physical Disability Law, USA, 2002).

Parry J., *Mental Disability Law A Primer* (5th ed., American Bar Association Commission on Mental and Physical Disability Law, USA, 1995).

Paul Robert E., "Confidentiality and Patients' Records: Balancing the Interests of Society and the Individual", Spring 1979 *The Journal of Psychiatry and Law* 49.

Pearce R.A., *The Succession Act 1965 A Commentary* (Incorporated Law Society of Ireland, Dublin, 1986).

Pedler M., *Mind the Law*, Mind's Evidence to the Governments Mental Health Act Review Team.

Perlin M., *Mental Disability Law Civil and Criminal*, Vols 1–3 (The Michie Company Virginia, 1991).

Petersen K., "Private Decisions and Public Scrutiny: Sterilisations and Minors in Australia and England" (1996) *Contemporary Issues in Law Medicine and Ethics*, pp.57–77.

Pierse R., *Road Traffic Law* (Butterworths (Ireland) Ltd, Dublin, 1995).

Power C., "The Equal Status Bill 1999 – Equal to the Task?", 2000 Vol. 5(6) *Bar Review* 267.

Quill E., *Torts in Ireland* (Gill and Macmillan, 1999).

Quinlivan S. and Keys M., "Official Indifference and Persistent Procrastination An Analysis of *Sinnott*" [2002] Vol. 2(2) *Judicial Studies Institute Journal* 163.

Quinn G., McDonagh M. and Kimber C., *Disability Discrimination Law in the United States, Australia and Canada* (Oak Tree Press, Dublin, 1993.

Quinn G., "Civil Commitment and the Right to Treatment under the European Convention on Human Rights: An Interpretation", *Harvard Human Rights Journal* Vol. 5 [1992] 1.

Quinn G. and Degener. T., *Human Rights and Disability: The Current Use and Future Potential of United Nations Human Rights Instruments in the Context of Disability* (United Nations, New York and Geneva, 2002).

Reppucci N.D. et al., *Children, Mental Health and the Law* (Sage Publications Inc, California, 1984).

Richardson Committee Report, *Report of the Expert Committee on Review of the Mental Health Act 1983*, HMSO November 1999.

Robertson G.B., *Mental Disability and the Law in Canada* (2nd ed., Carswell Thomson Professional Publishing, Toronto, 1994).

Robins J., *Fools and Mad A History of the Insane in Ireland* (Institute of Public Administration, Dublin, 1986).

Robinson D., "Crazy Situation", 2003 Jan/Feb *Law Society Gazette* 12.

Rosenthal E. and Rubenstein L.S., "International Human Rights Advocacy under the Principles for the Protection of Persons with Mental Illness" (1993) Vol. 16 *International Journal of Law and Psychiatry* pp. 257–300.

Rosenthal E. and Sundram C.J., *International Human Rights and Mental Health Legislation*, Paper submitted to World Health Organisation (10 February 2003).

Rubotham N., *The Application of Wardship to the Health Sector*.

Ruddy D. and Cottrell S., *Primary Education Management Manual* (Roundhall Sweet & Maxwell, Dublin, 2002).

Ryan E.F. and Magee P.P., *The Irish Criminal Process* (The Mercier Press, Dublin and Cork, 1983).

Ryan F.W., "Disability and the Right to Education: Defining the Constitutional 'Child'" [2002] Vol. 24 *Dublin University Law Journal* 98.

Saks E.R., "The Use of Mechanical Restraints in Psychiatric Hospitals" [1986] Vol. 95 *The Yale Law Journal* 1836.

Scott P.A., "Morally Autonomous Practice" (1998) Vol. 21(2) *Advances in Nursing Science* pp. 69–79.

Scottish Law Commission, *Incapable Adults* Report No. 151 Cm 2962 (September 1995).

Scottish Law Commission, *Mentally Disabled Adults – Legal Arrangements for Managing their Welfare and Finances*, Discussion Paper No. 94 (September 1991).

Seldon L. and Kierans T., *The Irish Human Rights Handbook* (Oak Tree Press, Dublin, 1994).

Shah, *The Law and Mental Health: Research and Policy* (Sage Publications, 1986).

Shannon G., "Babes in the Hood", 2003 November *Law Society Gazette* 12.

Shannon G., "Children Act 2001", Paper delivered to Children Act Conference 7 November 2002.

Shatter A.J., *Shatter's Family Law* (4th ed., Butterworths (Ireland) Ltd, Dublin, 1997).

Shaw Malcolm N., *International Law* (3rd ed., Cambridge University Press, 1991).

Shuhbotham B., "Illness and Incapacity in the Workplace", Vol. 1(1) *Irish Employment Law Journal* 6.

Slovenko R., "Disposition of the Insanity Acquittee", 1983 Spring *Journal of Psychiatry and Law* 97.

Smith J.C. and Hogan B., *Criminal Law Cases and Materials* (5th ed., Butterworths, London, 1993).

Smith J.C. and Hogan B., *Criminal Law* (7th ed., Butterworths, London, 1992).

Smith O., "Disability Discrimination and Employment: A Never Ending Legal Story" [2201] Vol. 23 *Dublin University Law Journal* 148.

Special Committee on Ageing United States Senate, *Working Paper on Protective Services for the Elderly* July 1977.

Spellman J., "Implications of Recent Decision on Pre-Discharge Assessment Process of Psychiatric Patients" (1996) *Medico-Legal Journal of Ireland* 25.

Spender Lynne (ed.), *Mental Health Rights Manual A Guide to the legal and human rights of people with a mental illness in New South Wales* (Redfern Legal Centre Publishing Ltd, New South Wales, 1995).

Spring R.L., *Patients, Psychiatrists and Lawyers: Law and the Mental Health System* (2nd ed., Anderson Publishing Co, Cincinatti, 1997).

Stone A. & Stromberg A., *Mental Health and Law: A System in Transition* (Jason Aronson Inc., New York, 1976).

Stromberg C.D. and Stone A., "A Model State Law on Civil Commitment of the Mentally Ill" [1983] Vol. 20 *Harvard Journal on Legislation* 275.

Stuart D., *Canadian Criminal Law A Treatise* (3rd ed., Carswell, Scarborough Ontario, 1995).

Study Group on the Development of the Psychiatric Services, Report of *The Psychiatric Services Planning for the Future* Pl. 3001Government Stationery Office, Dublin (December 1984).

Sundram C.J. (ed.), *Choice and Responsibility Legal and Ethical Dilemmas in Services for Persons with Mental Disabilities* (New York State Commission on Quality of Care for the Mentally Disabled, New York, 1994).

Sutherland P.J. and Gearty C.A., "Insanity and the European Court of Human Rights" [1992] *Criminal Law Review* 418.

Terrell, "Statutory Wills – Making Wills for People without Capacity", November/Decmber 2000 *Elderly Client Adviser* 18–20.

The Garda Siochana Guide (Dublin Incorporated Law Society of Ireland, 1991).

The Law Commission of New Zealand, *Community Safety: Mental Health and Criminal Justice Issues*, Report No. 30 (August 1994).

The Law Commission of New Zealand, *The Evidence of Children and other Vulnerable Witnesses*, Preliminary Paper No. 26 (October 1996).

The Law Reform Commission of the Australian Capital Territory, *Guardianship and Management of Property*, Report No. 52 (31 August 1989).

Thompson W.A.R., *Black's Medical Dictionary* Adam and Charles Black, London (1984).

Tomkin D. and Hanafin P., *Irish Medical Law* The Round Hall Press, Dublin (1995).

Tomkin D. and McAuley A., "Re A Ward of Court Legal Analysis" 1995 *Medico-Legal Journal of Ireland* 45.

Turner T. Madill M.F. and Solberg D., "Patient Advocacy: The Ontario Experience" [1984] 7 *International Journal of Law and Psychiatry* 329.

Twomey M., *Partnership Law* (Butterworths (Ireland) Ltd, 2000).

Unsworth C., *The Politics of Mental Health Legislation* (Clarendon Press, Oxford, 1987).

Walsh D., *Criminal Procedure* (Thomson Round Hall, Dublin, 2002).

Ward T., "Law, Common Sense and the Authority of Science: Expert Witnesses and Criminal Insanity in England, ca. 1840–1940" Vol. 6(3) *Social and Legal Studies* 343–362.

Watters L., "Attitudes of general practitioners to the psychiatric services" (1994) Vol. 11(1) *Irish Journal of Psychological Medicine* 44-46.

Webb M., "Comments from an Adult Psychiatric Service on the Mental Health Bill 1999" (2000) *Medico-Legal Journal of Ireland* 14.

Weisstub D.N. (ed.), *Law and Mental Health International Perspectives* (Oxford Pergamon Press Inc, New York, 1990).

Wells, "Whither Insanity?" [1983] *Criminal Law Review* 787.

Wexler D., *Mental Health Law* Plenum, New York (1981).

Whelan D "Some Procedural Aspects of Insanity Cases (2001) Vol. 11(3) *Irish Criminal Law Journal* 3.

Whelan D., "Criminal Charges against Mental Patients" (1995) *Irish Criminal Law Journal* Vol. 5(1) 67–89.

Whelan D., "Fitness to Plead and Insanity in the District Court" (2001) *Irish Criminal Law Journal* Vol 11(2) 2.

Williams, *Contract for Sale of Land and Title to Land* (4th ed., Butterworths, London, 1975).

Williams Glanville, *Textbook of Criminal Law* (Stevens & Sons, London, 1978).

Winfield and Jolowicz on Tort (14th ed., Sweet & Maxwell, London, 1998).

Winick B.J., *Therapeutic Jurisprudence Applied Essays on Mental Health Law* (Carolina Academic Press, Carolina, 1997).

Wood K., "Nullity and Divorce – The New Alternatives?" [1999] 2 *Irish Journal of Family Law* 12.

World Health Organisation, *Guidelines for the Promotion of Human Rights of Persons with Mental Disorders* (WHO Division of Mental Health and Prevention of Substance Abuse, Geneva, 1996).

World Health Organisation, *Mental Health Care Law: Ten Basic Principles* (WHO Division of Mental Health and Prevention of Substance Abuse, Geneva, 1996).

Yeates V., "In whose interests?", August 9, 1996, *New Law Journal* 1182.

Yeo S., "Rethinking the Incapacities of Insanity", *Irish Jurist* 275.

Young R., *Personal Autonomy – Beyond Negative and Positive Liberty* (Croom Helm Ltd, Kent, 1986).

Index

Central Mental Hospital (CMH), 41, 129, 142
discharge from, 386
transfer to 366, 408, 524
Child, *see also* **Guardianship, Minors** and **Wards of court**
definition of, 51, 89, 93
detention of, 144 *et seq., see also* **Detention** and **Involuntary admissions**
ascertainment of age of child, 150
conduct of proceedings, 149
court jurisdiction, 149
court reports on, 148
court's power to proceed in absence of child, 149
district court's powers to give directions, 152 *et seq.*
failure to deliver up child, 151
guardian *ad litem,* 148
health service executive and access to child, 151
party to proceedings as, 147
prohibition on publication/ broadcasting of proceedings, 150
service of documents, 150
welfare of, 147
treatment of, continuation of, 409
voluntary patient as, 89 *et seq., see also* **Voluntary admissions**
Chlorpromazine drug group, 22
Circuit Court, *see also* **District Court, High Court** and **Judicial process**
appeals to, 99, 149, 157, 174, 175, 314 *et seq.,* 367, 380, 406, 408, 416 *et seq.,* 420, 437, 438, 462 *et seq.,* 508 *et seq.*
damages awarded by, 78
in camera rule and, 417
jurisdiction of, 40, 345, 674 *et seq., see* **Wards of court**
proceedings in, 149
Civil rights, 69, 70, 285, 288, 760 *et seq., see also* **Constitutional rights, Human rights, Political rights** and **Solicitors**
civil duties, 761
jury service, 761

Clinical trials, 31, 295 *et seq., see also* **Treatment**
basic ethical standards for, 298
conditions for holding of, 298
conduct of, 295
consent to, 31, 261, 293, 296, 297
criteria for, 295
current irish law and, 295 *et seq.*
inducements, prohibition on, 297
medical practitioners' duties and, 298, 299
notification of matters before, 296
participant, definition of, 296
permission to carry out, 295
rewards for, prohibition on, 297
risks of, 296
Cognitive impairments, 1, 635
Communicate, right to, 155, 197 *et seq., see also* **Confidentiality, Constitutional rights, Information, Medical records** and **Privacy**
comparative law and, 200 *et seq.*
constitution and, 198
human rights and, 198 *et seq., see also* **Human rights**
international law and, 199
legislation and, 197 *et seq.*
undue censorship and, 197
Communication disorders, 1
Community care services, 49 *et seq., see also* **Health boards** and **Health Service Executive**
drugs payment scheme, 51 *et seq., see* **Drugs payment scheme**
free general medial practitioner services, 49, 50, *see* **Medical Card Holders**
free medicines, 50 *et seq.*
programme managers, 33
resource implications for, 459
Confidentiality, *see also* **Privacy**
breach of obligation of, 224
data protection and, 214 *et seq.*
data controller and, 215 *et seq.*
data processor, 215 *et seq.*
Data Protection Commissioner, 219, 221 *et seq.*
disclosures of medical information practice guide, 219 *et seq.*
objections to disclosure, 221
principles, 215, 223 *et seq.*

Patients—*contd.*
    courts, access to, *see* **Courts** and **Judicial process**
    definition of, 257
    detained, 22
        person of unsound mind, 22
        code of practice for, 31
        temporary, 22
    restraint of, 31, *see* **Restraints**
    seclusion of, 31, *see* **Restraints**
Persons of unsound mind
    admission to hospital, 136
    conveyance of to hospital, 132
    detention of, 22, 34, 65, 66, 72, 683, 777, *see also* **Detention**
    examination of, 135
    president of high court and, 656
    property of, 14 *et seq.*
    treatment of, 34, 35, 72, 131, 328, 451, *see also* **Treatment**
    voting and, 759
PET scan, *see* **Mental Illness**
Pharmacists
    capacity, 767, *see also* **Legal capacity**
Political rights, *see also* **Civil rights** and **Legal capacity**
    impact of incapacity on, 759 *et seq.*
    right to vote, 759
    public representation, 761
        membership of Dail Éireann, 761
President of the High Court, 334, *see also* **High Court**
    powers of, 15, 273, 334
Prisoners
    consent to treatment, 524, *see also* **Consent**
    European standards, 528 *et seq.*
    human rights and, 527, *see also* **Human rights**
    international standards, 534
    mental disability with, 521 *et seq.*
    prison rules, 526, 530
    psychiatric treatment in prison, 522
    transfer to central mental hospital, 524 *et seq.*
Privacy
    right to, 155, 632, *see* **Confidentially** and **Constitutional rights**

Psychiatric centres, *see also* **Approved Centres**
    approved centres, 340
        appeals against refusal, 343
        application for registration of, 341
        conditions attached to registration of, 342
        Minister of health and Children's powers and, 344 *et seq.*
        refusal of registration of, 341
        register of, 340
        residents, definition of, 342
    registration of, 340
Psychiatric review boards, 24
Psychiatric services, 33, 35
    approved institution, 33, 34, 36
    authorised institution, 34, 36
    mental health districts, 333
    mental hospital authorities, duties of, 33
    private charitable institutions, 33, 34, 36
    private institutions and provision of, 33, 34, 36
Psychiatric treatment, *see also* **Treatment,** and **Consultant Psychiatrist**
    consent to by voluntary patients, 29, 245 *et seq.*, 264, *see also* **Consent and voluntary admissions**
        capacity to give, 247 *et seq.*
        common law position and, 245
        freely given requirement, 246
        informed, 249 *et seq.*
        minors and, 247 *et seq.*, *see also* **Child**
        treatment without, 255
    detained patients and consent, 264 *et seq.*
    international principles and consent, 259 *et seq.*
    involuntary patients and consent, 255 *et seq.*, *see also* **Involuntary admissions**
        capacity to give, 258
        freely given, 257, 258
        informed, 258
Psychotic patients, 2, 22, 105, 245, 270, 284 *et seq.*, 319, 320, 614, 692
Psycho-surgery, 274 *et seq.*, *see also* **Anorexia nervosa, Psychiatric treatment, Psychotherapy, Schizophrenia** and **treatment**
    authorisation of by Mental Health Tribunal, 405 *et seq.*